CW00730951

POCKET

SCRABBLE®
BRAND Crossword Game

DICTIONARY

POCKET

SCRABBLE®
BRAND Crossword Game

DICTIONARY

Collins

HarperCollins Publishers
Westerhill Road
Bishopbriggs
Glasgow
G64 2QT
Great Britain

Second Edition 2008

Reprint 10 9 8 7 6 5 4 3 2

© HarperCollins Publishers 2004,
2008

ISBN 978-0-00-726108-6

Collins® is a registered trademark of
HarperCollins Publishers Limited

Scrabble® is a registered trademark
of J. W. Spear & Sons Ltd,
a subsidiary of Mattel, Inc.
© 2005 Mattel, Inc.

www.collinslanguage.com

A catalogue record for this book is
available from the British Library

This book is set in Collins Fedra, a
typeface specifically created for
Collins dictionaries by Peter Bil'ak

Printed in Italy by
Rotolito Lombarda S.p.A.

Contributors

Editors
Sandra Anderson
Kay Cullen
Penny Hands
Helen Hucker
Andrew Holmes
Mike Munro

Project Manager
Justin Crozier

For the Publisher
Morven Dooner
Elaine Higgleton
Lucy Cooper

Computing Support
Thomas Callan

Collins Corpus Programmer
Nigel Rochford

Typesetting
Wordcraft

Contents

Introduction

Collins Pocket Scrabble Dictionary – Every Word Counts

The *Collins Pocket Scrabble Dictionary* is the ideal reference book for people who play Scrabble for enjoyment, in a social or family setting. This dictionary doesn't include every word eligible for Scrabble, but does contain the most commonly used of the 260,000 words in *Collins Scrabble Words 2005*, the definitive Scrabble wordlist. The concise definitions in the *Pocket Scrabble Dictionary* allow players to check the meaning of words, as well as using the book for settling arguments during games.

The *Collins Pocket Scrabble Dictionary* contains only words of up to 15 letters in length, as longer words cannot be used in Scrabble. Because the dictionary is designed for family play, it does not include offensive terms. Such words are, however, included in *Collins Scrabble Words 2005*, the complete wordlist for tournaments and club competitions.

Word order

In the *Collins Pocket Scrabble Dictionary*, all words are listed in alphabetical order, rather than some being grouped at the base form as in a conventional dictionary. Where words are inflections of a base form, only the base form has a definition, but the inflections are listed alphabetically as individual entries for easy reference during a game. Base forms and inflections are shown in black; inflections are indented, with a cross-reference to the base form in blue.

Special Scrabble Words

To help family players learn and use some of the rarer and higher-scoring words in the game, the Collins Pocket Scrabble Dictionary includes a number of special panel entries. These are unusual words which are particularly useful in Scrabble, either because they use the high-scoring 'power tiles' (J, Q, X, and Z), or because they have only two or three letters. There are also panel entries at the start of every letter section, which offer advice on useful words beginning with that letter.

The *Collins Pocket Scrabble Dictionary* is designed to be useful to new players and Scrabble veterans alike – we hope you enjoy using it!

Forming Words

The key to successful Scrabble is constant awareness of the opportunities for forming words on the board. The obvious way to play a new word is to place it so that it intersects a word already on the board through a common letter:

Other methods of forming words, however, create more than one new word in the process, giving a higher score. The two main ways of doing this are 'hooking' and 'tagging'.

Hooking

Hooking involves 'hanging' one word on another – the word already on the board acts as a 'hook' on which the other word can be hung – changing the first word in the process. When you form a word by hooking, you add a letter to the beginning or end of a word on the board, transforming it into a longer word as you do so:

C_3	O_1	M_3	E_1	T_1	

In this example, you get the points for COMETS as well as for SERPENTS. Plurals ending in S provide some of the most obvious – and useful – end-hooks. But there are plenty of other end-hooks as well. There are also lots of useful front-hooks. Consider the following example:

If you happened to have CEFIKL among the letters on your rack, you could play the following, taking full advantage of the valuable X played by your opponent:

Here you get the 13 points for FOX as well as those for FICKLE. So you can see that hooking is generally a much more profitable method of word-formation than simply playing a word through one that is already on the board.

Obviously, only certain words can act as hooks. Some words cannot form other words by having a letter added to their front or back; these are known as 'blockers', as they prevent other players from adding words by hooking.

Tagging
Playing a word parallel to one already on the board, so that one or more tiles are in contact, is known as tagging. Tagging is more difficult than hooking because you need to form one additional word for each tile in contact with the word on the board. In most circumstances, these will be two-letter words, which is why short words are so vital to the game. The more two-letter words you know, the greater your opportunities for

fitting words onto the board through tagging – and of running up some impressive scores!

For example, consider the following situation (your opponent has started the game with SHAM, and you have EEHISTX on your rack):

You could play HEXES so that it also forms SH, HE, AX and ME (all valid two-letter words), thus adding the scores for these three words to the points you make from HEXES:

A particular advantage of tagging is that it allows you to benefit from valuable tiles twice in one go, as in the example above where X is used in both HEXES and AX.

Two-letter words are very important for tagging. The panel sections of this dictionary contain a number of unusual two-letter words: learning these is a good method of improving your game immediately!

ABBREVIATIONS USED IN THIS DICTIONARY

AD	anno Domini	Meteorol	Meteorology
adj	adjective	Mil	Military
adv	adverb	n	noun
Anat	Anatomy	N	North
Archit	Architecture	Naut	Nautical
Astrol	Astrology	NZ	New Zealand
Aust	Australia(n)	Obs	Obsolete
BC	before Christ	Offens	Offensive
Biol	Biology	orig.	originally
Brit	British	Photog	Photography
Chem	Chemistry	pl	plural
C of E	Church of England	prep	preposition
conj	conjunction	pron	pronoun
E	East	Psychol	Psychology
e.g.	for example	®	Trademark
esp.	especially	RC	Roman Catholic
etc.	et cetera	S	South
fem	feminine	S Afr	South Africa(n)
foll.	followed	Scot	Scottish
Geom	Geometry	sing	singular
Hist	History	US	United States
interj	interjection	usu.	usually
Lit	Literary	v	verb
masc	masculine	W	West
Med	Medicine	Zool	Zoology

Aa

A forms a two-letter word when followed by any one of A, B, D, E, G, H, I, M, N, R, S, T, W, X and Y – 15 letters out of 26 – so it's a really useful tile. There are also a number of short high-scoring words beginning with A. **Axe** (10 points) and **adze** (14 points) are good examples, but don't forget their US variants, **ax** (9 points) and **adz** (13 points). Also remember their plurals and the verb form **axed** (12 points). **Aye** (6) and **ay** (5) are handy for tight corners.

a *adj* indefinite article, used before a noun being mentioned for the first time

> **aa** aa *n* (**aas**). Aa is a type of volcanic rock. Aa scores 2 points, and is a good way of getting rid of annoying multiples of A.
> **aah** *interj*. Aah is a sound people make when they're pleased or amazed. Aah scores 6 points.
> **aal** *adj* Aal is a Scots word for **all**. Aal scores 3 points.

aardvark *n* (*pl* -s) S African anteater with long ears and snout

aardvarks *n* ▷ aardvark

ab *n* (*pl* -s) (*Informal*) (usually plural) abdominal muscle

> **aba** *noun* (**abas**). Cloth made from goat or camel hair. This is a useful word to remember for when you have more than one A on your rack. Aba scores 5 points.

aback *adv* startled or disconcerted

abacus (*pl* -es) *n* beads on a wire frame, used for doing calculations

abacuses *n* ▷ abacus

abalone (*pl* -s) [ab-a-**lone**-ee] *n* edible sea creature with a shell lined with mother of pearl

abalones *n* ▷ abalone

abandon *v* (-s, -ing, -ed) desert or leave (one's wife, children, etc.) ▶ *n* lack of inhibition > **abandonment** *n* (*pl* -s)

abandoned *adj* deserted ▶ *v* ▷ abandon

abandoning *v* ▷ abandon

abandonment *n* ▷ abandon

abandonments *n* ▷ abandon

abandons *v* ▷ abandon

abase *v* (-ses, -sing, -sed) humiliate or degrade (oneself) > **abasement** *n* (*pl* -s)

abased *v* ▷ abase

abasement *n* ▷ abase

abasements *n* ▷ abase

abases *v* ▷ abase

abashed *adj* embarrassed and ashamed

abasing *v* ▷ abase

abate *v* (-tes, -ting, -ted) make or become less strong > **abatement** *n* (*pl* -s)

abated *v* ▷ abate

abatement *n* ▷ abate

abatements *n* ▷ abate

abates *v* ▷ abate

abating *v* ▷ abate

abattoir [ab-a-**twahr**] *n* place where animals are killed for food (*pl* -s)

abattoirs *n* ▷ abattoir

> **abb** *noun* (**abbs**). Abb is yarn used in weaving. Remember this word for when you have two Bs on your rack, as there will probably already be an A on the board that you can use. Abb scores 7 points.

abbess *n* (*pl* -es) nun in charge of a convent

abbesses *n* ▷ abbess

abbey *n* (*pl* -s) dwelling place of, or a church belonging to, a community of monks or nuns

abbeys *n* ▷ abbey

abbot *n* (*pl* -s) head of an abbey of monks

abbots *n* ▷ abbot

abbreviate *v* (-tes, -ting, -ted) shorten (a word) by leaving out some letters

abbreviated *v* ▷ abbreviate

abbreviates *v* ▷ abbreviate

abbreviating *v* ▷ abbreviate

abbreviation *n* (*pl* -s) shortened form of a word or words

abbreviations *n* ▷ abbreviation

abdicate v (-tes, -ting, -ted) give up (the throne or a responsibility) > **abdication** n (pl -s)
  abdicated v ▷ abdicate
  abdicates v ▷ abdicate
  abdicating v ▷ abdicate
  abdication n ▷ abdicate
  abdications n ▷ abdicate
abdomen n (pl -s) part of the body containing the stomach and intestines > **abdominal** adj
  abdomens n ▷ abdomen
  abdominal adj ▷ abdomen
abduct v (-s, -ing, -ed) carry off, kidnap > **abduction** n (pl -s) > **abductor** n (pl -s)
  abducted v ▷ abduct
  abducting v ▷ abduct
  abduction n ▷ abduct
  abductions n ▷ abduct
  abductor n ▷ abduct
  abductors n ▷ abduct
  abducts v ▷ abduct
aberrant adj showing aberration
aberration n (pl -s) sudden change from what is normal, accurate, or correct
  aberrations n ▷ aberration
abet v (-s, -ting, -ted) help or encourage in wrongdoing > **abettor** n (pl -s)
  abets v ▷ abet
  abetted v ▷ abet
  abetting v ▷ abet
  abettor n ▷ abet
  abettors n ▷ abet
abeyance n (pl -s) not in use
  abeyances n ▷ abeyance
abhor v (-s, -horring, -horred) detest utterly > **abhorrence** n (pl -s)
  abhorred v ▷ abhor
  abhorrence n ▷ abhor
  abhorrences n ▷ abhor
abhorrent adj hateful, loathsome
  abhorring v ▷ abhor
  abhors v ▷ abhor
abide v (-des, -ding, -ded) endure, put up with
  abided v ▷ abide
  abides v ▷ abide
abiding adj lasting ▶ v ▷ abide
  abilities n ▷ ability
ability n (pl -ties) competence, power
abject adj utterly miserable > **abjectly** adv
  abjectly adv ▷ abject
abjure v (-res, -ring, -red) deny or renounce on oath
  abjured v ▷ abjure
  abjures v ▷ abjure
  abjuring v ▷ abjure

ablative n (pl -s) case of nouns in Latin and other languages, indicating source, agent, or instrument of action
  ablatives n ▷ ablative
ablaze adj burning fiercely
able adj (-r, -st) capable, competent > **ably** adv
  abler adj ▷ able
  ablest adj ▷ able
ablution n (pl -s) (usually plural) act of washing
  ablutions n ▷ ablution
  ably adv ▷ able
abnormal adj not normal or usual > **abnormally** adv > **abnormality** n (pl -ties)
  abnormalities n ▷ abnormal
  abnormality n ▷ abnormal
  abnormally adv ▷ abnormal
aboard adv, prep on, in, onto, or into (a ship, train, or plane)
abode n (pl -s) home, dwelling
  abodes n ▷ abode
abolish v (-shes, -shing, -shed) do away with > **abolition** n (pl -s)
  abolished v ▷ abolish
  abolishes v ▷ abolish
  abolishing v ▷ abolish
  abolition n ▷ abolish
abolitionist n (pl -s) person who wishes to do away with something, esp. slavery
  abolitionists n ▷ abolitionist
  abolitions n ▷ abolish
abominable adj detestable, very bad > **abominably** adv
  abominably adv ▷ abominable
abomination n (pl -s) someone or something that is detestable
  abominations n ▷ abomination
  aboriginal n, adj ▷ aborigine
  aboriginals n ▷ aborigine
aborigine, aboriginal [ab-or-rij-in-ee] n (pl -s) original inhabitant of a country or region, esp. (A-) Australia > **aboriginal** adj
  aborigines n ▷ aborigine
abort v (-s, -ing, -ed) have an abortion or perform an abortion on
  aborted v ▷ abort
  aborting v ▷ abort
abortion n (pl -s) operation to end a pregnancy
abortionist n (pl -s) person who performs abortions, esp. illegally
  abortionists n ▷ abortionist
  abortions n ▷ abortion
abortive adj unsuccessful
  aborts v ▷ abort
abound v (-s, -ing, -ed) be plentiful

> **abounding** *adj*
abounded *v* ▷ abound
abounding *v*, *adj* ▷ abound
abounds *v* ▷ abound
about *prep* concerning, on the subject of ▶ *adv* nearly, approximately
above *adv*, *prep* over or higher (than)
abracadabra *n* (*pl* -s) supposedly magic word
abracadabras *n* ▷ abracadabra
abrasion *n* (*pl* -s) scraped area on the skin
abrasions *n* ▷ abrasion
abrasive *adj* harsh and unpleasant in manner ▶ *n* (*pl* -s) substance for cleaning or polishing by rubbing
abrasives *n* ▷ abrasive
abreast *adv*, *adj* side by side
abridge *v* (-ges, -ging, -ged) shorten by using fewer words > **abridgment, abridgement** *n* (*pl* -s)
abridged *v* ▷ abridge
abridgement *n* ▷ abridge
abridgements *n* ▷ abridge
abridges *v* ▷ abridge
abridging *v* ▷ abridge
abridgment *n* ▷ abridge
abridgments *n* ▷ abridge
abroad *adv* to or in a foreign country
abrogate *v* (-tes, -ting, -ted) cancel (a law or agreement) formally > **abrogation** *n* (*pl* -s)
abrogated *v* ▷ abrogate
abrogates *v* ▷ abrogate
abrogating *v* ▷ abrogate
abrogation *n* ▷ abrogate
abrogations *n* ▷ abrogate
abrupt *adj* (-er, -est) sudden, unexpected > **abruptly** *adv* > **abruptness** *n* (*pl* -es)
abrupter *adj* ▷ abrupt
abruptest *adj* ▷ abrupt
abruptly *adv* ▷ abrupt
abruptness *n* ▷ abrupt
abruptnesses *n* ▷ abrupt
abs *n* ▷ ab
abscess *n* (*pl* abscesses) inflamed swelling containing pus
abscesses *n* ▷ abscess
abscond *v* (-s, -ing, -ed) leave secretly
absconded *v* ▷ abscond
absconding *v* ▷ abscond
absconds *v* ▷ abscond
abseil [ab-sale] *v* (-s, -ing, -ed) go down a steep drop by a rope fastened at the top and tied around one's body
abseiled *v* ▷ abseil
abseiling *v* ▷ abseil
abseils *v* ▷ abseil

absence *n* (*pl* -s) being away
absences *n* ▷ absence
absent *adj* not present ▶ *v* (-s, -ing, -ed) stay away > **absently** *adv*
absented *v* ▷ absent
absentee *n* (*pl* -s) person who should be present but is not
absenteeism *n* (*pl* -s) persistent absence from work or school
absenteeisms *n* ▷ absenteeism
absentees *n* ▷ absentee
absenting *v* ▷ absent
absently *adv* ▷ absent
absents *v* ▷ absent
absinthe *n* (*pl* -s) strong green aniseed-flavoured liqueur
absinthes *n* ▷ absinthe
absolute *adj* complete, perfect
absolutely *adv* completely ▶ *interj* certainly, yes
absolution *n* ▷ absolve
absolutions *n* ▷ absolve
absolutism *n* (*pl* -s) government by a ruler with unrestricted power
absolutisms *n* ▷ absolutism
absolve *v* (-ves, -ving, -ved) declare to be free from blame or sin > **absolution** *n* (*pl* -s)
absolved *v* ▷ absolve
absolves *v* ▷ absolve
absolving *v* ▷ absolve
absorb *v* (-s, -ing, -ed) soak up (a liquid) > **absorption** *n* (*pl* -s) > **absorbency** *n* (*pl* -s)
absorbed *v* ▷ absorb
absorbencies *n* ▷ absorb
absorbency *n* ▷ absorb
absorbent *adj* able to absorb liquid
absorbing *v* ▷ absorb
absorbs *v* ▷ absorb
absorption *n* ▷ absorb
absorptions *n* ▷ absorb
abstain *v* (-s, -ing, -ed) choose not to do something > **abstainer** *n* (*pl* -s)
abstained *v* ▷ abstain
abstainer *n* ▷ abstain
abstainers *n* ▷ abstain
abstaining *v* ▷ abstain
abstains *v* ▷ abstain
abstemious *adj* taking very little alcohol or food > **abstemiousness** *n* (*pl* -es)
abstemiousness *n* ▷ abstemious
abstemiousnesses *n* ▷ abstemious
abstention *n* (*pl* -s) abstaining, esp. from voting
abstentions *n* ▷ abstention
abstinence *n* (*pl* -s) abstaining, esp. from

drinking alcohol > **abstinent** *adj*
abstinences *n* ▷ abstinence
abstinent *adj* ▷ abstinence
abstract *adj* (-er, -est) existing as a quality or idea rather than a material object ▶ *n* (*pl* -s) summary ▶ *v* (-s, -ing, -ed) summarize > **abstraction** *n* (*pl* -s)
abstracted *adj* lost in thought *v* ▷ abstract
  abstracter *adj* ▷ abstract
  abstractest *adj* ▷ abstract
  abstracting *v* ▷ abstract
  abstraction *n* ▷ abstract
  abstractions *n* ▷ abstract
  abstracts *n*, *v* ▷ abstract
abstruse *adj* (-er, -est) not easy to understand
  abstruser *adj* ▷ abstruse
  abstrusest *adj* ▷ abstruse
absurd *adj* (-er, -est) incongruous or ridiculous > **absurdly** *adv* > **absurdity** *n* (*pl* -ties)
  absurder *adj* ▷ absurd
  absurdest *adj* ▷ absurd
  absurdities *n* ▷ absurd
  absurdity *n* ▷ absurd
  absurdly *adv* ▷ absurd
  abundance *n* ▷ abundant
  abundances *n* ▷ abundant
abundant *adj* plentiful > **abundantly** *adv* > **abundance** *n* (*pl* -s)
  abundantly *adv* ▷ abundant
abuse *v* (-ses, -sing, -sed) use wrongly ▶ *n* (*pl* -s) prolonged ill-treatment > **abuser** *n* (*pl* -s) > **abusive** *adj* > **abusively** *adv* > **abusiveness** *n* (-es)
  abused *v* ▷ abuse
  abuser *n* ▷ abuse
  abusers *n* ▷ abuse
  abuses *v*, *n* ▷ abuse
  abusing *v* ▷ abuse
  abusive *adj* ▷ abuse
  abusively *adv* ▷ abuse
  abusiveness *n* ▷ abuse
  abusivenesses *n* ▷ abuse
abut *v* (-s, abutting, abutted) be next to or touching
  abuts *v* ▷ abut
  abutted *v* ▷ abut
  abutting *v* ▷ abut

> **aby** *verb* (**abys abying abought**). Aby is an old word meaning to pay a penalty. If someone plays this word, remember that it can be expanded to **baby**, **abysmal** or **abyss**. Aby scores 8 points.

abysmal *adj* (*Informal*) extremely bad, awful > **abysmally** *adv*
  abysmally *adv* ▷ abysmal

abyss *n* (*pl* -es) very deep hole or chasm
  abysses *n* ▷ abyss
acacia [a-**kay**-sha] *n* (*pl* -s) tree or shrub with yellow or white flowers
  acacias *n* ▷ acacia
academic *adj* of an academy or university ▶ *n* (*pl* -s) lecturer or researcher at a university > **academically** *adv*
  academically *adv* ▷ academic
academician *n* (*pl* -s) member of an academy
  academicians *n* ▷ academician
  academics *n* ▷ academician
  academies *n* ▷ academy
academy *n* (*pl* -mies) society to advance arts or sciences
acanthus *n* (*pl* -es) prickly plant
  acanthuses *n* ▷ acanthus
accede *v* (-des, -ding, -ded) consent or agree (to)
  acceded *v* ▷ accede
  accedes *v* ▷ accede
  acceding *v* ▷ accede
accelerate *v* (-tes, -ting, -ted) (cause to) move faster > **acceleration** *n* (*pl* -s)
  accelerated *v* ▷ accelerate
  accelerates *v* ▷ accelerate
  accelerating *v* ▷ accelerate
  acceleration *n* ▷ accelerate
  accelerations *n* ▷ accelerate
accelerator *n* (*pl* -s) pedal in a motor vehicle to increase speed
  accelerators *n* ▷ accelerator
accent *n* (*pl* -s) distinctive style of pronunciation of a local, national, or social group ▶ *v* (-s, -ing, -ed) place emphasis on
  accented *v* ▷ accent
  accenting *v* ▷ accent
  accents *n*, *v* ▷ accent
accentuate *v* (-tes, -ting, -ted) stress, emphasize > **accentuation** *n* (*pl* -s)
  accentuated *v* ▷ accentuate
  accentuates *v* ▷ accentuate
  accentuating *v* ▷ accentuate
  accentuation *n* ▷ accentuate
  accentuations *n* ▷ accentuate
accept *v* (-s, -ing, -ed) receive willingly > **acceptance** *n* (*pl* -s)
  acceptabilities *n* ▷ acceptable
  acceptability *n* ▷ acceptable
acceptable *adj* tolerable > **acceptably** *adv* > **acceptability** *n* (*pl* -ties)
  acceptably *adv* ▷ acceptable
  acceptance *n* ▷ accept
  acceptances *n* ▷ accept
  accepted *v* ▷ accept

accepting v ▷ accept

accepts v ▷ accept

access n (pl -es) means of or right to approach or enter ▶ v (-es, -ing, -ed) obtain (data) from a computer

accessed v ▷ access

accesses n, v ▷ access

accessibilities n ▷ accessible

accessibility n ▷ accessible

accessible adj easy to reach > **accessibility** n (pl -**ties**)

accessing v ▷ access

accession n (pl -s) taking up of an office or position

accessions n ▷ accession

accessories n ▷ accessory

accessory n (pl -ries) supplementary part or object

accident n (pl -s) mishap, often causing injury

accidental adj happening by chance or unintentionally ▶ n (pl -s) (MUSIC) symbol indicating that a sharp, flat, or natural note is not a part of the key signature > **accidentally** adv

accidentally adv ▷ accidental

accidentals n ▷ accidental

accidents n ▷ accident

acclaim v (-s, -ing, -ed) applaud, praise ▶ n (pl -s) enthusiastic approval > **acclamation** n (pl -s)

acclaimed v ▷ acclaim

acclaiming v ▷ acclaim

acclaims v, n ▷ acclaim

acclamation n ▷ acclaim

acclamations n ▷ acclaim

acclimatization n ▷ acclimatize

acclimatizations n ▷ acclimatize

acclimatize v (-zes, -zing, -zed) adapt to a new climate or environment > **acclimatization** n (pl -s)

acclimatized v ▷ acclimatize

acclimatizes v ▷ acclimatize

acclimatizing v ▷ acclimatize

accolade n (pl -s) award, honour, or praise

accolades n ▷ accolade

accommodate v (-tes, -ting, -ted) provide with lodgings

accommodated v ▷ accommodate

accommodates v ▷ accommodate

accommodating adj obliging ▶ v ▷ accommodate

accommodation n (pl -s) house or room for living in

accommodations n ▷ accommodation

accompanied v ▷ accompany

accompanies v ▷ accompany

accompaniment n (pl -s) something that accompanies

accompaniments n ▷ accompaniment

accompanist n ▷ accompanist

accompanists n ▷ accompany

accompany v (-nies, -nying, -nied) go along with > **accompanist** n (pl -s)

accompanying v ▷ accompany

accomplice n (pl -s) person who helps another to commit a crime

accomplices n ▷ accomplice

accomplish v (-es, -ing, -ed) manage to do

accomplished adj expert, proficient ▶ v ▷ accomplish

accomplishes v ▷ accomplish

accomplishing v ▷ accomplish

accomplishment n (pl -s) completion

accomplishments n ▷ accomplishment

accord n (pl -s) agreement, harmony ▶ v (-s, -ing, -ed) fit in with

accordance n (pl -s) conforming to or according to

accordances n ▷ accordance

accorded v ▷ accord

according adv as stated by ▶ v ▷ accord

accordingly adv in an appropriate manner

accordion n (pl -s) portable musical instrument played by moving the two sides apart and together, and pressing a keyboard or buttons to produce the notes > **accordionist** n

accordionist n (pl -s) ▷ accordion

accordionists n ▷ accordion

accordions n ▷ accordion

accords v ▷ accord

accost v (-s, -ing, -ed) approach and speak to, often aggressively

accosted v ▷ accost

accosting v ▷ accost

accosts v ▷ accost

account n (pl -s) report, description ▶ v (-s, -ing, -ed) judge to be

accountabilities n ▷ accountable

accountability n ▷ accountable

accountable adj responsible to someone or for something > **accountability** n (pl -**ties**)

accountancies n ▷ accountant

accountancy n ▷ accountant

accountant n (pl -s) person who maintains and audits business accounts > **accountancy** n (pl -**cies**)

accountants n ▷ accountant

accounted v ▷ account

accounting n (pl -s) skill or practice of

maintaining and auditing business accounts
▶ v ▷ account
accountings n ▷ accounting
accounts n, v ▷ account
accoutrement n (pl -s) an item of clothing and equipment for a particular activity
accoutrements n ▷ accoutrement
accredited adj authorized, officially recognized
accretion [ak-**kree**-shun] n (pl -s) gradual growth
accretions n ▷ accretion
accrual n ▷ accrue
accruals n ▷ accrue
accrue v (-crues, -cruing, -crued) increase gradually > **accrual** n (pl -s)
accrued v ▷ accrue
accrues v ▷ accrue
accruing v ▷ accrue
accumulate v (-tes, -ting, -ted) gather together in increasing quantity
> **accumulation** n (pl -s) > **accumulative** adj
accumulated v ▷ accumulate
accumulates v ▷ accumulate
accumulating v ▷ accumulate
accumulation n ▷ accumulate
accumulations v ▷ accumulate
accumulative adj ▷ accumulate
accumulator n (pl -s) (BRIT & AUST) rechargeable electric battery
accumulators n ▷ accumulator
accuracies n ▷ accurate
accuracy n ▷ accurate
accurate adj exact, correct > **accurately** adv
> **accuracy** n (pl -cies)
accurately adv ▷ accurate
accursed adj under a curse
accusation n ▷ accuse
accusations n ▷ accuse
accusative n (pl -s) grammatical case indicating the direct object
accusatives n ▷ accusative
accusatory adj ▷ accuse
accuse v (-ses, -sing, -sed) charge with wrongdoing > **accused** n > **accuser** n (pl -s) > **accusing** adj > **accusation** n (pl -s) > **accusatory** adj
accused v ▷ accuse
accused n ▷ accuse
accuser n ▷ accuse
accusers n ▷ accuser
accuses v ▷ accuse
accusing v, adj ▷ accuse
accusing adj ▷ accuse
accustom v (-s, -ing, -ed) make used to

accustomed adj usual v ▷ accustom
accustoming v ▷ accustom
accustoms v ▷ accustom
ace n (pl -s) playing card with one symbol on it
▶ adj (Informal) excellent
acerbic [ass-**sir**-bik] adj harsh or bitter
> **acerbity** n (pl -ties)
acerbities n ▷ acerbic
acerbity n ▷ acerbic
aces n ▷ ace
acetate [**ass**-it-tate] n (pl -s) (CHEM) salt or ester of acetic acid
acetates n ▷ acetate
acetic [ass-**see**-tik] adj of or involving vinegar
acetone [**ass**-it-tone] n (pl -s) colourless liquid used as a solvent
acetones n ▷ acetone
acetylene [ass-**set**-ill-een] n (pl -s) colourless flammable gas used in welding metals
acetylenes n ▷ acetylene
ache n (pl -s) dull continuous pain ▶ v (-ches, -ching, -ched) be in or cause continuous dull pain
ached n ▷ ache
aches v, n ▷ ache
achieve v (-ves, -ving, -ved) gain by hard work or ability
achieved v ▷ achieve
achievement n (pl -s) something accomplished
achievements n ▷ achievement
achieves v ▷ achieve
achieving v ▷ achieve
aching v ▷ ache
achromatic adj colourless
acid n (pl -s) (CHEM) one of a class of compounds, corrosive and sour when dissolved in water, that combine with a base to form a salt ▶ adj containing acid > **acidic** adj > **acidify** v > **acidity** n (pl -ties)
acidic adj ▷ acid
acidify v ▷ acid
acidities n ▷ acid
acidity n ▷ acid
acids n ▷ acid
acknowledge v (-ges, -ging, -ged) admit, recognize > **acknowledgment,** **acknowledgement** n (pl -s)
acknowledged v ▷ acknowledge
acknowledgement n ▷ acknowledge
acknowledgements n ▷ acknowledge
acknowledges v ▷ acknowledge
acknowledging v ▷ acknowledge
acknowledgment n ▷ acknowledge
acknowledgments n ▷ acknowledge

acme [ak-mee] *n* (*pl* -s) highest point of achievement or excellence
　acmes *n* ▷ acme
acne [ak-nee] *n* (*pl* -s) pimply skin disease
　acnes *n* ▷ acne
acolyte *n* (*pl* -s) follower or attendant
　acolytes *n* ▷ acolyte
aconite *n* (*pl* -s) poisonous plant with hoodlike flowers
　aconites *n* ▷ aconite
acorn *n* (*pl* -s) nut of the oak tree
　acorns *n* ▷ acorn
acoustic *adj* of sound and hearing
　> **acoustically** *adv*
　acoustically *adv* ▷ acoustic
　acoustics *n* science of sounds
acquaint *v* (-s, -ing, -ed) make familiar, inform
　> **acquainted** *adj*
acquaintance *n* (*pl* -s) person known
　acquaintances *n* ▷ acquaintance
　acquainted *v*, *adj* ▷ acquaint
　acquainting *v* ▷ acquaint
　acquaints *v* ▷ acquaint
acquiesce [ak-wee-**ess**] *v* (-sces, -scing, -sced) agree to what someone wants
　> **acquiescence** *n* (*pl* -s) > **acquiescent** *adj*
　acquiesced *v* ▷ acquiesce
　acquiescence *n* ▷ acquiesce
　acquiescences *n* ▷ acquiesce
　acquiescent *adj* ▷ acquiesce
　acquiesces *v* ▷ acquiesce
　acquiescing *v* ▷ acquiesce
acquire *v* (-res, -ring, -red) gain, get
　acquired *v* ▷ acquire
　acquires *v* ▷ acquire
　acquiring *v* ▷ acquire
acquisition *n* (*pl* -s) thing acquired
　acquisitions *n* ▷ acquisition
acquisitive *adj* eager to gain material possessions > **acquisitiveness** *n* (*pl* -es)
　acquisitiveness *n* ▷ acquisitive
　acquisitivenesses *n* ▷ acquisitive
acquit *v* (-s, -quitting, -quitted) pronounce (someone) innocent > **acquittal** *n* (*pl* -s)
　acquits *v* ▷ acquit
　acquittal *n* ▷ acquit
　acquittals *n* ▷ acquit
　acquitted *v* ▷ acquit
　acquitting *v* ▷ acquit
acre *n* (*pl* -s) measure of land, 4840 square yards (4046.86 square metres)
acreage [ake-er-rij] *n* (*pl* -s) land area in acres
　acreages *n* ▷ acreage
　acres *n* ▷ acre
acrid [ak-rid] *adj* (-er, -est) pungent, bitter

acrider *adj* ▷ acrid
acridest *adj* ▷ acrid
acrimonies *n* ▷ acrimonious
acrimonious *adj* bitter in speech or manner
　> **acrimony** *n* (*pl* -ies)
　acrimony *n* ▷ acrimonious
acrobat *n* (*pl* -s) person skilled in gymnastic feats requiring agility and balance
　> **acrobatic** *adj*
　acrobatic *adj* ▷ acrobat
　acrobatics *pl n* acrobatic feats
　acrobats *n* ▷ acrobat
acronym *n* (*pl* -s) word formed from the initial letters of other words, such as NASA
　acronyms *n* ▷ acronym
across *adv*, *prep* from side to side (of)
acrostic *n* (*pl* -s) lines of writing in which the first or last letters of each line spell a word or saying
　acrostics *n* ▷ acrostic
acrylic *n* (*pl* -s) ▶ *adj* (synthetic fibre, paint, etc.) made from acrylic acid
　acrylics *n* ▷ acrylic
act *n* (*pl* -s) thing done ▶ *v* (-s, -ing, -ed) do something
　acted *v* ▷ act
acting *n* (*pl* -s) art of an actor ▶ *adj* temporarily performing the duties of ▶ *v* ▷ act
　actings *n* ▷ acting
actinium *n* (*pl* -s) (CHEM) radioactive chemical element
　actiniums *n* ▷ actinium
action *n* (*pl* -s) process of doing something
actionable *adj* giving grounds for a lawsuit
　actions *n* ▷ action
activate *v* (-tes, -ting, -ted) make active
　> **activation** *n* (*pl* -s) > **activator** *n* (*pl* -s)
　activated *v* ▷ activate
　activates *v* ▷ activate
　activating *v* ▷ activate
　activation *n* ▷ activate
　activations *n* ▷ activate
　activator *n* ▷ activate
　activators *n* ▷ activate
active *adj* moving, working > **actively** *adv*
　actively *adv* ▷ active
　activism *n* ▷ activist
　activisms *n* ▷ activist
activist *n* (*pl* -s) person who works energetically to achieve political or social goals > **activism** *n* (*pl* -s)
　activists *n* ▷ activist
　activities *n* ▷ activity
activity *n* (*pl* -ties) state of being active
actor *n* (*pl* -s) person who acts in a play, film,

etc.
actors n ▷ actor
actress n (pl **-es**) woman who acts in a play, film, etc.
actresses n ▷ actress
acts n, v ▷ act
actual adj existing in reality > **actuality** n (pl **-ties**)
actualities n ▷ actual
actuality n ▷ actual
actually adv really, indeed
actuarial adj ▷ actuary
actuaries n ▷ actuary
actuary n (pl **-ries**) statistician who calculates insurance risks > **actuarial** adj
actuate v (**-tes, -ting, -ted**) start up (a device)
actuated v ▷ actuate
actuates v ▷ actuate
actuating v ▷ actuate
acuities n ▷ acuity
acuity [ak-**kew**-it-ee] n (pl **-ties**) keenness of vision or thought
acumen [ak-**yew**-men] n (pl **-s**) ability to make good judgments
acumens n ▷ acumen
acupuncture n (pl **-s**) medical treatment involving the insertion of needles at various points on the body > **acupuncturist** n (pl **-s**)
acupunctures n ▷ acupuncture
acupuncturist n ▷ acupuncture
acupuncturists n ▷ acupuncture
acute adj (**-r, -st**) severe ▶ n (pl **-s**) accent (ˊ) over a letter to indicate the quality or length of its sound, as in café > **acutely** adv > **acuteness** n
acutely adv ▷ acute
acuteness n ▷ acute
acuter adj ▷ acute
acutes n ▷ acute
acutest adj ▷ acute
ad n (pl **-s**) (Informal) advertisement
adage n (pl **-s**) wise saying, proverb
adages n ▷ adage
adagio n (pl **-gios**) ▶ adv (MUSIC) (piece to be played) slowly and gracefully
adagios n ▷ adagio
adamant adj unshakable in determination or purpose > **adamantly** adv
adamantly adv ▷ adamant
adapt v (**-s, -ing, -ed**) alter for new use or new conditions > **adaptable** adj > **adaptability** n (pl **-ties**)
adaptabilities n ▷ adapt
adaptability n ▷ adapt
adaptable adj ▷ adapt

adaptation n (pl **-s**) thing produced by adapting something
adaptations n ▷ adaptation
adapted v ▷ adapt
adapter n ▷ adaptor
adapters n ▷ adaptor
adapting v ▷ adapt
adaptor, adapter n (pl **-s**) device for connecting several electrical appliances to a single socket
adaptors n ▷ adaptor
adapts v ▷ adapt
add v (**-s, -ing, -ed**) combine (numbers or quantities)
added v ▷ add
addenda n ▷ addendum
addendum n (pl **-da**) addition
adder n (pl **-s**) small poisonous snake
adders n ▷ adder
addict n (pl **-s**) person who is unable to stop taking drugs > **addicted** adj > **addiction** n (pl **-s**)
addicted adj ▷ addict
addiction n ▷ addict
addictions n ▷ addict
addictive adj causing addiction
addicts n ▷ addict
adding v ▷ add
addition n (pl **-s**) adding > **additional** adj > **additionally** adv
additional adj ▷ addition
additionally adv ▷ addition
additions n ▷ addition
additive n (pl **-s**) something added, esp. to a foodstuff, to improve it or prevent deterioration
additives n ▷ additive
addled adj confused or unable to think clearly
address n (pl **-es**) place where a person lives ▶ v (**-es, -ing, -ed**) mark the destination, as on an envelope
addressed v ▷ address
addressee n (pl **-s**) person addressed
addressees n ▷ addressee
addresses n, v ▷ address
addressing v ▷ address
adds v ▷ add
adduce v (**-ces, -cing, -uced**) mention something as evidence or proof
adduced v ▷ adduce
adduces v ▷ adduce
adducing v ▷ adduce
adenoid [**ad**-in-oid] n (pl **-s**) (usually plural) mass of tissue at the back of the throat
adenoidal adj having a nasal voice caused by

swollen adenoids
adenoids *n* ▷ adenoid
adept *adj* (-er, -est) ▶ *n* (*pl* -s) very skilful (person)
adepter *adj* ▷ adept
adeptest *adj* ▷ adept
adepts *n* ▷ adept
adequacies *n* ▷ adequate
adequacy *n* ▷ adequate
adequate *adj* sufficient, enough > **adequately**
adv > **adequacy** *n* (*pl* -ies)
adequately *adv* ▷ adequate
adherable *adj* ▷ adhere
adhere *v* (-res, -ring, -red) stick (to)
> **adherence** *n* (*pl* -ces)
adhered *v* ▷ adhere
adherence *n* ▷ adhere
adherences *n* ▷ adhere
adherent *n* (*pl* -s) devotee, follower
adherents *n* ▷ adherent
adheres *v* ▷ adhere
adhering *v* ▷ adhere
adhesion *n* (*pl* -s) sticking (to)
adhesions *n* ▷ adhesion
adhesive *n* (*pl* -s) substance used to stick
things together ▶ *adj* able to stick to things
adhesives *n* ▷ adhesive
adieu [a-dew] *interj* (Lit) farewell, goodbye
adipose *adj* of or containing fat
adjacent *adj* near or next (to)
adjectival *adj* ▷ adjective
adjective *n* (*pl* -es) word that adds information
about a noun or pronoun > **adjectival** *adj*
adjectives *n* ▷ adjective
adjoin *v* (-s, -ing, -ed) be next to > **adjoining** *adj*
adjoined *v* ▷ adjoin
adjoining *v, adj* ▷ adjoin
adjoins *v* ▷ adjoin
adjourn *v* (-s, -ing, -ed) close (a court) at the
end of a session > **adjournment** *n* (*pl* -s)
adjourned *v* ▷ adjourn
adjourning *v* ▷ adjourn
adjournment *n* ▷ adjourn
adjournments *n* ▷ adjourn
adjourns *v* ▷ adjourn
adjudge *v* (-ges, -ging, -ged) declare (to be)
adjudged *v* ▷ adjudge
adjudges *v* ▷ adjudge
adjudging *v* ▷ adjudge
adjudicate *v* (-tes, -ting, -ted) give a formal
decision on (a dispute) > **adjudication** *n* (*pl* -s)
> **adjudicator** *n* (*pl* -s)
adjudicated *v* ▷ adjudicate
adjudicates *v* ▷ adjudicate
adjudicating *v* ▷ adjudicate
adjudication *n* ▷ adjudicate

adjudications *n* ▷ adjudicate
adjudicator *n* ▷ adjudicate
adjudicators *n* ▷ adjudicate
adjunct *n* (*pl* -s) subordinate or additional
person or thing
adjuncts *n* ▷ adjunct
adjure *v* (-res, -ring, -red) command (to do)
adjured *v* ▷ adjure
adjures *v* ▷ adjure
adjuring *v* ▷ adjure
adjust *v* (-s, -ing, -ted) adapt to new
conditions > **adjustable** *adj* > **adjuster** *n* (*pl* -s)
> **adjustment** *n* (*pl* -s)
adjustable *adj* ▷ adjust
adjusted *v* ▷ adjust
adjuster *n* ▷ adjust
adjusters *n* ▷ adjust
adjustment *n* ▷ adjust
adjustments *n* ▷ adjust
adjusts *v* ▷ adjust
adjutant [aj-oo-tant] *n* (*pl* -s) army officer in
charge of routine administration
adjutants *n* ▷ adjutant
admin *n* (*pl* -s) (*Informal*) administration
administer *v* (-s, -ing, -ed) manage (business
affairs)
administered *v* ▷ administer
administering *v* ▷ administer
administers *v* ▷ administer
administrate *v* (-tes, -ting, -ated) manage (an
organization) > **administrator** *n* (*pl* -s)
administrated *v* ▷ administrate
administrates *v* ▷ administrate
administrating *v* ▷ administrate
administration *n* (*pl* -s) management of an
organization
administrations *n* ▷ administration
administrative *adj* of the management of an
organization
administrator *n* ▷ administrate
administrators *n* ▷ administrate
admins *n* ▷ admin
admirable *adj* ▷ admire
admirably *adv* ▷ admire
admiral *n* (*pl* -s) highest naval rank
admirals *n* ▷ admiral
admiralties *n* ▷ admiralty
admiralty *n* (*pl* -ties) the office or jurisdiction
of an admiral
admiration *n* ▷ admire
admirations *n* ▷ admire
admire *v* (-res, -ring, -red) regard with esteem
and approval > **admirable** *adj* > **admirably**
adv > **admiration** *n* (*pl* -s) > **admirer** *n* (*pl* -s)
> **admiring** *adj* > **admiringly** *adv*

admired v ▷ admire

admirer n ▷ admire

admirers n ▷ admire

admires v ▷ admire

admiring v, adj ▷ admire

admiringly adv ▷ admire

admissibilities n ▷ admissible

admissibility n ▷ admissible

admissible adj allowed to be brought in as
evidence in court > **admissibility** n (pl -ties)

admission n (pl -s) permission to enter

admissions n ▷ admission

admit v (-mits, -mitting, -mitted) confess,
acknowledge

admits v ▷ admit

admittance n (pl -s) permission to enter

admittances n ▷ admittance

admitted v ▷ admit

admittedly adv it must be agreed

admitting v ▷ admit

admixture n (pl -s) mixture

admixtures n ▷ admixture

admonish v (-es, -ing, -ed) reprove sternly
> **admonition** n (pl -s)

admonished v ▷ admonish

admonishes v ▷ admonish

admonishing v ▷ admonish

admonition n ▷ admonish

admonitions n ▷ admonish

ado n (pl -s) (Lit) fuss, trouble

adobe [ad-**oh**-bee] n (pl -s) sun-dried brick

adobes n ▷ adobe

adolescence n (pl -s) period between puberty
and adulthood

adolescences n ▷ adolescence

adolescent n (pl -s), adj (person) between
puberty and adulthood

adolescents n ▷ adolescent

adopt v (-s, -ing, -ed) take (someone else's
child) as one's own > **adoption** n (pl -s)

adopted v ▷ adopt

adopting v ▷ adopt

adoption n ▷ adopt

adoptions n ▷ adopt

adoptive adj related by adoption

adopts v ▷ adopt

adorable adj ▷ adore

adoration n ▷ adore

adorations n ▷ adore

adore v (-res, -ring, -red) love intensely
> **adorable** adj > **adoration** n (pl -s) > **adoring**
adj > **adoringly** adv

adored v ▷ adore

adores v ▷ adore

adoring v, adj ▷ adore

adoringly adv ▷ adore

adorn v (-s, -ing, -ed) decorate, embellish
> **adornment** n (pl -s)

adorned v ▷ adorn

adorning v ▷ adorn

adornment n ▷ adorn

adornments n ▷ adorn

adorns v ▷ adorn

ados n ▷ ado

adrenal [ad-**reen**-al] adj near the kidneys

adrenalin, adrenaline n (pl -s) hormone
secreted by the adrenal glands in response
to stress

adrenaline n ▷ adrenalin

adrenalines n ▷ adrenalin

adrenalins n ▷ adrenalin

adrenally adv ▷ adrenal

adrift adj, adv drifting

adroit adj quick and skilful > **adroitly** adv
> **adroitness** n

adroitly adv ▷ adroit

adroitness n ▷ adroit

ads n ▷ ad

adsorb v (-s, -ing, -ed) (of a gas or vapour)
condense and form a thin film on a surface
> **adsorption** n (pl -s)

adsorbed v ▷ adsorb

adsorbing v ▷ adsorb

adsorbs v ▷ adsorb

adsorption n ▷ adsorb

adsorptions n ▷ adsorb

adulation n (pl -s) uncritical admiration

adulations n ▷ adulation

adult adj fully grown, mature ▶ n (pl -s) adult
person or animal > **adulthood** n (pl -s)

adulterate v (-tes, -ting, -ted) spoil by adding
inferior material > **adulteration** n (pl -s)

adulterated v ▷ adulterate

adulterates v ▷ adulterate

adulterating v ▷ adulterate

adulteration n ▷ adulterate

adulterations n ▷ adulterate

adulterer n ▷ adultery

adulterers n ▷ adultery

adulteress n ▷ adultery

adulteresses n ▷ adultery

adulteries n ▷ adultery

adulterous adj ▷ adultery

adultery n (pl -teries) sexual unfaithfulness
of a husband or wife > **adulterer** n (pl -s)
> **adulteress** n (pl -es) > **adulterous** adj

adulthood n ▷ adult

adulthoods n ▷ adult

adults n ▷ adult

advance v (-ces, -cing, -ced) go or bring

forward ▶ n (pl -s) forward movement ▶ adj done or happening before an event

advanced adj at a late stage in development ▶ v ▷ advance

advancement n (pl advancements) promotion

  advancements n ▷ advancement

  advances v, n ▷ advance

  advancing v ▷ advance

advantage n (pl -s) more favourable position or state > **advantageous** adj > **advantageously** adv

  advantageous adj ▷ advantage

  advantageously adv ▷ advantage

  advantages n ▷ advantage

advent n (pl -s) arrival

adventitious adj added or appearing accidentally

  advents n ▷ advent

adventure n (pl -s) exciting and risky undertaking or exploit > **adventurous** adj

adventurer n (pl -s) person who unscrupulously seeks money or power

  adventurers n ▷ adventurer

  adventures n ▷ adventure

adventuress n (pl -es) woman who unscrupulously seeks money or power

  adventuresses n ▷ adventuress

  adventurous adj ▷ adventure

adverb n (pl -s) word that adds information about a verb, adjective, or other adverb > **adverbial** adj

  adverbial adj ▷ adverb

  adverbs n ▷ adverb

  adversaries n ▷ adversary

adversary [ad-verse-er-ree] n (pl -ries) opponent or enemy

adverse adj unfavourable > **adversely** adv

  adversely adv ▷ adverse

  adversities n ▷ adversity

adversity n (pl -ties) very difficult or hard circumstances

advert n (pl -s) (Informal) advertisement

advertise v (-ses, -sing, -sed) present or praise (goods or services) to the public in order to encourage sales > **advertiser** n (pl -s) > **advertising** adj, n (pl -s)

  advertised v ▷ advertise

advertisement n (pl -s) public announcement to sell goods or publicize an event

  advertisements n ▷ advertisement

  advertiser n ▷ advertise

  advertises v ▷ advertise

  advertising v, adj n ▷ advertise

  advertisings n ▷ advertise

  adverts n ▷ advert

advice n (pl -s) recommendation as to what to do

  advices n ▷ advice

  advisabilities n ▷ advisable

  advisability n ▷ advisable

advisable adj prudent, sensible > **advisability** n (pl -ties)

advise v (-ses, -sing, -sed) offer advice to

advised adj considered, thought-out ▶ v ▷ advise

advisedly adv deliberately

adviser, advisor n (pl -s) person who offers advice, e.g. on careers to students

  advisers n ▷ adviser

  advises v ▷ advise

  advising v ▷ advise

  advisor n ▷ adviser

  advisors n ▷ adviser

advisory adj giving advice

advocaat n (pl -s) liqueur with a raw egg base

  advocaats n ▷ advocaat

  advocacies n ▷ advocate

  advocacy n ▷ advocate

advocate v (-tes, -ting, -ted) propose or recommend ▶ n (pl -s) person who publicly supports a cause > **advocacy** n (pl -cies)

  advocated v ▷ advocate

  advocates v, n ▷ advocate

  advocating v ▷ advocate

  adz n ▷ adze

adze, adz n (pl adzes) tool with an arched blade at right angles to the handle

  adzed v ▷ adze

  adzes n ▷ adze

> **ae** adj. Ae is a Scots word that means **one**. This is a useful word to remember when you want to form words in two directions at once. Ae scores 2 points.

aegis [ee-jiss] n (pl -es) sponsorship, protection

  aegises n ▷ aegis

aeon [ee-on] n (pl -s) immeasurably long period of time

  aeons n ▷ aeon

aerate v (-tes, -ting, -ted) put gas into (a liquid), as when making a fizzy drink > **aeration** n (pl -s)

  aerated v ▷ aerate

  aerates v ▷ aerate

  aerating v ▷ aerate

  aeration n ▷ aerate

  aerations n ▷ aerate

aerial adj in, from, or operating in the air ▶ n (pl -ls) metal pole, wire, etc., for receiving or transmitting radio or TV signals

aerials n ▷ aerial
aerobatic adj ▷ aerobatics
aerobatics pl n stunt flying > **aerobatic** adj
aerobic adj ▷ aerobics
aerobics n exercises designed to increase the amount of oxygen in the blood > **aerobic** adj
aerodrome n (pl -s) small airport
aerodromes n ▷ aerodrome
aerodynamic adj ▷ aerodynamics
aerodynamics n study of how air flows around moving solid objects > **aerodynamic** adj
aerofoil n (pl -s) part of an aircraft, such as the wing, designed to give lift
aerofoils n ▷ aerofoil
aerogram n (pl -s) airmail letter on a single sheet of paper that seals to form an envelope
aerograms n ▷ aerogram
aeronautical adj ▷ aeronautics
aeronautics n study or practice of aircraft flight > **aeronautical** adj
aeroplane n (pl -s) powered flying vehicle with fixed wings
aeroplanes n ▷ aeroplane
aerosol n (pl -s) pressurized can from which a substance can be dispensed as a fine spray
aerosols n ▷ aerosol
aerospace n (pl -s) earth's atmosphere and space beyond
aerospaces n ▷ aerospace
aesthete [eess-theet] n (pl -s) person who has or affects an extravagant love of art > **aestheticism** n (pl -s)
aesthetes n ▷ aesthete
aesthetic [iss-thet-ik] adj relating to the appreciation of art and beauty > **aesthetically** adv
aesthetically adv ▷ aesthetic
aestheticism n ▷ aesthete
aestheticisms n ▷ aesthete
aesthetics n study of art, beauty, and good taste
aether n (pl -s) ▷ ether
aethers n ▷ aether
aetiologies n ▷ aetiology
aetiology [ee-tee-ol-a-jee] n (pl -gies) ▷ etiology
afar adv from or at a great distance
affabilities n ▷ affable
affability n ▷ affable
affable adj friendly and easy to talk to > **affably** adv > **affability** n (pl -ties)
affably adv ▷ affable
affair n (pl -s) event or happening
affairs n ▷ affair
affect[1] v (-s, -ing, -ed) act on, influence

affect[2] v (-s, -ing, -ed) put on a show of
affectation n (pl -s) attitude or manner put on to impress
affectations n ▷ affectation
affected adj displaying affectation ▶ v ▷ affect[1,2]
affecting v ▷ affect[1,2]
affection n (pl -s) fondness or love
affectionate adj loving > **affectionately** adv
affectionately adv ▷ affectionate
affections n ▷ affection
affects v ▷ affect[1,2]
affianced [af-fie-anst] adj (Old-fashioned) engaged to be married
affidavit [af-fid-dave-it] n (pl -s) written statement made on oath
affidavits n ▷ affidavit
affiliate v (-tes, -ting, -ted) (of a group) link up with a larger group > **affiliation** n (pl -s)
affiliated v ▷ affiliate
affiliates v ▷ affiliate
affiliating v ▷ affiliate
affiliation n ▷ affiliate
affiliations n ▷ affiliate
affinities n ▷ affinity
affinity n (pl -ties) close connection or liking
affirm v (-s, -ing, -ed) declare to be true > **affirmation** n (pl -s)
affirmation n ▷ affirm
affirmations n ▷ affirm
affirmative n (pl -s), adj (word or phrase) indicating agreement
affirmatives n ▷ affirmative
affirmed v ▷ affirm
affirming v ▷ affirm
affirms v ▷ affirm
affix v (-fixes, -fixing, -fixed) attach or fasten ▶ n (pl -fixes) word or syllable added to a word to change its meaning
affixed v ▷ affix
affixes v, n ▷ affix
affixing v ▷ affix
afflict v (-s, -ing, -ed) give pain or grief to > **affliction** n (pl -s)
afflicted v ▷ afflict
afflicting v ▷ afflict
affliction n ▷ afflict
afflictions n ▷ afflict
afflicts v ▷ afflict
affluence n (pl -s) wealth
affluences n ▷ affluence
affluent adj having plenty of money
afford v (-s, -ing, -ed) have enough money to buy > **affordable** adj
affordable adj ▷ afford

afforded v ▷ afford
affording v ▷ afford
affords v ▷ afford
afforest v (**-s, -ing, -ed**) plant trees on > **afforestation** n (pl **-s**)
afforestation n ▷ afforest
afforestations n ▷ afforest
afforested v ▷ afforest
afforesting v ▷ afforest
afforests v ▷ afforest
affray n (pl **-s**) (BRIT, AUST & NZ) (LAW) noisy fight, brawl
affrays n ▷ affray
affront v (**-s, -ing, -ed**), n (pl **-s**) insult
affronted v ▷ affront
affronting v ▷ affront
affronts v, n ▷ affront
afghan adj of Afghanistan or its language
aficionado [af-fish-yo-**nah**-do] n (pl **-dos**) enthusiastic fan of something or someone
aficionados n ▷ aficionado
afield adv far away
aflame adj burning
afloat adv, adj floating
afoot adv, adj happening, in operation
aforementioned adj referred to previously
aforesaid adj referred to previously
aforethought adj premeditated
afraid adj frightened
afresh adv again, anew
aft adv at or towards the rear of a ship or aircraft
after prep following in time or place ▶ conj at a later time than ▶ adv at a later time
afterbirth n (pl **-s**) material expelled from the womb after childbirth
afterbirths n ▷ afterbirth
aftercare n (pl **-s**) support given to a person discharged from a hospital or prison
aftercares n ▷ aftercare
aftereffect n (pl **-s**) result occurring some time after its cause
aftereffects n ▷ aftereffect
afterglow n (pl **-s**) glow left after a source of light has gone
afterglows n ▷ afterglow
afterlife n (pl **-lives**) life after death
afterlives n ▷ afterlife
aftermath n (pl **-s**) results of an event considered together
aftermaths n ▷ aftermath
afternoon n (pl **-s**) time between noon and evening
afternoons n ▷ afternoon
afters pl n (BRIT) (Informal) dessert

aftershave n (pl **-s**) lotion applied to the face after shaving
aftershaves n ▷ aftershave
afterthought n (pl **-s**) idea occurring later
afterthoughts n ▷ afterthought
afterward adv ▷ afterwards
afterwards, afterward adv later

> **ag** adj. Ag means to do with **agriculture**. This is a good short word to remember, as it can come in handy when you need to form words in more than one direction. Ag scores 3 points.

again adv once more
against prep in opposition or contrast to
agape adj (of the mouth) wide open
agaric n (pl **-s**) fungus with gills on the underside of the cap, such as a mushroom
agarics n ▷ agaric
agate [**ag**-git] n (pl **-s**) semiprecious form of quartz with striped colouring
agates n ▷ agate
age n (pl **-s**) length of time a person or thing has existed ▶ v (**-s, ageing** or **aging, -d**) make or grow old > **ageing, aging** n, adj
aged adj [**ay**-jid] old ▷ age
ageing v, n, adj ▷ age
ageless adj apparently never growing old
agencies n ▷ agency
agency n (pl **-cies**) organization providing a service
agenda n (pl **-s**) list of things to be dealt with, esp. at a meeting
agendas n ▷ agenda
agent n (pl **-s**) person acting on behalf of another
agents n ▷ agent
ages n, v ▷ age
agglomeration n (pl **-s**) confused mass or cluster
agglomerations n ▷ agglomeration
aggrandize v (**-zes, -zing, -zed**) make greater in size, power, or rank > **aggrandizement** n (pl **-s**)
aggrandized v ▷ aggrandize
aggrandizement n ▷ aggrandize
aggrandizements n ▷ aggrandize
aggrandizes v ▷ aggrandize
aggrandizing v ▷ aggrandize
aggravate v (**-tes, -ting, -ted**) make worse > **aggravating** adj > **aggravation** n (pl **-s**)
aggravated v ▷ aggravate
aggravates v ▷ aggravate
aggravating v, adj ▷ aggravate
aggravation n ▷ aggravate
aggravations n ▷ aggravate

aggregate n (pl -s) total ▶ adj gathered into a mass ▶ v (-tes, -ting, -ted) combine into a whole > **aggregation** n (pl -s)
  aggregated v ▷ aggregate
  aggregates n, v ▷ aggregate
  aggregating v ▷ aggregate
  aggregation n ▷ aggregate
  aggregations n ▷ aggregate
aggression n (pl -s) hostile behaviour
  > **aggressor** n (pl -s)
  aggressions n ▷ aggression
aggressive adj showing aggression
  > **aggressively** adv > **aggressiveness** n
  aggressively adv ▷ aggressive
  aggressiveness n ▷ aggressive
  aggressor n ▷ aggression
  aggressors n ▷ aggression
aggrieved adj upset and angry
aggro n (pl -s) (BRIT, AUST & NZ) (Slang) aggressive behaviour
  aggros n ▷ aggro
aghast adj overcome with amazement or horror
agile adj (-r, -st) nimble, quick-moving > **agility** n (pl -ties)
  agileness n ▷ agile
  agiler adj ▷ agile
  agilest adj ▷ agile
  agilities n ▷ agile
  agility n ▷ agile
aging v, n, adj ▷ age
agitate v (-tes, -ting, -ted) disturb or excite
  > **agitation** n (pl -s) > **agitator** n (pl -s)
  agitated v ▷ agitate
  agitates v ▷ agitate
  agitating v ▷ agitate
  agitation n ▷ agitate
  agitations n ▷ agitate
  agitator n ▷ agitate
  agitators n ▷ agitate
aglow adj glowing
agnostic n (pl -s) person who believes that it is impossible to know whether God exists ▶ adj of agnostics > **agnosticism** n (pl -s)
  agnosticism n ▷ agnostic
  agnosticisms n ▷ agnostic
  agnostics n ▷ agnostic
ago adv in the past
agog adj eager or curious
  agonies n ▷ agony
agonize v (-zes, -zing, -zed) worry greatly
  > **agonizing** adj
  agonized v ▷ agonize
  agonizes v ▷ agonize
  agonizing v, adj ▷ agonize

agony n (pl -nies) extreme physical or mental pain
agoraphobia n (pl -s) fear of open spaces
  > **agoraphobic** n (pl -s), adj
  agoraphobias n ▷ agoraphobia
  agoraphobic n, adj ▷ agoraphobia
  agoraphobics n ▷ agoraphobic
agrarian adj of land or agriculture
agree v (-s, -ing, -d) be of the same opinion
agreeable adj pleasant and enjoyable
  > **agreeably** adv
  agreeably adv ▷ agreeable
  agreed v ▷ agree
  agreeing v ▷ agree
agreement n (pl agreements) agreeing
  agreements n ▷ agreement
  agrees v ▷ agree
agricultural adj ▷ agriculture
  agriculturalist n ▷ agriculture
  agriculturalists n ▷ agriculture
agriculture n (pl -s) raising of crops and livestock > **agricultural** adj > **agriculturalist** n (pl -s)
  agricultures n ▷ agriculture
  agronomies n ▷ agronomy
  agronomist n ▷ agronomy
  agronomists n ▷ agronomy
agronomy [ag-**ron**-om-mee] n (pl -mies) science of soil management and crop production
  > **agronomist** n (pl -s)
aground adv onto the bottom of shallow water
ague [**aig**-yew] n (pl -s) (Old-fashioned) periodic fever with shivering
  agues n ▷ ague

  ah interj. Ah is a sound people make to show pleasure or pain. Ah scores 5 points, and is a good word to form as a result of playing a longer word.

ahead adv in front
ahoy interj shout used at sea to attract attention

  ai n (**ais**). An ai is a three-toed sloth. It's useful when trying to form several words at once. Ai scores 2 points.

aid v (-s, -ing, -ed) ▶ n (pl -s) (give) assistance or support
aide n (pl -s) assistant
  aided v ▷ aid
  aides n ▷ aide
  aiding v ▷ aid
  aids v, n ▷ aid
ail v (-s, -ing, -ed) trouble, afflict
  ailed v ▷ ail
aileron n (pl -s) movable flap on an aircraft

wing which controls rolling

ailerons n ▷ aileron

ailing adj sickly ▶ v ▷ ail

ailment n (pl -s) illness

ailments n ▷ ailment

ails v, n ▷ ail

aim v (-s, -ing, -ed) point (a weapon or missile) or direct (a blow or remark) at a target ▶ n (pl -s) aiming

aimed v ▷ aim

aiming v ▷ aim

aimless adj having no purpose > **aimlessly** adv

aimlessly adv ▷ aimless

aims v, n ▷ aim

air n (pl -s) mixture of gases forming the earth's atmosphere ▶ v (-s, -ing, -ed) make known publicly

airborne adj carried by air

airbrush n (pl -es) atomizer spraying paint by compressed air

airbrushes n ▷ airbrush

aircraft n any machine that flies, such as an aeroplane

aired v ▷ air

airfield n (pl -s) place where aircraft can land and take off

airfields n ▷ airfield

airier adj ▷ airy

airiest adj ▷ airy

airily adv ▷ airy

airing n (pl -s) exposure to air for drying or ventilation ▶ v ▷ air

airings n ▷ airing

airless adj stuffy

airlift n (pl -s) transport of troops or cargo by aircraft when other routes are blocked ▶ v (-s, -ing, -ed) transport by airlift

airlifted v ▷ airlift

airlifting v ▷ airlift

airlifts n, v ▷ airlift

airline n (pl -s) company providing scheduled flights for passengers and cargo

airliner n (pl -s) large passenger aircraft

airliners n ▷ airliner

airlines n ▷ airline

airlock n (pl -s) air bubble blocking the flow of liquid in a pipe

airlocks n ▷ airlock

airmail n system of sending mail by aircraft

airman n (pl -men) member of the air force

airmen n ▷ airman

airplay n (pl -s) broadcast performances of a record on radio

airplays n ▷ airplay

airport n (pl -s) airfield for civilian aircraft, with facilities for aircraft maintenance and passengers

airports n ▷ airport

airs n, v ▷ air

airship n (pl -s) lighter-than-air self-propelled aircraft

airships n ▷ airship

airspace n (pl -s) atmosphere above a country, regarded as its territory

airspaces n ▷ airspace

airstrip n (pl -s) cleared area where aircraft can take off and land

airstrips n ▷ airstrip

airtight adj sealed so that air cannot enter

airworthiness n ▷ airworthy

airworthinesses n ▷ airworthy

airworthy adj (of aircraft) fit to fly > **airworthiness** n (pl -es)

airy adj (-rier, -riest) well-ventilated > **airily** adv

aisle [rhymes with **mile**] n (pl -s) passageway separating seating areas in a church, theatre, etc., or row of shelves in a supermarket

aisles n ▷ aisle

ajar adj, adv (of a door) partly open

akimbo adv with hands on hips and elbows outwards

akin adj similar, related

▓ **al** conj. Al is an old word for **if** or **although**. Al scores 2 points.

alabaster n (pl -s) soft white translucent stone

alabasters n ▷ alabaster

alacrities n ▷ alacrity

alacrity n (pl -ies) speed, eagerness

alarm n (pl -s) sudden fear caused by awareness of danger ▶ v (-s, -ing, -med) fill with fear > **alarming** adj

alarmed v ▷ alarm

alarming v, adj ▷ alarm

alarmist n (pl -s) person who alarms others needlessly

alarmists n ▷ alarmist

alarms n, v ▷ alarm

alas adv unfortunately, regrettably

albatross n (pl -es) large sea bird with very long wings

albatrosses n ▷ albatross

albeit conj even though

albino n (pl -nos) person or animal with white skin and hair and pink eyes

albinos n ▷ albino

album n (pl -s) book with blank pages for keeping photographs or stamps in

albumen n (pl -s) egg white

albumens n ▷ albumen

albumin n (pl -s) protein found in blood

plasma, egg white, milk, and muscle
albumins n ▷ albumin
albums n ▷ album
alchemies n ▷ alchemy
alchemist n ▷ alchemy
alchemists n ▷ alchemy
alchemy n (pl -ies) medieval form of chemistry concerned with trying to turn base metals into gold and to find the elixir of life > **alchemist** n (pl -s)
alcohol n (pl -s) colourless flammable liquid present in intoxicating drinks
alcoholic adj of alcohol ▶ n (pl -s) person addicted to alcohol
alcoholics n ▷ alcoholic
alcoholism n (pl -s) addiction to alcohol
alcoholisms n ▷ alcoholism
alcohols n ▷ alcohol
alcopop n (pl -s) (BRIT, AUST & S AFR) (Informal) alcoholic drink that tastes like a soft drink
alcopops n ▷ alcopop
alcove n (pl -s) recess in the wall of a room
alcoves n ▷ alcove
aldehyde n (pl -s) one of a group of chemical compounds derived from alcohol by oxidation
aldehydes n ▷ aldehyde
alder n (pl -s) tree related to the birch
alderman n (pl -men) formerly, senior member of a local council
aldermen n ▷ alderman
alders n ▷ alder
ale n (pl -s) kind of beer
alert adj (-er, -est) watchful, attentive ▶ n (pl -s) warning of danger ▶ v (-s, -ing, -ed) warn of danger > **alertness** n (pl -es)
alerted v ▷ alert
alerter adj ▷ alert
alertest adj ▷ alert
alerting v ▷ alert
alertness n ▷ alert
alertnesses n ▷ alert
alerts n, v ▷ alert
ales n ▷ ale
alfalfa n (pl -s) kind of plant used to feed livestock
alfalfas n ▷ alfalfa
alfresco adv, adj in the open air
alga n (pl -e) (usually plural) plant which lives in or near water and has no true stems, leaves, or roots
algae [al-jee] n ▷ alga
algebra n (pl -s) branch of mathematics using symbols to represent numbers > **algebraic** adj
algebraic adj ▷ algebra

algebras n ▷ algebra
algorithm n (pl -s) logical arithmetical or computational procedure for solving a problem
algorithms n ▷ algorithm
alias adv also known as ▶ n (pl -ses) false name
aliases n ▷ alias
alibi n (pl -s) plea of being somewhere else when a crime was committed
alibis n ▷ alibi
alien adj foreign ▶ n (pl -s) foreigner
alienate v (-tes, -ting, -ted) cause to become hostile > **alienation** n (pl -s)
alienated v ▷ alienate
alienates v ▷ alienate
alienating v ▷ alienate
alienation n ▷ alienate
alienations n ▷ alienate
aliens n ▷ alien
alight¹ v (-s, -ing, -ed) step out of (a vehicle)
alight² adj on fire
alighted v ▷ alight¹
alighting v ▷ alight¹
alights v ▷ alight¹
align [a-line] v (-s, -ing, -ed) bring (a person or group) into agreement with the policy of another > **alignment** n (pl -s)
aligned v ▷ align
aligning v ▷ align
alignment n ▷ align
alignments n ▷ align
aligns v ▷ align
alike adj like, similar ▶ adv in the same way
alimentary adj of nutrition
alimonies n ▷ alimony
alimony n (pl -nies) allowance paid under a court order to a separated or divorced spouse
aliquot (MATHS) adj of or denoting an exact divisor of a number ▶ n (pl -s) exact divisor
aliquots n ▷ aliquot
alive adj living, in existence
alkali [alk-a-lie] n (pl -s) substance which combines with acid and neutralizes it to form a salt > **alkaline** adj > **alkalinity** n (pl -ties)
alkaline adj ▷ alkali
alkalinities n ▷ alkali
alkalinity n ▷ alkali
alkalis n ▷ alkali
alkaloid n (pl -s) any of a group of organic compounds containing nitrogen
alkaloids n ▷ alkaloid
all adj whole quantity or number (of) ▶ adv wholly, entirely
allay v (-s, -ing, -ed) reduce (fear or anger)
allayed v ▷ allay

allaying *v* ▷ allay
allays *v* ▷ allay
allegation *n* (*pl* -s) unproved accusation
  allegations *n* ▷ allegation
allege *v* (-ges, -ging, -ged) state without proof
  > **alleged** *adj* > **allegedly** *adv*
  alleged *v, adj* ▷ allege
  allegedly *adv* ▷ allege
  alleges *v* ▷ allege
allegiance *n* (*pl* -s) loyalty to a person, country,
  or cause
  allegiances *n* ▷ allegiance
  alleging *v* ▷ allege
  allegorical *adj* ▷ allegory
  allegories *n* ▷ allegory
allegory *n* (*pl* -ries) story with an underlying
  meaning as well as the literal one
  > **allegorical** *adj*
allegretto *n* (*pl* -s) ▶ *adv* (MUSIC) (piece to be
  played) fairly quickly or briskly
  allegrettos *n* ▷ allegretto
allegro *n* (*pl* -s) ▶ *adv* (MUSIC) (piece to be
  played) in a brisk lively manner
  allegros *n* ▷ allegro
alleluia *interj* ▷ hallelujah
allergen *n* (*pl* -s) substance capable of causing
  an allergic reaction
  allergens *n* ▷ allergen
allergic *adj* having or caused by an allergy
  allergies *n* ▷ allergy
allergy *n* (*pl* -gies) extreme sensitivity to a
  substance, which causes the body to react
  to it
alleviate *v* (-tes, -ting, -ted) lessen (pain or
  suffering) > **alleviation** *n* (*pl* -s)
  alleviated *v* ▷ alleviate
  alleviates *v* ▷ alleviate
  alleviating *v* ▷ alleviate
  alleviation *n* ▷ alleviate
  alleviations *n* ▷ alleviate
alley *n* (*pl* -s) narrow street or path
  alleys *n* ▷ alley
alliance *n* (*pl* -s) state of being allied
  alliances *n* ▷ alliance
  allied *v, adj* ▷ ally
  allies *n, v* ▷ ally
alligator *n* (*pl* -s) reptile of the crocodile family,
  found in the southern US and China
  alligators *n* ▷ alligator
alliteration *n* (*pl* -s) use of the same sound at
  the start of words occurring together, e.g.
  moody music > **alliterative** *adj*
  alliterations *n* ▷ alliteration
  alliterative *adj* ▷ alliteration
allocate *v* (-tes, -ting, -ted) assign to someone

or for a particular purpose > **allocation** *n*
  (*pl* -s)
  allocated *v* ▷ allocate
  allocates *v* ▷ allocate
  allocating *v* ▷ allocate
  allocation *n* ▷ allocate
  allocations *n* ▷ allocate
allot *v* (-lots, -lotting, -lotted) assign as a share
  or for a particular purpose
allotment *n* (*pl* -s) distribution
  allotments *n* ▷ allotment
allotrope *n* (*pl* -s) any of two or more physical
  forms in which an element can exist
  allotropes *n* ▷ allotrope
  allots *v* ▷ allot
  allotted *v* ▷ allot
  allotting *v* ▷ allot
allow *v* (-s, -ing, -ed) permit > **allowable** *adj*
  allowable *adj* ▷ allow
allowance *n* (*pl* -s) amount of money given at
  regular intervals
  allowances *n* ▷ allowance
  allowed *v* ▷ allow
  allowing *v* ▷ allow
  allows *v* ▷ allow
alloy *n* (*pl* -s) mixture of two or more metals ▶ *v*
  (-s, -ing, -ed) mix (metals)
  alloyed *v* ▷ alloy
  alloying *v* ▷ alloy
  alloys *n, v* ▷ alloy
allspice *n* (*pl* -s) spice made from the berries of
  a tropical American tree
  allspices *n* ▷ allspice
allude *v* (-des, -ding, -ded) (*foll. by* **to**) refer
  indirectly to
  alluded *v* ▷ allude
  alludes *v* ▷ allude
  alluding *v* ▷ allude
allure *n* (*pl* -s) attractiveness ▶ *v* (-s, -ing, -ed)
  entice or attract > **alluring** *adj*
  allured *v* ▷ allure
  allures *n, v* ▷ allure
  alluring *v, adj* ▷ allure
allusion *n* (*pl* -s) indirect reference > **allusive**
  adj
  allusions *n* ▷ allusion
  allusive *adj* ▷ allusion
  alluvial *adj* ▷ alluvium
alluvium *n* (*pl* -s) fertile soil deposited by
  flowing water > **alluvial** *adj*
  alluviums *n* ▷ alluvium
ally *n* (*pl* -lies) country, person, or group with
  an agreement to support another ▶ *v* (-lies,
  -lying, -lied) > **allied** *adj*
  allying *v* ▷ ally

almanac n (pl -s) yearly calendar with detailed information on phases of the moon, etc.
  almanacs n ▷ almanac
almighty adj having absolute power
almond n (pl -s) edible oval-shaped nut which grows on a small tree
  almonds n ▷ almond
  almondy adj ▷ almond
almoner n (pl -s) (BRIT) formerly, a hospital social worker
  almoners n ▷ almoner
almost adv very nearly
alms [ahmz] pl n (Old-fashioned) gifts to the poor
aloe n (pl -s) plant with fleshy spiny leaves
  aloes n ▷ aloe
aloft adv in the air
alone adj, adv without anyone or anything else
along prep over part or all the length of ▶ adv forward
alongside prep, adv beside (something)
aloof adj distant or haughty in manner
  > **aloofness** n (pl -es)
  aloofness n ▷ aloof
  aloofnesses n ▷ aloof
alopecia [al-loh-pee-sha] n (pl -s) loss of hair
  alopecias n ▷ alopecia
aloud adv in an audible voice
alpaca n (pl -s) Peruvian llama
  alpacas n ▷ alpaca
alpenstock n (pl -s) iron-tipped stick used by climbers
  alpenstocks n ▷ alpenstock
alpha n (pl -s) first letter in the Greek alphabet
alphabet n (pl -s) set of letters used in writing a language
alphabetical adj in the conventional order of the letters of an alphabet > **alphabetically** adv
  alphabetically adv ▷ alphabetical
alphabetize v (-zes, -zing, -zed) put in alphabetical order
  alphabetized v ▷ alphabetize
  alphabetizes v ▷ alphabetize
  alphabetizing v ▷ alphabetize
  alphabets n ▷ alphabet
  alphas n ▷ alpha
alpine adj of high mountains ▶ n (pl -s) mountain plant
  alpines n ▷ alpine
already adv before the present time
alright adj, interj all right
also adv in addition, too
altar n (pl -s) table used for Communion in Christian churches
altarpiece n (pl -s) work of art above and

behind the altar in some Christian churches
  altarpieces n ▷ altarpiece
  altars n ▷ altar
alter v (-s, -ing, -ed) make or become different
  > **alteration** n (pl -s)
  alteration n ▷ alter
  alterations n ▷ alter
altercation n (pl -s) heated argument
  altercations n ▷ altercation
  altered v ▷ alter
  altering v ▷ alter
alternate v (-tes, -ting, -ted) (cause to) occur by turns ▶ adj occurring by turns
  > **alternately** adv > **alternation** n (pl -s)
  alternated v ▷ alternate
  alternately adv ▷ alternate
  alternates v ▷ alternate
  alternating v ▷ alternate
  alternation n ▷ alternate
  alternations n ▷ alternate
alternative n (pl -s) one of two choices ▶ adj able to be done or used instead of something else > **alternatively** adv
  alternatively adv ▷ alternative
  alternatives n ▷ alternative
alternator n (pl -s) electric generator for producing alternating current
  alternators n ▷ alternator
  alters v ▷ alter
although conj despite the fact that
altimeter [al-**tim**-it-er] n (pl -s) instrument that measures altitude
  altimeters n ▷ altimeter
altitude n (pl -s) height above sea level
  altitudes n ▷ altitude
alto n (pl -s) (MUSIC) (singer with) the highest adult male voice
altogether adv entirely
  altos n ▷ alto
altruism n (pl -s) unselfish concern for the welfare of others > **altruist** n (pl -s) > **altruistic** adj > **altruistically** adv
  altruisms n ▷ altruism
  altruist n ▷ altruism
  altruists n ▷ altruism
  altruistic adj ▷ altruism
  altruistically adv ▷ altruism
aluminium n (pl -s) (CHEM) light silvery-white metal that does not rust
  aluminiums n ▷ aluminium
  alumna n ▷ alumnus
  alumnae n ▷ alumnus
  alumni n ▷ alumnus
alumnus [al-**lumm**-nuss] n (pl -ni) [-nie] graduate of a college > **alumna** [al-**lumm**-na]

▶ *n fem* (*pl* **-nae**) [-nee]
always *adv* at all times
alyssum *n* (*pl* **-s**) garden plant with small
yellow or white flowers
  alyssums *n* ▷ alyssum
am *v* ▷ be
amalgam *n* (*pl* **-s**) blend or combination
amalgamate *v* (**-tes, -ting, -ted**) combine or
unite > **amalgamation** *n* (*pl* **-s**)
  amalgamated *v* ▷ amalgamate
  amalgamates *v* ▷ amalgamate
  amalgamating *v* ▷ amalgamate
  amalgamation *n* ▷ amalgamate
  amalgamations *n* ▷ amalgamate
  amalgams *n* ▷ amalgam
amandla [ah-**mand**-lah] *n* (s AFR) political
slogan calling for power to the Black
population
  amandlas *n* ▷ amandla
  amanuenses *v* ▷ amanuensis
amanuensis [am-man-yew-**en**-siss] *n* (*pl* **-ses**)
[-seez] person who writes from dictation
amaranth *n* (*pl* **-s**) imaginary flower that
never fades
  amaranths *n* ▷ amaranth
amaryllis *n* (*pl* **-ses**) lily-like plant with large
red, pink, or white flowers
  amaryllises *n* ▷ amaryllis
amass *v* (**-ses, -sing, -sed**) collect or
accumulate
  amassed *v* ▷ amass
  amasses *v* ▷ amass
  amassing *v* ▷ amass
amateur *n* (*pl* **-s**) person who engages in a
sport or activity as a pastime rather than as
a profession
amateurish *adj* lacking skill > **amateurishly**
adv
  amateurishly *adv* ▷ amateurish
  amateurs *n* ▷ amateur
amatory *adj* relating to love
amaze *v* (**-zes, -zing, -zed**) surprise greatly,
astound > **amazing** *adj* > **amazingly** *adv*
> **amazement** *n* (*pl* **-s**)
  amazed *v* ▷ amaze
  amazement *n* ▷ amaze
  amazements *n* ▷ amaze
  amazes *v* ▷ amaze
  amazing *v, adj* ▷ amaze
  amazingly *adv* ▷ amaze
amazon *n* (*pl* **-s**) strong and powerful woman
> **amazonian** *adj*
  amazonian *adj* ▷ amazon
  amazons *n* ▷ amazon
ambassador *n* (*pl* **-s**) senior diplomat who

represents his or her country in another
country > **ambassadorial** *adj*
  ambassadorial *adj* ▷ ambassador
  ambassadors *n* ▷ ambassador
amber *n* (*pl* **-s**) clear yellowish fossil resin ▶ *adj*
brownish-yellow
ambergris [am-ber-**greece**] *n* (*pl* **-es**) waxy
substance secreted by the sperm whale, used
in making perfumes
  ambergrises *n* ▷ ambergris
  ambers *n* ▷ amber
ambidextrous *adj* able to use both hands with
equal ease
ambience *n* (*pl* **-s**) atmosphere of a place
  ambiences *n* ▷ ambience
ambient *adj* surrounding
  ambiguities *n* ▷ ambiguous
  ambiguity *n* ▷ ambiguous
ambiguous *adj* having more than one possible
meaning > **ambiguously** *adv* > **ambiguity**
n (*pl* **-ties**)
  ambiguously *adv* ▷ ambiguous
ambit *n* (*pl* **-s**) limits or boundary
ambition *n* (*pl* **-s**) desire for success
> **ambitious** *adj* > **ambitiously** *adv*
  ambitions *n* ▷ ambition
  ambitious *adj* ▷ ambition
  ambitiously *adv* ▷ ambition
  ambits *n* ▷ ambit
ambivalence *n* (*pl* **-s**) state of feeling two
conflicting emotions at the same time
> **ambivalent** *adj* > **ambivalently** *adv*
  ambivalences *n* ▷ ambivalence
  ambivalent *adj* ▷ ambivalence
  ambivalently *adv* ▷ ambivalence
amble *v* (**-les, -ling, -led**) walk at a leisurely
pace ▶ *n* (*pl* **-s**) leisurely walk or pace
  ambled *v* ▷ amble
  ambles *v, n* ▷ amble
  ambling *v* ▷ amble
ambrosia *n* (*pl* **-s**) (MYTH) food of the gods
> **ambrosial** *adj*
  ambrosial *adj* ▷ ambrosia
  ambrosias *n* ▷ ambrosia
ambulance *n* (*pl* **-s**) motor vehicle designed to
carry sick or injured people
  ambulances *n* ▷ ambulance
ambush *n* (*pl* **-es**) act of waiting in a concealed
position to make a surprise attack ▶ *v* (**-shes,
-shing, -shed**) attack from a concealed
position
  ambushed *v* ▷ ambush
  ambushes *n, v* ▷ ambush
  ambushing *v* ▷ ambush
ameliorate [am-**meal**-yor-rate] *v* (**-tes,**

-ting, -ted) make (something) better
> **amelioration** n (pl -s)
ameliorated v ▷ ameliorate
ameliorates v ▷ ameliorate
ameliorating v ▷ ameliorate
amelioration n ▷ ameliorate
ameliorations n ▷ ameliorate
amen interj so be it: used at the end of a prayer
amenable adj likely or willing to cooperate
amend v (-s, -ing, -ed) make small changes to correct or improve (something)
> **amendment** n (pl -s)
amended v ▷ amend
amending v ▷ amend
amendment n ▷ amend
amends pl n compensation for ▶ v ▷ amend
amenities n ▷ amenity
amenity n (pl -ties) useful or enjoyable feature
amethyst [am-myth-ist] n (pl -s) bluish-violet variety of quartz used as a gemstone
amethysts n ▷ amethyst
amiabilities n ▷ amiable
amiability n ▷ amiable
amiable adj friendly, pleasant-natured
> **amiably** adv > **amiability** n (pl -ties)
amiably adv ▷ amiable
amicable adj friendly > **amicably** adv
amicably adv ▷ amicable
amid, amidst prep in the middle of, among
amidships adv at or towards the middle of a ship
amidst prep ▷ amid
amiss adv wrongly, badly ▶ adj wrong, faulty
amities n ▷ amity
amity n (pl -ties) friendship
ammeter n (pl -s) instrument for measuring electric current
ammeters n ▷ ammeter
ammonia n (pl -s) strong-smelling alkaline gas containing hydrogen and nitrogen
ammonias n ▷ ammonia
ammonite n (pl -s) fossilized spiral shell of an extinct sea creature
ammonites n ▷ ammonite
ammunition n (pl -s) bullets, bombs, and shells that can be fired from or as a weapon
ammunitions n ▷ ammunition
amnesia n (pl -s) loss of memory > **amnesiac** adj, n (pl -s)
amnesiac adj, n ▷ amnesia
amnesiacs n ▷ amnesia
amnesias n ▷ amnesia
amnesties n ▷ amnesty
amnesty n (pl -ties) general pardon for offences against a government

amniocenteses n ▷ amniocentesis
amniocentesis n (pl -ses) removal of some amniotic fluid to test for possible abnormalities in a fetus
amoeba [am-mee-ba] n (pl -bae, -bas) microscopic single-celled animal able to change its shape
amoebae n ▷ amoeba
amoebas n ▷ amoeba
amok [a-muck, a-mock] adv in a violent frenzy
among, amongst prep in the midst of
amongst prep ▷ among
amoral [aim-mor-ral] adj without moral standards > **amorality** n (pl -ties)
amoralities n ▷ amoral
amorality n ▷ amoral
amorous adj feeling, showing, or relating to sexual love > **amorously** adv
amorously adv ▷ amorous
amorphous adj without distinct shape
amortize v (-zes, -zing, -zed) pay off (a debt) gradually by periodic transfers to a sinking fund
amortized v ▷ amortize
amortizes v ▷ amortize
amortizing v ▷ amortize
amount n (pl -s) extent or quantity ▶ v (-s, -ing, -ed) (foll. by to) be equal to or add up to
amounted v ▷ amount
amounting v ▷ amount
amounts n, v ▷ amount
amour n (pl -s) (secret) love affair
amours n ▷ amour
amp n (pl -s) ampere
ampere [am-pair] n (pl -s) basic unit of electric current
amperes n ▷ ampere
ampersand n (pl -s) the character (&) meaning and
ampersands n ▷ ampersand
amphetamine [am-fet-am-mean] n (pl -s) drug used as a stimulant
amphetamines n ▷ amphetamine
amphibian n (pl -s) animal that lives on land but breeds in water
amphibians n ▷ amphibian
amphibious adj living or operating both on land and in water
amphitheatre n (pl -s) open oval or circular building with tiers of seats rising round an arena
amphitheatres n ▷ amphitheatre
amphora [am-for-ra] n (pl -phorae) two-handled ancient Greek or Roman jar
amphorae n ▷ amphora

ample *adj* (**-r, -st**) more than sufficient > **amply** *adv*
  ampler *adj* ▷ ample
  amplest *adj* ▷ ample
  amplification *n* ▷ amplify
  amplifications *n* ▷ amplify
  amplified *v* ▷ amplify
amplifier *n* (*pl* -s) device used to amplify a current or sound signal
  amplifiers *n* ▷ amplifier
  amplifies *v* ▷ amplify
amplify *v* (**-fies, -fying, -fied**) increase the strength of (a current or sound signal) of > **amplification** *n* (*pl* -s)
  amplifying *v* ▷ amplify
amplitude *n* (*pl* -s) greatness of extent
  amplitudes *n* ▷ amplitude
  amply *adv* ▷ ample
ampoule *n* (*pl* -s) small sealed glass vessel containing liquid for injection
  ampoules *n* ▷ ampoule
  amps *n* ▷ amp
amputate *v* (**-tes, -ting, -ted**) cut off (a limb or part of a limb) for medical reasons > **amputation** *n* (*pl* -s)
  amputated *v* ▷ amputate
  amputates *v* ▷ amputate
  amputating *v* ▷ amputate
  amputation *n* ▷ amputate
  amputations *n* ▷ amputate
  amuck *adv* ▷ amok
amulet *n* (*pl* -s) something carried or worn as a protection against evil
  amulets *n* ▷ amulet
amuse *v* (**-ses, -sing, -sed**) cause to laugh or smile > **amusing** *adj*
  amused *v* ▷ amuse
amusement *n* (*pl* -s) state of being amused
  amusements *n* ▷ amusement
  amuses *v* ▷ amuse
  amusing *v, adj* ▷ amuse
an *adj* form of **a** used before vowels, and sometimes before *h*
anachronism [an-**nak**-kron-iz-zum] *n* (*pl* -s) person or thing placed in the wrong historical period or seeming to belong to another time > **anachronistic** *adj*
  anachronisms *n* ▷ anachronism
  anachronistic *adj* ▷ anachronism
anaconda *n* (*pl* -s) large S American snake which kills by constriction
  anacondas *n* ▷ anaconda
anaemia [an-**neem**-ee-a] *n* (*pl* -s) deficiency in the number of red blood cells
  anaemias *n* ▷ anaemia

anaemic *adj* having anaemia
anaesthesia [an-niss-**theez**-ee-a] *n* (*pl* -s) loss of bodily feeling
  anaesthesias *n* ▷ anaesthesia
anaesthetic [an-niss-**thet**-ik] *n* (*pl* -s), *adj* (substance) causing loss of bodily feeling
  anaesthetics *n* ▷ anaesthetic
anaesthetist [an-**neess**-thet-ist] *n* (*pl* -s) doctor trained to administer anaesthetics > **anaesthetize** *v* (**-zes, -zing, -zed**)
  anaesthetists *n* ▷ anaesthetist
  anaesthetize *v* ▷ anaesthetist
  anaesthetized *v* ▷ anaesthetist
  anaesthetizes *v* ▷ anaesthetist
  anaesthetizing *v* ▷ anaesthetist
anagram *n* (*pl* -s) word or phrase made by rearranging the letters of another word or phrase
  anagrams *n* ▷ anagram
anal [**ain**-al] *adj* of the anus
analgesia *n* (*pl* -s) absence of pain
  analgesias *n* ▷ analgesia
analgesic [an-nal-**jeez**-ik] *n* (*pl* -s) ▶ *adj* (drug) relieving pain
  analgesics *n* ▷ analgesic
  analogical *adj* ▷ analogy
  analogies *n* ▷ analogy
analogous *adj* similar in some respects
analogue *n* (*pl* -s) something that is similar in some respects to something else ▶ *adj* displaying information by means of a dial
  analogues *n* ▷ analogue
analogy *n* (*pl* -gies) similarity in some respects > **analogical** *adj*
analyse *v* (**-ses, -sing, -sed**) make an analysis of (something)
  analysed *v* ▷ analyse
  analyses *v* ▷ analyse ▶ *n* ▷ analysis
  analysing *v* ▷ analyse
analysis *n* (*pl* -ses) separation of a whole into its parts for study and interpretation > **analytical, analytic** *adj* > **analytically** *adv*
analyst *n* (*pl* -s) person skilled in analysis
  analysts *n* ▷ analyst
  analytic *adj* ▷ analysis
  analytical *adj* ▷ analysis
  analytically *adv* ▷ analysis
  anarchic *adj* ▷ anarchy
  anarchies *n* ▷ anarchy
anarchism *n* (*pl* -s) doctrine advocating the abolition of government
  anarchisms *n* ▷ anarchism
anarchist *n* (*pl* -s) person who advocates the abolition of government > **anarchistic** *adj*
  anarchistic *adj* ▷ anarchist

anarchists n ▷ anarchist

anarchy [an-ark-ee] n (pl -ies) lawlessness and disorder > **anarchic** adj

anathema [an-nath-im-a] n (pl -s) detested person or thing

anathemas n ▷ anathema

anatomical adj ▷ anatomy

anatomically adv ▷ anatomy

anatomies n ▷ anatomy

anatomist n (pl -s) expert in anatomy

anatomists n ▷ anatomist

anatomy n (pl -mies) science of the structure of the body > **anatomical** adj > **anatomically** adv

ancestor n (pl -s) person from whom one is descended > **ancestral** adj

ancestors n ▷ ancestor

ancestral adj ▷ ancestor

ancestries n ▷ ancestry

ancestry n (pl -ries) lineage or descent

anchor n (pl -s) heavy hooked device attached to a boat by a cable and dropped overboard to fasten the ship to the sea bottom ▶ v (-s, -ing, -ed) fasten with or as if with an anchor

anchorage n (pl -s) place where boats can be anchored

anchorages n ▷ anchorage

anchored v ▷ anchor

anchoring v ▷ anchor

anchorite n (pl -s) religious recluse

anchorites n ▷ anchorite

anchorman n (pl -men) broadcaster in a central studio who links up and presents items from outside camera units and other studios

anchormen n ▷ anchorman

anchors n, v ▷ anchor

anchorwoman n (pl -women) female broadcaster in a central studio who links up and presents items from outside camera units and other studios

anchorwomen n ▷ anchorwoman

anchovies n ▷ anchovy

anchovy [an-chov-ee] n (pl -vies) small strong-tasting fish

ancient adj dating from very long ago

ancients pl n people who lived very long ago

ancillary adj supporting the main work of an organization

and conj in addition to

andante [an-dan-tay] n (pl -s) ▶ adv (MUSIC) (piece to be played) moderately slowly

andantes n ▷ andante

andiron n (pl -s) iron stand for supporting logs in a fireplace

andirons n ▷ andiron

androgynous adj having both male and female characteristics

android n (pl -s) robot resembling a human

androids n ▷ android

anecdotal adj ▷ anecdote

anecdote n (pl -s) short amusing account of an incident > **anecdotal** adj

anecdotes n ▷ anecdote

anemometer n (pl -s) instrument for recording wind speed

anemometers n ▷ anemometer

anemone [an-nem-on-ee] n (pl -s) plant with white, purple, or red flowers

anemones n ▷ anemone

aneurism n ▷ aneurysm

aneurisms n ▷ aneurysm

aneurysm, aneurism [an-new-riz-zum] n (pl -s) permanent swelling of a blood vessel

aneurysms n ▷ aneurysm

anew adv once more

angel n (pl -s) spiritual being believed to be an attendant or messenger of God > **angelic** adj > **angelically** adv

angelic adj ▷ angel

angelica n (pl -s) aromatic plant

angelically adv ▷ angel

angelicas n ▷ angelica

angels n ▷ angel

angelus [an-jell-uss] n (pl -es) (in the Roman Catholic Church) prayers recited in the morning, at midday, and in the evening

angeluses n ▷ angelus

anger n (pl -s) fierce displeasure or extreme annoyance ▶ v (-s, -ing, -ed) make (someone) angry

angered v ▷ anger

angering v ▷ anger

angers n, v ▷ anger

angina [an-jine-a] n (pl -s) heart disorder causing sudden severe chest pains

anginas n ▷ angina

angle¹ n (pl -s) space between or shape formed by two lines or surfaces that meet ▶ v (-s, -ing, -ed) bend or place (something) at an angle

angle² v (-s, -ing, -ed) fish with a hook and line > **angling** n (pl -s)

angled v ▷ angle¹, ²

angler n (pl -s) person who fishes with a hook and line

anglers n ▷ angler

angles n ▷ angle¹ ▶ v ▷ angle¹, ²

anglicize v (-zes, -zing, -zed) make or become English in outlook, form, etc.

anglicized v ▷ anglicize

anglicizes v ▷ anglicize
anglicizing v ▷ anglicize
angling n ▷ angle² ▶ v ▷¹, ²
anglings n ▷ angle²
angophora n (pl -s) Australian tree related to the eucalyptus
  angophoras n ▷ angophora
angora n (pl -s) variety of goat, cat, or rabbit with long silky hair
  angoras n ▷ angora
  angrier adj ▷ angry
  angriest adj ▷ angry
  angrily adv ▷ angry
angry adj (-grier, -griest) full of anger > **angrily** adv
angst n feeling of anxiety
angstrom n (pl angstroms) unit of length used to measure wavelengths
  angstroms n ▷ angstrom
anguish n (pl -es) great mental pain > **anguished** adj
  anguished adj ▷ anguish
  anguishes n ▷ anguish
angular adj (of a person) lean and bony > **angularity** n (pl -ties)
  angularities n ▷ angular
  angularity n ▷ angular
anhydrous adj (CHEM) containing no water
aniline n (pl -s) colourless oily liquid used for making dyes, plastics, and explosives
  anilines n ▷ aniline
animal n (pl -s) living creature with specialized sense organs and capable of voluntary motion, esp. one other than a human being ▶ adj of animals
  animalian adj ▷ animal
  animals n ▷ animal
animate v (-tes, -ting, -ted) give life to ▶ adj having life > **animated** adj > **animator** n (pl -s)
  animated v, adj ▷ animate
  animates v ▷ animate
  animating v ▷ animate
animation n (pl -s) technique of making cartoon films
  animations n ▷ animation
  animator n ▷ animate
  animators n ▷ animate
animism n (pl -s) belief that natural objects possess souls > **animist** n (pl -s) adj > **animistic** adj
  animisms n ▷ animism
  animist n, adj ▷ animism
  animistic adj ▷ animism
  animists n ▷ animism
  animosities n ▷ animosity

animosity n (pl -ties) hostility, hatred
animus n (pl -es) hatred, animosity
  animuses n ▷ animus
anion [an-eye-on] n (pl -s) ion with negative charge
  anions n ▷ anion
anise [an-niss] n (pl -s) plant with liquorice-flavoured seeds
aniseed n (pl -s) liquorice-flavoured seeds of the anise plant
  aniseeds n ▷ aniseed
  anises n ▷ anise
ankle n (pl -s) joint between the foot and leg
  ankles n ▷ ankle
anklet n (pl -s) ornamental chain worn round the ankle
  anklets n ▷ anklet
annal n (usually plural) yearly record of events
  annals n ▷ annal
anneal v (-s, -ing, -ed) toughen (metal or glass) by heating and slow cooling
  annealed v ▷ anneal
  annealing v ▷ anneal
  anneals v ▷ anneal
annelid n (pl -s) worm with a segmented body, such as an earthworm
  annelids n ▷ annelid
annex v (-es, -ing, -ed) seize (territory) > **annexation** n (pl -s)
  annexation n ▷ annex
  annexations n ▷ annex
annexe n (pl -s) extension to a building
  annexed v ▷ annex
  annexes v ▷ annex ▶ n ▷ annexe
  annexing v ▷ annex
annihilate v (-tes, -ting, -ted) destroy utterly > **annihilation** n (pl -s)
  annihilated v ▷ annihilate
  annihilates v ▷ annihilate
  annihilating v ▷ annihilate
  annihilation n ▷ annihilate
  annihilations n ▷ annihilate
  anniversaries n ▷ anniversary
anniversary n (pl -ries) date on which something occurred in a previous year
annotate v (-tes, -ting, -ted) add notes to (a written work) > **annotation** n (pl -s)
  annotated v ▷ annotate
  annotates v ▷ annotate
  annotating v ▷ annotate
  annotation n ▷ annotate
  annotations n ▷ annotate
announce v (-ces, -cing, -ced) make known publicly > **announcement** n (pl -s)
  announced v ▷ announce

announcement *n* ▷ announce
announcements *n* ▷ announce
announcer *n* (*pl* -s) person who introduces radio or television programmes
announcers *n* ▷ announcer
announces *v* ▷ announce
announcing *v* ▷ announce
annoy *v* (-s, -ing, -ed) irritate or displease
> **annoyance** *n* (*pl* -s)
annoyance *n* ▷ annoy
annoyances *n* ▷ annoy
annoyed *v* ▷ annoy
annoying *v* ▷ annoy
annoys *v* ▷ annoy
annual *adj* happening once a year ▶ *n* (*pl* -s) plant that completes its life cycle in a year
> **annually** *adv*
annually *adv* ▷ annual
annuals *n* ▷ annual
annuities *n* ▷ annuity
annuity *n* (*pl* -ties) fixed sum paid every year
annul *v* (-ls, -lling, -lled) declare (something, esp. a marriage) invalid ▶ **annulment** *n* (*pl* -s)
annular [an-new-lar] *adj* ring-shaped
annulled *v* ▷ annul
annulling *v* ▷ annul
annulment *n* ▷ annul
annulments *n* ▷ annul
annuls *v* ▷ annul
anode *n* (*pl* -s) (ELECTRICITY) positive electrode in a battery, valve, etc.
anodes *n* ▷ anode
anodize *v* (-zes, -zing, -zed) coat (metal) with a protective oxide film by electrolysis
anodized *v* ▷ anodize
anodizes *v* ▷ anodize
anodizing *v* ▷ anodize
anodyne *n* (*pl* -s) something that relieves pain or distress ▶ *adj* relieving pain or distress
anodynes *n* ▷ anodyne
anoint *v* (-s, -ing, -ed) smear with oil as a sign of consecration
anointed *v* ▷ anoint
anointing *v* ▷ anoint
anoints *v* ▷ anoint
anomalies *n* ▷ anomaly
anomalous *adj* ▷ anomaly
anomaly [an-nom-a-lee] *n* (*pl* -lies) something that deviates from the normal, irregularity
> **anomalous** *adj*
anon *adv* (*Obs*) in a short time, soon
anonymity *n* ▷ anonymous
anonymous *adj* by someone whose name is unknown or withheld > **anonymously** *adv*
> **anonymity** *n*

anonymously *adv* ▷ anonymous
anorak *n* (*pl* -s) light waterproof hooded jacket
anoraks *n* ▷ anorak
anorexia *n* (*pl* -s) psychological disorder characterized by fear of becoming fat and refusal to eat > **anorexic** *adj, n*
anorexias *n* ▷ anorexia
anorexic *adj, n* ▷ anorexia
another *adj, pron* one more
answer *n* (*pl* -s) reply to a question, request, letter, etc. ▶ *v* (-s, -ing, -ed) give an answer (to)
answerable *adj* (foll. by **for** or **to**) responsible for or accountable to
answered *v* ▷ answer
answering *v* ▷ answer
answers *n, v* ▷ answer
ant *n* (*pl* -s) small insect living in highly organized colonies
antacid *n* (*pl* -s) substance that counteracts acidity, esp. in the stomach
antacids *n* ▷ antacid
antagonism *n* (*pl* -s) open opposition or hostility
antagonisms *n* ▷ antagonism
antagonist *n* (*pl* -s) opponent or adversary
> **antagonistic** *adj*
antagonistic *adj* ▷ antagonist
antagonists *n* ▷ antagonist
antagonize *v* (-zes, -zing, -zed) arouse hostility in, annoy
antagonized *v* ▷ antagonize
antagonizes *v* ▷ antagonize
antagonizing *v* ▷ antagonize
antarctic *n* area around the South Pole ▶ *adj* of this region
ante *n* (*pl* -s) player's stake in poker ▶ *v* (-tes, -teing, -ted or -teed) place (one's stake) in poker
anteater *n* (*pl* -s) mammal which feeds on ants by means of a long snout
anteaters *n* ▷ anteater
antecedent *n* (*pl* -s) event or circumstance happening or existing before another ▶ *adj* preceding, prior
antecedents *n* ▷ antecedent
anted *v* ▷ ante
antedate *v* (-tes, -ting, -ted) precede in time
antedated *v* ▷ antedate
antedates *v* ▷ antedate
antedating *v* ▷ antedate
antediluvian *adj* of the time before the biblical Flood
anteed *v* ▷ ante
anteing *v* ▷ ante
antelope *n* (*pl* -s) deerlike mammal with long

legs and horns

antelopes n ▷ antelope

antenatal adj during pregnancy, before birth

antenna n (pl -e) insect's feeler; (pl -s) aerial

antennae n ▷ antenna

antennas n ▷ antenna

anterior adj to the front

anteroom n (pl -s) small room leading into a larger one, often used as a waiting room

anterooms n ▷ anteroom

antes n, v ▷ ante

anthem n (pl -s) song of loyalty, esp. to a country

anthems n ▷ anthem

anther n (pl -s) part of a flower's stamen containing pollen

anthers n ▷ anther

anthologies n ▷ anthology

anthologist n ▷ anthology

anthologists n ▷ anthology

anthology n (pl -gies) collection of poems or other literary pieces by various authors > **anthologist** n (pl -s)

anthraces n ▷ anthrax

anthracite n (pl -s) hard coal burning slowly with little smoke or flame but intense heat

anthracites n ▷ anthracite

anthrax n (pl -thraces) dangerous disease of cattle and sheep, communicable to humans

anthropoid adj like a human ▶ n (pl -s) ape, such as a chimpanzee, that resembles a human

anthropoids n ▷ anthropoid

anthropological adj ▷ anthropology

anthropologies n ▷ anthropology

anthropologist n ▷ anthropology

anthropologists n ▷ anthropology

anthropology n (pl -ies) study of human origins, institutions, and beliefs > **anthropological** adj > **anthropologist** n (pl -s)

anthropomorphic adj attributing human form or personality to a god, animal, or object > **anthropomorphism** n (pl -s)

anthropomorphism n ▷ anthropomorphic

anthropomorphisms n ▷ anthropomorphic

antibiotic n (pl -s) chemical substance capable of destroying bacteria ▶ adj of antibiotics

antibiotics n ▷ antibiotic

antibodies n ▷ antibody

antibody n (pl -dies) protein produced in the blood, which destroys bacteria

anticipate v (-tes, -ting, -ted) foresee and act in advance of > **anticipation** n (pl -s) > **anticipatory** adj

anticipated v ▷ anticipate

anticipates v ▷ anticipate

anticipating v ▷ anticipate

anticipation n ▷ anticipate

anticipations n ▷ anticipate

anticipatory adj ▷ anticipate

anticlimax n (pl -es) disappointing conclusion to a series of events

anticlimaxes n ▷ anticlimax

anticlockwise adv, adj in the opposite direction to the rotation of the hands of a clock

antics pl n absurd acts or postures

anticyclone n (pl -s) area of moving air of high pressure in which the winds rotate outwards

anticyclones n ▷ anticyclone

antidote n (pl -s) substance that counteracts a poison

antidotes n ▷ antidote

antifreeze n (pl -s) liquid added to water to lower its freezing point, used esp. in car radiators

antifreezes n ▷ antifreeze

antigen [an-tee-jen] n (pl -s) substance, usu. a toxin, causing the blood to produce antibodies

antigens n ▷ antigen

antihero n (pl -roes) central character in a book, film, etc., who lacks the traditional heroic virtues

antiheroes n ▷ antihero

antihistamine n (pl -s) drug used to treat allergies

antihistamines n ▷ antihistamine

antimacassar n (pl -s) cloth put over a chair-back to prevent soiling

antimacassars n ▷ antimacassar

antimonies n ▷ antimony

antimony n (pl -ies) (CHEM) brittle silvery-white metallic element

antipathetic adj ▷ antipathy

antipathies n ▷ antipathy

antipathy [an-tip-a-thee] n (pl -thies) dislike, hostility > **antipathetic** adj

antiperspirant n (pl -s) substance used to reduce or prevent sweating

antiperspirants n ▷ antiperspirant

antiphon n (pl -s) hymn sung in alternate parts by two groups of singers > **antiphonal** adj

antiphonal adj ▷ antiphon

antiphons n ▷ antiphon

antipodean adj ▷ antipodes

antipodes [an-tip-pod-deez] pl n any two places diametrically opposite one another on the earth's surface > **antipodean** adj

antipyretic *adj* reducing fever ▶ *n* (*pl* -s) drug that reduces fever
antipyretics *n* ▷ antipyretic
antiquarian *adj* of or relating to antiquities or rare books ▶ *n* (*pl* -s) antiquary
antiquarians *n* ▷ antiquarian
antiquaries *n* ▷ antiquary
antiquary *n* (*pl* -ries) student or collector of antiques or ancient works of art
antiquated *adj* out-of-date
antique *n* (*pl* -s) object of an earlier period, valued for its beauty, workmanship, or age ▶ *adj* made in an earlier period
antiques *n* ▷ antique
antiquities *pl n* objects dating from ancient times ▶ *n* ▷ antiquity
antiquity *n* (*pl* -ties) great age
antiracism *n* (*pl* -s) policy of challenging racism and promoting racial tolerance
antiracisms *n* ▷ antiracism
antirrhinum *n* (*pl* -s) two-lipped flower of various colours
antirrhinums *n* ▷ antirrhinum
antiseptic *adj* preventing infection by killing germs ▶ *n* (*pl* -s) antiseptic substance
antiseptics *n* ▷ antiseptic
antisocial *adj* avoiding the company of other people
antistatic *adj* reducing the effects of static electricity
antitheses *n* ▷ antithesis
antithesis [an-tith-iss-iss] *n* (*pl* -ses) [-seez] exact opposite > **antithetical** *adj*
antithetical *adj* ▷ antithesis
antitoxin *n* (*pl* -s) (serum containing) an antibody that acts against a toxin
antitoxins *n* ▷ antitoxin
antitrust *adj* (AUST & S AFR) (of laws) opposing business monopolies
antler *n* (*pl* -s) branched horn of male deer
antlers *n* ▷ antler
antonym *n* (*pl* -s) word that means the opposite of another
antonyms *n* ▷ antonym
ants *n* ▷ ant
anus [ain-uss] *n* (*pl* -es) opening at the end of the alimentary canal, through which faeces are discharged
anuses *n* ▷ anus
anvil *n* (*pl* -s) heavy iron block on which metals are hammered into particular shapes
anvils *n* ▷ anvil
anxieties *n* ▷ anxiety
anxiety *n* (*pl* -ties) state of being anxious
anxious *adj* worried and tense > **anxiously** *adv*

anxiously *adv* ▷ anxious
any *adj*, *pron* one or some, no matter which ▶ *adv* at all > **anything** *pron*
anybody *pron* anyone
anyhow *adv* anyway
anyone *pron* any person
anything *pron* ▷ any
anyway *adv* at any rate, nevertheless
anywhere *adv* in, at, or to any place
aorta [eh-or-ta] *n* (*pl* -s) main artery of the body, carrying oxygen-rich blood from the heart
aortas *n* ▷ aorta
apace *adv* (Lit) swiftly
apalled *v* ▷ appal
apart *adv* to or in pieces
apartheid *n* (*pl* -s) former official government policy of racial segregation in S Africa
apartheids *n* ▷ apartheid
apartment *n* (*pl* -s) room in a building
apartments *n* ▷ apartment
apathetic *adj* ▷ apathy
apathy *n* (*pl* -thies) lack of interest or enthusiasm > **apathetic** *adj*
apethies *n* ▷ apathy
ape *n* (*pl* -s) tailless monkey such as the chimpanzee ▶ *v* (**apes, aping, aped**) imitate
aped *v* ▷ ape
aperient [ap-peer-ee-ent] *adj* having a mild laxative effect ▶ *n* (*pl* -s) mild laxative
aperients *n* ▷ aperient
aperitif [ap-per-rit-teef] *n* (*pl* -s) alcoholic drink taken before a meal
aperitifs *n* ▷ aperitif
apertural *adj* ▷ aperture
aperture *n* (*pl* -s) opening or hole
apertures *n* ▷ aperture
apes *n*, *v* ▷ ape
apex *n* (*pl* -es) highest point
apexes *n* ▷ apex
aphasia *n* disorder of the central nervous system that affects the ability to speak and understand words
aphid [eh-fid], **aphis** [eh-fiss] *n* (*pl* aphids) small insect which sucks the sap from plants
aphids *n* ▷ aphid
aphis *n* ▷ aphid
aphorism *n* (*pl* -s) short clever saying expressing a general truth
aphorisms *n* ▷ aphorism
aphrodisiac [af-roh-diz-zee-ak] *n* (*pl* -s) substance that arouses sexual desire ▶ *adj* arousing sexual desire
aphrodisiacs *n* ▷ aphrodisiac
apiaries *n* ▷ apiary
apiary *n* (*pl* -ries) place where bees are kept

apiculture n (pl -s) breeding and care of bees
  apicultures n ▷ apiculture
apiece adv each
  aping v ▷ ape
aplomb n (pl -s) calm self-possession
  aplombs n ▷ aplomb
apocalypse n (pl -s) end of the world
  > **apocalyptic** adj
  apocalypses n ▷ apocalypse
  apocalyptic adj ▷ apocalypse
apocryphal [ap-**pok**-rif-al] adj (of a story) of
  questionable authenticity
apogee [ap-oh-jee] n (pl -s) point of the moon's
  or a satellite's orbit that is farthest from
  the earth
  apogees n ▷ apogee
apologetic adj showing or expressing regret
  > **apologetically** adv
  apologetically adv ▷ apologetic
apologetics n branch of theology concerned
  with the reasoned defence of Christianity
  apologies n ▷ apology
apologist n (pl -s) person who formally
  defends a cause
  apologists n ▷ apologist
apologize v (-zes, -zing, -zed) make an apology
  apologized v ▷ apologize
  apologizes v ▷ apologize
  apologizing v ▷ apologize
apology n (pl -gies) expression of regret for
  wrongdoing
apoplectic adj of apoplexy
  apoplexies n ▷ apoplexy
apoplexy n (pl -xies) (MED) stroke
  apostasies n ▷ apostasy
apostasy [ap-poss-stass-ee] n (pl -sies)
  abandonment of one's religious faith or other
  belief > **apostate** n (pl -s) adj
  apostate n, adj ▷ apostasy
  apostates n ▷ apostasy
apostle n (pl -s) ardent supporter of a cause or
  movement > **apostolic** adj
  apostles n ▷ apostle
  apostolic adj ▷ apostle
apostrophe [ap-poss-trof-fee] n (pl -s)
  punctuation mark (') showing the omission
  of a letter or letters in a word, e.g. don't, or
  forming the possessive, e.g. Jill's car
  apostrophes n ▷ apostrophe
  apothecaries n ▷ apothecary
apothecary n (pl -ries) (Obs) chemist
  apotheoses n ▷ apotheosis
apotheosis [ap-poth-ee-oh-siss] n (pl -ses)
  [-seez] perfect example
appal v (-s, -lling, -lled) dismay, terrify

appalled v ▷ appal
appalling adj dreadful, terrible ▶ v ▷ appal
  appals v ▷ appal
apparatus n (pl -es) equipment for a particular
  purpose
  apparatuses n ▷ apparatus
apparel n (pl -s) (Old-fashioned) clothing
  apparels n ▷ apparel
apparent adj readily seen, obvious
  > **apparently** adv
  apparently adv ▷ apparent
apparition n (pl -s) ghost or ghostlike figure
  apparitions n ▷ apparition
appeal v (-s, -ing, -ed) make an earnest request
  ▶ n (pl -s) earnest request > **appealing** adj
  appealed v ▷ appeal
  appealing v, adj ▷ appeal
  appeals v, n ▷ appeal
appear v (-s, -ing, -ed) become visible or
  present
  appearance n (pl -s) appearing
  appearances n ▷ appearance
  appeared v ▷ appear
  appearing v ▷ appear
  appears v ▷ appear
appease v (-s, -ing, -ed) pacify (a person)
  by yielding to his or her demands
  > **appeasement** n (pl -s)
  appeased v ▷ appease
  appeasement n ▷ appeal
  appeasements n ▷ appeal
  appeases v ▷ appease
  appeasing v ▷ appease
appellant n (pl -s) person who makes an
  appeal to a higher court
  appellants n ▷ appellant
appellation n (pl -s) (Formal) name, title
  appellations n ▷ appellation
append v (-s, -ing, -ed) join on, add
appendage n (pl -s) thing joined on or added
  appendages n ▷ appendage
  appended v ▷ append
  appendices n ▷ appendix
appendicitis n (pl -es) inflammation of the
  appendix
  appendicitises n ▷ appendicitis
  appending v ▷ append
appendix n (pl -dices, -dixes) separate
  additional material at the end of a book
  appendixes n ▷ appendix
  appends v ▷ append
appertain v (-s, -ing, -ed) (foll. by **to**) belong to
  appertained v ▷ appertain
  appertaining v ▷ appertain
  appertains v ▷ appertain

appetite n (pl -s) desire for food or drink
  appetites n ▷ appetite
appetizer n (pl -s) thing eaten or drunk to
stimulate the appetite > **appetizing** adj
stimulating the appetite
  appetizers n ▷ appetizer
  appetizing adj ▷ appetizer
applaud v (-s, -ing, -ed) show approval of by
clapping one's hands
  applauded v ▷ applaud
  applauding v ▷ applaud
  applauds v ▷ applaud
applause n (pl -s) approval shown by clapping
one's hands
  applauses n ▷ applause
apple n (pl -s) round firm fleshy fruit that
grows on trees
  apples n ▷ apple
appliance n (pl -s) device with a specific
function
  appliances n ▷ appliance
  applicabilities n ▷ applicable
  applicability n ▷ applicable
applicable adj relevant, appropriate
> **applicability** n (pl -ties)
applicant n (pl -s) person who applies for
something
  applicants n ▷ applicant
application n (pl -s) formal request
  applications n ▷ application
applied adj (of a skill, science, etc.) put to
practical use ▶ v ▷ apply
  applies v ▷ apply
appliqué [ap-plee-kay] n (pl -s) kind of
decoration in which one material is cut out
and attached to another
  appliqués n ▷ appliqué
apply v (-plies, -plying, -plied) make a formal
request
  applying v ▷ apply
appoint v (-s, -ing, -ed) assign to a job or
position
  appointed v ▷ appoint
  appointing v ▷ appoint
appointment n (pl -s) arrangement to meet
a person
  appointments n ▷ appointment
  appoints v ▷ appoint
apportion v (-s, -ing, -ed) divide out in shares
  apportioned v ▷ apportion
  apportioning v ▷ apportion
  apportions v ▷ apportion
apposite adj suitable, apt
apposition n (pl -s) grammatical construction
in which two nouns or phrases referring to

the same thing are placed one after another
without a conjunction
  appositions n ▷ apposition
  appraisal n ▷ appraise
  appraisals n ▷ appraise
appraise v (-ses, -sing, -sed) estimate the
value or quality of > **appraisal** n (pl -s)
  appraised v ▷ appraise
  appraises v ▷ appraise
  appraising v ▷ appraise
appreciable adj enough to be noticed
> **appreciably** adv
  appreciably adv ▷ appreciable
appreciate v (-tes, -ting, -ted) value highly
> **appreciation** n (pl -s)
  appreciated v ▷ appreciate
  appreciates v ▷ appreciate
  appreciating v ▷ appreciate
  appreciation n ▷ appreciate
  appreciations n ▷ appreciate
appreciative adj feeling or showing
appreciation
apprehend v (-s, -ing, -ed) arrest and take into
custody
  apprehended v ▷ apprehend
  apprehending v ▷ apprehend
  apprehends v ▷ apprehend
apprehension n (pl -s) dread, anxiety
  apprehensions n ▷ apprehension
apprehensive adj fearful or anxious
apprentice n (pl -s) someone working for a
skilled person for a fixed period in order to
learn his or her trade ▶ v (-ces, -cing, -ced)
take or place (someone) as an apprentice
> **apprenticeship** n (pl -s)
  apprenticed v ▷ apprentice
  apprentices n, v ▷ apprentice
  apprenticing v ▷ apprentice
apprise v (-ses, -sing, -sed) make aware (of)
  apprised v ▷ apprise
  apprises v ▷ apprise
  apprising v ▷ apprise
appro n (pl -s) (BRIT, AUST, NZ & S AFR) (Informal)
on approval
approach v (-ches, -ching, -ched) come near or
nearer (to) ▶ n (pl -es) approaching or means
of approaching > **approachable** adj
  approachable adj ▷ approach
  approached v ▷ approach
  approaches v, n ▷ approach
  approaching v ▷ approach
approbation n (pl -s) approval
  approbations n ▷ approbation
appropriate adj suitable, fitting ▶ v (-tes,
-ting, -ted) take for oneself > **appropriately**

adv ▷ **appropriateness** *n* ▷ **appropriation** *n* (*pl* **-s**)

appropriated *v* ▷ appropriate

appropriately *adv* ▷ appropriate

appropriateness *n* ▷ appropriate

appropriates *v* ▷ appropriate

appropriating *v* ▷ appropriate

appropriation *n* ▷ appropriate

appropriations *n* ▷ appropriate

appros *n* ▷ appro

approval *n* (*pl* **-s**) consent

approvals *n* ▷ approval

approve *v* (**-ves, -ving, -ved**) consider good or right

approved *v* ▷ approve

approves *v* ▷ approve

approving *v* ▷ approve

approximate *adj* almost but not quite exact ▶ *v* (**-tes, -ting, -ted**) (foll. by **to**) come close to > **approximately** *adv* > **approximation** *n* (*pl* **-s**)

approximated *v* ▷ approximate

approximately *adv* ▷ approximate

approximates *v* ▷ approximate

approximating *v* ▷ approximate

approximation *n* ▷ approximate

approximations *n* ▷ approximate

appurtenance *n* (*pl* **-s**) a minor or additional feature

appurtenances *n* ▷ appurtenance

apricot *n* (*pl* **-s**) yellowish-orange juicy fruit like a small peach ▶ *adj* yellowish-orange

apricots *n* ▷ apricot

apron *n* (*pl* **-s**) garment worn over the front of the body to protect the clothes

apronlike *adj* ▷ apron

aprons *n* ▷ apron

apropos [ap-prop-**poh**] *adj, adv* appropriate(ly)

apse *n* (*pl* **-s**) arched or domed recess

apses *n* ▷ apse

apt *adj* having a specified tendency > **aptly** *adv* > **aptness** *n* (*pl* **-es**)

aptitude *n* (*pl* **-s**) natural ability

aptitudes *n* ▷ aptitude

aptly *adv* ▷ apt

aptness *n* ▷ apt

aptnesses *n* ▷ apt

aqualung *n* (*pl* **-s**) mouthpiece attached to air cylinders, worn for underwater swimming

aqualungs *n* ▷ aqualung

aquamarine *n* (*pl* **-s**) greenish-blue gemstone ▶ *adj* greenish-blue

aquamarines *n* ▷ aquamarine

aquaplane *n* (*pl* **-s**) board on which a person stands to be towed by a motorboat ▶ *v* (**-nes, -ning, -ned**) ride on an aquaplane

aquaplaned *v* ▷ aquaplane

aquaplanes *n, v* ▷ aquaplane

aquaplaning *v* ▷ aquaplane

aquaria *n* ▷ aquarium

aquarium *n* (*pl* **-s, -ria**) tank in which fish and other underwater creatures are kept

aquariums *n* ▷ aquarium

aquatic *adj* living in or near water

aquatics *pl n* water sports

aquatint *n* (*pl* **-s**) print like a watercolour, produced by etching copper

aquatints *n* ▷ aquatint

aqueduct *n* (*pl* **-s**) structure carrying water across a valley or river

aqueducts *n* ▷ aqueduct

aqueous *adj* of, like, or containing water

aqueously *adv* ▷ aqueous

aquiline *adj* (of a nose) curved like an eagle's beak

ar *n* (**ars**). Ar is the letter R. This is a good two-letter word to remember because it uses two very common tiles. Ar scores 2 points.

arabesque [ar-ab-**besk**] *n* (*pl* **-s**) ballet position in which one leg is raised behind and the arms are extended

arabesques *n* ▷ arabesque

arable *adj* suitable for growing crops on

arachnid [ar-**rak**-nid] *n* (*pl* **-s**) eight-legged invertebrate, such as a spider, scorpion, tick, or mite

arachnids *n* ▷ arachnid

arbiter *n* (*pl* **-s**) person empowered to judge in a dispute

arbiters *n* ▷ arbiter

arbitrarily *adv* ▷ arbitrary

arbitrary *adj* based on personal choice or chance, rather than reason > **arbitrarily** *adv*

arbitrate *v* ▷ arbitration

arbitrated *v* ▷ arbitration

arbitrates *v* ▷ arbitration

arbitrating *v* ▷ arbitration

arbitration *n* (*pl* **-s**) hearing and settling of a dispute by an impartial referee chosen by both sides > **arbitrate** *v* (**-tes, -ting, -ted**) > **arbitrator** *n* (*pl* **-s**)

arbitrations *n* ▷ arbitration

arbitrator *n* ▷ arbitration

arbitrators *n* ▷ arbitration

arboreal *adj* of or living in trees

arboreta *n* ▷ arboretum

arboretum [ahr-bore-**ee**-tum] *n* (*pl* **-ta**) place where rare trees or shrubs are cultivated

arboriculture *n* (*pl* **-s**) cultivation of trees or shrubs arboricultures n ▷ arboriculture

arbour n (pl -s) glade sheltered by trees
  arbours n ▷ arbour

arc n (pl -s) part of a circle or other curve ▸ v (-s, -ing, -ed) form an arc

arcade n (pl -s) covered passageway lined with shops
  arcades n ▷ arcade

arcane adj mysterious and secret
  arced v ▷ arc

arch¹ n (pl -es) curved structure supporting a bridge or roof ▸ v (-es, -ing, -ed) (cause to) form an arch

arch² adj (-er, -est) superior, knowing > **archly** adv > **archness** n (pl -es)

archaeological adj ▷ archaeology
archaeologies n ▷ archaeology
archaeologist n ▷ archaeology
archaeologists n ▷ archaeology

archaeology n (pl -ies) study of ancient cultures from their physical remains > **archaeological** adj > **archaeologist** n (pl -s)

archaic [ark-kay-ik] adj ancient > **archaism** [ark-kay-iz-zum] ▸ n (pl -s) archaic word or phrase

archaism n ▷ archaic
archaisms n ▷ archaic

archangel [ark-ain-jell] n (pl -s) chief angel
  archangels n ▷ archangel

archbishop n (pl -s) chief bishop
  archbishops n ▷ archbishop

archdeacon n (pl -s) priest ranking just below a bishop
  archdeacons n ▷ archdeacon

archdiocese n (pl -es) diocese of an archbishop
  archdioceses n ▷ archdiocese
  arched v ▷ arch¹

archer n (pl -s) person who shoots with a bow and arrow ▸ adj ▷ arch² > **archery** n (pl -ries)

archeries n ▷ archer
archers n ▷ archer
archery n ▷ archer
arches n, v ▷ arch¹
archest adj ▷ arch²
archetypal adj ▷ archetype

archetype [ark-ee-type] n (pl -s) perfect specimen > **archetypal** adj

archetypes n ▷ archetype
arching v ▷ arch¹

archipelago [ark-ee-**pel**-a-go] n (pl -gos) group of islands
  archipelagos n ▷ archipelago

architect n (pl -s) person qualified to design and supervise the construction of buildings
  architects n ▷ architect

architectural adj ▷ architecture

architecture n (pl -s) style in which a building is designed and built > **architectural** adj

architectures n ▷ architecture

architrave n (pl -s) (ARCHIT) beam that rests on columns
  architraves n ▷ architrave
  archival adj ▷ archive

archive [ark-ive] n (pl -s) (often pl) collection of records or documents > **archival** adj
  archives n ▷ archive

archivist [ark-iv-ist] n (pl -s) person in charge of archives
  archivists n ▷ archivist
  archly adv ▷ arch²
  archness n ▷ arch²
  archnesses n ▷ arch²

archway n (pl -s) passageway under an arch
  archways n ▷ archway
  arcing v ▷ arc
  arcs n, v ▷ arc

arctic n (pl -s) area around the North Pole ▸ adj of this region
  arctics n ▷ arctic

ardent adj passionate > **ardently** adv
  ardently adv ▷ ardent

ardour n (pl -s) passion
  ardours n ▷ ardour

arduous adj hard to accomplish, strenuous > **arduously** adv
  arduously adv ▷ arduous
  are¹ v ▷ be

are² n (pl -s) unit of measure, 100 square metres

area n (pl -s) part or region
  areas n ▷ area

arena n (pl -s) seated enclosure for sports events
  arenas n ▷ arena

areola n (pl -lae, -las) small circular area, such as the coloured ring around the human nipple
  areolae n ▷ areola
  areolas n ▷ areola
  ares n ▷ are²

argon n (pl -s) (CHEM) inert gas found in the air
  argons n ▷ argon

argot [ahr-go] n (pl -s) slang or jargon
  argots n ▷ argot

arguable adj ▷ argue
  arguably adv ▷ argue

argue v (-gues, -guing, -gued) try to prove by giving reasons > **arguable** adj > **arguably** adv
  argued v ▷ argue
  argues v ▷ argue

arguing v ▷ argue

argument n (pl -s) quarrel

argumentation n (pl -s) process of reasoning methodically

argumentations n ▷ argumentation

argumentative adj given to arguing

arguments n ▷ argument

aria [ah-ree-a] n (pl -s) elaborate song for solo voice, esp. one from an opera

arias n ▷ aria

arid adj parched, dry > **aridity** n (pl -ties)

aridities n ▷ arid

aridity n ▷ arid

aright adv rightly

arise v (arises, arising, arose, arisen) come about

arisen v ▷ arise

arises v ▷ arise

arising v ▷ arise

aristocracies n ▷ aristocracy

aristocracy n (pl -cies) highest social class

aristocrat n (pl -s) member of the aristocracy > **aristocratic** adj

aristocratic adj ▷ aristocrat

aristocrats n ▷ aristocrat

arithmetic n (pl -s) calculation by or of numbers ▶ adj of arithmetic > **arithmetical** adj > **arithmetically** adv

arithmetical adj ▷ arithmetic

arithmetically adv ▷ arithmetic

arithmetics n ▷ arithmetic

ark n (pl -s) (OLD TESTAMENT) boat built by Noah, which survived the Flood

arks n ▷ ark

arm[1] n (pl -s) either of the upper limbs from the shoulder to the wrist

arm[2] n (-s, -ing, -ed) supply with weapons

armada n (pl -s) large number of warships

armadas n ▷ armada

armadillo n (pl -s) small S American mammal covered in strong bony plates

armadillos n ▷ armadillo

armament n (pl -s) military weapons

armaments n ▷ armament

armature n (pl -s) revolving structure in an electric motor or generator, wound with coils carrying the current

armatures n ▷ armature

armchair n (pl -s) upholstered chair with side supports for the arms

armchairs n ▷ armchair

armed v ▷ arm[2]

armful n (pl -s) as much as can be held in the arms

armfuls n ▷ armful

armhole n (pl -s) opening in a garment

through which the arm passes

armholes n ▷ armhole

armies n ▷ army

arming v ▷ arm[2]

armistice [arm-miss-stiss] n (pl -s) agreed suspension of fighting

armistices n ▷ armistice

armour n (pl -s) metal clothing formerly worn to protect the body in battle

armourer n (pl -s) maker, repairer, or keeper of arms or armour

armourers n ▷ armourer

armouries n ▷ armoury

armours n ▷ armour

armoury n (pl -ries) place where weapons are stored

armpit n (pl -s) hollow under the arm at the shoulder

armpits n ▷ armpit

arms pl n weapons ▶ n ▷ arm[1] ▶ v ▷ arm[2]

army n (pl -mies) military land forces of a nation

aroma n (pl -s) pleasant smell > **aromatic** adj

aromas n ▷ aroma

aromatherapies n ▷ aromatherapy

aromatherapy n (pl -pies) massage with fragrant oils to relieve tension

aromatic adj ▷ aroma

arose v ▷ arise

around prep, adv on all sides (of)

arouse v (-ses, -sing, -sed) stimulate, make active

aroused v ▷ arouse

arouses v ▷ arouse

arousing v ▷ arouse

arpeggio [arp-pej-ee-oh] n (pl -s) (MUSIC) notes of a chord played or sung in quick succession

arpeggios n ▷ arpeggio

arraign [ar-rain] v (-s, -ing, -ed) bring (a prisoner) before a court to answer a charge > **arraignment** n (pl -s)

arraigned v ▷ arraign

arraigning v ▷ arraign

arraignment n ▷ arraign

arraignments n ▷ arraign

arraigns v ▷ arraign

arrange v (-ges, -ging, -ged) plan > **arrangement** n (pl -s)

arranged v ▷ arrange

arrangement n ▷ arrange

arrangements n ▷ arrange

arranges v ▷ arrange

arranging v ▷ arrange

arrant adj utter, downright

arras n (pl -es) tapestry wall-hanging

arrases n ▷ arras

array n (pl -s) impressive display or collection

(*Poetic*) ▶ v (**-s, -ing, -ed**) arrange in order
arrayed v ▷ array
arraying v ▷ array
arrays n, v ▷ array
arrear n (p -**s**) (usually plural) money owed
arrears n ▷ arrear
arrest v (**-s, -ing, -ed**) take (a person) into
custody ▶ n (pl -**s**) act of taking a person into
custody
arrested v ▷ arrest
arresting adj attracting attention, striking
▶ v ▷ arrest
arrests v, n ▷ arrest
arrival n (pl -**s**) arriving
arrivals n ▷ arrival
arrive v (**-ves, -ving, -ved**) reach a place or
destination
arrived v ▷ arrive
arrives v ▷ arrive
arriving v ▷ arrive
arrogance n ▷ arrogant
arrogances n ▷ arrogant
arrogant adj proud and overbearing
> **arrogantly** adv > **arrogance** n (pl -**s**)
arrogantly adv ▷ arrogant
arrogate v (**-tes, -ting, -ted**) claim or seize
without justification
arrogated v ▷ arrogate
arrogates v ▷ arrogate
arrogating v ▷ arrogate
arrow n (pl -**s**) pointed shaft shot from a bow
arrowhead n (pl -**s**) pointed tip of an arrow
arrowheads n ▷ arrowhead
arrowless adj ▷ arrow
arrowlike adj ▷ arrow
arrowroot n (pl -**s**) nutritious starch obtained
from the root of a W Indian plant
arrowroots n ▷ arrowroot
arrows n ▷ arrow
arsenal n (pl -**s**) place where arms and
ammunition are made or stored
arsenals n ▷ arsenal
arsenic n (pl -**s**) toxic grey element > **arsenical**
adj
arsenical adj ▷ arsenic
arsenics n ▷ arsenic
arson n (pl -**s**) crime of intentionally setting
property on fire > **arsonist** n (pl -**s**)
arsonist n ▷ arson
arsonists n ▷ arson
arsons n ▷ arson
art n (pl -**s**) creation of works of beauty, esp.
paintings or sculpture
artefact n (pl -**s**) something man-made
artefacts n ▷ artefact

arterial adj of an artery
arteries n ▷ artery
artery n (pl -**ries**) one of the tubes carrying
blood from the heart
artful adj cunning, wily > **artfully** adv
> **artfulness** n (pl -**es**)
artfully adv ▷ artful
artfulness n ▷ artful
artfulnesses n ▷ artful
arthritic adj, n ▷ arthritis
arthritics n ▷ arthritis
arthritis n (pl -**es**) painful inflammation of a
joint or joints > **arthritic** adj, n (pl -**s**)
arthritises n ▷ arthritis
arthropod n (pl -**s**) animal, such as an insect,
with jointed limbs and a segmented body
arthropods n ▷ arthropod
artichoke n (pl -**s**) flower head of a thistle-like
plant, cooked as a vegetable
artichokes n ▷ artichoke
article n (pl -**s**) written piece in a magazine or
newspaper
articled adj bound (as an apprentice) by a
written contract
articles n ▷ article
articulate adj able to express oneself clearly
and coherently ▶ v (**-tes, -ting, -ted**) speak or
say clearly and coherently > **articulately** adv
> **articulation** n (pl -**s**)
articulated adj jointed ▶ v ▷ articulate
articulates v ▷ articulate
articulating v ▷ articulate
articulation n ▷ articulate
articulations n ▷ articulate
artier adj ▷ arty
artiest adj ▷ arty
artifice n (pl -**s**) clever trick
artificer [art-**tiff**-iss-er] n (pl -**s**) craftsman
artificers n ▷ artificer
artifices n ▷ artifice
artificial adj man-made, not occurring
naturally > **artificially** adv > **artificiality** n
(pl -**ties**)
artificialities n ▷ artificial
artificiality n ▷ artificial
artificially adv ▷ artificial
artilleries n ▷ artillery
artillery n (pl -**ies**) large-calibre guns
artisan n (pl -**s**) skilled worker, craftsman
artisans n ▷ artisan
artist n (pl -**s**) person who produces works of
art, esp. paintings or sculpture > **artistic** adj
> **artistically** adv
artiste n (pl -**s**) professional entertainer such
as a singer or dancer

artistes *n* ▷ artiste
artistic *adj* ▷ artist
artistically *adv* ▷ artist
artistries *n* ▷ artistry
artistry *n* (*pl* -ries) artistic skill
artists *n* ▷ artist
artless *adj* free from deceit or cunning
> **artlessly** *adv*
artlessly *adv* ▷ artless
arts *n* ▷ art
arty *adj* (-tier, -tiest) (*Informal*) having an affected interest in art
arvie *n* (*pl* -s) (s AFR) (*Informal*) afternoon
arvies *n* ▷ arvie
as *conj* while, when ▶ *adv*, *conj* used to indicate amount or extent in comparisons ▶ *prep* in the role of, being
asafoetida *n* (*pl* -s) strong-smelling plant resin used as a spice in Eastern cookery
asafoetidas *n* ▷ asafoetida
asbestos *n* (*pl* -es) fibrous mineral which does not burn
asbestoses *n* ▷ asbestos, asbestosis
asbestosis *n* (*pl* -ses) lung disease caused by inhalation of asbestos fibre
ascend *v* (-s, -ing, -ed) go or move up
ascendancies *n* ▷ ascendancy
ascendancy *n* (*pl* -cies) condition of being dominant
ascendant *adj* dominant or influential
ascended *v* ▷ ascend
ascending *v* ▷ ascend
ascends *v* ▷ ascend
ascent *n* (*pl* -s) ascending
ascents *n* ▷ ascent
ascertain *v* (-s, -ing, -ed) find out definitely
> **ascertainable** *adj* > **ascertainment** *n* (*pl* -s)
ascertainable *adj* ▷ ascertain
ascertained *v* ▷ ascertain
ascertaining *v* ▷ ascertain
ascertainment *n* ▷ ascertain
ascertainments *n* ▷ ascertain
ascertains *v* ▷ ascertain
ascetic [ass-**set**-tik] *n* (*pl* -s) ▶ *adj* (person) abstaining from worldly pleasures and comforts > **asceticism** *n* (*pl* -s)
asceticism *n* ▷ ascetic
asceticisms *n* ▷ ascetic
ascetics *n* ▷ ascetic
ascribe *v* (-bes, -bing, -bed) attribute, as to a particular origin > **ascription** *n* (*pl* -s)
ascribed *v* ▷ ascribe
ascribes *v* ▷ ascribe
ascribing *v* ▷ ascribe
ascription *n* ▷ ascribe

ascriptions *n* ▷ ascribe
aseptic [eh-**sep**-tik] *adj* free from harmful bacteria
asexual [eh-**sex**-yew-al] *adj* without sex
> **asexually** *adv*
asexually *adv* ▷ asexual
ash[1] *n* (*pl* -es) powdery substance left when something is burnt
ash[2] *n* (*pl* -es) tree with grey bark
ashamed *adj* feeling shame
ashen *adj* pale with shock
ashes *n* ▷ ash[1, 2]
ashlar *n* (*pl* -s) square block of hewn stone used in building
ashlars *n* ▷ ashlar
ashore *adv* towards or on land
ashram *n* (*pl* -s) religious retreat where a Hindu holy man lives
ashrams *n* ▷ ashram
ashtray *n* (*pl* -s) receptacle for tobacco ash and cigarette butts
ashtrays *n* ▷ ashtray
aside *adv* to one side ▶ *n* (*pl* -s) remark not meant to be heard by everyone present
asides *n* ▷ aside
asinine *adj* stupid, idiotic
ask *v* (-s, -ing, -ed) say or write (something) in a form that requires an answer
askance [ass-**kanss**] *adv* with an oblique glance
asked *v* ▷ ask
askew *adv*, *adj* to one side, crooked
asking *v* ▷ ask
asks *v* ▷ ask
aslant *adv*, *prep* at a slant (to), slanting (across)
asleep *adj* sleeping
asp *n* (*pl* -s) small poisonous snake
asparagus *n* (*pl* -es) plant whose shoots are cooked as a vegetable
asparaguses *n* ▷ asparagus
aspect *n* (*pl* -s) feature or element
aspects *n* ▷ aspect
aspen *n* (*pl* -s) kind of poplar tree
aspens *n* ▷ aspen
asperities *n* ▷ asperity
asperity *n* (*pl* -ties) roughness of temper
aspersion *n* (*pl* -s) derogatory remark
aspersions *n* ▷ aspersion
asphalt *n* (*pl* -s) black hard tarlike substance used for road surfaces etc.
asphalts *n* ▷ asphalt
asphodel *n* (*pl* -s) plant with clusters of yellow or white flowers
asphodels *n* ▷ asphodel
asphyxia [ass-**fix**-ee-a] *n* (*pl* -s) suffocation
asphyxiate *v* (-tes, -ting, -ted) suffocate

> **asphyxiation** *n* (*pl* -s)
asphyxiated *v* ▷ asphyxiate
asphyxiates *v* ▷ asphyxiate
asphyxiating *v* ▷ asphyxiate
asphyxiation *n* ▷ asphyxiate
asphyxiations *n* ▷ asphyxiate
aspic *n* (*pl* -s) savoury jelly used to coat meat, eggs, fish, etc.
aspics *n* ▷ aspic
aspidistra *n* (*pl* -s) plant with long tapered leaves
aspidistras *n* ▷ aspidistra
aspirant *n* (*pl* -s) person who aspires
aspirants *n* ▷ aspirant
aspirate (PHONETICS) *v* (-tes, -ting, -ted) pronounce with an *h* sound ▶ *n* (*pl* -s) *h* sound
aspirated *v* ▷ aspirate
aspirates *v*, *n* ▷ aspirate
aspirating *v* ▷ aspirate
aspiration *n* (*pl* -s) strong desire or aim
aspirations *n* ▷ aspiration
aspire *v* (-res, -ring, -red) (*foll. by* **to**) yearn (for), hope (to do or be)
aspired *v* ▷ aspire
aspires *v* ▷ aspire
aspirin *n* (*pl* -s) drug used to relieve pain and fever
aspiring *v* ▷ aspire
aspirins *n* ▷ aspirin
asps *n* ▷ asp
ass *n* (*pl* -es) donkey
assail *v* (-s, -ing, -ed) attack violently
> **assailant** *n* (*pl* -s)
assailant *n* ▷ assail
assailants *n* ▷ assail
assailed *v* ▷ assail
assailing *v* ▷ assail
assails *v* ▷ assail
assassin *n* (*pl* -s) person who murders a prominent person
assassinate *v* (-tes, -ting, -ted) murder (a prominent person) > **assassination** *n* (*pl* -s)
assassinated *v* ▷ assassinate
assassinates *v* ▷ assassinate
assassinating *v* ▷ assassinate
assassination *n* ▷ assassinate
assassinations *n* ▷ assassinate
assassins *n* ▷ assassin
assault *n* (*pl* -ts) violent attack ▶ *v* (-s, -ing, -ed) attack violently
assaulted *v* ▷ assault
assaulting *v* ▷ assault
assaults *n*, *v* ▷ assault
assay *n* (*pl* -s) analysis of a substance, esp. a metal, to ascertain its purity ▶ *v* (-s, -ing, -ed)

assayed *v* ▷ assay
assaying *v* ▷ assay
assays *n*, *v* ▷ assay
assegai [ass-a-guy] *n* (*pl* -s) slender spear used in S Africa
assegais *n* ▷ assegai
assemblage *n* (*pl* -s) collection or group
assemblages *n* ▷ assemblage
assemble *v* (-bles, -bling, -bled) collect or congregate
assembled *v* ▷ assemble
assembles *v* ▷ assemble
assemblies *n* ▷ assembly
assembling *v* ▷ assemble
assembly *n* (*pl* -blies) assembled group
assent *n* (*pl* -s) agreement or consent ▶ *v* (-s, -ing, -ed) agree or consent
assented *v* ▷ assent
assenting *v* ▷ assent
assents *n*, *v* ▷ assent
assert *v* (-s, -ing, -ed) declare forcefully
> **assertion** *n* (*pl* -s) > **assertive** *adj*
> **assertively** *adv*
asserted *v* ▷ assert
asserting *v* ▷ assert
assertion *n* ▷ assert
assertions *n* ▷ assert
assertive *adj* ▷ assert
assertively *adv* ▷ assert
asserts *v* ▷ assert
asses *n* ▷ ass
assess *v* (-es, -ing, -ed) judge the worth or importance of > **assessment** *n* (*pl* -s)
> **assessor** *n* (*pl* -s)
assessed *v* ▷ assess
assesses *v* ▷ assess
assessing *v* ▷ assess
assessment *n* ▷ assess
assessments *n* ▷ assess
assessor *n* ▷ assess
assessors *n* ▷ assess
asset *n* (*pl* -s) valuable or useful person or thing
assets *n* ▷ asset
asseverate *v* (-tes, -ting, -ted) declare solemnly
asseverated *v* ▷ asseverate
asseverates *v* ▷ asseverate
asseverating *v* ▷ asseverate
assiduities *n* ▷ assiduous
assiduity *n* ▷ assiduous
assiduous *adj* hard-working > **assiduously** *adv*
> **assiduity** *n* (*pl* -ties)
assiduously *adv* ▷ assiduous
assign *v* (-s, -ing, -ed) appoint (someone) to a job or task

assignation *n* (*pl* -s) assigning
  assignations *n* ▷ assignation
  assigned *v* ▷ assign
  assigning *v* ▷ assign
assignment *n* (*pl* -s) task assigned
  assignments *n* ▷ assignment
  assigns *v* ▷ assign
  assimilable *adj* ▷ assimilate
assimilate *v* (-tes, -ting, -ted) learn and
  understand (information) > **assimilable** *adj*
  > **assimilation** *n* (*pl* -s)
  assimilated *v* ▷ assimilate
  assimilates *v* ▷ assimilate
  assimilating *v* ▷ assimilate
  assimilation *n* ▷ assimilate
  assimilations *n* ▷ assimilate
assist *v* (-s, -ing, -ed) give help or support
  > **assistance** *n* (*pl* -s)
  assistance *n* ▷ assist
  assistances *n* ▷ assist
assistant *n* (*pl* -s) helper ▶ *adj* junior or deputy
  assistants *n* ▷ assistant
  assisted *v* ▷ assist
  assisting *v* ▷ assist
  assists *v* ▷ assist
assizes *pl n* (BRIT) court sessions formerly held
  in each county of England and Wales
associate *v* (-tes, -ting, -ted) connect in the
  mind ▶ *n* (*pl* -s) partner in business ▶ *adj*
  having partial rights or subordinate status
  associated *v* ▷ associate
  associates *v, n* ▷ associate
  associating *v* ▷ associate
association *n* (*pl* -s) society or club
  associations *n* ▷ association
assonance *n* (*pl* -s) rhyming of vowel sounds
  but not consonants, as in *time* and *light*
  assonances *n* ▷ assonance
assorted *adj* consisting of various types mixed
  together
assortment *n* (*pl* -s) assorted mixture
  assortments *n* ▷ assortment
assuage [ass-**wage**] *v* (-ges, -ging, -ged) relieve
  (pain, grief, thirst, etc.)
  assuaged *v* ▷ assuage
  assuages *v* ▷ assuage
  assuaging *v* ▷ assuage
assume *v* (-mes, -ming, -med) take to be true
  without proof
  assumed *v* ▷ assume
  assumes *v* ▷ assume
  assuming *v* ▷ assume
assumption *n* (*pl* -s) thing assumed
  assumptions *n* ▷ assumption
assurance *n* (*pl* -s) assuring or being assured

  assurances *n* ▷ assurance
assure *v* (-res, -ring, -red) promise or
  guarantee
  assured *adj* confident ▶ *v* ▷ assure
  assuredly *adv* definitely
  assures *v* ▷ assure
  assuring *v* ▷ assure
astatine *n* (*pl* -s) (CHEM) radioactive
  nonmetallic element
  astatines *n* ▷ astatine
aster *n* (*pl* -s) plant with daisy-like flowers
asterisk *n* (*pl* -s) star-shaped symbol (∗) used
  in printing or writing to indicate a footnote
  etc. ▶ *v* (-s, -ing, -ed) mark with an asterisk
  asterisked *v* ▷ asterisk
  asterisking *v* ▷ asterisk
  asterisks *n, v* ▷ asterisk
astern *adv* at or towards the stern of a ship
asteroid *n* (*pl* -s) any of the small planets that
  orbit the sun between Mars and Jupiter
  asteroids *n* ▷ asteroid
  asters *n* ▷ aster
asthma [ass-ma] *n* (*pl* -s) illness causing
  difficulty in breathing > **asthmatic** *adj, n*
  (*pl* -s)
  asthmas *n* ▷ asthma
  asthmatic *adj, n* ▷ asthma
  asthmatics *n* ▷ asthma
astigmatism [eh-**stig**-mat-tiz-zum] *n* (*pl* -s)
  inability of a lens, esp. of the eye, to focus
  properly
  astigmatisms *n* ▷ astigmatism
astir *adj* (Old-fashioned) out of bed
astonish *v* (-es, -ing, -ed) surprise greatly
  > **astonishment** *n* (*pl* -s)
  astonished *v* ▷ astonish
  astonishes *v* ▷ astonish
  astonishing *v* ▷ astonish
  astonishment *n* ▷ astonish
  astonishments *n* ▷ astonish
astound *v* (-s, -ing, -ed) overwhelm with
  amazement > **astounding** *adj*
  astounded *v* ▷ astound
  astounding *v, adj* ▷ astound
  astounds *v* ▷ astound
astrakhan *n* (*pl* -s) dark curly fleece of lambs
  from Astrakhan in Russia
  astrakhans *n* ▷ astrakhan
astral *adj* of stars
astray *adv* off the right path
astride *adv, prep* with a leg on either side (of)
  astringencies *n* ▷ astringent
  astringency *n* ▷ astringent
astringent *adj* causing contraction of body
  tissue ▶ *n* (*pl* -s) astringent substance

> **astringency** n (pl **-cies**)
astringents n ▷astringent
astrolabe n (pl **-s**) instrument formerly used to measure the altitude of stars and planets
astrolabes n ▷astrolabe
astrologer n ▷astrology
astrologers n ▷astrology
astrological adj ▷astrology
astrologies n ▷astrology
astrology n (pl **-gies**) study of the alleged influence of the stars, planets, and moon on human affairs > **astrologer** n (pl **-s**)
> **astrological** adj
astronaut n (pl **-s**) person trained for travelling in space
astronautical adj ▷astronautics
astronautics n science and technology of space flight > **astronautical** adj
astronauts n ▷astronaut
astronomer n ▷astronomy
astronomers n ▷astronomy
astronomical adj very large > **astronomically** adv
astronomically adv ▷astronomical
astronomies n ▷astronomy
astronomy n (pl **-mies**) scientific study of heavenly bodies > **astronomer** n (pl **-s**)
astrophysical adj ▷astrophysics
astrophysicist n ▷astrophysics
astrophysicists n ▷astrophysics
astrophysics n science of the physical and chemical properties of stars, planets, etc.
> **astrophysical** adj > **astrophysicist** n (pl **-s**)
astute adj perceptive or shrewd > **astutely** adv
> **astuteness** n (pl **-es**)
astutely adv ▷astute
astuteness n ▷astute
astutenesses n ▷astute
asunder adv (Obs or poetic) into parts or pieces
asylum n (pl **-s**) refuge or sanctuary
asylums n ▷asylum
asymmetric adj ▷asymmetry
asymmetrical adj ▷asymmetry
asymmetries n ▷asymmetry
asymmetry n (pl **-tries**) lack of symmetry
> **asymmetrical, asymmetric** adj
asymptote [ass-im-tote] n (pl **-s**) straight line closely approached but never met by a curve
asymptotes n ▷asymptote
at prep indicating position in space or time, movement towards an object, etc.
atavism [at-a-viz-zum] n (pl **-s**) recurrence of a trait present in distant ancestors > **atavistic** adj
atavisms n ▷atavism
atavistic adj ▷atavism

ate v ▷eat
atheism [aith-ee-iz-zum] n (pl **-s**) belief that there is no God > **atheist** n (pl **-s**) > **atheistic** adj
atheisms n ▷atheism
atheist n ▷atheism
atheistic adj ▷atheism
atheists n ▷atheism
atherosclerosis n disease in which deposits of fat cause the walls of the arteries to thicken
athlete n (pl **-s**) person trained in or good at athletics
athletes n ▷athlete
athletic adj physically fit or strong
> **athletically** adv > **athleticism** n (pl **-s**)
athletically adv ▷athletic
athleticism n ▷athletic
athleticisms n ▷athletic
athletics pl n track-and-field sports such as running, jumping, throwing, etc.
athwart prep across ▶ adv transversely
atlas n (pl **-es**) book of maps
atlases n ▷atlas
atmosphere n (pl **-s**) mass of gases surrounding a heavenly body, esp. the earth
> **atmospheric** adj
atmospheres n ▷atmosphere
atmospheric adj ▷atmosphere
atmospherics pl n radio interference due to electrical disturbance in the atmosphere
atoll n (pl **-s**) ring-shaped coral reef enclosing a lagoon
atolls n ▷atoll
atom n (pl **-s**) smallest unit of matter which can take part in a chemical reaction
atomic adj of or using atomic bombs or atomic energy
atomize v (**-zes, -zing, -zed**) reduce to atoms or small particles
atomized v ▷atomize
atomizer n (pl **-s**) device for discharging a liquid in a fine spray
atomizers n ▷atomizer
atomizes v ▷atomize
atomizing v ▷atomize
atoms n ▷atom
atonal [eh-tone-al] adj (of music) not written in an established key
atone v (**-nes, -ning, -ned**) make amends (for sin or wrongdoing) > **atonement** n (pl **-s**)
atoned v ▷atone
atonement n ▷atone
atonements n ▷atone
atones v ▷atone
atoning v ▷atone

atop *prep* (*Lit*) on top of
  atria *n* ▷ atrium
atrium *n* (*pl* **atria**) upper chamber of either half of the heart
atrocious *adj* extremely cruel or wicked > **atrociously** *adv*
  atrociously *adv* ▷ atrocious
  atrocities *n* ▷ atrocity
atrocity *n* (*pl* **-ties**) wickedness
  atrophied *v* ▷ atrophy
  atrophies *n, v* ▷ atrophy
atrophy [at-trof-fee] *n* (*pl* **-phies**) wasting away of an organ or part ▶ *v* (**-phies, -phying, -phied**) (cause to) waste away
  atrophying *v* ▷ atrophy
attach *v* (**-es, -ing, -ed**) join, fasten, or connect > **attached** *adj* (foll. by **to**) fond of > **attachment** *n* (*pl* **-s**)
attaché [at-tash-shay] *n* (*pl* **-s**) specialist attached to a diplomatic mission
  attached *v, adj* ▷ attach
  attaches *v* ▷ attach
  attachés *n* ▷ attaché
  attaching *v* ▷ attach
attack *v* (**-s, -ing, -ed**) launch a physical assault (against) ▶ *n* (*pl* **-s**) act of attacking > **attacker** *n* (*pl* **-s**)
  attacked *v* ▷ attack
  attacker *n* ▷ attack
  attackers *n* ▷ attack
  attacking *v* ▷ attack
  attacks *v, n* ▷ attack
attain *v* (**-s, -ing, -ed**) achieve or accomplish (a task or aim) > **attainable** *adj*
  attainable *adj* ▷ attain
  attained *v* ▷ attain
  attaining *v* ▷ attain
attainment *n* (*pl* **-s**) accomplishment
  attainments *n* ▷ attainment
  attains *v* ▷ attain
attar *n* (*pl* **-s**) fragrant oil made from roses
  attars *n* ▷ attar
attempt *v* (**-s, -ing, -ed**) try, make an effort ▶ *n* (*pl* **-s**) effort or endeavour
  attempted *v* ▷ attempt
  attempting *v* ▷ attempt
  attempts *v, n* ▷ attempt
attend *v* (**-s, -ing, -ed**) be present at
attendance *n* (*pl* **-s**) attending
  attendances *n* ▷ attendance
attendant *n* (*pl* **-s**) person who assists, guides, or provides a service ▶ *adj* accompanying
  attendants *n* ▷ attendant
  attended *v* ▷ attend
  attending *v* ▷ attend

  attends *v* ▷ attend
attention *n* (*pl* **-s**) concentrated direction of the mind
  attentions *n* ▷ attention
attentive *adj* giving attention > **attentively** *adv* > **attentiveness** *n* (*pl* **-es**)
  attentively *adv* ▷ attentive
  attentiveness *n* ▷ attentive
  attentivenesses *n* ▷ attentive
attenuated *adj* weakened > **attenuation** *n* (*pl* **-s**)
  attenuation *n* ▷ attenuated
  attenuations *n* ▷ attenuated
attest *v* (**-s, -ing, -ed**) affirm the truth of, be proof of > **attestation** *n* (*pl* **-s**)
  attestation *n* ▷ attest
  attestations *n* ▷ attest
  attested *v* ▷ attest
  attesting *v* ▷ attest
  attests *v* ▷ attest
attic *n* (*pl* **-s**) space or room within the roof of a house
  attics *n* ▷ attic
attire *n* (*pl* **-s**) (*Formal*) fine or formal clothes
attired *adj* dressed in a specified way
  attires *n* ▷ attire
attitude *n* (*pl* **-s**) way of thinking and behaving
  attitudes *n* ▷ attitude
attorney *n* (*pl* **-s**) person legally appointed to act for another (US & S AFR)
  attorneys *n* ▷ attorney
attract *v* (**-s, -ing, -ed**) arouse the interest or admiration of
  attracted *v* ▷ attract
  attracting *v* ▷ attract
attraction *n* (*pl* **-s**) power to attract > **attractive** *adj* > **attractively** *adv* > **attractiveness** *n*
  attractions *n* ▷ attraction
  attractive *adj* ▷ attraction
  attractively *adv* ▷ attraction
  attractiveness *n* ▷ attraction
  attracts *v* ▷ attract
  attributable *adj* ▷ attribute
attribute *v* (**-tes, -ting, -ted**) (*usu.* foll. by **to**) regard as belonging to or produced by ▶ *n* (*pl* **-s**) quality or feature representative of a person or thing > **attributable** *adj* > **attribution** *n* (*pl* **-s**)
  attributed *v* ▷ attribute
  attributes *v, n* ▷ attribute
  attributing *v* ▷ attribute
attributive *adj* (GRAMMAR) (of an adjective) preceding the noun modified
attrition *n* (*pl* **-s**) constant wearing down to weaken or destroy

attritions n ▷ attrition

attune v (-nes, -ning, -ned) adjust or accustom (a person or thing)

attuned v ▷ attune

attunes v ▷ attune

attuning v ▷ attune

atypical [eh-tip-ik-al] adj not typical

aubergine [oh-bur-zheen] n (pl -s) (BRIT) dark purple tropical fruit, cooked as a vegetable

aubergines n ▷ aubergine

aubrietia [aw-bree-sha] n (pl -s) trailing plant with purple flowers

aubrietias n ▷ aubrietia

auburn adj (of hair) reddish-brown

auction n (pl -s) public sale in which articles are sold to the highest bidder ▶ v (-s, -ing, -ed) sell by auction

auctioned v ▷ auction

auctioneer n (pl -s) person who conducts an auction

auctioneers n ▷ auctioneer

auctioning v ▷ auction

auctions n, v ▷ auction

audacious adj recklessly bold or daring > **audaciously** adv > **audacity** n (pl -ties)

audaciously adv ▷ audacious

audacities n ▷ audacious

audacity n ▷ audacious

audibilities n ▷ audible

audibility n ▷ audible

audible adj loud enough to be heard > **audibly** adv > **audibility** n (pl -ties)

audibly adv ▷ audible

audience n (pl -s) group of spectators or listeners

audiences n ▷ audience

audio adj of sound or hearing > **audiovisual** adj (esp. of teaching aids) involving both sight and hearing

audiovisual adj ▷ audio

audit n (pl -s) official examination of business accounts ▶ v (-s, -ing, -ted) examine (business accounts) officially > **auditor** n (pl -s)

audited v ▷ audit

auditing v ▷ audit

audition n (pl -s) test of a performer's ability for a particular role or job ▶ v (-s, -ing, -ed) test or be tested in an audition

auditioned v ▷ audition

auditioning v ▷ audition

auditions n, v ▷ audition

auditor n ▷ audit

auditoria n ▷ auditorium

auditorium n (pl -riums, -ria) area of a concert hall or theatre where the audience sits

auditoriums n ▷ auditorium

auditors n ▷ audit

auditory adj of or relating to hearing

audits n, v ▷ audit

auf n (**aufs**). An auf is an elf-child left in place of a human baby. Auf scores 6 points.

auger n (pl -s) tool for boring holes

augers n ▷ auger

aught pron (Obs) anything whatever

augment v (-s, -ing, -ed) increase or enlarge > **augmentation** n (pl -s)

augmentation n ▷ augment

augmentations n ▷ augment

augmented v ▷ augment

augmenting v ▷ augment

augments v ▷ augment

augur v (-s, -ing, -ed) be a sign of (future events)

augured v ▷ augur

auguries n ▷ augury

auguring v ▷ augur

augurs v ▷ augur

augury n (pl -ries) foretelling of the future

august [aw-gust] adj dignified and imposing

auk n (pl -s) northern sea bird with short wings and black-and-white plumage

auks n ▷ auk

aunt n (pl -s) father's or mother's sister

auntie, aunty n (pl -ties) (Informal) aunt

aunties n ▷ auntie

aunts n ▷ aunt

aunty n ▷ auntie

aura n (pl -s) distinctive air or quality of a person or thing

aural adj of or using the ears or hearing

aurality n ▷ aura

auras n ▷ aura

aureola n ▷ aureole

aureolas n ▷ aureole

aureole, aureola n (pl -s) halo

aureoles n ▷ aureole

auricle n (pl -s) upper chamber of the heart > **auricular** adj

auricles n ▷ auricle

auricular adj ▷ auricle

aurochs n (pl aurochs) recently extinct European wild ox

aurora n (pl -ras, -rae) bands of light sometimes seen in the sky in polar regions

aurorae n ▷ aurora

auroras n ▷ aurora

auscultation n (pl -s) listening to the internal sounds of the body, usu. with a stethoscope, to help with diagnosis

auscultations n ▷ auscultation

auspice [**aw**-spiss] *n* (*pl* **-s**) (usually plural) patronage or guidance
auspices *n* ▷ auspice
auspicious *adj* showing signs of future success, favourable > **auspiciously** *adv*
auspiciously *adv* ▷ auspicious
austere *adj* (**-r, -st**) stern or severe > **austerely** *adv* > **austerity** *n* (*pl* **-ties**)
austerely *adv* ▷ austere
austerer *adj* ▷ austere
austerest *adj* ▷ austere
austerities *n* ▷ austere
austerity *n* ▷ austere
autarchies *n* ▷ autarchy
autarchy [**aw**-tar-kee] *n* (*pl* **-chies**) absolute power or autocracy
autarkies *n* ▷ autarky
autarky [**aw**-tar-kee] *n* (*pl* **-kies**) policy of economic self-sufficiency
authentic *adj* known to be real, genuine > **authentically** *adv* > **authenticity** *n* (*pl* **-ties**)
authentically *adv* ▷ authentic
authenticate *v* (**-tes, -ting, -ted**) establish as genuine > **authentication** *n* (*pl* **-s**)
authenticated *v* ▷ authenticate
authenticates *v* ▷ authenticate
authenticating *n* ▷ authenticate
authentication *n* ▷ authenticate
authentications *n* ▷ authenticate
authenticities *n* ▷ authentic
authenticity *n* ▷ authentic
author *n* (*pl* **-s**) writer of a book etc. > **authorship** *n* (*pl* **-s**)
authoritarian *n* (*pl* **-s**) ▶ *adj* (person) insisting on strict obedience to authority
authoritarians *n* ▷ authoritarian
authoritative *adj* recognized as being reliable > **authoritatively** *adv*
authoritatively *adv* ▷ authoritative
authorities *n* ▷ authority
authority *n* (*pl* **-ties**) power to command or control others
authorization *n* ▷ authorize
authorizations *n* ▷ authorize
authorize *v* (**-zes, -zing, -zed**) give authority to > **authorization** *n* (*pl* **-s**)
authorized *v* ▷ authorize
authorizes *v* ▷ authorize
authorizing *v* ▷ authorize
authors *n* ▷ author
authorship *n* ▷ author
authorships *n* ▷ author
autism *n* (*pl* **-s**) (PSYCHIATRY) disorder, usu. of children, characterized by lack of response to people and limited ability to communicate

autistic *adj*
autisms *n* ▷ autism
autistic *adj* ▷ autism
autobiographical *adj* ▷ autobiography
autobiographically *adv* ▷ autobiography
autobiographies *n* ▷ autobiography
autobiography *n* (*pl* **-phies**) account of a person's life written by that person > **autobiographical** *adj* > **autobiographically** *adv*
autocracies *n* ▷ autocracy
autocracy *n* (*pl* **-cies**) government by an autocrat
autocrat *n* (*pl* **-s**) ruler with absolute authority > **autocratic** *adj* > **autocratically** *adv*
autocratic *adj* ▷ autocrat
autocratically *adv* ▷ autocrat
autocrats *n* ▷ autocrat
autocross *n* (*pl* **-es**) motor-racing over a rough course
autocrosses *n* ▷ autocross
autocue *n* (*pl* autocues) ® electronic television prompting device displaying a speaker's script, unseen by the audience
autocues *n* ▷ autocue
autogiro, autogyro *n* (*pl* **-ros**) self-propelled aircraft resembling a helicopter but with an unpowered rotor
autogiros *n* ▷ autogiro
autograph *n* (*pl* **-s**) handwritten signature of a (famous) person ▶ *v* (**-s, -ing, -ed**) write one's signature on or in
autographed *v* ▷ autograph
autographing *v* ▷ autograph
autographs *n, v* ▷ autograph
autogyro *n* ▷ autogiro
autogyros *n* ▷ autogiro
automat *n* (*pl* **-s**) (US) vending machine
automate *v* (**-tes, -ting, -ted**) make (a manufacturing process) automatic > **automation** *n* (*pl* **-s**)
automated *v* ▷ automate
automates *v* ▷ automate
automatic *adj* (of a device) operating mechanically by itself ▶ *n* (*pl* **-s**) self-loading firearm > **automatically** *adv*
automatically *adv* ▷ automatic
automatics *n* ▷ automatic
automating *v* ▷ automate
automation *n* ▷ automate
automations *n* ▷ automate
automaton *n* (*pl* **-s**) robot
automatons *n* ▷ automaton
automats *n* ▷ automat
automobile *n* (*pl* **-s**) (US) motor car

automobiles *n* ▷ automobile
autonomies *n* ▷ autonomy
autonomous *adj* ▷ autonomy
autonomy *n* (*pl* **-mies**) self-government
> **autonomous** *adj*
autopsies *n* ▷ autopsy
autopsist *n* ▷ autopsy
autopsy *n* (*pl* **-sies**) examination of a corpse to determine the cause of death
autosuggestion *n* (*pl* **-s**) process in which a person unconsciously influences his or her own behaviour or beliefs
autosuggestions *n* ▷ autosuggestion
autumn *n* (*pl* **-s**) season between summer and winter > **autumnal** *adj*
autumnal *adj* ▷ autumn
autumns *n* ▷ autumn
auxiliaries *n* ▷ auxiliary
auxiliary *adj* secondary or supplementary ▶ *n* (*pl* **-ries**) person or thing that supplements or supports
avail *v* (**-s**, **-ing**, **-ed**) be of use or advantage (to) ▶ *n* (*pl* **-s**) use or advantage
availabilities *n* ▷ available
availability *n* ▷ available
available *adj* obtainable or accessible
> **availability** *n* (*pl* **-ties**)
availed *v* ▷ avail
availing *v* ▷ avail
avails *v*, *n* ▷ avail
avalanche *n* (*pl* **-s**) mass of snow or ice falling down a mountain
avalanches *n* ▷ avalanche
avarice [av-a-riss] *n* (*pl* **-s**) greed for wealth
> **avaricious** *adj*
avarices *n* ▷ avarice
avaricious *adj* ▷ avarice
avast *interj* (NAUT) stop
avatar *n* (*pl* **-s**) (HINDUISM) appearance of a god in animal or human form
avatars *n* ▷ avatar
avenge *v* (**-ges**, **-ging**, **-ged**) take revenge in retaliation for (harm done) or on behalf of (a person harmed) > **avenger** *n* (*pl* **-s**)
avenged *v* ▷ avenge
avenger *n* ▷ avenge
avengers *n* ▷ avenge
avenges *v* ▷ avenge
avenging *v* ▷ avenge
avenue *n* (*pl* **-s**) wide street
avenues *n* ▷ avenue
aver [av-vur] *v* (**avers**, **averring**, **averred**) state to be true
average *n* (*pl* **-s**) typical or normal amount or quality ▶ *adj* usual or typical ▶ *v* (**-ges**, **-ging**,

-ged) calculate the average of
averaged *v* ▷ average
averages *n*, *v* ▷ average
averred *v* ▷ aver
averring *v* ▷ aver
avers *v* ▷ aver
averages *n*, *v* ▷ average
averse *adj* (*usu. foll. by* **to**) disinclined or unwilling
aversion *n* (*pl* **-s**) strong dislike
aversions *n* ▷ aversion
avert *v* (**-s**, **-ing**, **-ed**) turn away
averted *v* ▷ avert
averting *v* ▷ avert
averts *v* ▷ avert
aviaries *n* ▷ aviary
aviary *n* (*pl* **-ries**) large enclosure for birds
aviation *n* (*pl* **-s**) art of flying aircraft > **aviator** *n* (*pl* **-s**)
aviations *n* ▷ aviation
aviator *n* ▷ aviation
aviators *n* ▷ aviation
aviatrice *n* ▷ aviation
avid *adj* (**-er**, **-est**) keen or enthusiastic > **avidly** *adv* > **avidity** *n* (*pl* **-ties**)
avider *adj* ▷ avid
avidest *adj* ▷ avid
avidities *n* ▷ avid
avidity *n* ▷ avid
avidly *adv* ▷ avid
avocado *n* (*pl* **-dos**) pear-shaped tropical fruit with a leathery green skin
avocados *n* ▷ avocado
avocation *n* (*pl* **-s**) (*Old-fashioned*) occupation
avocations *n* ▷ avocation
avocet *n* (*pl* **-s**) long-legged wading bird with a long slender upward-curving bill
avocets *n* ▷ avocet
avoid *v* (**-s**, **-ing**, **-ed**) prevent from happening
> **avoidable** *adj* > **avoidance** *n* (*pl* **-s**)
avoidable *adj* ▷ avoid
avoidance *n* ▷ avoid
avoidances *n* ▷ avoid
avoided *v* ▷ avoid
avoiding *v* ▷ avoid
avoids *v* ▷ avoid
avoirdupois [av-er-de-poise] *n* (*pl* **-es**) system of weights based on pounds and ounces
avoirdupoises *n* ▷ avoirdupois
avow *v* (**-s**, **-ing**, **-ed**) state or affirm > **avowal** *n* (*pl* **-s**) > **avowed** *adj* > **avowedly** *adv*
avowal *n* ▷ avow
avowals *n* ▷ avow
avowed *v*, *adj* ▷ avow
avowedly *adv* ▷ avow

avowing v ▷ avow
avows v ▷ avow
avuncular adj (of a man) friendly, helpful, and caring towards someone younger

> **aw** interj. A sound people make when they're feeling sorry for someone. Aw scores 5 points.

await v (-s, -ing, -ed) wait for
  awaited v ▷ await
  awaiting v ▷ await
  awaits v ▷ await
awake v (awakes, awaking, awoke, awoken) emerge or rouse from sleep ▶ adj not sleeping
awaken v (-s, -ing, -ed) awake
  awakened v ▷ awaken
  awakening v ▷ awaken
  awakens v ▷ awaken
  awakes v ▷ awake
  awaking v ▷ awake
award v (-s, -ing, -ed) give (something, such as a prize) formally ▶ n (pl -s) something awarded, such as a prize
  awarded v ▷ award
  awarding v ▷ award
  awards v, n ▷ award
aware adj having knowledge, informed > **awareness** n (pl -es)
  awareness n ▷ aware
  awarenesses n ▷ aware
awash adv washed over by water
away adv from a place ▶ adj not present
awe n (pl -s) wonder and respect mixed with dread ▶ v (awes, awing, awed) fill with awe
  awed v ▷ awe
  awes n, v ▷ awe
awesome adj inspiring awe
awestruck adj filled with awe
awful adj (-ller, -llest) very bad or unpleasant
  awfuller adj ▷ awful
  awfullest adj ▷ awful
awfully adv in an unpleasant way
awhile adv for a brief time
  awing v ▷ awe
awkward adj (-er, -est) clumsy or ungainly > **awkwardly** adv > **awkwardness** n (pl -es)
  awkwarder adj ▷ awkward
  awkwardest adj ▷ awkward
  awkwardly adv ▷ awkward
  awkwardness n ▷ awkward
  awkwardnesses n ▷ awkward
awl n (pl -s) pointed tool for piercing wood, leather, etc.
  awls n ▷ awl
awning n (pl -s) canvas roof supported by a frame to give protection against the weather

awnings n ▷ awning
awoke v ▷ awake
awoken v ▷ awake
awry [a-**rye**] adv, adj with a twist to one side, askew
ax n ▷ axe
axe, ax n (pl axes) tool with a sharp blade for felling trees or chopping wood (Informal) ▶ v (axes, axing, axed) (Informal) dismiss (employees), restrict (expenditure), or terminate (a project)
  axed v ▷ axe
  axes n, v ▷ axe, axis
  axial adj ▷ axis
axil n (pl -s) angle where the stalk of a leaf joins a stem
  axils n ▷ axil
  axing v ▷ axe
axiom n (pl -s) generally accepted principle
axiomatic adj self-evident
  axioms n ▷ axiom
axis n (pl axes) (imaginary) line round which a body can rotate or about which an object or geometrical figure is symmetrical > **axial** adj
axle n (pl -s) shaft on which a wheel or pair of wheels turns
  axles n ▷ axle
axolotl n (pl -s) aquatic salamander of central America
  axolotls n ▷ axolotl
  ay interj ▷ aye
ayatollah n (pl -s) Islamic religious leader in Iran
  ayatollahs n ▷ ayatollah
aye, ay interj yes ▶ n (pl -s) affirmative vote or voter
  ayes n ▷ aye
azalea [az-**zale**-ya] n (pl -s) garden shrub grown for its showy flowers
  azaleas n ▷ azalea
azimuth n (pl -s) arc of the sky between the zenith and the horizon
  azimuths n ▷ azimuth

> **azo** adj. Azo describes a kind of chemical. Azo scores 12 points, and so is a very high-scoring word for only three letters.
> **azulejo (azulejos).** An azulejo is a painted and glazed tile. Azulejo scores 23 points, and if you are lucky enough to have all seven letters needed for it, you'll get the 50-point bonus for using all of your tiles.

azure adj, n (pl -s) (of) the colour of a clear blue sky
  azures n ▷ azure

B b

B forms a two-letter word with every vowel except U – and with Y as well. With a B in your rack, you can play lots of short everyday words that will give you relatively high scores. The best of these is **box** (12 points), but don't forget **bay** (8), **by** (7), **bow** (8), **boy** (8), **buy** (8) and **bye** (8).

ba *n* (**bas**). A ba is the human soul in Egyptian mythology, shown in paintings as a bird with a human head. Ba scores 4 points.

baa *v* (**-s, -ing, -ed**) make the characteristic bleating sound of a sheep ▸ *n* (*pl* **-s**) cry made by a sheep
  baaed *v* ▷ baa
  baaing *v* ▷ baa
  baas *v, n* ▷ baa

babble *v* (**-les, -ling, -led**) talk excitedly or foolishly ▸ *n* (*pl* **-s**) muddled or foolish speech
  babbled *v* ▷ babble
  babbles *v, n* ▷ babble
  babbling *v* ▷ babble

babe *n* (*pl* **-s**) baby

babel *n* (*pl* **-s**) confused mixture of noises or voices
  babels *n* ▷ babel
  babes *n* ▷ babe
  babies *n* ▷ baby

baboon *n* (*pl* **-s**) large monkey with a pointed face and a long tail
  baboons *n* ▷ baboon

baby *n* (*pl* **-bies**) very young child or animal ▸ *adj* comparatively small of its type
  ▸ **babyish** *adj*
  babyish *adj* ▷ baby

babysitter *n* (*pl* **-s**) someone who looks after children when the parents are out
  babysitters *n* ▷ babysitter

baccarat [back-a-rah] *n* (*pl* **-s**) card game involving gambling
  baccarats *n* ▷ baccarat

bacchanalia [back-a-nail-ee-a] *n* (*pl* **-s**) wild drunken party or orgy
  bacchanalias *n* ▷ bacchanalia

bach [batch] (NZ) *n* (*pl* **-es**) small holiday cottage ▸ *v* (**-es, -ing, -ed**) look after oneself when one's spouse is away

bached *v* ▷ bach

bachelor *n* (*pl* **-s**) unmarried man
  bachelors *n* ▷ bachelor
  baches *n, v* ▷ bach
  baching *v* ▷ bach
  bacilli *n* ▷ bacillus

bacillus [bass-ill-luss] *n* (*pl* **-li**) [-lie] rod-shaped bacterium

back *n* (*pl* **-s**) rear part of the human body, from the neck to the pelvis ▸ *v* (**-s, -ing, -ed**) (cause to) move backwards ▸ *adv* at, to, or towards the rear

backbencher *n* (*pl* **-s**) Member of Parliament who does not hold office in the government or opposition
  backbenchers *n* ▷ backbencher

backbiting *n* (*pl* **-s**) spiteful talk about an absent person
  backbitings *n* ▷ backbiting

backbone *n* (*pl* **-s**) spinal column
  backbones *n* ▷ backbone

backchat *n* (*pl* **-s**) (*Informal*) impudent replies
  backchats *n* ▷ backchat

backcloth *n* (*pl* **-s**) painted curtain at the back of a stage set
  backcloths *n* ▷ backcloth

backdate *v* (**-tes, -ting, -ted**) make (a document) effective from a date earlier than its completion
  backdated *v* ▷ backdate
  backdates *v* ▷ backdate
  backdating *v* ▷ backdate

backdrop *n* (*pl* **-s**) painted curtain at the back of a stage set
  backdrops *n* ▷ backdrop
  backed *v* ▷ back

backer *n* (*pl* **-s**) person who gives financial support
  backers *n* ▷ backer

backfire *v* (**-res, -ring, -red**) (of a plan) fail to have the desired effect

backfired v ▷ backfire

backfires v ▷ backfire

backfiring v ▷ backfire

backgammon n (pl -s) game played with counters and dice

backgammons n ▷ backgammon

background n (pl -s) events or circumstances that help to explain something

backgrounds n ▷ background

backhand n (pl -s) (TENNIS ETC.) stroke played with the back of the hand facing the direction of the stroke

backhanded adj ambiguous or implying criticism

backhander n (pl -s) (Slang) bribe

backhanders n ▷ backhander

backhands n ▷ backhand

backing n (pl -s) support ▶ v ▷ back

backings n ▷ backing

backlash n (pl -es) sudden and adverse reaction

backlashes n ▷ backlash

backlog n (pl -s) accumulation of things to be dealt with

backlogs n ▷ backlog

backpack n (pl -s) large pack carried on the back

backpacks n ▷ backpack

backs n, v ▷ back

backside n (pl -s) (Informal) buttocks

backsides n ▷ backside

backslid v ▷ backslide

backslide v (-slides, -sliding, -slid) relapse into former bad habits > **backslider** n (pl -s)

backslider n ▷ backslide

backsliders n ▷ backslide

backslides v ▷ backslide

backsliding v ▷ backslide

backstage adv, adj behind the stage in a theatre

backstroke n (pl -s) swimming stroke performed on the back

backstrokes n ▷ backstroke

backtrack v (-s, -ing, -ed) return by the same route by which one has come

backtracked v ▷ backtrack

backtracking v ▷ backtrack

backtracks v ▷ backtrack

backup n (pl -s) support or reinforcement

backups n ▷ backup

backward adj directed towards the rear > **backwardness** n (pl -es)

backwardness n ▷ backward

backwardnesses n ▷ backwardness

backwards adv towards the rear

backwash n (pl -es) water washed backwards by the motion of a boat

backwashes n ▷ backwash

backwater n (pl -s) isolated or backward place or condition

backwaters n ▷ backwater

backwood n (pl -s) (usually plural) remote sparsely populated area

backwoods n ▷ backwood

bacon n (pl -s) salted or smoked pig meat

bacons n ▷ bacon

bacteria pl n (sing -rium) large group of microorganisms, many of which cause disease > **bacterial** adj

bacterial adj ▷ bacteria

bacteriologist n ▷ bacteriology

bacteriologists n ▷ bacteriology

bacteriology n study of bacteria > **bacteriologist** n (pl -s)

bacterium n ▷ bacteria

bad adj (**worse, worst**) of poor quality > **badly** adv > **badness** n (pl -es)

bade v ▷ bid

badge n (pl -s) emblem worn to show membership, rank, etc.

badger n (pl -s) nocturnal burrowing mammal of Europe, Asia, and N America with a black and white head ▶ v (-s, -ing, -ed) pester or harass

badgered v ▷ badger

badgering v ▷ badger

badgers n, v ▷ badger

badges n ▷ badge

badinage [bad-in-nahzh] n (pl -s) playful and witty conversation

badinages n ▷ badinage

badly adv ▷ bad

badminton n (pl -s) game played with rackets and a shuttlecock, which is hit back and forth over a high net

badmintons n ▷ badminton

badness n ▷ bad

badnesses n ▷ bad

baffle v (-les, -ling, -led) perplex or puzzle ▶ n (pl -s) device to limit or regulate the flow of fluid, light, or sound > **bafflement** n

baffled v ▷ baffle

bafflement n ▷ baffle

baffles v, n ▷ baffle

baffling v ▷ baffle

bag n (pl -s) flexible container with an opening at one end ▶ v (**bags, bagging, bagged**) put into a bag

bagatelle n (pl -s) something of little value

bagatelles *n* ▷ bagatelle

bagel *n* (*pl* -s) hard ring-shaped bread roll

bagels *n* ▷ bagel

baggage *n* (*pl* -s) suitcases packed for a journey

baggages *n* ▷ baggage

bagged *n* ▷ bag

baggier *adj* ▷ baggy

baggiest *adj* ▷ baggy

bagging *n* ▷ bag

baggy *adj* (-gier, -giest) (of clothes) hanging loosely

bagpipes *pl n* musical wind instrument with reed pipes and an inflatable bag

bags *n*, *v* ▷ bag

> **bah** *interj*. Bah is something people say when they are annoyed or disgusted. Bah scores 8 points.

bail[1] *n* (*pl* -s) (LAW) money deposited with a court as security for a person's reappearance in court ▶ *v* (-s, -ing, -ed) pay bail for (a person)

bail[2], **bale** *v* (-s, -ing, -ed) (foll. by out) remove (water) from (a boat) (*Informal*)

bail[3] *n* (*pl* -s) (CRICKET) either of two wooden bars across the tops of the stumps

bailed *v* ▷ bail[1, 2]

bailey *n* (*pl* -s) outermost wall or court of a castle

baileys *n* ▷ bailey

bailiff *n* (*pl* -s) sheriff's officer who serves writs and summonses

bailiffs *n* ▷ bailiff

bailing *v* ▷ bail[1, 2]

bails *n* ▷ bail[1, 3] ▶ *v* ▷ bail[1, 2]

bairn *n* (*pl* -s) (SCOT) child

bairns *n* ▷ bairn

bait *n* (*pl* -s) piece of food on a hook or in a trap to attract fish or animals ▶ *v* (-s, -ing, -ed) put a piece of food on or in (a hook or trap)

baited *v* ▷ bait

baiting *v* ▷ bait

baits *n*, *v* ▷ bait

baize *n* (*pl* -s) woollen fabric used to cover billiard and card tables

baizes *n* ▷ bait

bake *v* (-kes, -king, -ked) cook by dry heat as in an oven

baked *v* ▷ bake

baker *n* (*pl* -s) person whose business is to make or sell bread, cakes, etc.

bakeries *n* ▷ bakery

bakers *n* ▷ baker

bakery *n* (*pl* -eries) place where bread, cakes, etc. are baked or sold

bakes *v* ▷ bake

baking *v* ▷ bake

bakkie *n* (*pl* -s) (S AFR) small truck

bakkies *n* ▷ bakkie

balaclava *n* (*pl* -s) close-fitting woollen hood that covers the ears and neck

balaclavas *n* ▷ balaclava

balalaika *n* (*pl* -s) guitar-like musical instrument with a triangular body

balalaikas *n* ▷ balalaika

balance *n* (*pl* -s) state in which a weight or amount is evenly distributed ▶ *v* (-ces, -cing, -ced) weigh in a balance

balanced *v* ▷ balance

balances *n*, *v* ▷ balance

balancing *v* ▷ balance

balancings *n* ▷ balance

balconies *n* ▷ balcony

balcony *n* (*pl* -nies) platform on the outside of a building with a rail along the outer edge

bald *adj* (-er, -est) having little or no hair on the scalp > **baldness** *n* (*pl* -es)

balder *adj* ▷ bald

balderdash *n* (*pl* -es) stupid talk

balderdashes *n* ▷ balderdash

baldest *adj* ▷ bald

balding *adj* becoming bald

baldness *n* ▷ bald

baldnesses *n* ▷ bald

bale[1] *n* (*pl* -s) large bundle of hay or goods tightly bound together ▶ *v* (-les, -ling, -led) make or put into bales

bale[2] *v* ▷ bail[2]

baled *v* ▷ bail[1, 2]

baleful *adj* vindictive or menacing > **balefully** *adv*

balefully *adv* ▷ baleful

bales *n*, *v* ▷ bale[1, 2]

baling *v* ▷ bale[1, 2]

balk, baulk *v* (-s, -ing, -ed) be reluctant to (do something)

balked *v* ▷ balk

balking *v* ▷ balk

balks *v* ▷ balk

ball[1] *n* (*pl* -s) round or nearly round object, esp. one used in games ▶ *v* (-lls, -lling, -lled) form into a ball

ball[2] *n* (*pl* -s) formal social function for dancing > **ballroom** *n* (*pl* -s)

ballad *n* (*pl* -s) narrative poem or song

ballads *n* ▷ ballad

ballast *n* (*pl* -s) substance used to stabilize a ship when it is not carrying cargo

ballasts *n* ▷ ballast

balled *v* ▷ ball[1]

ballerina n (pl -s) female ballet dancer
  ballerinas n ▷ ballerina
ballet n (pl -s) classical style of expressive dancing based on conventional steps
  ballets n ▷ ballet
  balling v ▷ ball¹
  ballistic adj ▷ ballistics
ballistics n study of the flight of projectiles, such as bullets > **ballistic** adj
balloon n (pl -s) inflatable rubber bag used as a plaything or decoration ▶ v (-s, -ing, -ed) fly in a balloon > **balloonist** n (pl -s)
  ballooned v ▷ balloon
  ballooning v ▷ balloon
  balloonist n ▷ balloon
  balloonists n ▷ balloonist
  balloons n, v ▷ balloon
ballot n (pl -s) method of voting ▶ v (-lots, -loting, -loted) vote or ask for a vote from
  balloted v ▷ ballot
  balloting v ▷ ballot
  ballots n, v ▷ ballot
ballpoint n (pl -s) pen with a tiny ball bearing as a writing point
  ballpoints n ▷ ballpoint
  ballroom n ▷ ball²
  ballrooms n ▷ ball²
  balls n ▷ ball¹, ² v ▷ ball¹
ballyhoo n (pl -s) exaggerated fuss
  ballyhoos n ▷ ballyhoo
balm n (pl -s) aromatic substance used for healing and soothing
  balmier adj ▷ balmy
  balmiest adj ▷ balmy
  balms n ▷ balm
balmy adj (-mier, -miest) (of weather) mild and pleasant
baloney, boloney n (pl -s) (Informal) nonsense
  baloneys n ▷ baloney
balsa [bawl-sa] n (pl -s) very light wood from a tropical American tree
balsam n (pl -s) soothing ointment
  balsams n ▷ balsam
  balsas n ▷ balsa
baluster n (pl -s) set of posts supporting a rail
  balusters n ▷ baluster
balustrade n (pl -s) ornamental rail supported by balusters
  balustrades n ▷ balustrade
bamboo n (pl -s) tall treelike tropical grass with hollow stems
  bamboos n ▷ bamboo
bamboozle v (-zles, -zling, -zled) (Informal) cheat or mislead
  bamboozled v ▷ bamboozle

  bamboozles v ▷ bamboozle
  bamboozling v ▷ bamboozle
ban v (-s, -nning, -nned) prohibit or forbid officially ▶ n (pl -s) official prohibition
banal [ban-nahl] adj (-er, -est) ordinary and unoriginal > **banality** n (pl -ties)
  banaler adj ▷ banal
  banalest adj ▷ banal
  banalities n ▷ banal
  banality n ▷ banal
banana n (pl -s) yellow crescent-shaped fruit
  bananas n ▷ banana
band¹ n (pl -s) group of musicians playing together > **bandsman** n (pl -men)
band² n (pl -s) strip of some material, used to hold objects
bandage n (pl -s) piece of material used to cover a wound or wrap an injured limb ▶ v (-ges, -ging, -ged) cover with a bandage
  bandaged v ▷ bandage
  bandages n, v ▷ bandage
  bandaging v ▷ bandage
  bandana n ▷ bandanna
  bandanas n ▷ bandanna
bandanna, bandana n (pl -s) large brightly coloured handkerchief or neckerchief
  bandannas n ▷ bandanna
bandicoot n (pl -s) ratlike Australian marsupial
  bandicoots n ▷ bandicoot
  bandied v ▷ bandy
  bandier adj ▷ bandy
  bandies v ▷ bandy
  bandiest adj ▷ bandy
bandit n (pl -s) robber, esp. a member of an armed gang > **banditry** n
  banditry n ▷ bandit
  bandits n ▷ bandit
bandolier n (pl -s) shoulder belt for holding cartridges
  bandoliers n ▷ bandolier
  bands n ▷ band¹, ²
  bandsman n ▷ band¹
  bandsmen n ▷ band¹
bandstand n (pl -s) roofed outdoor platform for a band
  bandstands n ▷ bandstand
bandwagon n (pl -s) a party or movement that seems assured of success
  bandwagons n ▷ bandwagon
bandy adj (-dier, -diest) ▶ v (-dies, -dying, -died) exchange (words) in a heated manner
  bandying v ▷ bandy
bane n (pl -s) person or thing that causes misery or distress > **baneful** adj

baneful adj ▷ bane
banes n ▷ bane
bang n (pl -s) short loud explosive noise ▶ v (-s, -ging, -ged) hit or knock, esp. with a loud noise ▶ adv precisely
banged v ▷ bang
banger n (pl -s) (Informal) (BRIT & AUST) old decrepit car
bangers n ▷ banger
banging v ▷ bang
bangle n (pl -s) bracelet worn round the arm or the ankle
bangles n ▷ bangle
bangs n, v ▷ bang
banish v (-es, -ing, -ed) send (someone) into exile > **banishment** n (pl -s)
banished v ▷ banish
banishes v ▷ banish
banishing v ▷ banish
banishment n ▷ banish
banishments n ▷ banish
banisters, bannisters pl n railing supported by posts on a staircase

> **banjax** v (banjaxes, banjaxing, banjaxed). If you banjax something, you wreck or ruin it. This is a great word to remember, with its high-scoring combination of J and X. Look out for chances to form it from either **ban** or **ax**. Banjax scores 22 points.

banjo n (pl -jos, -joes) guitar-like musical instrument with a circular body
banjoes n ▷ banjo
banjos n ▷ banjo
bank¹ n (pl -s) institution offering services such as the safekeeping and lending of money ▶ v (-s, -ing, -ed) deposit (cash or cheques) in a bank > **banking** n
bank² n (pl -s) raised mass, esp. of earth ▶ v (-s, -ing, -ed) form into a bank
bank³ n (pl -s) arrangement of switches, keys, oars, etc. in a row or tiers
banked v ▷ bank¹, ²
banker n (pl -s) manager or owner of a bank
bankers n ▷ banker
banking v ▷ bank¹, ², ³ ▶ n ▷ bank¹
banknote n (pl -s) piece of paper money
banknotes n ▷ banknote
bankrupt n (pl -s) person declared by a court to be unable to pay his or her debts ▶ adj financially ruined ▶ v (-s, -ing, -ed) make bankrupt > **bankruptcy** n (pl -cies)
bankruptcies n ▷ bankrupt
bankruptcy n ▷ bankrupt
bankrupted v ▷ bankrupt

bankrupting v ▷ bankrupt
bankrupts n, v ▷ bankrupt
banks n ▷ bank¹, ², ³ ▶ v ▷ bank¹, ²
banksia n (pl -s) Australian evergreen tree or shrub
banksias n ▷ banksia
banned v ▷ ban
banner n (pl -s) long strip of cloth displaying a slogan, advertisement, etc.
banners n ▷ banner
banning v ▷ ban
bannisters pl n ▷ banisters
banns pl n public declaration, esp. in a church, of an intended marriage
banquet n (pl -s) elaborate formal dinner
banquets n ▷ banquet
bans v, n ▷ ban
banshee n (pl -s) (in Irish folklore) female spirit whose wailing warns of a coming death
banshees n ▷ banshee
bantam n (pl -s) small breed of chicken
bantams n ▷ bantam
bantamweight n (pl -s) boxer weighing up to 118lb (professional) or 54kg (amateur)
bantamweights n ▷ bantamweight
banter v (-s, -ing, -ed) tease jokingly ▶ n (pl -s) teasing or joking conversation
bantered v ▷ banter
bantering v ▷ banter
banters v, n ▷ banter
baobab [bay-oh-bab] n (pl -s) African tree with a thick trunk and angular branches
baobabs n ▷ baobab
baptism n (pl -s) Christian religious ceremony in which a person is immersed in or sprinkled with water as a sign of being cleansed from sin and accepted into the Church > **baptismal** adj
baptismal adj ▷ baptism
baptisms n ▷ baptism
baptist n (pl -s) member of a Protestant denomination that believes in adult baptism by immersion
baptists n ▷ baptist
baptize v (-zes, -zing, -zed) perform baptism on
baptized v ▷ baptize
baptizes v ▷ baptize
baptizing v ▷ baptize
bar¹ n (pl -s) rigid length of metal, wood, etc. ▶ v (bars, barring, barred) secure with a bar > **barman** (pl -men), **barmaid** (pl -s) ▶ n
bar² n (pl -s) unit of atmospheric pressure
barb n (pl -s) cutting remark > **barbed** adj
barbarian n (pl -s) member of a primitive or

uncivilized people

barbarians *n* ▷ barbarian

barbaric *adj* cruel or brutal

barbarism *n* (*pl* -s) condition of being backward or ignorant

barbarisms *n* ▷ barbarism

barbarities *n* ▷ barbarity

barbarity *n* (*pl* -ties) state of being barbaric or barbarous

barbarous *adj* uncivilized

barbecue *n* (*pl* -s) grill on which food is cooked over hot charcoal, usu. outdoors ▶ *v* (-cues, -cuing, -cued) cook (food) on a barbecue

barbecued *v* ▷ barbecue

barbecues *n, v* ▷ barbecue

barbecuing *v* ▷ barbecue

barbed *adj* ▷ barb

barber *n* (*pl* -s) person who cuts men's hair and shaves beards

barbers *n* ▷ barber

barbiturate *n* (*pl* -s) drug used as a sedative

barbiturates *n* ▷ barbiturate

barbs *n* ▷ barb

bard *n* (*pl* -s) (*Lit*) poet

bards *n* ▷ bard

bare *adj* (-r, -st) unclothed, naked ▶ *v* (-res, -ring, -red) uncover > **bareness** *n* (*pl* -es)

bareback *adj, adv* (of horse-riding) without a saddle

bared *v* ▷ bare

barefaced *adj* shameless or obvious

barely *adv* only just

bareness *n* ▷ bare

barenesses *n* ▷ bare

barer *adj* ▷ bare

bares *v* ▷ bare

barest *adj* ▷ bare

bargain *n* (*pl* -s) agreement establishing what each party will give, receive, or perform in a transaction ▶ *v* (-s, -ing, -ed) negotiate the terms of an agreement

bargained *v* ▷ bargain

bargaining *v* ▷ bargain

bargains *n, v* ▷ bargain

barge *n* (*pl* -s) flat-bottomed boat used to transport freight ▶ *v* (-ges, -ging, -ged) (*Informal*) push violently

barged *v* ▷ barge

barges *n, v* ▷ barge

barging *v* ▷ barge

baring *v* ▷ bare

barista [bar-ee-sta] *n* (*pl* -s) person who makes and sells coffee in a coffee bar

baristas *n* ▷ barista

baritone *n* (*pl* -s) (singer with) the second

lowest adult male voice

baritones *n* ▷ baritone

barium *n* (*pl* -s) (CHEM) soft white metallic element

bariums *n* ▷ barium

bark¹ *n* (*pl* -s) loud harsh cry of a dog ▶ *v* (-s, -ing, -ed) (of a dog) make its typical cry

bark² *n* (*pl* -s) tough outer layer of a tree

barked *v* ▷ bark¹

barking *v* ▷ bark¹

barks *n, v* ▷ bark¹ ▶ *n* ▷ bark²

barley *n* (*pl* -s) tall grasslike plant cultivated for grain

barleys *n* ▷ barley

barmaid *n* ▷ bar¹

barmaids *n* ▷ bar¹

barman *n* ▷ bar¹

barmen *n* ▷ bar¹

barmier *adj* ▷ barmy

barmiest *adj* ▷ barmy

barmy *adj* (-mier, -miest) (*Slang*) insane

barn *n* (*pl* -s) large building on a farm used for storing grain

barnacle *n* (*pl* -s) shellfish that lives attached to rocks, ship bottoms, etc.

barnacles *n* ▷ barnacle

barney *n* (*pl* -s) (*Informal*) noisy fight or argument

barneys *n* ▷ barney

barns *n* ▷ barn

barometer *n* (*pl* -s) instrument for measuring atmospheric pressure > **barometric** *adj*

barometers *n* ▷ barometer

barometric *adj* ▷ barometer

baron *n* (*pl* -s) member of the lowest rank of nobility > **baroness** *n* (*pl* -es) > **baronial** *adj*

baroness *n* ▷ baron

baronesses *n* ▷ baron

baronet *n* (*pl* baronets) commoner who holds the lowest hereditary British title

baronets *n* ▷ baronet

baronial *adj* ▷ baron

barons *n* ▷ baron

baroque [bar-rock] *n* (*pl* -s) highly ornate style of art, architecture, or music from the late 16th to the early 18th century ▶ *adj* ornate in style

baroques *n* ▷ baroque

barque [bark] *n* (*pl* -s) sailing ship, esp. one with three masts

barques *n* ▷ barque

barra *n* (*pl* -s) (AUST) (*Informal*) ▷ barramundi

barrack *v* (-s, -ing, -ed) criticize loudly or shout against (a team or speaker)

barracked *v* ▷ barrack

barracking v ▷ barrack
barracks v ▷ barrack ▶ pl n building used to accommodate military personnel
barracouta n (pl -s) large Pacific fish with a protruding lower jaw and strong teeth
  barracoutas n ▷ barracouta
barracuda n (pl barracuda) tropical sea fish
barrage [bar-rahzh] n (pl -s) continuous delivery of questions, complaints, etc.
  barrages n ▷ barrage
barramundi n (pl -s) edible Australian fish
  barramundis n ▷ barramundi
  barras n ▷ barra
  barred v ▷ bar¹
barrel n (pl -s) cylindrical container with rounded sides and flat ends
  barrels n ▷ barrel
barren adj (-er, -est) (of a woman or female animal) incapable of producing offspring
  > **barrenness** n (pl -es)
  barrener adj ▷ barren
  barrenest adj ▷ barren
  barrenness n ▷ barren
  barrennesses n ▷ barren
barricade n (pl -s) barrier, esp. one erected hastily for defence ▶ v (-des, -ding, -ded) erect a barricade across (an entrance)
  barricaded v ▷ barricade
  barricades n, v ▷ barricade
  barricading v ▷ barricade
barrier n (pl -s) anything that prevents access, progress, or union
  barriers n ▷ barrier
  barring v ▷ bar¹ ▶ prep except for
barrister n (pl -s) (BRIT, AUST & NZ) lawyer qualified to plead in a higher court
  barristers n ▷ barrister
barrow¹ n (pl -s) wheelbarrow
barrow² n (pl -s) mound of earth over a prehistoric tomb
  barrows n ▷ barrow¹, ²
  bars n ▷ bar¹, ² ▶ v ▷ bar¹
barter v (-s, -ing, -ed) trade (goods) in exchange for other goods ▶ n (pl -s) trade by the exchange of goods
  bartered v ▷ barter
  bartering v ▷ barter
  barters v, n ▷ barter
basalt [bass-awlt] n (pl -s) dark volcanic rock
  > **basaltic** adj
  basaltic adj ▷ basalt
  basalts n ▷ basalt
base¹ n (pl -s) bottom or supporting part of anything ▶ v (bases, basing, based) (foll. by on or upon) use as a basis (for) > **baseless** adj

base² adj (-r, -st) dishonourable or immoral
  > **baseness** n
baseball n (pl -s) team game in which runs are scored by hitting a ball with a bat then running round four bases
  baseballs n ▷ baseball
  based v ▷ base¹
  baseless adj ▷ base¹
basement n (pl -s) partly or wholly underground storey of a building
  basements n ▷ basement
  baseness n ▷ base²
  baser adj ▷ base²
  bases n ▷ base¹, basis ▶ v ▷ base¹
  basest adj ▷ base²
bash (Informal) v (-es, -ing, -ed) hit violently or forcefully ▶ n (pl bashes) heavy blow
  bashed v ▷ bash
  bashes v, n ▷ bash
bashful adj shy or modest > **bashfully** adv
  > **bashfulness** n
  bashfully adv ▷ bash
  bashfulness n ▷ bash
  bashing v ▷ bash
basic adj of or forming a base or basis
  > **basically** adv
  basically adv ▷ basic
basics pl n fundamental principles, facts, etc.
basil n (pl -s) aromatic herb used in cooking
basilica n (pl -s) rectangular church with a rounded end and two aisles
  basilicas n ▷ basilica
basilisk n (pl -s) legendary serpent said to kill by its breath or glance
  basilisks n ▷ basilisk
  basils n ▷ basil
basin n (pl -s) round open container
  basing v ▷ base¹
  basins n ▷ basin
basis n (pl -ses) fundamental principles etc. from which something is started or developed
bask v (-s, -ing, -ed) lie in or be exposed to something, esp. pleasant warmth
  basked v ▷ bask
basket n (pl -s) container made of interwoven strips of wood or cane > **basketry** n (pl -s)
basketball n (pl -s) team game in which points are scored by throwing the ball through a high horizontal hoop
  basketballs n ▷ basketball
  baskets n ▷ basket
  basketwork n ▷ basket
  basketworks n ▷ basket
  basking v ▷ bask

basks v ▷ bask

bass¹ [base] n (pl -es) (singer with) the lowest adult male voice ▶ adj of the lowest range of musical notes

bass² n (pl bass) edible sea fish

basses n ▷ bass¹

bassoon n (pl -s) low-pitched woodwind instrument

bassoons n ▷ bassoon

bastard n (pl -s) (Offens) obnoxious or despicable person

bastards n ▷ bastard

baste¹ v (bastes, basting, basted) moisten (meat) during cooking with hot fat

baste² v (bastes, basting, basted) sew with loose temporary stitches

basted v ▷ baste¹, ²

bastes v ▷ baste¹, ²

basting v ▷ baste¹, ²

bastion n (pl -s) projecting part of a fortification

bastions n ▷ bastion

bat¹ n (pl -s) any of various types of club used to hit the ball in certain sports ▶ v (bats, batting, batted) strike with or as if with a bat

bat² n (pl -s) nocturnal mouselike flying animal

batch n (pl -es) group of people or things dealt with at the same time

batches n ▷ batch

bath n (pl -s) large container in which to wash the body ▶ pl public swimming pool ▶ v (-s, -ing, -ed) wash in a bath

bathe v (-thes, -thing, -thed) swim in open water for pleasure > **bather** n (pl -s)

bathed v ▷ bath ▷ bathe

bather n ▷ bathe

bathers n ▷ bathe

bathes v ▷ bath ▷ bathe

bathing v ▷ bath ▷ bathe

bathos [bay-thoss] n (pl -es) sudden ludicrous change in speech or writing from a serious subject to a trivial one

bathoses n ▷ bathos

bathroom n (pl -s) room with a bath, sink, and usu. a toilet

bathrooms n ▷ bathe

baths n, v ▷ bath

batik [bat-teek] n (pl -s) process of printing fabric using wax to cover areas not to be dyed

batiks n ▷ batik

batman n (pl -men) officer's servant in the armed forces

batmen n ▷ batman

baton n (pl -s) thin stick used by the conductor of an orchestra

batons n ▷ baton

bats n ▷ bat¹, ² ▶ v ▷ bat¹

batsman n (pl -men) (CRICKET) person who bats or specializes in batting

batsmen n ▷ batsman

battalion n (pl -s) army unit consisting of three or more companies

battalions n ▷ battalion

batted v ▷ bat¹

batten n (pl -s) strip of wood fixed to something, esp. to hold it in place

battens n ▷ batten

batter¹ v (-s, -ing, -ed) hit repeatedly

batter² n (pl -s) mixture of flour, eggs, and milk, used in cooking

battered v ▷ batter¹

batteries n ▷ battery

battering v ▷ batter¹

batters v, n ▷ batter¹, ²

battery n (pl -teries) device that produces electricity in a torch, radio, etc. ▶ adj kept in series of cages for intensive rearing

battier adj ▷ batty

battiest adj ▷ batty

batting adj ▷ bat¹

battle n (pl -s) fight between large armed forces ▶ v (battles, battling, battled) struggle

battled v ▷ battle

battlement n (pl -s) wall with gaps along the top for firing through

battlements n ▷ battlement

battles n, v ▷ battle

battleship n (pl -s) large heavily armoured warship

battleships n ▷ battleship

battling v ▷ battle

batty adj (-tier, -tiest) (Slang) eccentric or crazy

bauble n (pl -s) trinket of little value

baubles n ▷ bauble

bauera n (pl -s) small evergreen Australian shrub

baueras n ▷ bauera

baulk v (-s, -ing, -ed) ▷ balk

baulked v ▷ baulk

baulking v ▷ baulk

baulks v ▷ baulk

bauxite n (pl -s) claylike substance that is the chief source of aluminium

bauxites n ▷ bauxite

bawdier adj ▷ bawdy

bawdiest adj ▷ bawdy

bawdy adj (-ier, -iest) (of writing etc.) containing humorous references to sex

bawl v (-s, -ing, -ed) shout or weep noisily

bawled v ▷ bawl

bawling v ▷ bawl

bawls v ▷ bawl

bay¹ n (pl -s) stretch of coastline that curves inwards

bay² n (pl -s) recess in a wall

bay³ v (-s, -ing, -ed) howl in deep prolonged tones

bay⁴ n (pl -s) Mediterranean laurel tree

bay⁵ adj, n (pl -s) reddish-brown (horse)

bayed v ▷ bay³

baying v ▷ bay³

bayonet n (pl -s) sharp blade that can be fixed to the end of a rifle ▶ v (-nets, -neting, -neted) stab with a bayonet

bayoneted v ▷ bayonet

bayoneting v ▷ bayonet

bayonets n, v ▷ bayonet

bays n ▷ bay¹, ², ⁴, ⁵ ▶ v³

bazaar n (pl -s) sale in aid of charity

bazaars n ▷ bazaar

bazooka n (pl -s) portable rocket launcher that fires an armour-piercing projectile

bazookas n ▷ bazooka

be v (present sing (1st person **am**) (2nd person **are**) (3rd person **is**) (present pl **are**) (past sing (1st person **was**) (2nd person **were**) (3rd person **was**) (past pl **were**) (present participle **being**) (past participle **been**) exist or live

beach n (pl -es) area of sand or pebbles on a shore ▶ v (-es, -ing, -ed) run or haul (a boat) onto a beach

beached v ▷ beach

beaches n, v ▷ beach

beachhead n (pl -s) beach captured by an attacking army on which troops can be landed

beachheads v ▷ beachhead

beaching v ▷ beach

beacon n (pl -s) fire or light on a hill or tower, used as a warning

beacons n ▷ beacon

bead n (pl -s) small piece of plastic, wood, etc., pierced for threading on a string to form a necklace etc. ▷ **beaded** adj

beaded n ▷ bead

beadier adj ▷ beady

beadiest adj ▷ beady

beadinesses n ▷ beady

beading n strip of moulding used for edging furniture

beads n ▷ bead

beady adj (-ier, -iest) small, round, and glittering

beagle n (pl -s) small hound with short legs and drooping ears

beagles n ▷ beagle

beak¹ n (pl -s) projecting horny jaws of a bird ▷ **beaky** adj (-ier, -iest)

beak² n (pl -s) (BRIT, AUST & NZ) (Slang) judge, magistrate, or headmaster

beaker n (pl -s) large drinking cup

beakers n ▷ beaker

beakier adj ▷ beak¹

beakiest adj ▷ beak¹

beaks n ▷ beak¹, ²

beaky adj ▷ beak¹

beam n (pl -s) broad smile ▶ v (-s, -ing, -ed) smile broadly

beamed v ▷ beam

beaming v ▷ beam

beams n, v ▷ beam

bean n (pl -s) seed or pod of various plants, eaten or used to make coffee etc.

beanie n (pl -s) close-fitting woollen hat

beanies n ▷ beanie

beans n ▷ bean

bear¹ v (bears, bearing, bore, borne) support or hold up (passive **born**) ▷ **bearable** adj

bear² n (pl -s) large heavy mammal with a shaggy coat

bearable adj ▷ bear¹

beard n (pl -s) hair growing on the lower parts of a man's face ▷ **bearded** adj

bearded adj ▷ beard

beards n ▷ beard

bearer n (pl -s) person who carries, presents, or upholds something

bearers n ▷ bearer

bearing n (pl -s) relevance (to) ▶ pl sense of one's own relative position ▶ v ▷ bear¹

bearings n ▷ bearing

bears v ▷ bear¹ ▶ n ▷ bear²

bearskin n (pl -s) tall fur helmet worn by some British soldiers

bearskins n ▷ bearskin

beast n (pl -s) large wild animal

beastliness n ▷ beastly

beastly adj unpleasant or disagreeable ▷ **beastliness** n

beasts n ▷ beast

beat v (beats, beating, beat, beaten or beat) hit hard and repeatedly ▶ n (pl beats) regular throb

beaten v ▷ beat

beatific adj displaying great happiness

beatification n ▷ beatify

beatifications n ▷ beatify

beatified v ▷ beatify

beatifies v ▷ beatify

beatify [bee-**at**-if-fie] v (-fies, -fying, -fied) (RC

CHURCH) declare (a dead person) to be among the blessed in heaven: the first step towards canonization > **beatification** *n* (*pl* -s)
  beatifying *v* ▷ beatify
  beating *v* ▷ beat
beatitude *n* (*pl* -s) (CHRISTIANITY) any of the blessings on the poor, meek, etc., in the Sermon on the Mount
  beatitudes *n* ▷ beatitude
  beats *v*, *n* ▷ beat
beau [boh] *n* (*pl* beaux, beaus) boyfriend or admirer
  beaus *n* ▷ beau
beautician *n* (*pl* -s) person who gives beauty treatments professionally
  beauticians *n* ▷ beautician
  beauties *n* ▷ beauty
  beautification *n* ▷ beautify
  beautified *v* ▷ beautify
  beautifies *v* ▷ beautify
beautiful *adj* very attractive to look at > **beautifully** *adv*
  beautifully *adv* ▷ beautiful
beautify *v* (-fies, -fying, -fied) make beautiful > **beautification** *n*
  beautifying *v* ▷ beautify
beauty *n* (*pl* -ties) combination of all the qualities of a person or thing that delight the senses and mind
  beaux *n* ▷ beau
beaver *n* (*pl* -s) amphibious rodent with a big flat tail
  beavers *n* ▷ beaver
becalmed *adj* (of a sailing ship) motionless through lack of wind
  became *v* ▷ become
because *conj* on account of the fact that
beck *n* (*pl* -s) (N ENGLISH) stream
beckon *v* (-s, -ing, -ed) summon with a gesture
  beckoned *v* ▷ beckon
  beckoning *v* ▷ beckon
  beckons *v* ▷ beckon
  becks *n* ▷ beck
become *v* (-coming, -came, -come) come to be
becoming *adj* attractive or pleasing
bed *n* (*pl* -s) piece of furniture on which to sleep > **bedroom** *n* (*pl* -s)
bedding *n* (*pl* -s) sheets and covers that are used on a bed
  beddings *n* ▷ bedding
bedevil *v* (-s, -illing, -illed) harass, confuse, or torment
  bedevilled *v* ▷ bedevil
  bedevilling *v* ▷ bedevil
  bedevils *v* ▷ bedevil

bedlam *n* (*pl* -s) noisy confused situation
  bedlams *n* ▷ bedlam
bedpan *n* (*pl* -s) shallow bowl used as a toilet by bedridden people
  bedpans *n* ▷ bedpan
bedraggled *adj* untidy, wet, or dirty
bedridden *adj* confined to bed because of illness or old age
bedrock *n* (*pl* -s) solid rock beneath the surface soil
  bedrocks *n* ▷ bedrock
  bedroom *n* ▷ bed
  bedrooms *n* ▷ bed
  beds *n* ▷ bed
bedsit, bedsitter *n* (*pl* -s) furnished sitting room with a bed
  bedsits *n* ▷ bedsit
  bedsitters *n* ▷ bedsit
bee *n* (*pl* -s) insect that makes wax and honey
beech *n* (*pl* -es) tree with a smooth greyish bark
  beeches *n* ▷ beech
beef *n* (*pl* beeves) flesh of a cow, bull, or ox
beefburger *n* (*pl* -s) flat grilled or fried cake of minced beef
  beefburgers *n* ▷ beefburger
beefeater *n* (*pl* -s) yeoman warder at the Tower of London
  beefeaters *n* ▷ beefeater
  beefier *adj* ▷ beefy
  beefiest *adj* ▷ beefy
beefy *adj* (-fier, -fiest) like beef
beehive *n* (*pl* -s) structure in which bees live
  beehives *n* ▷ beehive
  been *v* ▷ be
beep *n* (*pl* -s) high-pitched sound, like that of a car horn ▶ *v* (-s, -ing, -ed) (cause to) make this noise
  beeped *v* ▷ beep
  beeping *v* ▷ beep
  beeps *n*, *v* ▷ beep
beer *n* (*pl* -s) alcoholic drink brewed from malt and hops > **beery** (-ier, -iest) ▶ *adj*
  beerier *adj* ▷ beer
  beeriest *adj* ▷ beer
  beers *n* ▷ beer
  beery *adj* ▷ beer
  bees *n* ▷ bee
beeswax *n* (*pl* -es) wax secreted by bees, used in polishes etc.
  beeswaxes *n* ▷ beeswax
beet *n* (*pl* -s) plant with an edible root and leaves
beetle *n* (*pl* -s) insect with a hard wing cover on its back

beetles n ▷ beetle

beetroot n (pl -s) type of beet plant with a dark red root
  beetroots n ▷ beetroot

beets n ▷ beet

beeves n ▷ beef

befall v (-falls, -falling, -fell, -fallen) (Old-fashioned) happen to (someone)
  befallen v ▷ befall
  befalling v ▷ befall
  befalls v ▷ befall
  befell v ▷ befall

befit v (-fits, -fitting, -fitted) be appropriate or suitable for > **befitting** adj
  befits v ▷ befit
  befitted v ▷ befit
  befitting v, adj ▷ befit

before conj, prep adv indicating something earlier in time, in front of, or preferred to

beforehand adv in advance

befriend v (-s, -ing, -ed) become friends with
  befriended v ▷ befriend
  befriending v ▷ befriend
  befriends v ▷ befriend

beg v (begs, begging, begged) solicit (for money or food), esp. in the street
  began v ▷ begin
  begat v ▷ beget

beget v (-gets, -getting, -got or -gat; -gotten or -got) (Old-fashioned) cause or create
  begets v ▷ beget
  begetting v ▷ beget

beggar n (pl s) person who lives by begging > **beggarly** adj > **beggarliness** n
  beggarliness n ▷ beggar
  beggarly adj ▷ beggar
  beggars n ▷ beggar
  begged v ▷ beg
  begging v ▷ beg

begin v (-gins, -ginning, -gan, -gun) start > **beginning** n (pl -s)

beginner n (pl -s) person who has just started learning to do something
  beginners n ▷ begin
  beginning v, n ▷ begin
  begins v ▷ begin

begonia n (pl -s) tropical plant with waxy flowers
  begonias n ▷ begonia
  begot v ▷ beget
  begotten v ▷ beget

begrudge v (-grudges, -grudging, -grudged) envy (someone) the possession of something
  begrudged v ▷ begrudge
  begrudges v ▷ begrudge

begrudging v ▷ begrudge

begs v ▷ beg

beguile [big-gile] v (-guiles, -guiling, -guiled) cheat or mislead > **beguiling** adj
  beguiled v ▷ beguile
  beguiles v ▷ beguile
  beguiling v, adj ▷ beguile
  begun v ▷ begin

behalf n in the interest of or for the benefit of

behave v (-haves, -having, -haved) act or function in a particular way
  behaved v ▷ behave
  behaves v ▷ behave
  behaving v ▷ behave

behaviour n (pl -s) manner of behaving
  behaviours n ▷ behaviour

behead v (-s, -ing, -ed) remove the head from
  beheaded v ▷ behead
  beheading v ▷ behead
  beheads v ▷ behead
  beheld v ▷ behold

behest n (pl -s) order or earnest request
  behests n ▷ behest

behind prep, adv indicating position to the rear, lateness, responsibility, etc. ▶ n (pl -s) (Informal) buttocks
  behinds n ▷ behind

behold v (-holds, -holding, -held) (Old-fashioned) look (at) > **beholder** n (pl -s)

beholden adj indebted or obliged
  beholder n ▷ behold
  beholders n ▷ behold
  beholding v ▷ behold
  beholds v ▷ behold

behove v (-hoves, -hoving, -hoved) (Old-fashioned) be necessary or fitting for
  behoved v ▷ behove
  behoves v ▷ behove
  behoving v ▷ behove

beige adj pale brown

being n (pl -s) state or fact of existing ▶ v ▷ be
  beings n ▷ being

belabour v (-s, -ing, -ed) attack verbally or physically
  belaboured v ▷ belabour
  belabouring v ▷ belabour
  belabours v ▷ belabour

belated adj late or too late > **belatedly** adv
  belatedly adv ▷ belated

belch v (-es, -ing, -ed) expel wind from the stomach noisily through the mouth ▶ n (pl belches) act of belching
  belched v ▷ belch
  belches v, n ▷ belch
  belching v ▷ belch

beleaguered *adj* struggling against difficulties or criticism
  belfries *n* ▷ belfry
belfry *n* (*pl* -fries) part of a tower where bells are hung
belie *v* (belies, belying, belied) show to be untrue
  belied *v* ▷ belie
belief *n* (*pl* -s) faith or confidence
  beliefs *n* ▷ belief
  belies *v* ▷ belie
  believable *adj* ▷ believe
believe *v* (-lieves, -lieving, -lieved) accept as true or real ▷ **believable** *adj* > **believer** *n* (*pl* -s)
  believed *v* ▷ believe
  believer *n* ▷ believe
  believers *n* ▷ believe
  believes *v* ▷ believe
  believing *v* ▷ believe
belittle *v* (-ttles, -ttling, -ttled) treat as having little value or importance
  belittled *v* ▷ belittle
  belittles *v* ▷ belittle
  belittling *v* ▷ belittle
bell *n* (*pl* -s) hollow, usu. metal, cup-shaped instrument that emits a ringing sound when struck
belladonna *n* (*pl* -s) (drug obtained from) deadly nightshade
  belladonnas *n* ▷ belladonna
bellbird *n* (*pl* -s) Australasian bird with bell-like call
  bellbirds *n* ▷ bellbird
belle *n* (*pl* -s) beautiful woman, esp. the most attractive woman at a function
  belles *n* ▷ belle
bellicose *adj* warlike and aggressive
  bellied *v* ▷ belly
  bellies *n, v* ▷ belly
  belligerence *n* ▷ belligerent
belligerent *adj* hostile and aggressive ▶ *n* (*pl* -s) person or country engaged in war > **belligerence** *n*
  belligerents *n* ▷ belligerent
bellow *v* (-s, -ing, -ed) make a low deep cry like that of a bull ▶ *n* (*pl* -s) loud deep roar
  bellowed *v* ▷ bellow
  bellowing *v* ▷ bellow
bellows *v, n* ▷ bellow ▶ *pl n* instrument for pumping a stream of air into something
  bells *n* ▷ bell
belly *n* (*pl* -lies) part of the body of a vertebrate which contains the intestines ▶ *v* (-lies, -lying, -lied) (cause to) swell out
bellyful *n* (*pl* -s) (*Slang*) more than one can

tolerate
  bellyfuls *n* ▷ bellyful
  bellying *v* ▷ belly
belong *v* (-s, -ing, -ed) (*foll. by* **to**) be the property of
  belonged *v* ▷ belong
  belonging *v* ▷ belong
belongings *pl n* personal possessions
  belongs *v* ▷ belong
beloved *adj* dearly loved ▶ *n* (*pl* -s) person dearly loved
  beloveds *n* ▷ beloved
below *prep, adv* at or to a position lower than, under
belt *n* (*pl* -s) band of cloth, leather, etc., worn usu. around the waist ▶ *v* (-s, -ing, -ed) fasten with a belt
  belted *v* ▷ belt
  belting *v* ▷ belt
  belts *n, v* ▷ belt
  belying *v* ▷ belie
bemoan *v* (-s, -ing, -ed) express sorrow or dissatisfaction about
  bemoaned *v* ▷ bemoan
  bemoaning *v* ▷ bemoan
  bemoans *v* ▷ bemoan
bemused *adj* puzzled or confused
bench *n* (*pl* -es) long seat
  benches *n* ▷ bench
benchmark *n* (*pl* -s) criterion by which to measure something
  benchmarks *n* ▷ benchmark
bend *v* (-s, -ing, bent) (cause to) form a curve ▶ *n* curved part > **bendy** *adj* (-dier, -diest) > **bendiness** *n* (*pl* -es)
  bendier *adj* ▷ bend
  bendiest *adj* ▷ bend
  bendiness *n* ▷ bend
  bendinesses *n* ▷ bend
  bending *v* ▷ bend
bends *v* ▷ bend ▶ *pl n* (*Informal*) decompression sickness
  bendy *adj* ▷ bend
beneath *adv, prep* below
benediction *n* (*pl* -s) prayer for divine blessing
  benedictions *n* ▷ benediction
  benefaction *n* ▷ benefactor
  benefactions *n* ▷ benefactor
benefactor, benefactress *n* (*pl* -s, -esses) someone who supports a person or institution by giving money > **benefaction** *n* (*pl* -s)
  benefactors *n* ▷ benefactor
  benefactress *n* ▷ benefactor
  benefactresses *n* ▷ benefactor

beneficence n ▷ **beneficent**
beneficent [bin-**eff**-iss-ent] adj charitable or generous ▷ **beneficence** n
beneficial adj helpful or advantageous
beneficiaries n ▷ **beneficiary**
beneficiary n (pl -ciaries) person who gains or benefits
benefit n (pl -s) something that improves or promotes ▶ v (-s, -fiting, -fited) do or receive good
benefited v ▷ **benefit**
benefiting v ▷ **benefit**
benefits n, v ▷ **benefit**
benevolence n (pl -s) inclination to do good ▷ **benevolent** adj ▷ **benevolently** adv
benevolences n ▷ **benevolence**
benevolent adj ▷ **benevolence**
benevolently adv ▷ **benevolence**
benighted adj ignorant or uncultured
benign [bin-**nine**] adj showing kindliness ▷ **benignly** adv
benignly adv ▷ **benign**
bent v ▷ **bend** ▶ adj curved ▶ n (pl -s) personal inclination or aptitude
bento n (pl -s) thin lightweight box divided into compartments, which contain small separate dishes comprising a Japanese meal
bentos n ▷ **bento**
bents n ▷ **bent**
benzene n (pl -s) flammable poisonous liquid used as a solvent, insecticide, etc.
benzenes n ▷ **benzene**
bequeath v (-s, -ing, -ed) dispose of (property) as in a will
bequeathed v ▷ **bequeath**
bequeathing v ▷ **bequeath**
bequeaths v ▷ **bequeath**
bequest n (pl -s) legal gift of money or property by someone who has died
bequests n ▷ **bequest**
berate v (-ates, -ating, -ated) scold harshly
berated v ▷ **berate**
berates v ▷ **berate**
berating v ▷ **berate**
bereaved adj having recently lost a close friend or relative through death ▷ **bereavement** n (pl -s)
bereavements n ▷ **bereavement**
bereft adj (foll. by **of**) deprived
beret [ber-**ray**] n (pl -s) round flat close-fitting brimless cap
berets n ▷ **beret**
berg[1] n (pl -s) iceberg
berg[2] n (pl -s) (S AFR) mountain
bergamot n (pl -s) small Asian tree, the fruit of

which yields an oil used in perfumery
bergamots n ▷ **bergamot**
bergs n ▷ **berg**[1, 2]
beriberi n (pl -s) disease caused by vitamin B deficiency
beriberis n ▷ **beriberi**
berk n (pl -s) (BRIT, AUST & NZ) (Slang) stupid person
berks n ▷ **berk**
berm n (pl -s) (NZ) narrow grass strip between the road and the footpath in a residential area
berms n ▷ **berm**
berries n ▷ **berry**
berry n (pl -ries) small soft stoneless fruit
berserk adj violent or destructive
berth n (pl -s) bunk in a ship or train ▶ v (-s, -ing, -ed) dock (a ship)
berthed v ▷ **berth**
berthing v ▷ **berth**
berths n, v ▷ **berth**
beryl n (pl -s) hard transparent mineral
beryllium n (pl -s) (CHEM) toxic silvery-white metallic element
berylliums n ▷ **beryllium**
beryls n ▷ **beryl**
beseech v (-seeches, -seeching, -sought or -seeched) ask earnestly; beg
beseeched v ▷ **beseech**
beseeches v ▷ **beseech**
beseeching v ▷ **beseech**
beset v (-sets, -setting, -set) trouble or harass constantly
besets v ▷ **beset**
besetting v ▷ **beset**
beside prep at, by, or to the side of
besides adv, prep in addition
besiege v (-sieges, -sieging, -sieged) surround with military forces
besieged v ▷ **besiege**
besieges n ▷ **besiege**
besieging v ▷ **besiege**
besotted adj infatuated
besought v ▷ **beseech**
bespeak v (-speaks, -speaking, -spoke, -spoken) indicate or suggest
bespeaking v ▷ **bespeak**
bespeaks v ▷ **bespeak**
bespoke v ▷ **bespeak** ▶ adj (esp. of a suit) made to the customer's specifications
bespoken v ▷ **bespeak**
best adj most excellent of a particular group etc. ▶ adv in a manner surpassing all others ▶ n (pl -s) most outstanding or excellent person, thing, or group in a category

bestial *adj* brutal or savage ▷ **bestiality** *n* (*pl* -ities)
  bestialities *n* ▷ bestial
  bestiality *n* ▷ bestial
bestir *v* (-stirs, -stirring, -stirred) cause (oneself) to become active
  bestirred *v* ▷ bestir
  bestirring *v* ▷ bestir
  bestirs *v* ▷ bestir
bestow *v* (-s, -ing, -ed) present (a gift) or confer (an honour) ▷ **bestowal** *n* (*pl* -s)
  bestowal *n* ▷ bestow
  bestowals *n* ▷ bestow
  bestowed *v* ▷ bestow
  bestowing *v* ▷ bestow
  bestows *v* ▷ bestow
  bestridden *v* ▷ bestride
bestride *v* (-strides, -striding, -strode, -stridden) have or put a leg on either side of
  bestrides *v* ▷ bestride
  bestriding *v* ▷ bestride
  bestrode *v* ▷ bestride
  bests *n* ▷ best
bestseller *n* (*pl* -s) book or other product that has sold in great numbers
  bestsellers *n* ▷ bestseller
bet *n* (*pl* -s) the act of staking a sum of money or other stake on the outcome of an event ▷ *v* (bets, betting, bet *or* betted) make or place (a bet)
betel [bee-tl] *n* (*pl* -s) Asian climbing plant, the leaves and nuts of which can be chewed
  betels *n* ▷ betels
betide *v* (-tides, -tiding, -tided) happen (to)
  betided *v* ▷ betide
  betides *v* ▷ betide
  betiding *v* ▷ betide
betoken *v* (-s, -ing, -ed) indicate or signify
  betokened *v* ▷ betoken
  betokening *v* ▷ betoken
  betokens *v* ▷ betoken
betray *v* (-s, -ing, -ed) hand over or expose (one's nation, friend, etc.) treacherously to an enemy ▷ **betrayal** *n* (*pl* -s) ▷ **betrayer** *n* (*pl* -s)
  betrayal *n* ▷ betray
  betrayals *n* ▷ betray
  betrayed *v* ▷ betray
  betrayer *n* ▷ betray
  betrayers *n* ▷ betray
  betraying *v* ▷ betray
  betrays *v* ▷ betray
  betrothal *n* ▷ betrothed
  betrothals *n* ▷ betrothed
betrothed *adj* engaged to be married ▷ **betrothal** *n* (*pl* -s)

bets *n*, *v* ▷ bet
  betted *v* ▷ bet
better *adj* more excellent than others ▷ *adv* in a more excellent manner ▷ *pl n* one's superiors ▷ *v* (-s, -ing, -ed) improve upon
  bettered *v* ▷ better
  bettering *v* ▷ better
  betters *n*, *v* ▷ better
  betting *v* ▷ bet
bettong *n* (*pl* -s) short-nosed rat kangaroo
  bettongs *n* ▷ bettong
between *prep*, *adv* indicating position in the middle, alternatives, etc.
betwixt *prep*, *adv* (*Old-fashioned*) between
bevel *n* (*pl* -s) slanting edge ▷ *v* (-els, -elling, -elled) cut a bevel on (a piece of timber etc.)
  bevelled *v* ▷ bevel
  bevelling *v* ▷ bevel
  bevels *n*, *v* ▷ bevel
beverage *n* (*pl* -s) drink
  beverages *n* ▷ beverage
  bevies *n* ▷ bevy
bevy *n* (*pl* bevies) flock or group
bewail *v* (-s, -ing, -ed) express great sorrow over
  bewailed *v* ▷ bewail
  bewailing *v* ▷ bewail
  bewails *v* ▷ bewail
beware *v* (-wares, -waring, -wared) be on one's guard (against)
  bewared *v* ▷ beware
  bewares *v* ▷ beware
  bewaring *v* ▷ beware
bewilder *v* (-s, -ing, -ed) confuse utterly ▷ **bewildering** *adj* ▷ **bewilderment** *n* (*pl* -s)
  bewildered *v* ▷ bewilder
  bewildering *v*, *adj* ▷ bewilder
  bewilderment *n* ▷ bewilder
  bewilderments *n* ▷ bewilder
  bewilders *v* ▷ bewilder
bewitch *v* (-es, -ing, -ed) attract and fascinate ▷ **bewitching** *adj*
  bewitched *v* ▷ bewitch
  bewitches *v* ▷ bewitch
  bewitching *v*, *adj* ▷ bewitch

> **bey** *n* (**beys**). A bey was an official in the Ottoman empire, and scores 8 points.

beyond *prep* at or to a point on the other side of ▷ *adv* at or to the far side of something

> **bez** *n* (**bezes**). A bez is the second spike of a deer's antler. This is a really handy word when you have Z on your rack. Bez scores 14 points.

> **bezique** *n* (**beziques**). Bezique is a card game; if you're lucky enough to be able

▨▨▨ to play it, you'll score 27 points.

bi *adj, n (pl -s)* short for bisexual

biannual *adj* occurring twice a year
> **biannually** *adv*

  biannually *adv* ▷ **biannual**

bias *n (pl -es)* mental tendency, esp. prejudice
▶ *v (-ases, -asing, -ased or -asses or -assing or -ased)* cause to have a bias > **biased, biassed** *adj*

  biased *v* ▷ **bias**

  biases *n, v* ▷ **bias**

  biasing *v* ▷ **bias**

  biassed *v* ▷ **bias**

  biasses *n, v* ▷ **bias**

  biassing *v* ▷ **bias**

bib *n (pl -s)* piece of cloth or plastic worn to protect a young child's clothes when eating

bible *n (pl -s)* book regarded as authoritative
> **biblical** *adj*

  bibles *n* ▷ **bible**

  biblical *n* ▷ **bible**

  bibliographer *n* ▷ **bibliography**

  bibliographers *n* ▷ **bibliography**

  bibliographies *n* ▷ **bibliography**

bibliography *n (pl -phies)* list of books on a subject > **bibliographer** *n (pl -s)*

bibliophile *n (pl -s)* person who collects or is fond of books

  bibliophiles *n* ▷ **bibliophile**

  bibs *n* ▷ **bib**

bibulous *adj* addicted to alcohol

bicarbonate *n (pl -s)* salt of carbonic acid

  bicarbonates *n* ▷ **bicarbonate**

  bicentenaries *n* ▷ **bicentenary**

bicentenary *n (pl -naries)* 200th anniversary

biceps *n (pl -es)* muscle with two origins, esp. the muscle that flexes the forearm

bicker *v (-s, -ing, -ed)* argue over petty matters

  bickered *v* ▷ **bicker**

  bickering *v* ▷ **bicker**

  bickers *v* ▷ **bicker**

bicycle *n (pl -s)* vehicle with two wheels, one behind the other, pedalled by the rider

  bicycles *n* ▷ **bicycle**

bid *v (bids, bidding, bade, bidden)* say (a greeting) *(past bid)* ▶ *n (pl -s)* offer of a specified amount > **bidder** *n (pl -s)*

biddable *adj* obedient

  bidden *v* ▷ **bid**

  bidder *n* ▷ **bid**

  bidders *n* ▷ **bid**

bidding *n (pl -s)* command ▶ *v* ▷ **bid**

bide *v (bides, biding, bided)* wait patiently for an opportunity

  bided *v* ▷ **bide**

  bides *v* ▷ **bide**

bidet [bee-day] *n (pl -s)* low basin for washing the genital area

  bidets *n* ▷ **bidet**

  biding *v* ▷ **bide**

  bids *v, n* ▷ **bid**

biennial *adj* occurring every two years ▶ *n (pl -s)* plant that completes its life cycle in two years

  biennials *n* ▷ **biennial**

bier *n (pl -s)* stand on which a corpse or coffin rests before burial

  biers *n* ▷ **bier**

bifocals *pl n* spectacles with lenses permitting near and distant vision

big *adj (bigger, biggest)* of considerable size, height, number, or capacity ▶ *adv* on a grand scale

  bigamies *n* ▷ **bigamy**

  bigamist *n* ▷ **bigamy**

  bigamists *n* ▷ **bigamy**

  bigamous *adj* ▷ **bigamy**

  bigamously *adv* ▷ **bigamy**

bigamy *n (pl -mies)* crime of marrying a person while still legally married to someone else > **bigamist** *n (pl -s)* > **bigamous** *adj*
> **bigamously** *adv*

  bigger *adj* ▷ **big**

  biggest *adj* ▷ **big**

bighead *n (pl -s)* (*Informal*) conceited person
> **bigheaded** *adj*

  bigheaded *n* ▷ **bighead**

  bigheads *n* ▷ **bighead**

bigot *n (pl -s)* person who is intolerant, esp. regarding religion or race > **bigoted** *adj*
> **bigotry** *n (pl -tries)*

  bigoted *adj* ▷ **bigot**

  bigotries *n* ▷ **bigot**

  bigotry *n* ▷ **bigot**

  bigots *n* ▷ **bigot**

bigwig *n (pl -s)* (*Informal*) important person

  bigwigs *n* ▷ **bigwig**

▨▨▨ **bijou** *n* (**bijoux**). A bijou is an intricate trinket. The plural form, bijoux, uses an X and allows you to score 22 points.

bike *n (pl -s)* (*Informal*) bicycle or motorcycle

  bikes *n* ▷ **bike**

bikini *n (pl -s)* woman's brief two-piece swimming costume

  bikinis *n* ▷ **bikini**

bilateral *adj* affecting or undertaken by two parties > **bilaterally** *adv*

  bilaterally *adv* ▷ **bilateral**

  bilberries *n* ▷ **bilberry**

bilberry *n (pl -berries)* bluish-black edible berry

bilbies *n* ▷ bilby

bilby *n* (*pl* -**bies**) Australian marsupial with long pointed ears and grey fur

bile *n* (*pl* -**s**) bitter yellow fluid secreted by the liver

biles *n* ▷ bile

bilge *n* (*pl* -**s**) (*Informal*) nonsense

bilges *n* ▷ bilge

bilingual *adj* involving or using two languages

bilious *adj* sick, nauseous > **biliousness** *n*
biliousness *n* ▷ bilious

bill[1] *n* (*pl* -**s**) statement of money owed for goods or services supplied ▶ *v* (-**s**, -**ing**, -**ed**) send or present a bill to

bill[2] *n* (*pl* -**s**) bird's beak

billabong *n* (*pl* -**s**) (AUST) stagnant pool in an intermittent stream

billabongs *n* ▷ billabong

billed *v* ▷ bill[1]

billet *v* (-**lets**, -**leting**, -**leted**) assign a lodging to (a soldier) ▶ *n* (*pl* -**s**) accommodation for a soldier in civil lodgings

billeted *v* ▷ billet

billeting *v* ▷ billet

billets *v*, *n* ▷ billet

billhook *n* (*pl* -**s**) tool with a hooked blade, used for chopping etc.

billhooks *n* ▷ billhook

billiards *n* game played on a table with balls and a cue

billies *n* ▷ billy

billing *v* ▷ bill[1]

billion *n* (*pl* -**s**) one thousand million > **billionth** *adj*

billions *n* ▷ billion

billionth *adj* ▷ billion

billow *n* (*pl* -**s**) large sea wave ▶ *v* (-**s**, -**ing**, -**ed**) rise up or swell out > **billowy, billowing** *adj*

billowed *v* ▷ billow

billowing *v*, *adj* ▷ billow

billows *n*, *v* ▷ billow

billowy *adj* ▷ billow

bills *n* ▷ bill[1, 2] ▶ *v* ▷ bill[1]

billy, billycan *n* (*pl* -**lies**, -**s**) metal can or pot for cooking on a camp fire

billycan *n* ▷ billy

billycans *n* ▷ billy

biltong *n* (*pl* -**s**) (S AFR) strips of dried meat

biltongs *n* ▷ biltong

bimbo *n* (*pl* -**s**) (*Slang*) attractive but empty-headed young person, esp. a woman

bimbos *n* ▷ bimbo

bin *n* (*pl* -**s**) container for rubbish or for storing grain, coal, etc.

binary *adj* composed of two parts (MATHS)

(COMPUTERS)

bind *v* (**binds, binding, bound**) make secure with or as if with a rope ▶ *n* (*pl* -**s**) (*Informal*) annoying situation

binder *n* (*pl* -**s**) firm cover for holding loose sheets of paper together

binders *n* ▷ binder

binding *n* (*pl* -**s**) anything that binds or fastens ▶ *n* ▷ bind

bindings *n* ▷ binding

bindweed *n* (*pl* -**s**) plant that twines around a support

bindweeds *n* ▷ bindweed

binge *n* (*pl* -**s**) (*Informal*) bout of excessive indulgence, esp. in drink

binges *n* ▷ binge

bingo *n* (*pl* -**s**) gambling game in which numbers are called out and covered by the players on their individual cards

bingos *n* ▷ bingo

binoculars *pl n* optical instrument consisting of two small telescopes joined together

binomial *n* (*pl* -**s**), *adj* (mathematical expression) consisting of two terms

binomials *n* ▷ binomial

bins *n* ▷ bin

biochemistries *n* ▷ biochemistry

biochemistry *n* (*pl* -**ries**) study of the chemistry of living things > **biochemist** *n* (*pl* -**s**)

biochemists *n* ▷ biochemistry

biodegradable *adj* capable of being decomposed by natural means

biodiversities *n* ▷ biodiversity

biodiversity *n* (*pl* -**ities**) existence of a wide variety of species in their natural environment

biographer *n* (*pl* -**s**) person who writes an account of another person's life

biographers *n* ▷ biographer

biographical *n* ▷ biography

biographies *n* ▷ biography

biography *n* (*pl* -**phies**) account of a person's life by another person > **biographical** *adj*

biological *adj* of or relating to biology > **biologically** *adv*

biologically *adv* ▷ biological

biologies *n* ▷ biology

biologist *n* ▷ biology

biologists *n* ▷ biology

biology *n* (*pl* -**ogies**) study of living organisms > **biologist** *n* (*pl* -**s**)

biometric *adj* of any automated system using physiological or behavioural traits as a means of identification.

bionic *adj* having a part of the body that is operated electronically

biopsies *n* ▷ biopsy

biopsy *n* (*pl* -sies) examination of tissue from a living body

biotechnologies *n* ▷ biotechnology

biotechnology *n* (*pl* -ologies) use of microorganisms, such as cells or bacteria, in industry and technology

bioterrorism *n* (*pl* -s) use of viruses, bacteria, etc., by terrorists > **bioterrorist** *n* (*pl* -s)

bioterrorisms *n* ▷ bioterrorism

bioterrorists *n* ▷ bioterrorism

biped [bye-ped] *n* (*pl* -s) animal with two feet

bipeds *n* ▷ biped

biplane *n* (*pl* -s) aeroplane with two sets of wings, one above the other

biplanes *n* ▷ biplane

birch *n* (*pl* -es) tree with thin peeling bark

birches *n* ▷ birch

bird *n* (*pl* -s) creature with feathers and wings, most types of which can fly

birdie *n* (*pl* -s) (GOLF) score of one stroke under par for a hole

birdies *n* ▷ birdie

birds *n* ▷ bird

biretta *n* (*pl* -s) stiff square cap worn by the Catholic clergy

birettas *n* ▷ biretta

birth *n* (*pl* -s) process of bearing young; childbirth

birthday *n* (*pl* -s) anniversary of the day of one's birth

birthdays *n* ▷ birthday

birthmark *n* (*pl* -s) blemish on the skin formed before birth

birthmarks *n* ▷ birthmark

birthright *n* (*pl* -s) privileges or possessions that someone is entitled to as soon as he or she is born

birthrights *n* ▷ birthright

births *n* ▷ birth

bis *n* ▷ bi

biscuit *n* (*pl* -s) small flat dry sweet or plain cake

biscuits *n* ▷ biscuit

bisect *v* (-s, -ing, -ed) divide into two equal parts

bisected *v* ▷ bisect

bisecting *v* ▷ bisect

bisects *v* ▷ bisect

bisexual *adj* sexually attracted to both men and women > **bisexuality** *n* (*pl* -ties)

bisexualities *n* ▷ bisexual

bisexuality *n* ▷ bisexual

bishop *n* (*pl* -s) clergyman who governs a diocese

bishopric *n* (*pl* -s) diocese or office of a bishop

bishoprics *n* ▷ bishopric

bishops *n* ▷ bishop

bismuth *n* (*pl* -s) (CHEM) pinkish-white metallic element

bismuths *n* ▷ bismuth

bison *n* (*pl* -bison) large hairy animal of the cattle family, native to N America and Europe

bistro *n* (*pl* -s) small restaurant

bistros *n* ▷ bistro

bit¹ *n* (*pl* -s) small piece, portion, or quantity

bit² *n* (*pl* -s) metal mouthpiece on a bridle

bit3 *v* ▷ bite

bit3 *n* (*pl* -s) (MATHS) (COMPUTERS) single digit of binary notation, either 0 or 1

bitch *n* (*pl* -es) female dog, fox, or wolf ▶ *v* (-es, -ing, -ed) (*Informal*) complain or grumble > **bitchy** *adj* (-ier, -iest) > **bitchiness** *n*

bitched *v* ▷ bitch

bitches *n*, *v* ▷ bitch

bitchier *adj* ▷ bitch

bitchiest *adj* ▷ bitch

bitching *v* ▷ bitch

bitchy *adj* ▷ bitch

bite *v* (bites, biting, bit, bitten) grip, tear, or puncture the skin, as with the teeth or jaws ▶ *n* (*pl* -s) act of biting > **biter** *n* (*pl* -s)

biter *n* ▷ bite

biters *n* ▷ bite

bites *v*, *n* ▷ bite

biting *adj* piercing or keen ▶ *v* ▷ bite

bits *n* ▷ bit¹, ², 4

bitten *v* ▷ bite

bitter *adj* (-er, -est) having a sharp unpleasant taste ▶ *n* (*pl* -s) beer with a slightly bitter taste ▶ *pl* bitter-tasting alcoholic drink > **bitterly** *adv* > **bitterness** *n* (*pl* -es)

bitterer *adj* ▷ bitter

bitterest *adj* ▷ bitter

bitterly *adv* ▷ bitter

bittern *n* (*pl* -s) wading marsh bird with a booming call

bitterness *n* ▷ bitter

bitternesses *n* ▷ bitter

bitterns *n* ▷ bittern

bitters *n* ▷ bitter

bitumen *n* (*pl* -s) black sticky substance obtained from tar or petrol

bitumens *n* ▷ bitumen

bivalve *n* (*pl* -s) ▶ *adj* (marine mollusc) with two hinged segments to its shell

bivalves *n* ▷ bivalve

bivouac *n* (*pl* -s) temporary camp in the

open air ▶ v (-acs, -acking, -acked) camp in a bivouac
bivouacked v ▷ bivouac
bivouacking v ▷ bivouac
bivouacs n, v ▷ bivouac
bizarre adj odd or unusual > **bizarrely** adv > **bizarreness** n
bizarrely adv ▷ bizarre
bizarreness n ▷ bizarre
blab v (blabs, blabbing, blabbed) reveal (secrets) indiscreetly
blabbed v ▷ blab
blabbing v ▷ blab
blabs v ▷ blab
black adj (-er, -est) of the darkest colour, like coal ▶ n (pl -s) darkest colour ▶ v (-s, -ing, -ed) make black > **blackness** n
blackball v (-balls, -balling, -balled) exclude from a group ▶ n (pl -balls) (NZ) hard boiled sweet with black-and-white stripes
blackballed v ▷ blackball
blackballing v ▷ blackball
blackballs v, n ▷ blackball
blackberries n ▷ blackberry
blackberry n (pl -rries) small blackish edible fruit
blackbird n (pl -s) common European thrush
blackbirds n ▷ blackbird
blackboard n (pl -s) hard black surface used for writing on with chalk
blackboards n ▷ blackboard
blackboy n (pl -s) Australian plant with grasslike leaves and a spike of small white flowers
blackboys n ▷ blackboy
blackbutt n (pl -s) Australian eucalyptus tree with hard wood used as timber
blackbutts n ▷ blackbutt
blackcurrant n (pl -s) very small blackish edible fruit that grows in bunches
blackcurrants n ▷ blackcurrant
blacked v ▷ black
blacken v (-s, -ing, -ed) make or become black
blackened v ▷ blacken
blackening v ▷ blacken
blackens v ▷ blacken
blacker adj ▷ black
blackest adj ▷ black
blackfish n (pl blackfish) small dark Australian estuary fish
blackguard [blag-gard] n (pl -s) unprincipled person
blackguards n ▷ blackguard
blackhead n (pl -s) black-tipped plug of fatty matter clogging a skin pore

blackheads n ▷ blackhead
blacking v ▷ black
blackleg n (pl -s) person who continues to work during a strike
blacklegs n ▷ blackleg
blacklist n (pl -s) list of people or organizations considered untrustworthy etc.
blacklists n ▷ blacklist
blackmail n (pl -s) act of attempting to extort money by threats ▶ v (-s, -ing, -ed) (attempt to) obtain money by blackmail
blackmailed v ▷ blackmail
blackmailing v ▷ blackmail
blackmails n, v ▷ blackmail
blackness n ▷ black
blackout n (pl -s) extinguishing of all light as a precaution against an air attack
blackouts n ▷ blackout
blacks n, v ▷ black
blacksmith n (pl -s) person who works iron with a furnace, anvil, etc.
blacksmiths n ▷ blacksmith
bladder n (pl -s) sac in the body where urine is held
bladders n ▷ bladder
blade n (pl -s) cutting edge of a weapon or tool
blades n ▷ blade
blame v (-mes, -ming, -med) consider (someone) responsible for ▶ n (pl -s) responsibility for something that is wrong > **blameless** adj
blamed v ▷ blame
blameless adj ▷ blame
blames v, n ▷ blame
blameworthy adj deserving blame
blaming v ▷ blame
blanch v (-es, -ing, -ed) become white or pale
blanched v ▷ blanch
blanches v ▷ blanch
blanching v ▷ blanch
blancmange [blam-monzh] n (pl -s) jelly-like dessert made with milk
blancmanges n ▷ blancmange
bland adj (-er, -est) dull and uninteresting > **blandly** adv
blander adj ▷ bland
blandest adj ▷ bland
blandishments pl n flattery intended to coax or persuade
blandly adj ▷ bland
blank adj not written on ▶ n (pl -s) empty space > **blankly** adv
blanket n (pl -s) large thick cloth used as covering for a bed ▶ v (-s, -ing, -ed) cover as with a blanket

blanketed v ▷ blanket
blanketing v ▷ blanket
blankets n, v ▷ blanket
blankly adv ▷ blank
blanks n ▷ blank
blare v (**blares, blaring, blared**) sound loudly and harshly ▸ n (pl -s) loud harsh noise
blared v ▷ blare
blares v, n ▷ blare
blaring v ▷ blare
blarney n (pl -s) flattering talk
blarneys n ▷ blarney
blasé [blah-zay] adj indifferent or bored through familiarity
blaspheme v (**-phemes, -pheming, -phemed**) speak disrespectfully of (God or sacred things) > **blasphemy** n (pl -phemies) > **blasphemous** adj > **blasphemously** adv > **blasphemer** n (pl -s)
blasphemed v ▷ blaspheme
blasphemer n ▷ blaspheme
blasphemers n ▷ blaspheme
blasphemes v ▷ blaspheme
blasphemies n ▷ blaspheme
blaspheming v ▷ blaspheme
blasphemous v ▷ blaspheme
blasphemously v ▷ blaspheme
blast n (pl -s) explosion ▸ v (**-s, -ing, -ed**) blow up (a rock etc.) with explosives
blasted v ▷ blast
blasting v ▷ blast
blastoff n (pl -s) launching of a rocket
blastoffs n ▷ blastoff
blasts n, v ▷ blast
blatant adj glaringly obvious > **blatantly** adv
blatantly adv ▷ blatant
blaze[1] n (pl -s) strong fire or flame ▸ v (**-s, -ing, -d**) burn or shine brightly
blaze[2] n (pl -s) mark made on a tree to indicate a route
blazed v ▷ blaze[1]
blazer n (pl -s) lightweight jacket, often in the colours of a school etc.
blazers n ▷ blazer
blazes n ▷ blaze[1, 2] ▸ v ▷ blaze[1]
blazing v ▷ blaze[1]
blazon v (**-s, -ing, -ed**) proclaim publicly
blazoned v ▷ blazon
blazoning v ▷ blazon
blazons v ▷ blazon
bleach v (**-es, -ing, -ed**) make or become white or colourless ▸ n (pl -es) bleaching agent
bleached v ▷ bleach
bleaches v, n ▷ bleach
bleaching v ▷ bleach

bleak adj (**-er, -est**) exposed and barren > **bleakly** adv > **bleakness** n (pl -es)
bleaker adj ▷ bleak
bleakest adj ▷ bleak
bleakly adv ▷ bleak
bleakness n ▷ bleak
bleaknesses n ▷ bleak
blearier adj ▷ bleary
bleariest adj ▷ bleary
blearily adv ▷ bleary
bleariness n ▷ bleary
blearinesses n ▷ bleary
bleary adj (**-rier, -riest**) with eyes dimmed, as by tears or tiredness > **blearily** adv > **bleariness** n (pl -es)
bleat v (**-s, -ing, -ed**) (of a sheep, goat, or calf) utter its plaintive cry ▸ n (pl -s) cry of sheep, goats, and calves
bleated v ▷ bleat
bleating v ▷ bleat
bleats v, n ▷ bleat
bled v ▷ bleed
bleed v (**-s, -ing, bled**) lose or emit blood
bleeding v ▷ bleed
bleeds v ▷ bleed
bleep n (pl -s) short high-pitched sound made by an electrical device ▸ v (**-s, -ing, -ed**) make a bleeping sound
bleeped v ▷ bleep
bleeper n (pl -s) small portable radio receiver that makes a bleeping signal
bleepers n ▷ bleeper
bleeping v ▷ bleep
bleeps n, v ▷ bleep
blemish n (pl -es) defect or stain ▸ v (**-es, -ing, -ed**) spoil or tarnish
blemished v ▷ blemish
blemishes n, v ▷ blemish
blemishing v ▷ blemish
blench v (**-es, -ing, -ed**) shy away, as in fear
blenched v ▷ blench
blenches v ▷ blench
blenching v ▷ blench
blend v (**-s, -ing, -ed**) mix or mingle (components or ingredients) ▸ n (pl -s) mixture
blended v ▷ blend
blender n (pl -s) electrical appliance for puréeing vegetables etc.
blenders n ▷ blender
blending v ▷ blend
blends v, n ▷ blend
bless v (**-es, -ing, -ed**) make holy by means of a religious rite
blessed adj holy ▸ v ▷ blessed > **blessedness** n

blessedness *n* ▷ blessed

blesses *v* ▷ bless

blessing *n* (*pl* -s) invoking of divine aid ▶ *v*
▷ bless

blessings *n* ▷ blessing

blether (SCOT) *v* (-s, -ing, -ed) talk, esp. foolishly
or at length ▶ *n* (*pl* -s) conversation

blethered *v* ▷ blether

blethering *v* ▷ blether

blethers *v*, *n* ▷ blether

blew *v* ▷ blow¹

blight *n* (*pl* -s) person or thing that spoils or
prevents growth ▶ *v* (-s, -ing, -ed) frustrate or
disappoint

blighted *v* ▷ blight

blighter *n* (*pl* -s) (*Informal*) irritating person

blighters *n* ▷ blighter

blighting *v* ▷ blight

blights *n*, *v* ▷ blight

blimp *n* (*pl* -s) small airship

blimps *n* ▷ blimp

blind *adj* (-er, -est) unable to see ▶ *v* (-s, -ing,
-ed) deprive of sight ▶ *n* (*pl* -s) covering for a
window > **blindly** *adv* > **blindness** *n* (*pl* -es)

blinded *v* ▷ blind

blinder *adj* ▷ blind

blindest *adj* ▷ blind

blindfold *v* (-s, -ing, -ed) prevent (a person)
from seeing by covering the eyes ▶ *n* (*pl* -s)
piece of cloth used to cover the eyes

blindfolded *v* ▷ blindfold

blindfolding *v* ▷ blindfold

blindfolds *v*, *n* ▷ blindfold

blinding *adj*, *v* ▷ blind

blindly *adv* ▷ blind

blindness *n* ▷ blind

blindnesses *n* ▷ blind

blinds *v*, *n* ▷ blind

blink *v* (-s, -ing, -ed) close and immediately
reopen (the eyes) ▶ *n* (*pl* -s) act of blinking

blinked *v* ▷ blink

blinkers *pl n* leather flaps on a horse's bridle to
prevent sideways vision

blinking *v* ▷ blink

blinks *v*, *n* ▷ blink

blip *n* (*pl* -s) spot of light on a radar screen
indicating the position of an object

blips *n* ▷ blip

bliss *n* (*pl* -es) perfect happiness > **blissful** *adj*
> **blissfully** *adv*

blisses *n* ▷ bliss

blissful *adj* ▷ bliss

blissfully *adv* ▷ bliss

blister *n* (*pl* -s) small bubble on the skin ▶ *v* (-s,
-ing, -ed) (cause to) have blisters

blistered *v* ▷ blister

blistering *adj* (of weather) very hot ▶ *v* ▷ blister
> **blisteringly** *adv*

blisteringly *adv* ▷ blistering

blisters *n*, *v* ▷ blister

blithe *adj* (-r, -st) casual and indifferent
> **blithely** *adv* > **blitheness** *n* (*pl* -es)

blithely *adv* ▷ blithe

blitheness *n* ▷ blithe

blithenesses *n* ▷ blithe

blither *adj* ▷ blithe

blithest *adj* ▷ blithe

blitz *n* (*pl* -es) violent and sustained attack by
aircraft ▶ *v* (-es, -ing, -ed) attack suddenly and
intensively

blitzed *v* ▷ blitz

blitzes *n*, *v* ▷ blitz

blitzing *v* ▷ blitz

blizzard *n* (*pl* -s) blinding storm of wind and
snow

blizzards *n* ▷ blizzard

bloat *v* (-s, -ing, -ed) cause to swell, as with
liquid or air

bloated *v* ▷ bloat

bloater *n* (*pl* -s) (BRIT) salted smoked herring

bloaters *n* ▷ bloater

bloating *v* ▷ bloat

bloats *v* ▷ bloat

blob *n* (*pl* -s) soft mass or drop

blobs *n* ▷ blob

bloc *n* (*pl* -s) people or countries combined by a
common interest

block *n* (*pl* -s) large solid piece of wood, stone,
etc. ▶ *v* (-s, -ing, -ed) obstruct or impede by
introducing an obstacle > **blockage** *n* (*pl* -s)

blockade *n* (*pl* -s) sealing off of a place to
prevent the passage of goods ▶ *v* (-ades,
-ading, -aded) impose a blockade on

blockaded *v* ▷ blockade

blockades *n*, *v* ▷ blockade

blockading *v* ▷ blockade

blockage *n* ▷ block

blockages *n* ▷ block

blocked *v* ▷ block

blockhead *n* (*pl* -s) stupid person

blockheads *n* ▷ blockhead

blockie *n* (*pl* -s) (AUST) owner of a small
property, esp. a farm

blockies *n* ▷ blockie

blocking *v* ▷ block

blocks *n*, *v* ▷ block

blocs *n* ▷ bloc

blog *n* (*pl* -s) ▷ weblog

blogs *n* ▷ blog

bloke *n* (*pl* -s) (*Informal*) man

blokes n ▷ bloke
blonde, masc **blond** adj, n (pl **-es, -s**) fair-haired (person)
blondes n ▷ blonde
blonds n ▷ blonde
blood n (pl **-s**) red fluid that flows around the body > **bloodless** adj > **bloodlessness** n
bloodhound n (pl **-s**) large dog formerly used for tracking
bloodhounds n ▷ bloodhound
bloodied v ▷ bloody
bloodies v ▷ bloody
bloodily adv ▷ bloody
bloodiness n ▷ bloody
bloodless adj ▷ blood
bloodlessness n ▷ blood
bloods n ▷ blood
bloodshed n (pl **-s**) slaughter or killing
bloodsheds n ▷ bloodshed
bloodshot adj (of an eye) inflamed
bloodstream n (pl **-s**) flow of blood round the body
bloodstreams n ▷ bloodstream
bloodsucker n (pl **-s**) animal that sucks blood
bloodsuckers n ▷ bloodsucker
bloodthirstily adv ▷ bloodthirsty
bloodthirstiness n ▷ bloodthirsty
bloodthirsty adj taking pleasure in violence > **bloodthirstily** adv > **bloodthirstiness** n
bloody adj covered with blood ▶ adj, adv (Slang) extreme or extremely ▶ v (**-dies, -dying, -died**) stain with blood > **bloodily** adv > **bloodiness** n
bloodying v ▷ bloody
bloom n (pl **-s**) blossom on a flowering plant ▶ v (**-s, -ing, -ed**) bear flowers
bloomed v ▷ bloom
bloomer n (pl **-s**) (BRIT) (Informal) stupid mistake
bloomers n ▷ bloomer ▶ pl n woman's baggy knickers
blooming v ▷ bloom
blooms n, v ▷ bloom
blooper n (pl **-s**) (CHIEFLY US) (Informal) stupid mistake
bloopers n ▷ blooper
blossom n (pl **-s**) flowers of a plant ▶ v (**-s, -ing, -ed**) (of plants) flower
blossomed v ▷ blossom
blossoming v ▷ blossom
blossoms n, v ▷ blossom
blot n (pl **-s**) spot or stain ▶ v (**-s, -tting, -tted**) cause a blemish in or on > **blotter** n (pl **-s**)
blotch n (pl **-es**) discoloured area or stain > **blotchy** adj
blotches n ▷ blotch
blotchy adj ▷ blotch

blots n, v ▷ blot
blotted v ▷ blot
blotter n ▷ blot
blotters n ▷ blot
blotting v ▷ blot
blotto adj (BRIT, AUST & NZ) (Slang) extremely drunk
blouse n (pl **-s**) woman's shirtlike garment
blouses n ▷ blouse
blow[1] v (**-s, -ing, blew, blown**) (of air, the wind, etc.) move > **blower** n (pl **-s**)
blow[2] n (pl **-s**) hard hit
blower n ▷ blow[1]
blowers n ▷ blow[1]
blowie n (pl **blowies**) (AUST) (Informal) bluebottle
blowier n ▷ blowie
blowies n ▷ blowie
blowiest n ▷ blowy
blowing v ▷ blow[1]
blown v ▷ blow[1]
blowout n (pl **-s**) sudden loss of air in a tyre
blowouts n ▷ blowout
blows v ▷ blow[1] ▶ n ▷ blow[2]
blowsier n ▷ blowsy
blowsiest n ▷ blowsy
blowsy adj (**-sier, -siest**) fat, untidy, and red-faced
blowy adj (**-wier, -wiest**) windy
blubber n (pl **-s**) fat of whales, seals, etc. ▶ v (**-s, -ing, -ed**) sob without restraint
blubbered v ▷ blubber
blubbering v ▷ blubber
blubbers n, v ▷ blubber
bludge (Informal) v (**-s, -ging, -d**) (AUST & NZ) evade work (AUST & NZ) ▶ n (pl **-s**) (AUST) easy task
bludged v ▷ bludge
bludgeon n (pl **-s**) short thick club ▶ v (**-s, -ing, -ed**) hit with a bludgeon
bludgeoned v ▷ bludgeon
bludgeoning v ▷ bludgeon
bludgeons n, v ▷ bludgeon
bludger n (pl **-s**) person who scrounges
bludgers n ▷ bludger
bludges v, n ▷ bludge
bludging v ▷ bludge
blue n (pl **-s**) colour of a clear unclouded sky ▶ pl feeling of depression ▶ adj (**bluer, bluest**) of the colour blue > **bluish** adj
bluebell n (pl **-s**) flower with blue bell-shaped flowers
bluebells n ▷ bluebell
bluebottle n (pl **-s**) large fly with a dark-blue body
bluebottles n ▷ bluebottle

blueprint n (pl -s) photographic print of a plan
  blueprints n ▷ blueprint
  bluer adj ▷ blue
  blues n ▷ blue
  bluest adj ▷ blue

bluetongue n (pl -s) Australian lizard with a blue tongue
  bluetongues n ▷ bluetongue

bluff¹ v (-s, -ing, -ed) pretend to be confident in order to influence (someone) ▶ n (pl -s) act of bluffing

bluff² n (pl -s) steep cliff or bank ▶ adj good-naturedly frank and hearty
  bluffed v ▷ bluff¹
  bluffing v ▷ bluff¹
  bluffs v, n ▷ bluff¹, ²
  bluish adj ▷ blue

blunder n (pl -s) clumsy mistake ▶ v (-s, -ing, -ed) make a blunder

blunderbuss n (pl -es) obsolete gun with a wide flared muzzle
  blunderbusses n ▷ blunderbuss
  blundered v ▷ blunder
  blundering v ▷ blunder
  blunders n, v ▷ blunder

blunt adj (blunter, bluntest) not having a sharp edge or point ▶ v (-s, -ing, -ed) make less sharp > **bluntly** adv > **bluntness** n
  blunted v ▷ blunt
  blunter adj ▷ blunt
  bluntest adj ▷ blunt
  blunting v ▷ blunt
  bluntly adv ▷ blunt
  bluntness n ▷ blunt
  blunts v ▷ blunt

blur v (-s, -rring, -rred) make or become vague or less distinct ▶ n (pl -s) something vague, hazy, or indistinct > **blurry** adj (-rier, -rriest)

blurb n (pl -s) promotional description, as on the jacket of a book
  blurbs n ▷ blurb
  blurred v ▷ blur
  blurrier adj ▷ blur
  blurriest adj ▷ blur
  blurring v ▷ blur
  blurry adj ▷ blur
  blurs v, n ▷ blur

blurt v (-s, -ing, -ed) (foll. by **out**) utter suddenly and involuntarily
  blurted v ▷ blurt
  blurting v ▷ blurt
  blurts v ▷ blurt

blush v (-es, -ing, -ed) become red in the face, esp. from embarrassment or shame ▶ n (pl -es) reddening of the face

blushed v ▷ blush
blushes v, n ▷ blush
blushing v ▷ blush

bluster v (-s, -ing, -ed) speak loudly or in a bullying way ▶ n (pl -s) empty threats or protests
  blustered v ▷ bluster
  blusteriness n ▷ blustery
  blustering v ▷ bluster
  blusters v, n ▷ bluster

blustery adj (of weather) rough and windy > **blusteriness** n

> **bo** or **boh** interjection. Bo is an exclamation used to startle someone. Bo scores 4 points, while boh scores 8.

boa n (pl -s) large nonvenomous snake

boab [boh-ab] n (pl -s) (AUST) (Informal) ▷ baobab
  boabs n ▷ boab

boar n (pl -s) uncastrated male pig

board n (pl -s) long flat piece of sawn timber ▶ v (-s, -ing, -ed) go aboard (a train, aeroplane, etc.)
  boarded v ▷ board

boarder n (pl -s) person who pays rent in return for accommodation in someone else's home
  boarders n ▷ boarder
  boarding v ▷ board

boardroom n (pl -s) room where the board of a company meets
  boardrooms n ▷ boardroom
  boards n, v ▷ board
  boars n ▷ boar
  boas n ▷ boa

boast v (-s, -ing, -ed) speak too proudly about one's talents etc. ▶ n (pl -s) bragging statement > **boastful** adj > **boastfully** adv > **boastfulness** n
  boasted v ▷ boast
  boastful adj ▷ boast
  boastfully adv ▷ boast
  boastfulness n ▷ boast
  boasting v ▷ boast
  boasts v, n ▷ boast

boat n (pl -s) small vehicle for travelling across water > **boating** n

boater n (pl -s) flat straw hat
  boaters n ▷ boater
  boating n ▷ boat
  boats n ▷ boat

boatswain n (pl -s) ▷ bosun
  boatswains n ▷ boatswain

bob¹ v (bobs, bobbing, bobbed) move up and down repeatedly ▶ n (pl -s) short abrupt movement

bob² n (pl -s) hairstyle in which the hair is cut

short evenly all round the head ▶ v (**bobs, bobbing, bobbed**) cut (the hair) in a bob
bobbed v ▷ bob[1, 2]
bobbies n ▷ bobby
bobbin n (pl -s) reel on which thread is wound
bobbing v ▷ bob[1, 2]
bobbins n ▷ bobbin
bobble n (pl -s) small ball of material, usu. for decoration
bobbles n ▷ bobble
bobby n (pl -bies) (BRIT) (Informal) policeman
bobotie [ba-**boot**-ee] n (pl -s) (S AFR) dish of curried mince
boboties n ▷ bobotie
bobs v ▷ bob[1, 2] ▶ n[1, 2]
bobsleigh n (pl -s) sledge for racing down an icy track ▶ v (-s, -ing, -ed) ride on a bobsleigh
bobsleighed v ▷ bobsleigh
bobsleighing v ▷ bobsleigh
bobsleighs n, v ▷ bobsleigh
bode v (-s, -ding, -ed) be an omen of (good or ill)
boded v ▷ bode
bodes v ▷ bode
bodice n (pl -s) upper part of a dress
bodices n ▷ bodice
bodies n ▷ body
bodily adj relating to the body ▶ adv by taking hold of the body
boding v ▷ bode
bodkin n (pl -s) blunt large-eyed needle
bodkins n ▷ bodkin
body n (pl -dies) entire physical structure of an animal or human
bodyboard n (pl -s) small polystyrene surfboard
bodyboards n ▷ bodyboard
bodyguard n (pl -s) person or group of people employed to protect someone
bodyguards n ▷ bodyguard
bodywork n (pl -s) outer shell of a vehicle
bodyworks n ▷ bodywork
boerewors n (S AFR) spiced sausage
boffin n (pl -s) (BRIT, AUST, NZ & S AFR) (Informal) scientist or expert
boffins n ▷ boffin
bog n (pl -s) wet spongy ground > **boggy** adj (**boggier, boggiest**)
bogan n (pl -s) (AUST DATED & NZ) (Slang) youth who dresses and behaves rebelliously
bogans n ▷ bogan
bogey, bogy n (pl bogeys, bogies) something that worries or annoys
bogeys n ▷ bogey
boggier adj ▷ bog

boggiest adj ▷ bog
boggle v (**boggles, boggling, boggled**) be surprised, confused, or alarmed
boggled v ▷ boggle
boggles v ▷ boggle
boggling v ▷ boggle
boggy adj ▷ bog
bogies n ▷ bogey
bogong, bugong n (pl -s, -s) large nocturnal Australian moth
bogongs n ▷ bogong
bogs n ▷ bog
bogus adj not genuine
bogusnesses n ▷ bogus
bogy n (pl -gies) ▷ bogey
bohemian n (pl -s) ▶ adj (person) leading an unconventional life
bohemians n ▷ bohemian
boil[1] v (-s, -ing, -ed) (cause to) change from a liquid to a vapour so quickly that bubbles are formed ▶ n (pl -s) state or action of boiling
boil[2] n (pl -s) red pus-filled swelling on the skin
boiled v ▷ boil[1]
boiler n (pl -s) piece of equipment which provides hot water
boilers n ▷ boiler
boiling v ▷ boil[1, 2]
boils v, n ▷ boil[1, 2]
boisterous adj noisy and lively > **boisterously** adv > **boisterousness** n
boisterously adv ▷ boisterous
boisterousness n ▷ boisterous

■ **bok** n (**boks**). A bok is a goat or antelope. Bok scores 9 points.

bold adj (-er, -est) confident and fearless > **boldly** adv > **boldness** n (pl -es)
bolder adj ▷ bold
boldest adj ▷ bold
boldly adv ▷ bold
boldness n ▷ bold
boldnesses n ▷ bold
bole n (pl -s) tree trunk
bolero n (pl -s) (music for) traditional Spanish dance
boleros n ▷ bolero
boles n ▷ bole
bollard n (pl -s) short thick post used to prevent the passage of motor vehicles
bollards n ▷ bollard
boloney n (pl -s) ▷ baloney
boloneys n ▷ boloney
bolshie, bolshy adj (Informal) difficult or rebellious
bolshy n ▷ bolshie
bolster v (-s, -ing, -ed) support or strengthen

▶ *n* (*pl* **-s**) long narrow pillow
bolstered *v* ▷ bolster
bolstering *v* ▷ bolster
bolsters *v*, *n* ▷ bolster
bolt *n* (*pl* **-s**) sliding metal bar for fastening a door etc. ▶ *v* (**-s, -ing, -ed**) run away suddenly
bolted *v* ▷ bolt
bolting *v* ▷ bolt
bolts *n*, *v* ▷ bolt
bomb *n* (*pl* **-s**) container fitted with explosive material ▶ *v* (**-s, -ing, -ed**) attack with bombs
bombard *v* (**-s, -ing, -ed**) attack with heavy gunfire or bombs > **bombardment** *n* (*pl* **-s**)
bombarded *v* ▷ bombard
bombarding *v* ▷ bombard
bombardment *n* ▷ bombard
bombardments *n* ▷ bombard
bombards *n* ▷ bombard
bombast *n* (*pl* **-s**) pompous language > **bombastic** *adj*
bombastic *adj* ▷ bombast
bombasts *n* ▷ bombast
bombed *v* ▷ bomb
bomber *n* (*pl* **-s**) aircraft that drops bombs
bombers *n* ▷ bomber
bombing *v* ▷ bomb
bombs *n*, *v* ▷ bomb
bombshell *n* (*pl* **-s**) shocking or unwelcome surprise
bombshells *n* ▷ bombshell
bonanza *n* (*pl* **-s**) sudden good luck or wealth
bonanzas *n* ▷ bonanza
bond *n* (*pl* **-s**) something that binds, fastens or holds together ▶ *pl* something that restrains or imprisons ▶ *v* (**-s, -ing, -ed**) bind > **bonded** *adj*
bondage *n* (*pl* **-s**) slavery
bondages *n* ▷ bondage
bonded *v*, *adj* ▷ bond
bonding *v* ▷ bond
bonds *n*, *v* ▷ bond
bone *n* (*pl* **-s**) any of the hard parts in the body that form the skeleton ▶ *v* (**-s, -ing, -d**) remove the bones from (meat for cooking etc.) > **boneless** *adj*
boned *v* ▷ bone
boneless *adj* ▷ bone
bones *n*, *v* ▷ bone
bonfire *n* (*pl* **-s**) large outdoor fire
bonfires *n* ▷ bonfire
bongo *n* (*pl* **-gos, -goes**) small drum played with the fingers
bongoes *n* ▷ bongo
bongos *n* ▷ bongo
bonhomie [bon-om-ee] *n* (*pl* **-s**) cheerful

friendliness
bonhomies *n* ▷ bonhomie
boning *v* ▷ bone
bonito [ba-nee-toh] *n* (*pl* **-s**) small tunny-like marine food fish
bonitos *n* ▷ bonito
bonnet *n* (*pl* **-s**) metal cover over a vehicle's engine
bonnets *n* ▷ bonnet
bonnier *adj* ▷ bonny
bonniest *adj* ▷ bonny
bonnily *adv* ▷ bonny
bonny *adj* (**-nier, -niest**) (Scot) beautiful > **bonnily** *adv*
bonsai *n* (*pl* **bonsai**) ornamental miniature tree or shrub
bonus *n* (*pl* **-es**) something given, paid, or received above what is due or expected
bonuses *n* ▷ bonus
bony *adj* having many bones
boo *interj* shout of disapproval ▶ *v* (**-s, -ing, -ed**) shout 'boo' to show disapproval
boob (Slang) *n* (*pl* **-s**) foolish mistake
boobies *n* ▷ booby
boobook [boo-book] *n* (*pl* **-s**) small spotted Australian brown owl
boobooks *n* ▷ boobook
boobs *n* ▷ boob
booby *n* (*pl* **-bies**) foolish person
booed *v* ▷ boo
boogie *v* (**-s, -ing, -ied**) (Informal) dance to fast pop music
boogied *v* ▷ boogie
boogieing *v* ▷ boogie
boogies *v* ▷ boogie
booing *v* ▷ boo
book *n* (*pl* **-s**) number of pages bound together between covers ▶ *pl* record of transactions of a business or society ▶ *v* (**-s, -ing, -ed**) reserve (a place, passage, etc.) in advance
booked *n* ▷ book
booking *v* ▷ book
booklet *n* (*pl* **-s**) thin book with paper covers
booklets *v* ▷ booklet
bookmaker *n* (*pl* **-s**) person whose occupation is taking bets
bookmakers *n* ▷ bookmaker
bookmark *n* (*pl* **-s**) strip of material used to mark a place in a book ▶ *v* (**-s, -ing, -ed**) (COMPUTERS) identify and store (a website) so that one can return to it quickly and easily
bookmarked *v* ▷ bookmark
bookmarking *v* ▷ bookmark
bookmarks *n*, *v* ▷ bookmark
books *n*, *v* ▷ book

bookworm n (pl -s) person devoted to reading
  bookworms n ▷ bookworm
boom¹ v (-s, -ing, -ed) make a loud deep echoing sound ▶ n (pl -s) loud deep echoing sound
boom² n (pl -s) pole to which the foot of a sail is attached
  boomed v ▷ boom¹
boomer n (pl -s) (AUST) large male kangaroo
boomerang n (pl -s) curved wooden missile which can be made to return to the thrower ▶ v (-s, -ing, -ed) (of a plan) recoil unexpectedly
  boomeranged n ▷ boomerang
  boomeranging v ▷ boomerang
  boomerangs n, v ▷ boomerang
  boomers n ▷ boomer
  booming v ▷ boom¹
  booms v, n ▷ boom¹, ²
boon n (pl -s) something helpful or beneficial
  boongaries n ▷ boongary
boongary [boong-gar-ree] n (pl -garies) tree kangaroo of NE Queensland, Australia
  boons n ▷ boon
boor n (pl -s) rude or insensitive person > **boorish** adj > **boorishly** adv > **boorishness** n
  boorishly adv ▷ boor
  boorishness n ▷ boor
  boors n ▷ boor
  boos v ▷ boo
boost n (pl -s) encouragement or help ▶ v (-s, -ing, -ed) improve
  boosted v ▷ boost
booster n (pl -s) small additional injection of a vaccine
  boosters n ▷ booster
  boosting v ▷ boost
  boosts n, v ▷ boost
boot n (pl -s) outer covering for the foot that extends above the ankle ▶ v (-s, -ing, -ed) (Informal) kick
  booted v ▷ boot
bootee n (pl -s) baby's soft shoe
  bootees n ▷ bootee
booth n (pl -s) small partly enclosed cubicle
  booths n ▷ booth
  booties n ▷ booty
  booting v ▷ boot¹
bootleg adj produced, distributed, or sold illicitly ▶ v (-legs, -legging, -legged) make, carry, or sell (illicit goods) > **bootlegger** n (pl -s)
  bootlegged v ▷ bootleg
  bootlegger n ▷ bootleg
  bootleggers n ▷ bootleg

  bootlegging v ▷ bootleg
  bootlegs v ▷ bootleg
  boots n ▷ boot
booty n (pl -ties) valuable articles obtained as plunder
booze v (-zes, -zing, -zed) ▶ n (pl -s) (Informal) (consume) alcoholic drink > **boozy** adj (-zier, -ziest) > **boozily** adv
  boozed v ▷ booze
boozer n (pl -s) (Informal) person who is fond of drinking
  boozers n ▷ booze
  boozes v, n ▷ booze
  boozier adj ▷ booze
  booziest adj ▷ booze
  boozily adv ▷ booze
  boozing v ▷ booze
  boozy adj ▷ booze
bop v (-s, -pping, -pped) (Informal) dance to pop music
  bopped v ▷ bop
  bopping v ▷ bop
  bops v ▷ bop
bora n (pl -s) (AUST) Aboriginal ceremony
  boras n ▷ bora
borax n (pl -es) white mineral used in making glass
  boraxes n ▷ borax
border n (pl -s) dividing line between political or geographical regions ▶ v (-s, -ing, -ed) provide with a border
  bordered v ▷ border
  bordering v ▷ border
  borders n, v ▷ border
bore¹ v (-s, -ring, -d) make (a hole) with a drill etc. ▶ n (pl -s) (diameter of) the hollow of a gun barrel or other tube
bore² v (-s, -ring, -d) make weary by being dull or repetitious ▶ n dull or repetitious person or thing > **bored** adj > **boredom** n
bore³ n (pl -s) high wave in a narrow estuary, caused by the tide
bore⁴ v ▷ bear¹
  bored v, n ▷ bore¹, ²
boree [baw-ree] n (pl -s) (AUST) ▷ myall
  borees n ▷ boree
  bores n ▷ bore¹, ², ³ ▶ v ▷ bore¹, ²
  boring v ▷ bore¹, ²
born v ▷ bear¹ ▶ adj possessing certain qualities from birth
  borne v ▷ bear¹
boron n (pl -s) (CHEM) element used in hardening steel
boronia n (pl -s) Australian aromatic flowering shrub

boronias n ▷ boronia
borons n ▷ boron
borough n (pl -s) (CHIEFLY BRIT) town or district with its own council
boroughs n ▷ borough
borrow v (-s, -ing, -ed) obtain (something) temporarily > **borrower** n (pl -s)
borrowed v ▷ borrow
borrower n ▷ borrow
borrowers n ▷ borrow
borrowing v ▷ borrow
borrows v ▷ borrow
borstal n (pl -s) (formerly in Britain) prison for young criminals
borstals n ▷ borstal
borzoi n (pl -s) tall dog with a long silky coat
borzois n ▷ borzoi
bosh n (pl -es) (BRIT, AUST & NZ) (*Informal*) empty talk, nonsense
boshes n ▷ bosh
bosom n (pl -s) chest of a person, esp. the female breasts ▶ adj very dear
bosoms n ▷ bosom
boss[1] n (pl -es) person in charge of or employing others ▶ v (-es, -ing, -ed) be domineering towards > **bossy** adj > **bossiness** n
boss[2] n (pl -es) raised knob or stud
bossed v ▷ boss[1]
bosses n ▷ boss[1, 2] ▶ v ▷ boss[1]
bossiness n ▷ boss[1]
bossing v ▷ boss[1]
bossy adj ▷ boss[1]
bosun n (pl -s) officer responsible for the maintenance of a ship
bosuns n ▷ bosun
botanic adj ▷ botany
botanical adj ▷ botany
botanies n ▷ botany
botanist n ▷ botany
botanists n ▷ botany
botany n (pl -ies) study of plants > **botanical**, **botanic** adj > **botanist** n (pl -s)
botch v (-es, -ing, -ed) spoil through clumsiness ▶ n (pl -es) (also **botch-up**) (pl -s) badly done piece of work or repair
botched v ▷ botch
botches v, n ▷ botch
botching v ▷ botch
both adj, pron two considered together
bother v (-s, -ing, -ed) take the time or trouble ▶ n (pl -s) trouble, fuss, or difficulty > **bothersome** adj
bothered v ▷ bother
bothering v ▷ bother

bothers v, n ▷ bother
bothersome adj ▷ bother
bottle n (pl -s) container for holding liquids ▶ v (-s, -ttling, -d) put in a bottle
bottled v ▷ bottle
bottleneck n (pl -s) narrow stretch of road where traffic is held up
bottlenecks n ▷ bottleneck
bottles n, v ▷ bottle
bottling v ▷ bottle
bottom n (pl -s) lowest, deepest, or farthest removed part of a thing ▶ adj lowest or last > **bottomless** adj
bottomless adj ▷ bottom
bottoms n ▷ bottom
botulism n (pl -s) severe food poisoning
botulisms n ▷ botulism
boudoir [boo-dwahr] n (pl -s) woman's bedroom or private sitting room
boudoirs n ▷ boudoir
bougainvillea n (pl -s) climbing plant with red or purple flowers
bougainvilleas n ▷ bougainvillea
bough n (pl -s) large branch of a tree
boughs n ▷ bough
bought v ▷ buy
boulder n (pl -s) large rounded rock
boulders n ▷ boulder
boulevard n (pl -s) wide, usu. tree-lined, street
boulevards n ▷ boulevard
bounce v (-s, -cing, -d) (of a ball etc.) rebound from an impact (*Slang*) ▶ n (pl -s) act of rebounding
bounced v ▷ bounce
bouncer n (pl -s) person employed at a disco etc. to remove unwanted people
bouncers n ▷ bouncer
bounces v, n ▷ bounce
bouncing v ▷ bounce ▶ adj vigorous and robust
bound[1] v (-s, -ing, -ed) ▷ bind ▶ adj destined or certain
bound[2] v (-s, -ing, -ed) move forwards by jumps ▶ n (pl -s) jump upwards or forwards
bound[3] v (-s, -ing, -ed) form a boundary of ▶ pl n limit
bound[4] adj going or intending to go towards
boundaries n ▷ boundary
boundary n (pl -aries) dividing line that indicates the farthest limit
bounded v ▷ bound[2, 3]
bounding v ▷ bound[2, 3]
bounds v, n ▷ bound[2, 3]
bounteous adj ▷ bounty
bounties n ▷ bounty

bountiful adj ▷ bounty

bounty n (pl **-ties**) generosity > **bountiful, bounteous** adj

bouquet n (pl **-s**) bunch of flowers

bouquets n ▷ bouquet

bourbon [bur-bn] n (pl **-s**) whiskey made from maize

bourbons n ▷ bourbon

bourgeois [boor-zhwah] adj, n (pl **bourgeois**) middle-class (person)

bout n (pl **-s**) period of activity or illness

boutique n (pl **-s**) small clothes shop

boutiques n ▷ boutique

bouts n ▷ bout

bovine adj relating to cattle

bow[1] [rhymes with **now**] v (**-s, -ing, -ed**) lower (one's head) or bend (one's knee or body) as a sign of respect or shame ▶ n (pl **-s**) movement made when bowing

bow[2] [rhymes with **go**] n (pl **-s**) knot with two loops and loose ends

bow[3] [rhymes with **now**] n (pl **-s**) front end of a ship

bowdlerize v (**-zes, -zing, -zed**) remove words regarded as indecent from (a play, novel, etc.)

bowdlerized v ▷ bowdlerize

bowdlerizes v ▷ bowdlerize

bowdlerizing v ▷ bowdlerize

bowed v ▷ bow[1]

bowel n (pl **-s**) intestine, esp. the large intestine ▶ pl innermost part

bowels n ▷ bowel

bower n (pl **-s**) shady leafy shelter

bowerbird n (pl **-s**) songbird of Australia and New Guinea, the males of which build bower-like display grounds to attract females

bowerbirds n ▷ bowerbird

bowers n ▷ bower

bowing v ▷ bow[1]

bowl[1] n (pl **-s**) round container with an open top

bowl[2] n (pl **-s**) large heavy ball ▶ pl game played on smooth grass with wooden bowls ▶ v (**-s, -ing, -ed**) (CRICKET) send (a ball) towards the batsman

bowled v ▷ bowl[2]

bowlegged adj having legs that curve outwards at the knees

bowler[1] n (pl **-s**) (CRICKET) player who sends (a ball) towards the batsman

bowler[2] n (pl **-s**) stiff felt hat with a rounded crown

bowlers n ▷ bowler[1, 2]

bowling n game in which bowls are rolled at a group of pins ▶ v ▷ bowl[2]

bowls n ▷ bowl[1, 2] ▶ v ▷ bowl[2]

bows v ▷ bow[1] ▶ n ▷ bow[1, 2, 3]

box[1] n (pl **-es**) container with a firm flat base and sides ▶ v (**-es, -ing, -ed**) put into a box

box[2] v (**-es, -ing, -ed**) fight (an opponent) in a boxing match

box[3] n (pl **-es**) evergreen tree with shiny leaves bark

boxed v ▷ box[1, 2]

boxer n (pl **-s**) person who participates in the sport of boxing

boxers n ▷ boxer

boxes v ▷ box[1, 2] ▶ n ▷ box[1, 2, 3]

boxing n sport of fighting with the fists ▶ v ▷ box[1, 2]

boy n (pl **-s**) male child ▶ **boyish** adj ▶ **boyhood** n (pl **-s**)

boycott v (**-cotts, -cotting, -cotted**) refuse to deal with (an organization or country) ▶ n (pl **-s**) instance of boycotting

boycotted v ▷ boycott

boycotting v ▷ boycott

boycotts v, n ▷ boycott

boyfriend n (pl **-s**) male friend with whom a person is romantically or sexually involved

boyfriends n ▷ boyfriend

boyhood n ▷ boy

boyhoods n ▷ boy

boyish n ▷ boy

boys n ▷ boy

bra n (pl **-s**) woman's undergarment for supporting the breasts

braai n ▷ braaivlies

braaied v ▷ braaivlies

braaiing v ▷ braaivlies

braais n, v ▷ braaivlies

braaivlies [brye-flayss], **braai** (S AFR) n (pl **braais**) grill on which food is cooked over hot charcoal, usu. outdoors ▶ v (**braais, braaiing, braaied**) cook (food) in this way

brace n (pl **-s**) object fastened to something to straighten or support it ▶ pl straps worn over the shoulders to hold up trousers ▶ v (**-ces, -cing, -ced**) steady or prepare (oneself) for something unpleasant

braced n, v ▷ brace

bracelet n (pl **-s**) ornamental chain or band for the wrist

bracelets n ▷ bracelet

braces n, v ▷ brace

bracing adj refreshing and invigorating ▶ v ▷ brace

bracken n (pl **-s**) large fern

brackens n ▷ bracken

bracket n (pl **-s**) either of a pair of characters

used to enclose a section of writing ▶ *v* (**-ets,
-eting, -eted**) put in brackets
  bracketed *v* ▷ bracket
  bracketing *v* ▷ bracket
  brackets *n*, *v* ▷ bracket
brackish *adj* (of water) slightly salty
  > **brackishness** *n*
  brackishness *n* ▷ bracket
bract *n* (*pl* **-s**) leaf at the base of a flower
  bracts *n* ▷ bract
brag *v* (**-s, -gging, -gged**) speak arrogantly and
boastfully > **braggart** *n* (*pl* **-s**)
  braggart *n* ▷ brag
  braggarts *n* ▷ brag
  bragged *v* ▷ brag
  bragging *v* ▷ brag
  brags *v* ▷ brag
braid *v* (**-s, -ing, -ed**) interweave (hair, thread,
etc.) ▶ *n* (*pl* **-s**) length of hair etc. that has
been braided
  braided *v* ▷ braid
  braiding *v* ▷ braid
  braids *v*, *n* ▷ braid
braille *n* (*pl* **-s**) system of writing for the blind,
consisting of raised dots interpreted by
touch
  brailles *n* ▷ braille
brain *n* (*pl* **-s**) soft mass of nervous tissue in
the head ▶ *v* (**-s, -ing, -ed**) hit (someone) hard
on the head
brainchild *n* (*pl* **-children**) idea produced by
creative thought
  brainchildren *n* ▷ brainchild
  brained *v* ▷ brain
  brainier *adj* ▷ brainy
  brainiest *adj* ▷ brainy
  braininess *n* ▷ brainy
  braininesses *n* ▷ brainy
  braining *v* ▷ brain
brainless *adj* stupid
  brains *n*, *v* ▷ brain
brainwash *v* (**-es, -ing, -ed**) cause (a person) to
alter his or her beliefs, esp. by methods based
on isolation, sleeplessness, etc.
  brainwashed *v* ▷ brainwash
  brainwashes *v* ▷ brainwash
  brainwashing *v* ▷ brainwash
brainwave *n* (*pl* **-s**) sudden idea
  brainwaves *v* ▷ brainwave
brainy *adj* (**-nier, -niest**) (*Informal*) clever
  > **braininess** *n* (*pl* **-es**)
braise *v* (**-ses, -sing, -sed**) cook slowly in a
covered pan with a little liquid
  braised *v* ▷ braise
  braises *v* ▷ braise

braising *v* ▷ braise
brake *n* (*pl* **-s**) device for slowing or stopping
a vehicle ▶ *v* (**-kes, -king, -ked**) slow down or
stop by using a brake
  braked *v* ▷ brake
  brakes *n*, *v* ▷ brake
  braking *v* ▷ brake
bramble *n* (*pl* **-s**) prickly shrub that produces
blackberries
  brambles *n* ▷ bramble
bran *n* (*pl* **-s**) husks of cereal grain
branch *n* (*pl* **-es**) secondary stem of a tree ▶ *v*
(**-es, -ing, -ed**) (of stems, roots, etc.) divide,
then develop in different directions
  branched *n* ▷ branch
  branches *n*, *v* ▷ branch
  branching *v* ▷ branch
brand *n* (*pl* **-s**) particular product ▶ *v* (**-s, -ing,
-ed**) mark with a brand
  branded *v* ▷ brand
  brandies *n* ▷ brandy
  branding *v* ▷ brand
brandish *v* (**-es, -ing, -ed**) wave (a weapon etc.)
in a threatening way
  brandished *v* ▷ brandish
  brandishes *v* ▷ brandish
  brandishing *v* ▷ brandish
  brands *n*, *v* ▷ brand
brandy *n* (*pl* **-dies**) alcoholic spirit distilled
from wine
  brans *n* ▷ bran
  bras *n* ▷ bra
brash *adj* offensively loud, showy, or self-
confident > **brashness** *n*
  brashness *n* ▷ brash
brass *n* (*pl* **-es**) alloy of copper and zinc
  brasses *n* ▷ brass
  brassier *adj* ▷ brassy
brassiere *n* (*pl* **-s**) bra
  brassieres *n* ▷ brassiere
  brassiest *adj* ▷ brassy
  brassiness *adj* ▷ brassy
  brassinesses *adj* ▷ brassy
brassy *adj* (**-ssier, -ssiest**) brazen or flashy
  > **brassiness** *n* (*pl* **-es**)
brat *n* (*pl* **-s**) unruly child
  brats *n* ▷ brat
bravado *n* (*pl* **-oes**) showy display of self-
confidence
  bravadoes *n* ▷ bravado
brave *adj* (**-r, -st**) having or showing courage,
resolution, and daring ▶ *n* (*pl* **-s**) Native
American warrior ▶ *v* (**-ves, -ving, -ved**)
confront with resolution or courage
  > **bravery** *n* (*pl* **-ies**)

braved v ▷ brave

bravenesses n ▷ brave

braver adj ▷ brave

braveries n ▷ brave

bravery n ▷ brave

braves n, v ▷ brave

bravest adj ▷ brave

braving v ▷ brave

bravo interj well done!

brawl n (pl -s) noisy fight ▶ v (-s, -ing, -ed) fight noisily

brawled v ▷ brawl

brawling v ▷ brawl

brawls n, v ▷ brawl

brawn n (pl -s) physical strength > **brawny** (-nier, -niest) adj

brawnier adj ▷ brawn

brawniest adj ▷ brawn

brawns n ▷ brawn

brawny adj ▷ brawn

bray v (-s, -ing, -ed) (of a donkey) utter its loud harsh sound ▶ n (pl -s) donkey's loud harsh sound

brayed v ▷ bray

braying v ▷ bray

brays v, n ▷ bray

brazen adj shameless and bold ▶ v (-s, -ing, -ed) > **brazenly** adv > **brazenness** n

brazened v ▷ brazen

brazening v ▷ brazen

brazenly adv ▷ brazen

brazenness n ▷ brazen

brazens v ▷ brazen

brazier [bray-zee-er] n (pl -s) portable container for burning charcoal or coal

braziers n ▷ brazier

breach n (pl -es) breaking of a promise, obligation, etc. ▶ v (-es, -ing, -ed) break (a promise, law, etc.)

breached v ▷ breach

breaches n, v ▷ breach

breaching v ▷ breach

bread n (pl -s) food made by baking a mixture of flour and water or milk

breads n ▷ bread

breadth n (pl -s) extent of something from side to side

breadths n ▷ breadth

breadwinner n (pl -s) person whose earnings support a family

breadwinners n ▷ breadwinner

break v (breaks, breaking, broke, broken) separate or become separated into two or more pieces ▶ n (pl -s) act or result of breaking > **breakable** adj > **breakage** n (pl -s)

breakable adj ▷ break

breakage n ▷ break

breakages n ▷ break

breakdown n (pl -s) act or instance of breaking down

breakdowns n ▷ breakdown

breaker n (pl -s) large wave

breakers n ▷ breaker

breakfast v (-s, -ing, -ed) ▶ n (pl -s) (eat) the first meal of the day

breakfasted v ▷ breakfast

breakfasting v ▷ breakfast

breakfasts v, n ▷ breakfast

breaking v ▷ break

breakneck adj fast and dangerous

breaks v, n ▷ break

breakthrough n (pl -s) important development or discovery

breakthroughs n ▷ breakthrough

breakwater n (pl -s) wall that extends into the sea to protect a harbour or beach from the force of waves

breakwaters n ▷ breakwater

bream n (pl bream) silver freshwater fish

breast n (pl -s) either of the two soft fleshy milk-secreting glands on a woman's chest

breastbone n (pl -s) long flat bone in the front of the body, to which most of the ribs are attached

breastbones n ▷ breastbone

breasts n ▷ breast

breaststroke n (pl -s) swimming stroke in which the arms are extended in front of the head and swept back on either side

breaststrokes n ▷ breaststroke

breath n (pl -s) taking in and letting out of air during breathing > **breathless** adj > **breathlessly** adv > **breathlessness** n

breathalysed v ▷ breathalyser

breathalyser n (pl -s)® device for estimating the amount of alcohol in the breath > **breathalyse** v (-ses, -sing, -sed)

breathalysers n ▷ breathalyser

breathalyses v ▷ breathalyser

breathalysing v ▷ breathalyser

breathe v (-thes, -thing, -thed) take in oxygen and give out carbon dioxide > **breathing** n

breathed v ▷ breathe

breather n (pl -s) (Informal) short rest

breathers n ▷ breather

breathes v ▷ breathe

breathing v, n ▷ breathe

breathless adj ▷ breath

breathlessly adv ▷ breath

breathlessness n ▷ breath

breaths n ▷ breath

breathtaking adj causing awe or excitement

bred v ▷ breed

breech n (pl -es) buttocks

breeches pl n trousers extending to just below the knee ▶ n ▷ breech

breed v (-s, -ding, bred) produce new or improved strains of (domestic animals or plants) ▶ ▶ n (pl -s) group of animals etc. within a species that have certain clearly defined characteristics > **breeder** n (pl -s)

breeder n ▷ breed

breeders n ▷ breed

breeding n (pl -s) result of good upbringing or training ▶ v ▷ breed

breedings n ▷ breeding

breeds v, n ▷ breed

breeze n (pl -s) gentle wind ▶ v (-zes, -zing, -zed) move quickly or casually

breezed v ▷ breeze

breezes n, v ▷ breeze

breezier adj ▷ breezy

breeziest adj ▷ breezy

breezily adj ▷ breezy

breezing v ▷ breeze

breezy adj (-zier, -ziest) windy > **breezily** adv

brethren pl n (Old-fashioned) (used in religious contexts) brothers

brevities n ▷ brevity

brevity n (pl -ities) shortness

brew v (-s, -ing, -ed) make (beer etc.) by steeping, boiling, and fermentation ▶ n (pl -s) beverage produced by brewing

brewed v ▷ brew

brewer n (pl -s) person or company that brews beer

breweries n ▷ brewery

brewers n ▷ brewer

brewery n (pl -eries) place where beer etc. is brewed

brewing v ▷ brew

brews v, n ▷ brew

briar¹, brier n (pl -s) European shrub with a hard woody root

briar2 n (pl -s) ▷ brier¹

briars n ▷ briar¹, ²

bribe v (bribes, bribing, bribed) offer or give something to someone to gain favour, influence, etc. ▶ n (pl -s) something given or offered as a bribe > **bribery** n

bribed v ▷ bribe

bribes v, n ▷ bribe

bribing v ▷ bribe

brick n (pl -s) (rectangular block of) baked clay used in building ▶ v (-s, -ing, -ed) (foll. by up or over) build, enclose, or fill with bricks

bricked v ▷ brick

bricking v ▷ brick

bricklayer n (pl -s) person who builds with bricks

bricklayers n ▷ bricklayer

bricks n, v ▷ brick

bridal adj ▷ bride

bride n (pl -s) woman who has just been or is about to be married > **bridal** adj

bridegroom n (pl -s) man who has just been or is about to be married

bridegrooms n ▷ bridegroom

brides n ▷ bride

bridesmaid n (pl -s) girl or woman who attends a bride at her wedding

bridesmaids n ▷ bridesmaid

bridge¹ n (pl -s) structure for crossing a river etc. ▶ v (-dges, -dging, -dged) build a bridge over (something)

bridge² n (pl -s) card game based on whist, played between two pairs

bridged v ▷ bridge¹

bridgehead n (pl -s) fortified position at the end of a bridge nearest the enemy

bridgeheads n ▷ bridgehead

bridges n ▷ bridge¹, ² ▶ v ▷ bridge¹

bridging v ▷ bridge¹

bridle n (pl -s) headgear for controlling a horse ▶ v (-dles, -dling, -dled) show anger or indignation

bridled v ▷ bridle

bridles n, v ▷ bridle

bridling v ▷ bridle

brief adj (-er, -est) short in duration ▶ n (pl -s) condensed statement or written synopsis (also **briefing**) (pl -s) ▶ pl men's or women's underpants ▶ v (-s, -ing, -ed) give information and instructions to (a person) > **briefly** adv

briefcase n (pl -s) small flat case for carrying papers, books, etc.

briefcases n ▷ briefcase

briefed v ▷ brief

briefer adj ▷ brief

briefest adj ▷ brief

briefing v, n ▷ brief

briefings n ▷ brief

briefly adv ▷ brief

briefs n, v ▷ brief

brier¹, briar n (pl -s) wild rose with long thorny stems

brier² n (pl -s) ▷ briar¹

briers n ▷ brier¹, ²

brig n (pl -s) two-masted square-rigged ship

brigade n (pl -s) army unit smaller than a

division
brigades *n* ▷brigade
brigadier *n* (*pl* -s) high-ranking army officer
  brigadiers *n* ▷brigadier
brigalow *n* (*pl* -s) (AUST) type of acacia tree
  brigalows *n* ▷brigalow
brigand *n* (*pl* -s) (*Lit*) bandit
  brigands *n* ▷brigand
brigantine *n* (*pl* -s) two-masted sailing ship
  brigantines *n* ▷brigantine
bright *adj* (-er, -est) emitting or reflecting
much light > **brightly** *adv* > **brightness** *n*
> **brighten** *v* (-s, -ing, -ed)
  brighten *v* ▷bright
  brightened *v* ▷bright
  brightening *v* ▷bright
  brightens *v* ▷bright
  brighter *adj* ▷bright
  brightest *adj* ▷bright
  brightly *adj* ▷bright
  brigs *n* ▷brig
brilliance *n* ▷brilliant
brilliancy *n* ▷brilliant
brilliant *adj* shining with light > **brilliance**,
brilliancy *n* > **brilliantly** *adv*
  brilliantly *adv* ▷brilliant
brim *n* (*pl* -s) upper rim of a cup etc. ▶ *v* (brims,
brimming, brimmed) be full to the brim
  brimmed *v* ▷brim
  brimming *v* ▷brim
  brims *n, v* ▷brim
brimstone *n* (*pl* -s) (*Obs*) sulphur
  brimstones *n* ▷brimstone
brine *n* (*pl* -s) salt water
  brines *n* ▷brine
bring *v* (-s, -ing, brought) carry, convey, or take
to a designated place or person
  bringing *v* ▷bring
  brings *v* ▷bring
  brinier *adj* ▷briny
  briniest *adj* ▷briny
brinjal *n* (*pl* -s) (S AFR) aubergine
  brinjals *n* ▷brinjal
brink *n* (*pl* -s) edge of a steep place
  brinks *n* ▷brink
briny (brinier, briniest) *adj* very salty
brisk *adj* (-er, -est) lively and quick > **briskly** *adv*
  brisker *adj* ▷brisk
  briskest *adj* ▷brisk
brisket *n* (*pl* -s) beef from the breast of a cow
  briskets *n* ▷brisket
  briskly *adv* ▷brisk
bristle *n* (*pl* -s) short stiff hair ▶ *v* (-les, -ling,
-led) (cause to) stand up like bristles > **bristly**
adj (-lier, -liest)

bristled *v* ▷bristle
bristles *n, v* ▷bristle
bristlier *adj* ▷bristle
bristliest *adj* ▷bristle
bristling *v* ▷bristle
bristly *adj* ▷bristle
brit *n* (*pl* -s) (*Informal*) British person
  brits *n* ▷brit
brittle *adj* (-r, -st) hard but easily broken
> **brittleness** *n* (*pl* -es)
  brittleness *n* ▷brittle
  brittlenesses *n* ▷brittle
  brittler *adj* ▷brittle
  brittlest *adj* ▷brittle
broach *v* (-es, -ing, -ed) introduce (a topic) for
discussion
  broached *v* ▷broach
  broaches *v* ▷broach
  broaching *v* ▷broach
broad *adj* (-er, -est) having great breadth or
width > **broadly** *adv* > **broaden** *v* (-s, -ing, -ed)
broadband *n* (*pl* -s) telecommunication
transmission technique using a wide range
of frequencies
  broadbands *n* ▷broadband
broadcast *n* (*pl* -s) programme or
announcement on radio or television ▶ *v*
(-s, -ing, broadcast) transmit (a programme
or announcement) on radio or television
> **broadcaster** *n* (*pl* -s) > **broadcasting** *n*
  broadcaster *n* ▷broadcast
  broadcasters *n* ▷broadcast
  broadcasting *v, n* ▷broadcast
  broadcasts *n, v* ▷broadcast
broaden *v* ▷broad
  broadened *v* ▷broad
  broadening *v* ▷broad
  broadens *v* ▷broad
  broader *adj* ▷broad
  broadest *adj* ▷broad
  broadly *adv* ▷broad
broadminded *adj* tolerant
broadside *n* (*pl* -s) strong verbal or written
attack
  broadsides *n* ▷broadside
brocade *n* (*pl* -s) rich fabric woven with a
raised design
  brocades *n* ▷brocade
broccoli *n* (*pl* -s) type of cabbage with greenish
flower heads
  broccolis *n* ▷broccoli
brochure *n* (*pl* -s) booklet that contains
information about a product or service
  brochures *n* ▷brochure
broekies [brook-eez] *pl n* (S AFR) (*Informal*)

underpants

brogue[1] *n* (*pl* -**s**) sturdy walking shoe

brogue[2] *n* (*pl* -**s**) strong accent, esp. Irish

  brogues *n* ▷ **brogue**[1, 2]

broil *v* (-**s**, -**ing**, -**ed**) (AUST, NZ, US & CANADIAN) cook by direct heat under a grill

  broiled *v* ▷ **broil**

  broiling *v* ▷ **broil**

  broils *v* ▷ **broil**

broke *v* ▷ **break** ▶ *adj* (*Informal*) having no money

broken *v* ▷ **break** ▶ *adj* fractured or smashed

brokenhearted *adj* overwhelmed by grief

broker *n* (*pl* -**s**) agent who buys or sells goods, securities, etc.

  brokers *n* ▷ **broker**

brolga *n* (*pl* -**s**) large grey Australian crane with a trumpeting call

  brolgas *n* ▷ **brolga**

  brollies *n* ▷ **brolly**

brolly *n* (*pl* -**lies**) (*Informal*) umbrella

bromide *n* (*pl* -**s**) chemical compound used in medicine and photography

  bromides *n* ▷ **bromide**

bromine *n* (*pl* -**s**) (CHEM) dark red liquid element that gives off a pungent vapour

  bromines *n* ▷ **bromine**

  bronchi *n* ▷ **bronchus**

bronchial [bronk-ee-al] *adj* of the bronchi

bronchitis [bronk-**eye**-tiss] *n* inflammation of the bronchi

bronchus [bronk-uss] *n* (*pl* bronchi) [bronk-eye] either of the two branches of the windpipe

bronco *n* (*pl* -**s**) (in the US) wild or partially tamed pony

  broncos *n* ▷ **bronco**

brontosaurus *n* (*pl* -**es**) very large plant-eating four-footed dinosaur

  brontosauruses *n* ▷ **brontosaurus**

bronze *n* (*pl* -**s**) alloy of copper and tin ▶ *adj* made of, or coloured like, bronze ▶ *v* (-**zes**, -**zing**, -**zed**) (esp. of the skin) make or become brown

  bronzed *v* ▷ **bronze**

  bronzes *n*, *v* ▷ **bronze**

  bronzing *v* ▷ **bronze**

brooch *n* (*pl* -**es**) ornament with a pin, worn fastened to clothes

  brooches *n* ▷ **brooch**

brood *n* (*pl* -**s**) number of birds produced at one hatching ▶ *v* (-**s**, -**ing**, -**ed**) think long and unhappily > **broody** *adj* moody and sullen (*Informal*)

  brooded *v* ▷ **brood**

  brooding *v* ▷ **brood**

  broods *n*, *v* ▷ **brood**

  broody *adj* ▷ **brood**

brook[1] *n* (*pl* -**s**) small stream

brook[2] *v* (-**s**, -**ing**, -**ed**) bear or tolerate

  brooked *v* ▷ **brook**[2]

  brooking *v* ▷ **brook**[2]

  brooks *n* ▷ **brook**[1] ▶ *v* ▷ **brook**[2]

broom *n* (*pl* -**s**) long-handled sweeping brush

  brooms *n* ▷ **broom**

broomstick *n* (*pl* -**s**) handle of a broom

  broomsticks *n* ▷ **broomstick**

broth *n* (*pl* -**s**) soup, usu. containing vegetables

brothel *n* (*pl* -**s**) house where men pay to have sex with prostitutes

  brothels *n* ▷ **brothel**

brother *n* (*pl* -**s**) boy or man with the same parents as another person > **brotherly** *adj*

brotherhood *n* (*pl* -**s**) fellowship

  brotherhoods *n* ▷ **brotherhood**

  brotherly *adj* ▷ **brother**

  brothers *n* ▷ **brother**

  broths *n* ▷ **broth**

  brought *v* ▷ **bring**

brow *n* (*pl* -**s**) part of the face from the eyes to the hairline

browbeat *v* (-**s**, -**ing**, browbeat, -**en**) frighten (someone) with threats

  browbeaten *v* ▷ **browbeat**

  browbeating *v* ▷ **browbeat**

  browbeats *v* ▷ **browbeat**

brown *n* (*pl* -**s**) colour of earth or wood ▶ *adj* (-**er**, -**est**) of the colour brown ▶ *v* (-**s**, -**ing**, -**ed**) make or become brown > **brownish** *adj*

  browned *v* ▷ **brown**

  browner *adj* ▷ **brown**

  brownest *adj* ▷ **brown**

  browning *v* ▷ **brown**

  brownish *adj* ▷ **brown**

  browns *n*, *v* ▷ **brown**

  brows *n* ▷ **brow**

browse *v* (-**ses**, -**sing**, -**sed**) look through (a book or articles for sale) in a casual manner ▶ *n* (*pl* -**s**) instance of browsing

  browsed *v* ▷ **browse**

browser *n* (*pl* -**s**) (COMPUTERS) software package that enables a user to read hypertext, esp. on the Internet

  browsers *n* ▷ **browser**

  browses *v*, *n* ▷ **browse**

  browsing *v* ▷ **browse**

bruise *n* (*pl* -**s**) discoloured area on the skin caused by an injury ▶ *v* (-**ses**, -**sing**, -**sed**) cause a bruise on

  bruised *v* ▷ **bruise**

bruiser *n* (*pl* -**s**) strong tough person

bruisers n ▷ bruiser
bruises n, v ▷ bruise
bruising v ▷ bruise
brumbies n ▷ brumby
brumby n (pl -bies) (AUST) wild horse
brunch n (pl -es) (Informal) breakfast and lunch combined
brunches n ▷ brunch
brunette n (pl -s) girl or woman with dark brown hair
brunettes n ▷ brunette
brunt n (pl -s) main force or shock of a blow, attack, etc.
brunts n ▷ brunt
brush¹ n (pl -es) device made of bristles, wires, etc. used for cleaning, painting, etc. ▶ v (-es, -ing, -ed) clean, scrub, or paint with a brush
brush² n (pl -es) thick growth of shrubs
brushed v ▷ brush¹
brushes v ▷ brush¹ ▶ n ▷ brush¹, ²
brushing v ▷ brush¹
brusque adj (-r, -st) blunt or curt in manner or speech > **brusquely** adv > **brusqueness** n (pl -es)
brusquely adv ▷ brusque
brusqueness n ▷ brusque
brusquenesses n ▷ brusque
brusquer adj ▷ brusque
brusquest adj ▷ brusque
brutal adj cruel and vicious > **brutally** adv > **brutality** n (pl -ities) > **brutalize** v (-lizes, -lizing, -lized)
brutalities n ▷ brutal
brutality n ▷ brutal
brutalized v ▷ brutal
brutalizes v ▷ brutal
brutalizing v ▷ brutal
brutally adv ▷ brutal
brute n (pl -s) brutal person ▶ adj wholly instinctive or physical, like an animal
brutes n ▷ brute
brutish adj of or like an animal > **brutishly** adv > **brutishness** n
brutishly adv ▷ brutish
brutishness n ▷ brutish
bubble n (pl -s) ball of air in a liquid or solid ▶ v (-les, -ling, -led) form bubbles
bubbled v ▷ bubble
bubbles n, v ▷ bubble
bubblier adj ▷ bubbly
bubbliest adj ▷ bubbly
bubbling v ▷ bubble
bubbly adj (-lier, -liest) excited and lively
buccaneer n (pl -s) (HIST) pirate
buccaneers n ▷ buccaneer

buck¹ n (pl -s) male of the goat, hare, kangaroo, rabbit, and reindeer ▶ v (-s, -ing, -ed) (of a horse etc.) jump with legs stiff and back arched
buck² n (pl -s) (US, CANADIAN, AUST & NZ) (Slang) dollar
bucked v ▷ buck¹
bucket n (pl -s) open-topped round container with a handle ▶ v (-ets, -eting, -eted) rain heavily > **bucketful** n (pl -s)
bucketed v ▷ bucket
bucketful n ▷ bucket
bucketfuls n ▷ bucket
bucketing v ▷ bucket
buckets n, v ▷ bucket
bucking v ▷ buck¹
buckle n (pl -s) clasp for fastening a belt or strap ▶ v (-les, -ling, -led) fasten or be fastened with a buckle
buckled v ▷ buckle
buckles n, v ▷ buckle
buckling v ▷ buckle
bucks v ▷ buck¹ ▶ n ▷ buck¹, ²
buckshee adj (Slang) free
buckteeth pl n projecting upper front teeth > **buck-toothed** adj
buck-toothed adj ▷ buckteeth
buckwheat n (pl -s) small black grain used for making flour
buckwheats n ▷ buckwheat
bucolic [bew-koll-ik] adj of the countryside or country life
bud n (pl -s) swelling on a tree or plant that develops into a leaf or flower ▶ v (buds, budding, budded) produce buds
budded v ▷ bud
buddies n ▷ buddy
budding adj beginning to develop or grow ▶ v ▷ bud
buddleia n (pl -s) shrub with long spikes of purple flowers
buddleias n ▷ buddleia
buddy n (pl -dies) (Informal) friend
budge v (budges, budging, budged) move slightly
budged v ▷ budge
budgerigar n (pl -s) small cage bird bred in many different-coloured varieties
budgerigars n ▷ budgerigar
budges v ▷ budge
budget n (pl -s) financial plan for a period of time ▶ v (-ets, -eting, -eted) plan the expenditure of (money or time) ▶ adj cheap > **budgetary** adj
budgeted v ▷ budget

budgeting v ▷ budget

budgets n, v ▷ budget

budgie n (pl -s) (Informal) ▷ budgerigar

budgies n ▷ budgie

budging v ▷ budge

buds n, v ▷ bud

buff¹ adj dull yellowish-brown ▶ v (-s, -ing, -ed) clean or polish with soft material

buff² n (pl -s) (Informal) expert on or devotee of a given subject

buffalo n (pl -oes) type of cattle (us)

buffaloes n ▷ buffalo

buffed v ▷ buff¹

buffer n (pl -s) something that lessens shock or protects from damaging impact, circumstances, etc.

buffers n ▷ buffer

buffet¹ [boof-ay, buff-ay] n (pl -s) counter where drinks and snacks are served

buffet² [buff-it] v (-s, -feting, -feted) knock against or about

buffeted v ▷ buffet²

buffeting v ▷ buffet²

buffets n ▷ buffet¹ ▶ v ▷ buffet²

buffing v ▷ buff¹

buffoon n (pl -s) clown or fool ▶ **buffoonery** n (pl -ries)

buffooneries n ▷ buffoon

buffoonery n ▷ buffoon

buffoons n ▷ buffoon

buffs v ▷ buff¹ ▶ n ▷ buff²

bug n (pl -s) small insect ▶ v (bugs, bugging, bugged) (Informal) irritate (someone)

bugbear n (pl -s) thing that causes obsessive anxiety

bugbears n ▷ bugbear

bugged v ▷ bug

bugging v ▷ bug

bugle n (pl -s) instrument like a small trumpet ▷ **bugler** n (pl -s)

bugler n ▷ bugle

buglers n ▷ bugle

bugles n ▷ bugle

bugong n ▷ bogong

bugongs n ▷ bogong

bugs n, v ▷ bug

build v (builds, building, built) make, construct, or form by joining parts or materials ▶ n (pl -s) shape of the body ▷ **builder** n (pl -s)

builder n ▷ build

builders n ▷ build

building v ▷ build ▶ n (pl -s) structure with walls and a roof

buildings n ▷ building

builds v, n ▷ build

built v ▷ build

bulb n (pl -s) onion-shaped root which grows into a flower or plant

bulbous adj round and fat

bulbs n ▷ bulb

bulge n (pl -s) swelling on a normally flat surface ▶ v (bulges, bulging, bulged) swell outwards ▷ **bulging** adj

bulged v ▷ bulge

bulges n, v ▷ bulge

bulging v, adj ▷ bulge

bulimia n (pl -s) disorder characterized by compulsive overeating followed by vomiting ▷ **bulimic** adj, n (pl -s)

bulimias n ▷ bulimia

bulimic adj, n ▷ bulimia

bulimics n ▷ bulimia

bulk n (pl -s) size or volume, esp. when great ▷ **bulky** adj (-ier, -iest)

bulkhead n (pl -s) partition in a ship or aeroplane

bulkheads n ▷ bulkhead

bulkier adj ▷ bulk

bulkiest adj ▷ bulk

bulks n ▷ bulk

bulky adj ▷ bulk

bull¹ n (pl -s) male of some animals, such as cattle, elephants, and whales

bull² n (pl -s) (Informal) complete nonsense

bull³ n (pl -s) papal decree

bulldog n (pl -s) thickset dog with a broad head and a muscular body

bulldogs n ▷ bulldog

bulldoze v ▷ bulldozer

bulldozed v ▷ bulldozer

bulldozer n (pl -s) powerful tractor for moving earth ▷ **bulldoze** v (-zes, -zing, -zed)

bulldozers n ▷ bulldozer

bulldozes v ▷ bulldozer

bulldozing v ▷ bulldozer

bullet n (pl -s) small piece of metal fired from a gun

bulletin n (pl -s) short official report or announcement

bulletins n ▷ bulletin

bullets n ▷ bullet

bullfight n (pl -s) public show in which a matador kills a bull ▷ **bullfighter** n (pl -s)

bullfighter n ▷ bullfight

bullfighters n ▷ bullfight

bullfights n ▷ bullfight

bullied v ▷ bully

bullies n, v ▷ bully

bullion n (pl -s) gold or silver in the form of bars
bullions n ▷ bullion
bullock n (pl -s) castrated bull
bullocks n ▷ bullock
bulls n ▷ bull[1, 2, 3]
bullswool n (AUST DATED & NZ) (Slang) nonsense
bully n (pl -lies) person who hurts, persecutes,
or intimidates a weaker person ▶ v (-lies,
-lying, -lied) hurt, intimidate, or persecute (a
weaker person)
bullying v ▷ bully
bulrush n (pl -es) tall stiff reed
bulrushes n ▷ bulrush
bulwark n (pl -s) wall used as a fortification
bulwarks n ▷ bulwark
bum[1] n (pl -s) (Slang) buttocks or anus
bum[2] (Informal) n (pl -s) disreputable idler ▶ adj
of poor quality
bumble v (-bles, -bling, -bled) speak, do, or
move in a clumsy way > **bumbling** adj, n
bumblebee n (pl -s) large hairy bee
bumblebees n ▷ bumblebee
bumbled v ▷ bumble
bumbles v ▷ bumble
bumbling v, adj n ▷ bumble
bumf, bumph n (pl -s) (Informal) official
documents or forms
bumfs n ▷ bumf
bump v (-s, -ing, -ed) knock or strike with a jolt
▶ n (pl -s) dull thud from an impact or collision
> **bumpy** adj (-ier, -iest)
bumped v ▷ bump
bumper[1] n (pl -s) bar on the front and back of a
vehicle to protect against damage
bumper[2] adj unusually large or abundant
bumpers n ▷ bumper[1]
bumph n ▷ bumf
bumphs n ▷ bumf
bumpier adj ▷ bump
bumpiest adj ▷ bump
bumping v ▷ bump
bumpkin n (pl -s) awkward simple country
person
bumpkins n ▷ bumpkin
bumps v, n ▷ bump
bumptious adj offensively self-assertive
> **bumptiously** adv > **bumptiousness** n
bumptiously adj ▷ bumptious
bumptiousness adj ▷ bumptious
bumpy adj ▷ bump
bums n ▷ bum[1, 2]
bun n (pl -s) small sweet bread roll or cake
bunch n (pl -es) number of things growing,
fastened, or grouped together ▶ v (-es, -ing,
-ed) group or be grouped together in a bunch

bunched v ▷ bunch
bunches n, v ▷ bunch
bunching v ▷ bunch
bundle n (pl -s) number of things gathered
loosely together ▶ v (-dles, -dling, -dled) cause
to go roughly or unceremoniously
bundled v ▷ bundle
bundles n, v ▷ bundle
bundling v ▷ bundle
bung n (pl -s) stopper for a cask etc. ▶ v (-s, -ing,
-ed) (foll. by up) (Informal) close with a bung
bungalow n (pl -s) one-storey house
bungalows n ▷ bungalow
bunged v ▷ bung
bunging v ▷ bung
bungle v (-gles, -gling, -gled) spoil through
incompetence ▶ **bungler** n (pl -s) > **bungling**
adj, n
bungled v ▷ bungle
bungler n ▷ bungle
bunglers n ▷ bungle
bungles v ▷ bungle
bungling v, adj n ▷ bungle
bungs n, v ▷ bung
bunion n (pl -s) inflamed swelling on the big
toe
bunions n ▷ bunion
bunk[1] n (pl -s) narrow shelflike bed
bunk[2] n (pl -s) ▷ bunkum
bunk[3] (Slang) n (pl -s) (BRIT) make a hurried and
secret departure ▶ v (-s, -ing, -ed) (BRIT, NZ & S
AFR) be absent without permission
bunked v ▷ bunk[3]
bunker n (pl -s) sand-filled hollow forming an
obstacle on a golf course
bunkers n ▷ bunker
bunking v ▷ bunk[3]
bunks n ▷ bunk[1, 2, 3] ▶ v ▷ bunk[3]
bunkum n (pl -s) nonsense
bunkums n ▷ bunkum
bunnies n ▷ bunny
bunny n (pl -nies) child's word for a rabbit
buns n ▷ bun
bunting n (pl -s) decorative flags
buntings n ▷ bunting
bunya n (pl -s) tall dome-shaped Australian
coniferous tree
bunyas n ▷ bunya
bunyip n (pl -s) (AUST) legendary monster said
to live in swamps and lakes
bunyips n ▷ bunyip
buoy n (pl -s) floating marker anchored in the
sea ▶ v (-s, -ing, -ed) prevent from sinking
buoyancy n ▷ buoyant
buoyant adj able to float > **buoyancy** n

buoyed v ▷ buoy
buoying v ▷ buoy
buoys n, v ▷ buoy
bur n (pl -s) ▷ burr¹
burble v (-bles, -bling, -bled) make a bubbling sound
burbled v ▷ burble
burbles v ▷ burble
burbling v ▷ burble
burden¹ n (pl -s) heavy load ▶ v (-s, -ing, -ed) put a burden on > **burdensome** adj
burden² n (pl -s) theme of a speech etc.
burdened v ▷ burden¹
burdening v ▷ burden¹
burdens v ▷ burden¹ ▶ n ▷ burden¹,²
burdensome adj ▷ burden¹
bureau n (pl -reaus, -reaux) office that provides a service
bureaucracies n ▷ bureaucracy
bureaucracy n (pl -cies) administrative system based on complex rules and procedures > **bureaucrat** n (pl -s) > **bureaucratic** adj
bureaucrat n ▷ bureaucracy
bureaucratic adj ▷ bureaucracy
bureaucrats n ▷ bureaucracy
bureaus n ▷ bureau
bureaux n ▷ bureau
burgeon v (-s, -ing, -ed) develop or grow rapidly
burgeoned v ▷ burgeon
burgeoning v ▷ burgeon
burgeons v ▷ burgeon
burgh n (pl -s) Scottish borough
burghs n ▷ burgh
burglar n (pl -s) person who enters a building to commit a crime, esp. theft > **burglary** n (pl -glaries) > **burgle** v (burgles, burgling, burgled)
burglaries n ▷ burglar
burglars n ▷ burglar
burglary n ▷ burglar
burgled v ▷ burglar
burgles v ▷ burglar
burgling v ▷ burglar
burgundy adj dark-purplish red
burial n (pl -s) burying of a dead body
burials n ▷ burial
buried v ▷ bury
buries v ▷ bury
burlesque n (pl -s) artistic work which satirizes a subject by caricature
burlesques n ▷ burlesque
burlier adj ▷ burly
burliest adj ▷ burly
burly adj (-lier, -liest) (of a person) broad and strong

burn¹ v (-s, -ing, -t or -ed) be or set on fire ▶ n (pl burns) injury or mark caused by fire or exposure to heat
burn² n (pl -s) (Scot) small stream
burned v ▷ burn¹
burning adj intense ▶ v ▷ burn¹
burnish v (-es, -ing, -ed) make smooth and shiny by rubbing
burnished v ▷ burnish
burnishes v ▷ burnish
burnishing v ▷ burnish
burns n ▷ burn¹,² ▶ v ▷ burn¹
burnt v ▷ burn¹
burp v (-s, -ing, -ed) ▶ n (pl -s) (Informal) belch
burped v ▷ burp
burping v ▷ burp
burps v, n ▷ burp
burr¹, bur n (pl -s) head of a plant with prickles or hooks
burr² n (pl -s) soft trilling sound given to the letter r in some dialects
burrawang n (pl -s) Australian plant with fernlike leaves and an edible nut
burrawangs n ▷ burrawang
burrow n (pl -s) hole dug in the ground by a rabbit etc. ▶ v (-s, -ing, -ed) dig holes in the ground
burrowed v ▷ burrow
burrowing v ▷ burrow
burrows n, v ▷ burrow
burrs n ▷ burr¹,²
burs n ▷ bur
bursar n (pl -s) treasurer of a school, college, or university
bursaries n ▷ bursary
bursars n ▷ bursar
bursary n (pl -ries) scholarship
burst v (-s, -ing, burst) (cause to) break open or apart noisily and suddenly ▶ n (pl -s) instance of breaking open suddenly
bursting v ▷ burst
bursts v, n ▷ burst
bury v (buries, burying, buried) place in a grave
burying v ▷ bury
bus n (pl buses) large motor vehicle for carrying passengers ▶ v (busses, bussing, bussed) travel or transport by bus
busbies n ▷ busby
busby n (pl -bies) tall fur hat worn by some soldiers
buses n ▷ bus
bush n (pl -es) dense woody plant, smaller than a tree
bushbabies n ▷ bushbaby

bushbaby n (pl -babies) small African tree-living mammal with large eyes

bushel n (pl -s) obsolete unit of measure equal to 8 gallons (36.4 litres)

bushels n ▷ bushel

bushes n ▷ bush

bushier adj ▷ bushy

bushiest adj ▷ bushy

bushy adj (-shier, -shiest) (of hair) thick and shaggy

busied v ▷ busy

busier adj ▷ busy

busies v ▷ busy

busiest adj ▷ busy

business n (pl -es) purchase and sale of goods and services > **businessman** n (pl -men), **businesswoman** (pl -women)

businesses n ▷ business

businesslike adj efficient and methodical

businessman n ▷ business

businessmen n ▷ business

businesswoman n ▷ business

businesswomen n ▷ business

busk v (-s, -ing, -ed) act as a busker

busked v ▷ busk

busker n (pl -s) street entertainer

buskers n ▷ busker

busking v ▷ busk

busks v ▷ busk

bussed v ▷ bus

busses v ▷ bus

bussing v ▷ bus

bust[1] n (pl -s) woman's bosom

bust[2] (Informal) v (busts, busting, bust or **busted**) burst or break ▶ adj broken

bustard n (pl -s) bird with long strong legs, a heavy body, a long neck, and speckled plumage

bustards n ▷ bustard

busted v ▷ bust[2]

busting v ▷ bust[2]

bustle[1] v (-les, -ling, -led) hurry with a show of activity or energy ▶ n (pl -s) energetic and noisy activity > **bustling** adj

bustle[2] n (pl -s) cushion or framework formerly worn under the back of a woman's skirt to hold it out

bustled v ▷ bustle[1]

bustles v ▷ bustle[1] ▶ n ▷ bustle[1, 2]

bustling v, adj ▷ bustle[1]

busts n ▷ bust[1] ▶ v ▷ bust[2]

busy adj (busier, busiest) actively employed ▶ v (busies, busying, busied) keep (someone, esp. oneself) busy > **busily** adv

busybodies n ▷ busybody

busybody n (pl -bodies) meddlesome or nosy person

busying v ▷ busy

but conj contrary to expectation ▶ prep except ▶ adv only

butane n (pl -s) gas used for fuel

butanes n ▷ butane

butch adj (-er, -est) (Slang) markedly or aggressively masculine

butcher n (pl -s) person who slaughters animals or sells their meat ▶ v (-s, -ing, -ed) kill and prepare (animals) for meat > **butchery** n (pl -ries) adj ▷ butch

butcherbird n (pl -s) Australian magpie that impales its prey on thorns

butcherbirds n ▷ butcherbird

butchered v ▷ butcher

butcheries n ▷ butcher

butchering v ▷ butcher

butchers n, v ▷ butcher

butchery n ▷ butcher

butchest adj ▷ butch

butler n (pl -s) chief male servant

butlers n ▷ butler

butt[1] n (pl -s) thicker end of something

butt[2] n (pl -s) person or thing that is the target of ridicule

butt[3] v (-s, -ing, -ed) strike with the head or horns

butt[4] n (pl -s) large cask

butted v ▷ butt[3]

butter n (pl -s) edible fatty solid made by churning cream ▶ v (-s, -ing, -ed) put butter on > **buttery** adj

buttercup n (pl -s) small yellow flower

buttercups n ▷ buttercup

buttered v ▷ butter

butterfingers n (pl -s) (Informal) person who drops things by mistake

butterflies n ▷ butterfly

butterfly n (pl -flies) insect with brightly coloured wings

buttering v ▷ butter

buttermilk n (pl -s) sourish milk that remains after the butter has been separated from milk

buttermilks n ▷ buttermilks

butters n, v ▷ butter

butterscotch n (pl -es) kind of hard brittle toffee

butterscotches n ▷ butterscotch

buttery adj ▷ butter

butting v ▷ butt[3]

buttock n (pl -s) either of the two fleshy masses that form the human rump

buttocks n ▷ buttock

button n (pl -s) small disc or knob sewn to clothing, which can be passed through a slit in another piece of fabric to fasten them ▸ v (-s, -ing, -ed) fasten with buttons
   buttoned v ▷ button
buttonhole n (pl -s) slit in a garment through which a button is passed ▸ v (-holes, -holing, -holed) detain (someone) in conversation
   buttonholed v ▷ buttonhole
   buttonholes n, v ▷ buttonhole
   buttonholing v ▷ buttonhole
   buttoning v ▷ button
   buttons n, v ▷ button
buttress n (pl -es) structure to support a wall ▸ v (-es, -ing, -ed) support with, or as if with, a buttress
   buttressed v ▷ buttress
   buttresses n, v ▷ buttress
   buttressing v ▷ buttress
   butts n ▷ butt[1, 2, 4] ▸ v ▷ butt[3]
buxom adj (-er, -est) (of a woman) healthily plump and full-bosomed
   buxomer adj ▷ buxom
   buxomest adj ▷ buxom
buy v (-s, -ing, bought) acquire by paying money for ▸ n (pl -s) thing acquired through payment
buyer n (pl -s) customer
   buyers n ▷ buyer
   buying v ▷ buy
   buys v, n ▷ buy
buzz n (pl -es) rapidly vibrating humming sound (Informal) ▸ v (-es, -ing, -ed) make a humming sound > **buzzer** n (pl -s)
buzzard n (pl -s) bird of prey of the hawk family

   buzzards n ▷ buzzard
   buzzed v ▷ buzz
   buzzer n ▷ buzz
   buzzers n ▷ buzz
   buzzes n, v ▷ buzz
   buzzing v ▷ buzz
by prep indicating the doer of an action, nearness, movement past, time before or during which, etc. ▸ adv near
bye interj (Informal) goodbye
   byelaw n ▷ bylaw
   byelaws n ▷ bylaw
bygone adj past or former
bylaw, byelaw n (pl -s) rule made by a local authority
   bylaws n ▷ bylaw
bypass n (pl -es) main road built to avoid a city ▸ v (-es, -ing, -ed) go round or avoid
   bypassed v ▷ bypass
   bypasses n, v ▷ bypass
   bypassing v ▷ bypass
byre n (pl -s) (BRIT) shelter for cows
   byres n ▷ byre
bystander n (pl -s) person present but not involved
   bystanders n ▷ bystander
byte n (pl -s) (COMPUTERS) group of bits processed as one unit of data
   bytes n ▷ byte
byway n (pl -s) minor road
   byways n ▷ byway
byword n (pl -s) person or thing regarded as a perfect example of something
   bywords n ▷ byword

Cc

C can be a tricky letter to use, especially as it only forms a single two-letter word **ch**. But if you remember this, you won't waste time racking your brains for two-letter words. There are, however, plenty of good three-letter words beginning with C. **Cox** scores 12 points, while **caw**, **cow** and **coy** are each worth 8. It's also a good idea to remember the short words starting with C that don't contain any vowels: **cly** and **cwm** as well as **ch**.

cab n (pl -s) taxi

cabal [kab-**bal**] n (pl -s) small group of political plotters
   cabals n ▷ cabal

cabaret [**kab**-a-ray] n (pl -s) dancing and singing show in a nightclub
   cabarets n ▷ cabaret

cabbage n (pl -s) vegetable with a large head of green leaves
   cabbages n ▷ cabbage

cabbie, cabby n (pl -bies) (Informal) taxi driver
   cabbies n ▷ cabbie
   cabby ▷ cabbie

caber n (pl -s) tree trunk tossed in competition at Highland games
   cabers n ▷ caber

cabin n (pl -s) compartment in a ship or aircraft

cabinet n (pl -s) piece of furniture with drawers or shelves

cabinetmaker n (pl -s) person who makes fine furniture
   cabinetmakers n ▷ cabinetmaker
   cabinets n ▷ cabinet
   cabins n ▷ cabin

cable n (pl -s) strong thick rope ▶ v (-les, -ling, -led) send (someone) a message by cable
   cabled v ▷ cable
   cables n, v ▷ cable
   cabling v ▷ cable

caboodle n (Informal) the whole lot

cabriolet [kab-ree-oh-**lay**] n (pl -s) small horse-drawn carriage with a folding hood
   cabriolets n ▷ cabriolet
   cabs n ▷ cab

cacao [kak-**kah**-oh] n (pl -s) tropical tree with seed pods from which chocolate and cocoa are made
   cacaos n ▷ cacao

cache [kash] n (pl -s) hidden store of weapons or treasure
   caches n ▷ cache

cachet [**kash**-shay] n (pl -s) prestige, distinction
   cachets n ▷ cachet

cackle v (-les, -ling, -led) laugh shrilly ▶ n (pl -s) cackling noise
   cackled v ▷ cackle
   cackles v, n ▷ cackle
   cackling v ▷ cackle
   cacophonies n ▷ cacophony
   cacophonous adj ▷ cacophony

cacophony [kak-**koff**-on-ee] n (pl -phonies) harsh discordant sound > **cacophonous** adj
   cacti n ▷ cactus

cactus n (pl -tuses, -ti) fleshy desert plant with spines but no leaves
   cactuses n ▷ cactus

cad n (pl -s) (Old-fashioned) dishonourable man > **caddish** adj

cadaver [kad-**dav**-ver] n (pl -s) corpse

cadaverous adj pale, thin, and haggard
   cadavers n ▷ cadaver

caddie, caddy n (pl -dies) person who carries a golfer's clubs ▶ v (-dies, -dying, -died) act as a caddie
   caddies n ▷ caddie, caddy ▶ v ▷ caddie
   caddish adj ▷ cad

caddy n (pl -dies) small container for tea ▷ caddie

cadence [**kade**-enss] n (pl -s) rise and fall in the pitch of the voice
   cadences n ▷ cadence

cadenza n (pl -s) complex solo passage in a piece of music
   cadenzas n ▷ cadenza

cadet n (pl -s) young person training for the armed forces or police

cadets *n* ▷ cadet

cadge *v* (**cadges, cadging, cadged**) (*Informal*) get (something) by taking advantage of someone's generosity > **cadger** *n* (*pl* -**s**)

cadged *v* ▷ cadge

cadger *n* ▷ cadge

cadgers *n* ▷ cadge

cadges *v* ▷ cadge

cadging *v* ▷ cadge

cadmium *n* (*pl* -**s**) (CHEM) bluish-white metallic element used in alloys

cadmiums *n* ▷ cadmium

cadre [kah-der] *n* (*pl* -**s**) small group of people selected and trained to form the core of a political organization or military unit

cadres *n* ▷ cadre

cads *n* ▷ cad

caeca *n* ▷ caecum

caecum [**seek**-um] *n* (*pl* -**ca**) [-ka] pouch at the beginning of the large intestine

caesium *n* (*pl* -**s**) (CHEM) silvery-white metallic element used in photocells

caesiums *n* ▷ caesium

café *n* (*pl* -**s**) small or inexpensive restaurant serving light refreshments

cafés *n* ▷ café

cafeteria *n* (*pl* -**s**) self-service restaurant

cafeterias *n* ▷ cafeteria

caffeine *n* (*pl* -**s**) stimulant found in tea and coffee

caffeines *n* ▷ caffeine

caftan *n* (*pl* -**s**) ▷ kaftan

caftans *n* ▷ caftan

cage *n* (*pl* -**s**) enclosure of bars or wires, for keeping animals or birds

caged *adj* kept in a cage

cages *n* ▷ cage

cagey *adj* (**cagier, cagiest**) (*Informal*) reluctant to go into details

cagier *adj* ▷ cagey

cagiest *adj* ▷ cagey

cagoule *n* (*pl* -**s**) (BRIT) lightweight hooded waterproof jacket

cagoules *n* ▷ cagoule

cahoots *pl n* (*Informal*) conspiring together

cairn *n* (*pl* -**s**) mound of stones erected as a memorial or marker

cairns *n* ▷ cairn

cajole *v* (-**les**, -**ling**, -**led**) persuade by flattery > **cajolery** *n*

cajoled *v* ▷ cajole

cajolery *n* ▷ cajole

cajoles *v* ▷ cajole

cajoling *v* ▷ cajole

cake *n* (*pl* -**s**) sweet food baked from a mixture of flour, eggs, etc. ▶ *v* (**cakes, caking, caked**) form into a hardened mass or crust

caked *v* ▷ cake

cakes *n, v* ▷ cake

caking *v* ▷ cake

calamine *n* (*pl* -**s**) pink powder consisting chiefly of zinc oxide, used in skin lotions and ointments

calamines *n* ▷ calamine

calamities *n* ▷ calamity

calamitous *adj* ▷ calamity

calamity *n* (*pl* -**ties**) disaster > **calamitous** *adj*

calcification *v* ▷ calcify

calcified *v* ▷ calcify

calcifies *v* ▷ calcify

calcify *v* (-**fies**, -**fying**, -**fied**) harden by the depositing of calcium salts > **calcification** *n*

calcifying *v* ▷ calcify

calcium *n* (*pl* -**s**) (CHEM) silvery-white metallic element found in bones, teeth, limestone, and chalk

calciums *n* ▷ calcium

calculable *adj* ▷ calculate

calculate *v* (-**lates**, -**lating**, -**lated**) solve or find out by a mathematical procedure or by reasoning > **calculable** *adj* > **calculation** *n* (*pl* -**s**)

calculated *v* ▷ calculate

calculates *v* ▷ calculate

calculating *adj* selfishly scheming ▶ *v* ▷ calculate

calculation *n* ▷ calculate

calculations *n* ▷ calculate

calculator *n* (*pl* -**s**) small electronic device for making calculations

calculators *n* ▷ calculator

calculus *n* (*pl* -**es**) branch of mathematics dealing with infinitesimal changes to a variable number or quantity

calculuses *n* ▷ calculus

calendar *n* (*pl* -**s**) chart showing a year divided up into months, weeks, and days

calendars *n* ▷ calendar

calendula *n* (*pl* -**s**) marigold

calendulas *n* ▷ calendula

calf[1] *n* (*pl* **calves**) young cow, bull, elephant, whale, or seal

calf[2] *n* (*pl* **calves**) back of the leg between the ankle and knee

calibrate *v* (-**brates**, -**brating**, -**brated**) mark the scale or check the accuracy of (a measuring instrument) > **calibration** *n* (*pl* -**s**)

calibrated *v* ▷ calibrate

calibrates *v* ▷ calibrate

calibrating *v* ▷ calibrate

calibration n ▷ calibrate

calibrations n ▷ calibrate

calibre n (pl -s) person's ability or worth

calibres n ▷ calibre

calico n (pl -coes) white cotton fabric

calicoes n ▷ calico

caliph n (pl -s) (HIST) Muslim ruler

caliphs n ▷ caliph

call v (-s, -ing, -ed) name ▶ n (pl -s) cry, shout > **caller** n (pl -s)

called v ▷ call

caller n ▷ call

callers n ▷ call

calligrapher n ▷ calligraphy

calligraphers n ▷ calligraphy

calligraphies n ▷ calligraphy

calligraphy n (pl -phies) (art of) beautiful handwriting > **calligrapher** n (pl -s)

calling n (pl -s) vocation, profession ▶ v ▷ call

callings n ▷ calling

calliper n (pl -s) metal splint for supporting the leg

callipers n ▷ calliper

callisthenics pl n light keep-fit exercises

callous adj showing no concern for other people's feelings > **callously** adv > **callousness** n

calloused adj (of skin) thickened and hardened

callously adv ▷ callous

callousness adv ▷ callous

callow adj (-er, -est) young and inexperienced > **callowness** n (pl -es)

callower adj ▷ callow

callowest adj ▷ callow

callowness adv ▷ callow

callownesses adv ▷ callow

calls v, n ▷ call

callus n (pl -es) area of thick hardened skin

calluses n ▷ callus

calm adj (-er, -est) not agitated or excited ▶ n (pl -s) peaceful state ▶ v (-s, -ing, -ed) (often foll. by **down**) make or become calm > **calmly** adv > **calmness** n (pl -es)

calmed v ▷ calm

calmer adj ▷ calm

calmest adj ▷ calm

calming v ▷ calm

calmly adv ▷ calm

calmness adv ▷ calm

calmnesses adv ▷ calm

calms n, v ▷ calm

calorie n (pl -s) unit of measurement for the energy value of food

calories n ▷ calorie

calorific adj of calories or heat

calumnies n ▷ calumny

calumny n (pl -nies) false or malicious statement

calve v (calves, calving, calved) give birth to a calf

calved v ▷ calve

calves v ▷ calve ▶ n ▷ calf[1, 2]

calving v ▷ calve

calyces n ▷ calyx

calypso n (pl -s) West Indian song with improvised topical lyrics

calypsos n ▷ calypso

calyx n (pl calyxes, calyces) outer leaves that protect a flower bud

calyxes n ▷ calyx

cam n (pl -s) device that converts a circular motion to a to-and-fro motion

camaraderie n (pl -s) comradeship

camaraderies n ▷ camaraderie

camber n (pl -s) slight upward curve to the centre of a surface

cambers n ▷ camber

cambric n (pl -s) fine white linen fabric

cambrics n ▷ cambric

camcorder n (pl -s) combined portable video camera and recorder

camcorders n ▷ camcorder

came v ▷ come

camel n (pl -s) humped mammal that can survive long periods without food or water in desert regions

camellia [kam-**meal**-ya] n (pl -s) evergreen ornamental shrub with white, pink, or red flowers

camellias n ▷ camellia

camels n ▷ camel

cameo n (pl -s) brooch or ring with a profile head carved in relief

cameos n ▷ cameo

camera n (pl -s) apparatus used for taking photographs or pictures for television or cinema

cameraman n (pl -men) man who operates a camera for television or cinema

cameramen n ▷ cameraman

cameras n ▷ camera

camiknickers pl n (BRIT) woman's undergarment consisting of knickers attached to a camisole

camisole n (pl -s) woman's bodice-like garment

camisoles n ▷ camisole

camomile n (pl -s) aromatic plant, used to make herbal tea

camomiles n ▷ camomile

camouflage [kam-moo-flahzh] *n* (*pl* -s) use of natural surroundings or artificial aids to conceal or disguise something ▸ *v* (-lages, -flaging, -flaged) conceal by camouflage

camouflaged *v* ▷ camouflage

camouflages *n*, *v* ▷ camouflage

camouflaging *v* ▷ camouflage

camp¹ *n* (*pl* -s) (place for) temporary lodgings consisting of tents, huts, or cabins ▸ *v* (-s, -ing, -ed) stay in a camp > **camper** *n* (*pl* -s)

camp² *adj* (-er, -est) (*Informal*) effeminate or homosexual

campaign *n* (*pl* -s) series of coordinated activities designed to achieve a goal ▸ *v* (-s, -ing, -ed) take part in a campaign

campaigned *v* ▷ campaign

campaigning *v* ▷ campaign

campaigns *n*, *v* ▷ campaign

campanologies *n* ▷ campanology

campanology *n* (*pl* -gies) art of ringing bells

campanula *n* (*pl* -s) plant with blue or white bell-shaped flowers

campanulas *n* ▷ campanula

camped *v* ▷ camp¹

camper *n* ▷ camp¹ ▸ *adj* ▷ camp²

campers *n* ▷ camp¹

campest *adj* ▷ camp²

camphor *n* (*pl* -s) aromatic crystalline substance used medicinally and in mothballs

camphors *n* ▷ camphor

camping *v* ▷ camp¹

campion *n* (*pl* -s) red, pink, or white wild flower

campions *n* ▷ campion

camps *n*, *v* ▷ camp¹

campus *n* (*pl* -es) grounds of a university or college

campuses *n* ▷ campus

cams *n* ▷ cam

camshaft *n* (*pl* -s) part of an engine consisting of a rod to which cams are fixed

camshafts *n* ▷ camshaft

can¹ *v* (*past* could) be able to

can² *n* (*pl* -s) metal container for food or liquids ▸ *v* (cans, canning, canned) put (something) into a can

canal *n* (*pl* -s) artificial waterway

canals *n* ▷ canal

canapé [kan-nap-pay] *n* (*pl* -s) small piece of bread or toast with a savoury topping

canapés *n* ▷ canapé

canaries *n* ▷ canary

canary *n* (*pl* -ries) small yellow songbird often kept as a pet

canasta *n* (*pl* -s) card game like rummy, played with two packs

canastas *n* ▷ canasta

cancan *n* (*pl* -s) lively high-kicking dance performed by a female group

cancans *n* ▷ cancan

cancel *v* (-cels, -celling, -celled) stop (something that has been arranged) from taking place > **cancellation** *n* (*pl* -s)

cancellation *n* ▷ cancel

cancellations *n* ▷ cancel

cancelled *v* ▷ cancel

cancelling *v* ▷ cancel

cancels *v* ▷ cancel

cancer *n* (*pl* -s) serious disease resulting from a malignant growth or tumour > **cancerous** *adj*

cancerous *adj* ▷ cancer

cancers *n* ▷ cancer

candela [kan-**dee**-la] *n* (*pl* -s) unit of luminous intensity

candelabra *n* ▷ candelabrum

candelabrum *n* (*pl* -bra) large branched candle holder

candelas *n* ▷ candela

candid *adj* (-er, -est) honest and straightforward > **candidly** *adv* > **candidness** *n* (*pl* -es)

candidacies *n* ▷ candidate

candidacy *n* ▷ candidate

candidate *n* (*pl* -s) person seeking a job or position > **candidacy** (*pl* -acies), **candidature** *n* (*pl* -s)

candidates *n* ▷ candidate

candidature *n* ▷ candidate

candidatures *n* ▷ candidate

candider *adj* ▷ candid

candidest *adj* ▷ candid

candidly *adv* ▷ candid

candidness *n* ▷ candid

candidnesses *n* ▷ candid

candied *adj* coated with sugar

candies *n* ▷ candy

candle *n* (*pl* -s) stick of wax enclosing a wick, which is burned to produce light

candles *n* ▷ candle

candlestick *n* (*pl* -s) holder for a candle

candlesticks *n* ▷ candlestick

candlewick *n* (*pl* -s) cotton fabric with a tufted surface

candlewicks *n* ▷ candlewick

candour *n* (*pl* -s) honesty and straightforwardness

candours *n* ▷ candour

candy *n* (*pl* -dies) (*us*) sweet or sweets

candyfloss *n* (*pl* -es) light fluffy mass of spun sugar on a stick

candyflosses n ▷ **candyfloss**
cane n (pl **-s**) stem of the bamboo or similar plant ▶ v (**canes, caning, caned**) beat with a cane
  caned v ▷ **cane**
  canes n, v ▷ **cane**
canine adj of or like a dog ▶ n (pl **-s**) sharp pointed tooth between the incisors and the molars
  canines n ▷ **canine**
  caning v ▷ **cane**
canister n (pl **-s**) metal container
  canisters n ▷ **canister**
canker n (pl **-s**) ulceration, ulcerous disease
  cankers n ▷ **canker**
cannabis n (pl **-es**) Asian plant with tough fibres
  cannabises n ▷ **cannabis**
canned adj preserved in a can ▶ v ▷ **can²**
cannelloni pl n tubular pieces of pasta filled with meat etc.
  canneries n ▷ **cannery**
cannery n (pl **-ries**) factory where food is canned
cannibal n (pl **-s**) person who eats human flesh > **cannibalism** n
cannibalize v (**-lizes, -lizing, -lized**) use parts from (one machine) to repair another
  cannibalized v ▷ **cannibalize**
  cannibalizes v ▷ **cannibalize**
  cannibalizing v ▷ **cannibalize**
  cannibals n ▷ **cannibal**
  cannier adj ▷ **canny**
  canniest adj ▷ **canny**
  cannily adv ▷ **canny**
  canning v ▷ **can²**
cannon n (pl **-s**) large gun on wheels
cannonade n (pl **-s**) continuous heavy gunfire
  cannonades n ▷ **cannonade**
cannonball n (pl **-s**) heavy metal ball fired from a cannon
  cannonballs n ▷ **cannonball**
  cannons n ▷ **cannon**
cannot v can not
canny adj (**-nier, -niest**) shrewd, cautious > **cannily** adv
canoe n (pl **-s**) light narrow open boat propelled by a paddle or paddles > **canoeist** n (pl **-s**)
canoeing n sport of rowing in a canoe
  canoeist n ▷ **canoe**
  canoeists n ▷ **canoe**
  canoes n ▷ **canoe**
canon¹ n (pl **-s**) priest serving in a cathedral
canon² n (pl **-s**) Church decree regulating

morals or religious practices > **canonical** adj
canonical adj ▷ **canon²**
canonization n ▷ **canonize**
canonizations n ▷ **canonize**
canonize v (**-izes, -izing, -ized**) declare (a person) officially to be a saint > **canonization** n (pl **-s**)
  canonized v ▷ **canonize**
  canonizes v ▷ **canonize**
  canonizing v ▷ **canonize**
  canons n ▷ **canon¹, ²**
canoodle v (**-les, -ling, -led**) (Slang) kiss and cuddle
  canoodled v ▷ **canoodle**
  canoodles v ▷ **canoodle**
  canoodling v ▷ **canoodle**
canopied adj covered with a canopy
  canopies n ▷ **canopy**
canopy n (pl **-pies**) covering above a bed, door, etc
  cans n, v ▷ **can²**
cant¹ n (pl **-s**) insincere talk
cant² n (pl **-s**) tilted position ▶ v (**-s, -ing, -ed**) tilt, overturn
cantaloupe, cantaloup n (pl **-s**) kind of melon with sweet orange flesh
  cantaloupes n ▷ **cantaloupe**
  cantaloups n ▷ **cantaloupe**
cantankerous adj quarrelsome, bad-tempered
cantata n (pl **-s**) musical work consisting of arias, duets, and choruses
  cantatas n ▷ **cantata**
  canted v ▷ **cant²**
canteen n (pl **-s**) restaurant attached to a workplace or school
  canteens n ▷ **canteen**
canter n (pl **-s**) horse's gait between a trot and a gallop ▶ v (**-s, -ing, -ed**) move at a canter
  cantered v ▷ **canter**
  cantering v ▷ **canter**
  canters n, v ▷ **canter**
canticle n (pl **-s**) short hymn with words from the Bible
  canticles n ▷ **canticle**
cantilever n (pl **-s**) beam or girder fixed at one end only
  cantilevers n ▷ **cantilever**
  canting v ▷ **cant²**
canto n (pl **-s**) main division of a long poem
canton n (pl **-s**) political division of a country, esp. Switzerland
  cantons n ▷ **canton**
cantor n (pl **-s**) man employed to lead services in a synagogue

cantors n ▷ cantor

cantos n ▷ canto

cants n ▷ cant[1, 2] ▶ v ▷ cant[2]

canvas n (pl -es) heavy coarse cloth used for sails and tents, and for oil painting

canvases n ▷ canvas

canvass v (-es, -ing, -ed) try to get votes or support (from) ▶ n (pl -es) canvassing

canvassed v ▷ canvass

canvasses v, n ▷ canvass

canvassing v ▷ canvass

canyon n (pl -s) deep narrow valley

canyons n ▷ canyon

cap n (pl -s) soft close-fitting covering for the head ▶ v (**caps, capping, capped**) cover or top with something

capabilities n ▷ capable

capability n ▷ capable

capable adj (foll. by **of**) having the ability (for) > **capably** adv > **capability** n (pl -ties)

capably adv ▷ capable

capacious adj roomy

capacitance n (pl -s) (measure of) the ability of a system to store electrical charge

capacitances n ▷ capacit

capacities n ▷ capacity

capacitor n (pl -s) device for storing electrical charge

capacitors n ▷ capacitor

capacity n (pl -ties) ability to contain, absorb, or hold

caparisoned adj magnificently decorated

cape[1] n (pl -s) short cloak

cape[2] n (pl -s) large piece of land that juts out into the sea

caper n (pl -s) high-spirited prank ▶ v (-s, -ing, -ed) skip about

capercaillie, capercailzie [kap-per-**kale**-yee] n (pl -s) large black European grouse

capercaillies n ▷ capercaillie

capercailzie n ▷ capercaillie

capercailzies n ▷ capercaillie

capered v ▷ caper

capering v ▷ caper

capers pl n pickled flower buds of a Mediterranean shrub used in sauces ▶ n ▷ caper ▶ v ▷ caper

capes n ▷ cape[1, 2]

capillaries n ▷ capillary

capillary n (pl -laries) very fine blood vessel

capital[1] n (pl -s) chief city of a country ▶ adj involving or punishable by death

capital[2] n (pl -s) top part of a pillar

capitalism n (pl -s) economic system based on the private ownership of industry

capitalisms n ▷ capitalism

capitalist adj of capitalists or capitalism ▶ n (pl -s) supporter of capitalism > **capitalistic** adj

capitalistic adj ▷ capitalist

capitalists n ▷ capitalist

capitalize v (-lizes, -lizing, -lized) write or print (words) in capitals

capitalized v ▷ capitalize

capitalizes v ▷ capitalize

capitalizing v ▷ capitalize

capitals n ▷ capital[1, 2]

capitation n (pl -s) tax of a fixed amount per person

capitations n ▷ capitation

capitulate v (-lates, -lating, -lated) surrender on agreed terms > **capitulation** n (pl -s)

capitulated v ▷ capitulate

capitulates v ▷ capitulate

capitulating v ▷ capitulate

capitulation n ▷ capitulate

capitulations n ▷ capitulate

capon n (pl -s) castrated cock fowl fattened for eating

capons n ▷ capon

capped v ▷ cap

capping v ▷ cap

cappuccino [kap-poo-**cheen**-oh] n (pl -s) coffee with steamed milk, sprinkled with powdered chocolate

cappuccinos n ▷ cappuccino

caprice [kap-**reess**] n (pl -s) sudden change of attitude

caprices n ▷ caprice

capricious adj tending to have sudden changes of attitude > **capriciously** adv

capriciously adv ▷ capricious

caps n, v ▷ cap

capsicum n (pl -s) kind of pepper used as a vegetable or as a spice

capsicums n ▷ capsicum

capsize v (-sizes, -sizing, -sized) (of a boat) overturn accidentally

capsized v ▷ capsize

capsizes v ▷ capsize

capsizing v ▷ capsize

capstan n (pl -s) rotating cylinder round which a ship's rope is wound

capstans n ▷ capstan

capsule n (pl -s) soluble gelatine case containing a dose of medicine

capsules n ▷ capsule

captain n (pl -s) commander of a ship or civil aircraft ▶ v (-s, -ing, -ed) be captain of > **captaincy** n (pl -cies)

captaincies n ▷ captain

captaincy n (pl -s) ▷ captain
captained v ▷ captain
captaining v ▷ captain
captains n, v ▷ captain
caption n (pl -s) title or explanation accompanying an illustration ▶ v (-s, -ing, -ed) provide with a caption
captioned v ▷ caption
captioning v ▷ caption
captions n, v ▷ caption
captious adj tending to make trivial criticisms > **captiously** adv > **captiousness** n
captiously adv ▷ captious
captiousness n ▷ captious
captivate v (-ates, -ating, -ated) attract and hold the attention of > **captivating** adj
captivated v ▷ captivate
captivates v ▷ captivate
captivating adj, v ▷ captivate
captive n (pl -s) person kept in confinement ▶ adj kept in confinement > **captivity** n
captives n ▷ captive
captivity n ▷ captive
captor n (pl -s) person who captures a person or animal
captors n ▷ captor
capture v (-tures, -turing, -tured) take by force ▶ n (pl -s) capturing
captured v ▷ capture
captures v, n ▷ capture
capturing v ▷ capture
car n (pl -s) motor vehicle designed to carry a small number of people
carafe [kar-**raff**] n (pl -s) glass bottle for serving water or wine
carafes n ▷ carafe
caramel n (pl -s) chewy sweet made from sugar and milk
caramelize v (-izes, -izing, -ized) turn into caramel
caramelized v ▷ caramelize
caramelizes v ▷ caramelize
caramelizing v ▷ caramelize
caramels n ▷ caramel
carapace n (pl -s) hard upper shell of tortoises and crustaceans
carapaces n ▷ carapace
carat n (pl -s) unit of weight of precious stones
carats n ▷ carat
caravan n (pl -s) large enclosed vehicle for living in, designed to be towed by a car or horse
caravans n ▷ caravan
caraway n (pl -s) plant whose seeds are used as a spice

caraways n ▷ caraway
carbide n (pl -s) compound of carbon with a metal
carbides n ▷ carbide
carbine n (pl -s) light automatic rifle
carbines n ▷ carbine
carbohydrate n (pl -s) any of a large group of energy-producing compounds in food, such as sugars and starches
carbohydrates n ▷ carbohydrate
carbon n (pl -s) nonmetallic element occurring as charcoal, graphite, and diamond, found in all organic matter
carbonate n (pl -s) salt or ester of carbonic acid
carbonated adj (of a drink) containing carbon dioxide
carbonates n ▷ carbonate
carbonize v (-izes, -izing, -ized) turn into carbon as a result of heating
carbonized v ▷ carbonize
carbonizes v ▷ carbonize
carbonizing v ▷ carbonize
carbons n ▷ carbon
carbuncle n (pl -s) inflamed boil
carbuncles n ▷ carbuncle
carburettor n (pl -s) device which mixes petrol and air in an internal-combustion engine
carburettors n ▷ carburettor
carcase n ▷ carcass
carcases n ▷ carcass
carcass, carcase n (pl -es, -es) dead body of an animal
carcasses n ▷ carcass
carcinogen n (pl -s) substance that produces cancer > **carcinogenic** adj
carcinogenic adj ▷ carcinogen
carcinogens n ▷ carcinogen
carcinoma n (pl -s) malignant tumour
carcinomas n ▷ carcinoma
card n (pl -s) piece of thick stiff paper or cardboard used for identification, reference, or sending greetings or messages ▶ pl any card game, or card games in general
cardboard n (pl -s) thin stiff board made from paper pulp
cardboards n ▷ cardboard
cardiac adj of the heart
cardigan n (pl -s) knitted jacket
cardigans n ▷ cardigan
cardinal n (pl -s) any of the high-ranking clergymen of the RC Church who elect the Pope and act as his counsellors ▶ adj fundamentally important
cardinals n ▷ cardinal
cardiogram n (pl -s) electrocardiogram

cardiograms n ▷ cardiogram
cardiograph n (pl -s) electrocardiograph
cardiographs n ▷ cardiograph
cardiologist n ▷ cardiology
cardiologists n ▷ cardiology
cardiology n study of the heart and its
diseases > **cardiologist** n (pl -s)
cardiovascular adj of the heart and the blood
vessels
cards n ▷ card
cardsharp n (pl -s) professional card player
who cheats
cardsharps n ▷ cardsharp
care v (cares, caring, cared) be concerned ▶ n
(pl -s) careful attention, caution > **careful**
adj (-ller, -llest) > **carefully** adv > **carefulness**
n (pl -es) > **careless** adj > **carelessly** adv
> **carelessness** n
cared v ▷ care
careen v (-s, -ing, -ed) tilt over to one side
careened v ▷ careen
careening v ▷ careen
careens v ▷ careen
career n (pl -s) series of jobs in a profession or
occupation that a person has through their
life ▶ v (-s, -ing, -ed) rush in an uncontrolled
way
careered v ▷ career
careering v ▷ career
careerist n (pl -s) person who seeks
advancement by any possible means
careerists n ▷ careerist
careers n, v ▷ career
carefree adj without worry or responsibility
careful adj ▷ care
carefuller adj ▷ care
carefullest adj ▷ care
carefully adv ▷ care
carefulness n ▷ care
carefulnesses n ▷ care
careless adj ▷ care
carelessly adv ▷ care
carelessness adv ▷ care
cares v, n ▷ care
caress n (pl -es) gentle affectionate touch or
embrace ▶ v (-es, -ing, -ed) touch gently and
affectionately
caressed v ▷ caress
caresses n, v ▷ caress
caressing v ▷ caress
caret [kar-rett] n (pl -s) symbol (ʌ) indicating
a place in written or printed matter where
something is to be inserted
caretaker n (pl -s) person employed to look
after a place

caretakers n ▷ caretaker
carets n ▷ caret
careworn adj showing signs of worry
cargo n (pl -es) goods carried by a ship, aircraft,
etc.
cargoes n ▷ cargo
caribou n (pl -bou or -bous) large N American
reindeer
caribous n ▷ caribou
caricature n (pl -s) drawing or description of
a person that exaggerates features for comic
effect ▶ v (-tures, -turing, -tured) make a
caricature of
caricatured v ▷ caricature
caricatures n, v ▷ caricature
caricaturing v ▷ caricature
caries [care-reez] n (pl caries) tooth decay
carillon [kar-rill-yon] n (pl -s) set of bells played
by keyboard or mechanically
carillons n ▷ carillon
caring v ▷ care
cark v (-s, -ing, -ed) (AUST & NZ) (Slang) die
carked v ▷ cark
carking v ▷ cark
carks v ▷ cark
carmine adj vivid red
carnage n (pl -s) extensive slaughter of people
carnages n ▷ carnage
carnal adj of a sexual or sensual nature
> **carnally** adv
carnally adv ▷ carnal
carnation n (pl -s) cultivated plant with
fragrant white, pink, or red flowers
carnations n ▷ carnation
carnival n (pl -s) festive period with
processions, music, and dancing in the street
carnivals n ▷ carnival
carnivore n (pl -s) meat-eating animal
> **carnivorous** adj
carnivores n ▷ carnivore
carnivorous adj ▷ carnivore
carob n (pl -s) pod of a Mediterranean tree,
used as a chocolate substitute
carobs n ▷ carob
carol n (pl -s) joyful Christmas hymn ▶ v (-ls,
-lling, -lled) sing carols
carolled v ▷ carol
carolling v ▷ carol
carols n, v ▷ carol
carotid adj, n (pl -s) (of) either of the two
arteries supplying blood to the head
carotids n ▷ carotid
carouse v (-ouses, -ousing, -oused) have a
merry drinking party
caroused v ▷ carouse

carousel [kar-roo-**sell**] n (pl -s) revolving conveyor belt for luggage or photographic slides
   carousels n ▷ carousel
   carouses v ▷ carouse
   carousing v ▷ carouse

carp¹ n (pl carp) large freshwater fish

carp² v (-s, -ing, -ed) complain, find fault
   carped v ▷ carp²

carpel n (pl -s) female reproductive organ of a flowering plant
   carpels n ▷ carpel

carpenter n (pl -s) person who makes or repairs wooden structures > **carpentry** n
   carpenters n ▷ carpenter
   carpentry n ▷ carpenter

carpet n (pl -s) heavy fabric for covering floors ▶ v (-s, -ing, -ed) cover with a carpet
   carpeted v ▷ carpet
   carpeting v ▷ carpet
   carpets n, v ▷ carpet
   carpi n ▷ carpus
   carping v ▷ carp²
   carps v ▷ carp²

carpus n (pl -pi) set of eight bones of the wrist

carriage n (pl -s) one of the sections of a train for passengers
   carriages n ▷ carriage

carriageway n (pl -s) (BRIT) part of a road along which traffic passes in one direction
   carriageways n ▷ carriageway
   carried v ▷ carry

carrier n (pl -s) person or thing that carries something
   carriers n ▷ carrier
   carries v ▷ carry

carrion n (pl -s) dead and rotting flesh
   carrions n ▷ carrion

carrot n (pl -s) long tapering orange root vegetable
   carrots n ▷ carrot

carroty adj (of hair) reddish-orange

carry v (-ries, -rying, -ried) take from one place to another
   carrying v ▷ carry
   cars n ▷ car

cart n (pl -s) open two-wheeled horse-drawn vehicle for carrying goods or passengers ▶ v (-s, -ing, -ed) carry, usu. with some effort
   carted v ▷ cart

cartel n (pl -s) association of competing firms formed to fix prices
   cartels n ▷ cartel

carthorse n (pl -s) large heavily built horse
   carthorses n ▷ carthorse

cartilage n (pl -s) strong flexible tissue forming part of the skeleton > **cartilaginous** adj
   cartilages n ▷ cartilage
   cartilaginous n ▷ cartilage
   carting v ▷ cart

cartographer n ▷ cartography
   cartographers n ▷ cartography
   cartographic adj ▷ cartography
   cartographically adj ▷ cartography
   cartographies n ▷ cartography

cartography n (pl -ies) map making > **cartographer** n (pl -s) > **cartographic** adj > **cartographically** adv

carton n (pl -s) container made of cardboard or waxed paper
   cartons n ▷ carton

cartoon n (pl -s) humorous or satirical drawing > **cartoonist** n (pl -s)
   cartoonist n ▷ cartoon
   cartoonists n ▷ cartoon
   cartoons n ▷ cartoon

cartridge n (pl -s) casing containing an explosive charge and bullet for a gun
   cartridges n ▷ cartridge
   carts n, v ▷ cart

cartwheel n (pl -s) sideways somersault supported by the hands with legs outstretched
   cartwheels n ▷ cartwheel

carve v (carves, carving, carved) cut to form an object > **carving** n (pl -s)
   carved v ▷ carve
   carves v ▷ carve
   carving v, n ▷ carve
   carvings n ▷ carve

caryatid [kar-ree-**at**-id] n (pl -s) supporting column in the shape of a female figure
   caryatids n ▷ caryatid

casbah n (pl -s) citadel of a N African city
   casbahs n ▷ casbah

cascade n (pl -s) waterfall ▶ v (-cades, -cading, -caded) flow or fall in a cascade
   cascaded v ▷ cascade
   cascades n, v ▷ cascade
   cascading v ▷ cascade

case¹ n (pl -s) instance, example

case² n (pl -s) container, protective covering ▶ v (cases, casing, cased) (Slang) inspect (a building) with the intention of burgling it
   cased v ▷ case²

casement n (pl -s) window that is hinged on one side
   casements n ▷ casement
   cases n ▷ case¹, ² ▶ v ▷ case²

cash *n* banknotes and coins ▶ *v* (**-es, -ing, -ed**) obtain cash for
  cashed *v* ▷ **cash**
  cashes *v* ▷ **cash**
cashew *n* (*pl* **-s**) edible kidney-shaped nut
  cashews *n* ▷ **cashew**
cashier[1] *n* (*pl* **-s**) person responsible for handling cash in a bank, shop, etc.
cashier[2] *v* (**-s, -ing, -ed**) dismiss with dishonour from the armed forces
  cashiered *v* ▷ **cashier**[2]
  cashiering *v* ▷ **cashier**[2]
  cashiers *n* ▷ **cashier**[1] ▶ *v* ▷ **cashier**[2]
  cashing *v* ▷ **cash**
cashmere *n* (*pl* **-s**) fine soft wool obtained from goats
  cashmeres *n* ▷ **cashmere**
casing *n* (*pl* **-s**) protective case, covering ▶ *v* ▷ **case**[2]
  casings *n* ▷ **casing**
casino *n* (*pl* **-s**) public building or room where gambling games are played
  casinos *n* ▷ **casino**
cask *n* (*pl* **-s**) barrel used to hold alcoholic drink
casket *n* (*pl* **-s**) small box for valuables
  caskets *n* ▷ **casket**
  casks *n* ▷ **cask**
cassava *n* (*pl* **-s**) starch obtained from the roots of a tropical American plant, used to make tapioca
  cassavas *n* ▷ **cassava**
casserole *n* (*pl* **-s**) covered dish in which food is cooked slowly, usu. in an oven ▶ *v* (**-oles, -oling, -oled**) cook in a casserole
  casseroled *v* ▷ **casserole**
  casseroles *n, v* ▷ **casserole**
  casseroling *v* ▷ **casserole**
cassette *n* (*pl* **-s**) plastic case containing a reel of film or magnetic tape
  cassettes *n* ▷ **cassette**
cassock *n* (*pl* **-s**) long tunic, usu. black, worn by priests
  cassocks *n* ▷ **cassock**
  cassowaries *n* ▷ **cassowary**
cassowary *n* (*pl* **-waries**) large flightless bird of Australia and New Guinea
cast *n* (*pl* **-s**) actors in a play or film collectively ▶ *v* (**casts, casting, cast**) select (an actor) to play a part in a play or film
castanets *pl n* musical instrument, used by Spanish dancers, consisting of curved pieces of hollow wood clicked together in the hand
castaway *n* (*pl* **-s**) shipwrecked person
  castaways *n* ▷ **castaway**
caste *n* (*pl* **-s**) any of the hereditary classes into which Hindu society is divided
castellated *adj* having battlements
  castes *n* ▷ **caste**
castigate *v* (**-gates, -gating, -gated**) reprimand severely > **castigation** *n*
  castigated *v* ▷ **castigate**
  castigates *v* ▷ **castigate**
  castigating *v* ▷ **castigate**
  castigation *v* ▷ **castigate**
  casting *v* ▷ **cast**
castle *n* (*pl* **-s**) large fortified building, often built as a ruler's residence
  castles *n* ▷ **castle**
castoff *adj, n* (*pl* **-s**) discarded (person or thing)
  castoffs *n* ▷ **castoff**
castor *n* (*pl* **-s**) small swivelling wheel fixed to the bottom of a piece of furniture for easy moving
  castors *n* ▷ **castor**
castrate *v* (**-tes, -ting, -ted**) remove the testicles of > **castration** *n* (*pl* **-s**)
  castrated *v* ▷ **castrate**
  castrates *v* ▷ **castrate**
  castrating *v* ▷ **castrate**
  castration *n* ▷ **castrate**
  castrations *n* ▷ **castrate**
  casts *n, v* ▷ **cast**
casual *adj* careless, nonchalant > **casually** *adv*
  casually *adv* ▷ **casual**
  casualties *n* ▷ **casualty**
casualty *n* (*pl* **-ties**) person killed or injured in an accident or war
casuarina [kass-yew-a-**reen**-a] *n* (*pl* **-s**) Australian tree with jointed green branches
  casuarinas *n* ▷ **casuarina**
  casuistries *n* ▷ **casuistry**
casuistry *n* (*pl* **-ries**) reasoning that is misleading or oversubtle
cat *n* (*pl* **-s**) small domesticated furry mammal
cataclysm [kat-a-kliz-zum] *n* (*pl* **-s**) violent upheaval > **cataclysmic** *adj*
  cataclysmic *adj* ▷ **cataclysm**
  cataclysms *n* ▷ **cataclysm**
catacombs [kat-a-koomz] *pl n* underground burial place consisting of tunnels with recesses for tombs
catafalque [kat-a-falk] *n* (*pl* **-s**) raised platform on which a body lies in state before or during a funeral
  catafalques *n* ▷ **catafalque**
  catalepsies *n* ▷ **catalepsy**
catalepsy *n* (*pl* **-sies**) trancelike state in which the body is rigid > **cataleptic** *adj*
  cataleptic *adj* ▷ **catalepsy**
catalogue *n* (*pl* **-s**) book containing details of

items for sale ▸ v (-logues, -loguing, -logued) make a systematic list of
catalogued v ▷ catalogue
catalogues n, v ▷ catalogue
cataloguing v ▷ catalogue
catalyse v (-lyses, -lysing, -lysed) speed up (a chemical reaction) by a catalyst
catalysed v ▷ catalyse
catalyses v ▷ catalyse
catalysing v ▷ catalyse
catalysis n ▷ catalyst
catalyst n (pl -s) substance that speeds up a chemical reaction without itself changing > **catalysis** n > **catalytic** adj > **catalytically** adv
catalysts n ▷ catalyst
catalytic adj ▷ catalyst
catalytically adv ▷ catalyst
catamaran n (pl -s) boat with twin parallel hulls
catamarans n ▷ catamaran
catapult n (pl -s) Y-shaped device with a loop of elastic, used by children for firing stones ▸ v (-s, -ing, -ed) shoot forwards or upwards violently
catapulted v ▷ catapult
catapulting v ▷ catapult
catapults n, v ▷ catapult
cataract n (pl -s) eye disease in which the lens becomes opaque
cataracts n ▷ cataract
catarrh [kat-tar] n (pl -s) excessive mucus in the nose and throat, during or following a cold > **catarrhal** adj
catarrhal adj ▷ catarrh
catarrhs n ▷ catarrh
catastrophe [kat-ass-trof-fee] n (pl -s) great and sudden disaster > **catastrophic** adj > **catastrophically** adv
catastrophes n ▷ catastrophe
catastrophic adj ▷ catastrophe
catastrophically adv ▷ catastrophe
catcall n (pl -s) derisive whistle or cry
catcalls n ▷ catcall
catch v (catches, catching, caught) seize, capture ▸ n (pl -es) device for fastening a door, window, etc.
catches v, n ▷ catch
catchier adj ▷ catchy
catchiest adj ▷ catchy
catchily adv ▷ catchy
catchiness n ▷ catchy
catchinesses n ▷ catchy
catching adj infectious ▸ v ▷ catch
catchword n (pl -s) well-known and frequently used phrase

catchwords n ▷ catchword
catchy adj (-chier, -chiest) (of a tune) pleasant and easily remembered > **catchily** adv > **catchiness** n (pl -es)
catechism [kat-ti-kiz-zum] n (pl -s) instruction on the doctrine of a Christian Church in a series of questions and answers
catechisms n ▷ catechism
categorical adj absolutely clear and certain > **categorically** adv
categorically adv ▷ categorical
categories n ▷ category
categorization n ▷ categorize
categorizations n ▷ categorize
categorize v (-izes, -izing, -ized) put in a category > **categorization** n (pl -s)
categorized v ▷ categorize
categorizes v ▷ categorize
categorizing v ▷ categorize
category n (pl -ries) class, group
cater v (-s, -ing, -ed) provide what is needed or wanted, esp. food or services > **caterer** n (pl -s)
catered v ▷ cater
caterer n ▷ cater
caterers n ▷ cater
catering v ▷ cater
caterpillar n (pl -s) wormlike larva of a moth or butterfly
caterpillars n ▷ caterpillar
caters v ▷ cater
caterwaul v (-s, -ing, -ed) wail, yowl
caterwauled v ▷ caterwaul
caterwauling v ▷ caterwaul
caterwauls v ▷ caterwaul
catfish n (pl catfish, catfishes) fish with whisker-like barbels round the mouth
catfishes n ▷ catfish
catgut n (pl -s) strong cord used to string musical instruments and sports rackets
catguts n ▷ catgut
catharses n ▷ catharsis
catharsis [kath-thar-siss] n (pl -ses) relief of strong suppressed emotions > **cathartic** adj
cathartic adj ▷ catharsis
cathedral n (pl -s) principal church of a diocese
cathedrals n ▷ cathedral
catheter [kath-it-er] n (pl -s) tube inserted into a body cavity to drain fluid
catheters n ▷ catheter
cathode n (pl -s) negative electrode, by which electrons leave a circuit
cathodes n ▷ cathode
catholic adj (of tastes or interests) covering a wide range > **catholicism** n (pl -s)
catholicism n ▷ catholic

catholicisms n ▷ catholic
cation [kat-eye-on] n (pl -s) positively charged ion
cations n ▷ cation
catkin n (pl -s) drooping flower spike of certain trees
catkins n ▷ catkin
catnap n (pl -s) ▶ v (-naps, -napping, -napped) doze
catnapped v ▷ catnap
catnapping v ▷ catnap
catnaps n, v ▷ catnap
cats n ▷ cat
cattier adj ▷ catty
cattiest adj ▷ catty
cattily adv ▷ catty
cattiness n ▷ catty
cattle pl n domesticated cows and bulls
catty adj (cattier, cattiest) (Informal) spiteful > **cattily** adv > **cattiness** n
catwalk n (pl -s) narrow pathway or platform
catwalks n ▷ catwalk
caucus n (pl -es) local committee or faction of a political party
caught v ▷ catch
cauldron n (pl -s) large pot used for boiling
cauldrons n ▷ cauldron
cauliflower n (pl -s) vegetable with a large head of white flower buds surrounded by green leaves
cauliflowers n ▷ cauliflower
caulk v (-s, -ing, -ed) fill in (cracks) with paste etc.
caulked v ▷ caulk
caulking v ▷ caulk
caulks v ▷ caulk
causal adj of or being a cause > **causally** adv
causality n ▷ causation
causally adv ▷ causal
causation, causality n relationship of cause and effect
cause n (pl -s) something that produces a particular effect ▶ v (causes, causing, caused) be the cause of
caused v ▷ cause
causes n, v ▷ cause
causeway n (pl -s) raised path or road across water or marshland
causeways n ▷ causeway
causing v ▷ cause
caustic adj capable of burning by chemical action > **caustically** adv
caustically adv ▷ caustic
cauterize v (-izes, -izing, -ized) burn (a wound) with heat or a caustic agent to prevent

infection
cauterized v ▷ cauterize
cauterizes v ▷ cauterize
cauterizing v ▷ cauterize
caution n (pl -s) care, esp. in the face of danger ▶ v (-s, -ing, -ed) warn, advise
cautionary adj warning
cautioned v ▷ caution
cautioning v ▷ caution
cautions n, v ▷ caution
cautious adj showing caution > **cautiously** adv
cautiously adv ▷ cautious
cavalcade n (pl -s) procession of people on horseback or in cars
cavalcades n ▷ cavalcade
cavalier adj showing haughty disregard ▶ n (pl -s) (C-) supporter of Charles I in the English Civil War > **cavalierly** adv
cavalierly adv ▷ cavalier
cavaliers n ▷ cavalier
cavalries n ▷ cavalry
cavalry n (pl -ries) part of the army orig. on horseback, but now often using fast armoured vehicles
cave n (pl -s) hollow in the side of a hill or cliff
caveat [kav-vee-at] n (pl -s) warning
caveats n ▷ caveat
caveman n (pl -men) prehistoric cave dweller
cavemen n ▷ caveman
cavern n (pl -s) large cave > **cavernous** adj
cavernous adj ▷ cavern
caverns n ▷ cavern
caves n ▷ cave
caviar, caviare n (pl -s) salted sturgeon roe, regarded as a delicacy
caviare n ▷ caviar
caviares n ▷ caviar
caviars n ▷ caviar
cavil v (-ils, -illing, -illed) make petty objections ▶ n (pl -s) petty objection
cavilled v ▷ cavil
cavilling v ▷ cavil
cavils v, n ▷ cavil
caving n sport of exploring caves
cavities v ▷ cavity
cavity n (pl -ties) hollow space
cavort v (-s, -ing, -ed) skip about
cavorted v ▷ cavort
cavorting v ▷ cavort
cavorts v ▷ cavort
caw n (pl -s) cry of a crow, rook, or raven ▶ v (-s, -ing, -ed) make this cry
cawed v ▷ caw
cawing v ▷ caw

caws n, v ▷ caw

cay n (cays). A cay is a small low island. Cay scores 8 points.

cayman n (pl -s) S American reptile similar to an alligator

caymans n ▷ cayman

caz adj. Caz is a slang word for casual. It's a great word to have up your sleeve as it scores 14 points.

cazique n (caziques). A cazique is a chief among certain American Indian tribes. Cazique scores 27 points, and will earn you a 50-point bonus if you manage to use all of your tiles to form it.

cease v (ceases, ceasing, ceased) bring or come to an end > ceaseless adj > ceaselessly adv

ceased v ▷ cease

ceasefire n (pl -s) temporary truce

ceasefires n ▷ ceasefire

ceaseless adj ▷ cease

ceaselessly adv ▷ cease

ceases v ▷ cease

ceasing v ▷ cease

cedar n (pl -s) evergreen coniferous tree

cedars n ▷ cedar

cede v (cedes, ceding, ceded) surrender (territory or legal rights)

ceded v ▷ cede

cedes v ▷ cede

cedilla n (pl -s) character (.) placed under a c in some languages, to show that it is pronounced s, not k

cedillas n ▷ cedilla

ceding v ▷ cede

ceilidh [kay-lee] n (pl -s) informal social gathering for singing and dancing, esp. in Scotland

ceilidhs n ▷ ceilidh

ceiling n (pl -s) inner upper surface of a room

ceilings n ▷ ceiling

celandine n (pl -s) wild plant with yellow flowers

celandines n ▷ celandine

celebrant n (pl -s) person who performs a religious ceremony

celebrants n ▷ celebrant

celebrate v (-rates, -rating, -rated) hold festivities to mark (a happy event, anniversary, etc.) > celebration n (pl -s)

celebrated adj well known ▶ v ▷ celebrate

celebrates v ▷ celebrate

celebrating v ▷ celebrate

celebration n ▷ celebrate

celebrations n ▷ celebrate

celebrities n ▷ celebrity

celebrity n (pl -rities) famous person

celeriac [sill-ler-ee-ak] n (pl -s) variety of celery with a large turnip-like root

celeriacs n ▷ celeriac

celeries n ▷ celery

celerities n ▷ celerity

celerity [sill-ler-rit-tee] n (pl -ties) swiftness

celery n (pl -ries) vegetable with long green crisp edible stalks

celestial adj heavenly, divine > celestially adv

celestially adv ▷ celestial

celibacy n ▷ celibate

celibate adj unmarried or abstaining from sex, esp. because of a religious vow of chastity ▶ n (pl -s) celibate person > celibacy n

celibates n ▷ celibate

cell n (pl -s) smallest unit of an organism that is able to function independently

cellar n (pl -s) underground room for storage

cellars n ▷ cellar

cellist n ▷ cello

cellists n ▷ cello

cello [chell-oh] n (pl -s) large low-pitched instrument of the violin family > cellist n (pl -s)

cellophane n (pl -s)® thin transparent cellulose sheeting used as wrapping

cellophanes n ▷ cellophane

cellos n ▷ cello

cells n ▷ cell

cellular adj of or consisting of cells

celluloid n (pl -s) kind of plastic used to make toys and, formerly, photographic film

celluloids n ▷ celluloid

cellulose n (pl -s) main constituent of plant cell walls, used in making paper, plastics, etc.

celluloses n ▷ cellulose

cement n (pl -s) fine grey powder mixed with water and sand to make mortar or concrete ▶ v (-s, -ing, -ed) join, bind, or cover with cement

cemented v ▷ cement

cementing v ▷ cement

cements n, v ▷ cement

cemeteries n ▷ cemetery

cemetery n (pl -ries) place where dead people are buried

cenotaph n (pl -s) monument honouring soldiers who died in a war

cenotaphs n ▷ cenotaph

censer n (pl -s) container for burning incense

censers n ▷ censer

censor n (pl -s) person authorized to examine

films, books, etc., to ban or cut anything considered obscene or objectionable ▶ v (-s, -ing, -ed) ban or cut parts of (a film, book, etc.) > **censorship** n

censored v ▷ censor

censoring v ▷ censor

censorious adj harshly critical > **censoriously** adv

censoriously adv ▷ censorious

censors n, v ▷ censor

censorship n ▷ censor

censure n (pl -s) severe disapproval ▶ v (-sures, -suring, -sured) criticize severely

censured v ▷ censure

censures n, v ▷ censure

censuring v ▷ censure

census n (pl -es) official count of a population

censuses n ▷ census

cent n (pl -s) hundredth part of a monetary unit such as the dollar or euro

centaur n (pl -s) mythical creature with the head, arms, and torso of a man, and the lower body and legs of a horse

centaurs n ▷ centaur

centenarian n (pl -s) person at least 100 years old

centenarians n ▷ centenarian

centenaries n ▷ centenary

centenary [sen-teen-a-ree] n (CHIEFLY BRIT) (pl -naries) 100th anniversary or its celebration

centennial n (pl -s) 100th anniversary or its celebration

centennials n ▷ centennial

centigrade adj of the temperature in which water freezes at 0° and boils at 100°

centigram, centigramme n (pl -s) one hundredth of a gram

centigramme n ▷ centigram

centigrammes n ▷ centigram

centigrams n ▷ centigram

centilitre n (pl -s) one hundredth of a litre

centilitres n ▷ centilitre

centimetre n (pl -s) one hundredth of a metre

centimetres n ▷ centimetre

centipede n (pl -s) small wormlike creature with many legs

centipedes n ▷ centipede

central adj of, at, or forming the centre > **centrally** adv > **centrality** n

centralism n principle of central control of a country or organization > **centralist** n (pl -s)

centralist n ▷ centralism

centralists n ▷ centralism

centrality n ▷ central

centralization n ▷ centralize

centralizations n ▷ centralize

centralize v (-izes, -izing, -ized) bring under central control > **centralization** n (pl -s)

centralized v ▷ centralize

centralizes v ▷ centralize

centralizing v ▷ centralize

centrally adv ▷ central

centre n (pl -s) middle point or part (SPORT) ▶ v (centres, centring, centred) put in the centre of something

centred v ▷ centre

centres n, v ▷ centre

centrifugal adj moving away from a centre > **centrifugally** adv

centrifugally adv ▷ centrifugal

centrifuge n (pl -s) machine that separates substances by centrifugal force

centrifuges n ▷ centrifuge

centring v ▷ centre

centripetal adj moving towards a centre > **centripetally** adv

centripetally adv ▷ centripetal

centrist n (pl -s) person favouring political moderation

centrists n ▷ centrist

cents n ▷ cent

centuries n ▷ century

centurion n (pl -s) (in ancient Rome) officer commanding 100 men

centurions n ▷ centurion

century n (pl -ries) period of 100 years

cep n (ceps). A cep is an edible fungus. Cep scores 7 points.

cephalopod [seff-a-loh-pod] n (pl -s) sea mollusc with a head and tentacles, such as the octopus

cephalopods n ▷ cephalopod

ceramic n (pl -s) hard brittle material made by heating clay to a very high temperature ▶ pl art of producing ceramic objects ▶ adj made of ceramic

ceramics n ▷ ceramic

cereal n (pl -s) grass plant with edible grain, such as oat or wheat

cereals n ▷ cereal

cerebra n ▷ cerebrum

cerebral [ser-rib-ral, ser-reeb-ral] adj of the brain

cerebrum [serr-rib-rum] n (pl -brums, -bra) [-bra] main part of the brain

cerebrums n ▷ cerebrum

ceremonial adj ▷ ceremony

ceremonially adv ▷ ceremony

ceremonials n ▷ ceremony

ceremonies n ▷ ceremony

ceremonious adj excessively polite or formal

> **ceremoniously** adv

ceremoniously adv ▷ ceremonious

ceremony n (pl -nies) formal act or ritual

> **ceremonial** adj, n (pl -s) > **ceremonially** adv

cerise [ser-**reess**] adj cherry-red

certain adj (-er, -est) positive and confident

> **certainly** adv

certainer adj ▷ certain

certainest adj ▷ certain

certainly adv ▷ certain

certainties n ▷ certainty

certainty n (pl -ties) state of being sure

certifiable adj considered legally insane

> **certifiably** adv

certifiably n ▷ certifiable

certificate n (pl -s) official document stating the details of a birth, academic course, etc.

certificates n ▷ certificate

certification n ▷ certify

certifications n ▷ certify

certified v ▷ certify

certifies v ▷ certify

certify v (-fies, -fying, -fied) confirm, attest to

> **certification** n (pl -s)

certifying v ▷ certify

certitude n (pl -s) confidence, certainty

certitudes n ▷ certitude

cervical adj ▷ cervix

cervices n ▷ cervix

cervix n (pl cervixes, cervices) narrow entrance of the womb > **cervical** adj

cervixes n ▷ cervix

cessation n (pl -s) ceasing

cessations n ▷ cessation

cesspit, cesspool n (pl -s) covered tank or pit for sewage

cesspits n ▷ cesspit

cesspool n ▷ cesspit

cesspools n ▷ cesspit

cetacean [sit-**tay**-shun] n (pl -s) fish-shaped sea mammal such as a whale or dolphin

cetaceans n ▷ cetacean

> **ch** pron. This is an old dialect form of **I**. It's the only two-letter word that can be formed with the letter C, and it's a good word to remember because it doesn't use any vowels. Ch scores 7 points.
> **cha** n (**chas**). Cha is a slang word for **tea**. Cha scores 8 points.

chafe v (chafes, chafing, chafed) make sore or worn by rubbing

chafed v ▷ chafe

chafes v ▷ chafe

chaff¹ n (pl -s) grain husks

chaff² v (-s, -ing, -ed) (Old-fashioned) tease good-naturedly

chaffed v ▷ chaff²

chaffinch n (pl -es) small European songbird

chaffinches n ▷ chaffinch

chaffing v ▷ chaff²

chaffs n ▷ chaff¹ ▶ v ▷ chaff²

chafing v ▷ chafe

chagrin [shag-**grin**] n (pl -s) annoyance and disappointment

chagrined adj annoyed and disappointed

chagrins n ▷ chagrin

chain n (pl -s) flexible length of connected metal links ▶ v (-s, -ing, -ed) restrict or fasten with or as if with a chain

chained v ▷ chain

chaining v ▷ chain

chains n, v ▷ chain

chair n (pl -s) seat with a back, for one person ▶ v (-s, -ing, -ed) preside over (a meeting)

chaired v ▷ chair

chairing v ▷ chair

chairlift n (pl -s) series of chairs suspended from a moving cable for carrying people up a slope

chairlifts n ▷ chairlift

chairman, chairwoman n (pl -men, -women) person in charge of a company's board of directors or a meeting (also **chairperson**) (pl -s)

chairmen n ▷ chairman

chairperson n ▷ chairman

chairpersons n ▷ chairman

chairs n, v ▷ chair

chairwoman n ▷ chairman

chairwomen n ▷ chairman

chaise [shaze] n (pl -s) (HIST) light horse-drawn carriage

chaises n ▷ chaise

chalcedonies n ▷ chalcedony

chalcedony [kal-**sed**-don-ee] n (pl -nies) variety of quartz

chalet n (pl -s) kind of Swiss wooden house with a steeply sloping roof

chalets n ▷ chalet

chalice n (pl -s) large goblet

chalices n ▷ chalice

chalk n (pl -s) soft white rock consisting of calcium carbonate ▶ v (-s, -ing, -ed) draw or mark with chalk > **chalky** adj (-kier, -kiest)

chalked v ▷ chalk

chalkier adj ▷ chalk

chalkiest adj ▷ chalk

chalking v ▷ chalk

chalks n, v ▷ chalk

chalky adj ▷ chalk

challenge n (pl -s) demanding or stimulating situation ▸ v (-ges, -ging, -ged) issue a challenge to > **challenger** n (pl -s)

challenged adj disabled as specified ▸ v ▷ challenge

challenger n ▷ challenge

challengers n ▷ challenge

challenges n, v ▷ challenge

challenging v ▷ challenge

chamber n (pl -s) hall used for formal meetings (Old-fashioned) ▸ pl set of rooms used as offices by a barrister

chamberlain n (pl -s) (HIST) officer who managed the household of a king or nobleman

chamberlains n ▷ chamberlain

chambermaid n (pl -s) woman employed to clean bedrooms in a hotel

chambermaids n ▷ chambermaid

chambers n ▷ chamber

chameleon [kam-**meel**-yon] n (pl -s) small lizard that changes colour to blend in with its surroundings

chameleons n ▷ chameleon

chamfer [**cham**-fer] v (-s, -ing, -ed) bevel the edge of

chamfered v ▷ chamfer

chamfering v ▷ chamfer

chamfers v ▷ chamfer

chamois [**sham**-wah] n (pl -ois) small mountain antelope

chamomile [**kam**-mo-mile] n (pl -s) ▷ camomile

chamomiles n ▷ chamomile

champ[1] v (-s, -ing, -ed) chew noisily

champ[2] n (pl -s) ▷ champion

champagne n (pl -s) sparkling white French wine

champagnes n ▷ champagne

champed v ▷ champ[1]

champing v ▷ champ[1]

champion n (pl -s) overall winner of a competition (foll. by of) ▸ v (-s, -ing, -ed) support ▸ adj (Dialect) excellent > **championship** n (pl -s)

championed v ▷ champion

championing v ▷ champion

champions n, v ▷ champion

championship n ▷ champion

championships n ▷ champion

champs v ▷ champ[1] ▸ n ▷ champ[2]

chance n (pl -s) likelihood, probability ▸ v (chances, chancing, chanced) risk, hazard

chanced v ▷ chance

chancel n (pl -s) part of a church containing the altar and choir

chancellor n (pl -s) head of government in some European countries > **chancellorship** n (pl -s)

chancellors n ▷ chancellor

chancellorship n ▷ chancellor

chancellorships n ▷ chancellor

chancels n ▷ chancel

chances n, v ▷ chance

chancier adj ▷ chancy

chanciest adj ▷ chancy

chancing v ▷ chance

chancy adj (-cier, -ciest) uncertain, risky

chandelier [shan-dill-**eer**] n (pl -s) ornamental light with branches and holders for several candles or bulbs

chandeliers n ▷ chandelier

chandler n (pl -s) dealer, esp. in ships' supplies

chandlers n ▷ chandler

change n (pl -s) becoming different ▸ v (changes, changing, changed) make or become different

changeable adj changing often

changed v ▷ change

changeling n (pl -s) child believed to have been exchanged by fairies for another

changelings n ▷ changeling

changes n, v ▷ change

changing v ▷ change

channel n (pl -s) band of broadcasting frequencies ▸ v (-nels, -nelling, -nelled) direct or convey through a channel

channelled v ▷ channel

channelling v ▷ channel

channels n, v ▷ channel

chant v (-s, -ing, -ed) utter or sing (a slogan or psalm) ▸ n (pl -s) rhythmic or repetitious slogan

chanted v ▷ chant

chanter n (pl -s) (on bagpipes) pipe on which the melody is played

chanters n ▷ chanter

chanting v ▷ chant

chants v, n ▷ chant

chaos n complete disorder or confusion > **chaotic** adj > **chaotically** adv

chaotic adj ▷ chaos

chaotically adv ▷ chaos

chap n (pl -s) (Informal) man or boy

chapati, chapatti n (pl -s) (in Indian cookery) flat thin unleavened bread

chapatis n ▷ chapati

chapatti n ▷ chapati

chapattis n ▷ chapati

chapel n (pl -s) place of worship with its own altar, within a church

chapels n ▷ chapel

chaperone [shap-per-rone] n (pl -s) older person who accompanies and supervises a young person or young people on a social occasion ▶ v (-ones, -oning, -oned) act as a chaperone to

chaperoned v ▷ chaperone

chaperones n, v ▷ chaperone

chaperoning v ▷ chaperone

chaplain n (pl -s) clergyman attached to a chapel, military body, or institution > **chaplaincy** n (pl -cies)

chaplaincies n ▷ chaplain

chaplaincy n ▷ chaplain

chaplains n ▷ chaplain

chaplet n (pl -s) garland for the head

chaplets n ▷ chaplet

chapped adj (of the skin) raw and cracked, through exposure to cold

chaps n ▷ chap

chapter n (pl -s) division of a book

chapters n ▷ chapter

char¹ v (chars, charring, charred) blacken by partial burning

char² (BRIT) (Informal) n (pl -s) charwoman ▶ v (chars, charring, charred) clean other people's houses as a job

char³ n (BRIT) (Old-fashioned slang) tea

charabanc [shar-rab-bang] n (pl -s) (Old-fashioned) coach for sightseeing

charabancs n ▷ charabanc

character n (pl -s) combination of qualities distinguishing a person, group, or place

characteristic n (pl -s) distinguishing feature or quality ▶ adj typical > **characteristically** adv

characteristically n ▷ characteristic

characteristics n ▷ characteristic

characterization n ▷ characterize

characterizations n ▷ characterize

characterize v (-rizes, -rizing, -rized) be a characteristic of (foll. by as) > **characterization** n (pl -s)

characterized v ▷ characterize

characterizes v ▷ characterize

characterizing v ▷ characterize

characters n ▷ character

charade [shar-rahd] n (pl -s) absurd pretence ▶ pl game in which one team acts out a word or phrase, which the other team has to guess

charades n ▷ charade

charcoal n (pl -s) black substance formed by partially burning wood

charcoals n ▷ charcoal

charge v (charges, charging, charged) ask as a price ▶ n (pl -s) price charged > **chargeable** adj

chargeable adj ▷ charge

charged v ▷ charge

charger n (pl -s) device for charging an accumulator

chargers n ▷ charger

charges v, n ▷ charge

charging v ▷ charge

charier adj ▷ chary

chariest adj ▷ chary

chariot n (pl -s) two-wheeled horse-drawn vehicle used in ancient times in wars and races

charioteer n (pl -s) chariot driver

charioteers n ▷ charioteer

chariots n ▷ chariot

charisma [kar-rizz-ma] n (pl -s) person's power to attract or influence people > **charismatic** [kar-rizz-mat-ik] ▶ adj

charismas n ▷ charisma

charismatic adj ▷ charisma

charitable adj ▷ charity

charitably adv ▷ charity

charities n ▷ charity

charity n (pl -ties) organization that gives help, such as money or food, to those in need > **charitable** adj > **charitably** adv

charladies n ▷ charlady

charlady n (pl -ladies) (BRIT) (Informal) ▷ charwoman

charlatan [shar-lat-tan] n (pl -s) person who claims expertise that he or she does not have

charlatans n ▷ charlatan

charleston n (pl -s) lively dance of the 1920s

charlestons n ▷ charleston

charm n (pl -s) attractive quality ▶ v (-s, -ing, -ed) attract, delight > **charmer** n (pl -s)

charmed v ▷ charm

charmer n ▷ charm

charmers n ▷ charm

charming adj attractive ▶ v ▷ charm

charms n, v ▷ charm

charred v ▷ char¹, ²

charring v ▷ char¹, ²

chars v ▷ char¹, ² ▶ n ▷ char²

chart n (pl -s) graph, table, or diagram showing information ▶ v (-s, -ing, -ed) plot the course of

charted v ▷ chart

charter n (pl -s) document granting or demanding certain rights ▶ v (-s, -ing, -ed) hire by charter

chartered adj officially qualified to practise a profession ▶ v ▷ charter

chartering v ▷ charter

charters n, v ▷ charter
charting v ▷ chart
chartreuse [shar-**trerz**] n (pl -s) sweet-smelling green or yellow liqueur
chartreuses n ▷ chartreuse
charts n, v ▷ chart
charwoman n (pl charwomen) woman whose job is to clean other people's homes
charwomen n ▷ charwoman
chary [chair-ee] adj (-rier, -riest) wary, careful
chase[1] v (chases, chasing, chased) run after quickly in order to catch or drive away ▶ n (pl -s) chasing, pursuit
chase[2] v (chases, chasing, chased) engrave or emboss (metal)
chased v ▷ chase[1, 2]
chaser n (pl -s) milder drink drunk after another stronger one
chasers n ▷ chaser
chases v ▷ chase[1, 2] ▶ n ▷ chase[1]
chasing v ▷ chase[1, 2]
chasm [kaz-zum] n (pl -s) deep crack in the earth
chasms n ▷ chasm
chassis [shass-ee] n (pl -sis) frame, wheels, and mechanical parts of a vehicle
chaste adj (-r, -st) abstaining from sex outside marriage or altogether > **chastely** adv > **chasteness** n (pl -es) > **chastity** n (pl -ties)
chastely adv ▷ chaste
chasten [chase-en] v (-s, -ing, -ed) subdue by criticism
chastened v ▷ chasten
chasteness n ▷ chaste
chastenesses n ▷ chaste
chastening v ▷ chasten
chastens v ▷ chasten
chaster adj ▷ chaste
chastest adj ▷ chaste
chastise v (-ises, -ising, -ised) scold severely > **chastisement** n (pl -s)
chastised v ▷ chastise
chastisement n ▷ chastise
chastisements n ▷ chastise
chastises v ▷ chastise
chastising v ▷ chastise
chastities n ▷ chaste
chastity n ▷ chaste
chat n (pl -s) informal conversation ▶ v (chats, chatting, chatted) have an informal conversation > **chatty** adj (-tier, -ttiest) > **chattily** adv > **chattiness** n (pl -es)
chateau [shat-toe] n (pl -teaux, -teaus) French castle
chateaus n ▷ chateau

chateaux n ▷ chateau
chatelaine [shat-tell-lane] n (pl -s) (formerly) mistress of a large house or castle
chatelaines n ▷ chatelaine
chatroom n (pl -s) site on the Internet where users have group discussions by e-mail
chatrooms n ▷ chatroom
chats n, v ▷ chat
chatted v ▷ chat
chattel n (pl -s) (usually plural) possessions
chattels n ▷ chattel
chatter v (-s, -ing, -ed) speak quickly and continuously about unimportant things ▶ n (pl -s) idle talk
chatterbox n (pl -es) person who chatters a lot
chatterboxes n ▷ chatterbox
chattered v ▷ chatter
chattering v ▷ chatter
chatters v, n ▷ chatter
chattier adj ▷ chat
chattiest adj ▷ chat
chattily adv ▷ chat
chattiness n ▷ chat
chattinesses n ▷ chat
chatting v ▷ chat
chatty adj ▷ chat
chauffeur n (pl -s) person employed to drive a car for someone
chauffeurs n ▷ chauffeur
chauvinism [show-vin-iz-zum] n (pl -s) irrational belief that one's own country, race, group, or sex is superior > **chauvinist** n (pl -s) adj > **chauvinistic** adj > **chauvinistically** adv
chauvinisms n ▷ chauvinism
chauvinist n ▷ chauvinism
chauvinistic adj ▷ chauvinism
chauvinistically adv ▷ chauvinism
chauvinists n ▷ chauvinism
⬛ **che** pron. Like **ch**, che is an old dialect form of I. Che scores 8 points.
cheap adj (-er, -est) costing relatively little > **cheaply** adv
cheapen v (-s, -ing, -ed) lower the reputation of
cheapened v ▷ cheapen
cheapening v ▷ cheapen
cheapens v ▷ cheapen
cheaper adj ▷ cheap
cheapest adj ▷ cheap
cheaply adv ▷ cheap
cheapskate n (pl -s) (Informal) miserly person
cheapskates n ▷ cheapskate
cheat v (-s, -ing, -ed) act dishonestly to gain profit or advantage ▶ n (pl -s) person who cheats

cheated v ▷ cheat

cheating v ▷ cheat

cheats v, n ▷ cheat

check v (-s, -ing, -ed) examine, investigate ▶ n (pl -s) test to ensure accuracy or progress

checked v ▷ check

checking v ▷ check

checkmate n (pl -s) (CHESS) winning position in which an opponent's king is under attack and unable to escape ▶ v (-mates, -mating, -mated) (CHESS) place the king of (one's opponent) in checkmate

checkmated v ▷ checkmate

checkmates n, v ▷ checkmate

checkmating v ▷ checkmate

checkout n (pl -s) counter in a supermarket, where customers pay

checkouts n ▷ checkout

checks v, n ▷ check

checkup n (pl -s) thorough medical examination

checkups n ▷ checkup

cheddar n (pl -s) firm orange or yellowy-white cheese

cheddars n ▷ cheddar

cheek n (pl -s) either side of the face below the eye (Informal) ▶ v (-s, -ing, -ed) (BRIT, AUST & NZ) (Informal) speak impudently to

cheeked v ▷ cheek

cheekier adj ▷ cheeky

cheekiest adj ▷ cheeky

cheekily adv ▷ cheeky

cheekiness n ▷ cheeky

cheekinesses n ▷ cheeky

cheeking v ▷ cheek

cheeks n, v ▷ cheek

cheeky adj (-kier, -kiest) impudent, disrespectful > **cheekily** adv > **cheekiness** n (pl -es)

cheep n (pl -s) young bird's high-pitched cry ▶ v (-s, -ing, -ed) utter a cheep

cheeped v ▷ cheep

cheeping v ▷ cheep

cheeps n, v ▷ cheep

cheer v (-s, -ing, -ed) applaud or encourage with shouts ▶ n (pl -s) shout of applause or encouragement > **cheerful** adj (-ller, -llest) > **cheerfully** adv > **cheerfulness** n > **cheery** adj (-rier, -riest) > **cheerily** adv

cheered v ▷ cheer

cheerful adj ▷ cheer

cheerfuller adj ▷ cheer

cheerfullest adj ▷ cheer

cheerfully adv ▷ cheer

cheerfulness n ▷ cheer

cheerier adj ▷ cheer

cheeriest adj ▷ cheer

cheerily adv ▷ cheer

cheering v ▷ cheer

cheerio interj (Informal) goodbye ▶ n (pl -s) (AUST & NZ) small red cocktail sausage

cheerios n ▷ cheerio

cheerless adj dreary, gloomy > **cheerlessly** adv > **cheerlessness** n

cheerlessly adv ▷ cheerless

cheerlessness n ▷ cheerless

cheers v, n ▷ cheer

cheery adj ▷ cheer

cheese n (pl -s) food made from coagulated milk curd > **cheesy** adj (pl -sier, -siest) > **cheesily** adv > **cheesiness** n

cheeseburger n (pl -s) hamburger topped with melted cheese

cheeseburgers n ▷ cheeseburger

cheesecake n (pl -s) dessert with a biscuit-crumb base covered with a sweet cream-cheese mixture

cheesecakes n ▷ cheesecake

cheesecloth n (pl -s) light cotton cloth

cheesecloths n ▷ cheesecloth

cheeses n ▷ cheese

cheesier adj ▷ cheese

cheesiest adj ▷ cheese

cheesily adv ▷ cheese

cheesiness n ▷ cheese

cheesy adj ▷ cheese

cheetah n (pl -s) large fast-running spotted African wild cat

cheetahs n ▷ cheetah

chef n (pl -s) cook in a restaurant

chefs n ▷ chef

chemical n (pl -s) substance used in or resulting from a reaction involving changes to atoms or molecules ▶ adj of chemistry or chemicals > **chemically** adv

chemically adv ▷ chemical

chemicals n ▷ chemical

chemise [shem-**meez**] n (pl -s) (Old-fashioned) woman's loose-fitting slip

chemises n ▷ chemise

chemist n (pl -s) shop selling medicines and cosmetics

chemistries n ▷ chemistry

chemistry n (pl -ries) science of the composition, properties, and reactions of substances

chemists n ▷ chemist

chemotherapies n ▷ chemotherapy

chemotherapy n (pl -apies) treatment of disease, often cancer, using chemicals

chenille [shen-**neel**] n (pl -s) (fabric of) thick tufty yarn
chenilles n ▷ chenille
cheque n (pl -s) written order to one's bank to pay money from one's account
chequer n (pl chequers) piece used in Chinese chequers ▶ pl game of draughts
chequered adj marked by varied fortunes
chequers n ▷ chequer
cheques n ▷ cheque
cherish v (-es, -ing, -ed) cling to (an idea or feeling)
cherished v ▷ cherish
cherishes v ▷ cherish
cherishing v ▷ cherish
cheroot [sher-**root**] n (pl -s) cigar with both ends cut flat
cheroots n ▷ cheroot
cherries n ▷ cherry
cherry n (pl -ries) small red or black fruit with a stone ▶ adj deep red
cherub n (pl -s, -ubim) angel, often represented as a winged child > **cherubic** [cher-**rew**-bik] ▶ adj
cherubic adj ▷ cherub
cherubim n ▷ cherub
cherubs n ▷ cherub
chervil n (pl -s) aniseed-flavoured herb
chervils n ▷ chervil
chess n (pl -es) game for two players with 16 pieces each, played on a chequered board of 64 squares
chesses n ▷ chess
chessman n (pl -men) piece used in chess
chessmen n ▷ chessman
chest n (pl -s) front of the body, from neck to waist
chesterfield n (pl -s) couch with high padded sides and back
chesterfields n ▷ chesterfield
chestnut n (pl -s) reddish-brown edible nut (Informal) ▶ adj (of hair or a horse) reddish-brown
chestnuts n ▷ chestnut
chests n ▷ chest
chevron [shev-ron] n (pl -s) V-shaped pattern, esp. on the sleeve of a military uniform to indicate rank
chevrons n ▷ chevron
chew v (-s, -ing, -ed) grind (food) between the teeth
chewed v ▷ chew
chewier adj ▷ chewy
chewiest adj ▷ chewy
chewiness n ▷ chewy

chewinesses n ▷ chewy
chewing v ▷ chew
chews v ▷ chew
chewy adj (-ier, -iest) requiring a lot of chewing > **chewiness** n (pl -es)
■ **chi** n (**chis**). Chi is a letter of the Greek alphabet, and is worth 8 points.
chianti [kee-**ant**-ee] n (pl -s) dry red Italian wine
chiantis n ▷ chianti
chiaroscuro [kee-ah-roh-**skew**-roh] n (pl -s) distribution of light and shade in a picture
chiaroscuros n ▷ chiaroscuro
chic [**sheek**] adj (-er, -est) stylish, elegant ▶ n (pl -s) stylishness, elegance
chicane [shik-**kane**] n (pl -s) obstacle in a motor-racing circuit
chicaneries n ▷ chicanery
chicanery n (pl -eries) trickery, deception
chicanes n ▷ chicane
chicer adj ▷ chic
chicest adj ▷ chic
chick n (pl -s) baby bird
chicken n (pl -s) domestic fowl ▶ adj (Slang) cowardly
chickenpox n (pl -es) infectious disease with an itchy rash
chickenpoxes n ▷ chickenpox
chickens n ▷ chicken
chickpea n (pl -s) edible yellow pealike seed
chickpeas n ▷ chickpea
chicks n ▷ chick
chickweed n (pl -s) weed with small white flowers
chickweeds n ▷ chickweed
chicories n ▷ chicory
chicory n (pl -ries) plant whose leaves are used in salads
chics n ▷ chic
chid v ▷ chide
chidden v ▷ chide
chide v (chiding, chided or chid) (chid or chidden) rebuke, scold
chided v ▷ chide
chiding v ▷ chide
chief n (pl -s) head of a group of people ▶ adj most important
chiefly adv especially
chiefs n ▷ chief
chieftain n (pl -s) leader of a tribe
chieftains n ▷ chieftain
chiffon [**shif**-fon] n (pl -s) fine see-through fabric
chiffons n ▷ chiffon
chignon [**sheen**-yon] n (pl -s) knot of hair pinned up at the back of the head

chignons n ▷chignon

chihuahua [chee-**wah**-wah] n (pl **-s**) tiny short-haired dog
  chihuahuas n ▷chihuahua

chilblain n (pl **-s**) inflammation of the fingers or toes, caused by exposure to cold
  chilblains n ▷chilblain

child n (pl children) young human being, boy or girl **> childhood** n (pl **-s**) **> childless** adj **> childlessness** n

childbirth n (pl **-s**) giving birth to a child
  childbirths n ▷childbirth
  childhood n ▷child
  childhoods n ▷child

childish adj immature, silly **> childishly** adv **> childishness** n
  childishly adv ▷childish
  childishness n ▷childish
  childless adj ▷child
  childlessness n ▷child

childlike adj innocent, trustful
  children n ▷child

chili n ▷chilli
  chilies n ▷chilli

chill n (pl **-s**) feverish cold ▶ v (**-s, -ing, -ed**) make (something) cool or cold ▶ adj unpleasantly cold
  chilled v ▷chill

chilli, chili n (pl **-es**) small red or green hot-tasting capsicum pod, used in cooking
  chillier adj ▷chilly
  chillies n ▷chilli
  chilliest adj ▷chilly
  chilliness n ▷chilly
  chillinesses n ▷chilly
  chilling v ▷chill
  chills n, v ▷chill

chilly adj (**-lier, -liest**) moderately cold **> chilliness** n (pl **-es**)

chime n (pl **-s**) musical ringing sound of a bell or clock ▶ v (**-mes, -ming, -med**) make a musical ringing sound
  chimed v ▷chime

chimera [kime-**meer**-a] n (pl **-s**) unrealistic hope or idea
  chimeras n ▷chimera
  chimes n, v ▷chime
  chiming v ▷chime

chimney n (pl **-s**) hollow vertical structure for carrying away smoke from a fire
  chimneys n ▷chimney

chimp n (pl **-s**) (Informal) ▷chimpanzee

chimpanzee n (pl **-s**) intelligent black African ape
  chimpanzees n ▷chimpanzee

chimps n ▷chimp

chin n (pl **-s**) part of the face below the mouth

china n (pl **-s**) fine earthenware or porcelain
  chinas n ▷china

chinchilla n (pl **-s**) S American rodent bred for its soft grey fur
  chinchillas n ▷chinchilla

chine n (pl **-s**) cut of meat including part of the backbone
  chines n ▷chine

chink¹ n (pl **-s**) small narrow opening

chink² v (**-s, -ing, -ed**) ▶ n (pl **-s**) (make) a light ringing sound
  chinked v ▷chink²
  chinking v ▷chink²
  chinks n ▷chink¹,² ▶ v ▷chink²
  chins n ▷chin

chintz n (pl **-es**) printed cotton fabric with a glazed finish
  chintzes n ▷chintz

chinwag n (pl **-s**) (BRIT, AUST & NZ) (Informal) chat
  chinwags n ▷chinwag

chip n (pl **-s**) strip of potato, fried in deep fat ▶ v (**chips, chipping, chipped**) break small pieces from

chipboard n (pl **-s**) thin board made of compressed wood particles
  chipboards n ▷chipboard

chipmunk n (pl **-s**) small squirrel-like N American rodent with a striped back
  chipmunks n ▷chipmunk
  chipped v ▷chip

chippie n (pl **-s**) (BRIT, AUST & NZ) (Informal) carpenter
  chippies n ▷chippie
  chipping v ▷chip
  chips n, v ▷chip

chiropodist [kir-**rop**-pod-ist] n (pl **-s**) person who treats minor foot complaints **> chiropody** n
  chiropodists n ▷chiropodist
  chiropody n ▷chiropodist

chiropractic [kire-oh-**prak**-tik] n (pl **-s**) system of treating bodily disorders by manipulation of the spine **> chiropractor** n (pl **-s**)
  chiropractics n ▷chiropractic
  chiropractor n ▷chiropractic
  chiropractors n ▷chiropractic

chirp v (**-s, -ing, -ed**) (of a bird or insect) make a short high-pitched sound ▶ n (pl **-s**) chirping sound
  chirped v ▷chirp
  chirpier adj ▷chirpy
  chirpiest adj ▷chirpy
  chirpily adv ▷chirpy

chirpiness n ▷ chirpy
chirping v ▷ chirp
chirps v, n ▷ chirp
chirpy adj (-pier, -piest) (Informal) lively and cheerful > **chirpily** adv > **chirpiness** n
chisel n (pl -s) metal tool with a sharp end for shaping wood or stone ▶ v (-**els**, -**elling**, -**elled**) carve or form with a chisel
chiselled v ▷ chisel
chiselling v ▷ chisel
chisels n, v ▷ chisel
chit[1] n (pl -s) short official note, such as a receipt
chit[2] n (pl -s) (BRIT, AUST & NZ) (old-fashioned) pert or impudent girl
chitchat n (pl -s) chat, gossip
chitchats n ▷ chitchat
chits n ▷ chit[1, 2]
chitterlings pl n pig's intestines cooked as food
chivalries n ▷ chivalry
chivalrous adj ▷ chivalry
chivalrously adv ▷ chivalry
chivalry n (pl -ries) courteous behaviour, esp. by men towards women > **chivalrous** adj > **chivalrously** adv
chives pl n herb with a mild onion flavour
chivvied v ▷ chivvy
chivvies v ▷ chivvy
chivvy v (-vies, -vying, -vied) (Informal) harass, nag
chivvying v ▷ chivvy
chloride n (pl -s) compound of chlorine and another substance
chlorides n ▷ chloride
chlorinate v (-ates, -ating, -ated) disinfect (water) with chlorine > **chlorination** n
chlorinated v ▷ chlorinate
chlorinates v ▷ chlorinate
chlorinating v ▷ chlorinate
chlorination n ▷ chlorinate
chlorine n (pl -s) strong-smelling greenish-yellow gaseous element, used to disinfect water
chlorines n ▷ chlorine
chlorofluorocarbon n (pl -s) any of various gaseous compounds of carbon, hydrogen, chlorine, and fluorine, used in refrigerators and aerosol propellants, some of which break down the ozone in the atmosphere
chlorofluorocarbons n ▷ chlorofluorocarbon
chloroform n (pl -s) strong-smelling liquid formerly used as an anaesthetic
chloroforms n ▷ chloroform
chlorophyll n (pl -s) green colouring matter of plants, which enables them to convert sunlight into energy
chlorophylls n ▷ chlorophyll
chock n (pl -s) block or wedge used to prevent a heavy object from moving
chockablock adj completely full
chocks n ▷ chock
chocolate n (pl -s) sweet food made from cacao seeds ▶ adj dark brown
chocolates n ▷ chocolate
choice n (pl -s) choosing ▶ adj (**choicer**, **choicest**) of high quality
choicer adj ▷ choice
choices n ▷ choice
choicest adj ▷ choice
choir n (pl -s) organized group of singers, esp. in church
choirs n ▷ choir
choke v (**chokes**, **choking**, **choked**) hinder or stop the breathing of (a person) by strangling or smothering ▶ n (pl -s) device controlling the amount of air that is mixed with the fuel in a petrol engine
choked v ▷ choke
choker n (pl -s) tight-fitting necklace
chokers n ▷ choker
chokes v, n ▷ choke
choking v ▷ choke
cholera [kol-ler-a] n (pl -s) serious infectious disease causing severe vomiting and diarrhoea
choleras n ▷ cholera
choleric [kol-ler-ik] adj bad-tempered
cholesterol [kol-**lest**-er-oll] n (pl -s) fatty substance found in animal tissue, an excess of which can cause heart disease
cholesterols n ▷ cholesterol
chomp v (-**s**, -**ing**, -**ed**) chew noisily
chomped v ▷ chomp
chomping v ▷ chomp
chomps v ▷ chomp
chook n (pl -s) (AUST & NZ) hen or chicken
chooks n ▷ chook
choose v (**chooses**, **choosing**, **chose**, **chosen**) select from a number of alternatives
chooses v ▷ choose
choosier adj ▷ choosy
choosiest adj ▷ choosy
choosing v ▷ choose
choosy adj (-**sier**, -**siest**) (Informal) fussy, hard to please
chop[1] v (**chops**, **chopping**, **chopped**) cut with a blow from an axe or knife (BOXING) (KARATE) ▶ n (pl -s) cutting or sharp blow
chop[2] v (**chops**, **chopping**, **chopped**) change

one's mind repeatedly
chopped v ▷ chop[1, 2]
chopper n (pl -s) (Informal) helicopter
choppers n ▷ chopper
choppier adj ▷ choppy
choppiest adj ▷ choppy
choppiness n ▷ choppy
choppinesses n ▷ choppy
chopping v ▷ chop[1, 2]
choppy adj (-pier, -piest) (of the sea) fairly
rough > **choppiness** n (pl -es)
chops pl n (BRIT, AUST & NZ) (Informal) jaws,
cheeks ▶ v ▷ chop[1, 2] ▶ n ▷ chop[1]
chopsticks pl n pair of thin sticks used to eat
Chinese food
choral adj of a choir
chorale [kor-rahl] n (pl -s) slow stately hymn
tune
chorales n ▷ chorale
chord[1] n (pl -s) (MATHS) straight line joining two
points on a curve
chord[2] n (pl -s) simultaneous sounding of
three or more musical notes
chords n ▷ chord[1, 2]
chore n (pl -s) routine task
choreographer n ▷ choreography
choreographers n ▷ choreography
choreographic adj ▷ choreography
choreographies n ▷ choreography
choreography n (pl -phies) composition
of steps and movements for dancing
> **choreographer** n (pl -s) > **choreographic** adj
chores n ▷ chore
chorister n (pl -s) singer in a choir
choristers n ▷ chorister
chortle v (-tles, -tling, -tled) chuckle in
amusement ▶ n (pl -s) amused chuckle
chortled v ▷ chortle
chortles v, n ▷ chortle
chortling v ▷ chortle
chorus n (pl -es) large choir ▶ v (-es, -ing, -ed)
sing or say together
chorused v ▷ chorus
choruses n, v ▷ chorus
chorusing v ▷ chorus
chose v ▷ choose
chosen v ▷ choose
chow n (pl -s) thick-coated dog with a curled
tail, orig. from China
chowder n (pl -s) thick soup containing clams
or fish
chowders n ▷ chowder
chows n ▷ chow
christen v (-s, -ing, -ed) baptize > **christening**
n (pl -s)

christened v ▷ christen
christening v, n ▷ christen
christenings n ▷ christen
christens v ▷ christen
chromatic adj of colour or colours
> **chromatically** adv
chromatically adv ▷ chromatic
chromatographies n ▷ chromatic
chromatography n (pl -phies) separation and
analysis of the components of a substance
by slowly passing it through an adsorbing
material
chrome n ▷ chromium
chromes n ▷ chromium
chromium, chrome n (pl -s) (CHEM) grey
metallic element used in steel alloys and for
electroplating
chromiums n ▷ chromium
chromosome n (pl -s) microscopic gene-
carrying body in the nucleus of a cell
chromosomes n ▷ chromosome
chronic adj (of an illness) lasting a long time
> **chronically** adv
chronically adv ▷ chronic
chronicle n (pl -s) record of events in order of
occurrence ▶ v (-les, -ing, -led) record in or as
if in a chronicle > **chronicler** n (pl -s)
chronicled v ▷ chronicle
chronicler n ▷ chronicle
chroniclers n ▷ chronicle
chronicles v ▷ chronicle
chronicling v ▷ chronicle
chronological adj ▷ chronology
chronologically adv ▷ chronology
chronologies n ▷ chronology
chronology n (pl -gies) arrangement or list of
events in order of occurrence > **chronological**
adj > **chronologically** adv
chronometer n (pl -s) timepiece designed to
be accurate in all conditions
chronometers n ▷ chronometer
chrysalis [kriss-a-liss] n (pl -es) insect in the
stage between larva and adult, when it is in
a cocoon
chrysalises n ▷ chrysalis
chrysanthemum n (pl -s) garden flower with a
large head made up of thin petals
chrysanthemums n ▷ chrysanthemum
chub n (pl chub) European freshwater fish of
the carp family
chubbier adj ▷ chubby
chubbiest adj ▷ chubby
chubbiness n ▷ chubby
chubby adj (-bier, -biest) plump and round
> **chubbiness** n

chuck¹ v (-s, -ing, -ed) (*Informal*) throw
chuck² n (pl -s) cut of beef from the neck to the shoulder
  chucked v ▷ chuck¹
  chucking v ▷ chuck¹
chuckle v (-les, -ling, -led) laugh softly ▶ n (pl -s) soft laugh
  chuckled v ▷ chuckle
  chuckles v, n ▷ chuckle
  chuckling v ▷ chuckle
  chucks v ▷ chuck¹ ▶ n ▷ chuck²
chuffed adj (*Informal*) very pleased
chug n (pl -s) short dull sound like the noise of an engine ▶ v (chugs, chugging, chugged) operate or move with this sound
  chugged v ▷ chug
  chugging v ▷ chug
  chugs n, v ▷ chug
chukka n (pl -s) period of play in polo
  chukkas n ▷ chukka
chum (*Informal*) n (pl -s) close friend ▶ v (chums, chumming, chummed) form a close friendship with > **chummy** adj (-mier, -mmiest) > **chumminess** n (pl -es)
  chummed v ▷ chum
  chummier adj ▷ chum
  chummiest adj ▷ chum
  chumminess n ▷ chum
  chumminesses n ▷ chum
  chumming v ▷ chum
  chummy adj ▷ chum
chump n (pl -s) (*Informal*) stupid person
  chumps n ▷ chump
  chums n, v ▷ chum
chunk n (pl -s) thick solid piece
  chunkier adj ▷ chunky
  chunkiest adj ▷ chunky
  chunkiness n ▷ chunky
  chunkinesses n ▷ chunky
  chunks n ▷ chunk
chunky adj (-kier, -kiest) (of a person) broad and heavy > **chunkiness** n (pl -es)
church n (pl -s) building for public Christian worship
  churches n ▷ church
churchgoer n (pl -s) person who attends church regularly
  churchgoers n ▷ churchgoer
churchwarden n (pl -s) member of a congregation who assists the vicar
  churchwardens n ▷ churchwarden
churchyard n (pl -s) grounds round a church, used as a graveyard
  churchyards n ▷ churchyard
churlish adj surly and rude > **churlishly** adv

> **churlishness** n
churlishly adv ▷ churlish
  churlishness n ▷ churlish
churn n (pl -s) machine in which cream is shaken to make butter ▶ v (-s, -ing, -ed) stir (cream) vigorously to make butter
  churned v ▷ churn
  churning v ▷ churn
  churns n, v ▷ churn
chute¹ [shoot] n (pl -s) steep slope down which things may be slid
chute² n (pl -s) (*Informal*) ▷ parachute
  chutes n ▷ chute¹, ²
chutney n (pl -s) pickle made from fruit, vinegar, spices, and sugar
  chutneys n ▷ chutney
cicada [sik-kah-da] n (pl -s) large insect that makes a high-pitched drone
  cicadas n ▷ cicada
  cicatrices n ▷ cicatrix
cicatrix [sik-a-trix] n (pl -trices) scar
  cid (**cids**). A cid is a hero or commander. Cid scores 6 points.
cider n (pl -s) alcoholic drink made from fermented apple juice
  ciders n ▷ cider
cigar n (pl -s) roll of cured tobacco leaves for smoking
cigarette n (pl -s) thin roll of shredded tobacco in thin paper, for smoking
  cigarettes n ▷ cigarette
  cigars n ▷ cigar
cinch [sinch] n (pl -es) (*Informal*) easy task
  cinches n ▷ cinch
cinder n (pl -s) piece of material that will not burn, left after burning coal
  cinders n ▷ cinder
cinema n (pl -s) place for showing films
  > **cinematic** adj
  cinemas n ▷ cinema
  cinematic adj ▷ cinema
cinematographer n ▷ cinematography
  cinematographers n ▷ cinematography
cinematography n technique of making films
  > **cinematographer** n (pl -s)
cineraria n (pl -s) garden plant with daisy-like flowers
  cinerarias n ▷ cineraria
cinnamon n (pl -s) spice obtained from the bark of an Asian tree
  cinnamons n ▷ cinnamon
cipher, cypher [sife-er] n (pl -s) system of secret writing
  ciphers n ▷ cipher
circa [sir-ka] prep (LATIN) approximately, about

circle *n* (*pl* **-s**) perfectly round geometric figure, line, or shape ▶ *v* (**circles, circling, circled**) move in a circle (round)
  circled *v* ▷circle
  circles *n*, *v* ▷circle
circlet *n* (*pl* **-s**) circular ornament worn on the head
  circlets *n* ▷circlet
  circling *v* ▷circle
circuit *n* (*pl* **-s**) complete route or course, esp. a circular one
circuitous [sir-**kew**-it-uss] *adj* indirect and lengthy > **circuitously** *adv*
  circuitously *adv* ▷circuitous
circuitry [**sir**-kit-tree] *n* electrical circuit(s)
  circuits *n* ▷circuit
circular *adj* in the shape of a circle ▶ *n* (*pl* **-s**) letter for general distribution > **circularity** *n*
  circularity *n* ▷circular
  circulars *n* ▷circular
circulate *v* (**-lates, -lating, -lated**) send, go, or pass from place to place or person to person > **circulatory** *adj*
  circulated *v* ▷circulate
  circulates *v* ▷circulate
  circulating *v* ▷circulate
circulation *n* flow of blood around the body
  circulatory *adj* ▷circulate
circumcise *v* (**-cises, -cising, -cised**) remove the foreskin of > **circumcision** *n* (*pl* **-s**)
  circumcised *v* ▷circumcise
  circumcises *v* ▷circumcise
  circumcising *v* ▷circumcise
  circumcision *n* ▷circumcise
  circumcisions *n* ▷circumcise
circumference *n* (*pl* **-s**) boundary of a specified area or shape, esp. of a circle
  circumferences *n* ▷circumference
circumflex *n* (*pl* **-es**) mark (^) over a vowel to show that it is pronounced in a particular way
  circumflexes *n* ▷circumflex
circumlocution *n* (*pl* **-s**) indirect way of saying something
  circumlocutions *n* ▷circumlocution
circumnavigate *v* (**-gates, -gating, -gated**) sail right round > **circumnavigation** *n* (*pl* **-s**)
  circumnavigated *v* ▷circumnavigate
  circumnavigates *v* ▷circumnavigate
  circumnavigating *v* ▷circumnavigate
  circumnavigation *n* ▷circumnavigate
  circumnavigations *n* ▷circumnavigate
circumscribe *v* (**-scribes, -scribing, -scribed**) limit, restrict > **circumscription** *n* (*pl* **-s**)
  circumscribed *v* ▷circumscribe

  circumscribes *v* ▷circumscribe
  circumscribing *v* ▷circumscribe
  circumscription *n* ▷circumscribe
  circumscriptions *n* ▷circumscribe
circumspect *adj* cautious and careful not to take risks > **circumspectly** *adv* > **circumspection** *n*
  circumspection *n* ▷circumspect
  circumspectly *adv* ▷circumspect
circumstance *n* (*pl* **-s**) (*usu. pl*) occurrence or condition that accompanies or influences a person or event
  circumstances *n* ▷circumstance
circumstantial *adj* (of evidence) strongly suggesting something but not proving it
circumvent *v* (**-s, -ing, -ed**) avoid or get round (a rule etc.) > **circumvention** *n* (*pl* **-s**)
  circumvented *v* ▷circumvent
  circumventing *v* ▷circumvent
  circumvention *n* ▷circumvent
  circumventions *n* ▷circumvent
  circumvents *v* ▷circumvent
circus *n* (*pl* **-es**) (performance given by) a travelling company of acrobats, clowns, performing animals, etc.
  circuses *n* ▷circus
cirrhosis [sir-**roh**-siss] *n* serious liver disease, often caused by drinking too much alcohol > **cirrhotic** *adj*
  cirrhotic *adj* ▷cirrhosis
  cirri *n* ▷cirrus
cirrus *n* (*pl* **-ri**) high wispy cloud
cistern *n* (*pl* **-s**) water tank, esp. one that holds water for flushing a toilet
  cisterns *n* ▷cistern
citadel *n* (*pl* **-s**) fortress in a city
  citadels *n* ▷citadel
  citation *n* ▷cite
  citations *n* ▷cite
cite *v* (**cites, citing, cited**) quote, refer to > **citation** *n* (*pl* **-s**)
  cited *v* ▷cite
  cites *v* ▷cite
  cities *n* ▷city
  citing *v* ▷cite
citizen *n* (*pl* **-s**) native or naturalized member of a state or nation > **citizenship** *n* (*pl* **-s**)
  citizens *n* ▷citizen
  citizenship *n* ▷citizen
  citizenships *n* ▷citizen
city *n* (*pl* **-ties**) large or important town
civet [**siv**-vit] *n* (*pl* **-s**) spotted catlike African mammal
  civets *n* ▷civet
civic *adj* of a city or citizens

civics *n* study of the rights and responsibilities of citizenship

civil *adj* relating to the citizens of a state as opposed to the armed forces or the Church > **civilly** *adv*

civilian *n* (*pl* -s) ▶ *adj* (person) not belonging to the armed forces
    civilians *n* ▷ civilian
    civilities *n* ▷ civility

civility *n* (*pl* -ities) polite or courteous behaviour

civilization *n* (*pl* -s) high level of human cultural and social development
    civilizations *n* ▷ civilization

civilize *v* (-izes, -izing, -ized) refine or educate (a person)
    civilized *v* ▷ civilize
    civilizes *v* ▷ civilize
    civilizing *v* ▷ civilize
    civilly *adv* ▷ civil

civvies *pl n* (BRIT, AUST & NZ) (*Slang*) ordinary clothes that are not part of a uniform

clack *n* (*pl* -s) sound made by two hard objects striking each other ▶ *v* (-s, -ing, -ed) make this sound
    clacked *v* ▷ clack
    clacking *v* ▷ clack
    clacks *n*, *v* ▷ clack

clad *v* (clads, cladding, clad) ▷ clothe

cladding *n* (*pl* -s) material used to cover the outside of a building ▶ *v* ▷ clad
    claddings *n* ▷ cladding
    clads *v* ▷ clad

claim *v* (-s, -ing, -ed) assert as a fact ▶ *n* (*pl* -s) assertion that something is true > **claimant** *n* (*pl* -s)
    claimant *n* ▷ claim
    claimants *n* ▷ claim
    claimed *v* ▷ claim
    claiming *v* ▷ claim
    claims *v*, *n* ▷ claim

clairvoyance *n* (*pl* -s) power of perceiving things beyond the natural range of the senses > **clairvoyant** *n* (*pl* -s) *adj*
    clairvoyances *n* ▷ clairvoyance
    clairvoyant *n*, *adj* ▷ clairvoyance
    clairvoyants *n* ▷ clairvoyance

clam *n* (*pl* -s) edible shellfish with a hinged shell ▶ *v* (clams, clamming, clammed) (*Informal*) stop talking, esp. through nervousness

clamber *v* (-s, -ing, -ed) climb awkwardly
    clambered *v* ▷ clamber
    clambering *v* ▷ clamber
    clambers *v* ▷ clamber

clammed *v* ▷ clam
clammier *adj* ▷ clammy
clammiest *adj* ▷ clammy
clamming *v* ▷ clam

clammy *adj* (-mier, -miest) unpleasantly moist and sticky

clamour *n* (*pl* -s) loud protest ▶ *v* (-s, -ing, -ed) make a loud noise or outcry > **clamorous** *adj* > **clamorously** *adv* > **clamorousness** *n*
    clamoured *v* ▷ clamour
    clamouring *v* ▷ clamour
    clamorous *adj* ▷ clamour
    clamorously *adj* ▷ clamour
    clamorousness *n* ▷ clamour
    clamours *n*, *v* ▷ clamour

clamp *n* (*pl* -s) tool with movable jaws for holding things together tightly ▶ *v* (-s, -ing, -ed) fasten with a clamp
    clamped *v* ▷ clamp
    clamping *v* ▷ clamp
    clamps *n*, *v* ▷ clamp
    clams *v*, *n* ▷ clam

clan *n* (*pl* -s) group of families with a common ancestor, esp. among Scottish Highlanders

clandestine *adj* secret and concealed > **clandestinely** *adv*
    clandestinely *adv* ▷ clandestine

clang *v* (-s, -ing, -ed) make a loud ringing metallic sound ▶ *n* (*pl* -s) ringing metallic sound
    clanged *v* ▷ clang

clanger *n* (*pl* -s) (*Informal*) obvious mistake
    clangers *n* ▷ clanger
    clanging *v* ▷ clang

clangour *n* (*pl* -s) loud continuous clanging sound
    clangours *n* ▷ clangour
    clangs *v*, *n* ▷ clang

clank *n* (*pl* -s) harsh metallic sound ▶ *v* (-s, -ing, -ed) make such a sound
    clanked *v* ▷ clank
    clanking *v* ▷ clank
    clanks *n*, *v* ▷ clank

clannish *adj* (of a group) tending to exclude outsiders > **clannishness** *n*
    clannishness *n* ▷ clannish
    clans *n* ▷ clan

clap *v* (claps, clapping, clapped) applaud by hitting the palms of one's hands sharply together ▶ *n* (*pl* -s) act or sound of clapping
    clapped *v* ▷ clap

clapper *n* (*pl* -s) piece of metal inside a bell, which causes it to sound when struck against the side

clapperboard *n* (*pl* -s) pair of hinged boards

clapped together during filming to help in synchronizing sound and picture
clapperboards n ▷ clapperboard
clappers n ▷ clapper
clapping v ▷ clap
claps v, n ▷ clap
claptrap n (pl -s) (*Informal*) foolish or pretentious talk
claptraps n ▷ claptrap
claret [klar-rit] n (pl -s) dry red wine from Bordeaux
clarets n ▷ claret
clarification n ▷ clarify
clarifications n ▷ clarify
clarified v ▷ clarify
clarifies v ▷ clarify
clarify v (-fies, -fying, -fied) make (a matter) clear and unambiguous > **clarification** n (pl -s)
clarifying v ▷ clarify
clarinet n (pl -s) keyed woodwind instrument with a single reed > **clarinettist** n (pl -s)
clarinets n ▷ clarinet
clarinettist n ▷ clarinet
clarinettists n ▷ clarinet
clarion n (pl -s) obsolete high-pitched trumpet
clarions n ▷ clarion
clarities n ▷ clarity
clarity n (pl -ities) clearness
clash v (-es, -ing, -ed) come into conflict ▶ n (pl -es) fight, argument
clashed v ▷ clash
clashes v, n ▷ clash
clashing v ▷ clash
clasp n (pl -s) device for fastening things ▶ v (-s, -ing, -ed) grasp or embrace firmly
clasped v ▷ clasp
clasping v ▷ clasp
clasps n, v ▷ clasp
class n (pl -es) group of people sharing a similar social position ▶ v (-es, -ing, -ed) place in a class
classed v ▷ class
classes n, v ▷ class
classic adj being a typical example of something ▶ n (pl -s) author, artist, or work of art of recognized excellence ▶ pl study of ancient Greek and Roman literature and culture
classical adj of or in a restrained conservative style > **classically** adv
classically adv ▷ classical
classicism n artistic style showing emotional restraint and regularity of form > **classicist** n (pl -s)

classicist n ▷ classicism
classicists n ▷ classicism
classics n ▷ classic
classier adj ▷ classy
classiest adj ▷ classy
classifiable adj ▷ classify
classification n ▷ classify
classifications n ▷ classify
classified v ▷ classify
classifies v ▷ classify
classify v (-fies, -fying, -fied) divide into groups with similar characteristics > **classifiable** adj > **classification** n (pl -s)
classifying v ▷ classify
classing v ▷ class
classy adj (classier, classiest) (*Informal*) stylish and elegant
clatter v (-s, -ing, -ed) ▶ n (pl -s) (make) a rattling noise
clattered v ▷ clatter
clattering v ▷ clatter
clatters v, n ▷ clatter
clause n (pl -s) section of a legal document
clauses n ▷ clause
claustrophobia n (pl -s) abnormal fear of confined spaces > **claustrophobic** adj
claustrophobia n ▷ claustrophobia
claustrophobias n ▷ claustrophobia
claustrophobic adj ▷ claustrophobia
clavichord n (pl -s) early keyboard instrument
clavichords n ▷ clavichord
clavicle n (pl -s) > collarbone
clavicles n ▷ clavicle
claw n (pl -s) sharp hooked nail of a bird or beast ▶ v (-s, -ing, -ed) tear with claws or nails
clawed v ▷ claw
clawing v ▷ claw
claws n, v ▷ claw
clay n (pl -s) fine-grained earth, soft when moist and hardening when baked, used to make bricks and pottery > **clayey** adj
clayey adj ▷ clay
claymore n (pl -s) large two-edged sword formerly used by Scottish Highlanders
claymores n ▷ claymore
clays n ▷ clay
clean adj (-er, -est) free from dirt or impurities ▶ v (-s, -ing, -ed) make (something) free from dirt ▶ adv (*Not standard*) completely > **cleaner** n (pl -s) > **cleanly** adv > **cleanliness** n (pl -es)
cleaned v ▷ clean
cleaner n, adj ▷ clean
cleaners n ▷ clean
cleanest adj ▷ clean
cleaning v ▷ clean

cleanliness n ▷ clean

cleanlinesses n ▷ clean

cleanly adv ▷ clean

cleans v ▷ clean

cleanse v (-ses, -sing, -sed) make clean > **cleanser** n (pl -s)

cleansed v ▷ cleanse

cleanser n ▷ cleanse

cleansers n ▷ cleanse

cleanses v ▷ cleanse

cleansing v ▷ cleanse

clear adj (-er, -est) free from doubt or confusion ▶ adv out of the way ▶ v (-s, -ing, -ed) make or become clear > **clearly** adv

clearance n (pl -s) clearing

clearances n ▷ clear

cleared v ▷ clear

clearer adj ▷ clear

clearest adj ▷ clear

clearing n (pl -s) treeless area in a wood ▶ v ▷ clear

clearings n ▷ clearing

clearly adv ▷ clear

clears v ▷ clear

clearway n (pl -s) stretch of road on which motorists may stop in an emergency

clearways n ▷ clearway

cleat n (pl -s) wedge

cleats n ▷ cleat

cleavage n (pl -s) space between a woman's breasts, as revealed by a low-cut dress

cleavages n ▷ cleavage

cleave[1] v (-ves, -ving, cleft, -ved or clove) (cleft, cleaved or cloven) split apart

cleave[2] v (-ves, -ving, cleft, cleft) cling or stick

cleaved v ▷ cleave[1]

cleaver n (pl -s) butcher's heavy knife with a square blade

cleavers n ▷ cleaver

cleaves v ▷ cleave[1, 2]

cleaving v ▷ cleave[1, 2]

clef n (pl -s) (MUSIC) symbol at the beginning of a stave to show the pitch

clefs n ▷ clef

cleft n (pl -s) narrow opening or crack ▶ v ▷ cleave[1, 2]

clefted v ▷ cleft

clefting v ▷ cleft

clefts n, v ▷ cleft

clematis n climbing plant with large colourful flowers

clemencies n ▷ clemency

clemency n (pl -cies) kind or lenient treatment

clement adj (of weather) mild

clementine n (pl -s) small orange citrus fruit

clementines n ▷ clementine

clench v (-es, -ing, -ed) close or squeeze (one's teeth or fist) tightly

clenched v ▷ clench

clenches v ▷ clench

clenching v ▷ clench

clerestories n ▷ clerestory

clerestory [clear-store-ee] n (pl -ries) row of windows at the top of a wall above an adjoining roof

clergies n ▷ clergy

clergy n (pl clergies) priests and ministers as a group > **clergyman** n (pl -men)

clergyman n ▷ clergy

clergymen n ▷ clergy

cleric n (pl -s) member of the clergy

clerical adj of clerks or office work

clerics n ▷ cleric

clerk n (pl -s) employee in an office, bank, or court who keeps records, files, and accounts

clerks n ▷ clerk

clever adj (-er, -est) intelligent, quick at learning > **cleverly** adv > **cleverness** n (pl -es)

cleverer adj ▷ clever

cleverest adj ▷ clever

cleverly adv ▷ clever

cleverness n ▷ clever

clevernesses n ▷ clever

clianthus [klee-anth-us] n (pl -es) Australian or NZ plant with slender scarlet flowers

clianthuses n ▷ clianthus

cliché [klee-shay] n (pl -s) expression or idea that is no longer effective because of overuse > **clichéd** adj

clichéd n ▷ cliché

clichés n ▷ cliché

click n (pl -s) short sharp sound ▶ v (-s, -ing, -ed) make this sound

clicked v ▷ click

clicking v ▷ click

clicks n, v ▷ click

client n (pl -s) person who uses the services of a professional person or company

clientele [klee-on-tell] n (pl -s) clients collectively

clienteles n ▷ clientele

clients n ▷ client

cliff n (pl -s) steep rock face, esp. along the sea shore

cliffhanger n (pl -s) film, game, etc., that is tense and exciting because its outcome is uncertain

cliffhangers n ▷ cliffhanger

cliffs n ▷ cliff

climactic adj ▷ climax

climate n (pl -s) typical weather conditions of an area ▷ **climatic** adj
  climates n ▷ climate
  climatic adj ▷ climate
climax n (pl -es) most intense point of an experience, series of events, or story ▷ **climactic** adj
  climaxes n ▷ climax
climb v (-s, -ing, -ed) go up, ascend ▶ n (pl -s) climbing ▷ **climber** n (pl -s)
  climbed v ▷ climb
  climber n ▷ climb
  climbers n ▷ climb
  climbing v ▷ climb
  climbs v, n ▷ climb
clime n (pl -s) (Poetic) place or its climate
  climes n ▷ clime
clinch v (-es, -ing, -ed) settle (an argument or agreement) decisively
  clinched v ▷ clinch
clincher n (pl -s) (Informal) something decisive
  clinchers n ▷ clincher
  clinches v ▷ clinch
  clinching v ▷ clinch
cling v (clings, clinging, clung) hold tightly or stick closely
clingfilm n (pl -s) thin polythene material for wrapping food
  clingfilms n ▷ clingfilm
  clinging v ▷ cling
  clings v ▷ cling
clinic n (pl -s) building where outpatients receive medical treatment or advice
clinical adj of a clinic ▷ **clinically** adv
  clinically adv ▷ clinical
  clinics n ▷ clinic
clink¹ v (-s, -ing, -ed) ▶ n (pl -s) (make) a light sharp metallic sound
clink² n (pl -s) (BRIT, AUST & NZ) (Slang) prison
  clinked v ▷ clink¹
clinker n (pl -s) fused coal left over in a fire or furnace
  clinkers n ▷ clinker
  clinking v ▷ clink¹
  clinks n ▷ clink¹, ² ▶ v ▷ clink¹
clip¹ v (clips, clipping, clipped) cut with shears or scissors ▶ n (pl -s) short extract of a film
clip² n device for attaching or holding things together ▶ v (clips, clipping, clipped) attach or hold together with a clip
  clipped v ▷ clip¹, ²
clipper n (pl -s) fast commercial sailing ship
  clippers pl n tool for clipping ▶ n ▷ clipper
clipping n (-s) something cut out, esp. an article from a newspaper ▶ v ▷ clip¹, ²

  clippings n ▷ clipping
  clips n, v ▷ clip¹, ²
clique [kleek] n (pl -s) small exclusive group
  cliques n ▷ clique
  clitoral adj ▷ clitoris
clitoris [klit-or-iss] n (pl -es) small sexually sensitive organ at the front of the vulva ▷ **clitoral** adj
  clitorises n ▷ clitoris
cloak n (pl -s) loose sleeveless outer garment ▶ v (-s, -ing, -ed) cover or conceal
  cloaked v ▷ cloak
  cloaking v ▷ cloak
cloakroom n (pl -s) room where coats may be left temporarily
  cloakrooms n ▷ cloakroom
  cloaks n, v ▷ cloak
clobber¹ v (-s, -ing, -ed) (Informal) hit
clobber² n (pl -es) (BRIT, AUST & NZ) (Informal) belongings, esp. clothes
  clobbered v ▷ clobber¹
  clobbering v ▷ clobber¹
  clobbers v ▷ clobber¹ ▶ n ▷ clobber²
cloche [klosh] n (pl -s) cover to protect young plants
  cloches n ▷ cloche
clock n (pl -s) instrument for showing the time
  clocks n ▷ clock
clockwise adv, adj in the direction in which the hands of a clock rotate
clockwork n mechanism similar to the kind in a clock, used in wind-up toys
clod n (pl -s) lump of earth
  clods n ▷ clod
clog v (clogs, clogging, clogged) obstruct ▶ n (pl -s) wooden or wooden-soled shoe
  clogged v ▷ clog
  clogging v ▷ clog
  clogs v, n ▷ clog
cloister n (pl -s) covered pillared arcade, usu. in a monastery
cloistered adj sheltered
  cloisters n ▷ cloister
clone n (pl -s) animal or plant produced artificially from the cells of another animal or plant, and identical to the original (Informal) ▶ v (clones, cloning, cloned) produce as a clone
  cloned v ▷ clone
  clones n, v ▷ clone
  cloning v ▷ clone
close¹ v (-ses, -sing, -sed) [rhymes with **nose**] shut ▶ n (pl -s) end, conclusion
close² adj (-r, -st) [rhymes with **dose**] near ▶ adv closely, tightly ▷ **closely** adv ▷ **closeness** n

(pl **-es**)
closed v ▷ close¹
closely adv ▷ close²
closeness n ▷ close²
closenesses n ▷ close²
closer adj ▷ close²
closes v, n ▷ close¹
closest adj ▷ close²
closet n (pl **-s**) (US) cupboard ▶ adj private, secret ▶ v (**-s, -ing, -ed**) shut (oneself) away in private
  closeted v ▷ closet
  closeting v ▷ closet
  closets n, v ▷ closet
closing v ▷ close¹
closure n (pl **-s**) closing
  closures n ▷ closure
clot n (pl **-s**) soft thick lump formed from liquid ▶ v (**-s, -tting, -tted**) form soft thick lumps
cloth n (pl **-s**) (piece of) woven fabric
clothe v (**clothes, clothing, clothed** or **clad**) put clothes on
  clothed v ▷ clothe
clothes pl n articles of dress ▶ v ▷ clothe
clothing n clothes collectively ▶ v ▷ clothe
  cloths n ▷ cloth
  clots n, v ▷ clot
  clotted v ▷ clot
  clotting v ▷ clot
cloud n (pl **-s**) mass of condensed water vapour floating in the sky ▶ v (**-s, -ing, -ed**) (foll. by **over**) become cloudy > **cloudless** adj
cloudburst n (pl **-s**) heavy fall of rain
  cloudbursts n ▷ cloudburst
  clouded v ▷ cloud
  cloudier adj ▷ cloud
  cloudiest adj ▷ cloud
  cloudiness n ▷ cloudy
  clouding v ▷ cloud
  cloudless adj ▷ cloud
  clouds n, v ▷ cloud
cloudy adj (**-dier, -diest**) having a lot of clouds > **cloudiness** n
clout (Informal) n (pl **-s**) hard blow ▶ v (**-s, -ed, -ing**) hit hard
  clouted v ▷ clout
  clouting v ▷ clout
  clouts n, v ▷ clout
clove¹ n (pl **-s**) dried flower bud of a tropical tree, used as a spice
clove² n (pl **-s**) segment of a bulb of garlic
clove³ v ▷ cleave¹
  cloven v ▷ cleave¹
clover n (pl **-s**) plant with three-lobed leaves
  clovers n ▷ clover

cloves n ▷ clove¹, ²
clown n (pl **-s**) comic entertainer in a circus ▶ v (**-s, -ing, -ed**) behave foolishly > **clownish** adj > **clownishly** adv > **clownishness** n
  clowned v ▷ clown
  clowning v ▷ clown
  clownish adj ▷ clown
  clownishly adv ▷ clown
  clownishness n ▷ clown
  clowns n, v ▷ clown
club n (pl **-s**) association of people with common interests ▶ v (**clubs, clubbing, clubbed**) hit with a club
  clubbed v ▷ club
  clubbing v ▷ club
  clubs n, v ▷ club
cluck n (pl **-s**) low clicking noise made by a hen ▶ v (**-s, -ing, -ed**) make this noise
  clucked v ▷ cluck
  clucking v ▷ cluck
  clucks n, v ▷ cluck
clue n (pl **-s**) something that helps to solve a mystery or puzzle
clueless adj stupid > **cluelessly** adv > **cluelessness** n
  cluelessly adv ▷ clueless
  cluelessness n ▷ clueless
  clues n ▷ clue
clump n (pl **-s**) small group of things or people ▶ v (**-s, -ing, -ed**) walk heavily
  clumped v ▷ clump
  clumping v ▷ clump
  clumps n, v ▷ clump
  clumsier adj ▷ clumsy
  clumsiest adj ▷ clumsy
  clumsily adv ▷ clumsy
  clumsiness n ▷ clumsy
clumsy adj (**-sier, -siest**) lacking skill or physical coordination > **clumsily** adv > **clumsiness** n
  clung v ▷ cling
clunk n (pl **-s**) dull metallic sound ▶ v (**-s, -ing, -ed**) make such a sound
  clunked v ▷ clunk
  clunking v ▷ clunk
  clunks n, v ▷ clunk
cluster n (pl **-s**) small close group ▶ v (**-s, -ing, -ed**) gather in clusters
  clustered v ▷ cluster
  clustering v ▷ cluster
  clusters n, v ▷ cluster
clutch¹ v (**-es, -ing, -ed**) grasp tightly (foll. by **at**) ▶ n (pl **-es**) device enabling two revolving shafts to be connected and disconnected, esp. in a motor vehicle

clutch² n (pl -es) set of eggs laid at the same time
clutched v ▷ clutch¹
clutches v ▷ clutch¹ ▷ n ▷ clutch¹, ²
clutching v ▷ clutch¹
clutter v (-s, -ing, -ed) scatter objects about (a place) untidily ▶ n (pl -s) untidy mess
cluttered v ▷ clutter
cluttering v ▷ clutter
clutters v, n ▷ clutter

cly verb (**clys, clying, clyed**). Cly is an old word meaning steal. The various forms of this word can be useful when you are short of vowels. Cly scores 8 points.

coach n (pl -es) long-distance bus ▶ v (-es, -ing, -ed) train, teach
coached v ▷ coach
coaches n, v ▷ coach
coaching v ▷ coach
coagulant n (pl -s) substance causing coagulation
coagulants n ▷ coagulant
coagulate [koh-**ag**-yew-late] v (-lates, -lating, -lated) change from a liquid to a semisolid mass > **coagulation** n (pl -s)
coagulated v ▷ coagulate
coagulates v ▷ coagulate
coagulating v ▷ coagulate
coagulation n ▷ coagulate
coagulations n ▷ coagulate
coal n (pl -s) black rock consisting mainly of carbon, used as fuel
coalesce [koh-a-**less**] v (-lesces, -lescing, -lesced) come together, merge > **coalescence** n (pl -s)
coalesced v ▷ coalesce
coalescence n ▷ coalesce
coalescences n ▷ coalesce
coalesces v ▷ coalesce
coalescing v ▷ coalesce
coalfield n (pl -s) area with coal under the ground
coalfields n ▷ coalfield
coalition [koh-a-**lish**-un] n (pl -s) temporary alliance, esp. between political parties
coalitions n ▷ coalition
coals n ▷ coal
coarse adj (-r, -st) rough in texture > **coarsely** adv > **coarseness** n (pl -es) > **coarsen** v (-s, -ing, -ed)
coarsely adv ▷ coarse
coarsen v ▷ coarse
coarsened v ▷ coarse
coarseness n ▷ coarse
coarsenesses n ▷ coarse

coarsening v ▷ coarse
coarsens v ▷ coarse
coarser adj ▷ coarse
coarsest adj ▷ coarse
coast n (pl -s) place where the land meets the sea ▶ v (-s, -ing, -ed) move by momentum, without the use of power > **coastal** adj
coastal adj ▷ coast
coasted v ▷ coast
coaster n (pl -s) small mat placed under a glass
coasters n ▷ coaster
coastguard n (pl -s) organization that aids ships and swimmers in trouble and prevents smuggling
coastguards n ▷ coastguard
coasting v ▷ coast
coastline n (pl -s) outline of a coast
coastlines n ▷ coastline
coasts n, v ▷ coast
coat n (pl -s) outer garment with long sleeves ▶ v (-s, -ing, -ed) cover with a layer
coated v ▷ coat
coating n (pl -s) covering layer ▶ v ▷ coat
coatings n ▷ coating
coats n, v ▷ coat
coax v (-es, -ing, -ed) persuade gently
coaxed v ▷ coax
coaxes v ▷ coax
coaxial [koh-**ax**-ee-al] adj (of a cable) transmitting by means of two concentric conductors separated by an insulator
coaxing v ▷ coax
cob n (pl -s) stalk of an ear of maize
cobalt n (pl -s) (CHEM) brittle silvery-white metallic element
cobalts n ▷ cobalt
cobber n (pl -s) (AUST & OLD-FASHIONED NZ) (Informal) friend
cobbers n ▷ cobber
cobble n (pl -s) cobblestone
cobbler n (pl -s) shoe mender
cobblers n ▷ cobbler
cobbles n ▷ cobble
cobblestone n (pl -s) rounded stone used for paving
cobblestones n ▷ cobblestone
cobia [koh-bee-a] n (pl -s) large dark-striped game fish of tropical and subtropical seas
cobias n ▷ cobia
cobra n (pl -s) venomous hooded snake of Asia and Africa
cobras n ▷ cobra
cobs n ▷ cob
cobweb n (pl -s) spider's web
cobwebs n ▷ cobweb

cocaine *n* (*pl* -s) addictive drug used as a narcotic and as an anaesthetic
cocaines *n* ▷ cocaine
coccyges *n* ▷ coccyx
coccyx [kok-six] *n* (*pl* coccyges) [kok-**sije**-eez] bone at the base of the spinal column
cochineal *n* (*pl* -s) red dye obtained from a Mexican insect, used for food colouring
cochineals *n* ▷ cochineal
cock *n* (*pl* -s) male bird, esp. of domestic fowl ▶ *v* (-s, -ing, -ed) draw back (the hammer of a gun) to firing position
cockade *n* (*pl* -s) feather or rosette worn on a hat as a badge
cockades *n* ▷ cockade
cockateel *n* ▷ cockatiel
cockateels *n* ▷ cockatiel
cockatiel, cockateel *n* (*pl* -s) crested Australian parrot with a greyish-brown and yellow plumage
cockatiels *n* ▷ cockatiel
cockatoo *n* (*pl* -s) crested parrot of Australia or the East Indies
cockatoos *n* ▷ cockatoo
cocked *v* ▷ cock
cockerel *n* (*pl* -s) young domestic cock
cockerels *n* ▷ cockerel
cockeyed *adj* (*Informal*) crooked, askew
cockie, cocky *n* (*pl* -kies) (AUST & NZ) (*Informal*) farmer
cockier *adj* ▷ cocky
cockies *n* ▷ cockie
cockiest *adj* ▷ cocky
cockily *adv* ▷ cocky
cockiness *n* ▷ cocky
cocking *v* ▷ cock
cockle *n* (*pl* -s) edible shellfish
cockles *n* ▷ cockle
cockney *n* (*pl* -s) native of the East End of London
cockneys *n* ▷ cockney
cockpit *n* (*pl* -s) pilot's compartment in an aircraft
cockpits *n* ▷ cockpit
cockroach *n* (*pl* -es) beetle-like insect which is a household pest
cockroaches *n* ▷ cockroach
cocks *n*, *v* ▷ cock
cocksure *adj* overconfident, arrogant
cocktail *n* (*pl* -s) mixed alcoholic drink
cocktails *n* ▷ cocktail
cocky *adj* (cockier, cockiest) conceited and overconfident ▶ *n* ▷ cockie > **cockily** *adv* > **cockiness** *n*
cocoa *n* (*pl* -s) powder made from the seed of

the cacao tree
cocoas *n* ▷ cocoa
coconut *n* (*pl* -s) large hard fruit of a type of palm tree
coconuts *n* ▷ coconut
cocoon *n* (*pl* -s) silky protective covering of a silkworm ▶ *v* (-s, -ing, -ed) wrap up tightly for protection
cocooned *v* ▷ cocoon
cocooning *v* ▷ cocoon
cocoons *n*, *v* ▷ cocoon
cod *n* (*pl* cod) large food fish of the North Atlantic
coda *n* (*pl* -s) final part of a musical composition
codas *n* ▷ coda
coddle *v* (coddles, coddling, coddled) pamper, overprotect
coddled *v* ▷ coddle
coddles *v* ▷ coddle
coddling *v* ▷ coddle
code *n* (*pl* -s) system of letters, symbols, or prearranged signals by which messages can be communicated secretly or briefly ▶ *v* (codes, coding, coded) put into code
coded *v* ▷ code
codeine [kode-een] *n* (*pl* -s) drug used as a painkiller
codeines *v* ▷ codeine
codes *n*, *v* ▷ code
codex *n* (*pl* codices) volume of manuscripts of an ancient text
codger *n* (*pl* -s) (BRIT, AUST & NZ) (*Informal*) old man
codgers *n* ▷ codger
codices *n* ▷ codex
codicil [kode-iss-ill] *n* (*pl* -s) addition to a will
codicils *n* ▷ codicil
codification *n* ▷ codify
codifications *n* ▷ codify
codified *v* ▷ codify
codifies *v* ▷ codify
codify *v* (-fies, -fying, -fied) organize (rules or procedures) systematically > **codification** *n* (*pl* -s)
codifying *v* ▷ codify
coding *v* ▷ code
coeducation *n* education of boys and girls together > **coeducational** *adj*
coeducational *adj* ▷ coeducation
coefficient *n* (*pl* -s) (MATHS) number or constant placed before and multiplying a quantity
coefficients *n* ▷ coefficient
coelacanth [seel-a-kanth] *n* (*pl* -s) primitive marine fish

coelacanths n ▷ coelacanth
coerce [koh-urss] v (-ces, -cing, -ced) compel, force > **coercion** n > **coercive** adj
coerced v ▷ coerce
coerces v ▷ coerce
coercing v ▷ coerce
coercion n ▷ coerce
coercive adj ▷ coerce
coeval [koh-eev-al] adj, n (pl -s) contemporary
coevals n ▷ coeval
coexist v (-s, -ing, -ed) exist together, esp. peacefully despite differences > **coexistence** n
coexisted v ▷ coexist
coexistence n ▷ coexist
coexisting v ▷ coexist
coexists v ▷ coexist
coffee n (pl -s) drink made from the roasted and ground seeds of a tropical shrub ▶ adj medium-brown
coffees n ▷ coffee
coffer n (pl -s) chest for valuables ▶ pl store of money
coffers n ▷ coffer
coffin n (pl -s) box in which a corpse is buried or cremated
coffins n ▷ coffin
cog n (pl -s) one of the teeth on the rim of a gearwheel
cogency n ▷ cogent
cogent [koh-jent] adj forcefully convincing > **cogency** n > **cogently** adv
cogently n ▷ cogent
cogitate [koj-it-tate] v (-tates, -tating, -tated) think deeply about > **cogitation** n (pl -s)
cogitated v ▷ cogitate
cogitates v ▷ cogitate
cogitating v ▷ cogitate
cogitation n ▷ cogitate
cogitations n ▷ cogitate
cognac [kon-yak] n (pl -s) French brandy
cognacs n ▷ cognac
cognate adj derived from a common original form
cognition n (pl -s) act or experience of knowing or acquiring knowledge > **cognitive** adj
cognitions n ▷ cognition
cognitive adj ▷ cognition
cognizance n (pl -s) knowledge, understanding > **cognizant** adj
cognizances n ▷ cognizance
cognizant adj ▷ cognizance
cognoscenti [kon-yo-shen-tee] pl n connoisseurs

cogs n ▷ cog
cohabit v (-s, -ing, -ed) live together as husband and wife without being married > **cohabitation** n (pl -s)
cohabitation n ▷ cohabit
cohabitations n ▷ cohabit
cohabited v ▷ cohabit
cohabiting v ▷ cohabit
cohabits v ▷ cohabit
cohere v (-heres, -hering, -hered) hold or stick together
cohered v ▷ cohere
coherence n ▷ cohere
coherent adj logical and consistent > **coherence** n > **coherently** adv
coherently n ▷ coherent
coheres v ▷ cohere
cohering v ▷ cohere
cohesion n sticking together
cohesive adj sticking together to form a whole
cohort n (pl -s) band of associates
cohorts n ▷ cohort
coiffeur n ▷ coiffure
coiffeurs n ▷ coiffure
coiffeuse n ▷ coiffure
coiffeuses n ▷ coiffure
coiffure n (pl -s) hairstyle > **coiffeur, coiffeuse** n (pl -s) hairdresser
coiffures n ▷ coiffure
coil v (-s, -ing, -ed) wind in loops ▶ n (pl -s) something coiled
coiled v ▷ coil
coiling v ▷ coil
coils v, n ▷ coil
coin n (pl -s) piece of metal money ▶ v (-s, -ing, -ed) invent (a word or phrase)
coinage n (pl -s) coins collectively
coinages n ▷ coinage
coincide v (-cides, -ciding, -cided) happen at the same time
coincided v ▷ coincide
coincidence n (pl -s) occurrence of simultaneous or apparently connected events
coincidences n ▷ coincidence
coincident adj in agreement
coincidental adj resulting from coincidence > **coincidentally** adv
coincidentally adv ▷ coincidental
coincides v ▷ coincide
coinciding v ▷ coincide
coined v ▷ coin
coining v ▷ coin
coins n, v ▷ coin
coir n (pl -s) coconut fibre, used for matting

coirs *n* ▷ coir

coital *adj* ▷ coitus

coition *n* ▷ coitus

coitions *n* ▷ coitus

coitus [koh-it-uss], **coition** [koh-**ish**-un] *n* (*pl* -s) sexual intercourse > **coital** *adj*

coke[1] *n* (*pl* -s) solid fuel left after gas has been distilled from coal

coke[2] *n* (*pl* -s) (*Slang*) cocaine

cokes *n* ▷ coke[1, 2]

col *n* (*pl* -s) high mountain pass

cola *n* (*pl* -s) dark brown fizzy soft drink

colander *n* (*pl* -s) perforated bowl for straining or rinsing foods

colanders *n* ▷ colander

colas *n* ▷ cola

cold *adj* (-er, -est) lacking heat ▶ *n* (*pl* -s) lack of heat > **coldly** *adv* > **coldness** *n* (*pl* -es)

colder *adj* ▷ cold

coldest *adj* ▷ cold

coldly *adv* ▷ cold

coldness *n* ▷ cold

coldnesses *n* ▷ cold

colds *n* ▷ cold

coleslaw *n* (*pl* -s) salad dish of shredded raw cabbage in a dressing

coleslaws *n* ▷ coleslaw

coley *n* (*pl* -s) codlike food fish of the N Atlantic

coleys *n* ▷ coley

colic *n* (*pl* -s) severe pains in the stomach and bowels > **colicky** *adj* (-ckier, -ckiest)

colickier *adj* ▷ colic

colickiest *adj* ▷ colic

colicky *adj* ▷ colic

colics *n* ▷ colic

colitis [koh-**lie**-tiss] *n* inflammation of the colon

collaborate *v* (-ates, -ating, -ated) work with another on a project > **collaboration** *n* (*pl* -s) > **collaborative** *adj* > **collaboratively** *adv* > **collaborator** *n* (*pl* -s)

collaborated *v* ▷ collaborate

collaborates *v* ▷ collaborate

collaborating *v* ▷ collaborate

collaboration *n* ▷ collaborate

collaborations *n* ▷ collaborate

collaborative *adj* ▷ collaborate

collaboratively *adv* ▷ collaborate

collaborator *n* ▷ collaborate

collaborators *n* ▷ collaborate

collage [kol-**lahzh**] *n* (*pl* -s) art form in which various materials or objects are glued onto a surface

collages *n* ▷ collage

collapse *v* (-lapses, -lapsing, -lapsed) fall down

suddenly ▶ *n* (*pl* -s) collapsing > **collapsible** *adj*

collapsed *v* ▷ collapse

collapses *v*, *n* ▷ collapse

collapsible *adj* ▷ collapse

collapsing *v* ▷ collapse

collar *n* (*pl* -s) part of a garment round the neck ▶ *v* (-s, -ing, -ed) (BRIT, AUST & NZ) (*Informal*) seize, arrest

collarbone *n* (*pl* -s) bone joining the shoulder blade to the breastbone

collarbones *n* ▷ collarbone

collared *v* ▷ collar

collaring *v* ▷ collar

collars *n*, *v* ▷ collar

collate *v* (-lates, -lating, -lated) gather together, examine, and put in order

collated *v* ▷ collate

collateral *n* (*pl* -s) security pledged for the repayment of a loan

collaterals *n* ▷ collateral

collates *v* ▷ collate

collating *v* ▷ collate

collation *n* (*pl* -s) collating

collations *n* ▷ collation

colleague *n* (*pl* -s) fellow worker, esp. in a profession

colleagues *n* ▷ colleague

collect[1] *v* (-s, -ing, -ed) gather together > **collector** *n* (*pl* -s)

collect[2] *n* (*pl* -s) short prayer

collected *adj* calm and controlled ▶ *v* ▷ collect[1] > **collectedly** *adv* > **collectedness** *n*

collectedly *adv* ▷ collected

collectedness *n* ▷ collected

collecting *v* ▷ collect[1]

collection *n* (*pl* -s) things collected

collections *n* ▷ collection

collective *adj* of or done by a group ▶ *n* (*pl* -s) group of people working together on an enterprise and sharing the benefits from it > **collectively** *adv*

collectively *adv* ▷ collective

collectives *n* ▷ collective

collects *v* ▷ collect[1] ▶ *n* ▷ collect[2]

colleen *n* (*pl* -s) (IRISH) girl

colleens *n* ▷ colleen

college *n* (*pl* -s) place of higher education > **collegiate** *adj*

colleges *n* ▷ college

collegiate *adj* ▷ college

collide *v* (-lides, -liding, -lided) crash together violently > **collision** *n* (*pl* -s)

collided *v* ▷ collide

collides *v* ▷ collide

colliding *v* ▷ collide

collie *n* (*pl* -s) silky-haired sheepdog
collier *n* (*pl* -s) coal miner
  collieries *n* ▷ colliery
  colliers *n* ▷ collier
colliery *n* (*pl* -lieries) coal mine
  collies *n* ▷ collie
  collision *n* ▷ collide
  collisions *n* ▷ collide
collocate *v* (-cates, -cating, -cated) (of words) occur together regularly > **collocation** *n* (*pl* -s)
  collocated *v* ▷ collocate
  collocates *v* ▷ collocate
  collocating *v* ▷ collocate
  collocation *n* ▷ collocate
  collocations *n* ▷ collocate
colloid *n* (*pl* -s) suspension of particles in a solution
  colloids *n* ▷ colloid
colloquial *adj* suitable for informal speech or writing > **colloquially** *adv*
colloquialism *n* (*pl* -s) colloquial word or phrase
  colloquialisms *n* ▷ colloquialism
  colloquially *adv* ▷ colloquial
collude *v* (-ludes, -luding, -luded) act in collusion
  colluded *v* ▷ collude
  colludes *v* ▷ collude
  colluding *v* ▷ collude
collusion *n* (*pl* -s) secret or illegal cooperation
  collusions *n* ▷ collusion
collywobbles *pl n* (*Slang*) nervousness
cologne *n* (*pl* -s) mild perfume
  colognes *n* ▷ cologne
colon¹ *n* (*pl* -s) punctuation mark (:)
colon² *n* (*pl* -s) part of the large intestine connected to the rectum
colonel *n* (*pl* -s) senior commissioned army or air-force officer
  colonels *n* ▷ colonel
colonial *adj, n* (*pl* -s) (inhabitant) of a colony
colonialism *n* policy of acquiring and maintaining colonies
  colonials *n* ▷ colonial
  colonies *n* ▷ colony
colonist *n* (*pl* -s) settler in a colony
  colonists *n* ▷ colonist
  colonization *n* ▷ colonize
  colonizations *n* ▷ colonize
colonize *v* (-izes, -izing, -ized) make into a colony > **colonization** *n* (*pl* -s)
  colonized *v* ▷ colonize
  colonizes *v* ▷ colonize
  colonizing *v* ▷ colonize
colonnade *n* (*pl* -s) row of columns

colonnades *n* ▷ colonnade
colons *n* ▷ colon¹, ²
colony *n* (*pl* -nies) group of people who settle in a new country but remain under the rule of their homeland
coloration *n* (*pl* -s) arrangement of colours
  colorations *n* ▷ coloration
colossally *adv* ▷ colossal
colossal *adj* very large > **colossally** *adv*
  colossi *n* ▷ colossus
colossus *n* (*pl* -si, -suses) huge statue
  colossuses *n* ▷ colossus
  colostomies *n* ▷ colostomy
colostomy *n* (*pl* -mies) operation to form an opening from the colon to the surface of the body, for emptying the bowel
colour *n* (*pl* -s) appearance of things as a result of reflecting light ▶ *pl* flag of a country or regiment (*SPORT*) ▶ *v* (-s, -ing, -ed) apply colour to > **colourless** *adj* > **colourlessly** *adv*
coloured *adj* having colour ▶ *v* ▷ colour
colourful *adj* with bright or varied colours > **colourfully** *adv*
  colourfully *adv* ▷ colourful
  colouring *v* ▷ colour
  colourless *adj* ▷ colour
  colourlessly *adv* ▷ colour
  colours *n, v* ▷ colour
  cols *n* ▷ col
colt *n* (*pl* -s) young male horse
  colts *n* ▷ colt
columbine *n* (*pl* -s) garden flower with five petals
  columbines *n* ▷ columbine
column *n* (*pl* -s) pillar
columnist *n* (*pl* -s) journalist who writes a regular feature in a newspaper
  columnists *n* ▷ columnist
  columns *n* ▷ column
coma *n* (*pl* -s) state of deep unconsciousness
  comas *n* ▷ coma
comatose *adj* in a coma
comb *n* (*pl* -s) toothed implement for arranging the hair ▶ *v* (-s, -ing, -ed) use a comb on
combat *n* (*pl* -s) ▶ *v* (-s, -ing, -ed) fight, struggle > **combatant** *n* (*pl* -s) > **combative** *adj* > **combativeness** *n*
  combatant *n* ▷ combat
  combatants *n* ▷ combat
  combated *v* ▷ combat
  combating *v* ▷ combat
  combats *n, v* ▷ combat
  combed *v* ▷ comb
combination *n* (*pl* -s) combining ▶ *pl* (*BRIT*) old-

fashioned undergarment with long sleeves and long legs

combinations n ▷ combination

combine v (-bines, -bining, -bined) join together ▶ n (pl -s) association of people or firms for a common purpose

combined v ▷ combine

combines v, n ▷ combine

combing v ▷ comb

combining v ▷ combine

combs n, v ▷ comb

combustible adj burning easily

combustion n (pl -s) process of burning

combustions n ▷ combustion

come v (comes, coming, came, come) move towards a place, arrive

comeback n (pl -s) (Informal) return to a former position

comebacks n ▷ comeback

comedian, comedienne n (pl -s) entertainer who tells jokes

comedians n ▷ comedian

comedienne n ▷ comedian

comediennes n ▷ comedian

comedies n ▷ comedy

comedown n (pl -s) decline in status

comedowns n ▷ comedown

comedy n (pl -dies) humorous play, film, or programme

comelier adj ▷ comely

comeliest adj ▷ comely

comeliness n ▷ comely

comely adj (-lier, -liest) (Old-fashioned) nice-looking > **comeliness** n

comes v ▷ come

comestibles pl n (Formal) food

comet n (pl -s) heavenly body with a long luminous tail

comets n ▷ comet

comeuppance n (Informal) deserved punishment

comfier adj ▷ comfy

comfiest adj ▷ comfy

comfit n (pl -s) (Old-fashioned) sugar-coated sweet

comfits n ▷ comfit

comfort n (pl -s) physical ease or wellbeing ▶ v (-s, -ing, -ed) soothe, console > **comforter** n (pl -s)

comfortable adj giving comfort > **comfortably** adv

comfortably adv ▷ comfortable

comforted v ▷ comfort

comforter n ▷ comfort

comforters n ▷ comfort

comforting v ▷ comfort

comforts n, v ▷ comfort

comfrey n (pl -s) tall plant with bell-shaped flowers

comfreys n ▷ comfrey

comfy adj (-fier, -fiest) (Informal) comfortable

comic adj humorous, funny ▶ n (pl -s) comedian

comical adj amusing > **comically** adv

comically adv ▷ comical

comics n ▷ comic

coming v ▷ come

comma n (pl -s) punctuation mark (,)

command v (-s, -ing, -ed) order ▶ n (pl -s) authoritative instruction that something must be done

commandant n (pl -s) officer commanding a military group

commandants n ▷ commandant

commanded v ▷ command

commandeer v (-s, -ing, -ed) seize for military use

commandeered v ▷ commandeer

commandeering v ▷ commandeer

commandeers v ▷ commandeer

commander n (pl -s) military officer in command of a group or operation

commanders n ▷ commander

commanding v ▷ command

commandment n (pl -s) command from God

commandments n ▷ commandment

commando n (pl -dos, -does) (member of) a military unit trained for swift raids in enemy territory

commandoes n ▷ commando

commandos n ▷ commando

commands v, n ▷ command

commas n ▷ comma

commemorate v (-rates, -rating, -rated) honour the memory of > **commemoration** n (pl -s) > **commemorative** adj

commemorated v ▷ commemorate

commemorates v ▷ commemorate

commemorating v ▷ commemorate

commemoration n ▷ commemorate

commemorations n ▷ commemorate

commemorative adj ▷ commemorate

commence v (-mences, -mencing, -menced) begin > **commencement** n (pl -s)

commenced v ▷ commence

commencement n ▷ commence

commencements n ▷ commence

commences v ▷ commence

commencing v ▷ commence

commend v (-s, -ing, -ed) praise

> **commendable** *adj* > **commendably** *adv*
> **commendation** *n (pl* -s)
commendable *adj* ▷ commend
commendably *adv* ▷ commend
commendation *n* ▷ commend
commendations *n* ▷ commend
commended *v* ▷ commend
commending *v* ▷ commend
commends *v* ▷ commend
commensurable *adj* measurable by the same standards
commensurate *adj* corresponding in degree, size, or value
comment *n (pl* -s) remark ▶ *v* (-s, -ing, -ed) make a comment
commentaries *n* ▷ commentary
commentary *n (pl* -taries) spoken accompaniment to a broadcast or film
commentate *v* (-tates, -tating, -tated) provide a commentary > **commentator** *n (pl* -s)
commentated *v* ▷ commentate
commentates *v* ▷ commentate
commentating *v* ▷ commentate
commentator *n* ▷ commentate
commentators *n* ▷ commentate
commented *v* ▷ comment
commenting *v* ▷ comment
comments *n, v* ▷ comment
commerce *n (pl* -s) buying and selling, trade
commerces *n* ▷ commerce
commercial *adj* of commerce ▶ *n (pl* -s) television or radio advertisement
commercialization *n* ▷ commercialize
commercialize *v* (-izes, -izing, -ized) make commercial > **commercialization** *n*
commercialized *v* ▷ commercialize
commercializes *v* ▷ commercialize
commercializing *v* ▷ commercialize
commercials *n* ▷ commercial
commiserate *v* (-rates, -rating, -rated) (*foll. by* with) express sympathy (for) > **commiseration** *n (pl* -s)
commiserated *v* ▷ commiserate
commiserates *v* ▷ commiserate
commiserating *v* ▷ commiserate
commiseration *n* ▷ commiserate
commiserations *n* ▷ commiserate
commissar *n (pl* -s) (formerly) official responsible for political education in Communist countries
commissariat *n (pl* -s) (BRIT, AUST & NZ) military department in charge of food supplies
commissariats *n* ▷ commissariat
commissars *n* ▷ commissar

commission *n (pl* -s) piece of work that an artist is asked to do (MIL) ▶ *v* (-s, -ing, -ed) place an order for
commissionaire *n (pl* -s) uniformed doorman at a hotel, theatre, etc.
commissionaires *n* ▷ commissionaire
commissioned *v* ▷ commission
commissioner *n (pl* -s) appointed official in a government department
commissioners *n* ▷ commissioner
commissioning *v* ▷ commission
commissions *n, v* ▷ commission
commit *v* (-mits, -mitting, -mitted) perform (a crime or error)
commitment *n (pl* -s) dedication to a cause
commitments *n* ▷ commitment
commits *v* ▷ commit
committal *n (pl* -s) sending someone to prison or hospital
committals *n* ▷ committal
committed *v* ▷ commit
committee *n (pl* -s) group of people appointed to perform a specified service or function
committees *n* ▷ committee
committing *v* ▷ commit
commode *n (pl* -s) seat with a hinged flap concealing a chamber pot
commodes *n* ▷ commode
commodious *adj* roomy
commodities *n* ▷ commodity
commodity *n (pl* -ities) something that can be bought or sold
commodore *n (pl* -s) senior commissioned officer in the navy
commodores *n* ▷ commodore
common *adj* (-er, -est) occurring often ▶ *n (pl* -s) area of grassy land belonging to a community > **commonly** *adv*
commoner *n (pl* -s) person who does not belong to the nobility ▶ *adj* ▷ common
commoners *n* ▷ commoner
commonest *adj* ▷ common
commonly *adv* ▷ common
commonplace *adj* ordinary, everyday ▶ *n (pl* -s) trite remark
commonplaces *n* ▷ commonplace
commons *n* ▷ common
commonwealth *n (pl* -s) state or nation viewed politically
commonwealths *n* ▷ commonwealth
commotion *n (pl* -s) noisy disturbance
commotions *n* ▷ commotion
communal *adj* shared > **communally** *adv*
communally *n* ▷ communal
commune¹ *n (pl* -s) group of people who live

together and share everything

commune² v (-munes, -muning, -muned) (foll. by **with**) feel very close (to)

communed v ▷ commune²

communes n ▷ commune¹ ▷ v ▷ commune²

communicable adj (of a disease) able to be passed on

communicant n (pl -s) person who receives Communion

communicants n ▷ communicant

communicate v (-cates, -cating, -cated) make known or share (information, thoughts, or feelings)

communicated v ▷ communicate

communicates v ▷ communicate

communicating adj (of a door) joining two rooms ▶ v ▷ communicate

communication n communicating ▶ pl (-s) means of travelling or sending messages

communications n ▷ communication

communicative adj talking freely

communing v ▷ commune²

communion n (pl -s) sharing of thoughts or feelings

communions n ▷ communion

communiqué [kom-mune-ik-kay] n (pl -s) official announcement

communiqués n ▷ communiqué

communism n belief that all property and means of production should be shared by the community ▷ **communist** n (pl -s) adj

communists n ▷ communism

communities n ▷ community

community n (pl -ties) all the people living in one district

commutator n (pl -s) device used to change alternating electric current into direct current

commutators n ▷ commutator

commute v (-mutes, -muting, -muted) travel daily to and from work

commuted v ▷ commute

commuter n (pl -s) person who commutes to and from work

commuters n ▷ commuter

commutes v ▷ commute

commuting v ▷ commute

compact¹ adj (-er, -est) closely packed ▶ n (pl -s) small flat case containing a mirror and face powder ▶ v (-s, -ing, -ed) pack closely together ▷ **compactly** adv ▷ **compactness** n

compact² n (pl -s) contract, agreement

compacted v ▷ compact¹

compacter adj ▷ compact¹

compactest adj ▷ compact¹

compacting v ▷ compact¹

compactly adv ▷ compact¹

compactness n ▷ compact¹

compacts n ▷ compact¹, ² ▷ v ▷ compact¹

companies n ▷ company

companion n (pl -s) person who associates with or accompanies someone ▷ **companionship** n (pl -s)

companionable adj friendly ▷ **companionably** adv

companionably adv ▷ companionable

companions n ▷ companion

companionship n ▷ companion

companionships n ▷ companion

companionway n (pl -s) ladder linking the decks of a ship

companionways n ▷ companionway

company n (pl -nies) business organization

comparability n ▷ compare

comparable adj ▷ compare

comparative adj relative ▶ n (pl -s) (GRAMMAR) comparative form of a word ▷ **comparatively** adv

comparatively adv ▷ comparative

comparatives n ▷ comparative

compare v (-pares, -paring, -pared) examine (things) and point out the resemblances or differences (foll. by **to**) (foll. by **with**) ▷ **comparable** adj ▷ **comparability** n

compared v ▷ compare

compares v ▷ compare

comparing v ▷ compare

comparison n (pl -s) comparing

comparisons n ▷ comparison

compartment n (pl -s) section of a railway carriage

compartments n ▷ compartment

compass n (pl -es) instrument for showing direction, with a needle that points north ▶ pl hinged instrument for drawing circles

compasses n ▷ compass

compassion n pity, sympathy ▷ **compassionate** adj ▷ **compassionately** adv

compassionate adj ▷ compassion

compassionately adj ▷ compassion

compatibility n ▷ compatible

compatible adj able to exist, work, or be used together ▷ **compatibility** n

compatriot n (pl -s) fellow countryman or countrywoman

compatriots n ▷ compatriot

compel v (-pels, -pelling, -pelled) force (to be or do)

compelled v ▷ compel

compelling v ▷ compel

compels v ▷ compel

compendia n ▷ compendium

compendious adj brief but comprehensive

compendium n (pl -diums, -dia) selection of board games in one box

compendiums n ▷ compendium

compensate v (-sates, -sating, -sated) make amends to (someone), esp. for injury or loss (foll. by **for**) > **compensatory** adj

compensated v ▷ compensate

compensates v ▷ compensate

compensating v ▷ compensate

compensation n (pl -s) payment to make up for loss or injury

compensations n ▷ compensation

compensatory adj ▷ compensate

compere n (pl -s) person who presents a stage, radio, or television show ▶ v (-peres, -pering, -pered) be the compere of

compered v ▷ compere

comperes n, v ▷ compere

compering v ▷ compere

compete v (-petes, -peting, -peted) try to win or achieve (a prize, profit, etc.) > **competitive** adj > **competitively** adv > **competitiveness** n > **competitor** n (pl -s)

competed v ▷ compete

competence n ▷ competent

competent adj having the skill or knowledge to do something well > **competently** adv > **competence** n

competently adv ▷ competent

competes v ▷ compete

competing v ▷ compete

competition n (pl -s) competing

competitions n ▷ competition

competitive adj ▷ compete

competitively adv ▷ compete

competitiveness n ▷ compete

competitor n ▷ compete

competitors n ▷ compete

compilation n ▷ compile

compilations n ▷ compile

compile v (-piles, -piling, -piled) collect and arrange (information), esp. to make a book > **compilation** n (pl -s) > **compiler** n (pl -s)

compiled v ▷ compile

compiler n ▷ compile

compilers n ▷ compile

compiles v ▷ compile

compiling v ▷ compile

complacencies n ▷ complacent

complacency n ▷ complacent

complacent adj self-satisfied > **complacently** (pl -cies) adv > **complacency** n

complacently adv ▷ complacent

complain v (-s, -ing, -ed) express resentment or displeasure

complainant n (pl -s) (LAW) plaintiff

complainants n ▷ complainant

complained v ▷ complain

complaining v ▷ complain

complains v ▷ complain

complaint n (pl -s) complaining

complaints n ▷ complaint

complaisance n ▷ complaisant

complaisant [kom-play-zant] adj willing to please > **complaisance** n

complement n (pl -s) thing that completes something (GRAMMAR) ▶ v (-s, -ing, -ed) make complete > **complementary** adj

complementary adj ▷ complement

complemented v ▷ complement

complementing v ▷ complement

complements n, v ▷ complement

complete adj thorough, absolute ▶ v (-pletes, -pleting, -pleted) finish > **completeness** n > **completely** adv

completed v ▷ complete

completely adv ▷ complete

completeness n ▷ complete

completes v ▷ complete

completing v ▷ complete

completion n finishing

complex adj (-er, -est) made up of parts ▶ n (pl -es) whole made up of parts > **complexity** n (pl -ities)

complexer adj ▷ complex

complexes n ▷ complex

complexest adj ▷ complex

complexion n (pl -s) skin of the face

complexions n ▷ complexion

complexities n ▷ complexity

complexity n ▷ complex

compliance n (pl -s) complying > **compliant** adj

compliances n ▷ compliance

compliant adj ▷ compliance

complicate v (-cates, -cating, -cated) make or become complex or difficult to deal with > **complication** n (pl -s)

complicated v ▷ complicate

complicates v ▷ complicate

complicating v ▷ complicate

complication n ▷ complicate

complications n ▷ complicate

complicities n ▷ complicity

complicity n (pl -ities) fact of being an accomplice in a crime

complied v ▷ comply

complies *v* ▷ comply
compliment *n* (*pl* -s) expression of praise ▶ *pl* formal greetings ▶ *v* (-s, -ing, -ed) praise
complimentary *adj* expressing praise
complimented *v* ▷ compliment
complimenting *v* ▷ compliment
compliments *n, v* ▷ compliment
compline *n* (*pl* -s) last service of the day in the Roman Catholic Church
complines *n* ▷ compline
comply *v* (-plies, -plying, -plied) (*foll. by* **with**) act in accordance (with)
complying *v* ▷ comply
component *n* (*pl* -s) ▶ *adj* (being) part of a whole
components *n* ▷ component
comport *v* (-s, -ing, -ed) (*Formal*) behave (oneself) in a specified way
comported *v* ▷ comport
comporting *v* ▷ comport
comports *v* ▷ comport
compose *v* (-poses, -posing, -posed) put together
composed *v* ▷ compose
composer *n* (*pl* -s) person who writes music
composers *n* ▷ composer
composes *v* ▷ compose
composing *v* ▷ compose
composite *n* (*pl* -s) ▶ *adj* (something) made up of separate parts
composites *n* ▷ composite
composition *n* (*pl* -s) way that something is put together or arranged
compositions *n* ▷ composition
compositor *n* (*pl* -s) person who arranges type for printing
compositors *n* ▷ compositor
compost *n* (*pl* -s) decayed plants used as a fertilizer
composts *n* ▷ compost
composure *n* calmness
compote *n* (*pl* -s) fruit stewed with sugar
compotes *n* ▷ compote
compound[1] *n* (*pl* -s) ▶ *adj* (thing, esp. chemical) made up of two or more combined parts or elements ▶ *v* (-s, -ing, -ed) combine or make by combining
compound[2] *n* (*pl* -s) fenced enclosure containing buildings
compounded *v* ▷ compound[1]
compounding *v* ▷ compound[1]
compounds *v* ▷ compound[1] ▶ *n* ▷ compound[1, 2]
comprehend *v* (-s, -ing, -ed) understand
  > **comprehensible** *adj* > **comprehensibly** *adv*
  > **comprehension** *n* (*pl* -s)

comprehended *v* ▷ comprehend
comprehending *v* ▷ comprehend
comprehends *v* ▷ comprehend
comprehensible *adj* ▷ comprehend
comprehensibly *adv* ▷ comprehend
comprehension *n* ▷ comprehend
comprehensions *n* ▷ comprehend
comprehensive *adj* of broad scope, fully inclusive ▶ *n* (*pl* -s) (BRIT) comprehensive school > **comprehensively** *adv*
  > **comprehensiveness** *n*
comprehensively *adv* ▷ comprehensive
comprehensiveness *n* ▷ comprehensive
comprehensives *n* ▷ comprehensive
compress *v* (-es, -ing, -ed) [kum-**press**] squeeze together ▶ *n* (*pl* -es) [kom-**press**] pad applied to stop bleeding or cool inflammation
  > **compression** *n* (*pl* -s)
compressed *v* ▷ compress
compresses *v, n* ▷ compress
compressing *v* ▷ compress
compression *n* ▷ compress
compressions *n* ▷ compress
compressor *n* (*pl* -s) machine that compresses gas or air
compressors *n* ▷ compressor
comprise *v* (-ises, -ising, -ised) be made up of or make up
comprised *v* ▷ comprise
comprises *v* ▷ comprise
comprising *v* ▷ comprise
compromise [kom-prom-mize] *n* (*pl* -s) settlement reached by concessions on each side ▶ *v* (-ises, -ising, -ised) settle a dispute by making concessions
compromised *v* ▷ compromise
compromises *n, v* ▷ compromise
compromising *v* ▷ compromise
comptroller *n* (*pl* -s) (in titles) financial controller
comptrollers *n* ▷ comptroller
compulsion *n* (*pl* -s) irresistible urge
  > **compulsive** *adj* > **compulsively** *adv*
compulsions *n* ▷ compulsion
compulsive *adj* ▷ compulsion
compulsively *adv* ▷ compulsion
compulsorily *adv* ▷ compulsory
compulsoriness *n* ▷ compulsory
compulsory *adj* required by rules or laws
  > **compulsorily** *adv* > **compulsoriness** *n*
compunction *n* (*pl* -s) feeling of guilt or shame
compunctions *n* ▷ compunction
computation *n* ▷ compute
computations *n* ▷ compute
compute *v* (-putes, -puting, -puted) calculate,

esp. using a computer > **computation** n (pl -s)
computed v ▷ compute
computer n (pl -s) electronic machine that
stores and processes data > **computerize** v
(-izes, -izing, -ized) adapt (a system) to be
handled by computer > **computerization**
n (pl -s)
computerization n ▷ computerize
computerizations v ▷ computerize
computerized v ▷ computerize
computerizes v ▷ computerize
computerizing v ▷ computerize
computers n ▷ computer
computes v ▷ compute
computing v ▷ compute
comrade n (pl -s) fellow member of a union or
socialist political party > **comradeship** n
comrades n ▷ comrade
comradeship n ▷ comrade
con¹ (Informal) n (pl -s) ▷ **confidence trick** ▶ v
(cons, conning, conned) deceive, swindle
con² n (pl -s) ▷ **pro¹**
concatenation n (pl -s) series of linked events
concatenations n ▷ concatenation
concave adj curving inwards
conceal v (-s, -ing, -ed) cover and hide
> **concealment** n
concealed v ▷ conceal
concealing v ▷ conceal
concealment n ▷ conceal
conceals v ▷ conceal
concede v (-cedes, -ceding, -ceded) admit to
be true
conceded v ▷ concede
concedes v ▷ concede
conceding v ▷ concede
conceit n (pl -s) too high an opinion of
oneself > **conceited** adj > **conceitedly** adv
> **conceitedness** n
conceited adj ▷ conceit
conceitedly adv ▷ conceit
conceitedness adv ▷ conceit
conceits n ▷ conceit
conceivable adj imaginable, possible
> **conceivably** adv
conceivably adv ▷ conceivable
conceive v (-ceives, -ceiving, -ceived) imagine,
think
conceived v ▷ conceive
conceives v ▷ conceive
conceiving v ▷ conceive
concentrate v (-rates, -rating, -rated) fix one's
attention or efforts on something ▶ n (pl -s)
concentrated liquid
concentrated v ▷ concentrate

concentrates v, n ▷ concentrate
concentrating v ▷ concentrate
concentration n (pl -s) concentrating
concentrations n ▷ concentration
concentric adj having the same centre
concept n (pl -s) abstract or general idea
conception n (pl -s) general idea
conceptions n ▷ conception
concepts n ▷ concept
conceptual adj of or based on concepts
> **conceptually** adv
conceptualize v (-izes, -izing, -ized) form a
concept of
conceptualized v ▷ conceptualize
conceptualizes v ▷ conceptualize
conceptualizing v ▷ conceptualize
conceptually adv ▷ conceptual
concern n (pl -s) anxiety, worry ▶ v (-s, -ing, -ed)
worry (someone)
concerned adj interested, involved ▶ v
▷ concern
concerning prep about, regarding ▶ v
▷ concern
concerns n, v ▷ concern
concert n (pl -s) musical entertainment
concerted adj done together
concerti n ▷ concerto
concertina n (pl -s) small musical instrument
similar to an accordion ▶ v (-nas, -naing,
-naed) collapse or fold up like a concertina
concertinaed v ▷ concertina
concertinaing v ▷ concertina
concertinas n, v ▷ concertina
concerto [kon-**chair**-toe] n (pl -tos, -ti) large-
scale composition for a solo instrument and
orchestra
concertos n ▷ concerto
concerts n ▷ concert
concession n (pl -s) grant of rights, land, or
property > **concessionary** adj
concessionary adj ▷ concession
concessions n ▷ concession
conch n (pl -s) shellfish with a large spiral shell
conchs n ▷ conch
concierge [kon-see-**airzh**] n (pl -s) (in France)
caretaker in a block of flats
concierges n ▷ concierge
conciliate v (-ates, -ating, -ated) try to end
a disagreement (with) > **conciliation** n
> **conciliator** n (pl -s)
conciliated v ▷ conciliate
conciliates v ▷ conciliate
conciliating v ▷ conciliate
conciliation n ▷ conciliate
conciliator n ▷ conciliate

conciliators *n* ▷ conciliate

conciliatory *adj* intended to end a disagreement

concise *adj* (-r, -st) brief and to the point
> **concisely** *adv* > **concision, conciseness** *n* (*pl* -s, -es)

concisely *adv* ▷ concise

conciseness *n* ▷ concise

concisenesses *n* ▷ concise

conciser *adj* ▷ concise

concisest *adj* ▷ concise

concision *n* ▷ concise

concisions *n* ▷ concise

conclave *n* (*pl* -s) secret meeting

conclaves *n* ▷ conclave

conclude *v* (-cludes, -cluding, -cluded) decide by reasoning

concluded *v* ▷ conclude

concludes *v* ▷ conclude

concluding *v* ▷ conclude

conclusion *n* (*pl* -s) decision based on reasoning

conclusions *n* ▷ conclusion

conclusive *adj* ending doubt, convincing
> **conclusively** *adv*

conclusively *adv* ▷ conclusive

concoct *v* (-s, -ing, -ed) make up (a story or plan) > **concoction** *n* (*pl* -s)

concocted *v* ▷ concoct

concocting *v* ▷ concoct

concoction *n* ▷ concoct

concoctions *n* ▷ concoct

concocts *v* ▷ concoct

concomitant *adj* existing along with something else

concord *n* (*pl* -s) state of peaceful agreement, harmony

concordance *n* (*pl* -s) similarity or consistency

concordances *n* ▷ concordance

concordant *adj* agreeing > **concordantly** *adv*

concordantly *adv* ▷ concordant

concords *n* ▷ concord

concourse *n* (*pl* -s) large open public place where people can gather

concourses *n* ▷ concourse

concrete *n* (*pl* -s) mixture of cement, sand, stone, and water, used in building ▶ *adj* made of concrete

concretes *n* ▷ concrete

concubine [kon-**kew**-bine] *n* (*pl* -s) (HIST) woman living in a man's house but not married to him and kept for his sexual pleasure

concubines *n* ▷ concubine

concupiscence [kon-**kew**-piss-enss] *n* (Formal) lust

concur *v* (-curs, -curring, -curred) agree
> **concurrence** *n* (*pl* -s)

concurred *v* ▷ concur

concurrence *n* ▷ concur

concurrent *adj* happening at the same time or place

concurrently *adv* at the same time

concurring *v* ▷ concur

concurs *v* ▷ concur

concussed *adj* having concussion

concussion *n* (*pl* -s) period of unconsciousness caused by a blow to the head

concussions *n* ▷ concussion

condemn *v* (-s, -ing, -ed) express disapproval of > **condemnation** *n* (*pl* -s) > **condemnatory** *adj*

condemnation *n* ▷ condemn

condemnations *n* ▷ condemn

condemnatory *adj* ▷ condemn

condemned *v* ▷ condemn

condemning *v* ▷ condemn

condemns *v* ▷ condemn

condensation *n* ▷ condense

condense *v* (-denses, -densing, -densed) make shorter > **condensation** *n*

condensed *v* ▷ condense

condenser *n* (*pl* -s) (ELECTRICITY) capacitor

condensers *n* ▷ condenser

condenses *v* ▷ condense

condensing *v* ▷ condense

condescend *v* (-s, -ing, -ed) behave patronizingly towards someone
> **condescension** *n*

condescended *v* ▷ condescend

condescending *v* ▷ condescend

condescends *v* ▷ condescend

condescension *n* ▷ condescend

condiment *n* (*pl* -s) seasoning for food, such as salt or pepper

condiments *n* ▷ condiment

condition *n* (*pl* -s) particular state of being ▶ *pl* circumstances ▶ *v* (-s, -ed, -ing) train or influence to behave in a particular way

conditional *adj* depending on circumstances
> **conditionally** *adv*

conditionally *adv* ▷ conditional

conditioned *v* ▷ condition

conditioner *n* (*pl* -s) thick liquid used when washing to make hair or clothes feel softer

conditioning *v* ▷ condition

conditioners *n* ▷ condition

conditions *n*, *v* ▷ condition

condolence *n* (*pl* -s) sympathy ▶ *pl* expression of sympathy

condolences n ▷ condolence
condom n (pl -s) rubber sheath worn on the penis or in the vagina during sexual intercourse to prevent conception or infection
condominium n (pl -s) (AUST, US & CANADIAN) block of flats in which each flat is owned by the occupant
condominiums n ▷ condominium
condoms n ▷ condom
condone v (-dones, -doning, -doned) overlook or forgive (wrongdoing)
condoned v ▷ condone
condones v ▷ condone
condoning v ▷ condone
condor n (pl -s) large vulture of S America
condors n ▷ condor
conducive adj (foll. by to) likely to lead (to)
conduct n (pl -s) management of an activity
   ▶ v (-s, -ing, -ed) carry out (a task)
conducted v ▷ conduct
conducting v ▷ conduct
conduction n transmission of heat or electricity
conductive adj ▷ conductivity
conductivities n ▷ conductivity
conductivity n (pl -vities) ability to transmit heat or electricity > **conductive** adj
conductor n (pl -s) person who conducts musicians, fem **conductress** ▶ n (pl -es)
conductors n ▷ conductor
conductress n ▷ conductor
conductresses n ▷ conductor
conducts n, v ▷ conduct
conduit [kon-dew-it] n (pl -s) channel or tube for fluid or cables
conduits n ▷ conduit
cone n (pl -s) object with a circular base, tapering to a point
cones n ▷ cone
coney n (pl -s) ▷ cony
coneys n ▷ coney
confab n (pl -s) (Informal) conversation (also confabulation)
confabs n ▷ confab
confabulation n ▷ confab
confabulations n ▷ confab
confection n (pl -s) any sweet food (Old-fashioned)
confectioner n (pl -s) maker or seller of confectionery
confectioneries n ▷ confectionery
confectioners n ▷ confectioner
confectionery n (pl -eries) sweets
confections n ▷ confection

confederacies n ▷ confederacy
confederacy n (pl -cies) union of states or people for a common purpose
confederate n (pl -s) member of a confederacy ▶ adj united, allied ▶ v (-rates, -rating, -rated) unite in a confederacy
confederated v ▷ confederate
confederates n, v ▷ confederate
confederating v ▷ confederate
confederation n (pl -s) alliance of political units
confederations n ▷ confederation
confer v (-fers, -ferring, -ferred) discuss together
conference n (pl -s) meeting for discussion
conferences n ▷ conference
conferment n (pl -s) granting, giving
conferments n ▷ conferment
conferred v ▷ confer
conferring v ▷ confer
confers v ▷ confer
confess v (-es, -ing, -ed) admit (a fault or crime)
confessed v ▷ confess
confesses v ▷ confess
confessing v ▷ confess
confession n (pl -s) something confessed
confessional n (pl -s) small stall in which a priest hears confessions
confessionals n ▷ confessional
confessions n ▷ confession
confessor n (pl -s) priest who hears confessions
confessors n ▷ confessor
confetti n (pl -s) small pieces of coloured paper thrown at weddings
confettis n ▷ confetti
confidant n (pl -s) person confided in > **confidante** n fem (pl -s)
confidante n ▷ confidant
confidantes n ▷ confidant
confidants n ▷ confidant
confide v (-fides, -fiding, -fided) tell someone (a secret)
confided v ▷ confide
confidence n (pl -s) trust
confidences n ▷ confidence
confident adj sure, esp. of oneself > **confidently** adv
confidential adj private, secret > **confidentially** adv > **confidentiality** n
confidentiality n ▷ confidential
confidentially adv ▷ confidential
confidently adv ▷ confident
confides v ▷ confide

confiding v ▷ confide
configuration n (pl -s) arrangement of parts
  configurations n ▷ configuration
confine v (-fines, -fining, -fined) keep within
  bounds
  confined v ▷ confine
confinement n (pl -s) being confined
confines pl n boundaries, limits ▶ v ▷ confine
  confining v ▷ confine
confirm v (-s, -ing, -ed) prove to be true
confirmation n (pl -s) confirming
  confirmations n ▷ confirmation
confirmed adj firmly established in a habit or
  condition ▶ v ▷ confirm
  confirming v ▷ confirm
  confirms v ▷ confirm
confiscate v (-cates, -cating, -cated) seize
  (property) by authority > **confiscation** n (pl -s)
  confiscated v ▷ confiscate
  confiscates v ▷ confiscate
  confiscating v ▷ confiscate
  confiscation n ▷ confiscate
  confiscations n ▷ confiscate
conflagration n (pl -s) large destructive fire
  conflagrations n ▷ conflagration
conflate v (-ates, -ating, -ated) combine or
  blend into a whole > **conflation** n (pl -s)
  conflated v ▷ conflate
  conflates v ▷ conflate
  conflating v ▷ conflate
  conflation n ▷ conflate
  conflations n ▷ conflate
conflict n (pl -s) disagreement ▶ v (-s, -ing, -ed)
  be incompatible
  conflicted v ▷ conflict
  conflicting v ▷ conflict
  conflicts n, v ▷ conflict
confluence n (pl -s) place where two rivers join
  confluences n ▷ confluence
conform v (-s, -ing, -ed) comply with accepted
  standards or customs (foll. by **to** or **with**)
  conformed v ▷ conform
  conforming v ▷ conform
conformist n (pl -s) ▶ adj (person) complying
  with accepted standards or customs
  conformists n ▷ conformist
  conformities n ▷ conformity
conformity n (pl -ities) compliance with
  accepted standards or customs
  conforms v ▷ conform
confound v (-s, -ing, -ed) astound, bewilder
confounded adj (Old-fashioned) damned ▶ v
  ▷ confound > **confoundedly** adv
  confoundedly adv ▷ confounded
  confounding v ▷ confound

confounds v ▷ confound
confront v (-s, -ing, -ed) come face to face with
confrontation n (pl -s) serious argument
  > **confrontational** adj
  confrontational adj ▷ confrontation
  confrontations n ▷ confrontation
  confronted v ▷ confront
  confronting v ▷ confront
  confronts v ▷ confront
confuse v (-fuses, -fusing, -fused) mix up
  > **confusion** n (pl -s)
  confused v ▷ confuse
  confuses v ▷ confuse
  confusing v ▷ confuse
  confusion n ▷ confuse
  confusions n ▷ confuse
confute v (-futes, -futing, -futed) prove wrong
  confuted v ▷ confute
  confutes v ▷ confute
  confuting v ▷ confute
conga n (pl -s) dance performed by a number of
  people in single file
  congas n ▷ conga
congeal v (-s, -ing, -ed) (of a liquid) become
  thick and sticky
  congealed v ▷ congeal
  congealing v ▷ congeal
  congeals v ▷ congeal
congenial adj pleasant, agreeable
  > **congeniality** n > **congenially** adv
  congeniality n ▷ congenial
  congenially adv ▷ congenial
congenital adj (of a condition) existing from
  birth > **congenitally** adv
  congenitally adv ▷ congenital
conger n (pl -s) large sea eel
  congers n ▷ conger
congested adj crowded to excess
  > **congestion** n
  congestion n ▷ congested
conglomerate n (pl -s) large corporation made
  up of many companies ▶ v (-rates, -rating,
  -rated) form into a mass ▶ adj made up of
  several different elements > **conglomeration**
  n (pl -s)
  conglomerated v ▷ conglomerate
  conglomerates n, v ▷ conglomerate
  conglomerating v ▷ conglomerate
  conglomeration n ▷ conglomerate
  conglomerations n ▷ conglomerate
congratulate v (-lates, -lating, -lated) express
  one's pleasure to (someone) at his or her
  good fortune or success > **congratulations** pl
  n, interj > **congratulatory** adj
  congratulated v ▷ congratulate

congratulates v ▷ congratulate
congratulating v ▷ congratulate
congratulations n ▷ congratulate
congratulatory adj ▷ congratulate
congregate v (-gates, -gating, -gated) gather together in a crowd
congregated v ▷ congregate
congregates v ▷ congregate
congregating v ▷ congregate
congregation n (pl -s) people who attend a church > **congregational** adj
congregational adj ▷ congregation
congregations n ▷ congregation
congress n (pl congresses) formal meeting for discussion > **congressional** adj
congresses n ▷ congress
congressional n ▷ congress
congressman, congresswoman n (pl -men, -women) member of Congress
congressmen n ▷ congressman
congresswoman n ▷ congressman
congresswomen n ▷ congressman
congruence n ▷ congruent
congruent adj similar, corresponding > **congruence** n
conical adj cone-shaped
conies n ▷ cony
conifer n (pl -s) cone-bearing tree, such as the fir or pine > **coniferous** adj
coniferous adj ▷ conifer
conifers n ▷ conifer
conjectural adj ▷ conjecture
conjecture n (pl -s) ▶ v (-tures, -turing, -tured) guess > **conjectural** adj
conjectured v ▷ conjecture
conjectures n, v ▷ conjecture
conjecturing v ▷ conjecture
conjugal adj of marriage > **conjugally** adv
conjugally adv ▷ conjugal
conjugate v (-gates, -gating, -gated) give the inflections of (a verb)
conjugated v ▷ conjugate
conjugates v ▷ conjugate
conjugating v ▷ conjugate
conjugation n (pl -s) complete set of inflections of a verb
conjugations n ▷ conjugation
conjunction n (pl -s) combination
conjunctions n ▷ conjunction
conjunctiva n (pl -s) the membrane covering the eyeball and inner eyelid
conjunctivas n ▷ conjunctiva
conjunctivitis n inflammation of the conjunctiva
conjure v (-jures, -juring, -jured) perform

tricks that appear to be magic > **conjuror** n (pl -s)
conjured v ▷ conjure
conjures v ▷ conjure
conjuring v ▷ conjure
conjuror n ▷ conjure
conjurors n ▷ conjure
conk n (pl -s) (BRIT, AUST & NZ) (Slang) nose
conker n (pl -s) (Informal) nut of the horse chestnut
conkers n ▷ conker
conks n ▷ conk
connect v (-s, -ing, -ed) join together > **connection, connexion** n (pl -s) relationship, association > **connective** adj
connected v ▷ connect
connecting v ▷ connect
connection n ▷ connect
connections n ▷ connect
connective n ▷ connect
connects v ▷ connect
conned v ▷ con[1]
connexion n ▷ connect
connexions n ▷ connect
conning v ▷ con[1]
connivance n ▷ connive
connivances n ▷ connive
connive v (-nives, -niving, -nived) (foll. by at) allow (wrongdoing) by ignoring it > **connivance** n (pl -s)
connived v ▷ connive
connives v ▷ connive
conniving v ▷ connive
connoisseur [kon-noss-**sir**] n (pl -s) person with special knowledge of the arts, food, or drink
connoisseurs n ▷ connoisseur
connotation n (pl -s) associated idea conveyed by a word > **connote** v (-notes, -noting, -noted)
connotations n ▷ connotation
connoted v ▷ connotation
connotes v ▷ connotation
connoting v ▷ connotation
connubial adj (Formal) of marriage
conquer v (-s, -ing, -ed) defeat > **conqueror** n (pl -s)
conquered v ▷ conquer
conquering v ▷ conquer
conqueror n ▷ conquer
conquerors n ▷ conquer
conquers v ▷ conquer
conquest n (pl -s) conquering
conquests n ▷ conquest
cons n ▷ con[1, 2]
conscience n (pl -s) sense of right or wrong as

regards thoughts and actions
consciences *n* ▷ conscience
conscientious *adj* painstaking
> **conscientiously** *adv*
conscientiously *adv* ▷ conscientious
conscious *adj* alert and awake > **consciously**
adv > **consciousness** *n*
consciously *adv* ▷ conscious
consciousness *n* ▷ conscious
conscript *n* (*pl* -s) person enrolled for
compulsory military service ▶ *v* (-s, -ing, -ed)
enrol (someone) for compulsory military
service > **conscription** *n* (*pl* -s)
conscripted *v* ▷ conscript
conscripting *v* ▷ conscript
conscription *n* ▷ conscript
conscriptions *n* ▷ conscript
conscripts *n*, *v* ▷ conscript
consecrate *v* (-rates, -rating, -rated) make
sacred > **consecration** *n* (*pl* -s)
consecrated *v* ▷ consecrate
consecrates *v* ▷ consecrate
consecrating *v* ▷ consecrate
consecration *n* ▷ consecrate
consecrations *n* ▷ consecrate
consecutive *adj* in unbroken succession
> **consecutively** *adv*
consecutively *adv* ▷ consecutive
consensus *n* general agreement
consent *n* (*pl* -s) agreement, permission ▶ *v* (-s,
-ing, -ed) (*foll. by* to) permit, agree to
consented *v* ▷ consent
consenting *v* ▷ consent
consents *v*, *n* ▷ consent
consequence *n* (*pl* -s) result, effect
consequences *n* ▷ consequence
consequent *adj* resulting
consequential *adj* important
consequently *adv* as a result, therefore
conservancies *n* ▷ conservancy
conservancy *n* (*pl* -cies) environmental
conservation
conservation *n* (*pl* -s) protection of
natural resources and the environment
> **conservationist** *n* (*pl* -s)
conservationist *n* ▷ conservation
conservationists *n* ▷ conservation
conservations *n* ▷ conservation
conservatism *n* ▷ conservative
conservative *adj* opposing change ▶ *n* (*pl* -s)
conservative person > **conservatively** *adv*
> **conservatism** *n*
conservatively *adv* ▷ conservative
conservatives *n* ▷ conservative
conservatoire [kon-**serv**-a-twahr] *n* (*pl* -s)

school of music
conservatoires *n* ▷ conservatoire
conservatories *n* ▷ conservatory
conservatory *n* (*pl* -ries) room with glass walls
and a glass roof, attached to a house
conserve *v* (-serves, -serving, -served) protect
from harm, decay, or loss ▶ *n* (*pl* -s) jam
containing large pieces of fruit
conserved *v* ▷ conserve
conserves *v*, *n* ▷ conserve
conserving *v* ▷ conserve
consider *v* (-s, -ing, -ed) regard as
considerable *adj* large in amount or degree
> **considerably** *adv*
considerably *adv* ▷ considerable
considerate *adj* thoughtful towards others
> **considerately** *adv*
considerately *adv* ▷ considerate
consideration *n* (*pl* -s) careful thought
considerations *n* ▷ consideration
considered *v* ▷ consider
considering *prep* taking (a specified fact) into
account ▶ *v* ▷ consider
considers *v* ▷ consider
consign *v* (-s, -ing, -ed) put somewhere
consigned *v* ▷ consign
consigning *v* ▷ consign
consignment *n* (*pl* -s) shipment of goods
consignments *n* ▷ consignment
consigns *v* ▷ consign
consist *v* (-s, -ing, -ed) be made up of
consisted *v* ▷ consist
consistencies *n* ▷ consistency
consistency *n* (*pl* -cies) being consistent
consistent *adj* unchanging, constant (*foll. by*
with) > **consistently** *adv*
consistently *adv* ▷ consistent
consisting *v* ▷ consist
consists *v* ▷ consist
consolation *n* (*pl* -s) consoling
consolations *n* ▷ consolation
console[1] *v* (-soles, -soling, -soled) comfort in
distress
console[2] *n* (*pl* -s) panel of controls for
electronic equipment
consoled *v* ▷ console[1]
consoles *v* ▷ console[1] ▶ *n* ▷ console[2]
consolidate *v* (-dates, -dating, -dated)
make or become stronger or more stable
> **consolidation** *n* (*pl* -s)
consolidated *v* ▷ consolidate
consolidates *v* ▷ consolidate
consolidating *v* ▷ consolidate
consolidation *n* ▷ consolidate
consolidations *n* ▷ consolidate

consoling v ▷ console[1]
consommé [kon-som-may] n (pl -s) thin clear meat soup
consommés n ▷ consommé
consonance n agreement, harmony
consonant n (pl -s) speech sound made by partially or completely blocking the breath stream, such as b or f ▶ adj (foll. by with) agreeing (with) > **consonantly** adv
consonantly adv ▷ consonant
consonants n ▷ consonant
consort v (-s, -ing, -ed) (foll. by with) keep company (with) ▶ n (pl -s) husband or wife of a monarch
consorted v ▷ consort
consortia n ▷ consortium
consorting v ▷ consort
consortium n (pl -tia) association of business firms
consorts v, n ▷ consort
conspectus n (pl -es) (Formal) survey or summary
conspectuses n ▷ conspectus
conspicuous adj clearly visible > **conspicuously** adv > **conspicuousness** n
conspicuously adv ▷ conspectus
conspicuousness n ▷ conspectus
conspiracies n ▷ conspiracy
conspiracy n (pl -cies) conspiring > **conspirator** n (pl -s) > **conspiratorial** adj
conspirator n ▷ conspiracy
conspiratorial adj ▷ conspiracy
conspirators n ▷ conspiracy
conspire v (-spires, -spiring, -spired) plan a crime together in secret
conspired v ▷ conspire
conspires v ▷ conspire
conspiring v ▷ conspire
constable n (pl -s) police officer of the lowest rank
constables n ▷ constable
constabularies n ▷ constabulary
constabulary n (pl -laries) police force of an area
constancy n ▷ constant
constant adj continuous ▶ n (pl -s) unvarying quantity > **constantly** adv > **constancy** n
constantly adv ▷ constant
constants n ▷ constant
constellation n (pl -s) group of stars
constellations n ▷ constellation
consternation n anxiety or dismay
constipated adj having constipation
constipation n difficulty in defecating
constituencies n ▷ constituency

constituency n (pl -cies) area represented by a Member of Parliament
constituent n (pl -s) member of a constituency ▶ adj forming part of a whole
constituents n ▷ constituent
constitute v (-tutes, -tuting, -tuted) form, make up
constituted v ▷ constitute
constitutes v ▷ constitute
constituting v ▷ constitute
constitution n (pl -s) principles on which a state is governed
constitutional adj of a constitution ▶ n (pl -s) walk taken for exercise > **constitutionally** adv
constitutionally adv ▷ constitutional
constitutionals n ▷ constitutional
constitutions n ▷ constitution
constrain v (-s, -ing, -ed) compel, force > **constraint** n (pl -s)
constrained v ▷ constrain
constraining v ▷ constrain
constrains v ▷ constrain
constraint n ▷ constrain
constraints n ▷ constrain
constrict v (-s, -ing, -ed) make narrower by squeezing > **constriction** n (pl -s) > **constrictive** adj
constricted v ▷ constrict
constricting v ▷ constrict
constriction n ▷ constrict
constrictions n ▷ constrict
constrictive adj ▷ constrict
constrictor n (pl -s) large snake that squeezes its prey to death
constrictors n ▷ constrictor
constricts v ▷ constrict
construct v (-s, -ing, -ed) build or put together
constructed v ▷ construct
constructing v ▷ construct
construction n (pl -s) constructing
constructions n ▷ construction
constructive adj (of advice, criticism, etc.) useful and helpful > **constructively** adv
constructively adv ▷ constructive
constructs v ▷ construct
construe v (-strues, -struing, -strued) interpret
construed v ▷ construe
construes v ▷ construe
construing v ▷ construe
consul n (pl -s) official representing a state in a foreign country > **consular** adj > **consulship** n (pl -s)
consular adj ▷ consul
consulate n (pl -s) workplace or position of

a consul

consulates n ▷ consulate

consuls n ▷ consul

consulship n ▷ consul

consulships n ▷ consul

consult v (-s, -ing, -ed) go to for advice or information

consultancies n ▷ consultancy

consultancy n (pl -cies) work or position of a consultant

consultant n (pl -s) specialist doctor with a senior position in a hospital

consultants n ▷ consultant

consultation n (pl -s) (meeting for) consulting

consultations n ▷ consultation

consultative adj giving advice

consulted v ▷ consult

consulting v ▷ consult

consults v ▷ consult

consume v (-sumes, -suming, -sumed) eat or drink

consumed v ▷ consume

consumer n (pl -s) person who buys goods or uses services

consumers n ▷ consumer

consumes v ▷ consume

consuming v ▷ consume

consummate [kon-sum-mate] v (-mates, -mating, -mated) make (a marriage) legal by sexual intercourse ▶ adj [kon-**sum**-mit] supremely skilled > **consummately** adv > **consummation** n (pl -s)

consummated v ▷ consummate

consummately adv ▷ consummate

consummates v ▷ consummate

consummating v ▷ consummate

consummation n ▷ consummate

consummations n ▷ consummate

consumption n (pl -s) amount consumed

consumptions n ▷ consumption

consumptive n (pl -s) ▶ adj (Old-fashioned) (person) having tuberculosis

consumptives n ▷ consumptive

contact n (pl -s) communicating ▶ v (-s, -ing, -ed) get in touch with

contacted v ▷ contact

contacting v ▷ contact

contacts n, v ▷ contact

contagion n (pl -s) passing on of disease by contact

contagions n ▷ contagion

contagious adj spreading by contact, catching

contain v (-s, -ing, -ed) hold or be capable of holding

contained v ▷ contain

container n (pl -s) object used to hold or store things in

containers n ▷ container

containing v ▷ contain

containment n prevention of the spread of something harmful

contains v ▷ contain

contaminant n (pl -s) contaminating substance

contaminants n ▷ contaminant

contaminate v (-nates, -nating, -nated) make impure, pollute > **contamination** n (pl -s)

contaminated v ▷ contaminate

contaminates v ▷ contaminate

contaminating v ▷ contaminate

contamination n ▷ contaminate

contaminations n ▷ contaminate

contemplate v (-lates, -lating, -lated) think deeply > **contemplation** n (pl -s) > **contemplative** adj

contemplated v ▷ contemplate

contemplates v ▷ contemplate

contemplating v ▷ contemplate

contemplation n ▷ contemplate

contemplations n ▷ contemplate

contemplative adj ▷ contemplate

contemporaneous adj happening at the same time

contemporaries n ▷ contemporary

contemporary adj present-day, modern ▶ n (pl -raries) person or thing living or occurring at the same time as another

contempt n (pl -s) dislike and disregard

contemptible adj deserving contempt > **contemptibly** adv

contemptibly adv ▷ contemptible

contempts n ▷ contempt

contemptuous adj showing contempt > **contemptuously** adv

contemptuously adv ▷ contemptuous

contend v (-s, -ing, -ed) (foll. by **with**) deal with

contended v ▷ contend

contender n (pl -s) competitor, esp. a strong one

contenders n ▷ contender

contending v ▷ contend

contends v ▷ contend

content[1] n (pl -s) meaning or substance of a piece of writing ▶ pl what something contains

content[2] adj satisfied with things as they are ▶ v (-s, -ing, -ed) make (someone) content ▶ n happiness and satisfaction > **contented** adj > **contentedly** adv > **contentment** n

contented v, adj ▷ content²
contentedly adv ▷ content²
contenting v ▷ content²
contention n (pl -s) disagreement or dispute
contentions n ▷ contention
contentious adj causing disagreement
> **contentiously** adv > **contentiousness** n
contentiously adv ▷ contentious
contentiousness n ▷ contentious
contentment n ▷ content²
contents n ▷ content¹ ▶ v ▷ content²
contest n (pl -s) competition or struggle ▶ v (-s, -ing, -ed) dispute, object to > **contestant** n (pl -s)
contestant n ▷ contest
contestants n ▷ contest
contested v ▷ contest
contesting v ▷ contest
contests n, v ▷ contest
context n (pl -s) circumstances of an event or fact > **contextual** adj
contexts n ▷ context
contextual adj ▷ context
contiguous adj very near or touching
> **contiguously** adv
contiguously adv ▷ contiguous
continence n ▷ continent²
continent¹ n (pl -s) one of the earth's large masses of land > **continental** adj
> **continentally** adv
continent² adj able to control one's bladder and bowels > **continence** n
continental adj ▷ continent¹
continentally adv ▷ continent¹
continents n ▷ continent¹
contingencies n ▷ contingency
contingency n (pl -cies) something that may happen
contingent n (pl -s) group of people that represents or is part of a larger group ▶ adj (foll. by on) dependent on (something uncertain)
contingents n ▷ contingent
continua n ▷ continuum
continual adj constant > **continually** adv
continually adv ▷ continual
continuance n continuing
continuation n (pl -s) continuing
continuations n ▷ continuation
continue v (-tinues, -tinuing, -tinued) (cause to) remain in a condition or place
continued v ▷ continue
continues v ▷ continue
continuing v ▷ continue
continuities n ▷ continuity

continuity n (pl -ities) smooth development or sequence
continuo n (pl -s) (MUSIC) continuous bass part, usu. played on a keyboard instrument
continuos n ▷ continuo
continuous adj continuing uninterrupted
> **continuously** adv
continuously adv ▷ continuous
continuum n (pl -tinua, -tinuums) continuous series
continuums n ▷ continuum
contort v (-s, -ing, -ed) twist out of shape
> **contortion** n (pl -s)
contorted v ▷ contort
contorting v ▷ contort
contortion n ▷ contort
contortionist n (pl -s) performer who contorts his or her body to entertain
contortionists n ▷ contortionist
contortions n ▷ contort
contorts v ▷ contort
contour n (pl -s) outline
contours n ▷ contour
contraband n, adj smuggled (goods)
contraception n (pl -s) prevention of pregnancy by artificial means
contraceptions n ▷ contraception
contraceptive n (pl -s) device used or pill taken to prevent pregnancy ▶ adj preventing pregnancy
contraceptives n ▷ contraceptive
contract n (pl -s) (document setting out) a formal agreement ▶ v (-s, -ing, -ed) make a formal agreement (to do something)
> **contraction** n (pl -s) > **contractual** adj
> **contractually** adv
contracted v ▷ contract
contracting v ▷ contract
contraction n ▷ contract
contractions n ▷ contract
contractor n (pl -s) firm that supplies materials or labour
contractors n ▷ contractor
contracts n, v ▷ contract
contractual adj ▷ contract
contractually adv ▷ contract
contradict v (-s, -ing, -ed) declare the opposite of (a statement) to be true > **contradiction** n (pl -s) > **contradictory** adj
contradicted v ▷ contradict
contradicting v ▷ contradict
contradiction n ▷ contradict
contradictions n ▷ contradict
contradictory adj ▷ contradict
contradicts v ▷ contradict

contraflow n (pl -s) flow of traffic going alongside but in an opposite direction to the usual flow
contraflows n ▷ contraflow
contralto n (pl -s) (singer with) the lowest female voice
contraltos n ▷ contralto
contraption n (pl -s) strange-looking device
contraptions n ▷ contraption
contrapuntal adj (MUSIC) of or in counterpoint
> **contrapuntally** adv
contrapuntally adv ▷ contrapuntal
contraries n ▷ contrary
contrarily adv ▷ contrary
contrariness n ▷ contrary
contrariwise adv ▷ contrary
contrary n (pl -aries) complete opposite
▶ adj opposed, completely different ▶ adv in opposition > **contrarily** adv > **contrariness** n
> **contrariwise** adv
contrast n (pl -s) obvious difference ▶ v (-s, -ing, -ed) compare in order to show differences (foll. by **with**)
contrasted v ▷ contrast
contrasting v ▷ contrast
contrasts n, v ▷ contrast
contravene v (-venes, -vening, -vened) break (a rule or law) > **contravention** n (pl -s)
contravened v ▷ contravene
contravenes v ▷ contravene
contravening v ▷ contravene
contravention n ▷ contravene
contraventions n ▷ contravene
contretemps [kon-tra-tahn] n (pl -temps) embarrassing minor disagreement
contribute v (-butes, -buting, -buted) give for a common purpose or fund (foll. by **to**)
> **contribution** n (pl -s) > **contributor** n (pl -s)
> **contributory** adj
contributed v ▷ contribute
contributes v ▷ contribute
contributing v ▷ contribute
contribution n ▷ contribute
contributions n ▷ contribute
contributor n ▷ contribute
contributors n ▷ contribute
contributory adj ▷ contribute
contrite adj sorry and apologetic > **contritely** adv > **contrition** n
contritely adv ▷ contrite
contrition n ▷ contrite
contrivance n (pl -s) device
contrivances n ▷ contrivance
contrive v (-trives, -triving, -trived) make happen

contrived adj planned or artificial ▶ v
▷ contrive
contrives v ▷ contrive
contriving v ▷ contrive
control n (pl -s) power to direct something ▶ pl instruments used to operate a machine ▶ v (-trols, -trolling, -trolled) have power over
> **controllable** adj > **controller** n (pl -s)
controllable adj ▷ control
controlled v ▷ control
controller n ▷ control
controllers n ▷ control
controlling v ▷ control
controls n, v ▷ control
controversial adj causing controversy
> **controversially** adv
controversially adv ▷ controversial
controversies adv ▷ controversy
controversy n (pl -sies) fierce argument or debate
contumelies n ▷ contumely
contumely [kon-tume-mill-ee] n (pl -melies) (Lit) scornful or insulting treatment
contusion n (pl -s) (Formal) bruise
contusions n ▷ contusion
conundrum n (pl -s) riddle
conundrums n ▷ conundrum
conurbation n (pl -s) large urban area formed by the growth and merging of towns
conurbations n ▷ conurbation
convalesce v (-lesces, -lescing, -lesced) recover after an illness or operation
> **convalescence** n (pl -s) > **convalescent** n (pl -s) adj
convalesced v ▷ convalesce
convalescence n ▷ convalesce
convalescences n ▷ convalesce
convalescent n ▷ convalesce
convalescents n ▷ convalesce
convalesces v ▷ convalesce
convalescing v ▷ convalesce
convection n (pl -s) transmission of heat in liquids or gases by the circulation of currents
convections n ▷ convection
convector n (pl -s) heater that gives out hot air
convectors n ▷ convector
convene v (-venes, -vening, -vened) gather or summon for a formal meeting
convened v ▷ convene
convener, convenor n (pl -s) person who calls a meeting
conveners n ▷ convener
convenes v ▷ convene
convenience n (pl -s) quality of being convenient

conveniences n ▷ convenience
convenient adj suitable or opportune
> **conveniently** adv
conveniently adv ▷ convenient
convening v ▷ convene
convenor n ▷ convener
convenors n ▷ convener
convent n (pl -s) building where nuns live
convention n (pl -s) widely accepted view of proper behaviour
conventional adj (unthinkingly) following the accepted customs > **conventionally** adv
> **conventionality** n
conventionality n ▷ conventional
conventionally adv ▷ conventional
conventions n ▷ convention
convents n ▷ convent
converge v (-verges, -verging, -verged) meet or join > **convergence** n
converged v ▷ converge
converges v ▷ converge
converging v ▷ converge
conversant adj having knowledge or experience of
conversation n (pl -s) informal talk
> **conversational** adj
conversational adj ▷ conversation
conversationalist n (pl -s) person with a specified ability at conversation
conversationalists n ▷ conversationalist
conversations n ▷ conversation
converse[1] v (-verses, -versing, versed) have a conversation
converse[2] adj, n (pl -s) opposite or contrary
> **conversely** adv
conversed v ▷ converse[1]
conversely adv ▷ converse[2]
converses v ▷ converse[1] ▶ n ▷ converse[2]
conversing v ▷ converse[1]
conversion n (pl -s) (thing resulting from) converting
conversions n ▷ conversion
convert v (-s, -ing, ed) change in form, character, or function ▶ n (pl -s) person who has converted to a different belief or religion
converted v ▷ convert
convertible adj capable of being converted ▶ n (pl -s) car with a folding or removable roof
convertibles n ▷ convertible
converting v ▷ convert
converts v, n ▷ convert
convex adj curving outwards
convey v (-s, -ing, -ed) communicate (information)
conveyance n (pl -s) (Old-fashioned) vehicle

conveyances n ▷ conveyance
conveyancing n branch of law dealing with the transfer of ownership of property
conveyed v ▷ convey
conveying v ▷ convey
conveys v ▷ convey
convict v (-s, -ing, -ed) declare guilty ▶ n (pl -s) person serving a prison sentence
convicted v ▷ convict
convicting v ▷ convict
conviction n (pl -s) firm belief
convictions n ▷ conviction
convicts v, n ▷ convict
convince v (-vinces, -vincing, -vinced) persuade by argument or evidence
> **convincing** adj > **convincingly** adv
convinced v ▷ convince
convinces v ▷ convince
convincing v, adj ▷ convince
convincingly adv ▷ convince
convivial adj sociable, lively > **conviviality** n
> **convivially** adv
conviviality n ▷ convivial
convivially adv ▷ convivial
convocation n (pl -s) calling together
convocations n ▷ convocation
convoke v (-vokes, -voking, -voked) call together
convoked v ▷ convoke
convokes v ▷ convoke
convoking v ▷ convoke
convoluted adj coiled, twisted > **convolution** n (pl -s)
convolution n ▷ convoluted
convolutions n ▷ convoluted
convolvulus n (pl -es) twining plant with funnel-shaped flowers
convolvuluses n ▷ convolvulus
convoy n (pl -s) group of vehicles or ships travelling together
convoys n ▷ convoy
convulse v (-vulses, -vulsing, -vulsed) (of part of the body) undergo violent spasms (Informal) > **convulsive** adj > **convulsively** adv
convulsed v ▷ convulse
convulses v ▷ convulse
convulsing v ▷ convulse
convulsion n (pl -s) violent muscular spasm ▶ pl uncontrollable laughter
convulsions n ▷ convulsion
convulsive adj ▷ convulse
convulsively adv ▷ convulse
cony, coney n (pl conies, -s) (BRIT) rabbit
coo v (coos, cooing, cooed) (of a dove or pigeon) make a soft murmuring sound

cooed v ▷ coo
cooee *interj* (BRIT, AUST & NZ) call to attract attention
cooing v ▷ coo
cook v (-s, -ing, -ed) prepare (food) by heating ▶ n (pl -s) person who cooks food
  cooked v ▷ cook
cooker n (pl -s) (CHIEFLY BRIT) apparatus for cooking heated by gas or electricity
  cookers n ▷ cooker
cookery n art of cooking
cookie n (pl -s) (US) biscuit
  cookies n ▷ cookie
  cooking v ▷ cook
  cooks v, n ▷ cook
cool *adj* (-er, -est) moderately cold (*Informal*) ▶ v (-s, -ing, -ed) make or become cool ▶ n (pl -s) coolness > **coolly** *adv* > **coolness** n (pl -es)
coolant n (pl -s) fluid used to cool machinery while it is working
  coolants n ▷ coolant
  cooled v ▷ cool
cooler n (pl -s) container for making or keeping things cool ▶ *adj* ▷ cool
  coolers n ▷ cooler
  coolest *adj* ▷ cool
coolibah n (pl -s) Australian eucalypt that grows beside rivers
  coolibahs n ▷ coolibah
  cooling v ▷ cool
  coolly *adv* ▷ cool
  coolness n ▷ cool
  coolnesses n ▷ cool
  cools v, n ▷ cool
coomb, coombe n (pl -s) (S ENGLISH) short valley or deep hollow
  coombe n ▷ coomb
  coombes n ▷ coomb
  coombs n ▷ coomb
coop¹ n (pl -s) cage or pen for poultry
coop² [koh-op] n (pl -s) (BRIT, US & AUST) (shop run by) a cooperative society
cooper n (pl -s) person who makes or repairs barrels
cooperate v (-rates, -rating, -rated) work or act together > **cooperation** n
  cooperated v ▷ cooperate
  cooperates v ▷ cooperate
  cooperating v ▷ cooperate
  cooperation n ▷ cooperate
cooperative *adj* willing to cooperate ▶ n (pl -s) cooperative organization
  cooperatives n ▷ cooperative
  coopers n ▷ cooper
  coops n ▷ coop¹, ²

coopt [koh-opt] v (-s, -ing, -ed) add (someone) to a group by the agreement of the existing members
  coopted v ▷ coopt
  coopting v ▷ coopt
  coopts v ▷ coopt
coordinate v (-nates, -nating, -nated) bring together and cause to work together efficiently ▶ n (pl -s) (MATHS) any of a set of numbers defining the location of a point ▶ *pl* clothes designed to be worn together > **coordination** n > **coordinator** n (pl -s)
  coordinated v ▷ coordinate
  coordinates v, n ▷ coordinate
  coordinating v ▷ coordinate
  coordination n ▷ coordinate
  coordinator n ▷ coordinate
  coordinators n ▷ coordinate
  coos v ▷ coo
coot n (pl -s) small black water bird
  coots n ▷ coot
cop (*Slang*) n (pl -s) policeman ▶ v (cops, copping, copped) take or seize
cope¹ v (cops, coping, coped) (*often foll. by* **with**) deal successfully (with)
cope² n (pl -s) large ceremonial cloak worn by some Christian priests
  coped v ▷ cope¹
  copes v ▷ cope¹ ▶ n ▷ cope²
  copied v ▷ copy
  copies n, v ▷ copy
  coping v ▷ cope¹ ▶ n (pl -s) sloping top row of a wall
  copings n ▷ coping
copious [kope-ee-uss] *adj* abundant, plentiful > **copiously** *adv*
  copiously *adv* ▷ copious
  copped v ▷ cop
copper¹ n (pl -s) soft reddish-brown metal
copper² n (pl -s) (BRIT) (*Slang*) policeman
copperplate n (pl -s) fine handwriting style
  copperplates n ▷ copperplate
  coppers n ▷ copper¹, ²
coppice, copse n (pl -s) small group of trees growing close together
  coppices n ▷ coppice
  copping v ▷ cop
copra n (pl -s) dried oil-yielding kernel of the coconut
  copras n ▷ copra
  cops n, v ▷ cop
  copse n ▷ coppice
  copses n ▷ coppice
copulate v (-lates, -lating, -lated) have sexual intercourse > **copulation** n (pl -s)

copulated v ▷ copulate
copulates v ▷ copulate
copulating v ▷ copulate
copulation n ▷ copulate
copulations n ▷ copulate
copy n (pl copies) thing made to look exactly like another ▶ v (copies, copying, copied) make a copy of
copying v ▷ copy
copyright n (pl -s) exclusive legal right to reproduce and control a book, work of art, etc. ▶ v (-s, -ing, -ed) take out a copyright on ▶ adj protected by copyright
copyrighted v ▷ copyright
copyrighting v ▷ copyright
copyrights n, v ▷ copyright
copywriter n (pl -s) person who writes advertising copy
copywriters n ▷ copywriter
coquette n (pl -s) woman who flirts
> **coquettish** adj
coquettes n ▷ coquette
coquettish adj ▷ coquette
coracle n (pl -s) small round boat of wicker covered with skins
coracles n ▷ coracle
coral n (pl -s) hard substance formed from the skeletons of very small sea animals ▶ adj orange-pink
corals n ▷ coral
cord n (pl -s) thin rope or thick string ▶ pl corduroy trousers
cordial adj warm and friendly ▶ n (pl -s) drink with a fruit base > **cordially** adv > **cordiality** n
cordiality n ▷ cordial
cordially adv ▷ cordial
cordials n ▷ cordial
cordite n (pl -s) explosive used in guns and bombs
cordites n ▷ cordite
cordon n (pl -s) chain of police, soldiers, etc., guarding an area
cordons n ▷ cordon
cords n ▷ cord
corduroy n (pl -s) cotton fabric with a velvety ribbed surface
corduroys n ▷ corduroy
core n (pl -s) central part of certain fruits, containing the seeds ▶ v (cores, coring, cored) remove the core from
cored v ▷ core
corella n (pl -s) white Australian cockatoo
corellas n ▷ corella
cores n, v ▷ core
corgi n (pl -s) short-legged sturdy dog

corgis n ▷ corgi
coriander n (pl -s) plant grown for its aromatic seeds and leaves
corianders n ▷ coriander
coring v ▷ core
cork n (pl -s) thick light bark of a Mediterranean oak ▶ v (-s, -ing, -ed) seal with a cork
corkage n (pl -s) restaurant's charge for serving wine bought elsewhere
corkages n ▷ corkage
corked v ▷ cork
corking v ▷ cork
corks n, v ▷ cork
corkscrew n (pl -s) spiral metal tool for pulling corks from bottles
corkscrews n ▷ corkscrew
corm n (pl -s) bulblike underground stem of certain plants
cormorant n (pl -s) large dark-coloured long-necked sea bird
cormorants n ▷ cormorant
corms n ▷ corm
corn¹ n (pl -s) cereal plant such as wheat or oats
corn² n (pl -s) painful hard skin on the toe
cornea [korn-ee-a] n (pl -neas, -neae) transparent membrane covering the eyeball
> **corneal** adj
corneae n ▷ cornea
corneal adj ▷ cornea
corneas n ▷ cornea
corner n (pl -s) area or angle where two converging lines or surfaces meet (SPORT) ▶ v (-s, -ing, -ed) force into a difficult or inescapable position
cornered v ▷ corner
cornering v ▷ corner
corners n, v ▷ corner
cornerstone n (pl -s) indispensable part or basis
cornerstones n ▷ cornerstone
cornet n (pl -s) brass instrument similar to the trumpet
cornets n ▷ cornet
cornflakes pl n breakfast cereal made from toasted maize
cornflour n (pl -s) (CHIEFLY BRIT) fine maize flour
cornflours n ▷ cornflour
cornflower n (pl -s) plant with blue flowers
cornflowers n ▷ cornflower
cornice n (pl -s) decorative moulding round the top of a wall
cornices n ▷ cornice
cornier adj ▷ corny
corniest adj ▷ corny

corns *n* ▷ corn[1, 2]

cornucopia [korn-yew-**kope**-ee-a] *n* (*pl* -s) great abundance

cornucopias *n* ▷ cornucopia

corny (-nier, -niest) *adj* (*Slang*) unoriginal or oversentimental

corolla *n* (*pl* -s) petals of a flower collectively

corollaries *n* ▷ corollary

corollary *n* (*pl* -laries) idea, fact, or proposition which is the natural result of something else

corollas *n* ▷ corolla

corona *n* (*pl* -nas, -nae) ring of light round the moon or sun

coronae *n* ▷ corona

coronaries *n* ▷ coronary

coronary [kor-ron-a-ree] *adj* of the arteries surrounding the heart ▶ *n* (*pl* -naries)

coronas *n* ▷ corona

coronation *n* (*pl* -s) ceremony of crowning a monarch

coronations *n* ▷ coronation

coroner *n* (*pl* -s) (BRIT, AUST & NZ) official responsible for the investigation of violent, sudden, or suspicious deaths

coroners *n* ▷ coroner

coronet *n* (*pl* -s) small crown

coronets *n* ▷ coronet

corpora *n* ▷ corpus

corporal[1] *n* (*pl* -s) noncommissioned officer in an army

corporal[2] *adj* of the body > corporally *adv*

corporally *adv* ▷ corporal[2]

corporals *n* ▷ corporal[1]

corporate *adj* of business corporations

corporation *n* (*pl* -s) large business or company

corporations *n* ▷ corporation

corporeal [kore-**pore**-ee-al] *adj* physical or tangible

corps [kore] *n* (*pl* corps) military unit with a specific function

corpse *n* (*pl* -s) dead body

corpses *n* ▷ corpse

corpulence *n* ▷ corpulent

corpulent *adj* fat or plump > corpulence *n*

corpus *n* (*pl* corpora) collection of writings, esp. by a single author

corpuscle *n* (*pl* -s) red or white blood cell

corpuscles *n* ▷ corpuscle

corral (us) *n* (*pl* -s) enclosure for cattle or horses ▶ *v* (-rals, -ralling, -ralled) put in a corral

corralled *v* ▷ corral

corralling *v* ▷ corral

corrals *n*, *v* ▷ corral

correct *adj* free from error, true ▶ *v* (-s, -ing, -ed)

put right > correctly *adv* > correctness *n*

corrected *v* ▷ correct

correcting *v* ▷ correct

correction *n* (*pl* -s) correcting

corrections *n* ▷ correction

corrective *adj* intended to put right something wrong

correctly *adv* ▷ correct

correctness *n* ▷ correct

corrects *v* ▷ correct

correlate *v* (-lates, -lating, -lated) place or be placed in a mutual relationship > correlation *n* (*pl* -s)

correlated *v* ▷ correlate

correlates *v* ▷ correlate

correlating *v* ▷ correlate

correlation *n* ▷ correlate

correlations *n* ▷ correlate

correspond *v* (-s, -ing, -ed) be consistent or compatible (with) > corresponding *adj* > correspondingly *adv*

corresponded *v* ▷ correspond

correspondence *n* communication by letters

correspondent *n* (*pl* -s) person employed by a newspaper etc. to report on a special subject or from a foreign country

correspondents *n* ▷ correspondent

corresponding *v*, *adj* ▷ correspond

correspondingly *adv* ▷ correspond

corresponds *v* ▷ correspond

corridor *n* (*pl* -s) passage in a building or train

corridors *n* ▷ corridor

corrigenda *n* ▷ corrigendum

corrigendum [kor-rij-end-um] *n* (*pl* -da) error to be corrected

corroborate *v* (-rates, -rating, -rated) support (a fact or opinion) by giving proof > corroboration *n* (*pl* -s) > corroborative *adj*

corroborated *v* ▷ corroborate

corroborates *v* ▷ corroborate

corroborating *v* ▷ corroborate

corroboration *n* ▷ corroborate

corroborations *n* ▷ corroborate

corroborative *adj* ▷ corroborate

corroboree *n* (*pl* -s) (AUST) Aboriginal gathering or dance

corroborees *n* ▷ corroboree

corrode *v* (-rodes, -roding, -roded) eat or be eaten away by chemical action or rust > corrosion *n* > corrosive *adj* > corrosively *adv* > corrosiveness *n*

corroded *v* ▷ corrode

corrodes *v* ▷ corrode

corroding *v* ▷ corrode

corrosion *n* ▷ corrode

corrosive v ▷ corrode
corrosively adv ▷ corrode
corrosiveness n ▷ corrode
corrugated adj folded into alternate grooves and ridges
corrupt adj (-er, -est) open to or involving bribery ▶ v (-s, -ing, -ed) make corrupt > **corruptly** adv > **corruption** n > **corruptible** adj
corrupted v ▷ corrupt
corrupter adj ▷ corrupt
corruptest adj ▷ corrupt
corruptible adj ▷ corrupt
corrupting v ▷ corrupt
corruption n ▷ corrupt
corruptly adv ▷ corrupt
corrupts v ▷ corrupt
corsage [kor-**sahzh**] n (pl -s) small bouquet worn on the bodice of a dress
corsages n ▷ corsage
corsair n (pl -s) pirate
corsairs n ▷ corsair
corset n (pl -s) women's close-fitting undergarment worn to shape the torso
corsets n ▷ corset
cortege [kor-**tayzh**] n (pl -s) funeral procession
corteges n ▷ cortege
cortex n (pl -tices) (ANAT) outer layer of the brain or other internal organ > **cortical** adj
cortical adj ▷ cortex
cortices n ▷ cortex
cortisone n (pl -s) steroid hormone used to treat various diseases
cortisones n ▷ cortisone
corundum n (pl -s) hard mineral used as an abrasive
corundums n ▷ corundum
coruscate v (-cates, -cating, -cated) (Formal) sparkle
coruscated v ▷ coruscate
coruscates v ▷ coruscate
coruscating v ▷ coruscate
corvette n (pl -s) lightly armed escort warship
corvettes n ▷ corvette
cosh n (pl -es) (BRIT) heavy blunt weapon ▶ v (-es, -ing, -ed) hit with a cosh
coshed v, n ▷ cosh
coshes v ▷ cosh
coshing v ▷ cosh
cosier adj ▷ cosy
cosies adj ▷ cosy
cosiest adj ▷ cosy
cosily adv ▷ cosy
cosine [**koh**-sine] n (pl -s) (in trigonometry) ratio of the length of the adjacent side to that

of the hypotenuse in a right-angled triangle
cosines n ▷ cosine
cosiness n ▷ cosy
cosmetic n (pl -s) preparation used to improve the appearance of a person's skin ▶ adj improving the appearance only
cosmetics n ▷ cosmetic
cosmic adj of the whole universe > **cosmically** adv
cosmically adv ▷ cosmic
cosmological adj ▷ cosmology
cosmologist n ▷ cosmology
cosmologists n ▷ cosmology
cosmology n study of the origin and nature of the universe > **cosmological** adj > **cosmologist** n (pl -s)
cosmonaut n (pl -s) Russian name for an astronaut
cosmonauts n ▷ cosmonaut
cosmopolitan adj composed of people or elements from many countries ▶ n (pl -s) cosmopolitan person > **cosmopolitanism** n
cosmopolitanism n ▷ cosmopolitan
cosmopolitans n ▷ cosmopolitan
cosmos n (pl cosmos) the universe
cossack n (pl -s) member of a S Russian people famous as horsemen and dancers
cossacks n ▷ cossack
cosset v (-s, -ing, -ed) pamper
cosseted v ▷ cosset
cosseting v ▷ cosset
cossets v ▷ cosset
cost n (pl -s) amount of money, time, labour, etc., required for something ▶ pl expenses of a lawsuit ▶ v (costs, costing, cost) have as its cost
costermonger n (pl -s) (BRIT) person who sells fruit and vegetables from a street barrow
costermongers n ▷ costermonger
costing v ▷ cost
costlier adj ▷ costly
costliest adj ▷ costly
costliness n ▷ costly
costlinesses n ▷ costly
costly adj (-lier, -liest) expensive > **costliness** n (pl -es)
costs n, v ▷ cost
costume n (pl -s) style of dress of a particular place or time, or for a particular activity
costumes n ▷ costume
costumier n (pl -s) maker or seller of costumes
costumiers n ▷ costumier
cosy adj (-sier, -siest) warm and snug ▶ n (pl -sies) cover for keeping things warm > **cosily** adv > **cosiness** n

cot *n* (*pl* -s) baby's bed with high sides

cote *n* (*pl* -s) shelter for birds or animals

coterie [kote-er-ee] *n* (*pl* -s) exclusive group, clique
  coteries *n* ▷ coterie
  cotes *n* ▷ cote

cotoneaster [kot-tone-ee-ass-ter] *n* (*pl* -s) garden shrub with red berries
  cotoneasters *n* ▷ cotoneaster
  cots *n* ▷ cot

cottage *n* (*pl* -s) small house in the country
  cottages *n* ▷ cottage

cotter *n* (*pl* -s) pin or wedge used to secure machine parts
  cotters *n* ▷ cotter

cotton *n* (*pl* -s) white downy fibre covering the seeds of a tropical plant **> cottony** *adj*
  cottons *n* ▷ cotton
  cottony *adj* ▷ cotton

cotyledon [kot-ill-ee-don] *n* (*pl* -s) first leaf of a plant embryo
  cotyledons *n* ▷ cotyledon

couch *n* (*pl* couches) piece of upholstered furniture for seating more than one person ▶ *v* (-es, -ing, -ed) express in a particular way
  couched *v* ▷ couch
  couches *n*, *v* ▷ couch

couchette [koo-shett] *n* (*pl* -s) bed converted from seats on a train or ship
  couchettes *n* ▷ couchette
  couching *v* ▷ couch

cougan *n* (*pl* -s) (AUST) (Slang) drunk and rowdy person
  cougans *n* ▷ cougan

cougar *n* (*pl* -s) puma
  cougars *n* ▷ cougar

cough *v* (-s, -ing, -ed) expel air from the lungs abruptly and noisily ▶ *n* (*pl* -s) act or sound of coughing
  coughed *v* ▷ cough
  coughing *v* ▷ cough
  coughs *v*, *n* ▷ cough
  could *v* ▷ can¹

coulomb [koo-lom] *n* (*pl* -s) SI unit of electric charge
  coulombs *n* ▷ coulomb

coulter *n* (*pl* -s) blade at the front of a ploughshare
  coulters *n* ▷ coulter

council *n* (*pl* -s) group meeting for discussion or consultation ▶ *adj* of or by a council

councillor *n* (*pl* -s) member of a council
  councillors *n* ▷ councillor
  councils *n* ▷ council

counsel *n* (*pl* -s) advice or guidance ▶ *v* (-sels, -selling, -selled) give guidance to **> counsellor** *n* (*pl* -s)
  counselled *v* ▷ counsel
  counselling *v* ▷ counsel
  counsellor *n* ▷ counsel
  counsellors *n* ▷ counsel
  counsels *n*, *v* ▷ counsel

count¹ *v* (-s, -ing, -ed) say numbers in order ▶ *n* (*pl* -s) counting

count² *n* (*pl* -s) European nobleman

countdown *n* (*pl* -s) counting backwards to zero of the seconds before an event
  countdowns *n* ▷ countdown
  counted *v* ▷ count¹

countenance *n* (*pl* -s) (expression of) the face ▶ *v* (-nances, -nancing, -nanced) allow or tolerate
  countenanced *v* ▷ countenance
  countenances *n*, *v* ▷ countenance
  countenancing *v* ▷ countenance

counter¹ *n* (*pl* -s) long flat surface in a bank or shop, on which business is transacted

counter² *v* (-s, -ing, -ed) oppose, retaliate against ▶ *adv* in the opposite direction ▶ *n* (*pl* -s) opposing or retaliatory action

counteract *v* (-s, -ing, -ed) act against or neutralize **> counteraction** *n*
  counteracted *v* ▷ counteract
  counteracting *v* ▷ counteract
  counteraction *n* ▷ counteract
  counteracts *v* ▷ counteract

counterattack *n* (*pl* -s) ▶ *v* (-s, -ing, -ed) attack in response to an attack
  counterattacked *v* ▷ counterattack
  counterattacking *v* ▷ counterattack
  counterattacks *n*, *v* ▷ counterattack

counterbalance *n* (*pl* -s) weight or force balancing or neutralizing another ▶ *v* (-ces, -cing, -ced) act as a counterbalance to
  counterbalanced *v* ▷ counterbalance
  counterbalances *n*, *v* ▷ counterbalance
  counterbalancing *v* ▷ counterbalance

counterblast *n* (*pl* -s) aggressive response to a verbal attack
  counterblasts *n* ▷ counterblast
  countered *v* ▷ counter

counterfeit *adj* fake, forged ▶ *n* (*pl* -s) fake, forgery ▶ *v* (-s, -ing, -ed) fake, forge
  counterfeited *v* ▷ counterfeit
  counterfeiting *v* ▷ counterfeit
  counterfeits *n*, *v* ▷ counterfeit

counterfoil *n* (*pl* -s) part of a cheque or receipt kept as a record
  counterfoils *n* ▷ counterfoil
  countering *v* ▷ counter

countermand v (-s, -ing, -ed) cancel (a previous order)
  countermanded v ▷ countermand
  countermanding v ▷ countermand
  countermands v ▷ countermand
counterpane n (pl -s) bed covering
  counterpanes n ▷ counterpane
counterpart n (pl -s) person or thing complementary to or corresponding to another
  counterparts n ▷ counterpart
counterpoint n (pl -s) (MUSIC) technique of combining melodies
  counterpoints n ▷ counterpoint
counterpoise n (pl -s) ▶ v (-ses, -sing, -sed) counterbalance
  counterpoised v ▷ counterpoise
  counterpoises n, v ▷ counterpoise
  counterpoising v ▷ counterpoise
counterproductive adj having an effect opposite to the one intended
counters n ▷ counter¹, ² ▶ v ▷ counter²
  countersank v ▷ countersink
countersign v (-s, -ing, -ed) sign (a document already signed by someone) as confirmation
  countersigned v ▷ countersign
  countersigning v ▷ countersign
  countersigns v ▷ countersign
countersink v (-sinks, -sinking, -sank, -sunk) drive (a screw) into a shaped hole so that its head is below the surface
  countersinking v ▷ countersink
  countersinks v ▷ countersink
  countersunk v ▷ countersink
countertenor n (pl -s) male alto
  countertenors n ▷ countertenor
counterterrorism n measures to prevent terrorist attacks or eradicate terrorist groups
countess n (pl -es) woman holding the rank of count or earl
  countesses n ▷ countess
  counties n ▷ county
  counting v ▷ count¹
countless adj too many to count
  countries n ▷ country
countrified adj rustic in manner or appearance
country n (pl -tries) nation
countryman, countrywoman n (pl -men, -women) person from one's native land
  countrymen n ▷ countryman
countryside n land away from cities
  countrywoman n ▷ countryman
  countrywomen n ▷ countryman
  counts v ▷ count¹ ▶ n ▷ count¹, ²

county n (pl -ties) (in some countries) division of a country
coup [koo] n (pl -s) successful action
coupé [koo-pay] n (pl -s) sports car with two doors and a sloping fixed roof
  coupés n ▷ coupé
couple n (pl -s) two people who are married or romantically involved ▶ v (-ples, -pling, -pled) connect, associate
  coupled v ▷ couple
  couples n, v ▷ couple
couplet n (pl -s) two consecutive lines of verse, usu. rhyming and of the same metre
  couplets n ▷ couplet
coupling n (pl -s) device for connecting things, such as railway carriages ▶ v ▷ couple
  couplings n ▷ coupling
coupon n (pl -s) piece of paper entitling the holder to a discount or gift
  coupons n ▷ coupon
  coups n ▷ coup
courage n ability to face danger or pain without fear > **courageous** adj > **courageously** adv
  courageous adj ▷ courage
  courageously adv ▷ courage
courgette n (pl -s) type of small vegetable marrow
  courgettes n ▷ courgette
courier n (pl -s) person employed to look after holiday-makers
  couriers n ▷ courier
course n (pl -s) series of lessons or medical treatment ▶ v (-ses, -sing, -sed) (of liquid) run swiftly
  coursed v ▷ course
  courses n, v ▷ course
  coursing v ▷ course
court n (pl -s) body which decides legal cases ▶ v (-s, -ing, -ed) (Old-fashioned) try to gain the love of
  courted v ▷ court
courteous adj polite > **courteously** adv
  courteously adv ▷ courteous
courtesan [kor-tiz-zan] n (pl -s) (HIST) mistress or high-class prostitute
  courtesans n ▷ courtesan
  courtesies n ▷ courtesy
courtesy n (pl -sies) politeness, good manners
courtier n (pl -s) attendant at a royal court
  courtiers n ▷ courtier
  courting v ▷ court
  courtlier adj ▷ courtly
  courtliest adj ▷ courtly
  courtliness n ▷ courtly

courtlinesses *n* ▷ courtly
courtly *adj* (-lier, -liest) ceremoniously polite
> **courtliness** *n* (*pl* -es)
courts *n*, *v* ▷ court
courtship *n* (*pl* -s) courting of an intended
spouse or mate
courtships *n* ▷ courtship
courtyard *n* (*pl* -s) paved space enclosed by
buildings or walls
courtyards *n* ▷ courtyard
cousin *n* (*pl* -s) child of one's uncle or aunt
cousins *n* ▷ cousin
couture [koo-**toor**] *n* (*pl* -s) high-fashion
designing and dressmaking
coutures *n* ▷ couture
couturier *n* (*pl* -s) person who designs
women's fashion clothes
couturiers *n* ▷ couturier
cove *n* (*pl* -s) small bay or inlet
coven [**kuv**-ven] *n* (*pl* -s) meeting of witches
covenant [**kuv**-ven-ant] *n* (*pl* -s) contract ▶ *v* (-s,
-ing, -ed) agree by a covenant
covenanted *v* ▷ covenant
covenanting *v* ▷ covenant
covenants *n*, *v* ▷ covenant
covens *n* ▷ coven
cover *v* (-s, -ing, -ed) place something over, to
protect or conceal ▶ *n* (*pl* -s) anything that
covers
coverage *n* amount or extent covered
covered *v* ▷ cover
covering *v* ▷ cover
coverlet *n* (*pl* -s) bed cover
coverlets *v* ▷ coverlet
covers *v*, *n* ▷ cover
covert *adj* concealed, secret ▶ *n* (*pl* -s) thicket
giving shelter to game birds or animals
> **covertly** *adv*
covertly *adv* ▷ covert
coverts *n* ▷ covert
coves *n* ▷ cove
covet *v* (-s, -ing, -ed) long to possess (what
belongs to someone else) > **covetous** *adj*
> **covetousness** *n*
coveted *v* ▷ covet
coveting *v* ▷ covet
covetous *adj* ▷ covet
covetousness *n* ▷ covet
covets *v* ▷ covet
covey [**kuv**-vee] *n* (*pl* -s) small flock of grouse
or partridge
coveys *n* ▷ covey
cow[1] *n* (*pl* -s) mature female of cattle and of
certain other mammals, such as the elephant
or seal

cow[2] *v* (-s, -ing, -ed) intimidate, subdue
coward *n* (*pl* -s) person who lacks courage
> **cowardly** *adj* > **cowardliness** *n*
cowardice *n* lack of courage
cowardliness *n* ▷ coward
cowardly *adj* ▷ coward
cowards *n* ▷ coward
cowboy *n* (*pl* -s) (in the US) ranch worker who
herds and tends cattle, usu. on horseback
cowboys *n* ▷ cowboy
cowed *v* ▷ cow**[2]**
cower *v* (-s, -ing, -ed) cringe in fear
cowered *v* ▷ cower
cowering *v* ▷ cower
cowers *v* ▷ cower
cowing *v* ▷ cow**[2]**
cowl *n* (*pl* -s) loose hood
cowling *n* (*pl* -s) cover on an engine
cowlings *n* ▷ cowling
cowls *n* ▷ cowl
cowrie *n* (*pl* -s) brightly-marked sea shell
cowries *n* ▷ cowrie
cows *n* ▷ cow**[1]** ▶ *v* ▷ cow**[2]**
cowslip *n* (*pl* -s) small yellow wild European
flower
cowslips *n* ▷ cowslip
cox *n* (*pl* -es) coxswain ▶ *v* (-es, -ing, -ed) act as
cox of (a boat)
coxed *v* ▷ cox
coxes *n*, *v* ▷ cox
coxing *v* ▷ cox
coxswain [**kok**-sn] *n* (*pl* -s) person who steers
a rowing boat
coxswains *n* ▷ coxswain
coy *adj* (-er, -est) affectedly shy or modest
> **coyly** *adv* > **coyness** *n* (*pl* -es)
coyer *adj* ▷ coy
coyest *adj* ▷ coy
coyly *adv* ▷ coy
coyness *n* ▷ coy
coynesses *n* ▷ coy
coyote [koy-**ote**-ee] *n* (*pl* -s) prairie wolf of N
America
coyotes *n* ▷ coyote
coypu *n* (*pl* -s) beaver-like aquatic rodent
native to S America, bred for its fur
coypus *n* ▷ coypu

> **coz** *n* (**cozes**). Coz is an old word for
> **cousin**, and a good one to know as it
> scores 14 points.

cozen *v* (-s, -ing, -ed) (Lit) cheat, trick
cozened *v* ▷ cozen
cozening *v* ▷ cozen
cozens *v* ▷ cozen
crab *n* (*pl* -s) edible shellfish with ten legs, the

first pair modified into pincers

crabbed *adj* (of handwriting) hard to read (*also* **crabby**) (**crabbier, crabbiest**)

crabbier *adj* ▷ crabbed

crabbiest *adj* ▷ crabbed

crabby *adj* ▷ crabbed

crabs *n* ▷ crab

crack *v* (**-s, -ing, -ed**) break or split partially ▶ *n* (*pl* **-s**) sudden sharp noise ▶ *adj* (*Informal*) first-rate, excellent

crackdown *n* (*pl* **-s**) severe disciplinary measures

crackdowns *n* ▷ crackdown

cracked *v* ▷ crack

cracker *n* (*pl* **-s**) thin dry biscuit

crackers *n* ▷ cracker ▶ *adj* (*Slang*) insane

cracking *adj* very good ▶ *v* ▷ crack

crackle *v* (**-ckles, -ckling, -ckled**) make small sharp popping noises ▶ *n* (*pl* **-ckles**) crackling sound

crackled *v* ▷ crackle

crackles *v, n* ▷ crackle

crackling *n* crackle ▶ *v* ▷ crackle

crackpot *n* (*pl* **-s**) ▶ *adj* (*Informal*) eccentric (person)

crackpots *n* ▷ crackpot

cracks *v, n* ▷ crack

cradle *n* (*pl* **-s**) baby's bed on rockers ▶ *v* (**-dles, -dling, -dled**) hold gently as if in a cradle

cradled *v* ▷ cradle

cradles *n, v* ▷ cradle

cradling *v* ▷ cradle

craft *n* (*pl* **-s**) occupation requiring skill with the hands

craftier *adj* ▷ crafty

craftiest *adj* ▷ crafty

craftily *adv* ▷ crafty

craftiness *n* ▷ crafty

craftinesses *n* ▷ crafty

crafts *n* ▷ craft

craftsman, craftswoman *n* (*pl* **-men, -women**) skilled worker > **craftsmanship** *n* (*pl* **-s**)

craftsmanship *n* ▷ craftsman

craftsmanships *n* ▷ craftsman

craftsmen *n* ▷ craftsman

craftswoman *n* ▷ craftsman

craftswomen *n* ▷ craftsman

crafty *adj* (**-tier, -tiest**) skilled in deception > **craftily** *adv* > **craftiness** *n* (*pl* **-es**)

crag *n* (*pl* **-s**) steep rugged rock > **craggy** *adj* (**-gier, -ggiest**)

craggier *adj* ▷ crag

craggiest *adj* ▷ crag

craggy *adj* ▷ crag

crags *n* ▷ crag

cram *v* (**-s, -mming, -mmed**) force into too small a space

crammed *v* ▷ cram

cramming *v* ▷ cram

cramp¹ *n* (*pl* **-s**) painful muscular contraction

cramp² *v* (**-s, -ing, -ed**) confine, restrict

cramped *v* ▷ cramp²

cramping *v* ▷ cramp²

crampon *n* (*pl* **-s**) spiked plate strapped to a boot for climbing on ice

crampons *n* ▷ crampon

cramps *n* ▷ cramp¹ ▶ *v* ▷ cramp²

crams *v* ▷ cram

cranberries *n* ▷ cranberry

cranberry *n* (*pl* **-berries**) sour edible red berry

crane *n* (*pl* **-s**) machine for lifting and moving heavy weights ▶ *v* (**cranes, craning, craned**) stretch (one's neck) to see something

craned *v* ▷ crane

cranes *n, v* ▷ crane

crania *n* ▷ cranium

cranial *adj* ▷ cranium

craning *v* ▷ crane

cranium *n* (*pl* **-niums, -nia**) (ANAT) skull > **cranial** *adj*

craniums *n* ▷ cranium

crank *n* (*pl* **-s**) arm projecting at right angles from a shaft, for transmitting or converting motion (*Informal*) ▶ *v* (**-s, -ing, -ed**) start (an engine) with a crank

cranked *v* ▷ crank

crankier *adj* ▷ cranky

crankiest *adj* ▷ cranky

cranking *v* ▷ crank

cranks *n, v* ▷ crank

crankshaft *n* (*pl* **-s**) shaft driven by a crank

crankshafts *n* ▷ crankshaft

cranky *adj* (**-kier, -kiest**) (*Informal*) eccentric

crannies *n* ▷ cranny

cranny *n* (*pl* **-nies**) narrow opening

crape *n* (*pl* **-s**) ▷ crepe

crapes *n* ▷ crepe

craps *n* gambling game played with two dice

crash *n* (*pl* **-es**) collision involving a vehicle or vehicles ▶ *v* (**-es, -ing, -ed**) (cause to) collide violently with a vehicle, a stationary object, or the ground

crashed *v* ▷ crash

crashes *n, v* ▷ crash

crashing *v* ▷ crash

crass *adj* (**-er, -est**) stupid and insensitive > **crassly** *adv* > **crassness** *n* (*pl* **-es**)

crasser *adj* ▷ crass

crassest *adj* ▷ crass

crassly adv ▷ crass

crassness n ▷ crass

crassnesses n ▷ crass

crate n (pl -s) large wooden container for packing goods

crater n (pl -s) very large hole in the ground or in the surface of the moon

craters n ▷ crater

crates n ▷ crate

cravat n (pl -s) man's scarf worn like a tie

cravats n ▷ cravat

crave v (craves, craving, craved) desire intensely > **craving** n (pl -s)

craved v ▷ crave

craven adj cowardly

craves v ▷ crave

craving n, v ▷ crave

cravings n ▷ crave

crawfish n (pl crawfish) ▷ crayfish

crawl v (-s, -ing, -ed) move on one's hands and knees ▶ n (pl -s) crawling motion or pace > **crawler** n (pl -s)

crawled v ▷ crawl

crawler n ▷ crawl

crawlers n ▷ crawl

crawling v ▷ crawl

crawls v, n ▷ crawl

crayfish n (pl crayfish) edible shellfish like a lobster

crayon v (-s, -ing, -ed), n (pl -s) (draw or colour with) a stick or pencil of coloured wax or clay

crayoned v ▷ crayon

crayoning v ▷ crayon

crayons v, n ▷ crayon

craze n (pl -s) short-lived fashion or enthusiasm

crazed adj wild and uncontrolled

crazes n ▷ craze

crazier adj ▷ crazy

craziest adj ▷ crazy

crazily adv ▷ crazy

craziness n ▷ crazy

crazinesses n ▷ crazy

crazy adj (-zier, -ziest) ridiculous > **crazily** adv > **craziness** n (pl -es)

creak v, n (pl -s) (make) a harsh squeaking sound > **creaky** adj (-kier, -kiest)

creakier adj ▷ creak

creakiest adj ▷ creak

creaks n ▷ creak

creaky adj ▷ creak

cream n (pl -s) fatty part of milk ▶ adj yellowish-white ▶ v (-s, -ing, -ed) beat to a creamy consistency > **creamy** adj > **creaminess** n

creamed v ▷ cream

creaminess n ▷ cream

creaming v ▷ cream

creams n, v ▷ cream

creamy adj ▷ cream

crease n (pl -s) line made by folding or pressing ▶ v (creases, creasing, creased) crush or line

creased v ▷ crease

creases n, v ▷ crease

creasing v ▷ crease

create v (creates, creating, created) make, cause to exist > **creation** n (pl -s) > **creator** n (pl -s)

created v ▷ create

creates v ▷ create

creating v ▷ create

creation n ▷ create

creations n ▷ create

creative adj imaginative or inventive > **creatively** adv > **creativity** n

creatively adv ▷ creative

creativity n ▷ creative

creator n ▷ create

creators n ▷ create

creature n (pl -s) animal, person, or other being

creatures n ▷ creature

crèche n (pl -s) place where small children are looked after while their parents are working, shopping, etc.

crèches n ▷ crèche

credence n (pl -s) belief in the truth or accuracy of a statement

credences n ▷ credence

credentials pl n document giving evidence of a person's identity or qualifications

credibility n ▷ credible

credible adj believable > **credibly** adv > **credibility** n

credibly adv ▷ credible

credit n (pl -s) system of allowing customers to receive goods and pay later ▶ v (-s, -ing, -ed) enter as a credit in an account

creditable adj praiseworthy > **creditably** adv

creditably adv ▷ creditable

credited v ▷ credit

crediting v ▷ credit

creditor n (pl -s) person to whom money is owed

creditors n ▷ creditor

credits n, v ▷ credit

credulity n ▷ credulous

credulous adj too willing to believe > **credulity** n > **credulously** adv

credulously adv ▷ credulous

creed n (pl -s) statement or system of (Christian) beliefs or principles
   creeds n ▷ creed

creek n (pl -s) narrow inlet or bay (AUST, NZ, US & CANADIAN)
   creeks n ▷ creek

creel n (pl -s) wicker basket used by anglers
   creels n ▷ creel

creep v (creeps, creeping, crept) move quietly and cautiously ▶ n (pl -s) (Slang) obnoxious or servile person

creeper n (pl -s) creeping plant
   creepers n ▷ creeper
   creepier adj ▷ creepy
   creepiest adj ▷ creepy
   creepily adv ▷ creepy
   creepiness n ▷ creepy
   creepinesses n ▷ creepy
   creeping v ▷ creep
   creeps v, n ▷ creep

creepy adj (-pier, -piest) (Informal) causing a feeling of fear or disgust > **creepily** adv > **creepiness** n (pl -es)

cremate v (-mates, -mating, -mated) burn (a corpse) to ash > **cremation** n (pl -s)
   cremated v ▷ cremate
   cremates v ▷ cremate
   cremating v ▷ cremate
   cremation n ▷ cremate
   cremations n ▷ cremate
   crematoria n ▷ crematorium

crematorium n (pl -iums, -ia) building where corpses are cremated
   crematoriums n ▷ crematorium

crenellated adj having battlements

creole n (pl -s) language developed from a mixture of languages
   creoles n ▷ creole

creosote n (pl -s) dark oily liquid made from coal tar and used for preserving wood ▶ v (-sotes, -soting, -soted) treat with creosote
   creosoted v ▷ creosote
   creosotes n, v ▷ creosote
   creosoting v ▷ creosote

crepe, crape [krayp] n (pl -s) fabric or rubber with a crinkled texture
   crepes n ▷ crepe
   crept v ▷ creep

crepuscular adj (Lit) of or like twilight

crescendo [krish-end-oh] n (pl -s) gradual increase in loudness, esp. in music
   crescendos n ▷ crescendo

crescent n (pl -s) (curved shape of) the moon as seen in its first or last quarter
   crescents n ▷ crescent

cress n (pl -es) plant with strong-tasting leaves, used in salads
   cresses n ▷ cress

crest n (pl -s) top of a mountain, hill, or wave > **crested** adj
   crested adj ▷ crest

crestfallen adj disheartened
   crests n ▷ crest

cretin n (pl -s) (Informal) stupid person > **cretinous** adj
   cretinous adj ▷ cretin
   cretins n ▷ cretin

crevasse n (pl -s) deep open crack in a glacier
   crevasses n ▷ crevasse

crevice n (pl -s) narrow crack or gap in rock
   crevices n ▷ crevice

crew n (pl -s) people who work on a ship or aircraft (Informal) ▶ v (-s, -ing, -ed) serve as a crew member (on)
   crewed v ▷ crew

crewel n (pl -s) fine worsted yarn used in embroidery
   crewels n ▷ crewel
   crewing v ▷ crew
   crews n, v ▷ crew

crib n (pl -s) piece of writing stolen from elsewhere ▶ v (cribs, cribbing, cribbed) copy (someone's work) dishonestly

cribbage n card game for two to four players
   cribbed v ▷ crib
   cribbing v ▷ crib
   cribs n, v ▷ crib

crick n (pl -s) muscle spasm or cramp in the back or neck ▶ v (-s, -ing, -ed) cause a crick in
   cricked v ▷ crick

cricket¹ n (pl -s) outdoor game played with bats, a ball, and wickets by two teams of eleven > **cricketer** n (pl -s)

cricket² n (pl -s) chirping insect like a grasshopper
   cricketer n ▷ cricket¹
   cricketers n ▷ cricket¹
   crickets n ▷ cricket¹, ²
   cricking v ▷ crick
   cricks n, v ▷ crick
   cried v ▷ cry
   cries v ▷ cry

crime n (pl -s) unlawful act
   crimes n ▷ crime

criminal n (pl -s) person guilty of a crime ▶ adj of crime > **criminally** adv > **criminality** n
   criminality n ▷ criminal
   criminally adv ▷ criminal
   criminals n ▷ criminal
   criminologist n ▷ criminology

criminologists n ▷ criminology
criminology n study of crime > **criminologist** n (pl -s)
crimp v (-s, -ing, -ed) fold or press into ridges
  crimped v ▷ crimp
  crimping v ▷ crimp
  crimps v ▷ crimp
crimson adj deep purplish-red
cringe v (cringes, cringing, cringed) flinch in fear
  cringed v ▷ cringe
  cringes v ▷ cringe
  cringing v ▷ cringe
crinkle v (-kles, -kling, -kled) ▶ n (pl -s) wrinkle, crease, or fold
  crinkled v ▷ crinkle
  crinkles v, n ▷ crinkle
  crinkling v ▷ crinkle
crinoline n (pl -s) hooped petticoat
  crinolines n ▷ crinoline
cripple n (pl -s) person who is lame or disabled ▶ v (-pples, -ppling, -ppled) make lame or disabled
  crippled v ▷ cripple
  cripples n, v ▷ cripple
  crippling v ▷ cripple
  crises n ▷ crisis
crisis n (pl -ses) crucial stage, turning point
crisp adj (-er, -est) fresh and firm ▶ n (pl -s) (BRIT) very thin slice of potato fried till crunchy > **crisply** adv > **crispness** n (pl -es)
crispbread n (pl -s) thin dry biscuit
  crispbreads n ▷ crispbread
  crisper adj ▷ crisp
  crispest adj ▷ crisp
  crispier adj ▷ crisp
  crispiest adj ▷ crisp
  crisply adv ▷ crisp
  crispness adv ▷ crisp
  crispnesses adv ▷ crisp
  crisps n ▷ crisp
crispy adj (-pier, -piest) hard and crunchy
crisscross v (-es, -ing, -ed) move in or mark with a crosswise pattern ▶ adj (of lines) crossing in different directions
  crisscrossed v ▷ crisscross
  crisscrosses v ▷ crisscross
  crisscrossing v ▷ crisscross
  criteria n ▷ criterion
criterion n (pl -ria) standard of judgment
critic n (pl -s) professional judge of any of the arts
critical adj very important or dangerous > **critically** adv
  critically adv ▷ critical

criticism n (pl -s) fault-finding
  criticisms n ▷ criticism
criticize v (-cizes, -cizing, -cized) find fault with
  criticized v ▷ criticize
  criticizes v ▷ criticize
  criticizing v ▷ criticize
  critics n ▷ critic
critique n (pl -s) critical essay
  critiques n ▷ critique
croak v (-s, -ing, -ed) (of a frog or crow) give a low hoarse cry ▶ n (pl -s) low hoarse sound
  croaked v ▷ croak
  croakiness n ▷ croaky
  croaking v ▷ croak
  croaks v, n ▷ croak
croaky adj hoarse > **croakiness** n
crochet [kroh-shay] v (-chets, -cheting, -cheted) make by looping and intertwining yarn with a hooked needle ▶ n (pl -s) work made in this way
  crocheted v ▷ crochet
  crocheting v ▷ crochet
  crochets v, n ▷ crochet
crock^1 n (pl -s) earthenware pot or jar
crock^2 n (pl -s) (BRIT, AUST & NZ) (Informal) old or decrepit person or thing
crockery n dishes
  crocks n ▷ crock$^{1, 2}$
crocodile n (pl -s) large amphibious tropical reptile
  crocodiles n ▷ crocodile
crocus n (pl -cuses) small plant with yellow, white, or purple flowers in spring
  crocuses n ▷ crocus
croft n (pl -s) small farm worked by one family in Scotland > **crofter** n (pl -s)
  crofter n ▷ croft
  crofters n ▷ croft
  crofts n ▷ croft
croissant [krwah-son] n (pl -s) rich flaky crescent-shaped roll
  croissants n ▷ croissant
cromlech n (pl -s) (BRIT) circle of prehistoric standing stones
  cromlechs n ▷ cromlech
crone n (pl -s) witchlike old woman
  crones n ▷ crone
  cronies n ▷ crony
crony n (pl -nies) close friend
crook n (pl -s) (Informal) criminal ▶ adj (AUST & NZ) (Slang) unwell, injured
crooked adj bent or twisted > **crookedly** adv > **crookedness** n
  crookedly adv ▷ crooked

crookedness *n* ▷ crooked
crooks *n* ▷ crook
croon *v* (-s, -ing, -ed) sing, hum, or speak in a soft low tone
crooned *v* ▷ croon
crooner *n* (*pl* -s) male singer of sentimental ballads
crooners *n* ▷ crooner
crooning *v* ▷ croon
croons *v* ▷ croon
crop *n* (*pl* -s) cultivated plant ▶ *v* (**crops, cropping, cropped**) cut very short ▷ **cropper** *n* (*pl* -s)
cropped *v* ▷ crop
cropper *n* ▷ crop
croppers *n* ▷ crop
cropping *v* ▷ crop
crops *n*, *v* ▷ crop
croquet [kroh-kay] *n* (*pl* -s) game played on a lawn in which balls are hit through hoops
croquets *n* ▷ croquet
croquette [kroh-kett] *n* (*pl* -s) fried cake of potato, meat, or fish
croquettes *n* ▷ croquette
crosier *n* (*pl* -s) ▷ crozier
crosiers *n* ▷ crosier
cross *v* (-es, -ing, -ed) move or go across (something) ▶ *n* (*pl* -es) structure, symbol, or mark of two intersecting lines ▶ *adj* (-er, -est) angry, annoyed ▷ **crossly** *adv* ▷ **crossness** *n* (*pl* -es)
crossbar *n* (*pl* -s) horizontal bar across goalposts or on a bicycle
crossbars *n* ▷ crossbar
crossbow *n* (*pl* -s) weapon consisting of a bow fixed across a wooden stock
crossbows *n* ▷ crossbow
crossbred *adj* bred from two different types of animal or plant
crossbreed *n* (*pl* -s) crossbred animal or plant
crossbreeds *n* ▷ crossbreed
crossed *v* ▷ cross
crosser *adj* ▷ cross
crosses *v*, *n* ▷ cross
crossest *adj* ▷ cross
crossfire *n* (*pl* -s) gunfire crossing another line of fire
crossfires *n* ▷ crossfire
crossing *n* (*pl* -s) place where a street may be crossed safely ▶ *v* ▷ cross
crossings *n* ▷ crossing
crossly *adv* ▷ cross
crossness *n* ▷ cross
crossnesses *n* ▷ cross
crossroads *n* place where roads intersect

crosswise *adj*, *adv* across
crossword *n* (*pl* -s) puzzle in which words suggested by clues are written into a grid of squares
crosswords *n* ▷ crossword
crotch *n* (*pl* -es) part of the body between the tops of the legs
crotches *n* ▷ crotch
crotchet *n* (*pl* -s) musical note half the length of a minim
crotchetier *adj* ▷ crotchety
crotchetiest *adj* ▷ crotchety
crotchets *n* ▷ crotchet
crotchety *adj* (-tier, -tiest) (*Informal*) bad-tempered
crouch *v* (-es, -ing, -ed) bend low with the legs and body close ▶ *n* (*pl* -es) this position
crouched *v* ▷ crouch
crouches *v*, *n* ▷ crouch
crouching *v* ▷ crouch
croup[1] [kroop] *n* (*pl* -s) throat disease of children, with a cough
croup[2] [kroop] *n* (*pl* -s) hind quarters of a horse
croupier [kroop-ee-ay] *n* (*pl* -s) person who collects bets and pays out winnings at a gambling table in a casino
croupiers *n* ▷ croupier
croups *n* ▷ croup[1, 2]
crouton *n* (*pl* -s) small piece of fried or toasted bread served in soup
croutons *n* ▷ crouton
crow[1] *n* (*pl* -s) large black bird with a harsh call
crow[2] *v* (-s, -ing, -ed) (of a cock) make a shrill squawking sound
crowbar *n* (*pl* -s) iron bar used as a lever
crowbars *n* ▷ crowbar
crowd *n* (*pl* -s) large group of people or things ▶ *v* (-s, -ing, -ed) gather together in large numbers
crowded *v* ▷ crowd
crowding *v* ▷ crowd
crowds *n*, *v* ▷ crowd
crowed *v* ▷ crow[2]
crowing *v* ▷ crow[2]
crown *n* (*pl* -s) monarch's headdress of gold and jewels ▶ *v* (-s, -ing, -ed) put a crown on the head of (someone) to proclaim him or her monarch
crowned *v* ▷ crown
crowning *v* ▷ crown
crowns *n*, *v* ▷ crown
crows *n* ▷ crow[1] ▶ *v* ▷ crow[2]
crozier, crosier *n* (*pl* -s) bishop's hooked staff
croziers *n* ▷ crozier
crucial *adj* very important ▷ **crucially** *adv*

crucially *adv* ▷ crucial
crucible *n* (*pl* -s) pot in which metals are melted
crucibles *n* ▷ crucible
crucified *v* ▷ crucify
crucifies *v* ▷ crucify
crucifix *n* (*pl* -es) model of Christ on the Cross
crucifixes *n* ▷ crucify
crucifixion *n* (*pl* -s) crucifying
crucifixions *n* ▷ crucifixion
cruciform *adj* cross-shaped
crucify *v* (-fies, -fying, -fied) put to death by fastening to a cross
crucifying *v* ▷ crucify
crude *adj* (-r, -st) rough and simple ▶ **crudely** *adv* ▶ **crudeness** *n* (*pl* -es) ▶ **crudity** *n* (*pl* -ties)
crudely *adv* ▷ crude
crudeness *n* ▷ crude
crudenesses *n* ▷ crude
cruder *adj* ▷ crude
crudest *adj* ▷ crude
crudities *n* ▷ crude
crudity *n* ▷ crude
cruel *adj* (-ller, -llest) delighting in others' pain ▶ **cruelly** *adv* ▶ **cruelty** *n* (*pl* -ties)
crueller *adj* ▷ cruel
cruellest *adj* ▷ cruel
cruelly *adv* ▷ cruel
cruelties *n* ▷ cruel
cruelty *n* ▷ cruel
cruet *n* (*pl* -s) small container for salt, pepper, etc., at table
cruets *n* ▷ cruet
cruise *n* (*pl* -s) sail for pleasure ▶ *v* (**cruises**, **cruising**, **cruised**) sail from place to place for pleasure
cruised *v* ▷ cruise
cruiser *n* (*pl* -s) fast warship
cruisers *n* ▷ cruiser
cruises *n*, *v* ▷ cruise
cruising *v* ▷ cruise
crumb *n* (*pl* -s) small fragment of bread or other dry food
crumble *v* (-bles, -bling, -bled) break into fragments ▶ *n* (*pl* -s) pudding of stewed fruit with a crumbly topping ▶ **crumbly** *adj* (-blier, -bliest)
crumbled *v* ▷ crumble
crumbles *v*, *n* ▷ crumble
crumblier *adj* ▷ crumble
crumbliest *adj* ▷ crumble
crumbling *v* ▷ crumble
crumbly *adj* ▷ crumble
crumbs *n* ▷ crumb
crummier *adj* ▷ crummy

crummiest *adj* ▷ crummy
crummy *adj* (-mier, -miest) (*Slang*) of poor quality
crumpet *n* (*pl* -s) round soft yeast cake, eaten buttered
crumpets *n* ▷ crumpet
crumple *v* (-ples, -pling, -pled) crush, crease ▶ **crumpled** *adj*
crumpled *v*, *adj* ▷ crumple
crumples *v* ▷ crumple
crumpling *v* ▷ crumple
crunch *v* (-es, -ing, -ed) bite or chew with a noisy crushing sound ▶ *n* (*pl* -es) crunching sound (*Informal*) ▶ **crunchy** *adj* (-chier, -chiest)
crunched *v* ▷ crunch
crunches *v*, *n* ▷ crunch
crunchier *adj* ▷ crunch
crunchiest *adj* ▷ crunch
crunching *v* ▷ crunch
crunchy *adj* ▷ crunch
crupper *n* (*pl* -s) strap that passes from the back of a saddle under a horse's tail
cruppers *n* ▷ crupper
crusade *n* (*pl* -s) medieval Christian war to recover the Holy Land from the Muslims ▶ *v* (-sades, -sading, -saded) take part in a crusade
crusaded *v* ▷ crusade
crusader *n* (*pl* -s) person who took part in the medieval Christian war to recover the Holy Land from the Muslims
crusaders *n* ▷ crusader
crusades *n*, *v* ▷ crusade
crusading *v* ▷ crusade
crush *v* (-es, -ing, -ed) compress so as to injure, break, or crumple ▶ *n* (*pl* -es) dense crowd
crushed *v* ▷ crush
crushes *v*, *n* ▷ crush
crushing *v* ▷ crush
crust *n* (*pl* -s) hard outer part of something, esp. bread ▶ *v* (-s, -ing, -ed) cover with or form a crust
crustacean *n* (*pl* -s) hard-shelled, usu. aquatic animal with several pairs of legs, such as the crab or lobster
crustaceans *n* ▷ crustacean
crusted *v* ▷ crust
crustier *adj* ▷ crusty
crustiest *adj* ▷ crusty
crusting *v* ▷ crust
crusts *n*, *v* ▷ crust
crusty *adj* (-tier, -tiest) having a crust
crutch *n* (*pl* -es) long sticklike support with a rest for the armpit, used by a lame person
crutches *n* ▷ crutch

crux *n* (*pl* **-es**) crucial or decisive point
  cruxes *n* ▷ crux
cry *v* (**cries, crying, cried**) shed tears ▶ *n* (*pl* **cries**) fit of weeping
  crybabies *n* ▷ crybaby
crybaby *n* (*pl* **-babies**) person, esp. a child, who cries too readily
  crying *v* ▷ cry
  cryogenic *adj* ▷ cryogenics
cryogenics *n* branch of physics concerned with very low temperatures > **cryogenic** *adj*
crypt *n* (*pl* **-s**) vault under a church, esp. one used as a burial place
cryptic *adj* obscure in meaning, secret > **cryptically** *adv*
  cryptographer *n* ▷ cryptography
  cryptographers *n* ▷ cryptography
cryptography *n* art of writing in and deciphering codes > **cryptographer** *n* (*pl* **-s**)
  crypts *n* ▷ crypt
crystal *n* (*pl* **-s**) (single grain of) a symmetrically shaped solid formed naturally by some substances ▶ *adj* bright and clear
crystalline *adj* of or like crystal or crystals
  crystallization *n* ▷ crystallize
  crystallizations *n* ▷ crystallize
crystallize *v* (**-lizes, -lizing, -lized**) make or become definite > **crystallization** *n* (*pl* **-s**)
  crystallized *v* ▷ crystallize
  crystallizes *v* ▷ crystallize
  crystallizing *v* ▷ crystallize
  crystals *n* ▷ crystal
cub *n* (*pl* **-s**) young wild animal such as a bear or fox ▶ *v* (**cubs, cubbing, cubbed**) give birth to cubs
  cubbed *v* ▷ cub
  cubbing *v* ▷ cub
cubbyhole *n* (*pl* **-s**) small enclosed space or room
  cubbyholes *n* ▷ cubbyhole
cube *n* (*pl* **-s**) object with six equal square sides ▶ *v* (**cubes, cubing, cubed**) cut into cubes
  cubed *v* ▷ cube
  cubes *n, v* ▷ cube
cubic *adj* having three dimensions
cubicle *n* (*pl* **-s**) enclosed part of a large room, screened for privacy
  cubicles *n* ▷ cubicle
  cubing *v* ▷ cube
cubism *n* style of art in which objects are represented by geometrical shapes > **cubist** *adj, n* (*pl* **-s**)
  cubists *n* ▷ cubist
  cubs *n, v* ▷ cub
cuckold *n* (*pl* **-s**) man whose wife has been unfaithful ▶ *v* (**-s, -ing, -ed**) be unfaithful to (one's husband)
  cuckolded *v* ▷ cuckold
  cuckolding *v* ▷ cuckold
  cuckolds *n, v* ▷ cuckold
cuckoo *n* (*pl* **-s**) migratory bird with a characteristic two-note call, which lays its eggs in the nests of other birds ▶ *adj* (*Informal*) insane or foolish
  cuckoos *n* ▷ cuckoo
cucumber *n* (*pl* **-s**) long green-skinned fleshy fruit used in salads
  cucumbers *n* ▷ cucumber
cud *n* (*pl* **-s**) partially digested food which a ruminant brings back into its mouth to chew again
cuddle *v* (**cuddles, cuddling, cuddled**) ▶ *n* (*pl* **-s**) hug > **cuddly** *adj* (**-lier, -liest**)
  cuddled *v* ▷ cuddle
  cuddles *v, n* ▷ cuddle
  cuddlier *adj* ▷ cuddle
  cuddliest *adj* ▷ cuddle
  cuddling *v* ▷ cuddle
  cuddly *adj* ▷ cuddle
cudgel *n* (*pl* **-s**) short thick stick used as a weapon
  cudgels *n* ▷ cudgel
  cuds *n* ▷ cud
cue[1] *n* (*pl* **-s**) signal to an actor or musician to begin speaking or playing ▶ *v* (**cues, cueing, cued**) give a cue to
cue[2] *n* long tapering stick used in billiards, snooker, or pool ▶ *v* (**cues, cueing, cued**) hit (a ball) with a cue
  cued *v* ▷ cue[1, 2]
  cueing *v* ▷ cue[1, 2]
  cues *n, v* ▷ cue[1, 2]
cuff[1] *n* (*pl* **-s**) end of a sleeve
cuff[2] (BRIT, AUST & NZ) *v* (**-s, -ing, -ed**) hit with an open hand ▶ *n* (*pl* **-s**) blow with an open hand
  cuffed *v* ▷ cuff[2]
  cuffing *v* ▷ cuff[2]
  cuffs *n* ▷ cuff[1, 2], *v* ▷ cuff[2]
cuisine [quiz-zeen] *n* (*pl* **-s**) style of cooking
  cuisines *n* ▷ cuisine
culinary *adj* of kitchens or cookery
cull *v* (**-s, -ing, -ed**) choose, gather ▶ *n* (*pl* **-s**) culling
  culled *v* ▷ cull
  culling *v* ▷ cull
  culls *v, n* ▷ cull
culminate *v* (**-nates, -nating, -nated**) reach the highest point or climax > **culmination** *n* (*pl* **-s**)
  culminated *v* ▷ culminate

culminates v ▷ culminate
culminating v ▷ culminate
culmination n ▷ culminate
culminations n ▷ culminate
culottes pl n women's knee-length trousers cut to look like a skirt
culpabilities n ▷ culpable
culpability n ▷ culpable
culpable adj deserving blame > **culpability** n (pl -**ties**)> **culpably** adv
culpably adv ▷ culpable
culprit n (pl -**s**) person guilty of an offence or misdeed
culprits n ▷ culprit
cult n (pl -**s**) specific system of worship
cultivate v (-**vates, -vating, -vated**) prepare (land) to grow crops > **cultivation** n
cultivated adj well-educated ▶ v ▷ cultivate
cultivates v ▷ cultivate
cultivating v ▷ cultivate
cultivation n ▷ cultivate
cults n ▷ cult
cultural adj ▷ culture
culturally adv ▷ culture
culture n (pl -**s**) ideas, customs, and art of a particular society > **cultural** adj > **culturally** adv
cultured adj showing good taste or manners
cultures n ▷ culture
culvert n (pl -**s**) drain under a road or railway
culverts n ▷ culvert
cumbersome adj awkward because of size or shape
cumin, cummin n (pl -**s**) sweet-smelling seeds of a Mediterranean plant, used in cooking
cumins n ▷ cumin
cummerbund n (pl -**s**) wide sash worn round the waist
cummerbunds n ▷ cummerbund
cummin n ▷ cumin
cummins n ▷ cumin
cumulative adj increasing steadily > **cumulatively** adv
cumulatively adv ▷ cumulative
cumuli n ▷ cumulus
cumulus [kew-**myew**-luss] n (pl -**li**) thick white or dark grey cloud
cuneiform [kew-**nif**-form] n, adj (written in) an ancient system of writing using wedge-shaped characters
cunjevoi n (pl -**s**) (AUST) plant of tropical Asia and Australia with small flowers, cultivated for its edible rhizome
cunjevois n ▷ cunjevoi
cunning adj clever at deceiving ▶ n cleverness at deceiving > **cunningly** adv
cunningly adv ▷ cunning
cup n (pl -**s**) small bowl-shaped drinking container with a handle ▶ v (**cups, cupping, cupped**) form (one's hands) into the shape of a cup > **cupful** n (pl -**s**)
cupboard n (pl -**s**) piece of furniture or alcove with a door, for storage
cupboards n ▷ cupboard
cupful n ▷ cup
cupfuls n ▷ cup
cupidity [kew-**pid**-it-ee] n greed for money or possessions
cupola [kew-pol-la] n (pl -**s**) domed roof or ceiling
cupolas n ▷ cupola
cupped v ▷ cup
cupping v ▷ cup
cups n, v ▷ cup
cur n (pl -**s**) (Lit) mongrel dog
curable adj ▷ cure
curaçao [kew-rah-so] n orange-flavoured liqueur
curacies n ▷ curacy
curacy [kew-rah-see] n (pl -**cies**) work or position of a curate
curare [kew-**rah**-ree] n (pl -**s**) poisonous resin of a S American tree, used as a muscle relaxant in medicine
curares n ▷ curare
curate n (pl -**s**) clergyman who assists a parish priest
curates n ▷ curate
curative adj, n (pl -**s**) (something) able to cure
curatives n ▷ curative
curator n (pl -**s**) person in charge of a museum or art gallery > **curatorship** n (pl -**s**)
curators n ▷ curator
curatorship n ▷ curator
curatorships n ▷ curator
curb n (pl -**s**) something that restrains ▶ v (-**s, -ing, -ed**) control, restrain
curbed v ▷ curb
curbing v ▷ curb
curbs n, v ▷ curb
curd n (pl -**s**) coagulated milk, used to make cheese
curdle v (-**dles, -dling, -dled**) turn into curd, coagulate
curdled v ▷ curdle
curdles v ▷ curdle
curdling v ▷ curdle
curds n ▷ curd
cure v (**cures, curing, cured**) get rid of (an illness or problem) ▶ n (pl -**s**) (treatment

causing) curing of an illness or person
> **curable** adj
cured v ▷ cure
cures v, n ▷ cure
curettage n ▷ curette
curettages n ▷ curette
curette n (pl -s) surgical instrument for scraping tissue from body cavities ▶ v (**curettes, curetting, curetted**) scrape with a curette > **curettage** n (pl -s)
curetted v ▷ curette
curettes n, v ▷ curette
curetting v ▷ curette
curfew n (pl -s) law ordering people to stay inside their homes after a specific time at night
curfews n ▷ curfew
curie n (pl -s) standard unit of radioactivity
curies n ▷ curie
curing v ▷ cure
curio n rare or unusual object valued as a collector's item
curios n ▷ curio
curiosities n ▷ curiosity
curiosity n eagerness to know or find out (pl -**ties**)
curiously adv ▷ curious
curious adj eager to learn or know > **curiously** adv
curl n (pl -s) curved piece of hair ▶ v (-**s, -ing, -ed**) make (hair) into curls or (of hair) grow in curls > **curler** n (pl -s) > **curly** adj (-**lier, -liest**)
curled v ▷ curl
curler n ▷ curl
curlers n ▷ curl
curlew n (pl -s) long-billed wading bird
curlews n ▷ curlew
curlier adj ▷ curl
curliest adj ▷ curl
curling n game like bowls, played with heavy stones on ice ▶ v ▷ curl
curls n, v ▷ curl
curly adj ▷ curl
curmudgeon n (pl -s) bad-tempered person > **curmudgeonly** adj
curmudgeonly adj ▷ curmudgeon
curmudgeons n ▷ curmudgeon
currajong n (pl -s) ▷ kurrajong
currajongs n ▷ currajong
currant n (pl -s) small dried grape
currants n ▷ currant
currawong n (pl -s) Australian songbird
currawongs n ▷ currawong
currencies n ▷ currency
currency n (pl -**cies**) money in use in a

particular country
current adj of the immediate present ▶ n (pl -s) flow of water or air in one direction > **currently** adv
currently adv ▷ current
currents n ▷ current
curricula n ▷ curriculum
curriculum n (pl -**la, -lums**) all the courses of study offered by a school or college
curriculums n ▷ curriculum
curried v ▷ curry[1, 2]
curries n ▷ curry[1] ▶ v ▷ curry[1, 2]
curry[1] n (pl -**ries**) Indian dish of meat or vegetables in a hot spicy sauce ▶ v (-**ries, -rying, -ried**) prepare (food) with curry powder
curry[2] v (-**ries, -rying, -ried**) groom (a horse)
currying v ▷ curry[1, 2]
curs n ▷ cur
curse v (**curses, cursing, cursed**) swear (at) ▶ n (pl -s) swearword > **cursed** adj
cursed adj, v ▷ curse
curses v, n ▷ curse
cursing v ▷ curse
cursive adj, n (pl -s) (handwriting) done with joined letters > **cursively** adv
cursively adv ▷ cursive
cursives n ▷ cursive
cursor n (pl -s) movable point of light that shows a specific position on a visual display unit
cursorily adv ▷ cursory
cursoriness n ▷ cursory
cursors n ▷ cursor
cursory adj quick and superficial > **cursorily** adv > **cursoriness** n
curt adj (-**er, -est**) brief and rather rude > **curtly** adv > **curtness** n (pl -es)
curtail v (-**s, -ing, -ed**) cut short > **curtailment** n (pl -s)
curtailed v ▷ curtail
curtailing v ▷ curtail
curtailment n ▷ curtail
curtailments n ▷ curtail
curtails v ▷ curtail
curtain n (pl -s) piece of cloth hung at a window or opening as a screen ▶ v (-**s, -ing, -ed**) provide with curtains
curtained v ▷ curtain
curtaining v ▷ curtain
curtains n, v ▷ curtain
curter adj ▷ curt
curtest adj ▷ curt
curtly adv ▷ curt
curtness n ▷ curt

curtnesses *n* ▷ curt
curtsey *n* ▷ curtsy
curtseyed *v* ▷ curtsy
curtseying *v* ▷ curtsy
curtseys *n, v* ▷ curtsy
curtsied *v* ▷ curtsy
curtsies *n, v* ▷ curtsy
curtsy, curtsey *n* (*pl* -**sies**, -**seys**) woman's gesture of respect made by bending the knees and bowing the head ▶ *v* (-**sies**, -**seys**, -**sying**, -**sied** *or* -**seying**) (-**seyed**) make a curtsy
curtsying *v* ▷ curtsy
curvaceous *adj* (*Informal*) (of a woman) having a shapely body
curvature *n* (*pl* -**s**) curved shape
curvatures *n* ▷ curvature
curve *n* (*pl* -**s**) continuously bending line with no straight parts ▶ *v* (**curves, curving, curved**) form or move in a curve > **curvy** *adj* (-**vier, -viest**)
curved *v* ▷ curve
curves *n, v* ▷ curve
curvier *adj* ▷ curve
curviest *adj* ▷ curve
curvilinear *adj* consisting of or bounded by a curve
curving *v* ▷ curve
curvy *adj* ▷ curve
cuscus *n* (*pl* -**ses**) large Australian nocturnal possum
cuscuses *n* ▷ cuscus
cushier *adj* ▷ cushy
cushiest *adj* ▷ cushy
cushion *n* (*pl* -**s**) bag filled with soft material, to make a seat more comfortable ▶ *v* (-**s, -ing, -ed**) lessen the effects of
cushioned *v* ▷ cushion
cushioning *v* ▷ cushion
cushions *n, v* ▷ cushion
cushy *adj* (**cushier, cushiest**) (*Informal*) easy
cusp *n* (*pl* -**s**) pointed end, esp. on a tooth
cusps (*Informal*) *n* (*pl* -**es**) curse, oath ▶ *v* (-**es, -ing, -ed**) swear (at)
cussed [kuss-id] *adj* (*Informal*) obstinate ▶ *v* ▷ cuss > **cussedly** *adv* > **cussedness** *n*
cussedly *adv* ▷ cussed
cussedness *n* ▷ cussed
cusses *n, v* ▷ cuss
cussing *v* ▷ cuss
custard *n* (*pl* -**s**) sweet yellow sauce made from milk and eggs
custards *n* ▷ custard
custodial *adj* ▷ custody

custodian *n* (*pl* -**s**) person in charge of a public building
custodians *n* ▷ custodian
custodies *n* ▷ custody
custody *n* (*pl* -**dies**) protective care > **custodial** *adj*
custom *n* (*pl* -**s**) long-established activity or action ▶ *pl* duty charged on imports or exports
customarily *adv* ▷ customary
customary *adj* usual > **customarily** *adv*
customer *n* (*pl* **s**) person who buys goods or services
customers *n* ▷ customer
customs *n* ▷ custom
cut *v* (**cuts, cutting, cut**) open up, penetrate, wound, or divide with a sharp instrument ▶ *n* (*pl* -**s**) stroke or incision made by cutting
cutaneous [kew-**tane**-ee-uss] *adj* of the skin
cute *adj* (**cuter, cutest**) appealing or attractive > **cutely** *adv* > **cuteness** *n*
cutely *adv* ▷ cute
cuteness *n* ▷ cute
cuter *adj* ▷ cute
cutest *adj* ▷ cute
cuticle *n* (*pl* -**s**) skin at the base of a fingernail or toenail
cuticles *n* ▷ cuticle
cutlass *n* (*pl* -**es**) curved one-edged sword formerly used by sailors
cutlasses *n* ▷ cutlass
cutler *n* (*pl* -**s**) maker of cutlery
cutlers *n* ▷ cutler
cutlery *n* knives, forks, and spoons
cutlet *n* (*pl* -**s**) small piece of meat like a chop
cutlets *n* ▷ cutlet
cuts *v, n* ▷ cut
cutter *n* (*pl* -**s**) person or tool that cuts
cutters *n* ▷ cutter
cutting *n* (*pl* -**s**) article cut from a newspaper or magazine ▶ *adj* (of a remark) hurtful ▶ *v* ▷ cut > **cuttingly** *adv*
cuttingly *adv* ▷ cutting
cuttings *n* ▷ cutting
cuttlefish *n* (*pl* **cuttlefish**) squidlike sea mollusc

> **cuz** *n* (**cuzzes**). Like **coz**, cuz is an old word for **cousin**. You need a blank tile for the second Z if you're going to play the plural. Cuz scores 14 points.
> **cwm** *n* (**cwms**). Cwm is a Welsh word for a valley. It's a useful one to remember because it doesn't contain any vowels. Cwm scores 10 points.

cyanide *n* (*pl* -**s**) extremely poisonous chemical

compound

cyanides n ▷ cyanide

cybernetics n branch of science in which electronic and mechanical systems are studied and compared to biological systems

cyberspace n place said to contain all the data stored in computers

cyclamen [**sik**-la-men] n (pl **-s**) plant with red, pink, or white flowers

cyclamens n ▷ cyclamen

cycle v (**cycles, cycling, cycled**) ride a bicycle ▶ n (pl **-s**) (BRIT, AUST & NZ) bicycle

cycled v ▷ cycle

cycles v, n ▷ cycle

cyclic adj ▷ cyclical

cyclical, cyclic adj occurring in cycles > **cyclically** adv

cyclically adv ▷ cyclical

cycling v ▷ cycle

cyclist n (pl **-s**) person who rides a bicycle

cyclists n ▷ cyclist

cyclone n (pl **-s**) violent wind moving round a central area

cyclones n ▷ cyclone

cyclotron n (pl **-s**) apparatus that accelerates charged particles by means of a strong vertical magnetic field

cyclotrons n ▷ cyclotron

cygnet n (pl **-s**) young swan

cygnets n ▷ cygnet

cylinder n (pl **-s**) solid or hollow body with straight sides and circular ends > **cylindrical** adj

cylinders n ▷ cylinder

cylindrical adj ▷ cylinder

cymbal n (pl **-s**) percussion instrument consisting of a brass plate which is struck

against another or hit with a stick

cymbals n ▷ cymbal

cynic [**sin**-ik] n (pl **-s**) person who believes that people always act selfishly > **cynical** adj > **cynically** adv > **cynicism** n

cynical adj ▷ cynic

cynically adv ▷ cynic

cynicism n ▷ cynic

cynics n ▷ cynic

cynosure [**sin**-oh-zyure] n (pl **-s**) centre of attention

cynosures n ▷ cynosure

cypher n (pl **-s**) ▷ cipher

cyphers n ▷ cypher

cypress n (pl **-es**) evergreen tree with dark green leaves

cypresses n ▷ cypress

cyst [**sist**] n (pl **-s**) (abnormal) sac in the body containing fluid or soft matter > **cystic** adj

cystic adj ▷ cyst

cystitis [siss-**tite**-iss] n inflammation of the bladder

cysts n ▷ cyst

cytological adj ▷ cytology

cytologically adv ▷ cytology

cytologies n ▷ cytology

cytologist n ▷ cytology

cytologists n ▷ cytology

cytology [site-**ol**-a-jee] n (pl **-logies**) study of plant and animal cells > **cytological** adj > **cytologically** adv > **cytologist** n (pl **-s**)

czar [**zahr**] n (pl **-s**) ▷ tsar > **czarism** n > **czarist** adj, n (pl **-s**)

czarism n ▷ czar

czarist n ▷ czar

czarists n ▷ czar

czars n ▷ czar

Dd

D only starts a handful of two-letter words, but it does form a two-letter word before every vowel except U. There are plenty of good three-letter words beginning with D, particularly those with a Y or W: **day**, **dye** and **dew** are worth 7 points each, for example.

da n (**das**). A da is a Burmese knife. Da scores 3 points.

dab¹ v (**-s, -bbing, -bbed**) pat lightly ▶ n (pl **-s**) small amount of something soft or moist

dab² n (pl **-s**) small European flatfish with rough scales

   dabbed v ▷ dab¹

   dabbing v ▷ dab¹

dabble v (**-les, -ling, -led**) be involved in something superficially > **dabbler** n (pl **-s**)

   dabbled v ▷ dabble

   dabbler n ▷ dabble

   dabblers n ▷ dabble

   dabbles v ▷ dabble

   dabbling v ▷ dabble

   dabs n ▷ dab¹, ² ▶ v ▷ dab¹

dace n (pl dace) small European freshwater fish

dachshund n (pl **-s**) dog with a long body and short legs

   dachshunds n ▷ dachshund

dad n (pl **-s**) (Informal) father

   daddies n ▷ daddy

daddy n (pl **-dies**) (Informal) father

dado [day-doe] n (pl **-does, -dos**) lower part of an interior wall, below a rail, decorated differently from the upper part

   dadoes n ▷ dado

   dados n ▷ dado

   dads n ▷ dad

daffodil n (pl **-s**) yellow trumpet-shaped flower that blooms in spring

   daffodils n ▷ daffodil

daft adj (**-er, -est**) (Informal) foolish or crazy > **daftness** n (pl **-es**)

   dafter adj ▷ daft

   daftest adj ▷ daft

   daftness n ▷ daft

   daftnesses n ▷ daft

dag (NZ) n (pl **-s**) dried dung on a sheep's rear (Informal) ▶ v (**-s, -gging, -gged**) remove the dags from a sheep

dagga n (pl **-s**) (S AFR) (Informal) cannabis

   daggas n ▷ dagga

   dagged v ▷ dag

dagger n (pl **-s**) short knifelike weapon with a pointed blade

   daggers n ▷ dagger

   daggier adj ▷ daggy

   daggiest adj ▷ daggy

   dagging v ▷ dag

daggy adj (**-ggier, -ggiest**) (NZ) (Informal) amusing

   dags n, v ▷ dag

daguerreotype [dag-**gair**-oh-type] n (pl **-s**) type of early photograph produced on chemically treated silver

   daguerreotypes n ▷ daguerreotype

dahlia [day-lya] n (pl **-s**) brightly coloured garden flower

   dahlias n ▷ dahlia

   dailies n ▷ daily

daily adj occurring every day or every weekday ▶ adv every day ▶ n (pl **-lies**) daily newspaper

   daintier adj ▷ dainty

   daintiest adj ▷ dainty

   daintily adv ▷ dainty

dainty adj (**-tier, -tiest**) delicate or elegant > **daintily** adv

daiquiri [dak-eer-ee] n (pl **-s**) iced drink containing rum, lime juice, and sugar

   daiquiris n ▷ daiquiri

   dairies n ▷ dairy

dairy n (pl **-s**) place for the processing or sale of milk and its products ▶ adj of milk or its products

dais [day-iss, dayss] n (pl **-es**) raised platform in a hall, used by a speaker

   daises n ▷ dais

   daisies n ▷ daisy

daisy n (pl **-sies**) small wild flower with a

yellow centre and white petals

dak n (daks) A dak is an old Indian mail or transport system. This is a good word to know if you have a K on your rack but can't think of a longer word in which to use it. Dak scores 8 points.

dale n (pl -s) (esp. in N England) valley
 dales n ▷ dale

dalliance n (pl -s) flirtation
 dalliances n ▷ dalliance
 dallied v ▷ dally
 dallies v ▷ dally

dally v (-lies, -lying, -lied) waste time
 dallying v ▷ dally

dalmatian n (pl -s) large dog with a white coat and black spots
 dalmatians n ▷ dalmatian

dam¹ n (pl -s) barrier built across a river to create a lake ▶ v (dams, damming, dammed) build a dam across (a river)

dam² n (pl -s) mother of an animal such as a sheep or horse

damage v (-ages, -aging, -aged) harm, spoil ▶ n (pl -s) harm to a person or thing ▶ pl money awarded as compensation for injury or loss
 damaged v ▷ damage
 damages v, n ▷ damage
 damaging v ▷ damage

damask n (pl -s) fabric with a pattern woven into it, used for tablecloths etc.
 damasks n ▷ damask

dame n (pl -s) (CHIEFLY US & CANADIAN) (Slang) woman
 dames n ▷ dame
 dammed v ▷ dam¹
 damming v ▷ dam¹

damn interj (Slang) exclamation of annoyance ▶ adv, adj (also **damned**) (Slang) extreme(ly) ▶ v (-s, -ing, -ed) condemn as bad or worthless > **damnation** interj, n (pl -s)

damnable adj annoying > **damnably** adv
 damnably adv ▷ damnable
 damnation interj, n ▷ damn
 damnations n ▷ damn
 damned v ▷ damn

damning adj proving or suggesting guilt ▶ v ▷ damn
 damns v ▷ damn

damp adj (-er, -est) slightly wet ▶ n (pl -s) slight wetness, moisture ▶ v (-s, -ing, -ed) (also **dampen**) (-s, -ing, -ed) make damp (foll. by down) > **damply** adv > **dampness** n
 damped v ▷ damp
 dampen v ▷ dampen
 dampened v ▷ dampen

dampening v ▷ dampen
 dampens v ▷ dampen

damper n (pl -s) movable plate to regulate the draught in a fire ▶ adj ▷ damp
 dampers n ▷ damper
 dampest adj ▷ damp
 damping v ▷ damp
 damply adv ▷ damp
 dampness n ▷ damp
 damps v, n ▷ damp
 dams n ▷ dam¹, ² ▶ v ▷ dam¹

damsel n (pl -s) (Old-fashioned) young woman
 damsels n ▷ damsel

damson n (pl -s) small blue-black plumlike fruit
 damsons n ▷ damson

dance v (dances, dancing, danced) move the feet and body rhythmically in time to music ▶ n (pl -s) series of steps and movements in time to music > **dancer** n (pl -s)
 danced v ▷ dance
 dancer n ▷ dance
 dancers n ▷ dance
 dances v, n ▷ dance
 dancing v ▷ dance

dandelion n (pl -s) yellow-flowered wild plant
 dandelions n ▷ dandelion

dander n (pl -s) (Slang) anger
 danders n ▷ dander
 dandier adj ▷ dandy
 dandies n ▷ dandy
 dandiest adj ▷ dandy
 dandified adj ▷ dandy

dandle v (-dles, -dling, -dled) move (a child) up and down on one's knee
 dandled v ▷ dandle
 dandles v ▷ dandle
 dandling v ▷ dandle

dandruff n (pl -s) loose scales of dry dead skin shed from the scalp
 dandruffs n ▷ dandruff

dandy n (pl -dies) man who is overconcerned with the elegance of his appearance ▶ adj (-dier, -diest) (Informal) very good > **dandified** adj

danger n (pl -s) possibility of being injured or killed > **dangerously** adv
 dangerous adj ▷ danger
 dangerously adv ▷ danger
 dangers n ▷ danger

dangle v (-gles, -gling, -gled) hang loosely
 dangled v ▷ dangle
 dangles v ▷ dangle
 dangling v ▷ dangle

dank adj (-er, -est) unpleasantly damp and

chilly > **dankly** adv > **dankness** n (pl -es)
> **danker** adj ▷ dank
> **dankest** adj ▷ dank
> **dankly** adv ▷ dank
> **dankness** n ▷ dank
> **danknesses** n ▷ dank

dapper adj (-er, -est) (of a man) neat in appearance > **dapperly** adv > **dapperness** n (pl -es)
> **dapperer** adj ▷ dapper
> **dapperest** adj ▷ dapper
> **dapperly** adv ▷ dapper
> **dapperness** n ▷ dapper
> **dappernesses** n ▷ dapper

dappled adj marked with spots of a different colour

dare v (dares, daring, dared) be courageous enough to try (to do something) ▶ n (pl -s) challenge to do something risky
> **dared** v ▷ dare

daredevil adj, n (pl -s) recklessly bold (person)
> **daredevils** n ▷ daredevil
> **dares** v, n ▷ dare

daring adj willing to take risks ▶ n courage to do dangerous things ▶ v ▷ dare > **daringly** adv
> **daringly** adv ▷ daring

dark adj (-er, -est) having little or no light ▶ n (pl -s) absence of light > **darkly** adv > **darkness** n (pl -es) > **darken** v (-s, -ing, -ed)
> **darken** v ▷ dark
> **darkened** v ▷ dark
> **darkening** v ▷ dark
> **darkens** v ▷ dark
> **darker** adj ▷ dark
> **darkest** adj ▷ dark
> **darkly** adv ▷ dark
> **darkness** n ▷ dark
> **darknesses** n ▷ dark

darkroom n (pl -s) darkened room for processing photographic film
> **darkrooms** n ▷ darkroom
> **darks** n ▷ dark

darling n (pl -s) much-loved person ▶ adj much-loved
> **darlings** n ▷ darling

darn[1] v (-s, -ing, -ed) mend (a garment) with a series of interwoven stitches ▶ n (pl -s) patch of darned work

darn[2] interj, adv, adj, v (-s, -ing, -ed) (Euphemistic) damn
> **darned** v ▷ darn[1, 2]
> **darning** v ▷ darn[1, 2]
> **darns** v ▷ darn[1, 2] ▶ n ▷ darn[1]

dart n (pl -s) small narrow pointed missile that is thrown or shot, esp. in the game of

darts ▶ pl game in which darts are thrown at a circular numbered board ▶ v (-s, -ing, -ed) move or direct quickly and suddenly
> **darted** v ▷ dart
> **darting** v ▷ dart
> **darts** n, v ▷ dart

dash v (-es, -ing, -ed) move quickly ▶ n (pl -es) sudden quick movement

dashboard n (pl -s) instrument panel in a vehicle
> **dashboards** n ▷ dashboard
> **dashed** v ▷ dash
> **dashes** v, n ▷ dash

dashing adj stylish and attractive ▶ v ▷ dash > **dashingly** adv
> **dashingly** adv ▷ dashing

dassie n (pl -s) (S AFR) type of hoofed rodent-like animal (also **hyrax**)
> **dassies** n ▷ dassie
> **dastardliness** n ▷ dastardly

dastardly adj wicked and cowardly > **dastardliness** n
> **dastardliness** n ▷ dastardly

dasyure [dass-ee-your] n (pl -s) small marsupial of Australia, New Guinea, and adjacent islands
> **dasyures** n ▷ dasyure

data n information consisting of observations, measurements, or facts

date[1] n (pl -s) specified day of the month ▶ v (dates, dating, dated) mark with the date

date[2] n (pl -s) dark-brown sweet-tasting fruit of the date palm

dated adj old-fashioned ▶ v ▷ date[1]
> **dates** n ▷ date[1, 2] ▶ v ▷ date[1]
> **dating** v ▷ date[1]

dative n (pl -s) (in certain languages) the form of the noun that expresses the indirect object
> **datives** n ▷ dative

datum n (pl data) single piece of information in the form of a fact or statistic

daub v (-s, -ing, -ed) smear or spread quickly or clumsily
> **daubed** v ▷ daub
> **daubing** v ▷ daub
> **daubs** v ▷ daub

daughter n (pl -s) female child > **daughterly** adj
> **daughterly** adj ▷ daughter
> **daughters** n ▷ daughter

daunting adj intimidating or worrying > **dauntingly** adv
> **dauntingly** adv ▷ daunting

dauntless adj fearless > **dauntlessly** adv > **dauntlessness** n
> **dauntlessly** adv ▷ dauntless
> **dauntlessness** n ▷ dauntless

dauphin [doe-fan] n (pl -s) (formerly) eldest son of the king of France
  dauphins n ▷ dauphin

davenport n (pl -s) (CHIEFLY BRIT) small writing table with drawers
  davenports n ▷ davenport

davit [dav-vit] n (pl -s) crane, usu. one of a pair, at a ship's side, for lowering and hoisting a lifeboat
  davits n ▷ davit

  ■ **daw** n (daws). A daw is another name for a **jackdaw**. Daw scores 7 points.

dawdle v (-dles, -dling, -dled) walk slowly, lag behind
  dawdled v ▷ dawdle
  dawdles v ▷ dawdle
  dawdling v ▷ dawdle

dawn n (pl -s) daybreak ▶ v (-s, -ing, -ed) begin to grow light
  dawned v ▷ dawn
  dawning v ▷ dawn
  dawns n, v ▷ dawn

day n (pl -s) period of 24 hours

daybreak n time in the morning when light first appears

daydream n (pl -s) pleasant fantasy indulged in while awake ▶ v (-s, -ing, -ed) indulge in idle fantasy > **daydreamer** n (pl -s)
  daydreamed v ▷ daydream
  daydreamer n ▷ daydream
  daydreamers n ▷ daydream
  daydreaming v ▷ daydream
  daydreams n, v ▷ daydream

daylight n light from the sun
  days n ▷ day

daze v (dazes, dazing, dazed) stun, by a blow or shock ▶ n (pl -s) state of confusion or shock
  dazed v ▷ daze
  dazes v, n ▷ daze
  dazing v ▷ daze

dazzle v (-zles, -zling, -zled) impress greatly ▶ n (pl -s) bright light that dazzles > **dazzling** adj > **dazzlingly** adv
  dazzled v ▷ dazzle
  dazzles v, n ▷ dazzle
  dazzling v, adj ▷ dazzle
  dazzlingly adv ▷ dazzle

  ■ **de** prep. De means of or from. This is a useful little word to fit in when trying to form several words at once. De scores 3 points.

deacon n (pl -s) (CHRISTIANITY) ordained minister ranking immediately below a priest
  deacons n ▷ deacon

dead adj (-er, -est) no longer alive ▶ n (pl -s) period during which coldness or darkness is most intense ▶ adv extremely

deadbeat n (pl -s) (Informal) lazy useless person
  deadbeats n ▷ deadbeat

deaden v (-s, -ing, -ed) make less intense
  deadened v ▷ deaden
  deadening v ▷ deaden
  deadens v ▷ deaden
  deader adj ▷ dead
  deadest adj ▷ dead
  deadlier adj ▷ deadly
  deadliest adj ▷ deadly

deadline n (pl -s) time limit
  deadlines n ▷ deadline
  deadliness n ▷ deadly

deadlock n (pl -s) point in a dispute at which no agreement can be reached > **deadlocked** adj
  deadlocked adj ▷ deadlock
  deadlocks n ▷ deadlock

deadly adj (-lier, -liest) likely to cause death ▶ adv extremely > **deadliness** n

deadpan adj, adv showing no emotion or expression
  deads n ▷ dead

deaf adj (-er, -est) unable to hear > **deafness** n (pl -es)

deafen v (-s, -ing, -ed) make deaf, esp. temporarily
  deafened v ▷ deafen
  deafening v ▷ deafen
  deafens v ▷ deafen
  deafer adj ▷ deaf
  deafest adj ▷ deaf
  deafness n ▷ deaf
  deafnesses n ▷ deaf

deal[1] n (pl -s) agreement or transaction ▶ v (deals, dealing, dealt) inflict (a blow) on > **dealer** n (pl -s)

deal[2] n (pl -s) plank of fir or pine wood
  dealer n ▷ deal[1]
  dealers n ▷ deal[1]
  dealing v ▷ deal[1]

dealings pl n transactions or business relations
  deals v ▷ deal[1] ▶ n ▷ deal[1, 2]
  dealt v ▷ deal[1]

dean n (pl -s) chief administrative official of a college or university faculty
  deaneries n ▷ deanery

deanery n (pl -eries) office or residence of a dean
  deans n ▷ dean

dear n (pl -s) someone regarded with affection ▶ adj (-er, -est) much-loved > **dearly** adv

> **dearness** n (pl -es)
dearer adj ▷ dear
dearest adj ▷ dear
dearly adv ▷ dear
dearness n ▷ dear
dearnesses n ▷ dear
dears n ▷ dear
dearth [dirth] n (pl -s) inadequate amount, scarcity
dearths n ▷ dearth
death n (pl -s) permanent end of life in a person or animal
deathly adj, adv like death
deaths n ▷ death
deb n (pl -s) (Informal) debutante
debacle [day-bah-kl] n (pl -s) disastrous failure
debacles n ▷ debacle
debar v (-bars, -barring, -barred) prevent, bar
debarred v ▷ debar
debarring v ▷ debar
debars v ▷ debar
debase v (-bases, -basing, -based) lower in value, quality, or character > **debasement** n (pl -s)
debased v ▷ debase
debasement n ▷ debase
debasements n ▷ debase
debases v ▷ debase
debasing v ▷ debase
debatable adj not absolutely certain > **debatably** adv
debate n (pl -s) discussion ▶ v (-bates, -bating, -bated) discuss formally
debated v ▷ debate
debates n, v ▷ debate
debating v ▷ debate
debauch [dib-bawch] v (-es, -ing, -ed) make (someone) bad or corrupt, esp. sexually > **debauchery** n (pl -eries)
debauched adj immoral, sexually corrupt ▶ v ▷ debauch
debaucheries n ▷ debauch
debauchery n ▷ debauch
debauches v ▷ debauch
debauching v ▷ debauch
debenture n (pl -s) long-term bond bearing fixed interest, issued by a company or a government agency
debentures n ▷ debenture
debilitate v (-tates, -tating, -tated) weaken, make feeble > **debilitation** n
debilitated v ▷ debilitate
debilitates v ▷ debilitate
debilitating v ▷ debilitate
debilitation n ▷ debilitate

debilities n ▷ debility
debility n (pl -ities) weakness, infirmity
debit n (pl -s) acknowledgment of a sum owing by entry on the left side of an account ▶ v (-s, -ing, -ed) charge (an account) with a debt
debited v ▷ debit
debiting v ▷ debit
debits n, v ▷ debit
debonair adj (of a man) charming and refined
debouch v (-es, -ing, -ed) move out from a narrow place to a wider one
debouched v ▷ debouch
debouches v ▷ debouch
debouching v ▷ debouch
debrief v (-s, -ing, -ed) receive a report from (a soldier, diplomat, etc.) after an event > **debriefing** n (pl -s)
debriefed v ▷ debrief
debriefing v, n ▷ debrief
debriefings n ▷ debrief
debriefs v ▷ debrief
debris [deb-ree] n fragments of something destroyed
debs n ▷ deb
debt n (pl -s) something owed, esp. money > **debtor** n (pl -s)
debtor n ▷ debt
debtors n ▷ debt
debts n ▷ debt
debunk v (-s, -ing, -ed) (Informal) expose the falseness of
debunked v ▷ debunk
debunking v ▷ debunk
debunks v ▷ debunk
debut [day-byoo] n (pl -s) first public appearance of a performer
debutante [day-byoo-tont] n (pl -s) young upper-class woman being formally presented to society
debutantes n ▷ debutante
debuts n ▷ debut
decade n (pl -s) period of ten years
decadence n (pl -s) deterioration in morality or culture > **decadent** adj > **decadently** adv
decadences n ▷ decadence
decadent adj ▷ decadence
decadently adv ▷ decadence
decades n ▷ decade
decaffeinated [dee-kaf-fin-ate-id] adj (of coffee, tea, or cola) with caffeine removed
decagon n (pl -s) geometric figure with ten faces > **decagonal** adj
decagonal adj ▷ decagon
decagons n ▷ decagon
decahedral adj ▷ decahedron

decahedron [deck-a-**heed**-ron] *n* (*pl* -s) solid
figure with ten sides > **decahedral** *adj*
  decahedrons *n* ▷ decahedron
decamp *v* (-s, -ing, -ed) depart secretly or
suddenly
  decamped *v* ▷ decamp
  decamping *v* ▷ decamp
  decamps *v* ▷ decamp
decant *v* (-s, -ing, -ed) pour (a liquid) from one
container to another
  decanted *v* ▷ decant
decanter *n* (*pl* -s) stoppered bottle for wine
or spirits
  decanters *n* ▷ decanter
  decanting *v* ▷ decant
  decants *v* ▷ decant
decapitate *v* (-tates, -tating, -tated) behead
  > **decapitation** *n* (*pl* -s)
  decapitated *v* ▷ decapitate
  decapitates *v* ▷ decapitate
  decapitating *v* ▷ decapitate
  decapitation *n* ▷ decapitate
  decapitations *n* ▷ decapitate
decathlete *n* ▷ decathlon
  decathletes *n* ▷ decathlon
decathlon *n* (*pl* -s) athletic contest with ten
events > **decathlete** *n* (*pl* -s)
  decathlons *n* ▷ decathlon
decay *v* (-s, -ing, -ed) become weaker or more
corrupt ▶ *n* (*pl* -s) process of decaying
  decayed *v* ▷ decay
  decaying *v* ▷ decay
  decays *v*, *n* ▷ decay
decease *n* (*pl* -s) (*Formal*) death
  deceases *n* ▷ decease
deceased *adj* (*Formal*) dead
deceit *n* (*pl* -s) behaviour intended to deceive
  > **deceitful** *adj* > **deceitfully** *adv*
  deceitful *adj* ▷ deceit
  deceitfully *adv* ▷ deceit
  deceits *n* ▷ deceit
deceive *v* (-ceives, -ceiving, -ceived) mislead
by lying > **deceiver** *n* (*pl* -s)
  deceived *v* ▷ deceive
  deceiver *n* ▷ deceive
  deceivers *n* ▷ deceive
  deceives *v* ▷ deceive
  deceiving *v* ▷ deceive
decelerate *v* (-rates, -rating, -rated) slow
down > **deceleration** *n* (*pl* -s)
  decelerated *v* ▷ decelerate
  decelerates *v* ▷ decelerate
  decelerating *v* ▷ decelerate
  deceleration *n* ▷ decelerate
  decelerations *n* ▷ decelerate

decencies *n* ▷ decent
decency *n* ▷ decent
decent *adj* (-er, -est) (of a person) polite and
morally acceptable > **decently** *adv* > **decency**
n (*pl* -cies)
  decenter *adj* ▷ decent
  decentest *adj* ▷ decent
  decently *adv* ▷ decent
  decentralization *n* ▷ decentralize
decentralize *v* (-lizes, -lizing, -lized)
reorganize into smaller local units
  > **decentralization** *n*
  decentralized *v* ▷ decentralize
  decentralizes *v* ▷ decentralize
  decentralizing *v* ▷ decentralize
deception *n* (*pl* -s) deceiving
  deceptions *n* ▷ deception
deceptive *adj* likely or designed to deceive
  > **deceptively** *adv* > **deceptiveness** *n*
  deceptively *adv* ▷ deceptive
  deceptiveness *n* ▷ deceptive
decibel *n* (*pl* -s) unit for measuring the
intensity of sound
  decibels *n* ▷ decibel
decide *v* (-cides, -ciding, -cided) (cause to)
reach a decision
decided *adj* unmistakable ▶ *v* ▷ decide
  > **decidedly** *adv*
  decidedly *adv* ▷ decided
  decides *v* ▷ decide
  deciding *v* ▷ decide
deciduous *adj* (of a tree) shedding its leaves
annually
decimal *n* (*pl* -s) fraction written in the form
of a dot followed by one or more numbers
  ▶ *adj* relating to or using powers of ten
  > **decimalization** *n* > **decimally** *adv*
  decimalization *n* ▷ decimal
  decimally *adv* ▷ decimal
  decimals *n* ▷ decimal
decimate *v* (-mates, -mating, -mated) destroy
or kill a large proportion of > **decimation**
n (*pl* -s)
  decimated *v* ▷ decimate
  decimates *v* ▷ decimate
  decimating *v* ▷ decimate
  decimation *n* ▷ decimate
  decimations *n* ▷ decimate
decipher *v* (-s, -ing, -ed) work out the
meaning of (something illegible or in code)
  > **decipherable** *adj*
  decipherable *adj* ▷ decipher
  deciphered *v* ▷ decipher
  deciphering *v* ▷ decipher
  deciphers *v* ▷ decipher

decision n (pl -s) judgment, conclusion, or resolution
  decisions n ▷ decision
decisive adj having a definite influence
  > **decisively** adv > **decisiveness** n
  decisively adv ▷ decisive
  decisiveness n ▷ decisive
deck n (pl -s) area of a ship that forms a floor
decking n wooden platform in a garden
  decks n ▷ deck
declaim v (-s, -ing, -ed) speak loudly and dramatically > **declamation** n (pl -s)
  > **declamatory** adj
  declaimed v ▷ declaim
  declaiming v ▷ declaim
  declaims v ▷ declaim
  declamation n ▷ declaim
  declamations n ▷ declaim
  declamatory adj ▷ declaim
  declaration n ▷ declare
  declarations n ▷ declare
  declaratory adj ▷ declare
declare v (-clares, -claring, -clared) state firmly and forcefully > **declaration** n (pl -s)
  > **declaratory** adj
  declared v ▷ declare
  declares v ▷ declare
  declaring v ▷ declare
declension n (pl -s) (GRAMMAR) changes in the form of nouns, pronouns, or adjectives to show case, number, and gender
  declensions n ▷ declension
decline v (-clines, -clining, -clined) become smaller, weaker, or less important ▶ n (pl -s) gradual weakening or loss
  declined v ▷ decline
  declines v, n ▷ decline
  declining v ▷ decline
  declivities n ▷ declivity
declivity n (pl -ties) downward slope
declutch v (-es, -ing, -ed) disengage the clutch of a motor vehicle
  declutched v ▷ declutch
  declutches v ▷ declutch
  declutching v ▷ declutch
decoct v (-s, -ing, -ed) extract the essence from (a substance) by boiling > **decoction** n (pl -s)
  decocted v ▷ decoct
  decocting v ▷ decoct
  decoction n ▷ decoct
  decoctions n ▷ decoct
  decocts v ▷ decoct
decode v (-codes, -coding, -coded) convert from code into ordinary language > **decoder** n (pl -s)

  decoded v ▷ decode
  decoder n ▷ decode
  decoders n ▷ decode
  decodes v ▷ decode
  decoding v ▷ decode
décolleté [day-kol-tay] adj (of a woman's garment) low-cut
decommission v (-s, -ing, -ed) dismantle (a nuclear reactor, weapon, etc.) which is no longer needed
  decommissioned v ▷ decommission
  decommissioning v ▷ decommission
  decommissions v ▷ decommission
decompose v (-poses, -posing, -posed) be broken down through chemical or bacterial action > **decomposition** n (pl -s)
  decomposed v ▷ decompose
  decomposes v ▷ decompose
  decomposing v ▷ decompose
  decomposition n ▷ decompose
  decompositions n ▷ decompose
decompress v (-presses, -pressing, -pressed) free from pressure > **decompression** n (pl -s)
  decompressed v ▷ decompress
  decompresses v ▷ decompress
  decompressing v ▷ decompress
  decompression n ▷ decompress
  decompressions n ▷ decompress
decongestant n (pl -s) medicine that relieves nasal congestion
  decongestants n ▷ decongestant
decontaminate v (-nates, -nating, -nated) make safe by removing poisons, radioactivity, etc. > **decontamination** n (pl -s)
  decontaminated v ▷ decontaminate
  decontaminates v ▷ decontaminate
  decontaminating v ▷ decontaminate
  decontamination n ▷ decontaminate
  decontaminations n ▷ decontaminate
decor [day-core] n (pl -s) style in which a room or house is decorated
decorate v (-rates, -rating, -rated) make more attractive by adding something ornamental
  > **decoration** n (pl -s) > **decorative** adj
  > **decorator** n (pl -s)
  decorated v ▷ decorate
  decorates v ▷ decorate
  decorating v ▷ decorate
  decoration n ▷ decorate
  decorations n ▷ decorate
  decorator n ▷ decorate
  decorators n ▷ decorate
decorous [dek-a-russ] adj polite, calm, and sensible in behaviour > **decorously** adv
  > **decorousness** n

decorously adv ▷ decorous

decorousness n ▷ decorous

decors n ▷ decor

decorum [dik-core-um] n (pl -s) polite and socially correct behaviour

decorums n ▷ decorum

decoy n (pl -s) person or thing used to lure someone into danger ▶ v (-s, -ing, -ed) lure away by means of a trick

decoyed v ▷ decoy

decoying v ▷ decoy

decoys n, v ▷ decoy

decrease v (-creases, -creasing, -creased) make or become less ▶ n (pl -s) lessening, reduction

decreased v ▷ decrease

decreases v, n ▷ decrease

decreasing v ▷ decrease

decree n (pl -s) law made by someone in authority ▶ v (-crees, -creeing, -creed) order by decree

decreed v ▷ decree

decreeing v ▷ decree

decrees n, v ▷ decree

decrepit adj weakened or worn out by age or long use ▷ **decrepitude** n (pl -s)

decrepitude n ▷ decrepit

decrepitudes n ▷ decrepit

decried v ▷ decry

decries v ▷ decry

decry v (-cries, -crying, -cried) express disapproval of

decrying v ▷ decry

dedicate v (-cates, -cating, -cated) commit (oneself or one's time) wholly to a special purpose or cause ▷ **dedication** n (pl -s)

dedicated adj devoted to a particular purpose or cause ▶ v ▷ dedicate

dedicates v ▷ dedicate

dedicating v ▷ dedicate

dedication n ▷ dedicate

dedications n ▷ dedicate

deduce v (-duces, -ducing, -duced) reach (a conclusion) by reasoning from evidence ▷ **deducible** adj

deduced v ▷ deduce

deduces v ▷ deduce

deducible adj ▷ deduce

deducing v ▷ deduce

deduct v (-s, -ing, -ed) subtract

deducted v ▷ deduct

deducting v ▷ deduct

deduction n (pl -s) deducting ▷ **deductive** adj

deductions n ▷ deduction

deductive adj ▷ deduction

deducts v ▷ deduct

deed n (pl -s) something that is done

deeds n ▷ deed

deem v (-s, -ing, -ed) consider, judge

deemed v ▷ deem

deeming v ▷ deem

deems v ▷ deem

deep adj (-er, -est) extending or situated far down, inwards, backwards, or sideways ▷ **deepen** v (-s, -ing, -ed)

deepen v ▷ deep

deepened v ▷ deep

deepening v ▷ deep

deepens v ▷ deep

deeper adj ▷ deep

deepest adj ▷ deep

deepfreeze n (pl -s) ▷ freezer

deepfreezes n ▷ deepfreeze

deeply adv profoundly or intensely

deer n (pl deer) large wild animal, the male of which has antlers

deerstalker n (pl -s) cloth hat with peaks at the back and front and earflaps

deerstalkers n ▷ deerstalker

deface v (-faces, -facing, -faced) deliberately spoil the appearance of ▷ **defacement** n (pl -s)

defaced v ▷ deface

defacement n ▷ deface

defacements n ▷ deface

defaces v ▷ deface

defacing v ▷ deface

defamation n ▷ defame

defamations n ▷ defame

defamatory adj ▷ defame

defame v (-fames, -faming, -famed) attack the good reputation of ▷ **defamation** n (pl -s) ▷ **defamatory** [dif-fam-a-tree] adj

defamed v ▷ defame

defames v ▷ defame

defaming v ▷ defame

default n (pl -s) failure to do something ▶ v (-s, -ing, -ed) fail to fulfil an obligation ▷ **defaulter** n (pl -s)

defaulted v ▷ default

defaulter n ▷ default

defaulters n ▷ default

defaulting v ▷ default

defaults n, v ▷ default

defeat v (-s, -ing, -ed) win a victory over ▶ n (pl -s) defeating

defeated v ▷ defeat

defeating v ▷ defeat

defeatism n ready acceptance or expectation of defeat ▷ **defeatist** adj, n (pl -s)

defeatist n, adj ▷ defeatism

defeatists *n* ▷defeatism

defeats *v*, *n* ▷defeat

defecate *v* (-**cates**, -**cating**, -**cated**) discharge waste from the body through the anus > **defecation** *n* (*pl* -**s**)

defecated *v* ▷defecate

defecates *v* ▷defecate

defecating *v* ▷defecate

defecation *n* ▷defecate

defecations *n* ▷defecate

defect *n* (*pl* -**s**) imperfection, blemish ▶ *v* (-**s**, -**ing**, -**ed**) desert one's cause or country to join the opposing forces > **defection** *n* (*pl* -**s**) > **defector** *n* (*pl* -**s**)

defected *v* ▷defect

defecting *v* ▷defect

defection *n* ▷defect

defections *n* ▷defect

defective *adj* imperfect, faulty > **defectiveness** *n*

defectiveness *n* ▷defective

defector *n* ▷defect

defectors *n* ▷defect

defects *n*, *v* ▷defect

defence *n* (*pl* -**s**) resistance against attack > **defenceless** *adj*

defenceless *adj* ▷defence

defences *n* ▷defence

defend *v* (-**s**, -**ing**, -**ed**) protect from harm or danger

defendant *n* (*pl* -**s**) person accused of a crime

defendants *n* ▷defendant

defended *v* ▷defend

defender *n* (*pl* -**s**) person who supports someone or something in the face of criticism

defenders *n* ▷defender

defending *v* ▷defend

defends *v* ▷defend

defensibilities *n* ▷defensible

defensibility *n* ▷defensible

defensible *adj* capable of being defended because believed to be right > **defensibility** *n* (*pl* -**ities**)

defensive *adj* intended for defence > **defensively** *adv*

defensively *adv* ▷defensive

defer[1] *v* (-**fers**, -**ferring**, -**ferred**) delay (something) until a future time > **deferment**, **deferral** *n* (*pl* -**s**)

defer[2] *v* (-**fers**, -**ferring**, -**ferred**) (*foll. by* **to**) comply with the wishes (of)

deference *n* polite and respectful behaviour > **deferential** *adj* > **deferentially** *adv*

deferential *adj* ▷deference

deferentially *adv* ▷deference

deferment *n* ▷defer[1]

deferments *n* ▷defer[1]

deferral *n* ▷defer[1]

deferrals *n* ▷defer[1]

deferred *v* ▷defer[1, 2]

deferring *v* ▷defer[1, 2]

defers *v* ▷defer[1, 2]

defiance *n* ▷defy

defiances *n* ▷defy

defiant *adj* ▷defy

defiantly *adv* ▷defy

deficiencies *n* ▷deficiency

deficiency *n* (*pl* -**cies**) state of being deficient

deficient *adj* lacking some essential thing or quality > **deficiently** *adv*

deficiently *adv* ▷deficient

deficit *n* (*pl* -**s**) amount by which a sum of money is too small

deficits *n* ▷deficit

defied *v* ▷defy

defies *v* ▷defy

defile[1] *v* (-**files**, -**filing**, -**filed**) treat (something sacred or important) without respect > **defilement** *n* (*pl* -**s**)

defile[2] *n* (*pl* -**s**) narrow valley or pass

defiled *v* ▷defile[1]

defilement *n* ▷defile[1]

defilements *n* ▷defile[1]

defiles *v* ▷defile[1] ▶ *n* ▷defile[1, 2]

defiling *v* ▷defile[1]

definable *adj* ▷define

define *v* (-**fines**, -**fining**, -**fined**) state precisely the meaning of > **definable** *adj*

defined *v* ▷define

defines *v* ▷define

defining *v* ▷define

definite *adj* firm, clear, and precise > **definitely** *adv*

definitely *adv* ▷definite

definition *n* (*pl* -**s**) statement of the meaning of a word or phrase

definitions *n* ▷definition

definitive *adj* providing an unquestionable conclusion > **definitively** *adv*

definitively *adv* ▷definitive

deflate *v* (-**flates**, -**flating**, -**flated**) (cause to) collapse through the release of air

deflated *v* ▷deflate

deflates *v* ▷deflate

deflating *v* ▷deflate

deflation *n* (*pl* -**s**) (ECONOMICS) reduction in economic activity resulting in lower output and investment > **deflationary** *adj*

deflationary *adj* ▷deflation

deflations *n* ▷ deflation
deflect *v* (-flects, -flecting, -flected) (cause to) turn aside from a course > **deflection** *n* (*pl* -s) > **deflector** *n* (*pl* -s)
deflected *v* ▷ deflect
deflecting *v* ▷ deflect
deflection *n* ▷ deflect
deflections *n* ▷ deflect
deflector *n* ▷ deflect
deflectors *n* ▷ deflect
deflects *v* ▷ deflect
deflower *v* (-flowers, -flowering, -flowered) (*Lit*) deprive (a woman) of her virginity
deflowered *v* ▷ deflower
deflowering *v* ▷ deflower
deflowers *v* ▷ deflower
defoliant *n* ▷ defoliate
defoliants *n* ▷ defoliate
defoliate *v* (-ates, -ating, -ated) deprive (a plant) of its leaves > **defoliant** *n* (*pl* -s) > **defoliation** *n* (*pl* -s)
defoliated *v* ▷ defoliate
defoliates *v* ▷ defoliate
defoliating *v* ▷ defoliate
defoliation *n* ▷ defoliate
defoliations *n* ▷ defoliate
deforestation *n* (*pl* -s) destruction of all the trees in an area
deforestations *n* ▷ deforestation
deform *v* (-s, -ing, -ed) put out of shape or spoil the appearance of > **deformation** *n* (*pl* -s) > **deformity** *n* (*pl* -ties)
deformation *n* ▷ deform
deformations *n* ▷ deform
deformed *v* ▷ deform
deforming *v* ▷ deform
deformities *n* ▷ deform
deformity *n* ▷ deform
deforms *v* ▷ deform
defraud *v* (-s, -ing, -ed) cheat out of money, property, etc.
defrauded *v* ▷ defraud
defrauding *v* ▷ defraud
defrauds *v* ▷ defraud
defray *v* (-s, -ing, -ed) provide money for (costs or expenses)
defrayed *v* ▷ defray
defraying *v* ▷ defray
defrays *v* ▷ defray
defrock *v* (-s, -ing, -ed) deprive (a priest) of priestly status
defrocked *v* ▷ defrock
defrocking *v* ▷ defrock
defrocks *v* ▷ defrock
defrost *v* (-s, -ing, -ed) make or become free of ice
defrosted *v* ▷ defrost
defrosting *v* ▷ defrost
defrosts *v* ▷ defrost
deft *adj* quick and skilful in movement > **deftly** *adv* > **deftness** *n* (*pl* -es)
deftly *adv* ▷ deft
deftness *n* ▷ deft
deftnesses *n* ▷ deft
defunct *adj* no longer existing or operative
defuse *v* (-fuses, -fusing, -fused) remove the fuse of (an explosive device)
defused *v* ▷ defuse
defuses *v* ▷ defuse
defusing *v* ▷ defuse
defy *v* (-fies, -fying, -fied) resist openly and boldly > **defiance** *n* (*pl* -s) > **defiant** *adj* > **defiantly** *adv*
defying *v* ▷ defy
degeneracies *n* ▷ degeneracy
degeneracy *n* (*pl* -acies) degenerate behaviour
degenerate *adj* having deteriorated to a lower mental, moral, or physical level ▶ *n* (*pl* -s) degenerate person ▶ *v* (-ates, -ating, -ated) become degenerate > **degeneration** *n* (*pl* -s)
degenerated *v* ▷ degenerate
degenerates *n*, *v* ▷ degenerate
degenerating *v* ▷ degenerate
degeneration *n* ▷ degenerate
degenerations *n* ▷ degenerate
degradation *n* ▷ degrade
degradations *n* ▷ degrade
degrade *v* (-grades, -grading, -graded) reduce to dishonour or disgrace (CHEM) > **degradation** *n* (*pl* -s)
degraded *v* ▷ degrade
degrades *v* ▷ degrade
degrading *v* ▷ degrade
degree *n* (*pl* -s) stage in a scale of relative amount or intensity
degrees *n* ▷ degree
dehumanization *n* ▷ dehumanize
dehumanizations *n* ▷ dehumanize
dehumanize *v* (-izes, -izing, -ized) deprive of human qualities > **dehumanization** *n* (*pl* -s)
dehumanized *v* ▷ dehumanize
dehumanizes *v* ▷ dehumanize
dehumanizing *v* ▷ dehumanize
dehydrate *v* (-ates, -ating, -ated) remove water from (food) to preserve it > **dehydration** *n* (*pl* -s)
dehydrated *v* ▷ dehydrate
dehydrates *v* ▷ dehydrate
dehydrating *v* ▷ dehydrate
dehydration *n* ▷ dehydrate

dehydrations n ▷ dehydrate

deification n ▷ deify

deifications n ▷ deify

deified v ▷ deify

deifies v ▷ deify

deify [**day**-if-fie] v (**-fies, -fying, -fied**) treat or worship as a god > **deification** n (pl **-s**)

deifying v ▷ deify

deign [dane] v (**-s, -ing, -ed**) agree (to do something), but as if doing someone a favour

deigned v ▷ deign

deigning v ▷ deign

deigns v ▷ deign

deities n ▷ deity

deity [**dee**-it-ee, **day**-it-ee] n (pl **-ties**) god or goddess

dejected adj unhappy > **dejectedly** adv > **dejection** n (pl **-s**)

dejectedly adv ▷ dejected

dejection n ▷ dejected

dejections n ▷ dejected

dekko n (pl **-s**) (BRIT, AUST & NZ) (Slang) look

dekkos n ▷ dekko

delay v (**-s, -ing, -ed**) put off to a later time ▸ n (pl **-s**) act of delaying

delayed v ▷ delay

delaying v ▷ delay

delays v, n ▷ delay

delectable adj delightful, very attractive

delectation n (pl **-s**) (Formal) great pleasure

delectations n ▷ delectation

delegate n (pl **-s**) person chosen to represent others, esp. at a meeting ▸ v (**-gates, -gating, -gated**) entrust (duties or powers) to someone

delegated v ▷ delegate

delegates n, v ▷ delegate

delegating v ▷ delegate

delegation n (pl **-s**) group chosen to represent others

delegations n ▷ delegation

delete v (**-letes, -leting, -leted**) remove (something written or printed) > **deletion** n (pl **-s**)

deleted v ▷ delete

deleterious [del-lit-**eer**-ee-uss] adj harmful, injurious

deletes v ▷ delete

deleting v ▷ delete

deletion n ▷ deletion

deletions n ▷ deletion

deliberate adj planned in advance, intentional ▸ v (**-ates, -ating, -ated**) think something over > **deliberately** adv > **deliberation** n (pl **-s**) > **deliberative** adj

deliberated v ▷ deliberate

deliberately adv ▷ deliberate

deliberates v ▷ deliberate

deliberating v ▷ deliberate

deliberation n ▷ deliberate

deliberations n ▷ deliberate

deliberative adj ▷ deliberate

delicacies n ▷ delicacy

delicacy n (pl **-cies**) being delicate

delicate adj fine or subtle in quality or workmanship > **delicately** adv

delicately adv ▷ delicate

delicatessen n (pl **-s**) shop selling imported or unusual foods, often already cooked or prepared

delicatessens n ▷ delicatessen

delicious adj very appealing to taste or smell > **deliciously** adv > **deliciousness** n

deliciously adv ▷ delicious

deliciousness n ▷ delicious

delight n (pl **-s**) (source of) great pleasure ▸ v (**-s, -ing, -ed**) please greatly > **delightful** adj > **delightfully** adv

delighted v ▷ delight

delightful adj ▷ delight

delightfully adv ▷ delight

delighting v ▷ delight

delights n, v ▷ delight

delimit v (**-s, -ing, -ed**) mark or lay down the limits of > **delimitation** n (pl **-s**)

delimitation n ▷ delimit

delimitations n ▷ delimit

delimited v ▷ delimit

delimiting v ▷ delimit

delimits v ▷ delimit

delineate [dill-**lin**-ee-ate] v (**-ates, -ating, -ated**) show by drawing > **delineation** n (pl **-s**)

delineated v ▷ delineate

delineates v ▷ delineate

delineating v ▷ delineate

delineation n ▷ delineate

delineations n ▷ delineate

delinquencies n ▷ delinquent

delinquency n ▷ delinquent

delinquent n (pl **-s**) someone, esp. a young person, who repeatedly breaks the law ▸ adj repeatedly breaking the law > **delinquency** n (pl **-cies**)

delinquents n ▷ delinquent

delirious adj ▷ delirium

deliriously adv ▷ delirium

delirium n (pl **-s**) state of excitement and mental confusion, often with hallucinations > **delirious** adj > **deliriously** adv

deliriums n ▷ delirium

deliver v (**-s, -ing, -ed**) carry (goods etc.) to a destination
deliverance n (pl **-s**) rescue from captivity or evil
deliverances n ▷ **deliverance**
delivered v ▷ **deliver**
deliveries n ▷ **delivery**
delivering v ▷ **deliver**
delivers v ▷ **deliver**
delivery n (pl **-eries**) delivering
dell n (pl **-s**) (CHIEFLY BRIT) small wooded hollow
dells n ▷ **dell**
delphinium n (pl **-s**) large garden plant with blue flowers
delphiniums n ▷ **delphinium**
delta n (pl **-s**) fourth letter in the Greek alphabet
deltas n ▷ **delta**
delude v (**-ludes, -luding, -luded**) deceive
deluded v ▷ **delude**
deludes v ▷ **delude**
deluding v ▷ **delude**
deluge [del-lyooj] n (pl **-s**) great flood ▶ v (**-luges, -luging, -luged**) flood
deluged v ▷ **deluge**
deluges n, v ▷ **deluge**
deluging v ▷ **deluge**
delusion n (pl **-s**) mistaken idea or belief > **delusive** adj
delusions n ▷ **delusion**
delusive adj ▷ **delusion**
delve v (**delves, delving, delved**) research deeply (for information)
delved v ▷ **delve**
delves v ▷ **delve**
delving v ▷ **delve**
demagogic adj ▷ **demagogue**
demagogics v ▷ **demagogue**
demagogue n (pl **-s**) political agitator who appeals to the prejudice and passions of the mob > **demagogic** adj > **demagogy** n (pl **-gies**)
demagogues n ▷ **demagogue**
demagogy ▷ **demagogue**
demand v (**-s, -ing, -ed**) request forcefully ▶ n (pl **-s**) forceful request
demanded v ▷ **demand**
demanding adj requiring a lot of time or effort ▶ v ▷ **demand**
demands v, n ▷ **demand**
demarcation n (pl **-s**) (Formal) establishing limits or boundaries, esp. between the work performed by different trade unions
demarcations n ▷ **demarcation**
demean v (**-s, -ing, -ed**) do something unworthy of one's status or character

demeaned v ▷ **demean**
demeaning v ▷ **demean**
demeanour n (pl **-s**) way a person behaves
demeanours n ▷ **demeanour**
demeans v ▷ **demean**
demented adj mad > **dementedly** adv
dementedly adv ▷ **demented**
dementia [dim-**men**-sha] n (pl **-s**) state of serious mental deterioration
dementias n ▷ **dementia**
demerit n (pl **-s**) fault, disadvantage
demerits n ▷ **demerit**
demesne [dim-**mane**] n (pl **-s**) land surrounding a house
demesnes n ▷ **demesne**
demijohn n (pl **-s**) large bottle with a short neck, often encased in wicker
demijohns n ▷ **demijohn**
demilitarization n ▷ **demilitarize**
demilitarizations n ▷ **demilitarize**
demilitarize v (**-izes, -izing, -ized**) remove the military forces from > **demilitarization** n (pl **-s**)
demilitarized v ▷ **demilitarize**
demilitarizes v ▷ **demilitarize**
demilitarizing v ▷ **demilitarize**
demimonde n (pl **-s**) (esp. in the 19th century) class of women considered to be outside respectable society because of promiscuity
demimondes n ▷ **demimonde**
demise n (pl **-s**) eventual failure (of something successful)
demises n ▷ **demise**
demo n (pl **-s**) (Informal) demonstration, organized expression of public opinion
demob v (**-mobs, -mobbing, -mobbed**) (BRIT, AUST & NZ) (Informal) demobilize
demobbed v ▷ **demob**
demobbing v ▷ **demob**
demobilization n ▷ **demobilize**
demobilizations n ▷ **demobilize**
demobilize v (**-izes, -izing, -ized**) release from the armed forces > **demobilization** n (pl **-s**)
demobilized v ▷ **demobilize**
demobilizes v ▷ **demobilize**
demobilizing v ▷ **demobilize**
demobs v ▷ **demob**
democracies n ▷ **democracy**
democracy n (pl **-cies**) government by the people or their elected representatives
democrat n (pl **-s**) advocate of democracy
democratic adj of democracy > **democratically** adv
democratically adv ▷ **democratic**

democrats *n* ▷ democrat
demographer *n* ▷ demography
demographers *n* ▷ demography
demographic *adj* ▷ demography
demographies *n* ▷ demography
demography *n* (*pl* -phies) study of population statistics, such as births and deaths
> **demographer** *n* (*pl* -s) > **demographic** *adj*
demolish *v* (-es, -ing, -ed) knock down or destroy (a building) > **demolition** *n* (*pl* -s)
demolished *v* ▷ demolish
demolishes *v* ▷ demolish
demolishing *v* ▷ demolish
demolition *n* ▷ demolish
demolitions *n* ▷ demolish
demon *n* (*pl* -s) evil spirit
demoniac *adj* ▷ demonic
demoniacal *adj* ▷ demonic
demoniacally *adv* ▷ demonic
demonic *adj* evil > **demoniac, demoniacal** *adj* appearing to be possessed by a devil
> **demoniacally** *adv*
demonologies *n* ▷ demonology
demonologist *n* ▷ demonology
demonologists *n* ▷ demonology
demonology *n* (*pl* -logies) study of demons
> **demonologist** *n* (*pl* -s)
demons *n* ▷ demon
demonstrable *adj* able to be proved
> **demonstrably** *adv*
demonstrably *adv* ▷ demonstrable
demonstrate *v* (-rates, -rating, -rated) show or prove by reasoning or evidence
demonstrated *v* ▷ demonstrate
demonstrates *v* ▷ demonstrate
demonstrating *v* ▷ demonstrate
demonstration *n* (*pl* -s) organized expression of public opinion
demonstrations *n* ▷ demonstration
demonstrative *adj* tending to show one's feelings unreservedly > **demonstratively** *adv*
demonstratively *adv* ▷ demonstrative
demonstrator *n* (*pl* -s) person who demonstrates how a device or machine works
demonstrators *n* ▷ demonstrator
demoralization *n* ▷ demoralize
demoralizations *n* ▷ demoralize
demoralize *v* (-lizes, -lizing, -lized) undermine the morale of > **demoralization** *n* (*pl* -s)
demoralized *v* ▷ demoralize
demoralizes *v* ▷ demoralize
demoralizing *v* ▷ demoralize
demos *n* ▷ demo
demote *v* (-motes, -moting, -moted) reduce in

status or rank > **demotion** *n* (*pl* -s)
demoted *v* ▷ demote
demotes *v* ▷ demote
demoting *v* ▷ demote
demotion *n* ▷ demote
demotions *n* ▷ demote
demur *v* (-murs, -murring, -murred) show reluctance
demure *adj* (-r, -st) quiet, reserved, and rather shy > **demurely** *adv*
demurely *adv* ▷ demure
demurer *adj* ▷ demure
demurest *adj* ▷ demure
demurred *v* ▷ demur
demurring *v* ▷ demur
demurs *v* ▷ demur
den *n* (*pl* -s) home of a wild animal
denationalization *n* ▷ denationalize
denationalizations *n* ▷ denationalize
denationalize *v* (-lizes, -lizing, -lized) transfer (an industry) from public to private ownership > **denationalization** *n* (*pl* -s)
denationalized *v* ▷ denationalize
denationalizes *v* ▷ denationalize
denationalizing *v* ▷ denationalize
denature *v* (-tures, -turing, -tured) change the nature of
denatured *v* ▷ denature
denatures *v* ▷ denature
denaturing *v* ▷ denature
deniable *adj* ▷ deny
deniably *adv* ▷ deny
denial *n* (*pl* -s) statement that something is not true
denials *n* ▷ denial
denied *v* ▷ deny
denier [den-yer] *n* (*pl* -s) unit of weight used to measure the fineness of nylon or silk
deniers *n* ▷ denier
denies *v* ▷ deny
denigrate *v* (-grates, -grating, -grated) criticize unfairly > **denigration** *n* (*pl* -s)
denigrated *v* ▷ denigrate
denigrates *v* ▷ denigrate
denigrating *v* ▷ denigrate
denigration *n* ▷ denigrate
denigrations *n* ▷ denigrate
denim *n* (*pl* -s) hard-wearing cotton fabric, usu. blue ▶ *pl* jeans made of denim
denims *n* ▷ denim
denizen *n* (*pl* -s) inhabitant
denizens *n* ▷ denizen
denominate *v* (-nates, -nating, -nated) give a specific name to
denominated *v* ▷ denominate

denominates v ▷ denominate

denominating v ▷ denominate

denomination n (pl -s) group having a distinctive interpretation of a religious faith > **denominational** adj

denominational adj ▷ denomination

denominations n ▷ denomination

denominator n (pl -s) number below the line in a fraction

denominators n ▷ denominator

denotation n ▷ denote

denotations n ▷ denote

denote v (-notes, -noting, -noted) be a sign of > **denotation** n (pl -s)

denoted v ▷ denote

denotes v ▷ denote

denoting v ▷ denote

denouement [day-noo-mon] n (pl -s) final outcome or solution in a play or book

denouements n ▷ denouement

denounce v (-ces, -cing, -ced) speak vehemently against

denounced v ▷ denounce

denounces v ▷ denounce

denouncing v ▷ denounce

dens n ▷ den

dense adj (-r, -st) closely packed > **densely** adv

densely adv ▷ dense

denser adj ▷ dense

densest adj ▷ dense

densities n ▷ density

density n (pl -ties) degree to which something is filled or occupied

dent n (pl -s) hollow in the surface of something, made by hitting it ▶ v (-s, -ing, -ed) make a dent in

dental adj of teeth or dentistry

dented v ▷ dent

dentine [den-teen] n (pl -s) hard dense tissue forming the bulk of a tooth

dentines n ▷ dentine

denting v ▷ dent

dentist n (pl -s) person qualified to practise dentistry

dentistries n ▷ dentistry

dentistry n (pl -ries) branch of medicine concerned with the teeth and gums

dentists n ▷ dentist

dents n, v ▷ dent

denture n (pl -s) false tooth

dentures n ▷ denture

denude v (-nudes, -nuding, -nuded) remove the covering or protection from

denuded v ▷ denude

denudes v ▷ denude

denuding v ▷ denude

denunciation n (pl -s) open condemnation

denunciations n ▷ denunciation

deny v (-nies, -nying, -nied) declare to be untrue > **deniable** adj > **deniably** adv

denying v ▷ deny

deodorant n (pl -s) substance applied to the body to mask the smell of perspiration

deodorants n ▷ deodorant

deodorize v (-izes, -izing, -ized) remove or disguise the smell of

deodorized v ▷ deodorize

deodorizes v ▷ deodorize

deodorizing v ▷ deodorize

depart v (-s, -ing, -ed) leave > **departed** > **departure** n (pl -s)

departed adj (Euphemistic) dead ▶ v ▷ depart

departing v ▷ depart

department n (pl -s) specialized division of a large organization > **departmental** adj

departmental adj ▷ department

departments n ▷ department

departs v ▷ depart

departure n ▷ depart

departures n ▷ depart

depend v (-s, -ing, -ed) (foll. by on) put trust (in) > **dependable** adj > **dependably** adv > **dependability** n (pl -ities)

dependabilities n ▷ depend

dependability n ▷ depend

dependable adj ▷ depend

dependably adv ▷ depend

dependant n (pl -s) person who depends on another for financial support

dependants n ▷ dependant

depended v ▷ depend

dependence n (pl -s) state of being dependent

dependences n ▷ dependence

dependencies n ▷ dependency

dependency n (pl -cies) country controlled by another country

dependent adj depending on someone or something > **dependently** adv

dependently adv ▷ dependent

depending v ▷ depend

depends v ▷ depend

depict v (-s, -ing, -ed) produce a picture of > **depiction** n (pl -s)

depicted v ▷ depict

depicting v ▷ depict

depiction n ▷ depict

depictions n ▷ depict

depicts v ▷ depict

depilatories n ▷ depilatory

depilatory [dip-**pill**-a-tree] n (pl -tories) ▶ adj

(substance) designed to remove unwanted hair

deplete *v* (**-letes, -leting, -leted**) use up > **depletion** *n* (*pl* **-s**)
  depleted *v* ▷ deplete
  depletes *v* ▷ deplete
  depleting *v* ▷ deplete
  depletion *n* ▷ deplete
  depletions *n* ▷ deplete

deplorable *adj* very bad or unpleasant > **deplorably** *adv*
  deplorably *adv* ▷ deplorable

deplore *v* (**-lores, -loring, -lored**) condemn strongly
  deplored *v* ▷ deplore
  deplores *v* ▷ deplore
  deploring *v* ▷ deplore

deploy *v* (**-s, -ing, -ed**) organize (troops or resources) into a position ready for immediate action > **deployment** *n* (*pl* **-s**)
  deployed *v* ▷ deploy
  deploying *v* ▷ deploy
  deployment *n* ▷ deploy
  deployments *n* ▷ deploy
  deploys *v* ▷ deploy

depopulate *v* (**-lates, -lating, -lated**) reduce the population of > **depopulation** *n* (*pl* **-s**)
  depopulated *v* ▷ depopulate
  depopulates *v* ▷ depopulate
  depopulating *v* ▷ depopulate
  depopulation *n* ▷ depopulate
  depopulations *n* ▷ depopulate

deport *v* (**-s, -ing, -ed**) remove forcibly from a country > **deportation** *n* (*pl* **-s**) > **deportee** *n* (*pl* **-s**)
  deportation *n* ▷ deport
  deportations *n* ▷ deport
  deported *v* ▷ deport
  deportee *n* ▷ deport
  deportees *n* ▷ deport
  deporting *v* ▷ deport

deportment *n* (*pl* **-s**) way in which a person moves or stands
  deportments *n* ▷ deportment
  deports *v* ▷ deport

depose *v* (**-poses, -posing, -posed**) remove from an office or position of power
  deposed *v* ▷ depose
  deposes *v* ▷ depose
  deposing *v* ▷ depose

deposit *v* (**-s, -ing, -ed**) put down ▶ *n* (*pl* **-s**) sum of money paid into a bank account > **depositor** *n* (*pl* **-s**)
  depositaries *n* ▷ depositary

depositary *n* (*pl* **-aries**) person to whom something is entrusted for safety
  deposited *v* ▷ deposit
  depositing *v* ▷ deposit

deposition *n* (*pl* **-s**) (LAW) sworn statement of a witness used in court in his or her absence
  depositions *n* ▷ deposition
  depositor *n* ▷ deposit
  depositories *n* ▷ deposit
  depositors *n* ▷ deposit

depository *n* (*pl* **-ories**) store for furniture etc.
  deposits *v*, *n* ▷ deposit

depot [**dep**-oh] *n* (*pl* **-s**) building where goods or vehicles are kept when not in use
  depots *n* ▷ depot

depraved *adj* morally bad > **depravity** *n* (*pl* **-ities**)
  depravities *n* ▷ depraved
  depravity *n* ▷ depraved

deprecate *v* (**-cates, -cating, -cated**) express disapproval of > **deprecation** *n* (*pl* **-s**) > **deprecatory** *adj*
  deprecated *v* ▷ deprecate
  deprecates *v* ▷ deprecate
  deprecating *v* ▷ deprecate
  deprecation *n* ▷ deprecate
  deprecations *n* ▷ deprecate
  deprecatory *adj* ▷ deprecate

depreciate *v* (**-ates, -ating, -ated**) decline in value or price > **depreciation** *n* (*pl* **-s**)
  depreciated *v* ▷ depreciate
  depreciates *v* ▷ depreciate
  depreciating *v* ▷ depreciate
  depreciation *n* ▷ depreciate
  depreciations *n* ▷ depreciate

depredation *n* (*pl* **-s**) plundering
  depredations *n* ▷ depredation

depress *v* (**-es, -ing, -ed**) make sad > **depressing** *adj* > **depressingly** *adv*

depressant *n* (*pl* **-s**) ▶ *adj* (drug) able to reduce nervous activity
  depressants *n* ▷ depressant
  depressed *v* ▷ depress
  depresses *v* ▷ depress
  depressing *v*, *adj* ▷ depress
  depressingly *adv* ▷ depress

depression *n* (*pl* **-s**) mental state in which a person has feelings of gloom and inadequacy
  depressions *n* ▷ depression

depressive *adj* tending to cause depression ▶ *n* (*pl* **-s**) person who suffers from depression > **depressively** *adv*
  depressively *adv* ▷ depressive
  depressives *n* ▷ depressive
  deprivation *n* ▷ deprive
  deprivations *n* ▷ deprive

deprive v (**-rives, -riving, -rived**) (foll. by **of**) prevent from (having or enjoying) > **deprivation** n (pl **-s**)

deprived adj lacking adequate living conditions, education, etc. ▶ v ▷ **deprive**

deprives v ▷ **deprive**

depriving v ▷ **deprive**

depth n (pl **-s**) distance downwards, backwards, or inwards

depths n ▷ **depth**

deputation n (pl **-s**) body of people appointed to represent others

deputations n ▷ **deputation**

depute v (**-putes, -puting, -puted**) appoint (someone) to act on one's behalf

deputed v ▷ **depute**

deputes v ▷ **depute**

deputies n ▷ **deputy**

deputing v ▷ **depute**

deputize v (**-izes, -izing, -ized**) act as deputy

deputized v ▷ **deputize**

deputizes v ▷ **deputize**

deputizing v ▷ **deputize**

deputy n (pl **-ties**) person appointed to act on behalf of another

derail v (**-s, -ing, -ed**) cause (a train) to go off the rails > **derailment** n (pl **-s**)

derailed v ▷ **derail**

derailing v ▷ **derail**

derailment n ▷ **derail**

derailments n ▷ **derail**

derails v ▷ **derail**

deranged adj insane or uncontrolled > **derangement** n (pl **-s**)

derangement n ▷ **derange**

derangements n ▷ **derange**

derbies n ▷ **derby**

derby [dah-bee] n (pl **-bies**) sporting event between teams from the same area ▶ n any of various horse races

deregulate v (**-ates, -ating, -ated**) remove regulations or controls from > **deregulation** n (pl **-s**)

deregulated v ▷ **deregulate**

deregulates v ▷ **deregulate**

deregulating v ▷ **deregulate**

deregulation n ▷ **deregulate**

deregulations n ▷ **deregulate**

derelict adj unused and falling into ruins ▶ n (pl **-s**) social outcast, vagrant

dereliction n (pl **-s**) state of being abandoned

derelictions n ▷ **dereliction**

derelicts n ▷ **derelict**

deride v (**-rides, -riding, -rided**) treat with contempt or ridicule > **derision** n (pl **-s**)

derided v ▷ **deride**

derides v ▷ **deride**

deriding v ▷ **deride**

derision n ▷ **deride**

derisions n ▷ **deride**

derisive adj mocking, scornful > **derisively** adv > **derisiveness** n

derisively adv ▷ **derisive**

derisiveness n ▷ **derisive**

derisory adj too small or inadequate to be considered seriously

derivation n ▷ **derive**

derivations n ▷ **derive**

derivative adj word, idea, etc., derived from another > **derivatively** adv

derivatively adv ▷ **derivative**

derive v (**-rives, -riving, -rived**) (foll. by **from**) take or develop (from) > **derivation** n (pl **-s**)

derived v ▷ **derive**

derives v ▷ **derive**

deriving v ▷ **derive**

dermatitis n inflammation of the skin

dermatologies n ▷ **dermatology**

dermatologist n ▷ **dermatology**

dermatologists n ▷ **dermatology**

dermatology n (pl **-ogies**) branch of medicine concerned with the skin > **dermatologist** n (pl **-s**)

derogatorily adv ▷ **derogatory**

derogatory [dir-**rog**-a-tree] adj intentionally offensive > **derogatorily** adv

derrick n (pl **-s**) simple crane

derricks n ▷ **derrick**

derv n (pl **-s**) (BRIT) diesel oil, when used for road transport

dervish n (pl **-es**) member of a Muslim religious order noted for a frenzied whirling dance

dervishes n ▷ **dervish**

dervs n ▷ **derv**

descant n (pl **-s**) (MUSIC) tune played or sung above a basic melody

descants n ▷ **descant**

descend v (**-s, -ing, -ed**) move down (a slope etc.)

descendant n (pl **-s**) person or animal descended from an individual, race, or species

descendants n ▷ **descendant**

descended v ▷ **descend**

descendent adj descending

descending v ▷ **descend**

descends v ▷ **descend**

descent n (pl **-s**) descending

descents n ▷ **descent**

describe v (**-ribes, -ribing, -ribed**) give an account of (something or someone) in words
described v ▷ describe
describes v ▷ describe
describing v ▷ describe
descried v ▷ descry
descries v ▷ descry
description n (pl **-s**) statement that describes something or someone > **descriptive** adj
> **descriptively** adv > **descriptiveness** n
descriptions n ▷ description
descriptive adj ▷ description
descriptively adv ▷ description
descriptiveness n ▷ description
descry v (**-scries, -scrying, -scried**) catch sight of
descrying v ▷ descry
desecrate v (**-rates, -rating, -rated**) damage or insult (something sacred) > **desecration** n (pl **-s**)
desecrated v ▷ desecrate
desecrates v ▷ desecrate
desecrating v ▷ desecrate
desecration n ▷ desecrate
desecrations n ▷ desecrate
desegregate v (**-gates, -gating, -gated**) end racial segregation in > **desegregation** n (pl **-s**)
desegregated v ▷ desegregate
desegregates v ▷ desegregate
desegregating v ▷ desegregate
desegregation n ▷ desegregate
desegregations n ▷ desegregate
deselect v (**-s, -ing, -ed**) (BRIT) (POLITICS) refuse to select (an MP) for re-election > **deselection** n (pl **-s**)
deselected v ▷ deselect
deselecting v ▷ deselect
deselection n ▷ deselect
deselections n ▷ deselect
deselects v ▷ deselect
desert[1] n (pl **-s**) region with little or no vegetation because of low rainfall
desert[2] v (**-s, -ing, -ed**) abandon (a person or place) without intending to return > **deserter** n (pl **-s**) > **desertion** n (pl **-s**)
deserted v ▷ desert[2]
deserter n ▷ desert[2]
deserters n ▷ desert[2]
deserting v ▷ desert[2]
desertion n ▷ desert[2]
desertions n ▷ desert[2]
deserts n ▷ desert[1] ▶ pl n the punishment one deserves ▶ v ▷ desert[2]
deserve v (**-serves, -serving, -served**) be entitled to or worthy of

deserved adj rightfully earned ▶ v ▷ deserve
> **deservedly** adv
deservedly adv ▷ deserved
deserves v ▷ deserve
deserving adj worthy of help, praise, or reward ▶ v ▷ deserve
deshabille [day-zab-**beel**] n (pl **-s**) state of being partly dressed
deshabilles n ▷ deshabille
desiccate v (**-siccates, -siccating, -siccated**) remove most of the water from > **desiccation** n (pl **-s**)
desiccated v ▷ desiccate
desiccates v ▷ desiccate
desiccating v ▷ desiccate
desiccation n ▷ desiccate
desiccations n ▷ desiccate
design v (**-s, -ing, -ed**) work out the structure or form of (something), by making a sketch or plans ▶ n (pl **-s**) preliminary drawing
designate [**dez**-zig-nate] v (**-nates, -nating, -nated**) give a name to ▶ adj appointed but not yet in office
designated v ▷ designate
designates v ▷ designate
designating v ▷ designate
designation n (pl **-s**) name
designations n ▷ designation
designed v ▷ design
designedly [dee-**zine**-id-lee] adv intentionally
designer n (pl **-s**) person who draws up original sketches or plans from which things are made ▶ adj designed by a well-known designer
designers n ▷ designer
designing adj cunning and scheming ▶ v ▷ design
designs v, n ▷ design
desirabilities n ▷ desirable
desirability n ▷ desirable
desirable adj worth having > **desirability** n (pl **-ities**) > **desirably** adv
desirably adv ▷ desirable
desire v (**-sires, -siring, -sired**) want very much ▶ n (pl **-s**) wish, longing
desired v ▷ desire
desires v, n ▷ desire
desiring v ▷ desire
desist v (**-s, -ing, -ed**) (foll. by **from**) stop (doing something)
desisted v ▷ desist
desisting v ▷ desist
desists v ▷ desist
desk n (pl **-s**) piece of furniture with a writing surface and drawers

desks n ▷ desk

desktop adj (of a computer) small enough to use at a desk

desolate adj uninhabited and bleak ▶ v (-lates, -lating, -lated) deprive of inhabitants > **desolately** adv > **desolateness** n > **desolation** n (pl -s)

desolated v ▷ desolate

desolately adv ▷ desolate

desolateness n ▷ desolate

desolates v ▷ desolate

desolating v ▷ desolate

desolation n ▷ desolate

desolations n ▷ desolate

despair n (pl -s) total loss of hope ▶ v (-s, -ing, -ed) lose hope > **despairingly** adv

despaired v ▷ despair

despairing v ▷ despair

despairingly adv ▷ despair

despairs n, v ▷ despair

despatch v (-es, -ing, -ed) ▶ n (pl -es) ▷ dispatch

despatched v ▷ despatch

despatches v, n ▷ despatch

despatching v ▷ despatch

desperado n (pl -does, -dos) reckless person ready to commit any violent illegal act

desperadoes v ▷ desperado

desperados v ▷ desperado

desperate adj in despair and reckless > **desperately** adv > **desperateness** n > **desperation** n (pl -s)

desperately adv ▷ desperate

desperateness n ▷ desperate

desperation n ▷ desperate

desperations n ▷ desperate

despicable adj deserving contempt > **despicably** adv

despicably adv ▷ despicable

despise v (-pises, -pising, -pised) regard with contempt

despised v ▷ despise

despises v ▷ despise

despising v ▷ despise

despite prep in spite of

despoil v (-s, -ing, -ed) (Formal) plunder > **despoliation** n (pl -s)

despoiled v ▷ despoil

despoiling v ▷ despoil

despoils v ▷ despoil

despoliation n ▷ despoil

despoliations n ▷ despoil

despondencies n ▷ despondent

despondency n ▷ despondent

despondent adj unhappy > **despondently** adv > **despondency** n (pl -cies)

despondently adv ▷ despondent

despot n (pl -s) person in power who acts unfairly or cruelly > **despotic** adj > **despotically** adv

despotic adj ▷ despot

despotically adv ▷ despot

despotism n (pl -s) unfair or cruel government or behaviour

despotisms n ▷ despotism

despots n ▷ despot

dessert n (pl -s) sweet course served at the end of a meal

desserts n ▷ dessert

dessertspoon n (pl -s) spoon between a tablespoon and a teaspoon in size

dessertspoons n ▷ dessertspoon

destination n (pl -s) place to which someone or something is going

destinations n ▷ destination

destined adj certain to be or to do something

destinies n ▷ destiny

destiny n (pl -nies) future marked out for a person or thing

destitute adj having no money or possessions > **destitution** n

destitution n ▷ destitute

destroy v (-s, -ing, -ed) ruin, demolish

destroyed v ▷ destroy

destroyer n (pl -s) small heavily armed warship

destroyers n ▷ destroyer

destroying v ▷ destroy

destroys v ▷ destroy

destruction n (pl -s) destroying

destructions n ▷ destruction

destructive adj (capable of) causing destruction > **destructively** adv > **destructiveness** n

destructively adv ▷ destructive

destructiveness n ▷ destructive

desuetude [diss-**syoo**-it-tude] n (pl -s) condition of not being in use

desuetudes n ▷ desuetude

desultorily adv ▷ desultory

desultoriness n ▷ desultory

desultory [**dez**-zl-tree] adj jumping from one thing to another, disconnected > **desultorily** adv > **desultoriness** n

detach v (-es, -ing, -ed) disengage and separate > **detachable** adj

detachable adj ▷ detach

detached adj (BRIT, AUST & S AFR) (of a house) not joined to another house ▶ v ▷ detach

detaches v ▷ detach

detaching v ▷ detach

detachment n (pl -s) lack of emotional

involvement

detachments n ▷ detachment

detail n (pl -s) individual piece of information
▶ v (-s, -ing, -ed) list fully

detailed v ▷ detail

detailing v ▷ detail

details n, v ▷ detail

detain v (-s, -ing, -ed) delay (someone)
> **detainee** n (pl -s)

detained v ▷ detain

detainee n ▷ detain

detainees n ▷ detain

detaining v ▷ detain

detains v ▷ detain

detect v (-s, -ing, -ed) notice > **detectable** adj
> **detection** n (pl -s)

detectable adj ▷ detect

detected v ▷ detect

detecting v ▷ detect

detection n ▷ detect

detections n ▷ detect

detective n (pl -s) policeman or private agent
who investigates crime

detectives n ▷ detective

detector n (pl -s) instrument used to find
something

detectors n ▷ detector

detects v ▷ detect

detente [day-tont] n (pl -s) easing of tension
between nations

detentes n ▷ detente

detention n (pl -s) imprisonment

detentions n ▷ detention

deter v (-ters, -terring, -terred) discourage
(someone) from doing something by
instilling fear or doubt

detergent n (pl -s) chemical substance for
washing clothes or dishes

detergents n ▷ detergent

deteriorate v (-rates, -rating, -rated) become
worse > **deterioration** n (pl -s)

deteriorated v ▷ deteriorate

deteriorates v ▷ deteriorate

deteriorating v ▷ deteriorate

deterioration n ▷ deteriorate

deteriorations n ▷ deteriorate

determinant n (pl -s) factor that determines

determinants n ▷ determinant

determinate adj definitely limited or fixed
> **determinateness** n

determinateness n ▷ determinate

determination n (pl -s) being determined or
resolute

determinations n ▷ determination

determine v (-mines, -mining, -mined) settle

(an argument or a question) conclusively

determined adj firmly decided, unable to be
dissuaded ▶ v ▷ determine > **determinedly**
adv

determiner n (pl -s) (GRAMMAR) word that
determines the object to which a noun
phrase refers

determiners n ▷ determiner

determines v ▷ determine

determining v ▷ determine

determinism n theory that human choice
is not free, but decided by past events
> **determinist** n (pl -s) adj

determinist n ▷ determinism

determinists n ▷ determinism

deterred v ▷ deter

deterrent n (pl -s) something that deters ▶ adj
tending to deter

deterrents n ▷ deterrent

deterring v ▷ deter

deters v ▷ deter

detest v (-s, -ing, -ed) dislike intensely
> **detestable** adj > **detestably** adv
> **detestation** n (pl -s)

detestable adj ▷ detest

detestably adv ▷ detest

detestation n ▷ detest

detestations n ▷ detest

detested v ▷ detest

detesting v ▷ detest

detests v ▷ detest

dethrone v (-rones, -roning, -roned) remove
from a throne or position of power

dethroned v ▷ dethrone

dethrones v ▷ dethrone

dethroning v ▷ dethrone

detonate v (-nates, -nating, -nated) explode
> **detonation** n (pl -s)

detonated v ▷ detonate

detonates v ▷ detonate

detonating v ▷ detonate

detonation n ▷ detonate

detonations n ▷ detonate

detonator n (pl -s) small amount of explosive,
or a device, used to set off an explosion

detonators n ▷ detonator

detour n (pl -s) route that is not the most
direct one

detours n ▷ detour

detract v (-s, -ing, -ed) (foll. by **from**) make
(something) seem less good > **detractor** n
(pl -s)

detracted v ▷ detract

detracting v ▷ detract

detractor n ▷ detract

detractors n ▷ detract
detracts v ▷ detract
detriment n (pl -s) disadvantage or damage > **detrimental** adj > **detrimentally** adv
detrimental adj ▷ detract
detrimentally adv ▷ detract
detriments n ▷ detract
detritus [dit-trite-uss] n loose mass of stones and silt worn away from rocks
deuce [dyewss] n (pl -s) (TENNIS) score of forty all
deuces n ▷ deuce

deus n (di). Deus is a Latin word for a god. Its plural, di, is a very handy word to know when trying to form several words at once. Di scores 3 points.

deuterium n (pl -s) isotope of hydrogen twice as heavy as the normal atom
deuteriums n ▷ deuterium

dev n (devs). A dev is a Hindu god. Dev scores 7 points.

devaluation n ▷ devalue
devaluations n ▷ devalue
devalue v (-lues, -luing, -lued) reduce the exchange value of (a currency) > **devaluation** n (pl -s)
devalued v ▷ devalue
devalues v ▷ devalue
devaluing v ▷ devalue
devastate v (-tates, -tating, -tated) destroy > **devastation** n (pl -s)
devastated adj shocked and extremely upset ▶ v ▷ devastate
devastates v ▷ devastate
devastating v ▷ devastate
devastation n ▷ devastate
devastations n ▷ devastate
develop v (-s, -ing, -ed) grow or bring to a later, more elaborate, or more advanced stage > **development** n (pl -s)
developed v ▷ develop
developer n (pl -s) person who develops property
developers n ▷ developer
developing v ▷ develop
development n ▷ develop
developments n ▷ develop
develops v ▷ develop
deviance n ▷ deviant
deviances n ▷ deviant
deviant n (pl -s) ▶ adj (person) deviating from what is considered acceptable behaviour > **deviance** n (pl -s)
deviants n ▷ deviant
deviate v (-ates, -ating, -ated) differ from others in belief or thought > **deviation** n (pl -s)

deviated v ▷ deviate
deviates v ▷ deviate
deviating v ▷ deviate
deviation n ▷ deviate
deviations n ▷ deviate
device n (pl -s) machine or tool used for a specific task
devices n ▷ device
devil n (pl -s) evil spirit (Informal) ▶ v (-ils, -illing, -illed) prepare (food) with a highly flavoured spiced mixture
devilish adj cruel or unpleasant ▶ adv (also **devilishly**) (Informal) extremely
devilishly adv ▷ devilish
devilled v ▷ devil
devilling v ▷ devil
devil-may-care adj carefree and cheerful
devilment n (pl -s) mischievous conduct
devilments n ▷ devilment
devilries n ▷ devilry
devilry n (pl -ries) mischievousness
devils n, v ▷ devil
devious adj insincere and dishonest > **deviously** adv > **deviousness** n
deviously adv ▷ devious
deviousness n ▷ devious
devise v (-vises, -vising, -vised) work out (something) in one's mind
devised v ▷ devise
devises v ▷ devise
devising v ▷ devise
devoid adj (foll. by **of**) completely lacking (in)
devolution n (pl -s) transfer of authority from a central government to regional governments
devolutions n ▷ devolution
devolve v (-volves, -volving, -volved) (foll. by **on** or **to**) pass (power or duties) or (of power or duties) be passed to a successor or substitute
devolved v ▷ devolve
devolves v ▷ devolve
devolving v ▷ devolve
devote v (-votes, -voting, -voted) apply or dedicate to a particular purpose
devoted adj showing loyalty or devotion ▶ v ▷ devote > **devotedly** adv
devotedly adv ▷ devoted
devotee n (pl -s) person who is very enthusiastic about something
devotees n ▷ devotee
devotes v ▷ devote
devoting v ▷ devote
devotion n (pl -s) strong affection for or loyalty to someone or something ▶ pl prayers > **devotional** adj

devotional adj ▷ devotion
devotions adj ▷ devotion
devour v (-s, -ing, -ed) eat greedily
devoured v ▷ devour
devouring v ▷ devour
devours v ▷ devour
devout adj deeply religious > **devoutly** adv
> **devoutness** n
devoutly adv ▷ devout
devoutness n ▷ devout
dew n (pl -s) drops of water that form on the
ground at night from vapour in the air > **dewy**
adj (-wier, -wiest)
dewier adj ▷ dew
dewiest adj ▷ dew
dewlap n (pl -s) loose fold of skin hanging
under the throat in dogs, cattle, etc.
dewlaps n ▷ dewlap
dews n ▷ dew
dewy adj ▷ dew

> **dex** n (**dexes**). Dex is a slang word for a
kind of amphetamine. This is an easy
way to pick up a some points after
another player has used an X. Dex
scores 11 points.

dexterities n ▷ dexterity
dexterity n (pl -ities) skill in using one's hands
> **dexterous** adj > **dexterously** adv
dexterous adj ▷ dexterity
dexterously adv ▷ dexterity
dextrose n (pl -s) glucose occurring in fruit,
honey, and the blood of animals
dextroses n ▷ dextrose

> **dey** n (**deys**). A dey is an Ottoman
governor. Dey scores 7 points.

diabetes [die-a-**beet**-eez] n disorder in which
an abnormal amount of urine containing
an excess of sugar is excreted > **diabetic** n
(pl -s) adj
diabetic n ▷ diabetes
diabetics n ▷ diabetes
diabolic adj of the Devil
diabolical adj (Informal) extremely bad
> **diabolically** adv > **diabolicalness** n
diabolically adv ▷ diabolical
diabolicalness n ▷ diabolical
diabolism n witchcraft, devil worship
> **diabolist** n (pl -s)
diabolist n ▷ diabolism
diabolists n ▷ diabolism
diaconate n (pl -s) position or period of office
of a deacon
diaconates n ▷ diaconate
diacritic n (pl -s) sign above or below a
character to indicate phonetic value or stress

diacritics n ▷ diacritic
diadem n (pl -s) (Old-fashioned) crown
diadems n ▷ diadem
diaereses n ▷ diaeresis
diaeresis n (pl -ses) mark (¨) placed over
a vowel to show that it is pronounced
separately from the preceding one, for
example in Noël
diagnosed v ▷ diagnosis
diagnoses n, v ▷ diagnosis
diagnosis [die-ag-**no**-siss] n (pl -ses) [-seez]
discovery and identification of diseases from
the examination of symptoms > **diagnose** v
(-noses, -nosing, -nosed) > **diagnostic** adj
diagnostic adj ▷ diagnosis
diagonal adj from corner to corner ▶ n (pl -s)
diagonal line > **diagonally** adv
diagonally adv ▷ diagonal
diagonals n ▷ diagonal
diagram n (pl -s) sketch showing the form or
workings of something > **diagrammatic** adj
diagrammatic adj ▷ diagram
diagrams n ▷ diagram
dial n (pl -s) face of a clock or watch ▶ v (dials,
dialling, dialled) operate the dial or buttons
on a telephone in order to contact (a number)
dialect n (pl -s) form of a language spoken in
a particular area > **dialectal** adj > **dialectally**
adv
dialectal adj ▷ dialect
dialectally adv ▷ dialect
dialectic n (pl -s) logical debate by question
and answer to resolve differences between
two views > **dialectical** adj > **dialectically** adv
dialectical adj ▷ dialectic
dialectically adv ▷ dialectic
dialectics n ▷ dialectic
dialects n ▷ dialect
dialled v ▷ dial
dialling v ▷ dial
dialogue n (pl -s) conversation between two
people, esp. in a book, film, or play
dialogues n ▷ dialogue
dials n, v ▷ dial
dialyses n ▷ dialysis
dialysis [die-**al**-iss-iss] n (pl -ses) (MED) filtering
of blood through a membrane to remove
waste products
diamanté [die-a-man-tee] adj decorated with
artificial jewels or sequins
diameter n (pl -s) (length of) a straight line
through the centre of a circle or sphere
diameters n ▷ diameter
diametric, diametrical adj of a diameter

> **diametrically** adv
diametrical adj ▷ diametric
diametrically adv ▷ diametric
diamond n (pl -s) exceptionally hard, usu. colourless, precious stone
diamonds n ▷ diamond
diaper n (pl -s) (US) nappy
diapers n ▷ diaper
diaphanous [die-**af**-fan-ous] adj fine and almost transparent > **diaphanously** adv
diaphanously adv ▷ diaphanous
diaphragm [**die**-a-fram] n (pl -s) muscular partition that separates the abdominal cavity and chest cavity
diaphragms n ▷ diaphragm
diaries n ▷ diary
diarist n ▷ diary
diarists n ▷ diary
diarrhoea [die-a-**ree**-a] n (pl -s) frequent discharge of abnormally liquid faeces
diarrhoeas n ▷ diarrhoea
diary n (pl -ries) (book for) a record of daily events, appointments, or observations > **diarist** n (pl -s)
diatribe n (pl -s) bitter critical attack
diatribes n ▷ diatribe
dibble n (pl -s) small hand tool used to make holes in the ground for seeds or plants
dibbles n ▷ dibble
dice n (pl dice) small cube each of whose sides has a different number of spots (1 to 6), used in games of chance ▶ v (dices, dicing, diced) cut (food) into small cubes
diced v ▷ dice
dices v ▷ dice
dicey adj (dicier, diciest) (Informal) dangerous or risky
dichotomies n ▷ dichotomy
dichotomy [die-**kot**-a-mee] n (pl -mies) division into two opposed groups or parts
dicier adj ▷ dice
diciest adj ▷ dice
dicing v ▷ dice
dickier adj ▷ dicky²
dickies n ▷ dicky¹
dickiest adj ▷ dicky²
dicky¹ n (pl dickies) false shirt front
dicky² adj (dickier, dickiest) (Informal) shaky or weak
dickybird n (pl -s) child's word for a bird
dickybirds n ▷ dickybird
dicta n ▷ dictum
dictate v (-tes, -ting, -ted) say aloud for someone else to write down (foll. by to) ▶ n (pl -s) authoritative command > **dictation**

n (pl -s)
dictated v ▷ dictate
dictates v, n ▷ dictate
dictating v ▷ dictate
dictation n ▷ dictate
dictations n ▷ dictate
dictator n (pl -s) ruler who has complete power > **dictatorship** n (pl -s)
dictatorial adj like a dictator > **dictatorially** adv
dictatorially adv ▷ dictatorial
dictators n ▷ dictator
dictatorship n ▷ dictator
dictatorships n ▷ dictator
diction n (pl -s) manner of pronouncing words and sounds
dictionaries n ▷ dictionary
dictionary n (pl -aries) book consisting of an alphabetical list of words with their meanings
dictions n ▷ diction
dictum n (pl -tums, -ta) formal statement
dictums n ▷ dictum
did v ▷ do
didactic adj intended to instruct > **didactically** adv
didactically adv ▷ didactic
diddle v (-dles, -dling, -dled) (Informal) swindle
diddled v ▷ diddle
diddles v ▷ diddle
diddling v ▷ diddle
didgeridoo n (pl -s) Australian musical instrument made from a long hollow piece of wood
didgeridoos n ▷ didgeridoo
didn't did not
die¹ v (dies, dying, died) (of a person, animal, or plant) cease all biological activity permanently
die² n (pl -s) shaped block used to cut or form metal
died v ▷ die¹
diehard n (pl -s) person who resists change
diehards n ▷ diehard
diereses n ▷ dieresis
dieresis [die-**air**-iss-iss] n (pl -ses) [-seez] ▷ diaeresis
dies v ▷ die¹ ▶ n ▷ die²
diesel n (pl -s) diesel engine
diesels n ▷ diesel
diet¹ n (pl -s) food that a person or animal regularly eats ▶ v (-s, -ing, -ed) follow a special diet so as to lose weight ▶ adj (of food) suitable for a weight-reduction diet > **dietary** adj > **dieter** n (pl -s)

diet² n (pl -s) parliament of some countries
  dietary adj ▷ diet
  dieted v ▷ diet
  dieter n ▷ diet
  dieters n ▷ diet
dietetic adj prepared for special dietary requirements
dietetics n study of diet and nutrition
dietician n (pl -s) person who specializes in dietetics
  dieticians n ▷ dietician
  dieting v ▷ diet
  diets v ▷ diet¹ ▶ n ▷ diet¹, ²
differ v (-s, -ing, -ed) be unlike
  differed v ▷ differ
difference n (pl -s) state of being unlike
  differences n ▷ difference
different adj unlike > **differently** adv
differential adj of or using a difference ▶ n (pl -s) factor that differentiates between two comparable things > **differentially** adv
  differentially adv ▷ differential
  differentials n ▷ differential
differentiate v, v (-te, -ting, -ted) perceive or show the difference (between) > **differentiation** n (pl -s)
  differentiated v ▷ differentiate
  differentiates v ▷ differentiate
  differentiating v ▷ differentiate
  differentiation n ▷ differentiate
  differentiations n ▷ differentiate
  differently n ▷ different
  differing v ▷ differ
  differs v ▷ differ
difficult adj requiring effort or skill to do or understand > **difficultly** adv > **difficulty** n (pl -ties)
  difficulties n ▷ difficult
  difficultly adv ▷ difficult
  difficulty n ▷ difficult
  diffidence n ▷ diffident
  diffidences n ▷ diffident
diffident adj lacking self-confidence > **diffidence** n (pl -s) > **diffidently** adv
  diffidently adv ▷ diffident
diffraction n (pl -s) (PHYSICS) deviation in the direction of a wave at the edge of an obstacle in its path
  diffractions n ▷ diffraction
diffuse v (-fuses, -fusing, -fused) spread over a wide area ▶ adj widely spread > **diffusely** adv > **diffuseness** n > **diffusion** n (pl -s)
  diffused v ▷ diffuse
  diffusely adv ▷ diffuse
  diffuseness n ▷ diffuse

  diffuses v ▷ diffuse
  diffusing v ▷ diffuse
  diffusion n ▷ diffuse
  diffusions n ▷ diffuse
dig v (digs, digging, dug) cut into, break up, and turn over or remove (earth), esp. with a spade ▶ n (pl -s) digging ▶ pl (pl -s) (BRIT, AUST & S AFR) (Informal) lodgings
digest v (-s, -ing, -ed) subject to a process of digestion ▶ n (pl -s) shortened version of a book, report, or article > **digestible** adj > **digestibility** n > **digestive** adj > **digestively** adv
  digested v ▷ digest
  digestibility n ▷ digest
  digestible adj ▷ digest
  digesting v ▷ digest
digestion n (pl -s) (body's system for) breaking down food into easily absorbed substances
  digestions n ▷ digestion
  digestive adj ▷ digest
  digestively adv ▷ digest
  digests v, n ▷ digest
digger n (pl -s) machine used for digging
  diggers n ▷ digger
  digging v ▷ dig
  diggings n ▷ dig
digit [dij-it] n (pl -s) finger or toe
digital adj displaying information as numbers rather than with hands and a dial > **digitally** adv
digitalis n drug made from foxglove leaves, used as a heart stimulant
  digitally adv ▷ digital
  digits n ▷ digit
  dignified n ▷ dignify
  dignifies n ▷ dignify
dignify v (-s, -ing, -ed) add distinction to
  dignifying v ▷ dignify
  dignitaries n ▷ dignitary
dignitary n (pl -aries) person of high official position
  dignities n ▷ dignity
dignity n (pl -ties) serious, calm, and controlled behaviour or manner
digress v (-es, -ing, -ed) depart from the main subject in speech or writing > **digression** n (pl -s)
  digressed v ▷ digress
  digresses v ▷ digress
  digressing v ▷ digress
  digression n ▷ digress
  digressions n ▷ digress
  digs v, n ▷ dig
dike n (pl -s) ▷ dyke

dikes n ▷ dike

dilapidated adj (of a building) having fallen into ruin > **dilapidation** n (pl -s)

dilapidation n ▷ dilapidated

dilapidations n ▷ dilapidated

dilatation n ▷ dilate

dilatations n ▷ dilate

dilate v (-lates, -lating, -lated) make or become wider or larger > **dilation, dilatation** n (pl -s)

dilated v ▷ dilate

dilates v ▷ dilate

dilating v ▷ dilate

dilation n ▷ dilate

dilations n ▷ dilate

dilatorily adv ▷ dilatory

dilatoriness n ▷ dilatory

dilatory [dill-a-tree] adj tending or intended to waste time > **dilatorily** adv > **dilatoriness** n

dilemma n (pl -s) situation offering a choice between two equally undesirable alternatives

dilemmas n ▷ dilemma

dilettante [dill-it-**tan**-tee] n (pl -tantes, -tanti) person whose interest in a subject is superficial rather than serious > **dilettantism** n

dilettantes n ▷ dilettante

dilettanti n ▷ dilettante

dilettantism n ▷ dilettante

diligence n ▷ diligent

diligent adj careful and persevering in carrying out duties > **diligently** adv > **diligence** n

diligently adv ▷ diligent

dill n (pl -s) sweet-smelling herb

dills n ▷ dill

dilute v (-lutes, -luting, -luted) make (a liquid) less concentrated, esp. by adding water > **dilution** n (pl -s)

diluted v ▷ dilute

dilutes v ▷ dilute

diluting v ▷ dilute

dilution n ▷ dilute

dilutions n ▷ dilute

diluvial, diluvian adj of a flood, esp. the great Flood described in the Old Testament

diluvian adj ▷ diluvial

dim adj (dimmer, dimmest) badly lit ▶ v (dims, dimming, dimmed) make or become dim > **dimly** adv > **dimness** n

dime n (pl -s) coin of the US and Canada, worth ten cents

dimension n (pl -s) measurement of the size of something in a particular direction

dimensions n ▷ dimension

dimes n ▷ dime

diminish v (-es, -ing, -ed) make or become smaller, fewer, or less > **diminution** n (pl -s)

diminished v ▷ diminish

diminishes v ▷ diminish

diminishing v ▷ diminish

diminuendo n (pl -s) (MUSIC) gradual decrease in loudness

diminuendos n ▷ diminuendo

diminution n ▷ diminish

diminutions n ▷ diminish

diminutive adj very small ▶ n (pl -s) word or affix which implies smallness or unimportance > **diminutively** adv > **diminutiveness** n

diminutively adv ▷ diminutive

diminutiveness n ▷ diminutive

diminutives n ▷ diminutive

dimly adv ▷ dim

dimmed v ▷ dim

dimmer n (pl -s) device for dimming an electric light ▶ adj ▷ dim

dimmers n ▷ dimmer

dimmest adj ▷ dim

dimming v ▷ dim

dimness n ▷ dim

dimple n (pl -s) small natural dent, esp. in the cheeks or chin ▶ v (-ples, -pling, -pled) produce dimples by smiling

dimpled v ▷ dimple

dimples n, v ▷ dimple

dimpling v ▷ dimple

dims v ▷ dim

din n (pl -s) loud unpleasant confused noise ▶ v (dins, dinning, dinned) (foll. by **into**) instil (something) into someone by constant repetition

dinar [dee-**nahr**] n (pl -s) monetary unit of various Balkan, Middle Eastern, and North African countries

dinars n ▷ dinar

dine v (dines, dining, dined) eat dinner

dined v ▷ dine

diner n (pl -s) person eating a meal

diners n ▷ diner

dines v ▷ dine

ding n (pl -s) (AUST DATED & NZ) (Informal) small dent in a vehicle

dinghies n ▷ dinghy

dinghy [ding-ee] n (pl -ghies) small boat, powered by sails, oars, or a motor

dingier adj ▷ dingy

dingiest adj ▷ dingy

dinginess n ▷ dingy

dingo n (pl -goes) Australian wild dog

dingoes n ▷ dingo

dings n ▷ dingo

dingy [din-jee] adj (-gier, -giest) (BRIT, AUST & NZ) dull and drab > **dinginess** n

dining v ▷ dine

dinkier adj ▷ dinky

dinkiest adj ▷ dinky

dinkum adj (AUST & NZ) (Informal) genuine or right

dinky adj (-kier, -kiest) (BRIT, AUST & NZ) (Informal) small and neat

dinned v ▷ din

dinner n (pl -s) main meal of the day, eaten either in the evening or at midday

dinners n ▷ dinner

dinning v ▷ din

dinosaur n (pl -s) type of extinct prehistoric reptile, many of which were of gigantic size

dinosaurs n ▷ dinosaur

dins n, v ▷ din

dint n (pl -s) means

dints n ▷ dint

diocesan adj ▷ diocese

diocese [die-a-siss] n (pl -s) district over which a bishop has control > **diocesan** adj

dioceses n ▷ diocese

diode n (pl -s) semiconductor device for converting alternating current to direct current

diodes n ▷ diode

dioptre [die-op-ter] n (pl -s) unit for measuring the refractive power of a lens

dioptres n ▷ dioptre

dioxide n (pl -s) oxide containing two oxygen atoms per molecule

dioxides n ▷ dioxide

dip v (dips, dipping, dipped) plunge quickly or briefly into a liquid ▶ n (pl -s) dipping

diphtheria [dif-theer-ya] n (pl -s) contagious disease producing fever and difficulty in breathing and swallowing

diphtherias n ▷ diphtheria

diphthong n (pl -s) union of two vowel sounds in a single compound sound

diphthongs n ▷ diphthong

diploma n (pl -s) qualification awarded by a college on successful completion of a course

diplomacies n ▷ diplomacy

diplomacy n (pl -macies) conduct of the relations between nations by peaceful means

diplomas n ▷ diploma

diplomat n (pl -s) official engaged in diplomacy

diplomatic adj of diplomacy > **diplomatically** adv

diplomatically adv ▷ diplomatic

diplomats n ▷ diplomat

dipped v ▷ dip

dipper n (pl -s) ladle used for dipping

dippers n ▷ dipper

dipping v ▷ dip

diprotodont [die-pro-toe-dont] n (pl -s) marsupial with fewer than three upper incisor teeth on each side of the jaw

diprotodonts n ▷ diprotodont

dips v, n ▷ dip

dipsomania n (pl -s) compulsive craving for alcohol > **dipsomaniac** n (pl -s) adj

dipsomaniac n, adj ▷ dipsomania

dipsomaniacs n ▷ dipsomania

dipsomanias n ▷ dipsomania

diptych [dip-tik] n (pl -s) painting on two hinged panels

diptychs n ▷ diptych

dire adj (-er, -est) disastrous, urgent, or terrible > **direly** adv > **direness** n (pl -es)

direct adj (of a route) shortest, straight ▶ adv in a direct manner ▶ v (-s, -ing, -ed) lead and organize > **directness** n

directed v ▷ direct

directing v ▷ direct

direction n (pl -s) course or line along which a person or thing moves, points, or lies ▶ pl instructions for doing something or for reaching a place > **directional** adj

directional adj ▷ direction

directions n ▷ direction

directive n (pl -s) instruction, order

directives n ▷ directive

directly adv in a direct manner ▶ conj as soon as

directness n ▷ direct

director n (pl -s) person or thing that directs or controls > **directorial** adj > **directorship** n (pl -s)

directorate n (pl -s) board of directors

directorates n ▷ directorate

directorial adj ▷ director

directories n ▷ directory

directors n ▷ director

directorship n ▷ director

directorships n ▷ director

directory n (pl -ries) book listing names, addresses, and telephone numbers

directs v ▷ direct

direly adv ▷ dire

direness n ▷ dire

direnesses n ▷ dire

direr adj ▷ dire

direst adj ▷ dire

dirge *n* (*pl* **-s**) slow sad song of mourning
  dirges *n* ▷ dirge
dirigible [dir-rij-jib-bl] *adj* able to be steered ▶ *n*
  (*pl* **-s**) airship
  dirigibles *n* ▷ dirigible
dirk *n* (*pl* **-s**) dagger, formerly worn by Scottish
  Highlanders
  dirks *n* ▷ dirk
dirndl *n* (*pl* **-s**) full gathered skirt originating
  from Tyrolean peasant wear
  dirndls *n* ▷ dirndl
dirt *n* (*pl* **-s**) unclean substance, filth
  dirtied *v* ▷ dirty
  dirtier *adj* ▷ dirty
  dirties *v* ▷ dirty
  dirtiest *adj* ▷ dirty
  dirtily *adv* ▷ dirty
  dirtiness *n* ▷ dirty
  dirts *n* ▷ dirt
dirty *adj* (**dirtier, dirtiest**) covered or marked
  with dirt ▶ *v* (**dirties, dirtying, dirtied**) make
  dirty > **dirtily** *adv* > **dirtiness** *n*
  dirtying *v* ▷ dirty
  disabilities *n* ▷ disability
disability *n* (*pl* **-ties**) condition of being
  disabled
disable *v* (**-bles, -bling, -bled**) make ineffective,
  unfit, or incapable > **disablement** *n*
disabled *adj* lacking a physical power, such as
  the ability to walk ▶ *v* ▷ disable
  disablement *n* ▷ disable
  disables *v* ▷ disable
  disabling *v* ▷ disable
disabuse *v* (**-buses, -busing, -bused**) (*foll. by* **of**)
  rid (someone) of a mistaken idea
  disabused *v* ▷ disabuse
  disabuses *v* ▷ disabuse
  disabusing *v* ▷ disabuse
disadvantage *n* (*pl* **-s**) unfavourable or
  harmful circumstance > **disadvantageous**
  adj > **disadvantageously** *adv*
  > **disadvantageousness** *n*
disadvantaged *adj* socially or economically
  deprived
  disadvantageous *adj* ▷ disadvantage
  disadvantageously *adv* ▷ disadvantage
  disadvantageousness *n* ▷ disadvantage
  disadvantages *n* ▷ disadvantage
disaffected *adj* having lost loyalty to or
  affection for someone or something
  > **disaffectedly** *adv* > **disaffection** *n* (*pl* **-s**)
  disaffectedly *adv* ▷ disaffected
  disaffection *n* ▷ disaffected
  disaffections *n* ▷ disaffected
disagree *v* (**-grees, -greeing, -greed**) argue

or have different opinions > **disagreement**
  n (*pl* **-s**)
disagreeable *adj* unpleasant
  > **disagreeableness** *n* > **disagreeably** *adv*
  disagreeableness *n* ▷ disagreeable
  disagreeably *adv* ▷ disagreeable
  disagreed *v* ▷ disagree
  disagreeing *v* ▷ disagree
  disagreement *n* ▷ disagree
  disagreements *n* ▷ disagree
  disagrees *v* ▷ disagree
disallow *v* (**-s, -ing, -ed**) reject as untrue or
  invalid
  disallowed *v* ▷ disallow
  disallowing *v* ▷ disallow
  disallows *v* ▷ disallow
disappear *v* (**-s, -ing, -ed**) cease to be visible
  > **disappearance** *n* (*pl* **-s**)
  disappearance *n* ▷ disappear
  disappearances *n* ▷ disappear
  disappeared *v* ▷ disappear
  disappearing *v* ▷ disappear
  disappears *v* ▷ disappear
disappoint *v* (**-s, -ing, -ed**) fail to meet the
  expectations or hopes of > **disappointingly**
  adv
  disappointed *v* ▷ disappoint
  disappointing *v* ▷ disappoint
  disappointingly *adv* ▷ disappoint
disappointment *n* (*pl* **-s**) feeling of being
  disappointed
  disappointments *n* ▷ disappointment
  disappoints *v* ▷ disappoint
disapprobation *n* (*pl* **-s**) disapproval
  disapprobations *n* ▷ disapprobation
  disapproval *n* ▷ disapprove
  disapprovals *n* ▷ disapprove
disapprove *v* (**-proves, -proving, -proved**) (*foll.*
  by **of**) consider wrong or bad > **disapproval**
  n (*pl* **-s**)
  disapproved *v* ▷ disapprove
  disapproves *v* ▷ disapprove
  disapproving *v* ▷ disapprove
disarm *v* (**-s, -ing, -ed**) deprive of weapons
  > **disarmament** *n* (*pl* **-s**)
  disarmament *n* ▷ disarm
  disarmaments *n* ▷ disarm
  disarmed *v* ▷ disarm
disarming *adj* removing hostility or suspicion
  ▶ *v* ▷ disarm > **disarmingly** *adv*
  disarmingly *adv* ▷ disarming
  disarms *v* ▷ disarm
disarrange *v* (**-ranges, -ranging, -ranged**)
  throw into disorder
  disarranged *v* ▷ disarrange

disarranges v ▷ disarrange

disarranging v ▷ disarrange

disarray n (pl -s) confusion and lack of discipline

disarrays n ▷ disarray

disaster n (pl -s) occurrence that causes great distress or destruction > **disastrous** adj > **disastrously** adv

disasters n ▷ disaster

disastrous adj ▷ disaster

disastrously adv ▷ disaster

disavow v (-s, -ing, -ed) deny connection with or responsibility for > **disavowal** n (pl -s)

disavowal n ▷ disavow

disavowals n ▷ disavow

disavowed v ▷ disavow

disavowing v ▷ disavow

disavows v ▷ disavow

disband v (-s, -ing, -ed) (cause to) cease to function as a group

disbanded v ▷ disband

disbanding v ▷ disband

disbands v ▷ disband

disbelief n ▷ disbelieve

disbelieve v (-lieves, -lieving, -lieved) reject as false (foll. by **in**) > **disbelief** n

disbelieved v ▷ disbelieve

disbelieves v ▷ disbelieve

disbelieving v ▷ disbelieve

disburse v (-burses, -bursing, -bursed) pay out > **disbursement** n (pl -s)

disbursed v ▷ disburse

disbursement n ▷ disburse

disbursements n ▷ disburse

disburses v ▷ disburse

disbursing v ▷ disburse

disc n (pl -s) flat circular object ▷ **disk**

discard v (-s, -ing, -ed) get rid of (something or someone) as useless or undesirable

discarded v ▷ discard

discarding v ▷ discard

discards v ▷ discard

discern v (-s, -ing, -ed) see or be aware of (something) clearly > **discernible** adj > **discernibly** adv > **discernment** n (pl -s)

discerned v ▷ discern

discernible adj ▷ discern

discernibly adv ▷ discern

discerning adj having good judgment ▶ v ▷ discern

discernment n ▷ discern

discernments n ▷ discern

discerns v ▷ discern

discharge v (-charges, -charging, -charged) release, allow to go ▶ n (pl -s) substance that comes out from a place

discharged v ▷ discharge

discharges v, n ▷ discharge

discharging v ▷ discharge

disciple [diss-**sipe**-pl] n (pl -s) follower of the doctrines of a teacher, esp. Jesus Christ

disciples n ▷ disciple

disciplinarian n (pl -s) person who practises strict discipline

disciplinarians n ▷ disciplinarian

disciplinary adj ▷ discipline

discipline n (pl -s) practice of imposing strict rules of behaviour ▶ v (-plines, -plining, -plined) attempt to improve the behaviour of (oneself or another) by training or rules > **disciplinary** adj

disciplined adj able to behave and work in a controlled way ▶ v ▷ discipline

disciplines n, v ▷ discipline

disciplining v ▷ discipline

disclaimed v ▷ disclaimer

disclaimer n (pl -s) statement denying responsibility > **disclaim** v (-s, -ing, -ed)

disclaimers n ▷ disclaimer

disclaiming v ▷ disclaimer

disclaims v ▷ disclaimer

disclose v (-closes, -closing, -closed) make known > **disclosure** n (pl -s)

disclosed v ▷ disclose

discloses v ▷ disclose

disclosing v ▷ disclose

disclosure n ▷ disclose

disclosures n ▷ disclose

disco n (pl -s) nightclub where people dance to amplified pop records

discoloration n ▷ discolour

discolorations n ▷ discolour

discolour v (-s, -ing, -ed) change in colour, fade > **discoloration** n (pl -s)

discoloured v ▷ discolour

discolouring v ▷ discolour

discolours v ▷ discolour

discomfit v (-s, -ing, -ed) make uneasy or confused > **discomfiture** n (pl -s)

discomfited v ▷ discomfit

discomfiting v ▷ discomfit

discomfits v ▷ discomfit

discomfiture n ▷ discomfit

discomfitures n ▷ discomfit

discomfort n (pl -s) inconvenience, distress, or mild pain

discomforts n ▷ discomfort

discommode v (-modes, -moding, -moded) cause inconvenience to

discommoded v ▷ discommode

discommodes v ▷ discommode
discommoding v ▷ discommode
disconcert v (-s, -ing, -ed) embarrass or upset
disconcerted v ▷ disconcert
disconcerting v ▷ disconcert
disconcerts v ▷ disconcert
disconnect v (-s, -ing, -ed) undo or break
the connection between (two things)
> **disconnection** n (pl -s)
disconnected adj (of speech or ideas) not
logically connected ▶ v ▷ disconnect
disconnecting v ▷ disconnect
disconnection n ▷ disconnect
disconnections n ▷ disconnect
disconnects v ▷ disconnect
disconsolate adj sad beyond comfort
> **disconsolately** adv
disconsolately adv ▷ disconsolate
discontent n (pl -s) lack of contentment
> **discontented** adj > **discontentedly** adv
discontented adj ▷ discontent
discontentedly adv ▷ discontent
discontents n ▷ discontent
discontinue v (-nues, -nuing, -nued) come or
bring to an end
discontinued v ▷ discontinue
discontinues v ▷ discontinue
discontinuing v ▷ discontinue
discontinuities n ▷ discontinuous
discontinuity n ▷ discontinuous
discontinuous adj characterized by
interruptions > **discontinuity** n (pl -nuities)
discord n (pl -s) lack of agreement or
harmony between people > **discordant** adj
> **discordantly** adv > **discordance** n (pl -s)
discordance n ▷ discord
discordances n ▷ discord
discordant adj ▷ discord
discordantly adv ▷ discord
discords n ▷ discord
discos n ▷ disco
discotheque n (pl -s) ▷ disco
discotheques n ▷ discotheque
discount v (-s, -ing, -ed) take no account of
(something) because it is considered to be
unreliable, prejudiced, or irrelevant ▶ n (pl -s)
deduction from the full price of something
discounted v ▷ discount
discounting v ▷ discount
discounts v, n ▷ discount
discourage v (-rages, -raging, -raged)
deprive of the will to persist in something
> **discouragement** n (pl -s)
discouraged v ▷ discourage
discouragement n ▷ discourage

discouragements n ▷ discourage
discourages v ▷ discourage
discouraging v ▷ discourage
discourse n (pl -s) conversation ▶ v (-ses, -sing,
-sed) (foll. by on) speak or write (about) at
length
discoursed v ▷ discourse
discourses n, v ▷ discourse
discoursing v ▷ discourse
discourteous adj showing bad manners
> **discourteously** adv > **discourtesy** n (pl
-esies)
discourteously adv ▷ discourteous
discourtesies n ▷ discourteous
discourtesy n ▷ discourteous
discover v (-s, -ing, -ed) be the first to find or to
find out about > **discoverer** n (pl -s)
discovered v ▷ discover
discoverer n ▷ discover
discoverers n ▷ discover
discoveries n ▷ discovery
discovering v ▷ discover
discovers v ▷ discover
discovery n (pl -eries) discovering
discredit v (-s, -ing, -ed) damage the
reputation of ▶ n (pl -s) damage to someone's
reputation
discreditable adj bringing shame
discredited v ▷ discredit
discrediting v ▷ discredit
discredits v, n ▷ discredit
discreet adj (-er, -est) careful to avoid
embarrassment, esp. by keeping confidences
secret > **discreetly** adv > **discreetness** n (pl -es)
discreeter adj ▷ discreet
discreetest adj ▷ discreet
discreetly adv ▷ discreet
discreetness n ▷ discreet
discreetnesses n ▷ discreet
discrepancies n ▷ discrepancy
discrepancy n (pl -cies) conflict or variation
between facts, figures, or claims
discrete adj (-r, -st) separate, distinct
> **discretely** adv > **discreteness** n (pl -es)
discretely adv ▷ discrete
discreteness n ▷ discrete
discretenesses n ▷ discrete
discreter adj ▷ discrete
discretest adj ▷ discrete
discretion n (pl -s) quality of behaving in a
discreet way > **discretionary** adj
discretionary adj ▷ discretion
discretions n ▷ discretion
discriminate v (-nates, -nating, -nated)
(foll. by against or in favour of) single

out (a particular person or group) for worse or better treatment than others > **discrimination** n (pl -s)

discriminated v ▷ discriminate

discriminates v ▷ discriminate

discriminating adj showing good taste and judgment ▶ v ▷ discriminate

discrimination n ▷ discriminate

discriminations n ▷ discriminate

discriminatory adj based on prejudice

discs n ▷ disc

discursive adj passing from one topic to another > **discursively** adv > **discursiveness** n

discursively adv ▷ discursive

discursiveness n ▷ discursive

discus n (pl -es) heavy disc-shaped object thrown in sports competitions

discuses n ▷ discus

discuss v (-es, -ing, -ed) consider (something) by talking it over > **discussion** n (pl -s)

discussed v ▷ discuss

discusses v ▷ discuss

discussing v ▷ discuss

discussion n ▷ discuss

discussions n ▷ discuss

disdain n feeling of superiority and dislike ▶ v (-s, -ing, -ed) refuse with disdain ▶ **disdainful** adj > **disdainfully** adv

disdained v ▷ disdain

disdainful adj ▷ disdain

disdainfully adv ▷ disdain

disdaining v ▷ disdain

disdains v ▷ disdain

disease n (pl -s) illness, sickness > **diseased** adj

diseased n ▷ disease

diseases n ▷ disease

disembark v (-s, -ing, -ed) get off a ship, aircraft, or bus > **disembarkation** n (pl -s)

disembarkation n ▷ disembark

disembarkations n ▷ disembark

disembarked v ▷ disembark

disembarking v ▷ disembark

disembarks v ▷ disembark

disembodied adj lacking a body

disembowel v (-els, -elling, -elled) remove the entrails of

disembowelled v ▷ disembowel

disembowelling v ▷ disembowel

disembowels v ▷ disembowel

disenchanted adj disappointed and disillusioned > **disenchantment** n (pl -s)

disenchantment n ▷ disenchant

disenchantments n ▷ disenchant

disenfranchise, disfranchise v (-ises, -ising, -ised) deprive (someone) of the right

to vote or of other rights of citizenship > **disenfranchisement** n (pl -s)

disenfranchised v ▷ disenfranchise

disenfranchisement n ▷ disenfranchise

disenfranchisements n ▷ disenfranchise

disenfranchises v ▷ disenfranchise

disenfranchising v ▷ disenfranchise

disengage v (-gages, -gaging, -gaged) release from a connection > **disengagement** n (pl -s)

disengaged v ▷ disengage

disengagement n ▷ disengage

disengagements n ▷ disengage

disengages v ▷ disengage

disengaging v ▷ disengage

disentangle v (-tangles, -tangling, -tangled) release from entanglement or confusion

disentangled v ▷ disentangle

disentangles v ▷ disentangle

disentangling v ▷ disentangle

disfavour n (pl -s) disapproval or dislike

disfavours n ▷ disfavour

disfigure v (-gures, -guring, -gured) spoil the appearance of > **disfigurement** n (pl -s)

disfigured v ▷ disfigure

disfigurement n ▷ disfigure

disfigurements n ▷ disfigure

disfigures v ▷ disfigure

disfiguring v ▷ disfigure

disfranchise v (-ises, -ising, -ised) ▷ disenfranchise

disfranchised v ▷ disfranchise

disfranchises v ▷ disfranchise

disfranchising v ▷ disfranchise

disgorge v (-gorges, -gorging, -gorged) empty out, discharge

disgorged v ▷ disgorge

disgorges v ▷ disgorge

disgorging v ▷ disgorge

disgrace n (pl -s) condition of shame, loss of reputation, or dishonour ▶ v (-graces, -gracing, -graced) bring shame upon (oneself or others) > **disgraceful** adj > **disgracefully** adv

disgraced v ▷ disgrace

disgraceful adj ▷ disgrace

disgracefully adv ▷ disgrace

disgraces n, v ▷ disgrace

disgracing v ▷ disgrace

disgruntled adj sulky or discontented > **disgruntlement** n

disgruntlement n ▷ disgruntled

disguise v (-guises, -guising, -guised) change the appearance or manner in order to conceal the identity of (someone or something) ▶ n (pl -s) mask, costume, or manner that

disguises
disguised v ▷ disguise
disguises v, n ▷ disguise
disguising v ▷ disguise
disgust n (pl -s) great loathing or distaste ▶ v (-s, -ing, -ed) sicken, fill with loathing
disgusted v ▷ disgust
disgusting v ▷ disgust
disgusts v ▷ disgust
dish n (pl -es) shallow container used for holding or serving food
dishabille [diss-a-beel] n (pl -s) ▷ deshabille
dishabilles n ▷ dishabille
dishcloth n (pl -s) cloth for washing dishes
dishcloths n ▷ dishcloth
dishearten v (-s, -ing, -ed) weaken or destroy the hope, courage, or enthusiasm of
disheartened v ▷ dishearten
disheartening v ▷ dishearten
disheartens v ▷ dishearten
dishes n ▷ dish
dishevelled adj (of a person's hair, clothes, or general appearance) disordered and untidy
dishonest adj not honest or fair > **dishonestly** adv > **dishonesty** n (pl -ties)
dishonesties n ▷ dishonest
dishonestly adv ▷ dishonest
dishonesty n ▷ dishonest
dishonour v (-s, -ing, -ed) treat with disrespect ▶ n (pl -s) lack of respect > **dishonourable** adj > **dishonourably** adv
dishonourable adj ▷ dishonour
dishonourably adv ▷ dishonour
dishonoured v ▷ dishonour
dishonouring v ▷ dishonour
dishonours v, n ▷ dishonour
disillusion v (-s, -ing, -ed) destroy the illusions or false ideas of (also **disillusionment**) ▶ n (pl -s) state of being disillusioned
disillusioned v ▷ disillusion
disillusioning v ▷ disillusion
disillusionment n ▷ disillusion
disillusionments n ▷ disillusion
disillusions v, n ▷ disillusion
disincentive n (pl -s) something that acts as a deterrent
disincentives n ▷ disincentive
disinclination n ▷ disinclined
disinclinations n ▷ disinclined
disinclined adj unwilling, reluctant > **disinclination** n (pl -s)
disinfect v (-s, -ing, -ed) rid of harmful germs, chemically > **disinfection** n (pl -s)
disinfectant n (pl -s) substance that destroys harmful germs

disinfectants n ▷ disinfectant
disinfected v ▷ disinfect
disinfecting v ▷ disinfect
disinfection n ▷ disinfect
disinfections n ▷ disinfect
disinfects v ▷ disinfect
disinformation n false information intended to mislead
disingenuous adj not sincere > **disingenuously** adv > **disingenuousness** n
disingenuously adv ▷ disingenuous
disingenuousness n ▷ disingenuous
disinherit v (-s, -ing, -ed) (LAW) deprive (an heir) of inheritance > **disinheritance** n (pl -s)
disinheritance n ▷ disinherit
disinheritances n ▷ disinherit
disinherited v ▷ disinherit
disinheriting v ▷ disinherit
disinherits v ▷ disinherit
disintegrate v (-rates, -rating, -rated) break up > **disintegration** n (pl -s)
disintegrated v ▷ disintegrate
disintegrates v ▷ disintegrate
disintegrating v ▷ disintegrate
disintegration n ▷ disintegrate
disintegrations n ▷ disintegrate
disinter v (-ters, -terring, -terred) dig up
disinterest n ▷ disinterested
disinterested adj free from bias or involvement > **disinterest** n > **disinterestedly** adv > **disinterestedness** n
disinterestedly adv ▷ disinterested
disinterestedness n ▷ disinterested
disinterred v ▷ disinter
disinterring v ▷ disinter
disinters v ▷ disinter
disjointed adj having no coherence, disconnected > **disjointedly** adv
disjointedly adv ▷ disjointed
disk n (pl -s) (COMPUTERS) storage device, consisting of a stack of plates coated with a magnetic layer, which rotates rapidly as a single unit
disks n ▷ disk
dislike v (-likes, -liking, -liked) consider unpleasant or disagreeable ▶ n (pl -s) feeling of not liking something or someone
disliked v ▷ dislike
dislikes v, n ▷ dislike
disliking v ▷ dislike
dislocate v (-cates, -cating, -cated) displace (a bone or joint) from its normal position > **dislocation** n (pl -s)
dislocated v ▷ dislocate
dislocates v ▷ dislocate

dislocating *v* ▷ dislocate
dislocation *n* ▷ dislocate
dislocations *n* ▷ dislocate
dislodge *v* (-lodges, -lodging, -lodged) remove (something) from a previously fixed position
dislodged *v* ▷ dislodge
dislodges *v* ▷ dislodge
dislodging *v* ▷ dislodge
disloyal *adj* not loyal, deserting one's allegiance ▷ **disloyalty** *n* (*pl* -ties)
disloyalties *n* ▷ disloyalty
dismal *adj* gloomy and depressing ▷ **dismally** *adv* ▷ **dismalness** *n*
dismally *adv* ▷ dismal
dismalness *n* ▷ dismal
dismantle *v* (-mantles, -mantling, -mantled) take apart piece by piece
dismantled *v* ▷ dismantle
dismantles *v* ▷ dismantle
dismantling *v* ▷ dismantle
dismay *v* (-s, -ing, -ed) fill with alarm or depression ▶ *n* (*pl* -s) alarm mixed with sadness
dismayed *v* ▷ dismay
dismaying *v* ▷ dismay
dismays *v*, *n* ▷ dismay
dismember *v* (-s, -ing, -ed) remove the limbs of ▷ **dismemberment** *n* (*pl* -s)
dismembered *v* ▷ dismember
dismembering *v* ▷ dismember
dismemberment *n* ▷ dismember
dismemberments *n* ▷ dismember
dismembers *v* ▷ dismember
dismiss *v* (-es, -ing, -ed) remove (an employee) from a job ▷ **dismissal** *n* (*pl* -s)
dismissal *n* ▷ dismiss
dismissals *n* ▷ dismiss
dismissed *v* ▷ dismiss
dismisses *v* ▷ dismiss
dismissing *v* ▷ dismiss
dismissive *adj* scornful, contemptuous
dismount *v* (-s, -ing, -ed) get off a horse or bicycle
dismounted *v* ▷ dismount
dismounting *v* ▷ dismount
dismounts *v* ▷ dismount
disobedience *n* ▷ disobey
disobedient *adj* ▷ disobey
disobediently *adv* ▷ disobey
disobey *v* (-s, -ing, -ed) neglect or refuse to obey ▷ **disobedient** *adj* ▷ **disobediently** *adv* ▷ **disobedience** *n*
disobeyed *v* ▷ disobey
disobeying *v* ▷ disobey
disobeys *v* ▷ disobey

disobliging *adj* unwilling to help
disorder *n* (*pl* -s) state of untidiness and disorganization
disordered *adj* untidy
disorderliness *n* ▷ disorderly
disorderly *adj* untidy and disorganized ▷ **disorderliness** *n*
disorders *n* ▷ disorder
disorganization *n* ▷ disorganize
disorganizations *n* ▷ disorganize
disorganize *v* (-nizes, -nizing, -nized) disrupt the arrangement or system of ▷ **disorganization** *n* (*pl* -s)
disorganized *v* ▷ disorganize
disorganizes *v* ▷ disorganize
disorganizing *v* ▷ disorganize
disorientate, disorient *v* (-tates, -tating, -tated, -s, -ing, -ed) cause (someone) to lose his or her bearings ▷ **disorientation** *n* (*pl* -s)
disorientated *v* ▷ disorientate
disorientates *v* ▷ disorientate
disorientating *v* ▷ disorientate
disorientation *n* ▷ disorientate
disorientations *n* ▷ disorientate
disoriented *v* ▷ disorientate
disorienting *v* ▷ disorientate
disorients *v* ▷ disorientate
disown *v* (-s, -ing, -ed) deny any connection with (someone)
disowned *v* ▷ disown
disowning *v* ▷ disown
disowns *v* ▷ disown
disparage *v* (-rages, -raging, -raged) speak contemptuously of ▷ **disparagement** *n* (*pl* -s)
disparaged *v* ▷ disparage
disparagement *n* ▷ disparage
disparagements *n* ▷ disparage
disparages *v* ▷ disparage
disparaging *v* ▷ disparage
disparate *adj* completely different ▷ **disparately** *adv* ▷ **disparateness** *n* ▷ **disparity** *n* (*pl* -ities)
disparately *adv* ▷ disparate
disparateness *n* ▷ disparate
disparities *n* ▷ disparate
disparity *n* ▷ disparate
dispassionate *adj* not influenced by emotion ▷ **dispassionately** *adv*
dispassionately *adv* ▷ dispassionate
dispatch *v* (-es, -ing, -ed) send off to a destination or to perform a task ▶ *n* (*pl* -es) official communication or report, sent in haste
dispatched *v* ▷ dispatch
dispatches *v*, *n* ▷ dispatch

dispatching v ▷ dispatch
dispel v (-pels, -pelling, -pelled) destroy or remove
dispelled v ▷ dispel
dispelling v ▷ dispel
dispels v ▷ dispel
dispensability n ▷ dispensable
dispensable adj not essential > **dispensability** n
dispensaries n ▷ dispensary
dispensary n (pl -saries) place where medicine is dispensed
dispensation n (pl -s) dispensing
dispensations n ▷ dispensation
dispense v (-penses, -pensing, -pensed) distribute in portions > **dispenser** n (pl -s)
dispensed v ▷ dispense
dispenser n ▷ dispense
dispensers n ▷ dispense
dispenses v ▷ dispense
dispensing v ▷ dispense
dispersal n ▷ disperse
dispersals n ▷ disperse
disperse v (-perses, -persing, -persed) scatter over a wide area > **dispersal, dispersion** n (pl -s)
dispersed v ▷ disperse
disperses v ▷ disperse
dispersing v ▷ disperse
dispersion n ▷ disperse
dispersions n ▷ disperse
dispirit v (-s, -ing, -ed) make downhearted
dispirited v ▷ dispirit
dispiriting v ▷ dispirit
dispirits v ▷ dispirit
displace v (-places, -placing, -placed) move from the usual location > **displacement** n (pl -s)
displaced v ▷ displace
displacement n ▷ displace
displacements n ▷ displace
displaces v ▷ displace
displacing v ▷ displace
display v (-s, -ing, -ed) make visible or noticeable ▶ n (pl -s) displaying
displayed v ▷ display
displaying v ▷ display
displays v, n ▷ display
displease v (-ses, -sing, -sed) annoy or upset > **displeasure** n (pl -s)
displeased v ▷ displease
displeases v ▷ displease
displeasing v ▷ displease
displeasure n ▷ displease
displeasures n ▷ displease

disport v (-s, -ing, -ed) indulge oneself in pleasure
disported v ▷ disport
disporting v ▷ disport
disports v ▷ disport
disposability n ▷ disposable
disposable adj designed to be thrown away after use > **disposability** n
disposal n (pl -s) getting rid of something
disposals n ▷ disposal
dispose v (-poses, -posing, -posed) place in a certain order
disposed adj willing or eager ▶ v ▷ dispose
disposes v ▷ dispose
disposing v ▷ dispose
disposition n (pl -s) person's usual temperament
dispositions n ▷ disposition
dispossess v (-es, -ing, -ed) (foll. by of) deprive (someone) of (a possession) > **dispossession** n (pl -s)
dispossessed v ▷ dispossess
dispossesses v ▷ dispossess
dispossessing v ▷ dispossess
dispossession n ▷ dispossess
dispossessions n ▷ dispossess
disproportion n (pl -s) lack of proportion or equality
disproportionate adj out of proportion > **disproportionately** adv
disproportionately adv ▷ disproportionate
disproportions n ▷ disproportion
disprove v (-proves, -proving, -proved) show (an assertion or claim) to be incorrect
disproved v ▷ disprove
disproves v ▷ disprove
disproving v ▷ disprove
dispute n (pl -s) disagreement, argument ▶ v (-putes, -puting, -puted) argue about (something)
disputed v ▷ dispute
disputes n, v ▷ dispute
disputing v ▷ dispute
disqualification n ▷ disqualify
disqualifications n ▷ disqualify
disqualified v ▷ disqualify
disqualifies v ▷ disqualify
disqualify v (-fies, -fying, -fied) stop (someone) officially from taking part in something for wrongdoing > **disqualification** n (pl -s)
disqualifying v ▷ disqualify
disquiet n (pl -s) feeling of anxiety ▶ v (-s, -ing, -ed) make (someone) anxious > **disquietude** n (pl -s)

disquieted v ▷ disquiet

disquieting v ▷ disquiet

disquiets v, n ▷ disquiet

disquietude n ▷ disquiet

disquietudes n ▷ disquiet

disregard v (-s, -ing, -ed) give little or no attention to ▶ n (pl -s) lack of attention or respect

disregarded v ▷ disregard

disregarding v ▷ disregard

disregards v, n ▷ disregard

disrepair n (pl -s) condition of being worn out or in poor working order

disrepairs n ▷ disrepair

disreputable adj having or causing a bad reputation > **disreputably** adv

disreputably adv ▷ disreputable

disrepute n (pl -s) loss or lack of good reputation

disreputes n ▷ disrepute

disrespect n (pl -s) lack of respect > **disrespectful** adj > **disrespectfully** adv

disrespectful adj ▷ disrespect

disrespectfully adv ▷ disrespect

disrespects n ▷ disrespect

disrobe v (-robes, -robing, -robed) undress

disrobed v ▷ disrobe

disrobes v ▷ disrobe

disrobing v ▷ disrobe

disrupt v (-s, -ing, -ed) interrupt the progress of > **disruption** n (pl -s) > **disruptive** adj

disrupted v ▷ disrupt

disrupting v ▷ disrupt

disruption n ▷ disrupt

disruptions n ▷ disrupt

disruptive adj ▷ disrupt

disrupts v ▷ disrupt

dissatisfaction n ▷ dissatisfied

dissatisfactions n ▷ dissatisfied

dissatisfied adj not pleased or contented > **dissatisfaction** n (pl -s)

dissect v (-s, -ing, -ed) cut open (a corpse) to examine it > **dissection** n (pl -s)

dissected v ▷ dissect

dissecting v ▷ dissect

dissection n ▷ dissect

dissections n ▷ dissect

dissects v ▷ dissect

dissemble v (-bles, -bling, -bled) conceal one's real motives or emotions by pretence

dissembled v ▷ dissemble

dissembles v ▷ dissemble

dissembling v ▷ dissemble

disseminate v (-nates, -nating, -nated) spread (information) > **dissemination** n (pl -s)

disseminated v ▷ disseminate

disseminates v ▷ disseminate

disseminating v ▷ disseminate

dissemination n ▷ disseminate

disseminations n ▷ disseminate

dissension n ▷ dissent

dissensions n ▷ dissent

dissent v (-s, -ing, -ed) disagree ▶ n (pl -s) disagreement > **dissension** n (pl -s) > **dissenter** n (pl -s)

dissented v ▷ dissent

dissenter n ▷ dissent

dissenters n ▷ dissent

dissenting v ▷ dissent

dissents v ▷ dissent

dissertation n (pl -s) written thesis, usu. required for a higher university degree

dissertations n ▷ dissertation

disservice n (pl -s) harmful action

disservices n ▷ disservice

dissidence n ▷ dissident

dissidences n ▷ dissident

dissident n (pl -s) person who disagrees with and criticizes the government ▶ adj disagreeing with the government > **dissidence** n (pl -s)

dissidents n ▷ dissident

dissimilar adj not alike, different > **dissimilarity** n (pl -ities)

dissimilarities n ▷ dissimilar

dissimilarity n ▷ dissimilar

dissimulate v (-lates, -lating, -lated) conceal one's real feelings by pretence > **dissimulation** n (pl -s)

dissimulated v ▷ dissimulate

dissimulates v ▷ dissimulate

dissimulating v ▷ dissimulate

dissimulation n ▷ dissimulate

dissimulations n ▷ dissimulate

dissipate v (-pates, -pating, -pated) waste or squander > **dissipation** n (pl -s)

dissipated adj showing signs of overindulgence in alcohol and other physical pleasures ▶ v ▷ dissipate

dissipates v ▷ dissipate

dissipating v ▷ dissipate

dissipation n ▷ dissipate

dissipations n ▷ dissipate

dissociate v (-ciates, -ciating, -ciated) regard or treat as separate > **dissociation** n (pl -s)

dissociated v ▷ dissociate

dissociates v ▷ dissociate

dissociating v ▷ dissociate

dissociation n ▷ dissociate

dissociations n ▷ dissociate

dissolute adj leading an immoral life
> **dissolutely** adv > **dissoluteness** n
  dissolutely adv > dissolute
  dissoluteness n > dissolute
dissolution n (pl -s) official breaking up of
an organization or institution, such as
Parliament
  dissolutions n > dissolution
dissolve v (-solves, -solving, -solved) (cause to)
become liquid
  dissolved v > dissolve
  dissolves v > dissolve
  dissolving v > dissolve
dissonance n (pl -s) lack of agreement or
harmony > **dissonant** adj
  dissonances n > dissonance
  dissonant adj > dissonance
dissuade v (-suades, -suading, -suaded)
deter (someone) by persuasion from doing
something > **dissuasion** n (pl -s)
  dissuaded v > dissuade
  dissuades v > dissuade
  dissuading v > dissuade
  dissuasion n > dissuade
  dissuasions n > dissuade
distaff n (pl -s) rod on which wool etc. is
wound for spinning
  distaffs n > distaff
distance n (pl -s) space between two points
  distances n > distance
distant adj far apart > **distantly** adv
  distantly adv > distant
distaste n (pl -s) dislike, disgust
distasteful adj unpleasant, offensive
> **distastefulness** n
  distastefulness n > distasteful
  distastes n > distaste
distemper[1] n (pl -s) highly contagious viral
disease of dogs
distemper[2] n (pl -s) paint mixed with water,
glue, etc., used for painting walls
  distempers n > distemper[1, 2]
distend v (-s, -ing, -ed) (of part of the body)
swell > **distension** n (pl -s)
  distended v > distend
  distending v > distend
  distends v > distend
  distension n > distend
  distensions n > distend
distil v (-tils, -tilling, -tilled) subject to or
obtain by distillation
  distillate n > distillation
  distillates n > distillation
distillation n (pl -s) process of evaporating
a liquid and condensing its vapour (also

distillate) (pl -s)
  distillations n > distillation
  distilled v > distil
distiller n (pl -s) person or company that
makes strong alcoholic drink, esp. whisky
  distilleries n > distillery
  distillers n > distiller
distillery n (pl -leries) place where a strong
alcoholic drink, esp. whisky, is made
  distilling v > distil
  distils v > distil
distinct adj (-er, -est) not the same > **distinctly**
adv > **distinctness** n (pl -es)
  distincter adj > distinct
  distinctest adj > distinct
distinction n (pl -s) act of distinguishing
  distinctions n > distinction
distinctive adj easily recognizable
> **distinctively** adv > **distinctiveness** n
  distinctively adv > distinctive
  distinctiveness n > distinctive
  distinctly adv > distinct
  distinctness n > distinct
  distinctnesses n > distinct
distinguish v (-es, -ing, -ed) (usu. foll. by
between) make, show, or recognize a
difference (between) > **distinguishable** adj
  distinguishable adj > distinguish
distinguished adj dignified in appearance ▶ v
  > distinguish
  distinguishes v > distinguish
  distinguishing v > distinguish
distort v (-s, -ing, -ed) misrepresent (the truth
or facts) > **distortion** n (pl -s)
  distorted v > distort
  distorting v > distort
  distortion n > distort
  distortions n > distort
  distorts v > distort
distract v (-s, -ing, -ed) draw the attention
of (a person) away from something
> **distraction** n (pl -s)
distracted adj unable to concentrate,
preoccupied ▶ v > distract > **distractedly** adv
  distractedly adv > distracted
  distracting v > distract
  distraction n > distract
  distractions n > distract
  distracts v > distract
distrait [diss-**tray**] adj absent-minded or
preoccupied
distraught [diss-**trawt**] adj extremely anxious
or agitated
distress n (pl -es) extreme unhappiness ▶ v
(-es, -ing, -ed) upset badly > **distressing** adj

> **distressingly** *adv*

distressed *adj* extremely upset ▶ *v* ▷ distress
　distresses *n, v* ▷ distress
　distressing *v, adj* ▷ distress
　distressingly *adv* ▷ distress

distribute *v* (-butes, -buting, -buted) hand out or deliver > **distributive** *adj* > **distributively** *adv*
　distributed *v* ▷ distribute
　distributes *v* ▷ distribute
　distributing *v* ▷ distribute

distribution *n* (*pl* -s) distributing
　distributions *n* ▷ distribution
　distributive *adj* ▷ distribute
　distributively *adv* ▷ distribute

distributor *n* (*pl* -s) wholesaler who distributes goods to retailers in a specific area
　distributors *n* ▷ distributor

district *n* (*pl* -s) area of land regarded as an administrative or geographical unit
　districts *n* ▷ district

distrust *v* (-s, -ing, -ed) regard as untrustworthy ▶ *n* (*pl* -s) feeling of suspicion or doubt > **distrustful** *adj*
　distrusted *v* ▷ distrust
　distrustful *adj* ▷ distrust
　distrusting *v* ▷ distrust
　distrusts *v, n* ▷ distrust

disturb *v* (-s, -ing, -ed) intrude on > **disturbance** *n* (*pl* -s) > **disturbing** *adj* > **disturbingly** *adv*
　disturbance *n* ▷ disturb
　disturbances *n* ▷ disturb

disturbed *adj* (PSYCHIATRY) emotionally upset or maladjusted ▶ *v* ▷ disturb
　disturbing *v, adj* ▷ disturb
　disturbingly *adv* ▷ disturb
　disturbs *v* ▷ disturb

disunite *v* (-nites, -niting, -nited) cause disagreement among > **disunity** *n* (*pl* -ities)
　disunited *v* ▷ disunite
　disunites *v* ▷ disunite
　disunities *n* ▷ disunite
　disuniting *v* ▷ disunite
　disunity *n* ▷ disunite

disuse *n* (*pl* -s) state of being no longer used > **disused** *adj*
　disused *adj* ▷ disuse
　disuses *n* ▷ disuse

ditch *n* (*pl* -es) narrow channel dug in the earth for drainage or irrigation ▶ *v* (-es, -ing, -ed) (*Slang*) abandon
　ditched *v* ▷ ditch
　ditches *n, v* ▷ ditch

ditching *v* ▷ ditch

dither *v* (-s, -ing, -ed) be uncertain or indecisive ▶ *n* (*pl* -s) state of indecision or agitation > **ditherer** *n* (*pl* -s) > **dithery** *adj* > **ditheriness** *n*
　dithered *v* ▷ dither
　ditheriness *n* ▷ dither
　dithering *v* ▷ dither
　dithers *v, n* ▷ dither
　dithery *adj* ▷ dither
　ditties *n* ▷ ditty

ditto *n* (*pl* -tos) the same ▶ *adv* in the same way
　dittos *n* ▷ ditto

ditty *n* (*pl* -ties) short simple poem or song

diuretic [die-yoor-**et**-ik] *n* (*pl* -s) drug that increases the flow of urine
　diuretics *n* ▷ diuretic

diurnal [die-**urn**-al] *adj* happening during the day or daily > **diurnally** *adv*
　diurnally *adv* ▷ diurnal

diva *n* (*pl* -s) distinguished female singer

divan *n* (*pl* -s) low backless bed
　divans *n* ▷ divan
　divas *n* ▷ diva

dive *v* (dives, diving, dived) plunge headfirst into water (*foll. by* in *or* into) ▶ *n* (*pl* -s) diving
　dived *v* ▷ dive

diver *n* (*pl* -s) person who works or explores underwater

diverge *v* (-verges, -verging, -verged) separate and go in different directions > **divergence** *n* (*pl* -s) > **divergent** *adj*
　diverged *v* ▷ diverge
　divergence *n* ▷ diverge
　divergences *n* ▷ diverge
　divergent *adj* ▷ diverge
　diverges *v* ▷ diverge
　diverging *v* ▷ diverge

divers *adj* (*Old-fashioned*) various ▶ *n* ▷ diver

diverse *adj* having variety, assorted > **diversely** *adv* > **diversify** *v* (-fies, -fying, -fied) > **diversification** *n* (*pl* -s)
　diversely *adv* ▷ diverse
　diversification *n* ▷ diverse
　diversifications *n* ▷ diverse
　diversified *v* ▷ diverse
　diversifies *v* ▷ diverse
　diversify *v* ▷ diverse
　diversifying *v* ▷ diverse

diversion *n* (*pl* -s) official detour used by traffic when a main route is closed > **diversionary** *adj*
　diversionary *adj* ▷ diversion
　diversions *n* ▷ diversion
　diversities *n* ▷ diversity

diversity n (pl **-ties**) quality of being different or varied

divert v (**-s, -ing, -ed**) change the direction of
 diverted v ▷ divert
 diverting v ▷ divert
 diverts v ▷ divert
 dives v, n ▷ dive

divest v (**-s, -ing, -ed**) strip (of clothes)
 divested v ▷ divest
 divesting v ▷ divest
 divests v ▷ divest

divide v (**-vides, -viding, -vided**) separate into parts ▸ n (pl **-s**) division, split
 divided v ▷ divide

dividend n (pl **-s**) sum of money representing part of the profit made, paid by a company to its shareholders
 dividends n ▷ dividend

divider n (pl **-s**) screen used to divide a room into separate areas ▸ pl compasses with two pointed points, used for measuring or dividing lines
 dividers n ▷ divider
 divides v, n ▷ divide
 dividing v ▷ divide

divination n (pl **-s**) art of discovering future events, as though by supernatural powers
 divinations n ▷ divine

divine adj (**-r, -st**) of God or a god ▸ v (**-nes, -ning, -ned**) discover (something) by intuition or guessing > **divinely** adv
 divined v ▷ divine
 divinely adv ▷ divine
 diviner adj ▷ divine
 divines v ▷ divine
 divinest adj ▷ divine
 diving v ▷ dive
 divining v ▷ divine
 divinities n ▷ divinity

divinity n study of religion (pl **-ties**)
 divisibility n ▷ divisible

divisible adj > **divisibility** n

division n (pl **-s**) dividing, sharing out

divisional adj of a division in an organization > **divisionally** adv
 divisionally adv ▷ divisional
 divisions n ▷ division

divisive adj tending to cause disagreement > **divisively** adv > **divisiveness** n
 divisively adv ▷ divisive
 divisiveness n ▷ divisive

divisor n (pl **-s**) number to be divided into another number
 divisors n ▷ divisor

divorce n (pl **-s**) legal ending of a marriage ▸ v

(**-ces, -cing, -ced**) legally end one's marriage (to)
 divorcé n ▷ divorcée
 divorced v ▷ divorce

divorcée, masc **divorcé** n (pl **-s**) person who is divorced
 divorcées n ▷ divorcée
 divorces n, v ▷ divorce
 divorcés n ▷ divorcée
 divorcing v ▷ divorce

divulge v (**-ges, -ging, -ged**) make known, disclose > **divulgence** n (pl **-s**)
 divulged v ▷ divulge
 divulgence n ▷ divulge
 divulgences n ▷ divulge
 divulges v ▷ divulge
 divulging v ▷ divulge

dizzied v ▷ dizzy
 dizzier adj ▷ dizzy
 dizzies v ▷ dizzy
 dizziest adj ▷ dizzy
 dizzily adv ▷ dizzy
 dizziness n ▷ dizzy

dizzy adj (**-zier, -ziest**) having or causing a whirling sensation ▸ v (**-zies, -zying, -zied**) make dizzy > **dizzily** adv > **dizziness** n
 dizzying v ▷ dizzy

do v (**does, doing, did, done**) perform or complete (a deed or action) ▸ n (pl **dos, do's**) (Informal) party, celebration

docile adj (**-r, -st**) (of a person or animal) easily controlled > **docilely** adv > **docility** n (pl **-ties**)
 docilely adv ▷ docile
 dociler adj ▷ docile
 docilest adj ▷ docile
 docilities n ▷ docile
 docility n ▷ docile

dock[1] n (pl **-s**) enclosed area of water where ships are loaded, unloaded, or repaired ▸ v (**-s, -ing, -ed**) bring or be brought into dock

dock[2] v (**docks, docking, docked**) deduct money from (a person's wages)

dock[3] n (pl **-s**) enclosed space in a court of law where the accused person sits or stands

dock[4] n (pl **-s**) weed with broad leaves
 docked v ▷ dock

docker n (pl **-s**) (BRIT) person employed to load and unload ships
 dockers n ▷ docker

docket n (pl **dockets**) label on a package or other delivery, stating contents, delivery instructions, etc.
 dockets n ▷ docket
 docking v ▷ dock
 docks n ▷ dock[1, 3, 4] ▸ v ▷ dock[1, 2]

dockyard *n* (*pl* **-s**) place where ships are built or repaired
  dockyards *n* ▷ dockyard
doctor *n* (*pl* **-s**) person licensed to practise medicine ▶ *v* (**-s, -ing, -ed**) alter in order to deceive > **doctoral** *adj*
  doctoral *adj* ▷ doctor
doctorate *n* (*pl* **-s**) highest academic degree in any field of knowledge
  doctorates *n* ▷ doctorate
  doctored *v* ▷ doctor
  doctoring *v* ▷ doctor
  doctors *n, v* ▷ doctor
doctrinaire *adj* stubbornly insistent on the application of a theory without regard to practicality
doctrinal *adj* of doctrines > **doctrinally** *adv*
  doctrinally *adv* ▷ doctrinal
doctrine *n* (*pl* **-s**) body of teachings of a religious, political, or philosophical group
  doctrines *n* ▷ doctrine
document *n* (*pl* **-s**) piece of paper providing an official record of something ▶ *v* (**-s, -ing, -ed**) record or report (something) in detail > **documentation** *n* (*pl* **-s**)
  documentaries *n* ▷ documentary
documentary *n* (*pl* **-ries**) film or television programme presenting the facts about a particular subject ▶ *adj* (of evidence) based on documents
  documentation *n* ▷ document
  documentations *n* ▷ document
  documented *v* ▷ document
  documenting *v* ▷ document
  documents *n, v* ▷ document
dodder *v* (**-s, -ing, -ed**) move unsteadily > **doddery** *adj* (**-rier, -riest**)
  doddered *v* ▷ dodder
  dodderier *adj* ▷ dodder
  dodderiest *adj* ▷ dodder
  doddering *v* ▷ dodder
  dodders *v* ▷ dodder
  doddery *adj* ▷ dodder
dodecagon [doe-**deck**-a-gon] *n* (*pl* **-s**) geometric figure with twelve sides
  dodecagons *n* ▷ dodecagon
dodge *v* (**dodges, dodging, dodged**) avoid (a blow, being seen, etc.) by moving suddenly ▶ *n* (*pl* **-s**) cunning or deceitful trick
  dodged *v* ▷ dodge
dodger *n* (*pl* **-s**) person who evades a responsibility or duty
  dodgers *n* ▷ dodger
  dodges *v, n* ▷ dodge
  dodgier *adj* ▷ dodgy

dodgiest *adj* ▷ dodgy
  dodging *v* ▷ dodge
dodgy *adj* (**-gier, -giest**) (*Informal*) dangerous, risky
dodo *n* (*pl* **-s, -es**) large flightless extinct bird
  dodoes *n* ▷ dodo
  dodos *n* ▷ dodo
doe *n* (*pl* **-s**) female deer, hare, or rabbit
  does *n* ▷ doe ▶ *v* ▷ do
doesn't does not
doff *v* (**-s, -ing, -ed**) take off or lift (one's hat) in polite greeting
  doffed *v* ▷ doff
  doffing *v* ▷ doff
  doffs *v* ▷ doff
dog *n* (*pl* **-s**) domesticated four-legged mammal of many different breeds ▶ *v* (**dogs, dogging, dogged**) follow (someone) closely
dogcart *n* (*pl* **-s**) light horse-drawn two-wheeled cart
  dogcarts *n* ▷ dogcart
doge [doje] *n* (*pl* **-s**) (formerly) chief magistrate of Venice or Genoa
dogeared *adj* (of a book) having pages folded down at the corner
  doges *n* ▷ doge
dogfight *n* (*pl* **-s**) close-quarters combat between fighter aircraft
  dogfights *n* ▷ dogfight
dogfish *n* (*pl* **-es**) small shark
  dogfishes *n* ▷ dogfish
dogged [dog-gid] *adj* obstinately determined ▶ *v* ▷ dog > **doggedly** *adv* > **doggedness** *n* (*pl* **-es**)
  doggedly *adv* ▷ dogged
  doggedness *n* ▷ dogged
  doggednesses *n* ▷ dogged
doggerel *n* (*pl* **-s**) poorly written poetry, usu. comic
  doggerels *n* ▷ doggerel
  doggie *n* ▷ doggy
  doggies *n* ▷ doggy
  dogging *v* ▷ dog
doggo *adv* (*Informal*) in hiding and keeping quiet
doggy, doggie *n* (*pl* **-gies**) child's word for a dog
doghouse *n* (*pl* **-s**) (US) kennel
  doghouses *n* ▷ doghouse
dogleg *n* (*pl* **-s**) sharp bend
  doglegs *n* ▷ dogleg
dogma *n* (*pl* **-s**) doctrine or system of doctrines proclaimed by authority as true > **dogmatic** *adj* habitually stating one's opinions forcefully or arrogantly > **dogmatically** *adv*

> **dogmatism** n

dogmas n ▷ dogma

dogs n, v ▷ dog

dogsbodies n ▷ dogsbody

dogsbody n (pl -bodies) (Informal) person who carries out boring tasks for others

> **doh** interj. Doh is a sound people make when things go wrong. Doh scores 7 points.

doilies n ▷ doily

doily n (pl -lies) decorative lacy paper mat, laid on a plate

doing v ▷ do

doldrums pl n depressed state of mind

dole n (pl -s) (BRIT, AUST & NZ) (Informal) money received from the state while unemployed ▶ v (**doles, doling, doled**) (foll. by **out**) distribute in small quantities

doled v ▷ dole

doleful adj dreary, unhappy > **dolefully** adv > **dolefulness** n

dolefully adv ▷ doleful

dolefulness n ▷ doleful

doles v, n ▷ dole

doling v ▷ dole

doll n (pl -s) small model of a human being, used as a toy

dollar n (pl -s) standard monetary unit of many countries

dollars n ▷ dollar

dollies n ▷ dolly

dollop n (pl -s) (Informal) lump (of food)

dollops n ▷ dollop

dolls n ▷ doll

dolly n (pl -lies) child's word for a doll

dolmen n (pl -s) prehistoric monument consisting of a horizontal stone supported by vertical stones

dolmens n ▷ dolmen

dolomite n (pl -s) mineral consisting of calcium magnesium carbonate

dolomites n ▷ dolomite

dolorous adj sad, mournful > **dolorously** adv

dolorously adv ▷ dolorous

dolphin n (pl -s) sea mammal of the whale family, with a beaklike snout

dolphinaria n ▷ dolphinarium

dolphinarium n (pl -ariums, -aria) aquarium for dolphins

dolphinariums n ▷ dolphinarium

dolphins n ▷ dolphin

dolt n (pl -s) stupid person > **doltish** adj > **doltishness** n

doltish adj ▷ dolt

doltishness n ▷ dolt

dolts n ▷ dolt

domain n (pl -s) field of knowledge or activity

domains n ▷ domain

dome n (pl -s) rounded roof built on a circular base > **domed** adj

domes n ▷ dome

domestic adj of one's own country or a specific country ▶ n (pl -s) person whose job is to do housework in someone else's house > **domestically** adv > **domesticity** n

domestically adv ▷ domestic

domesticate v (-cates, -cating, -cated) bring or keep (a wild animal or plant) under control or cultivation > **domestication** n (pl -s)

domesticated v ▷ domesticate

domesticates v ▷ domesticate

domesticating v ▷ domesticate

domestication n ▷ domesticate

domestications n ▷ domesticate

domesticity n ▷ domestic

domestics n ▷ domestic

domicile [dom-miss-ile] n (pl -s) place where one lives

domiciles n ▷ domicile

dominance n ▷ dominant

dominances n ▷ dominant

dominant adj having authority or influence > **dominance** n (pl -s)

dominate v (-nates, -nating, -nated) control or govern > **domination** n (pl -s)

dominated v ▷ dominate

dominates v ▷ dominate

dominating v ▷ dominate

domination n ▷ dominate

dominations n ▷ dominate

domineering adj forceful and arrogant

dominion n (pl -s) control or authority

dominions n ▷ dominion

domino n (pl -noes) small rectangular block marked with dots, used in dominoes ▶ pl game in which dominoes with matching halves are laid together

dominoes n ▷ domino

don¹ v (**dons, donning, donned**) put on (clothing)

don² n (pl -s) (BRIT) member of the teaching staff at a university or college

donate v (-nates, -nating, -nated) give, esp. to a charity or organization

donated v ▷ donate

donates v ▷ donate

donating v ▷ donate

donation n (pl -s) donating

donations n ▷ donation

done v ▷ do

donga [dong-ga] *n* (*pl* **-s**) (S AFR, AUST & NZ) steep-sided gully created by soil erosion
  dongas *n* ▷ donga
donkey *n* (*pl* **-s**) long-eared member of the horse family
  donkeys *n* ▷ donkey
donkeywork *n* (*pl* **-s**) tedious hard work
  donkeyworks *n* ▷ donkeywork
  donned *v* ▷ don¹
  donning *v* ▷ don¹
donnish *adj* serious and academic
  > **donnishness** *n* (*pl* **-es**)
  donnishness *n* ▷ donnish
  donnishnesses *n* ▷ donnish
donor *n* (*pl* **-s**) (MED) person who gives blood or organs for use in the treatment of another person
  donors *n* ▷ donor
  dons *v* ▷ don¹ ▶ *n* ▷ don²
doodle *v* (**-dles, -dling, -dled**) scribble or draw aimlessly ▶ *n* (*pl* **-s**) shape or picture drawn aimlessly
  doodled *v* ▷ doodle
  doodles *v, n* ▷ doodle
  doodling *v* ▷ doodle
doom *n* (*pl* **-s**) death or a terrible fate ▶ *v* (**-s, -ing, -ed**) destine or condemn to death or a terrible fate
  doomed *v* ▷ doom
  dooming *v* ▷ doom
  dooms *n, v* ▷ doom
doomsday *n* (*pl* **-s**) (CHRISTIANITY) day on which the Last Judgment will occur
  doomsdays *n* ▷ doomsday
door *n* (*pl* **-s**) hinged or sliding panel for closing the entrance to a building, room, etc.
doormat *n* (*pl* **-s**) mat for wiping dirt from shoes before going indoors
  doormats *n* ▷ doormat
  doors *n* ▷ door
doorway *n* (*pl* **-s**) opening into a building or room
  doorways *n* ▷ doorway
dope *n* (*pl* **-s**) (Slang) illegal drug, usu. cannabis ▶ *v* (**dopes, doping, doped**) give a drug to, esp. in order to improve performance in a race
  doped *v* ▷ dope
  dopes *n, v* ▷ dope
dopey, dopy (**dopier, dopiest**) *adj* half-asleep, drowsy
  dopier *adj* ▷ dopey
  dopiest *adj* ▷ dopey
  doping *v* ▷ dope
  dopy *adj* ▷ dopey
  dorb *n* ▷ dorba

dorba *n* (*pl* **-s**) (AUST) (Slang) stupid, inept, or clumsy person (*also* **dorb**) (*pl* **-s**)
  dorbas *n* ▷ dorba
  dorbs *n* ▷ dorba
  dories *n* ▷ dory
dork *n* (*pl* **-s**) (Slang) stupid person
  dorks *n* ▷ dork
  dormancy *n* ▷ dormant
dormant *adj* temporarily quiet, inactive, or not being used > **dormancy** *n*
dormer *n* (*pl* **-s**) window that sticks out from a sloping roof
  dormers *n* ▷ dormer
  dormice *n* ▷ dormouse
  dormitories *n* ▷ dormitory
dormitory *n* (*pl* **-ries**) large room, esp. at a school, containing several beds
dormouse *n* (*pl* **-mice**) small mouselike rodent with a furry tail
dorp *n* (*pl* **-s**) (S AFR) small town
  dorps *n* ▷ dorp
dorsal *adj* of or on the back
dory *n* (*pl* **-ries**) spiny-finned edible sea fish
  dos *n* ▷ do
  do's *n* ▷ do
dosage *n* (*pl* **-s**) size of a dose
  dosages *n* ▷ dosage
dose *n* (*pl* **-s**) specific quantity of a medicine taken at one time ▶ *v* (**doses, dosing, dosed**) give a dose to
  dosed *v* ▷ dose
  doses *n, v* ▷ dose
  dosing *v* ▷ dose
doss *v* (**-es, -ing, -ed**) (Slang) sleep in an uncomfortable place
  dossed *v* ▷ doss
  dosses *v* ▷ doss
dosshouse *n* (*pl* **-s**) (BRIT & S AFR) (Slang) cheap lodging house for homeless people
  dosshouses *n* ▷ dosshouse
dossier [doss-ee-ay] *n* (*pl* **-s**) collection of documents about a subject or person
  dossiers *n* ▷ dossier
  dossing *v* ▷ doss
dot *n* (*pl* **-s**) small round mark ▶ *v* (**dots, dotting, dotted**) mark with a dot
dotage *n* (*pl* **-s**) weakness as a result of old age
  dotages *n* ▷ dotage
dotcom *n* (*pl* **-s**) company that does most of its business on the Internet
  dotcoms *n* ▷ dotcom
dote *v* (**dotes, doting, doted**) love to an excessive degree
  doted *v* ▷ dote
  dotes *v* ▷ dote

doting v ▷ dote
dots n, v ▷ dot
dotted v ▷ dot
dottier adj ▷ dotty
dottiest adj ▷ dotty
dottily adv ▷ dotty
dottiness n ▷ dotty
dottinesses n ▷ dotty
dotting v ▷ dot
dotty adj (-tier, -tiest) (Slang) rather eccentric > **dottily** adv > **dottiness** n (pl -es)
double adj as much again in number, amount, size, etc. ▶ adv twice over ▶ n (pl -s) twice the number, amount, size, etc. ▶ pl game between two pairs of players ▶ v (-bles, -bling, -bled) make or become twice as much or as many > **doubly** adv
doubled v ▷ double
doubles n, v ▷ double
doublet [dub-lit] n (pl -s) (HIST) man's close-fitting jacket, with or without sleeves
doublets n ▷ doublet
doubling v ▷ double
doubloon n (pl -s) former Spanish gold coin
doubloons n ▷ doubloon
doubly adv ▷ double
doubt n (pl -s) uncertainty about the truth, facts, or existence of something ▶ v (-s, -ing, -ed) question the truth of > **doubter** n (pl -s)
doubted v ▷ doubt
doubter n ▷ doubt
doubters n ▷ doubt
doubtful adj unlikely > **doubtfully** adv
doubtfully adv ▷ doubtful
doubting v ▷ doubt
doubtless adv probably or certainly > **doubtlessly** adv
doubtlessly adv ▷ doubtless
doubts n, v ▷ doubt
douche [doosh] n (pl -s) (instrument for applying) a stream of water directed onto or into the body for cleansing or medical purposes ▶ v (-es, -ing, -ed) cleanse or treat by means of a douche
douched v ▷ douche
douches n, v ▷ douche
douching v ▷ douche
dough n (pl -s) thick mixture of flour and water or milk, used for making bread etc.
doughnut n (pl -s) small cake of sweetened dough fried in deep fat
doughnuts n ▷ doughnut
doughs n ▷ dough
doughtier adj ▷ doughty
doughtiest adj ▷ doughty

doughtily adv ▷ doughty
doughtiness n ▷ doughty
doughtinesses n ▷ doughty
doughty [dowt-ee] adj (-tier, -tiest) (Old-fashioned) brave and determined > **doughtily** adv > **doughtiness** n (pl -es)
dour [doo-er] adj (-er, -est) sullen and unfriendly > **dourly** adv > **dourness** n (pl -es)
dourer adj ▷ dour
dourest adj ▷ dour
dourly adv ▷ dour
dourness n ▷ dour
dournesses n ▷ dour
douse [rhymes with **mouse**] v (-ses, -sing, -sed) drench with water or other liquid
doused v ▷ douse
douses v ▷ douse
dousing v ▷ douse
dove n (pl -s) bird with a heavy body, small head, and short legs
dovecot n ▷ dovecote
dovecote, dovecot n (pl -s) structure for housing pigeons
dovecotes n ▷ dovecote
dovecots n ▷ dovecote
doves n ▷ dove
dovetail n (pl -s) joint containing wedge-shaped tenons ▶ v (-s, -ing, -ed) fit together neatly
dovetailed v ▷ dovetail
dovetailing v ▷ dovetail
dovetails v ▷ dovetail

▪ **dow** n (**dows**). A **dow** is an Arab ship. **Dow** scores 7 points.

dowager n (pl -s) widow possessing property or a title obtained from her husband
dowagers n ▷ dowager
dowdier adj ▷ dowdy
dowdiest adj ▷ dowdy
dowdily adv ▷ dowdy
dowdiness n ▷ dowdy
dowdy adj (-dier, -diest) dull and old-fashioned > **dowdily** adv > **dowdiness** n
dowel n (pl -s) wooden or metal peg that fits into two corresponding holes to join two adjacent parts
dowels n ▷ dowel
dower n (pl -s) life interest in a part of her husband's estate allotted to a widow by law
dowers n ▷ dower
down¹ prep, adv indicating movement to or position in a lower place ▶ adv indicating completion of an action, lessening of intensity, etc. ▶ adj depressed, unhappy ▶ v (-s, -ing, -ed) (Informal) drink quickly

down² n (pl -s) soft fine feathers > **downiness** n
> **downy** adj (-nier, -niest)

downbeat adj (informal) gloomy

downcast adj sad, dejected
  downed v ▷ down¹

downfall n (pl -s) (cause of) a sudden loss of
position or reputation
  downfalls n ▷ downfall

downgrade v (-grades, -grading, -graded)
reduce in importance or value
  downgraded v ▷ downgrade
  downgrades v ▷ downgrade
  downgrading v ▷ downgrade

downhearted adj sad and discouraged
> **downheartedly** adv
  downheartedly adv ▷ downhearted

downhill adj going or sloping down ▶ adv
towards the bottom of a hill
  downier adj ▷ down²
  downiest adj ▷ down²
  downiness n ▷ down²
  downing v ▷ down¹

download v (-s, -ing, -ed) transfer (data) from
the memory of one computer to that of
another, especially over the Internet ▶ n (pl -s)
file transferred in such a way
  downloaded v ▷ download
  downloading v ▷ download
  downloads v, n ▷ download

downpour n (pl -s) heavy fall of rain
  downpours n ▷ downpour

downright adj, adv extreme(ly)

downs pl n low grassy hills, esp. in S England
  ▶ v ▷ down¹ ▶ n ▷ down²

downstairs adv to or on a lower floor ▶ n lower
or ground floor

downtrodden adj oppressed and lacking the
will to resist

downward adj, adv (descending) from a higher
to a lower level, condition, or position

downwards adv from a higher to a lower level,
condition, or position

downy adj ▷ down²

dowries n ▷ dowry

dowry n (pl -ries) property brought by a
woman to her husband at marriage

dowse [rhymes with cows] v (-ses, -sing, -sed)
search for underground water or minerals
using a divining rod
  dowsed v ▷ dowse
  dowses v ▷ dowse
  dowsing v ▷ dowse
  doxologies n ▷ doxology

doxology n (pl -gies) short hymn of praise
to God

doy n (**doys**). Doy is a dialect word for a
beloved person. Doy scores 7 points.

doyen [doy-en] n (pl -s) senior member of a
group, profession, or society > **doyenne**
[doy-en] ▶ n fem
  doyenne n ▷ doyen
  doyennes n ▷ doyen
  doyens n ▷ doyen

doze v (dozes, dozing, dozed) sleep lightly or
briefly ▶ n (pl -s) short sleep
  dozed v ▷ doze

dozen adj, n (pl -s) twelve > **dozenth** adj
  dozens n ▷ dozen
  dozenth adj ▷ dozen
  dozes v, n ▷ doze
  dozier adj ▷ dozy
  doziest adj ▷ dozy
  dozily adv ▷ dozy
  doziness n ▷ dozy
  dozing v ▷ doze

dozy adj (dozier, doziest) feeling sleepy
> **dozily** adv > **doziness** adv

drab adj (drabber, drabbest) dull and dreary
> **drably** adv > **drabness** n (pl -es)
  drabber adj ▷ drab
  drabbest adj ▷ drab
  drably adv ▷ drab
  drabness n ▷ drab
  drabnesses n ▷ drab

drachm [dram] n (pl -s) (BRIT) one eighth of a
fluid ounce

drachma n (pl -mas, -mae) former monetary
unit of Greece
  drachmae n ▷ drachma
  drachmas n ▷ drachma
  drachms n ▷ drachm

draconian adj severe, harsh

draft n (pl -s) plan, sketch, or drawing of
something (US & AUST) ▶ v (-s, -ing, -ed) draw
up an outline or plan of
  drafted v ▷ draft
  drafting v ▷ draft
  drafts n, v ▷ draft

drag v (-s, -gging, -gged) pull with force, esp.
along the ground (foll. by **on** or **out**) ▶ n (pl -s)
person or thing that slows up progress
  dragged v ▷ drag
  dragging v ▷ drag

dragnet n (pl -s) net used to scour the bottom
of a pond or river to search for something
  dragnets n ▷ dragnet

dragon n (pl -s) mythical fire-breathing
monster like a huge lizard
  dragonflies n ▷ dragonfly

dragonfly n (pl -flies) brightly coloured insect

with a long slender body and two pairs of wings

dragons n ▷ dragon

dragoon n (pl -s) heavily armed cavalryman ▶ v (-s, -ing, -ed) coerce, force

dragooned v ▷ dragoon

dragooning v ▷ dragoon

dragoons n, v ▷ dragoon

drags v, n ▷ drag

drain n (pl -s) pipe or channel that carries off water or sewage ▶ v (-s, -ing, -ed) draw off or remove liquid from

drainage n (pl -s) system of drains

drainages n ▷ drainage

drained v ▷ drain

draining v ▷ drain

drains n, v ▷ drain

drake n (pl -s) male duck

drakes n ▷ drake

dram n (pl -s) small amount of a strong alcoholic drink, esp. whisky

drama n (pl -s) serious play for theatre, television, or radio

dramas n ▷ drama

dramatic adj of or like drama > **dramatically** adv

dramatically adv ▷ dramatic

dramatist n (pl -s) person who writes plays

dramatists n ▷ dramatist

dramatization n ▷ dramatize

dramatizations n ▷ dramatize

dramatize v (-tizes, -izing, -tized) rewrite (a book) in the form of a play > **dramatization** n (pl -s)

dramatized v ▷ dramatize

dramatizes v ▷ dramatize

dramatizing v ▷ dramatize

drams n ▷ dram

drank v ▷ drink

drape v (drapes, draping, draped) cover with material, usu. in folds ▶ n (pl -s) (AUST, US & CANADIAN) piece of cloth hung at a window or opening as a screen

draped v ▷ drape

draper n (pl -s) (BRIT) person who sells fabrics and sewing materials

draperies n ▷ drapery

drapers n ▷ draper

drapery n (pl -peries) fabric or clothing arranged and draped

drapes v, n ▷ drape

draping v ▷ drape

drastic adj strong and severe > **drastically** adv

drastically adv ▷ drastic

draught n (pl -s) current of cold air, esp. in an

enclosed space ▶ pl game for two players using a chessboard and twelve draughts each ▶ adj (of an animal) used for pulling heavy loads

draughtier adj ▷ draughty

draughtiest adj ▷ draughty

draughtiness n ▷ draughty

draughts n ▷ draught

draughtsman n (pl -men) person employed to prepare detailed scale drawings of machinery, buildings, etc. > **draughtsmanship** n

draughtsmanship n ▷ draughtsman

draughtsmen n ▷ draughtsman

draughty adj (-tier, -tiest) exposed to draughts of air > **draughtiness** n

draw v (draws, drawing, drew, drawn) sketch (a figure, picture, etc.) with a pencil or pen ▶ n (pl -s) raffle or lottery

drawback n (pl -s) disadvantage

drawbacks n ▷ drawback

drawbridge n (pl -s) bridge that may be raised to prevent access or to enable vessels to pass

drawbridges n ▷ drawbridge

drawer n (pl -s) sliding box-shaped part of a piece of furniture, used for storage ▶ pl (Old-fashioned) undergarment worn on the lower part of the body

drawers n ▷ drawer

drawing n (pl -s) picture or plan made by means of lines on a surface ▶ v ▷ draw

drawl v (-s, -ing, -ed) speak slowly, with long vowel sounds ▶ n (pl drawls) drawling manner of speech

drawled v ▷ drawl

drawling v ▷ drawl

drawls v ▷ drawl

drawls n ▷ drawl

drawn v ▷ draw ▶ adj haggard, tired, or tense in appearance

draws n, v ▷ draw

drawstring n (pl -s) cord run through a hem around an opening, so that when it is pulled tighter, the opening closes

drawstrings n ▷ drawstring

dray n (pl -s) low cart used for carrying heavy loads

drays n ▷ dray

dread v (-s, -ing, -ed) anticipate with apprehension or fear ▶ n (pl -s) great fear

dreaded v ▷ dread

dreadful adj very disagreeable or shocking > **dreadfully** adv

dreadfully adv ▷ dreadful

dreading v ▷ dread

dreadlocks *pl n* hair worn in the Rastafarian style of tightly twisted strands
  dreads *v*, *n* ▷ **dread**
dream *n* (*pl* **-s**) imagined series of events experienced in the mind while asleep (*Informal*) ▶ *v* (**-s**, **-ing**, **-ed** *or* **-t**) see imaginary pictures in the mind while asleep (*often foll. by* **of** *or* **about**) (*foll. by* **of**) ▶ *adj* ideal
  > **dreamer** *n* (*pl* **-s**)
  dreamed *v* ▷ **dream**
  dreamer *n* ▷ **dream**
  dreamers *n* ▷ **dream**
  dreamier *adj* ▷ **dreamy**
  dreamiest *adj* ▷ **dreamy**
  dreamily *adv* ▷ **dreamy**
  dreaminess *n* ▷ **dreamy**
  dreaminesses *n* ▷ **dreamy**
  dreaming *v* ▷ **dream**
  dreams *n*, *v* ▷ **dream**
  dreamt *v* ▷ **dream**
dreamy *adj* (**-mier**, **-miest**) vague or impractical > **dreamily** *adv* > **dreaminess** *n* (*pl* **-es**)
  drearier *adj* ▷ **dreary**
  dreariest *adj* ▷ **dreary**
  drearily *adv* ▷ **dreary**
  dreariness *n* ▷ **dreary**
dreary *adj* (**drearier**, **dreariest**) dull, boring > **drearily** *adv* > **dreariness** *n*
dredge¹ *v* (**dredges**, **dredging**, **dredged**) clear or search (a river bed or harbour) by removing silt or mud
dredge² *v* (**dredges**, **dredging**, **dredged**) sprinkle (food) with flour etc.
  dredged *v* ▷ **dredge**¹, ²
dredger *n* (*pl* **-s**) boat fitted with machinery for dredging
  dredgers *n* ▷ **dredger**
  dredges *v* ▷ **dredge**¹, ²
  dredging *v* ▷ **dredge**¹, ²
dregs *pl n* solid particles that settle at the bottom of some liquids
drench *v* (**-es**, **-ing**, **-ed**) make completely wet
  drenched *v* ▷ **drench**
  drenches *v* ▷ **drench**
  drenching *v* ▷ **drench**
dress *n* (*pl* **-es**) one-piece garment for a woman or girl, consisting of a skirt and bodice and sometimes sleeves ▶ *v* (**-es**, **-ing**, **-ed**) put clothes on
dressage [dress-ahzh] *n* (*pl* **-s**) training of a horse to perform manoeuvres in response to the rider's body signals
  dressages *n* ▷ **dressage**
  dressed *v* ▷ **dress**

dresser¹ *n* (*pl* **-s**) piece of furniture with shelves and with cupboards, for storing or displaying dishes
dresser² *n* (*pl* **-s**) (THEATRE) person employed to assist actors with their costumes
  dressers *n* ▷ **dresser**¹, ²
  dresses *n*, *v* ▷ **dress**
  dressier *adj* ▷ **dressy**
  dressiest *adj* ▷ **dressy**
  dressiness *n* ▷ **dressy**
  dressinesses *n* ▷ **dressy**
dressing *n* (*pl* **-s**) sauce for salad ▶ *v* ▷ **dress**
  dressings *n* ▷ **dressing**
dressmaker *n* (*pl* **-s**) person who makes women's clothes > **dressmaking** *n*
  dressmakers *n* ▷ **dressmaker**
  dressmaking *n* ▷ **dressmaker**
dressy *adj* (**-ssier**, **-ssiest**) (of clothes) elegant > **dressiness** *n* (*pl* **-es**)
  drew *v* ▷ **draw**
drey *n* (*pl* **-s**) squirrel's nest
  dreys *n* ▷ **drey**
dribble *v* (**-les**, **-ling**, **-led**) (allow to) flow in drops ▶ *n* (*pl* **-s**) small quantity of liquid falling in drops > **dribbler** *n* (*pl* **-s**)
  dribbled *v* ▷ **dribble**
  dribbler *n* ▷ **dribble**
  dribblers *n* ▷ **dribble**
  dribbles *v*, *n* ▷ **dribble**
  dribbling *v* ▷ **dribble**
  dried *v* ▷ **dry**
  drier¹ *adj* ▷ **dry**
  drier² *n* (*pl* **-s**) ▷ **dryer**
  driers *n* ▷ **drier²**
  dries *v* ▷ **dry**
  driest *adj* ▷ **dry**
drift *v* (**-s**, **-ing**, **-ed**) be carried along by currents of air or water ▶ *n* (*pl* **-s**) something piled up by the wind or current, such as a snowdrift
  drifted *v* ▷ **drift**
drifter *n* (*pl* **-s**) person who moves aimlessly from place to place or job to job
  drifters *n* ▷ **drifter**
  drifting *v* ▷ **drift**
  drifts *v*, *n* ▷ **drift**
driftwood *n* (*pl* **-s**) wood floating on or washed ashore by the sea
  driftwoods *n* ▷ **driftwood**
drill¹ *n* (*pl* **-s**) tool or machine for boring holes ▶ *v* (**-s**, **-ing**, **-ed**) bore a hole in (something) with or as if with a drill
drill² *n* (*pl* **-s**) machine for sowing seed in rows
drill³ *n* (*pl* **-s**) hard-wearing cotton cloth
  drilled *v* ▷ **drill¹**

drilling v ▷ drill¹
drills n ▷ drill¹˒², ³ ▶ v ▷ drill¹
drily adv ▷ dry
drink v (drinks, drinking, drank, drunk) swallow (a liquid) ▶ n (pl -s) (portion of) a liquid suitable for drinking > **drinkable** adj > **drinker** n (pl -s)
drinkable adj ▷ drink
drinker n ▷ drink
drinkers n ▷ drink
drinking v ▷ drink
drinks v, n ▷ drink
drip v (drips, dripping, dripped) (let) fall in drops ▶ n (pl -s) falling of drops of liquid
dripped v ▷ drip
dripping n (pl -s) fat that comes from meat while it is being roasted or fried ▶ v ▷ drip
drippings n ▷ dripping
drips v, n ▷ drip
drive v (drives, driving, drove, driven) guide the movement of (a vehicle) ▶ n (pl -s) journey by car, van, etc.; path for vehicles (also **driveway**) (pl -s)
drivel n (pl -s) foolish talk ▶ v (-els, -elling, -elled) speak foolishly
drivelled v ▷ drivel
drivelling v ▷ drivel
drivels v, n ▷ drivel
driven v ▷ drive
driver n (pl -s) person who drives a vehicle
drivers n ▷ driver
drives v, n ▷ drive
driveway n ▷ drive
driveways n ▷ drive
driving v ▷ drive
drizzle n (pl -s) very light rain ▶ v (-zles, -zling, -zled) rain lightly > **drizzly** adj
drizzled v ▷ drizzle
drizzles n, v ▷ drizzle
drizzling v ▷ drizzle
drizzly adj ▷ drizzle
droll adj (-er, -est) quaintly amusing > **drolly** adv > **drollery** n (pl -ries) > **drollness** n (pl -es)
droller adj ▷ droll
drolleries n ▷ droll
drollery n ▷ droll
drollest adj ▷ droll
drollness n ▷ droll
drollnesses n ▷ droll
drolly adv ▷ droll
dromedaries n ▷ dromedary
dromedary [drom-mid-er-ee] n (pl -daries) camel with a single hump
drone¹ n (pl -s) male bee
drone² v (drones, droned, droning) ▶ n (pl -s)

(make) a monotonous low dull sound
droned v ▷ drone²
drones n ▷ drone¹˒² ▶ v ▷ drone²
drongo n (pl -gos) tropical songbird with a glossy black plumage, a forked tail, and a stout bill
drongos n ▷ drongo
droning v ▷ drone²
drool v (-s, -ing, -ed) (foll. by **over**) show excessive enthusiasm (for)
drooled v ▷ drool
drooling v ▷ drool
drools v ▷ drool
droop v (-s, -ing, -ed) hang downwards loosely > **droopy** adj (-pier, -piest)
drooped v ▷ droop
droopier adj ▷ droop
droopiest adj ▷ droop
drooping v ▷ droop
droops v ▷ droop
droopy adj ▷ droop
drop v (-s, -pping, -pped) (allow to) fall vertically ▶ n (pl -s) small quantity of liquid forming a round shape ▶ pl liquid medication applied in small drops > **droplet** n (pl -s)
droplet n ▷ drop
droplets n ▷ drop
dropout n (pl -s) person who rejects conventional society
dropouts n ▷ dropout
dropped v ▷ drop
dropping v ▷ drop
droppings pl n faeces of certain animals, such as rabbits or birds
drops v, n ▷ drop
dropsical adj ▷ dropsy
dropsies n ▷ dropsy
dropsy n (pl -sies) illness in which watery fluid collects in the body > **dropsical** adj
dross n (pl -es) scum formed on the surfaces of molten metals
drosses n ▷ dross
drought n (pl -s) prolonged shortage of rainfall
droughts n ▷ drought
drove¹ v ▷ drive
drove² n (pl -s) very large group, esp. of people
drover n (pl -s) person who drives sheep or cattle
drovers n ▷ drover
droves n ▷ drove²
drown v (-s, -ing, -ed) die or kill by immersion in liquid
drowned v ▷ drown
drowning v ▷ drown
drowns v ▷ drown

drowse v (-ses, -sing, -sed) be sleepy, dull, or sluggish ▸ **drowsy** adj (-sier, -siest) ▸ **drowsily** adv ▸ **drowsiness** n (pl -es)
  drowsed v ▷ drowse
  drowses v ▷ drowse
  drowsier adj ▷ drowse
  drowsiest adj ▷ drowse
  drowsily adv ▷ drowse
  drowsiness n ▷ drowse
  drowsinesses n ▷ drowse
  drowsing v ▷ drowse
  drowsy adj ▷ drowse
drubbing n (pl -s) utter defeat in a contest etc.
  drubbings n ▷ drubbing
drudge n (pl -s) person who works hard at uninteresting tasks ▸ **drudgery** n (pl -eries)
  drudgeries n ▷ drudge
  drudgery n ▷ drudge
  drudges n ▷ drudge
drug n (pl -s) substance used in the treatment or prevention of disease ▸ v (drugs, drugging, drugged) give a drug to (a person or animal) to cause sleepiness or unconsciousness
  drugged v ▷ drug
  drugging v ▷ drug
  drugs v, n ▷ drug
drugstore n (pl -s) (us) pharmacy where a wide range of goods are available
  drugstores n ▷ drugstore
druid n (pl -s) member of an ancient order of Celtic priests ▸ **druidic, druidical** adj
  druidic adj ▷ druid
  druidical adj ▷ druid
  druids adj ▷ druid
drum n (pl -s) percussion instrument sounded by striking a membrane stretched across the opening of a hollow cylinder ▸ v (drums, drumming, drummed) play (music) on a drum
  drummed v ▷ drum
drummer n (pl -s) person who plays a drum or drums
  drummers n ▷ drummer
  drumming v ▷ drum
  drums n, v ▷ drum
drumstick n (pl -s) stick used for playing a drum
  drumsticks n ▷ drumstick
drunk v ▷ drink ▸ adj (-er, -est) intoxicated with alcohol to the extent of losing control over normal functions ▸ n (pl -s) person who is drunk or who frequently gets drunk
drunkard n (pl -s) person who frequently gets drunk
  drunkards n ▷ drunkard

drunken adj drunk or frequently drunk ▸ **drunkenly** adv ▸ **drunkenness** n (pl -es)
  drunkenly adv ▷ drunken
  drunkenness n ▷ drunken
  drunkennesses n ▷ drunken
  drunker adj ▷ drunk
  drunkest adj ▷ drunk
  drunks n ▷ drunk
dry adj (drier, driest or dryer, dryest) lacking moisture ▸ v (dries, drying, dried) make or become dry ▸ **drily, dryly** adv ▸ **dryness** n (pl -es)
dryad n (pl -s) wood nymph
  dryads n ▷ dryad
dryer, drier n (pl -s) apparatus for removing moisture
  dryer adj ▷ dry
  dryers n ▷ dryer
  dryest adj ▷ dry
  drying v ▷ dry
  dryly adv ▷ dry
  dryness n ▷ dry
  drynesses n ▷ dry

> **dso** n (**dsos**). Dso is one of several spelling for a Tibetan animal bred from yaks and cattle. The other forms are **dzo, zho** and **zo**, and it's worth remembering all of them. Dso scores 4 points.

dual adj having two parts, functions, or aspects ▸ **duality** n (pl -ities) ▸ **dually** adv
  dualities n ▷ dual
  duality n ▷ dual
  dually adv ▷ dual
dub¹ v (dubs, dubbing, dubbed) give (a person or place) a name or nickname
dub² v (dubs, dubbing, dubbed) provide (a film) with a new soundtrack, esp. in a different language
  dubbed v ▷ dub¹, ²
dubbin n (pl -s) (BRIT) thick grease applied to leather to soften and waterproof it
  dubbing v ▷ dub¹, ²
  dubbins n ▷ dubbin
  dubieties n ▷ dubious
  dubiety n ▷ dubious
dubious [dew-bee-uss] adj feeling or causing doubt ▸ **dubiously** adv ▸ **dubiousness** n ▸ **dubiety** [dew-by-it-ee] n (pl -ities)
  dubiously adv ▷ dubious
  dubiousness n ▷ dubious
  dubs v ▷ dub¹, ²
ducal [duke-al] adj of a duke
ducat [duck-it] n (pl -s) former European gold or silver coin

ducats n ▷ ducat

duchess n (pl -es) woman who holds the rank of duke

duchesse n (pl -s) (NZ) dressing table with a mirror

duchesses n ▷ duchess, duchesse

duchies n ▷ duchy

duchy n (pl duchies) territory of a duke or duchess

duck¹ n (pl -s) water bird with short legs, webbed feet, and a broad blunt bill

duck² v (-s, -ing, -ed) move (the head or body) quickly downwards, to avoid being seen or to dodge a blow

ducked v ▷ duck²

ducking v ▷ duck²

duckling n (pl -s) baby duck

ducklings n ▷ duckling

ducks n ▷ duck¹ ▶ v ▷ duck²

duct n (pl -s) tube, pipe, or channel through which liquid or gas is conveyed

ductile adj (of a metal) able to be shaped into sheets or wires

ducts n ▷ duct

dud (Informal) n (pl -s) ineffectual person or thing ▶ adj bad or useless

dude n (pl -s) (US) (Informal) man

dudes n ▷ dude

dudgeon n (pl -s) anger, resentment

dudgeons n ▷ dudgeon

duds n ▷ dud

due adj expected or scheduled to be present or arrive ▶ n (pl -s) something that is owed or required ▶ pl charges for membership of a club or organization ▶ adv directly or exactly

duel n (pl -s) formal fight with deadly weapons between two people, to settle a quarrel ▶ v (-s, -lling, -lled) fight in a duel > **duellist** n (pl -s)

duelled v ▷ duel

duelling v ▷ duel

duellist n ▷ duel

duellists n ▷ duel

duels n, v ▷ duel

dues n ▷ due

duet n (pl -s) piece of music for two performers

duets n ▷ duet

duff adj (-er, -est) (CHIEFLY BRIT) broken or useless

duffel, duffle n (pl -s) heavy woollen cloth

duffels n ▷ duffel

duffer n (pl -s) (Informal) dull or incompetent person ▶ adj ▷ duff

duffers n ▷ duffer

duffest adj ▷ duff

duffle n ▷ duffel

duffles n ▷ duffel

dug¹ v ▷ dig

dug² n (pl -s) teat or udder

dugite [doo-gyte] n (pl -s) medium-sized Australian venomous snake

dugites n ▷ dugite

dugong n (pl -s) whalelike mammal of tropical waters

dugongs n ▷ dugong

dugout n (pl -s) (BRIT) (at a sports ground) covered bench where managers and substitutes sit

dugouts n ▷ dugout

dugs n ▷ dug²

duke n (pl -s) nobleman of the highest rank > **dukedom** n (pl -s)

dukedom n ▷ duke

dukedoms n ▷ duke

dukes n ▷ duke

dulcet [dull-sit] adj (of a sound) soothing or pleasant

dulcimer n (pl -s) tuned percussion instrument consisting of a set of strings stretched over a sounding board and struck with hammers

dulcimers n ▷ dulcimer

dull adj (-er, -est) not interesting ▶ v (-s, -ing, -ed) make or become dull > **dullness** n (pl -es) > **dully** adv

dullard n (pl -s) dull or stupid person

dullards n ▷ dullard

dulled v ▷ dull

duller adj ▷ dull

dullest adj ▷ dull

dulling v ▷ dull

dullness n ▷ dull

dullnesses n ▷ dull

dulls v ▷ dull

dully adv ▷ dull

duly adv in a proper manner

dumb adj (dumber, dumbest) lacking the power to speak > **dumbly** adv > **dumbness** n

dumbbell n (pl -s) short bar with a heavy ball or disc at each end, used for physical exercise

dumbbells n ▷ dumbbell

dumber adj ▷ dumb

dumbest adj ▷ dumb

dumbfounded adj speechless with astonishment

dumbly adv ▷ dumb

dumbness n ▷ dumb

dumdum n (pl -s) soft-nosed bullet that expands on impact and causes serious wounds

dumdums n ▷ dumdum

dummies n ▷ dummy

dummy n (pl **-mies**) figure representing the human form, used for displaying clothes etc. ▶ adj imitation, substitute

dump v (**-s, -ing, -ed**) drop or let fall in a careless manner ▶ n (pl **-s**) place where waste materials are left

dumped v ▷ dump

dumpier adj ▷ dumpy

dumpiest adj ▷ dumpy

dumpily adv ▷ dumpy

dumpiness n ▷ dumpy

dumping v ▷ dump

dumpling n (pl **-s**) small ball of dough cooked and served with stew

dumplings n ▷ dumpling

dumps v, n ▷ dump

dumpy adj (**dumpier, dumpiest**) short and plump > **dumpily** adv > **dumpiness** n

dun (**dunner, dunnest**) adj brownish-grey

dunce n (pl **-s**) person who is stupid or slow to learn

dunces n ▷ dunce

dunderhead n (pl **-s**) slow-witted person

dunderheads n ▷ dunderhead

dune n (pl **-s**) mound or ridge of drifted sand

dunes n ▷ dune

dung n (pl **-s**) faeces from animals such as cattle

dungarees pl n trousers with a bib attached

dungeon n (pl **-s**) underground prison cell

dungeons n ▷ dungeon

dungs n ▷ dung

dunk v (**-s, -ing, -ed**) dip (a biscuit or bread) in a drink or soup before eating it

dunked v ▷ dunk

dunking v ▷ dunk

dunks v ▷ dunk

dunner adj ▷ dun

dunnest adj ▷ dun

dunnies n ▷ dunny

dunny n (pl **-nies**) (AUST & OLD-FASHIONED NZ) (Informal) toilet

duo n (pl **-s**) pair of performers

duodena n ▷ duodenum

duodenal adj ▷ duodenum

duodenum [dew-oh-**deen**-um] n (pl **-na, -nums**) first part of the small intestine, just below the stomach > **duodenal** adj

duodenums n ▷ duodenum

duos n ▷ duo

dupe v (**dupes, duping, duped**) deceive or cheat ▶ n (pl **-s**) person who is easily deceived

duped v ▷ dupe

dupes v, n ▷ dupe

duping v ▷ dupe

duple adj (MUSIC) having two beats in a bar

duplex n (pl **-es**) (CHIEFLY US) apartment on two floors

duplexes n ▷ duplex

duplicate adj copied exactly from an original ▶ n (pl **-s**) exact copy ▶ v (**-cates, -cating, -cated**) make an exact copy of > **duplication** n (pl **-s**) > **duplicator** n (pl **-s**)

duplicated v ▷ duplicate

duplicates n, v ▷ duplicate

duplicating v ▷ duplicate

duplication n ▷ duplicate

duplications n ▷ duplicate

duplicator n ▷ duplicate

duplicators n ▷ duplicate

duplicities n ▷ duplicity

duplicity n (pl **-ities**) deceitful behaviour

durability n ▷ durable

durable adj long-lasting > **durability** n > **durably** adv

durables pl n goods that require infrequent replacement

durably adv ▷ durable

duration n (pl **-s**) length of time that something lasts

durations n ▷ duration

duress n compulsion by use of force or threats

during prep throughout or within the limit of (a period of time)

dusk n (pl **-s**) time just before nightfall, when it is almost dark

duskier adj ▷ dusky

duskiest adj ▷ dusky

duskily adv ▷ dusky

duskiness n ▷ dusky

dusks n ▷ dusk

dusky adj (**duskier, duskiest**) dark in colour > **duskily** adv > **duskiness** n

dust n (pl **-s**) small dry particles of earth, sand, or dirt ▶ v (**-s, -ing, -ed**) remove dust from (furniture) by wiping

dustbin n (pl **-s**) large container for household rubbish

dustbins n ▷ dustbin

dusted v ▷ dust

duster n (pl **-s**) cloth used for dusting

dusters n ▷ duster

dustier adj ▷ dusty

dustiest adj ▷ dusty

dusting v ▷ dust

dustman n (pl **-men**) (BRIT) man whose job is to collect household rubbish

dustmen n ▷ dustman

dustpan n (pl **-s**) short-handled shovel into which dust is swept from floors

dustpans n ▷ dustpan

dusts n, v ▷ dust

dusty adj (dustier, dustiest) covered with dust

dutiability n ▷ dutiable

dutiable adj (of goods) requiring payment of duty ▷ **dutiability** n

duties n ▷ duty

dutiful adj doing what is expected ▷ **dutifully** adv

dutifully adv ▷ dutiful

duty n (pl -ties) work or a task performed as part of one's job

duvet [doo-vay] n (pl -s) kind of quilt used in bed instead of a top sheet and blankets

duvets n ▷ duvet

dux n (duces). A dux is the top pupil in a school. This is a handy word to have ready if someone else has played a word containing X. Dux scores 11 points.

dwang n (pl -s) (NZ & S AFR) short piece of wood inserted in a timber-framed wall

dwangs n ▷ dwang

dwarf n (pl dwarfs, dwarves) person who is smaller than average ▶ adj (of an animal or plant) much smaller than the usual size for the species ▶ v (dwarfs, dwarfing or dwarfed) cause (someone or something) to seem small being much larger

dwarfed v ▷ dwarf

dwarfing v ▷ dwarf

dwarfs n, v ▷ dwarf

dwarves n ▷ dwarf

dwell v (dwells, dwelling, dwelt or dwelled) live, reside

dwelled v ▷ dwell

dweller n (pl -s) person who lives in a specified place

dwellers n ▷ dweller

dwelling n (pl -s) place of residence ▶ v ▷ dwell

dwellings n ▷ dwelling

dwells v ▷ dwell

dwelt v ▷ dwell

dwindle v (-dles, -dling, -dled) grow less in size, strength, or number

dwindled v ▷ dwindle

dwindles v ▷ dwindle

dwindling v ▷ dwindle

dye n (pl -s) colouring substance ▶ v (dyes, dyeing, dyed) colour (hair or fabric) by applying a dye ▷ **dyer** n (pl -s)

dyed v ▷ dye

dyeing v ▷ dye

dyer n ▷ dye

dyers n ▷ dye

dyes n, v ▷ dye

dying v ▷ die¹

dyke n (pl -s) wall built to prevent flooding

dykes n ▷ dyke

dynamic adj full of energy, ambition, and new ideas ▷ **dynamically** adv

dynamically adv ▷ dynamic

dynamics n branch of mechanics concerned with the forces that change or produce the motions of bodies ▶ pl forces that produce change in a system

dynamism n great energy and enthusiasm

dynamite n (pl -s) explosive made of nitroglycerine ▶ v (-mites, -miting, -mited) blow (something) up with dynamite

dynamited v ▷ dynamite

dynamites n, v ▷ dynamite

dynamiting v ▷ dynamite

dynamo n (pl -s) device for converting mechanical energy into electrical energy

dynamos n ▷ dynamo

dynastic adj ▷ dynasty

dynasties n ▷ dynasty

dynasty n (pl -ties) sequence of hereditary rulers ▷ **dynastic** adj

dysenteries n ▷ dysentery

dysentery n (pl -teries) infection of the intestine causing severe diarrhoea

dysfunction n (pl -s) (MED) disturbance or abnormality in the function of an organ or part ▷ **dysfunctional** adj ▷ **dysfunctionally** adv

dysfunctional adj ▷ dysfunction

dysfunctionally adv ▷ dysfunction

dysfunctions n ▷ dysfunction

dyslexia n (pl -s) disorder causing impaired ability to read ▷ **dyslexic** adj

dyslexias n ▷ dyslexia

dyslexic adj ▷ dyslexia

dysmenorrhoea n (pl -s) painful menstruation

dysmenorrhoeas n ▷ dysmenorrhoea

dyspepsia n (pl -s) indigestion ▷ **dyspeptic** adj

dyspepsias n ▷ dyspepsia

dyspeptic adj ▷ dyspepsia

dystrophic adj ▷ dystrophy

dystrophies n ▷ dystrophy

dystrophy [diss-trof-fee] n (pl -phies) wasting disorder ▷ **dystrophic** adj

dzho *n* (**dzhos**). A dzho is one of several ways of spelling the name of a Tibetan animal bred from yaks and cattle. This spelling is less useful than the others (**dso, dzo, zho** and **zo**) because it has four letters rather than two or three. It is, however, a very useful word to know when someone else has played zho, as you can use D to hook another word onto zho, or just to take advantage of the Z already on the board. Dzho scores 17 points.

dzo *n* (**dzos**). Dzo is one of several spelling for a Tibetan animal bred from yaks and cattle. The other forms are **dso, dzho, zho** and **zo,** and it's worth remembering all of them. Dzo scores 13 points.

Ee

E is the most common tile in the game and, while it is only worth one point, as the most frequent letter in English it is extremely useful. Many words contain two or more Es, so, unlike many tiles, it's good to have several Es on your rack. Keep in mind three-letter words formed by two Es either side of a consonant, like **eye**, **ewe** and **eve** (6 points each), and **eke** (7). E can also be handy for getting rid of double consonants: think of words like **egg** or **ebb** (each 5 points). E also combines well with K: as well as **eke**, we have **elk** and **eek** (both 7), and **ewk** (10). If you have an X on your rack, E offers you all kinds of options: just think of all the words that begin with ex-, like **exhaust** (17), which will give you a 50-point bonus if you use all of your tiles to form it. And don't forget **ex** itself, a nice little word that earns you 9 points.

ea n (**eas**). Ea is a dialect word for a river. This word won't earn you many points, but it does provide many opportunities to play longer words that form ea in the process. Ea scores 2 points.

each adj, pron every (one) taken separately

eager adj (**-er**, **-est**) showing or feeling great desire, keen > **eagerly** adv > **eagerness** n (pl **-es**)

  eagerer adj ▷ eager
  eagerest adj ▷ eager
  eagerly adv ▷ eager
  eagerness n ▷ eager
  eagernesses n ▷ eager

eagle n (pl **-s**) large bird of prey with keen eyesight

  eagles n ▷ eagle

eaglet n (pl **-s**) young eagle

  eaglets n ▷ eaglet

ear[1] n (pl **-s**) organ of hearing, esp. the external part of it

ear[2] n (pl **-s**) head of corn

earache n (pl **-s**) pain in the ear

  earaches n ▷ earache

earbash v (**-es**, **-ing**, **-ed**) (AUST & NZ) (Informal) talk incessantly > **earbashing** n (pl **-s**)

  earbashed n ▷ earbash
  earbashes n ▷ earbash
  earbashing v, n ▷ earbash
  earbashings n ▷ earbash

eardrum n (pl **-s**) thin piece of skin inside the ear which enables one to hear sounds

  eardrums n ▷ eardrum

earl n (pl **-s**) British nobleman ranking next below a marquess > **earldom** n (pl **-s**)

  earldom n ▷ earl
  earldoms n ▷ earl

earlier adj, adv ▷ early

earliest adj, adv ▷ early

  earls n ▷ earl

early adj, adv (**-ier**, **-iest**) before the expected or usual time

earmark v (**-s**, **-ing**, **-ed**) set (something) aside for a specific purpose

  earmarked v ▷ earmark
  earmarking v ▷ earmark
  earmarks v ▷ earmark

earn v (**-s**, **-ing**, **-ed**) obtain by work or merit

  earned v ▷ earn

earnest[1] adj serious and sincere > **earnestly** adv

earnest[2] n (pl **-s**) part payment given in advance, esp. to confirm a contract

  earnests n ▷ earnest[2]
  earning v ▷ earn

earnings pl n money earned

  earns v ▷ earn

earphone n (pl **-s**) receiver for a radio etc., held to or put in the ear

  earphones n ▷ earphone

earring n (pl **-s**) ornament for the lobe of the ear

  earrings n ▷ earring
  ears n ▷ ear[1, 2]

earshot n (pl **-s**) hearing range

  earshots n ▷ earshot

earth n (pl **-s**) land, the ground ▶ v (**-s**, **-ing**, **-ed**)

connect (a circuit) to earth
  earthed v ▷ **earth**
earthen adj made of baked clay or earth
earthenware n (pl -s) pottery made of baked
clay
  earthenwares n ▷ **earthenwares**
  earthier adj ▷ **earthy**
  earthiest adj ▷ **earthy**
  earthing v ▷ **earth**
earthly adj conceivable or possible
earthquake n (pl -s) violent vibration of the
earth's surface
  earthquakes n ▷ **earthquake**
  earths n, v ▷ **earth**
earthwork n (pl -s) fortification made of earth
  earthworks n ▷ **earthwork**
earthworm n (pl -s) worm which burrows in
the soil
  earthworms n ▷ **earthworm**
earthy adj (-thier, -thiest) coarse or crude
earwig n (pl -s) small insect with a pincer-like
tail
  earwigs n ▷ **earwig**
ease n (pl -ses) freedom from difficulty,
discomfort, or worry ▶ v (-ses, -sing, -sed)
give bodily or mental ease to
  eased v ▷ **ease**
easel n (pl -s) frame to support an artist's
canvas or a blackboard
  easels n ▷ **easel**
  eases n, v ▷ **ease**
  easier adj ▷ **easy**
  easily adv ▷ **easy**
  easiest adj ▷ **easy**
  easiness n ▷ **easy**
  easinesses n ▷ **easy**
  easing v ▷ **ease**
east n (pl -s) (direction towards) the part of
the horizon where the sun rises ▶ adj to or
in the east ▶ adv in, to, or towards the east
> **easterly** adj > **eastern** adj > **eastward** adj,
adv > **eastwards** adv
  easterly adj ▷ **east**
  eastern adj ▷ **east**
  easts n ▷ **east**
  eastward adj, adv ▷ **east**
  eastwards adj, adv ▷ **east**
easy adj (-ier, -iest) not needing much work or
effort > **easily** adv > **easiness** n (pl -s)
eat v (eats, eating, ate, eaten) take (food) into
the mouth and swallow it
eatable adj fit or suitable for eating
  eaten v ▷ **eat**
  eating v ▷ **eat**
  eats v ▷ **eat**

eaves pl n overhanging edges of a roof
eavesdrop v (-s, -pping, -pped) listen secretly
to a private conversation > **eavesdropper** n
(pl -s) > **eavesdropping** n (pl -s)
  eavesdropped v ▷ **eavesdrop**
  eavesdropper n ▷ **eavesdrop**
  eavesdroppers n ▷ **eavesdrop**
  eavesdropping v, n ▷ **eavesdrop**
  eavesdroppings n ▷ **eavesdrop**
  eavesdrops v ▷ **eavesdrop**
ebb v (-s, -ing, -ed) (of tide water) flow back ▶ n
(pl -s) flowing back of the tide
  ebbed v ▷ **ebb**
  ebbing v ▷ **ebb**
  ebbs v, n ▷ **ebb**
  ebonies n ▷ **ebony**
ebony n (pl -ies) hard black wood ▶ adj deep
black
  ebullience n ▷ **ebullient**
  ebulliences n ▷ **ebullient**
ebullient adj full of enthusiasm or excitement
> **ebullience** n (pl -s)
eccentric adj odd or unconventional ▶ n (pl
-s) eccentric person > **eccentrically** adv
> **eccentricity** n (pl -ies)
  eccentrically adv ▷ **eccentric**
  eccentricities n ▷ **eccentric**
  eccentricity n ▷ **eccentric**
  eccentrics n ▷ **eccentric**
ecclesiastic n (pl -s) member of the clergy ▶ adj
(also **ecclesiastical**) of the Christian Church
or clergy
  ecclesiastical adj ▷ **ecclesiastic**
  ecclesiastics n ▷ **ecclesiastic**

> **ech** v (**echs, eching, eched**). Ech is
> an old word that Shakespeare uses,
> and means **eke**. It's a good one to
> have ready if you have C and H but no
> obvious place to play them. Ech scores
> 8 points.

echelon [esh-a-lon] n (pl -s) level of power or
responsibility
  echelons n ▷ **echelon**
echidna [ik-**kid**-na] n (pl -nas, -nae) [-nee]
Australian spiny egg-laying mammal
  echidnae n ▷ **echidna**
  echidnas n ▷ **echidna**
echo n (pl -es) repetition of sounds by
reflection of sound waves off a surface ▶ v
(-s, -ing, -ed) repeat or be repeated as an
echo
  echoed v ▷ **echo**
  echoes v, n ▷ **echo**
  echoing v ▷ **echo**
éclair n (pl -s) finger-shaped pastry filled with

cream and covered with chocolate
  éclairs n ▷ éclair
éclat [ake-**lah**] n brilliant success
eclectic adj selecting from various styles, ideas, or sources > **eclecticism** n (pl -s)
  eclecticism n ▷ eclectic
  eclecticisms n ▷ eclectic
eclipse n (pl -es) temporary obscuring of one star or planet by another ▶ v (-ses, -sing, -sed) surpass or outclass
  eclipsed v ▷ eclipse
  eclipses v ▷ eclipse
  eclipsing v ▷ eclipse
ecliptic n (pl -s) apparent path of the sun
  ecliptics n ▷ ecliptic
ecological adj of ecology > **ecologically** adv
  ecologically adv ▷ ecological
  ecologist n ▷ ecology
  ecologists n ▷ ecology
ecology n study of the relationships between living things and their environment > **ecologist** n (pl -s)
economic adj of economics
economical adj not wasteful, thrifty > **economically** adv
  economically adv ▷ economical
economics n social science concerned with the production and consumption of goods and services
  economies n ▷ economy
economist n (pl -s) specialist in economics
  economists n ▷ economist
economize v (-izes, -izing, -ized) reduce expense or waste
  economized v ▷ economize
  economizes v ▷ economize
  economizing v ▷ economize
economy n (pl -ies) system of interrelationship of money, industry, and employment in a country
ecosystem n (pl -s) system involving interactions between a community and its environment
  ecosystems n ▷ ecosystem
ecru adj pale creamy-brown
  ecstasies n ▷ ecstasy
ecstasy n (pl -ies) state of intense delight > **ecstatic** adj > **ecstatically** adv
  ecstatic adj ▷ ecstasy
  ecstatically adv ▷ ecstasy
ectoplasm n (pl -s) (SPIRITUALISM) substance that supposedly is emitted from the body of a medium during a trance
  ectoplasms n ▷ ectoplasm
ecumenical adj of the Christian Church

throughout the world
eczema [ek-sim-a] n (pl s) skin disease causing intense itching
  eczemas n ▷ eczema
  eddied v ▷ eddy
  eddies n, v ▷ eddy
eddy n (pl eddies) circular movement of air, water, etc. ▶ v (eddies, eddying, eddied) move with a circular motion
  eddying v ▷ eddy
edelweiss [ade-il-vice] n (pl -es) alpine plant with white flowers
  edelweisses n ▷ edelweiss
edge n (pl -s) border or line where something ends or begins ▶ v (edges, edging, edged) provide an edge or border for
  edged v ▷ edge
  edges n, v ▷ edge
edgeways adv with the edge forwards or uppermost
  edgier adj ▷ edgy
  edgiest adj ▷ edgy
  edging v ▷ edge ▶ n (pl -s) anything placed along an edge to finish it
  edgings n ▷ edging
edgy adj (edgier, edgiest) nervous or irritable
  edibilities n ▷ edible
  edibility n ▷ edible
edible adj fit to be eaten > **edibility** n (pl -ties)
edict [ee-dikt] n (pl -s) order issued by an authority
  edicts n ▷ edict
  edification n ▷ edify
  edifications n ▷ edify
edifice [ed-if-iss] n (pl -s) large building
  edifices n ▷ edifice
  edified v ▷ edify
  edifies v ▷ edify
edify [ed-if-fie] v (-fies, -fying, -fied) improve morally by instruction > **edification** n (pl -s)
  edifying v ▷ edify
edit v (-s, -ing, -ed) prepare (a book, film, etc.) for publication or broadcast
  edited v ▷ edit
  editing v ▷ edit
  editings n ▷ edit
edition n (pl -s) number of copies of a new publication printed at one time
  editions n ▷ edition
editor n (pl -s) person who edits
editorial n (pl -s) newspaper article stating the opinion of the editor ▶ adj of editing or editors
  editorials n ▷ editorial
  editors n ▷ editor

edits v ▷ edit
educate v (-tes, -ting, -ted) teach ▷ **education** n (pl -s) ▷ **educational** adj ▷ **educationally** adv
educated v ▷ educate
educates v ▷ educate
educating v ▷ educate
educational adj ▷ educate
educationalist n (pl -s) expert in the theory of education
educationalists n ▷ educationalist
educationally adv ▷ educate
educations n ▷ educate
educative adj educating

> **ee** n (**een**). Ee is a Scots word for eye. While this word won't earn you a big score on its own, it can be very useful when you're trying to form several words at once. Ee scores 2 points.
> **eek** interj. Eek is a noise that people make when they are startled or frightened. Eek scores 7 points.

eel n (pl -s) snakelike fish
eels n ▷ eel
eerie adj (-ier, -iest) uncannily frightening or disturbing ▷ **eerily** adv
eerier adj ▷ eerie
eeriest adj ▷ eerie
eerily adv ▷ eerie

> **ef** n (**efs**). Ef is the letter F, and is a handy word to know when you want to play a longer word parallel to a word that's already on the board. Ef scores 5 points.

efface v (-ces, -cing, -ced) remove by rubbing > **effacement** n (pl -s)
effaced v ▷ efface
effacement n ▷ efface
effacements n ▷ efface
effaces v ▷ efface
effacing v ▷ efface
effect n (pl -s) change or result caused by someone or something ▶ pl personal belongings ▶ v (-s, -ing, -ed) cause to happen, accomplish
effected v ▷ effect
effecting v ▷ effect
effective adj producing a desired result > **effectively** adv
effectively adv ▷ effective
effects n, v ▷ effect
effectual adj producing the intended result > **effectually** adv
effectually adv ▷ effectual
effeminacies n ▷ effeminate
effeminacy n ▷ effeminate
effeminate adj (of a man) displaying

characteristics thought to be typical of a woman > **effeminacy** n (pl -ies)
effervescence n ▷ effervescent
effervescences n ▷ effervescent
effervescent adj (of a liquid) giving off bubbles of gas > **effervescence** n (pl -s)
effete [if-**feet**] adj powerless, feeble
efficacies n ▷ efficacious
efficacious adj producing the intended result > **efficacy** n (pl -ies)
efficacy n ▷ efficacious
efficiencies n ▷ efficient
efficiency n ▷ efficient
efficient adj functioning effectively with little waste of effort > **efficiently** adv > **efficiency** n (pl -ies)
efficiently adv ▷ efficient
effigies n ▷ effigy
effigy [**ef**-fij-ee] n (pl -ies) image or likeness of a person
efflorescence n (pl -s) flowering
efflorescences n ▷ efflorescence
effluent n (pl -s) liquid discharged as waste
effluents n ▷ effluent
effluvia n ▷ effluvium
effluvium n (pl -via) unpleasant smell, as of decaying matter or gaseous waste
effort n (pl -s) physical or mental exertion > **effortless** adj
effortless adj ▷ effort
efforts n ▷ effort
effronteries n ▷ effrontery
effrontery n (pl -ies) brazen impudence
effusion n (pl -s) unrestrained outburst
effusions n ▷ effusion
effusive adj openly emotional, demonstrative > **effusively** adv
effusively adv ▷ effusive
egalitarian adj upholding the equality of all people ▶ n (pl -s) person who holds egalitarian beliefs > **egalitarianism** n (pl -s)
egalitarianism n ▷ egalitarian
egalitarianisms n ▷ egalitarian
egalitarians n ▷ egalitarian
egg[1] n (pl -s) oval or round object laid by the females of birds and other creatures, containing a developing embryo
egg[2] v (-s, -ing, -ed) encourage or incite, esp. to do wrong
egged v ▷ egg[2]
egghead n (pl -s) (Informal) intellectual person
eggheads n ▷ egghead
egging v ▷ egg[2]
eggplant n (pl -s) (US, CANADIAN, AUST & NZ) aubergine

eggplants n ▷ eggplant

eggs n, v ▷ egg¹, ²

ego n (pl -s) the conscious mind of an individual

egocentric adj self-centred

egoism, egotism n excessive concern for one's own interests > **egoist, egotist** n (pl -s) > **egoistic, egotistic** adj

egoist n ▷ egoism

egoistic adj ▷ egoism

egoists n ▷ egoism

egos n ▷ ego

egotist n ▷ egoism

egotistic adj ▷ egoism

egotists n ▷ egoism

egregious [ig-**greej**-uss] adj outstandingly bad

egress [ee-gress] n (pl -es) departure

egresses n ▷ egress

egret [ee-grit] n (pl -s) lesser white heron

egrets n ▷ egret

eider n (pl -s) Arctic duck

eiderdown n (pl -s) quilt (orig. stuffed with eider feathers)

eiderdowns n ▷ eiderdown

eiders n ▷ eider

eight adj, n (pl -s) one more than seven

eighteen adj, n (pl -s) eight and ten > **eighteenth** adj, n (pl -s)

eighteens n ▷ eighteen

eighteenth adj, n ▷ eighteen

eighteenths n ▷ eighteen

eighth adj, n (pl -s) (of) number eight in a series

eighths n ▷ eighth

eighties n ▷ eighty

eightieth n ▷ eighty

eightieths n ▷ eighty

eights n ▷ eight

eighty adj, n (pl -ies) eight times ten > **eightieth** adj, n (pl -s)

eisteddfod [ice-sted-fod] n (pl -s) Welsh festival with competitions in music and other performing arts

eisteddfods n ▷ eisteddfod

either adj, pron one or the other (of two) ▶ conj used preceding two or more possibilities joined by or ▶ adv likewise

ejaculate v (-tes, -ting, -ted) eject (semen) > **ejaculation** n (pl -s)

ejaculated v ▷ ejaculate

ejaculates v ▷ ejaculate

ejaculating v ▷ ejaculate

ejaculation n ▷ ejaculate

ejaculations n ▷ ejaculate

eject v (-s, -ing, -ed) force out, expel > **ejection** n (pl -s) > **ejector** n (pl -s)

ejected v ▷ eject

ejecting v ▷ eject

ejection n ▷ eject

ejections n ▷ eject

ejector n ▷ eject

ejectors n ▷ eject

ejects v ▷ eject

eke v (ekes, eking, eked) (usu. foll. by **out**) make (a living) with difficulty

eked v ▷ eke

ekes v ▷ eke

eking v ▷ eke

elaborate adj with a lot of fine detail ▶ v (-tes, -ting, -ted) expand upon > **elaboration** n (pl -s)

elaborated v ▷ elaborate

elaborates v ▷ elaborate

elaborating v ▷ elaborate

elaboration n ▷ elaborate

elaborations n ▷ elaborate

élan [ale-an] n (pl -s) style and vigour

eland [eel-and] n (pl -s) large antelope of southern Africa

elands n ▷ eland

élans n ▷ élan

elapse v (-ses, -sing, -sed) (of time) pass by

elapsed v ▷ elapse

elapses v ▷ elapse

elapsing v ▷ elapse

elastic adj resuming normal shape after distortion ▶ n (pl -s) tape or fabric containing interwoven strands of flexible rubber > **elasticity** n (pl -ies)

elasticities n ▷ elastic

elasticity n ▷ elastic

elastics n ▷ elastic

elate v (-tes, -ting, -ted) make extremely happy and excited > **elation** n (pl -s)

elated v ▷ elate

elates v ▷ elate

elating v ▷ elate

elation n ▷ elate

elations n ▷ elate

elbow n (pl -s) joint between the upper arm and the forearm ▶ v (-s, -ing, -ed) shove or strike with the elbow

elbowed v ▷ elbow

elbowing v ▷ elbow

elbows n, v ▷ elbow

elder¹ adj older ▶ n (pl -s) older person

elder² n (pl -s) small tree with white flowers and black berries

elderly adj (fairly) old

elders n ▷ elder¹, ²

eldest adj oldest

eldritch *adj* (SCOT) weird, uncanny
elect *v* (-s, -ing, -ed) choose by voting ▶ *adj*
appointed but not yet in office
  elected *v* ▷ elect
  electing *v* ▷ elect
election *n* (*pl* -s) choosing of representatives
by voting
electioneering *n* (*pl* -s) active participation in
a political campaign
  electioneerings *n* ▷ electioneering
  elections *n* ▷ election
elective *adj* chosen by election
elector *n* (*pl* -s) someone who has the right to
vote in an election > **electoral** *adj*
  electoral *adj* ▷ elector
electorate *n* (*pl* -s) people who have the right
to vote
  electorates *n* ▷ electorate
  electors *n* ▷ elector
electric *adj* produced by, transmitting, or
powered by electricity
electrical *adj* using or concerning electricity
electrician *n* (*pl* -s) person trained to install
and repair electrical equipment
  electricians *n* ▷ electrician
  electricities *n* ▷ electricity
electricity *n* (*pl* -ies) form of energy associated
with stationary or moving electrons or other
charged particles
electrics *pl n* (BRIT) electric appliances
  electrification *n* ▷ electrify
  electrifications *n* ▷ electrify
  electrified *v* ▷ electrify
  electrifies *v* ▷ electrify
electrify *v* (-fies, -fying, -fied) adapt for
operation by electric power > **electrification**
n
  electrifying *v* ▷ electrify
electrocute *v* (-tes, -ting, -ted) kill or injure by
electricity > **electrocution** *n* (*pl* -s)
  electrocuted *v* ▷ electrocute
  electrocutes *v* ▷ electrocute
  electrocuting *v* ▷ electrocute
  electrocution *n* ▷ electrocute
  electrocutions *n* ▷ electrocute
electrode *n* (*pl* -s) conductor through which
an electric current enters or leaves a battery,
vacuum tube, etc
  electrodes *n* ▷ electrode
electrodynamics *n* branch of physics
concerned with the interactions between
electrical and mechanical forces
  electrolyses *n* ▷ electrolysis
electrolysis [ill-lek-**troll**-iss-iss] *n* (*pl* -ses)
conduction of electricity by an electrolyte,

esp. to induce chemical change
electrolyte *n* (*pl* -s) solution or molten
substance that conducts electricity
  > **electrolytic** *adj*
  electrolytes *n* ▷ electrolyte
  electrolytic *adj* ▷ electrolyte
electromagnet *n* (*pl* -s) magnet containing a
coil of wire through which an electric current
is passed
electromagnetic *adj* of or operated by an
electomagnet
  electromagnets *n* ▷ electromagnet
electron *n* (*pl* -s) elementary particle in all
atoms that has a negative electrical charge
electronic *adj* (of a device) dependent on the
action of electrons
electronics *n* technology concerned with
the development of electronic devices and
circuits
  electrons *n* ▷ electron
electronvolt *n* (*pl* -s) unit of energy used in
nuclear physics
  electronvolts *n* ▷ electronvolt
electroplate *v* (-tes, -ting, -ted) coat with
silver etc. by electrolysis
  electroplated *v* ▷ electroplate
  electroplates *v* ▷ electroplate
  electroplating *v* ▷ electroplate
  elects *v* ▷ elect
  elegance *n* ▷ elegant
  elegances *n* ▷ elegant
elegant *adj* pleasing or graceful in dress, style,
or design > **elegance** *n* (*pl* -s)
elegiac *adj* mournful or plaintive
  elegies *n* ▷ elegy
elegy [el-lij-ee] *n* (*pl* -ies) mournful poem, esp. a
lament for the dead
element *n* (*pl* -s) component part ▶ *pl* basic
principles of something
elemental *adj* of primitive natural forces or
passions
elementary *adj* simple and straightforward
  elements *n* ▷ element
elephant *n* (*pl* -s) huge four-footed thick-
skinned animal with ivory tusks and a long
trunk
elephantiasis [el-lee-fan-**tie**-a-siss] *n* disease
with hardening of the skin and enlargement
of the legs etc.
elephantine *adj* unwieldy, clumsy
  elephants *n* ▷ elephant
elevate *v* (-ates, -ating, -ated) raise in rank
or status
  elevated *v* ▷ elevate
  elevates *v* ▷ elevate

elevating v ▷ elevate
elevation n (pl -s) raising
elevator n (pl -s) (AUST, US & CANADIAN) lift for carrying people
  elevators n ▷ elevator
eleven adj, n (pl -s) one more than ten
  elevens n ▷ eleven
elevenses n (BRIT & S AFR) (Informal) mid-morning snack
eleventh adj, n (pl -s) (of) number eleven in a series
  elevenths n ▷ eleventh
elf n (pl elves) (in folklore) small mischievous fairy
elfin adj small and delicate
elicit v (-s, -ing, -ed) bring about (a response or reaction)
  elicited v ▷ elicit
  eliciting v ▷ elicit
  elicits v ▷ elicit
elide v (-des, -ding, -ded) omit (a vowel or syllable) from a spoken word > **elision** n (pl -s)
  elided v ▷ elide
  elides v ▷ elide
  eliding v ▷ elide
  eligibilities n ▷ eligible
  eligibility n ▷ eligible
eligible adj meeting the requirements or qualifications needed > **eligibility** n (pl -ties)
eliminate v (-tes, -ting, -ted) get rid of > **elimination** n (pl -s)
  eliminated v ▷ eliminate
  eliminates v ▷ eliminate
  eliminating v ▷ eliminate
  elimination n ▷ eliminate
  eliminations n ▷ eliminate
  elision n ▷ elide
  elisions n ▷ elide
elite [ill-eet] n (pl -s) most powerful, rich, or gifted members of a group
  elites n ▷ elite
elitism n (pl -s) belief that society should be governed by a small group of superior people > **elitist** n, adj (pl -s)
  elitisms n ▷ elitism
  elitists n ▷ elitist
elixir [ill-ix-er] n (pl -s) imaginary liquid that can prolong life or turn base metals into gold
  elixirs n ▷ elixir
elk n (pl -s) large deer of N Europe and Asia
  elks n ▷ elk
ellipse n (pl -ses) oval shape
  ellipses n ▷ ellipse, ellipsis
ellipsis n (pl -ses) omission of letters or words in a sentence

elliptical adj oval-shaped
elm n (pl -s) tree with serrated leaves
  elms n ▷ elm
elocution n (pl -s) art of speaking clearly in public
  elocutions n ▷ elocution
elongate [eel-long-gate] v (-tes, -ting, -ted) make or become longer > **elongation** n (pl -s)
  elongated v ▷ elongate
  elongates v ▷ elongate
  elongating v ▷ elongate
  elongation n ▷ elongate
  elongations n ▷ elongate
elope v (-s, -ing, -ed) (of two people) run away secretly to get married > **elopement** n (pl -s)
  eloped v ▷ elope
  elopement n ▷ elope
  elopements n ▷ elope
  elopes v ▷ elope
  eloping v ▷ elope
eloquence n (pl -s) fluent powerful use of language > **eloquent** adj > **eloquently** adv
  eloquencies n ▷ eloquence
  eloquent adj ▷ eloquence
  eloquently adv ▷ eloquence
else adv in addition or more
elsewhere adv in or to another place
elucidate v (-tes, -ting, -ted) make (something difficult) clear > **elucidation** n (pl -s)
  elucidated v ▷ elucidate
  elucidates v ▷ elucidate
  elucidating v ▷ elucidate
  elucidation n ▷ elucidate
  elucidations n ▷ elucidate
elude v (-s, -ing, -ed) escape from by cleverness or quickness
  eluded v ▷ elude
  eludes v ▷ elude
  eluding v ▷ elude
elusive adj difficult to catch or remember
elver n (pl -s) young eel
  elvers n ▷ elver
  elves n ▷ elf
emaciated [im-mace-ee-ate-id] adj abnormally thin > **emaciation** n (pl -s)
  emaciation n ▷ emaciated
  emaciations n ▷ emaciated
emanate [em-a-nate] v (-tes, -ting, -ted) issue, proceed from a source > **emanation** n (pl -s)
  emanated v ▷ emanate
  emanates v ▷ emanate
  emanating v ▷ emanate
  emanation n ▷ emanate
  emanations n ▷ emanate
emancipate v (-tes, -ting, -ted) free

from social, political, or legal restraints
> **emancipation** n (pl -s)
emancipated v ▷ emancipate
emancipates v ▷ emancipate
emancipating v ▷ emancipate
emancipation n ▷ emancipate
emancipations n ▷ emancipate
emasculate v (-tes, -ting, -ted) deprive of
power > **emasculation** n (pl -s)
emasculated v ▷ emasculate
emasculates v ▷ emasculate
emasculating v ▷ emasculate
emasculation n ▷ emasculate
emasculations n ▷ emasculate
embalm v (-s, -ing, -ed) preserve (a corpse)
from decay by the use of chemicals etc.
embalmed v ▷ embalm
embalming v ▷ embalm
embalms v ▷ embalm
embankment n (pl -s) man-made ridge that
carries a road or railway or holds back water
embankments n ▷ embankment
embargo n (pl -oes) order by a government
prohibiting trade with a country ▶ v (-oes,
-oing, -oed) put an embargo on
embargoed v ▷ embargo
embargoes n, v ▷ embargo
embargoing v ▷ embargo
embark v (-s, -ing, -ed) board a ship or aircraft
(foll. by **on**) > **embarkation** n (-s)
embarkation n ▷ embark
embarkations n ▷ embark
embarked v ▷ embark
embarking v ▷ embark
embarks v ▷ embark
embarrass v (-es, -ing, -ed) cause to feel self-
conscious or ashamed > **embarrassed** adj
> **embarrassing** adj > **embarrassment** n (pl -s)
embarrassed v, adj ▷ embarrass
embarrasses v ▷ embarrass
embarrassing v, adj ▷ embarrass
embarrassment n ▷ embarrass
embarrassments n ▷ embarrass
embassies n ▷ embassy
embassy n (pl -ies) offices or official residence
of an ambassador
embattled adj having a lot of difficulties
embed v (-s, -dding, -dded) fix firmly in
something solid
embedded adj (of a journalist) assigned
to accompany an active military unit ▶ v
▷ embed
embedding v ▷ embed
embeds v ▷ embed
embellish v (-es, -ing, -ed) decorate

> **embellishment** n (pl -s)
embellished v ▷ embellish
embellishes v ▷ embellish
embellishing v ▷ embellish
embellishment n ▷ embellish
embellishments n ▷ embellish
ember n (pl -s) glowing piece of wood or coal
in a dying fire
embers n ▷ ember
embezzle v (-s, -ing, -ed) steal money that has
been entrusted to one > **embezzlement** n (pl
-s) > **embezzler** n (pl -s)
embezzled v ▷ embezzle
embezzlement n ▷ embezzle
embezzlements n ▷ embezzle
embezzler n ▷ embezzle
embezzlers n ▷ embezzle
embezzles v ▷ embezzle
embezzling v ▷ embezzle
embittered adj feeling anger as a result of
misfortune
emblazon v (-s, -ing, -ed) decorate with bright
colours
emblazoned v ▷ emblazon
emblazoning v ▷ emblazon
emblazons v ▷ emblazon
emblem n (pl -s) object or design that
symbolizes a quality, type, or group
> **emblematic** adj
emblematic adj ▷ emblem
emblems n ▷ emblem
embodied v ▷ embody
embodies v ▷ embody
embodiment n ▷ embody
embodiments n ▷ embody
embody v (-dies, -dying, -died) be an example
or expression of > **embodiment** n (pl -s)
embodying v ▷ embody
embolden v (-s, -ing, -ed) encourage
(someone)
emboldened v ▷ embolden
emboldening v ▷ embolden
emboldens v ▷ embolden
embolism n (pl -s) blocking of a blood vessel by
a blood clot or air bubble
embolisms n ▷ embolism
embossed adj (of a design or pattern)
standing out from a surface
embrace v (-es, -cing, -ced) clasp in the arms,
hug ▶ n (pl -s) act of embracing
embraced v ▷ embrace
embraces v, n ▷ embrace
embracing v ▷ embrace
embrasure n (pl -s) door or window having
splayed sides so that the opening is larger

on the inside
embrasures *n* ▷ embrasure
embrocation *n* (*pl* -s) lotion for rubbing into the skin to relieve pain
embrocations *n* ▷ embrocation
embroider *v* (-s, -ing, -ed) decorate with needlework > **embroidery** *n* (*pl* -ies)
embroidered *v* ▷ embroider
embroideries *n* ▷ embroider
embroidering *v* ▷ embroider
embroiders *v* ▷ embroider
embroidery *n* ▷ embroider
embroil *v* (-s, -ing, -ed) involve (a person) in problems
embroiled *v* ▷ embroil
embroiling *v* ▷ embroil
embroils *v* ▷ embroil
embryo [em-bree-oh] *n* (*pl* -s) unborn creature in the early stages of development > **embryology** *n* (*pl* -ies)
embryologies *n* ▷ embryo
embryology *n* ▷ embryo
embryonic *adj* at an early stage
embryos *n* ▷ embryo
emend *v* (-s, -ing, -ed) remove errors from > **emendation** *n* (*pl* emendations)
emendation *n* ▷ emend
emendations *n* ▷ emend
emended *v* ▷ emend
emending *v* ▷ emend
emends *v* ▷ emend
emerald *n* (*pl* -s) bright green precious stone ▶ *adj* bright green
emeralds *n* ▷ emerald
emerge *v* (-ges, -ging, -ged) come into view > **emergence** *n* (*pl* -s) > **emergent** *adj*
emerged *v* ▷ emerge
emergence *n* ▷ emerge
emergences *n* ▷ emerge
emergencies *n* ▷ emergency
emergency *n* (*pl* -ies) sudden unforeseen occurrence needing immediate action
emergent *adj* ▷ emerge
emerges *v* ▷ emerge
emerging *v* ▷ emerge
emeries *n* ▷ emery
emeritus [im-mer-rit-uss] *adj* retired, but retaining an honorary title
emery *n* (*pl* -ies) hard mineral used for smoothing and polishing
emetic [im-met-ik] *n* (*pl* -s) substance that causes vomiting ▶ *adj* causing vomiting
emetics *n* ▷ emetic
emigrant *n* ▷ emigrate
emigrants *n* ▷ emigrate

emigrate *v* (-tes, -ting, -ted) go and settle in another country > **emigrant** *n* (*pl* -s) > **emigration** *n* (*pl* -s)
emigrated *v* ▷ emigrate
emigrates *v* ▷ emigrate
emigrating *v* ▷ emigrate
emigration *n* ▷ emigrate
emigrations *n* ▷ emigrate
émigré [em-mig-gray] *n* (*pl* -s) someone who has left his native country for political reasons
émigrés *n* ▷ émigré
eminence *n* (*pl* -s) position of superiority or fame
eminences *n* ▷ eminence
eminent *adj* distinguished, well-known > **eminently** *adv*
eminently *adv* ▷ eminent
emir [em-meer] *n* (*pl* -s) Muslim ruler
emirate *n* (*pl* -s) country ruled by an emir
emirates *n* ▷ emirate
emirs *n* ▷ emir
emissaries *n* ▷ emissary
emissary *n* (*pl* -ies) agent sent on a mission by a government
emission *n* ▷ emit
emissions ▷ emit
emit *v* (-s, -tting, -tted) give out (heat, light, or a smell) > **emission** *n* (*pl* -s)
emits *v* ▷ emit
emitted *v* ▷ emit
emitting *v* ▷ emit
emollient *adj* softening, soothing ▶ *n* (*pl* -s) substance which softens or soothes the skin
emollients *n* ▷ emollient
emolument *n* (*pl* -s) (*formal*) fees or wages from employment
emoluments *n* ▷ emolument
emoticon [i-mote-i-kon] *n* (*pl* -s) (COMPUTERS) ▷ smiley
emoticons *n* ▷ emoticon
emotion *n* (*pl* -s) strong feeling
emotional *adj* readily affected by or appealing to the emotions > **emotionally** *adv*
emotionally *adv* ▷ emotional
emotions *n* ▷ emotion
emotive *adj* tending to arouse emotion
empathies *n* ▷ empathy
empathy *n* (*pl* -ies) ability to understand someone else's feelings as if they were one's own
emperor *n* (*pl* -s) ruler of an empire > **empress** *n fem* (*pl* -es)
emperors *n* ▷ emperor
emphases *n* ▷ emphasis

emphasis n (pl -ses) special importance or significance ▷ **emphasize** v (-s, -ing, -ed)

emphasize v ▷ emphasis

emphasized v ▷ emphasis

emphasizes v ▷ emphasis

emphasizing v ▷ emphasis

emphatic adj showing emphasis ▷ **emphatically** adv

emphatically adv ▷ emphatic

emphysema [em-fiss-**see**-ma] n (pl -s) condition in which the air sacs of the lungs are grossly enlarged, causing breathlessness

emphysemas n ▷ emphysema

empire n (pl -s) group of territories under the rule of one state or person

empires n ▷ empire

empirical adj relying on experiment or experience, not on theory ▷ **empirically** adv

empirically adv ▷ empirical

empiricism n (pl -s) doctrine that all knowledge derives from experience ▷ **empiricist** n (pl -s)

empiricisms n ▷ empiricism

empiricist n ▷ empiricism

empiricists n ▷ empiricism

emplacement n (pl -s) prepared position for a gun

emplacements n ▷ emplacement

employ v (-s, -ing, -ed) hire (a person) ▶ n (pl -s) state of being employed ▷ **employee** n (pl -s)

employed v ▷ employ

employee n ▷ employ

employees n ▷ employ

employer n (pl -s) person or organization that employs someone

employers n ▷ employer

employing v ▷ employ

employment n (pl -s) state of being employed

employments n ▷ employment

employs v, n ▷ employ

emporia n ▷ emporium

emporium n (pl -riums, -ria) (Old-fashioned) large general shop

emporiums n ▷ emporia

empower v (-s, -ing, -ed) enable, authorize

empowered v ▷ empower

empowering v ▷ empower

empowers v ▷ empower

empress n ▷ emperor

empresses n ▷ emperor

emptied v ▷ empty

emptier adj ▷ empty

empties pl n empty boxes, bottles, etc. ▶ v ▷ empty

emptiest adj ▷ empty

emptiness n ▷ empty

emptinesses n ▷ empty

empty adj (-ier, -iest) containing nothing ▶ v (-ies, -ying, -ied) make or become empty ▷ **emptiness** n (pl -es)

emptying v ▷ empty

emu n (pl -s) large Australian flightless bird with long legs

emulate v (-tes, -ting, -ted) attempt to equal or surpass by imitating ▷ **emulation** n (pl -s)

emulated v ▷ emulate

emulates v ▷ emulate

emulating v ▷ emulate

emulation n ▷ emulate

emulations n ▷ emulate

emulsified v ▷ emulsify

emulsifier n ▷ emulsify

emulsifiers n ▷ emulsify

emulsifies v ▷ emulsify

emulsify v (-fies, -fying, -fied) (of two liquids) join together or join (two liquids) together ▷ **emulsifier** n (pl -s)

emulsifying v ▷ emulsify

emulsion n (pl -s) light-sensitive coating on photographic film ▶ v (-s, -ing, -ed) paint with emulsion paint

emulsioned v ▷ emulsion

emulsioning v ▷ emulsion

emulsions n, v ▷ emulsion

emus n ▷ emu

enable v (-les, -ling, -led) provide (a person) with the means, opportunity, or authority (to do something)

enabled v ▷ enable

enables v ▷ enable

enabling v ▷ enable

enact v (-s, -ing, -ed) establish by law ▷ **enactment** n (pl -s)

enacted v ▷ enact

enacting v ▷ enact

enactment n ▷ enact

enactments n ▷ enact

enacts v ▷ enact

enamel n (pl -s) glasslike coating applied to metal etc. to preserve the surface ▶ v (-s, -lling, -lled) cover with enamel

enamelled v ▷ enamel

enamelling v ▷ enamel

enamels v ▷ enamel

enamoured adj inspired with love

encamp v (-s, -ing, -ed) set up in a camp ▷ **encampment** n (pl -s)

encamped v ▷ encamp

encamping v ▷ encamp

encampment n ▷ encamp

encampments n ▷ encamp
encamps v ▷ encamp
encapsulate v (-tes, -ting, -ted) summarize
  encapsulated v ▷ encapsulate
  encapsulates v ▷ encapsulate
  encapsulating v ▷ encapsulate
encephalitis [en-sef-a-**lite**-iss] n (pl -es)
  inflammation of the brain
  encephalitises n ▷ encephalitis
enchant v (-s, -ing, -ed) delight and fascinate
  > **enchantment** n (pl -s) > **enchanter** n (pl -s)
  > **enchantress** n fem (pl -es)
  enchanted v ▷ enchant
  enchanter n ▷ enchant
  enchanters n ▷ enchant
  enchanting v ▷ enchant
  enchantment n ▷ enchant
  enchantments n ▷ enchant
  enchantress n ▷ enchant
  enchantresses n ▷ enchant
  enchants v ▷ enchant
encircle v (-s, -ling, -led) form a circle around
  > **encirclement** n (pl -s)
  encircled v ▷ encircle
  encirclement n ▷ encircle
  encirclements n ▷ encircle
  encircles v ▷ encircle
  encircling v ▷ encircle
enclave n (pl -s) part of a country entirely
  surrounded by foreign territory
  enclaves n ▷ enclave
enclose v (-s, -sing, -sed) surround completely
  > **enclosure** n (pl -s)
  enclosed v ▷ enclose
  encloses v ▷ enclose
  enclosing v ▷ enclose
  enclosure n ▷ enclose
  enclosures n ▷ enclose
encomia n ▷ encomium
encomium n (pl -miums, -mia) formal
  expression of praise
  encomiums n ▷ encomiums
encompass v (-es, -ing, -ed) surround
  encompassed v ▷ encompass
  encompasses v ▷ encompass
  encompassing v ▷ encompass
encore interj again, once more ▶ n (pl -s) extra
  performance due to enthusiastic demand
  encores n ▷ encore
encounter v (-s, -ing, -ed) meet unexpectedly
  ▶ n (pl -s) unexpected meeting
  encountered v ▷ encounter
  encountering v ▷ encounter
  encounters v, n ▷ encounter
encourage v (-ges, -ging, -ged) inspire with

confidence > **encouragement** n (pl -s)
  encouraged v ▷ encourage
  encouragement n ▷ encourage
  encouragements n ▷ encourage
  encourages v ▷ encourage
  encouraging v ▷ encourage
encroach v (-es, -ing, -ed) intrude gradually
  on a person's rights or land > **encroachment**
  n (pl -s)
  encroached v ▷ encroach
  encroaches v ▷ encroach
  encroaching v ▷ encroach
  encroachment n ▷ encroach
  encroachments n ▷ encroach
encrust v (-s, -ing, -ed) cover with a layer of
  something
  encrusted v ▷ encrust
  encrusting v ▷ encrust
  encrusts v ▷ encrust
encumber v (-s, -ing, -ed) hinder or impede
  encumbered v ▷ encumber
  encumbering v ▷ encumber
  encumbers v ▷ encumber
encumbrance n (pl -s) something that
  impedes or is burdensome
  encumbrances n ▷ encumbrance
encyclical [en-**sik**-lik-kl] n (pl -s) letter sent by
  the Pope to all bishops
  encyclicals n ▷ encyclical
  encyclopaedia n ▷ encyclopedia
  encyclopaedias n ▷ encyclopedia
  encyclopaedic adj ▷ encyclopedia
encyclopedia, encyclopaedia n (pl -s) book
  or set of books containing facts about
  many subjects, usu. in alphabetical order
  > **encyclopedic, encyclopaedic** adj
  encyclopedias n ▷ encyclopedia
  encyclopedic adj ▷ encyclopedia
end n (pl -s) furthest point or part ▶ v (-s, -ing,
  -ed) bring or come to a finish > **ending** n (pl -s)
  > **endless** adj
endanger v (-s, -ing, -ed) put in danger
  endangered v ▷ endanger
  endangering v ▷ endanger
  endangers v ▷ endanger
endear v (-s, -ing, -ed) cause to be liked
  > **endearing** adj
  endeared v ▷ endear
  endearing v, adj ▷ endear
endearment n (pl -s) affectionate word or
  phrase
  endearments n ▷ endearment
  endears v ▷ endear
endeavour v (-s, -ing, -ed) try ▶ n (pl -s) effort
  endeavoured v ▷ endeavour

endeavouring v ▷ endeavour
endeavours v, n ▷ endeavour
ended v ▷ end
endemic adj present within a localized area or peculiar to a particular group of people
ending v, n ▷ end
endings n ▷ end
endive n (pl -s) curly-leaved plant used in salads
endives n ▷ endive
endless adj ▷ end
endocrine adj relating to the glands which secrete hormones directly into the bloodstream
endogenous [en-dodge-in-uss] adj originating from within
endorse v (-ses, -sing, -sed) give approval to > **endorsement** n (pl -s)
endorsed v ▷ endorse
endorsement n ▷ endorse
endorsements n ▷ endorse
endorses v ▷ endorse
endorsing v ▷ endorse
endow v (-s, -ing, -ed) provide permanent income for > **endowment** n (pl -s)
endowed v ▷ endow
endowing v ▷ endow
endowment v ▷ endow
endowments v ▷ endow
endows v ▷ endow
ends n, v ▷ end
endurable adj ▷ endure
endurance n (pl -s) act or power of enduring
endurances n ▷ endurance
endure v (-res, -ring, -red) bear (hardship) patiently > **endurable** adj
endured v ▷ endure
endures v ▷ endure
enduring v ▷ endure
endways adv having the end forwards or upwards
enema [en-im-a] n (pl -s) medicine injected into the rectum to empty the bowels
enemas n ▷ enema
enemies n ▷ enemy
enemy n (pl -ies) hostile person or nation, opponent
energetic adj ▷ energy
energetically adv ▷ energy
energies n ▷ energy
energize v (-izes, -izing, -ized) give vigour to
energized v ▷ energize
energizes v ▷ energize
energizing v ▷ energize
energy n (pl -ies) capacity for intense activity

> **energetic** adj > **energetically** adv
enervate v (-tes, -ting, -ted) deprive of strength or vitality > **enervation** n (pl -s)
enervated v ▷ enervate
enervates v ▷ enervate
enervating v ▷ enervate
enervation n ▷ enervate
enervations n ▷ enervate
enfeeble v (-les, -ling, -led) weaken
enfeebled v ▷ enfeeble
enfeebles v ▷ enfeeble
enfeebling v ▷ enfeeble
enfold v (-s, -ing, -ed) cover by wrapping something around
enfolded v ▷ enfold
enfolding v ▷ enfold
enfolds v ▷ enfold
enforce v (-ces, -cing, -ced) impose obedience (to a law etc.) > **enforceable** adj > **enforcement** n (pl -s)
enforced v ▷ enforce
enforcement n ▷ enforce
enforcements n ▷ enforce
enforces v ▷ enforce
enforcing v ▷ enforce
enfranchise v (-ses, -sing, -sed) grant (a person) the right to vote > **enfranchisement** n (pl -s)
enfranchised v ▷ enfranchise
enfranchisement n ▷ enfranchise
enfranchisements n ▷ enfranchise
enfranchises v ▷ enfranchise
enfranchising v ▷ enfranchise
engage v (-ges, -ging, -ged) take part, participate > **engagement** n (pl -s)
engaged adj pledged to be married ▶ v ▷ engage
engagement n ▷ engage
engagements n ▷ engage
engages v ▷ engage
engaging adj charming ▶ v ▷ engage
engender v (-s, -ing, -ed) produce, cause to occur
engendered v ▷ engender
engendering v ▷ engender
engenders v ▷ engender
engine n (pl -s) any machine which converts energy into mechanical work
engineer n (pl -s) person trained in any branch of engineering ▶ v (-s, -ing, -ed) plan in a clever manner
engineered v ▷ engineer
engineering v ▷ engineer ▶ n (pl -s) profession of applying scientific principles to the design and construction of engines, cars, buildings,

or machines

engineerings n ▷ engineering

engineers n, v ▷ engineer

engines n ▷ engine

English n (pl -es) official language of Britain, Ireland, Australia, New Zealand, South Africa, Canada, the US, and several other countries ▶ adj relating to England

Englishes n ▷ English

engrave v (-ves, -ving, -ved) carve (a design) onto a hard surface > **engraver** n (pl -s)

engraved v ▷ engrave

engraver n ▷ engrave

engravers n ▷ engrave

engraves v ▷ engrave

engraving v ▷ engrave ▶ n (pl -s) print made from an engraved plate

engravings n ▷ engraving

engross [en-**groce**] v (-es, -ing, -ed) occupy the attention of (a person) completely

engrossed v ▷ engross

engrosses v ▷ engross

engrossing v ▷ engross

engulf v (-s, -ing, -ed) cover or surround completely

engulfed v ▷ engulf

engulfing v ▷ engulf

engulfs v ▷ engulf

enhance v (-s, -ing, -ed) increase in quality, value, or attractiveness > **enhancement** n (pl -s)

enhanced v ▷ enhance

enhancement n ▷ enhance

enhancements n ▷ enhance

enhances v ▷ enhance

enhancing v ▷ enhance

enigma n (pl -s) puzzling thing or person > **enigmatic** adj > **enigmatically** adv

enigmas n ▷ enigma

enigmatic adj ▷ enigma

enigmatically adv ▷ enigma

enjoin v (-s, -ing, -ed) order (someone) to do something

enjoined v ▷ enjoin

enjoining v ▷ enjoin

enjoins v ▷ enjoin

enjoy v (-s, -ing, -ed) take joy in > **enjoyable** adj > **enjoyment** n (pl -s)

enjoyable adj ▷ enjoy

enjoyed v ▷ enjoy

enjoying v ▷ enjoy

enjoyment n ▷ enjoy

enjoyments n ▷ enjoy

enjoys v ▷ enjoy

enlarge v (-ges, -ging, -ged) make or grow

larger (foll. by **on**) > **enlargement** n (pl -s)

enlarged v ▷ enlarge

enlargement n ▷ enlarge

enlargements n ▷ enlarge

enlarges v ▷ enlarge

enlarging v ▷ enlarge

enlighten v (-s, -ing, -ed) give information to > **enlightenment** n (pl -s)

enlightened v ▷ enlighten

enlightening v ▷ enlighten

enlightenment n ▷ enlighten

enlightenments n ▷ enlighten

enlightens v ▷ enlighten

enlist v (-s, -ing, -ed) enter the armed forces > **enlistment** n (pl -s)

enlisted v ▷ enlist

enlisting v ▷ enlist

enlistment n ▷ enlist

enlistments n ▷ enlist

enlists v ▷ enlist

enliven v (-s, -ing, -ed) make lively or cheerful

enlivened v ▷ enliven

enlivening v ▷ enliven

enlivens v ▷ enliven

enmeshed adj deeply involved

enmities n ▷ enmity

enmity n (pl -ies) ill will, hatred

ennoble v (-s, -ing, -ed) make noble, elevate

ennobled v ▷ ennoble

ennobles v ▷ ennoble

ennobling v ▷ ennoble

ennui [on-**nwee**] n (pl -s) boredom, dissatisfaction

ennuis n ▷ ennui

enormities n ▷ enormity

enormity n (pl -ies) great wickedness

enormous adj very big, vast

enough adj as much or as many as necessary ▶ pron sufficient quantity ▶ adv sufficiently

enquire v (-res, -ring, -red) ▷ inquire > **enquiry** n (pl -ies)

enquired v ▷ enquire

enquires v ▷ enquire

enquiries n ▷ enquire

enquiring v ▷ enquire

enquiry n ▷ enquire

enraptured adj filled with delight and fascination

enrich v (-es, -ing, -ed) improve in quality

enriched v ▷ enrich

enriches v ▷ enrich

enriching v ▷ enrich

enrol v (-s, -lling, -lled) (cause to) become a member > **enrolment** n (pl -s)

enrolled v ▷ enrol
enrolling v ▷ enrol
enrolment n ▷ enrol
enrolments n ▷ enrol
enrols v ▷ enrol
ensconce v (-ces, -cing, -ced) settle firmly or comfortably
ensconced v ▷ ensconce
ensconces v ▷ ensconce
ensconcing v ▷ ensconce
ensemble [on-**som**-bl] n (pl -s) all the parts of something taken together
ensembles n ▷ ensemble
enshrine v (-nes, -ning, -ned) cherish or treasure
enshrined v ▷ enshrine
enshrines v ▷ enshrine
enshrining v ▷ enshrine
ensign n (pl -s) naval flag
ensigns n ▷ ensign
enslave v (-ves, -ving, -ved) make a slave of (someone) > **enslavement** n (pl -s)
enslaved v ▷ enslave
enslavement n ▷ enslave
enslavements n ▷ enslave
enslaves v ▷ enslave
enslaving v ▷ enslave
ensnare v (-res, -ring, -red) catch in or as if in a snare
ensnared v ▷ ensnare
ensnares v ▷ ensnare
ensnaring v ▷ ensnare
ensue v (-sues, -suing, -sued) come next, result
ensued v ▷ ensue
ensues v ▷ ensue
ensuing v ▷ ensue
ensure v (-re, -ring, -red) make certain or sure
ensured v ▷ ensure
ensures v ▷ ensure
ensuring v ▷ ensure
entail v (-s, -ing, -ed) bring about or impose inevitably
entailed v ▷ entail
entailing v ▷ entail
entails v ▷ entail
entangle v (-les, -ling, -led) catch or involve in or as if in a tangle > **entanglement** n (pl -s)
entangled v ▷ entangle
entanglement n ▷ entangle
entanglements n ▷ entangle
entangles v ▷ entangle
entangling v ▷ entangle
entente [on-**tont**] n (pl -s) friendly understanding between nations
ententes n ▷ entente

enter v (-s, -ing, -ed) come or go in
entered v ▷ enter
enteric [en-**ter**-ik] adj intestinal
entering v ▷ enter
enteritis [en-ter-**rite**-iss] n (pl -es) inflammation of the intestine, causing diarrhoea
enteritises n ▷ enteritis
enterprise n (pl -s) company or firm
enterprises n ▷ enterprise
enterprising adj full of boldness and initiative
enters v ▷ enter
entertain v (-s, -ing, -ed) amuse > **entertainer** n (pl -s) > **entertainment** n (pl -s)
entertained v ▷ entertain
entertainer n ▷ entertain
entertainers n ▷ entertain
entertaining v ▷ entertain
entertainment n ▷ entertain
entertainments n ▷ entertain
entertains v ▷ entertain
enthral [en-**thrawl**] v (-s, -lling, -lled) hold the attention of > **enthralling** adj
enthralled v ▷ enthral
enthralling v, adj ▷ enthral
enthrals v ▷ enthral
enthuse v (-s, -ing, -ed) (cause to) show enthusiasm
enthused v ▷ enthuse
enthuses v ▷ enthuse
enthusiasm n (pl -s) ardent interest, eagerness
enthusiasms n ▷ enthusiasm
enthusiast n (pl -s) ardent supporter of something > **enthusiastic** adj > **enthusiastically** adv
enthusiastic adj ▷ enthusiast
enthusiastically adv ▷ enthusiast
enthusiasts n ▷ enthusiast
enthusing v ▷ enthuse
entice v (-ces, -cing, -ced) attract by exciting hope or desire, tempt > **enticement** n (pl -s)
enticed v ▷ entice
enticement n ▷ entice
enticements n ▷ entice
entices v ▷ entice
enticing v ▷ entice
entire adj including every detail, part, or aspect of something > **entirely** adv > **entirety** n (pl -ties)
entirely adv ▷ entire
entireties n ▷ entire
entirety n ▷ entire
entities n ▷ entity
entitle v (-les, -ling, -led) give a right to > **entitlement** n (pl -s)

entitled *v* ▷ entitle
entitlement *n* ▷ entitle
entitlements *n* ▷ entitle
entitles *v* ▷ entitle
entitling *v* ▷ entitle
entity *n* (*pl* -ties) separate distinct thing
entomological *adj* ▷ entomology
entomologies *n* ▷ entomology
entomologist *n* ▷ entomology
entomologists *n* ▷ entomology
entomology *n* (*pl* -ies) study of insects
 > **entomological** *adj* > **entomologist** *n* (*pl* -s)
entourage [on-toor-ahzh] *n* (*pl* -s) group of
 people who assist an important person
entourages *n* ▷ entourage
entrails *pl n* intestines
entrance¹ *n* (*pl* -s) way into a place
entrance² *v* (-s, -ing, -ed) delight
 entranced *v* ▷ entrance²
 entrances *n* ▷ entrance¹ ▶ *v* ▷ entrance²
 entrancing *v* ▷ entrance²
entrant *n* (*pl* -s) person who enters a
 university, contest, etc.
 entrants *n* ▷ entrant
entreat *v* (-s, -ing, -ed) ask earnestly
 entreated *v* ▷ entreat
 entreaties *n* ▷ entreaty
 entreating *v* ▷ entreat
 entreats *v* ▷ entreat
entreaty *n* (*pl* -ties) earnest request
entrée [on-tray] *n* (*pl* -s) dish served before a
 main course
 entrées *n* ▷ entrée
entrench *v* (-es, -ing, -ed) establish firmly
 > **entrenchment** *n* (*pl* -s)
 entrenched *v* ▷ entrench
 entrenches *v* ▷ entrench
 entrenching *v* ▷ entrench
 entrenchment *n* ▷ entrench
 entrenchments *n* ▷ entrench
entrepreneur *n* (*pl* -s) business person
 who attempts to make a profit by risk and
 initiative
 entrepreneurs *n* ▷ entrepreneur
 entries *n* ▷ entry
 entropies *n* ▷ entropy
entropy [en-trop-ee] *n* (*pl* -ies) lack of
 organization
entrust *v* (-s, -ing, -ed) put into the care or
 protection of
 entrusted *v* ▷ entrust
 entrusting *v* ▷ entrust
 entrusts *v* ▷ entrust
entry *n* (*pl* -ies) entrance
entwine *v* (-s, -ing, -ed) twist together or

around
 entwined *v* ▷ entwine
 entwines *v* ▷ entwine
 entwining *v* ▷ entwine
enumerate *v* (-tes, -ting, -ted) name one by
 one > **enumeration** *n* (*pl* -s)
 enumerated *v* ▷ enumerate
 enumerates *v* ▷ enumerate
 enumerating *v* ▷ enumerate
 enumeration *n* ▷ enumerate
 enumerations *n* ▷ enumerate
 enuncation *n* ▷ enunciate
enunciate *v* (-tes, -ting, -ted) pronounce
 clearly > **enunciation** *n* (*pl* -s)
 enunciated *v* ▷ enunciate
 enunciates *v* ▷ enunciate
 enunciating *v* ▷ enunciate
 enunciation *n* ▷ enunciate
 enunciations *n* ▷ enunciate
envelop *v* (-s, -ing, -ed) wrap up, enclose
 > **envelopment** *n* (*pl* -s)
envelope *n* (*pl* -s) folded gummed paper cover
 for a letter
 enveloped *v* ▷ envelop
 envelopes *n* ▷ envelope
 enveloping *v* ▷ envelop
 envelopment *n* ▷ envelop
 envelopments *n* ▷ envelop
 envelops *v* ▷ envelop
enviable *adj* arousing envy, fortunate
 envied *v* ▷ envy
 envies *n, v* ▷ envy
envious *adj* full of envy
environment [en-vire-on-ment] *n* (*pl* -s)
 external conditions and surroundings
 in which people, animals, or plants live
 > **environmental** *adj*
 environmental *adj* ▷ environment
environmentalist *n* (*pl* -s) person concerned
 with the protection of the natural
 environment
 environmentalists *n* ▷ environmentalist
 environments *n* ▷ environment
environs *pl n* surrounding area, esp. of a town
envisage *v* (-ges, -ging, -ged) conceive of as a
 possibility
 envisaged *v* ▷ envisage
 envisages *v* ▷ envisage
 envisaging *v* ▷ envisage
envoy *n* (*pl* -s) messenger
 envoys *n* ▷ envoy
envy *n* (*pl* -ies) feeling of discontent aroused by
 another's good fortune ▶ *v* (-ies, -ying, -ied)
 grudge (another's good fortune, success, or
 qualities)

envying v ▷ envy

enzyme n (pl -s) any of a group of complex proteins that act as catalysts in specific biochemical reactions
  enzymes n ▷ enzyme

eolithic adj of the early part of the Stone Age

epaulette n (pl -s) shoulder ornament on a uniform
  epaulettes n ▷ epaulette

ephemeral adj short-lived

epic n (pl -s) long poem, book, or film about heroic events or actions ▶ adj very impressive or ambitious

epicentre n (pl -s) point on the earth's surface immediately above the origin of an earthquake
  epicentres n ▷ epicentre
  epics n ▷ epic

epicure n (pl -s) person who enjoys good food and drink

epicurean adj devoted to sensual pleasures, esp. food and drink ▶ n (pl -s) epicure
  epicureans n ▷ epicurean
  epicures n ▷ epicure

epidemic n (pl -s) widespread occurrence of a disease
  epidemics n ▷ epidemic

epidermis n (pl -ses) outer layer of the skin
  epidermises n ▷ epidermis

epidural [ep-pid-**dure**-al] adj, n (pl -s) (of) spinal anaesthetic injected to relieve pain during childbirth
  epidurals n ▷ epidural

epiglottis n (pl -ses) thin flap that covers the opening of the larynx during swallowing
  epiglottises n ▷ epiglottis

epigram n (pl -s) short witty remark or poem > **epigrammatic** adj
  epigrammatic adj ▷ epigram
  epigrams n ▷ epigram

epigraph n (pl -s) quotation at the start of a book
  epigraphs n ▷ epigraph
  epilepsies n ▷ epilepsy

epilepsy n (pl -ies) disorder of the nervous system causing loss of consciousness and sometimes convulsions

epileptic adj of or having epilepsy ▶ n (pl -s) person who has epilepsy
  epileptics n ▷ epileptic

epilogue n (pl -s) short speech or poem at the end of a literary work, esp. a play
  epilogues n ▷ epilogue
  epiphanies n ▷ epiphany

epiphany n (pl -ies) a moment of great or sudden realization

episcopal [ip-**piss**-kop-al] adj of or governed by bishops

episcopalian adj advocating Church government by bishops ▶ n (pl -s) advocate of such Church government
  episcopalians n ▷ episcopalian

episode n (pl -s) incident in a series of incidents
  episodes n ▷ episode

episodic adj occurring at irregular intervals
  epistemological adj ▷ epistemology
  epistemologies n ▷ epistemology

epistemology [ips-iss-stem-**ol**-a-jee] n (pl -ies) study of the source, nature, and limitations of knowledge > **epistemological** adj

epistle n (pl -s) letter, esp. of an apostle > **epistolary** adj
  epistles n ▷ epistle
  epistolary adj ▷ epistle

epitaph n (pl -s) commemorative inscription on a tomb
  epitaphs n ▷ epitaph

epithet n (pl -s) descriptive word or name
  epithets n ▷ epithet

epitome [ip-**pit**-a-mee] n (pl -s) typical example
  epitomes n ▷ epitome

epitomize v (-izes, -izing, -ized) be the epitome of
  epitomized v ▷ epitomize
  epitomizes v ▷ epitomize
  epitomizing v ▷ epitomize

epoch [ee-pok] n (pl -s) period of notable events
  epochs n ▷ epoch

eponymous [ip-pon-im-uss] adj after whom a book, play, etc. is named

equable [ek-wab-bl] adj even-tempered > **equably** adv
  equably adv ▷ equable

equal adj identical in size, quantity, degree, etc. ▶ n (pl -s) person or thing equal to another ▶ v (-s, -lling, -lled) be equal to > **equally** adv
  equalities n ▷ equality

equality n (pl -ies) state of being equal
  equalization n ▷ equalize
  equalizations n ▷ equalize

equalize v (-lizes, -lizing, -lized) make or become equal > **equalization** n (pl -s)
  equalized v ▷ equalize
  equalizes v ▷ equalize
  equalizing v ▷ equalize
  equalled v ▷ equal
  equalling v ▷ equal
  equally adv ▷ equal
  equals n, v ▷ equal

equanimities *n* ▷ equanimity
equanimity *n* (*pl* -ies) calmness of mind
equate *v* (-tes, -ting, -ted) make or regard as equivalent
equated *v* ▷ equate
equates *v* ▷ equate
equating *v* ▷ equate
equation *n* (*pl* -s) mathematical statement that two expressions are equal
equations *n* ▷ equation
equator *n* (*pl* -s) imaginary circle round the earth, equidistant from the poles > **equatorial** *adj*
equatorial *adj* ▷ equator
equators *n* ▷ equator
equerries *n* ▷ equerry
equerry [ek-kwer-ee] *n* (*pl* -ies) (BRIT) officer who acts as an attendant to a member of a royal family
equestrian *adj* of horses and riding
equidistant *adj* equally distant
equilateral *adj* having equal sides
equilibria *n* ▷ equilibriums
equilibrium *n* (*pl* -ria) steadiness or stability
equine *adj* of or like a horse
equinoctial *adj* ▷ equinox
equinox *n* (*pl* -es) time of year when day and night are of equal length > **equinoctial** *adj*
equinoxes *n* ▷ equinox
equip *v* (-s, -pping, -pped) provide with supplies, components, etc.
equipment *n* (*pl* -s) set of tools or devices used for a particular purpose
equipments *n* ▷ equipment
equipoise *n* (*pl* -s) perfect balance
equipoises *n* ▷ equipoise
equipped *v* ▷ equip
equipping *v* ▷ equip
equips *v* ▷ equips
equitable *adj* fair and reasonable > **equitably** *adv*
equitably *adv* ▷ equitable
equities *n* ▷ equity
equity *n* (*pl* -ties) fairness ▸ *pl* interest of ordinary shareholders in a company
equivalence *n* ▷ equivalent
equivalences *n* ▷ equivalent
equivalent *adj* equal in value ▸ *n* (*pl* -s) something that is equivalent > **equivalence** *n* (*pl* -s)
equivalents *n* ▷ equivalent
equivocal *adj* ambiguous > **equivocally** *adv*
equivocally *adv* ▷ equivocal
equivocate *v* (-tes, -ting, -ted) use vague or ambiguous language to mislead people

> **equivocation** *n* (*pl* -s)
equivocated *v* ▷ equivocate
equivocates *v* ▷ equivocate
equivocating *v* ▷ equivocate
equivocation *n* ▷ equivocate
equivocations *n* ▷ equivocate
era *n* (*pl* -s) period of time considered as distinctive
eradicate *v* (-tes, -ting, -ted) destroy completely > **eradication** *n* (*pl* -s)
eradicated *v* ▷ eradicate
eradicates *v* ▷ eradicate
eradicating *v* ▷ eradicate
eradication *n* ▷ eradicate
eradications *n* ▷ eradicate
eras *n* ▷ era
erase *v* (-ses, -sing, -sed) rub out
erased *v* ▷ erase
eraser *n* (*pl* -s) object for erasing something written
erasers *n* ▷ eraser
erases *v* ▷ erase
erasing *v* ▷ erase
erasure *n* (*pl* -s) erasing
erasures *n* ▷ erasure
ere *prep, conj* (*Poetic*) before
erect *v* (-s, -ing, -ed) build ▸ *adj* upright > **erection** *n* (*pl* -s)
erected *v* ▷ erect
erectile *adj* capable of becoming erect from sexual excitement
erecting *v* ▷ erect
erection *n* ▷ erect
erections *n* ▷ erect
erects *v* ▷ erect
erg *n* (*pl* -s) unit of work or energy
ergonomic *adj* ▷ ergonomics
ergonomics *n* (*pl* study of the relationship between workers and their environment > **ergonomic** *adj*
ergot *n* (*pl* -s) fungal disease of cereal
ergots *n* ▷ ergot
ergs *n* ▷ erg
ermine *n* (*pl* -s) stoat in northern regions
ermines *n* ▷ ermine
erode *v* (-s, -ing, -ed) wear away > **erosion** *n* (*pl* -s)
eroded *v* ▷ erode
erodes *v* ▷ erode
eroding *v* ▷ erode
erogenous [ir-roj-in-uss] *adj* sensitive to sexual stimulation
erosion *n* ▷ erode
erosions *n* ▷ erode
erotic *adj* relating to sexual pleasure or desire

> **eroticism** n (pl -s)
erotica n sexual literature or art
  eroticism n ▷ erotic
  eroticisms n ▷ erotic
err v (-s, -ing, -ed) make a mistake
errand n (pl -s) short trip to do something for
someone
  errands n ▷ errand
errant adj behaving in a manner considered to
be unacceptable
  errata n ▷ erratum
erratic adj irregular or unpredictable
> **erratically** adv
  erratically adv ▷ erratic
erratum n (pl -ta) error in writing or printing
  erred v ▷ err
  erring v ▷ err
erroneous adj incorrect, mistaken
error n (pl -s) mistake, inaccuracy, or
misjudgment
  errors n ▷ error
  errs v ▷ err
ersatz [air-zats] adj made in imitation
erstwhile adj former
erudite adj having great academic knowledge
> **erudition** n (pl -s)
  erudition v ▷ erudite
  eruditions n ▷ erudite
erupt v (-s, -ing, -ed) eject (steam, water, or
volcanic material) violently > **eruption** n
(pl -s)
  erupted v ▷ erupt
  erupting v ▷ erupt
  eruption n ▷ erupt
  eruptions n ▷ erupt
  erupts v ▷ erupt
erysipelas [err-riss-**sip**-pel-ass] n (pl -es) acute
skin infection causing purplish patches
  erysipelases n ▷ erysipelas

> **es** n (**eses**). Es is the letter S. This is a
> useful word when you want to play
> a high-scoring word that will touch
> words already on the board. Es scores
> 2 points.

escalate v (-tes, -ting, -ted) increase in extent
or intensity > **escalation** n (pl -s)
  escalated v ▷ escalate
  escalates v ▷ escalate
  escalating v ▷ escalate
  escalation n ▷ escalate
  escalations n ▷ escalate
escalator n (pl -s) moving staircase
  escalators n ▷ escalator
escalope [ess-kal-lop] n (pl -s) thin slice of meat,
esp. veal

  escalopes n ▷ escalope
escapade n (pl -s) mischievous adventure
  escapades n ▷ escapade
escape v (-pes, -ping, -ped) get free (of) ▶ n (pl
-s) act of escaping
  escaped v ▷ escape
escapee n (pl -s) person who has escaped
  escapees n ▷ escapee
  escapes v, n ▷ escape
  escaping v ▷ escape
escapism n (pl -s) taking refuge in fantasy to
avoid unpleasant reality
  escapisms n ▷ escapism
  escapologies n ▷ escapologist
escapologist n (pl -s) entertainer who
specializes in freeing himself from
confinement > **escapology** n (pl -ies)
  escapologists n ▷ escapologist
  escapology n ▷ escapologist
escarpment n (pl -s) steep face of a ridge or
mountain
  escarpments n ▷ escarpment
eschew [iss-**chew**] v (-s, -ing, -ed) abstain
from, avoid
  eschewed v ▷ eschew
  eschewing v ▷ eschew
  eschews v ▷ eschew
escort n (pl -s) people or vehicles
accompanying another person for protection
or as an honour ▶ v (-s, -ing, -ed) act as an
escort to
  escorted v ▷ escort
  escorting v ▷ escort
  escorts n, v ▷ escort
escudo [ess-**kyoo**-doe] n (pl -dos) former
monetary unit of Portugal
  escudos n ▷ escudo
escutcheon n (pl -s) shield with a coat of arms
  escutcheons n ▷ escutcheon
esoteric [ee-so-**ter**-rik] adj understood by
only a small number of people with special
knowledge
espadrille [ess-pad-drill] n (pl -s) light canvas
shoe with a braided cord sole
  espadrilles n ▷ espadrille
espalier [ess-**pal**-yer] n (pl -s) shrub or fruit tree
trained to grow flat
  espaliers n ▷ espalier
esparto n (pl -s) grass of S Europe and N Africa
used for making rope etc.
  espartos n ▷ esparto
especial adj (Formal) special
especially adv particularly
  espied v ▷ espy
  espies v ▷ espy

espionage [ess-pyon-ahzh] *n* (*pl* -s) spying
  espionages *n* ▷ espionage
esplanade *n* (*pl* -s) wide open road used as a
  public promenade
  esplanades *n* ▷ esplanade
espousal *n* ▷ espouse
  espousals *n* ▷ espouse
espouse *v* (-ses, -sing, -sed) adopt or give
  support to (a cause etc.) > **espousal** *n* (*pl* -s)
  espoused *v* ▷ espouse
  espouses *v* ▷ espouse
  espousing *v* ▷ espouse
espresso *n* (*pl* -s) strong coffee made by forcing
  steam or boiling water through ground
  coffee beans
  espressos *n* ▷ espresso
esprit [ess-pree] *n* (*pl* -s) spirit, liveliness, or wit
  esprits *n* ▷ esprit
espy *v* (-ies, -ying, -ied) catch sight of
  espying *v* ▷ espy
esquire *n* (*pl* -s) courtesy title placed after a
  man's name
  esquires *n* ▷ esquire
essay *n* (*pl* -s) short literary composition ▶ *v*
  (-s, -ing, -ed) attempt > **essayist** *n* (*pl* -s)
  essayed *v* ▷ essay
  essaying *v* ▷ essay
  essayist *n* ▷ essay
  essayists *n* ▷ essay
  essays *n*, *v* ▷ essay
essence *n* (*pl* -s) most important feature of a
  thing which determines its identity
  essences *n* ▷ essence
essential *adj* vitally important ▶ *n* (*pl* -s)
  something fundamental or indispensable
  > **essentially** *adv*
  essentially *adv* ▷ essential
  essentials *n* ▷ essential
establish *v* (-es, -ing, -ed) set up on a
  permanent basis
  established *v* ▷ establish
  establishes *v* ▷ establish
  establishing *v* ▷ establish
establishment *n* (*pl* -s) act of establishing
  establishments *n* ▷ establishment
estate *n* (*pl* -s) landed property
  estates *n* ▷ estate
esteem *n* (*pl* -s) high regard ▶ *v* (-s, -ing, -ed)
  think highly of
  esteemed *v* ▷ esteem
  esteeming *v* ▷ esteem
  esteems *n*, *v* ▷ esteem
ester *n* (*pl* -s) (CHEM) compound produced by
  the reaction between an acid and an alcohol
  esters *n* ▷ ester

estimable *adj* worthy of respect
estimate *v* (-tes, -ting, -ted) calculate roughly
  ▶ *n* (*pl* -s) approximate calculation
  estimated *v* ▷ estimate
  estimates *v*, *n* ▷ estimate
  estimating *v* ▷ estimate
estimation *n* (*pl* -s) considered opinion
  estimations *n* ▷ estimation
estranged *adj* no longer living with one's
  spouse > **estrangement** *n* (*pl* -s)
  estrangement *n* ▷ estranged
  estrangements *n* ▷ estranged
estuaries *n* ▷ estuary
estuary *n* (*pl* --ies) mouth of a river
etch *v* (-es, -ing, -ed) wear away or cut the
  surface of (metal, glass, etc.) with acid
  > **etching** *n* (*pl* -s)
  etched *v* ▷ etch
  etches *v* ▷ etch
  etching *v*, *n* ▷ etch
eternal *adj* without beginning or end
  > **eternally** *adv*
  eternally *adv* ▷ eternal
  eternities *n* ▷ eternity
eternity *n* (*pl* -ies) infinite time
ether *n* (*pl* -s) colourless sweet-smelling liquid
  used as an anaesthetic
ethereal [eth-eer-ee-al] *adj* extremely delicate
  ethers *n* ▷ ether
ethic *n* (*pl* -s) moral principle > **ethical** *adj*
  > **ethically** *adv*
  ethical *adj* ▷ ethic
  ethically *adv* ▷ ethic
  ethics *n* ▷ ethic
ethnic *adj* relating to a people or group that
  shares a culture, religion, or language
  ethnological *adj* ▷ ethnology
  ethnologies *n* ▷ ethnology
  ethnologist *n* ▷ ethnology
  ethnologists *n* ▷ ethnology
ethnology *n* (*pl* -ies) study of human races
  > **ethnological** *adj* > **ethnologist** *n* (*pl* -s)
ethos [eeth-oss] *n* (*pl* -es) distinctive spirit and
  attitudes of a people, culture, etc.
  ethoses *n* ▷ ethos
ethyl [eeth-ile] *adj* of, consisting of, or
  containing the hydrocarbon group C_2H_5
ethylene *n* (*pl* -s) poisonous gas used as an
  anaesthetic and as fuel
  ethylenes *n* ▷ ethylene
etiolate [ee-tee-oh-late] *v* (-tes, -ting, -ted)
  become pale and weak (BOTANY)
  etiolated *v* ▷ etiolate
  etiolates *v* ▷ etiolate
  etiolating *v* ▷ etiolate

etiologies n ▷ etiology

etiology n (pl -ies) study of the causes of diseases

etiquette n (pl -s) conventional code of conduct

etiquettes n ▷ etiquette

étude [ay-tewd] n (pl -s) short musical composition for a solo instrument, esp. intended as a technical exercise

études n ▷ étude

etymological adj ▷ etymology

etymologies n ▷ etymology

etymology n (pl -gies) study of the sources and development of words > **etymological** adj

eucalypt n ▷ eucalyptus

eucalypts n ▷ eucalyptus

eucalyptus, eucalypt n (pl -ses, -s) tree, mainly grown in Australia, that provides timber, gum, and medicinal oil from the leaves

eucalyptuses n ▷ eucalyptus

eugenics [yew-jen-iks] n (pl study of methods of improving the human race

eulogies n ▷ eulogy

eulogistic adj ▷ euology

eulogize v (-s, -ing, -ed) praise (a person or thing) highly in speech or writing

eulogized v ▷ eulogize

eulogizes v ▷ eulogize

eulogizing v ▷ eulogize

eulogy n (pl -ies) speech or writing in praise of a person > **eulogistic** adj

eunuch n (pl -s) castrated man, esp. (formerly) a guard in a harem

eunuchs n ▷ eunuch

euphemism n (pl -s) inoffensive word or phrase substituted for one considered offensive or upsetting > **euphemistic** adj > **euphemistically** adv

euphemisms n ▷ euphemism

euphemistic ▷ euphemism

euphemistically ▷ euphemism

euphonies n ▷ euphony

euphonious adj pleasing to the ear

euphonium n (pl -s) brass musical instrument, tenor tuba

euphoniums n ▷ euphonium

euphony n (pl -nies) pleasing sound

euphoria n (pl -s) sense of elation > **euphoric** adj

euphorias n ▷ euphoria

euphoric adj ▷ euphoria

eureka [yew-reek-a] interj exclamation of triumph at finding something

euro n (pl -s) unit of the single currency of the European Union

euros n ▷ euro

euthanasia n (pl -s) act of killing someone painlessly, esp. to relieve his or her suffering

euthanasias n ▷ euthanasia

evacuate v (-tes, -ting, -ted) send (someone) away from a place of danger > **evacuation** n (pl -s) > **evacuee** n (pl -s)

evacuated v ▷ evacuate

evacuates v ▷ evacuate

evacuating v ▷ evacuate

evacuation n ▷ evacuate

evacuations n ▷ evacuate

evacuee n ▷ evacuate

evacuees n ▷ evacuate

evade v (-des, -ding, -ded) get away from or avoid > **evasion** n (pl -s)

evaded v ▷ evade

evades v ▷ evade

evading v ▷ evade

evaluate v (-tes, -ting, -ted) find or judge the value of > **evaluation** n (pl -s)

evaluated v ▷ evaluate

evaluates v ▷ evaluate

evaluating v ▷ evaluate

evaluation n ▷ evaluate

evaluations n ▷ evaluate

evanescence n ▷ evanescent

evanescences n ▷ evanescent

evanescent adj quickly fading away > **evanescence** n (pl -s)

evangelical adj of or according to gospel teaching ▶ n (pl -s) member of an evangelical sect > **evangelicalism** n (pl -s)

evangelicalism n ▷ evangelical

evangelicalisms n ▷ evangelical

evangelicals n ▷ evangelical

evangelism n (pl -s) teaching and spreading of the Christian gospel

evangelisms n ▷ evangelism

evangelist n (pl -s) writer of one of the four gospels

evangelists n ▷ evangelist

evangelization n ▷ evangelize

evangelizations n ▷ evangelize

evangelize v (-zes, -zing, -zed) preach the gospel > **evangelization** n (pl -s)

evangelized v ▷ evangelize

evangelizes v ▷ evangelize

evangelizing v ▷ evangelize

evaporate v (-tes, -ing, -ted) change from a liquid or solid to a vapour > **evaporation** n (pl -s)

evaporated v ▷ evaporate

evaporates v ▷ evaporate

evaporating v ▷ evaporate
evaporation n ▷ evaporate
evaporations n ▷ evaporate
evasion n ▷ evade
evasions n ▷ evade
evasive adj not straightforward > **evasively** adv
evasively adv ▷ evasive
evasiveness n ▷ evasive
eve n (pl -s) evening or day before some special event
even (-er, -est) adj flat or smooth (foll. by **with**) ▶ adv equally ▶ v (-s, -ing, -ed) make even
evened v ▷ even
evener adj ▷ even
evenest adj ▷ even
evening n (pl -s) end of the day or early part of the night ▶ adj of or in the evening ▶ v ▷ even
evenings n ▷ evening
evens v ▷ even
evensong n (pl -s) evening prayer
evensongs n ▷ evensong
event n (pl -s) anything that takes place
eventful adj full of exciting incidents
eventing n (pl -s) (BRIT, AUST & NZ) riding competitions, usu. involving cross-country, jumping, and dressage
eventings n ▷ eventing
events n ▷ event
eventual adj ultimate
eventualities n ▷ eventuality
eventuality n (pl -ies) possible event
eventually adv at the end of a situation or process
ever adv at any time > **everlasting** adj
evergreen adj, n (pl -s) (tree or shrub) having leaves throughout the year
evergreens n ▷ evergreen
everlasting adj ▷ ever
evermore adv for all time to come
every adj each without exception
everybody pron every person
everyday adj usual or ordinary
everyone pron every person
everything pron all things
everywhere adv in all places
eves n ▷ eve
evict v (-s, -ing, -ed) legally expel (someone) from his or her home > **eviction** n (pl -s)
evicted v ▷ evict
evicting v ▷ evict
eviction n ▷ evict
evictions n ▷ evict
evicts v ▷ evict
evidence n (pl -s) ground for belief ▶ v (-ces,

-cing, -ced) demonstrate, prove
evidenced v ▷ evidence
evidences n, v ▷ evidence
evidencing v ▷ evidence
evident adj easily seen or understood > **evidently** adv
evidential adj of, serving as, or based on evidence
evidently adv ▷ evident
evil n (pl -s) wickedness ▶ adj (-ller, -llest) harmful > **evilly** adv
evildoer n (pl -s) wicked person
evildoers n ▷ evildoer
eviller adj ▷ evil
evillest adj ▷ evil
evilly adv ▷ evil
evils n ▷ evil
evince v (-s, -ing, -ed) make evident
evinced v ▷ evince
evinces v ▷ evince
evincing v ▷ evince
eviscerate v (-tes, -ting, -ted) disembowel > **evisceration** n (pl -s)
eviscerated v ▷ eviscerate
eviscerates v ▷ eviscerate
eviscerating v ▷ eviscerate
evisceration n ▷ eviscerate
eviscerations n ▷ eviscerate
evocation n ▷ evoke
evocations n ▷ evoke
evocative adj ▷ evoke
evoke v (-s, -ing, -ed) call or summon up (a memory, feeling, etc.) > **evocation** n (pl -s) > **evocative** adj
evoked v ▷ evoke
evokes v ▷ evoke
evoking v ▷ evoke
evolution n (pl -s) gradual change in the characteristics of living things over successive generations, esp. to a more complex form > **evolutionary** adj
evolutionary n ▷ evolution
evolutions n ▷ evolution
evolve v (-kes, -king, -ked) develop gradually
evolved v ▷ evolve
evolves v ▷ evolve
evolving v ▷ evolve
ewe n (pl -s) female sheep
ewer n (pl -s) large jug with a wide mouth
ewers n ▷ ewer
ewes n ▷ ewe

> **ewk** n (**ewks**). Ewk is a dialect word for **itch**. It's a handy little word and a good one to remember in case you end up with both K and W, as you're very likely

to be able to play it from an E already on the board. Ewk scores 10 points.

ex n (pl -es) (*Informal*) former wife or husband

exacerbate [ig-zass-er-bate] v (-tes, -ting, -ted) make (pain, emotion, or a situation) worse > **exacerbation** n (pl -s)

  exacerbated v ▷ exacerbate

  exacerbates v ▷ exacerbate

  exacerbating v ▷ exacerbate

  exacerbation n ▷ exacerbate

  exacerbations n ▷ exacerbate

exact adj (-er, -est) correct and complete in every detail ▶ v (-s, -ing, -ed) demand (payment or obedience) > **exactness** n (pl -es) > **exactitude** n (pl -s)

  exacted v ▷ exact

  exacter adj ▷ exact

  exactest adj ▷ exact

exacting adj making rigorous or excessive demands ▶ v ▷ exact

  exactitude n ▷ exact

  exactitudes n ▷ exact

exactly adv precisely, in every respect

  exactness n ▷ exact

  exactnesses n ▷ exact

  exacts v ▷ exact

exaggerate v (-tes, -ting, -ted) regard or represent as greater than is true > **exaggeratedly** adv > **exaggeration** n (pl -s)

  exaggerated v ▷ exaggerate

  exaggeratedly adv ▷ exaggerate

  exaggerates v ▷ exaggerate

  exaggerating v ▷ exaggerate

  exaggeration n ▷ exaggerate

  exaggerations n ▷ exaggerate

exalt v (-s, -ing, -ed) praise highly > **exalted** adj > **exaltation** n (pl -s)

  exaltation n ▷ exalt

  exaltations n ▷ exalt

  exalted v, adj ▷ exalt

  exalting v ▷ exalt

  exalts v ▷ exalt

exam n (pl -s) ▷ examination

examination n (pl -s) examining

  examinations n ▷ examination

examine v (-nes, -ning, -ned) look at closely > **examinee** n (pl -s) > **examiner** n (pl -s)

  examined v ▷ examine

  examinee n ▷ examine

  examinees n ▷ examine

  examiner n ▷ examine

  examiners n ▷ examine

  examines v ▷ examine

  examining v ▷ examine

example n (pl -s) specimen typical of its group

  examples n ▷ example

  exams n ▷ exam

exasperate v (-tes, -ting, -ted) cause great irritation to > **exasperation** n (pl -s)

  exasperated v ▷ exasperate

  exasperates v ▷ exasperate

  exasperating v ▷ exasperate

  exasperation v ▷ exasperate

  exasperations v ▷ exasperate

excavate v (-tes, -ting, -ted) unearth buried objects from (a piece of land) methodically to learn about the past > **excavation** n (pl -s)

  excavated v ▷ excavate

  excavates v ▷ excavate

  excavating v ▷ excavate

  excavation n ▷ excavate

  excavations n ▷ excavate

excavator n (pl -s) large machine used for digging

  excavators n ▷ excavator

exceed v (-s, -ing, -ed) be greater than

  exceeded v ▷ exceed

  exceeding v ▷ exceed

exceedingly adv very

  exceeds v ▷ exceed

excel v (-s, -lling, -lled) be superior to

  excelled v ▷ excel

  excellence n ▷ excellent

  excellences n ▷ excellent

excellent adj exceptionally good > **excellence** n (pl -s)

  excelling v ▷ excel

  excels v ▷ excel

except prep (*sometimes foll. by* **for**) other than, not including ▶ v (-s, -ing, -ed) not include

  excepted v ▷ except

excepting prep except ▶ v ▷ except

exception n (pl -s) excepting

exceptional adj not ordinary

  exceptions n ▷ exception

  excepts v ▷ except

excerpt n (pl -s) passage taken from a book, speech, etc.

  excerpts n ▷ excerpt

excess n (pl -es) state or act of exceeding the permitted limits > **excessive** adj > **excessively** adv

  excesses n ▷ excess

  excessive adj ▷ excess

  excessively adv ▷ excess

exchange v (-ges, -ging, -ged) give or receive (something) in return for something else ▶ n (pl -s) act of exchanging > **exchangeable** adj

  exchangeable adj ▷ exchange

  exchanged v ▷ exchange

exchanges v, n ▷ exchange
exchanging v ▷ exchange
exchequer n (pl -s) (BRIT) government department in charge of state money
exchequers n ▷ exchequer
excise v (-ses, -sing, -sed) cut out or away > excision n (pl -s)
excised v ▷ excise
excises v ▷ excise
excising v ▷ excise
excision n ▷ excise
excisions n ▷ excise
excitabilities n ▷ excitable
excitability n ▷ excitable
excitable adj easily excited > excitability n (pl -s)
excite v (-s, -ing, -ed) arouse to strong emotion > excitement n (pl -s)
excited v ▷ excite
excitement n ▷ excite
excitements n ▷ excite
excites v ▷ excite
exciting v ▷ excite
exclaim v (-s, -ing, -ed) speak suddenly, cry out > exclamation n > exclamatory adj
exclaimed v ▷ exclaim
exclaiming v ▷ exclaim
exclaims v ▷ exclaim
exclamation n ▷ exclaim
exclamations n ▷ exclaim
exclamatory adj ▷ exclaim
exclude v (-s, -ing, -ed) keep out, leave out > exclusion n (pl -s)
excluded v ▷ exclude
excludes v ▷ exclude
excluding v ▷ exclude
exclusion n ▷ exclude
exclusions n ▷ exclude
exclusive adj excluding everything else ► n (pl -s) story reported in only one newspaper > exclusively adv > exclusivity n (pl -ies) > exclusiveness n (pl -es)
exclusively adv ▷ exclusive
exclusiveness n ▷ exclusive
exclusivenesses n ▷ exclusive
exclusives n ▷ exclusive
exclusivities n ▷ exclusive
exclusivity n ▷ exclusive
excommunicate v (-tes, -ting, -ted) exclude from membership and the sacraments of the Church > excommunication n (pl -s)
excommunicated v ▷ excommunicate
excommunicates v ▷ excommunicate
excommunicating v ▷ excommunicate
excommunication n ▷ excommunicate

excommunications n ▷ excommunicate
excoriate v (-tes, -ting, -ted) censure severely > excoriation n (pl -s)
excoriated v ▷ excoriate
excoriates v ▷ excoriate
excoriating v ▷ excoriate
excoriation n ▷ excoriate
excoriations n ▷ excoriate
excrement n (pl -s) waste matter discharged from the body
excrements n ▷ excrement
excrescence n (pl -s) lump or growth on the surface of an animal or plant
excrescences n ▷ excrescence
excreta [ik-skree-ta] n excrement
excrete v (-tes, -ting, -ted) discharge (waste matter) from the body > excretion n (pl -s) > excretory adj
excreted v ▷ excrete
excretes v ▷ excrete
excreting v ▷ excrete
excretion n ▷ excrete
excretions n ▷ excrete
excretory adj ▷ excrete
excruciating adj agonizing > excruciatingly adv
excruciatingly adv ▷ excruciating
exculpate v (-tes, -ting, -ted) free from blame or guilt
exculpated v ▷ exculpate
exculpates v ▷ exculpate
exculpating v ▷ exculpate
excursion n (pl -s) short journey, esp. for pleasure
excursions n ▷ excursion
excusable adj ▷ excuse
excuse n (pl -s) explanation offered to justify (a fault etc.) ► v (-ses, -sing, -sed) put forward a reason or justification for (a fault etc.) > excusable adj
excused v ▷ excuse
excuses n, v ▷ excuse
excusing v ▷ excuse
execrable [eks-sik-rab-bl] adj of very poor quality
execute v (-tes, -ting, -ted) put (a condemned person) to death > execution n (pl -s) > executioner n (pl -s)
executed v ▷ execute
executes v ▷ execute
executing v ▷ execute
execution n ▷ execute
executioner n ▷ execute
executioners n ▷ execute
executions n ▷ execute

executive n (pl -s) person or group in an administrative position ▶ adj having the function of carrying out plans, orders, laws, etc.

executives n ▷ executive

executor n (pl -s) person appointed to perform the instructions of a will

executors n ▷ executor

executrices n ▷ executrix

executrix n (pl -ixes, -ices) woman appointed to perform the instructions of a will

executrixes n ▷ executrix

exegeses n ▷ exegesis

exegesis [eks-sij-jee-siss] n (pl -ses) [-seez] explanation of a text, esp. of the Bible

exemplar n (pl -s) person or thing to be copied, model

exemplars n ▷ exemplar

exemplary adj being a good example

exemplification n ▷ exemplify

exemplifications n ▷ exemplify

exemplified v ▷ exemplify

exemplifies v ▷ exemplify

exemplify v (-ies, -fying, -ied) show an example of > **exemplification** n (pl -s)

exemplifying v ▷ exemplify

exempt adj not subject to an obligation etc. ▶ v (-s, -ing, -ed) release from an obligation etc. > **exemption** n (pl -s)

exempted v ▷ exempt

exempting v ▷ exempt

exemption n ▷ exempt

exemptions n ▷ exempt

exempts v ▷ exempt

> **exequy** n (**exequies**). An exequy is a funeral rite. This is a great word if you have the tiles for it, combining X and Q. Even better, if you have all the letters for the plural, exequies, and can play it, you'll score an extra 50 points for using all your tiles. Exequy scores 25 points.

exercise n (pl -s) activity to train the body or mind ▶ v (-ses, -sing, -sed) make use of

exercised v ▷ exercise

exercises n, v ▷ exercise

exercising v ▷ exercise

exert v (-s, -ing, -ed) use (influence, authority, etc.) forcefully or effectively > **exertion** n (pl -s)

exerted v ▷ exert

exerting v ▷ exert

exertion n ▷ exert

exertions n ▷ exert

exerts v ▷ exert

exes n ▷ ex

exeunt [eks-see-unt] (LATIN) they go out: used as a stage direction

exhalation n ▷ exhale

exhalations n ▷ exhale

exhale v (-les, -ling, -led) breathe out > **exhalation** n (pl -s)

exhaled v ▷ exhale

exhales v ▷ exhale

exhaling v ▷ exhale

exhaust v (-s, -ing, -ed) tire out ▶ n (pl -s) gases ejected from an engine as waste products

exhausted v ▷ exhaust

exhausting v ▷ exhaust

exhaustion n (pl -s) extreme tiredness

exhaustions n ▷ exhaustion

exhaustive adj comprehensive > **exhaustively** adv

exhaustively adv ▷ exhaustive

exhausts v, n ▷ exhaust

exhibit v (-s, -ing, -ed) display to the public ▶ n (pl -s) object exhibited to the public (LAW) > **exhibitor** n (pl -s)

exhibited v ▷ exhibit

exhibiting v ▷ exhibit

exhibition n (pl -s) public display of art, skills, etc.

exhibitionism n (pl -s) compulsive desire to draw attention to oneself > **exhibitionist** n (pl -s)

exhibitionisms n ▷ exhibitionism

exhibitionist n ▷ exhibitionism

exhibitionists n ▷ exhibitionism

exhibitions n ▷ exhibition

exhibitor n ▷ exhibit

exhibitors n ▷ exhibit

exhibits v, n ▷ exhibit

exhilarate v (-tes, -ting, -ted) make lively and cheerful > **exhilaration** n (pl -s)

exhilarated v ▷ exhilarate

exhilarates v ▷ exhilarate

exhilarating v ▷ exhilarate

exhilaration n ▷ exhilarate

exhilarations n ▷ exhilarate

exhort v (-s, -ing, -ed) urge earnestly > **exhortation** n (pl -s)

exhortation n ▷ exhort

exhortations n ▷ exhort

exhorted v ▷ exhort

exhorting v ▷ exhort

exhorts v ▷ exhort

exhumation n ▷ exhume

exhumations n ▷ exhume

exhume [ig-zyume] v (-mes, -ming, -med) dig up (something buried, esp. a corpse) > **exhumation** n (pl -s)

exhumed v ▷ exhume
exhumes v ▷ exhume
exhuming v ▷ exhume
exigencies n ▷ exigency
exigency n (pl -cies) urgent demand or need
 > **exigent** adj
exigent adj ▷ exigency
exiguous adj scanty or meagre
exile n (pl -s) prolonged, usu. enforced, absence
 from one's country ▶ v (-les, -ling, -led) expel
 from one's country
exiled v ▷ exile
exiles n ▷ exile
exiles n, v ▷ exile
exiling v ▷ exile
exist v (-s, -ing, -ed) have being or reality
 > **existence** n (pl -s) > **existent** adj
existed v ▷ exist
existence n ▷ exist
existences n ▷ exist
existent adj ▷ exist
existential adj of or relating to existence, esp.
 human existence
existentialism n (pl -s) philosophical
 movement stressing the personal experience
 and responsibility of the individual, who
 is seen as a free agent > **existentialist** adj,
 n (pl -s)
existentialisms n ▷ existentialism
existentialist adj, n ▷ existentialism
existentialists n ▷ existentialism
existing v ▷ exist
exists v ▷ exist
exit n (pl -s) way out ▶ v (-s, -ing, -ed) go out
exited v ▷ exit
exiting v ▷ exit
exits n, v ▷ exit

 exo adj. Exo is an informal Australian
 way of saying excellent. This is a great
 little word as it allows you to combine
 X with two of the most common tiles
 in the game, E and O. Exo scores 10
 points.

exocrine adj relating to a gland, such as the
 sweat gland, that secretes externally through
 a duct
exodus [eks-so-duss] n (pl -es) departure of a
 large number of people
exoduses n ▷ exodus
exonerate v (-tes, -ting, -ted) free from blame
 or a criminal charge > **exoneration** n (pl -s)
exonerates v ▷ exonerate
exonerated v ▷ exonerate
exonerating v ▷ exonerate
exoneration v ▷ exonerate

exonerations v ▷ exonerate
exorbitant adj (of prices, demands, etc.)
 excessive, immoderate > **exorbitantly** adv
exorbitantly adv ▷ exorbitant
exorcism n ▷ exorcize
exorcisms n ▷ exorcize
exorcist n ▷ exorcize
exorcists n ▷ exorcize
exorcize v (-zes, -zing, -zed) expel (evil spirits)
 by prayers and religious rites > **exorcism** n (pl
 -s) > **exorcist** n (pl -s)
exorcized v ▷ exorcize
exorcizes v ▷ exorcize
exorcizing v ▷ exorcize
exotic adj having a strange allure or beauty ▶ n
 (pl -s) non-native plant > **exotically** adv
exotica pl n (collection of) exotic objects
exotically adv ▷ exotic
exotics n ▷ exotic
expand v (-s, -ing, -ed) make or become larger
 (foll. by **on**) > **expansion** n (pl -s)
expanded v ▷ expand
expanding v ▷ expand
expands v ▷ expand
expanse n (pl -s) uninterrupted wide area
expanses n ▷ expanse
expansion n ▷ expand
expansions n ▷ expand
expansive adj wide or extensive
expat adj, n (pl -s) short for expatriate
expatiate [iks-**pay**-shee-ate] v (-tes, -ting, -ted)
 (foll. by **on**) speak or write at great length (on)
expatiated v ▷ expatiate
expatiates v ▷ expatiate
expatiating v ▷ expatiate
expatriate [eks-**pat**-ree-it] adj living outside
 one's native country ▶ n (pl -s) person
 living outside his or her native country
 > **expatriation** n (pl -s)
expatriates n ▷ expatriate
expatriation n ▷ expatriate
expatriations n ▷ expatriate
expats n ▷ expat
expect v (-s, -ing, -ed) regard as probable
expectancies n ▷ expectancy
expectancy n (pl -ies) something expected on
 the basis of an average
expectant adj expecting or hopeful
 > **expectantly** adv
expectantly adv ▷ expectant
expectation n (pl -s) act or state of expecting
expectations n ▷ expectation
expected v ▷ expect
expecting v ▷ expect
expectorant n (pl -s) medicine that helps

to bring up phlegm from the respiratory passages

expectorants *n* ▷ expectorant

expectorate *v* (-tes, -ting, -ted) spit out (phlegm etc.) > **expectoration** *n* (*pl* -s)

expectorated *v* ▷ expectorate

expectorates *v* ▷ expectorate

expectorating *v* ▷ expectorate

expectoration *n* ▷ expectorate

expectorations *n* ▷ expectorate

expects *v* ▷ expect

expediencies *n* ▷ expedient

expediency *n* ▷ expedient

expedient *n* (*pl* -s) something that achieves a particular purpose ▶ *adj* suitable to the circumstances, appropriate > **expediency** *n* (*pl* -ies)

expedients *n* ▷ expedient

expedite *v* (-s, -ing, -ed) hasten the progress of

expedited *v* ▷ expedite

expedites *v* ▷ expedite

expediting *v* ▷ expedite

expedition *n* (*pl* -s) organized journey, esp. for exploration

expeditionary *adj* relating to an expedition, esp. a military one

expeditions *n* ▷ expedition

expeditious *adj* done quickly and efficiently

expel *v* (-s, -lling, -lled) drive out with force > **expulsion** *n* (*pl* -s)

expelled *v* ▷ expel

expelling *v* ▷ expel

expels *v* ▷ expel

expend *v* (-s, -ing, -ed) spend, use up

expendable *adj* able to be sacrificed to achieve an objective

expended *v* ▷ expend

expending *v* ▷ expend

expenditure *n* (*pl* -s) something expended, esp. money

expenditures *n* ▷ expenditure

expends *v* ▷ expend

expense *n* (*pl* -s) cost ▶ *pl* charges, outlay incurred

expenses *n* ▷ expense

expensive *adj* high-priced

experience *n* (*pl* -s) direct personal participation ▶ *v* (-ces, -cing, -ced) participate in

experienced *v* ▷ experience ▶ *adj* skilful from extensive participation

experiences *n*, *v* ▷ experience

experiencing *v* ▷ experience

experiment *n* (*pl* experiments) test to provide evidence to prove or disprove a theory

▶ *v* (-s, -ing, -ed) carry out an experiment > **experimental** *adj* > **experimentally** *adv* > **experimentation** *n* (*pl* -s)

experimental *adj* ▷ experiment

experimentally *adv* ▷ experiment

experimentation *n* ▷ experiment

experimentations *n* ▷ experiment

experimented *v* ▷ experiment

experimenting *v* ▷ experiment

experiments *n*, *v* ▷ experiment

expert *n* (*pl* -s) person with extensive skill or knowledge in a particular field ▶ *adj* skilful or knowledgeable

expertise [eks-per-**teez**] *n* (*pl* -s) special skill or knowledge

expertises *n* ▷ expertise

experts *n* ▷ expert

expiate *v* (-tes, -ting, -ted) make amends for > **expiation** *n* (*pl* -s)

expiated *v* ▷ expiate

expiates *v* ▷ expiate

expiating *v* ▷ expiate

expiation *n* ▷ expiate

expiations *n* ▷ expiate

expiration *n* ▷ expire

expirations *n* ▷ expire

expire *v* (-res, -ring, -red) finish or run out (*Lit*) > **expiration** *n* (*pl* -s)

expired *v* ▷ expire

expires *v* ▷ expire

expiries *n* ▷ expiry

expiring *v* ▷ expire

expiry *n* (*pl* -ies) end, esp. of a contract period

explain *v* (-s, -ing, -ed) make clear and intelligible > **explanation** *n* (*pl* -s) > **explanatory** *adj*

explained *v* ▷ explain

explaining *v* ▷ explain

explains *v* ▷ explain

explanation *n* ▷ explain

explanations *n* ▷ explain

explanatory *adj* ▷ explain

expletive *n* (*pl* -s) swearword

expletives *n* ▷ expletive

explicable *adj* able to be explained

explicate *v* (-tes, -ting, -ted) (*Formal*) explain > **explication** *n* (*pl* -s)

explicated *v* ▷ explicate

explicates *v* ▷ explicate

explicating *v* ▷ explicate

explication *n* ▷ explicate

explications *n* ▷ explicate

explicit *adj* precisely and clearly expressed > **explicitly** *adv*

explicitly *adv* ▷ explicit

explode v (-des, -ding, -ded) burst with great violence, blow up > **explosion** n (pl -s)
  exploded v ▷ explode
  explodes v ▷ explode
  exploding v ▷ explode
exploit v (pl -s) take advantage of for one's own purposes ▶ n (pl -s) notable feat or deed > **exploitation** n (pl -s) > **exploiter** n (pl -s)
  exploitation n ▷ exploit
  exploitations n ▷ exploit
  exploited v ▷ exploit
  exploiter n ▷ exploit
  exploiters n ▷ exploit
  exploiting v ▷ exploit
  exploits v, n ▷ exploit
  exploration n ▷ explore
  explorations n ▷ explore
  exploratory adj ▷ explore
explore v (-res, -ring, -red) investigate > **exploration** n (pl -s) > **exploratory** adj > **explorer** n (pl -s)
  explored v ▷ explore
  explorer n ▷ explore
  explorers n ▷ explore
  explores v ▷ explore
  exploring v ▷ explore
  explosion n ▷ explode
  explosions n ▷ explode
explosive adj tending to explode ▶ n (pl -s) substance that causes explosions
  explosives n ▷ explosive
expo n (pl -s) (Informal) exposition, large public exhibition
exponent n (pl -s) person who advocates an idea, cause, etc.
exponential adj (Informal) very rapid > **exponentially** adv
  exponentially adv ▷ exponential
  exponents n ▷ exponent
export n (pl -s) selling or shipping of goods to a foreign country ▶ v (-s, -ing, -ed) sell or ship (goods) to a foreign country > **exporter** n (pl -s)
  exported v ▷ export
  exporter n ▷ export
  exporters n ▷ export
  exporting v ▷ export
  exports n, v ▷ export
  expos n ▷ expo
expose v (-ses, -sing, -sed) uncover or reveal > **exposure** n (pl -s) exposing
exposé [iks-**pose**-ay] n (pl -s) bringing of a crime, scandal, etc. to public notice
  exposed v ▷ expose
  exposes v ▷ expose

  exposés n ▷ exposé
  exposing v ▷ expose
  exposition n ▷ expound
  expositions n ▷ expound
expostulate v (-tes, -ting, -ted) (foll. by with) reason (with), esp. to dissuade
  expostulated v ▷ expostulate
  expostulates v ▷ expostulate
  expostulating v ▷ expostulate
  exposure n ▷ expose
  exposures n ▷ expose
expound v (-s, -ing, -ed) explain in detail > **exposition** n (pl -s) explanation
  expounded v ▷ expound
  expounding v ▷ expound
  expounds v ▷ expound
express v (-es, -ing, -ed) put into words ▶ adj explicitly stated ▶ n (pl -es) fast train or bus stopping at only a few stations ▶ adv by express delivery
  expressed v ▷ express
  expresses v, n ▷ express
  expressing v ▷ express
expression n (pl -s) expressing > **expressionless** adj > **expressive** adj
expressionism n (pl -s) early 20th-century artistic movement which sought to express emotions rather than represent the physical world > **expressionist** adj, n (pl -s)
  expressionisms n ▷ expressionism
  expressionist adj, n ▷ expressionism
  expressionists n ▷ expressionism
  expressionless adj ▷ expression
  expressions n ▷ expression
  expressive adj ▷ expression
expropriate v (-tes, -ting, -ted) deprive an owner of (property) > **expropriation** n (pl -s)
  expropriated v ▷ expropriate
  expropriates v ▷ expropriate
  expropriating v ▷ expropriate
  expropriation n ▷ expropriate
  expropriations n ▷ expropriate
  expulsion n ▷ expel
  expulsions n ▷ expel
expunge v (-ges, -ging, -ged) delete, erase, blot out
  expunged v ▷ expunge
  expunges v ▷ expunge
  expunging v ▷ expunge
expurgate v (-tes, -ting, -ted) remove objectionable parts from (a book etc.)
  expurgated v ▷ expurgate
  expurgates v ▷ expurgate
  expurgating v ▷ expurgate
exquisite adj of extreme beauty or delicacy

> **exquisitely** *adv*
exquisitely *adv* ▷ exquisite
extant *adj* still existing
extemporize *v* (-zes, -zing, -zed) speak, perform, or compose without preparation
extemporized *v* ▷ extemporize
extemporizes *v* ▷ extemporize
extemporizing *v* ▷ extemporize
extend *v* (-s, -ing, -ed) draw out or be drawn out, stretch (*foll. by* **to**) > **extendable** *adj*
extendable *adj* ▷ extend
extended *v* ▷ extend
extending *v* ▷ extend
extends *v* ▷ extend
extension *n* (*pl* -s) room or rooms added to an existing building
extensions *n* ▷ extension
extensive *adj* having a large extent, widespread
extensor *n* (*pl* -s) muscle that extends a part of the body
extensors *n* ▷ extensor
extent *n* (*pl* -s) range over which something extends, area
extents *n* ▷ extent
extenuate *v* (-tes, -ting, -ted) make (an offence or fault) less blameworthy
> **extenuation** *n* (*pl* -s)
extenuated *v* ▷ extenuate
extenuates *v* ▷ extenuate
extenuating *v* ▷ extenuate
extenuation *n* ▷ extenuate
extenuations *n* ▷ extenuate
exterior *n* (*pl* -s) part or surface on the outside ▶ *adj* of, on, or coming from the outside
exteriors *n* ▷ exterior
exterminate *v* (-tes, -ting, -ted) destroy (animals or people) completely
> **extermination** *n* (*pl* -s) > **exterminator** *n* (*pl* -s)
exterminated *v* ▷ exterminate
exterminates *v* ▷ exterminate
exterminating *v* ▷ exterminate
extermination *n* ▷ exterminate
exterminations *n* ▷ exterminate
exterminator *n* ▷ exterminate
exterminators *n* ▷ exterminate
external *adj* of, situated on, or coming from the outside > **externally** *adv*
externally *adv* ▷ external
extinct *adj* having died out > **extinction** *n* (*pl* -s)
extinction *n* ▷ extinct
extinctions *n* ▷ extinct
extinguish *v* (-es, -ing, -ed) put out (a fire or light)
extinguished *v* ▷ extinguish
extinguisher *n* (*pl* -s) device for extinguishing a fire or light
extinguishers *n* ▷ extinguisher
extinguishes *v* ▷ extinguish
extinguishing *v* ▷ extinguish
extirpate *v* (-tes, -ting, -ted) destroy utterly
extirpated *v* ▷ extirpate
extirpates *v* ▷ extirpate
extirpating *v* ▷ extirpate
extol *v* (-s, -lling, -lled) praise highly
extolled *v* ▷ extol
extolling *v* ▷ extol
extols *v* ▷ extol
extort *v* (-s, -ing, -ed) get (something) by force or threats > **extortion** *n* (*pl* -s)
extorted *v* ▷ extort
extorting *v* ▷ extort
extortion *n* ▷ extort
extortionate *adj* (of prices) excessive
extortions *n* ▷ extort
extorts *v* ▷ extort
extra *adj* more than is usual, expected or needed ▶ *n* (*pl* -s) additional person or thing ▶ *adv* unusually or exceptionally
extract *v* (-s, -ing, -ed) pull out by force ▶ *n* (*pl* -s) something extracted, such as a passage from a book etc. > **extraction** *n* (*pl* -s) > **extractor** (*pl* -s) *n*
extracted *v* ▷ extract
extracting *v* ▷ extract
extraction *n* ▷ extract
extractions *n* ▷ extract
extractor *n* ▷ extract
extractors *n* ▷ extract
extracts *n*, *v* ▷ extract
extradite *v* (-tes, -ting, -ted) send (an accused person) back to his or her own country for trial > **extradition** *n* (*pl* -s)
extradited *v* ▷ extradite
extradites *v* ▷ extradite
extraditing *v* ▷ extradite
extradition *n* ▷ extradite
extraditions *n* ▷ extradite
extramural *adj* connected with but outside the normal courses of a university or college
extraneous [iks-**train**-ee-uss] *adj* irrelevant
extraordinarily *adv* ▷ extraordinary
extraordinary *adj* very unusual
> **extraordinarily** *adv*
extrapolate *v* (-tes, -ting, -ted) infer (something not known) from the known facts (MATHS) > **extrapolation** *n* (*pl* -s)
extrapolated *v* ▷ extrapolate

extrapolates v ▷ extrapolate
extrapolating v ▷ extrapolate
extrapolation n ▷ extrapolate
extrapolations n ▷ extrapolate
extras n ▷ extra
extrasensory adj beyond the normal range of the senses
extravagance n ▷ extravagant
extravagances n ▷ extravagant
extravagant adj spending money excessively > **extravagance** n (pl -s)
extravaganza n (pl -s) elaborate and lavish entertainment, display, etc.
extravaganzas n ▷ extravaganza
extreme adj of a high or the highest degree or intensity ▶ n (pl -s) either of the two limits of a scale or range > **extremely** adv
extremely adv ▷ extreme
extremes n ▷ extreme
extremist n (pl -s) person who favours immoderate methods ▶ adj holding extreme opinions
extremists n ▷ extremist
extremities n ▷ extremity
extremity n (pl -ies) farthest point
extricate v (-tes, -ting, -ted) free from complication or difficulty > **extrication** n (pl -s)
extricated v ▷ extricate
extricates v ▷ extricate
extricating v ▷ extricate
extrication n ▷ extricate
extrications n ▷ extricate
extrovert adj lively and outgoing ▶ n (pl -s) extrovert person
extroverts n ▷ extrovert
extrude v (-des, -ding, -ded) squeeze or force out > **extrusion** n (pl -s)
extruded v ▷ extrude
extrudes v ▷ extrude
extruding v ▷ extrude
extrusion n ▷ extrude
extrusions n ▷ extrude
exuberance n ▷ exuberant
exuberances n ▷ exuberant
exuberant adj high-spirited > **exuberance** n (pl -s)
exude v (-s, -ing, -ed) (of a liquid or smell) seep or flow out slowly and steadily

exuded v ▷ exude
exudes v ▷ exude
exuding v ▷ exude
exult v (-s, -ing, -ed) be joyful or jubilant > **exultation** n (pl -s) > **exultant** adj
exultant adj ▷ exult
exultation n ▷ exult
exultations n ▷ exult
exulted v ▷ exult
exulting v ▷ exult
exults v ▷ exult
eye n (pl -s) organ of sight ▶ v (-s, eyeing or **eying, eyed**) look at carefully or warily > **eyeless** adj
eyeball n (pl -s) ball-shaped part of the eye
eyeballs n ▷ eyeball
eyebrow n (pl -s) line of hair on the bony ridge above the eye
eyebrows n ▷ eyebrow
eyed v ▷ eye
eyeglass n (pl -es) lens for aiding defective vision
eyeglasses n ▷ eyeglass
eyeing v ▷ eye
eyelash n (pl -es) short hair that grows out from the eyelid
eyelashes n ▷ eyelash
eyeless adj ▷ eye
eyelet n (pl -s) small hole for a lace or cord to be passed through
eyelets n ▷ eyelet
eyelid n (pl -s) fold of skin that covers the eye when it is closed
eyelids n ▷ eyelid
eyeliner n (pl -s) cosmetic used to outline the eyes
eyeliners n ▷ eyeliner
eyes n, v ▷ eye
eyesight n (pl -s) ability to see
eyesights n ▷ eyesight
eyesore n (pl -s) ugly object
eyesores n ▷ eyesore
eyewitness n (pl -es) person who was present at an event and can describe what happened
eyewitnesses n ▷ eyewitness
eying v ▷ eye
eyrie n (pl -s) nest of an eagle
eyries n ▷ eyrie

Ff

F can be an awkward letter in Scrabble: there are only two two-letter words beginning with F, for example (**fa** and **fy**). But if you're aware of this, you won't waste time trying to think of other two-letter words. There are also quite a few words that combine F with X or Z, allowing high scores particularly if you can hit a bonus square with them. **Fax**, **fix** and **fox** are good examples (13 points each), and don't forgets **fez** (15). If you have a blank tile, you can use it for the second Z in **fuzz** (15) or **fuzzy** (19). **Fey**, **fly** and **fry** can also be useful (9 each).

fa n (**fas**) Fa is the musical note F. This word isn't going to win you a game on its own, but it's useful when you're trying to form several words at once. Fa scores 5 points.
  fab adj Fab is a short form of **fabulous**. Fab scores 8 points.
fable n (pl -s) story with a moral
fabled adj made famous in legend
  fables n ▷ fable
fabric n (pl -s) knitted or woven cloth
fabricate v (-tes, -ting, -ted) make up (a story or lie) > **fabrication** n (pl -s)
  fabricated v ▷ fabricate
  fabricates v ▷ fabricate
  fabricating v ▷ fabricate
  fabrication n ▷ fabricate
  fabrications n ▷ fabricate
  fabrics n ▷ fabric
fabulous adj (Informal) excellent > **fabulously** adv
  fabulously adv ▷ fabulous
facade [fas-**sahd**] n (pl -s) front of a building
  facades n ▷ facade
face n (pl -s) front of the head ▸ v (-ces, -cing, -ced) look or turn towards
  faced v ▷ face
faceless adj impersonal, anonymous
  faces n, v ▷ face
facet n (pl -s) aspect
facetious [fas-**see**-shuss] adj funny or trying to be funny, esp. at inappropriate times
  facets n ▷ facet
  facia n (pl -ciae) ▷ fascia
  faciae n ▷ fascia
facial adj of the face ▸ n (pl -s) beauty treatment for the face

  facials n ▷ facial
facile [**fas**-sile] adj (of a remark, argument, etc.) superficial and showing lack of real thought
facilitate v (-tes, -ting, -ted) make easy > **facilitation** n (pl -s)
  facilitated v ▷ facilitate
  facilitates v ▷ facilitate
  facilitating v ▷ facilitate
  facilitation n ▷ facilitate
  facilitations n ▷ facilitate
  facilities n ▷ facility
facility n (pl -ties) skill ▸ pl means or equipment for an activity
  facing v ▷ face
facing n (pl -s) lining or covering for decoration or reinforcement ▸ pl contrasting collar and cuffs on a jacket
  facings n ▷ facing
facsimile [fak-**sim**-ill-ee] n (pl -s) exact copy
  facsimiles n ▷ facsimile
fact n (pl -s) event or thing known to have happened or existed > **factual** adj
faction n (pl -s) (dissenting) minority group within a larger body
  factions n ▷ faction
factious adj of or producing factions
factitious adj artificial
factor n (pl -s) element contributing to a result
factorial n (pl -s) product of all the integers from one to a given number
  factorials n ▷ factorial
  factories n ▷ factory
factorize v (-zes, -zing, -zed) calculate the factors of (a number)
  factorized v ▷ factorize
  factorizes v ▷ factorize
  factorizing v ▷ factorize

factors n ▷ factor

factory n (pl -ies) building where goods are manufactured

factotum n (pl -s) person employed to do all sorts of work

  factotums n ▷ factotum

facts n ▷ fact

factual adj ▷ fact

faculties n ▷ faculty

faculty n (pl -ties) physical or mental ability

fad n (pl -s) short-lived fashion > **faddy** (-ddier, -ddiest), **faddish** adj

  faddier adj ▷ fad

  faddiest adj ▷ fad

  faddish adj ▷ fad

  faddy adj ▷ fad

fade v (-des, -ding, -ded) (cause to) lose brightness, colour, or strength

  faded v ▷ fade

  fades v ▷ fade

  fading v ▷ fade

  fads n ▷ fad

faecal adj ▷ faeces

faeces [fee-seez] pl n waste matter discharged from the anus > **faecal** [fee-kl] ▶ adj

fag¹ n (pl -s) (Informal) boring task (BRIT) ▶ v (-gs, -gging, -gged) (BRIT) do menial chores in a public school

  fagged v ▷ fag¹

  fagging v ▷ fag¹

fag² n (BRIT) (Slang) cigarette

faggot n (pl -s) (BRIT, AUST & NZ) ball of chopped liver, herbs, and bread

  faggots n ▷ faggot

  fags n, v ▷ fag¹, ²

faïence [fie-ence] n (pl -s) tin-glazed earthenware

  faïences n ▷ faïence

fail v (-s, -ing, -ed) be unsuccessful ▶ n (pl -s) instance of not passing an exam or test

  failed v ▷ fail

failing n (pl -s) weak point ▶ prep in the absence of ▶ v ▷ fail

  failings n ▷ failing

  fails v, n ▷ fail

failure n (pl -s) act or instance of failing

  failures n ▷ failure

fain adv (Obs) gladly

faint adj lacking clarity, brightness, or volume ▶ v (-s, -ing, -ed) lose consciousness temporarily ▶ n (pl -s) temporary loss of consciousness

  fainted v ▷ faint

  fainting v ▷ faint

  faints v, n ▷ faint

fair¹ adj (-er, -est) unbiased and reasonable ▶ adv fairly > **fairness** n (pl -s)

  fairer adj ▷ fair¹

  fairest adj ▷ fair¹

fair² n (pl -s) travelling entertainment with sideshows, rides, and amusements

fairground n (pl -s) open space used for a fair

  fairgrounds n ▷ fairground

  fairies n ▷ fairy

fairly adv moderately

  fairness n ▷ fair¹

  fairnesses n ▷ fair¹

  fairs n ▷ fair¹, ²

fairway n (pl -s) (GOLF) smooth area between the tee and the green

  fairways n ▷ fairway

fairy n (pl -ries) imaginary small creature with magic powers > **fairyland** n (pl -s)

  fairyland n ▷ fairy

  fairylands n ▷ fairy

faith n (pl -s) strong belief, esp. without proof

faithful adj loyal > **faithfully** adv

  faithfully adv ▷ faithful

faithless adj disloyal or dishonest

  faiths n ▷ faith

fake v (-kes, -king, -ked) cause something not genuine to appear real or more valuable by fraud ▶ n (pl -s) person, thing, or act that is not genuine ▶ adj not genuine

  faked v ▷ fake

  fakes v, n ▷ fake

  faking v ▷ fake

fakir [fay-keer] n (pl -s) Muslim who spurns worldly possessions

  fakirs n ▷ fakir

falcon n (pl -s) small bird of prey

  falconer n ▷ falconry

  falconers n ▷ falconry

  falconries n ▷ falconry

falconry n (pl -ries) art of training falcons > **falconer** n (pl -s)

  falcons n ▷ falcon

fall v (-s, -ing, fell, fallen) drop from a higher to a lower place through the force of gravity ▶ n (pl -s) falling

  fallacies n ▷ fallacy

  fallacious adj ▷ fallacy

fallacy n (pl -cies) false belief > **fallacious** adj

  fallen v ▷ fall

  fallibilities n ▷ fallible

  fallibility n ▷ fallible

fallible adj (of a person) liable to make mistakes > **fallibility** n (pl -ties)

  falling v ▷ fall

fallout n (pl -s) radioactive particles spread as

a result of a nuclear explosion
  fallouts n ▷ fallout
fallow adj (of land) ploughed but left unseeded
  to regain fertility
  falls v, n ▷ fall
false adj (-r, -st) not true or correct ▷ **falsely** adv
  ▷ **falseness** n (pl -es) **falsity** n (pl -ties)
falsehood n (pl -s) quality of being untrue
  falsehoods n ▷ falsehood
  falsely adv ▷ false
  falseness n ▷ false
  falsenesses n ▷ false
  falser adj ▷ false
  falsest adj ▷ false
falsetto n (pl -tos) voice pitched higher than
  one's natural range
  falsettos n ▷ falsetto
  falsification n ▷ falsify
  falsifications n ▷ falsify
  falsified v ▷ falsify
  falsifies v ▷ falsify
falsify v (-fies, -fying, -fied) alter fraudulently
  ▷ **falsification** n (pl -s)
  falsifying v ▷ falsify
  falsities n ▷ false
  falsity n ▷ false
falter v (-s, -ing, -ed) be hesitant, weak, or
  unsure
  faltered v ▷ falter
  faltering v ▷ falter
  falters v ▷ falter
fame n (pl -s) state of being widely known or
  recognized
  famed adj famous
  famed adj ▷ fame
  fames n ▷ fame
  familial adj ▷ family
familiar adj well-known ▶ n (pl -s) demon
  supposed to attend a witch ▷ **familiarly** adv
  ▷ **familiarity** n (pl -ties)
  familiarities n ▷ familiarity
  familiarity n ▷ familiarity
familiarize (-zes, -zing, -zed) v acquaint fully
  with a particular subject ▷ **familiarization**
  n (pl -s)
  familiarization n ▷ familiarize
  familiarizations n ▷ familiarize
  familiarized v ▷ familiarize
  familiarizes v ▷ familiarize
  familiarizing v ▷ familiarize
  familiarly adv ▷ familiar
  familiars n ▷ familiar
  families n ▷ family
family n (pl -lies) group of parents and their
  children ▶ adj suitable for parents and

children together ▷ **familial** adj
famine n (pl -s) severe shortage of food
  famines n ▷ famine
famished adj very hungry
famous adj very well-known
famously adv (Informal) excellently
fan[1] n (pl -s) hand-held or mechanical object
  used to create a current of air for ventilation
  or cooling ▶ v (-s, -nning, -nned) blow or cool
  with a fan
fan[2] n (pl -s) (Informal) devotee of a pop star,
  sport, or hobby
fanatic n (pl -s) person who is excessively
  enthusiastic about something ▷ **fanatical** adj
  ▷ **fanatically** adv **fanaticism** n (pl -s)
  fanatical adj ▷ fanatic
  fanatically adv ▷ fanatic
  fanaticism n ▷ fanatic
  fanaticisms n ▷ fanatic
  fanatics n ▷ fanatic
fanbase n (pl -s) body of admirers of a
  particular pop singer, sports team, etc
  fanbases n ▷ fanbase
  fancied v ▷ fancy
  fancier adj ▷ fancy
  fancies n, v ▷ fancy
  fanciest adj ▷ fancy
fanciful adj not based on fact ▷ **fancifully** adv
  fancifully adv ▷ fanciful
fancy adj (-cier, -ciest) elaborate, not plain ▶ n
  (pl -cies) sudden irrational liking or desire
  ▶ v (-cies, -cying, -cied) (Informal) be sexually
  attracted to
fancy-free adj not in love
  fancying v ▷ fancy
fandango n (pl -os) lively Spanish dance
  fandangos n ▷ fandango
fanfare n (pl -s) short loud tune played on brass
  instruments
  fanfares n ▷ fanfare
fang n (pl -s) snake's tooth which injects
  poison
  fangs n ▷ fang
  fanned v ▷ fan
  fanning n ▷ fan
  fans n, v ▷ fan
fantail n (pl -s) small New Zealand bird with a
  tail like a fan
  fantails n ▷ fantail
fantasia n (pl -s) musical composition of an
  improvised nature
  fantasias n ▷ fantasia
  fantasies n ▷ fantasy
fantasize v (-zes, -zing, -zed) indulge in
  daydreams

fantasized v ▷ fantasize
fantasizes v ▷ fantasize
fantasizing v ▷ fantasize
fantastic adj (Informal) very good
> **fantastically** adv
fantastically adv ▷ fantastic
fantasy n (pl -sies) far-fetched notion
far adv (farther or further, farthest or furthest)
   at, to, or from a great distance ▶ adj remote in
   space or time
farad n (pl -s) unit of electrical capacitance
farads n ▷ farad
farce n (pl -s) boisterous comedy
farces n ▷ farce
farcical adj ludicrous > **farcically** adv
farcically adv ▷ farcical
fare n (pl -s) charge for a passenger's journey
   ▶ v (-res, -ring, -red) get on (as specified)
fared v ▷ fare
fares n, v ▷ fare
farewell interj goodbye ▶ n (pl -s) act of saying
   goodbye and leaving ▶ v (-s, -ing, -ed) (NZ) say
   goodbye
farewelled v ▷ farewell
farewelling v ▷ farewell
farewells n, v ▷ farewell
farinaceous adj containing starch or having a
   starchy texture
faring v ▷ fare
farm n (pl -s) area of land for growing crops or
   rearing livestock ▶ v (-s, -ing, -ed) cultivate
   (land) > **farmhouse** n (pl -s) > **farmyard** n (pl -s)
farmed v ▷ farm
farmer n (pl -s) person who owns or runs a
   farm
farmers n ▷ farmer
farmhouse n ▷ farm
farmhouses n ▷ farm
farming v ▷ farm
farms n, v ▷ farm
farmstead n (pl -s) farm and its buildings
farmsteads n ▷ farmstead
farmyard n ▷ farm
farmyards n ▷ farm
farrago [far-rah-go] n (pl -gos, -goes) jumbled
   mixture of things
farragoes n ▷ farrago
farragos n ▷ farrago
farrier n (pl -s) person who shoes horses
farriers n ▷ farrier
farrow n (pl -s) litter of piglets ▶ v (-s, -ing, -ed)
   (of a sow) give birth
farrowed v ▷ farrow
farrowing v ▷ farrow
farrows n, v ▷ farrow

farther, farthest adv, adj ▷ far
farthing n (pl -s) former British coin
   equivalent to a quarter of a penny
farthings n ▷ farthing
fascia [fay-shya] n (pl -ciae, -cias) outer surface
   of a dashboard
fasciae n ▷ fascia
fascias n ▷ fascia
fascinate v (-tes, -ting, -ted) attract
   and interest strongly > **fascinating** adj
   > **fascination** n (pl -s)
fascinated v ▷ fascinate
fascinates v ▷ fascinate
fascinating v, adj ▷ fascinate
fascination n ▷ fascinate
fascinations n ▷ fascinate
fascism [fash-iz-zum] n (pl -s) right-wing
   totalitarian political system characterized
   by state control and extreme nationalism
   > **fascist** adj, n (pl -s)
fascisms n ▷ fascism
fascist n ▷ fascism
fascists n ▷ fascism
fashion n (pl -s) style in clothes, hairstyle, etc.,
   popular at a particular time ▶ v (-s, -ing, -ed)
   form or make into a particular shape
fashionable adj currently popular
   > **fashionably** adv
fashionably adv ▷ fashionable
fashioned v ▷ fashion
fashioning v ▷ fashion
fashions n, v ▷ fashion
fast¹ adj (-er, -est) (capable of) acting or
   moving quickly ▶ adv quickly
fast² v (-s, -ing, -ed) go without food, esp. for
   religious reasons ▶ n (pl -s) period of fasting
fasted v ▷ fast²
fasten v (-s, -ing, -ed) make or become firmly
   fixed or joined
fastened v ▷ fasten
fastener n (pl -s) device that fastens
fasteners n ▷ fastener
fastening v ▷ fasten ▶ n (pl -s) device that
   fastens
fastenings n ▷ fastening
fastens v ▷ fasten
faster adj ▷ fast¹
fastest adj ▷ fast¹
fastidious adj very fussy about details
   > **fastidiously** adv > **fastidiousness** n
fastidiously adv ▷ fastidious
fastidiousness n ▷ fastidious
fastidiousnesses n ▷ fastidious
fasting v ▷ fast²
fastness n (pl -es) fortress, safe place

fastnesses n ▷ fastness

fasts v, n ▷ fast²

fat adj (-er, -est) having excess flesh on the body ▶ n (pl -s) extra flesh on the body >**fatness** n (pl -es)

fatal adj causing death or ruin >**fatally** adv

fatalism n (pl -s) belief that all events are predetermined and people are powerless to change their destinies >**fatalist** n (pl -s) >**fatalistic** adj

fatalisms n ▷ fatalism

fatalist n ▷ fatalism

fatalistic adj ▷ fatalism

fatalists n ▷ fatalism

fatalities n ▷ fatality

fatality n (pl -ties) death caused by an accident or disaster

fatally adv ▷ fatal

fate n (pl -s) power supposed to predetermine events

fated adj destined

fateful adj having important, usu. disastrous, consequences

fates n ▷ fate

fathead n (pl -s) (Informal) stupid person >**fat-headed** adj

fatheaded adj ▷ fathead

fatheads n ▷ fathead

father n (pl -s) male parent ▶ v (-s, -ing, -ed) be the father of (offspring) >**fatherhood** n (pl -s) >**fatherless** adj >**fatherly** adj

fathered v ▷ father

fatherhood n ▷ father

fatherhoods n ▷ fatherhood

fathering v ▷ father

fatherland n one's native country

fatherlands n ▷ fatherland

fatherless adj ▷ father

fatherly adj ▷ father

fathers n, v ▷ father

fathom n (pl -s) unit of length, used in navigation, equal to six feet (1.83 metres) ▶ v (-s, -ing, -ed) understand >**fathomable** adj

fathomable adj ▷ fathom

fathomed v ▷ fathom

fathoming v ▷ fathom

fathomless adj too deep or difficult to fathom

fathoms n, v ▷ fathom

fatigue [fat-**eeg**] n (pl -s) extreme physical or mental tiredness ▶ v (-gues, -guing, -gued) tire out

fatigued v ▷ fatigue

fatigues v, n ▷ fatigue

fatiguing v ▷ fatigue

fatness n ▷ fat

fatnesses n ▷ fat

fats n ▷ fat

fatten v (-s, -ing, -ed) (cause to) become fat

fattened v ▷ fatten

fattening v ▷ fatten

fattens v ▷ fatten

fattier adj ▷ fatty

fattiest adj ▷ fatty

fatty adj (-ier, -iest) containing fat

fatuities n ▷ fatuous

fatuity n ▷ fatuous

fatuous adj foolish >**fatuously** adv >**fatuity** n (pl -s)

fatuously adv ▷ fatuous

faucet [**faw**-set] n (pl -s) (US) tap

faucets n ▷ faucet

fault n (pl -s) responsibility for something wrong ▶ v (-s, -ing, -ed) criticize or blame >**faulty** adj (-tier, -tiest) >**faultless** adj >**faultlessly** adv

faulted v ▷ fault

faultier adj ▷ fault

faultiest adj ▷ fault

faulting v ▷ fault

faultless adj ▷ fault

faultlessly adv ▷ fault

faults v ▷ fault

faulty n ▷ fault

faun n (pl -s) (in Roman legend) creature with a human face and torso and a goat's horns and legs

fauna n (pl -as, -ae) animals of a given place or time

faunae n ▷ fauna

faunas n ▷ fauna

fauns n ▷ faun

favour n (pl -s) approving attitude ▶ v (-s, -ing, -ed) prefer

favourable adj encouraging or advantageous >**favourably** adv

favourably adv ▷ favourable

favoured v ▷ favour

favouring v ▷ favour

favourite adj most liked ▶ n (pl -s) preferred person or thing

favourites n ▷ favourite

favouritism n (pl -s) practice of giving special treatment to a person or group

favouritisms n ▷ favouritism

favours n, v ▷ favour

> **faw** n (**faws**). A faw is a gypsy. This is a good word for taking advantage of a nearby bonus square. Faw scores 9 points.

fawn¹ n (pl -s) young deer ▶ adj light yellowish-brown

fawn² v (-s, -ing, -ed) (foll. by **on**) seek attention from (someone) by insincere flattery

fawned v ▷ fawn²

fawning v ▷ fawn²

fawns n, v ▷ fawn¹, ²

fax n (pl -es) electronic system for sending facsimiles of documents by telephone ▶ v (-xes, -xing, -xed) send (a document) by this system

faxed n ▷ fax

faxes n, v ▷ fax

faxing v ▷ fax

> **fay** n (fays). A fay is a fairy. This is a fairly high-scoring short word. Fay scores 9 points.

fealties n ▷ fealty

fealty n (pl -ies) (in feudal society) subordinate's loyalty to his ruler or lord

fear n (pl -s) distress or alarm caused by impending danger or pain ▶ v (-s, -ing, -ed) be afraid of (something or someone) > **fearless** adj > **fearlessly** adv

feared v ▷ fear

fearful adj feeling fear (Informal) > **fearfully** adv

fearfully adv ▷ fearful

fearing v ▷ fear

fearless n ▷ fear

fearlessly adv ▷ fear

fears n, v ▷ fear

fearsome adj terrifying

feasibilities n ▷ feasible

feasibility n ▷ feasible

feasible adj able to be done, possible > **feasibly** adv > **feasibility** n (pl -s)

feasibly adv ▷ feasible

feast n (pl -s) lavish meal ▶ v (-s, -ing, -ed) eat a feast

feasted v ▷ feast

feasting v ▷ feast

feasts n, v ▷ feast

feat n (pl -s) remarkable, skilful, or daring action

feather n (pl -s) one of the barbed shafts forming the plumage of birds ▶ v (-s, -ing, -ed) fit or cover with feathers > **feathered** adj > **feathery** adj (-rier, -riest)

feathered v, adj ▷ feather

featherier adj ▷ feather

featheriest adj ▷ feather

feathering v ▷ feather

feathers n, v ▷ feather

featherweight n (pl -s) boxer weighing up to 126lb (professional) or 57kg (amateur)

featherweights n ▷ featherweight

feathery adj ▷ feather

featliness n ▷ feat

feats n ▷ feat

feature n (pl -s) part of the face, such as the eyes ▶ v (-res, -ring, -red) have as a feature or be a feature in > **featureless** adj

featured v ▷ feature

featureless adj ▷ feature

features n, v ▷ feature

featuring v ▷ feature

febrile [fee-brile] adj feverish

feckless adj ineffectual or irresponsible

fecund adj fertile > **fecundity** n (pl -ties)

fecundities n ▷ fecund

fecundity n ▷ fecund

fed v ▷ feed

federal adj of a system in which power is divided between one central government and several regional governments > **federalism** n (pl -s) > **federalist** n (pl -s)

federalism n ▷ federal

federalisms n ▷ federal

federalist n ▷ federal

federalists n ▷ federal

federate v (-tes, -ting, -ted) unite in a federation

federated v ▷ federate

federates v ▷ federate

federating v ▷ federate

federation n (pl -s) union of several states, provinces, etc.

federations n ▷ federation

fedora [fid-or-a] n (pl -s) man's soft hat with a brim

fedoras n ▷ fedora

fee n (pl -s) charge paid to be allowed to do something

feeble adj (-r, -st) lacking physical or mental power > **feebleness** n (pl -es) > **feebly** adv

feebleminded adj unable to think or understand effectively

feebleness n ▷ feeble

feeblenesses n ▷ feeble

feebler adj ▷ feeble

feeblest adj ▷ feeble

feebly adv ▷ feeble

feed v (-s, -ing, fed) give food to ▶ n (pl -s) act of feeding

feedback n (pl -s) information received in response to something done

feedbacks n ▷ feedback

feeder n (pl -s) road or railway line linking outlying areas to the main traffic network

feeders n ▷ feeder

feeding *v* ▷ feed
feeds *v, n* ▷ feed
feel *v* (-s, -ing, felt) have a physical or emotional sensation of ▶ *n* (*pl* -s) act of feeling
feeler *n* (*pl* -s) organ of touch in some animals
feelers *n* ▷ feeler
feeling *n* (*pl* -s) emotional reaction
feelings *n* ▷ feeling ▶ *v* ▷ feel
feels *v, n* ▷ feel
fees *n* ▷ fee
feet *n* ▷ foot
feign [fane] *v* (-s, -ing, -ed) pretend
feigned *v* ▷ feign
feigning *v* ▷ feign
feigns *v* ▷ feign
feint[1] [faint] *n* (*pl* -s) sham attack or blow meant to distract an opponent ▶ *v* (-s, -ing, -ed) make a feint
feint[2] [faint] *n* (*pl* -s) narrow lines on ruled paper
feinted *v* ▷ feint[1]
feinting *v* ▷ feint[1]
feints *n, v* ▷ feint[1, 2]
feldspar *n* (*pl* -s) hard mineral that is the main constituent of igneous rocks
feldspars *n* ▷ feldspar
felicitations *pl n* congratulations
felicities *n* ▷ felicity
felicitous *adj* ▷ felicity
felicity *n* (*pl* -ties) happiness > **felicitous** *adj*
feline *adj* of cats ▶ *n* (*pl* -s) member of the cat family
felines *n* ▷ feline
fell[1] *v* ▷ fall
fell[2] *v* (-s, -ing, -ed) cut down (a tree)
fell[3] *adj* (-er, -est) deadly
fell[4] *n* (*pl* -s) (SCOT & N ENGLISH) mountain, hill, or moor
felled *v* ▷ fell[2]
feller *adj* ▷ fell[3]
fellest *adj* ▷ fell[3]
felling *v* ▷ fell[2]
felloe *n* (*pl* -oes) (segment of) the rim of a wheel
felloes *n* ▷ felloe
fellow *n* (*pl* -s) man or boy ▶ *adj* in the same group or condition
fellows *n* ▷ fellow
fellowship *n* (*pl* -s) sharing of aims or interests
fellowships *n* ▷ fellowship
fells *v, n* ▷ fell[2, 4]
felon *n* (*pl* -s) (CRIMINAL LAW) (formerly) person guilty of a felony
felonies *n* ▷ felony

felonious *adj* ▷ felony
felons *n* ▷ felon
felony *n* (*pl* -nies) serious crime > **felonious** *adj*
felspar *n* (*pl* -s) ▷ feldspar
felspars *n* ▷ felspar
felt[1] *v* ▷ feel
felt[2] *n* (*pl* -s) matted fabric made by bonding fibres by pressure
felts *n* ▷ felt[2]
female *adj* of the sex which bears offspring ▶ *n* (*pl* -s) female person or animal
females *n* ▷ female
feminine *adj* having qualities traditionally regarded as suitable for, or typical of, women > **femininity** *n* (*pl* -ties)
femininities *n* ▷ feminine
femininity *n* ▷ feminine
feminism *n* (*pl* -s) advocacy of equal rights for women > **feminist** *adj, n* (*pl* -s)
feminisms *n* ▷ feminism
feminist *n* ▷ feminism
feminists *n* ▷ feminism
femoral *adj* of the thigh
femur [fee-mer] *n* (*pl* -s) thighbone
femurs *n* ▷ femur
fen *n* (*pl* -s) (BRIT) low-lying flat marshy land
fence *n* (*pl* -s) barrier of posts linked by wire or wood, enclosing an area ▶ *v* (-ces, -cing, -ced) enclose with or as if with a fence
fenced *v* ▷ fence
fencer *n* ▷ fencing
fencers *n* ▷ fencing
fences *n, v* ▷ fence
fencing *n* (*pl* -s) sport of fighting with swords ▶ *v* ▷ fence > **fencer** *n* (*pl* -s)
fencings *n* ▷ fencing
fend *v* (-s, -ing, -ed) provide (for oneself)
fended *v* ▷ fend
fender *n* (*pl* -s) low metal frame in front of a fireplace
fenders *n* ▷ fender
fending *v* ▷ fend
fends *v* ▷ fend
fennel *n* (*pl* -s) fragrant plant whose seeds, leaves, and root are used in cookery
fennels *n* ▷ fennel
fens *n* ▷ fen
fenugreek *n* (*pl* -s) Mediterranean plant grown for its heavily scented seeds
fenugreeks *n* ▷ fenugreek
feral *adj* wild
ferment *n* (*pl* -s) commotion, unrest ▶ *v* (-s, -ing, -ed) undergo or cause to undergo fermentation
fermentation *n* (*pl* -s) reaction in which

an organic molecule splits into simpler substances, esp. the conversion of sugar to alcohol

fermentations n ▷ fermentation
fermented n ▷ ferment
fermenting v ▷ ferment
ferments n, v ▷ ferment
fern n (pl -s) flowerless plant with fine fronds
ferns n ▷ fern
ferocious adj savagely fierce or cruel > **ferocity** n (pl -ties)
ferocities n ▷ ferocious
ferocity n ▷ ferocious
ferret n (pl -s) tamed polecat used to catch rabbits or rats ▶ v (-s, -ing, -ed) hunt with ferrets
ferreted v ▷ ferret
ferreting v ▷ ferret
ferrets n, v ▷ ferret
ferric, ferrous adj of or containing iron
ferried v ▷ ferry
ferries n, v ▷ ferry
ferrous adj ▷ ferric
ferry n (pl -rries) boat for transporting people and vehicles ▶ v (-rries, -rrying, -rried) carry by ferry > **ferryman** n (pl -men)
ferrying v ▷ ferry
ferryman n ▷ ferry
ferrymen n ▷ ferry
fertile adj capable of producing young, crops, or vegetation > **fertility** n (pl -ties)
fertilities n ▷ fertile
fertility n ▷ fertile
fertilization n ▷ fertilize
fertilizations n ▷ fertilize
fertilize v (-zes, -zing, -zed) provide (an animal or plant) with sperm or pollen to bring about fertilization > **fertilization** n (pl -s)
fertilized v ▷ fertilize
fertilizer n (pl -s) substance added to the soil to increase its productivity
fertilizers n ▷ fertilizer
fertilizes v ▷ fertilize
fertilizing v ▷ fertilize
fervent, fervid adj intensely passionate and sincere > **fervently** adv
fervently adv ▷ fervent
fervid adj ▷ fervent
fervour n (pl -s) intensity of feeling
fervours n ▷ fervour
fescue n (pl -s) pasture and lawn grass with stiff narrow leaves
fescues n ▷ fescue
fester v (-s, -ing, -ed) grow worse and increasingly hostile

festered v ▷ fester
festering v ▷ fester
festers v ▷ fester
festival n (pl -s) organized series of special events or performances
festivals n ▷ festival
festive adj of or like a celebration
festivities n ▷ festivity
festivity n (pl -ties) happy celebration ▶ pl celebrations
festoon v (-s, -ing, -ed) hang decorations in loops
festooned v ▷ festoon
festooning v ▷ festoon
festoons v ▷ festoon
feta n (pl -as) white salty Greek cheese
fetal adj ▷ fetus
fetas n ▷ feta
fetch v (-es, -ing, -ed) go after and bring back (Informal)
fetched v ▷ fetch
fetches v ▷ fetch
fetching v ▷ fetch ▶ adj attractive
fete [fate] n (pl -s) gala, bazaar, etc., usu. held outdoors ▶ v (-tes, -ting, -ted) honour or entertain regally
feted v ▷ fete
fetes n, v ▷ fete
fetid adj (-er, -est) stinking
fetider adj ▷ fetid
fetidest adj ▷ fetid
feting v ▷ fete
fetish n (pl -es) form of behaviour in which sexual pleasure is derived from looking at or handling an inanimate object > **fetishism** n (pl -s) > **fetishist** (pl -s) n
fetishes n ▷ fetish
fetishism n ▷ fetish
fetishisms n ▷ fetish
fetishist n ▷ fetish
fetishists n ▷ fetish
fetlock n (pl -s) projection behind and above a horse's hoof
fetlocks n ▷ fetlock
fetter n (pl -s) chain or shackle for the foot ▶ pl restrictions ▶ v (-s, -ing, -ed) restrict
fettered v ▷ fetter
fettering v ▷ fetter
fetters n, v ▷ fetter
fettle n (pl -s) state of health or spirits
fettles n ▷ fettle
fetus [fee-tuss] n (pl -tuses) embryo of a mammal in the later stages of development > **fetal** adj
fetuses n ▷ fetus

feu *n* (*pl* -s) (in Scotland) right of use of land in return for a fixed annual payment

feud *n* (*pl* -s) long bitter hostility between two people or groups ▸ *v* (-s, -ing, -ed) carry on a feud

feudal *adj* of or like feudalism

feudalism *n* (*pl* -s) medieval system in which people held land from a lord, and in return worked and fought for him

  feudalisms *n* ▷ feudalism

  feuded *v* ▷ feud

  feuding *v* ▷ feud

  feuds *n, v* ▷ feud

  feus *n* ▷ feu

fever *n* (*pl* -s) (illness causing) high body temperature > **fevered** *adj*

  fevered *adj* ▷ fever

feverish *adj* suffering from fever > **feverishly** *adv*

  feverishly *adv* ▷ feverish

  fevers *n* ▷ fever

few *adj* (-er, -est) not many

  fewer *adj* ▷ few

  fewest *adj* ▷ few

fey *adj* (-er, -est) whimsically strange

  feyer *adj* ▷ fey

  feyest *adj* ▷ fey

fez *n* (*pl* fezzes) brimless tasselled cap, orig. from Turkey

  fezzes *n* ▷ fez

fiancé [fee-on-say] *n* (*pl* -cés) man engaged to be married ▸ *n fem* (*pl* -cées)

  fiancée *n* ▷ fiancé

  fiancées *n* ▷ fiancé

  fiancés *n* ▷ fiancé

fiasco *n* (*pl* -cos, -coes) ridiculous or humiliating failure

  fiascoes *n* ▷ fiasco

  fiascos *n* ▷ fiasco

fiat [fee-at] *n* (*pl* -s) arbitrary order

  fiats *n* ▷ fiat

fib *n* (*pl* -s) trivial lie ▸ *v* (-s, -bbing, -bbed) tell a lie > **fibber** *n* (*pl* -s)

  fibbed *v* ▷ fib

  fibber *n* ▷ fib

  fibbers *n* ▷ fib

  fibbing *v* ▷ fib

fibre *n* (*pl* -s) thread that can be spun into yarn > **fibrous** *adj*

fibreglass *n* (*pl* -es) material made of fine glass fibres

  fibreglasses *n* ▷ fibreglass

  fibres *n* ▷ fibre

fibro *n* (*pl* -ros) (AUST) mixture of cement and asbestos fibre, used in sheets for building

(also **fibrocement**)

fibroid [fibe-royd] *n* (*pl* -s) benign tumour composed of fibrous connective tissue

  fibroids *n* ▷ fibroid

  fibros *n* ▷ fibro

  fibrosites *n* ▷ fibrositis

fibrositis [fibe-roh-site-iss] *n* (*pl* -es) inflammation of the tissues of muscle sheaths

  fibrous *adj* ▷ fibre

  fibs *n, v* ▷ fib

fibula *n* (*pl* -lae, -las) slender outer bone of the lower leg

  fibulae *n* ▷ fibula

  fibulas *n* ▷ fibula

fiche [feesh] *n* (*pl* -s) sheet of film for storing publications in miniaturized form

  fiches *n* ▷ fiche

fickle *adj* changeable, inconstant > **fickleness** *n* (*pl* -ess)

  fickleness *n* ▷ fickle

  ficklenesses *n* ▷ fickle

fiction *n* (*pl* -s) literary works of the imagination, such as novels > **fictional** *adj*

  fictional *adj* ▷ fiction

fictionalize *v* (-zes, -zing, -zed) turn into fiction

  fictionalized *v* ▷ fictionalize

  fictionalizes *v* ▷ fictionalize

  fictionalizing *v* ▷ fictionalize

  fictions *n* ▷ fiction

fictitious *adj* not genuine

fiddle *n* (*pl* -s) violin (*Informal*) ▸ *v* (-les, -ling, -led) play the violin

  fiddled *v* ▷ fiddle

  fiddles *n, v* ▷ fiddle

fiddlesticks *interj* expression of annoyance or disagreement

  fiddlier *adj* ▷ fiddly

  fiddliest *adj* ▷ fiddly

  fiddling *v* ▷ fiddle ▸ *adj* trivial

fiddly *adj* (-lier, -liest) awkward to do or use

  fidelities *n* ▷ fidelity

fidelity *n* (*pl* -ies) faithfulness

fidget *v* (-s, -ing, -ed) move about restlessly ▸ *n* (*pl* -s) person who fidgets ▸ *pl* restlessness > **fidgety** *adj* (-tier, -tiest)

  fidgeted *v* ▷ fidget

  fidgetier *adj* ▷ fidget

  fidgetiest *adj* ▷ fidget

  fidgeting *v* ▷ fidget

  fidgets *v, n* ▷ fidget

  fidgety *adj* ▷ fidget

  fiduciaries *n* ▷ fiduciary

fiduciary [fid-yew-she-er-ee] (LAW) *n* (*pl* -ies)

person bound to act for someone else's benefit, as a trustee ▸ *adj* of a trust or trustee

fief [feef] *n* (*pl* -s) (HIST) land granted by a lord in return for war service
fiefs *n* ▷ fief

field *n* (*pl* -s) enclosed piece of agricultural land ▸ *v* (-s, -ing, -ed) (SPORT) catch and return (a ball)
fielded *v* ▷ field
fielder *n* (*pl* -s) (SPORT) player whose task is to field the ball
fielders *n* ▷ fielder
fieldfare *n* (*pl* -s) type of large Old World thrush
fieldfares *n* ▷ fieldfare
fielding *v* ▷ field
fields *n*, *v* ▷ field
fieldwork *n* (*pl* -s) investigation made in the field as opposed to the classroom or the laboratory
fieldworks *n* ▷ fieldwork
fiend [feend] *n* (*pl* -s) evil spirit (*Informal*) > **fiendish** *adj* > **fiendishly** *adv*
fiendish *adj* ▷ fiend
fiendishly *adv* ▷ fiend
fiends *n* ▷ fiend
fierce *adj* (-r, -st) wild or aggressive > **fiercely** *adv* > **fierceness** *n* (*pl* -es)
fiercely *adv* ▷ fierce
fierceness *n* ▷ fierce
fiercenesses *n* ▷ fierce
fiercer *adj* ▷ fierce
fiercest *adj* ▷ fierce
fierier *adj* ▷ fiery
fieriest *adj* ▷ fiery
fiery *adj* (-rier, -riest) consisting of or like fire
fiesta *n* (*pl* -s) religious festival, carnival
fiestas *n* ▷ fiesta
fife *n* (*pl* -s) small high-pitched flute
fifes *n* ▷ fife
fifteen *adj*, *n* (*pl* -s) five and ten > **fifteenth** *adj*, *n* (*pl* -s)
fifteens *n* ▷ fifteen
fifteenth *adj*, *n* ▷ fifteen
fifteenths *n* ▷ fifteenth
fifth *adj*, *n* (*pl* -s) (of) number five in a series
fifths *n* ▷ fifth
fifties *n* ▷ fifty
fiftieth *adj*, *n* ▷ fifty
fiftieths *n* ▷ fifty
fifty *adj*, *n* (*pl* -ties) five times ten > **fiftieth** *adj*, *n* (*pl* -s)
fig *n* (*pl* -s) soft pear-shaped fruit
fight *v* (-s, -ing, fought) struggle (against) in battle or physical combat ▸ *n* (*pl* -s) aggressive conflict between two (groups of) people

fighter *n* (*pl* -s) boxer
fighters *n* ▷ fighter
fighting *v* ▷ fight
fights *n*, *v* ▷ fight
figment *n* (*pl* -s) something imagined
figments *n* ▷ figment
figs *n* ▷ fig
figurative *adj* (of language) abstract, imaginative, or symbolic > **figuratively** *adv*
figuratively *adv* ▷ figurative
figure *n* (*pl* -s) numerical symbol (MATHS) ▸ *v* (-res, -ring, -red) consider, conclude
figured *v* ▷ figure
figurehead *n* (*pl* -s) nominal leader
figureheads *n* ▷ figurehead
figures *n*, *v* ▷ figure
figurine *n* (*pl* -s) statuette
figurines *n* ▷ figurine
figuring *v* ▷ figure
filament *n* (*pl* -s) fine wire in a light bulb that gives out light
filaments *n* ▷ filament
filbert *n* (*pl* -s) hazelnut
filberts *n* ▷ filbert
filch *v* (-es, -ing, -ed) steal (small amounts)
filched *v* ▷ filch
filches *v* ▷ filch
filching *v* ▷ filch
file[1] *n* (*pl* -s) box or folder used to keep documents in order ▸ *v* (-les, -ling, -led) place (a document) in a file
file[2] *n* (*pl* -s) tool with a roughened blade for smoothing or shaping ▸ *v* (-les, -ling, -led) shape or smooth with a file
filed *v* ▷ file[1, 2]
files *n*, *v* ▷ file[1, 2]
filial *adj* of or befitting a son or daughter
filibuster *n* (*pl* -s) obstruction of legislation by making long speeches ▸ *v* (-s, -ing, -ed) obstruct (legislation) with such delaying tactics
filibustered *v* ▷ filibuster
filibustering *v* ▷ filibuster
filibusters *n*, *v* ▷ filibuster
filigree *n* (*pl* -s) delicate ornamental work of gold or silver wire ▸ *adj* made of filigree
filigrees *n* ▷ filigree
filing *v* ▷ file[1, 2]
filings *pl n* shavings removed by a file
fill *v* (-s, -ing, -ed) make or become full
filled *v* ▷ fill
filler *n* (*pl* -s) substance that fills a gap or increases bulk
fillers *n* ▷ filler
fillet *n* (*pl* -s) boneless piece of meat or fish ▸ *v*

(-s, -ing, -ed) remove the bones from

filleted v ▷ fillet

filleting v ▷ fillet

fillets n, v ▷ fillet

fillies n ▷ filly

filling n (pl -s) substance that fills a gap or cavity, esp. in a tooth ▶ adj (of food) substantial and satisfying ▶ v ▷ fill

fillings n ▷ filling

fillip n (pl -s) something that adds stimulation or enjoyment

fillips n ▷ fillip

fills v ▷ fill

filly n (pl -lies) young female horse

film n (pl -s) sequence of images projected on a screen, creating the illusion of movement ▶ v (-s, -ing, -ed) photograph with a movie or video camera ▶ adj connected with films or the cinema

filmed v ▷ film

filmier adj ▷ filmy

filmiest adj ▷ filmy

filming v ▷ film

films n, v ▷ film

filmy adj (-mier, -miest) very thin, delicate

filter n (pl -s) material or device permitting fluid to pass but retaining solid particles ▶ v (-s, -ing, -ed) remove impurities from (a substance) with a filter

filtered v ▷ filter

filtering v ▷ filter

filters n, v ▷ filter

filth n (pl -s) disgusting dirt > **filthy** adj (-thier, -thiest) > **filthiness** n (pl -es)

filthier adj ▷ filth

filthiest adj ▷ filth

filthiness n ▷ filth

filthinesses n ▷ filth

filths n ▷ filth

filthy adj ▷ filth

filtrate n (pl -s) filtered gas or liquid ▶ v (-tes, -ting, -ted) remove impurities with a filter > **filtration** n (pl -s)

filtrated v ▷ filtrate

filtrates n, v ▷ filtrate

filtrating v ▷ filtrate

filtration n ▷ filtrate

filtrations n ▷ filtrate

fin n (pl -s) projection from a fish's body enabling it to balance and swim

finagle [fin-**nay**-gl] v (-les, -ling, -led) get or achieve by craftiness or trickery

finagled v ▷ finagle

finagles v ▷ finagle

finagling v ▷ finagle

final adj at the end ▶ n (pl -s) deciding contest between winners of previous rounds in a competition ▶ pl (BRIT & S AFR) last examinations in an educational course > **finally** adv > **finality** n (pl -ties)

finale [fin-**nah**-lee] n (pl -s) n concluding part of a dramatic performance or musical work

finales n ▷ finale

finalist n (pl -s) competitor in a final

finalists n ▷ finalist

finalities n ▷ final

finality n ▷ final

finalize v (-zes, -zing, -zed) put into final form

finalized v ▷ finalize

finalizes v ▷ finalize

finalizing v ▷ finalize

finally adv ▷ final

finals n ▷ final

finance v (-ces, -cing, -ced) provide or obtain funds for ▶ n (pl -s) management of money, loans, or credits ▶ pl money resources > **financial** adj > **financially** adv

financed v ▷ finance

finances v, n ▷ finance

financial adj ▷ finance

financially adv ▷ finance

financier n (pl -s) person involved in large-scale financial business

financiers n ▷ financier

financing v ▷ finance

finch n (pl -es) small songbird with a short strong beak

finches n ▷ finch

find v (-s, -ing, found) discover by chance ▶ n (pl -s) person or thing found, esp. when valuable > **finder** n (pl -s)

finder n ▷ find

finders n ▷ find

finding n (pl -s) conclusion from an investigation ▶ v ▷ find

findings n ▷ finding

finds v, n ▷ find

fine[1] adj (-r, -st) very good > **finely** adv > **fineness** n (pl -es)

fine[2] n (pl -s) payment imposed as a penalty ▶ v (-nes, -ning, -ned) impose a fine on

fined v ▷ fine[2]

finely adv ▷ fine[1]

fineness n ▷ fine[1]

finenesses n ▷ fine[1]

finer adj ▷ fine[1]

fineries n ▷ finery

finery n (pl -ries) showy clothing

fines n, v ▷ fine[1, 2]

finesse [fin-**ness**] n (pl -s) delicate skill

finesses n ▷ finesse
finest adj ▷ fine¹
finger n (pl -s) one of the four long jointed parts of the hand ▶ v (-s, -ing, -ed) touch or handle with the fingers
fingerboard n part of a stringed instrument against which the strings are pressed
fingerboards n ▷ fingerboard
fingered v ▷ finger
fingering n technique of using the fingers in playing a musical instrument ▶ v ▷ finger
fingerprint n (pl -s) impression of the ridges on the tip of the finger ▶ v take the fingerprints of (someone)
fingerprints n ▷ fingerprint
fingers n, v ▷ finger
finickier adj ▷ finicky
finickiest adj ▷ finicky
finicky adj (-ckier, -ckiest) excessively particular, fussy
fining v ▷ fine
finish v (-es, -ing, -ed) bring to an end, stop ▶ n (pl -es) end, last part
finished v ▷ finish
finishes v, n ▷ finish
finishing v ▷ finish
finite adj having limits in space, time, or size
fins n ▷ fin
fiord n (pl -s) ▷ fjord
fiords n ▷ fiord
fir n (pl -s) pyramid-shaped tree with needle-like leaves and erect cones
fire n (pl -s) state of combustion producing heat, flames, and smoke ▶ v (-res, -ring, -red) operate (a weapon) so that a bullet or missile is released
firearm n (pl -s) rifle, pistol, or shotgun
firearms n ▷ firearms
firebrand n (pl -s) person who causes unrest
firebrands n ▷ firebrand
firebreak n strip of cleared land to stop the advance of a fire
firebreaks n ▷ firebreak
fired v ▷ fire
firedamp n (pl -s) explosive gas, composed mainly of methane, formed in mines
firedamps n ▷ firedamp
firefighter n (pl -s) member of a fire brigade
firefighters n ▷ firefighter
fireflies n ▷ firefly
firefly n (pl -flies) beetle that glows in the dark
fireguard n (pl -s) protective grating in front of a fire
fireguards n ▷ fireguard
fireplace n (pl -s) recess in a room for a fire

fireplaces n ▷ fireplace
fires n, v ▷ fire
firewall n (pl -s) (COMPUTERS) computer that prevents unauthorized access to a computer network from the Internet
firewalls n ▷ firewall
firework n (pl -s) device containing chemicals that is ignited to produce spectacular explosions and coloured sparks ▶ pl show of fireworks
fireworks n ▷ firework
firing v ▷ fire
firm¹ adj (-er, -est) not soft or yielding ▶ adv in an unyielding manner ▶ v (-s, -ing, -ed) make or become firm > **firmly** adv > **firmness** n (pl -es)
firm² n (pl -s) business company
firmament n (pl -s) (Lit) sky or the heavens
firmaments n ▷ firmament
firmed v ▷ firm¹
firmer adj ▷ firm¹
firmest adj ▷ firm¹
firming v ▷ firm¹
firmly adv ▷ firm¹
firmness n ▷ firm¹
firmnesses n ▷ firm¹
firms v, n ▷ firm¹, ²
firs n ▷ fir
first adj earliest in time or order ▶ n (pl -s) person or thing coming before all others ▶ adv before anything else > **firstly** adv
firsthand adj, adv (obtained) directly from the original source
firstly adv ▷ first
firsts n ▷ first
firth n (pl -s) narrow inlet of the sea, esp. in Scotland
firths n ▷ firth
fiscal adj of government finances, esp. taxes
fish n (pl fish, fishes) cold-blooded vertebrate with gills, that lives in water ▶ v (-es, -ing, -ed) try to catch fish
fished v ▷ fish
fisheries n ▷ fishery
fisherman n (pl -men) person who catches fish for a living or for pleasure
fishermen n ▷ fisherman
fishery n (pl -ries) area of the sea used for fishing
fishes n, v ▷ fish
fishfinger n (pl -s) oblong piece of fish covered in breadcrumbs
fishfingers n ▷ fishfinger
fishier adj ▷ fishy
fishiest adj ▷ fishy

fishing v ▷ fish

fishmeal n (pl -s) dried ground fish used as animal feed or fertilizer

fishmeals n ▷ fishmeal

fishmonger n (pl -s) seller of fish

fishmongers n ▷ fishmonger

fishnet n (pl -s) open mesh fabric

fishnets n ▷ fishnet

fishplate n (pl -s) metal plate holding rails together

fishplates n ▷ fishplate

fishwife n (pl -wives) coarse scolding woman

fishwives n ▷ fishwife

fishy adj (-shier, -shiest) of or like fish

fissile adj capable of undergoing nuclear fission

fission n (pl -s) splitting > **fissionable** adj

fissionable adj ▷ fission

fissions n ▷ fission

fissure [fish-er] n (pl -s) long narrow cleft or crack

fissures n ▷ fissure

fist n (pl -s) clenched hand

fisticuffs pl n fighting with the fists

fists n ▷ fist

fit[1] v (-s, -tting, -tted) be appropriate or suitable for ▸ adj appropriate ▸ n (-tter, -ttest) (pl -s) way in which something fits > **fitness** n (pl -es)

fit[2] n (pl -s) sudden attack or convulsion, such as an epileptic seizure

fitful adj occurring in irregular spells > **fitfully** adv

fitfully adv ▷ fitful

fitment n (pl -s) detachable part of the furnishings of a room

fitments n ▷ fitment

fitness n ▷ fit[1]

fitnesses n ▷ fit[1]

fits v, n ▷ fit[1, 2]

fitted v ▷ fit[1]

fitter n (pl -s) person skilled in the installation and adjustment of machinery ▸ adj ▷ fit[1]

fitters n ▷ fitter

fittest adj ▷ fit[1]

fitting adj appropriate, suitable ▸ n (pl -s) accessory or part ▸ pl furnishings and accessories in a building ▸ v ▷ fit

fittings n ▷ fitting

five adj, n (pl -s) one more than four

fiver n (pl -s) (Informal) five-pound note

fivers n ▷ fiver

fives n ball game resembling squash but played with bats or the hands ▸ n ▷ five

fix v (-xes, -xing, -xed) make or become firm, stable, or secure ▸ n (pl -es) (Informal) difficult situation > **fixed** adj > **fixedly** adv steadily

fixated adj obsessed

fixation n (pl -s) obsessive interest in something

fixations n ▷ fixation

fixative n (pl -s) liquid used to preserve or hold things in place

fixatives n ▷ fixative

fixed v, adj ▷ fix

fixedly adv ▷ fix

fixer n (pl -s) solution used to make a photographic image permanent

fixers n ▷ fixer

fixes v, n ▷ fix

fixing v ▷ fix

fixture n (pl -s) permanently fitted piece of household equipment

fixtures n ▷ fixture

fizz v (-es, -ing, -ed) make a hissing or bubbling noise ▸ n (pl -es) hissing or bubbling noise > **fizzy** adj (-zier, -zziest)

fizzed v ▷ fizz

fizzes v ▷ fizz

fizzier adj ▷ fizz

fizziest adj ▷ fizz

fizzinesses n ▷ fizz

fizzing v ▷ fizz

fizzle v (-les, -ling, -led) make a weak hissing or bubbling sound

fizzled v ▷ fizzle

fizzles v ▷ fizzle

fizzling v ▷ fizzle

fizzy adj ▷ fizz

fjord [fee-**ord**] n (pl -s) long narrow inlet of the sea between cliffs, esp. in Norway

fjords n ▷ fjord

flab n (pl -s) (Informal) unsightly body fat

flabbergasted adj completely astonished

flabbier adj ▷ flabby

flabbiest adj ▷ flabby

flabby adj (-bbier, -bbiest) having flabby flesh

flabs n ▷ flab

flaccid [**flas**-sid] adj (-er, -est) soft and limp > **flaccidity** n (pl -ties)

flaccider adj ▷ flaccid

flaccidest adj ▷ flaccid

flaccidities n ▷ flaccid

flaccidity n ▷ flaccid

flag[1] n (pl -s) piece of cloth attached to a pole as an emblem or signal ▸ v (-s, -gging, -gged) mark with a flag or sticker

flag[2] v (-s, -gging, -gged) lose enthusiasm or vigour

flag[3], **flagstone** (pl -s) n flat paving-stone

flagellant *n* (*pl* -s) person who whips himself or herself
   flagellants *n* ▷ flagellant
flagellate [flaj-a-late] *v* (-tes, -ting, -ted) whip, esp. in religious penance or for sexual pleasure > **flagellation** *n* (*pl* -s)
   flagellated *v* ▷ flagellate
   flagellates *v* ▷ flagellate
   flagellating *v* ▷ flagellate
   flagellation *n* ▷ flagellate
   flagellations *n* ▷ flagellate
flageolet [flaj-a-let] *n* (*pl* -s) small instrument like a recorder
   flageolets *n* ▷ flageolet
flagged *adj* paved with flagstones ▶ *v* ▷ flag[1, 2]
   flagged *v* ▷ flag[1, 2]
   flagging *v* ▷ flag[1, 2]
flagon *n* (*pl* -s) wide bottle for wine or cider
   flagons *n* ▷ flagon
flagpole, flagstaff (*pl* -s) *n* pole for a flag
   flagpoles *n* ▷ flagpole
flagrant [flayg-rant] *adj* openly outrageous > **flagrantly** *adv*
   flagrantly *adv* ▷ flagrant
   flagrantnesses *n* ▷ flagrant
   flags *v*, *n* ▷ flag[1, 2, 3]
flagship *n* (*pl* -s) admiral's ship
   flagships *n* ▷ flagship
   flagstaff *n* ▷ flagpole
   flagstaffs *n* ▷ flagpole
   flagstone *n* ▷ flag[3]
   flagstones *n* ▷ flag[3]
flail *v* (-s, -ing, -ed) wave about wildly ▶ *n* (*pl* -s) tool formerly used for threshing grain
   flailed *v* ▷ flail
   flailing *v* ▷ flail
   flails *v*, *n* ▷ flail
flair *n* (*pl* -s) natural ability
   flairs *n* ▷ flair
flak *n* (*pl* -s) anti-aircraft fire
flake[1] *n* (*pl* -s) small thin piece, esp. chipped off something ▶ *v* (-kes, -king, -ked) peel off in flakes > **flaky** *adj* (-kier, -kiest)
flake[2] *n* (*pl* -s) (in Australia) the commercial name for the meat of the gummy shark
   flaked *v* ▷ flake
   flakes *v*, *n* ▷ flake[1, 2]
   flakier *adj* ▷ flaky
   flakiest *adj* ▷ flaky
   flaking *v* ▷ flake
   flaks *n* ▷ flak
   flaky *adj* ▷ flake[1]
flambé [flahm-bay] *v* (-bés, -béing, -béed) cook or serve (food) in flaming brandy
   flambéed *v* ▷ flambé

   flambéing *v* ▷ flambé
   flambés *v* ▷ flambé
   flamboyances *n* ▷ flamboyant
flamboyant *adj* behaving in a very noticeable, extravagant way > **flamboyance** *n* (*pl* -s)
   flamboyance *n* ▷ flamboyant
flame *n* (*pl* -s) luminous burning gas coming from burning material ▶ *v* (-mes, -ming, -med) burn brightly
   flamed *v* ▷ flame
flamenco *n* (*pl* -cos) rhythmical Spanish dance accompanied by a guitar and vocalist
   flamencos *n* ▷ flamenco
   flames *n*, *v* ▷ flame
   flaming *v* ▷ flame
flamingo *n* (*pl* -gos, -goes) large pink wading bird with a long neck and legs
   flamingoes *n* ▷ flamingo
   flamingos *n* ▷ flamingo
   flammabilities *n* ▷ flammable
   flammability *n* ▷ flammable
flammable *adj* easily set on fire > **flammability** *n* (*pl* -ties)
flan *n* (*pl* -s) open sweet or savoury tart
flange *n* (*pl* -s) projecting rim or collar
   flanges *n* ▷ flange
flank *n* (*pl* -s) part of the side between the hips and ribs ▶ *v* (-s, -ing, -ed) be at or move along the side of
   flanked *v* ▷ flank
   flanking *v* ▷ flank
   flanks *n*, *v* ▷ flank
flannel *n* (*pl* -s) (BRIT) small piece of cloth for washing the face ▶ *pl* trousers made of flannel ▶ *v* (-s, -nelling, -nelled) (*Informal*) talk evasively
flannelette *n* (*pl* -s) cotton imitation of flannel
   flannelettes *n* ▷ flannelette
   flannelled *v* ▷ flannel
   flannelling *v* ▷ flannel
   flannels *n*, *v* ▷ flannel
   flans *n* ▷ flan
flap *v* (-s, -pping, -pped) move back and forwards or up and down ▶ *n* (*pl* -s) action or sound of flapping
flapjack *n* (*pl* -s) chewy biscuit made with oats
   flapjacks *n* ▷ flapjack
   flapped *v* ▷ flap
   flapping *v* ▷ flap
   flaps *v*, *n* ▷ flap
flare *v* (-res, -ring, -red) blaze with a sudden unsteady flame ▶ *n* (*pl* -s) sudden unsteady flame ▶ *pl* flared trousers
flared *adj* (of a skirt or trousers) becoming wider towards the hem ▶ *v* ▷ flare

flares v, n ▷ flare

flaring v ▷ flare

flash n (pl -es) sudden burst of light or flame ▶ v (-es, -ing, -ed) (cause to) burst into flame

flashback n (pl -s) scene in a book, play, or film, that shows earlier events

flashbacks n ▷ flashback

flashed v ▷ flash

flasher n (pl -s) (Slang) man who exposes himself indecently

flashers n ▷ flasher

flashes n, v ▷ flash

flashier adj ▷ flashy

flashiest adj ▷ flashy

flashing n (pl -s) watertight material used to cover joins in a roof ▶ v ▷ flash

flashings n ▷ flashing

flashlight n (pl -s) (US) torch

flashlights n ▷ flashlight

flashy adj (-shier, -shiest) vulgarly showy

flask n (pl -s) ▷ **vacuum flask** flat bottle for carrying alcoholic drink in the pocket

flasks n ▷ flask

flat[1] adj (-tter, -ttest) level and horizontal ▶ adv in or into a flat position ▶ n (pl -s) (MUSIC) symbol lowering the pitch of a note by a semitone > **flatly** adv > **flatness** n (pl -es) > **flatten** v (-s, -ing, -ed)

flat[2] n (pl -s) set of rooms for living in which are part of a larger building ▶ v (-s, -tting, -tted) (AUST & NZ) live in a flat

flatfish n (pl -fish, -fishes) sea fish, such as the sole, which has a flat body

flatfishes n ▷ flatfish

flatlet n (pl -s) (BRIT, AUST & S AFR) small flat

flatlets n ▷ flatlet

flatly adv ▷ flat[1]

flatmate n (pl -s) person with whom one shares a flat

flatmates n ▷ flatmate

flatness n ▷ flat[1]

flatnesses n ▷ flat[1]

flat-pack adj (of furniture, etc.) supplied in pieces in a flat box for assembly by the buyer

flats n, v ▷ flat[1, 2]

flatted v ▷ flat[2]

flatten v ▷ flat[1]

flattened v ▷ flat[1]

flattening v ▷ flat[1]

flatter[1] v (-s, -ing, -ed) praise insincerely > **flatterer** n (pl -s) > **flattery** n (pl -ries)

flatter[2] adj ▷ flat[1]

flattered v ▷ flatter[1]

flatterer n ▷ flatter

flatterers n ▷ flatter

flatteries n ▷ flatter

flattering v ▷ flatter[1]

flatters v ▷ flatter[1]

flattery n ▷ flatter

flattest adj ▷ flat[1]

flattie n (pl -s) (NZ & S AFR) (Informal) flat tyre

flatties n ▷ flattie

flatting v ▷ flat[2]

flatulence n ▷ flatulent

flatulences n ▷ flatulent

flatulent adj suffering from or caused by too much gas in the intestines > **flatulence** n (pl -s)

flaunt v (-s, -ing, -ed) display (oneself or one's possessions) arrogantly

flaunted v ▷ flaunt

flaunting v ▷ flaunt

flaunts v ▷ flaunt

flautist n (pl -s) flute player

flautists n ▷ flautist

flavour n (pl -s) distinctive taste ▶ v (-s, -ing, -ed) give flavour to > **flavourless** adj

flavoured v ▷ flavour

flavouring n (pl -s) substance used to flavour food ▶ v ▷ flavour

flavourings n ▷ flavouring

flavourless adj ▷ flavour

flavours n, v ▷ flavour

flaw n (pl -s) imperfection or blemish > **flawed** adj > **flawless** adj

flawed adj ▷ flaw

flawless adj ▷ flaw

flaws n ▷ flaw

flax n (pl -es) plant grown for its stem fibres and seeds

flaxen adj (of hair) pale yellow

flaxes n ▷ flax

flay v (-s, -ing, -ed) strip the skin off

flayed v ▷ flay

flaying v ▷ flay

flays v ▷ flay

flea n (pl -s) small wingless jumping bloodsucking insect

fleapit n (pl -s) (Informal) shabby cinema or theatre

fleapits n ▷ fleapit

fleas n ▷ flea

fleck n (pl -s) small mark, streak, or speck ▶ v (-s, -ing, -ed) speckle

flecked n ▷ fleck

flecking v ▷ fleck

flecks n, v ▷ fleck

fled v ▷ flee

fledged adj (of young birds) able to fly

fledgelings n ▷ fledgling

fledgling, fledgeling (*pl* -s) *n* young bird ▶ *adj* new or inexperienced
  fledglings *n* ▷ fledgling
flee *v* (-lees, -leeing, fled) run away (from)
fleece *n* (*pl* -s) sheep's coat of wool ▶ *v* (-ces, -cing, -ced) defraud or overcharge
  fleeced *v* ▷ fleece
  fleeces *n*, *v* ▷ fleece
  fleecier *adj* ▷ fleecy
  fleeciest *adj* ▷ fleecy
  fleecing *v* ▷ fleece
fleecy *adj* (-cier, -ciest) made of or like fleece
  fleeing *v* ▷ flee
  flees *v* ▷ flee
fleet¹ *n* (*pl* -s) number of warships organized as a unit
fleet² *adj* swift in movement
fleeting *adj* rapid and soon passing
  > **fleetingly** *adv*
  fleetingly *adv* ▷ fleeting
  fleets *n* ▷ fleet
flesh *n* (*pl* -es) soft part of a human or animal body (*Informal*)
  fleshes *n* ▷ flesh
  fleshier *adj* ▷ fleshy
  fleshiest *adj* ▷ fleshy
fleshly *adj* carnal
fleshy *adj* (-shier, -shiest) plump
  flew *v* ▷ fly¹
flex *n* (*pl* -xes) flexible insulated electric cable ▶ *v* (-xes, -xing, -xed) bend
  flexed *v* ▷ flex
  flexes *n*, *v* ▷ flex
  flexibility *n* ▷ flexible
flexible *adj* easily bent > **flexibly** *adv*
  > **flexibility** *n* (*pl* -ties)
  flexibilities *n* ▷ flexible
  flexibly *adv* ▷ flexible
  flexing *v* ▷ flex
flexitime, flextime *n* (*pl* -s) system permitting variation in starting and finishing times of work
  flexitimes *n* ▷ flexitime
  flextimes *n* ▷ flexitime
flick *v* (-s, -ing, -ed) touch or move with the finger or hand in a quick movement ▶ *n* (*pl* -s) tap or quick stroke ▶ *pl* (*Slang*) the cinema
  flicked *v* ▷ flick
flicker *v* (-s, -ing, -ed) shine unsteadily or intermittently ▶ *n* (*pl* -s) unsteady brief light
  flickered *v* ▷ flicker
  flickering *v* ▷ flicker
  flickers *v*, *n* ▷ flicker
  flicking *v* ▷ flick
  flicks *v*, *n* ▷ flick

flier¹ *adj* ▷ fly³
flier² *n* ▷ flyer
fliers *n* ▷ flyer
flies *v*, *n* ▷ fly¹, ²
fliest *adj* ▷ fly³
flight¹ *n* (*pl* -s) journey by air
flight² *n* (*pl* -s) act of running away
  flightier *adj* ▷ flighty
  flightiest *adj* ▷ flighty
flightless *adj* (of certain birds or insects) unable to fly
  flights *n* ▷ flight¹, ²
flighty *adj* (-tier, -tiest) frivolous and fickle
  flimsier *adj* ▷ flimsy
  flimsiest *adj* ▷ flimsy
  flimsily *adv* ▷ flimsy
  flimsiness *n* ▷ flimsy
  flimsinesses *n* ▷ flimsy
flimsy *adj* (-sier, -siest) not strong or substantial > **flimsily** *adv* > **flimsiness** *n* (*pl* -es)
flinch *v* (-es, -ing, -ed) draw back or wince, as from pain
  flinched *v* ▷ flinch
  flinches *v* ▷ flinch
  flinching *v* ▷ flinch
fling *v* (-s, -ing, flung) throw, send, or move forcefully or hurriedly ▶ *n* (*pl* -s) spell of self-indulgent enjoyment
  flinging *v* ▷ fling
  flings *v*, *n* ▷ fling
flint *n* (*pl* -s) hard grey stone
  flintier *adj* ▷ flinty
  flintiest *adj* ▷ flinty
  flints *n* ▷ flint
flinty (-tier, -tiest) *adj* cruel
flip *v* (-s, -pping, -pped) throw (something small or light) carelessly ▶ *adj* (*Informal*) flippant
  flippancies *n* ▷ flippant
  flippancy *n* ▷ flippant
flippant *adj* treating serious things lightly
  > **flippancy** *n* (*pl* -cies)
  flipped *v* ▷ flip
flipper (*pl* -s) *n* limb of a sea animal adapted for swimming
  flippers *n* ▷ flipper
  flipping *v* ▷ flip
  flips *v* ▷ flip
flirt *v* (-s, -ing, -ed) behave as if sexually attracted to someone ▶ *n* (*pl* -s) person who flirts > **flirtation** *n* (*pl* -s) > **flirtatious** *adj*
  flirtation *n* ▷ flirt
  flirtations *n* ▷ flirt
  flirtatious *adj* ▷ flirt

flirted *v* ▷ flirt

flirting *v* ▷ flirt

flirts *v*, *n* ▷ flirt

flit *v* (-s, -tting, -tted) move lightly and rapidly ▶ *n* (*pl* -s) act of flitting

flits *v*, *n* ▷ flit

flitted *v* ▷ flit

flitting *v* ▷ flit

float *v* (-s, -ing, -ed) rest on the surface of a liquid ▶ *n* (*pl* -s) light object used to help someone or something float

floated *v* ▷ float

floating *adj* moving about, changing ▶ *v* ▷ float

floats *v*, *n* ▷ float

flock[1] *n* (*pl* -s) number of animals of one kind together ▶ *v* (-s, -ing, -ed) gather in a crowd

flock[2] *n* (*pl* -s) wool or cotton waste used as stuffing ▶ *adj* (of wallpaper) with a velvety raised pattern

flocked *v* ▷ flock[1]

flocking *v* ▷ flock[1]

flocks *n*, *v* ▷ flock[1, 2]

floe *n* (*pl* -s) sheet of floating ice

floes *n* ▷ floe

flog *v* (-s, -gging, -gged) beat with a whip or stick > **flogging** *n* (*pl* -s)

flogged *v* ▷ flog

flogging *v*, *n* ▷ flog

floggings *n* ▷ flog

flogs *v* ▷ flog

flood *n* (*pl* -s) overflow of water onto a normally dry area ▶ *v* (-s, -ing, -ed) cover or become covered with water

flooded *v* ▷ flood

floodgate *n* (*pl* -s) gate used to control the flow of water

floodgates *n* ▷ floodgate

flooding *v* ▷ flood

floodlight *n* (*pl* -s) lamp that casts a broad intense beam of light ▶ *v* (-lights, -lighting, -lit) illuminate by floodlight

floodlighting *v* ▷ floodlight

floodlights *n*, *v* ▷ floodlight

floodlit *v* ▷ floodlight

floods *n*, *v* ▷ flood

floor *n* (*pl* -s) lower surface of a room ▶ *v* (-s, -ing, -ed) knock down

floored *adj* covered with a floor ▶ *v* ▷ floor

flooring *n* (*pl* -s) material for floors ▶ *v* ▷ floor

floorings *n* ▷ flooring

floors *n*, *v* ▷ floor

floozies *n* ▷ floozy

floozy *n* (*pl* -zies) (*Old-fashioned slang*) disreputable woman

flop *v* (-s, -pping, -pped) bend, fall, or collapse loosely or carelessly ▶ *n* (*pl* -s) failure

flopped *v* ▷ flop

floppier *adj* ▷ floppy

floppies *n* ▷ floppy

floppiest *adj* ▷ floppy

flopping *v* ▷ flop

floppy *adj* (-ppier, -ppiest) hanging downwards, loose ▶ *n* (*pl* -ppies) (COMPUTERS) a flexible magnetic disk that stores information

flops *v*, *n* ▷ flop

flora *n* (*pl* -s) plants of a given place or time

floral *adj* consisting of or decorated with flowers

floras *n* ▷ flora

floret *n* (*pl* -s) small flower forming part of a composite flower head

florets *n* ▷ floret

floribunda *n* (*pl* -s) type of rose whose flowers grow in large clusters

floribundas *n* ▷ floribunda

florid *adj* (-er, -est) with a red or flushed complexion

florider *adj* ▷ florid

floridest *adj* ▷ florid

florin *n* (*pl* -s) former British and Australian coin

florins *n* ▷ florin

florist *n* (*pl* -s) seller of flowers

florists *n* ▷ florist

floss *n* (*pl* -es) fine silky fibres

flosses *n* ▷ floss

flotation *n* (*pl* -s) launching or financing of a business enterprise

flotations *n* ▷ flotation

flotilla *n* (*pl* -s) small fleet or fleet of small ships

flotillas *n* ▷ flotilla

flotsam *n* (*pl* -s) floating wreckage

flotsams *n* ▷ flotsam

flounce[1] *v* (-ces, -cing, -ced) go with emphatic movements ▶ *n* (*pl* -s) flouncing movement

flounce[2] *n* (*pl* -s) ornamental frill on a garment

flounced *v* ▷ flounce

flounces *v*, *n* ▷ flounce[1, 2]

flouncing *v* ▷ flounce

flounder[1] *v* (-s, -ing, -ed) move with difficulty, as in mud

flounder[2] *n* (*pl* -s) edible flatfish

floundered *v* ▷ flounder

floundering *v* ▷ flounder

flounders *v*, *n* ▷ flounder[1, 2]

flour *n* (*pl* -s) powder made by grinding grain, esp. wheat ▶ *v* (-s, -ing, -ed) sprinkle with flour > **floury** *adj* (-rier, -riest)

floured v ▷ flour
flourier adj ▷ flour
flouriest adj ▷ flour
flouring v ▷ flour
flourish v (-es, -ing, -ed) be active, successful, or widespread ▶ n (pl -es) dramatic waving motion > **flourishing** adj
flourished v ▷ flourish
flourishes v, n ▷ flourish
flourishing n, adj ▷ flourish
flours n, v ▷ flour
floury adj ▷ flour
flout v (-s, -ing, -ed) deliberately disobey (a rule, law, etc.)
flouted v ▷ flout
flouting v ▷ flout
flouts v ▷ flout
flow v (-s, -ing, -ed) (of liquid) move in a stream ▶ n (pl -s) act, rate, or manner of flowing
flowed v ▷ flow
flower n (pl -s) part of a plant that produces seeds ▶ v (-s, -ing, -ed) produce flowers, bloom
flowerbed n (pl -s) piece of ground for growing flowers
flowerbeds n ▷ flowerbed
flowered adj decorated with a floral design ▶ v ▷ flower
flowerier adj ▷ flowery
floweriest adj ▷ flowery
flowering v ▷ flower
flowers n, v ▷ flower
flowery adj (-rier, -riest) decorated with a floral design
flowing v ▷ flow
flown v ▷ fly[1]
flows v, n ▷ flow
flu n (pl flus) ▷ influenza
fluctuate v (-tes, -ting, -ted) change frequently and erratically > **fluctuation** n (pl -s)
fluctuated v ▷ fluctuate
fluctuates v ▷ fluctuate
fluctuating v ▷ fluctuate
fluctuation n ▷ fluctuate
fluctuations n ▷ fluctuate
flue n (pl -s) passage or pipe for smoke or hot air
fluencies n ▷ fluent
fluency n ▷ fluent
fluent adj able to speak or write with ease > **fluently** adv > **fluency** n (pl -cies)
fluently adv ▷ fluent
flues n ▷ flue
fluff n (pl -s) soft fibres ▶ v (-s, -ing, -ed) make

or become soft and puffy > **fluffy** adj (-ffier, -ffiest)
fluffed v ▷ fluff
fluffier adj ▷ fluff
fluffiest adj ▷ fluff
fluffing v ▷ fluff
fluffs n, v ▷ fluff
fluffy adj ▷ fluff
fluid n (pl -s) substance able to flow and change its shape; a liquid or a gas ▶ adj able to flow or change shape easily > **fluidity** n (pl -ies)
fluidities n ▷ fluid
fluidity n ▷ fluid
fluids n ▷ fluid
fluke[1] n (pl -s) accidental stroke of luck
fluke[2] (pl -s) n flat triangular point of an anchor
fluke[3] (pl -s) n parasitic worm
flukes n ▷ fluke[1, 2, 3]
flume n (pl -s) narrow sloping channel for water
flumes n ▷ flume
flummox v (-xes, -xing, -xed) puzzle or confuse
flummoxed v ▷ flummox
flummoxes v ▷ flummox
flummoxing v ▷ flummox
flung v ▷ fling
flunk v (flunks, flunking, flunked) (US, AUST, NZ & S AFR) (Informal) fail
flunked v ▷ flunk
flunkey n ▷ flunky
flunkeys n ▷ flunky
flunkies n ▷ flunky
flunking v ▷ flunk
flunks v ▷ flunk
flunky, flunkey n (pl -kies, -keys) servile person
fluoresce v (-ces, -cing, -ced) exhibit fluorescence
fluoresced v ▷ fluoresce
fluorescence n (pl -s) emission of light from a substance bombarded by particles, such as electrons, or by radiation
fluorescences n ▷ fluorescence
fluorescent adj of or resembling fluorescence
fluoresces v ▷ fluoresce
fluorescing v ▷ fluoresce
fluoridate v (-tes, -ting, -ted) add fluoride to (water) as protection against tooth decay > **fluoridation** n (pl -s)
fluoridated v ▷ fluoridate
fluoridates v ▷ fluoridate
fluoridating v ▷ fluoridate
fluoridation n ▷ fluoridate
fluoridations n ▷ fluoridate

fluoride n (pl -s) compound containing fluorine
fluorides n ▷ fluoride
fluorine n (pl -s) (CHEM) toxic yellow gas, most reactive of all the elements
fluorines n ▷ fluorine
flurried v ▷ flurry
flurries n, v ▷ flurry
flurry n (pl -rries) sudden commotion ▶ v (-rries, -rrying, -rried) confuse
flus n ▷ flu
flush[1] v (-es, -ing, -ed) blush or cause to blush ▶ n (pl -es) blush
flush[2] adj level with the surrounding surface
flush[3] v (-es, -ing, -ed) drive out of a hiding place
flush[4] n (pl -es) (in card games) hand all of one suit
flushed v ▷ flush[1,3]
flushes v, n ▷ flush[1,3,4]
flushing v ▷ flush[1,3]
fluster v (-s, -ing, -ed) make nervous or upset ▶ n (pl -s) nervous or upset state
flustered v ▷ fluster
flustering v ▷ fluster
flusters v, n ▷ fluster
flute n (pl -s) wind instrument consisting of a tube with sound holes and a mouth hole in the side
fluted adj having decorative grooves
flutes n ▷ flute
flutter v (-s, -ing, -ed) wave rapidly ▶ n (pl -s) flapping movement
fluttered v ▷ flutter
fluttering v ▷ flutter
flutters v, n ▷ flutter
fluvial adj of rivers
flux n (pl -es) constant change or instability
fluxes n ▷ flux
fly[1] v (flying, flew, flown) move through the air on wings or in an aircraft ▶ n (pl flies) (often pl (BRIT) fastening at the front of trousers ▶ pl space above a stage, used for storage
fly[2] n (pl flies) two-winged insect
fly[3] adj (flier, fliest) (Slang) sharp and cunning
flycatcher n (pl -s) small insect-eating songbird
flycatchers n ▷ flycatcher
flyer, flier n (pl -s) n small advertising leaflet
flyers n ▷ flyer
flying adj hurried and brief ▶ v ▷ fly
flyleaf n (pl -leaves) blank leaf at the beginning or end of a book
flyleaves n ▷ flyleaf
flyover n (pl -s) road passing over another by a bridge
flyovers n ▷ flyover
flypaper n (pl -s) paper with a sticky poisonous coating, used to kill flies
flypapers n ▷ flypaper
flyweight n (pl -s) boxer weighing up to 112lb (professional) or 51kg (amateur)
flyweights n ▷ flyweight
flywheel (pl -s) n heavy wheel regulating the speed of a machine
flywheels n ▷ flywheel
foal n (pl -s) young of a horse or related animal ▶ v (-s, -ing, -ed) give birth to a foal
foaled v ▷ foal
foaling v ▷ foal
foals n, v ▷ foal
foam n (pl -s) mass of small bubbles on a liquid ▶ v (-s, -ing, -ed) produce foam > **foamy** adj (-ier, -iest)
foamed v ▷ foam
foamier adj ▷ foam
foamiest adj ▷ foam
foaming v ▷ foam
foams n, v ▷ foam
foamy adj ▷ foam
fob n (pl -s) short watch chain
fobs n ▷ fob
focal adj of or at a focus
foci n ▷ focus
fo'c's'le n (pl fo'c's'les) ▷ forecastle
fo'c's'les n ▷ fo'c's'le
focus n (pl -cuses, -ci) [-sɥe] point at which light or sound waves converge ▶ v (-cuses, -cusing, -cused or -cusses, -cussing, -cussed) bring or come into focus
focused v ▷ focus
focuses n, v ▷ focus
focusing v ▷ focus
focussed v ▷ focus
focussing ▷ focus
fodder n (pl -s) feed for livestock
fodders n ▷ fodder
foe n (pl foes) enemy, opponent
foes n ▷ foe
foetid adj (-er, -est) ▷ fetid
foetider adj ▷ foetid
foetidest adj ▷ foetid
foetus n (pl -tuses) ▷ fetus
foetuses n ▷ foetus
fog n (pl -s) mass of condensed water vapour in the lower air, often greatly reducing visibility ▶ v (-s, fogging, fogged) cover with steam > **foggy** adj (-ggier, -ggiest)
fogey, fogy n (pl -geys, -gies) old-fashioned person

fogeys n ▷ fogey
fogged v ▷ fog
foggier adj ▷ fog
foggiest adj ▷ fog
fogging v ▷ fog
foggy adj ▷ fog
foghorn n (pl -s) large horn sounded to warn ships in fog
foghorns n ▷ foghorn
fogies n ▷ fogey
fogs n ▷ fog
fogy n ▷ fogey
foible n (pl -s) minor weakness or slight peculiarity
foibles n ▷ foible
foil¹ v (-s, -ing, -ed) ruin (someone's plan)
foil² n (pl -s) metal in a thin sheet, esp. for wrapping food
foil³ n (pl -s) light slender flexible sword tipped with a button
foiled v ▷ foil
foiling v ▷ foil
foils v, n ▷ foil¹, ², ³
foist v (-s, -ing, -ed) (foll. by on or upon) force or impose on
foisted v ▷ foist
foisting v ▷ foist
foists v ▷ foist
fold¹ v (-s, -ing, -ed) bend so that one part covers another ▶ n (pl -s) folded piece or part
fold² n (pl -s) (BRIT, AUST & S AFR) enclosure for sheep
folded v ▷ fold
folder n (pl -s) piece of folded cardboard for holding loose papers
folders n ▷ folder
folding v ▷ fold
folds v, n ▷ fold¹, ²
foliage n (pl -s) leaves
foliages n ▷ foliage
foliation n (pl -s) process of producing leaves
foliations n ▷ foliation
folio n (pl -lios) sheet of paper folded in half to make two leaves of a book
folios n ▷ folio
folk n (pl -s) people in general ▶ pl relatives
folklore n (pl -s) traditional beliefs and stories of a people
folklores n ▷ folklore
folks n ▷ folk
folksier adj ▷ folksy
folksiest adj ▷ folksy
folksy adj (-sier, -siest) simple and unpretentious
follicle n (pl -s) small cavity in the body, esp.

one from which a hair grows
follicles n ▷ follicle
follies n ▷ folly
follow v (-s, -ing, -ed) go or come after
followed v ▷ follow
follower n (pl -s) disciple or supporter
followers n ▷ follower
following adj about to be mentioned ▶ n (pl -s) group of supporters ▶ prep as a result of ▶ v ▷ follow
followings n ▷ following
follows v ▷ follow
folly n (pl -llies) foolishness
foment [foam-ent] v (-s, -ing, -ed) encourage or stir up (trouble)
fomented v ▷ foment
fomenting v ▷ foment
foments v ▷ foment
fond adj (-er, -est) tender, loving > **fondly** adv > **fondness** n (pl -es)
fondant n (pl -s) (sweet made from) flavoured paste of sugar and water
fondants n ▷ fondant
fonder adj ▷ fond
fondest adj ▷ fond
fondle v (-les, -ling, -led) caress
fondled v ▷ fondle
fondles v ▷ fondle
fondling v ▷ fondle
fondly adv ▷ fond
fondness n ▷ fond
fondnesses n ▷ fond
fondue n (pl -dues) Swiss dish of a hot melted cheese sauce into which pieces of bread are dipped
fondues n ▷ fondue
font¹ n (pl -s) bowl in a church for baptismal water
font² (pl -s) n set of printing type of one style and size
fontanelle n (pl -s) soft membranous gap between the bones of a baby's skull
fontanelles n ▷ fontanelle
fonts n ▷ font¹, ²
food n (pl -dies) what one eats, solid nourishment
foodie n (pl -s) (Informal) gourmet
foodies n ▷ foodie
foods n ▷ food
foodstuff n (pl -s) substance used as food
foodstuffs n ▷ foodstuff
fool¹ n (pl -s) person lacking sense or judgment (HIST) ▶ v (-s, -ing, -ed) deceive (someone)
fool² (pl -s) n dessert of puréed fruit mixed with cream

fooled v ▷ fool
fooleries n ▷ foolery
foolery n (pl -ries) foolish behaviour
foolhardiness n ▷ foolhardy
foolhardinesses n ▷ foolhardy
foolhardy adj recklessly adventurous
> **foolhardiness** n (pl -es)
fooling v ▷ fool
foolish adj (-er, -est) unwise, silly, or absurd
> **foolishly** adv > **foolishness** n (pl -es)
foolisher adj ▷ foolish
foolishest adj ▷ foolish
foolishly adv ▷ foolish
foolishness n ▷ foolish
foolishnesses n ▷ foolish
foolproof adj unable to fail
fools n, v ▷ fool[1, 2]
foolscap n (pl -s) size of paper, 34.3 × 43.2 centimetres
foolscaps n ▷ foolscap
foot n (pl feet) part of the leg below the ankle
footage n (pl -s) amount of film used
footages n ▷ footage
football n (pl -s) game played by two teams of eleven players kicking a ball in an attempt to score goals > **footballer** n (pl -s)
footballer n ▷ football
footballers n ▷ footballs
footballs n ▷ football
footbridge n (pl -s) bridge for pedestrians
footbridges n ▷ footbridge
footfall n (pl -s) sound of a footstep
footfalls n ▷ footfall
foothills pl n hills at the foot of a mountain
foothold n (pl -s) secure position from which progress may be made
footholds n ▷ foothold
footing n (pl -s) basis or foundation
footings n ▷ footing
footlight pl n light at the front of a stage
footlights pl n ▷ footlight
footling adj (CHIEFLY BRIT) (Informal) trivial
footloose adj free from ties
footman n (pl -men) male servant in uniform
footmen n ▷ footman
footnote n note printed at the foot of a page
footnotes n ▷ footnote
footpath n (pl -s) narrow path for walkers only
footpaths n ▷ footpath
footplate n (pl -s) platform in the cab of a locomotive for the driver
footplates n ▷ footplate
footprint n (pl -s) mark left by a foot
footprints n ▷ footprint
footsie n (pl -s) (Informal) flirtation involving

the touching together of feet
footsies n ▷ footsie
footstep n step in walking
footsteps n ▷ footstep
footstool n (pl -s) low stool used to rest the feet on while sitting
footstools n ▷ footstool
footwear n (pl -s) anything worn to cover the feet
footwears n ▷ footwear
footwork n (pl -s) skilful use of the feet, as in sport or dancing
footworks n ▷ footwork
fop n (pl -s) man excessively concerned with fashion > **foppery** n (pl -ies) > **foppish** adj
fopperies n ▷ fop
foppery n ▷ fop
foppish n ▷ fop
fops n ▷ fop
for prep indicating a person intended to benefit from or receive something, span of time or distance, person or thing represented by someone, etc. ▶ conj because
forage v (-ges, -ging, -ged) search about (for) ▶ n (pl -s) food for cattle or horses
foraged v ▷ forage
forages v, n ▷ forage
foraging v ▷ forage
foray n (pl -s) brief raid or attack
forays n ▷ foray
forbade v ▷ forbid
forbear v (-s, -ing, forbore, forborne) cease or refrain (from doing something)
forbearance n (pl -s) tolerance, patience
forbearances n ▷ forbearance
forbearing v ▷ forbear
forbears v ▷ forbear
forbid v (-s, -dding, forbade, forbidden) prohibit, refuse to allow > **forbidden** adj
forbidden v, adj ▷ forbid
forbidding adj severe, threatening ▶ v ▷ forbid
forbids v ▷ forbid
forbore v ▷ forbear
forborne v ▷ forbear
force n (pl -s) strength or power ▶ v (-ces, -cing, -ced) compel, make (someone) do something
forced adj compulsory ▶ v ▷ force
forceful adj emphatic and confident
> **forcefully** adv
forceps pl n surgical pincers
forces n, v ▷ force
forcible adj involving physical force or violence
> **forcibly** adv
forcibly adv ▷ forcible

forging v ▷force

ford n (pl -s) shallow place where a river may be crossed ▶ v (-s, -ing, -ed) cross (a river) at a ford
forded v ▷ford
fording v ▷ford
fords n, v ▷ford

fore adj in, at, or towards the front ▶ n (pl -s) front part

forearm[1] n (pl -s) arm from the wrist to the elbow

forearm[2] v (-s, -ing, -ed) prepare beforehand
forearmed v ▷forearm[2]
forearming v ▷forearm[2]
forearms n, v ▷forearm[1, 2]

forebear n (pl -s) ancestor
forebears n ▷forebear

foreboding n (pl -s) feeling that something bad is about to happen
forebodings n ▷foreboding

forecast v (-casts, -casting, -cast or -casted) predict (weather, events, etc.) ▶ n (pl -s) prediction
forecasted v ▷forecast
forecasting v ▷forecast

forecastle [foke-sl] n (pl -s) raised front part of a ship
forecastles n ▷forecastle
forecasts n, v ▷forecast

foreclose v (-ses, -sing, -sed) take possession of (property bought with borrowed money which has not been repaid) > **foreclosure** n (pl -s)
foreclosed v ▷foreclose
forecloses v ▷foreclose
foreclosing v ▷foreclose
foreclosure n ▷foreclose
foreclosures n ▷foreclose

forecourt n (pl -s) courtyard or open space in front of a building
forecourts n ▷forecourt

forefather n (pl -s) ancestor
forefathers n ▷forefather

forefinger n (pl -s) finger next to the thumb
forefingers n ▷forefinger

forefront n (pl -s) most active or prominent position
forefronts n ▷forefront

foregather v (-s, -ing, -ed) meet together or assemble
foregathered v ▷foregather
foregathering v ▷foregather
foregathers v ▷foregather

forego v (-goes, -going, -went, -gone) ▷forgo
foregoes v ▷forego

foregoing adj going before, preceding ▶ v ▷forego

foregone v ▷forego

foreground n (pl -s) part of a view, esp. in a picture, nearest the observer
foregrounds n ▷foreground

forehand n (pl -s) (TENNIS ETC.) stroke played with the palm of the hand facing forward
forehands n ▷forehand

forehead n (pl -s) part of the face above the eyebrows
foreheads n ▷forehead

foreign adj not of, or in, one's own country > **foreigner** n (pl -s)
foreigner n ▷foreign
foreigners n ▷foreign

foreleg n (pl -s) either of the front legs of an animal
forelegs n ▷foreleg

forelock n (pl -s) lock of hair over the forehead
forelocks n ▷forelock

foreman n (pl -men) person in charge of a group of workers

foremast n (pl -s) mast nearest the bow of a ship
foremasts n ▷foremast
foremen n ▷foreman

foremost adj, adv first in time, place, or importance

forename n (pl -s) first name
forenames n ▷forename

forenoon n (pl -s) (CHIEFLY US & CANADIAN) morning
forenoons n ▷forenoon

forensic adj used in or connected with courts of law

foreplay n (pl -s) sexual stimulation before intercourse
foreplays n ▷foreplay

forerunner n (pl -s) person or thing that goes before, precursor
forerunners n ▷forerunner
fores n ▷fore

foresail n (pl -s) main sail on the foremast of a ship
foresails n ▷foresail
foresaw v ▷foresee

foresee v (-sees, -seeing, -saw, -seen) see or know beforehand > **foreseeable** adj
foreseeable adj ▷foresee
foreseeing v ▷foresee
foreseen v ▷foresee
foresees v ▷foresee

foreshadow v (-s, -ing, -ed) show or indicate beforehand

foreshadowed v ▷ foreshadow
foreshadowing v ▷ foreshadow
foreshadows v ▷ foreshadow
foreshore n (pl -s) part of the shore between high- and low-tide marks
foreshores n ▷ foreshore
foreshorten v (-s, -ing, -ed) represent (an object) in a picture as shorter than it really is, in accordance with perspective
foreshortened v ▷ foreshorten
foreshortening v ▷ foreshorten
foreshortens v ▷ foreshorten
foresight n (pl -s) ability to anticipate and provide for future needs
foresights n ▷ foresight
foreskin n (pl -s) fold of skin covering the tip of the penis
foreskins n ▷ foreskin
forest n (pl -s) large area with a thick growth of trees > **forested** adj
forestall v (-s, -ing, -ed) prevent or guard against in advance
forestalled v ▷ forestall
forestalling v ▷ forestall
forestalls v ▷ forestall
forested adj ▷ forest
forester n (pl -s) person skilled in forestry
foresters n ▷ foresters
forestries n ▷ forestry
forestry n (pl -ries) science of planting and caring for trees
forests n ▷ forest
foretaste n (pl -s) early limited experience of something to come
foretastes n ▷ foretaste
foretell v (-s, f-ing, -told) tell or indicate beforehand
foretelling v ▷ foretell
foretells v ▷ foretell
foretold v ▷ foretell
forethought n (pl -s) thoughtful planning for future events
forethoughts n ▷ forethought
foretold v ▷ foretell
forever adv without end
forewarn v (-s, -ing, -ed) warn beforehand
forewarned v ▷ forewarn
forewarning v ▷ forewarn
forewarns v ▷ forewarn
forewent v ▷ forego
foreword n (pl -s) introduction to a book
forewords n ▷ foreword
forfeit [for-fit] n (pl -s) thing lost or given up as a penalty for a fault or mistake ▶ v (-s, -ing, -ed) lose as a forfeit ▶ adj lost as a forfeit > **forfeiture** n (pl -s)

forfeited v ▷ forfeit
forfeiting v ▷ forfeit
forfeits n, v ▷ forfeit
forfeiture n ▷ forfeit
forfeitures n ▷ forfeit
forgave v ▷ forgive
forge[1] n (pl -s) place where metal is worked, smithy ▶ v (-ges, -ging, -ged) make a fraudulent imitation of (something)
forge[2] v (-ges, -ging, -ged) advance steadily
forged n ▷ forge[1, 2]
forger n (pl -s) person who makes an illegal copy of something
forgeries n ▷ forgery
forgers n ▷ forger
forgery n (pl -ries) illegal copy of something
forges v, n ▷ forge[1, 2]
forget v (-s, -getting, -got, -gotten) fail to remember
forgetful adj tending to forget > **forgetfulness** n (pl -es)
forgetfulness n ▷ forgetful
forgetfulnesses n ▷ forgetful
forgets v ▷ forget
forgetting v ▷ forget
forging v ▷ forge[1, 2]
forgive v (-giving, -gave, -given) cease to blame or hold resentment against, pardon > **forgiveness** n (pl -es)
forgiven v ▷ forgive
forgiveness n ▷ forgive
forgivenesses n ▷ forgive
forgiving v ▷ forgive
forgo v (-goes, -going, -went, -gone) do without or give up
forgoes v ▷ forgo
forgoing v ▷ forgo
forgone v ▷ forgo
forgot v ▷ forget
forgotten v ▷ forget
fork n (pl -s) tool for eating food, with prongs and a handle ▶ v (-s, -ing, -ed) pick up, dig, etc. with a fork > **forked** adj
forked v, adj ▷ fork
forking v ▷ fork
forks n, v ▷ fork
forlorn adj lonely and unhappy > **forlornly** adv
forlornly adv ▷ forlorn
form n (pl -s) shape or appearance ▶ v (-s, -ing, -ed) give a (particular) shape to or take a (particular) shape > **formless** adj
formal adj of or characterized by established conventions of ceremony and behaviour > **formally** adv
formaldehyde [for-**mal**-de-hide] n (pl -s)

colourless pungent gas
formaldehydes n ▷ formaldehyde
formalin n (pl -s) solution of formaldehyde in water, used as a disinfectant or a preservative for biological specimens
formalins n ▷ formalin
formalities n ▷ formality
formality n (pl -ties) requirement of custom or etiquette
formalize v (-zes, -zing, -zed) make official or formal
formalized v ▷ formalize
formalizes v ▷ formalize
formalizing v ▷ formalize
formally adv ▷ formal
format n (pl -s) style in which something is arranged ▶ v (-s, -matting, -matted) arrange in a format
formation n (pl -s) forming
formations n ▷ formation
formative adj of or relating to development
formativenesses n ▷ formative
formats n, v ▷ format
formatted v ▷ format
formatting v ▷ format
formed v ▷ form
former adj of an earlier time, previous
> **formerly** adv
formerly adv ▷ former
formidable adj frightening because difficult to overcome or manage > **formidably** adv
formidably adv ▷ formidable
forming v ▷ form
formless adj ▷ form
forms n, v ▷ form
formula n (pl -las, -lae) group of numbers, letters, or symbols expressing a scientific or mathematical rule > **formulaic** adj
formulae n ▷ formula
formulaic adj ▷ formula
formulas n ▷ formula
formulate v (-tes, -ting, -ted) plan or describe precisely and clearly > **formulation** n (pl -s) ▸
formulated v ▷ formulate
formulates v ▷ formulate
formulating v ▷ formulate
formulation n ▷ formulate
formulations n ▷ formulate
fornicate v (-tes, -ting, -ted) have sexual intercourse without being married
> **fornication** n (pl -s) > **fornicator** n (pl -s)
fornicated v ▷ fornicate
fornicates v ▷ fornicate
fornicating v ▷ fornicate
fornication n ▷ fornicate

fornications n ▷ fornicate
fornicator n ▷ fornicate
fornicators n ▷ fornicate
forsake v (-sakes, -saking, -sook, -saken) withdraw support or friendship from
forsaken v ▷ forsake
forsakes v ▷ forsake
forsaking v ▷ forsake
forsook v ▷ forsake
forsooth adv (Obs) indeed
forswear v (-s, -swearing, -swore, -sworn) renounce or reject
forswearing v ▷ forswear
forswears v ▷ forswear
forswore v ▷ forswear
forsworn v ▷ forswear
forsythia [for-**syth**-ee-a] n (pl -as) shrub with yellow flowers in spring
forsythias n ▷ forsythia
fort n (pl -s) fortified building or place
forte¹ [for-tay] n (pl -s) thing at which a person excels
forte² [for-tay] adv (MUSIC) loudly
fortes n ▷ forte
forth adv forwards, out, or away
forthcoming adj about to appear or happen
forthright adj direct and outspoken
forthwith adv at once
forties n ▷ forty
fortieth adj, n ▷ forty
fortieths n ▷ forty
fortifications n ▷ fortify
fortified v ▷ fortify
fortifies v ▷ fortify
fortify v (-fies, -fying, -fied) make (a place) defensible, as by building walls
> **fortification** n (pl -s)
fortification n ▷ fortify
fortifying v ▷ fortify
fortissimo adv (MUSIC) very loudly
fortitude n (pl -s) courage in adversity or pain
fortitudes n ▷ fortitude
fortnight n (pl -s) two weeks > **fortnightly** adv, adj
fortnightly adv, adj ▷ fortnight
fortnights n ▷ fortnight
fortress n (pl -es) large fort or fortified town
fortresses n ▷ fortress
forts n ▷ fort
fortuitous [for-**tyew**-it-uss] adj happening by (lucky) chance > **fortuitously** adv
fortuitously adv ▷ fortuitous
fortunate adj having good luck > **fortunately** adv
fortunately adv ▷ fortunate

fortune n (pl -s) luck, esp. when favourable ▸ pl person's destiny
   fortunes n ▷ fortune
forty adj, n (pl -ties) four times ten > **fortieth** adj, n (pl -s)
forum n (pl -ums) meeting or medium for open discussion or debate
   forums n ▷ forum
forward adj directed or moving ahead ▸ n (pl -s) attacking player in various team games, such as soccer or hockey ▸ adv forwards ▸ v (-s, -ing, -ed) send (a letter etc.) on to an ultimate destination
   forwarded v ▷ forward
   forwarding v ▷ forward
forwards adv towards or at a place further ahead in space or time ▸ n, v ▷ forward
fossick v (-s, -ing, -ed) (AUST & NZ) search, esp. for gold or precious stones
   fossicked v ▷ fossick
   fossicking v ▷ fossick
   fossicks v ▷ fossick
fossil n (pl -s) hardened remains of a prehistoric animal or plant preserved in rock
fossilize v (-zes, -zing, -zed) turn into a fossil
   fossilized v ▷ fossilize
   fossilizes v ▷ fossilize
   fossilizing v ▷ fossilize
   fossils n ▷ fossil
foster v (-s, -ing, -ed) promote the growth or development of ▸ adj of or involved in fostering a child
   fostered v ▷ foster
   fostering v ▷ foster
   fosters v ▷ foster
fought v ▷ fight
foul adj (-er, -est) loathsome or offensive ▸ n (pl -s) (SPORT) violation of the rules ▸ v (-s, -ing, -ed) make dirty or polluted
   fouled v ▷ foul
   fouler adj ▷ foul
   foulest adj ▷ foul
   fouling v ▷ foul
foulmouthed adj habitually using foul language
   fouls n, v ▷ foul
found¹ v ▷ find
found² v (-s, -ing, -ed) establish or bring into being (foll. by **on** or **upon**) > **founder** n (pl -s)
found³ v (-s, -ing, -ed) cast (metal or glass) by melting and setting in a mould
foundation n (pl -s) basis or base
   foundations n ▷ foundation
   founded v ▷ found², ³
   founder¹ n ▷ found²

founder² v (-s, -ing, -ed) break down or fail
   foundered v ▷ founder
   foundering v ▷ founder
   founders¹ n ▷ found²
   founders² v ▷ founder
   founding v ▷ found², ³
foundling n (pl -s) (CHIEFLY BRIT) abandoned baby
   foundlings n ▷ foundling
   foundries n ▷ foundry
foundry n (pl -dries) place where metal is melted and cast
   founds v ▷ found², ³
fount¹ n (pl -s) (Lit) fountain
fount² (pl -s) n set of printing type of one style and size
fountain n (pl -s) jet of water
fountainhead n (pl -s) original source
   fountainheads n ▷ fountainhead
   fountains n ▷ fountain
   founts n ▷ fount¹, ²
four adj, n (pl -s) one more than three
   fours n ▷ four
foursome n group of four people
   foursomes n (pl -s) ▷ foursome
fourteen adj, n (pl -s) four and ten > **fourteenth** adj, n (pl -s)
   fourteens n ▷ fourteen
   fourteenth adj, n ▷ fourteen
   fourteenths n ▷ fourteen
fourth adj, n (pl -s) (of) number four in a series ▸ n quarter
   fourths n ▷ fourth
fowl n (pl -s) domestic cock or hen
   fowls n ▷ fowl
fox n (pl -es) reddish-brown bushy-tailed animal of the dog family ▸ v (-s, -ing, -ed) (Informal) perplex or deceive
   foxed v ▷ fox
   foxes n, v ▷ fox
foxglove n (pl -s) tall plant with purple or white flowers
   foxgloves n ▷ foxglove
foxhole n (pl -s) (MIL) small pit dug for protection
   foxholes n ▷ foxhole
foxhound n (pl -s) dog bred for hunting foxes
   foxhounds n ▷ foxhound
   foxier adj ▷ foxy
   foxiest adj ▷ foxy
   foxing v ▷ fox
foxtrot n (pl -s) ballroom dance with slow and quick steps
   foxtrots n ▷ foxtrot
foxy adj (-xier, -xiest) of or like a fox, esp. in

craftiness

foy *n* (**foys**). Foy is an old dialect word meaning a farewell meal or gift. This unusual word can be useful when there is little space to form longer words. Foy scores 9 points.

foyer [foy-ay] *n* (*pl* -s) entrance hall in a theatre, cinema, or hotel
   foyers *n* ▷ foyer
fracas [frak-ah] *n* (*pl* -es) noisy quarrel
   fracases *n* ▷ fracas
fraction *n* (*pl* -s) numerical quantity that is not a whole number > **fractional** *adj*
   > **fractionally** *adv*
   fractional *adj* ▷ fraction
   fractionally *adv* ▷ fraction
   fractions *n* ▷ fraction
fractious *adj* easily upset and angered
fracture *n* (*pl* -s) breaking, esp. of a bone ▶ *v* (-**res, -ring, -red**) break
   fractured *v* ▷ fracture
   fractures *n, v* ▷ fracture
   fracturing *v* ▷ fracture
fragile *adj* easily broken or damaged > **fragility** *n* (*pl* -**lities**)
   fragilities *n* ▷ fragile
   fragility *n* ▷ fragile
fragment *n* (*pl* -s) piece broken off ▶ *v* (-**s, -ing, -ed**) break into pieces > **fragmentary** *adj*
   > **fragmentation** *n* (*pl* -s)
   fragmentary *adj* ▷ fragment
   fragmentation *n* ▷ fragment
   fragmentations *n* ▷ fragment
   fragmented *v* ▷ fragment
   fragmenting *v* ▷ fragment
   fragments *n, v* ▷ fragment
fragrance *n* (*pl* -s) pleasant smell
   fragrances *n* ▷ fragrance
fragrant *adj* sweet-smelling
frail *adj* (-**er, -est**) physically weak
   frailer *adj* ▷ frail
   frailest *adj* ▷ frail
   frailities *n* ▷ frailty
frailty *n* (*pl* -**ties**) physical or moral weakness
frame *n* (*pl* -s) structure giving shape or support ▶ *v* (-**mes, -ming, -med**) put together, construct
   framed *v* ▷ frame
   frames *n, v* ▷ frame
framework *n* (*pl* -s) supporting structure
   frameworks *n* ▷ framework
   framing *v* ▷ frame
franc *n* (*pl* -s) monetary unit of Switzerland, various African countries, and formerly of France and Belgium

franchise *n* (*pl* -s) right to vote
   franchises *n* ▷ franchise
francium *n* (*pl* -s) (CHEM) radioactive metallic element
   franciums *n* ▷ francium
   francs *n* ▷ franc
frangipani [fran-jee-**pah**-nee] *n* (*pl* -**nis**) Australian evergreen tree with large yellow fragrant flowers
   frangipanis *n* ▷ frangipani
frank *adj* (-**er, -est**) honest and straightforward in speech or attitude ▶ *n* (*pl* -s) official mark on a letter permitting delivery ▶ *v* (-**s, -ing, -ed**) put such a mark on (a letter) > **frankly** *adv*
   > **frankness** *n* (*pl* -**es**)
   franked *v* ▷ frank
   franker *adj* ▷ frank
   frankest *adj* ▷ frank
frankfurter *n* (*pl* -s) smoked sausage
   frankfurters *n* ▷ frankfurter
frankincense *n* (*pl* -**es**) aromatic gum resin burned as incense
   frankincenses *n* ▷ frankincense
   franking *v* ▷ frank
   frankly *adv* ▷ frank
   frankness *n* ▷ frank
   franknesses *n* ▷ frank
   franks *n, v* ▷ frank
frantic *adj* distracted with rage, grief, joy, etc.
   > **frantically** *adv*
   frantically *adv* ▷ frantic
fraternal *adj* of a brother, brotherly
   > **fraternally** *adv*
   fraternally *adv* ▷ fraternal
fraternity *n* (*pl* -**ties**) group of people with shared interests, aims, etc. (US)
fraternize *v* associate on friendly terms
   > **fraternization** *n*
fratricide *n* (*pl* -s) crime of killing one's brother
   fratricides *n* ▷ fratricide
frau [rhymes with **how**] *n* (*pl* **fraus, frauen**) married German woman
fraud *n* (*pl* -s) (criminal) deception, swindle
   > **fraudulent** *adj* > **fraudulence** *n* (*pl* -s)
   frauds *n* ▷ fraud
   fraudulence *n* ▷ fraud
   fraudulences *n* ▷ fraud
   fraudulent *adj* ▷ fraud
   frauen *n* ▷ frau
fraught [frawt] *adj* (-**er, -est**) tense or anxious
   fraughter *adj* ▷ fraught
   fraughtest *adj* ▷ fraught
fräulein [**froy**-line] *n* (*pl* -**leins, -lein**) unmarried German woman
   fräuleins *n* ▷ fräulein
   fraus *n* ▷ frau

fray[1] *n* (*pl* -s) (BRIT, AUST & NZ) noisy quarrel
fray[2] *v* (-s, -ing, -ed) make or become ragged at the edge
  frayed *v* ▷ fray[2]
  fraying *v* ▷ fray[2]
  frays *n*, *v* ▷ fray[1, 2]
frazzle *n* (*pl* -s) (*Informal*) exhausted state
  frazzles *n* ▷ frazzle
freak *n* (*pl* -s) abnormal person or thing ▶ *adj* abnormal > **freakish** *adj*
  freakish *adj* ▷ freak
  freaks *n* ▷ freak
freckle *n* (*pl* -s) small brown spot on the skin
freckled *adj* marked with freckles
  freckles *n* ▷ freckle
free *adj* (freer, freest) able to act at will, not compelled or restrained ▶ *v* (frees, freeing, freed) release, liberate > **freely** *adv*
  freed *v* ▷ free
freedom *n* (*pl* -s) being free
  freedoms *n* ▷ freedom
freehand *adj* drawn without guiding instruments
freehold *n* (*pl* -s) tenure of land for life without restrictions > **freeholder** *n* (*pl* -s)
  freeholder *n* ▷ freehold
  freeholders *n* ▷ freehold
  freeholds *n* ▷ freehold
  freeing *v* ▷ free
freelance *adj*, *n* (*pl* -s) (of) a self-employed person doing specific pieces of work for various employers
  freelances *n* ▷ freelance
freeloader *n* (*pl* -s) (*Slang*) habitual scrounger
  freeloaders *n* ▷ freeloader
  freely *adv* ▷ free
freemason *n* (*pl* -s) member of a secret fraternity pledged to help each other
  freemasons *n* ▷ freemason
  freer *adj* ▷ free
  frees *v* ▷ free
freesia *n* (*pl* -s) plant with fragrant tubular flowers
  freesias *n* ▷ freesia
  freest *adj* ▷ free
freeway *n* (*pl* -s) (US & AUST) motorway
  freeways *n* ▷ freeway
freewheel *v* (-s, -ing, -ed) travel downhill on a bicycle without pedalling
  freewheeled *v* ▷ freewheel
  freewheeling *v* ▷ freewheel
  freewheels *v* ▷ freewheel
freeze *v* (-zes, -zing, froze, frozen) change from a liquid to a solid by the reduction of temperature, as water to ice ▶ *n* period of very cold weather
freezer *n* (*pl* -s) insulated cabinet for cold-storage of perishable foods
  freezers *n* ▷ freezer
  freezes *v* ▷ freeze
  freezing *adj* (*Informal*) very cold ▶ *v* ▷ freeze
freight [frate] *n* (*pl* -s) commercial transport of goods ▶ *v* (-s, -ing, -ed) send by freight
  freighted *v* ▷ freight
freighter *n* (*pl* -s) ship or aircraft for transporting goods
  freighters *n* ▷ freighter
  freighting *v* ▷ freight
  freights *n*, *v* ▷ freight
frenetic [frin-net-ik] *adj* uncontrolled, excited > **frenetically** *adv*
  frenetically *adv* ▷ frenetic
  freneticnesses *n* ▷ frenetic
  frenzied *adj* ▷ frenzy
  frenziedly *adv* ▷ frenzy
  frenzies *n* ▷ frenzy
frenzy *n* (*pl* -zies) violent mental derangement > **frenzied** *adj* > **frenziedly** *adv*
  frequencies *n* ▷ frequency
frequency *n* (*pl* -cies) rate of occurrence
frequent *adj* happening often ▶ *v* (-s, -ing, -ed) visit habitually > **frequently** *adv*
  frequented *v* ▷ frequent
  frequenting *v* ▷ frequent
  frequently *adv* ▷ frequent
  frequents *n* ▷ frequent
fresco *n* (*pl* -coes, -cos) watercolour painting done on wet plaster on a wall
  frescoes *n* ▷ fresco
  frescos *n* ▷ fresco
fresh *adj* (-er, -est) newly made, acquired, etc. > **freshly** *adv* > **freshness** *n* (*pl* -es)
freshen *v* (-s, -ing, -ed) make or become fresh or fresher
  freshened *v* ▷ freshen
  freshening *v* ▷ freshen
  freshens *v* ▷ freshen
fresher *n* (*pl* -s) first-year student ▶ *adj* ▷ fresh
  freshers *n* ▷ fresher
  freshest *adj* ▷ fresh
  freshly *adv* ▷ fresh
freshman *n* (*pl* -men) (BRIT & US) first-year student
  freshmen *n* ▷ freshman
  freshness *n* ▷ fresh
  freshnesses *n* ▷ fresh
fret[1] *v* (-s, -tting, -tted) be worried
fret[2] *n* (*pl* -s) small bar on the fingerboard of a guitar etc.
fretful *adj* irritable

frets n ▷ fret[1, 2]

fretsaw n (pl -s) fine saw with a narrow blade, used for fretwork

fretsaws n ▷ fretsaw

fretted v ▷ fret[1]

fretting v ▷ fret[1]

fretwork n (pl -s) decorative carving in wood

fretworks n ▷ fretwork

friable adj easily crumbled

friar n (pl -s) member of a male Roman Catholic religious order

friaries n ▷ friary

friars n ▷ friar

friary n (pl -ries) house of friars

fricassee n (pl -s) stewed meat served in a thick white sauce

fricassees n ▷ fricassee

friction n (pl -s) resistance met with by a body moving over another > **frictional** adj

frictional adj ▷ friction

frictions n ▷ friction

fridge n (pl -s) apparatus in which food and drinks are kept cool

fridges n ▷ fridge

fried v ▷ fry[1]

friend n (pl -s) person whom one knows well and likes > **friendless** adj > **friendship** n (pl -s)

friendless adj ▷ friend

friendlier adj ▷ friendly

friendlies n ▷ friendly

friendliest adj ▷ friendly

friendliness n ▷ friendly

friendlinesses n ▷ friendly

friendly adj (-lier, -liest) showing or expressing liking ▶ n (pl -lies) (SPORT) match played for its own sake and not as part of a competition > **friendliness** n (pl -es)

friends n ▷ friend

friendship n ▷ friend

friendships n ▷ friend

fries v, n ▷ fry[1]

Friesian [free-zhan] n (pl -s) breed of black-and-white dairy cattle

Friesians n ▷ Friesian

frieze [freeze] n (pl -s) ornamental band on a wall

friezes n ▷ frieze

frigate [frig-it] n (pl -s) medium-sized fast warship

frigates n ▷ frigate

fright n (pl -s) sudden fear or alarm

frighten v (-s, -ing, -ed) scare or terrify > **frightening** adj

frightened v ▷ frighten

frightened v ▷ frighten

frightening v, adj ▷ frighten

frightful adj horrifying (Informal) > **frightfully** adv

frightfully adv ▷ frightful

frights n ▷ fright

frigid [frij-id] adj (of a woman) sexually unresponsive > **frigidity** n (pl -ties)

frigidities n ▷ frigid

frigidity n ▷ frigid

frill n (pl -s) gathered strip of fabric attached at one edge ▶ pl superfluous decorations or details > **frilled** adj > **frilly** adj (-ier, -iest)

frilled adj ▷ frill

frillier adj ▷ frill

frilliest adj ▷ frill

frills n ▷ frill

frilly adj ▷ frill

fringe n (pl -es) hair cut short and hanging over the forehead ▶ v (-ges, -ging, -ged) decorate with a fringe ▶ adj (of theatre) unofficial or unconventional > **fringed** adj

fringed v, adj ▷ fringe

fringes n, v ▷ fringe

fringing v ▷ fringe

fripperies n ▷ frippery

frippery n (pl -ries) useless ornamentation

frisk v (-s, -ing, -ed) move or leap playfully

frisked v ▷ frisk

friskier adj ▷ frisky

friskiest adj ▷ frisky

frisking v ▷ frisk

frisks v ▷ frisk

frisky adj (-kier, -kiest) lively or high-spirited

frisson [frees-sonn] n (pl -s) shiver of fear or excitement

frissons n ▷ frisson

fritter n (pl -s) piece of food fried in batter

fritters n ▷ fritter

frivolities n ▷ frivolous

frivolity n ▷ frivolous

frivolous adj not serious or sensible > **frivolity** n (pl -ties)

frizz v (-es, -ing, -ed) form (hair) into stiff wiry curls > **frizzy** adj (-zzier, -zziest)

frizzed v ▷ frizz

frizzes v ▷ frizz

frizzier adj ▷ frizz

frizziest adj ▷ frizz

frizzing v ▷ frizz

frizzle v (-les, -ling, -led) cook or heat until crisp and shrivelled

frizzled v ▷ frizzle

frizzles v ▷ frizzle

frizzling v ▷ frizzle

frizzy adj ▷ frizz

frock n (pl -s) dress
  frocks n ▷ frock
frog n (pl -s) smooth-skinned tailless
  amphibian with long back legs used for
  jumping
frogman n (pl -men) swimmer with a rubber
  suit and breathing equipment for working
  underwater
  frogmen n ▷ frogman
  frogs n ▷ frog
frogspawn n (pl -s) jelly-like substance
  containing frog's eggs
  frogspawns n ▷ frogspawn
frolic v (-lics, -licking, -licked) run and play
  in a lively way ▶ n (pl -s) lively and merry
  behaviour
  frolicked v ▷ frolic
  frolicking v ▷ frolic
  frolics v, n ▷ frolic
frolicsome adj playful
from prep indicating the point of departure,
  source, distance, cause, change of state, etc.
frond n (pl -s) long leaf or leaflike part of a fern,
  palm, or seaweed
  fronds n ▷ frond
front n (pl -s) fore part ▶ adj of or at the front ▶ v
  (-s, -ing, -ed) face (onto) > **frontal** adj
frontage n (pl -s) facade of a building
  frontages n ▷ frontage
  frontal adj ▷ front
  fronted v ▷ front
frontier n (pl -s) area of a country bordering
  on another
  frontiers n ▷ frontier
  fronting v ▷ front
frontispiece n (pl -s) illustration facing the
  title page of a book
  frontispieces n ▷ frontispiece
frontrunner (pl -s) n (Informal) person regarded
  as most likely to win a race, election, etc.
  frontrunners n ▷ frontrunner
  fronts n, v ▷ front
frost n (pl -s) white frozen dew or mist ▶ v (-s,
  -ing, -ed) become covered with frost
frostbite n destruction of tissue, esp. of the
  fingers or ears, by cold (pl -s) > **frostbitten** adj
  frostbites n ▷ frostbite
  frostbitten adj ▷ frostbite
  frosted v ▷ frost ▶ adj (of glass) having a rough
  surface to make it opaque
  frostier adj ▷ frosty
  frostiest adj ▷ frosty
  frostily adv ▷ frosty
  frostiness n ▷ frosty
  frostinesses n ▷ frosty

frosting v ▷ frost ▶ n (pl -s) (CHIEFLY US) sugar
  icing
  frostings n ▷ frosting
  frosts n, v ▷ frost
frosty adj (-tier, -tiest) characterized or
  covered by frost > **frostily** adv > **frostiness**
  n (pl -es)
froth n (pl -s) mass of small bubbles ▶ v (-s, -ing,
  -ed) foam > **frothy** adj (-thier, -thiest)
  frothed v ▷ froth
  frothier adj ▷ froth
  frothiest adj ▷ froth
  frothing v ▷ froth
  froths n, v ▷ froth
  frothy adj ▷ froth
  frowiest adj ▷ frowzy
frown v (-s, -ing, -ed) wrinkle one's brows in
  worry, anger, or thought ▶ n (pl -s) frowning
  expression
  frowned v ▷ frown
  frowning v ▷ frown
  frowns v, n ▷ frown
  frowsier adj ▷ frowzy
  frowsiest adj ▷ frowzy
  frowstier adj ▷ frowsty
  frowstiest adj ▷ frowsty
frowsty adj (-ier, -iest) (BRIT) stale or musty
  frowzier adj ▷ frowzy
frowzy, frowsy adj (-zier, -ziest) dirty or
  unkempt
  froze v ▷ freeze
  frozen v ▷ freeze
frugal adj thrifty, sparing > **frugally** adv
  > **frugality** n (pl -ties)
  frugalities n ▷ frugal
  frugality n ▷ frugal
  frugally adv ▷ frugal
fruit n (pl -s) part of a plant containing seeds,
  esp. if edible ▶ v (-s, -ing, -ed) bear fruit
  fruited v ▷ fruit
fruiterer n (pl -s) person who sells fruit
  fruiterers n ▷ fruiterer
fruitful adj useful or productive > **fruitfully** adv
  fruitfully adv ▷ fruitful
  fruitier adj ▷ fruity
  fruitiest adj ▷ fruity
  fruiting v ▷ fruit
fruition [froo-ish-on] n (pl -s) fulfilment of
  something worked for or desired
  fruitions n ▷ fruition
fruitless adj useless or unproductive
  > **fruitlessly** adv
  fruitlessly adv ▷ fruitless
  fruits n, v ▷ fruit
fruity adj (-tier, -tiest) of or like fruit

frump n (pl -s) dowdy woman > **frumpy** adj
(-pier, -piest)
 frumpier adj ▷ frump
 frumpiest adj ▷ frump
 frumps n ▷ frump
 frumpy adj ▷ frump
frustrate v (-tes, -ting, -ted) upset or
anger > **frustrated** adj > **frustrating** adj
> **frustration** n (pl -s)
 frustrated v, adj ▷ frustrate
 frustrates v ▷ frustrate
 frustrating v, adj ▷ frustrate
 frustration n ▷ frustrate
 frustrations n ▷ frustrate
fry¹ v (-ries, -rying, -ried) cook or be cooked in
fat or oil ▶ n (pl fries) potato chip
fry² n young fishes
 frying v ▷ fry
fuchsia [fyew-sha] n (pl -s) ornamental shrub
with hanging flowers
 fuchsias n ▷ fuchsia
fuddle v (-les, -ling, -led) cause to be
intoxicated or confused > **fuddled** adj
 fuddled v, adj ▷ fuddle
 fuddles v ▷ fuddle
 fuddling v ▷ fuddle
fudge¹ n (pl -s) soft caramel-like sweet
fudge² v (-ges, -ging, -ged) avoid making a
firm statement or decision
 fudged v ▷ fudge²
 fudges n, v ▷ fudge¹, ²
 fudging v ▷ fudge²
fuel n (pl -s) substance burned or treated to
produce heat or power ▶ v (-s, -lling, -lled)
provide with fuel
 fuelled v ▷ fuel
 fuelling v ▷ fuel
 fuels n, v ▷ fuel
fug n (pl -s) hot stale atmosphere > **fuggy** adj
(-ggier, -ggiest)
 fuggier adj ▷ fug
 fuggiest adj ▷ fug
 fuggy adj ▷ fug
fugitive [fyew-jit-iv] n (pl -s) person who flees,
esp. from arrest or pursuit ▶ adj fleeing
 fugitives n ▷ fugitive
 fugs n ▷ fug
fugue [fyewg] n (pl -s) musical composition in
which a theme is repeated in different parts
 fugues n ▷ fugue
 fulcra n ▷ fulcrum
fulcrum n (pl -crums, -cra) pivot about which
a lever turns
 fulcrums n ▷ fulcrum
fulfil v (-s, -lling, -lled) bring about the

achievement of (a desire or promise)
> **fulfilment** n (pl -s)
 fulfilled n ▷ fulfil
 fulfilling v ▷ fulfil
 fulfilment n ▷ fulfil
 fulfilments n ▷ fulfil
 fulfils v ▷ fulfil
full adj (-er, -est) containing as much or as
many as possible ▶ adv completely > **fully** adv
> **fullness** n (pl -es)
 fuller adj ▷ full
 fullest adj ▷ full
 fullness n ▷ full
 fullnesses n ▷ full
 fully adv ▷ full
fulmar n (pl -s) Arctic sea bird
 fulmars n ▷ fulmar
fulminate v (-tes, -ting, -ted) (foll. by **against**)
criticize or denounce angrily
 fulminated v ▷ fulminate
 fulminates v ▷ fulminate
 fulminating v ▷ fulminate
fulsome adj distastefully excessive or
insincere
fumble v (-les, -ling, -led) handle awkwardly
▶ n (pl -s) act of fumbling
 fumbled v ▷ fumble
 fumbles n, v ▷ fumble
 fumbling v ▷ fumble
fume v (-s, -ing, -ed) be very angry ▶ pl n
pungent smoke or vapour
 fumed v ▷ fume
 fumes v, n ▷ fume
fumigate [fyew-mig-gate] v (-tes, -ting, -ted)
disinfect with fumes > **fumigation** n (pl -s)
 fumigated v ▷ fumigate
 fumigates v ▷ fumigate
 fumigating v ▷ fumigate
 fumigation n ▷ fumigate
 fumigations n ▷ fuminate
 fuming v ▷ fume
fun n (pl -s) enjoyment or amusement
function n (pl -s) purpose something exists for
▶ v (-s, -ing, -ed) operate or work (foll. by **as**)
functional adj of or as a function
> **functionally** adv
 functionally adv ▷ functional
 functionaries n ▷ functionary
functionary n (pl -ries) official
 functioned v ▷ function
 functioning v ▷ function
 functions n, v ▷ function
fund n (pl -s) stock of money for a special
purpose ▶ pl money resources ▶ v (-s, -ing,
-ed) provide money to > **funding** n (pl -s)

fundamental *adj* essential or primary ▶ *n* (*pl* -s) basic rule or fact > **fundamentally** *adv*
fundamentalism *n* (*pl* -s) literal or strict interpretation of a religion > **fundamentalist** *adj*, *n* (*pl* -s)
fundamentalisms *n* ▷ fundamentalism
fundamentalist *adj*, *n* ▷ fundamentalism
fundamentalists *n* ▷ fundamentalism
fundamentally *adv* ▷ fundamental
fundamentals *n* ▷ fundamental
funded *v* ▷ fund
fundi *n* (*pl* -dis) (s AFR) expert or boffin
funding *v*, *n* ▷ fund
fundings *n* ▷ fund
fundis *n* ▷ fundi
funds *n*, *v* ▷ fund
funeral *n* (*pl* -s) ceremony of burying or cremating a dead person
funerals *n* ▷ funeral
funerary *adj* of or for a funeral
funereal [fyew-neer-ee-al] *adj* gloomy or sombre
funfair *n* (*pl* -s) entertainment with machines to ride on and stalls
funfairs *n* ▷ funfair
fungal *adj* ▷ fungus
fungi *n* ▷ fungus
fungicide *n* (*pl* -s) substance that destroys fungi
fungicides *n* ▷ fungicides
fungous *adj* ▷ fungus
fungus *n* (*pl* -gi, -guses) plant without leaves, flowers, or roots, such as a mushroom or mould > **fungal, fungous** *adj*
funguses *n* ▷ fungus
funicular *n* (*pl* -s) cable railway on a mountainside or cliff
funiculars *n* ▷ funicular
funk[1] *n* (*pl* -s) style of dance music with a strong beat
funk[2] (*Informal*) *n* nervous or fearful state ▶ *v* (-s, -ing, -ed) avoid (doing something) through fear
funked *v* ▷ funk
funkier *adj* ▷ funky
funkiest *adj* ▷ funky
funking *v* ▷ funk
funks *n*, *v* ▷ funk[1, 2]
funky *adj* (-kier, -kiest) (of music) having a strong beat
funnel *n* (*pl* -s) cone-shaped tube for pouring liquids into a narrow opening ▶ *v* (-s, -lling, -lled) (cause to) move through or as if through a funnel
funnelled *v* ▷ funnel

funnelling *v* ▷ funnel
funnels *n*, *v* ▷ funnel
funnier *adj* ▷ funny
funniest *adj* ▷ funny
funnily *adv* ▷ funny
funny *adj* (-nnier, -nniest) comical, humorous > **funnily** *adv*
funs *n* ▷ fun
fur *n* (*pl* -s) soft hair of a mammal ▶ *v* (-s, -rring, -rred) cover or become covered with fur > **furry** (-rrier, -rriest) ▶ *adj*
furbish *v* (-es, -ing, -ed) smarten up
furbished *v* ▷ furbish
furbishes *v* ▷ furbish
furbishing *v* ▷ furbish
furies *n* ▷ fury
furious *adj* very angry > **furiously** *adv*
furiously *adv* ▷ furious
furl *v* (-s, -ing, -ed) roll up and fasten (a sail, umbrella, or flag)
furled *v* ▷ furl
furling *v* ▷ furl
furlong *n* (*pl* -s) unit of length equal to 220 yards (201.168 metres)
furlongs *n* ▷ furlongs
furlough [fur-loh] *n* (*pl* -s) leave of absence
furloughs *n* ▷ furlough
furls *v* ▷ furl
furnace *n* (*pl* -s) enclosed chamber containing a very hot fire
furnaces *n* ▷ furnace
furnish *v* (-es, -ing, -ed) provide (a house or room) with furniture
furnished *v* ▷ furnish
furnishes *v* ▷ furnish
furnishing *v* ▷ furnish
furnishings *pl n* furniture, carpets, and fittings
furniture *n* (*pl* -s) large movable articles such as chairs and wardrobes
furnitures *n* ▷ furniture
furore [fyew-ror-ee] *n* (*pl* -s) very excited or angry reaction
furores *n* ▷ furore
furred *v* ▷ fur
furrier *n* (*pl* -s) dealer in furs ▶ *adj* ▷ fur
furriers *n* ▷ furrier
furriest *adj* ▷ fur
furring *v* ▷ fur
furrow *n* (*pl* -s) trench made by a plough ▶ *v* (-s, -ing, -ed) make or become wrinkled
furrowed *v* ▷ furrow
furrowing *v* ▷ furrow
furrows *n*, *v* ▷ furrow
furry *adj* ▷ fur

furrying v ▷ flurry

furs n, v ▷ fur

further adv in addition ▶ adj additional ▶ v (-s, -ing, -ed) assist the progress of > **furtherance** n (pl -s)

furtherance n ▷ further

furtherances n ▷ further

furthered v ▷ further

furthering v ▷ further

furthermore adv besides

furthermost adj most distant

furthers v ▷ further

furthest adv to the greatest distance or extent ▶ adj most distant

furtive adj sly and secretive > **furtively** adv

furtively adv ▷ furtive

fury n (pl -ries) wild anger

furze n (pl -s) gorse

furzes n ▷ furze

fuse¹ n (pl -s) cord containing an explosive for detonating a bomb

fuse² n (pl -s) safety device for electric circuits, containing a wire that melts and breaks the connection when the circuit is overloaded ▶ v (-s, -sing, -sed) (cause to) fail as a result of a blown fuse

fused v ▷ fuse

fuselage [fyew-zill-lahzh] n (pl -s) body of an aircraft

fuselages n ▷ fuselage

fuses v, n ▷ fuse

fusilier [fyew-zill-leer] n (pl -s) soldier of certain regiments

fusiliers n ▷ fusilier

fusillade [fyew-zill-lade] n (pl -s) continuous discharge of firearms

fusillades n ▷ fusillade

fusing v ▷ fuse

fusion n (pl -s) melting ▶ adj of a style of cooking that combines traditional Western techniques and ingredients with those used in Eastern cuisine

fusions n ▷ fusion

fuss n (pl -es) needless activity or worry ▶ v (-es, -ing, -ed) make a fuss

fussed v ▷ fuss

fusses n, v ▷ fuss

fussier adj ▷ fussy

fussiest adj ▷ fussy

fussily adv ▷ fussy

fussiness n ▷ fussy

fussinesses n ▷ fussy

fussing v ▷ fuss

fussy adj (-ssier, -ssiest) inclined to fuss > **fussily** adv > **fussiness** n (pl -es)

fustier adj ▷ fusty

fustiest adj ▷ fusty

fustiness n ▷ fusty

fustinesses n ▷ fusty

fusty adj (-tier, -tiest) stale-smelling > **fustiness** n (pl -es)

futile adj unsuccessful or useless > **futility** n (pl -ties)

futilities n ▷ futile

futility n ▷ futile

futon [foo-tonn] n (pl -s) Japanese-style bed

futons n ▷ futon

future n (pl -s) time to come ▶ adj yet to come or be

futures n ▷ future

futuristic adj of a design appearing to belong to some future time

fuzz¹ n (pl -es) mass of fine or curly hairs or fibres

fuzz² n (Slang) police

fuzzes n ▷ fuzz¹

fuzzier adj ▷ fuzzy

fuzziest adj ▷ fuzzy

fuzzily adv ▷ fuzzy

fuzziness n ▷ fuzzy

fuzzinesses n ▷ fuzzy

fuzzy adj (-zzier, -zziest) of, like, or covered with fuzz > **fuzzily** adv > **fuzziness** n (pl -es)

fy interj. Fy is an old word that people said when they were disgusted or dismayed. This very unusual word can be really useful when you're trying to form words in more than one direction. Fy scores 8 points.

Gg

Only three two-letter words begin with G (**gi, go** and **gu**). Knowing these will save you worrying about other possibilities. There are quite a few short words beginning with G that use Y, which can prove very useful. These include **gay, gey, goy** and **guy** (7 points each), as well as **gym** and **gyp** (9 points each).

gab *n* (*pl* -s) ▶ *v* (-s, -ing, -ed) (*Informal*) talk or chatter
  gababouts *n* ▷ gadabout
gabardine, gaberdine *n* (*pl* -s) strong twill cloth used esp. for raincoats
  gabardines *n* ▷ gabardine
  gabbed *v* ▷ gab
  gabbier *adj* ▷ gabby
  gabbiest *adj* ▷ gabby
  gabbing *v* ▷ gab
gabble *v* (-s, -ing, -ed) speak rapidly and indistinctly ▶ *n* (*pl* -s) rapid indistinct speech
  gabbled *v* ▷ gabble
  gabbles *v*, *n* ▷ gabble
  gabbling *v* ▷ gabble
gabby *adj* (-bier, -bbiest) (*Informal*) talkative
gable *n* (*pl* -s) triangular upper part of a wall between sloping roofs > **gabled** *adj*
  gabled *adj* ▷ gable
  gables *n* ▷ gable
  gabs *n*, *v* ▷ gab
gad *v* (-s, -dding, -dded) go around in search of pleasure
gadabout *n* (*pl* -s) pleasure-seeker
  gadded *v* ▷ gad
  gadding *v* ▷ gad
  gadflies *n* ▷ gadfly
gadfly *n* (*pl* -flies) fly that bites cattle
gadget *n* (*pl* -s) small mechanical device or appliance
  gadgetries *n* ▷ gadgetry
gadgetry *n* (*pl* -ries) gadgets
  gadgets *n* ▷ gadget
  gads *v* ▷ gad
gaff *n* (*pl* -s) stick with an iron hook for landing large fish
gaffe *n* (*pl* -s) social blunder
gaffer *n* (*pl* -s) (BRIT) (*Informal*) foreman or boss

  gaffers *n* ▷ gaffer
  gaffes *n* ▷ gaffe
  gaffs *n* ▷ gaff
gag¹ *v* (-s, -gging, -gged) choke or retch ▶ *n* (*pl* -s) cloth etc. put into or tied across the mouth
gag² *n* (*pl* -s) (*Informal*) joke
gaga [gah-gah] *adj* (*Slang*) senile
  gagged *v* ▷ gag¹
  gagging *v* ▷ gag¹
gaggle *n* (*pl* -s) (*Informal*) disorderly crowd
  gaggles *n* ▷ gaggle
  gags *v*, *n* ▷ gag¹, ²
  gaieties *n* ▷ gaiety
gaiety *n* (*pl* -ties) cheerfulness
gaily *adv* merrily
gain *v* (-s, -ing, -ed) acquire or obtain ▶ *n* (*pl* -s) profit or advantage
  gained *v* ▷ gain
gainful *adj* useful or profitable > **gainfully** *adv*
  gainfully *adv* ▷ gainful
  gaining *v* ▷ gain
  gains *v*, *n* ▷ gain
  gainsaid *v* ▷ gainsay
gainsay *v* (-s, -ing, -said) deny or contradict
  gainsaying *v* ▷ gainsay
  gainsays *v* ▷ gainsay
gait *n* (*pl* -s) manner of walking
gaiter *n* (*pl* -s) cloth or leather covering for the lower leg
  gaiters *n* ▷ gaiter
  gaits *n* ▷ gait
gala [gah-la] *n* (*pl* -s) festival
  galactic *adj* ▷ galaxy
  galas *n* ▷ gala
  galaxies *n* ▷ galaxy
galaxy *n* (*pl* -xies) system of stars > **galactic** *adj*
gale *n* (*pl* -s) strong wind
  gales *n* ▷ gale

gall¹ [gawl] n (pl -s) (Informal) impudence

gall² [gawl] v (-s, -ing, -ed) annoy

gall³ [gawl] n (pl -s) abnormal outgrowth on a tree or plant

gallant adj (-er, -est) brave and noble
> **gallantly** adv
  gallanter adj ▷ gallant
  gallantest adj ▷ gallant
  gallantly adv ▷ gallant
  gallantries n ▷ gallantry

gallantry n (pl -tries) showy, attentive treatment of women
  galled v ▷ gall²

galleon n (pl -s) large three-masted sailing ship of the 15th-17th centuries
  galleons n ▷ galleon
  galleries n ▷ gallery

gallery n (pl -ries) room or building for displaying works of art

galley n (pl -s) kitchen of a ship or aircraft
  galleys n ▷ galley
  galling v ▷ gall²

gallium n (pl -iums) (CHEM) soft grey metallic element used in semiconductors
  galliums n ▷ gallium

gallivant v (-s, -ing, -ed) go about in search of pleasure
  gallivanted v ▷ gallivant
  gallivanting v ▷ gallivant
  gallivants v ▷ gallivant

gallon n (pl -s) liquid measure of eight pints, equal to 4.55 litres
  gallons n ▷ gallon

gallop n (pl -s) horse's fastest pace ▶ v (-s, -ing, -ed) go or ride at a gallop
  galloped v ▷ gallop
  galloping v ▷ gallop
  gallops n, v ▷ gallop

gallows n (pl -ses) wooden structure used for hanging criminals
  gallowses n ▷ gallows
  galls v, n ▷ gall¹, ², ³

gallstone n (pl -s) hard mass formed in the gall bladder or its ducts
  gallstones n ▷ gallstone

galore adv in abundance

galoshes pl n (BRIT, AUST & NZ) waterproof overshoes

galumph v (-s, -ing, -ed) (BRIT, AUST & NZ) (Informal) leap or move about clumsily
  galumphed v ▷ galumph
  galumphing v ▷ galumph
  galumphs v ▷ galumph

galvanic adj of or producing an electric current generated by chemical means

galvanize v (-zes, -zing, -zed) stimulate into action
  galvanized v ▷ galvanize
  galvanizes v ▷ galvanize
  galvanizing v ▷ galvanize

gambit n (pl -s) opening line or move intended to secure an advantage (CHESS)
  gambits n ▷ gambit

gamble v (-les, -ling, -led) play games of chance to win money ▶ n (pl -s) risky undertaking > **gambler** n (pl -s) > **gambling** n (pl -s)
  gambled v ▷ gamble
  gambler n ▷ gamble
  gamblers n ▷ gamble
  gambles v, n ▷ gamble
  gambling v, n ▷ gamble
  gamblings n ▷ gamble

gamboge [gam-boje] n (pl -s) gum resin used as a yellow pigment and purgative
  gamboges n ▷ gamboge

gambol v (-s, -bolling, -bolled) jump about playfully, frolic ▶ n (pl -s) frolic
  gambolled v ▷ gambol
  gambolling v ▷ gambol
  gambols v, n ▷ gambol

game¹ n (pl -s) amusement or pastime ▶ v (-mes, -ming, -med) gamble ▶ adj (-er, -est) brave > **gamely** adv

game² adj (-er, -est) (BRIT, AUST & NZ) lame, crippled
  gamed v ▷ game¹

gamekeeper n (pl -s) (BRIT, AUST & S AFR) person employed to breed game and prevent poaching
  gamekeepers n ▷ gamekeeper
  gamely adv ▷ game¹

gamer n person who plays computer games ▶ adj ▷ game¹, ²
  gamers n ▷ gamer
  games n, v ▷ game¹

gamesmanship n (-s) art of winning by cunning practices without actually cheating
  gamesmanships n ▷ gamesmanship
  gamest adj ▷ game¹, ²

gamete n (pl -s) (BIOL) reproductive cell
  gametes n ▷ gamete

gamine [gam-een] n (pl -s) slim boyish young woman
  gamines n ▷ gamine

gaming n gambling ▶ v ▷ game¹

gamma n (pl -s) third letter of the Greek alphabet
  gammas n ▷ gamma
  gammier adj ▷ gammy

gammiest *adj* ▷ **gammy**
gammon *n* (*pl* **-s**) cured or smoked ham
 gammons *n* ▷ **gammon**
gammy *adj* (**-mier**, **-miest**) ▷ **game²**
gamut *n* (*pl* **-s**) whole range or scale (of music, emotions, etc.)
 gamuts *n* ▷ **gamut**
gander *n* (*pl* **-s**) male goose
 ganders *n* ▷ **gander**
gang *n* (*pl* **-s**) (criminal) group
gangland *n* (*pl* **-s**) criminal underworld
 ganglands *n* ▷ **gangland**
gangling *adj* lanky and awkward
ganglion *n* (*pl* **-s**) group of nerve cells
 ganglions *n* ▷ **ganglion**
gangplank *n* (*pl* **-s**) portable bridge for boarding or leaving a ship
 gangplanks *n* ▷ **gangplank**
gangrene *n* (*pl* **-s**) decay of body tissue as a result of disease or injury > **gangrenous** *adj*
 gangrenes *n* ▷ **gangrene**
 gangs *n* ▷ **gang**
gangster *n* (*pl* **-s**) member of a criminal gang
 gangsters *n* ▷ **gangster**
gangway *n* (*pl* **-s**) passage between rows of seats
 gangways *n* ▷ **gangway**
gannet *n* (*pl* **-s**) large sea bird
 gannets *n* ▷ **gannet**
 gantries *n* ▷ **gantry**
gantry *n* (*pl* **-ries**) structure supporting something such as a crane or rocket
 gaol [jayl] *n* (*pl* **-s**) ▷ **jail**
 gaols *n* ▷ **gaol**
gap *n* (*pl* **-s**) break or opening > **gappy** *adj* (**-ppier**, **-ppiest**)
gape *v* (**-pes**, **-ping**, **-ped**) stare in wonder > **gaping** *adj*
 gaped *v* ▷ **gape**
 gapes *v* ▷ **gape**
 gaping *v*, *adj* ▷ **gape**
 gappier *adj* ▷ **gap**
 gappiest *adj* ▷ **gap**
 gappy *adj* ▷ **gap**
 gaps *n* ▷ **gap**
garage *n* (*pl* **-s**) building used to house cars ▶ *v* (**-ges**, **-ging**, **-ged**) put or keep a car in a garage
 garaged *v* ▷ **garage**
 garages *n*, *v* ▷ **garage**
 garaging *v* ▷ **garage**
garb *n* (*pl* **-s**) clothes ▶ *v* (**-s**, **-ing**, **-ed**) clothe
garbage *n* (*pl* **-s**) rubbish
 garbages *n* ▷ **garbage**
 garbed *v* ▷ **garb**
 garbing *v* ▷ **garb**

garbled *adj* (of a story etc.) jumbled and confused
 garbs *n*, *v* ▷ **garb**
garden *n* (*pl* **-s**) piece of land for growing flowers, fruit, or vegetables ▶ *pl* ornamental park ▶ *v* (**-s**, **-ing**, **-ed**) cultivate a garden > **gardener** *n* (*pl* **-s**) > **gardening** *n* (*pl* **-s**)
 gardened *v* ▷ **garden**
gardenia [gar-**deen**-ya] *n* (*pl* **-s**) large fragrant white waxy flower
 gardenias *n* ▷ **gardenia**
 gardening *v* ▷ **garden**
 gardens *n*, *v* ▷ **garden**
garfish *n* (*pl* **-fishes**) freshwater fish with a long body and very long toothed jaws
 garfishes *n* ▷ **garfish**
gargantuan *adj* huge
gargle *v* (**-les**, **-ling**, **-led**) wash the throat with (a liquid) by breathing out slowly through the liquid ▶ *n* (*pl* **-s**) liquid used for gargling
 gargled *v* ▷ **gargle**
 gargles *v*, *n* ▷ **gargle**
 gargling *v* ▷ **gargle**
gargoyle *n* (*pl* **-s**) waterspout carved in the form of a grotesque face, esp. on a church
 gargoyles *n* ▷ **gargoyle**
garish *adj* crudely bright or colourful > **garishly** *adv* > **garishness** *n* (*pl* **-es**)
 garishly *adv* > **garishness**
 garishness *n* ▷ **garish**
 garishnesses *n* ▷ **garish**
garland *n* (*pl* **-s**) wreath of flowers worn or hung as a decoration ▶ *v* (**-s**, **-ing**, **-ed**) decorate with garlands
 garlanded *v* ▷ **garland**
 garlanding *v* ▷ **garland**
 garlands *n*, *v* ▷ **garland**
garlic *n* (*pl* **-s**) pungent bulb of a plant of the onion family, used in cooking
 garlics *n* ▷ **garlic**
garment *n* (*pl* **-s**) article of clothing ▶ *pl* clothes
 garments *n* ▷ **garment**
garner *v* (**-s**, **-ing**, **-ed**) collect or store
 garnered *v* ▷ **garner**
 garnering *v* ▷ **garner**
 garners *v* ▷ **garner**
garnet *n* (*pl* **-s**) red semiprecious stone
 garnets *n* ▷ **garnet**
garnish *v* (**-es**, **-ing**, **-ed**) decorate (food) ▶ *n* (*pl* **-es**) decoration for food
 garnished *v* ▷ **garnish**
 garnishes *v*, *n* ▷ **garnish**
 garnishing *v* ▷ **garnish**
 garotte *n* ▷ **garrotte**
 garotted *v* ▷ **garrotte**

garottes n, v ▷ garrotte
garotting v ▷ garrotte
garret n (pl -s) attic in a house
garrets n ▷ garret
garrison n (pl -s) troops stationed in a town or fort ▶ v (-s, -ing, -ed) station troops in
garrisoned v ▷ garrison
garrisoning v ▷ garrison
garrisons n, v ▷ garrison
garrotte, garotte n (pl -s) Spanish method of execution by strangling ▶ v (-tes, -ting, -ted) kill by this method
garrotted v ▷ garrotte
garrottes n, v ▷ garrotte
garrotting v ▷ garrotte
garrulous adj talkative
garter n (pl -s) band worn round the leg to hold up a sock or stocking
garters n ▷ garter
gas n (pl gases, gasses) airlike substance that is not liquid or solid ▶ v (gases, gasses, gassing, gassed) poison or render unconscious with gas
gasbag n (pl -s) (Informal) person who talks too much
gasbags n ▷ gasbag
gaseous adj of or like gas
gases n, v ▷ gas
gash v (-es, -ing, -ed) make a long deep cut in ▶ n (pl -es) long deep cut
gashed v ▷ gash
gashes v, n ▷ gash
gashing v ▷ gash
gasholder, gasometer [gas-som-it-er] (pl -s) n large tank for storing gas
gasholders n ▷ gasholder
gasket n (pl -s) piece of rubber etc. placed between the faces of a metal joint to act as a seal
gaskets n ▷ gasket
gasoline n (pl -s) (US) petrol
gasolines n ▷ gasoline
gasometers n ▷ gasholder
gasp v (-s, -ing, -ed) draw in breath sharply or with difficulty ▶ n (pl -s) convulsive intake of breath
gasped v ▷ gasp
gasping v ▷ gasp
gasps v, n ▷ gasp
gassed v ▷ gas
gasses n, v ▷ gas
gassier adj ▷ gassy
gassiest adj ▷ gassy
gassing v ▷ gas
gassy adj (-ssier, -ssiest) filled with gas

gastric adj of the stomach
gastritis n (pl -tes) inflammation of the stomach lining
gastritises n ▷ gastritis
gastroenteritis n inflammation of the stomach and intestines
gastronomies n ▷ gastronomy
gastronomy n (pl -mies) art of good eating > **gastronomic** adj
gastropod n (pl -s) mollusc, such as a snail, with a single flattened muscular foot
gastropodans n ▷ gastropod
gastropods n ▷ gastropod
gate n (pl -s) movable barrier, usu. hinged, in a wall or fence
gâteau [gat-toe] n (pl -teaux) [-toes] rich elaborate cake
gâteaux n ▷ gâteau
gatecrash v (-es, -ing, -ed) enter (a party) uninvited
gatecrashed v ▷ gatecrash
gatecrashes v ▷ gatecrash
gatecrashing v ▷ gatecrash
gatehouse n (pl -s) building at a gateway
gatehouses n ▷ gatehouse
gates n ▷ gate
gateway n (pl -s) entrance with a gate
gateways n ▷ gateway
gather v (-s, -ing, -ed) assemble
gathered v ▷ gather
gathering n (pl -s) assembly ▶ v ▷ gather
gatherings n ▷ gathering
gathers pl n gathered folds in material ▶ v ▷ gather
gauche [gohsh] adj (-r, -st) socially awkward > **gaucheness** n (pl -es)
gaucheness n ▷ gauche
gauchenesses n ▷ gauche
gaucher adj ▷ gauche
gauchest adj ▷ gauche
gaucho [gow-choh] n (pl -hos) S American cowboy
gauchos n ▷ gaucho
gaudier adj ▷ gaudy
gaudiest adj ▷ gaudy
gaudily adv ▷ gaudy
gaudiness n ▷ gaudy
gaudinesses n ▷ gaudy
gaudy adj (-dier, -diest) vulgarly bright or colourful > **gaudily** adv > **gaudiness** n (pl -es)
gauge [gayj] v (-ges, -ging, -ged) estimate or judge ▶ n (pl -s) measuring instrument
gauged v ▷ gauge
gauges v, n ▷ gauge
gauging v ▷ gauge

gaunt *adj* (-er, -est) lean and haggard
> **gauntness** *n* (*pl* -es)
  gaunter *adj* ▷ gaunt
  gauntest *adj* ▷ gaunt
gauntlet *n* (*pl* -s) heavy glove with a long cuff
  gauntlets *n* ▷ gauntlet
  gauntness *n* ▷ gaunt
  gauntnesses *n* ▷ gaunt
gauze *n* (*pl* -s) transparent loosely-woven
fabric, often used for surgical dressings
> **gauzy** *adj* (-zier, -ziest)
  gauzes *n* ▷ gauze
  gauzier *adj* ▷ gauze
  gauziest *adj* ▷ gauze
  gauzy *adj* ▷ gauze
  gave *v* ▷ give
gavel [gav-el] *n* (*pl* -s) small hammer used by a
judge, etc. to call for attention
  gavels *n* ▷ gavel
gavotte *n* (*pl* -s) old formal dance
  gavottes *n* ▷ gavotte
gawk *v* (-s, -ing, -ed) stare stupidly
  gawked *v* ▷ gawk
  gawkier *adj* ▷ gawky
  gawkiest *adj* ▷ gawky
  gawkiness *n* ▷ gawky
  gawkinesses *n* ▷ gawky
  gawking *v* ▷ gawk
  gawks *v* ▷ gawk
gawky *adj* (-kier, -kiest) clumsy or awkward
> **gawkiness** *n* (*pl* -es)
gawp *v* (-s, -ing, -ed) (*Slang*) stare stupidly
  gawped *v* ▷ gawp
  gawping *v* ▷ gawp
  gawps *v* ▷ gawp
gay *adj* (-er, -est) homosexual ▶ *n* (*pl* -s)
homosexual
  gayer *adj* ▷ gay
  gayest *adj* ▷ gay
gayness *n* (*pl* -es) homosexuality
  gaynesses *n* ▷ gayness
  gays *n* ▷ gay
gaze *v* (-zes, -zing, -zed) look fixedly ▶ *n* (*pl* -s)
fixed look
gazebo [gaz-zee-boh] *n* (*pl* -bos, -boes)
summerhouse with a good view
  gazeboes *n* ▷ gazebo
  gazebos *n* ▷ gazebo
  gazed *v* ▷ gaze
gazelle *n* (*pl* -s) small graceful antelope
  gazelles *n* ▷ gazelle
  gazes *v*, *n* ▷ gaze
gazette *n* (*pl* -s) official publication containing
announcements
gazetteer *n* (part of) a book that lists and

describes places
  gazetteers *n* ▷ gazetteer
  gazettes *n* ▷ gazette
gazillion *n* (*pl* -s) (*Informal*) extremely large,
unspecified amount
gazillionaire *n* (*Informal*) enormously rich
person
  gazillionaires *n* ▷ gazillionaire
  gazillions *n* ▷ gazillion
  gazing *v* ▷ gaze
  gazings *n* ▷ gaze
gazump *v* (-s, -ing, -ed) (BRIT & AUST) raise the
price of a property after verbally agreeing it
with (a prospective buyer)
  gazumped *v* ▷ gazump
  gazumping *v* ▷ gazump
  gazumps *v* ▷ gazump
gear *n* (*pl* -s) set of toothed wheels connecting
with another or with a rack to change the
direction or speed of transmitted motion
▶ *v* (-s, -ing, -ed) prepare or organize for
something
gearbox *n* (*pl* -es) case enclosing a set of gears
in a motor vehicle
  gearboxes *n* ▷ gearbox
  geared *v* ▷ gear
  gearing *v* ▷ gear
  gears *n*, *v* ▷ gear
gecko *n* (*pl* -kos, -koes) small tropical lizard
  geckoes *n* ▷ gecko
  geckos *n* ▷ gecko
geebung [gee-bung] *n* (*pl* -s) Australian tree or
shrub with an edible but tasteless fruit
  geebungs *n* ▷ geebung
geek *n* (*pl* -s) (*Informal*) boring, unattractive
person > **geeky** *adj* (-kier, -kiest)
  geekier *adj* ▷ geek
  geekiest *adj* ▷ geek
  geeks *n* ▷ geek
  geeky *adj* ▷ geek
geelbek *n* (*pl* -s) (S AFR) edible marine fish
  geelbeks *n* ▷ geelbek
  geese *n* ▷ goose
geezer *n* (*pl* -s) (BRIT, AUST & NZ) (*Informal*) man
  geezers *n* ▷ geezer
geisha [gay-sha] *n* (*pl* -sha, -shas) (in Japan)
professional female companion for men
  geishas *n* ▷ geisha
gel [jell] *n* (*pl* -s) jelly-like substance, esp. one
used to secure a hairstyle ▶ *v* (-s, gelling,
gelled) form a gel
gelatine [jel-at-teen], **gelatin** *n* (*pl* -s)
substance made by boiling animal bones
  gelatines *n* ▷ gelatine
gelatinous [jel-at-in-uss] *adj* of or like jelly

geld v (**gelds, gelding, gelded**) castrate
  gelded v ▷**geld**
gelding n (pl **-s**) castrated horse ▶ v ▷**geld**
  geldings n ▷**gelding**
  gelds v ▷**geld**
gelignite n (pl **-s**) type of dynamite used for
  blasting
  gelignites v ▷**gelignite**
  gelled v ▷**gell**
  gelling v ▷**gell**
  gels n, v ▷**gel**
gem n (pl **-s**) precious stone or jewel
gemfish (pl **-fishes**) n Australian food fish
  gemfishes n ▷**gemfish**
  gems n ▷**gem**
gen n (pl **-s**) (Informal) information
gendarme [zhohn-darm] n (pl **-s**) member of
  the French police force
  gendarmes n ▷**gendarme**
gender n (pl **-s**) state of being male or female
  genders n ▷**gender**
gene [jean] n (pl **-s**) part of a cell which
  determines inherited characteristics
  genealogical adj ▷**genealogy**
  genealogies n ▷**genealogy**
  genealogist n ▷**genealogy**
  genealogists n ▷**genealogy**
genealogy [jean-ee-**al**-a-gee] n (pl **-gies**) (study
  of) the history and descent of a family or
  families > **genealogical** adj > **genealogist**
  n (pl **-s**)
  genera [jen-er-a] ▷**genus**
general adj common or widespread ▶ n (pl **-s**)
  very senior army officer > **generally** adv
  generalities n ▷**generality**
generality n (pl **-ties**) general principle
  generalization n ▷**generalize**
  generalizations n ▷**generalize**
generalize v (**-zes, -zing, -zed**) draw general
  conclusions > **generalization** n (pl **-s**)
  generalized v ▷**generalize**
  generalizes v ▷**generalize**
  generalizing v ▷**generalize**
  generalnesses n ▷**general**
  generally adv ▷**general**
  generals n ▷**general**
generate v (**-tes, -ting, -ted**) produce or bring
  into being
  generated v ▷**generate**
  generates v ▷**generate**
  generating v ▷**generate**
generation n (pl **-s**) all the people born about
  the same time
  generations n ▷**generation**
generative adj capable of producing

generator n (pl **-s**) machine for converting
  mechanical energy into electrical energy
  generators n ▷**generator**
generic [jin-**ner**-ik] adj of a class, group, or
  genus > **generically** adv
  generically adv ▷**generic**
  generosities n ▷**generous**
  generosity n ▷**generous**
generous adj free in giving > **generously** adv
  > **generosity** n (pl **-ties**)
  generously adv ▷**generous**
  genes n ▷**gene**
  geneses n ▷**genesis**
genesis [jen-iss-iss] n (pl **-ses**) [-iss-eez]
  beginning or origin
genetic [jin-**net**-tik] adj of genes or genetics
  geneticist n ▷**genetics**
  geneticists n ▷**genetics**
genetics n study of heredity and variation in
  organisms > **geneticist** n (pl **-s**)
genial [jean-ee-al] adj cheerful and friendly
  > **genially** adv > **geniality** n (pl **-ties**)
  genialities n ▷**genial**
  geniality n ▷**genial**
  genially adv ▷**genial**
genie [jean-ee] n (pl **-s**) (in fairy tales) servant
  who appears by magic and grants wishes
  genies n ▷**genie**
genital adj of the sexual organs or
  reproduction
  genitalia n ▷**genitals**
genitals, genitalia [jen-it-**ail**-ya] pl n external
  sexual organs
genitive n (pl **-s**) grammatical case indicating
  possession or association
  genitives n ▷**genitive**
genius [jean-yuss] n (pl **-es**) (person with)
  exceptional ability in a particular field
  geniuses n ▷**genius**
genocide [jen-no-side] n (pl **-s**) murder of a race
  of people
  genocides n ▷**genocide**
genre [zhohn-ra] n (pl **-s**) style of literary,
  musical, or artistic work
  genres n ▷**genre**
  gens n ▷**gen**
gent n (pl **-s**) (BRIT, AUST & NZ) (Informal)
  gentleman
genteel adj (**-er, -est**) affectedly proper and
  polite > **genteelly** adv
  genteeler adj ▷**genteel**
  genteelest adj ▷**genteel**
  genteelly adv ▷**genteel**
gentian [jen-shun] n (pl **-s**) mountain plant
  with deep blue flowers

gentians *n* ▷ gentian
gentile *adj, n* (*pl* -s) non-Jewish (person)
  gentiles *n* ▷ gentile
gentle *adj* (-r, -st) mild or kindly > **gentleness** *n*
  (*pl* -es) > **gently** *adv*
gentleman *n* (*pl* -men) polite well-bred man
  > **gentlemanly** *adj* > **gentlewoman** *n fem* (*pl*
  -women)
  gentlemanly *adj* ▷ gentleman
  gentlemen *n* ▷ gentleman
  gentleness *n* ▷ gentle
  gentlenesses *n* ▷ gentle
  gentler *adj* ▷ gentle
  gentlest *adj* ▷ gentle
  gentlewoman *n* ▷ gentleman
  gentlewomen *n* ▷ gentleman
  gently *adv* ▷ gentle
  gentries *n* ▷ gentry
  gentries *n* ▷ gentry
gentrification *n* (*pl* -s) taking-over of a
  traditionally working-class area by middle-
  class incomers
  > **gentrify** *v* (-fies, -fying, -fied)
  gentrifications *n* ▷ gentrification
  gentrified *v* ▷ gentrification
  gentrifies *v* ▷ gentrification
  gentrifying *v* ▷ gentrification
gentry *n* (*pl* -ies) people just below the nobility
  in social rank
gents *n* men's public toilet ▶ *n* ▷ gent
genuflect *v* (-s, -ing, -ed) bend the knee
  as a sign of reverence or deference
  > **genuflection, genuflexion** *n* (*pl* -s)
  genuflected *v* ▷ genuflect
  genuflecting *v* ▷ genuflect
  genuflection *n* ▷ genuflect
  genuflections *n* ▷ genuflect
  genuflects *v* ▷ genuflect
  genuflexion *n* ▷ genuflect
  genuflexions *n* ▷ genuflect
genuine *adj* not fake, authentic > **genuinely**
  adv > **genuineness** *n* (-es)
  genuinely *adv* ▷ genuine
  genuineness *n* ▷ genuine
  genuinenesses *n* ▷ genuine
genus [jean-uss] *n* (*pl* genera) group into which
  a family of animals or plants is divided
geocentric *adj* having the earth as a centre
  geographer *n* ▷ geography
  geographers *n* ▷ geography
  geographic *adj* ▷ geography
  geographical *adj* ▷ geography
  geographically *adv* ▷ geography
  geographies *n* ▷ geography
geography *n* (*pl* -phies) study of the earth's

physical features, climate, population,
etc. > **geographer** *n* (*pl* -s) > **geographical,
geographic** *adj* > **geographically** *adv*
  geological *adj* ▷ geology
  geologically *adv* ▷ geology
  geologies *n* ▷ geology
  geologist *n* ▷ geology
  geologists *n* ▷ geology
geology *n* (*pl* -gies) study of the earth's origin,
  structure, and composition
  > **geological** *adj* > **geologically** *adv*
  > **geologist** *n* (*pl* -s)
  geometric *adj* ▷ geometry
  geometrical *adj* ▷ geometry
  geometrically *adv* ▷ geometry
  geometries *n* ▷ geometry
geometry *n* (*pl* -tries) branch of mathematics
  dealing with points, lines, curves, and
  surfaces > **geometric, geometrical** *adj*
  > **geometrically** *adv*
geostationary *adj* (of a satellite) orbiting
  so as to remain over the same point of the
  earth's surface
geothermal *adj* of or using the heat in the
  earth's interior
geranium *n* (*pl* -s) cultivated plant with red,
  pink, or white flowers
  geraniums *n* ▷ geranium
gerbil [jer-bill] *n* (*pl* -s) burrowing desert rodent
  of Asia and Africa
  gerbils *n* ▷ gerbil
geriatric *adj, n* (*pl* -s) old (person)
geriatrics *n* (*pl* branch of medicine dealing
  with old age and its diseases
  ▶ *n* ▷ geriatric
germ *n* (*pl* -s) microbe, esp. one causing
  disease
germane *adj* relevant to
germanium *n* (*pl* -s) (CHEM) brittle grey
  element that is a semiconductor
  germaniums *n* ▷ germanium
germinal *adj* of or in the earliest stage of
  development
germinate *v* (-tes, -ting, -ted) (cause to)
  sprout or begin to grow
  > **germination** *n* (*pl* -s)
  germinated *v* ▷ germinate
  germinates *v* ▷ germinate
  germinating *v* ▷ germinate
  germination *n* ▷ germinate
  germinations *n* ▷ germinate
  germs *n* ▷ germ
gerrymandering *n* (*pl* -s) alteration of voting
  constituencies in order to give an unfair
  advantage to one party

gerrymanderings n ▷ gerrymandering
gerund [jer-rund] n (pl -s) noun formed from a verb
gerunds n ▷ gerund
gestation n (pl -s) (period of) carrying of young in the womb between conception and birth
gestations n ▷ gestation
gesticulate v (-tes, -ting, -ted) make expressive movements with the hands and arms > **gesticulation** n (pl -s)
gesticulated v ▷ gesticulate
gesticulates v ▷ gesticulate
gesticulating v ▷ gesticulate
gesticulation n ▷ gesticulate
gesticulations n ▷ gesticulate
gesture n (pl -s) movement to convey meaning ▶ v (-res, -ring, -red) gesticulate
gestured v ▷ gesture
gestures n, v ▷ gesture
gesturing v ▷ gesture
get v (-s, -tting, got) obtain or receive
getaway adj, n (pl -s) (used in) escape
getaways n ▷ getaway
gets v ▷ get
getting v ▷ get

> **gey** adv. Gey is a Scots word meaning **very.** If you have a G and a Y, it's highly likley that there will be an E you can use somewhere on the board. Gey scores 7 points.

geyser [geez-er] n (pl -s) spring that discharges steam and hot water (BRIT & S AFR)
geysers n ▷ geyser
ghastlier adj ▷ ghastly
ghastliest adj ▷ ghastly
ghastliness n ▷ ghastly
ghastlinesses n ▷ ghastly
ghastly adj (-lier, -liest) (Informal) unpleasant > **ghastliness** n (pl -es)
ghat n (pl -s) (in India) steps leading down to a river
ghats n ▷ ghat
ghee [gee] n (pl -s) (in Indian cookery) clarified butter
ghees n ▷ ghee
gherkin n (pl -s) small pickled cucumber
gherkins n ▷ gherkin
ghetto n (pl -ttos, -ttoes) slum area inhabited by a deprived minority
ghettoblaster n (Informal) large portable cassette recorder or CD player
ghettoblasters n ▷ ghettoblaster
ghettoes n ▷ ghetto
ghettos n ▷ ghetto

ghillie n (pl -s) ▷ gillie
ghillies n ▷ ghillie
ghost n (pl -s) disembodied spirit of a dead person ▶ v (-s, -ing, -ed) ghostwrite > **ghostly** adj (-ier, -iest)
ghosted v ▷ ghost
ghosting v ▷ ghost
ghostlier adj ▷ ghost
ghostliest adj ▷ ghost
ghostly adj ▷ ghost
ghosts n, v ▷ ghost
ghostwriter n (pl -s) writer of a book or article on behalf of another person who is credited as the author
ghostwriters n ▷ ghostwriter
ghoul [gool] n (pl -s) person with morbid interests > **ghoulish** adj
ghoulish adj ▷ ghoul
ghouls n ▷ ghoul

> **gi** n. A gi is a suit worn by judo or karate practitioners. Gi is one of only three two-letter words beginning with G, and so is worth knowing. Gi scores 3 points.

giant n (pl -s) mythical being of superhuman size ▶ adj huge
giants n ▷ giant
gibber[1] [jib-ber] v (-s, -ing, -ed) speak or utter rapidly and unintelligibly
gibber[2] [gib-ber] n (pl -s) (AUST) boulder
gibbered v ▷ gibber[1]
gibbering v ▷ gibber[1]
gibberish n rapid unintelligible talk
gibbers n, v ▷ gibber[1, 2]
gibbet [jib-bit] n (pl -s) gallows for displaying executed criminals
gibbets n ▷ gibbet
gibbon [gib-bon] n (pl -s) agile tree-dwelling ape of S Asia
gibbons n ▷ gibbon
gibbous adj (of the moon) more than half but less than fully illuminated
gibe [jibe] v, n (pl -s) ▷ jibe[1]
gibes n ▷ gibe
giblets [jib-lets] pl n gizzard, liver, heart, and neck of a fowl
gidday, g'day interj (AUST & NZ) expression of greeting
giddier adj ▷ giddy
giddiest adj ▷ giddy
giddily adv ▷ giddy
giddiness n ▷ giddy
giddinesses n ▷ giddy
giddy adj (-ddier, -ddiest) having or causing a feeling of dizziness > **giddily** adv > **giddiness**

n (*pl* -**es**)

gift *n* (*pl* -**s**) present ▶ *v* (-**s**, -**ing**, -**ed**) make a present of

gifted *adj* talented ▶ *v* ▷ **gift**

  gifting *v* ▷ **gift**

  gifts *n*, *v* ▷ **gift**

gig¹ *n* (*pl* -**s**) single performance by pop or jazz musicians ▶ *v* (-**s**, -**gging**, -**gged**) play a gig or gigs

gig² (*pl* -**s**) *n* light two-wheeled horse-drawn carriage

gigantic *adj* enormous

  giganticnesses *n* ▷ **gigantic**

  gigged *v* ▷ **gig¹**

  gigging *v* ▷ **gig¹**

giggle *v* (-**les**, -**ling**, -**led**) laugh nervously or foolishly ▶ *n* (*pl* -**s**) such a laugh > **giggly** *adj* (-**lier**, -**liest**)

  giggled *v* ▷ **giggle**

  giggles *v*, *n* ▷ **giggle**

  gigglier *adj* ▷ **giggle**

  giggliest *adj* ▷ **giggle**

  giggling *v* ▷ **giggle**

  giggly *adj* ▷ **giggle**

gigolo [jig-a-lo] *n* (*pl* -**los**) man paid by an older woman to be her escort or lover

  gigolos *n* ▷ **gigolo**

gigot *n* (*pl* -**s**) (CHIEFLY BRIT) leg of lamb or mutton

  gigots *n* ▷ **gigot**

  gigs *n*, *v* ▷ **gig¹, ²**

gild *v* (-**s**, -**ing**, -**ed** *or* **gilt**) put a thin layer of gold on

  gilded *v* ▷ **gild**

  gilding *v* ▷ **gild**

  gilds *v* ▷ **gild**

gill [jill] *n* (*pl* -**s**) liquid measure of quarter of a pint, equal to 0.142 litres

gillie *n* (*pl* -**s**) (in Scotland) attendant for hunting or fishing

  gillies *n* ▷ **gillie**

gills [gillz] *pl n* breathing organs in fish and other water creatures ▶ *n* ▷ **gill**

gilt *adj* covered with a thin layer of gold ▶ *n* (*pl* -**s**) thin layer of gold used as decoration ▶ *v* ▷ **gild**

  gilts *n* ▷ **gilt**

gimbals *pl n* set of pivoted rings which allow nautical instruments to remain horizontal

gimcrack [jim-krak] *adj* showy but cheap

gimlet [gim-let] *n* (*pl* -**s**) small tool with a screwlike tip for boring holes in wood

  gimlets *n* ▷ **gimlet**

gimmick *n* (*pl* -**s**) something designed to attract attention or publicity > **gimmickry** *n*

(*pl* -**ries**) > **gimmicky** *adj* (-**ier**, -**iest**)

  gimmickier *adj* ▷ **gimmick**

  gimmickiest *adj* ▷ **gimmick**

  gimmickries *n* ▷ **gimmick**

  gimmickry *n* ▷ **gimmick**

  gimmicks *n* ▷ **gimmick**

  gimmicky *adj* ▷ **gimmick**

gin¹ *n* (*pl* -**s**) spirit flavoured with juniper berries

gin² *n* (*pl* -**s**) wire noose used to trap small animals

gin³ *n* (*pl* -**s**) (AUST) (*Offens*) Aboriginal woman

ginger *n* (*pl* -**s**) root of a tropical plant, used as a spice > **gingery** *adj*

gingerbread *n* (*pl* -**s**) moist cake flavoured with ginger

  gingerbreads *n* ▷ **gingerbread**

gingerly *adv* cautiously

  gingers *n* ▷ **ginger**

  gingery *adj* ▷ **ginger**

gingham *n* (*pl* -**s**) cotton cloth, usu. checked or striped

  ginghams *n* ▷ **gingham**

gingivitis [jin-jiv-**vite**-iss] *n* (*pl* -**tes**) inflammation of the gums

  gingivitises *n* ▷ **gingivitis**

ginkgo [**gink**-go] *n* (*pl* -**goes**) ornamental Chinese tree

  ginkgoes *n* ▷ **ginkgo**

  gins *n* ▷ **gin¹, ², ³**

ginseng [jin-seng] *n* (*pl* -**s**) (root of) a plant believed to have tonic and energy-giving properties

  ginsengs *n* ▷ **ginseng**

  gipsies *n* ▷ **gipsy**

  gipsy *n* (*pl* -**sies**) ▷ **gypsy**

giraffe *n* (*pl* -**s**) African ruminant mammal with a spotted yellow skin and long neck and legs

  giraffes *n* ▷ **giraffe**

gird *v* (-**s**, **girding**, **girded** *or* **girt**) put a belt round

  girded *v* ▷ **gird**

girder *n* (*pl* -**s**) large metal beam

  girders *n* ▷ **girder**

  girding *v* ▷ **gird**

girdle¹ *n* (*pl* -**s**) woman's elastic corset ▶ *v* (-**les**, -**ling**, -**led**) surround or encircle

girdle² *n* (*pl* -**s**) (SCOT) griddle

  girdled *v* ▷ **girdle¹**

  girdles *v*, *n* ▷ **girdle¹, ²**

  girdling *v* ▷ **girdle¹**

  girds *v* ▷ **gird**

girl *n* (*pl* -**s**) female child (*Informal*) > **girlhood** *n* > **girlish** *adj*

girlfriend n (pl -s) girl or woman with whom a person is romantically or sexually involved
girlfriends n ▷ girlfriend
girlhood n ▷ girl
girlhoods n ▷ girl
girlie, girly adj (Informal) featuring photographs of naked or scantily clad women
girlish adj ▷ girl
girls n ▷ girl
girly n ▷ girlie
giro [jire-oh] n (pl -os) (in some countries) system of transferring money within a post office or bank directly from one account to another
giros n ▷ giro
girt v ▷ gird
girth n (pl -s) measurement round something
girths n ▷ girth
gist [jist] n (pl -s) substance or main point of a matter
gists n ▷ gist
give v (-s, giving, gave, given) present (something) to another person ▶ n (pl -s) resilience or elasticity
giveaway n (pl -s) something that reveals hidden feelings or intentions ▶ adj very cheap or free
giveaways n ▷ giveaway
given v ▷ give
gives v, n ▷ give
giving v ▷ give
gizzard n (pl -s) part of a bird's stomach
gizzards n ▷ gizzard

> **gju** n (**gjus**). A gju (also spelt **gu**) is a kind of violin from Shetland. This unusual term is a great little word, especially when there's not much space on the board. Gju scores 11 points.

glacé [glass-say] adj preserved in a thick sugary syrup
glacial adj of ice or glaciers
glaciated adj covered with or affected by glaciers > **glaciation** n (pl -s)
glaciation n ▷ glaciated
glaciations n ▷ glaciated
glacier n (pl -s) slow-moving mass of ice formed by accumulated snow
glaciers n ▷ glacier
glad adj (-dder, -ddest) pleased and happy > **gladly** adv > **gladness** n (pl -es)
gladden v (-s, -ing, -ed) make glad
gladdened v ▷ gladden
gladdening v ▷ gladden

gladdens v ▷ gladden
gladder adj ▷ glad
gladdest adj ▷ glad
glade n (pl -s) open space in a forest
glades n ▷ glade
gladiator n (pl -s) (in ancient Rome) man trained to fight in arenas to provide entertainment
gladiators n ▷ gladiator
gladioli n ▷ gladiolus
gladiolus n (pl -lus, -li, -luses) garden plant with sword-shaped leaves
gladioluses n ▷ gladiolus
gladly adv ▷ glad
gladness n ▷ glad
gladnesses n ▷ glad
gladwrap ® (AUST, NZ & S AFR) n (pl -wraps) thin polythene material for wrapping food ▶ v (-wraps, -wrapping, -wrapped) wrap in gladwrap
gladwrapped v ▷ gladwrap
gladwrapping v ▷ gladwrap
gladwraps n, v ▷ gladwrap
glamorize v ▷ glamorous
glamorized v ▷ glamorous
glamorizes v ▷ glamorous
glamorizing v ▷ glamorous
glamorous adj alluring > **glamorize** v (-zes, -zing, -zed)
glamour n (pl -s) alluring charm or fascination
glamours n ▷ glamour
glance v (-ces, -cing, -ced) look rapidly or briefly ▶ n (pl -s) brief look
glanced v ▷ glance
glances v, n ▷ glance
gland n (pl -s) organ that produces and secretes substances in the body > **glandular** adj
glands n ▷ gland
glandular adj ▷ gland
glare v (-res, -ring, -red) stare angrily ▶ n (pl -s) angry stare
glared v ▷ glare
glares v, n ▷ glare
glaring adj conspicuous ▶ v ▷ glare > **glaringly** adv
glaringly adv ▷ glaring
glass n (pl -es) hard brittle, usu. transparent substance consisting of metal silicates or similar compounds ▶ pl spectacles
glasses n ▷ glass
glasshouse n greenhouse
glasshouses n ▷ glasshouse

glassier *adj* ▷ glassy
glassiest *adj* ▷ glassy
glassy *adj* (-ssier, -ssiest) like glass
glaucoma *n* (*pl* -s) eye disease
glaucomas *n* ▷ glaucoma
glaze *v* (-zes, -zing, -zed) fit or cover with glass
▶ *n* (*pl* -s) transparent coating
glazed *v* ▷ glaze
glazes *v*, *n* ▷ glaze
glazier (*pl* -s) *n* person who fits windows
with glass
glaziers *n* ▷ glazier
glazing *v* ▷ glaze
gleam *n* (*pl* -s) small beam or glow of light ▶ *v*
(-s, -ing, -ed) emit a gleam > **gleaming** *adj*
gleamed *v* ▷ gleam
gleaming *v*, *adj* ▷ gleam
gleams *n*, *v* ▷ gleam
glean *v* (-s, -ing, -ed) gather (facts etc.) bit by
bit > **gleaner** *n* (*pl* -s)
gleaned *v* ▷ glean
gleaner *n* ▷ glean
gleaners *n* ▷ glean
gleaning *v* ▷ glean
gleans *v* ▷ glean
glee *n* (*pl* -s) triumph and delight > **gleeful** *adj*
> **gleefully** *adv*
gleeful *adj* ▷ glee
gleefully *adv* ▷ glee
glees *n* ▷ glee
glen *n* (*pl* -s) deep narrow valley, esp. in
Scotland
glens *n* ▷ glen
glib *adj* (-bber, -bbest) fluent but insincere or
superficial > **glibly** *adv* > **glibness** *n* (*pl* -es)
glibber *adj* ▷ glib
glibbest *adj* ▷ glib
glibly *adv* ▷ glib
glibness *n* ▷ glib
glibnesses *n* ▷ glib
glide *v* (-des, -ding, -ded) move easily and
smoothly ▶ *n* (*pl* -s) smooth easy movement
glided *v* ▷ glide
glider *n* (AUST) flying phalanger
gliders *n* ▷ glider
glides *n* ▷ glide
gliding *n* sport of flying gliders ▶ *v* ▷ glide
glimmer *v* (-s, -ing, -ed) shine faintly, flicker
▶ *n* (*pl* -s) faint gleam
glimmered *v* ▷ glimmer
glimmering *v* ▷ glimmer
glimmers *v*, *n* ▷ glimmer
glimpse *n* (*pl* -s) brief or incomplete view ▶ *v*
(-ses, -sing, -sed) catch a glimpse of
glimpsed *v* ▷ glimpse

glimpses *n*, *v* ▷ glimpse
glimpsing *v* ▷ glimpse
glint *v* (-s, -ing, -ed) gleam brightly ▶ *n* (*pl* -s)
bright gleam
glinted *v* ▷ glint
glinting *v* ▷ glint
glints *v*, *n* ▷ glint
glissando *n* (*pl* -dos) (MUSIC) slide between
two notes in which all intermediate notes
are played
glissandos *n* ▷ glissando
glisten *v* (-s, -ing, -ed) gleam by reflecting light
glistened *v* ▷ glisten
glistening *v* ▷ glisten
glistens *v* ▷ glisten
glitch *n* (*pl* -es) small problem that stops
something from working properly
glitches *n* ▷ glitch
glitter *v* (-s, -ing, -ed) shine with bright flashes
▶ *n* (*pl* -s) sparkle or brilliance
glittered *v* ▷ glitter
glittering *v* ▷ glitter
glitters *v*, *n* ▷ glitter
gloaming *n* (*pl* -s) (SCOT) (*poetic*) twilight
gloamings *n* ▷ gloaming
gloat *v* (-s, -ing, -ed) regard one's own good
fortune or the misfortune of others with
smug or malicious pleasure
gloated *v* ▷ gloat
gloating *v* ▷ gloat
gloats *v* ▷ gloat
glob *n* (*pl* -s) rounded mass of thick fluid
global *adj* worldwide > **globally** *adv*
globalization *n* (*pl* -s) process by which
a company, etc., expands to operate
internationally
globalizations *n* ▷ globalization
globally *adv* ▷ global
globe *n* (*pl* globes) sphere with a map of the
earth on it
globes *n* ▷ globe
globetrotter *n* habitual worldwide traveller
> **globetrotting** *adj*, *n* (*pl* -s)
globetrotters *n* ▷ globetrotter
globetrotting *v* ▷ globetrotter
globetrottings *n* ▷ globetrotter
globs *n* ▷ glob
globular *adj* ▷ globule
globule *n* (*pl* -s) small round drop > **globular** *adj*
globules *n* ▷ globule
glockenspiel *n* (*pl* -s) percussion instrument
consisting of small metal bars played with
hammers
glockenspiels *n* ▷ glockenspiel
gloom *n* (*pl* glooms) melancholy or depression

> **gloomy** adj (**-mier, -miest**) > **gloomily** adv
gloomier adj ▷ gloom
gloomiest adj ▷ gloom
gloomily adv ▷ gloom
glooms n ▷ gloom
gloomy adj ▷ gloom
gloried v ▷ glory
glories n, v ▷ glory
glorification n ▷ glorify
glorifications n ▷ glorify
glorified v ▷ glorify
glorifies v ▷ glorify
glorify v (**-fies, -fying, -fied**) make (something) seem more worthy than it is > **glorification** n (pl **-s**)
glorifying v ▷ glorify
glorious adj brilliantly beautiful > **gloriously** adv
gloriously adv ▷ glorious
glory n (pl **-ries**) praise or honour ▶ v (**-ries, -rying, -ried**) (foll. by **in**) triumph or exalt
glorying v ▷ glory
gloss[1] n (pl **-es**) surface shine or lustre
gloss[2] n (pl **-es**) explanatory comment added to the text of a book ▶ v (**-es, -ing, -ed**) add glosses to
glossaries n ▷ glossary
glossary n (pl **-ries**) list of special or technical words with definitions
glossed v ▷ gloss[2]
glosses n, v ▷ gloss[1, 2]
glossier adj ▷ glossy
glossiest adj ▷ glossy
glossily adv ▷ glossy
glossiness n ▷ glossy
glossinesses n ▷ glossy
glossing v ▷ gloss[2]
glossy adj (**-ssier, -ssiest**) smooth and shiny > **glossily** adv > **glossiness** n (pl **-es**)
glottal adj of the glottis
glottides n ▷ glottis
glottis n (pl **-tises, -tides**) vocal cords and the space between them
glottises n ▷ glottis
glove n (pl **-s**) covering for the hand with individual sheaths for each finger and the thumb
gloved adj covered by a glove or gloves
gloves n ▷ glove
glow v (**-s, -ing, -ed**) emit light and heat without flames ▶ n (pl **-s**) glowing light
glowed v ▷ glow
glower [rhymes with **power**] v (**-s, -ing, -ed**) ▶ n (pl **-s**) scowl
glowered v ▷ glower

glowering v ▷ glower
glowers v, n ▷ glower
glowing v ▷ glow
glows v, n ▷ glow
glowworm n (pl **-s**) insect giving out a green light
glowworms n ▷ glowworm
gloxinia n (pl **-s**) tropical plant with large bell-shaped flowers
gloxinias n ▷ gloxinia
glucose n (pl **-s**) kind of sugar found in fruit
glucoses n ▷ glucose
glue n (pl **glues**) natural or synthetic sticky substance used as an adhesive ▶ v (**glues, gluing** or **glueing, glued**) fasten with glue > **gluey** adj
glued v ▷ glue
glueing v ▷ glue
glues n, v ▷ glue
gluey adj ▷ glue
gluier adj ▷ glue
gluiest adj ▷ glue
gluing v ▷ glue
glum adj (**-mmer, -mmest**) sullen or gloomy > **glumly** adv
glumly adv ▷ glum
glummer adj ▷ glum
glummest adj ▷ glum
glut n (pl **-s**) excessive supply ▶ v (**-s, -tting, -tted**) oversupply
gluten [gloo-ten] n (pl **-s**) protein found in cereal grain
glutens n ▷ gluten
glutinous [gloo-tin-uss] adj sticky or gluey
gluts n, v ▷ glut
glutted v ▷ glut
glutting v ▷ glut
glutton n (pl **-s**) greedy person > **gluttonous** adj > **gluttony** n (pl **-nies**)
gluttonies n ▷ glutton
gluttonous adj ▷ glutton
gluttons n ▷ glutton
gluttony n ▷ glutton
glycerine, glycerin n (pl **-s**) colourless sweet liquid used widely in chemistry and industry
glycerines n ▷ glycerine
glycerins n ▷ glycerine
glycerol [gliss-ser-ol] n (pl **-s**) ▷ glycerine
glycerols n ▷ glycerol
gnarled adj rough, twisted, and knobbly
gnash v (**-es, -ing, -ed**) grind (the teeth) together in anger or pain
gnashed v ▷ gnash
gnashes v ▷ gnash
gnashing v ▷ gnash

gnat n (pl -s) small biting two-winged fly
  gnats n ▷ gnat
gnaw v (-s, -ing, -ed or **gnawn**) bite or chew
  steadily
  gnawed v ▷ gnaw
  gnaws v ▷ gnaw
gneiss n (pl -es) coarse-grained metamorphic
  rock
  gneisses n ▷ gneiss
gnome n (pl -s) imaginary creature like a little
  old man
  gnomes n ▷ gnome
gnomic [no-mik] adj of pithy sayings
gnu [noo] n (pl -s) oxlike S African antelope
  gnus n ▷ gnu
go v (**going**, **went**, **gone**) move to or from a
  place (pl **gos**) ▶ n attempt
goad v (-s, -ing, -ed) provoke (someone) to
  take some kind of action, usu. in anger ▶ n (pl
  -s) spur or provocation
  goaded v ▷ goad
  goading v ▷ goad
  goads v, n ▷ goad
goal n (pl -s) (SPORT) posts through which
  the ball or puck has to be propelled to
  score
goalie n (pl -s) (Informal) goalkeeper
  goalies n ▷ goalie
goalkeeper n (pl -s) player whose task is to
  stop shots entering the goal
  goalkeepers n ▷ goalkeeper
goalpost (pl -s) n one of the two posts marking
  the limit of a goal
  goalposts n ▷ goalpost
  goals n ▷ goal
goanna n (pl -s) large Australian lizard
  goannas n ▷ goanna
goat n (pl -s) sure-footed ruminant animal
  with horns
goatee n (pl -s) pointed tuftlike beard
  goatees n ▷ goatee
  goats n ▷ goat
gob n (pl -s) lump of a soft substance (BRIT,
  AUST & NZ)
gobbet n (pl -s) lump, esp. of food
  gobbets n ▷ gobbet
gobble[1] v (-les, -ling, -led) eat hastily and
  greedily
gobble[2] n (pl -s) rapid gurgling cry of the
  male turkey ▶ v (-les, -ling, -led) make this
  noise
  gobbled v ▷ gobble[1, 2]
  gobbledegooks n ▷ gobbledegook
  gobbledygooks n ▷ gobbledegook
  gobbles v, n ▷ gobble[1, 2]

gobbledegook, gobbledygook n (pl -s)
  unintelligible (official) language or jargon
  gobbling v ▷ gobble[1, 2]
  gobies n ▷ goby
goblet n (pl -s) drinking cup without handles
  goblets n ▷ goblet
goblin n (pl -s) (in folklore) small malevolent
  creature
  goblins n ▷ goblin
  gobs n ▷ gob
goby n (pl -by, -bies) small spiny-finned
  fish
god n (pl -s) spirit or being worshipped as
  having supernatural power
  > **godlike** adj
godchild n (pl -s) child for whom a person
  stands as godparent
  > **goddaughter** n (pl -s)
  > **godson** n (pl -s)
  goddaughter n ▷ godchild
  goddaughters n ▷ godchild
goddess n fem (pl -es) female god
  goddesses n ▷ goddess
godetia n (pl -s) plant with showy flowers
  godetias n ▷ godetia
godfather n (pl -s) male godparent
  > **godmother** n (pl -s)
  godfathers n ▷ godfather
godforsaken adj desolate or dismal
  godlier adj ▷ godly
  godliest adj ▷ godly
  godlike adj ▷ god
  godliness n ▷ godly
  godlinesses n ▷ godly
godly adj (-lier, -liest) devout or pious
  > **godliness** n (pl -es)
  godmother n ▷ godfather
  godmothers n ▷ godfather
godparent n (pl -s) person who promises at
  a child's baptism to bring the child up as a
  Christian
  godparents n ▷ godparent
  gods n ▷ god
godsend n (pl -s) something unexpected but
  welcome
  godsends n ▷ godsend
  godson n ▷ godchild
  godsons n ▷ godchild
gogga n (pl -s) (S AFR) (Informal) any small insect
  goggas n ▷ gogga
goggle v (-les, -ling, -led) (of the eyes) bulge
  goggled v ▷ goggle
goggles pl n protective spectacles ▶ v ▷ goggle
  goggling v ▷ goggle
going n (pl -s) condition of the ground for

walking or riding over ▶ *adj* thriving ▶ *v* ▷ go

goings *n* ▷ going

goitre [goy-ter] *n* (*pl* -s) swelling of the thyroid gland in the neck

goitres *n* ▷ goitre

gold *n* (*pl* -s) yellow precious metal ▶ *adj* made of gold

goldcrest *n* (*pl* -s) small bird with a yellow crown

goldcrests *n* ▷ goldcrest

golden *adj* made of gold

goldfinch *n* (*pl* -es) kind of finch, the male of which has yellow-and-black wings

goldfinches *n* ▷ goldfinch

goldfish *n* (*pl* -es) orange fish kept in ponds or aquariums

goldfishes *n* ▷ goldfish

golds *n* ▷ gold

golf *n* (*pl* -s) outdoor game in which a ball is struck with clubs into a series of holes ▶ *v* (-s, -ing, -ed) play golf > **golfer** *n* (*pl* -s)

golfed *v* ▷ golf

golfer *n* ▷ golf

golfers *n* ▷ golf

golfing *v* ▷ golf

golfs *n*, *v* ▷ golf

golliwog *n* (*pl* -s) soft black-faced doll

golliwogs *n* ▷ golliwog

gonad *n* (*pl* -s) organ producing reproductive cells, such as a testicle or ovary

gonads *n* ▷ gonad

gondola *n* (*pl* -s) long narrow boat used in Venice

gondolas *n* ▷ gondola

gondolier *n* (*pl* -s) person who propels a gondola

gondoliers *n* ▷ gondoliers

gone *v* ▷ go

goner *n* (*pl* -s) (*Informal*) person or thing beyond help or recovery

goners *n* ▷ goner

gong *n* (*pl* -s) rimmed metal disc that produces a note when struck

gongs *n* ▷ gong

gonorrhoea [gon-or-**ree**-a] *n* (*pl* -s) venereal disease with a discharge from the genitals

gonorrhoeas *n* ▷ gonorrhoea

good *adj* (**better**, **best**) giving pleasure ▶ *n* benefit ▶ *pl* merchandise > **goodness** *n* (*pl* -es)

goodbye *interj*, *n* (*pl* -s) expression used on parting

goodbyes *n* ▷ goodbye

goodies *n* ▷ goody

goodly *adj* considerable

goodness *n* ▷ good

goodnesses *n* ▷ good

goodwill *n* (*pl* -s) kindly feeling

goodwills *n* ▷ goodwill

goody *n* (*pl* -dies) (*Informal*) hero in a book or film

gooey *adj* (**gooier**, **gooiest**) (*Informal*) sticky and soft

goof (*Informal*) *n* (*pl* -s) mistake ▶ *v* (-s, -ing, -ed) make a mistake

goofed *v* ▷ goof

goofing *v* ▷ goof

goofs *n*, *v* ▷ goof

googlies *n* ▷ googly

googly *n* (*pl* -lies) (CRICKET) ball that spins unexpectedly from off to leg on the bounce

gooier *adj* ▷ gooey

gooiest *adj* ▷ gooey

goon *n* (*pl* -s) (*Informal*) stupid person

goons *n* ▷ goon

goose *n* (*pl* **geese**) web-footed bird like a large duck

gooseberries *n* ▷ gooseberry

gooseberry *n* (*pl* -ries) edible yellowy-green berry

gopher [**go**-fer] *n* (*pl* -s) American burrowing rodent

gophers *n* ▷ gopher

gore¹ *n* (*pl* -s) blood from a wound

gore² *v* (-res, -ring, -red) pierce with horns

gored *v* ▷ gore²

gores *n*, *v* ▷ gore¹, ²

gorge *n* (*pl* -s) deep narrow valley ▶ *v* (-ges, -ging, -ged) eat greedily

gorged *v* ▷ gorge

gorgeous *adj* strikingly beautiful or attractive (*Informal*) > **gorgeously** *adv*

gorgeously *adv* ▷ gorgeous

gorges *n*, *v* ▷ gorge

gorging *v* ▷ gorge

gorgon *n* (*pl* -s) terrifying or repulsive woman

gorgons *n* ▷ gorgon

gorier *adj* ▷ gory

goriest *adj* ▷ gory

gorilla *n* (*pl* -s) largest of the apes, found in Africa

gorillas *n* ▷ gorilla

goring *v* ▷ gore²

gormless *adj* (*Informal*) stupid

gorse *n* (*pl* -s) prickly yellow-flowered shrub

gorses *n* ▷ gorse

gory *adj* (-rier, -riest) horrific or bloodthirsty

gos *n* ▷ go

goshawk *n* (*pl* -s) large hawk

goshawks *n* ▷ goshawk

gosling *n* (*pl* -s) young goose

goslings *n* ▷ gosling

gospel *n* (*pl* -s) any of the first four books of the New Testament

gospels *n* ▷ gospel

gossamer *n* (*pl* -s) very fine fabric

gossamers *n* ▷ gossamer

gossip *n* (*pl* -s) idle talk, esp. about other people ▶ *v* (-s, -ing, -ed) engage in gossip > **gossipy** *adj* (-ier, -iest)

gossiped *v* ▷ gossip

gossipier *adj* ▷ gossip

gossipiest *adj* ▷ gossip

gossiping *v* ▷ gossip

gossips *n*, *v* ▷ gossip

gossipy *adj* ▷ gossip

got *v* ▷ get

gouache *n* (*pl* -s) (painting using) watercolours mixed with glue

gouaches *n* ▷ gouache

gouge [gowj] *v* (-ges, -ging, -ged) scoop or force out ▶ *n* (*pl* -s) hole or groove

gouged *v* ▷ gouge

gouges *v*, *n* ▷ gouge

gouging *v* ▷ gouge

goulash [goo-lash] *n* (*pl* -es) rich stew seasoned with paprika

goulashes *n* ▷ goulash

gourd [goord] *n* (*pl* -s) fleshy fruit of a climbing plant

gourds *n* ▷ gourd

gourmand [goor-mand] *n* (*pl* -s) person who is very keen on food and drink

gourmands *n* ▷ gourmand

gourmet [goor-may] *n* (*pl* -s) connoisseur of food and drink

gourmets *n* ▷ gourmet

gout [gowt] *n* (*pl* -s) disease causing inflammation of the joints

gouts *n* ▷ gout

govern *v* (-s, -ing, -ed) rule, direct, or control > **governable** *adj*

governable *adj* ▷ govern

governance *n* (*pl* -s) governing

governances *n* ▷ governance

governed *v* ▷ govern

governess *n* (*pl* -es) woman teacher in a private household

governesses *n* ▷ governess

governing *v* ▷ govern

government *n* (*pl* -s) executive policy-making body of a state > **governmental** *adj*

governmental *adj* ▷ government

governments *n* ▷ government

governor *n* (*pl* -s) official governing a province or state

governors *n* ▷ governor

governs *v* ▷ govern

gown *n* (*pl* -s) woman's long formal dress

gowns *n* ▷ gown

goy *n* (*pl* -yim, -ys) (*Slang*) Jewish word for a non-Jew

goyim *n* ▷ goy

goys *n* ▷ goy

> **gox** *n* (**goxes**). Gox is a short word meaning gaseous oxygen. This unusual word can come in very useful, especially if you can use it to hit a bonus square. Gox scores 11 points.
>
> **goy** *n* (**goyim**) or (**goys**). Goy is a Yiddish word for someone who isn't Jewish. For a short word, this earns you a reasonable number of points, and the two plural forms can come in useful too. Goy scores 7 points.

grab *v* (-s, -bbing, -bbed) grasp suddenly, snatch ▶ *n* sudden snatch

grabbed *v* ▷ grab

grabbing *v* ▷ grab

grabs *v* ▷ grab

grace *n* (*pl* -s) beauty and elegance ▶ *v* (-ces, -cing, -ced) add grace to > **graceful** *adj* > **gracefully** *adv* > **graceless** *adj*

graced *v* ▷ grace

graceful *adj* ▷ grace

gracefully *adv* ▷ grace

graceless *adj* ▷ grace

graces *n*, *v* ▷ grace

gracing *v* ▷ grace

gracious *adj* kind and courteous > **graciously** *adv*

graciously *adv* ▷ gracious

gradation *n* (*pl* -s) (stage in) a series of degrees or steps

gradations *n* ▷ gradation

grade *n* (*pl* -s) place on a scale of quality, rank, or size ▶ *v* (-des, -ding, -ded) arrange in grades

graded *v* ▷ grade

grades *n*, *v* ▷ grade

gradient *n* (*pl* -s) (degree of) slope

gradients *n* ▷ gradient

grading *v* ▷ grade

gradual *adj* occurring, developing, or moving in small stages > **gradually** *adv*

gradually *adv* ▷ gradual

graduate *v* (-tes, -ting, -ted) receive a degree or diploma ▶ *n* (*pl* -s) holder of a degree > **graduation** *n* (*pl* -s)

graduated v ▷ graduate

graduates v, n ▷ graduate

graduating v ▷ graduate

graduation n ▷ graduate

graduations n ▷ graduate

graffiti [graf-**fee**-tee] pl n words or drawings scribbled or sprayed on walls etc.

graft¹ n (pl -s) surgical transplant of skin or tissue ▸ v (-s, -ing, -ed) transplant (living tissue) surgically

graft² (BRIT) (Informal) n hard work ▸ v work hard > **grafter** n (pl -s)

grafted v ▷ graft¹, ²

grafter n ▷ graft

grafters n ▷ graft

grafting v ▷ graft¹, ²

grafts n, v ▷ graft¹, ²

grain n (pl -s) seedlike fruit of a cereal plant > **grainy** adj (-ier, -iest)

grainier adj ▷ grain

grainiest adj ▷ grain

grains n ▷ grain

grainy adj ▷ grain

gram, gramme n (pl -s) metric unit of mass equal to one thousandth of a kilogram

grammar n (pl -s) branch of linguistics dealing with the form, function, and order of words > **grammarian** n (pl -s)

grammarian n ▷ grammar

grammarians n ▷ grammar

grammars n ▷ grammar

grammatical adj according to the rules of grammar > **grammatically** adv

grammatically adv ▷ grammatical

gramophone n (pl -s) old-fashioned type of record player

gramophones n ▷ gramophone

grampus n (pl -es) dolphin-like mammal

grampuses n ▷ grampus

grams n ▷ gram

gran n (pl -s) (BRIT, AUST & NZ) (Informal) grandmother

granaries n ▷ granary

granary n (pl -ries) storehouse for grain

grand adj large or impressive, imposing ▸ n (pl -s) (Slang) thousand pounds or dollars

grandchild n (pl -children) child of one's child

grandchildren n ▷ grandchild

granddaughter n (pl -s) female grandchild

granddaughters n ▷ granddaughter

grandee n (pl -s) person of high station

grandees n ▷ grandee

grandeur n (pl -s) magnificence

grandeurs n ▷ grandeur

grandfather n (pl -s) male grandparent

grandfathers n ▷ grandfather

grandiloquences n ▷ grandiloquent

grandiloquent adj using pompous language > **grandiloquence** n (pl -s)

grandiloquence n ▷ grandiloquent

grandiose adj imposing > **grandiosity** n (pl -ties)

grandiosities n ▷ grandiose

grandiosity n ▷ grandiose

grandmother n (pl -s) female grandparent

grandmothers n ▷ grandmother

grandparent n (pl -s) parent of one's parent

grandparents n ▷ grandparent

grands n ▷ grand

grandson n (pl -s) male grandchild

grandsons n ▷ grandson

grandstand n (pl -s) terraced block of seats giving the best view at a sports ground

grandstands n ▷ grandstand

grange n (pl -s) (BRIT) country house with farm buildings

granges n ▷ grange

granite [**gran**-nit] n (pl -s) very hard igneous rock often used in building

granites n ▷ granite

grannies n ▷ granny

granny, grannie n (pl -nies) (Informal) grandmother

grans n ▷ gran

grant v (-s, -ing, -ed) consent to fulfil (a request) ▸ n (pl -s) sum of money provided by a government for a specific purpose, such as education

granted v ▷ grant

granting v ▷ grant

grants v, n ▷ grant

granular adj of or like grains

granulated adj (of sugar) in the form of coarse grains

granule n (pl -s) small grain

granules n ▷ granule

grape n (pl -s) small juicy green or purple berry, eaten raw or used to produce wine, raisins, currants, or sultanas

grapefruit n (pl -s) large round yellow citrus fruit

grapefruits n ▷ grapefruit

grapes n ▷ grape

grapevine n (pl -s) grape-bearing vine

grapevines n ▷ grapevine

graph n (pl -s) drawing showing the relation of different numbers or quantities plotted against a set of axes

graphic adj vividly descriptive > **graphically** adv

graphically adv ▷ graphic
graphics pl n diagrams, graphs, etc., esp. as used on a television programme or computer screen
graphite n (pl -s) soft black form of carbon, used in pencil leads
  graphites n ▷ graphite
  graphologies n ▷ graphology
  graphologist n ▷ graphology
  graphologists n ▷ graphology
graphology n (pl -gies) study of handwriting > **graphologist** n (pl -s)
  graphs n ▷ graph
grapnel n (pl -s) device with several hooks, used to grasp or secure things
  grapnels n ▷ grapnel
grapple v (-les, -ling, -led) try to cope with (something difficult)
  grappled v ▷ grapple
  grapples v ▷ grapple
  grappling v ▷ grapple
grasp v (-s, -ing, -ed) grip something firmly ▶ n (pl -s) grip or clasp
  grasped v ▷ grasp
grasping adj greedy or avaricious ▶ v ▷ grasp
  grasps v, n ▷ grasp
grass n (pl -es) common type of plant with jointed stems and long narrow leaves, including cereals and bamboo ▶ v (-es, -ing, -ed) cover with grass > **grassy** adj (-ssier, -ssiest)
  grassed v ▷ grass
  grasses n, v ▷ grass
grasshopper n (pl -s) jumping insect with long hind legs
  grasshoppers n ▷ grasshopper
  grassier adj ▷ grass
  grassiest adj ▷ grass
  grassing v ▷ grass
grassroots adj of the ordinary members of a group, rather than its leaders
  grassy adj ▷ grass
grate¹ v (-tes, -ting, -ted) rub into small bits on a rough surface > **grater** n (pl -s)
grate² n (pl -s) framework of metal bars for holding fuel in a fireplace
  grated v ▷ grate¹
grateful adj feeling or showing gratitude > **gratefully** adv
  gratefully adv ▷ grateful
  grater n ▷ grate¹
  graters n ▷ grate¹
  grates v, n ▷ grate¹, ²
  gratification n ▷ gratify
  gratifications n ▷ gratify

  gratified v ▷ gratify
  gratifies v ▷ gratify
gratify v (-fies, -fying, -fied) satisfy or please > **gratification** n (pl -s)
  gratifying v ▷ gratify
grating n (pl -s) framework of metal bars covering an opening ▶ adj harsh or rasping ▶ v ▷ grate¹
  gratings n ▷ grating
gratis adv, adj free, for nothing
gratitude n (pl -s) feeling of being thankful for a favour or gift
  gratitudes n ▷ gratitude
  gratuities n ▷ gratuity
gratuitous adj unjustified > **gratuitously** adv
  gratuitously adv ▷ gratuitous
gratuity n (pl -ies) money given for services rendered, tip
grave¹ n (pl -s) hole for burying a corpse
grave² adj causing concern > **gravely** adv
grave³ [rhymes with **halve**] n (pl -s) accent (`) over a vowel to indicate a special pronunciation
gravel n (pl -s) mixture of small stones and coarse sand
gravelled adj covered with gravel
  gravellier adj ▷ gravelly
  gravelliest adj ▷ gravelly
gravelly adj (-llier, -lliest) covered with gravel
  gravels n ▷ gravel
  gravely adv ▷ grave²
graven adj carved or engraved
  graves n ▷ grave¹, ³
gravestone n (pl -s) stone marking a grave
  gravestones n ▷ gravestone
graveyard n (pl -s) cemetery
  graveyards n ▷ graveyard
gravid [grav-id] adj (MED) pregnant
  gravies n ▷ gravy
gravitate v (-tes, -ting, -ted) be influenced or drawn towards > **gravitation** n (pl -s) > **gravitational** adj
  gravitated v ▷ gravitate
  gravitates v ▷ gravitate
  gravitating v ▷ gravitate
  gravitation n ▷ gravitate
  gravitational adj ▷ gravitate
  gravitations n ▷ gravitate
  gravities n ▷ gravity
gravity n (pl -ties) force of attraction of one object for another, esp. of objects to the earth
gravy n (pl -vies) juices from meat in cooking
  grawing v ▷ gnaw
  grawn v ▷ gnaw
gray adj (-er, -est) (CHIEFLY US) grey

grayer *adj* ▷ gray
grayest *adj* ▷ gray
grayling *n* (*pl* -s) fish of the salmon family
graylings *n* ▷ grayling
graze[1] *v* (-zes, -zing, -zed) feed on grass
graze[2] *v* (-zes, -zing, -zed) scratch or scrape the skin ▶ *n* (*pl* -s) slight scratch or scrape
grazed *v* ▷ graze[1,2]
grazes *v*, *n* ▷ graze[1,2]
grazing *v* ▷ graze[1,2]
grease *n* (*pl* -s) soft melted animal fat ▶ *v* (-ses, -sing, -sed) apply grease to
greased *v* ▷ grease
greasepaint *n* (*pl* -s) theatrical make-up
greasepaints *n* ▷ greasepaint
greases *n*, *v* ▷ grease
greasier *adj* ▷ greasy
greasiest *adj* ▷ greasy
greasiness *n* ▷ greasy
greasinesses *n* ▷ greasy
greasing *v* ▷ grease
greasy *adj* (-sier, -siest) covered with or containing grease > **greasiness** *n* (*pl* -s)
great *adj* (-er, -est) large in size or number (*Informal*) > **greatly** *adv* > **greatness** *n* (*pl* -es)
greatcoat *n* (*pl* -s) heavy overcoat
greatcoats *n* ▷ greatcoat
greater *adj* ▷ great
greatest *adj* ▷ great
greatly *adv* ▷ great
greatness *n* ▷ great
greatnesses *n* ▷ great
greave *n* (*pl* -s) piece of armour for the shin
greaves *n* ▷ greave
grebe *n* (*pl* -s) diving water bird
grebes *n* ▷ grebe
greed *n* (*pl* -s) excessive desire for food, wealth, etc. > **greedy** *adj* (-dier, -diest) > **greedily** *adv* > **greediness** *n* (*pl* -es)
greedier *adj* ▷ greed
greediest *adj* ▷ greed
greedily *adv* ▷ greed
greediness *n* ▷ greed
greedinesses *n* ▷ greed
greeds *n* ▷ greed
greedy *adj* ▷ greed
green *adj* (-er, -est) of a colour between blue and yellow ▶ *n* (*pl* -s) colour between blue and yellow ▶ *pl* green vegetables ▶ *v* (-s, -ing, -ed) make or become green > **greenness** *n* (*pl* -es) > **greenish, greeny** *adj*
greened *v* ▷ green
greener *adj* ▷ green
greeneries *n* ▷ greenery
greenery *n* (*pl* -ries) vegetation

greenest *adj* ▷ green
greenfinch *n* (*pl* -es) European finch with dull green plumage in the male
greenfinches *n* ▷ greenfinch
greenflies *n* ▷ greenfly
greenfly *n* (*pl* -flies) green aphid, a common garden pest
greengage *n* (*pl* -s) sweet green plum
greengages *n* ▷ greengage
greengrocer *n* (*pl* -s) (BRIT) shopkeeper selling vegetables and fruit
greengrocer *n* ▷ greengrocers
greenhorn *n* (*pl* -s) (CHIEFLY US) novice
greenhorns *n* ▷ greenhorn
greenhouse *n* (*pl* -s) glass building for rearing plants
greenhouses *n* ▷ greenhouse
greening *v* ▷ green
greenish *adj* ▷ green
greenness *n* ▷ green
greennesses *n* ▷ green
greens *n*, *v* ▷ green
greenshank (*pl* -s) *n* large European sandpiper
greenshanks *n* ▷ greenshanks
greenstone *n* (*pl* -s) (NZ) type of green jade used for Maori ornaments
greenstones *n* ▷ greenstone
greeny *adj* ▷ green
greet *v* (-s, -ing, -ed) meet with expressions of welcome > **greeting** *n* (*pl* -s)
greeted *v* ▷ greet
greeting *v*, *n* ▷ greet
greetings *n* ▷ greet
greets *v* ▷ greet
gregarious *adj* fond of company
gremlin *n* (*pl* -s) imaginary being blamed for mechanical malfunctions
gremlins *n* ▷ gremlin
grenade *n* (*pl* -s) small bomb thrown by hand or fired from a rifle
grenades *n* ▷ grenade
grenadier *n* (*pl* -s) soldier of a regiment formerly trained to throw grenades
grenadiers *n* ▷ grenadier
grenadine [gren-a-**deen**] *n* (*pl* -s) syrup made from pomegranates
grenadines *n* ▷ grenadine
grevillea *n* (*pl* -s) any of various Australian evergreen trees and shrubs
grevilleas *n* ▷ grevillea
grew *v* ▷ grow
grey *adj* (-er, -est) of a colour between black and white ▶ *n* (*pl* -s) grey colour
greyer *adj* ▷ grey
greyest *adj* ▷ grey

greyhound n (pl -s) swift slender dog used in racing
  greyhounds n ▷ greyhound
greying adj (of hair) turning grey > **greyish** adj > **greyness** n (pl -es)
  greyish adj ▷ grey
  greyness n ▷ grey
  greynesses n ▷ grey
  greys n ▷ grey
grid n (pl -s) network of horizontal and vertical lines, bars, etc.
griddle n (pl -s) flat iron plate for cooking
  griddles n ▷ griddle
gridiron n (pl -s) frame of metal bars for grilling food
  gridirons n ▷ gridiron
gridlock n (pl -s) situation where traffic is not moving > **gridlocked** adj
  gridlocked adj ▷ gridlock
  gridlocks n ▷ gridlock
  grids n ▷ grid
grief n (pl -s) deep sadness
  griefs n ▷ grief
grievance (pl -s) n real or imaginary cause for complaint
  grievances n ▷ grievances
grieve v (-ves, -ving, -ved) (cause to) feel grief
  grieved v ▷ grieve
  grieves v ▷ grieve
  grieving adj ▷ grieve
grievous adj very severe or painful
griffin n (pl -s) mythical monster with an eagle's head and wings and a lion's body
  griffins n ▷ griffin
grill n (pl -s) device on a cooker that radiates heat downwards ▶ v (-s, -ing, -ed) cook under a grill
grille, grill n (pl -s) grating over an opening
  grilled v ▷ grill
  grilles n ▷ grille
grilling n (pl -s) relentless questioning ▶ v ▷ grill
  grillings n ▷ grilling
  grills[1] n, v ▷ grill
  grills[2] n ▷ grille
grilse [grillss] n (pl -s) salmon on its first return from the sea to fresh water
  grilses n ▷ grilse
grim adj (-mmer, -mmest) stern > **grimly** adv > **grimness** n (pl -es)
grimace n (pl -s) ugly or distorted facial expression of pain, disgust, etc. ▶ v (-ces, -cing, -ced) make a grimace
  grimaced v ▷ grimace
  grimaces n, v ▷ grimace

  grimacing v ▷ grimace
grime n (pl -s) ingrained dirt ▶ v (-mes, -ming, -med) make very dirty > **grimy** adj (-mier, -miest)
  grimed v ▷ grime
  grimes n, v ▷ grime
  grimier adj ▷ grime
  grimiest adj ▷ grime
  griming v ▷ grime
  grimly adv ▷ grim
  grimmer adj ▷ grim
  grimmest adj ▷ grim
  grimness n ▷ grim
  grimnesses n ▷ grim
  grimy adj ▷ grime
grin v (-s, -nning, -nned) smile broadly, showing the teeth ▶ n (-s) broad smile
grind v (-s, -ing, ground) crush or rub to a powder ▶ n (pl -s) (Informal) hard work
  grinding v ▷ grind
  grinds v, n ▷ grind
grindstone n (pl -s) stone used for grinding
  grindstones n ▷ grindstone
  grinned v ▷ grin
  grinning v ▷ grin
  grins v, n ▷ grin
grip n (pl -s) firm hold or grasp (US) ▶ v (-s, -pping, -pped) grasp or hold tightly > **gripping** adj
gripe v (-pes, -ping, -ped) (Informal) complain persistently ▶ n (pl -s) (Informal) complaint
  griped v ▷ gripe
  gripes v, n ▷ gripe
  griping v ▷ gripe
  gripped v ▷ grip
  gripping v, adj ▷ grip
  grips n, v ▷ grip
  grislier adj ▷ grisly
  grisliest adj ▷ grisly
grisly adj (-lier, -liest) horrifying or ghastly
grist n (pl -s) grain for grinding
gristle n (pl -s) tough stringy animal tissue found in meat > **gristly** adj (-lier, -liest)
  gristles n ▷ gristle
  gristlier adj ▷ gristle
  gristliest adj ▷ gristle
  gristly adj ▷ gristle
  grists n ▷ grist
grit n (pl -s) rough particles of sand ▶ pl coarsely ground grain ▶ v (-s, -tting, -tted) spread grit on (an icy road etc.) > **gritty** adj (-tier, -ttiest) > **grittiness** n (pl -es)
  grits v ▷ grit
  gritted v ▷ grit
  grittier adj ▷ grit

grittiest *adj* ▷ grit
grittiness *n* ▷ grit
grittinesses *n* ▷ grit
gritting *v* ▷ grit
gritty *adj* ▷ grit
grizzle *v* (-les, -ling, -led) (BRIT, AUST & NZ) (*Informal*) whine or complain
grizzled *adj* grey-haired ▶ *v* ▷ grizzle
grizzles *v* ▷ grizzle
grizzlies *n* ▷ grizzly
grizzling *v* ▷ grizzle
grizzly *n* (*pl* -lies) large American bear
groan *n* (*pl* -s) deep sound of grief or pain ▶ *v* (-s, -ing, -ed) utter a groan
groaned *v* ▷ groan
groaning *v* ▷ groan
groans *n*, *v* ▷ groan
groat *n* (*pl* -s) (HIST) fourpenny piece
groats *n* ▷ groat
grocer *n* (*pl* -s) shopkeeper selling foodstuffs
groceries *n* ▷ grocery
grocers *n* ▷ grocer
grocery *n* (*pl* -ceries) business or premises of a grocer ▶ *pl* goods sold by a grocer
grog *n* (*pl* -s) (BRIT, AUST & NZ) spirit, usu. rum, and water
groggier *adj* ▷ groggy
groggiest *adj* ▷ groggy
groggy *adj* (-ggier, -ggiest) (*Informal*) faint, shaky, or dizzy
grogs *n* ▷ grog
groin *n* (*pl* -s) place where the legs join the abdomen
groins *n* ▷ groin
grommet *n* (*pl* -s) ring or eyelet
grommets *n* ▷ grommet
groom *n* (*pl* -s) person who looks after horses ▶ *v* (-s, -ing, -ed) make or keep one's clothes and appearance neat and tidy
groomed *v* ▷ groom
grooming *v* ▷ groom
grooms *n*, *v* ▷ groom
groove *n* (*pl* -s) long narrow channel in a surface
grooves *n* ▷ groove
grope *v* (-pes, -ping, -ped) feel about or search uncertainly > **groping** *n* (*pl* -s)
groped *v* ▷ grope
gropes *v* ▷ grope
groping *v*, *n* ▷ grope
gropings *n* ▷ grope
gross *adj* flagrant ▶ *n* (*pl* -es) twelve dozen ▶ *v* (-es, -ing, -ed) make as total revenue before deductions > **grossly** *adv* > **grossness** *n* (*pl* -es)
grossed *v* ▷ gross

grosses *n*, *v* ▷ gross
grossing *v* ▷ gross
grossly *adv* ▷ gross
grossness *n* ▷ gross
grossnesses *n* ▷ gross
grotesque [grow-**tesk**] *adj* (-quer, -quest) strangely distorted ▶ *n* (*pl* -s) grotesque person or thing > **grotesquely** *adv*
grotesquely *adv* ▷ grotesque
grotesquer *adj* ▷ grotesque
grotesques *n* ▷ grotesque
grotesquest *adj* ▷ grotesque
grottier *adj* ▷ grotty
grottiest *adj* ▷ grotty
grotto *n* (*pl* -ttoes, -ttos) small picturesque cave
grottoes *n* ▷ grotto
grottos *n* ▷ grotto
grotty *adj* (-ttier, -ttiest) (*Informal*) nasty or in bad condition
grouch (*Informal*) *v* (-es, -ing, -ed) grumble or complain ▶ *n* (*pl* -es) person who is always complaining > **grouchy** *adj* (-chier, -chiest)
grouched *v* ▷ grouch
grouches *v*, *n* ▷ grouch
grouchier *adj* ▷ grouch
grouchiest *adj* ▷ grouch
grouching *v* ▷ grouch
grouchy *adj* ▷ grouch
ground¹ *n* (*pl* -s) surface of the earth ▶ *pl* enclosed land round a house ▶ *v* (-s, -ing, -ed) base or establish
ground² *v* ▷ grind
groundbreaking *adj* innovative
grounded *v* ▷ ground¹
grounding *n* (*pl* -s) basic knowledge of a subject ▶ *v* ▷ ground¹
groundings *n* ▷ grounding
groundless *adj* without reason
groundnut *n* (*pl* -s) peanut
groundnuts *n* ▷ groundnut
grounds *n*, *v* ▷ ground¹
groundsheet *n* (*pl* -s) waterproof sheet put on the ground under a tent
groundsheets *n* ▷ groundsheet
groundsman *n* (*pl* -men) person employed to maintain a sports ground or park
groundsmen *n* ▷ groundsman
groundswell *n* (*pl* -s) rapidly developing general feeling or opinion
groundswells *n* ▷ groundswell
groundwork *n* (*pl* -s) preliminary work
groundworks *n* ▷ groundwork
group *n* (*pl* -s) number of people or things regarded as a unit ▶ *v* (-s, -ing, -ed) place or

form into a group
grouped v ▷ group
grouping v ▷ group
groups n, v ▷ group
grouse¹ n (pl -s) stocky game bird
grouse² v (-ses, -sing, -sed) grumble or complain ▶ n (pl -s) complaint
groused v ▷ grouse²
grouses n, v ▷ grouse¹, ²
grousing v ▷ grouse²
grout n (pl -s) thin mortar ▶ v (-s, -ing, -ed) fill up with grout
grouted v ▷ grout
grouting v ▷ grout
grouts n, v ▷ grout
grove n (pl -s) small group of trees
grovel [grov-el] v (-s, -elling, -elled) behave humbly in order to win a superior's favour
grovelled v ▷ grovel
grovelling v ▷ grovel
grovels v ▷ grovel
groves n ▷ grove
grow v (-s, growing, grew, grown) develop physically
growing v ▷ grow
growl v (-s, -ing, -ed) make a low rumbling sound ▶ n (pl -s) growling sound
growled v ▷ growl
growling v ▷ growl
growls n, v ▷ growl
grown v ▷ grow
grownup adj, n (pl -s) adult
grownups n ▷ grownup
grows v ▷ grow
growth n (pl -s) growing
growths n ▷ growth
groyne n (pl -s) wall built from the shore to control erosion
groynes n ▷ groyne
grub n (pl -s) legless insect larva ▶ v (-s, -bbing, -bbed) search carefully for something by digging or by moving things about
grubbed v ▷ grub
grubbier adj ▷ grubby
grubbiest adj ▷ grubby
grubbiness n ▷ grubby
grubbinesses n ▷ grubby
grubbing v ▷ grub
grubby adj (-bbier, -bbiest) dirty > **grubbiness** n (pl -es)
grubs n, v ▷ grub
grudge v (-ges, -ging, -ged) be unwilling to give or allow ▶ n (pl -s) resentment
grudged v ▷ grudge
grudges v, n ▷ grudge

grudging v ▷ grudge
gruel n (pl -s) thin porridge
gruelling adj exhausting or severe
gruels n ▷ gruel
gruesome adj (-er, -est) causing horror and disgust
gruesomer adj ▷ gruesome
gruesomest adj ▷ gruesome
gruff adj (-er, -est) rough or surly in manner or voice > **gruffly** adv > **gruffness** n (pl -es)
gruffer adj ▷ gruff
gruffest adj ▷ gruff
gruffly adv ▷ gruff
gruffness n ▷ gruff
gruffnesses n ▷ gruff
grumble v (-les, -ling, -led) complain ▶ n (pl -s) complaint > **grumbler** n (pl -s) > **grumbling** adj, n (pl -s)
grumbled v ▷ grumble
grumbler n ▷ grumble
grumblers n ▷ grumble
grumbles v, n ▷ grumble
grumbling v, n ▷ grumble
grumblings n ▷ grumble
grumpier adj ▷ grumpy
grumpiest adj ▷ grumpy
grumpily adv ▷ grumpy
grumpiness n ▷ grumpy
grumpinesses n ▷ grumpy
grumpy adj (-pier, -piest) bad-tempered > **grumpily** adv > **grumpiness** n (pl -es)
grunge n (pl -s) style of rock music with a fuzzy guitar sound
grunges n ▷ grunge
grunt v (-s, -ing, -ed) make a low short gruff sound, like a pig ▶ n (pl -s) pig's sound
grunted v ▷ grunt
grunting v ▷ grunt
grunts v, n ▷ grunt
gryphon n (pl -s) ▷ griffin
gryphons n ▷ gryphon

> **gu** n (**gus**). A gu (also spelt **gju**) is a kind of violin from Shetland. This is one of only three two-letter words beginning with G, and so is a good one to remember. Gu scores 3 points.

guano [gwah-no] n (pl -nos) dried sea-bird manure, used as fertilizer
guanos n ▷ guano
guarantee n (pl -s) formal assurance, esp. in writing, that a product will meet certain standards ▶ v (-s, -teeing, -teed) give a guarantee
guaranteed v ▷ guarantee
guaranteeing v ▷ guarantee

guarantees n, v ▷ guarantee
guarantor n (pl -s) person who gives or is bound by a guarantee
guarantors n ▷ guarantor
guard v (-s, -ing, -ed) watch over to protect or to prevent escape ▶ n (pl -s) person or group that guards ▶ (G-) pl regiment with ceremonial duties
guarded adj cautious or noncommittal ▶ v ▷ guard > **guardedly** adv
guardedly adv ▷ guarded
guardian n (pl -s) keeper or protector > **guardianship** n (pl -s)
guardians n ▷ guardian
guardianship n ▷ guardian
guardianships n ▷ guardian
guarding v ▷ guard
guards v, n ▷ guard
guardsman n (pl -s) member of the Guards
guardsmen n ▷ guardsman
guava [gwah-va] n (pl -s) yellow-skinned tropical American fruit
guavas n ▷ guava
gudgeon n (pl -s) small freshwater fish
gudgeons n ▷ gudgeon
guerillas n ▷ guerrilla
guerrilla, guerilla n (pl -s) member of an unofficial armed force fighting regular forces
guerrillas n ▷ guerrilla
guess v (-es, -ing, -ed) estimate or draw a conclusion without proper knowledge ▶ n (pl -es) estimate or conclusion reached by guessing
guessed v ▷ guess
guesses v, n ▷ guess
guessing v ▷ guess
guesswork n (pl -s) process or results of guessing
guessworks n ▷ guesswork
guest n (pl -s) person entertained at another's house or at another's expense ▶ v (-s, -ing, -ed) appear as a visiting player or performer
guested v ▷ guest
guesthouse n (pl -s) boarding house
guesthouses n ▷ guesthouse
guesting v ▷ guest
guests n, v ▷ guest
guff n (pl -s) (BRIT, AUST & NZ) (Slang) nonsense
guffaw n (pl -s) crude noisy laugh ▶ v (-s, -ing, -ed) laugh in this way
guffawed v ▷ guffaw
guffawing v ▷ guffaw
guffaws n, v ▷ guffaw
guffs n ▷ guff
guidance n (pl -s) leadership, instruction, or advice

guidances n ▷ guidance
guide n (pl -s) person who conducts tour expeditions ▶ v (-s, -ing, -ed) act as a guide for
guided v ▷ guide
guideline n set principle for doing something
guidelines n ▷ guideline
guides n, v ▷ guide
guiding v ▷ guide
guild n (pl -s) organization or club
guilder n (pl -s) former monetary unit of the Netherlands
guilders n ▷ guilder
guilds n ▷ guild
guile [gile] n (pl -s) cunning or deceit > **guileful** adj > **guileless** adj
guileful adj ▷ guile
guileless adj ▷ guile
guiles n ▷ guile
guillemot [gil-lee-mot] n (pl -s) black-and-white diving sea bird of N hemisphere
guillemots n ▷ guillemot
guillotine n (pl -s) machine for beheading people ▶ v (-s, -ing, -ed) behead by guillotine
guillotined v ▷ guillotine
guillotines n, v ▷ guillotine
guillotining v ▷ guillotine
guilt n (pl -s) fact or state of having done wrong
guiltier adj ▷ guilty
guiltiest adj ▷ guilty
guiltily adv ▷ guilty
guiltless adj innocent
guilts n ▷ guilt
guilty adj (-tier, -tiest) responsible for an offence or misdeed > **guiltily** adv
guinea n (pl -s) former British monetary unit worth 21 shillings (1.05 pounds)
guineas n ▷ guinea
guise [rhymes with size] n (pl -s) false appearance
guises n ▷ guise
guitar n (pl -s) stringed instrument with a flat back and a long neck, played by plucking or strumming > **guitarist** n
guitarist n ▷ guitar
guitarists n ▷ guitar
guitars n ▷ guitar
gulch n (pl -es) (US) deep narrow valley
gulches n ▷ gulch
gulf n (pl -s) large deep bay
gulfs n ▷ gulf
gull n (pl -s) long-winged sea bird
gullet n (pl -s) muscular tube through which food passes from the mouth to the stomach
gullets n ▷ gullet

gullibilities n ▷ gullible
gullibility n ▷ gullible
gullible adj easily tricked > **gullibility** n (pl -ties)
gullies n ▷ gully
gulls n ▷ gull
gully n (pl -llies) channel cut by running water
gulp v (-s, -ing, -ed) swallow hastily ▶ n (pl -s) gulping
gulped v ▷ gulp
gulping v ▷ gulp
gulps v, n ▷ gulp
gum¹ n (pl -s) firm flesh in which the teeth are set
gum² n (pl -s) sticky substance obtained from certain trees ▶ v (-s, -mming, -mmed) stick with gum
gumboot n (pl -s) (CHIEFLY BRIT) Wellington boot
gumboots n ▷ gumboot
gumdrop n (pl -s) hard jelly-like sweet
gumdrops n ▷ gumdrop
gummed v ▷ gum²
gummier adj ▷ gummy¹,²
gummiest adj ▷ gummy¹,²
gumming v ▷ gum²
gummy¹ adj (-mmier, -mmiest) toothless
gummy² adj (-mmier, -mmiest) sticky
gumption n (pl -s) (Informal) resourcefulness
gumptions n ▷ gumption
gums n, v ▷ gum¹,²
gun n (pl -s) weapon with a metal tube from which missiles are fired by explosion ▶ v (-s, -nning, -nned) cause (an engine) to run at high speed
gunboat n (pl -s) small warship
gunboats n ▷ gunboat
gunge n (pl -s) (Informal) sticky unpleasant substance > **gungy** adj (-gier, -giest)
gunges n ▷ gunge
gungier adj ▷ gung
gungiest adj ▷ gung
gungy adj ▷ gung
gunman n (pl -men) armed criminal
gunmen n ▷ gunman
gunmetal n (pl -s) alloy of copper, tin, and zinc ▶ adj dark grey
gunmetals n ▷ gunmetal
gunned v ▷ gun
gunnel n ▷ gunwale
gunnels n ▷ gunwale
gunner n (pl -s) artillery soldier
gunneries n ▷ gunnery
gunners n ▷ gunner
gunnery n (pl -ries) use or science of large guns
gunnies n ▷ gunny

gunning v ▷ gun
gunny n (pl -ies) strong coarse fabric used for sacks
gunpowder n (pl -s) explosive mixture of potassium nitrate, sulphur, and charcoal
gunpowders n ▷ gunpowder
gunrunner n ▷ gunrunning
gunrunners n ▷ gunrunning
gunrunning n (pl -s) smuggling of guns and ammunition > **gunrunner** n (pl -s)
gunrunnings n ▷ gunrunning
guns n, v ▷ gun
gunshot n (pl -s) shot or range of a gun
gunshots n ▷ gunshot
gunwale, gunnel [gun-nel] n (pl -s) top of a ship's side
gunwales n ▷ gunwale
gunyah n (pl -s) (AUST) hut or shelter in the bush
gunyahs n ▷ gunyah
guppies n ▷ guppy
guppy n (pl -ppies) small colourful aquarium fish
gurgle v (-les, -ling, -led) ▶ n (pl -s) (make) a bubbling noise
gurgled v ▷ gurgle
gurgles v, n ▷ gurgle
gurgling v ▷ gurgle
guru n (pl -s) Hindu or Sikh religious teacher or leader
gurus n ▷ guru
gush v (-es, -ing, -ed) flow out suddenly and profusely ▶ n (pl -es) sudden copious flow
gushed v ▷ gush
gusher n (pl -s) spurting oil well
gushers n ▷ gusher
gushes v, n ▷ gush
gushing v ▷ gush
gusset n (pl -s) piece of material sewn into a garment to strengthen it
gussets n ▷ gusset
gust n (pl -s) sudden blast of wind ▶ v (-s, -ing, -ed) blow in gusts > **gusty** adj (-tier, -tiest)
gusted v ▷ gust
gustier adj ▷ gust
gustiest adj ▷ gust
gusting v ▷ gust
gusto n (pl -tos) enjoyment or zest
gustos n ▷ gusto
gusts n, v ▷ gust
gusty adj ▷ gust
gut n (pl -s) intestine (Informal) ▷ catgut ▶ pl internal organs ▶ v (-s, -tting, -tted) remove the guts from ▶ adj basic or instinctive
guts n ▷ gut
gutsier adj ▷ gutsy

gutsiest adj ▷ gutsy
gutsy adj (-sier, -siest) (*Informal*) courageous
gutted adj (BRIT, AUST & NZ) (*Informal*) disappointed and upset ▶ v ▷ gut
gutter n (pl -s) shallow channel for carrying away water from a roof or roadside ▶ v (-s, -ing, -ed) (of a candle) burn unsteadily, with wax running down the sides
guttered v ▷ gutter
guttering n material for gutters ▶ v ▷ gutter
gutters n, v ▷ gutter
guttersnipe n (pl -s) (BRIT) neglected slum child
guttersnipes n ▷ guttersnipe
gutting v ▷ gut
guttural adj (of a sound) produced at the back of the throat
gutturalnesses n ▷ guttural
guy[1] n (pl -s) (*Informal*) man or boy
guy[2] n (pl -s) rope or chain to steady or secure something
guys n ▷ guy[1, 2]
guzzle v (-les, -ling, -led) eat or drink greedily
guzzled v ▷ guzzle
guzzles v ▷ guzzle
guzzling v ▷ guzzle
gybe [jibe] v (-bes, -bing, -bed) (of a fore-and-aft sail) swing suddenly from one side to the other
gybed v ▷ gybe
gybes v ▷ gybe
gybing v ▷ gybe
gym n (pl -s) gymnasium
gymkhana [jim-**kah**-na] n (pl -s) horse-riding competition
gymkhanas n ▷ gymkhana
gymnasium n (pl -s) large room with equipment for physical training
gymnasiums n ▷ gymnasium
gymnast n (pl -s) expert in gymnastics
gymnastic n ▷ gymnastics
gymnastics pl n exercises to develop strength and agility > **gymnastic** adj
gymnasts n ▷ gymnast

gyms n ▷ gym
gynaecological adj ▷ gynaecology
gynaecologies n ▷ gynaecology
gynaecologist n ▷ gynaecology
gynaecologists n ▷ gynaecology
gynaecology [guy-nee-**kol**-la-jee] n (pl -ies) branch of medicine dealing with diseases and conditions specific to women > **gynaecological** adj > **gynaecologist** n (pl -s)

> **gyp** n (**gyps, gypping, gyped**). Gyp is a slang word meaning to cheat or swindle. This word and its inflections can be very useful when there is a word ending in Y on the board. Gyp scores 9 points.

gypsies n ▷ gypsy
gypsophila n (pl -s) garden plant with small white flowers
gypsophilas n ▷ gypsophila
gypsum n (pl -s) chalklike mineral used to make plaster of Paris
gypsums n ▷ gypsy
gypsy n (pl -sies) member of a travelling people found throughout Europe
gypsyhood n ▷ gypsy
gyrate [jire-**rate**] v (-tes, -ting, -ted) rotate or spiral about a point or axis > **gyration** n (pl -s)
gyrated v ▷ gyrate
gyrates v ▷ gyrate
gyrating v ▷ gyrate
gyration n ▷ gyrate
gyrations n ▷ gyrate
gyratory adj gyrating
gyrocompass n (pl -es) compass using a gyroscope
gyrocompasses n ▷ gyrocompass
gyroscope [jire-oh-skohp] n (pl -s) disc rotating on an axis that can turn in any direction, so the disc maintains the same position regardless of the movement of the surrounding structure > **gyroscopic** adj
gyroscopes n ▷ gyroscope
gyroscopic adj ▷ gyroscope

H h

H forms a two-letter word in front of every vowel except U (and you can make **uh** with U), making it a versatile tile when you want to form words in more than one direction. As H is worth 4 points on its own, you can earn some very high scores by doing this: even **ha, he, hi** and **ho** will give 5 points each. There are lots of good short words beginning with H, like **haw, hew, how, hay, hey** and **hoy** (9 each).

ha *interj.* Ha is a sound people make to express triumph or surprise. This gives a reasonable score for a two-letter word, and is a good one to form when making a longer word in another direction at the same time. Ha scores 5 points.

haberdasher *n* (*pl* -s) (BRIT, AUST & NZ) dealer in small articles used for sewing
> **haberdashery** *n* (*pl* -ries)
haberdasheries *n* ▷ haberdasher
haberdashers *n* ▷ haberdasher
haberdashery *n* ▷ haberdasher

habit *n* (*pl* -s) established way of behaving

habitable *adj* fit to be lived in

habitat *n* (*pl* -s) natural home of an animal or plant

habitation *n* (*pl* -s) (occupation of) a dwelling place
habitations *n* ▷ habitation
habitats *n* ▷ habitat
habits *n* ▷ habit

habitual *adj* done regularly and repeatedly
> **habitually** *adv*
habitually *adv* ▷ habitual

habituate *v* (-tes, -ting, -ted) accustom
> **habituation** *n* (*pl* -s)
habituated *v* ▷ habituate
habituates *v* ▷ habituate
habituating *v* ▷ habituate
habituation *n* ▷ habituate
habituations *n* ▷ habituate

habitué [hab-**it**-yew-ay] *n* (*pl* -s) frequent visitor to a place
habitués *n* ▷ habitué

hacienda [hass-ee-**end**-a] *n* (*pl* -s) ranch or large estate in Latin America
haciendas *n* ▷ hacienda

hack¹ *v* (-s, -ing, -ed) cut or chop violently (BRIT

& NZ) (*Informal*)

hack² *n* (*pl* -s) (inferior) writer or journalist
hacked *v* ▷ hack¹

hacker *n* (*pl* -s) (*Slang*) computer enthusiast, esp. one who breaks into the computer system of a company or government
hackers *n* ▷ hacker
hacking *v* ▷ hack¹

hackles *pl n* hairs on the neck and back of an animal

hackney *n* (*pl* -s) (BRIT) taxi

hackneyed *adj* (of a word or phrase) unoriginal and overused
hackneys *n* ▷ hackney
hacks *v* ▷ hack¹ ▶ *n* ▷ hack²

hacksaw *n* (*pl* -s) small saw for cutting metal
hacksaws *n* ▷ hacksaw
had *v* ▷ have

haddock *n* (*pl* -s) edible sea fish of N Atlantic
haddocks *n* ▷ haddock

hadj *n* (*pl* -es) ▷ hajj
hadjes *n* ▷ hadj
haematologies *n* ▷ haematology

haematology *n* (*pl* -gies) study of blood and its diseases

haemoglobin [hee-moh-**globe**-in] *n* (*pl* -s) protein found in red blood cells which carries oxygen
haemoglobins *n* ▷ haemoglobin

haemophilia [hee-moh-**fill**-lee-a] *n* (*pl* -s) hereditary illness in which the blood does not clot > **haemophiliac** *n* (*pl* -s)
haemophiliac *n* ▷ haemophilia
haemophiliacs *n* ▷ haemophilia
haemophilias *n* ▷ haemophilia

haemorrhage [**hem**-or-ij] *n* (*pl* -ges) heavy bleeding ▶ *v* (-ges, -ging, -ged) bleed heavily
haemorrhaged *v* ▷ haemorrhage
haemorrhages *n, v* ▷ haemorrhage

haemorrhaging v ▷ haemorrhage

haemorrhoids [hem-or-oydz] pl n swollen veins in the anus (also **piles**)

hafnium n (pl -s) (CHEM) metallic element found in zirconium ores

hafniums n ▷ hafnium

haft n (pl -s) handle of an axe, knife, or dagger

hafts n ▷ haft

hag n (pl -s) ugly old woman

haggard adj looking tired and ill

haggis n (pl -es) Scottish dish made from sheep's offal, oatmeal, suet, and seasonings, boiled in a bag made from the sheep's stomach

haggises n ▷ haggis

haggle v (-les, -ling, -led) bargain or wrangle over a price

haggled v ▷ haggle

haggles v ▷ haggle

haggling v ▷ haggle

hagiographies n ▷ hagiography

hagiography n (pl -phies) writing about the lives of the saints

hags n ▷ hag

hail[1] n (pl -s) (shower of) small pellets of ice ▶ v (-s, -ing, -ed) fall as or like hail ▶ **hailstone** n (pl -s)

hail[2] v (-s, -ing, -ed) call out to, greet

hailed v ▷ hail[1, 2]

hailing v ▷ hail[1, 2]

hails v ▷ hail[1, 2] ▶ n ▷ hail[1]

hailstone n ▷ hail[1]

hailstones n ▷ hail[1]

hair n (pl hairs) threadlike growth on the skin

hairclip n (pl -s) small bent metal hairpin

hairclips n ▷ hairclip

hairdo n (pl -s) (Informal) hairstyle

hairdos n ▷ hairdo

hairdresser n (pl -s) person who cuts and styles hair

hairdressers n ▷ hairdresser

hairgrip n (BRIT) (pl -s) ▷ hairclip

hairgrips n ▷ hairgrip

hairier adj ▷ hairy

hairiest adj ▷ hairy

hairiness n ▷ hairy

hairinesses n ▷ hairy

hairline n (pl -s) edge of hair at the top of the forehead ▶ adj very fine or narrow

hairlines n ▷ hairline

hairpin n (pl -s) U-shaped wire used to hold the hair in place

hairpins n ▷ hairpin

hairs n ▷ hair

hairsplitting n (pl -s) ▶ adj making petty distinctions

hairsplittings n ▷ hairsplitting

hairstyle n (pl -s) cut and arrangement of a person's hair

hairstyles n ▷ hairstyle

hairy adj (-rier, -riest) covered with hair > **hairiness** n (pl -es)

> **haj** n. Haj is the same as **hajj**. This is a very useful word, especially when there isn't much space on the board. Remember that this spelling doesn't have a plural form. Haj scores 13 points.

hajj n (pl -es) pilgrimage a Muslim makes to Mecca

hajjes n ▷ hajj

haka n (pl -s) (NZ) ceremonial Maori dance with chanting

hakas n ▷ haka

hake n (pl hakes) edible sea fish of N hemisphere (AUST) ▷ barracouta

hakea [hah-kee-a] n (pl -s) Australian tree or shrub with hard woody fruit

hakeas n ▷ hakea

hakes n ▷ hake

halal n (pl -s) meat from animals slaughtered according to Muslim law

halals n ▷ halal

halberd n (pl -s) (HIST) spear with an axe blade

halberds n ▷ halberd

halcyon [hal-see-on] adj peaceful and happy

hale adj (-ler, -lest) healthy, robust

haler adj ▷ hale

halest adj ▷ hale

half n (pl -lves) either of two equal parts ▶ adj denoting one of two equal parts ▶ adv to the extent of half

halfhearted adj unenthusiastic

halflife n (pl -ves) time taken for half the atoms in radioactive material to decay

halflives n ▷ halflife

halfpennies n ▷ halfpenny

halfpenny [hayp-nee] n (pl -nnies) former British coin worth half an old penny

halftime n (pl -s) (SPORT) short rest period between two halves of a game

halftimes n ▷ halftime

halftone n (pl -s) illustration showing lights and shadows by means of very small dots

halftones n ▷ halftone

halfway adv, adj at or half the distance

halfwit n (pl -s) foolish or stupid person

halfwits n ▷ halfwit

halibut n (pl halibuts) large edible flatfish of N Atlantic

halibuts n ▷ halibut

halitosis n (pl **-ises**) unpleasant-smelling breath
   halitosises n ▷ halitosis
hall n (pl **-s**) (also **hallway**) entrance passage
hallelujah [hal-ee-**loo**-ya] interj exclamation of praise to God
hallmark n (pl **-s**) typical feature ▶ v (**-s, -ing, -ed**) stamp with a hallmark
   hallmarked v ▷ hallmark
   hallmarking v ▷ hallmark
   hallmarks n, v ▷ hallmark
   hallo interj ▷ hello
hallowed adj regarded as holy
Halloween, Hallowe'en n (pl **-s**) October 31, celebrated by children by dressing up as ghosts, witches, etc.
   Halloweens n ▷ Halloween
   halls n ▷ hall
hallucinate v (**-tes, -ting, -ted**) seem to see something that is not really there > **hallucination** n (pl **-s**) > **hallucinatory** adj
   hallucinated v ▷ hallucinate
   hallucinates v ▷ hallucinate
   hallucinating v ▷ hallucinate
   hallucination n ▷ hallucinate
   hallucinations n ▷ hallucinate
   hallucinatory adj ▷ hallucinate
hallucinogen n (pl **-s**) drug that causes hallucinations > **hallucinogenic** adj
   hallucinogenic adj ▷ hallucinogen
   hallucinogens n ▷ hallucinogen
halo [**hay**-loh] n (pl **-loes, -los**) ring of light round the head of a sacred figure
   haloes n ▷ halo
halogen [**hal**-oh-jen] n (pl **-s**) (CHEM) any of a group of nonmetallic elements including chlorine and iodine
   halogens n ▷ halogen
   halos n ▷ halo
halt v (**-s, -ing, -ed**) come or bring to a stop ▶ n (pl **-s**) temporary stop
   halted v ▷ halt
halter n (pl **-s**) strap round a horse's head with a rope to lead it with
halterneck n (pl **-s**) woman's top or dress with a strap fastened at the back of the neck
   halternecks n ▷ halterneck
   halters n ▷ halter
halting adj hesitant, uncertain ▶ v ▷ halt
   halts v, n ▷ halt
halve v (**-ves, -ving, -ved**) divide in half
   halved v ▷ halve
   halves v ▷ halve ▶ n ▷ half
   halving v ▷ halve
halyard n (pl **-s**) rope for raising a ship's sail or flag
   halyards n ▷ halyard
ham[1] n (pl **-s**) smoked or salted meat from a pig's thigh
ham[2] (Informal) n (pl **-s**) amateur radio operator ▶ v (**-s, -mming, -mmed**) overact
hamburger n (pl **-s**) minced beef shaped into a flat disc, cooked and usu. served in a bread roll
   hamburgers n ▷ hamburger
hamlet n (pl **-s**) small village
   hamlets n ▷ hamlet
   hammed v ▷ ham[2]
hammer n (pl **-s**) tool with a heavy metal head and a wooden handle, used to drive in nails etc. ▶ v (**-s, -ing, -ed**) hit (as if) with a hammer
   hammered v ▷ hammer
hammerhead n (pl **-s**) shark with a wide flattened head
   hammerheads n ▷ hammerhead
   hammering v ▷ hammer
   hammers n, v ▷ hammer
   hamming v ▷ ham[2]
hammock n (pl **-s**) hanging bed made of canvas or net
   hammocks n ▷ hammock
hamper[1] v (**-s, -ing, -ed**) make it difficult for (someone or something) to move or progress
hamper[2] n (pl **-s**) large basket with a lid
   hampered v ▷ hamper[1]
   hampering v ▷ hamper[1]
   hampers v, n ▷ hamper[1, 2]
   hams n, v ▷ ham[1, 2]
hamster n (pl **-s**) small rodent with a short tail and cheek pouches
   hamsters n ▷ hamster
hamstring n (pl **-s**) tendon at the back of the knee ▶ v (**-s, -ing, -rung**) make it difficult for (someone) to take any action
   hamstringing v ▷ hamstring
   hamstrings n, v ▷ hamstring
   hamstrung v ▷ hamstring
hand n (pl **-s**) part of the body at the end of the arm, consisting of a palm, four fingers, and a thumb ▶ v (**-s, -ing, -ed**) pass, give
handbag n (pl **-s**) woman's small bag for carrying personal articles in
   handbags n ▷ handbag
handbill n (pl **-s**) small printed notice
   handbills n ▷ handbill
handbook n (pl **-s**) small reference or instruction book
   handbooks n ▷ handbook
handcuff n (pl **-s**) one of a linked pair of metal rings designed to be locked round a

prisoner's wrists by the police ▶ v (-s, -ing, -ed) put handcuffs on
handcuffed v ▷ handcuff
handcuffing v ▷ handcuff
handcuffs n, v ▷ handcuff
handed v ▷ hand
handful n (pl -s) amount that can be held in the hand
handfuls n ▷ handful
handheld adj (of a film camera) held rather than mounted, as in close-up action shots ▶ n (pl -s) computer that can be held in the hand
handhelds n ▷ handheld
handicap n (pl -s) physical or mental disability ▶ v (-s, -pping, -pped) make it difficult for (someone) to do something
handicapped v ▷ handicap
handicapping v ▷ handicap
handicaps n, v ▷ handicap
handicraft n (pl -s) objects made by hand
handicrafts n ▷ handicraft
handier adj ▷ handy
handiest adj ▷ handy
handily adv ▷ handy
handing v ▷ hand
handiwork n (pl -s) result of someone's work or activity
handiworks n ▷ handiwork
handkerchief n (pl -s) small square of fabric used to wipe the nose
handkerchiefs n ▷ handkerchief
handle n (pl -s) part of an object that is held so that it can be used ▶ v (-les, -ling, -led) hold, feel, or move with the hands
handlebars pl n curved metal bar used to steer a cycle
handled v ▷ handle
handler n (pl -s) person who controls an animal
handlers n ▷ handler
handles n, v ▷ handle
handling v ▷ handle
handout n (pl -s) clothing, food, or money given to a needy person
handouts n ▷ handout
hands n, v ▷ hand
handsome adj (esp. of a man) good-looking
handstand n (pl -s) act of supporting the body on the hands in an upside-down position
handstands n ▷ handstand
handwriting n (pl -s) (style of) writing by hand
handwritings n ▷ handwriting
handy adj (-dier, -diest) convenient, useful > **handily** adv
handyman n (pl -men) man who is good at

making or repairing things
handymen n ▷ handyman
hang v (-s, -ing, hung or hanged) attach or be attached at the top with the lower part free
hangar n (pl -s) large shed for storing aircraft
hangars n ▷ hangar
hangdog adj guilty, ashamed
hanged v ▷ hang
hanger n (pl -s) curved piece of wood, wire, or plastic, with a hook, for hanging up clothes (also **coat hanger**)
hangers n ▷ hanger
hangi n (pl -gi, -gis) (NZ) Maori oven consisting of a hole in the ground filled with hot stones
hanging v ▷ hang
hangis n ▷ hangi
hangman n (pl -men) man who executes people by hanging
hangmen n ▷ hangman
hangover n (pl -s) headache and nausea as a result of drinking too much alcohol
hangovers n ▷ hangover
hangs v ▷ hang
hangup n (pl -s) (Informal) emotional or psychological problem
hangups n ▷ hangup
hank n (pl -s) coil, esp. of yarn
hanker v (-s, -ing, -ed) (foll. by **after** or **for**) desire intensely
hankered v ▷ hanker
hankering v ▷ hanker
hankers v ▷ hanker
hankie n ▷ hanky
hankies n ▷ hanky
hanks n ▷ hank
hanky, hankie n (pl hankies) (Informal) handkerchief
haphazard adj not organized or planned > **haphazardly** adv
haphazardly adv ▷ haphazard
hapless adj unlucky
happen v (-s, -ing, -ed) take place, occur
happened v ▷ happen
happening n (pl -s) event, occurrence ▶ v ▷ happen
happenings n ▷ happening
happens v ▷ happen
happier adj ▷ happy
happiest adj ▷ happy
happily adv ▷ happy
happiness n ▷ happy
happinesses n ▷ happiness
happy adj (-ppier, -ppiest) feeling or causing joy > **happily** adv > **happiness** n (pl -es)
harangue v (-gues, -guing, -gued) address

angrily or forcefully ▶ n (pl -**gues**) angry or forceful speech

harangued v ▷ harangue

harangues v, n ▷ harangue

haranguing v ▷ harangue

harass v (-**es**, -**ing**, -**ssed**) annoy or trouble constantly > **harassed** adj > **harassment** n (pl -s)

harassed v, adj ▷ harass

harasses v ▷ harass

harassing v ▷ harass

harassment n ▷ harass

harassments n ▷ harassment

harbinger [har-binj-a] n (pl -s) someone or something that announces the approach of something

harbingers n ▷ harbinger

harbour n (pl -s) sheltered port ▶ v (-s, -ing, -ed) maintain secretly in the mind

harboured v ▷ harbour

harbouring v ▷ harbour

harbours n, v ▷ harbour

hard adj firm, solid, or rigid ▶ adv with great energy or effort > **harden** v (-s, -ing, -ed) > **hardness** n (pl -es)

hardboard n (pl -s) thin stiff board made of compressed sawdust and wood chips

hardboards n ▷ hardboard

harden v ▷ hard

hardened v ▷ hard

hardening v ▷ hard

hardens v ▷ hard

hardfill n (pl -s) (NZ & S AFR) stone waste material used for landscaping

hardfills n ▷ hardfill

hardheaded adj shrewd, practical

hardhearted adj unsympathetic, uncaring

hardier adj ▷ hardy

hardiest adj ▷ hardy

hardiness n ▷ hardy

hardinesses n ▷ hardy

hardly adv scarcely or not at all

hardness n ▷ hard

hardnesses n ▷ hard

hardship n (pl -s) suffering

hardships n ▷ hardship

hardware n (pl -s) metal tools or implements

hardwares n ▷ hardware

hardwood n (pl -s) wood of a broadleaved tree such as oak or ash

hardwoods n ▷ hardwood

hardy adj (-**dier**, -**diest**) able to stand difficult conditions > **hardiness** n (pl -es)

hare n (pl -s) animal like a large rabbit, with longer ears and legs ▶ v (-**res**, -**ring**, -**red**) (usu.

foll. by **off**) run (away) quickly

harebell n (pl -s) blue bell-shaped flower

harebells n ▷ harebell

harebrained adj foolish or impractical

hared v ▷ hare

harelip n (pl -s) slight split in the upper lip

harelips n ▷ harelip

harem n (pl -s) (apartments of) a Muslim man's wives and concubines

harems n ▷ harem

hares v, n ▷ hare

haring v ▷ hare

hark v (-s, -ing, -ed) (Old-fashioned) listen

harked v ▷ hark

harking v ▷ hark

harks v ▷ hark

harlequin n (pl -s) stock comic character with a diamond-patterned costume and mask ▶ adj in many colours

harlequins n ▷ harlequin

harlot n (pl -s) (Lit) prostitute

harlots n ▷ harlot

harm v (-s, -ing, -ed) injure physically, mentally, or morally ▶ n (pl -s) physical, mental, or moral injury > **harmful** adj > **harmless** adj

harmed v ▷ harm

harmful adj ▷ harm

harming v ▷ harm

harmless adj ▷ harm

harmonic adj of harmony

harmonica n (pl -s) small wind instrument played by sucking and blowing

harmonicas n ▷ harmonica

harmonics n science of musical sounds

harmonies n ▷ harmony

harmonious adj ▷ harmony

harmoniously adv ▷ harmony

harmonium n (pl -s) keyboard instrument like a small organ

harmoniums n ▷ harmonium

harmonization v ▷ harmonize

harmonizations v ▷ harmonize

harmonize v (-**zes**, -**zing**, -**zed**) blend well together > **harmonization** n (pl -s)

harmonized v ▷ harmonize

harmonizes v ▷ harmonize

harmonizing v ▷ harmonize

harmony n (pl -**nies**) peaceful agreement and cooperation > **harmonious** adj > **harmoniously** adv

harms v, n ▷ harm

harness n (pl -s) arrangement of straps for attaching a horse to a cart or plough ▶ v (-**es**, -**ing**, -**ed**) put a harness on

harnessed v ▷ harness

harnesses n, v ▷ harness

harnessing v ▷ harness

harp n (pl -s) large triangular stringed instrument played with the fingers > **harpist** n (pl -s)

harpies n ▷ harpy

harpist n ▷ harp

harpists n ▷ harp

harpoon n (pl -s) barbed spear attached to a rope used for hunting whales ▶ v (-s, -ing, -ed) spear with a harpoon

harpooned v ▷ harpoon

harpooning v ▷ harpoon

harpoons n, v ▷ harpoon

harps n ▷ harp

harpsichord n (pl -s) stringed keyboard instrument

harpsichords n ▷ harpsichord

harpy n (pl -pies) nasty or bad-tempered woman

harridan n (pl -s) nagging or vicious woman

harridans n ▷ harridan

harried v ▷ harry

harrier n (pl -s) cross-country runner

harriers n ▷ harrier

harries v ▷ harry

harrow n (pl -s) implement used to break up lumps of soil ▶ v (-s, -ing, -ed) draw a harrow over

harrowed v ▷ harrow

harrowing adj very distressing ▶ v ▷ harrow

harrows n, v ▷ harrow

harry v (-rries, -rrying, -rried) keep asking (someone) to do something, pester

harrying v ▷ harry

harsh adj severe and difficult to cope with > **harshly** adv > **harshness** n (pl -es)

harshly adv ▷ harsh

harshness n ▷ harsh

harshnesses n ▷ harsh

hart n (pl -s) adult male deer

harts n ▷ hart

harvest n (pl -s) (season for) the gathering of crops ▶ v (-s, -ing, -ed) gather (a ripened crop) > **harvester** n (pl -s)

harvested v ▷ harvest

harvester n ▷ harvest

harvesters n ▷ harvest

harvesting v ▷ harvest

harvests n, v ▷ harvest

has v ▷ have

hash¹ n (pl -es) dish of diced cooked meat and vegetables reheated

hash² n (pl -es) (Informal) hashish

hashes n ▷ hash¹, ²

hashish [hash-eesh] n (pl -es) drug made from the cannabis plant, smoked for its intoxicating effects

hashishes n ▷ hashish

hasp n (pl -s) clasp that fits over a staple and is secured by a bolt or padlock, used as a fastening

hasps n ▷ hasp

hassle (Informal) n (pl -s) trouble, bother ▶ v (-les, -ling, -led) bother or annoy

hassled v ▷ hassle

hassles n, v ▷ hassle

hassling v ▷ hassle

hassock n (pl -s) cushion for kneeling on in church

hassocks n ▷ hassock

haste n (pl -s) (excessive) quickness

hasten v (-s, -ing, -ed) (cause to) hurry

hastened v ▷ hasten

hastening n ▷ hasten

hastens n ▷ hasten

hastes n ▷ haste

hastier adj ▷ hasty

hastiest adj ▷ hasty

hastily adv ▷ hasty

hasty adj (-tier, -tiest) (too) quick > **hastily** adv

hat n (pl -s) covering for the head, often with a brim, usu. worn to give protection from the weather

hatch¹ v (-es, -ing, -ed) (cause to) emerge from an egg

hatch² n (pl -es) hinged door covering an opening in a floor or wall

hatchback n (pl -s) car with a lifting door at the back

hatchbacks n ▷ hatchback

hatched v ▷ hatch¹

hatches v ▷ hatch¹ ▶ n ▷ hatch²

hatchet n (pl -s) small axe

hatchets n ▷ hatchet

hatching v ▷ hatch¹

hatchway n (pl -s) opening in the deck of a ship

hatchways n ▷ hatchway

hate v (-tes, -ting, -ted) dislike intensely ▶ n (pl -s) intense dislike > **hater** n (pl -s)

hated v ▷ hate

hateful adj causing or deserving hate

hater n ▷ hate

haters n ▷ hate

hates v, n ▷ hate

hating v ▷ hate

hatred n (pl -s) intense dislike

hatreds n ▷ hatred

hats n ▷ hat
haughtier adj ▷ haughty
haughtiest adj ▷ haughty
haughtily adv ▷ haughty
haughtiness n ▷ haughty
haughtinesses n ▷ haughty
haughty adj (-tier, -tiest) proud, arrogant
> **haughtily** adv > **haughtiness** n (pl -es)
haul v (-s, -ing, -ed) pull or drag with effort ▶ n
(pl -s) amount gained by effort or theft
haulage n (pl -s) (charge for) transporting
goods
haulages n ▷ haulage
hauled v ▷ haul
haulier n (pl -s) firm or person that transports
goods by road
hauliers n ▷ haulier
hauling v ▷ haul
hauls v, n ▷ haul
haunch n (pl -es) human hip or fleshy
hindquarter of an animal
haunches n ▷ haunch
haunt v (-s, -ing, -ed) visit in the form of a
ghost ▶ n (pl -s) place visited frequently
haunted adj frequented by ghosts ▶ v ▷ haunt
haunting adj memorably beautiful or sad ▶ v
▷ haunt
haunts v, n ▷ haunt
hauteur [oat-ur] n (pl -s) haughtiness
hauteurs n ▷ hauteur
have v (has, having, had) possess, hold
haven n (pl -s) place of safety
havens n ▷ haven
haversack n (pl -s) canvas bag carried on the
back or shoulder
haversacks n ▷ haversack
having v ▷ have
havoc n (pl -s) disorder and confusion
havocs n ▷ havoc
haw n (pl -s) hawthorn berry
hawk[1] n (pl -s) bird of prey with a short hooked
bill and very good eyesight > **hawkish**,
hawklike adj
hawk[2] v (-s, -ing, -ed) offer (goods) for sale in
the street or door-to-door > **hawker** n (pl -s)
hawk[3] v (-s, -ing, -ed) cough noisily
hawked v ▷ hawk[2,3]
hawker n ▷ hawk[2]
hawkers n ▷ hawk[2]
hawk-eyed adj having very good eyesight
hawking v ▷ hawk[2,3]
hawkish adj ▷ hawk[1]
hawks n ▷ hawk[1] ▶ v ▷ hawk[2,3]
hawlike adj ▷ hawk[1]
haws n ▷ haw

hawser n (pl -s) large rope used on a ship
hawsers n ▷ hawser
hawthorn n (pl -s) thorny shrub or tree
hawthorns n ▷ hawthorn
hay n (pl hays) grass cut and dried as fodder
hays n ▷ hay
haystack n (pl -s) large pile of stored hay
haystacks n ▷ haystack
haywire adj (Informal) not functioning properly
hazard n (pl -s) something that could be
dangerous ▶ v (-s, -ing, -ed) put in danger
> **hazardous** adj
hazarded v ▷ hazard
hazarding v ▷ hazard
hazardous adj ▷ hazard
hazards n, v ▷ hazard
haze n (pl -s) mist, often caused by heat
hazel n (pl -s) small tree producing edible nuts
▶ adj (of eyes) greenish-brown > **hazelnut**
n (pl -s)
hazelnut n ▷ hazel
hazelnuts n ▷ hazel
hazels n ▷ hazel
hazes n ▷ haze
hazier adj ▷ hazy
haziest adj ▷ hazy
hazy adj (-zier, -ziest) not clear, misty
he pron refers to: male person or animal ▶ n (pl
-s) male person or animal
head n (pl -s) upper or front part of the body,
containing the sense organs and the brain
▶ adj chief, principal ▶ v (-s, -ing, -ed) be at the
top or front of
headache n (pl -s) continuous pain in the head
headaches n ▷ headache
headboard n (pl -s) vertical board at the top
end of a bed
headboards n ▷ headboard
headdress n (pl -s) decorative head covering
headdresses n ▷ headdress
headed v ▷ head
header n (pl -s) striking a ball with the head
headers n ▷ header
headhunt v (-s, -ing, -ed) (of a company)
approach and offer a job to (a person working
for a rival company) > **headhunter** n (pl -s)
headhunted v ▷ headhunt
headhunter n ▷ headhunt
headhunters n ▷ headhunt
headhunting v ▷ headhunt
headhunts v ▷ headhunt
headier adj ▷ heady
headiest adj ▷ heady
heading n (pl -s) title written or printed at the
top of a page ▶ v ▷ head

headings *n* ▷ heading
headland *n* (*pl* -s) area of land jutting out into the sea
headlands *n* ▷ headland
headlight *n* (*pl* -s) powerful light on the front of a vehicle
headlights *n* ▷ headlight
headline *n* (*pl* -s) title at the top of a newspaper article, esp. on the front page
headlines *n* ▷ headline ▶ *pl n* main points of a news broadcast
headlong *adv, adj* with the head first
headphones *pl n* two small loudspeakers held against the ears
headquarters *pl n* centre from which operations are directed
heads *adv* (*Informal*) with the side of a coin which has a portrait of a head on it uppermost ▶ *n, v* ▷ head
headstone *n* (*pl* -s) memorial stone on a grave
headstones *n* ▷ headstone
headstrong *adj* self-willed, obstinate
headway *n* (*pl* -s) progress
headways *n* ▷ headway
headwind *n* (*pl* -s) wind blowing against the course of an aircraft or ship
headwinds *n* ▷ headwind
heady *adj* (-dier, -diest) intoxicating or exciting
heal *v* (-s, -ing, -ed) make or become well
> **healer** *n* (*pl* -s)
healed *v* ▷ heal
healer *n* ▷ heal
healers *n* ▷ heal
healing *v* ▷ heal
heals *v* ▷ heal
health *n* (*pl* -s) normal (good) condition of someone's body
healthier *adj* ▷ healthy
healthiest *adj* ▷ healthy
healthily *adv* ▷ healthy
healths *n* ▷ health
healthy *adj* (-thier, -thiest) having good health
> **healthily** *adv*
heap *n* (*pl* -s) pile of things one on top of another ▶ *v* (-s, -ing, -ed) gather into a pile
heaped *v* ▷ heap
heaping *v* ▷ heap
heaps *n, v* ▷ heap
hear *v* (-s, -ing, heard) perceive (a sound) by ear
> **hearer** *n* (*pl* -s)
heard *v* ▷ hear
hearer *n* ▷ hear
hearers *n* ▷ hear
hearing *n* (*pl* -s) ability to hear ▶ *v* ▷ hear

hearings *n* ▷ hearing
hears *v* ▷ hear
hearsay *n* (*pl* -s) gossip, rumour
hearsays *n* ▷ hearsay
hearse *n* (*pl* -s) funeral car used to carry a coffin
hearses *n* ▷ hearse
heart *n* (*pl* -s) organ that pumps blood round the body
heartache *n* (*pl* -s) intense anguish
heartaches *n* ▷ heartache
heartbeat *n* (*pl* -s) one complete pulsation of the heart
heartbeats *n* ▷ heartbeat
heartbreak *n* (*pl* -s) intense grief
heartbreaks *n* ▷ heartbreak
heartburn *n* (*pl* -s) burning sensation in the chest caused by indigestion
heartburns *n* ▷ heartburn
hearten *v* (-s, -ing, -ed) encourage, make cheerful
heartened *v* ▷ hearten
heartening *v* ▷ hearten
heartens *v* ▷ hearten
heartfelt *adj* felt sincerely or strongly
hearth *n* (*pl* -s) floor of a fireplace
hearths *n* ▷ hearth
heartier *adj* ▷ hearty
heartiest *adj* ▷ hearty
heartily *adv* ▷ hearty
heartless *adj* cruel, unkind
heartrending *adj* causing great sorrow
hearts *n* ▷ heart
heartthrob *n* (*pl* -s) (*Slang*) very attractive man, esp. a film or pop star
heartthrobs *n* ▷ heartthrob
hearty *adj* (-tier, -tiest) substantial, nourishing > **heartily** *adv*
heat *v* (-s, -ing, -ed) make or become hot ▶ *n* (*pl* -s) state of being hot > **heater** *n* (*pl* -s)
heated *v* ▷ heat ▶ *adj* angry and excited
> **heatedly** *adv*
heatedly *adv* ▷ heated
heater *n* ▷ heat
heaters *n* ▷ heat
heath *n* (*pl* -s) (BRIT) area of open uncultivated land
heathen *adj, n* (*pl* -s) (of) a person who does not believe in an established religion
heathens *n* ▷ heathen
heather *n* (*pl* -s) low-growing plant with small purple, pinkish, or white flowers, growing on heaths and mountains
heathers *n* ▷ heather
heaths *n* ▷ heath
heating *v* ▷ heat

heats v, n ▷ heat

heave v (-ves, -ving, -ved) lift with effort ▶ n (pl -s) heaving

heaved v ▷ heave

heaven n (pl -s) place believed to be the home of God, where good people go when they die

heavenly adj of or like heaven

heavens n ▷ heaven

heaves v, n ▷ heave

heavier adj ▷ heavy

heaviest adj ▷ heavy

heavily adv ▷ heavy

heaviness n ▷ heavy

heavinesses n ▷ heavy

heaving v ▷ heave

heavy adj (-vier, -viest) of great weight > **heavily** adv > **heaviness** n (pl -es)

heavyweight n (pl -s) boxer weighing over 175lb (professional) or 81kg (amateur)

heavyweights n ▷ heavyweight

heckle v (-les, -ling, -led) interrupt (a public speaker) with comments, questions, or taunts > **heckler** n (pl -s)

heckled v ▷ heckle

heckler n ▷ heckle

hecklers n ▷ heckle

heckles v ▷ heckle

heckling v ▷ heckle

hectare n (pl -s) one hundred ares or 10 000 square metres (2.471 acres)

hectares n ▷ hectare

hectic adj rushed or busy

hector v (-s, -ing, -ed) bully

hectored v ▷ hector

hectoring v ▷ hector

hectors v ▷ hector

hedge n (pl -s) row of bushes forming a barrier or boundary ▶ v (-ges, -ging, -ged) be evasive or noncommittal

hedged v ▷ hedge

hedgehog n (pl -s) small mammal with a protective covering of spines

hedgehogs n ▷ hedgehog

hedgerow n (pl -s) bushes forming a hedge

hedgerows n ▷ hedgerow

hedges n, v ▷ hedge

hedging v ▷ hedge

hedonism n (pl -s) doctrine that pleasure is the most important thing in life > **hedonist** n (pl -s) > **hedonistic** adj

hedonisms n ▷ hedonism

hedonist n ▷ hedonism

hedonistic n ▷ hedonism

hedonists n ▷ hedonism

heed n (pl -s) careful attention ▶ v (-s, -ing, -ed)

pay careful attention to

heeded v ▷ heed

heeding v ▷ heed

heedless adj taking no notice of

heeds v, n ▷ heed

heel[1] n (pl -s) back part of the foot ▶ v (-s, -ing, -ed) repair the heel of (a shoe)

heel[2] v (-s, -ing, -ed) (foll. by **over**) lean to one side

heeled v ▷ heel[1, 2]

heeler n (pl -s) (AUST & NZ) dog that herds cattle by biting at their heels

heelers n ▷ heeler

heeling v ▷ heel[1, 2]

heels n ▷ heel[1] ▶ v ▷ heel[1, 2]

heftier adj ▷ hefty

heftiest adj ▷ hefty

hefty adj (-tier, -tiest) large, heavy, or strong

hegemonies n ▷ hegemony

hegemony [hig-**em**-on-ee] n (pl -nies) political domination

hegira n (pl -s) Mohammed's flight from Mecca to Medina in 622 AD

hegiras n ▷ hegira

heifer [**hef**-fer] n (pl -s) young cow

heifers n ▷ heifer

height n (pl -s) distance from base to top

heighten v (-s, -ing, -ed) make or become higher or more intense

heightened v ▷ heighten

heightening v ▷ heighten

heightens v ▷ heighten

heights n ▷ height

heinous adj evil and shocking

heir n (pl -s) person entitled to inherit property or rank > **heiress** n fem (pl -es)

heiresses n ▷ heiress

heirloom n (pl -s) object that has belonged to a family for generations

heirlooms n ▷ heirloom

heirs n ▷ heir

held v ▷ hold[1]

helical adj spiral

helices n ▷ helix

helicopter n (pl -s) aircraft lifted and propelled by rotating overhead blades

helicopters n ▷ helicopter

heliotrope n (pl -s) plant with purple flowers ▶ adj light purple

heliotropes n ▷ heliotrope

heliport n (pl -s) airport for helicopters

heliports n ▷ heliport

helium [**heel**-ee-um] n (pl -s) (CHEM) very light colourless odourless gas

heliums n ▷ helium

helix [heel-iks] *n* (*pl* **-ices, -ixes**) spiral
  helixes *n* ▷helix

hell *n* (*pl* **-s**) place believed to be where wicked people go when they die ▷ **hellish** *adj*

hellbent *adj* (*foll. by* **on**) intent
  hellish *adj* ▷hell

hello *interj* expression of greeting or surprise
  hells *n* ▷hell

helm *n* (*pl* **-s**) tiller or wheel for steering a ship

helmet *n* (*pl* **-s**) hard hat worn for protection
  helmets *n* ▷helmet
  helms *n* ▷helm

help *v* (**-s, -ing, -ed**) make something easier, better, or quicker for (someone) ▶ *n* (*pl* **-s**) assistance or support > **helper** *n* (*pl* **-s**) > **helpful** *adj*
  helped *v* ▷help
  helper *n* ▷help
  helpers *n* ▷help
  helpful *adj* ▷help

helping *n* (*pl* **-s**) single portion of food ▶ *v* ▷help
  helpings *n* ▷helping

helpless *adj* weak or incapable > **helplessly** *adv*
  helplessly *adv* ▷helpless

helpline *n* (*pl* **-s**) telephone line set aside for callers to contact an organization for help with a problem
  helplines *n* ▷helpline

helpmate *n* (*pl* **-s**) companion and helper, esp. a husband or wife
  helpmates *n* ▷helpmate
  helps *v, n* ▷help

hem *n* (*pl* **-s**) bottom edge of a garment, folded under and stitched down ▶ *v* (**-s, -mming, -mmed**) provide with a hem

hemisphere *n* (*pl* **-s**) half of a sphere, esp. the earth > **hemispherical** *adj*
  hemispheres *n* ▷hemisphere

hemline *n* (*pl* **-s**) level to which the hem of a skirt hangs
  hemlines *n* ▷hemline

hemlock *n* (*pl* **-s**) poison made from a plant with spotted stems and small white flowers
  hemlocks *n* ▷hemlock
  hemmed *v* ▷hem
  hemming *v* ▷hem

hemp *n* (*pl* **-s**) (*also* **cannabis**) Asian plant with tough fibres
  hemps *n* ▷hemp
  hems *n, v* ▷hem

hen *n* (*pl* **-s**) female domestic fowl

hence *conj* for this reason ▶ *adv* from this time

henceforth *adv* from now on

henchman *n* (*pl* **-men**) person employed by someone powerful to carry out orders
  henchmen *n* ▷henchman

henna *n* (*pl* **-s**) reddish dye made from a shrub or tree ▶ *v* (**-s, -ing, -ed**) dye (the hair) with henna
  hennaed *v* ▷henna
  hennaing *v* ▷henna
  hennas *n, v* ▷henna

henpecked *adj* (of a man) dominated by his wife
  henries *n* ▷henry

henry *n* (*pl* **-ries, -rys**) unit of electrical inductance
  henrys *n* ▷henry
  hens *n* ▷hen

hepatitis *n* (*pl* **-es**) inflammation of the liver
  hepatitises *n* ▷hepatitis

heptagon *n* (*pl* **-s**) geometric figure with seven sides
  heptagons *n* ▷heptagon

heptathlon *n* (*pl* **-s**) athletic contest for women, involving seven events
  heptathlons *n* ▷heptathlon

her *pron* refers to a female person or animal or anything personified as feminine when the object of a sentence or clause ▶ *adj* belonging to her

herald *n* (*pl* **-s**) person who announces important news ▶ *v* (**-s, -ing, -ed**) signal the approach of
  heralded *v* ▷herald
  heraldic *adj* ▷heraldry
  heralding *v* ▷herald
  heraldries *n* ▷heraldry

heraldry *n* (*pl* **-ries**) study of coats of arms and family trees > **heraldic** *adj*
  heralds *n, v* ▷herald

herb *n* (*pl* **-s**) plant used for flavouring in cookery, and in medicine > **herbal** *adj*

herbaceous *adj* (of a plant) soft-stemmed
  herbal *adj* ▷herb

herbalist *n* (*pl* **-s**) person who grows or specializes in the use of medicinal herbs
  herbalists *n* ▷herbalist

herbicide *n* (*pl* **-s**) chemical used to destroy plants, esp. weeds
  herbicides *n* ▷herbicide

herbivore *n* (*pl* **-s**) animal that eats only plants > **herbivorous** [her-biv-or-uss] ▶ *adj*
  herbivores *n* ▷herbivore
  herbivorous *adj* ▷herbivore
  herbs *n* ▷herb

herculean [her-kew-lee-an] *adj* requiring great strength or effort

herd *n* (*pl* **-s**) group of animals feeding and

living together ▸ v (-s, -ing, -ed) collect into
a herd
herded v ▷ herd
herding v ▷ herd
herds n, v ▷ herd
herdsman n (pl -men) man who looks after a
herd of animals
herdsmen n ▷ herd
here adv in, at, or to this place or point
hereabouts adv near here
hereafter adv after this point or time
hereby adv by means of or as a result of this
hereditary adj passed on genetically from one
generation to another
heredities n ▷ heredity
heredity [hir-**red**-it-ee] n (pl -ties) passing on
of characteristics from one generation to
another
herein adv in this place, matter, or document
heresies n ▷ heresy
heresy [**herr**-iss-ee] n (pl -sies) opinion contrary
to accepted opinion or belief
heretic [**herr**-it-ik] n (pl -s) person who holds
unorthodox opinions > **heretical** [hir-**ret**-ik-al]
▸ adj
heretical n ▷ heretic
heretics n ▷ heretic
herewith adv with this
heritage n (pl -s) something inherited
heritages n ▷ heritage
hermaphrodite [her-**maf**-roe-dite] n (pl -s)
animal, plant, or person with both male and
female reproductive organs
hermaphrodites n ▷ hermaphrodite
hermetic adj sealed so as to be airtight
> **hermetically** adv
hermetically adv ▷ hermetic
hermit n (pl -s) person living in solitude, esp.
for religious reasons
hermitage n (pl -s) home of a hermit
hermitages n ▷ hermitage
hermits n ▷ hermit
hernia n (pl -s) protrusion of an organ or part
through the lining of the surrounding body
cavity
hernias n ▷ hernia
hero n (pl -es) principal character in a film,
book, etc. > **heroine** n fem (pl -s) > **heroism**
[**herr**-oh-izz-um] n (pl -s)
heroes n ▷ hero
heroic adj courageous > **heroically** adv
heroically adv ▷ heroic
heroics pl n extravagant behaviour
heroin n (pl -s) highly addictive drug derived
from morphine

heroine n ▷ hero
heroines n ▷ hero
heroins n ▷ heroin
heroism n ▷ hero
heroisms n ▷ hero
heron n (pl -s) long-legged wading bird
herons n ▷ heron
herpes [**her**-peez] n (pl -es) any of several
inflammatory skin diseases, including
shingles and cold sores
herpeses n ▷ herpes
herring n (pl -s) important food fish of
northern seas
herringbone n (pl -s) pattern of zigzag lines
herringbones n ▷ herringbone
herrings n ▷ herring
hertz n (pl -es) (PHYSICS) unit of frequency
hertzes n ▷ hertz
hes n ▷ he
hesitancies n ▷ hesitant
hesitancy n ▷ hesitant
hesitant adj undecided or wavering
> **hesitantly** adv > **hesitancy** n (pl -cies)
hesitantly adv ▷ hesitant
hesitate v (-tes, -ting, -ted) be slow or
uncertain in doing something > **hesitation**
n (pl -s)
hesitated v ▷ hesitate
hesitates v ▷ hesitate
hesitating v ▷ hesitate
hesitation n ▷ hesitate
hesitations n ▷ hesitate
hessian n (pl -s) coarse jute fabric
hessians n ▷ hessian
heterodox adj differing from accepted
doctrines or beliefs > **heterodoxy** n (pl -xies)
heterodoxies n ▷ heterodox
heterodoxy n ▷ heterodox
heterogeneities n ▷ heterogeneous
heterogeneity n ▷ heterogeneous
heterogeneous [het-er-oh-**jean**-ee-uss]
adj composed of diverse elements
> **heterogeneity** n (pl -ties)
heterosexual n (pl -s) person sexually
attracted to members of the opposite sex
▸ adj > **heterosexuality** n (pl -ties)
heterosexualities n ▷ heterosexual
heterosexuality n ▷ heterosexual
heterosexuals n ▷ heterosexual
heuristic [hew-rist-ik] adj involving learning by
investigation
hew v (-s, -ing, -ed or hewn) cut with an axe
hewed v ▷ hew
hewing v ▷ hew
hewn v ▷ hew

hews v ▷ hew

hex n hexes. A hex is a curse or spell. This is a really useful word to remember when you have an X, as there is likely to be an E or H on the board already.

hexagon n (pl -s) geometrical figure with six sides > **hexagonal** adj

hexagonal adj ▷ hexagon

hexagons n ▷ hexagon

hey interj expression of surprise or for catching attention

heyday n (pl -s) time of greatest success, prime

heydays n ▷ heyday

hi interj. Hi is an informal word for **hello**. This everyday word is worth keeping in mind when you want to form a word adjacent to a parallel word below or above. Hi scores 5 points.

hiatus [hie-ay-tuss] n (pl -tuses, -tus) pause or interruption in continuity

hiatuses n ▷ hiatus

hibernate v (-tes, -ting, -ted) (of an animal) pass the winter as if in a deep sleep > **hibernation** n (pl -s)

hibernated v ▷ hibernate

hibernates v ▷ hibernate

hibernating v ▷ hibernate

hibernation n ▷ hibernate

hibernations n ▷ hibernate

hibiscus n (pl -cuses) tropical plant with large brightly coloured flowers

hibiscuses n ▷ hibiscus

hiccough n, v (pl -s) hiccup

hiccoughed v ▷ hiccup

hiccoughing v ▷ hiccup

hiccoughs n, v ▷ hiccup

hiccup, hiccough n (pl -s) spasm of the breathing muscles with a sharp coughlike sound (Informal) ▶ v (-s, -pping, -pped) make a hiccup

hiccupped v ▷ hiccup

hiccupping v ▷ hiccup

hiccups n, v ▷ hiccup

hick n (pl -s) (US, AUST & NZ) (Informal) unsophisticated country person

hickories n ▷ hickory

hickory n (pl -ries) N American nut-bearing tree

hicks n ▷ hick

hid v ▷ hide¹

hidden v ▷ hide¹

hide¹ v (-des, -ding, hid, hidden) put (oneself or an object) somewhere difficult to see or find ▶ n (pl -s) place of concealment, esp. for a bird-watcher

hide² n (pl -s) skin of an animal

hidebound adj unwilling to accept new ideas

hideous [hid-ee-uss] adj ugly, revolting > **hideously** adv

hideously adv ▷ hideous

hideout n (pl -s) place to hide in

hideouts n ▷ hideout

hides v ▷ hide¹ ▶ n ▷ hide¹, ²

hiding n (pl -s) (Slang) severe beating ▶ v ▷ hide¹

hidings n ▷ hiding

hierarchical adj ▷ hierarchy

hierarchies n ▷ hierarchy

hierarchy [hire-ark-ee] n (pl -chies) system of people or things arranged in a graded order > **hierarchical** adj

hieroglyphic [hire-oh-gliff-ik] adj of a form of writing using picture symbols, as used in ancient Egypt ▶ n (pl -s) symbol that is difficult to decipher (also **hieroglyph**)

hieroglyphics n ▷ hieroglyphic

high adj (-er, -est) of a great height ▶ adv at or to a high level > **highly** adv

highbrow adj, n (pl -s) intellectual and serious (person)

highbrows n ▷ highbrow

higher adj ▷ high

highest adj ▷ high

highlands pl n area of high ground

highlight n (pl -s) outstanding part or feature ▶ v (-s, -ing, -ed) give emphasis to

highlighted v ▷ highlight

highlighting v ▷ highlight

highlights n, v ▷ highlight

highly adv ▷ high

highway n (pl -s) (US, AUST & NZ) main road

highwayman n (pl -men) (formerly) robber, usu. on horseback, who robbed travellers at gunpoint

highwaymen n ▷ highwayman

highways n ▷ highway

hijack v (-s, -ing, -ed) seize control of (an aircraft or other vehicle) while travelling > **hijacker** n (pl -s)

hijacked v ▷ hijack

hijacker n ▷ hijack

hijackers n ▷ hijack

hijacking n ▷ hijack

hijacks v ▷ hijack

hike n (pl -s) long walk in the country, esp. for pleasure ▶ v (-kes, -king, -ked) go for a long walk > **hiker** n (pl -s)

hiked v ▷ hike

hiker n ▷ hike

hikers n ▷ hike

hikes *n, v* ▷ hike
hiking *v* ▷ hike
hilarious *adj* very funny > **hilariously** *adv*
> **hilarity** *n* (*pl* -ties)
hilariously *adv* ▷ hilarious
hilarities *n* ▷ hilarious
hilarity *n* ▷ hilarious
hill *n* (*pl* -s) raised part of the earth's surface,
less high than a mountain > **hilly** *adj* (-llier,
-lliest)
hillbillies *n* ▷ hillbilly
hillbilly *n* (*pl* -llies) (us) unsophisticated
country person
hillier *adj* ▷ hill
hilliest *adj* ▷ hill
hillock *n* (*pl* -s) small hill
hillocks *n* ▷ hillock
hills *n* ▷ hill
hilly *adj* ▷ hill
hilt *n* (*pl* -s) handle of a sword or knife
hilts *n* ▷ hilt
him *pron* refers to a male person or animal
when the object of a sentence or clause
hind[1] *adj* (-er, -most) situated at the back
hind[2] *n* (*pl* -s) female deer
hinder *adj* ▷ hind[1] ▶ *v* (-s, -ing, -ed) get in the
way of > **hindrance** *n* (*pl* -s)
hindered *v* ▷ hinder
hindering *v* ▷ hinder
hinders *v* ▷ hinder
hindmost *adj* ▷ hind[1]
hindrance *n* ▷ hinder
hindrances *n* ▷ hinder
hinds *n* ▷ hind[2]
hinge *n* (*pl* -s) device for holding together two
parts so that one can swing freely ▶ *v* (-ges,
-ging, -ged) (foll. by **on**) depend (on)
hinged *v* ▷ hinge
hinges *n, v* ▷ hinge
hinging *v* ▷ hinge
hint *n* (*pl* -s) indirect suggestion ▶ *v* (-s, -ing,
-ed) suggest indirectly
hinted *v* ▷ hint
hinterland *n* (*pl* -s) land lying behind a coast or
near a city, esp. a port
hinterlands *n* ▷ hinterland
hinting *v* ▷ hint
hints *n, v* ▷ hint
hip[1] *n* (*pl* -s) either side of the body between
the pelvis and the thigh
hip[2] *n* (*pl* -s) rosehip
hippie *adj, n* (*pl* -s) ▷ hippy
hippies *n* ▷ hippie
hippo *n* (*pl* -ppos) (Informal) hippopotamus
hippodrome *n* (*pl* -s) music hall, variety
theatre, or circus
hippodromes *n* ▷ hippodrome
hippopotami *n* ▷ hippopotamus
hippopotamus *n* (*pl* -muses, -mi) large African
mammal with thick wrinkled skin, living
near rivers
hippopotamuses *n* ▷ hippopotamus
hippos *n* ▷ hippo
hippy *adj, n* (*pl* -ppies) (esp. in the 1960s) (of)
a person whose behaviour and dress imply a
rejection of conventional values
hips *n* ▷ hip[1, 2]
hire *v* (-res, -ring, -red) pay to have temporary
use of ▶ *n* (*pl* -s) hiring
hired *v* ▷ hire
hireling *n* (*pl* -s) person who works only for
wages
hirelings *n* ▷ hireling
hires *v, n* ▷ hire
hiring *v* ▷ hire
hirsute [her-suit] *adj* hairy
his *pron, adj* (something) belonging to him
hiss *n* (*pl* -es) sound like that of a long *s* (as an
expression of contempt) ▶ *v* (-es, -ing, -ed)
utter a hiss
hissed *v* ▷ hiss
hisses *n, v* ▷ hiss
hissing *v* ▷ hiss
histamine [hiss-ta-meen] *n* (*pl* -s) substance
released by the body tissues in allergic
reactions
histamines *n* ▷ histamine
histogram *n* (*pl* -s) statistical graph in which
the frequency of values is represented by
vertical bars of varying heights and widths
histograms *n* ▷ histogram
histologies *n* ▷ histology
histology *n* (*pl* -gies) study of the tissues of an
animal or plant
historian *n* (*pl* -s) writer of history
historians *n* ▷ historian
historic *adj* famous or significant in history
historical *adj* occurring in the past
> **historically** *adv*
historically *adv* ▷ historical
histories *n* ▷ history
history *n* (*pl* -ries) (record or account of) past
events and developments
histrionic *adj* excessively dramatic
histrionics *pl n* excessively dramatic
behaviour
hit *v* (-s, -tting, hit) strike, touch forcefully ▶ *n*
(*pl* -s) hitting ▶ *adj* sometimes successful and
sometimes not
hitch *n* (*pl* -es) minor problem ▶ *v* (-es, -ing, -ed)

(*Informal*) obtain (a lift) by hitchhiking
hitched v ▷ hitch
hitches n, v ▷ hitch
hitchhike v (-kes, -king, -ked) travel by obtaining free lifts ▷ **hitchhiker** n (pl -s)
  hitchhiked n ▷ hitchhike
  hitchhiker n ▷ hitchhike
  hitchhikers n ▷ hitchhike
  hitchhikes n ▷ hitchhike
  hitchhiking n ▷ hitchhike
  hitching v ▷ hitch
hither adv (Old-fashioned) to or towards this place
hitherto adv until this time
  hits n, v ▷ hit
  hitting v ▷ hit
hive n (pl -s) ▷ beehive
  hives n ▷ hive

> **hm** or **hmm** *interj.* This is a noise that people make when they are thinking or considering something. Both forms of this word are useful because neither contains a vowel, which is great if you have no vowels on your rack. Hm scores 5 points, while hmm scores 8. **ho** *interj.* Ho is a noise people make when they laugh. This little word is useful when you want to go in two directions at once. It's also worth remembering that ho is oh backwards: if you can't use one, you might be able to use the other. Ho scores 5 points.

hoard n (pl -s) store hidden away for future use ▶ v (-s, -ing, -ed) save or store ▷ **hoarder** n (pl -s)
  hoarded v ▷ hoard
  hoarder n ▷ hoard
  hoarders n ▷ hoard
hoarding n (pl -s) large board for displaying advertisements ▶ v ▷ hoard
  hoardings n ▷ hoarding
  hoards n, v ▷ hoard
hoarfrost n (pl -s) white ground frost
  hoarfrosts n ▷ hoarfrost
  hoarier adj ▷ hoary
  hoariest adj ▷ hoary
hoarse adj (-ser, -sest) (of a voice) rough and unclear ▷ **hoarsely** adv ▷ **hoarseness** n (pl -es)
  hoarsely adv ▷ hoarse
  hoarseness n ▷ hoarse
  hoarsenesses n ▷ hoarse
  hoarsest adj ▷ hoarse
  hoarsest adj ▷ hoarse
hoary adj (-rier, -riest) grey or white(-haired)
hoax n (pl -es) deception or trick ▶ v (-es, -ing,

-ed) deceive or play a trick upon ▷ **hoaxer** n
  hoaxed v ▷ hoax
  hoaxer n ▷ hoax
  hoaxers n ▷ hoax
  hoaxes n, v ▷ hoax
  hoaxing v ▷ hoax
hob n (pl -s) (BRIT) flat top part of a cooker, or a separate flat surface, containing gas or electric rings for cooking on
  hobbies n ▷ hobby
hobble v (-les, -ling, -led) walk lamely
  hobbled v ▷ hobble
  hobbles v ▷ hobble
  hobbling v ▷ hobble
hobby n (pl -bbies) activity pursued in one's spare time
hobbyhorse n (pl -s) favourite topic
  hobbyhorses n ▷ hobbyhorse
hobgoblin n (pl -s) mischievous goblin
  hobgoblins n ▷ hobgoblin
hobnob v (-s, -nobbing, -nobbed) (foll. by **with**) be on friendly terms (with)
  hobnobbed v ▷ hobnob
  hobnobbing v ▷ hobnob
  hobnobs v ▷ hobnob
hobo n (pl -s) (US, AUST & NZ) tramp or vagrant
  hobos n ▷ hobo
  hobs n ▷ hob
hock¹ n (pl -s) joint in the back leg of an animal such as a horse that corresponds to the human ankle
hock² n (pl -s) white German wine
hock³ v (-s, -ing, -ed) (Informal) pawn
  hocked v ▷ hock
hockey n (pl -s) team game played on a field with a ball and curved sticks
  hockeys n ▷ hockey
  hocking v ▷ hock
  hocks n ▷ hock¹, ² ▶ v ▷ hock³
hod n (pl -s) open wooden box attached to a pole, for carrying bricks or mortar
  hods n ▷ hod
hoe n (pl -s) long-handled tool used for loosening soil or weeding ▶ v (-oes, -oeing, -oed) scrape or weed with a hoe
  hoed v ▷ hoe
  hoeing v ▷ hoe
  hoes n, v ▷ hoe
hog n (pl -s) castrated male pig (Informal) ▶ v (-s, -gging, -gged) (Informal) take more than one's share of
  hogged v ▷ hog
  hogging v ▷ hog
hogmanay n (pl -s) (in Scotland) New Year's Eve

hogmanays *n* ▷ hogmanay

hogs *n, v* ▷ hog

hogshead *n* (*pl* -s) large cask

hogsheads *n* ▷ hogshead

hogwash *n* (*pl* -es) (*Informal*) nonsense

hogwashes *n* ▷ hogwash

hoick *v* (-s, -ing, -ed) raise abruptly and sharply

hoicked *v* ▷ hoick

hoicking *v* ▷ hoick

hoicks *v* ▷ hoick

hoist *v* (-s, -ing, -ed) raise or lift up ▶ *n* (*pl* -s) device for lifting things

hoisted *v* ▷ hoist

hoisting *v* ▷ hoist

hoists *v, n* ▷ hoist

hold¹ *v* (-s, -ing, held) keep or support in or with the hands or arms ▶ *n* (*pl* -s) act or way of holding ▶ **holder** *n* (*pl* -s)

hold² *n* (*pl* -s) cargo compartment in a ship or aircraft

holdall *n* (*pl* -s) large strong travelling bag

holdalls *n* ▷ holdall

holder *n* ▷ hold¹

holders *n* ▷ hold¹

holding *n* (*pl* -s) property, such as land or stocks and shares ▶ *v* ▷ hold¹

holds *n* ▷ hold¹, ² ▶ *v* ▷ hold¹

holdup *n* (*pl* -s) armed robbery

holdups *n* ▷ holdup

hole *n* (*pl* -s) area hollowed out in a solid ▶ *v* (-les, -ling, -led) make holes in

holed *v* ▷ hole

holes *n, v* ▷ hole

holiday *n* (*pl* -s) time spent away from home for rest or recreation

holidays *n* ▷ holiday

holier *adj* ▷ holy

holiest *adj* ▷ holy

holiness *n* (*pl* -es) state of being holy

holinesses *n* ▷ holiness

holing *v* ▷ hole

holisms *n* ▷ holism

holistic *adj* considering the complete person, physically and mentally, in the treatment of an illness ▶ **holism** *n* (*pl* -s)

hollies *n* ▷ holly

holloganism *n* ▷ hooligan

hollow *adj* having a hole or space inside ▶ *n* (*pl* -s) cavity or space ▶ *v* (-s, -ing, -ed) form a hollow in

hollowed *v* ▷ hollow

hollowing *v* ▷ hollow

hollows *n, v* ▷ hollow

holly *n* (*pl* -llies) evergreen tree with prickly leaves and red berries

hollyhock *n* (*pl* -s) tall garden plant with spikes of colourful flowers

hollyhocks *n* ▷ hollyhock

holocaust *n* (*pl* -s) destruction or loss of life on a massive scale

holocausts *n* ▷ holocaust

hologram *n* (*pl* -s) three-dimensional photographic image

holograms *n* ▷ hologram

holograph *n* (*pl* -s) document handwritten by the author

holographs *n* ▷ holograph

holster *n* (*pl* -s) leather case for a pistol, hung from a belt

holsters *n* ▷ holster

holy *adj* (-lier, -liest) of God or a god

homage *n* (*pl* -s) show of respect or honour towards someone or something

homages *n* ▷ homage

home *n* (*pl* -s) place where one lives ▶ *adj* of one's home, birthplace, or native country (SPORT) ▶ *adv* to or at home ▶ *v* (-mes, -ming, -med) (*foll. by* in *or* in on) direct towards (a point or target) > **homeward** *adj, adv* > **homewards** *adv*

homed *v* ▷ home

homeland *n* (*pl* -s) country from which a person's ancestors came

homelands *n* ▷ homeland

homeless *adj* having nowhere to live ▶ *pl n* people who have nowhere to live > **homelessness** *n* (*pl* -es)

homelessness *n* ▷ homeless

homelessnesses *n* ▷ homeless

homelier *adj* ▷ homely

homeliest *adj* ▷ homely

homely *adj* (-lier, -liest) simple, ordinary, and comfortable

homemade *adj* made at home or on the premises

homeopath *n* (*pl* -s) person who practises homeopathy > **homeopathic** *adj*

homeopathic *adj* ▷ homeopath

homeopathies *n* ▷ homeopathy

homeopaths *n* ▷ homeopath

homeopathy [home-ee-**op**-ath-ee] *n* (*pl* -thies) treatment of disease by small doses of a drug that produces symptoms of the disease in healthy people

homes *n, v* ▷ home

homesick *adj* sad because missing one's home and family > **homesickness** *n* (*pl* -es)

homesickness *n* ▷ homesick

homesicknesses *n* ▷ homesick

homeward *adj, adv* ▷ home

homewards *adv* ▷ home
homework *n* (*pl* -s) school work done at home
homeworks *n* ▷ homework
homicidal *adj* ▷ homicide
homicide *n* (*pl* -s) killing of a human being > **homicidal** *adj*
homicides *n* ▷ homicide
homilies *n* ▷ homily
homily *n* (*pl* -lies) speech telling people how they should behave
homing *v* ▷ home
hominid *n* (*pl* -s) man or any extinct forerunner of man
hominids *n* ▷ hominid
homogeneities *n* ▷ homogeneous
homogeneity *n* ▷ homogeneous
homogeneous [home-oh-**jean**-ee-uss] *adj* formed of similar parts > **homogeneity** *n* (*pl* -ties)
homogenize *v* (-zes, -zing, -zed) break up fat globules in (milk or cream) to distribute them evenly
homogenized *v* ▷ homogenize
homogenizes *v* ▷ homogenize
homogenizing *v* ▷ homogenize
homograph *n* (*pl* -s) word spelt the same as another, but with a different meaning
homographs *n* ▷ homograph
homologous [hom-ol-log-uss] *adj* having a related or similar position or structure
homonym *n* (*pl* -s) word spelt or pronounced the same as another, but with a different meaning
homonyms *n* ▷ homonym
homophobia *n* (*pl* -s) hatred or fear of homosexuals > **homophobic** *adj*
homophobias *n* ▷ homophobia
homophobic *adj* ▷ homophobia
homophone *n* (*pl* -s) word pronounced the same as another, but with a different meaning or spelling
homophones *n* ▷ homophone
homosexual *n* (*pl* -s) ▶ *adj* (person) sexually attracted to members of the same sex > **homosexuality** *n* (*pl* -ties)
homosexualities *n* ▷ homosexual
homosexuality *n* ▷ homosexual
homosexuals *n* ▷ homosexual
hone *v* (-nes, -ning, -ned) sharpen
honed *v* ▷ hone
hones *v* ▷ hone
honest *adj* (-er, -est) truthful and moral > **honestly** *adv*
honester *adj* ▷ honest
honestest *adj* ▷ honest

honesties *n* ▷ honesty
honestly *adv* ▷ honest
honesty *n* (*pl* -ties) quality of being honest
honey *n* (*pl* -s) sweet edible sticky substance made by bees from nectar
honeycomb *n* (*pl* -s) waxy structure of six-sided cells in which honey is stored by bees in a beehive
honeycombs *n* ▷ honeycomb
honeymoon *n* (*pl* -s) holiday taken by a newly married couple
honeymoons *n* ▷ honeymoon
honeys *n* ▷ honey
honeysuckle *n* (*pl* -s) climbing shrub with sweet-smelling flowers
honeysuckles *n* ▷ honeysuckle
hongi [hong-jee] *n* (*pl* -s) (NZ) Maori greeting in which people touch noses
hongis *n* ▷ hongi
honing *v* ▷ hone
honk *n* (*pl* -s) sound made by a car horn ▶ *v* (-s, -ing, -ed) (cause to) make this sound
honked *v* ▷ honk
honking *v* ▷ honk
honks *n*, *v* ▷ honk
honorary *adj* held or given only as an honour
honorific *adj* showing respect
honour *n* (*pl* -s) sense of honesty and fairness ▶ *v* (-s, -ing, -ed) give praise and attention to
honourable *adj* worthy of respect or esteem > **honourably** *adv*
honourably *adv* ▷ honourable
honoured *v* ▷ honour
honouring *v* ▷ honour
honours *n*, *v* ▷ honour ▶ *pl n* university degree of a higher standard than an ordinary degree
hood[1] *n* (*pl* -s) head covering, often attached to a coat or jacket
hood[2] *n* (*pl* -s) (CHIEFLY US) (*Slang*) hoodlum
hooded *adj* (of a garment) having a hood
hoodlum *n* (*pl* -s) (*Slang*) violent criminal, gangster
hoodlums *n* ▷ hoodlum
hoodoo *n* (*pl* -s) (cause of) bad luck
hoodoos *n* ▷ hoodoo
hoods *n* ▷ hood[1, 2]
hoodwink *v* (-s, -ing, -ed) trick, deceive
hoodwinked *v* ▷ hoodwink
hoodwinking *v* ▷ hoodwink
hoodwinks *v* ▷ hoodwink
hoof *n* (*pl* hooves, hoofs) horny covering of the foot of a horse, deer, etc.
hoofs *n* ▷ hoof
hook *n* (*pl* -s) curved piece of metal, plastic, etc., used to hang, hold, or pull something

▶ v (-s, -ing, -ed) fasten or catch (as if) with a hook

hookah n (pl -s) oriental pipe in which smoke is drawn through water and a long tube
   hookahs n ▷ hookah

hooked adj bent like a hook ▶ v ▷ hook

hooker n (pl -s) (CHIEFLY US) (Slang) prostitute
   hookers n ▷ hooher
   hooking v ▷ hook
   hooks n, v ▷ hook

hookup n (pl -s) linking of radio or television stations
   hookups n ▷ hookup

hookworm n (pl -s) blood-sucking worm with hooked mouthparts
   hookworms n ▷ hookworm

hooligan n (pl -s) rowdy young person
   > **hooliganism** n (pl -s)
   hooliganisms n ▷ hooligan
   hooligans n ▷ hooligan

hoon n (pl -s) (AUST & NZ) (Slang) loutish youth who drives irresponsibly
   hoons n ▷ hoon

hoop n (pl -s) rigid circular band, used esp. as a child's toy or for animals to jump through in the circus

hoopla n (pl -s) fairground game in which hoops are thrown over objects in an attempt to win them
   hooplas n ▷ hoopla
   hoops n ▷ hoop
   hooray interj ▷ hurrah

hoot n (pl -s) sound of a car horn ▶ v (-s, -ing, -ed) sound (a car horn)
   hooted v ▷ hoot

hooter n (pl -s) device that hoots
   hooters n ▷ hooter
   hooting v ▷ hoot
   hoots n, v ▷ hoot

hoover n ® (pl -s) vacuum cleaner ▶ v (-s, -ing, -ed) clean with a vacuum cleaner
   hoovered v ▷ hoover
   hoovering v ▷ hoover
   hoovers n, v ▷ hoover
   hooves n ▷ hoof

hop¹ v (-s, -pping, -pped) jump on one foot ▶ n (pl -s) instance of hopping

hop² n (pl -s) (often pl) climbing plant, the dried flowers of which are used to make beer

hope v (-pes, -ping, -ped) want (something) to happen or to be true ▶ n (pl -s) expectation of something desired > **hopeless** adj
   hoped v ▷ hope

hopeful adj having, expressing, or inspiring hope ▶ n (pl -s) person considered to be on the brink of success

hopefully adv in a hopeful manner
   hopefuls adj ▷ hopeful
   hopefuls n ▷ hopeful
   hopeless adj ▷ hope
   hopes v, n ▷ hope
   hoping v ▷ hope
   hopped v ▷ hop¹

hopper n (pl -s) container for storing substances such as grain or sand
   hoppers n ▷ hopper
   hopping v ▷ hop¹
   hops n ▷ hop¹, ² ▶ v ▷ hop¹

hopscotch n (pl -es) children's game of hopping in a pattern drawn on the ground
   hopscotches n ▷ hopscotch

horde n (pl -s) large crowd
   hordes n ▷ horde

horizon n (pl -s) apparent line that divides the earth and the sky
   horizons n ▷ horizon ▶ pl n limits of scope, interest, or knowledge

horizontal adj parallel to the horizon, level, flat > **horizontally** adv
   horizontally adv ▷ horizontal
   hormonal adj ▷ hormone

hormone n (pl -s) substance secreted by certain glands which stimulates certain organs of the body > **hormonal** adj
   hormones n ▷ hormone

horn n (pl -s) one of a pair of bony growths sticking out of the heads of cattle, sheep, etc. > **horned** adj

hornbeam n (pl -s) tree with smooth grey bark
   hornbeams n ▷ hornbeam

hornbill n (pl -s) bird with a bony growth on its large beak
   hornbills n ▷ hornbill

hornblende n (pl -s) mineral containing aluminium, calcium, sodium, magnesium, and iron
   hornblendes n ▷ hornblende
   horned adj ▷ horn

hornet n (pl -s) large wasp with a severe sting
   hornets n ▷ hornet

hornpipe n (pl -s) (music for) a solo dance, traditionally performed by sailors
   hornpipes n ▷ hornpipe
   horns n ▷ horn

horny adj (-nier, -niest) of or like horn

horoscope n (pl -s) prediction of a person's future based on the positions of the planets, sun, and moon at his or her birth
   horoscopes n ▷ horoscope

horrendous adj very unpleasant and shocking

horrible *adj* disagreeable, unpleasant
> **horribly** *adv*
  horribly *adv* ▷ horrible
horrid *adj* disagreeable, unpleasant
horrific *adj* causing horror
  horrified *v* ▷ horrify
  horrifies *v* ▷ horrify
horrify *v* (-fies, -fying, -fied) cause to feel horror or shock
  horrifying *v* ▷ horrify
horror *n* (*pl* -s) (thing or person causing) terror or hatred
  horrors *n* ▷ horror
horse *n* (*pl* -s) large animal with hooves, a mane, and a tail, used for riding and pulling carts etc.
  horseflies *n* ▷ horsefly
horsefly *n* (*pl* -flies) large bloodsucking fly
horsehair *n* (*pl* -s) hair from the tail or mane of a horse
  horsehairs *n* ▷ horsehair
horseman *n* (*pl* -men) person riding a horse
  horsemen *n* ▷ horseman
horseplay *n* (*pl* -s) rough or rowdy play
  horseplays *n* ▷ horseplay
horsepower *n* (*pl* -s) unit of power (equivalent to 745.7 watts), used to measure the power of an engine
  horsepowers *n* ▷ horsepower
horseradish *n* (*pl* -es) strong-tasting root of a plant, usu. made into a sauce
  horseradishes *n* ▷ horseradish
  horses *n* ▷ horse
horseshoe *n* (*pl* -s) protective U-shaped piece of iron nailed to a horse's hoof, regarded as a symbol of good luck
  horseshoes *n* ▷ horseshoe
horsewoman *n* (*pl* -men) woman riding a horse
  horsewomen *n* ▷ horsewoman
horsey, horsy *adj* (-sier, -siest) very keen on horses
  horsier *adj* ▷ horsey
  horsiest *adj* ▷ horsey
  horsy *adj* ▷ horsey
horticultural *adj* ▷ horticulture
  horticulturalist *n* ▷ horticulture
  horticulturalists *n* ▷ horticulture
horticulture *n* (*pl* -s) art or science of cultivating gardens ▶ **horticultural** *adj*
> **horticulturalist, horticulturist** *n* (*pl* -s)
  horticultures *n* ▷ horticulture
  horticulturist *n* ▷ horticulture
  horticulturists *n* ▷ horticulture
hosanna *interj* exclamation of praise to God

hose¹ *n* (*pl* -s) flexible pipe for conveying liquid ▶ *v* (-ses, -sing, -sed) water with a hose
hose² *n* (*pl* -s) stockings, socks, and tights
  hosed *v* ▷ hose¹
  hoses *n*, *v* ▷ hose¹, ² ▶ *v* ▷ hose¹
  hosieries *n* ▷ hosiery
hosiery *n* (*pl* -ries) stockings, socks, and tights collectively
  hosing *v* ▷ hose¹
hospice [hoss-piss] *n* (*pl* -s) nursing home for the terminally ill
  hospices *n* ▷ hospice
hospitable *adj* welcoming to strangers or guests
hospital *n* (*pl* -s) place where people who are ill are looked after and treated
  hospitalities *n* ▷ hospitality
  hospitalities *n* ▷ hospitality
hospitality *n* (*pl* -ties) kindness in welcoming strangers or guests
  hospitalization *n* ▷ hospitalize
  hospitalizations *n* ▷ hospitalize
hospitalize *v* (-izes, -izing, -ized) send or admit to hospital > **hospitalization** *n* (*pl* -s)
  hospitalized *v* ▷ hospitalize
  hospitalizes *v* ▷ hospitalize
  hospitalizing *v* ▷ hospitalize
  hospitals *n* ▷ hospital
host¹ *n* (*pl* -s) man who entertains guests, esp. in his own home ▶ *v* (-s, -ing, -ed) be the host of
host² *n* (*pl* -s) large number
hostage *n* (*pl* -s) person who is illegally held prisoner until certain demands are met by other people
  hostages *n* ▷ hostage
  hosted *v* ▷ host¹
hostel *n* (*pl* -s) building providing accommodation at a low cost for a specific group of people such as students, travellers, homeless people, etc.
  hostelries *n* ▷ hostelry
hostelry *n* (*pl* -ries) (*Old-fashioned or facetious*) inn, pub
  hostels *n* ▷ hostel
hostess *n* (*pl* -es) woman who entertains guests, esp. in her own home
  hostesses *n* ▷ hostess
hostile *adj* unfriendly
  hostilities *n* ▷ hostility ▶ *pl n* acts of warfare
hostility *n* (*pl* -ties) unfriendly and aggressive feelings or behaviour
  hosting *v* ▷ host¹
  hosts *n* ▷ host¹, ² ▶ *v* ▷ host¹
hot *adj* (-tter, -ttest) having a high

temperature in trouble > **hotly** adv

hotbed n (pl -s) any place encouraging a particular activity
hotbeds n ▷ hotbed

hotchpotch n (pl -es) jumbled mixture
hotchpotches n ▷ hotchpotch

hotel n (pl -s) commercial establishment providing lodging and meals

hotelier n (pl -s) owner or manager of a hotel
hoteliers n ▷ hotelier
hotels n ▷ hotel

hotfoot adv (Informal) quickly and eagerly

hotheaded adj rash, having a hot temper

hothouse n (pl -s) greenhouse
hothouses n ▷ hothouse

hotline n (pl -s) direct telephone link for emergency use
hotlines n ▷ hotline

hotly adv ▷ hot

hotplate n (pl -s) heated metal surface on an electric cooker
hotplates n ▷ hotplate
hotter adj ▷ hot
hottest adj ▷ hot

hound n (pl -s) hunting dog ▶ v (-s, -ing, -ed) pursue relentlessly
hounded v ▷ hound
hounding v ▷ hound
hounds n, v ▷ hound

hour n (pl -s) twenty-fourth part of a day, sixty minutes

hourglass n (pl -es) device with two glass compartments, containing a quantity of sand that takes an hour to trickle from the top section to the bottom one
hourglasses n ▷ hourglass

houri n (pl -s) (ISLAM) any of the nymphs of paradise
houris n ▷ houri

hourly adj, adv (happening) every hour

hours pl n n period regularly appointed for work or business ▶ n ▷ hour

house n (pl -s) building used as a home ▶ v (-ses, -sing, -sed) give accommodation to

houseboat n (pl -s) stationary boat used as a home
houseboats n ▷ houseboat

housebreaker n (pl -s) burglar
housebreakers n ▷ housebreaker

housecoat n (pl -s) woman's long loose coat-shaped garment for wearing at home
housecoats n ▷ housecoat

housed v ▷ house

household n (pl -s) all the people living in a house

householder n (pl -s) person who owns or rents a house
householders n ▷ householder
households n ▷ household

housekeeper n (pl -s) person employed to run someone else's household
housekeepers n ▷ housekeeper

housekeeping n (pl -s) (money for) running a household
housekeepings n ▷ housekeeping

housemaid n (pl -s) female servant employed to do housework
housemaids n ▷ housemaid

houses n, v ▷ house

housewarming n (pl -s) party to celebrate moving into a new home
housewarmings n ▷ housewarming

housewife n (pl -wives) woman who runs her own household and does not have a job
housewives n ▷ housewife

housework n (pl -s) work of running a home, such as cleaning, cooking, and shopping
houseworks n ▷ housework

housing n (pl -s) (providing of) houses ▶ v ▷ house
housings n ▷ housing

hovea n (pl -s) Australian plant with purple flowers
hoveas n ▷ hovea

hovel n (pl -s) small dirty house or hut
hovels n ▷ hovel

hover v (-s, -ing, -red) (of a bird etc.) remain suspended in one place in the air

hovercraft n (pl -s) vehicle which can travel over both land and sea on a cushion of air
hovercrafts n ▷ hovercraft
hovered v ▷ hover
hovering v ▷ hover
hovers v ▷ hover

how adv in what way, by what means

howdah n (pl -s) canopied seat on an elephant's back
howdahs n ▷ howdah

however adv nevertheless

howitzer n (pl -s) large gun firing shells at a steep angle
howitzers n ▷ howitzer

howl n (pl -s) loud wailing cry ▶ v (-s, -ing, -ed) utter a howl
howled v ▷ howl

howler n (pl -s) (Informal) stupid mistake
howlers n ▷ howler
howling v ▷ howl
howls n, v ▷ howl

hoyden n (pl -s) (Old-fashioned) wild or

boisterous girl

hoydens n ▷ hoyden

hox v (**hoxes, hoxing, hoxed**). This is a word found in Shakespeare's plays, and means to cut a horse's hamstring. This unusual word is a handy one to remember if you draw an X. Hox scores 12 points.

hub n (pl -s) centre of a wheel, through which the axle passes

hubbies n ▷ hubby

hubbub n (pl -s) confused noise of many voices

hubbubs n ▷ hubbub

hubby n (pl -bbies) (Informal) husband

hubris [hew-briss] n (pl -es) (Formal) pride, arrogance

hubrises n ▷ hubris

hubs n ▷ hub

huckster n (pl -s) person using aggressive methods of selling

hucksters n ▷ huckster

huddle v (-les, -ling, -led) hunch (oneself) through cold or fear ▶ n (pl -s) small group

huddled v ▷ huddle

huddles n, v ▷ huddle

huddling v ▷ huddle

hue n (pl -s) colour, shade

hues n ▷ hue

huff n (pl -s) passing mood of anger or resentment ▶ v (-s, -ing, -ed) blow or puff heavily ▶ **huffy** adj (-fier, -ffiest) > **huffily** adv

huffed v ▷ huff

huffier adj ▷ huff

huffiest adj ▷ huff

huffily adv ▷ huff

huffing v ▷ huff

huffs n, v ▷ huff

huffy adj ▷ huff

hug v (-s, -gging, -gged) clasp tightly in the arms, usu. with affection ▶ n (pl -s) tight or fond embrace

huge adj (-r, -st) very big > **hugely** adv

huger adj ▷ huge

hugest adj ▷ huge

hugged v ▷ hug

hugging v ▷ hug

hugs n, v ▷ hug

huh interj exclamation of derision, bewilderment, or inquiry

hui [hoo-ee] n (pl **huies**) (NZ) meeting of Maori people

huies n ▷ hui

hula n (pl -s) swaying Hawaiian dance

hulas n ▷ hula

hulk n (pl -s) body of an abandoned ship

hulking adj bulky, unwieldy

hulks n ▷ hulk

hull n (pl -s) main body of a boat ▶ v (-s, -ing, -ed) remove the hulls from

hullabaloo n (pl -loos) loud confused noise or clamour

hullabaloos n ▷ hullabaloo

hulled v ▷ hull

hulling v ▷ hull

hulls n, v ▷ hull

hum v (-s, -mming, -mmed) make a low continuous vibrating sound ▶ n (pl -s) humming sound

human adj of or typical of people ▶ n (pl -s) human being

humane adj (-r, -st) kind or merciful > **humanely** adv

humanely adv ▷ humane

humaner adj ▷ humane

humanest adj ▷ humane

humanism n (pl -s) belief in human effort rather than religion > **humanist** n (pl -s)

humanisms n ▷ humanism

humanist n ▷ humanism

humanists n ▷ humanism

humanitarian adj, n (pl -s) (person) having the interests of humankind at heart

humanitarians n ▷ humanitarian

humanities n ▷ humanity ▶ pl n study of literature, philosophy, and the arts

humanity n (pl -ties) human race

humanize v (-zes, -zing, -zed) make human or humane

humanized v ▷ humanize

humanizes v ▷ humanize

humanizing v ▷ humanize

humankind n (pl -s) human race

humankinds n ▷ humankind

humanly adv by human powers or means

humans n ▷ human

humble adj (-r, -st) conscious of one's failings ▶ v (-les, -ling, -led) cause to feel humble, humiliate > **humbly** adv

humbled v ▷ humble

humbler adj ▷ humble

humbles v ▷ humble

humblest adj ▷ humble

humbling v ▷ humble

humbly adv ▷ humble

humbug n (pl -s) (BRIT) hard striped peppermint sweet

humbugs n ▷ humbug

humdinger n (pl -s) (Slang) excellent person or thing

humdingers n ▷ humdinger

humdrum *adj* ordinary, dull

humeri *n* ▷ humerus

humerus [hew-mer-uss] *n* (*pl* -**meri**) [-mer-rye] bone from the shoulder to the elbow

humid *adj* (-**er**, -**est**) damp and hot > **humidity** *n* (*pl* -**ties**) **humidify** *v* (-**fies**, -**fying**, -**fied**)

humider *adj* ▷ humid

humidest *adj* ▷ humid

humidified *v* ▷ humid

humidifier *n* (*pl* -**s**) device for increasing the amount of water vapour in the air in a room

humidifiers *n* ▷ humidifier

humidifies *v* ▷ humid

humidifying *v* ▷ humidify

humidities *n* ▷ humid

humidity *n* ▷ humid

humiliate *v* (-**tes**, -**ting**, -**ted**) lower the dignity or hurt the pride of > **humiliating** *adj* > **humiliation** *n* (*pl* -**s**)

humiliated *v* ▷ humiliate

humiliates *v* ▷ humiliate

humiliating *v*, *adj* ▷ humiliate

humiliation *n* ▷ humiliate

humiliations *n* ▷ humiliate

humilities *n* ▷ humility

humility *n* (*pl* humilities) quality of being humble

hummed *v* ▷ hum

humming *v* ▷ hum

hummingbird *n* (*pl* -**s**) very small American bird whose powerful wings make a humming noise as they vibrate

hummingbirds *n* ▷ hummingbird

hummock *n* (*pl* -**s**) very small hill

hummocks *n* ▷ hummock

humorist *n* (*pl* -**s**) writer or entertainer who uses humour in his or her work

humorists *n* ▷ humorist

humorous *adj* ▷ humour

humorously *adj* ▷ humour

humour *n* (*pl* -**s**) ability to say or perceive things that are amusing ▶ *v* (-**s**, -**ing**, -**ed**) be kind and indulgent to > **humorous** *adj* > **humorously** *adv*

humoured *v* ▷ humour

humouring *v* ▷ humour

humours *n*, *v* ▷ humour

hump *n* (*pl* -**s**) raised piece of ground ▶ *v* (-**s**, -**ing**, -**ed**) (*Slang*) carry or heave

humped *v* ▷ hump

humping *v* ▷ hump

humps *n*, *v* ▷ hump

hums *v*, *n* ▷ hum

humus [hew-muss] *n* (*pl* -**es**) decomposing vegetable and animal mould in the soil

humuses *n* ▷ humus

hunch *n* (*pl* -**es**) feeling or suspicion not based on facts ▶ *v* (-**es**, -**ing**, -**ed**) draw (one's shoulders) up or together

hunchback *n* (*pl* -**s**) (*Offens*) person with an abnormal curvature of the spine

hunchbacks *n* ▷ hunchback

hunched *v* ▷ hunch

hunches *n*, *v* ▷ hunch

hunching *v* ▷ hunch

hundred *adj* ten times ten ▶ *n* (*pl* -**s**) (*often pl*) large but unspecified number > **hundredth** *adj*, *n* (*pl* -**s**)

hundreds *n* ▷ hundred

hundredth *n* ▷ hundred

hundredths *n* ▷ hundred

hundredweight *n* (*pl* -**s**) (BRIT) unit of weight of 112 pounds (50.8 kilograms)

hundredweights *n* ▷ hundredweight

hung *v* ▷ hang ▶ *adj* (of a parliament or jury) with no side having a clear majority

hunger *n* (*pl* -**s**) discomfort or weakness from lack of food ▶ *v* (-**s**, -**ing**, -**ed**) (*foll. by* **for**) want very much

hungered *v* ▷ hunger

hungering *v* ▷ hunger

hungers *n*, *v* ▷ hunger

hungrier *adj* ▷ hungry

hungriest *adj* ▷ hungry

hungrily *adv* ▷ hungry

hungry *adj* (-**rier**, -**riest**) desiring food (*foll. by* **for**) > **hungrily** *adv*

hunk *n* (*pl* -**s**) large piece

hunks *n* ▷ hunk

hunt *v* (-**s**, -**ing**, -**ed**) seek out and kill (wild animals) for food or sport ▶ *n* (*pl* -**s**) hunting

huntaway *n* (*pl* -**s**) (NZ) sheepdog trained to drive sheep by barking

huntaways *n* ▷ huntaway

hunted *v* ▷ hunt

hunter *n* (*pl* -**s**) person or animal that hunts wild animals for food or sport

hunters *n* ▷ hunter

hunting *v* ▷ hunt

hunts *v*, *n* ▷ hunt

huntsman *n* (*pl* -**men**) man who hunts wild animals, esp. foxes

huntsmen *n* ▷ huntsman

hurdle *n* (*pl* -**s**) (SPORT) light barrier for jumping over in some races ▶ *v* (-**les**, -**ling**, -**led**) jump over (something) > **hurdler** *n* (*pl* -**s**)

hurdled *v* ▷ hurdle

hurdler *n* ▷ hurdle

hurdlers *n* ▷ hurdle

hurdles *n*, *v* ▷ hurdle ▶ *pl n* race involving

hurdles
hurdling v ▷ hurdle
hurl v (-s, -ing, -ed) throw or utter forcefully
hurled v ▷ hurl
hurley n ▷ hurling
hurleys n ▷ hurling
hurling, hurley n (pl -s) Irish game like hockey
▶ v ▷ hurl
hurlings n ▷ hurling
hurls v ▷ hurl
hurrah, hurray interj exclamation of joy or applause
hurricane n (pl -s) very strong, often destructive, wind or storm
hurricanes n ▷ hurricane
hurried v ▷ hurry
hurriedly adv ▷ hurry
hurries v, n ▷ hurry
hurry v (-ries, -rying, -ried) (cause to) move or act very quickly ▶ n (pl -ries) doing something quickly or the need to do something quickly
> **hurriedly** adv
hurrying v ▷ hurry
hurt v (-s, -ing, hurt) cause physical or mental pain to ▶ n (pl -s) physical or mental pain
hurtful adj unkind
hurting v ▷ hurt
hurtle v (-les, -ling, -led) move quickly or violently
hurtled v ▷ hurtle
hurtles v ▷ hurtle
hurtling v ▷ hurtle
hurts v, n ▷ hurt
husband n (pl -s) woman's partner in marriage ▶ v (-s, -ing, -ed) use economically
husbanded v ▷ husband
husbanding v ▷ husband
husbandries n ▷ husbandry
husbandry n (pl -ries) farming
husbands n, v ▷ husband
hush v (-es, -ing, -ed) make or be silent ▶ n (pl -es) stillness or silence
hushed v ▷ hush
hushes v, n ▷ hush
hushing v ▷ hush
husk n (pl -s) outer covering of certain seeds and fruits ▶ v (-s, -ing, -ed) remove the husk from
husked v ▷ husk
huskier adj ▷ husky¹
huskies n ▷ husky²
huskiest adj ▷ husky¹
huskily adv ▷ husky¹
husking v ▷ husk

husks n, v ▷ husk
husky¹ adj (-kier, -kiest) slightly hoarse
> **huskily** adv
husky² n (pl -kies) Arctic sledge dog with thick hair and a curled tail
hussar [hoo-**zar**] n (pl -s) (HIST) lightly armed cavalry soldier
hussars n ▷ hussar
hussies n ▷ hussy
hussy n (pl -sies) immodest or promiscuous woman
hustings pl n political campaigns and speeches before an election
hustle v (-les, -ling, -led) push about, jostle ▶ n (pl -les) lively activity or bustle
hustled v ▷ hustle
hustles v, n ▷ hustle
hustling v ▷ hustle
hut n (pl -s) small house, shelter, or shed
hutch n (pl -es) cage for pet rabbits etc.
hutches n ▷ hutch
huts n ▷ hut
hyacinth n (pl -s) sweet-smelling spring flower that grows from a bulb
hyacinths n ▷ hyacinth
hyaena n (pl -s) ▷ hyena
hyaenas n ▷ hyena
hybrid n (pl -s) offspring of two plants or animals of different species ▶ adj of mixed origin
hybrids n ▷ hybrid
hydra n (pl -s) mythical many-headed water serpent
hydrangea n (pl -s) ornamental shrub with clusters of pink, blue, or white flowers
hydrangeas n ▷ hydrangea
hydrant n (pl -s) outlet from a water main with a nozzle for a hose
hydrants n ▷ hydrant
hydras n ▷ hydra
hydrate n (pl -tes) chemical compound of water with another substance
hydrates n ▷ hydrate
hydraulic adj operated by pressure forced through a pipe by a liquid such as water or oil
hydraulically adv ▷ hydraulics
hydraulics n study of the mechanical properties of fluids as they apply to practical engineering > **hydraulically** adv
hydro¹ n (pl -s) hotel offering facilities for hydropathy
hydro² adj ▷ hydroelectric
hydrocarbon n (pl -s) compound of hydrogen and carbon
hydrocarbons n ▷ hydrocarbon

hydroelectric *adj* of the generation of electricity by water pressure

hydrofoil *n* (*pl* -**s**) fast light boat with its hull raised out of the water on one or more pairs of fins
  hydrofoils *n* ▷ hydrofoil

hydrogen *n* (*pl* -**s**) (CHEM) light flammable colourless gas that combines with oxygen to form water
  hydrogens *n* ▷ hydrogen
  hydrolyses *n* ▷ hydrolysis

hydrolysis [hie-**drol**-iss-iss] *n* (*pl* -**yses**) decomposition of a chemical compound reacting with water

hydrometer [hie-**drom**-it-er] *n* (*pl* -**s**) instrument for measuring the density of a liquid
  hydrometers *n* ▷ hydrometer
  hydropathies *n* ▷ hydropathy

hydropathy *n* (*pl* -**thies**) method of treating disease by the use of large quantities of water both internally and externally

hydrophobia *n* (*pl* -**s**) rabies
  hydrophobias *n* ▷ hydrophobia

hydroplane *n* (*pl* -**s**) light motorboat that skims the water
  hydroplanes *n* ▷ hydroplane

hydroponics *n* method of growing plants in water rather than soil
  hydros *n* ▷ hydro¹
  hydrotherapies *n* ▷ hydrotherapy

hydrotherapy *n* (*pl* -**pies**) (MED) treatment of certain diseases by exercise in water

hyena *n* (*pl* -**s**) scavenging doglike mammal of Africa and S Asia
  hyenas *n* ▷ hyena

hygiene *n* (*pl* -**s**) principles and practice of health and cleanliness > **hygienic** *adj*
 > **hygienically** *adv*
  hygienic *adj* ▷ hygiene
  hygienically *adj* ▷ hygiene

hymen *n* (*pl* -**s**) membrane partly covering the opening of a girl's vagina, which breaks before puberty or at the first occurrence of sexual intercourse
  hymens *n* ▷ hymen

hymn *n* (*pl* -**s**) Christian song of praise sung to God or a saint

hymnal *n* (*pl* -**s**) book of hymns (*also* **hymn book**)
  hymnals *n* ▷ hymnal
  hymns *n* ▷ hymn

hype *n* (*pl* -**s**) intensive or exaggerated publicity or sales promotion ▶ *v* (-**pes**, -**ping**, -**ped**) promote (a product) using intensive or exaggerated publicity

  hyped *v* ▷ hype

hyper *adj* (*Informal*) overactive or overexcited

hyperbola [hie-**per**-bol-a] *n* (*pl* -**s**) (GEOM) curve produced when a cone is cut by a plane at a steeper angle to its base than its side
  hyperbolas *n* ▷ hyperbola

hyperbole [hie-**per**-bol-ee] *n* (*pl* -**s**) deliberate exaggeration for effect
 > **hyperbolic** *adj*
  hyperboles *n* ▷ hyperbole
  hyperbolic *adj* ▷ hyperbole

hyperlink (COMPUTERS) *n* (*pl* -**s**) link from a hypertext file that gives users instant access to related material in another file ▶ *v* (-**s**, -**ing**, -**ed**) link (files) in this way
  hyperlinked *v* ▷ hyperlink
  hyperlinking *v* ▷ hyperlink
  hyperlinks *v*, *n* ▷ hyperlink

hypermarket *n* (*pl* -**s**) huge self-service store
  hypermarkets *n* ▷ hypermarket

hypersensitive *adj* extremely sensitive to certain drugs, extremes of temperature, etc.

hypersonic *adj* having a speed of at least five times the speed of sound

hypertension *n* (*pl* -**s**) very high blood pressure
  hypertensions *n* ▷ hypertension
  hypertensions *n* ▷ hypertension

hypertext *n* (*pl* -**s**) computer software and hardware that allows users to store and view text and move between related items easily
  hypertexts *n* ▷ hypertext
  hypes *n*, *v* ▷ hype

hyphen *n* (*pl* -**s**) punctuation mark (-) indicating that two words or syllables are connected

hyphenated *adj* (of two words or syllables) having a hyphen between them
 > **hyphenation** *n* (*pl* -**s**)
  hyphenation *n* ▷ hyphenated
  hyphenations *n* ▷ hyphenated
  hyphens *n* ▷ hyphen
  hyping *v* ▷ hype
  hypnoses *n* ▷ hypnosis

hypnosis *n* (*pl* -**noses**) artificially induced state of relaxation in which the mind is more than usually receptive to suggestion

hypnotic *adj* of or (as if) producing hypnosis

hypnotism *n* (*pl* -**s**) inducing hypnosis in someone > **hypnotist** *n* (*pl* -**s**) > **hypnotize** *v* (-**tizes**, -**tizing**, -**tized**)
  hypnotisms *n* ▷ hypnotism
  hypnotist *n* ▷ hypnotism
  hypnotists *n* ▷ hypnotism
  hypnotize *v* ▷ hypnotism

hypnotized v ▷ hypnotism
hypnotizes v ▷ hypnotism
hypnotizing v ▷ hypnotism
hypoallergenic adj (of cosmetics) not likely to cause an allergic reaction
hypochondria n (pl -s) undue preoccupation with one's health > **hypochondriac** n (pl -s)
hypochondriac n ▷ hypochondria
hypochondriacs n ▷ hypochondria
hypochondrias n ▷ hypochondria
hypocrisies n ▷ hypocrisy
hypocrisy [hip-ok-rass-ee] n (pl -sies) (instance of) pretence of having standards or beliefs that are contrary to one's real character or actual behaviour
hypocrite [hip-oh-krit] n (pl -s) person who pretends to be what he or she is not > **hypocritical** adj > **hypocritically** adv
hypocrites n ▷ hypocrite
hypocritical adj ▷ hypocrite
hypocritically adv ▷ hypocrite
hypodermic adj, n (pl -s) (denoting) a syringe or needle used to inject a drug beneath the skin
hypodermics n ▷ hypodermic
hypotension n (pl -s) very low blood pressure
hypotenuse [hie-pot-a-news] n (pl -s) side of a right-angled triangle opposite the right angle
hypotenuses n ▷ hypotenuse
hypothermia n (pl -s) condition in which a person's body temperature is dangerously low as a result of prolonged exposure to severe cold
hypothermias n ▷ hypothermia
hypotheses n ▷ hypothesis
hypothesis [hie-poth-iss-iss] n (pl -ses) [-seez] suggested but unproved explanation of something
hypothetical adj based on assumption rather than fact or reality > **hypothetically** adv
hypothetically adj ▷ hypothetical
hyraces n ▷ hyrax
hyrax n (pl -raxes or -races) type of hoofed rodent-like animal of Africa and Asia
hyraxes n ▷ hyrax
hysterectomies n ▷ hysterectomy
hysterectomy n (pl -mies) surgical removal of the womb
hysteria n (pl -s) state of uncontrolled excitement, anger, or panic > **hysterical** adj > **hysterically** adv
hysterias n ▷ hysteria
hysterical adj ▷ hysteria
hysterically adj ▷ hysteria
hysterics pl n attack of hysteria

I i

The letter I can prove a difficult tile to use effectively in Scrabble. It's one of the most common tiles in the game, so you often end up with two or more on your rack, but it can be hard to get rid of. Where I does come in very useful, though, is in the number of everyday short words that can be formed from it, which are very helpful when you need to form short words in addition to the main word that you want to play. These words include **in**, **is**, **it** (2 points each), **id** (3) and **if** (5). Other handy words are **icy** (8), **ivy** (9) and **imp** (7). Don't forget the three-letter words that use K: **ilk**, **ink** and **irk** (7 each).

ibex [ibe-eks] *n* (*pl* -es) wild goat of N with large backward-curving horns
  ibexes *n* ▷ ibex
ibis [ibe-iss] *n* (*pl* -es) large wading bird with long legs
  ibises *n* ▷ ibis
ice *n* (*pl* -s) frozen water ▶ *v* (-ces, -cing, -ced) (foll. by **up** or **over**) become covered with ice
iceberg *n* (*pl* -s) large floating mass of ice
  icebergs *n* ▷ iceberg
icebox *n* (*pl* -es) (us) refrigerator
  iceboxes *n* ▷ icebox
icecap *n* (*pl* -s) mass of ice permanently covering an area
  icecaps *n* ▷ icecap
iced *adj* covered with icing ▶ *v* ▷ ice
  ices *v*, *n* ▷ ice

> **ich** *pron.* Ich is an old dialect form of I. This is a useful little word that is worth remembering because of its unusual combination of letters and relatively high score. Ich scores 8 points.

  ichthyologies *n* ▷ ichthyology
ichthyology [ik-thi-ol-a-jee] *n* (*pl* -gies) scientific study of fish
icicle *n* (*pl* -s) tapering spike of ice hanging where water has dripped
  icicles *n* ▷ icicle
  icier *adj* ▷ icy
  iciest *adj* ▷ icy
  icily *adv* ▷ icy
  iciness *n* ▷ icy
  icinesses *n* ▷ icy
icing *v* ▷ ice ▶ *n* (*pl* -s) mixture of sugar and water etc., used to cover and decorate cakes
  icings *n* ▷ icing

> **ick** *interj.* Ick is something that people say when they encounter something unpleasant or disgusting. Ick is a good word to remember because, in addition to being useful when there's little space, it's one of the highest-scoring three-letter word beginning with I. Ick scores 9 points.

icon *n* (*pl* -s) picture of Christ or another religious figure, regarded as holy in the Orthodox Church
iconoclast *n* (*pl* -s) person who attacks established ideas or principles > **iconoclastic** *adj*
  iconoclastic *adj* ▷ iconoclastic
  iconoclasts *n* ▷ iconoclast
  icons *n* ▷ icon
icy *adj* (-cier, -ciest) very cold > **icily** *adv* > **iciness** *n* (*pl* -es)
id *n* (*pl* -s) (PSYCHOANALYSIS) the mind's instinctive unconscious energies

> **ide** *n* (**ides**). An ide is a kind of fish. This combination of letters is a good one to keep in mind because it is both a suffix that can be added to words already on the board and a word in its own right. Ide scores 4 points.

idea *n* (*pl* -s) plan or thought formed in the mind
ideal *adj* most suitable ▶ *n* (*pl* -s) conception of something that is perfect > **idealist** *n* (*pl* -s) > **idealistically** *adv* > **ideally** *adv*
idealism *n* (*pl* -s) tendency to seek perfection in everything
  idealisms *n* ▷ idealism
  idealist *n* ▷ ideal
  idealistic *adj* ▷ ideal
  idealists *n* ▷ ideal

idealization *n* ▷ idealize
idealizations *n* ▷ idealize
idealize *v* (-izes, -izing, -ized) regard or portray as perfect or nearly perfect > **idealization** *n* (*pl* -s)
idealized *n* ▷ idealize
idealizes *n* ▷ idealize
idealizing *n* ▷ idealize
ideally *adv* ▷ ideal
ideals *n* ▷ ideal
ideas *n* ▷ idea
idem *pron, adj* (LATIN) the same: used to refer to an article, chapter, or book already quoted
identical *adj* exactly the same > **identically** *adv*
identically *adv* ▷ identical
identifiable *adj* ▷ identify
identification *n* ▷ identify
identifications *n* ▷ identify
identified *v* ▷ identify
identifies *v* ▷ identify
identify *v* (-fies, -fying, -fied) prove or recognize as being a certain person or thing > **identifiable** *adj* > **identification** *n* (*pl* -s)
identifying *v* ▷ identify
identities *n* ▷ identity
identity *n* (*pl* -ties) state of being a specified person or thing
ideological *adj* ▷ ideology
ideologies *n* ▷ ideology
ideologist *n* ▷ ideology
ideologists *n* ▷ ideology
ideology *n* (*pl* -gies) body of ideas and beliefs of a group, nation, etc. > **ideological** *adj* > **ideologist** *n* (*pl* -s)
idiocies *n* ▷ idiocy
idiocy *n* (*pl* -cies) utter stupidity
idiom *n* (*pl* -s) group of words which when used together have a different meaning from the words individually > **idiomatic** *adj* > **idiomatically** *adv*
idiomatic *adj* ▷ idiom
idiomatically *adv* ▷ idiom
idioms *n* ▷ idiom
idiosyncrasies *n* ▷ idiosyncrasy
idiosyncrasy *n* (*pl* -sies) personal peculiarity of mind, habit, or behaviour
idiot *n* (*pl* -s) foolish or stupid person > **idiotic** *adj* > **idiotically** *adv*
idiotic *adj* ▷ idiot
idiotically *adv* ▷ idiot
idiots *n* ▷ idiot
idle *adj* not doing anything ▶ *v* (-les, -ling, -led) (*usu. foll. by away*) spend (time) doing very little > **idleness** *n* (*pl* -s) > **idler** *n* (*pl* -s) > **idly** *adv*

idled *v* ▷ idle
idleness *n* ▷ idle
idlenesses *n* ▷ idle
idler *n* ▷ idle
idlers *n* ▷ idle
idles *v* ▷ idle
idling *v* ▷ idle
idly *adj* ▷ idle
idol *n* (*pl* -s) object of excessive devotion
idolatries *n* ▷ idolatry
idolatrous *adj* ▷ idolatry
idolatry *n* (*pl* -ries) worship of idols > **idolatrous** *adj*
idolize *v* (-izes, -izing, -ized) love or admire excessively
idolized *v* ▷ idolize
idolizes *v* ▷ idolize
idolizing *v* ▷ idolize
idols *n* ▷ idol
ids *n* ▷ id
idyll [id-ill] *n* (*pl* -s) scene or time of great peace and happiness > **idyllic** *adj* > **idyllically** *adv*
idyllic *adj* ▷ idyll
idyllically *adj* ▷ idyll
idylls *n* ▷ idyll
if *conj* on the condition or supposition that ▶ *n* (*pl* -s) uncertainty or doubt

> **iff** *conj*. Iff is a word used in logic to mean if and only if. This word is worth remembering: not only can it come in handy when there isn't much space on the board, but it's also one of the highest-scoring three-letter word beginning with I. Iff scores 9 points.

iffy *adj* (*Informal*) doubtful, uncertain
ifs *n* ▷ if
igloo *n* (*pl* -loos) dome-shaped Inuit house made of snow and ice
igloos *n* ▷ igloo
igneous [ig-nee-uss] *adj* (of rock) formed as molten rock cools and hardens
ignite *v* (-tes, -ting, -ted) catch fire or set fire to
ignited *v* ▷ ignite
ignites *v* ▷ ignite
igniting *v* ▷ ignite
ignition *n* (*pl* -s) system that ignites the fuel-and-air mixture to start an engine
ignitions *n* ▷ ignition
ignoble *adj* dishonourable
ignominies *n* ▷ ignominy
ignominious *adj* ▷ ignominy
ignominiously *adj* ▷ ignominy
ignominy [ig-nom-in-ee] *n* (*pl* -nies) humiliating disgrace > **ignominious** *adj* > **ignominiously** *adv*

ignoramus n (pl -muses) ignorant person
ignoramuses n ▷ ignoramus
ignorance n ▷ ignorant
ignorances n ▷ ignorance
ignorant adj lacking knowledge > **ignorance** n (pl -s)
ignore v (-res, -ring, -red) refuse to notice, disregard deliberately
ignored v ▷ ignore
ignores v ▷ ignore
ignoring v ▷ ignore
iguana n (pl -s) large tropical American lizard
iguanas n ▷ iguana
ileum n (pl -s) lowest part of the small intestine
ileums n ▷ ileum
ilk n (pl -s) type
ilks n ▷ ilk
ill adj not in good health ▶ n (pl -s) evil, harm ▶ adv badly > **illness** n (pl -s)
illegal adj against the law > **illegally** adv > **illegality** n (pl -ties)
illegalities n ▷ illegal
illegality n ▷ illegal
illegally adv ▷ illegal
illegible adj unable to be read or deciphered
illegitimacies n ▷ illegitimate
illegitimacy n ▷ illegitimate
illegitimate adj born of parents not married to each other > **illegitimacy** n (pl -s)
illicit adj illegal
illiteracies n ▷ illiterate
illiteracy n ▷ illiterate
illiterate n (pl -s) ▶ adj (person) unable to read or write > **illiteracy** n (pl -s)
illiterates n ▷ illiterate
illness n ▷ ill
illnesses n ▷ ill
illogical adj unreasonable > **illogicality** n (pl -lities)
illogicalities adj ▷ illogical
illogicality adj ▷ illogical
ills n ▷ ill
illuminate v (-tes, -ting, -ted) light up > **illumination** n (pl -s) > **illuminating** adj
illuminated v ▷ illuminate
illuminates v ▷ illuminate
illuminating adj, v ▷ illuminate
illumination n ▷ illuminate
illuminations n ▷ illuminate
illusion n (pl -s) deceptive appearance or belief
illusionist n (pl -s) conjuror
illusionists n ▷ illusionist
illusions n ▷ illusion
illusory adj seeming to be true, but actually false

illustrate v (-tes, -ting, -ted) explain by use of examples > **illustrative** adj > **illustrator** n (pl -s)
illustrated v ▷ illustrate
illustrates v ▷ illustrate
illustrating v ▷ illustrate
illustration n (pl -s) picture or diagram
illustrations n ▷ illustrate
illustrative adj ▷ illustrate
illustrator n ▷ illustrate
illustrators n ▷ illustrate
illustrious adj famous and distinguished
image n (pl -s) mental picture of someone or something
imageries n ▷ imagery
imagery n (pl -ries) images collectively, esp. in the arts
images n ▷ image
imaginable adj ▷ imagine
imaginary adj existing only in the imagination
imagination n (pl -s) ability to make mental images of things that may not exist in real life
imaginations n ▷ imagination
imaginative adj having or showing a lot of creative mental ability > **imaginatively** adv
imaginatively adv ▷ imaginative
imagine v (-nes, -ning, -ned) form a mental image of > **imaginable** adj
imagined v ▷ imagine
imagines v ▷ imagine ▶ n ▷ imago
imagining v ▷ imagine
imago [im-**may**-go] n (pl -goes, -gines) [im-**maj**-in-ees] sexually mature adult insect
imagoes n ▷ imago
imam n (pl -s) leader of prayers in a mosque
imams n ▷ imam
imbalance n (pl -s) lack of balance or proportion
imbalances n ▷ imbalance
imbecile [imb-ess-eel] n (pl -s) stupid person ▶ adj (also **imbecilic**) stupid or senseless > **imbecility** n (pl -ties)
imbeciles n ▷ imbecile
imbecilic adj ▷ imbecile
imbecilities n ▷ imbecile
imbecility n ▷ imbecile
imbibe v (-bes, -bing, -bed) drink (alcoholic drinks)
imbibed v ▷ imbibe
imbibes v ▷ imbibe
imbibing v ▷ imbibe
imbroglio [imb-**role**-ee-oh] n (pl -ios) confusing and complicated situation

imbroglios n ▷ imbroglio
imbue v (-ues, -uing, -ued) (usu. foll. by **with**) fill or inspire with (ideals or principles)
  imbued v ▷ imbue
  imbues v ▷ imbue
  imbuing v ▷ imbue
imitate v (-tes, -ting, -ted) take as a model > **imitative** adj > **imitator** n (pl -s)
  imitated v ▷ imitate
  imitates v ▷ imitate
  imitating v ▷ imitate
imitation n (pl -s) copy of an original
  imitations n ▷ imitation
  imitative adj ▷ imitate
  imitator n ▷ imitate
  imitators n ▷ imitate
immaculate adj completely clean or tidy > **immaculately** adv
  immaculately adv ▷ immaculate
  immanence n ▷ immanent
  immanences n ▷ immanent
immanent adj present within and throughout something > **immanence** n (pl -s)
immaterial adj not important, not relevant
immature adj not fully developed > **immaturity** n (pl -ties)
  immaturities n ▷ immature
  immaturity n ▷ immature
  immediacies n ▷ immediate
  immediacy n ▷ immediate
immediate adj occurring at once > **immediately** adv > **immediacy** n (pl -cies)
  immediately adv ▷ immediate
immemorial adj longer than anyone can remember
immense adj extremely large > **immensity** n (pl -ties)
immensely adv to a very great degree
  immensities n ▷ immense
  immensity n ▷ immense
immerse v (-ses, -sing, -sed) involve deeply, engross > **immersion** n (pl -s)
  immersed v ▷ immerse
  immerses v ▷ immerse
  immersing v ▷ immerse
  immersion n ▷ immerse
  immersions n ▷ immerse
  immigrant n ▷ immigration
  immigrants n ▷ immigration
immigration n (pl -s) coming to a foreign country in order to settle there > **immigrant** n (pl -s)
  immigrations n ▷ immigration
  imminence n ▷ imminent
  imminences n ▷ imminent

imminent adj about to happen > **imminently** adv > **imminence** n (pl -s)
  imminently adv ▷ imminent
immobile adj not moving > **immobility** n (pl -ties)
  immobilities adj ▷ immobile
  immobility adj ▷ immobile
immobilize v (-izes, -izing, -ized) make unable to move or work
  immobilized v ▷ immobilize
  immobilizes v ▷ immobilize
  immobilizing v ▷ immobilize
immoderate adj excessive or unreasonable
immolate v (-tes, -ting, -ted) kill as a sacrifice > **immolation** n (pl -s)
  immolated v ▷ immolate
  immolates v ▷ immolate
  immolating v ▷ immolate
  immolation n ▷ immolate
  immolations n ▷ immolate
immoral adj morally wrong, corrupt > **immorality** n (pl -ties)
  immoralities n ▷ immoral
  immorality n ▷ immoral
immortal adj living forever ▶ n (pl -s) person whose fame will last for all time > **immortality** n (pl -s) > **immortalize** v (-lizes, -lizing, -lized)
  immortalities n ▷ immortal
  immortality n ▷ immortal
  immortalized v ▷ immortal
  immortalizes v ▷ immortal
  immortalizing v ▷ immortal
  immortals n ▷ immortal
immune adj protected against a specific disease
  immunities n ▷ immunity
immunity n (pl -ties) ability to resist disease
  immunization n ▷ immunize
  immunizations n ▷ immunize
immunize v (-izes, -izing, -ized) make immune to a disease > **immunization** n (pl -s)
  immunized v ▷ immunize
  immunizes v ▷ immunize
  immunizing v ▷ immunize
  immunodeficiencies n ▷ immunodeficiency
immunodeficiency n (pl -cies) deficiency in or breakdown of a person's ability to fight diseases
  immunological adj ▷ immunology
  immunologies n ▷ immunology
  immunologist n ▷ immunology
  immunologists n ▷ immunology
immunology n (pl -gies) branch of medicine concerned with the study of immunity

> **immunological** *adj* > **immunologist** *n* (*pl* -s)
immutabilities *n* ▷ immutable
immutability *n* ▷ immutable
immutable [im-**mute**-a-bl] *adj* unchangeable
> **immutability** *n* (*pl* -ties)
imp *n* (*pl* -s) (in folklore) mischievous small
creature with magical powers
impact *n* (*pl* -s) strong effect ▶ *v* (-s, -ing, -ed)
press firmly into something
impacted *v* ▷ impact
impacting *v* ▷ impact
impacts *n*, *v* ▷ impact
impair *v* (-s, -ing, -ed) weaken or damage
> **impairment** *n* (*pl* -s)
impaired *v* ▷ impair
impairing *v* ▷ impair
impairment *n* ▷ impair
impairments *n* ▷ impair
impairs *v* ▷ impair
impala [im-**ah**-la] *n* (*pl* -s) southern African
antelope
impalas *n* ▷ impala
impale *v* (-les, -ling, -led) pierce with a sharp
object
impaled *v* ▷ impale
impales *v* ▷ impale
impaling *v* ▷ impale
impalpable *adj* difficult to define or
understand
impart *v* (-s, -ing, -ed) communicate
(information)
imparted *v* ▷ impart
impartial *adj* not favouring one side or the
other > **impartially** *adv* > **impartiality** *n* (*pl*
-ties)
impartialities *n* ▷ impartial
impartiality *n* ▷ impartial
impartially *adv* ▷ impartial
imparting *v* ▷ impart
imparts *v* ▷ impart
impassable *adj* (of a road etc.) impossible to
travel through or over
impasse [am-**pass**] *n* (*pl* -s) situation in which
progress is impossible
impasses *n* ▷ impasse
impassioned *adj* full of emotion
impassive *adj* showing no emotion, calm
impatience *n* ▷ impatient
impatiences *n* ▷ impatient
impatient *adj* irritable at any delay or
difficulty > **impatiently** *adv* > **impatience**
n (*pl* -s)
impatiently *adv* ▷ impatient
impeach *v* (-es, -ing, -ed) charge with a serious
crime against the state > **impeachment** *n*

(*pl* -s)
impeached *v* ▷ impeach
impeaches *v* ▷ impeach
impeaching *v* ▷ impeach
impeachment *n* ▷ impeach
impeachments *n* ▷ impeach
impeccable *adj* without fault, excellent
> **impeccably** *adv*
impeccably *adv* ▷ impeccable
impecunious *adj* penniless, poor
impedance [imp-**eed**-anss] *n* (*pl* -s) (ELECTRICITY)
measure of the opposition to the flow of an
alternating current
impedances *n* ▷ impedance
impede *v* (-des, -ding, -ded) hinder in action
or progress
impeded *v* ▷ impede
impedes *v* ▷ impede
impediment *n* (*pl* -s) something that makes
action, speech, or progress difficult
impedimenta *pl n* objects impeding progress,
esp. baggage or equipment
impediments *n* ▷ impediment
impeding *v* ▷ impede
impel *v* (-s, -lling, -lled) push or force
(someone) to do something
impelled *v* ▷ impel
impelling *v* ▷ impel
impels *v* ▷ impel
impending *adj* (esp. of something bad) about
to happen
impenetrable *adj* impossible to get through
imperative *adj* extremely urgent, vital ▶ *n* (*pl*
-s) (GRAMMAR) imperative mood
imperatives *n* ▷ imperative
imperceptible *adj* too slight or gradual to be
noticed > **imperceptibly** *adv*
imperceptibly *adv* ▷ imperceptible
imperfect *adj* having faults or mistakes ▶ *n* (*pl*
-s) (GRAMMAR) imperfect tense > **imperfection**
n (*pl* -s)
imperfection *n* ▷ imperfect
imperfections *n* ▷ imperfect
imperfects *n* ▷ imperfect
imperial *adj* of or like an empire or emperor
imperialism *n* (*pl* -s) rule by one country over
many others > **imperialist** *adj*, *n* (*pl* -s)
imperialisms *n* ▷ imperialism
imperialist *adj*, *n* ▷ imperial
imperialists *n* ▷ imperialist
imperil *v* (-s, -lling, -lled) put in danger
imperilled *v* ▷ imperil
imperilling *v* ▷ imperil
imperils *v* ▷ imperil
imperious *adj* proud and domineering

impersonal *adj* not relating to any particular person, objective ▷ **impersonality** *n* (*pl* -ties)
impersonalities *n* ▷ impersonal
impersonality *n* ▷ impersonal
impersonate *v* (-tes, -ting, -ted) pretend to be (another person) ▷ **impersonation** *n* (*pl* -s) ▷ **impersonator** *n* (*pl* -s)
impersonated *v* ▷ impersonate
impersonates *v* ▷ impersonate
impersonating *v* ▷ impersonate
impersonation *n* ▷ impersonate
impersonations *n* ▷ impersonate
impersonator *n* ▷ impersonate
impersonators *n* ▷ impersonate
impertinence *n* ▷ impertinent
impertinences *n* ▷ impertinent
impertinent *adj* disrespectful or rude ▷ **impertinently** *adv* ▷ **impertinence** *n* (*pl* -s)
impertinently *adv* ▷ impertinent
imperturbable *adj* calm, not excitable
impervious *adj* (foll. by to) not letting (water etc.) through
impetigo [imp-it-**tie**-go] *n* (*pl* -s) contagious skin disease
impetigos *n* ▷ impetigo
impetuosities *n* ▷ impetuous
impetuosity *n* ▷ impetuous
impetuous *adj* done or acting without thought, rash ▷ **impetuously** *adv* ▷ **impetuosity** *n* (*pl* -ties)
impetuously *adv* ▷ impetuous
impetus [imp-it-uss] *n* (*pl* -es) incentive, impulse
impetuses *n* ▷ impetus
impinge *v* (-ges, -ging, -ged) (foll. by on) affect or restrict
impinged *v* ▷ impinge
impinges *v* ▷ impinge
impinging *v* ▷ impinge
impious [imp-ee-uss] *adj* showing a lack of respect or reverence
impish *adj* mischievous
implacabilities *n* ▷ implacable
implacability *n* ▷ implacable
implacable *adj* not prepared to be appeased, unyielding ▷ **implacably** *adv* ▷ **implacability** *n* (*pl* -ties)
implacably *adv* ▷ implacable
implant *n* (*pl* -s) (MED) something put into someone's body, usu. by surgical operation ▶ *v* (-s, -ing, -ed) put (something) into someone's body, usu. by surgical operation ▷ **implantation** *n* (*pl* -s)
implantation *n* ▷ implant
implantations *n* ▷ implant

implanted *v* ▷ implant
implanting *v* ▷ implant
implants *n*, *v* ▷ implant
implement *v* (-s, -ing, -ed) carry out (instructions etc.) ▶ *n* (*pl* -s) tool, instrument ▷ **implementation** *n* (*pl* -s)
implementation *n* ▷ implement
implementations *n* ▷ implement
implemented *v* ▷ implement
implementing *v* ▷ implement
implements *v*, *n* ▷ implement
implicate *v* (-tes, -ting, -ted) show to be involved, esp. in a crime
implicated *v* ▷ implicate
implicates *v* ▷ implicate
implicating *v* ▷ implicate
implication *n* (*pl* -s) something implied
implications *n* ▷ implication
implicit *adj* expressed indirectly ▷ **implicitly** *adv*
implicitly *adv* ▷ implicit
implied *v* ▷ imply
implies *v* ▷ imply
implore *v* (-res, -ring, -red) beg earnestly
implored *v* ▷ implore
implores *v* ▷ implore
imploring *v* ▷ implore
imply *v* (-lies, -lying, -lied) indicate by hinting, suggest
implying *v* ▷ imply
impolitic *adj* unwise or inadvisable
imponderable *n* (*pl* -s) ▶ *adj* (something) impossible to assess
imponderables *n* ▷ imponderable
import *v* (-s, -ing, -ed) bring in (goods) from another country ▶ *n* (*pl* -s) something imported ▷ **importation** *n* (*pl* -s) ▷ **importer** *n* (*pl* -s)
importance *n* ▷ important
importances *n* ▷ important
important *adj* of great significance or value ▷ **importance** *n* (*pl* -s)
importation *n* ▷ import
importations *n* ▷ import
imported *v* ▷ import
importer *n* ▷ import
importers *n* ▷ import
importing *v* ▷ import
imports *v*, *n* ▷ import
importunate *adj* persistent or demanding
importune *v* (-nes, -ning, -ned) harass with persistent requests ▷ **importunity** *n* (*pl* -ties)
importuned *v* ▷ importune
importunes *v* ▷ importune
importuning *v* ▷ importune

importunities *n* ▷ importune
importunity *n* ▷ importune
impose *v* (-ses, -sing, -sed) force the acceptance of
  imposed *v* ▷ impose
  imposes *v* ▷ impose
imposing *adj* grand, impressive ▶ *v* ▷ impose
imposition *n* (*pl* -s) unreasonable demand
  impositions *n* ▷ imposition
  impossibilities *n* ▷ impossible
  impossibility *n* ▷ impossible
impossible *adj* not able to be done or to happen > **impossibly** *adv* > **impossibility** *n* (*pl* -ties)
  impossibly *adv* ▷ impossible
imposter, impostor *n* (*pl* -s) person who cheats or swindles by pretending to be someone else
  imposters *n* ▷ imposter
  impostor *n* ▷ imposter
  impostors *n* ▷ imposter
  impotence *n* ▷ impotent
  impotences *n* ▷ impotent
impotent [imp-a-tent] *adj* powerless > **impotence** *n* (*pl* -s) > **impotently** *adv*
  impotently *adv* ▷ impotent
impound *v* (-s, -ing, -ed) take legal possession of, confiscate
  impounded *v* ▷ impound
  impounding *v* ▷ impound
  impounds *v* ▷ impound
impoverish *v* (-es, -ing, -ed) make poor or weak > **impoverishment** *n* (*pl* -s)
  impoverished *v* ▷ impoverish
  impoverishes *v* ▷ impoverish
  impoverishing *v* ▷ impoverish
  impoverishment *n* ▷ impoverish
  impoverishments *n* ▷ impoverish
impracticable *adj* incapable of being put into practice
impractical *adj* not sensible
imprecation *n* (*pl* -s) curse
  imprecations *n* ▷ imprecation
  impregnabilities *n* ▷ impregnable
  impregnability *n* ▷ impregnable
impregnable *adj* impossible to break into > **impregnability** *n* (*pl* -ties)
impregnate *v* (-tes, -ting, -ted) saturate, spread all through > **impregnation** *n* (*pl* -s)
  impregnated *v* ▷ impregnate
  impregnates *v* ▷ impregnate
  impregnating *v* ▷ impregnate
  impregnation *n* ▷ impregnate
  impregnations *n* ▷ impregnate
impresario *n* (*pl* -s) person who runs theatre performances, concerts, etc.
  impresarios *n* ▷ impresario
impress *v* (-es, -ing, -ed) affect strongly, usu. favourably
  impressed *v* ▷ impress
  impresses *v* ▷ impress
  impressing *v* ▷ impress
impression *n* (*pl* -s) effect, esp. a strong or favourable one
impressionable *adj* easily impressed or influenced
impressionism *n* (*pl* -s) art style that gives a general effect or mood rather than form or structure > **impressionist** *n* (*pl* -s) > **impressionistic** *adj*
  impressionisms *n* ▷ impressionism
  impressionist *n* ▷ impressionism
  impressionistic *adj* ▷ impressionism
  impressionists *n* ▷ impressionism
  impressions *n* ▷ impression
impressive *adj* making a strong impression, esp. through size, importance, or quality
imprimatur [imp-rim-**ah**-ter] *n* (*pl* -s) official approval to print a book
  imprimaturs *n* ▷ imprimatur
imprint *n* (*pl* -s) mark made by printing or stamping ▶ *v* (-s, -ing, -ed) produce (a mark) by printing or stamping
  imprinted *v* ▷ imprint
  imprinting *v* ▷ imprint
  imprints *n*, *v* ▷ imprint
imprison *v* (-s, -ing, -ed) put in prison > **imprisonment** *n* (*pl* -s)
  imprisoned *v* ▷ imprison
  imprisoning *v* ▷ imprison
  imprisonment *n* ▷ imprison
  imprisonments *n* ▷ imprisonment
  imprisons *v* ▷ imprison
  improbabilities *n* ▷ improbable
  improbability *n* ▷ improbable
improbable *adj* not likely to be true or to happen > **improbability** *n* (*pl* -ties)
impromptu *adj* without planning or preparation
improper *adj* indecent
  improprieties *n* ▷ impropriety
impropriety [imp-roe-**pry**-a-tee] *n* (*pl* -ties) unsuitable or slightly improper behaviour
improve *v* (-ves, -ving, -ved) make or become better > **improvement** *n* (*pl* -s)
  improved *v* ▷ improve
  improvement *n* ▷ improvement
  improvements *n* ▷ improvement
  improves *v* ▷ improve
  improvidence *n* ▷ improvident

improvidences n ▷ improvident
improvident adj not planning for future needs
> **improvidence** n (pl -s)
improving v ▷ improve
improvisation n ▷ improvise
improvisations n ▷ improvise
improvise v (-ises, -sing, -sed) make use
of whatever materials are available
> **improvisation** n (pl -s)
improvised v ▷ improvise
improvises v ▷ improvise
improvising v ▷ improvise
imps n ▷ imp
impudence n ▷ impudent
impudences n ▷ impudent
impudent adj cheeky, disrespectful
> **impudently** adv > **impudence** n (pl -s)
impudently adv ▷ impudently
impugn [imp-yoon] v (-s, -ing, -ed) challenge
the truth or validity of
impugned v ▷ impugn
impugning v ▷ impugn
impugns v ▷ impugn
impulse n (pl -s) sudden urge to do something
> **impulsive** adj acting or done without
careful consideration > **impulsively** adv
impulses n ▷ impulse
impulsive adj ▷ impulse
impulsively adv ▷ impulse
impunities n ▷ impunity
impunity [imp-yoon-it-ee] n (pl -ties) without
punishment
impure adj having dirty or unwanted
substances mixed in > **impurity** n (pl -ties)
impurities n ▷ impure
impurity n ▷ impure
imputation n ▷ impute
imputations n ▷ impute
impute v (-tes, -ting, -ted) attribute
responsibility to > **imputation** n (pl -s)
imputed v ▷ impute
imputes v ▷ impute
imputing v ▷ impute
in prep indicating position inside, state or
situation, etc. ▶ adv indicating position
inside, entry into, etc. ▶ adj fashionable
inabilities n ▷ inability
inability n (pl -ties) lack of means or skill to do
something
inaccuracies n ▷ inaccurate
inaccuracy n ▷ inaccurate
inaccurate adj not correct > **inaccuracy** n
(pl -cies)
inadequacies n ▷ inadequate
inadequacy n ▷ inadequate

inadequate adj not enough > **inadequacy** n
(pl -cies)
inadvertent adj unintentional
> **inadvertently** adv
inadvertently adv ▷ inadvertent
inalienable adj not able to be taken away
inane adj senseless, silly > **inanity** n (pl -ties)
inanimate adj not living
inanities n ▷ inane
inanity n ▷ inane
inappropriate adj not suitable
inarticulate adj unable to express oneself
clearly or well
inaugural adj ▷ inaugurate
inaugurate v (-tes, -ting, -ted) open or begin
the use of, esp. with ceremony > **inaugural**
adj > **inauguration** n (pl -s)
inaugurated v ▷ inaugurate
inaugurates v ▷ inaugurate
inaugurating v ▷ inaugurate
inauguration n ▷ inaugurate
inaugurations n ▷ inaugurate
inauspicious adj unlucky, likely to have an
unfavourable outcome
inboard adj (of a boat's engine) inside the hull
inborn adj existing from birth, natural
inbred adj produced as a result of inbreeding
inbreeding n (pl -s) breeding of animals or
people that are closely related
inbreedings n ▷ inbreeding
inbuilt adj present from the start
incalculable adj too great to be estimated
incandescence n ▷ incandescent
incandescences n ▷ incandescent
incandescent adj glowing with heat
> **incandescence** n (pl -s)
incantation n (pl -s) ritual chanting of magic
words or sounds
incantations n ▷ incantation
incapable adj (foll. by of) unable (to do
something)
incapacitate v (-tates, -tating, -tated) deprive
of strength or ability > **incapacity** n (pl -ties)
incapacitated v ▷ incapacitate
incapacitates v ▷ incapacitate
incapacitating v ▷ incapacitate
incapacities n ▷ incapacitate
incapacity n ▷ incapacitate
incarcerate v (-tes, -ting, -ted) imprison
> **incarceration** n (pl -s)
incarcerated v ▷ incarcerate
incarcerates v ▷ incarcerate
incarcerating v ▷ incarcerate
incarceration n ▷ incarcerate
incarcerations n ▷ incarcerate

incarnate *adj* in human form > **incarnation**
n (*pl* **-s**)
  incarnation *n* ▷ incarnate
  incarnations *n* ▷ incarnate
  incendiaries *n* ▷ incendiary
incendiary [in-**send**-ya-ree] *adj* (of a bomb,
attack, etc.) designed to cause fires ► *n* (*pl*
-ries) bomb designed to cause fires
incense¹ *v* (**-ses, -sing, -sed**) make very angry
incense² *n* (*pl* **incenses**) substance that gives
off a sweet perfume when burned
  incensed *v* ▷ incense¹
  incenses *v* ▷ incense¹ ► *n* ▷ incense²
  incensing *v* ▷ incense¹
incentive *n* (*pl* **-s**) something that encourages
effort or action
  incentives *n* ▷ incentive
inception *n* (*pl* **-s**) beginning
  inceptions *n* ▷ inception
incessant *adj* never stopping > **incessantly** *adv*
  incessantly *adv* ▷ incessant
incest *n* (*pl* **-s**) sexual intercourse between
two people too closely related to marry
> **incestuous** *adj*
  incests *n* ▷ incest
  incestuous *adj* ▷ incest
inch *n* (*pl* **-es**) unit of length equal to one
twelfth of a foot or 2.54 centimetres ► *v*
(**-ches, -ching, -ched**) move slowly and
gradually
  inched *v* ▷ inch
  inches *v, n* ▷ inch
  inching *v* ▷ inch
inchoate [in-**koe**-ate] *adj* just begun and not
yet properly developed
incidence *n* (*pl* **-s**) extent or frequency of
occurrence
  incidences *n* ▷ incidence
incident *n* (*pl* **-s**) something that happens
incidental *adj* occurring in connection with
or resulting from something more important
> **incidentally** *adv*
  incidentally *adv* ▷ incidental
  incidents *n* ▷ incident
incinerate *v* (**-tes, -ting, -ted**) burn to ashes
> **incineration** *n* (*pl* **-s**)
  incinerated *v* ▷ incinerate
  incinerates *v* ▷ incinerate
  incinerating *v* ▷ incinerate
  incineration *n* ▷ incinerate
  incinerations *n* ▷ incinerate
incinerator *n* (*pl* **-s**) furnace for burning
rubbish
  incinerators *n* ▷ incinerator
incipient *adj* just starting to appear or happen

incise *v* (**-ses, -sing, -sed**) cut into with a sharp
tool > **incision** *n* (*pl* **-s**)
  incised *v* ▷ incise
  incises *v* ▷ incise
  incising *v* ▷ incise
  incision *n* ▷ incise
  incisions *n* ▷ incise
incisive *adj* direct and forceful
incisor *n* (*pl* **-s**) front tooth, used for biting
into food
  incisors *n* ▷ incisor
incite *v* (**-tes, -ting, -ted**) stir up, provoke
> **incitement** *n* (*pl* **-s**)
  incited *v* ▷ incite
  incitement *n* ▷ incite
  incitements *n* ▷ incite
  incites *v* ▷ incite
  inciting *v* ▷ incite
  incivilities *n* ▷ incivility
incivility *n* (*pl* **-ties**) rudeness or a rude remark
inclement *adj* (of weather) stormy or severe
inclination *n* (*pl* **-s**) liking, tendency, or
preference
  inclinations *n* ▷ inclination
incline *v* (**-nes, -ning, -ned**) lean, slope ► *n* (*pl*
-s) slope
  inclined *v* ▷ incline
  inclines *v, n* ▷ incline
  inclining *v* ▷ incline
include *v* (**-des, -ding, -ded**) have as part of the
whole > **inclusion** *n* (*pl* **-s**)
  included *v* ▷ include
  includes *v* ▷ include
  including *v* ▷ include
  inclusion *n* ▷ include
  inclusions *n* ▷ include
inclusive *adj* including everything (specified)
> **inclusively** *adv*
  inclusively *adv* ▷ inclusive
incognito [in-kog-**nee**-toe] *adj, adv* having
adopted a false identity ► *n* (*pl* **-tos**) false
identity
  incognitos *n* ▷ incognito
  incoherence *n* ▷ incoherent
  incoherences *n* ▷ incoherent
incoherent *adj* unclear and impossible
to understand > **incoherence** *n* (*pl* **-s**)
> **incoherently** *adv*
  incoherently *adv* ▷ incoherent
income *n* (*pl* **-s**) amount of money earned from
work, investments, etc.
  incomes *n* ▷ income
incoming *adj* coming in
incommode *v* (**-des, -ding, -ded**) cause
inconvenience to

incommoded v ▷ incommode
incommodes v ▷ incommode
incommoding v ▷ incommode
incommunicado adj, adv deprived of communication with other people
incomparable adj beyond comparison, unequalled > **incomparably** adv
incomparably adv ▷ incomparable
incompatibilities n ▷ incompatible
incompatibility n ▷ incompatible
incompatible adj inconsistent or conflicting > **incompatibility** n (pl -ties)
incompetence n ▷ incompetent
incompetences n ▷ incompetent
incompetent adj not having the necessary ability or skill to do something > **incompetence** n (pl -s)
inconceivable adj extremely unlikely, unimaginable
inconclusive adj not giving a final decision or result
incongruities n ▷ incongruous
incongruity n ▷ incongruous
incongruous adj inappropriate or out of place > **incongruously** adv > **incongruity** n (pl -ties)
incongruously adv ▷ incongruous
inconsequential adj unimportant, insignificant
inconsiderable adj fairly large
inconstant adj liable to change one's loyalties or opinions
incontinence n ▷ incontinent
incontinences n ▷ incontinent
incontinent adj unable to control one's bladder or bowels > **incontinence** n (pl -s)
incontrovertible adj impossible to deny or disprove
inconvenience n (pl -s) trouble or difficulty ▶ v (-ces, -ncing, -nced) cause trouble or difficulty to > **inconvenient** adj
inconvenienced v ▷ inconvenience
inconveniences n, v ▷ inconvenience
inconveniencing v ▷ inconvenience
inconvenient adj ▷ inconvenience
incorporate v (-tes, -ting, -ted) include or be included as part of a larger unit
incorporated v ▷ incorporate
incorporates v ▷ incorporate
incorporating v ▷ incorporate
incorporeal adj without material form
incorrigible adj beyond correction or reform
incorruptible adj too honest to be bribed or corrupted
increase v (-ses, -sing, -sed) make or become greater in size, number, etc. ▶ n (pl -s) rise in

number, size, etc. > **increasingly** adv
increased v ▷ increase
increases v, n ▷ increase
increasing n ▷ increase
increasingly adv ▷ increase
incredible adj hard to believe or imagine > **incredibly** adv
incredibly adv ▷ incredible
incredulities n ▷ incredulous
incredulity n ▷ incredulous
incredulous adj not willing to believe something > **incredulity** n (pl -ties)
increment n (pl -s) increase in money or value, esp. a regular salary increase > **incremental** adj
incremental adj ▷ increment
increments n ▷ increment
incriminate v (-tes, -ting, -ted) make (someone) seem guilty of a crime > **incriminating** adj
incriminated v ▷ incriminate
incriminates v ▷ incriminate
incriminating v, adj ▷ incriminate
incubate [in-cube-ate] v (-tes, -ting, -ted) (of a bird) hatch (eggs) by sitting on them > **incubation** n (pl -s)
incubated v ▷ incubate
incubates v ▷ incubate
incubating v ▷ incubate
incubation n ▷ incubate
incubations n ▷ incubate
incubator n (pl -s) heated enclosed apparatus for rearing premature babies
incubators n ▷ incubator
incubi n ▷ incubus
incubus [in-cube-uss] n (pl -bi, -buses) (in folklore) demon believed to have sex with sleeping women
incubuses n ▷ incubus
inculcate v (-tes, -ting, -ted) fix in someone's mind by constant repetition > **inculcation** n (pl -s)
inculcated v ▷ inculcate
inculcates v ▷ inculcate
inculcating v ▷ inculcate
inculcation n ▷ inculcate
inculcations n ▷ inculcate
incumbencies n ▷ incumbent
incumbency n ▷ incumbent
incumbent n (pl -s) person holding a particular office or position ▶ adj it is the duty of > **incumbency** n (pl -cies)
incumbents n ▷ incumbent
incur v (-s, -rring, -rred) cause (something unpleasant) to happen

incurable *adj* not able to be cured ▷ **incurably**
adv
  incurably *adv* ▷ incurable
incurious *adj* showing no curiosity or interest
  incurred *v* ▷ incur
  incurring *v* ▷ incur
  incurs *v* ▷ incur
incursion *n* (*pl* -s) sudden brief invasion
  incursions *n* ▷ incursion
indebted *adj* owing gratitude for help or
favours ▷ **indebtedness** *n* (*pl* -es)
  indebtedness *n* ▷ indebted
  indebtednesses *n* ▷ indebted
  indecencies *n* ▷ indecent
  indecency *n* ▷ indecent
indecent *adj* morally or sexually offensive
▷ **indecently** *adv* ▷ **indecency** *n* (*pl* -cies)
  indecently *adv* ▷ indecent
indecipherable *adj* impossible to read
indeed *adv* really, certainly ▶ *interj* expression
of indignation or surprise
indefatigable *adj* never getting tired
▷ **indefatigably** *adv*
  indefatigably *adv* ▷ indefatigable
indefensible *adj* unable to be justified
indefinite *adj* without exact limits
▷ **indefinitely** *adv*
  indefinitely *adv* ▷ indefinite
indelible *adj* impossible to erase or remove
▷ **indelibly** *adv*
  indelibly *adv* ▷ indelible
indelicate *adj* offensive or embarrassing
  indemnified *v* ▷ indemnify
  indemnifies *v* ▷ indemnify
indemnify *v* (-fies, -fying, -fied) secure against
loss, damage, or liability
  indemnifying *v* ▷ indemnify
  indemnities *n* ▷ indemnity
indemnity *n* (*pl* -ties) insurance against loss
or damage
indent *v* (-s, -ing, -ed) start (a line of writing)
further from the margin than the other lines
indentation *n* (*pl* -s) dent in a surface or edge
  indentations *n* ▷ indentation
  indented *v* ▷ indent
  indenting *v* ▷ indent
  indents *v* ▷ indent
indenture *n* (*pl* -s) contract, esp. one binding
an apprentice to his or her employer
  indentures *n* ▷ indenture
  independence *n* ▷ independent
  independences *n* ▷ independent
independent *adj* free from the control or
influence of others ▶ *n* (*pl* -s) politician
who does not represent any political party

▷ **independently** *adv* ▷ **independence** *n* (*pl* -s)
  independently *adsv* ▷ independent
  independents *n* ▷ independent
indescribable *adj* too intense or extreme for
words ▷ **indescribably** *adv*
  indescribably *adv* ▷ indescribable
  indeterminacies *n* ▷ indeterminate
  indeterminacy *n* ▷ indeterminate
indeterminate *adj* uncertain in extent,
amount, or nature ▷ **indeterminacy** *n* (*pl* -cies)
index *n* (*pl* -dices) [in-diss-eez] alphabetical list
of names or subjects dealt with in a book ▶ *v*
(-dexes, -dexing, -dexed) provide (a book)
with an index
  indexed *v* ▷ index
  indexes *n* ▷ index
  indexing *v* ▷ index
indicate *v* (-tes, -ting, -ted) be a sign or
symptom of ▷ **indication** *n* (*pl* -s)
  indicated *v* ▷ indicate
  indicates *v* ▷ indicate
  indicating *v* ▷ indicate
  indication *n* ▷ indicate
  indications *n* ▷ indicate
indicative *adj* (foll. by **of**) suggesting ▶ *n* (*pl* -s)
(GRAMMAR) indicative mood
  indicatives *n* ▷ indicative
indicator *n* (*pl* -s) something acting as a sign
or indication
  indicators *n* ▷ indicator
  indices *n* ▷ index
indict [in-dite] *v* (-s, -ing, -ed) formally charge
with a crime ▷ **indictable** *adj* ▷ **indictment**
n (*pl* -s)
  indictable *adj* ▷ indict
  indicted *v* ▷ indict
  indicting *v* ▷ indict
  indictment *n* ▷ indict
  indictments *n* ▷ indict
  indicts *v* ▷ indict
indie *adj* (Informal) (of rock music) released by
an independent record company
  indifference *n* ▷ indifferent
  indifferences *n* ▷ indifferent
indifferent *adj* showing no interest or concern
▷ **indifference** *n* (*pl* -s) ▷ **indifferently** *adv*
  indifferently *adv* ▷ indifferent
  indigence *n* ▷ indigent
  indigences *n* ▷ indigent
indigenous [in-**dij**-in-uss] *adj* born in or natural
to a country
indigent *adj* extremely poor ▷ **indigence** *n*
(*pl* -s)
  indigestible *adj* ▷ indigestion
indigestion *n* (*pl* -s) (discomfort or pain

caused by) difficulty in digesting food
> **indigestible** adj
indigestions n ▷ indigestion
indignant adj feeling or showing indignation
> **indignantly** adv
indignantly adv ▷ indignant
indignation n (pl -s) anger at something
unfair or wrong
indignations n ▷ indignation
indignities n ▷ indignity
indignity n (pl -ties) embarrassing or
humiliating treatment
indigo adj deep violet-blue ▶ n (pl -s) dye of
this colour
indigos n ▷ indigo
indirect adj done or caused by someone or
something else
indiscreet adj incautious or tactless
in revealing secrets > **indiscreetly** adv
> **indiscretion** n (pl -s)
indiscreetly adv ▷ indiscreet
indiscretion n ▷ indiscreet
indiscretions n ▷ indiscreet
indiscriminate adj showing lack of careful
thought
indispensable adj absolutely essential
indisposed adj unwell, ill > **indisposition** n
(pl -s)
indisposition n ▷ indisposed
indispositions n ▷ indisposed
indisputable adj beyond doubt > **indisputably**
adv
indisputably adv ▷ indisputable
indissoluble adj permanent
indium n (pl -s) (CHEM) soft silvery-white
metallic element
indiums n ▷ indium
individual adj characteristic of or meant for a
single person or thing ▶ n (pl -s) single person
or thing > **individually** adv > **individuality**
n (pl -ties)
individualism n (pl -s) principle of living one's
life in one's own way > **individualist** n (pl -s)
> **individualistic** adj
individualisms n ▷ individualism
individualist n ▷ individualism
individualistic adj ▷ individualism
individualists n ▷ individualism
individualities n ▷ individual
individuality n ▷ individual
individually adv ▷ individual
individuals n ▷ individual
indoctrinate v (-tes, -ting, -ted) teach
(someone) to accept a doctrine or belief
uncritically > **indoctrination** n (pl -s)

indoctrinated v ▷ indoctrinate
indoctrinates v ▷ indoctrinate
indoctrinating v ▷ indoctrinate
indoctrination n ▷ indoctrinate
indoctrinations n ▷ indoctrinate
indolence n ▷ indolent
indolences n ▷ indolent
indolent adj lazy > **indolence** n (pl -s)
indomitable adj too strong to be defeated or
discouraged > **indomitably** adv
indomitably adv ▷ indomitable
indoor adj inside a building > **indoors** adv
indoors adv ▷ indoor
indubitable adj beyond doubt, certain
> **indubitably** adv
indubitably adv ▷ indubitable
induce v (-ces, -cing, -ced) persuade or
influence
induced v ▷ induce
inducement n (pl -s) something used to
persuade someone to do something
inducements n ▷ inducement
induces v ▷ induce
inducing v ▷ induce
induct v (-s, -ing, -ed) formally install
(someone, esp. a clergyman) in office
inductance n (pl -s) property of an electric
circuit creating voltage by a change of
current
inductances n ▷ inductance
inducted v ▷ induct
inducting v ▷ induct
induction n (pl -s) reasoning process by
which general conclusions are drawn from
particular instances > **inductive** adj
inductions n ▷ induction
inductive adj ▷ induction
inducts v ▷ induct
indulge v (-ges, -ging, -ged) allow oneself
pleasure > **indulgent** adj > **indulgently** adv
indulged v ▷ indulge
indulgence n (pl -s) something allowed
because it gives pleasure
indulgences n ▷ indulgence
indulgent adj ▷ indulge
indulgently adj ▷ indulge
indulges v ▷ indulge
indulging v ▷ indulge
industrial adj of, used in, or employed in
industry
industrialization n ▷ industrialize
industrializations n ▷ industrialize
industrialize v (-izes, -izing, -ized) develop
large-scale industry in (a country or region)
> **industrialization** n (pl -s)

industrialized *v* ▷ industrialize
industrializes *v* ▷ industrialize
industrializing *v* ▷ industrialize
industries *n* ▷ industry
industrious *adj* ▷ industry
industry *n* (*pl* -**tries**) manufacture of goods
> **industrious** *adj* hard-working
inebriate *n* (*pl* -**s**) ▶ *adj* (person who is)
habitually drunk
inebriated *adj* drunk > **inebriation** *n* (*pl* -**s**)
inebriates *n* ▷ inebriate
inebriation *n* ▷ inebriated
inebriations *n* ▷ inebriated
inedible *adj* not fit to be eaten
ineffable *adj* too great for words > **ineffably**
adv
ineffably *adv* ▷ ineffable
ineffectual *adj* having very little effect
ineligible *adj* not qualified for or entitled to
something
ineluctable *adj* impossible to avoid
inept *adj* clumsy, lacking skill > **ineptitude**
n (*pl* -**s**)
ineptitude *n* ▷ inept
ineptitudes *n* ▷ inept
inequitable *adj* unfair
ineradicable *adj* impossible to remove
inert *adj* without the power of motion or
resistance > **inertness** *n* (*pl* -**es**)
inertia *n* (*pl* -**s**) feeling of unwillingness to do
anything
inertias *n* ▷ inertia
inertness *n* ▷ inert
inertnesses *n* ▷ inert
inescapable *adj* unavoidable
inestimable *adj* too great to be estimated
> **inestimably** *adv*
inestimably *adv* ▷ inestimable
inevitabilities *n* ▷ inevitable
inevitability *n* ▷ inevitable
inevitable *adj* unavoidable, sure to happen
> **inevitably** *adv* > **inevitability** *n* (*pl* -**ties**)
inevitably *adv* ▷ inevitable
inexorable *adj* unable to be prevented from
continuing or progressing > **inexorably** *adv*
inexorably *adv* ▷ inexorable
inexpert *adj* lacking skill
inexplicable *adj* impossible to explain
> **inexplicably** *adv*
inexplicably *adv* ▷ inexplicable
inextricable *adj* impossible to escape from
infallibilities *adv* ▷ infallible
infallibility *adv* ▷ infallible
infallible *adj* never wrong > **infallibly** *adv*
> **infallibility** *n* (*pl* -**ties**)

infallibly *adv* ▷ infallible
infamies *n* ▷ infamous
infamous [in-fam-uss] *adj* well-known for
something bad > **infamously** *adv* > **infamy**
n (*pl* -**mies**)
infamously *adv* ▷ infamous
infamy *n* ▷ infamous
infancies *n* ▷ infancy
infancy *n* (*pl* -**cies**) early childhood
infant *n* (*pl* -**s**) very young child
infanticide *n* (*pl* -**s**) murder of an infant
infanticides *n* ▷ infanticide
infantile *adj* childish
infantries *n* ▷ infantry
infantry *n* (*pl* -**ries**) soldiers who fight on foot
infants *n* ▷ infant
infatuated *adj* feeling intense unreasoning
passion
infatuation *n* (*pl* -**s**) intense unreasoning
passion
infatuations *n* ▷ infatuation
infect *v* (-**s**, -**ing**, -**ed**) affect with a disease
> **infection** *n* (*pl* -**s**)
infected *v* ▷ infect
infecting *v* ▷ infect
infection *n* ▷ infect
infections *n* ▷ infect
infectious *adj* (of a disease) spreading without
actual contact
infects *v* ▷ infect
infer *v* (-**s**, -**rring**, -**rred**) work out from
evidence > **inference** *n* (*pl* -**s**)
inference *n* ▷ infer
inferences *n* ▷ infer
inferior *adj* lower in quality, position, or status
▶ *n* (*pl* -**s**) person of lower position or status
> **inferiority** *n* (*pl* -**ties**)
inferiorities *n* ▷ inferior
inferiority *n* ▷ inferior
inferiors *n* ▷ inferior
infernal *adj* of hell (*Informal*) > **infernally** *adv*
infernally *adv* ▷ infernal
inferno *n* (*pl* -**s**) intense raging fire
infernos *n* ▷ inferno
inferred *v* ▷ infer
inferring *v* ▷ infer
infers *v* ▷ infer
infertile *adj* unable to produce offspring
> **infertility** *n* (*pl* -**ties**)
infertilities *n* ▷ infertile
infertility *n* ▷ infertile
infest *v* (-**s**, -**ing**, -**ed**) inhabit or overrun in
unpleasantly large numbers > **infestation**
n (*pl* -**s**)
infestation *n* ▷ infest

infestations *n* ▷ infest
infested *v* ▷ infest
infesting *v* ▷ infest
infests *v* ▷ infest
infidel *n* (*pl* -s) person with no religion
　infidelities *n* ▷ infidelity
infidelity *n* (*pl* -ties) (act of) sexual
　unfaithfulness to one's husband, wife, or lover
　infidels *n* ▷ infidel
infighting *n* (*pl* -s) quarrelling within a group
　infightings *n* ▷ infighting
infiltrate *v* (-tes, -ting, -ted) enter gradually
　and secretly > **infiltration** *n* (*pl* -s) > **infiltrator**
　n (*pl* -s)
　infiltrated *v* ▷ infiltrate
　infiltrates *v* ▷ infiltrate
　infiltrating *v* ▷ infiltrate
　infiltration *n* ▷ infiltrate
　infiltrations *n* ▷ infiltrate
　infiltrator *n* ▷ infiltrate
　infiltrators *n* ▷ infiltrate
infinite [in-fin-it] *adj* without any limit or end
　> **infinitely** *adv*
　infinitely *adv* ▷ infinite
infinitesimal *adj* extremely small
　infinities *n* ▷ infinity
infinitive *n* (*pl* -s) (GRAMMAR) form of a verb not
　showing tense, person, or number
　infinitives *n* ▷ infinitive
infinity *n* (*pl* -ties) endless space, time, or
　number
infirm *adj* physically or mentally weak
　> **infirmity** *n* (*pl* -ties)
　infirmaries *n* ▷ infirmary
infirmary *n* (*pl* -ries) hospital
　infirmities *n* ▷ infirm
　infirmity *n* ▷ infirm
inflame *v* (-mes, -ming, -med) make angry
　or excited
inflamed *adj* (of part of the body) red, swollen,
　and painful because of infection ▶ *v* ▷ inflame
　> **inflammation** *n* (*pl* -s)
　inflames *v* ▷ inflame
　inflaming *v* ▷ inflame
inflammable *adj* easily set on fire
　inflammation *n* ▷ inflamed
　inflammations *n* ▷ inflamed
inflammatory *adj* likely to provoke anger
inflatable *adj* able to be inflated ▶ *n* (*pl* -s)
　plastic or rubber object which can be inflated
　inflatables *n* ▷ inflatable
inflate *v* (-tes, -ting, -ted) expand by filling
　with air or gas
　inflated *v* ▷ inflate
　inflates *v* ▷ inflate

inflating *v* ▷ inflate
inflation *n* (*pl* -s) inflating > **inflationary** *adj*
　inflationary *adj* ▷ inflationary
　inflations *n* ▷ inflation
inflection, inflexion *n* (*pl* -s) change in the
　pitch of the voice
　inflections *n* ▷ inflection
　inflexibilities *n* ▷ inflexible
　inflexibility *n* ▷ inflexible
inflexible *adj* unwilling to be persuaded,
　obstinate > **inflexibly** *adv* > **inflexibility** *n*
　(*pl* -ties)
　inflexibly *n* ▷ inflexibly
　inflexion *n* ▷ inflection
　inflexions *n* ▷ inflection
inflict *v* (-s, -ing, -ed) impose (something
　unpleasant) on > **infliction** *n* (*pl* -s)
　inflicted *v* ▷ inflict
　inflicting *v* ▷ inflict
　infliction *n* ▷ inflict
　inflictions *n* ▷ inflict
　inflicts *v* ▷ inflict
inflorescence *n* (*pl* -s) (BOTANY) arrangement of
　flowers on a stem
　inflorescences *n* ▷ inflorescence
influence *n* (*pl* -s) effect of one person or thing
　on another ▶ *v* (-ces, -cing, -ced) have an
　effect on > **influential** *adj*
　influenced *v* ▷ influence
　influences *n, v* ▷ influence
　influencing *v* ▷ influence
　influential *adj* ▷ influence
influenza *n* (*pl* -s) contagious viral disease
　causing headaches, muscle pains, and fever
　influenzas *n* ▷ influenza
influx *n* (*pl* -es) arrival or entry of many people
　or things
　influxes *n* ▷ influx
info *n* (*pl* -s) (*Informal*) information
inform *v* (-s, -ing, -ed) tell
informal *adj* relaxed and friendly > **informally**
　adv > **informality** *n* (*pl* -s)
　informalities *n* ▷ informal
　informality *n* ▷ informal
　informally *adv* ▷ informal
informant *n* (*pl* -s) person who gives
　information
　informants *n* ▷ informant
information *n* (*pl* -s) knowledge or facts
　informations *n* ▷ information
informative *adj* giving useful information
　informed *v* ▷ inform
informer *n* (*pl* -s) person who informs to the
　police
　informers *n* ▷ informer

informing *v* ▷ inform
informs *v* ▷ inform
infos *n* ▷ info
infrared *adj* of or using rays below the red end of the visible spectrum
infrastructure *n* (*pl* -s) basic facilities, services, and equipment needed for a country or organization to function properly
infrastructures *n* ▷ infrastructure
infringe *v* (-ges, -ging, -ged) break (a law or agreement) > **infringement** *n* (*pl* -s)
infringed *v* ▷ infringe
infringement *n* ▷ infringe
infringements *n* ▷ infringe
infringes *v* ▷ infringe
infringing *v* ▷ infringe
infuriate *v* (-tes, -ting, -ted) make very angry
infuriated *v* ▷ infuriate
infuriates *v* ▷ infuriate
infuriating *v* ▷ infuriate
infuse *v* (-ses, -sing, -sed) fill (with an emotion or quality) > **infusion** *n* (*pl* -s) infusing
infused *v* ▷ infuse
infuses *v* ▷ infuse
infusing *v* ▷ infuse
infusion *n* ▷ infuse
infusions *n* ▷ infuse
ingenious [in-**jean**-ee-uss] *adj* showing cleverness and originality > **ingeniously** *adv* > **ingenuity** [in-jen-**new**-it-ee] *n* (*pl* -ties)
ingeniously *adv* ▷ ingenious
ingénue [an-jay-new] *n* (*pl* -s) naive young woman, esp. as a role played by an actress
ingénues *n* ▷ ingénue
ingenuities *n* ▷ ingenious
ingenuity *n* ▷ ingenious
ingenuous [in-**jen**-new-uss] *adj* unsophisticated and trusting > **ingenuously** *adv*
ingenuously *adv* ▷ ingenuously
ingest *v* (-s, -ing, -ed) take (food or liquid) into the body > **ingestion** *n* (*pl* -s)
ingested *v* ▷ ingest
ingesting *v* ▷ ingest
ingestion *n* ▷ ingest
ingestions *n* ▷ ingest
ingests *v* ▷ ingest
inglorious *adj* dishonourable, shameful
ingot *n* (*pl* -s) oblong block of cast metal
ingots *n* ▷ ingot
ingrained *adj* firmly fixed
ingratiate *v* (-iates, -iating, -iated) try to make (oneself) popular with someone > **ingratiating** *adj* > **ingratiatingly** *adv*
ingratiated *v* ▷ ingratiate
ingratiates *v* ▷ ingratiate

ingratiating *v, adj* ▷ ingratiate
ingratiatingly *adv* ▷ ingratiatingly
ingredient *n* (*pl* -s) component of a mixture or compound
ingredients *n* ▷ ingredient
ingress *n* (*pl* -es) act or right of entering
ingresses *n* ▷ ingress
ingrowing *adj* (of a toenail) growing abnormally into the flesh
inhabit *v* (-s, -ing, -ed) live in > **inhabitable** *adj* > **inhabitant** *n* (*pl* -s)
inhabitable *adj* ▷ inhabitable
inhabitant *n* ▷ inhabit
inhabitants *n* ▷ inhabit
inhabited *v* ▷ inhabit
inhabiting *v* ▷ inhabit
inhabits *v* ▷ inhabit
inhalant *n* (*pl* -s) medical preparation inhaled to help breathing problems
inhalants *n* ▷ inhalant
inhalations *n* ▷ inhalation
inhale *v* (-les, -ling, -led) breathe in (air, smoke, etc.) > **inhalation** *n* (*pl* -s)
inhaled *v* ▷ inhale
inhaler *n* (*pl* -s) container for an inhalant
inhalers *n* ▷ inhaler
inhales *v* ▷ inhale
inhaling *v* ▷ inhale
inherent *adj* existing as an inseparable part > **inherently** *adv*
inherently *adv* ▷ inherent
inherit *v* (-s, -ing, -ed) receive (money etc.) from someone who has died > **inheritance** *n* (*pl* -s) > **inheritor** *n* (*pl* -s)
inheritance *n* ▷ inherit
inheritances *n* ▷ inherit
inherited *v* ▷ inherit
inheriting *v* ▷ inherit
inheritor *n* ▷ inherit
inheritors *n* ▷ inherit
inherits *v* ▷ inherit
inhibit *v* (-s, -ing, -ed) restrain (an impulse or desire) > **inhibited** *adj*
inhibited *v, adj* ▷ inhibit
inhibiting *v* ▷ inhibit
inhibition *n* (*pl* -s) feeling of fear or embarrassment that stops one from behaving naturally
inhibitions *n* ▷ inhibition
inhibits *v* ▷ inhibit
inhospitable *adj* not welcoming, unfriendly
inhuman *adj* cruel or brutal
inhumane *adj* cruel or brutal > **inhumanity** *n* (*pl* -ties)
inhumanities *n* ▷ inhumane

inhumanity n ▷inhumane

inimical adj unfavourable or hostile

inimitable adj impossible to imitate, unique

iniquities n ▷iniquity

iniquitous adj ▷iniquity

iniquity n (pl -ties) injustice or wickedness
> iniquitous adj

initial adj first, at the beginning ▶ n (pl -s) first
letter, esp. of a person's name ▶ v (-s, -lling,
-lled) sign with one's initials > **initially** adv

initialled v ▷initial

initialling v ▷initial

initially adv ▷initial

initials n, v ▷initial

initiate v (-tes, -ting, -ted) begin or set
going ▶ n (pl -s) recently initiated person
> **initiation** n (pl -s) > **initiator** n (pl -s)

initiated v ▷initiate

initiates v, n ▷initiate

initiating v ▷initiate

initiation n ▷initiate

initiations n ▷initiate

initiative n (pl -ves) first step, commencing
move

initiatives n ▷initiative

initiator n ▷initiation

initiators n ▷initiation

inject v (-s, -ing, -ed) put (a fluid) into the body
with a syringe > **injection** n (pl -s)

injected v ▷inject

injecting v ▷inject

injection n ▷inject

injections n ▷inject

injects v ▷inject

injudicious adj showing poor judgment,
unwise

injunction n (pl -s) court order not to do
something

injunctions n ▷injunction

injure v (-res, -ring, -red) hurt physically or
mentally > **injury** n (pl -ries) > **injurious** adj

injured v ▷injure

injures v ▷injure

injuries n ▷injure

injuring v ▷injure

injurious adj ▷injure

injury n ▷injure

injustice n (pl -s) unfairness

injustices n ▷injustice

ink n (pl -s) coloured liquid used for writing or
printing ▶ v (-s, -ing, -ed) (foll. by in) mark in
ink (something already marked in pencil)

inked v ▷ink

inking v ▷ink

inkling n (pl -s) slight idea or suspicion

inklings n ▷inkling

inks v, n ▷ink

inky adj dark or black

inlaid adj set in another material so that the
surface is smooth

inland adj, adv in or towards the interior of a
country, away from the sea

inlay n (pl -s) inlaid substance or pattern

inlays n ▷inlay

inlet n (pl -s) narrow strip of water extending
from the sea into the land

inlets n ▷inlet

inmate n (pl -s) person living in an institution
such as a prison

inmates n ▷inmate

inmost adj innermost

inn n (pl -s) pub or small hotel, esp. in the
country > **innkeeper** n (pl -s)

innards pl n (Informal) internal organs

innate adj being part of someone's nature,
inborn

inner adj happening or located inside

innermost adj furthest inside

innings n (SPORT) player's or side's turn of
batting

innkeeper n ▷inn

innkeepers n ▷inn

innocence n ▷innocent

innocences n ▷innocent

innocent adj not guilty of a crime ▶ n (pl -s)
innocent person, esp. a child > **innocently** adv
> **innocence** n (pl -s)

innocently adv ▷innocent

innocents n ▷innocent

innocuous adj not harmful > **innocuously** adv

innocuously adv ▷innocuous

innovated v ▷innovation

innovates v ▷innovation

innovating v ▷innovation

innovation n (pl -s) new idea or method
> **innovate** v (-tes, -ting, -ted) > **innovative**
adj > **innovator** n (pl -s)

innovations n ▷innovation

innovative adj ▷innovation

innovator n ▷innovation

innovators n ▷innovation

inns n ▷inn

innuendo n (pl -does) (remark making) an
indirect reference to something rude or
unpleasant

innuendoes n ▷innuendo

innumerable adj too many to be counted

innumeracies n ▷innumerate

innumeracy n ▷innumerate

innumerate adj having no understanding

of mathematics or science > **innumeracy** *n*
(*pl* -**cies**)
inoculate *v* (-**tes**, -**ting**, -**ted**) protect
against disease by injecting with a vaccine
> **inoculation** *n* (*pl* -**s**)
inoculated *v* ▷ **inoculate**
inoculates *v* ▷ **inoculate**
inoculating *v* ▷ **inoculate**
inoculation *n* ▷ **inoculate**
inoculations *n* ▷ **inoculate**
inoperable *adj* (of a tumour or cancer) unable
to be surgically removed
inopportune *adj* badly timed, unsuitable
inordinate *adj* excessive
inorganic *adj* not having the characteristics of
living organisms
inpatient *n* (*pl* -**s**) patient who stays in a
hospital for treatment
inpatients *n* ▷ **inpatient**
input *n* (*pl* -**s**) resources put into a project etc.
▶ *v* (-**s**, -**tting**, -**put**) enter (data) in a computer
inputs *v*, *n* ▷ **input**
inputting *v*, *n* ▷ **input**
inquest *n* (*pl* -**s**) official inquiry into a sudden
death
inquests *n* ▷ **inquest**
inquire *v* (-**res**, -**ring**, -**red**) seek information or
ask (about) > **inquirer** *n* (*pl* -**s**)
inquired *v* ▷ **inquire**
inquirer *n* ▷ **inquire**
inquirers *n* ▷ **inquire**
inquires *v* ▷ **inquire**
inquiries *n* ▷ **inquiry**
inquiring *v* ▷ **inquire**
inquiry *n* (*pl* -**ries**) question
inquisition *n* (*pl* -**s**) thorough investigation
> **inquisitor** *n* (*pl* -**s**) > **inquisitorial** *adj*
inquisitions *n* ▷ **inquisition**
inquisitive *adj* excessively curious about
other people's affairs > **inquisitively** *adv*
inquisitively *adv* ▷ **inquisitive**
inquisitor *n* ▷ **inquisition**
inquisitorial *adj* ▷ **inquisition**
inquisitors *n* ▷ **inquisition**
inquorate *adj* without enough people present
to make a quorum
inroads *pl n* start affecting or reducing
insalubrious *adj* unpleasant, unhealthy, or
sordid
insane *adj* mentally ill > **insanely** *adv*
> **insanity** *n* (*pl* -**ties**)
insanely *adv* ▷ **insane**
insanitary *adj* dirty or unhealthy
insanities *n* ▷ **insane**
insanity *n* ▷ **insane**

insatiable [in-**saysh**-a-bl] *adj* unable to be
satisfied
inscribe *v* (-**bes**, -**bing**, -**bed**) write or carve
words on
inscribed *v* ▷ **inscribe**
inscribes *v* ▷ **inscribe**
inscribing *v* ▷ **inscribe**
inscription *n* (*pl* -**s**) words inscribed
inscriptions *n* ▷ **inscription**
inscrutable *adj* mysterious, enigmatic
> **inscrutably** *adv*
inscrutably *adv* ▷ **inscrutable**
insect *n* (*pl* -**s**) small animal with six legs and
usu. wings, such as an ant or fly
insecticide *n* (*pl* -**s**) substance for killing
insects
insecticides *n* ▷ **insecticide**
insectivorous *adj* insect-eating
insects *n* ▷ **insect**
insecure *adj* anxious, not confident
inseminated *v* ▷ **insemination**
inseminates *v* ▷ **insemination**
inseminating *v* ▷ **insemination**
insemination *n* (*pl* -**s**) putting semen into a
woman's or female animal's body to try to
make her pregnant > **inseminate** *v* (-**tes**,
-**ting**, -**ted**)
inseminations *n* ▷ **insemination**
insensate *adj* without sensation, unconscious
insensible *adj* unconscious, without feeling
insensitive *adj* unaware of or ignoring other
people's feelings > **insensitivity** *n* (*pl* -**ties**)
insensitivities *n* ▷ **insensitive**
insensitivity *n* ▷ **insensitive**
inseparable *adj* (of two people) spending
most of the time together
insert *v* (-**s**, -**ing**, -**ed**) put inside or include ▶ *n*
(*pl* -**s**) something inserted > **insertion** *n* (*pl* -**s**)
inserted *v* ▷ **insert**
inserting *v* ▷ **insert**
insertion *n* ▷ **insert**
insertions *n* ▷ **insert**
inserts *v*, *n* ▷ **insert**
inset *n* (*pl* -**s**) small picture inserted within a
larger one
insets *n* ▷ **inset**
inshore *adj* close to the shore ▶ *adj*, *adv*
towards the shore
inside *prep* in or to the interior of ▶ *adj* on or
of the inside ▶ *adv* on, in, or to the inside,
indoors ▶ *n* (*pl* -**s**) inner side, surface, or part
insider *n* (*pl* -**s**) member of a group who has
privileged knowledge about it
insiders *n* ▷ **insider**
insides *n* ▷ **inside** ▶ *pl n* (*Informal*) stomach

and bowels

insidious *adj* subtle or unseen but dangerous
> **insidiously** *adv*

insidiously *adv* ▷ **insidious**

insight *n* (*pl* -s) deep understanding

insights *n* ▷ **insight**

insignia *n* (*pl* -s) badge or emblem of honour or office

insignias *n* ▷ **insignia**

insignificance *n* ▷ **insignificant**

insignificances *n* ▷ **insignificant**

insignificant *adj* not important
> **insignificance** *n* ▷ **insignificant**

insincere *adj* showing false feelings, not genuine > **insincerely** *adv* > **insincerity** *n* (*pl* -ties)

insincerely *adv* ▷ **insincerely**

insincerities *n* ▷ **insincere**

insincerity *n* ▷ **insincere**

insinuate *v* (-tes, -ting, -ted) suggest indirectly > **insinuation** *n* (*pl* -s)

insinuated *v* ▷ **insinuate**

insinuates *v* ▷ **insinuate**

insinuating *v* ▷ **insinuate**

insinuation *n* ▷ **insinuate**

insinuations *n* ▷ **insinuate**

insipid *adj* lacking interest, spirit, or flavour

insist *v* (-s, -ing, -ed) demand or state firmly
> **insistent** *adj* making persistent demands
> **insistently** *adv* > **insistence** *n* (*pl* -s)

insisted *v* ▷ **insist**

insistence *n* ▷ **insist**

insistences *n* ▷ **insist**

insistent *adj* ▷ **insist**

insistently *adv* ▷ **insist**

insisting *v* ▷ **insist**

insists *v* ▷ **insist**

insole *n* (*pl* -s) inner sole of a shoe or boot

insolence *n* ▷ **insolent**

insolences *n* ▷ **insolent**

insolent *adj* rude and disrespectful
> **insolence** *n* (*pl* -s) > **insolently** *adv*

insolently *adv* ▷ **insolent**

insoles *n* ▷ **insole**

insoluble *adj* incapable of being solved

insolvencies *n* ▷ **insolvent**

insolvency *n* ▷ **insolvent**

insolvent *adj* unable to pay one's debts
> **insolvency** *n* (*pl* -cies)

insomnia *n* (*pl* -s) inability to sleep
> **insomniac** *n* (*pl* -s)

insomniac *n* ▷ **insomnia**

insomniacs *n* ▷ **insomnia**

insomnias *n* ▷ **insomnia**

insouciance *n* ▷ **insouciant**

insouciances *n* ▷ **insouciant**

insouciant *adj* carefree and unconcerned
> **insouciance** *n* (*pl* -s)

inspect *v* (-s, -ing, -ed) check closely or officially > **inspection** *n* (*pl* -s)

inspected *v* ▷ **inspect**

inspecting *v* ▷ **inspect**

inspection *n* ▷ **inspect**

inspections *n* ▷ **inspect**

inspector *n* (*pl* -s) person who inspects

inspectors *n* ▷ **inspector**

inspects *v* ▷ **inspect**

inspiration *n* (*pl* -s) creative influence or stimulus > **inspirational** *adj*

inspirational *adj* ▷ **inspiration**

inspirations *n* ▷ **inspiration**

inspire *v* (-res, -ring, -red) fill with enthusiasm, stimulate

inspired *v* ▷ **inspire**

inspires *v* ▷ **inspire**

inspiring *v* ▷ **inspire**

instabilities *n* ▷ **instability**

instability *n* (*pl* -ties) lack of steadiness or reliability

install *v* (-lls, -lling, -lled) put in and prepare (equipment) for use

installation *n* (*pl* -s) installing

installations *n* ▷ **installation**

installed *v* ▷ **install**

installing *v* ▷ **install**

installs *v* ▷ **install**

instalment *n* (*pl* -s) any of the portions of a thing presented or a debt paid in successive parts

instalments *n* ▷ **instalment**

instance *n* (*pl* -s) particular example ▶ *v* (-ces, -cing, -ced) mention as an example

instanced *v* ▷ **instance**

instances *n*, *v* ▷ **instance**

instancing *v* ▷ **instance**

instant *n* (*pl* -s) very brief time ▶ *adj* happening at once > **instantly** *adv*

instantaneous *adj* happening at once
> **instantaneously** *adv*

instantaneously *adv* ▷ **instantaneous**

instantly *adv* ▷ **instant**

instants *n* ▷ **instant**

instead *adv* as a replacement or substitute

instep *n* (*pl* -s) part of the foot forming the arch between the ankle and toes

insteps *n* ▷ **instep**

instigate *v* (-tes, -ting, -ted) cause to happen
> **instigation** *n* (*pl* -s) > **instigator** *n* (*pl* -s)

instigated *v* ▷ **instigate**

instigates *v* ▷ **instigate**

instigating v ▷ instigate
instigation n ▷ instigate
instigations n ▷ instigate
instigator n ▷ instigate
instigators n ▷ instigate
instil v (-s, -lling, -lled) introduce (an idea etc.) gradually into someone's mind
instilled v ▷ instil
instilling v ▷ instil
instils v ▷ instil
instinct n (pl -s) inborn tendency to behave in a certain way > **instinctive** adj > **instinctively** adv
instinctive adj ▷ instinct
instinctively adv ▷ instinct
instincts n ▷ instinct
institute n (pl -s) organization set up for a specific purpose, esp. research or teaching ▶ v (-tutes, -tuting, -tuted) start or establish
instituted v ▷ institute
institutes n, v ▷ institute
instituting v ▷ institute
institution n (pl -s) large important organization such as a university or bank > **institutional** adj > **institutionalize** v (-izes, -izing, -ized)
institutional adj ▷ institution
institutionalize v ▷ institution
institutionalized v ▷ institution
institutionalizes v ▷ institution
institutionalizing v ▷ institution
institutions n ▷ institution
instruct v (-s, -ing, -ed) order to do something > **instructor** n (pl -s)
instructed v ▷ instruct
instructing v ▷ instruct
instruction n (pl -s) order to do something
instructions n ▷ instruction ▶ pl n information on how to do or use something
instructive adj informative or helpful
instructor n ▷ instruct
instructors n ▷ instruct
instructs v ▷ instruct
instrument n (pl -s) tool used for particular work
instrumental adj (foll. by **in**) having an important function (in)
instrumentalist n (pl -s) player of a musical instrument
instrumentalists n ▷ instrumentalist
instrumentation n (pl -s) set of instruments in a car etc.
instrumentations n ▷ instrumentation
instruments n ▷ instrument
insubordinate adj not submissive to

authority > **insubordination** n (pl -s)
insubordination n ▷ insubordinate
insubordinations n ▷ insubordinate
insufferable adj unbearable
insular adj not open to new ideas, narrow-minded > **insularity** n (pl -ties)
insularities n ▷ insular
insularity n ▷ insular
insulate v (-tes, -ting, -ted) prevent or reduce the transfer of electricity, heat, or sound by surrounding or lining with a nonconducting material > **insulation** n (pl -s) > **insulator** n (pl -s)
insulated v ▷ insulate
insulates v ▷ insulate
insulating v ▷ insulate
insulation n ▷ insulate
insulations n ▷ insulate
insulator n ▷ insulate
insulators n ▷ insulate
insulin n (pl -s) hormone produced in the pancreas that controls the amount of sugar in the blood
insulins n ▷ insulin
insult v (-s, -ing, -ed) behave rudely to, offend ▶ n (pl -s) insulting remark or action > **insulting** adj
insulted v ▷ insult
insulting v, adj ▷ insult
insults v, n ▷ insult
insuperable adj impossible to overcome
insupportable adj impossible to tolerate
insurance n (pl -ces) agreement by which one makes regular payments to a company who pay an agreed sum if damage, loss, or death occurs
insurances n ▷ insurance
insure v (-res, -ring, -red) protect by insurance
insured v ▷ insure
insures v ▷ insure
insurgent n (pl -s) ▶ adj (person) in revolt against an established authority
insurgents n ▷ insurgent
insuring v ▷ insure
insurrection n (pl -s) rebellion
insurrections n ▷ insurrection
intact adj not changed or damaged in any way
intaglio [in-**tah**-lee-oh] n (pl -s) (gem carved with) an engraved design
intaglios n ▷ intaglio
intake n (pl -kes) amount or number taken in
intakes n ▷ intake
integer n (pl -s) positive or negative whole number or zero
integers n ▷ integer

integral adj being an essential part of a whole ▶ n (pl -s) (MATHS) sum of a large number of very small quantities
  integrals n ▷ integral
integrate v (-tes, -ting, -ted) combine into a whole ▶ **integration** n (pl -s)
  integrated v ▷ integrate
  integrates v ▷ integrate
  integrating v ▷ integrate
  integration n ▷ integrate
  integrations n ▷ integrate
  integrities n ▷ integrity
integrity n (pl -ties) quality of having high moral principles
intellect n (pl -s) power of thinking and reasoning
  intellects n ▷ intellect
intellectual adj of or appealing to the intellect ▶ n (pl -s) intellectual person ▶ **intellectually** adv
  intellectually adv ▷ intellectual
  intellectuals n ▷ intellectual
intelligence n (pl -s) quality of being intelligent
  intelligences n ▷ intelligence
intelligent adj able to understand, learn, and think things out quickly ▶ **intelligently** adv
  intelligently adv ▷ intelligent
intelligentsia n (pl -s) intellectual or cultured people in a society
  intelligentsias n ▷ intelligentsia
  intelligibilities n ▷ intelligibile
  intelligibility n ▷ intelligibile
intelligible adj able to be understood
  > **intelligibility** n (pl -ties)
  intemperance n ▷ intemperate
  intemperances n ▷ intemperate
intemperate adj unrestrained, uncontrolled
  > **intemperance** n (pl -s)
intend v (-s, -ing, -ed) propose or plan (to do something)
  intended v ▷ intend
  intending v ▷ intend
  intends v ▷ intend
intense adj of great strength or degree
  > **intensity** n (pl -ties)
  intensification n ▷ intensify
  intensifications n ▷ intensify
  intensified v ▷ intensify
  intensifies v ▷ intensify
intensify v (-fies, -fying, -fied) make or become more intense > **intensification** n (pl -s)
  intensifying v ▷ intensify
  intensities n ▷ intense
  intensity n ▷ intense

intensive adj using or needing concentrated effort or resources > **intensively** adv
  intensively adv ▷ intensive
intent n (pl -s) intention ▶ adj paying close attention > **intently** adv > **intentness** n (pl -s)
intention n (pl -s) something intended
intentional adj planned in advance, deliberate
  > **intentionally** adv
  intentionally adv ▷ intentional
  intentions n ▷ intention
  intently adv ▷ intent
  intentness n ▷ intent
  intentnesses n ▷ intent
  intents n ▷ intent
inter [in-ter] v (-s, -rring, -rred) bury (a corpse)
  > **interment** n (pl -s)
interact v (-s, -ing, -ed) act on or in close relation with each other > **interaction** n (pl -s)
  > **interactive** adj
  interacted v ▷ interact
  interacting v ▷ interact
  interaction n ▷ interact
  interactions n ▷ interact
  interactive adj ▷ interact
  interacts v ▷ interact
  interbred v ▷ interbreed
interbreed v (-s, -ing, -bred) breed within a related group
  interbreeding v ▷ interbreed
  interbreeds v ▷ interbreed
intercede v (-des, -ding, -ded) try to end a dispute between two people or groups
  > **intercession** n (pl -s)
  interceded v ▷ intercede
  intercedes v ▷ intercede
  interceding v ▷ intercede
intercept v (-s, -ing, -ed) seize or stop in transit > **interception** n (pl -s)
  intercepted v ▷ intercept
  intercepting v ▷ intercept
  interception n ▷ intercept
  interceptions n ▷ intercept
  intercepts v ▷ intercept
  intercession n ▷ intercede
  intercessions n ▷ intercede
interchange v (-ges, -ging, -ged) (cause to) exchange places ▶ n (pl -ges) motorway junction > **interchangeable** adj
  interchangeable adj ▷ interchange
  interchanged v ▷ interchange
  interchanges v, n ▷ interchange
  interchanging v ▷ interchange
intercom n (pl -s) internal communication system with loudspeakers
  intercoms n ▷ intercom

intercontinental adj travelling between or linking continents

intercourse n (pl -s) sexual intercourse

intercourses n ▷ intercourse

interdict n ▷ interdiction

interdiction, interdict n (pl -s) formal order forbidding something

interdictions n ▷ interdiction

interdicts n ▷ interdiction

interdisciplinary adj involving more than one branch of learning

interest n (pl -s) desire to know or hear more about something ▶ v (-s, -ing, -ed) arouse the interest of > **interesting** adj > **interestingly** adv

interested adj feeling or showing interest ▶ v ▷ interest

interesting v, adj ▷ interest

interestingly adv ▷ interest

interests n, v ▷ interest

interface n (pl -s) area where two things interact or link

interfaces n ▷ interface

interfere v (-res, -ring, -red) try to influence other people's affairs where one is not involved or wanted > **interfering** adj > **interference** n (pl -s) interfering

interfered v ▷ interfere

interference n ▷ interfere

interference n ▷ interfere

interferes v ▷ interfere

interfering v, adj ▷ interfere

interferon n (pl -s) protein that stops the development of an invading virus

interferons n ▷ interferon

interim adj temporary or provisional

interior n (pl -s) inside ▶ adj inside, inner

interiors n ▷ interior

interject v (-s, -ing, -ed) make (a remark) suddenly or as an interruption > **interjection** n (pl -s)

interjected v ▷ interject

interjecting v ▷ interject

interjection n ▷ interject

interjections n ▷ interject

interjects v ▷ interject

interlace v (-ces, -cing, -ced) join together as if by weaving

interlaced v ▷ interlace

interlaces v ▷ interlace

interlacing v ▷ interlace

interlink v (-s, -ing, -ed) connect together

interlinked v ▷ interlink

interlinking v ▷ interlink

interlinks v ▷ interlink

interlock v (-s, -ing, -ed) join firmly together

interlocked v ▷ interlock

interlocking v ▷ interlock

interlocks v ▷ interlock

interlocutor [in-ter-**lok**-yew-ter] n (pl -s) person who takes part in a conversation

interlocutors n ▷ interlocutor

interloper [**in**-ter-lope-er] n (pl -s) person in a place or situation where he or she has no right to be

interlopers n ▷ interloper

interlude n (pl -s) short rest or break in an activity or event

interludes n ▷ interlude

intermarriage n ▷ intermarry

intermarriages n ▷ intermarry

intermarried v ▷ intermarry

intermarries v ▷ intermarry

intermarry v (-rries, -rrying, -rried) (of families, races, or religions) become linked by marriage > **intermarriage** n (pl -s)

intermarrying v ▷ intermarry

intermediaries n ▷ intermediary

intermediary n (pl -ries) person trying to create agreement between others

intermediate adj coming between two points or extremes

interment n ▷ inter

interments n ▷ inter

intermezzo [in-ter-**met**-so] n (pl -s) short piece of music, esp. one performed between the acts of an opera

intermezzos n ▷ intermezzo

interminable adj seemingly endless because boring > **interminably** adv

interminably adv ▷ interminable

intermingle v (-les, -ling, -led) mix together

intermingled v ▷ intermingle

intermingles v ▷ intermingle

intermingling v ▷ intermingle

intermission n (pl -s) interval between parts of a play, film, etc.

intermissions n ▷ intermission

intermittent adj occurring at intervals > **intermittently** adv

intermittently adv ▷ intermittent

intern v (-s, -ing, -ed) imprison, esp. during a war ▶ n (pl -s) trainee doctor in a hospital > **internment** n (pl -s)

internal adj of or on the inside > **internally** adv

internally adv ▷ internal

international adj of or involving two or more countries ▶ n (pl -s) game or match between teams of different countries > **internationally** adv

internationally adv ▷ international
internationals n ▷ international
internecine adj mutually destructive
interned v ▷ intern
internee n (pl -s) person who is interned
internees n ▷ internee
interning v ▷ intern
internment n ▷ intern
internments n ▷ intern
interns v, n ▷ intern
interplanetary adj of or linking planets
interplay n (pl -s) action and reaction of two
things upon each other
interplays n ▷ interplay
interpolate [in-ter-pole-ate] v (-tes, -ting,
-ted) insert (a comment or passage) into a
conversation or text) > **interpolation** n (pl -s)
interpolated v ▷ interpolate
interpolates v ▷ interpolate
interpolating v ▷ interpolate
interpolation n ▷ interpolate
interpolations n ▷ interpolate
interpose v (-ses, -sing, -sed) insert between
or among things
interposed v ▷ interpose
interposes v ▷ interpose
interposing v ▷ interpose
interpret v (-s, -ing, -ed) explain the meaning
of > **interpretation** n (pl -s)
interpretation n ▷ interpret
interpretations n ▷ interpret
interpreted v ▷ interpret
interpreter n (pl -s) person who translates
orally from one language into another
interpreters n ▷ interpreter
interpreting v ▷ interpret
interprets v ▷ interpret
interred v ▷ inter
interregna n ▷ interregnum
interregnum n (pl -nums, -na) interval
between reigns
interregnums n ▷ interregnum
interring v ▷ inter
interrogate v (-tes, -ting, -ted) question
closely > **interrogation** n (pl -s)
interrogated v ▷ interrogate
interrogates v ▷ interrogate
interrogating v ▷ interrogate
interrogation n ▷ interrogate
interrogations n ▷ interrogate
interrogative adj questioning ▶ n (pl -s) word
used in asking a question, such as how or why
> **interrogator** n (pl -s)
interrogatives n ▷ interrogative
interrogator n ▷ interrogative

interrogators n ▷ interrogative
interrupt v (-s, -ing, -ed) break into (a
conversation etc.) > **interruption** n (pl -s)
interrupted v ▷ interrupt
interrupting v ▷ interrupt
interruption n ▷ interrupt
interruptions n ▷ interrupt
interrupts v ▷ interrupt
inters v ▷ inter
intersect v (-s, -ing, -ed) (of roads) meet and
cross > **intersection** n (pl -s)
intersected v ▷ intersect
intersecting v ▷ intersect
intersection n ▷ intersect
intersections n ▷ intersect
intersects v ▷ intersect
interspersed adj scattered (among, between,
or on)
interstellar adj between or among stars
interstice [in-ter-stiss] n (pl -ces) small crack or
gap between things
interstices n ▷ interstice
intertwine v (-nes, -ning, -ned) twist together
intertwined v ▷ intertwine
intertwines v ▷ intertwine
intertwining v ▷ intertwine
interval n (pl -s) time between two particular
moments or events
intervals n ▷ interval
intervene v (-nes, -ning, -ned) involve oneself
in a situation, esp. to prevent conflict
> **intervention** n (pl -s)
intervened v ▷ intervene
intervenes v ▷ intervene
intervening v ▷ intervene
intervention n ▷ intervene
interventions n ▷ intervene
interview n (pl -s) formal discussion, esp.
between a job-seeker and an employer ▶ v
(-s, -ing, -ed) conduct an interview with
> **interviewee** n (pl -s) > **interviewer** n (pl -s)
interviewed v ▷ interview
interviewee n ▷ interview
interviewees n ▷ interview
interviewer n ▷ interview
interviewers n ▷ interview
interviewing v ▷ interview
interviews n, v ▷ interview
interweave v (-ves, -ving, -wove, -woven)
weave together
interweaves v ▷ interweave
interweaving v ▷ interweave
interwove v ▷ interweave
interwoven v ▷ interweave
intestacies n ▷ intestate

intestacy *n* ▷ intestate
intestate *adj* not having made a will
    > intestacy *n* (*pl* -cies)
    intestinal *adj* ▷ intestine
    intestinally *adv* ▷ intestine
intestine *n* (*pl* -s) (*often pl*) lower part of the
    alimentary canal between the stomach and
    the anus > intestinal *adj* > intestinally *adv*
    intestines *n* ▷ intestine
    intimacies *n* ▷ intimate¹
    intimacy *n* ▷ intimate¹
intimate¹ *adj* having a close personal
    relationship ▶ *n* (*pl* -s) close friend
    > intimately *adv* > intimacy *n* (*pl* -cies)
intimate² *v* (-tes, -ting, -ted) hint at or suggest
    > intimation *n* (*pl* -s)
    intimated *v* ▷ intimate²
    intimately *adv* ▷ intimate¹
    intimates *n* ▷ intimate¹ ▶ *v* ▷ intimate²
    intimating *v* ▷ intimate²
    intimation *n* ▷ intimate²
    intimations *n* ▷ intimate²
intimidate *v* (-tes, -ting, -ted) subdue
    or influence by fear > intimidating *adj*
    > intimidation *n* (*pl* -s)
    intimidated *v* ▷ intimidate
    intimidates *v* ▷ intimidate
    intimidating *v, adj* ▷ intimidate
    intimidation *n* ▷ intimidate
    intimidations *n* ▷ intimidate
into *prep* indicating motion towards the centre,
    result of a change, division, etc.
intolerable *adj* more than can be endured
    > intolerably *adv*
    intolerably *adv* ▷ intolerable
    intolerance *n* ▷ intolerant
    intolerances *n* ▷ intolerant
intolerant *adj* refusing to accept practices
    and beliefs different from one's own
    > intolerance *n* (*pl* -s)
intonation *n* (*pl* -s) sound pattern produced by
    variations in the voice
    intonations *n* ▷ intonation
intone *v* (-nes, -ning, -ned) speak or recite in
    an unvarying tone of voice
    intoned *v* ▷ intone
    intones *v* ▷ intone
    intoning *v* ▷ intone
intoxicant *n* (*pl* -s) intoxicating drink
    intoxicants *n* ▷ intoxicant
intoxicate *v* (-tes, -ting, -ted) make drunk
    intoxicated *v* ▷ intoxicate
    intoxicates *v* ▷ intoxicate
    intoxicating *v* ▷ intoxicate
intoxication *n* (*pl* -s) state of being drunk

intoxications *n* ▷ intoxication
intractable *adj* (of a person) difficult to control
intranet *n* (*pl* -s) (COMPUTERS) internal network
    that makes use of Internet technology
    intranets *n* ▷ intranet
    intransigence *n* ▷ intransigent
    intransigences *n* ▷ intransigent
intransigent *adj* refusing to change one's
    attitude > intransigence *n* (*pl* -s)
intransitive *adj* (of a verb) not taking a direct
    object
intrauterine *adj* within the womb
intravenous [in-tra-vee-nuss] *adj* into a vein
    > intravenously *adv*
    intravenously *adv* ▷ intravenous
intrepid *adj* fearless, bold > intrepidity *n* (*pl*
    -ties)
    intrepidities *n* ▷ intrepid
    intrepidity *n* ▷ intrepid
    intricacies *n* ▷ intricate
    intricacy *n* ▷ intricate
intricate *adj* involved or complicated
    > intricately *adv* > intricacy *n* (*pl* -cies)
    intricately *adv* ▷ intricate
intrigue *v* (-gues, -guing, -gued) make
    interested or curious ▶ *n* (*pl* -gues) secret
    plotting > intriguing *adj*
    intrigued *v* ▷ intrigue
    intrigues *v, n* ▷ intrigue
    intriguing *v, adj* ▷ intrigue
intrinsic *adj* essential to the basic nature of
    something > intrinsically *adv*
    intrinsically *adv* ▷ intrinsic
introduce *v* (-ces, -cing, -ced) present
    (someone) by name (to another person)
    introduced *v* ▷ introduce
    introduces *v* ▷ introduce
    introducing *v* ▷ introduce
introduction *n* (*pl* -s) presentation of one
    person to another > introductory *adj*
    introductions *n* ▷ introduction
    introductory *adj* ▷ introduction
introspection *n* (*pl* -s) examination of one's
    own thoughts and feelings > introspective *adj*
    introspections *n* ▷ introspection
    introspective *adj* ▷ introspection
    introversion *n* ▷ introvert
    introversions *n* ▷ introvert
introvert *n* (*pl* -s) person concerned more
    with his or her thoughts and feelings than
    with the outside world > introverted *adj*
    > introversion *n* (*pl* -s)
    introverted *adj* ▷ introvert
    introverts *n* ▷ introvert
intrude *v* (-des, -ding, -ded) come in or join

in without being invited **> intrusion** *n (pl* **-s)** **> intrusive** *adj*

intruded *v ▷* intrude

intruder *n (pl* **-s)** person who enters a place without permission

intruders *n ▷* intruder

intrudes *v ▷* intrude

intruding *v ▷* intrude

intrusion *n ▷* intrude

intrusions *n ▷* intrude

intrusive *adj ▷* intrude

intuition *n (pl* **-s)** instinctive knowledge or insight without conscious reasoning **> intuitive** *adj* **> intuitively** *adv*

intuitions *n ▷* intuition

intuitive *adj ▷* intuition

intuitively *adv ▷* intuition

inundate *v (***-tes, -ting, -ted)** flood **> inundation** *n (pl* **-s)**

inundated *v ▷* inundate

inundates *v ▷* inundate

inundating *v ▷* inundate

inundation *n ▷* inundate

inundations *n ▷* inundate

inured *adj* accustomed, esp. to hardship or danger

invade *v (***-des, -ding, -ded)** enter (a country) by military force **> invader** *n (pl* **-s)**

invaded *v ▷* invade

invader *n ▷* invade

invaders *n ▷* invade

invades *v ▷* invade

invading *v ▷* invade

invalid[1] *adj, n (pl* **-s)** disabled or chronically ill (person) **▶** *v (***-s, -ing, -ed)** *(often foll. by* **out)** dismiss from active service because of illness or injury **> invalidity** *n (pl* **-ties)**

invalid[2] *adj* having no legal force

invalidate *v (***-tes, -ting, -ted)** make or show to be invalid

invalidated *v ▷* invalidate

invalidates *v ▷* invalidate

invalidating *v ▷* invalidate

invalided *v ▷* invalid[1]

invaliding *v ▷* invalid[1]

invalidities *n ▷* invalid[1]

invalidity *n ▷* invalid[1]

invalids *n, v ▷* invalid[1]

invaluable *adj* of very great value or worth

invasion *n (pl* **-s)** invading

invasions *n ▷* invasion

invective *n (pl* **-s)** abusive speech or writing

invectives *n ▷* invective

inveigh [in-**vay**] *v (***-s, -ing, -ed)** *(foll. by* **against)** criticize strongly

inveighed *v ▷* inveigh

inveighing *v ▷* inveigh

inveighs *v ▷* inveigh

inveigle *v (***-les, -ling, -led)** coax by cunning or trickery

inveigled *v ▷* inveigle

inveigles *v ▷* inveigle

inveigling *v ▷* inveigle

invent *v (***-s, -ing, -ed)** think up or create (something new)

invented *v ▷* invent

inventing *v ▷* invent

invention *n (pl* **-s)** something invented

inventive *adj* creative and resourceful **> inventiveness** *n (pl* **-s)** **> inventor** *n (pl* **-s)**

inventiveness *n ▷* inventive

inventivenesses *n ▷* inventive

inventor *n ▷* inventive

inventories *v ▷* inventory

inventors *n ▷* inventive

inventory *n (pl* **-ries)** detailed list of goods or furnishings

invents *v ▷* invent

inverse *adj* reversed in effect, sequence, direction, etc. **> inversely** *adv*

inversely *adv ▷* inverse

inversion *n ▷* invert

inversions *n ▷* invert

invert *v (***-s, -ing, -ed)** turn upside down or inside out **> inversion** *n (pl* **-s)**

invertebrate *n (pl* **-s)** animal with no backbone

invertebrates *n ▷* invertebrate

inverted *v ▷* invert

inverting *v ▷* invert

inverts *v ▷* invert

invest *v (***-s, -ing, -ed)** spend (money, time, etc.) on something with the expectation of profit

invested *v ▷* invest

investigate *v (***-tes, -ting, -ted)** inquire into, examine **> investigation** *n (pl* **-s)** **> investigative** *adj* **> investigator** *n (pl* **-s)**

investigated *v ▷* investigate

investigates *v ▷* investigate

investigating *v ▷* investigate

investigation *n ▷* investigate

investigations *n ▷* investigate

investigative *adj ▷* investigate

investigator *n ▷* investigate

investigators *n ▷* investigate

investing *v ▷* invest

investiture *n (pl* **-s)** formal installation of a person in an office or rank

investitures *n ▷* investiture

investment *n (pl* **-s)** money invested

> **investor** n (pl -s)
investments n ▷ investment
investor n ▷ investment
investors n ▷ investment
invests v ▷ invest
inveterate adj firmly established in a habit or condition
invidious adj likely to cause resentment
invigilate v (-tes, -ting, -ted) supervise people sitting an examination > **invigilator** n (pl -s)
invigilated v ▷ invigilate
invigilates v ▷ invigilate
invigilating v ▷ invigilate
invigilation n ▷ invigilate
invigilations n ▷ invigilate
invigilator n ▷ invigilate
invigilators n ▷ invigilate
invigorate v (-tes, -ting, -ted) give energy to, refresh
invigorated v ▷ invigorate
invigorates v ▷ invigorate
invigorating v ▷ invigorate
invincibilities n ▷ invincibile
invincibility n ▷ invincibile
invincible adj impossible to defeat
> **invincibility** n (pl -ties)
inviolable adj unable to be broken or violated
inviolate adj unharmed, unaffected
invisibilities n ▷ invisible
invisibility adv ▷ invisible
invisible adj not able to be seen > **invisibly** adv
> **invisibility** n (pl -ties)
invisibly adv ▷ invisible
invitation n ▷ invite
invitations n ▷ invite
invite v (-tes, -ting, -ted) request the company of ▶ n (pl -s) (Informal) invitation > **invitation** n (pl -s)
invited v ▷ invite
invites v, n ▷ invite
inviting adj tempting, attractive ▶ v ▷ invite
invocation n ▷ invoke
invocations n ▷ invoke
invoice v (-ces, -cing, -ced) ▶ n (pl -s) (present with) a bill for goods or services supplied
invoiced v ▷ invoice
invoices n, v ▷ invoice
invoicing v ▷ invoice
invoke v (-kes, -king, -ked) put (a law or penalty) into operation > **invocation** n (pl -s)
invoked v ▷ invoke
invokes v ▷ invoke
invoking v ▷ invoke
involuntarily adv ▷ involuntary
involuntary adj not done consciously,

unintentional > **involuntarily** adv
involve v (-lves, -lving, -lved) include as a necessary part > **involved** adj complicated
> **involvement** n (pl -s)
involved v, adj ▷ involve
involvement n ▷ involve
involvements n ▷ involve
involves v ▷ involve
involving v ▷ involve
invulnerable adj not able to be wounded or harmed
inward adj directed towards the middle ▶ adv (also **inwards**) towards the inside or middle
> **inwardly** adv
inwardly adv ▷ inward
inwards adv ▷ inward

> **io** n (ios). An io a cry of joy or grief. While io doesn't earn many points, it's useful when you want to form words in more than one direction: I and O are two of the most common tiles in the game, so there's a good chance that you'll be able to use io when forming a word in another direction. Io scores 2 points.

iodine n (pl -s) (CHEM) bluish-black element used in medicine and photography
iodines n ▷ iodine
iodize v (-izes, -izing, -ized) treat with iodine
iodized n ▷ iodize
iodizes n ▷ iodize
iodizing n ▷ iodize
ion n (pl -s) electrically charged atom > **ionic** adj
ionic adj ▷ ion
ionization n ▷ ionize
ionizations n ▷ ionize
ionize v (-izes, -izing, -ized) change into ions
> **ionization** n (pl -s)
ionized v ▷ ionize
ionizes v ▷ ionize
ionizing v ▷ ionize
ionosphere n (pl -s) region of ionized air in the upper atmosphere that reflects radio waves
ionospheres n ▷ ionosphere
ions n ▷ ion
iota n (pl -s) very small amount
iotas n ▷ iota
irascibilities n ▷ irascible
irascibility n ▷ irascible
irascible adj easily angered > **irascibility** n (pl -ties)
irate adj very angry
ire n (pl -s) (Lit) anger
ires n ▷ ire
iridescence n ▷ iridescent

iridescences *n* ▷ iridescent
iridescent *adj* having shimmering changing colours like a rainbow ▶ **iridescence** *n* (*pl* -s)
iridium *n* (*pl* -s) (CHEM) very hard corrosion-resistant metal
iridiums *n* ▷ iridium
iris *n* (*pl* -ses) coloured circular membrane of the eye containing the pupil
irises *n* ▷ iris
irk *v* (-s, -ing, -ed) irritate, annoy
irked *v* ▷ irk
irking *v* ▷ irk
irks *v* ▷ irk
irksome *adj* irritating, annoying
iron *n* (*pl* -s) strong silvery-white metallic element, widely used for structural and engineering purposes ▶ *adj* made of iron ▶ *v* (-s, -ing, -ed) smooth (clothes or fabric) with an iron
ironbark *n* (*pl* -s) Australian eucalyptus with hard rough bark
ironbarks *n* ▷ ironbark
ironed *v* ▷ iron
ironic, ironical *adj* using irony ▷ **ironically** *adv*
ironical *adj* ▷ ironic
ironically *adv* ▷ ironic
ironies *n* ▷ irony
ironing *n* (*pl* -s) clothes to be ironed ▶ *v* ▷ iron
ironings *n* ▷ ironing
ironmonger *n* (*pl* -s) shopkeeper or shop dealing in hardware ▷ **ironmongery** *n* (*pl* -ries)
ironmongeries *n* ▷ ironmonger
ironmongers *n* ▷ ironmonger
ironmongery *n* ▷ ironmonger
irons *n*, *v* ▷ iron ▶ *pl n* chains, restraints
ironstone *n* (*pl* -s) rock consisting mainly of iron ore
ironstones *n* ▷ ironstone
irony *n* (*pl* -nies) mildly sarcastic use of words to imply the opposite of what is said
irradiate *v* (-tes, -ting, -ted) subject to or treat with radiation ▷ **irradiation** *n* (*pl* -s)
irradiated *v* ▷ irradiate
irradiates *v* ▷ irradiate
irradiating *v* ▷ irradiate
irradiation *n* ▷ irradiate
irradiations *n* ▷ irradiate
irrational *adj* not based on or not using logical reasoning
irredeemable *adj* not able to be reformed or corrected
irreducible *adj* impossible to put in a simpler form
irrefutable *adj* impossible to deny or disprove

irregular *adj* not regular or even ▷ **irregularly** *adv* ▷ **irregularity** *n* (*pl* -ties)
irregularities *n* ▷ irregular
irregularity *n* ▷ irregular
irregularly *adv* ▷ irregular
irrelevance *n* ▷ irrelevant
irrelevances *n* ▷ irrelevant
irrelevant *adj* not connected with the matter in hand ▷ **irrelevantly** *adv* ▷ **irrelevance** *n* (*pl* -s)
irrelevantly *adv* ▷ irrelevant
irreparable *adj* not able to be repaired or put right ▷ **irreparably** *adv*
irreparably *adv* ▷ irreparable
irreplaceable *adj* impossible to replace
irreproachable *adj* blameless, faultless
irresistible *adj* too attractive or strong to resist ▷ **irresistibly** *adv*
irresistibly *adv* ▷ irresistible
irresponsibilities *n* ▷ irresponsible
irresponsibility *n* ▷ irresponsible
irresponsible *adj* not showing or not done with due care for the consequences of one's actions or attitudes ▷ **irresponsibility** *n* (*pl* -ties)
irreverence *n* ▷ irreverent
irreverences *n* ▷ irreverent
irreverent *adj* not showing due respect ▷ **irreverence** *n* (*pl* -s)
irreversible *adj* not able to be reversed or put right again ▷ **irreversibly** *adv*
irreversibly *adv* ▷ irreversible
irrevocable *adj* not possible to change or undo ▷ **irrevocably** *adv*
irrevocably *adv* ▷ irrevocable
irrigate *v* (-tes, -ting, -ted) supply (land) with water by artificial channels or pipes ▷ **irrigation** *n* (*pl* -s)
irrigated *v* ▷ irrigate
irrigates *v* ▷ irrigate
irrigating *v* ▷ irrigate
irrigation *n* ▷ irrigate
irrigations *n* ▷ irrigate
irritable *adj* easily annoyed ▷ **irritably** *adv*
irritably *adv* ▷ irritable
irritant *n* (*pl* -s) ▶ *adj* (person or thing) causing irritation
irritants *n* ▷ irritant
irritate *v* (-tes, -ting, -ted) annoy, anger ▷ **irritation** *n* (*pl* -s)
irritated *v* ▷ irritate
irritates *v* ▷ irritate
irritating *v* ▷ irritate
irritation *n* ▷ irritate
irritations *n* ▷ irritate

is v ▷ be

ish n (**ishes**). An ish is a word for an issue in Scots law. If you have I, S and H on your rack, remember that as well as adding **ish** to the end of many words, you can also play those letters as a word in its own right. Ish scores 6 points.

isinglass [ize-ing-glass] n (pl **-es**) kind of gelatine obtained from some freshwater fish
　isinglasses n ▷ isinglass

island n (pl **-s**) piece of land surrounded by water

islander n (pl **-s**) person who lives on an island
　islanders n ▷ islander
　islands n ▷ island

isle n (pl **-s**) (*Poetic*) island
　isles n ▷ isle

islet n small island
　islets n ▷ islet

ism n (**isms**). An ism is an informal word for a belief or doctrine. While **ism** can be added to the ends of many words as a suffix, it's worth remembering it as a word in its own right. Ism scores 5 points.

isobar [ice-oh-bar] n (pl **-s**) line on a map connecting places of equal atmospheric pressure
　isobars n ▷ isobar

isolate v (**-tes, -ting, -ted**) place apart or alone
　> **isolation** n (pl **-s**)
　isolated v ▷ isolate
　isolates v ▷ isolate
　isolating v ▷ isolate
　isolation n ▷ isolate

isolationism n (pl **-s**) policy of not participating in international affairs
　> **isolationist** n (pl **-s**) adj
　isolationisms n ▷ isolationism

isolationist n, adj ▷ isolationism
　isolationists n ▷ isolationsim
　isolations n ▷ isolate

isomer [ice-oh-mer] n (pl **-s**) substance whose molecules contain the same atoms as another but in a different arrangement
　isomers n ▷ isomer

isometric adj relating to muscular contraction without shortening of the muscle
　isometrics pl n isometric exercises

isotherm [ice-oh-therm] n (pl **-s**) line on a map connecting points of equal temperature
　isotherms n ▷ isotherm

isotope [ice-oh-tope] n (pl **-s**) one of two or more atoms with the same number of protons in the nucleus but a different number of neutrons
　isotopes n ▷ isotope

issue n (pl **-s**) topic of interest or discussion ▶ v (**-ssues, -ssuing, -ssued**) make (a statement etc.) publicly
　issued v ▷ issue
　issues n, v ▷ issue
　issuing v ▷ issue

isthmus [iss-muss] n (pl **-muses**) narrow strip of land connecting two areas of land
　isthmuses n ▷ isthmus

it pron refers to a nonhuman, animal, plant, or inanimate object ▶ **its** adj, pron belonging to it

italic adj (of printing type) sloping to the right

italicize v (**-izes, -izing, -ized**) put in italics
　italicized v ▷ italicize
　italicizes v ▷ italicize
　italicizing v ▷ italicize

italics pl n this type, used for emphasis

itch n (pl **-es**) skin irritation causing a desire to scratch ▶ v (**-es, -ing, -ed**) have an itch
　> **itchy** adj
　itched v ▷ itch
　itches n, v ▷ itch
　itching v ▷ itch
　itchy adj ▷ itch

item n (pl **-s**) single thing in a list or collection
　> **itemize** v (**-izes, -izing, -ized**) make a list of
　itemized n ▷ item
　itemizes n ▷ item
　itemizing n ▷ item
　items n ▷ item

iterate v (**-tes, -ting, -ted**) repeat > **iteration** n (pl **-s**)
　iterated v ▷ iterate
　iterates v ▷ iterate
　iterating v ▷ iterate
　iteration n ▷ iterate
　iterations n ▷ iterate

itinerant adj travelling from place to place
　itineraries n ▷ itinerary

itinerary n (pl **-aries**) detailed plan of a journey
　itself pron ▷ it
　ivies n ▷ ivy
　ivories n ▷ ivory

ivory n (pl **-ries**) hard white bony substance forming the tusks of elephants ▶ adj yellowish-white

ivy n (pl **-vies**) evergreen climbing plant

iwi [ee-wee] n (pl **-s**) (NZ) Maori tribe
　iwis n ▷ iwi

Jj

J is one of the best tiles to have in Scrabble, as it is worth 8 points on its own. J also forms a number of words with X and Z, allowing you to earn some huge scores if you get the right tiles to go with it. Even better, some of these words are seven letters in length, so the right combination of tiles will give you a 50-point bonus if you are lucky enough to have it on your rack. On the other hand, J isn't the easiest tile to use when forming words in different directions. There's only one two-letter word that begins with J **jo**. If you remember this, you won't waste time trying to think of others. As J has such a high value, look out for double- and triple-letter squares when playing it. There are plenty of good three-letter words starting with J: **jab** (12 points), **jam** (12), **jar** (10), **jaw** (13), **jay** (13), **jet** (10), **jib** (12), **jig** (11), **job** (12), **jog** (11), **jot** (10), **joy** (13), **jug** (11) and **jut** (10). In addition to these, there are other fantastic words beginning with J. **Jazz** (19) is very useful – you'll need a blank tile for the second Z, but if you can form it, you may also be able to play **jazzes** (21) or **jazzy** (23). **Jinx** (18) is also handy, and don't forget **jukebox** (27), which can be formed from **box** or **ox** if someone has played those.

---

jab v (-s, -bbing, -bbed) poke sharply ▶ n (pl -s)
  jabbed v ▷ jab
jabber v (-s, -ing, -ed) talk rapidly or incoherently
  jabbered v ▷ jabber
  jabbering v ▷ jabber
  jabbers v ▷ jabber
  jabbing v ▷ jab
jabiru n (pl -s) large white-and-black Australian stork
  jabirus n ▷ jabiru
  jabs v, n ▷ jab
jacaranda n (pl -s) tropical tree with sweet-smelling wood
  jacarandas n ▷ jacaranda
jack n (pl -s) device for raising a motor vehicle or other heavy object
  jacks n ▷ jack
jackal n (pl -s) doglike wild animal of Africa and Asia
  jackals n ▷ jackal
jackaroo, jackeroo n (pl -roos) (AUST) trainee on a sheep station
  jackaroos n ▷ jackaroo
jackass n (pl -es) fool
  jackasses n ▷ jackass
jackboot n (pl -s) high military boot
  jackboots n ▷ jackboot

jackdaw n (pl -s) black-and-grey Eurasian bird of the crow family
  jackdaws n ▷ jackdaw
  jackeroo n ▷ jackaroo
  jackeroos n ▷ jackaroo
jacket n (pl -s) short coat
  jackets n ▷ jacket
  jackings n ▷ jack
jackknife v (-s, -fing, -fed) (of an articulated truck) go out of control so that the trailer swings round at a sharp angle to the cab ▶ n (pl -knives) large clasp knife
  jackknifed v ▷ jackknife
  jackknifes v ▷ jackknife
  jackknifing v ▷ jackknife
  jackknives n ▷ jackknife
jackpot n (pl -s) largest prize that may be won in a game
  jackpots n ▷ jackpot
jacuzzi [jak-oo-zee] n ® (pl -s) circular bath with a device that swirls the water
  jacuzzis n ▷ jacuzzi
jade n (pl -s) ornamental semiprecious stone, usu. dark green ▶ adj bluish-green
jaded adj tired and unenthusiastic
  jades n ▷ jade
jagged [jag-gid] adj having an uneven edge

with sharp points

jaguar n (pl -s) large S American spotted cat
jaguars n ▷ jaguar

jail n (pl -s) prison ▶ v (-s, -ing, -ed) send to
prison > **jailer** n (pl -s)

jailbird n (pl -s) (Informal) person who has often
been in prison
jailbirds n ▷ jailbird

jailed v ▷ jail

jailer n ▷ jail

jailers n ▷ jail

jailing v ▷ jail

jails n, v ▷ jail

jalopies n ▷ jalopy

jalopy [jal-lop-ee] n (pl -pies) (Informal) old car

jam¹ v (-s, -mming, -mmed) pack tightly into a
place ▶ n (pl -s) hold-up of traffic

jam² n (pl -s) food made from fruit boiled with
sugar

jamb n (pl -s) side post of a door or window
frame

jamboree n (pl -s) large gathering or
celebration

jamborees n ▷ jamboree

jambs n ▷ jamb

jammed v ▷ jam¹

jamming v ▷ jam¹

jams v ▷ jam¹ ▶ n ▷ jam¹,²

jandal n (pl -s) (NZ) sandal with a strap between
the toes

jandals n ▷ jandal

jangle v (-les, -ling, -led) (cause to) make a
harsh ringing noise

jangled v ▷ jangle

jangles v ▷ jangle

jangling v ▷ jangle

janitor n (pl -s) caretaker of a school or other
building

janitors n ▷ janitor

> **janizar** or **janizary** n (**janizars,**
janizaries). A janizar was an elite
soldier in the armies of the Ottoman
Empire. This is a very useful word,
and will earn you a 50-point bonus if
you are able to use all your letters in
playing it. Also, if janizar is already on
the board, you have an opportunity to
earn a good score by adding an S, Y or
IES. Janizar scores 23 points.

japan n (pl -s) very hard varnish, usu. black ▶ v
(-s, -nning, -nned) cover with this varnish

japanned v ▷ japan

japanning v ▷ japan

japans n, v ▷ japan

jape n (pl -s) (Old-fashioned) joke or prank

japes n ▷ jape

japonica n (pl -s) shrub with red flowers

japonicas n ▷ japonica

jar¹ n (pl -s) wide-mouthed container, usu.
round and made of glass

jar² v (-s, -rring, -rred) have a disturbing or
unpleasant effect ▶ n (pl -s) jolt or shock

jargon n (pl -s) specialized technical language
of a particular subject

jargons n ▷ jargon

jarrah n (pl -s) Australian eucalyptus yielding
valuable timber

jarrahs n ▷ jarrah

jarred v ▷ jar²

jarring v ▷ jar²

jars v ▷ jar² ▶ n ▷ jar¹,²

jasmine n (pl -s) shrub with sweet-smelling
yellow or white flowers

jasmines n ▷ jasmine

jasper n (pl -s) red, yellow, dark green, or brown
variety of quartz

jaspers n ▷ jasper

jaundice n (pl -s) disease marked by
yellowness of the skin

jaundiced adj (of an attitude or opinion) bitter
or cynical

jaundices n ▷ jaundice

jaunt n (pl -s) short journey for pleasure

jauntier adj ▷ jaunty

jauntiest adj ▷ jaunty

jauntily adv ▷ jaunty

jaunts n ▷ jaunt

jaunty adj (-tier, -tiest) sprightly and cheerful
> **jauntily** adv

javelin n (pl -s) light spear thrown in sports
competitions

javelins n ▷ javelin

jaw n (pl -s) one of the bones in which the teeth
are set ▶ v (-s, -ing, -ed) (Slang) talk lengthily

> **jawbox** n (**jawboxes**) Jawbox is a
Scots word for a sink. Watch out for
opportunities to form this if someone
else has played either jaw or box, and
if jawbox itself is on the board, you can
earn 27 points just by making it plural
with es. Jawbox scores 25 points.

jawed v ▷ jaw

jawing v ▷ jaw

jaws n, v ▷ jaw ▶ pl n mouth

jay n (pl -s) bird with a pinkish body and blue-
and-black wings

jays n ▷ jay

jaywalker n (pl -s) person who crosses the
road in a careless or dangerous manner
> **jaywalking** n (pl -s)

jaywalkers n ▷ jaywalker
jaywalking n ▷ jaywalker
jaywalkings n ▷ jaywalker

jazy n (jazies). Jazy is an old word for a wig. This is a marvellous word, combining J and Z. If you get this combination and have either an A or a Y, look for the missing letter on the board, as it's highly likely to be there. Jazy scores 23 points.

jazz n (pl -es) kind of music with an exciting rhythm, usu. involving improvisation
jazzes n ▷ jazz
jazzier adj ▷ jazzy
jazziest adj ▷ jazzy
jazzy adj (-zier, -ziest) flashy or showy
jealous adj fearful of losing a partner or possession to a rival ▶ **jealously** adv ▶ **jealousy** n (pl -sies)
jealousies n ▷ jealous
jealously adv ▷ jealous
jealousy n ▷ jealous
jeans pl n casual denim trousers
jeer v (-s, -ing, -ed) scoff or deride ▶ n (pl -s) cry of derision
jeered v ▷ jeer
jeering v ▷ jeer
jeers v, n ▷ jeer
jejune adj simple or naive
jell v (-s, -ing, -ed) form into a jelly-like substance
jelled v ▷ jell
jellied adj prepared in a jelly
jelling v ▷ jell
jells v ▷ jell
jellies n ▷ jelly
jelly n (pl -llies) soft food made of liquid set with gelatine
jellyfish n (pl jellyfish) small jelly-like sea animal
jemmies n ▷ jemmy
jemmy n (pl -mmies) short steel crowbar used by burglars
jennies n ▷ jenny
jenny n (pl -nnies) female ass or wren
jeopardies n ▷ jeopardy
jeopardize v (-izes, -izing, -ized) place in danger
jeopardized n ▷ jeopardy
jeopardizes n ▷ jeopardy
jeopardizing n ▷ jeopardy
jeopardy n (pl -dies) danger
jerboa n (pl -s) small mouselike rodent with long hind legs
jerboas n ▷ jerboa

jerk v (-s, -ing, -ed) move or throw abruptly ▶ n (pl -s) sharp or abruptly stopped movement
jerked v ▷ jerk
jerkily adv ▷ jerky
jerkin n (pl -s) sleeveless jacket
jerkiness n ▷ jerky
jerkinesses n ▷ jerky
jerking v ▷ jerk
jerkins n ▷ jerkin
jerks v, n ▷ jerk
jerky adj sudden or abrupt ▶ **jerkily** adv ▶ **jerkiness** n (pl -s)

jerque v (jerques, jerquing, jerqued), n (jerquer, jerquers, jerquing, jerquings). Jerque means to search a ship for smuggled goods. If you have all the tiles for jerques, jerquer or jerqued, you'll get a 50-point bonus for using all your letters, which will give you a fantastic score. Jerque scores 22 points.

jersey n (pl -s) knitted jumper
jerseys n ▷ jersey
jest n (pl -s) ▶ v (-s, -ing, -ed) joke
jested v ▷ jest
jester n (pl -s) (HIST) professional clown at court
jesters n ▷ jester
jesting v ▷ jest
jests n, v ▷ jest
jet¹ n (pl -s) aircraft driven by jet propulsion ▶ v (-s, jetting, jetted) fly by jet aircraft
jet² n (pl -s) hard black mineral
jetboat n (pl -s) motorboat propelled by a jet of water
jetboats n ▷ jetboat
jets n ▷ jet¹,² ▶ v ▷ jet¹
jetsam n (pl -s) goods thrown overboard to lighten a ship
jetsams n ▷ jetsam
jetted v ▷ jet¹
jetties n ▷ jetty
jetting v ▷ jet¹
jettison v (-s, -ing, -ed) abandon
jettisoned v ▷ jettison
jettisoning v ▷ jettison
jettisons v ▷ jettison
jetty n (pl -ties) small pier

jeu (jeux). Jeu is the French word for **game** or **play**. The plural form, jeux, is a great little word, using both J and X particularly if you can play it on a double- or triple-word square. Jeux scores 18 points.

jewel n (pl -s) precious stone
jeweller n (pl -s) dealer in jewels
jewelleries n ▷ jewellery

jewellers n ▷ jeweller

jewellery n (pl -s) objects decorated with precious stones

jewels n ▷ jewel

jewfish n (pl jewfish) (AUST) freshwater catfish

> **jezail** n (**jezails**). A jezail is a kind of heavy Afghan musket. This word is potentially a very high scorer, as its plural uses seven tiles. If you can play all of these at once, you'll earn the 50-point bonus for a total of 73 points! Jezail scores 22 points.

jib¹ n (pl -s) triangular sail set in front of a mast

jib² v (-s, -bbing, -bbed) (of a horse, person, etc.) stop and refuse to go on

jib³ n (pl -s) projecting arm of a crane or derrick

jibbed v ▷ jib²

jibbing v ▷ jib²

jibe¹ n (pl -s) ▶ v (-jibes, -jibing, -jibed) taunt or jeer

jibed v ▷ jibe¹

jibes n, v ▷ jibe¹

jibing v ▷ jibe¹

jibs n ▷ jib¹,³ ▶ v ▷ jib²

jiffies n ▷ jiffy

jiffy n (pl -ffies) (Informal) very short period of time

jig n (pl -s) type of lively dance ▶ v (-s, -gging, -gged) make jerky up-and-down movements

jigged v ▷ jig

jigging v ▷ jig

jiggle v (-ggles, -ggling, -ggled) move up and down with short jerky movements

jiggled v ▷ jiggle

jiggles v ▷ jiggle

jiggling v ▷ jiggle

jigs n, v ▷ jig

jigsaw n (pl -s) (also jigsaw puzzle) picture cut into interlocking pieces, which the user tries to fit together again

jigsaws n ▷ jigsaw

jihad n (pl -s) Islamic holy war against unbelievers

jihads n ▷ jihad

jilt v (-s, -ing, -ed) leave or reject (one's lover)

jilted v ▷ jilt

jilting v ▷ jilt

jilts v ▷ jilt

jingle n (pl -s) catchy verse or song used in a radio or television advert ▶ v (-les, -ling, -led) (cause to) make a gentle ringing sound

jingled v ▷ jingle

jingles n, v ▷ jingle

jingling v ▷ jingle

jingoism n (pl -s) aggressive nationalism

> jingoistic adj

jingoisms n ▷ jingoism

jingoistic adj ▷ jingoism

jinks pl n boisterous merrymaking

jinn n ▷ jinni

jinni n (pl jinn) spirit in Muslim mythology

jinx n (pl -es) person or thing bringing bad luck ▶ v (-xes, -xing, -xed) be or put a jinx on

jinxed v ▷ jinx

jinxes n, v ▷ jinx

jinxing v ▷ jinx

jitters pl n worried nervousness

jittery adj nervous

jive n (pl -s) lively dance of the 1940s and '50s ▶ v (-ves, -ving, -ved) dance the jive

jived v ▷ jive

jives n, v ▷ jive

jiving v ▷ jive

> **jiz** n (**jizes**). Jiz is an old word for a wig. This is a very useful word for when you find yourself with J and Z but nothing else that looks promising: there will almost certainly be an I on the board around which you can form jiz. Jiz scores 19 points.

> **jizz** n (**jizzes**). A jizz is the combination of characteristics used to identify a bird or plant species. A blank tile is required to form jizz because it contains two Zs. If **jiz** is already on the board, a blank or a blank and ES will earn you 19 or 21 points. Jizz scores 19 points.

> **jo** n (**joes**). Jo is a Scots word for a sweetheart. This is the only two-letter word that starts with J, and is worth remembering for that reason. It's also a good word to form when playing in more than one direction at once. Jo scores 9 points.

job n (pl -s) occupation or paid employment

jobbing adj doing individual jobs for payment

jobless adj, pl n unemployed (people)

jobs n ▷ job

jockey n (pl -s) (professional) rider of racehorses ▶ v (-ys, -ying, -yed) manoeuvre to obtain an advantage

jockeyed v ▷ jockey

jockeying v ▷ jockey

jockeys n, v ▷ jockey

jockstrap n (pl -s) belt with a pouch to support the genitals, worn by male athletes

jockstraps n ▷ jockstrap

jocose [joke-kohss] adj playful or humorous

jocular adj fond of joking > jocularity n (pl

-ties) > **jocularly** adv
jocularities n ▷ jocular
jocularity n ▷ jocular
jocularly adv ▷ jocular
jocund [jok-kund] adj (Lit) merry or cheerful
jodhpurs pl n riding trousers, loose-fitting above the knee but tight below
joey n (pl **-ys**) (AUST) young kangaroo
joeys n ▷ joey
jog v (**-s, -gging, -gged**) run at a gentle pace, esp. for exercise ▶ n (pl **-s**) slow run > **jogger** n (pl **-s**) > **jogging** n (pl **-s**)
jogged v ▷ jog
jogger n ▷ jog
joggers n ▷ jog
jogging n, v ▷ jog
joggings n ▷ jog
joggle v (**-les, -ling, -led**) shake or move jerkily
joggled v ▷ joggle
joggles v ▷ joggle
joggling v ▷ joggle
jogs n, v ▷ jog
join v (**-s, -ing, -ed**) become a member (of) ▶ n (pl **-s**) place where two things are joined
joined v ▷ join
joiner n (pl **-s**) maker of finished woodwork
joineries n ▷ joinery
joiners n ▷ joiner
joinery n (pl **-ries**) joiner's work
joining v ▷ join
joins n, v ▷ join
joint adj shared by two or more ▶ n (pl **-s**) place where bones meet but can move ▶ v (**-s, -ing, -ed**) divide meat into joints > **jointed** adj > **jointly** adv
jointed v, adj ▷ joint
jointing v ▷ joint
jointly adv ▷ joint
joints n, v ▷ joint
joist n (pl **-s**) horizontal beam that helps support a floor or ceiling
joists n ▷ joist
jojoba [hoe-**hoe**-ba] n (pl **-s**) shrub of SW North America whose seeds yield oil used in cosmetics
jojobas n ▷ jojoba
joke n (pl **-s**) thing said or done to cause laughter ▶ v (**-kes, -king, -ked**) make jokes > **jokey** adj > **jokingly** adv
joked v ▷ joke
joker n (pl **-s**) person who jokes
jokers n ▷ joker
jokes n, v ▷ joke
jokey adj ▷ joke
joking v ▷ joke

jokingly adv ▷ joke
jollied v ▷ jolly
jollier adj ▷ jolly
jollies v ▷ jolly
jolliest adj ▷ jolly
jollities n ▷ jolly
jollity n ▷ jolly
jolly adj (**-llier, -lliest**) (of a person) happy and cheerful ▶ v (**-lies, -lying, -lied**) try to keep (someone) cheerful by flattery or coaxing > **jollity** n (pl **-ties**)
jollification n (pl **-s**) merrymaking
jollifications n ▷ jolly
jollying v ▷ jolly
jolt n (pl **-s**) unpleasant surprise or shock ▶ v (**-s, -ing, -ed**) surprise or shock
jolted v ▷ jolt
jolting v ▷ jolt
jolts n, v ▷ jolt
jonquil n (pl **-s**) fragrant narcissus
jonquils n ▷ jonquil
josh v (**-es, -ing, -ed**) (CHIEFLY US) (Slang) tease
joshed v ▷ josh
joshes v ▷ josh
joshing v ▷ josh
jostle v (**-les, -ling, -led**) knock or push against
jostled v ▷ jostle
jostles v ▷ jostle
jostling v ▷ jostle
jot v (**-s, -tting, -tted**) write briefly ▶ n (pl **-s**) very small amount
jotted v ▷ jot
jotting v ▷ jot
jotter n (pl **-s**) notebook
jotters n ▷ jotter
jottings pl n notes jotted down
jots v, n ▷ jot
joule [jool] n (pl **-s**) (PHYSICS) unit of work or energy
joules n ▷ joule
journal n (pl **-s**) daily newspaper or magazine
journalese n (pl **-s**) superficial style of writing, found in some newspapers
journaleses n ▷ journalese
journalism n (pl **-s**) writing in or editing of newspapers and magazines > **journalist** n (pl **-s**) > **journalistic** adj
journalisms n ▷ journalism
journalist n ▷ journalism
journalistic adj ▷ journalism
journalists n ▷ journalism
journals n ▷ journal
journey n (pl **-s**) act or process of travelling from one place to another ▶ v (**-s, -ing, -ed**) travel

journeyed *v* ▷ journey

journeying *v* ▷ journey

journeyman *n* (*pl* **-men**) qualified craftsman employed by another

journeymen *n* ▷ journeyman

journeys *n*, *v* ▷ journey

joust (HIST) *n* (*pl* **-s**) combat with lances between two mounted knights ▶ *v* (**-s**, **-ing**, **-ed**) fight on horseback using lances

jousted *v* ▷ joust

jousting *v* ▷ joust

jousts *n*, *v* ▷ joust

jovial *adj* happy and cheerful > **jovially** *adv* > **joviality** *n* (*pl* **-ties**)

jovialities *n* ▷ jovial

joviality *n* ▷ jovial

jovially *adv* ▷ jovial

jowl[1] *n* (*pl* **-s**) lower jaw

jowl[2] *n* (*pl* **-s**) fatty flesh hanging from the lower jaw

jowls *n* ▷ jowl[1, 2] ▶ *pl n* cheeks

joy *n* (*pl* **-s**) feeling of great delight or pleasure > **joyful** *adj* > **joyless** *adj*

joyful *adj* ▷ joy

joyless *adj* ▷ joy

joyous *adj* extremely happy and enthusiastic

joyride *n* ▷ joyriding

joyrider *n* ▷ joyriding

joyriders *n* ▷ joyriding

joyrides *n* ▷ joyriding

joyriding *n* (*pl* **-s**) driving for pleasure, esp. in a stolen car > **joyride** *n* (*pl* **-s**) > **joyrider** *n* (*pl* **-s**)

joyridings *n* ▷ joyriding

joystick *n* (*pl* **-s**) control device for an aircraft or computer

joysticks *n* ▷ joystick

joys *n* ▷ joy

jubilant *adj* feeling or expressing great joy > **jubilantly** *adv* > **jubilation** *n* (*pl* **-s**)

jubilantly *adv* ▷ jubilant

jubilation *n* ▷ jubilant

jubilations *n* ▷ jubilant

jubilee *n* (*pl* **-s**) special anniversary, esp. 25th (**silver jubilee**) or 50th (**golden jubilee**)

jubilees *n* ▷ jubilee

judder *v* (**-s**, **-ing**, **-ed**) vibrate violently ▶ *n* (*pl* **-s**) violent vibration

juddered *v* ▷ judder

juddering *v* ▷ judder

judders *v*, *n* ▷ judder

judge *n* (*pl* **-s**) public official who tries cases and passes sentence in a court of law ▶ *v* (**-dges**, **-dging**, **-dged**) act as a judge

judged *v* ▷ judge

judgement *n* ▷ judgment

judgements *n* ▷ judgment

judgemental *adj* ▷ judgment

judges *n*, *v* ▷ judge

judging *v* ▷ judge

judgment, judgement *n* (*pl* **-s**) opinion reached after careful thought > **judgmental**, **judgemental** *adj*

judgmental *adj* ▷ judgment

judgments *n* ▷ judgment

judicial *adj* of or by a court or judge > **judicially** *adv*

judicially *adv* ▷ judicial

judiciary *n* (*pl* **-ries**) system of courts and judges

judiciaries *n* ▷ judiciary

judicious *adj* well-judged and sensible > **judiciously** *adv*

judiciously *adv* ▷ judicious

judo *n* sport in which two opponents try to throw each other to the ground

jug *n* (*pl* **-s**) container for liquids, with a handle and small spout

juggernaut *n* (*pl* **-s**) (BRIT) large heavy truck

juggernauts *n* ▷ juggernaut

juggle *v* (**-les**, **-ling**, **-led**) throw and catch (several objects) so that most are in the air at the same time > **juggler** *n* (*pl* **-s**)

juggled *v* ▷ juggle

juggler *n* ▷ juggle

jugglers *n* ▷ juggle

juggles *v* ▷ juggle

juggling *v* ▷ juggle

jugs *n* ▷ jug

jugular *n* (*pl* **-s**) one of three large veins of the neck that return blood from the head to the heart

jugulars *n* ▷ jugular

juice *n* (*pl* **-s**) liquid part of vegetables, fruit, or meat

juices *n* ▷ juice

juicier *adj* ▷ juicy

juiciest *adj* ▷ juicy

juicy *adj* (**-cier**, **-ciest**) full of juice

jujitsu *n* (*pl* **-s**) Japanese art of wrestling and self-defence

jujitsus *n* ▷ jujitsu

juju *n* (*pl* **-s**) W African magic charm or fetish

jujus *n* ▷ juju

jukebox *n* (*pl* **-es**) coin-operated machine on which records, CDs, or videos can be played

jukeboxes *n* ▷ jukebox

julep *n* (*pl* **-s**) sweet alcoholic drink

juleps *n* ▷ julep

jumble *n* (*pl* **-s**) confused heap or state ▶ *v* (**-les**, **-ling**, **-led**) mix in a disordered way

jumbled v ▷ jumble

jumbles n, v ▷ jumble

jumbling v ▷ jumble

jumbo adj (Informal) very large ▶ n (pl -s) (also **jumbo jet**) large jet airliner

jumbos n ▷ jumbo

jumbuck n (pl -s) (AUST) (Old-fashioned slang) sheep

jumbucks n ▷ jumbuck

jump v (-s, -ing, -ed) leap or spring into the air using the leg muscles ▶ n (pl -s) act of jumping

jumped v ▷ jump

jumper n (pl -s) sweater or pullover

jumpers n ▷ jumper

jumpier adj ▷ jumpy

jumpiest adj ▷ jumpy

jumping v ▷ jump

jumpings n ▷ jump

jumps v, n ▷ jump

jumpy adj (-pier, -piest) nervous

junction n (pl -s) place where routes, railway lines, or roads meet

junctions n ▷ junction

juncture n (pl -s) point in time, esp. a critical one

junctures n ▷ juncture

jungle n (pl -s) tropical forest of dense tangled vegetation

jungles n ▷ jungle

junior adj of lower standing ▶ n (pl -s) junior person

juniors n ▷ junior

juniper n (pl -s) evergreen shrub with purple berries

junipers n ▷ juniper

junk[1] n (pl -s) discarded or useless objects

junk[2] n (pl -s) flat-bottomed Chinese sailing boat

junket n (pl -s) excursion by public officials paid for from public funds

junkets n ▷ junket

junkie, junky n (pl -kies) (Slang) drug addict

junkies n ▷ junkie

junks n ▷ junk[1, 2]

junky n ▷ junkie

junta n (pl -s) group of military officers holding power in a country, esp. after a coup

juntas n ▷ junta

juridical adj of law or the administration of justice

juries n ▷ jury

jurisdiction n (pl -s) right or power to administer justice and apply laws

jurisdictions n ▷ jurisdiction

jurisprudence n (pl -s) science or philosophy of law

jurisprudences n ▷ jurisprudence

jurist n (pl -s) expert in law

jurists n ▷ jurist

juror n (pl -s) member of a jury

jurors n ▷ juror

jury n (pl -ries) group of people sworn to deliver a verdict in a court of law

just adv very recently ▶ adj fair or impartial in action or judgment > **justly** adv > **justness** n (pl -s)

justice n (pl -s) quality of being just

justices n ▷ justice

justifiable adj ▷ justify

justifiably adv ▷ justify

justification n ▷ justify

justifications n ▷ justify

justified v ▷ justify

justifies v ▷ justify

justify v (-fies, -fying, -fied) prove right or reasonable > **justifiable** adj > **justifiably** adv > **justification** n (pl -s)

justifying v ▷ justify

justly adv ▷ just

justness n ▷ just

justnesses n ▷ just

jut v (-s, -tting, -tted) project or stick out

jute n (pl -s) plant fibre, used for rope, canvas, etc.

jutes n ▷ jute

juts v ▷ jut

jutted v ▷ jut

jutting v ▷ jut

juvenilia pl n works produced in an author's youth

juvenile adj young ▶ n (pl -s) young person or child

juveniles n ▷ juvenile

juxtapose v (-ses, -sing, -sed) put side by side > **juxtaposition** n (pl -s)

juxtaposed v ▷ juxtapose

juxtaposes v ▷ juxtapose

juxtaposing v ▷ juxtapose

juxtaposition n ▷ juxtapose

juxtapositions n ▷ juxtapose

jynx n (**jynxes**). A jynx is a kind of woodpecker. This unusual word is unique in combining J, Y and Z without using any vowels. Jynx scores 21 points.

Kk

Worth 5 points, K is a valuable tile to have in your rack. However, it's not the most useful tile for the short words that you need when forming words in different directions at the same time. There are only three two-letter words beginning with K: **ka**, **ko** and **ky**. Remembering these will stop you wasting time trying to think of others. There aren't very many three-letter words either, but remember **kak** (11 points), **keg** (8), **ken** (7), **key** (10), **kid** (8), **kin** (7), **kip** (9) and **kit (7)**.

ka n (**kas**). A ka is a supernatural being in ancient Egyptian mythology. Along with **ko** and **ky**, it's one of only three two-letter words starting with K. Ka scores 6 points.

kaftan n (pl **-s**) long loose Eastern garment
　kaftans n ▷ kaftan

kaiser [kize-er] n (pl **-s**) (HIST) German or Austro-Hungarian emperor
　kaisers n ▷ kaiser

kak n (pl **-s**) (S AFR) (Slang) faeces
　kaks n (offensive) ▷ kak

kalashnikov n (pl **-s**) Russian-made automatic rifle
　kalashnikovs n ▷ kalashnikov

kale n (pl **-s**) cabbage with crinkled leaves
　kales n ▷ kale

kaleidoscope n (pl **-s**) tube-shaped toy containing loose coloured pieces reflected by mirrors so that intricate patterns form when the tube is twisted ▷ **kaleidoscopic** adj
　kaleidoscopes n ▷ kaleidoscope
　kaleidoscopic adj ▷ kaleidoscope

kamikaze [kam-mee-**kah**-zee] n (pl **-s**) (in World War II) Japanese pilot who performed a suicide mission ▶ adj (of an action) undertaken in the knowledge that it will kill or injure the person performing it
　kamikazes n ▷ kamikaze

kangaroo n (pl **-s**) Australian marsupial which moves by jumping with its powerful hind legs
　kangaroos n ▷ kangaroo

kaolin n (pl **-s**) fine white clay used to make porcelain and in some medicines
　kaolins n ▷ kaolin

kapok n (pl **-s**) fluffy fibre from a tropical tree, used to stuff cushions etc.

kapoks n ▷ kapok

kaput [kap-**poot**] adj (Informal) ruined or broken

karaoke n (pl **-s**) form of entertainment in which people sing over a prerecorded backing tape
　karaokes n ▷ karaoke

karate n (pl **-s**) Japanese system of unarmed combat using blows with the feet, hands, elbows, and legs
　karates n ▷ karate

karma n (pl **-s**) (BUDDHISM, HINDUISM) person's actions affecting his or her fate in the next reincarnation
　karmas n ▷ karma

karri n (pl **-s**) Australian eucalypt
　karris n ▷ karri

katipo n (pl **-s**) small poisonous New Zealand spider
　katipos n ▷ katipo

kayak n (pl **-s**) Inuit canoe made of sealskins stretched over a frame
　kayaks n ▷ kayak

kebab n (pl **-s**) dish of small pieces of meat grilled on skewers
　kebabs n ▷ kebab

kedgeree n (pl **-s**) dish of fish with rice and eggs
　kedgerees n ▷ kedgeree

keel n (pl **-s**) main lengthways timber or steel support along the base of a ship
　keels n ▷ keel

keen[1] adj (**-er**, **-est**) eager or enthusiastic ▷ **keenly** adv ▷ **keenness** n

keen[2] v (**-s**, **-ing**, **-ed**) wail over the dead
　keened v ▷ keen[2]
　keener adj ▷ keen[1]
　keenest adj ▷ keen[1]
　keening v ▷ keen[2]

keenly *adv* ▷ **keen¹**
keenness *n* ▷ **keen¹**
keens *v* ▷ **keen²**
keep *v* (**-s, -ing, kept**) have or retain possession of ▶ *n* (**-s**) cost of food and everyday expenses
keeper *n* (**-s**) person who looks after animals in a zoo ▶ *n* ▷ **keeper**
keeping *v* ▷ **keep** ▶ *n* (**-s**) care or charge ▶ *n* ▷ **keeping** ▶ *v* ▷ **keep** ▶ *n* ▷ **keep** > **keepsake** *n* (**-s**) gift treasured for the sake of the giver
keepsakes *n* ▷ **keepsake**
keg *n* (*pl* **-s**) small metal beer barrel
kegs *n* ▷ **keg**
kelp *n* (*pl* **-s**) large brown seaweed
kelpie *n* (*pl* **-s**) Australian sheepdog with a smooth coat and upright ears
kelpies *n* ▷ **kelpie**
kelps *n* ▷ **kelp**
kelvin *n* (*pl* **-s**) SI unit of temperature
kelvins *n* ▷ **kelvin**
ken *v* (**-s, -nning, -nned** *or* **kent**) (SCOT) know
kenning *v* ▷ **ken**
kenned *v* ▷ **ken**
kendo *n* (*pl* **-s**) Japanese sport of fencing using wooden staves
kendos *n* ▷ **kendo**
kennel *n* (*pl* **-s**) hutlike shelter for a dog
kennels *n* ▷ **kennel**
kens *v* ▷ **ken**
kent *v* ▷ **ken**
kept *v* ▷ **keep**
keratin *n* (*pl* **-s**) fibrous protein found in the hair and nails
keratins *n* ▷ **keratin**
kerb *n* (*pl* **-s**) edging to a footpath
kerbs *n* ▷ **kerb**
kerchief *n* (*pl* **-s**) piece of cloth worn over the head or round the neck
kerchiefs *n* ▷ **kerchief**
kerfuffle *n* (*pl* **-s**) (*Informal*) commotion or disorder
kerfuffles *n* ▷ **kerfuffle**
kernel *n* (*pl* **-s**) seed of a nut, cereal, or fruit stone
kernels *n* ▷ **kernel**
kerosene *n* (*pl* **-s**) (US, CANADIAN, AUST & NZ) liquid mixture distilled from petroleum and used as a fuel or solvent
kerosenes *n* ▷ **kerosene**
kestrel *n* (*pl* **-s**) type of small falcon
kestrels *n* ▷ **kestrel**
ketch *n* (*pl* **-es**) two-masted sailing ship
ketches *n* ▷ **ketch**
ketchup *n* (*pl* **-s**) thick cold sauce, usu. made of tomatoes

ketchups *n* ▷ **ketchup**
kettle *n* (*pl* **-s**) container with a spout and handle used for boiling water
kettledrum *n* (*pl* **-s**) large bowl-shaped metal drum
kettledrums *n* ▷ **kettledrum**
kettles *n* ▷ **kettle**
key *n* (*pl* **-s**) device for operating a lock by moving a bolt ▶ *adj* of great importance ▶ *v* (**-s, -ing, -ed**) enter (text) using a keyboard
keyboard *n* (*pl* **-s**) set of keys on a piano, computer, etc. ▶ *v* (**-s, -ing, -ed**) enter (text) using a keyboard
keyboarded *v* ▷ **keyboard**
keyboarding *v* ▷ **keyboard**
keyboards *n, v* ▷ **keyboard**
keyed *v* ▷ **key**
keyhole *n* (*pl* **-s**) opening for inserting a key into a lock
keyholes *n* ▷ **keyhole**
keying *v* ▷ **key**
keyings *n* ▷ **key**
keynote *n* (*pl* **-s**) dominant idea of a speech etc.
keynotes *n* ▷ **keynote**
keys *n, v* ▷ **key**
keystone *n* (*pl* **-s**) most important part of a process, organization, etc.
keystones *n* ▷ **keystone**

> **kex** *n* (**kexes**). A kex is a hollow-stemmed plant. This is a great three-letter word, combining K with X. If you have these letters on your rack, you can be confident that there will be, or will soon be, an E on the board, around which you can form kex. Kex scores 14 points.

khaki *adj* dull yellowish-brown ▶ *n* (*pl* **-s**) hard-wearing fabric of this colour
khakis *n* ▷ **khaki**

> **khi** *n* (**khis**). Khi is a letter of the Greek alphabet, also spelt **chi**. This is one of the higher-scoring three-letter words starting with K, and so is worth remembering. Khi scores 10 points.

kibbutz *n* (*pl* **-im**) communal farm or factory in Israel
kibbutzim *n* ▷ **kibbutz**
kick *v* (**-s, -ing, -ed**) drive, push, or strike with the foot ▶ *n* (*pl* **kicks**) thrust or blow with the foot
kickback (*Informal*) *n* (*pl* **-s**) money paid illegally for favours done
kickbacks *n* ▷ **kickback**
kicked *v* ▷ **kick**

kicking n, v ▷ kick

kicks n, v ▷ kick

kid¹ n (pl -s) (Informal) child

kid² v (-s, -dding, -dded) (Informal) tease or deceive (someone)

kidded v ▷ kid²

kidding v ▷ kid²

kiddishnesses n ▷ kid¹,²

kidnap v (-s, -pping, -pped) seize and hold (a person) to ransom > **kidnapper** n (pl -s)

kidnapped n ▷ kidnap

kidnapper n ▷ kidnap

kidnappers n ▷ kidnap

kidnapping n ▷ kidnap

kidnaps n ▷ kidnap

kidney n (pl kidneys) either of the pair of organs that filter waste products from the blood to produce urine

kidneys n ▷ kidney

kids n ▷ kid¹ ▷ v ▷ kid²

kill v (-s, -ing, -ed) cause the death of (Informal) ▶ n (pl -s) act of killing > **killer** n (pl killers)

killed v ▷ kill

killer n ▷ kill

killers n ▷ kill

killing (Informal) adj very tiring ▶ n (pl -s) sudden financial success ▶ v ▷ kill

killings n ▷ killing

killjoy n (pl -s) person who spoils others' pleasure

killjoys n ▷ killjoy

kills v, n ▷ kill

kiln n (pl -s) oven for baking, drying, or processing pottery, bricks, etc.

kilns n ▷ kiln

kilobyte n (pl -s) (COMPUTERS) 1024 units of information

kilobytes n ▷ kilobyte

kilogram, kilogramme n (pl -s) one thousand grams

kilogrammes n ▷ kilogram

kilograms n ▷ kilogram

kilohertz n (pl -es) one thousand hertz

kilohertzes n ▷ kilohertz

kilometre n (pl -s) one thousand metres

kilometres n ▷ kilometre

kilowatt n (pl -s) (ELECTRICITY) one thousand watts

kilowatts n ▷ kilowatt

kilt n (pl -s) knee-length pleated tartan skirt worn orig. by Scottish Highlanders > **kilted** adj

kilted n ▷ kilt

kilts n ▷ kilt

kimono n (pl -s) loose wide-sleeved Japanese robe, fastened with a sash

kimonos n ▷ kimono

kin, kinsfolk n person's relatives collectively > **kinship** (pl -s) ▶ n

kind¹ adj (-er, -est) considerate, friendly, and helpful > **kindness** n (pl -es) > **kindliness** n (pl -es) > **kind-hearted** adj

kind² n (pl -s) class or group with common characteristics

kinder adj ▷ kind¹

kindergarten n (pl -s) class or school for children under six years old

kindergartens n ▷ kindergarten

kindest adj ▷ kind¹

kindhearted adj ▷ kind¹

kindies n ▷ kindy

kindliness n (pl -es) ▷ kind¹

kindlinesses n ▷ kind¹

kindle v (-les, -ling, -led) set (a fire) alight

kindled v ▷ kindle

kindles v ▷ kindle

kindling n (pl -s) dry wood or straw for starting fires ▶ v ▷ kindle

kindly adj having a warm-hearted nature ▶ adv in a considerate way

kindness n (pl -es) ▷ kind¹

kindnesses n ▷ kind¹

kinds n ▷ kind²

kindred adj having similar qualities ▶ n (pl -s) ▷ kin

kindy, kindie n (pl -dies) (AUST & NZ) (Informal) kindergarten

kinetic [kin-**net**-ik] adj relating to or caused by motion

king n (pl kings) male ruler of a monarchy > **kingship** n (pl -s)

kingdom n (pl -s) state ruled by a king or queen

kingdoms n ▷ kingdom

kings n ▷ king

kingship n (pl -s) ▷ king

kingships n ▷ king

kingfisher n (pl -s) small bird, often with a bright-coloured plumage, that dives for fish

kingfishers n ▷ kingfisher

kingpin n (pl -s) most important person in an organization

kingpins n ▷ kingpin

kink n (pl -s) twist or bend in rope, wire, etc.

kinks n ▷ kink

kinky adj (Slang) given to unusual sexual practices

kinships n ▷ kinship

kiosk n (pl -s) small booth selling drinks, cigarettes, newspapers, etc.

kiosks n ▷ kiosk

kip (*Informal*) *n* (*pl* -s) sleep ▶ *v* (-s, -pping, -pped) sleep
  kipped *v* ▷ **kip**

kipper *n* (*pl* -s) cleaned, salted, and smoked herring
  kippers *n* ▷ **kipper**
  kipping *v* ▷ **kip**
  kips *v* ▷ **kip**

kirk *n* (*pl* -s) (SCOT) church
  kirks *n* ▷ **kirk**

kismet *n* (*pl* -s) fate or destiny
  kismets *n* ▷ **kismet**

kiss *v* (-es, -ing, -ed) touch with the lips in affection or greeting ▶ *n* (*pl* -es) touch with the lips

kissagram *n* (*pl* -s) greetings service in which a messenger kisses the person celebrating
  kissagrams *n* ▷ **kissagram**
  kissed *v* ▷ **kiss**

kisser *n* (*pl* -s) (*Slang*) mouth or face
  kissers *n* ▷ **kisser**
  kisses *v*, *n* ▷ **kiss**
  kissing *v* ▷ **kiss**

kist *n* (*pl* -s) (S AFR) large wooden chest
  kists *n* ▷ **kist**

kit *n* (*pl* -s) outfit or equipment for a specific purpose

kitbag *n* (*pl* -s) bag for a soldier's or traveller's belongings
  kitbags *n* ▷ **kitbag**
  kits *n* ▷ **kit**

kitset *n* (*pl* -s) (NZ) unassembled pieces for constructing a piece of furniture

kitchen *n* (*pl* -s) room used for cooking

kitchenette *n* (*pl* -s) small kitchen
  kitchenettes *n* ▷ **kitchenette**
  kitchens *n* ▷ **kitchen**
  kitches *n* ▷ **kitch**

kite *n* (*pl* -s) light frame covered with a thin material flown on a string in the wind
  kites *n* ▷ **kite**

kith *n* (*pl* -s) friends and relatives
  kiths *n* ▷ **kith**

kitsch *n* (*pl* -es) art or literature with popular sentimental appeal

kitten *n* (*pl* -s) young cat

kittenish *adj* lively and flirtatious
  kittens *n* ▷ **kitten**
  kitties *n* ▷ **kitty**

kittiwake *n* (*pl* -s) type of seagull
  kittiwakes *n* ▷ **kittiwake**

kitty *n* (*pl* -ties) communal fund

kiwi *n* (*pl* -s) New Zealand flightless bird with a long beak and no tail
  kiwis *n* ▷ **kiwi**

klaxon *n* (*pl* -s) loud horn used on emergency vehicles as a warning signal
  klaxons *n* ▷ **klaxon**

kleptomania *n* (*pl* -s) compulsive tendency to steal > **kleptomaniac** *n* (*pl* -s)

kleptomaniac *n* (*pl* -s) ▷ **kleptomania**
  kleptomaniacs *n* ▷ **kleptomania**

kloof *n* (*pl* kloofs) (S AFR) mountain pass or gorge
  kloofs *n* ▷ **kloof**

knack *n* (*pl* knacks) skilful way of doing something
  knacks *n* ▷ **knack**

knacker *n* (*pl* -s) (BRIT) buyer of old horses for killing

knackered *adj* (*Slang*) extremely tired
  knackers *n* ▷ **knacker**

knapsack *n* (*pl* -s) soldier's or traveller's bag worn strapped on the back
  knapsacks *n* ▷ **knapsack**

knave *n* (*pl* -s) jack at cards (*Obs*)
  knaves *n* ▷ **knave**

knead *v* (-s, -ing, -ed) work (dough) into a smooth mixture with the hands
  kneaded *v* ▷ **knead**
  kneading *v* ▷ **knead**
  kneads *v* ▷ **knead**

knee *n* (*pl* knees) joint between thigh and lower leg ▶ *v* (-s, -ing, -d) strike or push with the knee

kneecap *n* (*pl* kneecaps) bone in front of the knee ▶ *v* (-pping, -pped) shoot in the kneecap
  kneed *v* ▷ **knee**
  kneeing *v* ▷ **knee**

kneejerk *adj* (of a reply or reaction) automatic and predictable

kneel *v* (-s, -ing, -ed *or* knelt) fall or rest on one's knees
  kneeled, knelt *v* ▷ **kneel**
  kneeling *v* ▷ **kneel**
  kneels *v* ▷ **kneel**
  knees *n*, *v* ▷ **knee**

knell *n* (*pl* -s) sound of a bell, esp. at a funeral or death
  knells *n* ▷ **knell**
  knelt *v* ▷ **kneel**
  knew *v* ▷ **know**

knickerbockers *pl n* loose-fitting short trousers gathered in at the knee

knickers *pl n* woman's or girl's undergarment covering the lower trunk and having legs or legholes

knife *n* (*pl* knives) cutting tool or weapon consisting of a sharp-edged blade with a handle ▶ *v* (-s, -ing, -ed) cut or stab with a

knife
knifed v ▷ knife
knifes v ▷ knife
knifing v ▷ knife
knight n (pl -s) man who has been given a knighthood ▶ v (-s, -ing, -ed) award a knighthood to > **knightly** adj > **knighthood** n (pl -s) honorary title given to a man by the British sovereign
knighted v ▷ knight
knighthoods n ▷ knighthood
knighting v ▷ knight
knights n, v ▷ knight
knit v (-s, -tting, -tted or knit) make (a garment) by interlocking a series of loops in wool or other yarn > **knitting** n (pl -s)
knits v ▷ knit
knitted v ▷ knit
knitting v ▷ knit
knittings n ▷ knit
knitwear n (pl -s) knitted clothes, such as sweaters
knitwears n ▷ knitwear
knives n ▷ knife
knob n (pl -s) rounded projection, such as a switch on a radio
knobblier adj ▷ knobbly
knobbliest adj ▷ knobbly
knobbly adj (-lier, -liest) covered with small bumps
knobkerrie n (pl -s) (S AFR) club with a rounded end
knobkerries n ▷ knobkerrie
knobs n ▷ knob
knock v (-s, -ing, -ed) give a blow or push to ▶ n (pl -s) blow or rap
knockabout adj (of comedy) boisterous
knockdown adj (of a price) very low
knocked v ▷ knock
knocker n (pl -s) metal fitting for knocking on a door
knockers n ▷ knocker
knocking v ▷ knock
knockout n (pl -s) blow that renders an opponent unconscious
knockouts n ▷ knockout
knocks v, n ▷ knock
knoll n (pl -s) small rounded hill
knolls n ▷ knoll
knot n (pl -s) fastening made by looping and pulling tight strands of string, cord, or rope ▶ v (-s, -tting, -tted) tie with or into a knot
knots n ▷ knot
knotted n ▷ knot

knotting n ▷ knot
knotty adj full of knots
know v (-s, -ing, knew, known) be or feel certain of the truth of (information etc.) > **knowable** adj
knowing v ▷ know ▶ adj suggesting secret knowledge
knowingly adv deliberately
knowhow n (pl -s) (Informal) ingenuity, aptitude, or skill
knowhows n ▷ know-how
knowledgable n ▷ knowledgeable
knowledge n (pl -s) facts or experiences known by a person
knowledgeable, knowledgable adj intelligent or well-informed
knowledges n ▷ knowledge
known v ▷ know
knows v ▷ know
knuckle n (pl -s) bone at the finger joint
knuckles n ▷ knuckle

> **ko** n (kos). A ko is a Maori digging-stick. This is worth remembering as, along with ka and ky, it's one of only three two-letter words starting with K. Ko scores 6 points.

koala n (pl -s) tree-dwelling Australian marsupial with dense grey fur
koalas n ▷ koala
kohl n (pl -s) cosmetic powder used to darken the edges of the eyelids
kohls n ▷ kohls
kookaburra n (pl -s) large Australian kingfisher with a cackling cry
kookaburras n ▷ kookaburra
koori n (pl -s) Australian Aborigine
kooris n ▷ koori
kopje, koppie n (pl -s) (S AFR) small hill
kopjes n ▷ kopje
kosher [koh-sher] adj conforming to Jewish religious law, esp. (of food) to Jewish dietary law ▶ n (pl -s) kosher food
koshers n ▷ kosher
kowhai n (pl -s) New Zealand tree with clusters of yellow flowers
kowhais n ▷ kowhai

> **kow** n (kows). A kow is a Scots word for a bunch of twigs. Kow is relatively high-scoring for a three-letter word, and so can be a good one to form when playing in more than one direction. Kow scores 10 points.

kowtow v (-s, -ing, -ed) be servile (towards)
kowtowed v ▷ kowtow

kowtowing v ▷ **kowtow**
kowtows v ▷ **kowtow**
kraal n (pl -s) S African village surrounded by a strong fence
  kraals n ▷ **kraal**
krill n small shrimplike sea creature(s)
krypton n (pl -s) (CHEM) colourless gas present in the atmosphere and used in fluorescent lights
  kryptons n ▷ **krypton**
kudos n (pl -es) fame or credit
  kudoses n ▷ **kudoses**
kugel [koog-el] n (pl -s) (S AFR) rich, fashion-conscious, materialistic young woman
  kugels n ▷ **kugel**
kumara n (pl -s) (NZ) tropical root vegetable with yellow flesh
  kumaras n ▷ **kumara**

kumquat [kumm-kwott] n (pl -s) citrus fruit resembling a tiny orange
  kumquats n ▷ **kumquat**
kurrajong n (pl -s) Australian tree or shrub with tough fibrous bark
  kurrajongs n ▷ **kurrajong**

> **ky** or **kye** n. Ky is a Scots word for **cows.** If you are playing a longer word beginning with K, you may be able to use ky to tag onto a word on the board that ends in Y. Ky scores 9 points.
>
> **kyu** n (**kyus**). A kyu is a beginner's grade in judo. The unusual combination of letters makes this a useful word to have when you have an unpromising set of letters on your rack. Kyu scores 10 points.

Ll

L can be a difficult letter to use well, especially when you need to play short words. Just three two-letter words begin with L: **la**, **li** and **lo**. Knowing this will save you valuable time in a game, especially when you are trying to fit words into a crowded board. There aren't a great number of three-letter words either, but don't forget common words like **lab** (5 points), **law** (6), **lay** (6), **low** (6) and **lye** (6). Try to remember the three-letter words that combine L with X: **lax**, **lex**, **lox** and **lux** (10 points each). These are particularly useful towards the end of a game if you have an X but little opportunity to play it.

la n (**las**). In music, la is the sixth note of a major scale. La is also spelt **lah**. La scores 2 points.

label n (pl **-s**) piece of card or other material fixed to an object to show its ownership, destination, etc. ▶ v (**-s, -lling, -lled**) give a label to
  labels n ▷ label

labia pl n (sing **-bium**) four liplike folds of skin forming part of the female genitals

labial [lay-bee-al] adj of the lips
  labium n ▷ labia

labor n (pl **-s**) (US & AUST) ▷ labour

laboratories n ▷ laboratory

laboratory n (pl **-ies**) building or room designed for scientific research or for the teaching of practical science

laborious adj involving great prolonged effort > **laboriously** adv
  laboriously adv ▷ laborious
  labors n ▷ labor

labour, (US & AUST) **labor** n (pl **-s**) physical work or exertion ▶ v (**-s, -ing, -ed**) work hard

laboured adj uttered or done with difficulty ▶ v ▷ labour
  labourednesses n ▷ laboured

labourer n (pl **-s**) person who labours, esp. someone doing manual work for wages
  labourers n ▷ labourer
  labouring v ▷ labour
  labours n, v ▷ labour

labrador n (pl **-s**) large retriever dog with a usu. gold or black coat
  labradors n ▷ labrador

laburnum n (pl **-s**) ornamental tree with yellow hanging flowers
  laburnums n ▷ laburnum

labyrinth [lab-er-inth] n (pl **-s**) complicated network of passages > **labyrinthine** adj
  labyrinthine adj ▷ labyrinth
  labyrinths n ▷ labyrinth

lace n (pl **-s**) delicate decorative fabric made from threads woven into an open weblike pattern ▶ v (**-ces, -cing, -ced**) fasten with laces
  laced v ▷ lace
  laces n, v ▷ lace
  lacing v ▷ lace

lacerate [lass-er-rate] v (**-tes, -ting, -ted**) tear (flesh) > **laceration** n (pl **-s**)
  lacerated v ▷ lacerate
  lacerates v ▷ lacerate
  lacerating v ▷ lacerate
  lacerations v ▷ lacerate

lachrymose adj tearful

lack n (pl **-s**) shortage or absence of something needed or wanted ▶ v (**-s, -ing, -ed**) need or be short of (something)

lackadaisical adj lazy and careless in a dreamy way
  lacked v ▷ lack

lackey n (pl **-s**) servile follower
  lackeys n ▷ lackey
  lacking v ▷ lack

lacklustre adj lacking brilliance or vitality

laconic adj using only a few words, terse > **laconically** adv
  laconically adv ▷ laconic

lacquer n (pl **-s**) hard varnish for wood or metal
  lacquers n ▷ lacquer

lacrimal adj of tears or the glands which produce them

lacrosse n (pl **-s**) sport in which teams catch

and throw a ball using long sticks with a pouched net at the end
lacks n, v ▷ **lack**
lactation n (pl -s) secretion of milk by female mammals to feed young
　lactations n ▷ **lactation**
lactic adj of or derived from milk
lactose n (pl -s) white crystalline sugar found in milk
　lactoses n ▷ **lactose**
lacuna [lak-kew-na] n (pl -e) gap or missing part, esp. in a document or series
　lacunosities n ▷ **lacuna**
lacy adj fine, like lace
lad n (pl -s) boy or young man
　lads n ▷ **lad**
ladder n (pl -s) frame of two poles connected by horizontal steps used for climbing ▶ v (-s, -ing, -ed) have or cause to have such a line of undone stitches
　laddered v ▷ **ladder**
　laddering v ▷ **ladder**
　ladders n, v ▷ **ladder**
laden adj loaded
ladle n (pl -s) spoon with a long handle and a large bowl, used for serving soup etc. ▶ v (-les, -ling, -led) serve out
　ladled v ▷ **ladle**
　ladles n, v ▷ **ladle**
　ladling v ▷ **ladle**
lady n (pl -dies) woman regarded as having characteristics of good breeding or high rank
ladybird n (pl -s) small red beetle with black spots
　ladybirds n ▷ **ladybird**
ladykiller n (pl -s) (Informal) man who is or thinks he is irresistible to women
　ladykillers n ▷ **ladykiller**
ladylike adj polite and dignified
lag[1] v (-s, -gging, -gged) go too slowly, fall behind ▶ n (pl -s) delay between events
lag[2] v (-s, -gging, -gged) wrap (a boiler, pipes, etc.) with insulating material
lag[3] n (pl -s) (BRIT, AUST & NZ) (Slang) convict
laggard n (pl -s) person who lags behind
　laggards n ▷ **laggard**
lagging n (pl -s) insulating material ▶ v ▷ **lag**[1,2]
　laggings n ▷ **lagging**
lager n (pl -s) light-bodied beer
　lagers n ▷ **lager**
lagoon n (pl -s) body of water cut off from the open sea by coral reefs or sand bars
　lagoons n ▷ **lagoon**
　lags n ▷ **lag**[1,3]
laid v ▷ **lay**[1]

lain v ▷ **lie**[2]
lair n (pl -s) resting place of an animal
　lairs n ▷ **lair**
laird n (pl -s) Scottish landowner
　lairds n ▷ **laird**
laity [lay-it-ee] n (pl -ties) people who are not members of the clergy
　laities n ▷ **laity**
lake[1] n (pl -s) expanse of water entirely surrounded by land > **lakeside** n (pl -s)
lake[2] n (pl -s) red pigment
　lakes n ▷ **lake**[1,2]
　lakesides n ▷ **lake**[1]
lama n (pl -s) Buddhist priest in Tibet or Mongolia
　lamas n ▷ **lama**
lamb n (pl -s) young sheep ▶ v (-s, -ing, -ed) (of sheep) give birth to a lamb or lambs > **lambskin** n (pl -s) > **lambswool** n (pl -s)
lambast, lambaste v (-s, -ing, -ed) beat or thrash
　lambasted v ▷ **lambast**
　lambasting v ▷ **lambast**
　lambasts v ▷ **lambast**
　lambed v ▷ **lamb**
lambent adj (Lit) (of a flame) flickering softly
　lambing v ▷ **lamb**
　lambs n, v ▷ **lamb**
　lambskin v ▷ **lamb**
　lambswool v ▷ **lamb**
lame adj (-er, -est) having an injured or disabled leg or foot ▶ v (-mes, -ming, -med) make lame > **lamely** adv > **lameness** n (pl -s)
lamé [lah-may] n (pl -s) ▶ adj (fabric) interwoven with gold or silver thread
　lamed v ▷ **lame**
　lamely adv ▷ **lame**
　lamenesses n ▷ **lame**
lament v (-s, -ing, -ed) feel or express sorrow (for) ▶ n (pl -s) passionate expression of grief > **lamentation** n (pl -s)
lamentable adj very disappointing
　lamentations v ▷ **lament**
lamented adj grieved for ▶ v ▷ **lament**
　lamenting v ▷ **lament**
　laments v, n ▷ **lament**
　lamer adj ▷ **lame**
　lames v ▷ **lame**
　lamés n ▷ **lamé**
　lamest adj ▷ **lame**
laminate v (-tes, -ting, -ted) make (a sheet of material) by sticking together thin sheets ▶ n (pl -s) laminated sheet > **laminated** adj
　laminated v, adj ▷ **laminate**
　laminates v, n ▷ **laminate**

laminating v ▷ laminate
laming v ▷ lame
lamington n (pl -s) (AUST & NZ) sponge cake coated with a sweet coating
  lamingtons n ▷ lamington
lamp n (pl -s) device which produces light from electricity, oil, or gas > **lampshade** (pl -s) ▶ n
lamppost n (pl -s) post supporting a lamp in the street
  lampposts n ▷ lamppost
  lamps n ▷ lamp
lampoon n (pl -s) humorous satire ridiculing someone ▶ v (-s, -ing, -ed) satirize or ridicule
  lampooned v ▷ lampoon
  lampooning v ▷ lampoon
  lampoons n, v ▷ lampoon
lamprey n (pl -s) eel-like fish with a round sucking mouth
  lampreys n ▷ lamprey
  lampshades n ▷ lamp
lance n (pl -s) long spear used by a mounted soldier ▶ v (-ces, -cing, -ced) pierce (a boil or abscess) with a lancet
  lanced v ▷ lance
lancer n (pl -s) formerly, cavalry soldier armed with a lance
  lancers n ▷ lancer
  lances n, v ▷ lance
  lancing v ▷ lance
lancet n (pl -s) pointed two-edged surgical knife
  lancets n ▷ lancet
land n (pl -s) solid part of the earth's surface ▶ v (-s, -ing, -ed) come or bring to earth after a flight, jump, or fall > **landless** adj
landau [lan-daw] n (pl -s) four-wheeled carriage with two folding hoods
  landaus n ▷ landau
landed adj possessing or consisting of lands ▶ v ▷ land
landfall n (pl -s) ship's first landing after a voyage
  landfalls n ▷ landfall
landing n (pl -s) floor area at the top of a flight of stairs ▶ v ▷ land
  landings n ▷ landing
landlocked adj completely surrounded by land
  lands n, v ▷ land
landlady n (pl -dies) woman who rents out land, houses, etc.
  landladies n ▷ landlady
  landless v ▷ land
landlord n (pl -s) man who rents out land, houses, etc.
  landlords n ▷ landlord

landlubber n (pl -s) person who is not experienced at sea
  landlubbers n ▷ landlubber
landmark n (pl -s) prominent object in or feature of a landscape
  landmarks n ▷ landmark
landscape n (pl -s) extensive piece of inland scenery seen from one place ▶ v (-pes, -ping, -ped) improve natural features of (a piece of land)
  landscaped v ▷ landscape
  landscapes n, v ▷ landscape
  landscaping v ▷ landscape
landslide (also **landslip**) n (pl -s) falling of soil, rock, etc. down the side of a mountain
  landslides n ▷ landslide
  landslip n ▷ landslide
  landslips n ▷ landslide ▶ adj nearest to or facing the land ▶ adv (also **landwards**) towards land
  landwards adv ▷ landward
lane n (pl -s) narrow road
  lanes n ▷ lane
language n (pl -s) system of sounds, symbols, etc. for communicating thought
  languages n ▷ language
languid adj lacking energy or enthusiasm > **languidly** adv
  languidly adv ▷ languid
languish v (-es, -ing, -ed) suffer neglect or hardship
  languished v ▷ languish
  languishes v ▷ languish
  languishing v ▷ languish
languor [lang-ger] n (pl -s) state of dreamy relaxation > **languorous** adj
  languorous n ▷ languor
  languors n ▷ languor
lank adj (-er, -est) (of hair) straight and limp
  lanker adj ▷ lank
  lankest adj ▷ lank
  lankier adj ▷ lanky
  lankiest adj ▷ lanky
lanky adj (-kier, -kiest) ungracefully tall and thin
lanolin n (pl -s) grease from sheep's wool used in ointments etc.
  lanolins n ▷ lanolin
lantana [lan-tay-na] n (pl -s) shrub with orange or yellow flowers, considered a weed in Australia
  lantanas n ▷ lantana
lantern n (pl -s) light in a transparent protective case
  lanterns n ▷ lantern

lanthanum n (pl **-s**) (CHEM) silvery-white metallic element
lanthanums n ▷ lanthanum
lanyard n (pl **-s**) cord worn round the neck to hold a knife or whistle
lanyards n ▷ lanyard
lap¹ n (pl **-s**) part between the waist and knees of a person when sitting
lap² n (pl **-s**) single circuit of a racecourse or track ▶ v (**-s, -pping, -pped**) overtake an opponent so as to be one or more circuits ahead
lap³ v (**-s, -pping, -pped**) (of waves) beat softly against (a shore etc.)
lapel [lap-**pel**] n (pl **-s**) part of the front of a coat or jacket folded back towards the shoulders
lapels n ▷ lapel
lapidary adj of or relating to stones
lapped v ▷ lap²,³
lapping v ▷ lap²,³
laps n ▷ lap¹,² ▶ v ▷ lap²,³
lapse n (pl **-s**) temporary drop in a standard, esp. through forgetfulness or carelessness ▶ v (**-ses, -sing, -sed**) drop in standard > **lapsed** adj
lapsed v ▷ lapse
lapses n, v ▷ lapse
lapsing v ▷ lapse
laptop adj (of a computer) small enough to fit on a user's lap ▶ n (pl **-s**) computer small enough to fit on a user's lap
laptops n ▷ laptop
lapwing n (pl **-s**) plover with a tuft of feathers on the head
lapwings n ▷ lapwing
larboard adj, n (pl **-s**) (Old-fashioned) port (side of a ship)
larboards n ▷ larboard
larcenies n ▷ larceny
larceny n (pl **-nies**) (LAW) theft
larch n (pl **-es**) deciduous coniferous tree
larches n ▷ larch
lard n (pl **-s**) soft white fat obtained from a pig ▶ v (**-s, -ing, -ed**) insert strips of bacon in (meat) before cooking
larded v ▷ lard
larder n (pl **-s**) storeroom for food
larders n ▷ larder
larding v ▷ lard
lards n, v ▷ lard
large adj (**-r, -st**) great in size, number, or extent > **largely** adv > **largish** adj
largely adv ▷ large
larger adj ▷ large
largess n (pl **-es**) ▷ largesse
largesse, largess [lar-**jess**] n (pl **-es**) generous

giving, esp. of money
largesses n ▷ largesse
largest adj ▷ large
largish adj ▷ large
largo n (pl **-s**) ▶ adv (MUSIC) (piece to be played) in a slow and dignified manner
largos n ▷ largo
lariat n (pl **-s**) lasso
lariats n ▷ lariat
lark¹ n (pl **-s**) small brown songbird, skylark
lark² n (pl **-s**) (Informal) harmless piece of mischief or fun
larkishnesses n ▷ lark²
larks n ▷ lark¹,²
larkspur n (pl **-s**) plant with spikes of blue, pink, or white flowers with spurs
larkspurs n ▷ larkspur
larrikin n (pl **-s**) (AUST & NZ) (Old-fashioned slang) mischievous or unruly person
larrikins n ▷ larrikin
larva n (pl **-e**) insect in an immature stage, often resembling a worm > **larval** adj
larval adj ▷ larva
larynges n ▷ larynx
laryngeal adj ▷ larynx
laryngitis n (pl **-ses**) inflammation of the larynx
laryngitises n ▷ laryngitis
larynx n (pl **-nges**) part of the throat containing the vocal cords > **laryngeal** adj
lasagne, lasagna [laz-**zan**-ya] n (pl **-s**) pasta in wide flat sheets
lasagnas n ▷ lasagne
lasagnes n ▷ lasagne
lascivious [lass-**iv**-ee-uss] adj showing or producing sexual desire > **lasciviously** adv
lasciviously adv ▷ lascivious
laser [**lay**-zer] n (pl **-s**) device that produces a very narrow intense beam of light, used for cutting hard materials and in surgery etc.
lasers n ▷ laser
lash¹ n (pl **-es**) eyelash ▶ v (**-es, -ing, -ed**) hit with a whip
lash² v (**-es, -ing, -ed**) fasten or bind tightly with cord etc.
lashed v ▷ lash¹,²
lashes n ▷ lash¹ ▶ v ▷ lash¹,²
lashing v ▷ lash¹,²
lashings pl n (Old-fashioned) large amounts
lass, lassie n (pl **-es, -s**) (SCOT & N ENGLISH) girl
lasses n ▷ lass
lassies n ▷ lass
lassitude n (pl **-s**) physical or mental weariness
lassitudes n ▷ lassitude
lasso [lass-**oo**] n (pl **-s, -es**) rope with a noose for

catching cattle and horses ▶ v (-s, -ing, -ed) catch with a lasso
lassoed v ▷ lasso
lassoes n ▷ lasso
lassoing v ▷ lasso
lassos n, v ▷ lasso
last[1] adj, adv coming at the end or after all others ▶ adj only remaining ▶ n (pl -s) last person or thing > **lastly** adv
last[2] v (-s, -ing, -ed) continue > **lasting** adj
last[3] n (pl -s) model of a foot on which shoes and boots are made or repaired
lasted v ▷ last[2]
lasting v, adj ▷ last[2]
lastly adv ▷ last[1]
lasts n ▷ last[1,3] ▶ v ▷ last[2]
latch n (pl -es) fastening for a door with a bar and lever ▶ v (-es, -ing, -ed) fasten with a latch
latched v ▷ latch
latches n, v ▷ latch
latching v ▷ latch
late adj (-r, -st) after the normal or expected time ▶ adv after the normal or expected time > **lateness** n (pl -es)
lately adv in recent times
latencies n ▷ latent
lateness n ▷ late
latenesses n ▷ late
latent adj hidden and not yet developed > **latency** n (pl -cies)
later adj ▷ late
lateral [lat-ter-al] adj of or relating to the side or sides > **laterally** adv
latest adj ▷ late
latex n (pl -es) milky fluid found in some plants, esp. the rubber tree, used in making rubber
latexes n ▷ latex
lath n (pl -s) thin strip of wood used to support plaster, tiles, etc.
laths n ▷ lath
lathe n (pl -s) machine for turning wood or metal while it is being shaped
lathes n ▷ lathe
lather n (pl -s) froth of soap and water ▶ v (-s, -ing, -ed) make frothy
lathered v ▷ lather
lathering v ▷ lather
lathers n, v ▷ lather
lathery adj (-rier, -riest) frothy
latherier adj ▷ lathery
latheriest adj ▷ lathery
latitude n (pl -s) angular distance measured in degrees N or S of the equator
latitudes n ▷ latitude
latrine n (pl -s) toilet in a barracks or camp

latrines n ▷ latrine
latter adj second of two > **latterly** adv
latter-day adj modern
latterly adv ▷ latter
lattice [lat-iss] n (pl -s) framework of intersecting strips of wood, metal, etc. > **latticed** adj
latticed adj ▷ lattice
lattices n ▷ lattice
laud v (-s, -ing, -ed) praise or glorify > **laudably** adv
laudable adj praiseworthy
laudably adv ▷ laudable
laudanum [lawd-a-num] n (pl -s) opium-based sedative
laudanums n ▷ laudanum
laudatory adj praising or glorifying
lauded v ▷ laud
lauding v ▷ laud
lauds v ▷ laud
laugh v (-s, -ing, -ed) make inarticulate sounds with the voice expressing amusement, merriment, or scorn ▶ n (pl -s) act or instance of laughing
laughable adj ▷ laugh
laughed v ▷ laugh
laughing v ▷ laugh
laughs v, n ▷ laugh
laughter n (pl -s) sound or action of laughing
laughters n ▷ laughter
launch[1] v (-es, -ing, -ed) put (a ship or boat) into the water, esp. for the first time ▶ n (pl -es) launching > **launcher** n (pl -s)
launch[2] n (pl -s) open motorboat
launched v ▷ launch[1]
launchers n ▷ launch[1]
launches v ▷ launch[1] ▶ n ▷ launch[1,2]
launches n ▷ launch[1]
launching v ▷ launch[1]
launder v (-s, -ing, -ed) wash and iron (clothes and linen)
launderette n ® (pl -s) shop with coin-operated washing and drying machines
laundered v ▷ launder
launderettes n ▷ launderette
laundering v ▷ launder
launders v ▷ launder
laundry n (pl -ries) clothes etc. for washing or which have recently been washed
laundries n ▷ laundry
laureate [lor-ee-at] adj (of a poet) appointed to the court of Britain
laurel n (pl -s) glossy-leaved shrub, bay tree ▶ pl wreath of laurel, an emblem of victory or merit

laurels n ▷ laurel
lava n (pl **-e**) molten rock thrown out by volcanoes, which hardens as it cools
  lavae n ▷ lava
lavatory n (pl **-ries**) toilet
  lavatories n ▷ lavatory
lavender n (pl **-s**) shrub with fragrant flowers ▶ adj bluish-purple
  lavenders n ▷ lavender
lavish adj great in quantity or richness ▶ v (**-es, -ing, -ed**) give or spend generously
  > **lavishly** adv
  lavished v ▷ lavish
  lavishes v ▷ lavish
  lavishing v ▷ lavish
  lavishly adv ▷ lavish
law n (pl **-s**) rule binding on a community
  > **lawfully** adv > **lawlessness** n (pl **-es**) > **law-breaker** n (pl **-s**)
lawful adj allowed by law
  lawfully adv ▷ law
lawless adj breaking the law, esp. violently
  lawlessness n ▷ law
  lawlessnesses n ▷ law
lawn[1] n (pl **-s**) area of tended and mown grass
lawn[2] n (pl **-s**) fine linen or cotton fabric
  lawns n ▷ lawn[1,2]
  laws n ▷ law
lawsuit n (pl **-s**) court case brought by one person or group against another
  lawsuits n ▷ lawsuit
lawyer n (pl **-s**) professionally qualified legal expert
  lawyers n ▷ lawyer
lax adj not strict ▶ **laxity** n (pl **-ties**)
laxative n (pl **-s**) ▶ adj (medicine) inducing the emptying of the bowels
  laxatives n ▷ laxative
  laxities n ▷ lax
  laxity n ▷ lax
lay[1] v (**-s, -ing, laid**) cause to lie
  lay[2] v ▷ lie[2]
lay[3] adj of or involving people who are not clergymen
lay[4] n (pl **-s**) short narrative poem designed to be sung
layabout n (pl **-s**) lazy person
  layabouts n ▷ layabout
layer n (pl **-s**) single thickness of some substance, as a cover or coating on a surface ▶ v (**-s, -ing, -ed**) form a layer > **layered** adj
  layered v, adj ▷ layer
  layering v ▷ layer
  layers n, v ▷ layer
layette n (pl **-s**) clothes for a newborn baby

layettes n ▷ layette
laying v ▷ lay[1]
layman n (pl **-men**) person who is not a member of the clergy
  laymen n ▷ layman
layout n (pl **-s**) arrangement, esp. of matter for printing or of a building
  layouts n ▷ layout
  lays v ▷ lay[1] ▶ n ▷ lay[4]
laze v (**-s, -ing, -ed**) be idle or lazy ▶ n (pl **-s**) time spent lazing
  lazed v ▷ laze
  lazes v, n ▷ laze
  lazily adv ▷ lazy
  laziness adv ▷ lazy
  lazinesses adv ▷ lazy
  lazing v ▷ laze
lazy adj (**-zier, -ziest**) not inclined to work or exert oneself > **lazily** adv > **laziness** n (pl **-s**)
lea n (pl **-s**) (Poetic) meadow
  leas n ▷ lea
leach v (**-es, -ing, -ed**) remove or be removed from a substance by a liquid passing through it
  leached v ▷ leach
  leaches v ▷ leach
  leaching v ▷ leach
lead[1] v (**-s, -ing, led**) guide or conduct ▶ n (pl **-s**) first or most prominent place ▶ adj acting as a leader or lead
lead[2] n (pl **-s**) soft heavy grey metal
leaded adj (of windows) made from many small panes of glass held together by lead strips
leaden adj heavy or sluggish
leader n (pl **-s**) person who leads > **leadership** n (pl **-s**)
  leaders n ▷ leader
  leaderships n ▷ leader
leading adj principal
  leads n ▷ lead[1,2] ▶ v ▷ lead[1]
leaf n (pl **leaves**) flat usu. green blade attached to the stem of a plant > **leafy** (**-fier, -fiest**) ▶ adj > **leafless** adj
  leafier adj ▷ leaf
  leafiest adj ▷ leaf
  leafless adj ▷ leaf
  leaflessnesses n ▷ leaf
leaflet n (pl **-s**) sheet of printed matter for distribution
  leaflets n ▷ leaflet
  leafy adj ▷ leaf
league[1] n (pl **-s**) association promoting the interests of its members
league[2] n (Obs) measure of distance, about

three miles

leagues n ▷ **league**[1,2]

leak n (pl **-s**) hole or defect that allows the escape or entrance of liquid, gas, radiation, etc. ▶ v (**-s, -ing, -ed**) let liquid etc. in or out > **leaky** (**-kier, -kiest**) ▶ adj

leakage n (pl **-s**) act or instance of leaking

leakages n ▷ **leakage**

leaked v ▷ **leak**

leakier adj ▷ **leak**

leakiest adj ▷ **leak**

leaking v ▷ **leak**

leaks n, v ▷ **leak**

leaky adj (**-kier, -kiest**) ▷ **leak**

lean[1] v (**-ing, -ed** or **leant**) rest against

lean[2] adj (**-er, -est**) thin but healthy-looking ▶ n (pl **-s**) lean part of meat ▶ **leanness** n (pl **-es**)

leaner adj ▷ **lean**

leanest adj ▷ **lean**

leaning n (pl **-s**) tendency ▶ v ▷ **lean**[1]

leanings n ▷ **leaning**

leanness n ▷ **lean**[2]

leannesses n ▷ **lean**[2]

leans v, n ▷ **lean**[1]

leant n ▷ **lean**[1]

leap v (**-s, -ing, leapt** or **-ed**) make a sudden powerful jump ▶ n (pl **-s**) sudden powerful jump

leaped v ▷ **leap**

leapfrog n (pl **-s**) game in which a player vaults over another bending down

leapfrogs n ▷ **leapfrog**

leaping v ▷ **leap**

leaps v, n ▷ **leap**

leapt v ▷ **leap**

learn v (**-s, -ing, -ed** or **learnt**) gain skill or knowledge by study, practice, or teaching > **learner** n (pl **-s**)

learned adj erudite, deeply read

learner n ▷ **learn**

learners n ▷ **learn**

learning n (pl **-s**) knowledge got by study ▶ v ▷ **learn**

learnings n ▷ **learning**

lease n (pl **-s**) contract by which land or property is rented for a stated time by the owner to a tenant ▶ v (**-ses, -sing, -sed**) let or rent by lease > **leaseholder** n (pl **-s**)

leasehold n, adj (land or property) held on lease

leaseholder n ▷ **lease**

leaseholders n ▷ **lease**

leaseholds n ▷ **leasehold**

leased v ▷ **lease**

leases n, v ▷ **lease**

leash n (pl **-es**) lead for a dog

leashes n ▷ **leash**

leasing v ▷ **lease**

least adj ▷ **little** smallest ▶ n smallest one ▶ adv in the smallest degree

leather n (pl **-s**) material made from specially treated animal skins ▶ adj made of leather ▶ v (**-s, -ing, -ed**) beat or thrash

leathered v ▷ **leather**

leatherier adj ▷ **leathery**

leatheriest adj ▷ **leathery**

leathering v ▷ **leather**

leathers n, v ▷ **leather**

leathery adj (**-rier, -riest**) like leather, tough

leave[1] v (**-s, -ing, left**) go away from

leave[2] n (pl **-s**) permission to be absent from work or duty

leaven [lev-ven] n substance that causes dough to rise ▶ v (**-s, -ing, -ed**) raise with leaven

leavens v ▷ **leaven**

leavening v ▷ **leaven**

leavened v ▷ **leaven**

leaves v ▷ **leave**

leaving v ▷ **leave**

lecher n (pl **-s**) man who has or shows excessive sexual desire > **lechery** n (pl **-ries**)

lecheries n ▷ **lechery**

lecherous [letch-er-uss] adj (of a man) having or showing excessive sexual desire

lechers n ▷ **lecher**

lectern n (pl **-s**) sloping reading desk, esp. in a church

lecterns n ▷ **lectern**

lecture n (pl **-s**) informative talk to an audience on a subject ▶ v (**-s, -ing, -ed**) give a talk

lectured v ▷ **lecture**

lecturer n (pl **-s**) person who lectures, esp. in a university or college

lecturers n ▷ **lecturer**

lectures n, v ▷ **lecture**

lectureship n (pl **-s**) appointment as a lecturer

lectureships n ▷ **lectureship**

lecturing v ▷ **lecture**

ledge n (pl **-s**) narrow shelf sticking out from a wall

ledger n (pl **-s**) book of debit and credit accounts of a firm

ledgers n ▷ **ledger**

ledges n ▷ **ledge**

lee n (pl **-s**) sheltered part or side ▶ adv towards this side

leech n (pl **-es**) species of bloodsucking worm

leeches n ▷ **leech**

leek n (pl **-s**) vegetable of the onion family with

a long bulb and thick stem
leeks n ▷ leek

leer v (**-s, -ing, -ed**) look or grin at in a sneering or suggestive manner ▶ n (pl **-s**) sneering or suggestive look or grin
  leered v ▷ leer
  leerier adj ▷ leery
  leeriest adj ▷ leery
  leering v ▷ leer
  leers v, n ▷ leer

leery adj (Informal) (**-rier, -riest**) suspicious or wary (of)

lees pl n sediment of wine ▶ n ▷ lee

leeward adj, n (pl **-s**) (on) the lee side
  leewards n ▷ leeward

leeway n (pl **-s**) room for free movement within limits
  leeways n ▷ leeway

left[1] adj of the side that faces west when the front faces north ▶ adv on or towards the left ▶ n (pl **-s**) left hand or part

left[2] v ▷ leave[1]

leftist n (pl **-s**) ▶ adj (person) of the political left
  leftists n ▷ leftist

leftover n (pl **-s**) unused portion of food or material
  leftovers n ▷ leftover
  lefts n ▷ left[1]

leg n (pl **-s**) one of the limbs on which a person or animal walks, runs, or stands
  legacies n ▷ legacy

legacy n (pl **-cies**) thing left in a will

legal adj established or permitted by law > **legally** adv > **legality** n (pl **-ties**) > **legalization** n (pl **-s**)
  legalities n ▷ legal
  legality n ▷ legal
  legalization n ▷ legal
  legalizations n ▷ legal

legalize v (**-zes, -zing, -zed**) make legal
  legalized adv ▷ legalize
  legalizes adv ▷ legalize
  legalizing adv ▷ legalize
  legally adv ▷ legal

legate n (pl **-s**) messenger or representative, esp. from the Pope

legatee n (pl **-s**) recipient of a legacy
  legatees n ▷ legatee
  legates n ▷ legate

legation n (pl **-s**) diplomatic minister and his staff
  legations n ▷ legation

legato [leg-**ah**-toe] n (pl **-s**), adv (MUSIC) (piece to be played) smoothly
  legatos n ▷ legato

legend n (pl **-s**) traditional story or myth

legendary adj famous
  legends n ▷ legend

legerdemain [lej-er-de-**main**] n (pl **-s**) sleight of hand
  legerdemains n ▷ legerdemain
  leggier adj ▷ leggy
  leggiest adj ▷ leggy

leggings pl n covering of leather or other material for the legs

leggy adj (**-gier, -giest**) having long legs
  legibilities n ▷ legible
  legibility n ▷ legible

legible adj easily read > **legibility** n (pl **-ties**) > **legibly** adv
  legibly adv ▷ legible

legion n (pl **-s**) large military force > **legionary** adj, n (pl **-ries**)
  legionaries n ▷ legion
  legionary adj, n ▷ legion

legionnaire n (pl **-s**) member of a legion
  legionnaires n ▷ legionnaire
  legions n ▷ legion

legislate v (**-tes, -ting, -ted**) make laws > **legislative** adj
  legislated v ▷ legislate
  legislates v ▷ legislate
  legislating v ▷ legislate

legislation n (pl **-s**) legislating
  legislations n ▷ legislation
  legislative v ▷ legislate

legislator n (pl **-s**) maker of laws
  legislators n ▷ legislator

legislature n (pl **-s**) body of people that makes, amends, or repeals laws
  legislatures n ▷ legislature
  legitimacies n ▷ legitimate
  legitimacy n ▷ legitimate

legitimate adj authorized by or in accordance with law ▶ v (**-tes, -ting, -ted**) make legitimate > **legitimacy** n (pl **-cies**) > **legitimately** adv
  legitimated v ▷ legitimate
  legitimately adv ▷ legitimate
  legitimates v ▷ legitimate
  legitimating v ▷ legitimate

legitimize v (**-zes, -zing, -zed**) make legitimate, legalize > **legitimization** n (pl **-s**)
  legitimization n ▷ legitimize
  legitimizations n ▷ legitimize
  legitimized v ▷ legitimize
  legitimizes v ▷ legitimize
  legitimizing v ▷ legitimize

legless adj without legs
  legs n ▷ leg

leguaan [leg-oo-ahn] *n* (*pl* **-s**) large S African
lizard
  leguaans *n* ▷ leguaan

legume *n* (*pl* **-s**) pod of a plant of the pea or
bean family ▶ *pl* peas or beans
  legumes *n* ▷ legume

leguminous *adj* (of plants) pod-bearing

lei *n* (*pl* **-s**) (in Hawaii) garland of flowers
  leis *n* ▷ lei

leisure *n* (*pl* **-s**) time for relaxation or hobbies

leisured *adj* with plenty of spare time

leisurely *adj* deliberate, unhurried ▶ *adv* slowly
  leisures *n* ▷ leisure

leitmotif [lite-mote-eef] *n* (*pl* **-s**) (MUSIC)
recurring theme associated with a person,
situation, or thought
  leitmotifs *n* ▷ leitmotif

lekker *adj* (S AFR) (*Slang*) attractive or nice

lemming *n* (*pl* **-s**) rodent of arctic regions,
reputed to run into the sea and drown during
mass migrations
  lemmings *n* ▷ lemming

lemon *n* (*pl* **-s**) yellow oval fruit that grows on
trees ▶ *adj* pale-yellow

lemonade *n* (*pl* **-s**) lemon-flavoured soft drink,
often fizzy
  lemonades *n* ▷ lemonade
  lemons *n* ▷ lemon

lemur *n* (*pl* **-s**) nocturnal animal like a small
monkey, found in Madagascar
  lemurs *n* ▷ lemur

lend *v* (**-s**, **-ing**, **lent**) give the temporary use of
> **lender** *n* (*pl* **-s**)
  lending *v* ▷ lend
  lender *n* ▷ lend
  lenders *n* ▷ lend
  lends *v* ▷ lend

length *n* (*pl* **-s**) extent or measurement from
end to end > **lengthily** *adv* > **lengthways**,
lengthwise *adj*, *adv*

lengthen *v* (**-s**, **-ing**, **-ed**) make or become
longer
  lengthened *v* ▷ lengthen
  lengthening *v* ▷ lengthen
  lengthens *v* ▷ lengthen
  lengthier *adj* ▷ length
  lengthiest *adj* ▷ length
  lengthily *adv* ▷ length
  lengths *n* ▷ length
  lengthways *adj*, *adv* ▷ length
  lengthwise *adj*, *adv* ▷ lengthen

lengthy *adj* (**-thier**, **-thiest**) very long or
tiresome

leniencies *n* ▷ lenient

leniency *n* ▷ lenient

lenient [lee-nee-ent] *adj* tolerant, not strict or
severe > **leniency** *n* (*pl* **-cies**) > **leniently** *adv*
  leniently *adv* ▷ lenient

lens *n* (*pl* **-es**) piece of glass or similar material
with one or both sides curved, used to bring
together or spread light rays in cameras,
spectacles, telescopes, etc.
  lenses *n* ▷ lens

lent *v* ▷ lend

lentil *n* (*pl* **-s**) edible seed of a leguminous
Asian plant
  lentils *n* ▷ lentil

lento *n* (*pl* **-tos**), *adv* (MUSIC) (piece to be played)
slowly
  lentos *n* ▷ lento
  Lents *n* ▷ Lent

leonine *adj* like a lion

leopard *n* (*pl* **-s**) large spotted carnivorous
animal of the cat family
  leopards *n* ▷ leopard

leotard *n* (*pl* **-s**) tight-fitting garment covering
the upper body, worn for dancing or exercise
  leotards *n* ▷ leotard

leper *n* (*pl* **-s**) person suffering from leprosy
  lepers *n* ▷ leper

lepidoptera *pl n* order of insects with four
wings covered with fine gossamer scales, as
moths and butterflies

lepidopterist *n* (*pl* **-s**) person who studies or
collects butterflies or moths
  lepidopterists *n* ▷ lepidopterist

leprechaun *n* (*pl* **-s**) mischievous elf of Irish
folklore
  leprechauns *n* ▷ leprechaun

leprosy *n* (*pl* **-sies**) disease attacking the
nerves and skin, resulting in loss of feeling in
the affected parts > **leprous** *adj*
  leprosies *n* ▷ leprosy
  leprous *adj* ▷ leprosy

lesbian *n* (*pl* **-s**) homosexual woman ▶ *adj* of
homosexual women > **lesbianism** *n* (*pl* **-s**)
  lesbians *n* ▷ lesbian
  lesbianisms *n* ▷ lesbian

lesion *n* (*pl* **-s**) structural change in an organ of
the body caused by illness or injury
  lesions *n* ▷ lesion

less *adj* smaller in extent, degree, or duration
▷ **little** ▶ *pron* smaller part or quantity ▶ *adv*
to a smaller extent or degree ▶ *prep* after
deducting, minus

lessee *n* (*pl* **-s**) person to whom a lease is
granted
  lessees *n* ▷ lessee

lessen *v* (**-s**, **-ing**, **-ed**) make or become smaller
or not as much

lessened v ▷ lessen

lessening v ▷ lessen

lessens v ▷ lessen

lesser adj not as great in quantity, size, or worth

lesson n (pl -s) single period of instruction in a subject

lessons n ▷ lesson

lest conj so as to prevent any possibility that

let¹ v (-s, -tting, let) allow, enable, or cause

let² n (pl -s) (TENNIS) minor infringement or obstruction of the ball requiring a replay of the point

letdown n (pl -s) disappointment

letdowns n ▷ letdown

lets v ▷ let¹ ▶ n ▷ let²

lethal adj deadly

lethargic adj ▷ lethargy

lethargically adv ▷ lethargy

lethargies n ▷ lethargy

lethargy n (pl -gies) sluggishness or dullness > **lethargic** adj > **lethargically** adv

letter n (pl -s) written message, usu. sent by post ▶ pl literary knowledge or ability > **lettering** n (pl -s)

lettered adj learned

letterhead n (pl -s) printed heading on stationery giving the sender's name and address

letterheads n ▷ letterhead

lettering n ▷ letter

letterings n ▷ letter

letters n ▷ letter

letting v ▷ let¹

lettuce n (pl -s) plant with large green leaves used in salads

lettuces n ▷ lettuce

leucocyte [loo-koh-site] n (pl -s) white blood cell

leucocytes n ▷ leucocyte

leukaemia [loo-kee-mee-a] n (pl -s) disease caused by uncontrolled overproduction of white blood cells

leukaemias n ▷ leukaemia

levee n (pl -s) (US) natural or artificial river embankment

levees n ▷ levee

level adj (-llest, -ller) horizontal ▶ v (-s, -lling, -lled, -ller) make even or horizontal ▶ n (pl -s) horizontal line or surface

levelled v ▷ level

leveller v ▷ level

levellest adj ▷ level

levelling v ▷ level

levels v, n ▷ level

lever n (pl -s) handle used to operate

machinery ▶ v (-s, -ing, -ed) prise or move with a lever

leverage n (pl -s) action or power of a lever

leverages n ▷ leverage

levered v ▷ lever

levering v ▷ lever

levers n, v ▷ lever

leveret [lev-ver-it] n (pl -s) young hare

leverets n ▷ leveret

leviathan [lev-vie-ath-an] n (pl -s) sea monster

leviathans n ▷ leviathan

levitate v (-tes, -ting, -ted) rise or cause to rise into the air

levitated v ▷ levitate

levitates v ▷ levitate

levitating v ▷ levitate

levitation n (pl -s) raising of a solid body into the air supernaturally

levitations n ▷ levitation

levities n ▷ levity

levity n (pl -ties) inclination to make a joke of serious matters

levy [lev-vee] v (-vies, -ing, -vied) impose and collect (a tax) ▶ n (pl -vies) imposition or collection of taxes

levied v ▷ levy

levies v, n ▷ levy

levying v ▷ levy

lewd adj (-er, -est) lustful or indecent > **lewdly** adv > **lewdness** n (pl -es)

lewder adj ▷ lewd

lewdest adj ▷ lewd

lewdly adv ▷ lewd

lewdness n ▷ lewd

lewdnesses n ▷ lewd

lex (**leges**). A lex is a system or body of laws. This is a really handy word when you have L and X, as there is likely to be an E available on the board. Lex scores 10 points.

lexical adj relating to the vocabulary of a language

lexicographer n (pl -s) writer of dictionaries

lexicographers n ▷ lexicographer

lexicography n ▷ lexicon

lexicographies n ▷ lexicon

lexicon n (pl -s) dictionary > **lexicography** n (pl -phies)

lexicons n ▷ lexicon

li n (**lis**). The li is a Chinese unit of length. This low-scoring word is worth knowing for when you want to form words in more than one direction at the same time. Li scores 2 points.

liability n (pl -ties) hindrance or disadvantage

liable *adj* legally obliged or responsible

liaise *v* (**-ses, -sing, -sed**) establish and maintain communication (with)
 liaised *v* ▷ liaise
 liaises *v* ▷ liaise
 liaising *v* ▷ liaise

liaison *n* (*pl* **-s**) communication and contact between groups
 liaisons *n* ▷ liaison

liana *n* (*pl* **-s**) climbing plant in tropical forests
 lianas *n* ▷ liana

liar *n* (*pl* **-s**) person who tells lies
 liars *n* ▷ liar

libation [lie-**bay**-shun] *n* (*pl* **-s**) drink poured as an offering to the gods
 libations *n* ▷ libation

libel *n* (*pl* **-s**) published statement falsely damaging a person's reputation ▶ *v* (**-s, -lling, -lled**) falsely damage the reputation of (someone) ▷ **libellous** *adj*
 libelled *v* ▷ libel
 libelling *v* ▷ libel
 libellous *adj* ▷ libel
 libels *n, v* ▷ libel

liberal *adj* having social and political views that favour progress and reform ▶ *n* (*pl* **-s**) person who has liberal ideas or opinions ▷ **liberally** *adv* ▷ **liberalization** *n* (*pl* **-s**)

liberalism *n* (*pl* **-s**) belief in democratic reforms and individual freedom
 liberalisms *n* ▷ liberalism
 liberalities *n* ▷ liberality

liberality *n* (*pl* **-ties**) generosity
 liberalization *n* ▷ liberal
 liberalizations *n* ▷ liberal

liberalize *v* (**-zes, -zing, -zed**) make (laws, a country, etc.) less restrictive
 liberalized *v* ▷ liberalize
 liberalizes *v* ▷ liberalize
 liberalizing *v* ▷ liberalize
 liberally *adv* ▷ liberal
 liberals *n* ▷ liberal

liberate *v* (**-tes, -ting, -ted**) set free ▷ **liberation** *n* (*pl* **-s**) ▷ **liberator** *n* (*pl* **-s**)
 liberated *v* ▷ liberate
 liberates *v* ▷ liberate
 liberating *v* ▷ liberate
 liberation *n* ▷ liberate
 liberations *n* ▷ liberate
 liberator *n* ▷ liberate
 liberators *n* ▷ liberate

libertarian *n* (*pl* **-s**) believer in freedom of thought and action ▶ *adj* having such a belief
 libertarians *n* ▷ libertarian

libertine [lib-er-teen] *n* (*pl* **-s**) morally dissolute person
 libertines *n* ▷ libertine
 liberties *n* ▷ liberty

liberty *n* (*pl* **-ties**) freedom

libidinous *adj* lustful

libido [lib-**ee**-doe] *n* (*pl* **-s**) psychic energy
 libidos *n* ▷ libido

librarian *n* (*pl* **-s**) keeper of or worker in a library ▷ **librarianship** *n* (*pl* **-s**)
 librarians *n* ▷ librarian
 librarianship *n* ▷ librarian
 librarianships *n* ▷ librarian
 libraries *n* ▷ library

library *n* (*pl* **-ries**) room or building where books are kept
 libretti *n* ▷ libretto
 librettist *n* ▷ libretto
 librettists *n* ▷ libretto

libretto *n* (*pl* **-ttos, -tti**) words of an opera ▷ **librettist** *n* (*pl* **-s**)
 librettos *n* ▷ libretto
 lice *n* ▷ louse

licence *n* (*pl* **-s**) document giving official permission to do something
 licences *n* ▷ licence

license *v* (**-ses, -sing, -sed**) grant a licence to ▷ **licensed** *adj*
 licensed *v, adj* ▷ license

licensee *n* (*pl* **-s**) holder of a licence
 licensees *n* ▷ licensee
 licenses *v* ▷ license
 licensing *v* ▷ license

licentiate *n* (*pl* **-s**) person licensed as competent to practise a profession
 licentiates *n* ▷ licentiate

licentious *adj* sexually unrestrained or promiscuous

lichen *n* (*pl* **-s**) small flowerless plant forming a crust on rocks, trees, etc.
 lichens *n* ▷ lichen

licit *adj* lawful, permitted
 licitnesses *n* ▷ licit

lick *v* (**-s, -ing, -ed**) pass the tongue over ▶ *n* (*pl* **-s**) licking
 licked *v* ▷ lick
 licking *v* ▷ lick
 licks *v, n* ▷ lick

licorice *n* (*pl* **-s**) ▷ liquorice
 licorices *n* ▷ licorice

lid *n* (*pl* **-s**) movable cover
 lids *n* ▷ lid

lido [**lee**-doe] *n* (*pl* **-s**) open-air centre for swimming and water sports
 lidos *n* ▷ lido

lie¹ *v* (**-s, lying, lied**) make a deliberately false

statement ▶ n (pl -s) deliberate falsehood
lie² v (-s, lying, lay, lain) place oneself or be in a horizontal position ▶ n (pl -s) way something lies
  lied¹ v ▷ **lie¹**
lied² [leed] n (pl **lieder**) (MUSIC) setting for voice and piano of a romantic poem
liege [leej] adj bound to give or receive feudal service ▶ n (pl -s) lord
  lieges n ▷ **liege**
lien n (pl -s) (LAW) right to hold another's property until a debt is paid
  liens n ▷ **lien**
  lies v, n ▷ **lie¹,²**
lieutenant [lef-ten-ant] n (pl -s) junior officer in the army or navy
  lieutenants n ▷ **lieutenant**
life n (pl **lives**) state of living beings, characterized by growth, reproduction, and response to stimuli > **lifelike** adj
lifeboat n (pl -s) boat used for rescuing people at sea
  lifeboats adj ▷ **lifeboat**
lifeless adj dead
  lifelike adj ▷ **life**
lifeline n (pl -s) means of contact or support
  lifelines n ▷ **lifeline**
lifelong adj lasting all of a person's life
lifestyle n (pl -s) particular attitudes, habits, etc.
  lifestyles n ▷ **lifestyle**
lifetime n (pl -s) length of time a person is alive
  lifetimes n ▷ **lifetime**
lift v (**lifts, lifting, lifted**) move upwards in position, status, volume, etc. ▶ n (pl **lifts**) cage raised and lowered in a vertical shaft to transport people or goods
liftoff n moment a rocket leaves the ground
  lifts v ▷ **lift**
  lifting v ▷ **lift**
  lifted v ▷ **lift**
  lifts n ▷ **lift**
ligament n (pl -s) band of tissue joining bones
  ligaments n ▷ **ligament**
ligature n (pl -s) link, bond, or tie
  ligatures n ▷ **ligature**
light¹ n (pl -s) electromagnetic radiation by which things are visible ▶ pl traffic lights ▶ adj bright ▶ v (-s, -ing, lit) ignite
light² adj (-er, -est) not heavy, weighing relatively little ▶ adv with little equipment or luggage ▶ v (-s, -ing, -ed, lit) (esp. of birds) settle after flight > **lightly** adv > **lightness** n (pl -s)
  lighted v ▷ **light²**

lighten¹ v (-s, -ing, -ed) make less dark
lighten² v (-s, -ing, -ed) make less heavy or burdensome
  lightened v ▷ **lighten¹,²**
  lightening v ▷ **lighten¹,²**
  lightens v ▷ **lighten¹,²**
  lighter adj ▷ **light²**
  lightest adj ▷ **light²**
lighthouse n (pl -s) tower with a light to guide ships
  lighthouses n ▷ **lighthouse**
lighting n (pl -s) apparatus for and use of artificial light in theatres, films, etc. ▶ v ▷ **light¹,²**
  lightings n ▷ **lighting**
lighter¹ n (pl -s) device for lighting cigarettes etc.
lighter² n (pl -s) flat-bottomed boat for unloading ships
  lighters n ▷ **lighter¹,²**
  lightly adv ▷ **light²**
  lightness n ▷ **light²**
  lightnesses n ▷ **light²**
lightning n (pl -s) visible discharge of electricity in the atmosphere ▶ adj fast and sudden
  lightnings n ▷ **lightning**
lights pl n lungs of animals as animal food ▶ n ▷ **light¹** ▶ v ▷ **light¹,²**
lightweight n (pl -s) ▶ adj (person) of little importance
  lightweights n ▷ **lightweight**
ligneous adj of or like wood
lignite [lig-nite] n (pl -s) woody textured rock used as fuel
  lignites n ▷ **lignite**
like¹ prep, conj adj, pron indicating similarity, comparison, etc.
like² v (-s, -ing, -ed) find enjoyable > **likeable, likable** adj > **liking** n fondness
  liked v ▷ **like**
liken v (-s, -ing, -ed) compare
  likelier adj ▷ **likely**
  likeliest adj ▷ **likely**
likelihood n (pl -s) probability
  likelihoods n ▷ **likelihood**
likely adj (-lier, -liest) tending or inclined ▶ adv probably
  likened v ▷ **liken**
likeness n resemblance
  likening v ▷ **liken**
  likens v ▷ **liken**
  likes v ▷ **like**
likewise adv similarly
  liking v ▷ **like**

lilac *n* (*pl* **-s**) shrub with pale mauve or white flowers ▶ *adj* light-purple

lilacs *n* ▷ lilac

lilt *n* (*pl* **-s**) pleasing musical quality in speaking > **lilting** *adj*

lilting *adj* ▷ lilt

lilts *n* ▷ lilt

lily *n* (*pl* **-lies**) plant which grows from a bulb and has large, often white, flowers

limb *n* (*pl* **-s**) arm, leg, or wing

limbs *n* ▷ limb

limber *adj* pliant or supple

limbo *n* (*pl* **-s**) West Indian dance in which dancers lean backwards to pass under a bar

limbos *n* ▷ limbo

lime¹ *n* (*pl* **-s**) calcium compound used as a fertilizer or in making cement

lime² *n* (*pl* **-s**) small green citrus fruit

lime³ *n* (*pl* **-s**) deciduous tree with heart-shaped leaves and fragrant flowers

limelight *n* (*pl* **-s**) glare of publicity

limelights *n* ▷ lime

limerick [lim-mer-ik] *n* (*pl* **-s**) humorous verse of five lines

limericks *n* ▷ limerick

limes *n* ▷ lime¹,²,³

limestone *n* (*pl* **-s**) sedimentary rock used in building

limestones *n* ▷ limestone

limey *n* (*pl* **-s**) (US) (*Slang*) British person

limeys *n* ▷ limey

limit *n* (*pl* **-s**) ultimate extent, degree, or amount of something ▶ *v* (**-s**, **-ing**, **-ed**) restrict or confine > **limitation** *n* (*pl* **-s**) > **limitless** *adj*

limitation *n* ▷ limit

limitations *n* ▷ limit

limited *v* ▷ limit

limiting *v* ▷ limit

limitless *v* ▷ limit

limits *n*, *v* ▷ limit

limousine *n* (*pl* **-s**) large luxurious car

limousines *n* ▷ limousine

limp¹ *v* (**-s**, **-ing**, **-ed**) walk with an uneven step ▶ *n* (*pl* **-s**) limping walk

limp² (**-er**, **-est**) *adj* without firmness or stiffness > **limply** *adv*

limped *v* ▷ limp¹

limper *adj* ▷ limp²

limpest *adj* ▷ limp²

limping *v* ▷ limp¹

limply *adv* ▷ limp²

limps *v*, *n* ▷ limp¹

limpet *n* (*pl* **-s**) shellfish which sticks tightly to rocks

limpets *n* ▷ limpet

limpid *adj* clear or transparent > **limpidity** *n* (*pl* **-ties**)

limpidities *n* ▷ limpid

limpidity *n* ▷ limpid

linchpin, lynchpin *n* (*pl* **-s**) pin to hold a wheel on its axle

linchpins *n* ▷ linchpin

linctus *n* (*pl* **-es**) syrupy cough medicine

linctuses *n* ▷ linctus

linden *n* (*pl* **-s**) ▷ lime³

lindens *n* ▷ linden

line¹ *n* (*pl* **-s**) long narrow mark ▶ *pl* words of a theatrical part ▶ *v* (**-s**, **-ing**, **-ed**) mark with lines

line² *v* (**-s**, **-ning**, **-ned**) give a lining to

lined *v* ▷ line¹,²

lines *n*, *v* ▷ line¹,²

lining *v* ▷ line¹,²

lineage [lin-ee-ij] *n* (*pl* **-s**) descent from an ancestor

lineages *n* ▷ lineage

lineament *n* (*pl* **-s**) facial feature

lineaments *n* ▷ lineament

linear [lin-ee-er] *adj* of or in lines

linen *n* (*pl* **-s**) cloth or thread made from flax

linens *n* ▷ linen

liner¹ *n* (*pl* **-s**) large passenger ship or aircraft

liner² *n* something used as a lining

liners *n* ▷ liner¹,²

linesman *n* (*pl* **-men**) (in some sports) an official who helps the referee or umpire

linesmen *n* ▷ linesman

ling¹ *n* slender food fish

ling² *n* (*pl* **lings**) heather

linger *v* (**-s**, **-ing**, **-ed**) delay or prolong departure

lingered *v* ▷ linger

lingerie [lan-zher-ee] *n* (*pl* **-s**) women's underwear or nightwear

lingeries *n* ▷ lingerie

lingering *v* ▷ linger

lingers *v* ▷ linger

lingo *n* (*pl* **-s**) (*Informal*) foreign or unfamiliar language or jargon

lingos *n* ▷ lingo

lings *n* ▷ ling²

lingual *adj* of the tongue

linguist *n* (*pl* **-s**) person skilled in foreign languages

linguistic *adj* of languages

linguistics *n* (*pl* **-s**) scientific study of language

linguists *n* ▷ linguist

liniment *n* (*pl* **-s**) medicated liquid rubbed on the skin to relieve pain or stiffness

liniments n ▷ liniment
lining n (pl -s) layer of cloth attached to the inside of a garment etc.
linings n ▷ lining
link n (pl -s) any of the rings forming a chain ▶ v (-s, -ing, -ed) connect with or as if with links
> **linkage** n (pl -s)
linkage n ▷ link
linkages n ▷ link
linked v ▷ link
linking v ▷ link
links pl n golf course, esp. one by the sea
links n, v ▷ link
linnet n (pl -s) songbird of the finch family
linnets n ▷ linnet
linoleum n (pl -s) floor covering of hessian or jute with a smooth decorative coating of powdered cork
linoleums n ▷ linoleum
linseed n (pl -s) seed of the flax plant
linseeds n ▷ linseeds
lint n (pl -s) soft material for dressing a wound
lintel n (pl -s) horizontal beam at the top of a door or window
lintels n ▷ lintel
lints n ▷ lint
lion n (pl -s) large animal of the cat family, the male of which has a shaggy mane > **lioness** n fem
lioness n ▷ lion
lions n ▷ lion
lip n (pl -s) either of the fleshy edges of the mouth
lips n ▷ lip
lipstick n (pl -s) cosmetic in stick form, for colouring the lips
liquefy v (-fies, -fying, -fied) make or become liquid > **liquefaction** n (pl -s)
liquefaction n ▷ liquefy
liquefactions n ▷ liquefy
liquefied v ▷ liquefy
liquefies v ▷ liquefy
liquefying v ▷ liquefy
liqueur [lik-cure] n (pl -s) flavoured and sweetened alcoholic spirit
liqueurs n ▷ liqueur
liquid n (pl -s) substance in a physical state which can change shape but not size ▶ adj of or being a liquid
liquidate v (-tes, -ting, -ted) pay (a debt)
> **liquidation** n (pl -s)
liquidated v ▷ liquidate
liquidates v ▷ liquidate
liquidating v ▷ liquidate
liquidation n ▷ liquidate

liquidations n ▷ liquidate
liquidities n ▷ liquidity
liquidator n (pl -s) official appointed to liquidate a business
liquidators n ▷ liquidator
liquidity n (pl -ties) state of being able to meet financial obligations ▶ v (-zes, -zing, -zed) make or become liquid
liquidized v ▷ liquidize
liquidizer n (pl -s) kitchen appliance that liquidizes food
liquidizers v ▷ liquidizer
liquidizes v ▷ liquidize
liquidizing v ▷ liquidize
liquids n ▷ liquid
liquor n (pl -s) alcoholic drink, esp. spirits
liquors n ▷ liquor
liquorice [lik-ker-iss] n (pl -s) black substance used in medicine and as a sweet
liquorices n ▷ liquorice
lira n (pl -re, -ras) monetary unit of Turkey and formerly of Italy
liras n ▷ lira
lire n ▷ lira
lisle [rhymes with **mile**] n (pl -s) strong fine cotton thread or fabric
lisles n ▷ lisle
lisp n (pl -s) speech defect in which s and z are pronounced th ▶ v (-s, -ing, -ed) speak or utter with a lisp
lisped v ▷ lisp
lisping v ▷ lisp
lisps n, v ▷ lisp
lissom, lissome adj supple, agile
lissome adj ▷ lissom
list[1] n (pl -s) item-by-item record of names or things, usu. written one below another ▶ v (-s, -ing, -ed) make a list of
list[2] v (-s, -ing, -ed) (of a ship) lean to one side ▶ n (pl -s) leaning to one side
listed v ▷ list[1,2]
listing v ▷ list[1,2]
lists n, v ▷ list[1,2]
listen v (-s, -ing, -ed) concentrate on hearing something > **listener** n (pl -s)
listened v ▷ listen
listener n ▷ listen
listeners n ▷ listen
listening v ▷ listen
listens v ▷ listen
listeriosis n (pl -ses) dangerous form of food poisoning
listerioses n ▷ listeriosis
listless adj lacking interest or energy
> **listlessly** adv

listlessly adv ▷ listless
lit v ▷ light[1,2]
litanies n ▷ litany
litany n (pl -nies) prayer with responses from the congregation
literacies n ▷ literacy
literacy n (pl -cies) ability to read and write
literal adj according to the explicit meaning of a word or text, not figurative > **literally** adv
literally adv ▷ literal
literary adj of or knowledgeable about literature
literate adj able to read and write
literati pl n literary people
literature n (pl -s) written works such as novels, plays, and poetry
literatures n ▷ literature
lithe adj (-ther, -thest) flexible or supple, pliant
lither adj ▷ lithe
lithest adj ▷ lithe
lithium n (pl -s) (CHEM) chemical element, the lightest known metal
lithograph n (pl -s) print made by lithography
lithographer n ▷ lithography
lithographers n ▷ lithography
lithographic adj ▷ lithography
lithographied v ▷ lithography
lithographies n, v ▷ lithography
lithographs n ▷ lithograph
lithography [lith-og-ra-fee] n (pl -phies) method of printing from a metal or stone surface in which the printing areas are made receptive to ink ▶ v (-phies, -ying, -phied) reproduce by lithography > **lithographer** n (pl -s) > **lithographic** adj
lithographying v ▷ lithography
litigant n (pl -s) person involved in a lawsuit
litigants n ▷ litigant
litigate v (-tes, -ting, -ted) bring or contest a law suit
litigated v ▷ litigate
litigates v ▷ litigate
litigating v ▷ litigate
litigation n (pl -s) legal action
litigations n ▷ litigation
litigious [lit-ij-uss] adj frequently going to law
litmus n (pl -es) blue dye turned red by acids and restored to blue by alkalis
litmuses n ▷ litmus
litotes [lie-toe-teez] n ironical understatement used for effect
litre n (pl -s) unit of liquid measure equal to 1000 cubic centimetres or 1.76 pints
litres n ▷ litre
litter n (pl -s) untidy rubbish dropped in public

places ▶ v (-s, -ing, -ed) strew with litter
littered v ▷ litter
littering v ▷ litter
litters n, v ▷ litter
little adj small or smaller than average
▶ adv not a lot ▶ n small amount, extent, or duration
littoral adj of or by the seashore ▶ n (pl -s) coastal district
littorals n ▷ littoral
liturgical n ▷ liturgy
liturgies n ▷ liturgy
liturgy n (pl -gies) prescribed form of public worship > **liturgical** adj
live[1] v (-s, -ing, -ed) be alive
live[2] adj living, alive ▶ adv in the form of a live performance > **liveliness** n (pl -es)
lived v ▷ live[1]
liveliness n ▷ live[2]
livelinesses n ▷ live[2]
lively adj full of life or vigour
livelihood n (pl livelihoods) occupation or employment
livelihoods n ▷ livelihood
lively adj full of life or vigour
liver[1] n (pl -s) organ secreting bile
liver[2] n (pl -s) person who lives in a specified way
liveried adj ▷ livery
liverish adj having a disorder of the liver
livers n ▷ liver[1,2]
livery n (pl -ries) distinctive dress, esp. a servant or servants > **liveried** adj
lives v ▷ live[1] ▶ n ▷ life
livestock n (pl -s) farm animals
livestocks n ▷ livestock
livid adj (Informal) (-er, -est) angry or furious
livider adj ▷ livid
lividest adj ▷ livid
living adj possessing life, not dead or inanimate ▶ n (pl -s) condition of being alive
▶ v ▷ live
livings n ▷ living
lizard n (pl -s) four-footed reptile with a long body and tail
lizards n ▷ lizard
llama n (pl -s) woolly animal of the camel family used as a beast of burden in S America
llamas n ▷ llama

> **lo** interj. Lo is a command that means look! Along with **la** and **li**, lo is one of just three two-letter words that begin with L. Lo scores 2 points.

loach n (pl -es) carplike freshwater fish
loaches n ▷ loach

load n (pl -s) burden or weight ▸ pl (Informal) lots ▸ v (-s, -ing, -ed) put a load on or into

loaded adj (of a question) containing a hidden trap or implication

loaded v, adj ▷ load

loads n, v ▷ load

loading v ▷ load

loaf[1] n (pl loaves) shaped mass of baked bread

loaf[2] v (-s, -ing, -ed) idle, loiter > **loafer** n (pl -s)

loafed v ▷ loaf[2]

loafer n ▷ loaf[2]

loafers n ▷ loaf[2]

loafing v ▷ loaf[2]

loafs v ▷ loaf[2]

loam n (pl -s) fertile soil

loams n ▷ loam

loan n (pl -s) money lent at interest ▸ v (-s, -ing, -ed) lend

loaned v ▷ loan

loaning v ▷ loan

loans n, v ▷ loan

loath, loth [rhymes with **both**] adj unwilling or reluctant (to)

loathe v (-s, -thing, -thed) hate, be disgusted by > **loathing** n (pl -s) > **loathsome** adj

loathed v ▷ loathe

loathes v ▷ loathe

loathing v, n ▷ loathe

loathings n ▷ loathe

loathsome adj ▷ loathe

loaves n ▷ loaf[1]

lob (SPORT) n (pl -s) ball struck or thrown in a high arc ▸ v (-s, -bbing, -bbed) strike or throw (a ball) in a high arc

lobbed v ▷ lob

lobbied v ▷ lobby

lobbies n, v ▷ lobby

lobbing v ▷ lob

lobby n (pl -bies) corridor into which rooms open ▸ v (-bies, -ing, -bied) try to influence (legislators) in the formulation of policy > **lobbyist** n

lobbying v ▷ lobby

lobe n (pl -s) rounded projection > **lobed** adj

lobed n ▷ lobe

lobelia n (pl -s) garden plant with blue, red, or white flowers

lobelias n ▷ lobelia

lobes n ▷ lobe

lobola [law-bawl-a] n (pl -s) (S AFR) (in African custom) price paid by a bridegroom's family to his bride's family

lobolas n ▷ lobola

lobotomy n (pl -mies) surgical incision into a lobe of the brain to treat mental disorders

lobotomies n ▷ lobotomy

lobs n, v ▷ lob

lobster n (pl -s) shellfish with a long tail and claws, which turns red when boiled

lobsters n ▷ lobster

local adj of or existing in a particular place ▸ n (pl -s) person belonging to a particular district > **locally** adv

locale [loh-kahl] n (pl -s) scene of an event

localities n ▷ locality

locality n (pl -ties) neighbourhood or area

localize v (-zes, -zing, -zed) restrict to a particular place

localized v ▷ localize

localizes v ▷ localize

localizing v ▷ localize

locally adv ▷ local

locals n ▷ local

locate v (-s, -ing, -ed) discover the whereabouts of

located v ▷ locate

locates v ▷ locate

locating v ▷ locate

location n (pl -s) site or position

locations n ▷ location

loch n (pl -s) (SCOT) lake

lochs n ▷ loch

loci n ▷ locus

lock[1] n (pl -s) appliance for fastening a door, case, etc. ▸ v (-s, -ing, -ed) fasten or become fastened securely

lock[2] n (pl -s) strand of hair

locked v ▷ lock[1]

locker n (pl -s) small cupboard with a lock

lockers n ▷ locker

locket n (pl -s) small hinged pendant for a portrait etc.

lockets n ▷ locket

locking v ▷ lock[1]

lockjaw n (pl -s) tetanus

lockjaws n ▷ lockjaw

locomotion n (pl -s) action or power of moving

locomotions n ▷ locomotion

locomotive n (pl -s) self-propelled engine for pulling trains ▸ adj of locomotion

locomotives n ▷ locomotive

lockout n (pl -s) closing of a workplace by an employer to force workers to accept terms

lockouts n ▷ lockout

locks n ▷ lock[1,2] ▸ v ▷ lock[1]

locksmith n (pl -s) person who makes and mends locks

locksmiths n ▷ locksmith

lockup n (pl -s) prison

lockups n ▷ lockup

locum n (pl -s) temporary stand-in for a doctor or clergyman
  locums n ▷ locum
locus [loh-kuss] n (pl -ci) [loh-sigh] area or place where something happens
locust n (pl -s) destructive African insect that flies in swarms and eats crops
  locusts n ▷ locust
lode n (pl -s) vein of ore
  lodes n ▷ lode
lodestar n (pl -s) star used in navigation or astronomy as a point of reference
  lodestars n ▷ lodestar
lodestone n (pl -s) magnetic iron ore
  lodestones n ▷ lodestone
lodge n (pl -s) (CHIEFLY BRIT) gatekeeper's house ▶ v (-dges, -dging, -dged) live in another's house at a fixed charge ▶ **lodger** n (pl -s)
  lodged v ▷ lodge
  lodger n ▷ lodge
  lodgers n ▷ lodge
  lodges n, v ▷ lodge
lodging n (pl -s) temporary residence ▶ pl rented room or rooms in another person's house ▶ v ▷ lodge
  lodgings n ▷ lodging
loft n (pl -s) space between the top storey and roof of a building ▶ v (-s, -ing, -ed) (SPORT) strike, throw, or kick (a ball) high into the air
  lofted v ▷ loft
  loftier adj ▷ lofty
  loftiest adj ▷ lofty
loftily adv haughtily
  lofting v ▷ loft
  lofts n, v ▷ loft
lofty adj (-tier, -tiest) of great height
log¹ n (pl -s) portion of a felled tree stripped of branches ▶ v (-s, -gging, -gged) saw logs from a tree
  log² n ▷ logarithm
loganberry n (pl -rries) purplish-red fruit, similar to a raspberry
  loganberries n ▷ loganberry
logarithm n (pl -s) one of a series of arithmetical functions used to make certain calculations easier
  logarithms n ▷ logarithm
logbook n (pl -s) book recording the details about a car or a ship's journeys
  logbooks n ▷ logbook
  logged v ▷ log¹
loggerheads pl n quarrelling, disputing
loggia [loj-ya] n (pl -s) covered gallery at the side of a building
  loggias n ▷ loggia

logging n (pl -s) work of cutting and transporting logs ▶ v ▷ log¹
  loggings n ▷ logging
logic n (pl -s) philosophy of reasoning > **logically** adv > **logician** n (pl -s)
logical adj of logic
  logically adv ▷ logic
  logician n ▷ logic
  logicians n ▷ logic
  logics n ▷ logic
  logistical adj ▷ logistics
logistics n detailed planning and organization of a large, esp. military, operation > **logistical, logistic** adj
logo [loh-go] n (pl -s) emblem used by a company or other organization
  logos n ▷ logo
  logs n ▷ log¹
loin n (pl -s) part of the body between the ribs and the hips
loincloth n (pl -s) piece of cloth covering the loins only
  loincloths n ▷ loincloth
  loins n ▷ loin
loiter v (-s, -ing, -ed) stand or wait aimlessly or idly
  loitered v ▷ loiter
  loitering v ▷ loiter
  loiters v ▷ loiter
loll v (-s, -ing, -ed) lounge lazily
  lolled v ▷ loll
  lollies n ▷ lolly
  lolling v ▷ loll
lollipop n (pl -s) boiled sweet on a small wooden stick
  lollipops n ▷ lollipop
  lolls v ▷ loll
lolly n (pl -llies) (Informal) lollipop or ice lolly
lone adj solitary > **lonesome** adj lonely
  loneliness n ▷ lonely
  lonelinesses n ▷ lonely
lonely adj sad because alone > **loneliness** n (pl -s)
loner n (pl -s) (Informal) person who prefers to be alone
  loners n ▷ -s
  lonesome adj ▷ lone
long¹ adj (-er, -est) having length, esp. great length, in space or time ▶ adv for an extensive period
long² v (-s, -ing, -ed) have a strong desire (for)
  longed v ▷ long²
  longer adj ▷ long¹
  longest adj ▷ long¹
  longevities n ▷ longevity

longevity [lon-**jev**-it-ee] *n* (*pl* **-ties**) long life
longhand *n* (*pl* **-s**) ordinary writing, not shorthand or typing
   longhands *n* ▷ longhand
longing *n* (*pl* **-s**) yearning ▶ *v* ▷ long²
   > **longingly** *adv*
   longingly *adv* ▷ longing
   longings *n* ▷ longing
longitude *n* (*pl* **-s**) distance east or west from a standard meridian
   longitudes *n* ▷ longitude
longitudinal *adj* of length or longitude
   longs *v* ▷ long²
longshoreman *n* (*pl* **-men**) (us) docker
   longshoremen *n* ▷ longshoreman
loo *n* (*pl* **-s**) (*Informal*) toilet
   loos *n* ▷ loo
loofah *n* (*pl* **-s**) sponge made from the dried pod of a gourd
   loofahs *n* ▷ loofah
look *v* (**-s**, **-ing**, **-ed**) direct the eyes or attention (towards) ▶ *n* (*pl* **-s**) instance of looking
lookalike *n* (*pl* **-s**) person who is the double of another
   lookalikes *n* ▷ lookalike
   looked *v* ▷ look
   looking *v* ▷ look
lookout *n* (*pl* **-s**) guard
   lookouts *n* ▷ lookout
   looks *v*, *n* ▷ look
loom¹ *n* (*pl* **-s**) machine for weaving cloth
loom² *v* (**-s**, **-ing**, **-ed**) appear dimly
   loomed *v* ▷ loom²
   looming *v* ▷ loom²
   looms *n* ▷ loom¹ ▶ *v* loom²
   loonies *n* ▷ loony
loony (*Slang*) *adj* (**-nier**, **-niest**) foolish or insane ▶ *n* (*pl* **-nies**) foolish or insane person
loop *n* (*pl* **-s**) rounded shape made by a curved line or rope crossing itself ▶ *v* (**-s**, **-ing**, **-ed**) form or fasten with a loop
   looped *v* ▷ loop
loophole *n* (*pl* **-s**) means of evading a rule without breaking it
   loopholes *n* ▷ loophole
   looping *v* ▷ loop
   loops *n*, *v* ▷ loop
loose *adj* (**-r**, **-est**) not tight, fastened, fixed, or tense ▶ *adv* in a loose manner ▶ *v* (**-s**, **-sing**, **-sed**) free > **loosely** *adv* > **looseness** *n* (*pl* **-s**)
   loosed *v* ▷ loose
   loosely *adv* ▷ loose
loosen *v* (**-s**, **-ing**, **-ed**) make loose
   loosened *v* ▷ loosen
   looseness *n* ▷ loose

   loosenesses *n* ▷ loose
   loosening *v* ▷ loosen
   loosens *v* ▷ loosen
   looser *adj* ▷ loose
   looses *v* ▷ loose
   loosest *adj* ▷ loose
   loosing *v* ▷ loose
loot *n*, *v* (**-s**, **-ing**, **-ed**) plunder ▶ *n* (*pl* **-s**) (*Informal*) money > **looter** *n* (*pl* **-s**) > **looting** *n* (*pl* **-s**)
   looted *v* ▷ loot
   looter *n* ▷ loot
   looters *n* ▷ loot
   looting *v*, *n* ▷ loot
   lootings *n* ▷ loot
   loots *v*, *n* ▷ loot
lop *v* (**-s**, **-pping**, **-pped**) cut away twigs and branches
lope *v* (**-s**, **-ing**, **-ed**) run with long easy strides
   loped *v* ▷ lope
   lopes *v* ▷ lope
   loping *v* ▷ lope
lopsided *adj* greater in height, weight, or size on one side
loquacious *adj* talkative > **loquacity** *n* (*pl* **-ties**)
   loquacities *n* ▷ loquacity
lord *n* (*pl* **-s**) person with power over others, such as a monarch or master
   lordlier *adj* ▷ lordly
   lordliest *adj* ▷ lordly
lordly *adj* (**-lier**, **-liest**) imperious, proud
   lords *n* ▷ lord
lore *n* (*pl* **-s**) body of traditions on a subject
   lores *n* ▷ lore
lorgnette [lor-**nyet**] *n* (*pl* **-s**) pair of spectacles mounted on a long handle
   lorgnettes *n* ▷ lorgnette
   lorries *n* ▷ lorry
lorikeet *n* (*pl* **-s**) small brightly coloured Australian parrot
   lorikeets *n* ▷ lorikeet
lorry *n* (*pl* **-rries**) (BRIT & S AFR) large vehicle for transporting loads by road
lose *v* (**-s**, **-sing**, **lost**) come to be without, esp. by accident or carelessness
loser *n* (*pl* **-s**) person or thing that loses
   losers *n* ▷ loser
   loses *v* ▷ lose
   losing *v* ▷ lose
loss *n* (*pl* **-es**) losing
   losses *n* ▷ loss
   lost *v* ▷ lose ▶ *adj* unable to find one's way
lot *pron* great number ▶ *n* (*pl* **-s**) collection of people or things
   lots *n* ▷ lot

loth adj ▷ loath

lotion n (pl -s) medical or cosmetic liquid for use on the skin
lotions n ▷ lotion

lottery n (pl -ries) method of raising money by selling tickets that win prizes by chance

lotto n (pl -s) game of chance like bingo
lottos n ▷ lotto

lotus n (pl -es) legendary plant whose fruit induces forgetfulness
lotuses n ▷ lotus

loud adj (-er, -est) relatively great in volume
> **loudly** adv ▷ **loudness** n (pl -es)
louder adj ▷ loud
loudest adj ▷ loud
loudly adv ▷ loud
loudness n ▷ loud
loudnesses n ▷ loud

loudspeaker n (pl -s) instrument for converting electrical signals into sound
loudspeakers n ▷ loudspeaker

lough n (pl -s) (IRISH) loch
loughs n ▷ lough

lounge n (pl -s) living room in a private house ▶ v (-s, -ging, -ged) sit, lie, or stand in a relaxed manner
lounged v ▷ lounge
lounges n, v ▷ lounge
lounging v ▷ lounge

lour v (-s, -ing, -ed) ▷ lower²
loured v ▷ lour
louring v ▷ lour
lours v ▷ lour

louse n (pl lice, louses) wingless parasitic insect
louses n ▷ louse
lousier adj ▷ lousy
lousiest adj ▷ lousy

lousy adj (-sier, -siest) (Slang) mean or unpleasant

lout n (pl -s) crude, oafish, or aggressive person
> **loutish** adj
loutish adj ▷ lout
louts n ▷ lout

louvre [loo-ver] n (pl -s) one of a set of parallel slats slanted to admit air but not rain
> **louvred** adj
louvred adj ▷ louvre
louvres n ▷ louvre

love v (-s, -ving, -ved) have a great affection for ▶ n (pl -s) great affection > **lovable, loveable** adj > **loveless** adj ▷ **lovemaking** n (pl -s)
lovable adj ▷ love
loveable adj ▷ love
lovebird n (pl -s) small parrot

lovebirds n ▷ lovebird
loved v ▷ love
loveless adj ▷ love
lovelier adj ▷ lovely
loveliest adj ▷ lovely

lovelorn adj miserable because of unhappiness in love

lovely adj (-lier, -liest) very attractive
lovemaking n ▷ love
lovemakings n ▷ love

lover n (pl -s) person having a sexual relationship outside marriage
lovers n ▷ lover
loves v, n ▷ love

loving adj affectionate, tender ▶ v ▷ love
> **lovingly** adv
lovingly adv ▷ loving

low¹ adj not tall, high, or elevated ▶ adv in or to a low position, level, or degree ▶ n (pl -s) low position, level, or degree > **lowland** n (pl -s)

low² n (pl -s) cry of cattle, moo ▶ v (-s, -ing, -ed) moo

lowbrow n (pl -s) ▶ adj (person) with nonintellectual tastes and interests
lowbrows n ▷ lowbrow

lowdown n (pl -s) (Informal) inside information
lowdowns n ▷ lowdown
lowed v ▷ low²

lower¹ adj (-est) below one or more other things ▶ v (-s, -ing, -ed) cause or allow to move down

lower², lour (of the sky or weather) look gloomy or threatening
lowered v ▷ lower¹,²
lowering v ▷ lower¹,²
lowers v ▷ lower¹,²
lowest adj ▷ lower
lowing v ▷ low²

lowland n (pl -s) low-lying country
lowlands n ▷ lowland
lowlier adj ▷ lowly
lowliest adj ▷ lowly
lowliness n ▷ lowly
lowlinesses n ▷ lowly

lowly adj (-lier, -liest) modest, humble
> **lowliness** n (pl -s)
lows n ▷ low¹,² ▶ v ▷ low²

> **lox** n (**loxes**). Lox is a kind of smoked salmon. This is a good word if you get have an X and L in the late stages of the game: there's likely to be a usable O on the board already. Lox scores 10 points.

loyal adj (-ler, -lest) faithful to one's friends, country, or government > **loyally** adv ▷ **loyalty** n (pl -ties) > **loyalist** n (pl -s)

loyalist n ▷ loyal
loyalists n ▷ loyal
loyaller adj ▷ loyal
loyallest adj ▷ loyal
loyally adv ▷ loyal
loyalties n ▷ loyal
loyalty n ▷ loyal
lozenge n (pl -s) medicated tablet held in the mouth until it dissolves
lozenges n ▷ lozenge
lubricate [loo-brik-ate] v (-tes, -ting, -ted) oil or grease to lessen friction > **lubrication** n (pl -s)
lubricant n (pl -s) lubricating substance, such as oil
lubricants n ▷ lubricant
lubricated v ▷ lubricate
lubricates v ▷ lubricate
lubricating v ▷ lubricate
lubrication n ▷ lubricate
lubrications n ▷ lubricate
lubricious adj (Lit) lewd
lucerne n (pl -s) fodder plant like clover, alfalfa
lucernes n ▷ lucerne
lucid adj clear and easily understood > **lucidly** adv > **lucidity** n (pl -ties)
lucidities n ▷ lucid
lucidity n ▷ lucid
lucidly adv ▷ lucid
luck n (pl -s) fortune, good or bad
luckily adv fortunately
luckless adj having bad luck
lucrative adj very profitable
lucre [loo-ker] n (pl -s) (Facetious) money
lucks n having bad luck
lucky adj having or bringing good luck
luderick n (pl -s) Australian fish, usu. black or dark brown in colour
ludericks n ▷ luderick
ludicrous adj absurd or ridiculous > **ludicrously** adv
ludicrously adv ▷ ludicrous
ludo n (pl -s) game played with dice and counters on a board
lug[1] v (-s, -gging, -gged) carry or drag with great effort
lug[2] n (pl -s) projection serving as a handle
luggage n (pl -s) traveller's cases, bags, etc.
luggages n projection serving as a handle ▷ luggage
lugs v ▷ lug[1] ▶ n ▷ lug[2]
lugubrious adj mournful, gloomy > **lugubriously** adv
lugubriously adv ▷ lugubrious
lugworm n (pl -s) large worm used as bait
lugworms n ▷ lugworm

lukewarm adj moderately warm, tepid
lull v (-s, -ing, -ed) soothe (someone) by soft sounds or motions ▶ n (pl -s) brief time of quiet in a storm etc.
lullabies n ▷ lullaby
lullaby n (pl -bies) quiet song to send a child to sleep
lulled v ▷ lull
lulling v ▷ lull
lulls v, n ▷ lull
lumbago [lum-bay-go] n (pl -s) pain in the lower back
lumbagos n ▷ lumbago
lumbar adj relating to the lower back
lumber[1] n (pl -s) (BRIT) unwanted disused household articles ▶ v (-s, -ing, -ed) (Informal) burden with something unpleasant
lumber[2] v move heavily and awkwardly > **lumbering** adj
lumbered v ▷ lumber[1,2]
lumbering v ▷ lumber[1,2] ▶ adj ▷ lumber[2]
lumberjack n (pl -s) (US) man who fells trees and prepares logs for transport
lumberjacks n ▷ lumberjack
lumbers n[1] ▶ v ▷ lumber[1,2]
luminary n (pl -s) famous person
luminescence n (pl -s) emission of light at low temperatures by any process other than burning
luminescences n ▷ luminescence
luminescent adj ▷ luminous
luminosities n ▷ luminous
luminosity n ▷ luminous
luminous adj reflecting or giving off light > **luminosity** n (pl -s) > **luminescent** adj
lump[1] n (pl -s) shapeless piece or mass ▶ v (-s, -ing, -ed) consider as a single group > **lumpy** adj (-pier, -piest)
lump[2] v (Informal) tolerate or put up with it
lumped v ▷ lump[1,2]
lumpier adj ▷ lump[1]
lumpiest adj ▷ lump[1]
lumping v ▷ lump[1,2]
lumps n, v ▷ lump[1,2]
lumpy adj ▷ lump[1]
lunar adj relating to the moon
lunacies n ▷ lunacy
lunatic adj foolish and irresponsible ▶ n (pl -s) foolish or annoying person > **lunacy** n (pl -cies)
lunatics n ▷ lunatic
lunch n (pl lunches) meal taken in the middle of the day ▶ v (-es, -ing, -ed) eat lunch
lunched v ▷ lunch
luncheon n (pl -s) formal lunch

luncheons *n* ▷ luncheon
lunches *n, v* ▷ lunch
lunching *v* ▷ lunch
lung *n* (*pl* -s) organ that allows an animal or bird to breathe air: humans have two lungs in the chest
lungfish *n* freshwater bony fish with an air-breathing lung of South America and Australia
lungs *n* ▷ lung
lunge *n* (*pl* -s) sudden forward motion ▶ *v* (-s, -ging, -ged) move with or make a lunge
lunged *v* ▷ lunge
lunges *n, v* ▷ lunge
lunging *v* ▷ lunge
lupin *n* (*pl* -s) garden plant with tall spikes of flowers
lupins *n* ▷ lupin
lupine *adj* like a wolf
lurch *v* (-es, -ing, -ed) tilt or lean suddenly to one side ▶ *n* (*pl* -s) lurching movement
lurched *v* ▷ lurch
lurcher *n* (*pl* -s) crossbred dog trained to hunt silently
lurchers *n* ▷ lurcher
lurches *v, n* ▷ lurch
lurching *v* ▷ lurch
lure *v* (-s, -red, -ring) tempt or attract by the promise of reward ▶ *n* (*pl* -s) person or thing that lures
lured *v* ▷ lure
lures *v, n* ▷ lure
luring *v* ▷ lure
lurid *adj* (-er, -est) vivid in shocking detail, sensational > **luridly** *adv*
lurider *adj* ▷ lurid
luridest *adj* ▷ lurid
luridly *adv* ▷ lurid
luring *v* ▷ lure
lurk *v* (-s, -ing, -ed) lie hidden or move stealthily, esp. for sinister purposes
lurked *v* ▷ lurk
lurking *v* ▷ lurk
lurks *v* ▷ lurk
luscious [lush-uss] *adj* extremely pleasurable to taste or smell
lush¹ *adj* (-er, -est) (of grass etc.) growing thickly and healthily
lush² *n* (*pl* -es) (*Slang*) alcoholic
lusher *adj* ▷ lush¹
lushes *n* ▷ lush²
lushest *adj* ▷ lush¹
lust *n* (*pl* -s) strong sexual desire ▶ *v* (-s, -ing, -ed) have passionate desire (for) > **lustful** *adj* > **lusty** *adj* vigorous, healthy > **lustily** *adv*

lusted *v* ▷ lust
lustful *adj* ▷ lust
lustier *adj* ▷ lusty
lustiest *adj* ▷ lusty
lustily *adv* ▷ lusty
lusting *v* ▷ lust
lustre *n* (*pl* -s) gloss, sheen
lustres *n* ▷ lustre
lustrous *adj* shining, luminous
lusts *n, v* ▷ lust
lusty *adj* (-tier, -tiest) vigorous, healthy
lute *n* (*pl* -s) ancient guitar-like musical instrument with a body shaped like a half pear
lutes *n* ▷ lute

> **lux** *n* (**lux**). A lux is a unit of illumination. This is a great word to know when you have an X but little opportunity to play it. Lux scores 10 points.

luxuriant *adj* rich and abundant > **luxuriance** *n* (*pl* -ces) > **luxuriantly** *adv*
luxuriance *n* ▷ luxuriant
luxuriances *n* ▷ luxuriant
luxuriantly *adv* ▷ luxuriant
luxuriate *v* (-tes, -ting, -ted) take self-indulgent pleasure (in)
luxuriated *v* ▷ luxuriate
luxuriates *v* ▷ luxuriate
luxuriating *v* ▷ luxuriate
luxurious *adj* full of luxury, sumptuous > **luxuriously** *adv*
luxuriously *adv* ▷ luxurious
luxury *n* (*pl* -ries) enjoyment of rich, very comfortable living ▶ *adj* of or providing luxury

> **luz** *n* (**luzzes**). In traditional Jewish writings, the luz was a bone that was supposed to be indestructible. This very unusual word is very useful, especially if you have a Z at the end of a game when there is little opportunity to use it in a longer word. Luz scores 12 points.

lychee [lie-chee] *n* (*pl* -s) Chinese fruit with a whitish juicy pulp
lychees *n* ▷ lychee
lye *n* (*pl* -s) caustic solution obtained by leaching wood ash
lyes *n* ▷ lye
lying *v* ▷ lie¹,²
lymph *n* (*pl* -s) colourless bodily fluid consisting mainly of white blood cells > **lymphatic** *adj*
lymphatic *adj* ▷ lymph
lymphocyte *n* (*pl* -s) type of white blood cell
lymphocytes *n* ▷ lymphocyte

lymphs *n* ▷ lymph
lynch *v* (**-es, -ing, -ed**) put to death without
  a trial
  lynched *v* ▷ lynch
  lynches *v* ▷ lynch
  lynching *v* ▷ lynch
  lynchpin *n* ▷ lynchpin
  lynchpins *n* ▷ lynchpin
lynx *n* (*pl* **-es**) animal of the cat family with
  tufted ears and a short tail
  lynxes *n* ▷ lynx

lyre *n* (*pl* **-s**) ancient musical instrument like a
  U-shaped harp
  lyres *n* ▷ lyre
lyric *adj* (of poetry) expressing personal
  emotion in songlike style ▶ *n* (*pl* **-s**) short
  poem in a songlike style > **lyrical** *adj* lyric
  lyrical *n* ▷ lyric
lyricist *n* (*pl* **-s**) person who writes the words of
  songs or musicals
  lyricists *n* ▷ lyricist
  lyrics *n* ▷ lyric

Mm

M is a very useful letter when you need to form short words as it starts a two-letter word with every vowel, as well as with Y and with another M. Remembering this allows you to use M effectively when you're forming a word parallel to, and in contact with, a word that is already on the board. M also combines well with X and Z, so there is a lot of potential for high-scoring words. Keep **max**, **mix** and **mux** (12 points each) in mind, as well as **miz** and **muz** (14 each). It's also worth remembering the three-letter words ending in W: **maw**, **mew** and **mow** (8 points each).

ma n (pl -s) (Informal) mother
mas n ▷ ma
mac n (pl -s) (BRIT) (Informal) mackintosh
macs n ▷ mac
macabre [mak-**kahb**-ra] adj strange and horrible, gruesome
macadam n (pl -s) road surface of pressed layers of small broken stones
macadams n ▷ macadam
macadamia n (pl -s) Australian tree with edible nuts
macadamias n ▷ macadamia
macaroni n (pl -s) pasta in short tube shapes
macaronis n ▷ macaroni
macaroon n (pl -s) small biscuit or cake made with ground almonds
macaroons n ▷ macaroon
macaw n (pl -s) large tropical American parrot
macaws n ▷ macaw
mace¹ n (pl -s) ceremonial staff of office
mace² n (pl -s) spice made from the dried husk of the nutmeg
maces n ▷ mace¹,²
macerate [**mass**-er-ate] v (-tes, -ting, -ted) soften by soaking > **maceration** n (pl -s)
macerated v ▷ macerate
macerates v ▷ macerate
macerating v ▷ macerate
maceration n ▷ macerate
macerations n ▷ macerate
machete [mash-**ett**-ee] n (pl -s) broad heavy knife used for cutting or as a weapon
machetes n ▷ machete
machinations [mak-in-**nay**-shunz] pl n cunning plots and ploys
machine n (pl -s) apparatus, usu. powered by electricity, designed to perform a particular

task ▶ v (-nes, -ning, -ned) make or produce by machine
machined v ▷ machine
machinegun v (-s, -nning, -nned) fire at with such a gun
machinegunned v ▷ machinegun
machinegunning v ▷ machinegun
machineguns v ▷ machinegun
machineries n ▷ machinery
machinery n (pl -ries) machines or machine parts collectively
machines n, v ▷ machine
machining v ▷ machine
machinist n (pl -s) person who operates a machine
machinists n ▷ machinist
machismo [mak-**izz**-moh] n (pl -s) exaggerated or strong masculinity
machismos n ▷ machismo
macho [**match**-oh] adj strongly or exaggeratedly masculine
mackerel n edible sea fish
mackintosh n (pl -es) waterproof raincoat of rubberized cloth
mackintoshes n ▷ mackintosh
macramé [mak-**rah**-mee] n (pl -s) ornamental work of knotted cord
macramés n ▷ macramé
macrobiotics n dietary system advocating whole grains and vegetables grown without chemical additives > **macrobiotic** adj
macrobiotic adj ▷ macrobiotics
macrocosm n (pl -s) the universe
macrocosms n ▷ macrocosm
mad adj (madder, maddest) mentally deranged, insane > **madly** adv > **madness** n (pl -es) > **madman** n (pl -men) > **madwoman**

*n (pl -***women**)

madam *n (pl* **madams**) polite form of address to a woman
  madams *n* ▷ **madam**

madame [mad-**dam**] *n (pl* **mesdames**) [may-dam] French title equivalent to *Mrs*

madcap *adj* foolish or reckless

madden *v* (**-s, -ed, -ing**) infuriate or irritate
  > **maddening** *adj*
  maddened *v* ▷ **madden**
  maddening *v* ▷ **madden** ▶ *adj* ▷ **madden**
  maddens *v* ▷ **madden**

madder *n (pl -***s**) climbing plant ▶ *adj* ▷ **mad**
  maddest *adj* ▷ **mad**
  made *v* ▷ **make**

madeira [mad-**deer**-a] *n (pl -***s**) fortified white wine
  madeiras *n* ▷ **madeira**

mademoiselle [mad-mwah-**zel**, maid-mwah-zel] *n (pl -***s**) French title equivalent to *Miss*
  mademoiselles *n* ▷ **mademoiselle**

madonna *n (pl -***s**) the Virgin Mary
  madly *adv* ▷ **mad**
  madman *n* ▷ **mad**
  madmen *n* ▷ **mad**
  madness *n* ▷ **mad**
  madnesses *n* ▷ **madness**
  madonnas *n* ▷ **madonna**

madrigal *n (pl -***s**) 16th–17th-century part song for unaccompanied voices
  madrigals *n* ▷ **madrigal**
  madwoman *n* ▷ **mad**
  madwomen *n* ▷ **mad**

maelstrom [**male**-strom] *n (pl -***s**) great whirlpool
  maelstroms *n* ▷ **maelstrom**
  maestri *n* ▷ **maestro**

maestro [**my**-stroh] *n (pl* **-tri, -tros**) outstanding musician or conductor
  maestros *n* ▷ **maestro**

mafia *n (pl -***s**) international secret criminal organization
  mafias *n* ▷ **mafia**
  mafiosi *n* ▷ **mafioso**

mafioso *n (pl* **-sos, -si**) member of the Mafia
  mafiosos *n* ▷ **mafioso**

magazine *n (pl -***s**) periodical publication with articles by different writers
  magazines *n* ▷ **magazine**

magenta [maj-**jen**-ta] *adj* deep purplish-red

maggot *n (pl -***s**) larva of an insect > **maggoty** *adj*
  maggots *n* ▷ **maggot**
  maggoty *adj* ▷ **maggot**

magi [**maje**-eye] *pl n* wise men from the East

who came to worship the infant Jesus

magic *n (pl -***s**) supposed art of invoking supernatural powers to influence events
  ▶ *adj (also* **magical**) of, using, or like magic
  > **magically** *adv*
  magical *adj* ▷ **magic**
  magically *adv* ▷ **magic**

magician *n (pl -***s**) conjuror
  magicians *n* ▷ **magician**
  magics *n* ▷ **magic**

magisterial *adj* commanding or authoritative

magistrate *n (pl -***s**) public officer administering the law
  magistrates *n* ▷ **magistrate**

magma *n (pl -***s**) molten rock inside the earth's crust
  magmas *n* ▷ **magma**

magnanimous *adj* noble and generous
  > **magnanimously** *adv* > **magnanimity** *n (pl* -**ties**)
  magnanimities *n* ▷ **magnanimous**
  magnanimity *n* ▷ **magnanimous**
  magnanimously *n* ▷ **magnanimous**

magnate *n (pl -***s**) influential or wealthy person, esp. in industry
  magnates *n* ▷ **magnate**

magnesia *n (pl -***s**) white tasteless substance used as an antacid and a laxative; magnesium oxide
  magnesias *n* ▷ **magnesia**

magnesium *n (pl -***s**) (CHEM) silvery-white metallic element
  magnesiums *n* ▷ **magnesium**

magnet *n (pl -***s**) piece of iron or steel capable of attracting iron and pointing north when suspended

magnetic *adj* having the properties of a magnet > **magnetically** *adv*
  magnetically *adv* ▷ **magnetic**

magnetism *n (pl -***s**) magnetic property
  magnetisms *n* ▷ **magnetism**

magnetize *v* (**-zes, -zed, -zing**) make into a magnet
  magnetized *v* ▷ **magnetize**
  magnetizes *v* ▷ **magnetize**
  magnetizing *v* ▷ **magnetize**
  magnets *n* ▷ **magnet**

magneto [mag-**nee**-toe] *n (pl -***s**) apparatus for ignition in an internal-combustion engine

magnificent *adj* splendid or impressive
  > **magnificently** *adv* > **magnificence** *n (pl -***s**)
  magnificence *n* ▷ **magnificent**
  magnificences *n* ▷ **magnificent**
  magnificently *adv* ▷ **magnificent**

magnify *v* (**-fies, -ing, -fied**) increase in

apparent size > **magnification** n (pl -s)

magnification n ▷ magnify

magnifications n ▷ magnify

magnified v ▷ magnify

magnifies v ▷ magnify

magnifying v ▷ magnify

magnitude n (pl -s) relative importance or size

magnitudes n ▷ magnitude

magnolia n (pl -s) shrub or tree with showy white or pink flowers

magnolias n ▷ magnolia

magnum n (pl s) large wine bottle holding about 1.5 litres

magnums n ▷ magnum

magpie n (pl -s) black-and-white bird

magpies n ▷ magpie

maharajah n (pl -s) former title of some Indian princes > **maharani** n fem (pl -s)

maharajahs n ▷ maharajah

maharani n ▷ maharajah

maharanis n ▷ maharajah

mahogany n (pl -nies) hard reddish-brown wood of several tropical trees

mahoganies n ▷ mahogany

mahout [ma-**howt**] n (pl s) (in India and the East Indies) elephant driver or keeper

mahouts n ▷ mahout

maid (also **maidservant**) n (pl -s) female servant

maiden n (pl -s) (Lit) young unmarried woman ▶ adj unmarried

maidenhair n (pl -s) fern with delicate fronds

maidenhairs n ▷ maidenhair

maidenhead n (pl -s) virginity

maidenheads n ▷ maidenhead

maidenly adj modest

maidens n ▷ maiden

maidishnesses n ▷ maid

maids n ▷ maid

maidservant n ▷ maid

maidservants n ▷ maid

mail[1] n (pl -s) letters and packages transported and delivered by the post office ▶ v (-s, -ing, -ed) send by mail

mail[2] n (pl -s) flexible armour of interlaced rings or links

mailbox n (pl -es) (US, CANADIAN & AUST) box into which letters and parcels are delivered

mailboxes n ▷ mailbox

mailed v ▷ mail[1]

mailing v ▷ mail[1]

mails n ▷ mail[1,2] ▶ v ▷ mail[2]

mailshot n (pl -s) (BRIT) posting of advertising material to many selected people at once

mailshots n ▷ mailshot

maim v (-s, -ing, -ed) cripple or mutilate

maimed v ▷ maim

maiming v ▷ maim

maims v ▷ maim

main adj chief or principal ▶ n (pl -s) principal pipe or line carrying water, gas, or electricity

mainframe n (pl -s) ▶ adj (COMPUTERS) (denoting) a high-speed general-purpose computer

mainframes n ▷ mainframe

mainland n (pl -s) stretch of land which forms the main part of a country

mainlands n ▷ mainland

mainly adv for the most part, chiefly

mainmast n (pl -s) chief mast of a ship

mainmasts n ▷ mainmast

mains n ▷ main

mainsail n (pl -s) largest sail on a mainmast

mainsails n ▷ mainsail

mainspring n (pl -s) chief cause or motive

mainsprings n ▷ mainspring

mainstay n (pl -s) chief support

mainstays n ▷ mainstay

mainstream adj (of) a prevailing cultural trend

maintain v (-s, -ing, -ed) continue or keep in existence

maintained v ▷ maintain

maintaining v ▷ maintain

maintains v ▷ maintain

maintenance n (pl -s) maintaining

maintenances n ▷ maintenance

maisonette n (pl -s) (BRIT) flat with more than one floor

maisonettes n ▷ maisonette

maize n (pl -s) type of corn with spikes of yellow grains

maizes n ▷ maize

majesty n (pl -ties) stateliness or grandeur > **majestic** adj > **majestically** adv

majestic adj ▷ majesty

majestically adv ▷ majesty

majesties n ▷ majesty

major adj greater in number, quality, or extent ▶ n (pl -s) middle-ranking army officer ▶ v (-s, -ing, -ed) (foll. by **in**) (US, CANADIAN, S AFR, AUST & NZ) do one's principal study in (a particular subject)

majordomo n (pl -s) chief steward of a great household

majordomos n ▷ majordomo

majored v ▷ major

majoring v ▷ major

majorities n ▷ majority

majority n (pl -ties) greater number

majors n, v ▷ major

make v (-kes, -king, made) create, construct, or establish ▶ n (pl -s) brand, type, or style

maker (pl -s) ▷ **makeweight** n (pl -s) something unimportant added to make up a lack

maker n ▷ make

makers n ▷ make

makes n, v ▷ make

makeshift adj serving as a temporary substitute

makeup n (pl -s) cosmetics

makeups n ▷ makeup

making v ▷ make ▶ n (pl -s) creation or production

makings n ▷ making

malachite [mal-a-kite] n (pl -s) green mineral

malachites n ▷ malachite

maladjusted adj (PSYCHOL) unable to meet the demands of society > **maladjustment** n (pl -s)

maladjustment n ▷ maladjusted

maladjustments n ▷ maladjusted

maladministration n (pl -s) inefficient or dishonest administration

maladministrations n ▷ maladministration

maladroit adj clumsy or awkward

malady n (pl -dies) disease or illness

maladies n ▷ malady

malaise [mal-laze] n (pl -s) vague feeling of unease, illness, or depression

malaises n ▷ malaise

malapropism n (pl -s) comical misuse of a word by confusion with one which sounds similar, e.g. I am not under the affluence of alcohol

malapropisms n ▷ malapropism

malaria n (pl -s) infectious disease caused by the bite of some mosquitoes > **malarial** adj

malarias n ▷ malaria

malarial adj ▷ malaria

malcontent n (pl -s) discontented person

malcontents n ▷ malcontent

male adj of the sex which can fertilize female reproductive cells ▶ n (pl males) male person or animal

males n ▷ male

malediction [mal-lid-dik-shun] n (pl -s) curse

maledictions n ▷ malediction

malefactor [mal-if-act-or] n (pl -s) criminal or wrongdoer

malefactors n ▷ malefactor

malevolent [mal-lev-a-lent] adj wishing evil to others > **malevolently** adv > **malevolence** n (pl -s)

malevolence n ▷ malevolent

malevolences n ▷ malevolent

malevolently adv ▷ malevolent

malfeasance [mal-fee-zanss] n (pl -s) misconduct, esp. by a public official

malfeasances n ▷ malfeasance

malformed adj misshapen or deformed > **malformation** n (pl -s)

malformation n ▷ malformed

malformations n ▷ malformed

malfunction v (-s, -ing, -ed) function imperfectly or fail to function ▶ n (pl -s) defective functioning or failure to function

malfunctioned v ▷ malfunction

malfunctioning v ▷ malfunction

malfunctions v, n ▷ malfunction

malice [mal-iss] n (pl -s) desire to cause harm to others > **malicious** adj > **maliciously** adv

malices n ▷ malice

malicious adj ▷ malice

maliciously adj ▷ malice

malign [mal-line] v (-s, -ing, -ed) slander or defame ▶ adj evil in influence or effect > **malignity** n (pl -nities) evil disposition

malignancies n ▷ malignant

malignancy n ▷ malignant

malignant [mal-lig-nant] adj seeking to harm others > **malignancy** n (pl -cies)

maligned v ▷ malign

maligning v ▷ malign

malignities n ▷ malign

malignity n ▷ malign

maligns v ▷ malign

malinger v (-s, -ing, -ed) feign illness to avoid work > **malingerer** n (pl -s)

malingered v ▷ malinger

malingerer n ▷ malinger

malingering v ▷ malinger

malingerers n ▷ malinger

malingers v ▷ malinger

mall [mawl] n (pl -s) street or shopping area closed to vehicles

mallard n wild duck

malleable [mal-lee-a-bl] adj capable of being hammered or pressed into shape > **malleability** n (pl -ties)

malleability n ▷ malleable

malleabilities n ▷ malleable

mallee n (pl -s) (AUST) low-growing eucalypt in dry regions

mallees n ▷ mallee

mallet n (pl -s) (wooden) hammer

mallets n ▷ mallet

mallow n (pl -s) plant with pink or purple flowers

mallows n ▷ mallow

malls *n* ▷ mall
malnutrition *n* (*pl* -s) inadequate nutrition
 malnutritions *n* ▷ malnutrition
malodorous [mal-**lode**-or-uss] *adj* bad-smelling
malpractice *n* (*pl* -s) immoral, illegal, or
 unethical professional conduct
 malpractices *n* ▷ malpractice
malt *n* (*pl* -s) grain, such as barley, prepared for
 use in making beer or whisky
 malts *n* ▷ malt
maltreat *v* (-s, -ing, -ed) treat badly
 > **maltreatment** *n* (*pl* -s)
 maltreated *v* ▷ maltreat
 maltreating *v* ▷ maltreat
 maltreatment *n* ▷ maltreat
 maltreatments *n* ▷ maltreat
 maltreats *v* ▷ maltreat
mama *n* (*pl* -s) (*Old-fashioned*) mother
 mamas *n* ▷ mama
mamba *n* (*pl* -s) deadly S African snake
 mambas *n* ▷ mamba
 mamma *n* (*pl* -s) ▷ mama
 mammas *n* ▷ mamma
mammal *n* (*pl* -s) animal of the type that
 suckles its young > **mammalian** *adj*
 mammalian *adj* ▷ mammal
 mammals *n* ▷ mammal
mammary *adj* of the breasts or milk-
 producing glands
mammon *n* (*pl* -s) wealth regarded as a source
 of evil
 mammons *n* ▷ mammon
mammoth *n* (*pl* -s) extinct elephant-like
 mammal ▶ *adj* colossal
 mammoths *n* ▷ mammoth
man *n* (*pl* men) adult male ▶ *v* (-s, -nning,
 -nned) supply with sufficient people for
 operation or defence > **manhood** *n* (*pl* -s)
mana *n* (*pl* -s) (NZ) authority, influence
manacle [**man**-a-kl] *n* (*pl* -s) handcuff or fetter
 ▶ *v* (-les, -ling, -led) handcuff or fetter
 manacled *v* ▷ manacle
 manacling *v* ▷ manacle
 manacles *n, v* ▷ manacle
manage *v* (-ges, -ging, -ged) succeed in doing
 > **manageable** *adj* > **management** *n* (*pl* -s)
 managers collectively
 manageable *adj* ▷ manage
 managed *v* ▷ manage
 managing *v* ▷ manage
 management *n* ▷ manage
 managements *n* ▷ manage
 manages *v* ▷ manage
manager *n* (*pl* -s) person in charge of a
 business, institution, actor, sports team, etc.

> **managerial** *adj*
manageress *n* (*pl* -es) woman in charge of a
 business, institution, actor, sports team, etc.
 manageresses *n* ▷ manager
 managerial *adj* ▷ manager
 managers *n* ▷ manager
manas *n* ▷ mana
manatee *n* (*pl* -s) large tropical plant-eating
 aquatic mammal
 manatees *n* ▷ manatee
mandarin *n* (*pl* -s) high-ranking government
 official
 mandarins *n* ▷ mandarin
mandate *n* (*pl* -s) official or authoritative
 command ▶ *v* (-tes, -ting, -ted) give authority
 to
 mandated *v* ▷ mandate
 mandates *n, v* ▷ mandate
 mandating *v* ▷ mandate
mandatory *adj* compulsory
mandible *n* (*pl* -s) lower jawbone or jawlike
 part
 mandibles *n* ▷ mandible
mandolin *n* (*pl* s) musical instrument with
 four pairs of strings
 mandolins *n* ▷ mandolin
mandrake *n* (*pl* -s) plant with a forked root,
 formerly used as a narcotic
 mandrakes *n* ▷ mandrake
mandrel *n* (*pl* -s) shaft on which work is held
 in a lathe
 mandrels *n* ▷ mandrel
mandrill *n* (*pl* -s) large blue-faced baboon
 mandrills *n* ▷ mandrill
mane *n* (*pl* -s) long hair on the neck of a horse,
 lion, etc.
 manes *n* ▷ mane
manful *adj* determined and brave > **manfully**
 adv
 manfully *adv* ▷ manful
manganese *n* (*pl* -s) (CHEM) brittle greyish-
 white metallic element
 manganeses *n* ▷ manganese
mange *n* (*pl* -s) skin disease of domestic
 animals
 manges *n* ▷ mange
mangelwurzel *n* (*pl* -s) variety of beet used as
 cattle food
 mangelwurzels *n* ▷ mangelwurzel
manger *n* (*pl* -s) eating trough in a stable or
 barn
 mangers *n* ▷ manger
mangetout [mawnzh-**too**] *n* (*pl* -s) variety of
 pea with an edible pod
 mangetouts *n* ▷ mangetout

mangier adj ▷ mangy
mangiest adj ▷ mangy
mangle[1] v (-les, -ling, -led) destroy by crushing and twisting
mangle[2] n (pl -s) machine with rollers for squeezing water from washed clothes ▶ v (-les, -ling, -led) put through a mangle
  mangled v ▷ mangle[1,2]
  mangling v ▷ mangle[1,2]
  mangles v ▷ mangle[1,2] ▶ n ▷ mangle[2]
mango n (pl -goes, -gos) tropical fruit with sweet juicy yellow flesh
  mangoes n ▷ mango
  mangos n ▷ mango
mangrove n (pl -s) tropical tree with exposed roots, which grows beside water
  mangroves n ▷ mangrove
mangy adj (-gier, -giest) having mange
manhandle v (-les, -ling, -led) treat roughly
  manhandled v ▷ manhandle
  manhandling v ▷ manhandle
  manhandles v ▷ manhandle
manhole n (pl -s) hole with a cover, through which a person can enter a drain or sewer
  manholes n ▷ manhole
  manhood n ▷ man
  manhoods n ▷ man
mania n (pl -s) extreme enthusiasm > **maniacal** [man-**eye**-a-kl] ▶ adj
maniac n (pl -s) mad person
  maniacal adj ▷ mania
  maniacs n ▷ mania
  manias n ▷ mania
manic adj affected by mania
manicure n (pl -s) cosmetic care of the fingernails and hands ▶ v (-res, -ring, -red) care for (the fingernails and hands) in this way > **manicurist** n (pl -s)
  manicured v ▷ manicure
  manicures n, v ▷ manicure
  manicuring v ▷ manicure
  manicurist n ▷ manicure
  manicurists n ▷ manicure
manifest adj easily noticed, obvious ▶ v (-s, -ing, -ed) show plainly ▶ n (pl -s) list of cargo or passengers for customs > **manifestation** n (pl -s)
  manifestation n ▷ manifest
  manifestations n ▷ manifest
  manifested v ▷ manifest
  manifesting v, n ▷ manifest
manifesto n (pl -tos, -toes) declaration of policy as issued by a political party
  manifestoes n ▷ manifesto
  manifestos n ▷ manifesto

manifests v ▷ manifest
manifold adj numerous and varied ▶ n (pl -s) pipe with several outlets, esp. in an internal-combustion engine
  manifolds n ▷ manifold
manikin n (pl -s) little man or dwarf
  manikins n ▷ manikin
manila, manilla n (pl -s) strong brown paper used for envelopes
  manilas n ▷ manila
  manillas n ▷ manila
manipulate v (-tes, -ting, -ted) handle skilfully > **manipulation** n (pl -s) > **manipulative** adj > **manipulator** n (pl -s)
  manipulated v ▷ manipulate
  manipulates v ▷ manipulate
  manipulating v ▷ manipulate
  manipulation n ▷ manipulate
  manipulations n ▷ manipulate
  manipulative adj ▷ manipulate
  manipulator n ▷ manipulate
  manipulators n ▷ manipulate
mankind n (pl -s) human beings collectively
  mankinds n ▷ mankind
  manlier adj ▷ manly
  manliest adj ▷ manly
  manliness n ▷ manly
  manlinesses n ▷ manly
manly adj (-lier, -liest) (possessing qualities) appropriate to a man > **manliness** n (pl -s)
manna n (pl -s) (BIBLE) miraculous food which sustained the Israelites in the wilderness
  mannas n ▷ manna
  manned v ▷ man
mannequin n (pl -s) woman who models clothes at a fashion show
  mannequins n ▷ mannequin
manner n (pl -s) way a thing happens or is done > **mannered** adj affected
  mannered adj ▷ manner
mannerism n (pl -s) person's distinctive habit or trait
  mannerisms n ▷ manner
  manners n ▷ manner
mannikin n (pl -s) ▷ manikin
  mannikins n ▷ manikin
  manning v ▷ man
mannish adj (of a woman) like a man
manoeuvre [man-**noo**-ver] n (pl -s) skilful movement military or naval exercises ▶ v (-res, -ring, -red) manipulate or contrive skilfully or cunningly > **manoeuvrable** adj
  manoeuvred v ▷ manoeuvre
manoeuvres n, v ▷ manoeuvre
  manoeuvring v ▷ manoeuvre

manor *n* (*pl* -s) (BRIT) large country house and its lands > **manorial** *adj*

manorial *adj* ▷ manor

manors *n* ▷ manor

manpower *n* (*pl* -s) available number of workers

manpowers *n* ▷ manpower

manqué [mong-kay] *adj* would-be

mans *v* ▷ man

manse *n* (*pl* -s) house provided for a minister in some religious denominations

manses *n* ▷ manse

manservant *n* (*pl* menservants) male servant, esp. a valet

mansion *n* (*pl* -s) large house

mansions *n* ▷ mansion

manslaughter *n* (*pl* -s) unlawful but unintentional killing of a person

manslaughters *n* ▷ manslaughter

mantel *n* (*pl* -s) structure round a fireplace

mantelpiece *n* (*pl* -es) shelf above a fireplace

mantelpieces *n* ▷ mantelpiece

mantels *n* ▷ mantel

mantilla *n* (*pl* -s) (in Spain) a lace scarf covering a woman's head and shoulders

mantillas *n* ▷ mantilla

mantis *n* (*pl* -ses, -tes) carnivorous insect like a grasshopper

mantes *n* ▷ mantis

mantises *n* ▷ mantis

mantle *n* (*pl* -s) loose cloak

mantles *n* ▷ mantle

mantra *n* (*pl* -s) (HINDUISM, BUDDHISM) any sacred word or syllable used as an object of concentration

mantras *n* ▷ mantra

manual *adj* of or done with the hands ▶ *n* (*pl* -s) handbook > **manually** *adv*

manually *adv* ▷ manual

manuals *n* ▷ manual

manufacture *v* (-res, -ring, -red) process or make (goods) on a large scale using machinery ▶ *n* (*pl* -s) process of manufacturing goods

manufactured *v* ▷ manufacture

manufacturer *n* (*pl* -s) company that manufactures goods

manufacturers *n* ▷ manufacturer

manufactures *v*, *n* ▷ manufacture

manufacturing *v* ▷ manufacture

manure *n* (*pl* -s) animal excrement used as a fertilizer

manures *n* ▷ manure

manuscript *n* (*pl* -s) book or document, orig. one written by hand

manuscripts *n* ▷ manuscript

many *adj* (more, most) numerous ▶ *n* large number

map *n* (*pl* -s) representation of the earth's surface or some part of it, showing geographical features ▶ *v* (-s, -pping, -pped) make a map of

maple *n* (*pl* -s) tree with broad leaves, a variety of which (**sugar maple**) yields sugar

maples *n* ▷ maple

mapped *v* ▷ map

mapping *v* ▷ map

maps *n*, *v* ▷ map

mar *v* (-s, -rring, -rred) spoil or impair

marabou *n* (*pl* -s) large black-and-white African stork

marabous *n* ▷ marabou

maraca [mar-**rak**-a] *n* (*pl* -s) shaken percussion instrument made from a gourd containing dried seeds etc.

maracas *n* ▷ maraca

marae *n* (*pl* -s) (NZ) enclosed space in front of a Maori meeting house

maraes *n* ▷ marae

marathon *n* (*pl* -s) long-distance race of 26 miles 385 yards (42.195 kilometres)

marathons *n* ▷ marathon

marauder *n* ▷ marauding

marauders *n* ▷ marauder

marauding *adj* wandering or raiding in search of plunder > **marauder** *n* (*pl* -s)

marble *n* (*pl* -s) kind of limestone with a mottled appearance, which can be highly polished ▶ **marbled** *adj* having a mottled appearance like marble

marbled *n* ▷ marble

marbles *n* ▷ marble

march[1] *v* (-es, -ing, -ed) walk with a military step ▶ *n* (*pl* -es) action of marching > **marcher** *n* (*pl* -s)

march[2] *n* (*pl* -s) border or frontier

marched *v* ▷ march[1]

marches *v* ▷ march[1] ▶ *n* ▷ march[1,2]

marching *v* ▷ march[1]

marchioness [marsh-on-**ness**] *n* (*pl* -es) woman holding the rank of marquis

marchionesses *n* ▷ marchioness

mare *n* (*pl* -s) female horse or zebra

mares *n* ▷ mare

margarine *n* (*pl* -s) butter substitute made from animal or vegetable fats

margarines *n* ▷ margarine

marge *n* (*pl* -s) (*Informal*) margarine

marges *n* ▷ marge

margin *n* (*pl* -s) edge or border > **marginal** *adj*

insignificant, unimportant > **marginally** adv
marginal adj ▷ margin
marginalize v (-zes, -zing, -zed) make or treat
as insignificant
marginalized v ▷ marginalize
marginalizes v ▷ marginalize
marginalizing v ▷ marginalize
margins n ▷ margin
marguerite n (pl -s) large daisy
marguerites n ▷ marguerite
marigold n (pl -s) plant with yellow or orange
flowers
marigolds n ▷ marigold
marijuana [mar-ree-**wah**-na] n (pl -s) dried
flowers and leaves of the cannabis plant,
used as a drug, esp. in cigarettes
marijuanas n ▷ marijuana
marina n (pl -s) harbour for yachts and other
pleasure boats
marinas n ▷ marina
marinade n (pl -s) seasoned liquid in which
fish or meat is soaked before cooking ▶ v
(-des, -ding, -ded) ▷ marinate
marinaded v ▷ marinade
marinades n, v ▷ marinade
marinading v ▷ marinade
marinate v (-tes, -ting, -ted) soak in marinade
marinated v ▷ marinate
marinates v ▷ marinate
marinating v ▷ marinate
marine adj of the sea or shipping ▶ n (pl -s)
(esp. in Britain and the US) soldier trained for
land and sea combat
mariner n (pl -s) sailor
mariners n ▷ mariner
marines n ▷ marine
marionette n (pl -s) puppet worked with
strings
marionettes n ▷ marionette
marital adj relating to marriage
maritime adj relating to shipping
marjoram n (pl -s) aromatic herb used for
seasoning food and in salads
marjorams n ▷ marjoram
mark¹ n (pl -s) line, dot, scar, etc. visible on
a surface ▶ v (-s, -ing, -ed) make a mark on
> **marked** adj noticeable > **markedly** adv
> **marker** n (pl -s)
mark² n ▷ Deutschmark
marked v, adj ▷ mark¹
markedly adv ▷ mark¹
marker n ▷ mark¹
markers n ▷ mark
marking v ▷ mark¹
marks n ▷ mark¹,² ▶ v ▷ mark¹

market n (pl -s) assembly or place for buying
and selling ▶ v (-s, -ing, -ed) offer or produce
for sale > **marketable** adj
marketable adj ▷ market
marketing n (pl -s) part of a business that
controls the way that goods or services are
sold
marketings n ▷ marketing
marketplace n (pl -s) market
marketplaces n ▷ marketplace
markets n, v ▷ market
marksman n (pl -men) person skilled at
shooting > **marksmanship** n (pl -s)
marksmanship n ▷ marksman
marksmanships n ▷ marksman
marksmen n ▷ marksman
marl n (pl -s) soil formed of clay and lime, used
as fertilizer
marls n ▷ marl
marlin n large food and game fish of warm and
tropical seas, with a very long upper jaw
marlinespike, marlinspike n (pl -s) pointed
hook used to separate strands of rope
marlinespikes n ▷ marlinespike
marlinspikes n ▷ marlinspike
marmalade n (pl -s) jam made from citrus
fruits
marmalades n ▷ marmalade
marmoreal adj of or like marble
marmoset n (pl -s) small bushy-tailed monkey
marmosets n ▷ marmoset
marmot n (pl -s) burrowing rodent
marmots n ▷ marmot
maroon¹ adj reddish-purple
maroon² v (-s, -ing, -ed) abandon ashore, esp.
on an island
marooned v ▷ maroon
marooning v ▷ maroon
maroons v ▷ maroon
marquee n (pl -s) large tent used for a party or
exhibition
marquees n ▷ marquee
marquess [mar-kwiss] n (pl -es) (BRIT)
nobleman of the rank below a duke
marquesses n ▷ marquess
marquetry n (pl -ries) ornamental inlaid work
of wood
marquetries n ▷ marquetry
marquis n (pl -es) (in some European
countries) nobleman of the rank above a
count
marquises n ▷ marquis
marred v ▷ mar
marriage n (pl -s) state of being married
> **marriageable** adj

marriageable *adj* ▷ marriage
marriages *n* ▷ marriage
married *v* ▷ marry
marries *v* ▷ marry
marring *v* ▷ mar
marrow *n* (*pl* -s) fatty substance inside bones
marrows *n* ▷ marrow
marry *v* (-ries, -ing, -ried) take as a husband or wife
marrying *v* ▷ marry
mars *v* ▷ mar
marsala [mar-**sah**-la] *n* (*pl* -s) dark sweet wine
marsh *n* (*pl* -es) low-lying wet land > **marshy** *adj* (-shier, -shiest)
marshal *n* (*pl* -s) officer of the highest rank ▶ *v* (-s, -shalling, -shalled) arrange in order
marshalled *v* ▷ marshal
marshalling *v* ▷ marshal
marshals *n*, *v* ▷ marshal
marshes *n* ▷ marsh
marshier *adj* ▷ marsh
marshiest *adj* ▷ marsh
marshmallow *n* (*pl* -s) spongy pink or white sweet
marshmallows *n* ▷ marshmallow
marshy *n* ▷ marsh
marsupial [mar-**soop**-ee-al] *n* (*pl* -s) animal that carries its young in a pouch
marsupialians *n* ▷ marsupial
marsupials *n* ▷ marsupial
mart *n* (*pl* -s) market
marts *n* ▷ mart
marten *n* (*pl* -s) weasel-like animal
martens *n* ▷ marten
martial *adj* of war, warlike
martian [**marsh**-an] *adj* of Mars ▶ *n* (*pl* -s) supposed inhabitant of Mars
martians *n* ▷ martian
martin *n* (*pl* -s) bird with a slightly forked tail
martins *n* ▷ martin
martinet *n* (*pl* -s) person who maintains strict discipline
martinets *n* ▷ martinet
martini *n* (*pl* -s) cocktail of vermouth and gin
martinis *n* ▷ martini
martyr *n* (*pl* -s) person who dies or suffers for his or her beliefs ▶ *v* (-s, -ing, -ed) make a martyr of > **martyrdom** *n* (*pl* -s)
martyrdom *n* ▷ martyr
martyrdoms *n* ▷ martyr
martyred *v* ▷ martyr
martyring *v* ▷ martyr
martyrs *n*, *v* ▷ martyr
marvel *v* (-s, -velling, -velled) be filled with wonder ▶ *n* wonderful thing

marvelled *v* ▷ marvel
marvelling *v* ▷ marvel
marvellous *adj* amazing
marvels *v* ▷ marvel
marzipan *n* (*pl* -s) paste of ground almonds, sugar, and egg whites
marzipans *n* ▷ marzipan
mascara *n* (*pl* -s) cosmetic for darkening the eyelashes
mascaras *n* ▷ mascara
mascot *n* (*pl* -s) person, animal, or thing supposed to bring good luck
mascots *n* ▷ mascot
masculine *adj* relating to males > **masculinity** *n* (*pl* -ties)
masculinities *n* ▷ masculine
masculinity *n* ▷ masculine
mash *n* (*pl* -es) (*Informal*) mashed potatoes ▶ *v* (-es, -ing, -ed) crush into a soft mass
mashed *v* ▷ mash
mashes *n*, *v* ▷ mash
mashing *v* ▷ mash
mask *n* (*pl* -s) covering for the face, as a disguise or protection ▶ *v* (-s, -ing, -ed) cover with a mask
masked *v* ▷ mask
masking *v* ▷ mask
masks *n*, *v* ▷ mask
masochism [**mass**-oh-kiz-zum] *n* (*pl* -s) condition in which (sexual) pleasure is obtained from feeling pain or from being humiliated > **masochist** *n* (*pl* -s) > **masochistic** *adj*
masochist *n* ▷ masochism
masochistic *n* ▷ masochism
masochists *n* ▷ masochism
mason *n* (*pl* -s) person who works with stone
masonic *adj* of Freemasonry
masonry *n* (*pl* -ries) stonework
masonries *n* (*pl* -ries) stonework
masons *n* ▷ mason
masque [**mask**] *n* (*pl* -s) (HIST) 16th–17th-century form of dramatic entertainment
masques *n* ▷ masque
masquerade [mask-er-**aid**] *n* (*pl* -s) deceptive show or pretence ▶ *v* (-des, -ding, -ded) pretend to be someone or something else
masqueraded *v* ▷ masquerade
masquerades *n*, *v* ▷ masquerade
masquerading *v* ▷ masquerade
mass *n* (*pl* -es) coherent body of matter ▶ *adj* large-scale ▶ *v* (-es, -ing, -ed) form into a mass
massacre [**mass**-a-ker] *n* (*pl* -s) indiscriminate killing of large numbers of people ▶ *v* (-res, -ring, -red) kill in large numbers

massacred v ▷ massacre

massacres n, v ▷ massacre

massacring v ▷ massacre

massage [mass-ahzh] n (pl -s) rubbing and kneading of parts of the body to reduce pain or stiffness ▶ v (-ges, -ging, -ged) give a massage to

massaged v ▷ massage

massages n, v ▷ massage

massaging v ▷ massage

massed v ▷ mass

masses n, v ▷ mass

masseur, fem **masseuse** n (pl -s) person who gives massages

masseurs n ▷ masseur

masseuse n ▷ masseuses

massing v ▷ mass

massive adj large and heavy

massif [mass-seef] n (pl -s) connected group of mountains

massifs n ▷ massif

mast[1] n (pl -s) tall pole for supporting something, esp. a ship's sails

mast[2] n (pl -s) fruit of the beech, oak, etc., used as pig fodder

masts n ▷ mast[1,2]

mastectomies n ▷ mastectomy

mastectomy [mass-tek-tom-ee] n (pl -mies) surgical removal of a breast

master n (pl -s) person in control, such as an employer or an owner of slaves or animals ▶ adj overall or controlling ▶ v (-s, -ing, -ed) acquire knowledge of or skill in

mastered v ▷ master

masterful adj domineering

masteries n ▷ mastery

mastering v ▷ master

masterly adj showing great skill

mastermind v plan and direct (a complex task) n person who plans and directs a complex task

masterpiece n outstanding work of art

masters n, v ▷ master

mastery n (pl -ries) expertise

mastic n (pl -s) gum obtained from certain trees

mastics n ▷ mastic

masticate v (-tes, -ting, -ted) chew > **mastication** n (pl -s)

masticated v ▷ masticate

masticates v ▷ masticate

masticating v ▷ masticate

mastication n ▷ masticate

mastications n ▷ masticate

mastiff n (pl -s) large dog

mastiffs n ▷ mastiff

mastitis n (pl -tises) inflammation of a breast or udder

mastitises n ▷ mastitis

mastodon n (pl -s) extinct elephant-like mammal

mastodons n ▷ mastodon

mastoid n (pl -s) projection of the bone behind the ear

mastoids n ▷ mastoid

masturbate v (-tes, -ting, -ted) fondle the genitals (of) > **masturbation** n (pl -s)

masturbated v ▷ masturbate

masturbates v ▷ masturbate

masturbating v ▷ masturbate

masturbation n ▷ masturbate

masturbations n ▷ masturbate

mat n (pl -s) piece of fabric used as a floor covering or to protect a surface ▶ v (-s, -tting, -tted) tangle or become tangled into a dense mass

matador n (pl -s) man who kills the bull in bullfights

matadors n ▷ matador

match[1] n (pl -es) contest in a game or sport ▶ v (-es, -ing, -ed) be exactly like, equal to, or in harmony with

match[2] n small stick with a tip which ignites when scraped on a rough surface > **matchbox** n (pl -es)

matchbox n ▷ match[2]

matchboxes n ▷ match[2]

matched v ▷ match[1]

matches v ▷ match[1] ▶ n ▷ match[1,2]

matching v ▷ match[1]

matchless adj unequalled

matchmaker n (pl -s) person who schemes to bring about a marriage > **matchmaking** n (pl -s) adj

matchmakers n ▷ matchmaker

matchmaking n ▷ matchmaker

matchmakings n ▷ matchmaker

matchstick n (pl -s) wooden part of a match ▶ adj (of drawn figures) thin and straight

matchsticks n ▷ matchstick

matchwood n (pl -s) small splinters

matchwoods n ▷ matchwood

mate[1] n (pl -s) (Informal) friend ▶ v (-tes, -ting, -ted) pair (animals) or (of animals) be paired for reproduction

mate[2] n (pl -s) checkmate ▶ v (-tes, -ting, -ted) (CHESS) checkmate

mated v ▷ mate[1,2]

mates n, v ▷ mate[1,2]

mating v ▷ mate[1,2]

material n (pl -s) substance of which a thing is made ▶ adj of matter or substance > **materialist** adj, n > **materialistic** adj
materialism n (pl -s) excessive interest in or desire for money and possessions
materialisms n ▷ materialism
materialist adj, n (pl -s) ▷ material
materialistic adj ▷ material
materialists n ▷ material
materialize v (-zes, -zing, -zed) actually happen > **materialization** n (pl -s)
materialization n ▷ materialize
materializations n ▷ materialize
materialized v ▷ materialize
materializes v ▷ materialize
materializing v ▷ materialize
materially adv considerably
materials n ▷ material
maternal adj of a mother ▶ adj of or for pregnant women
maternities n ▷ maternity
maternity n (pl -ties) motherhood
matey adj (-tier, -tiest) (BRIT) (Informal) friendly or intimate
mathematics n science of number, quantity, shape, and space > **mathematical** adj > **mathematically** adv > **mathematician** n (pl -s)
mathematical adj ▷ mathematics
mathematically adv ▷ mathematics
mathematician n ▷ mathematics
mathematicians n ▷ mathematics
maths n (Informal) mathematics
matier adj ▷ matey
matiest adj ▷ matey
matilda n (pl -s) (AUST HIST) swagman's bundle of belongings
matildas n ▷ matilda
matinée [**mat**-in-nay] n (pl -s) afternoon performance in a theatre or cinema
matinées n ▷ matinée
matins pl n early morning service in various Christian Churches
matriarch [**mate**-ree-ark] n (pl -s) female head of a tribe or family > **matriarchal** adj
matriarchal adj ▷ matriarch
matriarchies n ▷ matriarchy
matriarchs n ▷ matriarch
matriarchy n (pl -chies) society governed by a female, in which descent is traced through the female line
matrices n ▷ matrix
matricide n (pl -s) crime of killing one's mother
matricides n ▷ matricide
matriculate v (-tes, -ting, -ted) enrol or

be enrolled in a college or university > **matriculation** n (pl -s)
matriculated v ▷ matriculate
matriculates v ▷ matriculate
matriculating v ▷ matriculate
matriculation n ▷ matriculate
matriculations n ▷ matriculate
matrimonial adj ▷ matrimony
matrimonies n ▷ matrimony
matrimony n (pl -nies) marriage > **matrimonial** adj
matrix [**may**-trix] n (pl -trices) substance or situation in which something originates, takes form, or is enclosed
matron n (pl -s) staid or dignified married woman > **matronly** adj
matrons n ▷ matron
mats n, v ▷ mat
matt adj dull, not shiny
matted v ▷ mat
matter n (pl -s) substance of which something is made ▶ v (-s, -ing, -ed) be of importance
mattered v ▷ matter
mattering v ▷ matter
matters n, v ▷ matter
matting v ▷ mat
mattock n (pl -s) large pick with one of its blade ends flattened for loosening soil
mattocks n ▷ mattock
mattress n (pl -es) large stuffed flat case, often with springs, used on or as a bed
mattresses n ▷ mattress
mature adj fully developed or grown-up ▶ v (-res, -ring, -red) make or become mature > **maturation** n (pl -s)
maturation n ▷ mature
maturations n ▷ mature
matured v ▷ mature
matures v ▷ mature
maturing v ▷ mature
maturities n ▷ maturity
maturity n (pl -ties) state of being mature
maudlin adj foolishly or tearfully sentimental
maul v (-s, -ing, -ed) handle roughly
mauled v ▷ maul
mauling v ▷ maul
mauls v ▷ maul
maunder v (-s, -ing, -ed) talk or act aimlessly or idly
maundered v ▷ maunder
maundering v ▷ maunder
maunders v ▷ maunder
mausoleum [maw-so-**lee**-um] n (pl -s) stately tomb
mausoleums n ▷ mausoleum

mauve adj (-r, -est) pale purple
  mauver adj ▷ mauve
  mauvest adj ▷ mauve
maverick n (pl -s) ▶ adj independent and
  unorthodox (person)
  mavericks n ▷ maverick
maw n (pl -s) animal's mouth, throat, or
  stomach
  maws n ▷ maw
mawkish adj foolishly sentimental

max n (**maxes**). Max is a short form
of **maximum**. This is a useful word,
particularly if you find yourself with
an X toward the end of the game, with
limited opportunity to play it. Max
scores 12 points.

maxim n (pl -s) general truth or principle
  maxima n ▷ maximum
  maximal adj ▷ maxim
  maxims n ▷ maxim
maximum adj, n (pl -s, -ma) greatest possible
  (amount or number) > **maximal** adj
maximize v (-zes, -zing, -zed) increase to a
  maximum
  maximized v ▷ maximize
  maximizes v ▷ maximize
  maximizing v ▷ maximize
  maximums n ▷ maximum
may v (past tense **might**) used as an auxiliary to
  express possibility, permission, opportunity,
  etc.
may² n (pl -s) ▷ hawthorn
  mays n ▷ may²
maybe adv perhaps, possibly
mayday n (pl -s) international radio distress
  signal
  maydays n ▷ mayday
  mayflies n ▷ mayfly
mayfly n (pl -lies) short-lived aquatic insect
mayhem n (pl -s) violent destruction or
  confusion
  mayhems n ▷ mayhem
mayonnaise n (pl -s) creamy sauce of egg
  yolks, oil, and vinegar
  mayonnaises n ▷ mayonnaise
mayor n (pl -s) head of a municipality
  mayoralties n ▷ mayoralty
mayoralty n (pl -ies) (term of) office of a mayor
mayoress n (pl -es) mayor's wife
  mayoresses n ▷ mayoress
  mayors n ▷ mayor
maypole n (pl -s) pole set up for dancing round
  on the first day of May to celebrate spring
  maypoles n ▷ maypole
maze n (pl -s) complex network of paths or

lines designed to puzzle
  mazes n ▷ maze
mazurka n (pl -s) lively Polish dance
  mazurkas n ▷ mazurka
me pron ▷ I
mead n (pl -s) alcoholic drink made from honey
  meads n ▷ mead
meadow n (pl -s) piece of grassland
  meadows n ▷ meadow
meadowsweet n (pl -s) plant with dense
  heads of small fragrant flowers
  meadowseets n ▷ meadowsweet
meagre adj scanty or insufficient
meal¹ n (pl -s) occasion when food is served
  and eaten
meal² n (pl -s) grain ground to powder > **mealy**
  -lier, -liest) ▶ adj
mealie n (pl -s) (S AFR) maize
  mealier adj ▷ meal²
  mealies n ▷ mealie
  mealiest adj ▷ meal²
  meals n ▷ meal¹,²
  mealy adj ▷ meal²
mealymouthed adj not outspoken enough
mean¹ v (-s, -ing, meant) intend to convey or
  express > **meaningful** adj > **meaningless** adj
mean² adj (-er, -est) miserly, ungenerous, or
  petty > **meanly** adv > **meanness** n (pl -es)
mean³ n (pl -s) middle point between two
  extremes ▶ pl method by which something is
  done ▶ adj intermediate in size or quantity
  meaner adj ▷ mean²
  meanest adj ▷ mean²
meaning n (pl -s) sense, significance
  meaningful adj ▷ mean¹
  meaningless adj ▷ mean¹
  meanings n ▷ meaning
  meanly adv ▷ mean²
  meanness n ▷ mean²
  meannesses n ▷ mean²
  means v ▷ mean¹ ▶ n ▷ mean³
meander [mee-and-er] v (-s, -ing, -ed) follow a
  winding course ▶ n (pl -s) winding course
  meandered v ▷ meander
  meandering v ▷ meander
  meanders v, n ▷ meander
meantime n (pl -s) intervening period ▶ adv
  meanwhile
  meantimes n ▷ meantime
meanwhile adv during the intervening period
measles n infectious disease producing red
  spots
measly adj (Informal) meagre
measure n (pl -s) size or quantity ▶ v (-res,
  -ring, -red) determine the size or quantity of

> **measurable** *adj*
measurable *adj* ▷ measure
measured *adj* slow and steady ▶ *v* ▷ measure
measurement *n* (*pl* -s) measuring
measures *n*, *v* ▷ measure
measuring *v* ▷ measure
meat *n* (*pl* -s) animal flesh as food
meatier *adj* ▷ meaty
meatiest *adj* ▷ meaty
meats *n* ▷ meat
meaty *adj* (-tier, -tiest) (tasting) of or like meat
mechanic *n* (*pl* -s) person skilled in repairing or operating machinery
mechanical *adj* of or done by machines
> **mechanically** *adv*
mechanically *adv* ▷ mechanical
mechanics *n* scientific study of motion and force ▷ mechanic
mechanism *n* (*pl* -s) way a machine works
mechanisms *n* ▷ mechanism
mechanization *n* ▷ mechanize
mechanizations *n* ▷ mechanism
mechanize *v* (-zes, -zing, -zed) equip with machinery > **mechanization** *n* (*pl* -s)
mechanized *v* ▷ mechanize
mechanizes *v* ▷ mechanize
mechanizing *v* ▷ mechanize
medal *n* (*pl* -s) piece of metal with an inscription etc., given as a reward or memento
medallion *n* (*pl* -s) disc-shaped ornament worn on a chain round the neck
medallions *n* ▷ medallion
medallist *n* (*pl* -s) winner of a medal
medallists *n* ▷ medallist
medals *n* ▷ medal
meddle *v* (-les, -ling, -led) interfere annoyingly > **meddler** *n* (*pl* -s) > **meddlesome** *adj*
meddled *v* ▷ meddle
meddler *n* ▷ meddle
meddlers *n* ▷ meddle
meddles *v* ▷ meddle
meddlesome *adj* ▷ meddle
meddling *v* ▷ meddle
media *n* (*pl* -iae) ▷ medium the mass media collectively
mediae *n* ▷ media
mediaeval *adj* ▷ medieval
medial *adj* of or in the middle
median *adj*, *n* (*pl* -s) middle (point or line)
medians *n* ▷ median
mediate *v* (-tes, -ting, -ted) intervene in a dispute to bring about agreement > **mediation** *n* (*pl* -s) > **mediator** *n* (*pl* -s)
mediated *v* ▷ mediate

mediates *v* ▷ mediate
mediating *v* ▷ mediate
mediation *n* ▷ mediate
mediations *n* ▷ mediate
mediator *n* ▷ mediate
mediators *n* ▷ mediate
medic *n* (*pl* -s) (*Informal*) doctor or medical student
medics *n* ▷ medic
medical *adj* of the science of medicine ▶ *n* (*pl* -s) (*Informal*) medical examination
> **medically** *adv*
medically *adv* ▷ medical
medicals *n* ▷ medical
medicate *v* (-tes, -ting, -ted) treat with a medicinal substance
medicated *v* ▷ medicate
medicates *v* ▷ medicate
medicating *v* ▷ medicate
medication *n* (*pl* -s) (treatment with) a medicinal substance
medications *n* ▷ medication
medicine *n* (*pl* -s) substance used to treat disease
medicinal [med-**diss**-in-al] *adj* having therapeutic properties
medicines *n* ▷ medicine
medieval [med-ee-**eve**-al] *adj* of the Middle Ages
mediocre [mee-dee-**oak**-er] *adj* average in quality > **mediocrity** [mee-dee-**ok**-rit-ee] ▶ *n* (*pl* -ties)
mediocrities *n* ▷ mediocre
mediocrity *n* ▷ mediocre
meditate *v* (-tes, -ting, -ted) reflect deeply, esp. on spiritual matters > **meditation** *n* (*pl* -s) > **meditative** *adj* > **meditatively** *adv* > **meditator** *n* (*pl* -s)
meditated *v* ▷ meditate
meditates *v* ▷ meditate
meditating *v* ▷ meditate
meditation *n* ▷ meditate
meditations *n* ▷ meditate
meditative *adj* ▷ meditate
meditatively *adv* ▷ meditate
meditator *n* ▷ meditate
meditators *n* ▷ meditate
medium *adj* midway between extremes, average ▶ *n* (*pl* -dia, -diums) middle state, degree, or condition
mediums *n* ▷ medium
medlar *n* (*pl* -s) apple-like fruit of a small tree, eaten when it begins to decay
medlars *n* ▷ medlar
medley *n* (*pl* -s) miscellaneous mixture

medleys *n* ▷ medley
medulla [mid-**dull**-la] *n* (*pl* -las, -lae) marrow, pith, or inner tissue
  medullae *n* ▷ medulla
  medullas *n* ▷ medulla
meek *adj* (-er, -est) submissive or humble > **meekly** *adv* > **meekness** *n* (*pl* -es)
  meeker *adj* ▷ meek
  meekest *adj* ▷ meek
  meekly *adv* ▷ meek
  meekness *n* ▷ meek
  meeknesses *n* ▷ meek
meerkat *n* (*pl* -s) S African mongoose
  meerkats *n* ▷ meerkat
meerschaum [**meer**-shum] *n* (*pl* -s) white substance like clay
  meerschaums *n* ▷ meerschaum
meet[1] *v* (-s, meeting, met) come together (with) ▶ *n* (*pl* -s) meeting, esp. a sports meeting
meet[2] *adj* (-er, -est) (*Obs*) fit or suitable
  meeter *adj* ▷ meet[2]
  meetest *adj* ▷ meet[2]
meeting *n* (*pl* -s) coming together ▶ *v* ▷ meet[1]
  meets *v*, *n* ▷ meet[1]
megabyte *n* (*pl* -s) (COMPUTERS) 2^{20} or 1 048 576 bytes
  megabytes *n* ▷ megabyte
megahertz *n* one million hertz
megalith *n* (*pl* -s) great stone, esp. as part of a prehistoric monument > **megalithic** *adj*
  megalithic *adj* ▷ megalith
  megaliths *n* ▷ megalith
megalomania *n* (*pl* -s) craving for or mental delusions of power > **megalomaniac** *adj*, *n* (*pl* -s)
  megalomaniac *n* ▷ megalomania
  megalomaniacs *n* ▷ megalomania
  megalomanias *n* ▷ megalomania
megaphone *n* (*pl* -s) cone-shaped instrument used to amplify the voice
  megaphones *n* ▷ megaphone
megapode *n* (*pl* -s) bird of Australia, New Guinea, and adjacent islands
  megapodes *n* ▷ megapode
megaton *n* (*pl* -s) explosive power equal to that of one million tons of TNT
  megatons *n* ▷ megaton
melaleuca [mela-**loo**-ka] *n* (*pl* -s) Australian shrub or tree with a white trunk and black branches
  melaleucas *n* ▷ melaleuca
melancholia [mel-an-**kole**-lee-a] *n* (*pl* -s) state of depression
  melancholias *n* ▷ melancholia

melancholic *adj* ▷ melancholy
melancholies *n* ▷ melancholy
melancholy [**mel**-an-kol-lee] *n* (*pl* -lies) sadness or gloom ▶ *adj* sad or gloomy > **melancholic** *adj*, *n* (*pl* -s)
melange [may-**lahnzh**] *n* (*pl* -s) mixture
  melanges *n* ▷ melange
melanin *n* (*pl* -s) dark pigment found in the hair, skin, and eyes of humans and animals
  melanins *n* ▷ melanin
mêlée [**mel**-lay] *n* (*pl* -s) noisy confused fight or crowd
  mêlées *n* ▷ mêlée
mellifluous [mel-**lif**-flew-uss] *adj* (of sound) smooth and sweet
mellow *adj* soft, not harsh ▶ *v* (-s, -ing, -ed) make or become mellow
  mellowed *v* ▷ mellow
  mellowing *v* ▷ mellow
  mellows *v* ▷ mellow
melodic [mel-**lod**-ik] *adj* of melody
melodious [mel-**lode**-ee-uss] *adj* pleasing to the ear
melodrama *n* (*pl* -s) play full of extravagant action and emotion > **melodramatic** *adj*
  melodramas *n* ▷ melodrama
  melodramatic *adj* ▷ melodrama
melody *n* (*pl* -dies) series of musical notes which make a tune
melon *n* (*pl* -s) large round juicy fruit with a hard rind
  melons *n* ▷ melon
melt *v* (-s, -ing, -ed) (cause to) become liquid by heat
meltdown *n* (*pl* -s) (in a nuclear reactor) melting of the fuel rods, with the possible release of radiation
  meltdowns *n* ▷ meltdown
  melted *v* ▷ melt
  melting *v* ▷ melt
  melts *v* ▷ melt
member *n* (*pl* -s) individual making up a body or society > **membership** *n* (*pl* -s)
  members *n* ▷ member
  membership *n* ▷ member
  memberships *n* ▷ member
membrane *n* (*pl* -s) thin flexible tissue in a plant or animal body > **membranous** *adj*
  membranes *n* ▷ membrane
  membranous *adj* ▷ membrane
memento *n* (*pl* -tos, -toes) thing serving to remind, souvenir
  mementoes *n* ▷ memento
  mementos *n* ▷ memento
memo *n* (*pl* -s) ▷ memorandum

memos *n* ▷ memo
memoir [mem-wahr] *n* (*pl* -s) biography or historical account based on personal knowledge ▶ *pl* collection of these
  memoirs *n* ▷ memoir
memorable *adj* worth remembering, noteworthy > **memorably** *adv*
  memorably *adv* ▷ memorable
  memoranda *n* ▷ memorandum
memorandum *n* (*pl* -dums, -da) written record or communication within a business
  memorandums *n* ▷ memorandum
memorial *n* (*pl* -s) something serving to commemorate a person or thing ▶ *adj* serving as a memorial
  memorials *n* ▷ memorandum
memorize *v* (-zes, -zing, -zed) commit to memory
  memorized *v* ▷ memorize
  memorizes *v* ▷ memorize
  memorizing *v* ▷ memorize
memory *n* (*pl* -ries) ability to remember
men *n* ▷ man
menace *n* (*pl* -s) threat ▶ *v* (-ces, -cing, -ced) threaten, endanger > **menacing** *adj*
  menaced *v* ▷ menace
  menaces *n*, *v* ▷ menace
  menacing *v*, *adj* ▷ menace
ménage [may-nahzh] *n* (*pl* -s) household
  ménages *n* ▷ ménage
menagerie [min-**naj**-er-ee] *n* (*pl* -s) collection of wild animals for exhibition
  menageries *n* ▷ menagerie
mend *v* (-s, -ing, -ed) repair or patch ▶ *n* (*pl* -s) mended area
  mendacious *adj* ▷ mendacity
  mendacities *n* ▷ mendacity
mendacity *n* (*pl* -ties) (tendency to) untruthfulness > **mendacious** *adj*
  mended *v* ▷ mend
mendicant *adj* begging ▶ *n* (*pl* -s) beggar
  mendicants *n* ▷ mendicant
  mending *v* ▷ mend
  mends *v*, *n* ▷ mend
menhir [**men**-hear] *n* (*pl* -s) single upright prehistoric stone
  menhirs *n* ▷ menhir
menial [**mean**-nee-al] *adj* involving boring work of low status ▶ *n* (*pl* -s) person with a menial job
  menials *n* ▷ menial
meningitis [men-in-**jite**-iss] *n* (*pl* -es) inflammation of the membranes of the brain
  meningitises *n* ▷ meningitis
meniscus *n* (*pl* -ci) curved surface of a liquid

menisci *n* ▷ meniscus
  menopausal *adj* ▷ menopause
menopause *n* (*pl* -s) time when a woman's menstrual cycle ceases > **menopausal** *adj*
  menopauses *n* ▷ menopause
  menservants *n* ▷ manservant
menstruation *n* (*pl* -s) approximately monthly discharge of blood and cellular debris from the womb of a nonpregnant woman > **menstruate** *v* (-tes, -ting, -ted) > **menstrual** *adj*
  menstrual *adj* ▷ menstruation
  menstruated *v* ▷ menstruation
  menstruates *v* ▷ menstruation
  menstruating *v* ▷ menstruation
  menstruations *n* ▷ menstruation
mensuration *n* (*pl* -s) measuring, esp. in geometry
  mensurations *n* ▷ mensuration
mental *adj* of, in, or done by the mind > **mentally** *adv*
  mentalities *n* ▷ mentality
mentality *n* (*pl* -ties) way of thinking
  mentally *adv* ▷ mental
menthol *n* (*pl* -s) organic compound found in peppermint, used medicinally
  menthols *n* ▷ menthol
mention *v* (-s, -ing, -ed) refer to briefly ▶ *n* (*pl* -s) brief reference to a person or thing
  mentioned *v* ▷ mention
  mentioning *v* ▷ mention
  mentions *v*, *n* ▷ mention
mentor *n* (*pl* -s) adviser or guide
  mentors *n* ▷ mentor
menu *n* (*pl* -s) list of dishes to be served, or from which to order
  menus *n* ▷ menu
mercantile *adj* of trade or traders
  mercenaries *n* ▷ mercenary
mercenary *adj* influenced by greed ▶ *n* (*pl* -ries) hired soldier
  merchandises *n* ▷ merchandise
  merchandise *n* (*pl* -s) commodities
merchant *n* (*pl* -s) person engaged in trade, wholesale trader
  merchantman *n* (*pl* -men) trading ship
  merchantmen *n* ▷ merchantman
  merchants *n* ▷ merchant
merciful *adj* compassionate
  merciless *adj* ▷ mercy
mercurial *adj* lively, changeable
  mercuries *n* ▷ mercury
mercury *n* (*pl* -ries) (CHEM) silvery liquid metal
mercy *n* (*pl* -cies) compassionate treatment of an offender or enemy who is in one's power

> **merciless** adj

mere² adj (-r, -st) nothing more than > **merely** adv

mere² n (pl -s) (BRIT) (Obs) lake

merely adv ▷ **mere¹**

merer adj ▷ **mere¹**

meres n ▷ **mere²**

merest adj ▷ **mere¹**

meretricious adj superficially or garishly attractive but of no real value

merganser [mer-**gan**-ser] n (pl -s) large crested diving duck

mergansers n ▷ **merganser**

merge v (-ges, -ging, -ged) combine or blend

merged v ▷ **merge**

merger n (pl -s) combination of business firms into one

mergers n ▷ **merger**

merges v ▷ **merge**

merging v ▷ **merge**

mergings n ▷ **merge**

meridian n (pl -s) imaginary circle of the earth passing through both poles

meridians n ▷ **meridian**

meringue [mer-**rang**] n (pl -s) baked mixture of egg whites and sugar

meringues n ▷ **meringue**

merino n (pl -s) breed of sheep with soft wool

merinos n ▷ **merino**

merit n (pl -s) excellence or worth ▶ pl admirable qualities ▶ v (-s, -ing, -ed) deserve

merited v ▷ **merit**

meriting v ▷ **merit**

meritocracies n ▷ **meritocracy**

meritocracy [mer-it-**tok**-rass-ee] n (pl -s) rule by people of superior talent or intellect

meritorious adj deserving praise

merits n, v ▷ **merit**

merlin n (pl -s) small falcon

merlins n ▷ **merlin**

mermaid n (pl -s) imaginary sea creature with the upper part of a woman and the lower part of a fish

mermaids n ▷ **mermaid**

merrier adj ▷ **merry**

merriest adj ▷ **merry**

merrily adv ▷ **merry**

merriment n ▷ **merry**

merriments n ▷ **merry**

merry adj (-rier, -rriest) cheerful or jolly > **merrily** adv > **merriment** n (pl -s)

merrymaking n (pl -s) noisy, cheerful celebrations or fun

merrymakings n ▷ **merrymaking**

mesdames n ▷ **madame**

mesdemoiselles n ▷ **mademoiselle**

mesh n (pl -es) network or net ▶ v (-es, -ing, -ed) (of gear teeth) engage

meshed v ▷ **mesh**

meshes n, v ▷ **mesh**

meshing v ▷ **mesh**

mesmerize v (-zes, -zing, -zed) hold spellbound

mesmerized v ▷ **mesmerize**

mesmerizes v ▷ **mesmerize**

mesmerizing v ▷ **mesmerize**

meson [**mee**-zon] n (pl -s) elementary atomic particle

mesons n ▷ **meson**

mess n (pl -es) untidy or dirty confusion ▶ v (-es, -ing, -ed) muddle or dirty

message n (pl -s) communication sent

messages n ▷ **message**

messaging n (pl -s) sending and receiving of textual communications by mobile phone

messagings n ▷ **message**

messed v ▷ **mess**

messeigneurs n ▷ **monseigneur**

messenger n (pl -s) bearer of a message

messengers n ▷ **messenger**

messes n, v ▷ **mess**

messiah n (pl -s) promised deliverer > **messianic** adj

messiahs n ▷ **messiah**

messianic adj ▷ **messiah**

messier adj ▷ **messy**

messiest adj ▷ **messy**

messieurs n ▷ **monsieur**

messily adv ▷ **messy**

messing v ▷ **mess**

messy adj (-ssier, -ssiest) dirty, confused, or untidy > **messily** adv

met v ▷ **meet¹**

metabolic adj ▷ **metabolism**

metabolism [met-**tab**-oh-liz-zum] n (pl -s) chemical processes of a living body > **metabolic** adj

metabolisms n ▷ **metabolism**

metabolize v (-zes, -zing, -zed) produce or be produced by metabolism

metabolized v ▷ **metabolize**

metabolizes v ▷ **metabolize**

metabolizing v ▷ **metabolize**

metal n (pl -s) chemical element, such as iron or copper, that is malleable and capable of conducting heat and electricity > **metallic** adj

metallic adj ▷ **metal**

metallurgical adj ▷ **metallurgy**

metallurgist n ▷ **metallurgy**

metallurgists n ▷ **metallurgy**

metallurgy n (pl -gies) scientific study of the structure, properties, extraction, and refining of metals ▷ **metallurgical** adj ▷ **metallurgist** n (pl -s)
　metals n ▷ metal
metamorphic adj (of rocks) changed in texture or structure by heat and pressure
metamorphose v (-ses, -sing, -sed) transform
　metamorphosed v ▷ metamorphose
　metamorphoses n, v ▷ metamorphosis
　metamorphosing v ▷ metamorphose
metamorphosis [met-a-**more**-foss-is] n (pl -ses) [-foss-eez] change of form or character
metaphor n (pl -s) figure of speech in which a term is applied to something it does not literally denote in order to imply a resemblance ▷ **metaphorical** adj ▷ **metaphorically** adv
　metaphorically adv ▷ metaphor
　metaphors n ▷ metaphor
　metaphysical adj ▷ metaphysics
metaphysics n branch of philosophy concerned with being and knowing ▷ **metaphysical** adj
mete v (-tes, -ting, -ted) (usu. with **out**) deal out as punishment
　meted v ▷ mete
meteor n (pl -s) small fast-moving heavenly body, visible as a streak of incandescence if it enters the earth's atmosphere
meteoric [meet-ee-or-rik] adj of a meteor
meteorite n (pl -s) meteor that has fallen to earth
　meteorites n ▷ meteorite
　meteorological adj ▷ meteorology
　meteorologies n ▷ meteorology
　meteorologist n ▷ meteorology
　meteorologists n ▷ meteorology
meteorology n (pl -gies) study of the earth's atmosphere, esp. for weather forecasting ▷ **meteorological** adj ▷ **meteorologist** n (pl -s)
　meteors n ▷ meteor
meter n (pl -s) instrument for measuring and recording something, such as the consumption of gas or electricity ▶ v (-s, -ing, -ed) measure by meter
　meters n, v ▷ meter
　metes v ▷ mete
　meting v ▷ mete
methane n (pl -s) colourless inflammable gas
　methanes n ▷ methane
methanol n (pl -s) colourless poisonous liquid used as a solvent and fuel (also **methyl alcohol**)
　methanols n ▷ methanol

methinks v (past tense **methought**) (Obs) it seems to me
method n (pl -s) way or manner
methodical adj orderly ▷ **methodically** adv
　methodically adv ▷ methodical
　methodism n ▷ methodist
　methodisms n ▷ methodist
methodist n (pl -s) member of any of the Protestant churches originated by John Wesley and his followers ▶ adj of methodists or their Church ▷ methodism n (pl -s)
　methodists n ▷ methodist
　methodologies n ▷ methodology
methodology n (pl -gies) particular method or procedure
　methods n ▷ method
meths n (Informal) methylated spirits
methyl n (pl -s) (compound containing) a saturated hydrocarbon group of atoms
　methyls n ▷ methyl
meticulous adj very careful about details ▷ **meticulously** adv
　meticulously adv ▷ meticulous
métier [met-ee-ay] n (pl -s) profession or trade
　métiers n ▷ métier
　metonymies n ▷ metonymy
metonymy [mit-**on**-im-ee] n (pl -mies) figure of speech in which one thing is replaced by another associated with it, such as 'the Crown' for 'the queen'
metre n (pl -s) basic unit of length equal to about 1.094 yards (100 centimetres)
　metres n ▷ metre
metric adj of the decimal system of weights and measures based on the metre
metrical adj of measurement
metrication n (pl -s) conversion to the metric system
　metrications n ▷ metrication
metronome n (pl -s) instrument which marks musical time by means of a ticking pendulum
　metronomes n ▷ metronome
metropolis [mit-**trop**-oh-liss] n (pl -es) chief city of a country or region
　metropolises n ▷ metropolis
metropolitan adj of a metropolis
metrosexual adj, n (pl -s) (of) a heterosexual man who is preoccupied with his appearance
　metrosexuals n ▷ metrosexual
mettle n (pl -s) courage or spirit
　mettles n ▷ mettle
mew n (pl -s) cry of a cat ▶ v (-s, -ing, -ed) utter this cry
　mewed v ▷ mew
　mewing v ▷ mew

mews *n, v* ▷ mew

> **mezquit** *n* (**mezquit**). A mezquit is a small spiny tree or shrub. With its combination of Q and Z, mezquit is a very high-scoring word. As it contains seven letters, mezquit can earn you a bonus of 50 points if you manage to use all the letters on your rack to form it. Mezquit scores 28 points.

mezzanine [mez-zan-een] *n* (*pl* -s) intermediate storey, esp. between the ground and first floor
   mezzanines *n* ▷ mezzanine

mezzotint [met-so-tint] *n* (*pl* -s) method of engraving by scraping the roughened surface of a metal plate
   mezzotints *n* ▷ mezzotint

> **mi** *n* (**mis**). Mi is the third degree of a major scale in music. This isn't a high-scoring word, but can be very helpful when you want to form words in more than one direction. Mi scores 4 points.

miaow [mee-ow] *n* (*pl* -s) ▷ *v* (-s, -ing, -wed) ▷ mew
   miaowed *v* ▷ miaow
   miaowing *v* ▷ miaow
miaows *v, n* ▷ miaow
miasma [mee-azz-ma] *n* (*pl* -mata) unwholesome or foreboding atmosphere
   miasmata *n* ▷ miasma
mica [my-ka] *n* (*pl* -s) glasslike mineral used as an electrical insulator
   micas *n* ▷ mica
mice *n* ▷ mouse
microbe *n* (*pl* -s) minute organism, esp. one causing disease > **microbial** *adj*
   microbes *n* ▷ microbe
   microbial *adj* ▷ microbe
microchip *n* (*pl* -s) small wafer of silicon containing electronic circuits
   microchips *n* ▷ microchip
microcomputer *n* (*pl* -s) computer with a central processing unit contained in one or more silicon chips
   microcomputers *n* ▷ microcomputer
microcosm *n* (*pl* -s) miniature representation of something
   microcosms *n* ▷ microcosm
microfiche [my-kroh-feesh] *n* (*pl* -s) microfilm in sheet form
   microfiches *n* ▷ microfiche
microfilm *n* (*pl* -s) miniaturized recording of books or documents on a roll of film
   microfilms *n* ▷ microfilm
microlight *n* (*pl* -s) very small light private aircraft with large wings
   microlights *n* ▷ microlight
micrometer [my-krom-it-er] *n* (*pl* -s) instrument for measuring very small distances or angles
   micrometers *n* ▷ micrometer
micron [my-kron] *n* (*pl* -s) one millionth of a metre
   microns *n* ▷ micron
microorganism *n* (*pl* -ms) organism of microscopic size
   microorganisms *n* ▷ microorganism
microphone *n* (*pl* -s) instrument for amplifying or transmitting sounds
   microphones *n* ▷ microphone
microprocessor *n* (*pl* -s) integrated circuit acting as the central processing unit in a small computer
   microprocessors *n* ▷ microprocessor
microscope *n* (*pl* -s) instrument with lens(es) which produces a magnified image of a very small object > **microscopic** *adj* too small to be seen except with a microscope > **microscopically** *adv*
   microscopes *n* ▷ microscope
   microscopic *adj* ▷ microscope
   microscopically *adv* ▷ microscope
   microscopies *n* ▷ microscopy
microscopy *n* (*pl* -pies) use of a microscope
   microsurgeries *n* ▷ microsurgery
microsurgery *n* (*pl* -ries) intricate surgery using a special microscope and miniature precision instruments
microwave *n* (*pl* -s) electromagnetic wave with a wavelength of a few centimetres, used in radar and cooking ▶ *v* (-ves, -ving, -ved) cook in a microwave oven
   microwaved *v* ▷ microwave
   microwaves *n, v* ▷ microwave
   microwaving *v* ▷ microwave
mid *adj* intermediate, middle
midday *n* (*pl* -s) noon
   middays *n* ▷ midday
midden *n* (*pl* -s) (BRIT & AUST) dunghill or rubbish heap
   middens *n* ▷ midden
middle *adj* equidistant from two extremes ▶ *n* (*pl* -s) middle point or part
middleman *n* (*pl* -men) trader who buys from the producer and sells to the consumer
   middlemen *n* ▷ middleman
   middles *n* ▷ middle
middleweight *n* (*pl* -s) boxer weighing up to 160lb (professional) or 75kg (amateur)
   middleweights *n* ▷ middleweight

middling *adj* mediocre
midge *n* (*pl* -s) small mosquito-like insect
  midges *n* ▷ midge
midget *n* (*pl* -s) very small person or thing
  midgets *n* ▷ midget
midland *n* (*pl* -s) (BRIT, AUST & US) middle part
  of a country
  midlands *n* ▷ midland
midnight *n* (*pl* -s) twelve o'clock at night
  midnights *n* ▷ midnight
midriff *n* (*pl* -s) middle part of the body
  midriffs *n* ▷ midriff
midshipman *n* (*pl* -men) naval officer of the
  lowest commissioned rank
  midshipmen *n* ▷ midshipman
midsummer *n* (*pl* -s) middle of summer
  midsummers *n* ▷ midsummer
midway *adj*, *adv* halfway
midwife *n* (*pl* -wives) trained person who
  assists at childbirth > **midwifery** *n* (*pl* -ries)
  midwiferies *n* ▷ midwife
  midwifery *n* ▷ midwife
  midwives *n* ▷ midwife
midwinter *n* (*pl* -s) middle or depth of winter
  midwinters *n* ▷ midwinter
mien [**mean**] *n* (*pl* -s) (Lit) person's bearing,
  demeanour, or appearance
  miens *n* ▷ mien
miffed *adj* (Informal) offended or upset
might[1] ▷ may
might[2] *n* (*pl* -s) power or strength
  mightier *adj* ▷ mighty
  mightiest *adj* ▷ mighty
  mightily *adv* ▷ mighty
mighty *adj* (-tier, -tiest) powerful ▶ *adv* (US &
  AUST) (Informal) very > **mightily** *adv*
migraine [**mee**-grain] *n* (*pl* -s) severe headache,
  often with nausea and visual disturbances
  migraines *n* ▷ migraine
migrant *n* (*pl* -s) person or animal that moves
  from one place to another ▶ *adj* moving from
  one place to another
  migrants *n* ▷ migrant
migrate *v* (-tes, -ting, -ted) move from one
  place to settle in another > **migration** *n* (*pl* -s)
  migrated *v* ▷ migrate
  migrates *v* ▷ migrate
  migrating *v* ▷ migrate
  migration *n* ▷ migrate
  migrations *n* ▷ migrate
migratory *adj* (of an animal) migrating every
  year
mike *n* (*pl* -s) (Informal) microphone
  mikes *n* ▷ mike
milch *adj* (CHIEFLY BRIT) (of a cow) giving milk

mild *adj* (-er, -est) not strongly flavoured
  > **mildly** *adv* > **mildness** *n* (*pl* -es)
  milder *adj* ▷ mild
  mildest *adj* ▷ mild
mildew *n* (*pl* -s) destructive fungus on plants
  or things exposed to damp > **mildewed** *adj*
  mildewed *adj* ▷ mildew
  mildews *n* ▷ mildew
  mildly *adv* ▷ mild
  mildness *n* ▷ mild
  mildnesses *n* ▷ mild
mile *n* (*pl* -s) unit of length equal to 1760 yards
  or 1.609 kilometres
mileage *n* (*pl* -s) distance travelled in miles
  mileages *n* ▷ mileage
mileometer *n* (*pl* -s) (BRIT) device that records
  the number of miles a vehicle has travelled
  mileometers *n* ▷ mileometer
  miles *n* ▷ mile
milestone *n* (*pl* -s) significant event
  milestones *n* ▷ milestone
milieu [meal-**yer**] *n* (*pl* milieux, milieus) [meal-
  yerz] environment or surroundings
  milieus *n* ▷ milieu
  milieux *n* ▷ milieu
  militancies *n* ▷ militant
  militancy *n* ▷ militant
militant *adj* aggressive or vigorous in support
  of a cause > **militancy** *n* (*pl* -cies)
  militants *n* ▷ militant
  militaries *n* ▷ military
militarism *n* (*pl* -s) belief in the use of military
  force and methods
  militarisms *n* ▷ militarism
  militarist *n* ▷ military
  militarists *n* ▷ military
  militarized *adj* ▷ military
military *adj* of or for soldiers, armies, or war
  ▶ *n* (*pl* -ries) armed services > **militarist** *n* (*pl*
  -s) > **militarized** *adj*
militate *v* (-tes, -ting, -ted) (usu. with **against**
  or **for**) have a strong influence or effect
  militated *v* ▷ militate
  militates *v* ▷ militate
  militating *v* ▷ militate
militia [mill-**ish**-a] *n* (*pl* -s) military force of
  trained citizens for use in emergency only
  militias *n* ▷ militia
milk *n* (*pl* -s) white fluid produced by female
  mammals to feed their young ▶ *v* (-s, -ing, -ed)
  draw milk from > **milky** *adj* (-kier, -kiest)
  milked *v* ▷ milk
  milkier *adj* ▷ milk
  milkiest *adj* ▷ milk
  milking *v* ▷ milk

milkmaid n (pl -s) (esp. in former times) woman who milks cows
  milkmaids n ▷ milkmaid
milkman n (pl -men) (BRIT, AUST & NZ) man who delivers milk to people's houses
  milkmen n ▷ milkman
  milks n, v ▷ milk
milkshake n (pl -s) frothy flavoured cold milk drink
  milkshakes n ▷ milkshake
milksop n (pl -s) feeble man
  milksops n ▷ milk
  milky adj ▷ milk
mill n (pl -s) factory ▶ v (-s, -ing, -ed) grind, press, or process in or as if in a mill
  milled v ▷ mill
millennium n (pl -nnia, -nniums) period of a thousand years
  millennia n ▷ mill
  millenniums n ▷ mill
miller n (pl -s) person who works in a mill
  millers n ▷ miller
millet n (pl -s) type of cereal grass
  millets n ▷ millet
millibar n (pl -s) unit of atmospheric pressure
  millibars n ▷ millibar
millimetre n (pl -s) thousandth part of a metre
  millimetres n ▷ millimetre
milliner n (pl -s) maker or seller of women's hats > **millinery** n (pl -ries)
  millineries n ▷ milliner
  milliners n ▷ milliner
  millinery n ▷ milliner
  milling v ▷ mill
million n (pl -s) one thousand thousands
  > **millionth** adj, n (pl -s)
millionaire n (pl -s) person who owns at least a million pounds, dollars, etc.
  millionaires n ▷ millionaire
  millions n ▷ million
  millionths n ▷ million
millipede n (pl -s) small animal with a jointed body and many pairs of legs
  millipedes n ▷ millipede
  mills n, v ▷ mill
millstone n (pl -s) flat circular stone for grinding corn
  millstones n ▷ millstone
millwheel n (pl -s) waterwheel that drives a mill
  millwheels n ▷ millwheel
milometer n (pl -s) (BRIT) ▷ mileometer
  milometers n ▷ milometer
milt n (pl -s) sperm of fish
  milts n ▷ milt

mime n (pl -s) acting without the use of words
  ▶ v (-mes, -ming, -med) act in mime
  mimed v ▷ mime
  mimes n, v ▷ mime
  miming v ▷ mime
mimic v (-ics, -icking, -icked) imitate (a person or manner), esp. for satirical effect ▶ n (pl -s) person or animal that is good at mimicking
  > **mimicry** n (pl -ries)
  mimicked v ▷ mimic
  mimicking v ▷ mimic
  mimicry n ▷ mimic
  mimics n, v ▷ mimic
  mina n ▷ myna
  minas n ▷ myna
minaret n (pl -s) tall slender tower of a mosque
  minarets n ▷ minaret
mince v (-ces, -cing, -ced) cut or grind into very small pieces ▶ n (pl -s) minced meat
  minced v ▷ mince
mincemeat n (pl -s) sweet mixture of dried fruit and spices
  mincemeats n ▷ mincemeat
mincer n (pl -s) machine for mincing meat
  mincers n ▷ mince
  minces v, n ▷ mince
mincing adj affected in manner ▶ v ▷ mince
mind n (pl -s) thinking faculties ▶ v (-s, -ing, -ed) take offence at
minded adj having an inclination as specified
  ▶ v ▷ mind
minder n (pl -s) (Informal) aide or bodyguard
  minders n ▷ minder
mindful adj heedful
  minding v ▷ mind
mindless adj stupid
  minds n, v ▷ mind
mine[1] pron belonging to me
mine[2] n (pl -s) deep hole for digging out coal, ores, etc. ▶ v (-nes, -ning, -ned) dig for minerals
  mined v ▷ mine
minefield n (pl -s) area of land or water containing mines
  minefields n ▷ minefield
miner n (pl -s) person who works in a mine
mineral n (pl -s) naturally occurring inorganic substance, such as metal ▶ adj of, containing, or like minerals
  mineralogies n ▷ mineralogy
mineralogy [min-er-al-a-jee] n (pl -gies) study of minerals
  minerals n ▷ mineral
  miners n ▷ miner
  mines n, v ▷ mine

minestrone [min-ness-**strone**-ee] *n* (*pl* **-s**) soup containing vegetables and pasta
  minestrones *n* ▷ minestrone
minesweeper *n* (*pl* **-s**) ship for clearing away mines
  minesweepers *n* ▷ minesweeper
  mining *v* ▷ mine
minger *n* (*pl* **-s**) (BRIT) (*Informal*) unattractive person
  mingers *n* ▷ minger
  mingier *adj* ▷ mingy
  mingiest *adj* ▷ mingy
minging *adj* (BRIT) (*Informal*) unattractive or unpleasant
mingle *v* (**-les, -ling, -led**) mix or blend
  mingled *v* ▷ mingle
  mingles *v* ▷ mingle
  mingling *v* ▷ mingle
mingy *adj* (**-gier, -giest**) (*Informal*) miserly
mini *n* (*pl* **-s**) ▶ *adj* (**-ier, -iest**) (something) small or miniature
  minier *adj* ▷ mini
  miniest *adj* ▷ mini
  minis *n* ▷ mini
miniature *n* (*pl* **-s**) small portrait, model, or copy ▶ *adj* small-scale ▷ **miniaturist** *n* (*pl* **-s**)
  miniatures *n* ▷ miniature
  miniaturist *n* ▷ miniature
  miniaturists *n* ▷ miniature
miniaturize *v* (**-zes, -zing, -zed**) make to a very small scale
  miniaturized *v* ▷ miniaturize
  miniaturizes *v* ▷ miniaturize
  miniaturizing *v* ▷ miniaturize
minibar *n* (*pl* **-s**) selection of drinks and confectionery provided in a hotel room
minibus *n* (*pl* **-es**) small bus
  minibuses *n* ▷ minibus
minicab *n* (*pl* **-s**) (BRIT) ordinary car used as a taxi
  minicabs *n* ▷ minicab
minicomputer *n* (*pl* **-s**) computer smaller than a mainframe but more powerful than a microcomputer
  minicomputers *n* ▷ minicomputer
minidisc *n* (*pl* **-s**) small recordable compact disc
  minidiscs *n* ▷ minidisc
minim *n* (*pl* **-s**) (MUSIC) note half the length of a semibreve
  minima *n* ▷ minimum
minimal *adj* minimum
minimize *v* (**-zes, -zing, -zed**) reduce to a minimum
  minimized *v* ▷ minimize

  minimizes *v* ▷ minimize
  minimizing *v* ▷ minimize
  minims *n* ▷ minim
minimum *adj, n* (*pl* **-mums, -ma**) least possible (amount or number)
  minimums *n* ▷ minimum
minion *n* (*pl* **-s**) servile assistant
  minions *n* ▷ minion
miniseries *n* (*pl* **-ries**) TV programme shown in several parts, often on consecutive days
  miniseries *n* ▷ miniseries
minister *n* (*pl* **-s**) head of a government department ▶ *v* (**-s, -ing, -ed**) (*foll. by* **to**) attend to the needs of ▷ **ministerial** *adj*
  ministered *v* ▷ minister
  ministerial *adj* ▷ minister
  ministering *v* ▷ minister
  ministers *n, v* ▷ minister
ministration *n* (*pl* **-s**) giving of help
  ministrations *n* ▷ ministration
  ministries *n* ▷ ministry
ministry *n* (*pl* **-tries**) profession or duties of a clergyman
mink *n* stoatlike animal
minnow *n* (*pl* **-s**) small freshwater fish
  minnows *n* ▷ minnow
minor *adj* lesser ▶ *n* (*pl* **-s**) person regarded legally as a child
  minorities *n* ▷ minority
minority *n* (*pl* **-ties**) lesser number
  minors *n* ▷ minor
minster *n* (*pl* **-s**) (BRIT) cathedral or large church
  minsters *n* ▷ minster
minstrel *n* (*pl* **-s**) medieval singer or musician
  minstrels *n* ▷ minstrel
mint¹ *n* (*pl* **-s**) plant with aromatic leaves used for seasoning and flavouring
mint² *n* place where money is coined ▶ *v* (**-s, -ing, -ed**) make (coins)
  minted *v* ▷ mint²
  minting *v* ▷ mint²
  mints *n* ▷ mint¹,² ▶ *v* ▷²
minuet [min-new-**wet**] *n* (*pl* **-s**) stately dance
  minuets *n* ▷ minuet
minus *prep, adj* indicating subtraction ▶ *adj* less than zero ▶ *n* (*pl* **-es**) sign (-) denoting subtraction or a number less than zero
  minuses *n* ▷ minus
minuscule [min-niss-skyool] *adj* very small
minute¹ [min-it] *n* (*pl* **-s**) 60th part of an hour or degree ▶ *pl* record of the proceedings of a meeting ▶ *v* (**-tes, -ting, -ted**) record the minutes
minute² [my-**newt**] *adj* (**-r, -st**) very small
  ▷ **minutely** *adv*

minuted v ▷ minute¹
minutely adv ▷ minute²
minuter adj ▷ minute²
minutes n, v ▷ minute¹
minutest adj ▷ minute²
minutiae [my-**new**-shee-eye] pl n trifling or precise details
minuting v ▷ minute¹
minx n (pl -es) bold or flirtatious girl
minxes n ▷ minx
miracle n (pl -s) wonderful supernatural event
   > **miraculous** adj > **miraculously** adv
miracles n ▷ miracle
miraculous adj ▷ miracle
miraculously adv ▷ miracle
mirage [mir-**rahzh**] n (pl -s) optical illusion, esp. one caused by hot air
mirages n ▷ mirage
mire n (pl -s) swampy ground
mires n ▷ mire
mirror n (pl -s) coated glass surface for reflecting images ▶ v (-s, -ing, -ed) reflect in or as if in a mirror
mirrored v ▷ mirror
mirroring v ▷ mirror
mirrors n, v ▷ mirror
mirth n (pl -s) laughter, merriment, or gaiety
   > **mirthful** adj > **mirthless** adj
mirthful adv ▷ mirth
mirthless adj ▷ mirth
mirths n ▷ mirth
misadventure n (pl -s) unlucky chance
misadventures n ▷ misadventure
misanthrope [miz-zan-**thrope**] n (pl -s) person who dislikes people in general
   > **misanthropic** [miz-zan-**throp**-ik] ▶ adj
   > **misanthropy** [miz-**zan**-throp-ee] ▶ n (pl -pies)
misanthropes n ▷ misanthrope
misanthropies n ▷ misanthrope
misanthropic adj ▷ misanthrope
misanthropy n ▷ misanthrope
misapprehend v (-s, -ing, -ed) missunderstand > **misapprehension** n (pl -s)
misapprehended v ▷ misapprehend
misapprehending v ▷ misapprehend
misapprehends v ▷ misapprehend
misapprehension n ▷ misapprehend
misapprehensions n ▷ misapprehend
misappropriate v (-tes, -ting, -ted) take and use (money) dishonestly > **misappropriation** n (pl -s)
misappropriated v ▷ misappropriate
misappropriates v ▷ misappropriate
misappropriating v ▷ misappropriate
misappropriation n ▷ misappropriate

misappropriations n ▷ misappropriate
miscarriage n (pl -s) spontaneous premature expulsion of a fetus from the womb
miscarriages n ▷ miscarriage
miscarried v ▷ miscarry
miscarries v ▷ miscarry
miscarry v (-ries, -rying, -ried) have a miscarriage
miscarrying v ▷ miscarry
miscast v (-s, -ing, -cast) cast (a role or actor) in (a play or film) inappropriately
miscasting v ▷ miscast
miscasts v ▷ miscast
miscegenation [miss-ij-in-**nay**-shun] n (pl -s) interbreeding of races
miscegenations n ▷ miscegenation
miscellaneous [miss-sell-**lane**-ee-uss] adj mixed or assorted
miscellanies n ▷ miscellany
miscellany [miss-**sell**-a-nee] n (pl -nies) mixed assortment
mischance n (pl -es) unlucky event
mischances n ▷ mischance
mischief n (pl -s) annoying but not malicious behaviour
mischiefs n ▷ mischief
mischievous adj full of mischief
   > **mischievously** adv
mischievously adv ▷ mischievous
miscible [miss-sib-bl] adj able to be mixed
misconception n (pl -s) wrong idea or belief
misconceptions n ▷ misconception
misconduct n (pl -s) immoral or unethical behaviour
misconducts n ▷ misconduct
miscreant [miss-kree-ant] n (pl -s) wrongdoer
miscreants n ▷ miscreant
misdeed n (pl -s) wrongful act
misdeeds n ▷ misdeed
misdemeanour n (pl -s) minor wrongdoing
misdemeanours n ▷ misdemeanour
miser n (pl -s) person who hoards money and hates spending it > **miserly** adj
miserable adj very unhappy, wretched
miseries adj ▷ misery
miserly adj ▷ miser
misers n ▷ miser
misery n (pl -ries) great unhappiness
misfire v (-res, -ring, -red) (of a firearm or engine) fail to fire correctly
misfired v ▷ misfire
misfires v ▷ misfire
misfiring v ▷ misfire
misfit n (pl -s) person not suited to his or her social environment

misfits *n* ▷ misfit
misfortune *n* (*pl* -s) (piece of) bad luck
  misfortunes *n* ▷ misfortune
misgiving *n* (*pl* -s) feeling of fear or doubt
  misgivings *n* ▷ misgiving
misguided *adj* mistaken or unwise
mishandle *v* (-les, -ling, -led) handle badly or
  inefficiently
  mishandled *v* ▷ mishandle
  mishandles *v* ▷ mishandle
  mishandling *v* ▷ mishandle
mishap *n* (*pl* -s) minor accident
  mishaps *n* ▷ mishap
misinform *v* (-s, -ing, -ed) give incorrect
  information to > **misinformation** *n* (*pl* -s)
  misinformation *n* ▷ misinform
  misinformations *n* ▷ misinform
  misinformed *v* ▷ misinform
  misinforming *v* ▷ misinform
  misinforms *v* ▷ misinform
misjudge *v* (-ges, -ging, -ged) judge wrongly
  or unfairly > **misjudgment, misjudgement**
  n (*pl* -s)
  misjudged *v* ▷ misjudge
  misjudgement *n* ▷ misjudge
  misjudges *v* ▷ misjudge
  misjudging *v* ▷ misjudge
  misjudgment *n* ▷ misjudge
  mislaid *v* ▷ mislay
mislay *v* (-s, -ing, -laid) lose (something)
  temporarily
  mislaying *v* ▷ mislay
  mislays *v* ▷ mislay
mislead *v* (-s, -ing, -led) give false or confusing
  information to > **misleading** *adj*
  misleading *v*, *adj* ▷ mislead
  misleads *v* ▷ mislead
  misled *v* ▷ mislead
mismanage *v* (-ges, -ging, -ged) organize or
  run (something) badly > **mismanagement**
  n (*pl* -s)
  mismanaged *v* ▷ mismanage
  mismanagement *n* ▷ mismanage
  mismanagements *n* ▷ mismanage
  mismanages *v* ▷ mismanage
  mismanaging *v* ▷ mismanage
misnomer [miss-no-mer] *n* (*pl* -s) incorrect or
  unsuitable name
  misnomers *n* ▷ misnomer
misogyny [miss-oj-in-ee] *n* (*pl* -nies) hatred of
  women > **misogynist** *n* (*pl* -s)
  misogynies *n* ▷ misogyny
  misogynist *n* ▷ misogyny
  misogynists *n* ▷ misogyny
misplace *v* (-ces, -cing, -ced) mislay

misplaced *v* ▷ misplace
misplaces *v* ▷ misplace
misplacing *v* ▷ misplace
misprint *n* (*pl* -s) printing error
  misprints *n* ▷ misprint
misrepresent *v* (-s, -ing, -ed) represent
  wrongly or inaccurately
  misrepresented *v* ▷ misrepresent
  misrepresenting *v* ▷ misrepresent
  misrepresents *v* ▷ misrepresent
miss *v* (-es, -ing, -ed) fail to notice, hear,
  hit, reach, find, or catch ▶ *n* (*pl* -es) fact or
  instance of missing
  missed *v* ▷ miss
  misses *v*, *n* ▷ miss
missing *adj* lost or absent ▶ *v* ▷ miss
missal *n* (*pl* -s) book containing the prayers
  and rites of the Mass
  missals *n* ▷ missal
misshapen *adj* badly shaped, deformed
missile *n* (*pl* -s) object or weapon thrown,
  shot, or launched at a target
  missiles *n* ▷ missile
mission *n* (*pl* -s) specific task or duty
  missionaries *n* ▷ mission
missionary *n* (*pl* -ries) person sent abroad to
  do religious and social work
  missions *n* ▷ mission
missive *n* (*pl* -s) letter
  missives *n* ▷ missive
misspent *adj* wasted or misused
mist *n* (*pl* -s) thin fog
  mists *n* ▷ mist
mistake *n* (*pl* -s) error or blunder ▶ *v* (-takes,
  -taking, -took, -taken) misunderstand
  mistaken *v* ▷ mistake
  mistakes *n*, *v* ▷ mistake
  mistaking *v* ▷ mistake
mister *n* (*pl* -s) an informal form of address
  for a man
  misters *n* ▷ mister
mistier *adj* ▷ misty
mistiest *adj* ▷ misty
mistletoe *n* (*pl* -s) evergreen plant with white
  berries growing as a parasite on trees
  mistletoes *n* ▷ mistletoe
mistook *v* ▷ mistake
mistral *n* (*pl* -s) strong dry northerly wind of
  S France
  mistrals *n* ▷ mistral
mistress *n* (*pl* -es) woman who has a
  continuing sexual relationship with a
  married man
  mistresses *n* ▷ mistress
mistrial *n* (*pl* -s) (LAW) trial made void because

of some error

mistrials n (pl -s) ▷ mistrial

mistrust v (-s, -ing, -ed) have doubts or suspicions about ▶ n (pl -s) lack of trust
> **mistrustful** adj

mistrusted v ▷ mistrust

mistrustful adj ▷ mistrust

mistrusting v ▷ mistrust

mistrusts v, n ▷ mistrust

misty adj full of mist

misunderstand v (-stands, -standing, -stood) fail to understand properly
> **misunderstanding** n (pl -s)

misunderstanding v, n ▷ misunderstand

misunderstandings n ▷ misunderstand

misunderstands v ▷ misunderstand

misunderstood v ▷ misunderstand

misuse n (pl -s) incorrect, improper, or careless use ▶ v (-ses, -sing, -sed) use wrongly

misused v ▷ misuse

misuses n, v ▷ misuse

misusing v ▷ misuse

mite n (pl -s) very small spider-like animal

mites n ▷ mite

mitigate v (-tes, -ting, -ted) make less severe
> **mitigation** n (pl -s)

mitigated v ▷ mitigate

mitigating v ▷ mitigate

mitigates v ▷ mitigate

mitigation n ▷ mitigate

mitigations n ▷ mitigate

mitre [my-ter] n (pl -s) bishop's pointed headdress ▶ v (-res, -ring, -red) join with a mitre joint

mitred v ▷ mitre

mitres n, v ▷ mitre

mitring v ▷ mitre

mitt n (pl -s) baseball catcher's glove

mitts n ▷ mitt

mitten n (pl -s) glove with one section for the thumb and one for the four fingers together

mittens n ▷ mitten

mix v (-es, -ing, -ed) combine or blend into one mass ▶ n (pl -es) mixture > **mixed** adj > **mixup** n (pl -s) > **mixer** n (pl -s)

mixed v, adj ▷ mix

mixer n ▷ mix

mixers n ▷ mix

mixes v, n ▷ mix

mixing v ▷ mix

mixture n (pl -s) something mixed

mixtures n ▷ mixture

mixup n ▷ mix

mixups n ▷ mix

miz n (**mizzes**). Miz is an informal short form of **misery**. This is a useful word, giving a high score for three letters. Remember that you'll need a blank tile for the second Z if you want to form the plural. Miz scores 14 points.

mizzenmast n (pl -s) (on a vessel with three or more masts) third mast from the bow

mizzenmasts n ▷ mizzenmast

mm interj. Mm is a sound that people make to express satisfaction. This two-letter word with no vowels can be very handy when forming several words at once. Mm scores 6 points.

mnemonic [nim-on-ik] n (pl -s) ▶ adj (something, such as a rhyme) intended to help the memory

mnemonics n ▷ mnemonic

mo n (mos). Mo is an informal short form of **moment**. This word can come in handy when you are trying to play words in more than one direction at once. Mo scores 4 points.

moa n (pl -s) large extinct flightless New Zealand bird

moas n ▷ moa

moan n (pl -s) low cry of pain ▶ v (-s, -ing, -ed) make or utter with a moan

moaned v ▷ moan

moaning v ▷ moan

moans n, v ▷ moan

moat n (pl -s) deep wide ditch, esp. round a castle

moats n ▷ moat

mob n (pl -s) disorderly crowd ▶ v (-s, -bbing, -bbed) surround in a mob to acclaim or attack

mobbed v ▷ mob

mobbing v ▷ mob

mobs n, v ▷ mob

mobile adj able to move ▶ n (pl -s) hanging structure designed to move in air currents
> **mobility** n (pl -ties)

mobiles n ▷ mobile

mobilities n ▷ mobile

mobility n ▷ mobile

mobilization n ▷ mobilize

mobilizations n ▷ mobilize

mobilize v (-zes, -zing, -zed) (of the armed services) prepare for active service
> **mobilization** n (pl -s)

mobilized v ▷ mobilize

mobilizes v ▷ mobilize

mobilizing v ▷ mobilize

moccasin n (pl -s) soft leather shoe

moccasins n ▷ moccasin

mocha [mock-a] n (pl -s) kind of strong dark

coffee

mochas *n* ▷ mocha

mock *v* (-s, -ing, -ed) make fun of ▶ *adj* sham or imitation

  mocked *v* ▷ mock

  mockeries *n* ▷ mockery

mockery *n* (*pl* -ries) derision

  mocking *v* ▷ mock

mockingbird *n* (*pl* -s) N American bird which imitates other birds' songs

  mockingbirds *n* ▷ mockingbird

mocks *pl n* (*Informal*) (in England and Wales) practice exams taken before public exams ▶ *v* ▷ mock

mock-up *n* (*pl* -s) full-scale model for test or study

  mock-ups *n* ▷ mock-up

mode *n* (*pl* -s) method or manner

  modes *n* ▷ mode

model *n* (*pl* -s) (miniature) representation ▶ *v* (-s, -elling, -elled) make a model of

  modelled *n* ▷ model

  modelling *n* ▷ model

  models *n* ▷ model

modem [**mode**-em] *n* (*pl* -s) device for connecting two computers by a telephone line

  modems *n* ▷ modem

moderate *adj* not extreme ▶ *n* (*pl* -s) person of moderate views ▶ *v* (-tes, -ting, -ted) make or become less violent or extreme > **moderately** *adv* > **moderation** (*pl* -s) *n*

  moderated *v* ▷ moderate

  moderately *adv* ▷ moderate

  moderates *n*, *v* ▷ moderate

  moderating *v* ▷ moderate

  moderation *n* ▷ moderate

  moderations *n* ▷ moderate

moderator *n* (*pl* -s) (Presbyterian Church) minister appointed to preside over a Church court, general assembly, etc.

  moderators *n* ▷ moderate

modern *adj* (-est) of present or recent times > **modernity** *n* (*pl* -ties)

  moderner *adj* ▷ modern

  modernest *adj* ▷ modern

modernism *n* (*pl* -s) (support of) modern tendencies, thoughts, or styles > **modernist** *adj*, *n* (*pl* -s)

  modernism *n* ▷ modern

  modernisms *n* ▷ modern

  modernist *n* ▷ modern

  modernists *n* ▷ modern

  modernities *n* ▷ modern

  modernity *n* ▷ modern

modernization *n* ▷ modernize

modernizations *n* ▷ modernize

modernize *v* (-izes, -izing, -ized) bring up to date > **modernization** *n* (*pl* -s)

modest *adj* (-er, -est) not vain or boastful > **modestly** *adv* > **modesty** *n* (*pl* -s)

  modester *adj* ▷ modest

  modestest *adj* ▷ modest

  modesties *n* ▷ modest

  modestly *adv* ▷ modest

  modesty *n* ▷ modest

modicum *n* (*pl* -s) small quantity

  modicums *n* ▷ modicum

modify *v* (-fies, -fying, -fied) change slightly > **modification** *n* (*pl* -s)

  modified *v* ▷ modify

modifier *n* (*pl* -s) word that qualifies the sense of another

  modifiers *n* ▷ modifier

modish [**mode**-ish] *adj* in fashion

modulate *v* (-tes, -ting, -ted) vary in tone > **modulation** *n* (*pl* -s) > **modulator** *n* (*pl* -s)

  modulated *v* ▷ modulate

  modulates *v* ▷ modulate

  modulating *v* ▷ modulate

  modulation *n* ▷ modulate

  modulations *n* ▷ modulate

module *n* (*pl* -s) self-contained unit, section, or component with a specific function

  modules *n* ▷ module

mogul [**moh**-gl] *n* (*pl* -s) important or powerful person

  moguls *n* ▷ mogul

mohair *n* (*pl* -s) fine hair of the Angora goat

  mohairs *n* ▷ mohair

mohican *n* (*pl* -s) punk hairstyle with shaved sides and a stiff central strip of hair, often brightly coloured

  mohicans *n* ▷ mohican

  moieties *n* ▷ moieties

moiety [**moy**-it-ee] *n* (*pl* -ties) half

moist *adj* (-er, -est) slightly wet

moisten *v* (-s, -ing, -ed) make or become moist

  moistened *v* ▷ moisten

  moistening *v* ▷ moisten

  moistens *v* ▷ moisten

  moister *adj* ▷ moist

  moistest *adj* ▷ moist

moisture *n* (*pl* -s) liquid diffused as vapour or condensed in drops

  moistures *n* ▷ moisture

moisturize *v* (-zes, -zing, -zed) add moisture to (the skin etc.)

  moisturized *v* ▷ moisten

  moisturizes *v* ▷ moisten

moisturizing v ▷ moisten

molar n (pl -s) large back tooth used for grinding
  molars n ▷ molar

molasses n dark syrup, a by-product of sugar refining

mole¹ n (pl -s) small dark raised spot on the skin

mole² n (pl -s) small burrowing mammal

mole³ n (pl -s) unit of amount of substance

mole⁴ n (pl -s) breakwater

molecule [mol-lik-kyool] n (pl -s) simplest freely existing chemical unit, composed of two or more atoms ▷ **molecular** [mol-**lek**-yew-lar] ▶ adj
  molecular adj ▷ molecule
  molecules n ▷ molecule
  moles n ▷ mole¹,²,³,⁴

molest v (-s, -ing, -ed) interfere with sexually ▷ **molester** n (pl -s) ▷ **molestation** n (pl -s)
  molested v ▷ molest
  molester n ▷ molest
  molesters n ▷ molest
  molesting v ▷ molest
  molests v ▷ molest

moll n (pl -s) (Slang) gangster's female accomplice

  mollified v ▷ mollify
  mollifies v ▷ mollify

mollify v (-fies, -fying, -fied) pacify or soothe
  mollifying v ▷ mollify
  molls n ▷ moll

mollusc n (pl -s) soft-bodied, usu. hard-shelled, animal, such as a snail or oyster
  molluscs n ▷ mollusc

mollycoddle v (-les, -ling, -led) pamper
  mollycoddled v ▷ mollycoddle
  mollycoddles v ▷ mollycoddle
  mollycoddling v ▷ mollycoddle

molten adj liquefied or melted

molybdenum [mol-**lib**-din-um] n (pl -s) (CHEM) hard silvery-white metallic element
  molybdenums n ▷ molybdenum

moment n (pl -s) short space of time
  momenta n ▷ momentum
  momentarily adv ▷ momentary

momentary adj lasting only a moment ▷ **momentarily** adv

momentous [moh-**men**-tuss] adj of great significance
  moments n ▷ moment

momentum n (pl -ta) impetus of a moving body

monarch n (pl -s) sovereign ruler of a state ▷ **monarchical** adj

monarchical adj ▷ monarch
monarchies n ▷ monarchy
monarchist n (pl -s) supporter of monarchy
  monarchists n ▷ monarchist
  monarchs n ▷ monarch

monarchy n (pl -chies) government by or a state ruled by a sovereign
  monasteries n ▷ monastery

monastery n (pl -ries) residence of a community of monks ▷ **monasticism** n (pl -s)

monastic adj of monks, nuns, or monasteries
  monasticism n ▷ monastery
  monasticisms n ▷ monastery

monetarism n (pl -s) theory that inflation is caused by an increase in the money supply ▷ **monetarist** n (pl -s) adj
  monetarisms n ▷ monetarism
  monetarist n, adj ▷ monetarism
  monetarists n ▷ monetarism

monetary adj of money or currency

money n (pl -s) medium of exchange, coins or banknotes ▷ **moneyed, monied** adj rich
  moneyed adj ▷ money
  moneys n ▷ money

mongoose n (pl -s) stoatlike mammal of Asia and Africa that kills snakes
  mongooses n ▷ money

mongrel n (pl -s) animal, esp. a dog, of mixed breed ▶ adj of mixed breed or origin
  mongrels n ▷ mongrel
  monied adj ▷ money

monitor n (pl -s) person or device that checks, controls, warns, or keeps a record of something ▶ v (-s, -ing, -ed) watch and check on
  monitored v ▷ monitor
  monitoring v ▷ monitor
  monitors n, v ▷ monitor

monk n (pl -s) member of an all-male religious community bound by vows ▷ **monkish** adj

monkey n (pl -s) long-tailed primate ▶ v (-s, -ing, -ed) (usu. foll. by **about** or **around**) meddle or fool
  monkeyed v ▷ monkey
  monkeying v ▷ monkey
  monkeys n, v ▷ monkey
  monkish adj ▷ monk
  monks n ▷ monk

monochrome adj (PHOTOG) black-and-white

monocle n (pl -s) eyeglass for one eye only
  monocles n ▷ monocle
  monogamies n ▷ monogamy

monogamy n (pl -mies) custom of being married to one person at a time

monogram n (pl -s) design of combined

letters, esp. a person's initials
monograms n ▷ monogram
monograph n (pl -s) book or paper on a single subject
monographs n ▷ monograph
monolith n (pl -s) large upright block of stone
> **monolithic** adj
monolithic adj ▷ monolith
monoliths n ▷ monolith
monologue n (pl -s) long speech by one person
monologues n ▷ monologue
monomania n (pl -s) obsession with one thing
> **monomaniac** n, adj
monomaniac adj ▷ monomania
monomanias n ▷ monomania
monoplane n (pl -s) aeroplane with one pair of wings
monoplanes n ▷ monoplane
monopolies n ▷ monopoly
monopolize v (-zes, -zing, -zed) have or take exclusive possession of
monopolized v ▷ monopoly
monopolizes v ▷ monopoly
monopolizing v ▷ monopoly
monopoly n (pl -lies) exclusive possession of or right to do something
monorail n (pl -s) single-rail railway
monorails n ▷ monorail
monotheism n (pl -s) belief in only one God
> **monotheistic** adj
monotheisms n ▷ monorail
monotheistic adj ▷ monotheism
monotone n (pl -s) unvaried pitch in speech or sound > **monotony** n (pl -s)
monotones n ▷ monotone
monotonies n ▷ monotone
monotonous adj tedious due to lack of variety
> **monotonously** adv
monotonously adv ▷ monotous
monseigneur [mon-sen-**nyur**] n (pl messeigneurs) [may-sen-**nyur**] title of French prelates
monsieur [muss-**syur**] n (pl messieurs) [may-**syur**] French title of address equivalent to sir or Mr
monsignor n (pl -s) (RC CHURCH) title attached to certain offices
monsignors n ▷ monsignor
monsoon n (pl -s) seasonal wind of SE Asia
monsoons n ▷ monsoon
monster n (pl -s) imaginary, usu. frightening, beast ▶ adj huge
monsters n ▷ monster
monstrance n (pl -ces) (RC CHURCH) container in which the consecrated Host is exposed for

adoration
monstrances n ▷ monstrance
monstrocities n ▷ monstrosity
monstrosity n (pl -ties) large ugly thing
monstrous adj unnatural or ugly
> **monstrously** adv
monstrously adv ▷ monstrous
montage [mon-tahzh] n (pl -s) (making of) a picture composed from pieces of others
montages n ▷ montage
month n (pl -s) one of the twelve divisions of the calendar year
monthlies n ▷ monthly
monthly adj happening or payable once a month ▶ adv once a month ▶ n (pl -lies) monthly magazine
months n ▷ month
monument n (pl -s) something, esp. a building or statue, that commemorates something
monumental adj large, impressive, or lasting
> **monumentally** adv
monumentally adv ▷ monumental
monuments n ▷ monument
moo n (pl -s) long deep cry of a cow ▶ v (-s, -ing, -ed) make this noise
mooed v ▷ moo
mooing v ▷ moo
moos n, v ▷ moo
mooch v (-es, -ing, -ed) (Slang) loiter about aimlessly
mooched v ▷ mooch
mooches v ▷ mooch
mooching v ▷ mooch
mood¹ n (pl -s) temporary (gloomy) state of mind
mood² n (GRAMMAR) form of a verb indicating whether it expresses a fact, wish, supposition, or command
moodier adj ▷ moody
moodiest adj ▷ moody
moodily adv ▷ moody
moods n ▷ mood¹,²
moody adj (-dier, -iest) sullen or gloomy
> **moodily** adv
moon n (pl -s) natural satellite of the earth ▶ v (-s, -ing, -ed) (foll. by about or around) be idle in a listless or dreamy way
mooned v ▷ moon
mooning v ▷ moon
moonlight n (pl -s) light from the moon ▶ v (-s, -ing, -ed) (Informal) work at a secondary job, esp. illegally
moonlighted v ▷ moonlight
moonlighting v ▷ moonlight
moonlights n, v ▷ moonlight

moons n, v ▷ moon

moonshine n (pl -s) (US & CANADIAN) illicitly distilled whisky

moonshines n ▷ moonshine

moonstone n (pl -s) translucent semiprecious stone

moonstones n ▷ moonstone

moonstruck adj slightly mad or odd

moor[1] n (pl -s) (BRIT) tract of open uncultivated ground covered with grass and heather

moor[2] v (-s, -ing, -ed) secure (a ship) with ropes etc. > **mooring** n (pl -s)

moored v ▷ moor[2]

moorhen n (pl -s) small black water bird

moorhens n ▷ moorhen

mooring v, n ▷ moor[2]

moors n ▷ moor[1] ▷ v ▷ moor[2]

moose n large N American deer

moot adj (-er, -est) debatable ▶ v (-s, -ing, -ed) bring up for discussion

mooted v ▷ moot

mooter adj ▷ moot

mootest adj ▷ moot

mooting v ▷ moot

moots v ▷ moot

mop n (pl -s) long stick with twists of cotton or a sponge on the end, used for cleaning ▶ v (-s, -pping, -pped) clean or soak up with or as if with a mop

mope v (-pes, -ping, -ped) be gloomy and apathetic

moped n (pl -s) light motorized cycle ▶ v ▷ mope

mopeds v ▷ mope

mopes v ▷ mope

moping v ▷ mope

mopoke n (pl -s) small spotted owl of Australia and New Zealand

mopokes n ▷ mopoke

mopped v ▷ mop

mopping v ▷ mop

mops n, v ▷ mop

moraine n (pl -s) accumulated mass of debris deposited by a glacier

moraines n ▷ moraine

moral adj concerned with right and wrong conduct ▶ n (pl -s) lesson to be obtained from a story or event > **morally** adv

morale [mor-**rahl**] n (pl -s) degree of confidence or hope of a person or group

morales n ▷ morale

moralist n (pl -s) person with a strong sense of right and wrong

moralists n ▷ moralist

moralities n ▷ morality

morality n (pl -ties) good moral conduct

moralize v (-zes, -zing, -zed) make moral pronouncements

moralized v ▷ moralize

moralizes v ▷ moralize

moralizing v ▷ moralize

morally adv ▷ moral

morals n ▷ moral

morass n (pl -es) marsh

morasses n ▷ morass

moratoria n ▷ moratorium

moratorium n (pl -ria, -riums) legally authorized ban or delay

moratoriums n ▷ moratorium

moray n (pl -s) large voracious eel

morays n ▷ moray

morbid adj unduly interested in death or unpleasant events

mordant adj sarcastic or scathing ▶ n (pl -s) substance used to fix dyes

mordants n ▷ mordant

more adj greater in amount or degree ▷ much, many ▶ adv to a greater extent ▶ pron greater or additional amount or number

moreover adv in addition to what has already been said

mores [**more**-rayz] pl n customs and conventions embodying the fundamental values of a community

morgue n (pl -s) mortuary

morgues n ▷ morgue

moribund adj without force or vitality

morn n (pl morns) (Poetic) morning

morns n ▷ morn

morning n (pl -s) part of the day before noon

mornings n ▷ morning

morocco n (pl -s) goatskin leather

moroccos n ▷ morocco

moron n (pl -s) (Informal) foolish or stupid person > **moronic** adj

moronic adj ▷ moron

morons n ▷ moron

morose [mor-**rohss**] adj (-r, -st) sullen or moody

moroser adj ▷ morose

morosest adj ▷ morose

morphia n ▷ morphine

morphines n ▷ morphine

morphine, morphia n (pl -s) drug extracted from opium, used as an anaesthetic and sedative

morphological adj ▷ morphology

morphologies n ▷ morphology

morphology n (pl -gies) science of forms and structures of organisms or words > **morphological** adj

morrow n (pl -s) (*Poetic*) next day
morrows n ▷ morrow
morse n (pl -s) clasp or fastening
morsel n (pl -s) small piece, esp. of food
morsels n ▷ morsel
morses n ▷ morse
mortal adj subject to death ▶ n (pl -s) human being > **mortally** adv
mortalities n ▷ mortal
mortality n (pl -ties) state of being mortal
mortally adj ▷ mortal
mortals n ▷ mortal
mortar n (pl -s) small cannon with a short range
mortarboard n (pl -s) black square academic cap
mortarboards n ▷ mortarboard
mortars n ▷ mortar
mortgage n (pl -s) conditional pledging of property, esp. a house, as security for the repayment of a loan ▶ v (-ges, -ging, -ged) pledge (property) as security thus
mortgaged v ▷ mortgage
mortgagee n (pl -s) creditor in a mortgage
mortgagees n ▷ mortgagee
mortgages n, v ▷ mortgage
mortgaging v ▷ mortgage
mortgagor n (pl -s) debtor in a mortgage
mortgagors n ▷ mortgagor
mortice, mortise [**more**-tiss] n (pl -s) hole in a piece of wood or stone shaped to receive a matching projection on another piece
mortices n ▷ mortice
mortification n ▷ mortify
mortifications n ▷ mortify
mortified v ▷ mortify
mortifies v ▷ mortify
mortify v (-fies, -fying, -fied) humiliate > **mortification** n (pl -s)
mortifying v ▷ mortify
mortise n ▷ mortice
mortises n ▷ mortice
mortuaries n ▷ mortuary
mortuary n (pl -aries) building where corpses are kept before burial or cremation
mosaic [mow-**zay**-ik] n (pl -s) design or decoration using small pieces of coloured stone or glass
mosaics n ▷ mosaic
mosque n (pl -s) Muslim temple
mosques n ▷ mosque
mosquito n (pl -toes, -tos) blood-sucking flying insect
mosquitoes n ▷ mosquito
mosquitos n ▷ mosquito

moss n (pl -es) small flowerless plant growing in masses on moist surfaces > **mossy** adj (-ssier, -ssiest)
mosses n ▷ moss
mossier adj ▷ moss
mossiest adj ▷ moss
mossy adj (-ssier, -ssiest) ▷ moss
most n greatest number or degree ▷ adj greatest in number or degree ▷ **much, many** ▶ adv in the greatest degree
mostly adv for the most part, generally
motel n (pl -s) roadside hotel for motorists
motels n ▷ motel
motet n (pl -s) short sacred choral song
motets n ▷ motet
moth n (pl -s) nocturnal insect like a butterfly
mothball n (pl -s) small ball of camphor or naphthalene used to repel moths from stored clothes ▶ v (-ed, -ing, -ed) store (something operational) for future use
mothballed v ▷ moth
mothballing v ▷ moth
mothballs n, v ▷ moth
moths n ▷ moth
mother n (pl -s) female parent ▶ adj native or inborn ▶ v (-s, -ing, -ed) look after as a mother > **motherhood** n (pl -s) **motherly** adj > **motherless** adj
mothered v ▷ mother
motherhood n ▷ mother
motherhoods n ▷ mother
mothering v ▷ mother
motherless adj ▷ mother
motherly adj ▷ mother
mothers n, v ▷ mother
mothers-in-law n ▷ mother-in-law
motif [moh-**teef**] n (pl -s) (recurring) theme or design
motifs n ▷ motif
motion n (pl -s) process, action, or way of moving ▶ v (-s, -ing, -ed) direct (someone) by gesture
motioned v ▷ motion
motioning v ▷ motion
motionless adj not moving
motions n, v ▷ motion
motivate v (-tes, -ting, -ted) give incentive to > **motivation** n (pl -s)
motivated v ▷ motivate
motivates v ▷ motivate
motivating v ▷ motivate
motivation n ▷ motivate
motivations n ▷ motivate
motive n (pl -s) reason for a course of action ▶ adj causing motion

motives n ▷ motive

motley adj miscellaneous

motocross n (pl -es) motorcycle race over a rough course

motocrosses n ▷ motocross

motor n (pl -s) engine, esp. of a vehicle ▸ v (-s, -ing, -ed) travel by car > **motorized** adj equipped with a motor or motor transport > **motorbike** n (pl -s) > **motorboat** n (pl -s) > **motorcar** n (pl -s) > **motorcycle** n (pl -s) > **motorcyclist** n (pl -s)

motorbike n ▷ motor

motorbikes n ▷ motor

motorboat n ▷ motor

motorboats n ▷ motor

motorcar n ▷ motor

motorcars n ▷ motor

motorcycle n ▷ motor

motorcycles n ▷ motor

motorcyclist n ▷ motor

motorcyclists n ▷ motor

motored v ▷ motor

motoring v ▷ motor

motorist n (pl -s) driver of a car

motorists n ▷ motorist

motorized adj ▷ motor

motors n, v ▷ motor

motorway n (pl -s) main road for fast-moving traffic

motorways n ▷ motorway

mottled adj marked with blotches

motto n (pl -ttoes, -ttos) saying expressing an ideal or rule of conduct

mottoes n ▷ motto

mottos n ▷ motto

mould[1] n (pl -s) hollow container in which metal etc. is cast ▸ v (-s, -ing, -ed) shape

mould[2] n (pl -s) fungal growth caused by dampness

mould[3] n (pl -s) loose soil

moulded v ▷ mould[1]

moulder v (-s, -ing, -ed) decay into dust

mouldered v ▷ moulder

mouldering v ▷ moulder

moulders v ▷ moulder

mouldier adj ▷ mouldy

mouldiest adj ▷ mouldy

moulding n (pl -s) moulded ornamental edging ▸ v ▷ mould[1]

moulds n ▷ mould[1,2,3] ▸ v ▷ mould[1]

mouldy adj (-dier, -diest) stale or musty; dull or boring

moult v (-s, -ing, -ed) shed feathers, hair, or skin to make way for new growth ▸ n (pl -s) process of moulting

moulted v ▷ moult

moulting v ▷ moult

moults v, n ▷ moult

mound n (pl -s) heap, esp. of earth or stones

mounds n ▷ mound

mount v (-s, -ing, -ed) climb or ascend ▸ n (pl -s) backing or support on which something is fixed

mountain n (pl -s) hill of great size > **mountainous** adj full of mountains n (pl -s) person who climbs mountains > **mountaineering** n (pl -s)

mountaineering n ▷ mountaineer

mountaineerings n ▷ mountaineer

mountaineers n ▷ mountaineer

mountains n ▷ mountain

mountebank n (pl -s) charlatan or fake

mountebanks n ▷ mountebank

mounted v ▷ mount

mounting v ▷ mount

mounts v, n ▷ mount

mourn v (-s, -ing, -ed) feel or express sorrow for (a dead person or lost thing)

mourned v ▷ mourn

mourner n (pl mourners) person attending a funeral

mourners n ▷ mourner

mournful adj (-ler, -lest) sad or dismal > **mournfully** adv

mournfuller adj ▷ mournful

mournfullest adj ▷ mournful

mournfully adv ▷ mournful

mourning n (pl -s) grieving ▸ v ▷ mourn

mournings n ▷ mourning

mourns v ▷ mourn

mouse n (pl mice) small long-tailed rodent

mouser n (pl -s) cat used to catch mice

mousers n ▷ mouser

mousse n (pl -s) dish of flavoured cream whipped and set

mousses n ▷ mousse

moustache n (pl -s) hair on the upper lip

moustaches n ▷ moustache

mousy adj like a mouse, esp. in hair colour

mouth n (pl -s) opening in the head for eating and issuing sounds ▸ v (-s, -ing, -ed) form (words) with the lips without speaking

mouthed v ▷ mouth

mouthful n (pl -s) amount of food or drink put into the mouth at any one time when eating or drinking

mouthfuls n ▷ mouthful

mouthing v ▷ mouth

mouthpiece n (pl -s) part of a telephone into which a person speaks

mouthpieces n ▷ mouthpiece

mouths n, v ▷ mouth

move v (-ves, -ving, -ved) change in place or position ▶ n (pl -s) moving > **movable, moveable** adj

movement n (pl -s) action or process of moving

movements n ▷ movement

moved v ▷ move

moves v, n ▷ move

movie n (pl -s) (Informal) cinema film

movies n ▷ movie

moving v ▷ move

mow v (-s, -ing, -ed or **mown**) cut (grass or crops)

mowed v ▷ mow

mower n (pl -s) machine for cutting grass

mowers n ▷ mower

mowing v ▷ mow

mown v ▷ mow

mows v ▷ mow

> **moz** n (**mozes**). Moz is an old Australian slang word for a jinx or hex. This is an unusual word that is worth remembering as it can be very useful if you have a Z but little chance to play it on a crowded board. Moz scores 14 points.

mozzarella [mot-sa-rel-la] n (pl -s) moist white cheese originally made in Italy from buffalo milk

mozzarellas n ▷ mozzarella

> **mu** n (**mus**). Mu is the 12th letter in the Greek alphabet. This is a useful word to remember: it won't score you many points on its own, but it can be very helpful on a crowded board when you need to form words in different directions. Mu scores 4 points.

much adj (**more, most**) large amount or degree of ▶ n large amount or degree ▶ adv (**more, most**) to a great degree

mucilage [mew-sill-ij] n (pl -s) gum or glue

mucilages n ▷ mucilage

muck n (pl -s) dirt, filth > **mucky** adj

mucks n ▷ mucks

mucky adj ▷ mucks

mucus [mew-kuss] n (pl -s) slimy secretion of the mucous membranes

mucuses n ▷ mucus

mud n (pl -s) wet soft earth > **muddy** adj

muddier adj ▷ mud

muddiest adj ▷ mud

muddy adj (-dier, -diest) ▷ mud

mudguard n (pl -s) cover over a wheel to prevent mud or water being thrown up by it

mudguards n ▷ mudguard

muds n ▷ mud

muddle v (-les, -ling, -led) (often foll. by **up**) confuse ▶ n (pl -s) state of confusion

muddled v ▷ muddle

muddles v, n ▷ muddle

muddling v ▷ muddle

muesli [mewz-lee] n (pl -s) mixture of grain, nuts, and dried fruit, eaten with milk

mueslis n ▷ muesli

muezzin [moo-ezz-in] n (pl -s) official who summons Muslims to prayer

muezzins n ▷ muezzin

muff[1] n (pl -s) tube-shaped covering to keep the hands warm

muff[2] v (-s, -ing, -ed) bungle (an action)

muffed v ▷ muff

muffin n (pl -s) light round flat yeast cake

muffing v ▷ muff

muffins n ▷ muffin

muffs n ▷ muff[1] ▶ v ▷ muff[2]

muffle v (-les, -ling, -led) wrap up for warmth or to deaden sound

muffled v ▷ muffle

muffler n (pl -s) (BRIT) scarf

mufflers n ▷ muffle

muffles v ▷ muffle

muffling v ▷ muffle

mufti n (pl -s) civilian clothes worn by a person who usually wears a uniform

muftis n ▷ mufti

mug[1] n (pl -s) large drinking cup

mug[2] n (pl -s) (Slang) face ▶ v (-s, -gging, -gged) (Informal) attack in order to rob > **mugger** n (pl -s)

mug[3] v (-s, -gging, -gged) (foll. by **up**) (Informal) study hard

mugged v ▷ mug[2,3]

mugger v ▷ mug[2]

muggers v ▷ mug[2]

muggier adj ▷ muggy

muggiest adj ▷ muggy

mugging v ▷ mug[2,3]

muggins n (Informal) stupid or gullible person

muggy adj (-ggier, -ggiest) (of weather) damp and stifling

mugs n ▷ mug[1,2]

mulatto [mew-lat-toe] n (pl -tos, -toes) child of one Black and one White parent

mulattoes adj ▷ mulatto

mulattos adj ▷ mulatto

mulberries n ▷ mulberry

mulberry n (pl -rries) tree whose leaves are used to feed silkworms

mulch n (pl -es) mixture of wet straw, leaves, etc., used to protect the roots of plants ▶ v (-es, -ing, -ed) cover (land) with mulch
mulched v ▷ mulch
mulches n, v ▷ mulch
mulching v ▷ mulch
mule[1] n (pl -s) offspring of a horse and a donkey > **mulish** adj obstinate
mule[2] n backless shoe or slipper
mules n ▷ mule[1,2]
mulga n (pl -s) Australian acacia shrub growing in desert regions
mulgas n ▷ mulga
mulish adj ▷ mule[1]
mull v (-s, -ing, -ed) think (over) or ponder > **mulled** adj (of wine or ale) flavoured with sugar and spices and served hot
mullah n (pl -s) Muslim scholar, teacher, or religious leader
mullahs n ▷ mullah
mulled v, adj ▷ mull
mullet[1] n (pl -s) edible sea fish
mullet[2] n (pl -s) haircut in which the hair is short at the top and sides and long at the back
mullets n ▷ mullet[1,2]
mulling v ▷ mull
mulls v ▷ mull
mulligatawnies n ▷ mulligatawny
mulligatawny n (pl -nies) soup made with curry powder
mullion n (pl -s) vertical dividing bar in a window > **mullioned** adj
mullioned adj ▷ mullion
mullions n ▷ mullion
mulloway n (pl -s) large Australian sea fish, valued for sport and food
mulloways n ▷ mulloway
multifarious [mull-tee-**fare**-ee-uss] adj having many various parts
multiple adj having many parts ▶ n (pl -s) quantity which contains another an exact number of times
multiples n ▷ multiple
multiplex n (pl -es) purpose-built complex containing several cinemas and usu. restaurants and bars ▶ adj having many elements, complex
multiplexes n ▷ multiplex
multiplicities n ▷ multiplicity
multiplicity n (pl -ties) large number or great variety
multiply v (-lies, -lying, -lied) (cause to) increase in number, quantity, or degree > **multiplication** n (pl -s)

multiplicand n (pl -s) (MATHS) number to be multiplied
multiplicands n ▷ multiplicand
multiplication n ▷ multiply
multiplications n ▷ multiply
multiplied v ▷ multiply
multiplies v ▷ multiply
multiplying v ▷ multiply
multipurpose adj having many uses
multitude n (pl -s) great number
multitudes n ▷ multitude
multitudinous adj very numerous
mum n (pl -s) (Informal) mother
mums n ▷ mum
mumble v (-les, -ling, -led) speak indistinctly, mutter
mumbled v ▷ mumble
mumbles v ▷ mumble
mumbling v ▷ mumble
mummer n (pl -s) actor in a traditional English folk play or mime
mummers n ▷ mummer
mummies n ▷ mummer
mummified adj (of a body) preserved as a mummy
mummy[1] n (pl -mmies) body embalmed and wrapped for burial in ancient Egypt
mummy[2] n (pl -mmies) ▷ mother
mumps n infectious disease with swelling in the glands of the neck
munch v (-es, -ing, -ed) chew noisily and steadily
munched v ▷ munch
munches v ▷ munch
munching v ▷ munch
mundane adj everyday
municipal adj relating to a city or town
municipalities n ▷ municipality
municipality n (pl -ties) city or town with local self-government
munificence n ▷ munificent
munificences n ▷ munificent
munificent [mew-**niff**-fiss-sent] adj very generous > **munificence** n (pl -s)
muniments pl n title deeds or similar documents
munitions pl n military stores
munted adj (NZ) (Slang) destroyed or ruined
mural n (pl -s) painting on a wall
murals n ▷ mural
murder n (pl -s) unlawful intentional killing of a human being ▶ v (-s, -ing, -ed) kill in this way > **murderer, murderess** n (pl -s) > **murderous** adj
murdered v ▷ murder

murderer *n* ▷ **murder**
murderers *n* ▷ **murder**
murderess *n* ▷ **murder**
murderesses *n* ▷ **murder**
murdering *v* ▷ **murder**
murderous *adj* ▷ **murder**
murders *v, n* ▷ **murder**
murk *n* (*pl* **-s**) thick darkness
murkier *adj* ▷ **murky**
murkiest *adj* ▷ **murky**
murks *n* ▷ **murk**
murky *adj* (**-kier, -kiest**) dark or gloomy
murmur *v* (**-s, -ing, -ed**) speak or say in a quiet indistinct way ▶ *n* (*pl* **-s**) continuous low indistinct sound
murmured *v* ▷ **murmur**
murmuring *v* ▷ **murmur**
murmurs *v, n* ▷ **murmur**
muscle *n* (*pl* **-s**) tissue in the body which produces movement by contracting
muscles *n* ▷ **muscle**
muscular *adj* with well-developed muscles
muse *v* (**-ses, -sing, -sed**) ponder quietly
mused *v* ▷ **muse**
musing *v* ▷ **muse**
muses *v* ▷ **muse**
museum *n* (*pl* **-s**) building where natural, artistic, historical, or scientific objects are exhibited and preserved
museums *n* ▷ **museum**
mush *n* (*pl* **-es**) soft pulpy mass > **mushy** *adj* (**-shier, -shiest**)
mushes *n* ▷ **mush**
mushier *adj* ▷ **mush**
mushiest *adj* ▷ **mush**
mushroom *n* (*pl* **-s**) edible fungus with a stem and cap ▶ *v* (**-s, -ing, -ed**) grow rapidly
mushroomed *v* ▷ **mushroom**
mushrooming *v* ▷ **mushroom**
mushrooms *n, v* ▷ **mushroom**
mushy (**-shier, -shiest**) *adj* ▷ **mush**
music *n* (*pl* **-s**) art form using a melodious and harmonious combination of notes ▶ *n* (*pl* **-s**) play or film with songs and dancing > **musician** *n* (*pl* **-s**)
musical *adj* of or like music > **musically** *adv*
musically *adv* ▷ **musical**
musician *n* ▷ **music**
musicians *n* ▷ **music**
musicologies *n* ▷ **musicology**
musicologist *n* ▷ **musicology**
musicologists *n* ▷ **musicology**
musicology *n* (*pl* **-gies**) scientific study of music > **musicologist** *n* (*pl* **-s**)
musics *n* ▷ **music**

musk *n* (*pl* **-s**) scent obtained from a gland of the musk deer or produced synthetically > **musky** *adj* (**-kier, -kiest**)
musket *n* (*pl* **-s**) (HIST) long-barrelled gun > **musketeer** *n* (*pl* **-s**)
musketeer *n* ▷ **musket**
musketeers *n* ▷ **musket**
musketries *n* ▷ **musketry**
musketry *n* (*pl* **-ries**) (use of) muskets
muskets *n* ▷ **musket**
muskier *adj* ▷ **musk**
muskiest *adj* ▷ **musk**
muskrat *n* (*pl* **-s**) N American beaver-like rodent
muskrats *n* ▷ **muskrat**
musks *n* ▷ **musk**
musky *adj* (**-kier, -kiest**) ▷ **musk**
muslin *n* (*pl* **-s**) fine cotton fabric
muslins *n* ▷ **muslin**
mussel *n* (*pl* **-s**) edible shellfish with a dark hinged shell
mussels *n* ▷ **mussel**
must[1] *v* used as an auxiliary to express obligation, certainty, or resolution ▶ *n* (*pl* **-s**) essential or necessary thing
must[2] *n* (*pl* **-s**) newly pressed grape juice
musts *n* ▷ **must**[1,2]
mustang *n* (*pl* **-s**) wild horse of SW USA
mustangs *n* ▷ **mustang**
mustard *n* (*pl* **-s**) paste made from the powdered seeds of a plant, used as a condiment
mustards *n* ▷ **mustard**
muster *v* (**-s, -ing, -ed**) assemble ▶ *n* (*pl* **-s**) assembly of military personnel
mustered *v* ▷ **muster**
mustering *v* ▷ **muster**
musters *v, n* ▷ **muster**
mustier *adj* ▷ **musty**
mustiest *adj* ▷ **musty**
mustiness *n* ▷ **musty**
mustinesses *n* ▷ **musty**
musty *adj* (**mustier, mustiest**) smelling mouldy and stale > **mustiness** *n* (*pl* **-es**)
mutabilities *n* ▷ **mutable**
mutability *n* ▷ **mutable**
mutable [**mew**-tab-bl] *adj* liable to change > **mutability** *n* (*pl* **-ties**)
mutant *n* (*pl* **-s**) mutated animal, plant, etc.
mutants *n* ▷ **mutant**
mutate *v* (**-tes, -ting, -ted**) (cause to) undergo mutation
mutated *v* ▷ **mutate**
mutates *v* ▷ **mutate**
mutating *v* ▷ **mutate**

mutation n (pl -s) (genetic) change
  mutations n ▷ mutation
mute adj (-r, -st) silent ▶ n (pl -s) person who is unable to speak > **mutely** adv
muted adj (of sound or colour) softened
  mutely adv ▷ mute
  muter adj ▷ mute
  mutes n ▷ mute
  mutest adj ▷ mute
muti [moo-ti] n (pl -s) (S AFR) (Informal) medicine, esp. herbal medicine
  mutis n ▷ muti
mutilate [mew-till-ate] v (-tes, -ting, -ted) deprive of a limb or other part > **mutilation** n (pl -s)
  mutilated v ▷ mutilate
  mutilates v ▷ mutilate
  mutilating v ▷ mutilate
  mutilation n ▷ mutilate
  mutilations n ▷ mutilate
  mutineer n ▷ mutiny
  mutineers n ▷ mutiny
  mutinied v ▷ mutiny
  mutinies v ▷ mutiny
  mutinous n ▷ mutiny
mutiny [mew-tin-ee] n (pl -nies) rebellion against authority, esp. by soldiers or sailors ▶ v (-nies, -nying, -nied) commit mutiny > **mutineer** n (pl -s) > **mutinous** adj
  mutinying n ▷ mutiny
mutt n (pl -s) (Slang) mongrel dog
  mutts n ▷ mutt
mutter v (-s, -ing, -ed) utter or speak indistinctly ▶ n (pl -s) muttered sound or grumble
  muttered v ▷ mutter
  muttering v ▷ mutter
  mutters v, n ▷ mutter
mutton n (pl -s) flesh of sheep, used as food
  muttons n ▷ mutton
mutual [mew-chew-al] adj felt or expressed by each of two people about the other > **mutually** adv
  mutually adv ▷ mutual

> **mux** v (muxes, muxing, muxed). Mux is an old American word meaning to make a mess of something. This word is very useful not only because it contains an X, but because its verb forms can enable you to clear your rack of unpromising letters. Mux scores 12 points.
>
> **muzjik** n (muzjiks). A muzjik is a Russian peasant. This is a great high-scoring word, combining Z, J and K. If

you can play the plural using all of your tiles, you'll get a bonus of 50 points. Muzjik scores 28 points.

muzzle n (pl -s) animal's mouth and nose ▶ v (-les, -ling, -led) prevent from being heard or noticed
  muzzled v ▷ muzzle
  muzzles n, v ▷ muzzle
  muzzling v ▷ muzzle
muzzy adj (-zzier, -zziest) confused or muddled
my adj belonging to me
myall n (pl -s) Australian acacia with hard scented wood
  myalls n ▷ myall
mycology n (pl -gies) study of fungi
  mycologies n ▷ mycology
myna, mynah, mina n (pl -s) Asian bird which can mimic human speech
  mynah n ▷ myna
  mynahs n ▷ myna
  mynas n ▷ myna
myopia [my-oh-pee-a] n (pl -s) short-sightedness > **myopic** [my-op-ik] ▶ adj
  myopias n ▷ myopia
  myopic adj ▷ myopia
myriad [mir-ree-ad] adj innumerable ▶ n (pl -s) large indefinite number
  myriads n ▷ myriad
myrrh [mur] n (pl -s) aromatic gum used in perfume, incense, and medicine
  myrrhs n ▷ myrrh
myrtle [mur-tl] n (pl -s) flowering evergreen shrub
  myrtles n ▷ myrtle
  myself pron ▷ I
  mysteries n ▷ mystery
  mysterious adj ▷ mystery
  mysteriously adv ▷ mystery
mystery n (pl -ries) strange or inexplicable event or phenomenon > **mysterious** adj > **mysteriously** adv
mystic n (pl -s) person who seeks spiritual knowledge ▶ adj mystical > **mysticism** n (pl -s)
mystical adj having a spiritual or religious significance beyond human understanding
  mysticism n ▷ mystic
  mysticisms n ▷ mystic
  mystics n ▷ mystic
  mystification v ▷ mystify
  mystifications v ▷ mystify
  mystified v ▷ mystify
  mystifies v ▷ mystify
mystify v (-fies, -fying, -fied) bewilder or puzzle > **mystification** n (pl -s)
  mystifying v ▷ mystify

mystique [miss-**steek**] *n* (*pl* **-s**) aura of mystery or power
  mystiques *n* ▷ mystique
myth *n* (*pl* **-s**) tale with supernatural characters, usu. of how the world and mankind began > **mythical, mythic** *adj*
  mythic *adj* ▷ myth
  mythical *adj* ▷ myth

mythological *adj* ▷ mythology
  mythologies *n* ▷ mythology
mythology *n* (*pl* **-gies**) myths collectively
  > **mythological** *adj*
  myths *n* ▷ myth
  myxomatoses *n* ▷ myxomatosis
myxomatosis [mix-a-mat-**oh**-siss] *n* (*pl* **-ses**) contagious fatal viral disease of rabbits

Nn

Along with R and T, N is one of the most common consonants in Scrabble. As you'll often have it on your rack, it's well worth learning what N can do in different situations. N is useful when you need short words, as it begins two-letter words with every vowel except I, and with Y as well. There are plenty of three-letter words starting with N, but there aren't many high-scoring ones. Remember words like **nab** (5 points), **nag** (4), **nap** (5), **nay** (6), **new** (6), **nib** (5), **nob** (5), **nod** (4) and **now (6).**

na *interj.* Na is a Scots word for **no** or **not.** This word can be very convenient when you need to form words in different directions. Na scores 2 points.

naan *n* (*pl* **-s**) ▷ **nan bread**
  naans *n* ▷ **naan**

naartjie [nahr-chee] *n* (*pl* **-s**) (S AFR) tangerine
  naartjies *n* ▷ **naartjie**

nab *v* (**-s**, **-bbing**, **-bbed**) (*Informal*) arrest (someone)
  nabbed *v* ▷ **nab**
  nabbing *v* ▷ **nab**
  nabs *v* ▷ **nab**

nadir *n* (*pl* **-s**) point in the sky opposite the zenith
  nadiral *adj* ▷ **nadir**
  nadirs *n* ▷ **nadir**
  naevi *n* ▷ **naevus**

naff *adj* (**-er**, **-est**) (BRIT) (*Slang*) lacking quality or taste
  naffer *adj* ▷ **naff**
  naffest *adj* ▷ **naff**

nag¹ *v* (**-s**, **-gging**, **-gged**) scold or find fault constantly ▶ *n* (*pl* **-s**) person who nags
  > **nagging** *adj*, *n* (*pl* **-s**)

nag² *n* (*pl* **-s**) (*Informal*) old horse
  nagged *v* ▷ **nag¹**
  nagging *v*, *adj n* ▷ **nag¹**
  naggings *n* ▷ **nag¹**
  nags *v* ▷ **nag¹** ▶ *n* ▷ **nag¹, ²**

naiad [nye-ad] *n* (*pl* **-s**) (GREEK MYTH) nymph living in a lake or river
  naiads *n* ▷ **naiad**

nail *n* (*pl* **-s**) pointed piece of metal with a head, hit with a hammer to join two objects together ▶ *v* (**-s**, **-ing**, **-ed**) attach (something) with nails
  nailed *v* ▷ **nail**
  nailing *v* ▷ **nail**
  nails *n*, *v* ▷ **nail**

naive [nye-**eev**] *adj* (**-r**, **-st**) innocent and gullible > **naively** *adv* > **naivety** [nye-**eev**-tee] *n* (*pl* **-ties**), **naïveté** (*pl* **-s**)
  naively *adv* ▷ **naive**
  naiver *adj* ▷ **naive**
  naivest *adj* ▷ **naive**
  naïveté *n* ▷ **naive**
  naïvetés *n* ▷ **naive**
  naiveties *n* ▷ **naive**
  naivety *n* ▷ **naive**

naked *adj* (**-er**, **-est**) without clothes
  > **nakedness** *n* (*pl* **-es**)
  nakeder *adj* ▷ **naked**
  nakedest *adj* ▷ **naked**
  nakedness *n* ▷ **naked**
  nakednesses *n* ▷ **naked**

name *n* (*pl* **-s**) word by which a person or thing is known ▶ *v* (**-mes**, **-ming**, **-med**) give a name to
  named *v* ▷ **name**

nameless *adj* without a name

namely *adv* that is to say
  names *n*, *v* ▷ **name**

namesake *n* (*pl* **-s**) person with the same name as another
  namesakes *n* ▷ **namely**
  naming *v* ▷ **name**
  nannies *n* ▷ **nanny**

nanny *n* (*pl* **-nnies**) woman whose job is looking after young children

nap¹ *n* (*pl* **-s**) short sleep ▶ *v* (**-s**, **-pping**, **-pped**) have a short sleep

nap² *n* (*pl* **-s**) raised fibres of velvet or similar cloth

nap³ n (pl **-s**) card game similar to whist
napalm n (pl **-s**) highly inflammable jellied petrol, used in bombs
  napalms n ▷ **napalm**
nape n (pl **-s**) back of the neck
  napes n ▷ **nape**
naphtha n (pl **-s**) liquid mixture distilled from coal tar or petroleum, used as a solvent and in petrol
naphthalene n (pl **-s**) white crystalline product distilled from coal tar or petroleum, used in disinfectants, mothballs, and explosives
  naphthalenes n ▷ **naphthalene**
  naphthas n ▷ **naphtha**
napkin n (pl **-s**) piece of cloth or paper for wiping the mouth or protecting the clothes while eating
  napkins n ▷ **napkin**
  napped v ▷ **nap¹**
  nappies n ▷ **nappy**
  napping v ▷ **nap¹**
nappy n (pl **-pies**) piece of absorbent material fastened round a baby's lower torso to absorb urine and faeces
  naps n ▷ **nap¹** ▶ v ▷ **nap¹**
narcissism n (pl **-s**) exceptional interest in or admiration for oneself > **narcissistic** adj
  narcissisms n ▷ **narcissism**
  narcissistic adj ▷ **narcissism**
  narcissi n ▷ **narcissus**
narcissus n (pl **-cissi**) yellow, orange, or white flower related to the daffodil
  narcoses n ▷ **narcosis**
narcosis n (pl **-s**) effect of a narcotic
narcotic n (pl **-s**) ▶ adj (of) a drug, such as morphine or opium, which produces numbness and drowsiness, used medicinally but addictive
  narcotics n ▷ **narcotic**
nark (Slang) v (**-s, -ing, -ed**) annoy ▶ n (pl **-s**) informer or spy
  narked v ▷ **nark**
  narkier adj ▷ **narky**
  narkiest adj ▷ **narky**
  narking v ▷ **nark**
  narks v, n ▷ **nark**
narky adj (Slang) (**-kier, -kiest**) irritable or complaining
narrate v (**-tes, -ting, -ted**) tell (a story) > **narration** n (pl **-s**) > **narrator** n (pl **-s**)
  narrated v ▷ **narrate**
  narrates v ▷ **narrate**
  narrating v ▷ **narrate**
  narration n ▷ **narrate**

  narrations n ▷ **narrate**
narrative n (pl **-s**) account, story
  narratives n ▷ **narrative**
  narrator n ▷ **narrate**
  narrators n ▷ **narrate**
narrow adj (**-er, -est**) small in breadth in comparison to length ▶ v (**-s, -ing, -ed**) make or become narrow ▶ **narrowly** adv > **narrowness** n (pl **-es**)
  narrowed v ▷ **narrow**
  narrower adj ▷ **narrow**
  narrowest adj ▷ **narrow**
  narrowing v ▷ **narrow**
  narrowly adv ▷ **narrow**
  narrowness n ▷ **narrow**
  narrownesses n ▷ **narrow**
  narrows v ▷ **narrow** ▶ pl n narrow part of a strait, river, or current
narwhal n (pl **-s**) arctic whale with a long spiral tusk
  narwhals n ▷ **narwhal**
nasal adj of the nose > **nasally** adv
  nasally adv ▷ **nasal**
nascent adj starting to grow or develop
  nastier adj ▷ **nasty**
  nastiest adj ▷ **nasty**
  nastily adv ▷ **nasty**
  nastiness n ▷ **nasty**
  nastinesses n ▷ **nasty**
nasturtium n (pl **-s**) plant with yellow, red, or orange trumpet-shaped flowers
  nasturtiums n ▷ **nasturtium**
nasty adj (**-tier, -tiest**) unpleasant > **nastily** adv > **nastiness** n (pl **-es**)
natal adj of or relating to birth
nation n (pl **nations**) people of one or more cultures or races organized as a single state
  nations n ▷ **nation**
national adj characteristic of a particular nation ▶ n (pl **-s**) citizen of a nation > **nationally** adv
nationalism n (pl **-s**) policy of national independence > **nationalist** n (pl **-s**) adj
  nationalisms n ▷ **nationalism**
  nationalist n ▷ **nationalism**
  nationalists n ▷ **nationalism**
  nationalities n ▷ **nationality**
nationality n (pl **-ties**) fact of being a citizen of a particular nation
  nationalization n ▷ **nationalize**
  nationalizations n ▷ **nationalize**
nationalize v (**-izes, -izing, -ized**) put (an industry or a company) under state control > **nationalization** n (pl **-s**)
  nationalized v ▷ **nationalize**

nationalizes v ▷ **nationalize**
nationalizing v ▷ **nationalize**
nationally adv ▷ **national**
nationals n ▷ **national**
native adj relating to a place where a person was born ▶ n (pl -**s**) person born in a specified place
natives n ▷ **native**
nativities n ▷ **nativity**
nativity n (pl -**ties**) birth or origin
natter (Informal) v (-**s**, -**ing**, -**ed**) talk idly or chatter ▶ n (pl -**s**) long idle chat
nattered v ▷ **natter**
nattering v ▷ **natter**
natters v, n ▷ **natter**
nattier adj ▷ **natty**
nattiest adj ▷ **natty**
natty adj (-**tier**, -**ttiest**) (Informal) smart and spruce
natural adj normal or to be expected ▶ n (pl -**s**) person with an inborn talent or skill
naturalism n (pl -**s**) movement in art and literature advocating detailed realism > **naturalistic** adj
naturalisms n ▷ **naturalism**
naturalist n (pl -**s**) student of natural history
naturalistic n ▷ **naturalism**
naturalists n ▷ **naturalist**
naturalization n ▷ **naturalize**
naturalizations n ▷ **naturalize**
naturalize v (-**izes**, -**izing**, -**ized**) give citizenship to (a person born in another country) > **naturalization** n (pl -**s**)
naturalized v ▷ **naturalize**
naturalizes v ▷ **naturalize**
naturalizing v ▷ **naturalize**
naturally adv of course
naturals n ▷ **natural**
nature n (pl -**s**) whole system of the existence, forces, and events of the physical world that are not controlled by human beings
natures n ▷ **nature**
naturism n (pl -**s**) nudism > **naturist** n (pl -**s**)
naturisms n ▷ **naturism**
naturist n ▷ **naturism**
naturists n ▷ **naturism**
naught n (pl -**s**) (Lit) nothing
naughtier adj ▷ **naughty**
naughtiest adj ▷ **naughty**
naughtily adv ▷ **naughty**
naughtiness n ▷ **naughty**
naughtinesses n ▷ **naughty**
naughts n ▷ **naught**
naughty adj (-**tier**, -**tiest**) disobedient or mischievous > **naughtily** adv > **naughtiness**

n (pl -**es**)
nausea [naw-zee-a] n (pl -**s**) feeling of being about to vomit
nauseas n ▷ **nausea**
nauseate v (-**tes**, -**ting**, -**ted**) make (someone) feel sick
nauseated v ▷ **nauseate**
nauseates v ▷ **nauseate**
nauseating v ▷ **nauseate**
nauseous adj as if about to vomit
nautical adj of the sea or ships
nautili n ▷ **nautilus**
nautilus n (pl -**luses**, -**li**) shellfish with many tentacles
nautiluses n ▷ **nautilus**
naval adj ▷ **navy**
nave n (pl -**s**) long central part of a church
navel n (pl -**s**) hollow in the middle of the abdomen where the umbilical cord was attached
navels n ▷ **navel**
naves n ▷ **nave**
navies n ▷ **navy**
navigable adj wide, deep, or safe enough to be sailed through
navigate v (-**tes**, -**ting**, -**ted**) direct or plot the path or position of a ship, aircraft, or car > **navigation** n (pl -**s**) > **navigator** n (pl -**s**)
navigated v ▷ **navigate**
navigates v ▷ **navigate**
navigating v ▷ **navigate**
navigation n ▷ **navigate**
navigations n ▷ **navigate**
navigator n ▷ **navigate**
navigators n ▷ **navigate**
navvies n ▷ **navvy**
navvy n (pl -**vvies**) (BRIT) labourer employed on a road or a building site
navy n (pl -**vies**) branch of a country's armed services comprising warships with their crews and organization
nay interj (Obs) no

ne adv. Ne is an old word meaning **not**. This handy little word can be very helpful when you are trying to form several words at once. Ne scores 2 points.

neanderthal [nee-ann-der-tahl] adj of a type of primitive man that lived in Europe before 12 000 BC
near prep, adv adj (-**er**, -**est**) indicating a place or time not far away ▶ adj almost being the thing specified ▶ v (-**s**, -**ing**, -**ed**) draw close (to) > **nearness** n (pl -**es**)
nearby adj not far away

neared v ▷ near
nearer adj ▷ near
nearest adj ▷ near
nearing v ▷ near
nearly adv almost
nearness n ▷ near
nearnesses n ▷ near
nears v ▷ near
nearside n (pl -s) side of a vehicle that is nearer the kerb
nearsides n ▷ nearside
neat adj (**-er, -est**) tidy and clean > **neatly** adv > **neatness** n (pl **-es**)
neater adj ▷ neat
neatest adj ▷ neat
neatly adv ▷ neat
neatness n ▷ neat
neatnesses n ▷ neat
nebula n (pl **-lae**) (ASTRONOMY) hazy cloud of particles and gases > **nebulous** adj vague and unclear
nebulae n ▷ nebula
nebulous adj ▷ nebula
necessarily adv ▷ necessary
necessary adj needed to obtain the desired result > **necessarily** adv
necessitate v (**-tes, -ting, -ted**) compel or require
necessitated v ▷ necessitate
necessitates v ▷ necessitate
necessitating v ▷ necessitate
necessities n ▷ necessity
necessity n (pl **-ties**) circumstances that inevitably require a certain result
neck n (pl **-s**) part of the body joining the head to the shoulders ▶ v (**-s, -ing, -ed**) (Slang) kiss and cuddle
necked v ▷ neck
neckerchief n (pl **-s**) piece of cloth worn tied round the neck
neckerchiefs n ▷ neckerchief
necking v ▷ neck
necklace n (pl **-s**) decorative piece of jewellery worn around the neck
necklaces n ▷ necklace
necks n, v ▷ neck
necromancies n ▷ necromancy
necromancy n (pl **-cies**) communication with the dead
necropolis [neck-**rop**-pol-liss] n (pl **-ses**) cemetery
necropolises n ▷ necropolis
nectar n (pl **-s**) sweet liquid collected from flowers by bees
nectars n ▷ nectar

nectarine n (pl **-s**) smooth-skinned peach
nectarines n ▷ nectarine
née [nay] prep indicating the maiden name of a married woman
need v (**-s, -ing, -ed**) require or be in want of ▶ n (pl **-s**) condition of lacking something
needed v ▷ need
needful adj necessary or required
needier adj ▷ needy
neediest adj ▷ needy
needing v ▷ need
needle n (pl **-s**) thin pointed piece of metal with an eye through which thread is passed for sewing ▶ v (**-les, -ling, -led**) (Informal) goad or provoke
needled v ▷ needle
needles n, v ▷ needle
needless adj unnecessary
needlework n (pl **-s**) sewing and embroidery
needleworks n ▷ needlework
needling v ▷ needle
needs v, n ▷ need ▶ adv (preceded or foll. by **must**) necessarily
needy adj (**-dier, -diest**) poor, in need of financial support
nefarious [nif-**fair**-ee-uss] adj wicked
negate v (**-tes, -ting, -ted**) invalidate > **negation** n (pl **-s**)
negated v ▷ negate
negates v ▷ negate
negating v ▷ negate
negation n ▷ negate
negations n ▷ negate
negative adj expressing a denial or refusal ▶ n (pl **-s**) negative word or statement
negatives n ▷ negative
neglect v (**-s, -ing, -ed**) take no care of ▶ n (pl **-s**) neglecting or being neglected > **neglectful** adj
neglected v ▷ neglect
neglectful adj ▷ neglect
neglecting v ▷ neglect
neglects v, n ▷ neglect
negligee [neg-lee-zhay] n (pl **-s**) woman's lightweight usu. lace-trimmed dressing gown
negligees n ▷ negligee
negligence n (pl **-s**) neglect or carelessness > **negligent** adj > **negligently** adv
negligences n ▷ negligence
negligent adj ▷ negligence
negligently adv ▷ negligence
negligible adj so small or unimportant as to be not worth considering
negotiable adj ▷ negotiate

negotiate v (-**tes**, -**ting**, -**ted**) discuss in order to reach (an agreement) > **negotiation** n (pl -**s**) > **negotiator** n (pl -**s**) > **negotiable** adj

negotiated v ▷ **negotiate**

negotiates v ▷ **negotiate**

negotiating v ▷ **negotiate**

negotiation n ▷ **negotiate**

negotiations n ▷ **negotiate**

negotiator n ▷ **negotiate**

negotiators n ▷ **negotiate**

neigh n (pl -**s**) loud high-pitched sound made by a horse ▶ v (-**s**, -**ing**, -**ed**) make this sound

neighed v ▷ **neigh**

neighing v ▷ **neigh**

neighs n, v ▷ **neigh**

neighbour n (pl -**s**) person who lives or is situated near another

neighbourhood n (pl -**s**) district

neighbourhoods n ▷ **neighbourhood**

neighbouring adj situated nearby

neighbourly adj kind, friendly, and helpful

neighbours n ▷ **neighbour**

neither adj, pron not one nor the other ▶ conj not

nemeses n ▷ **nemesis**

nemesis [nem-miss-iss] n (pl -**ses**) retribution or vengeance

neo- combining form new, recent, or a modern form of

neolith n (pl -**s**) stone implement from the Neolithic age

neoliths n ▷ **neolith**

neologism [nee-ol-a-jiz-zum] n (pl -**s**) newly-coined word or an established word used in a new sense

neologisms n ▷ **neologism**

neon n (pl -**s**) (CHEM) colourless odourless gaseous element used in illuminated signs and lights

neons n ▷ **neon**

neophyte n (pl -**s**) beginner or novice

neophytes n ▷ **neophyte**

nephew n (pl -**s**) son of one's sister or brother

nephews n ▷ **nephew**

nephritis [nif-frite-tiss] n (pl -**tises**) inflammation of a kidney

nephritises n ▷ **nephritis**

nepotism [nep-a-tiz-zum] n (pl -**s**) favouritism in business shown to relatives and friends

nepotisms n ▷ **nepotism**

nerd n (pl -**s**) (Slang) boring person obsessed with a particular subject

nerds n ▷ **nerd**

nerve n (pl -**s**) cordlike bundle of fibres that conducts impulses between the brain and other parts of the body

nerveless adj numb, without feeling

nerves n ▷ **nerve** ▶ pl n anxiety or tension

nervier adj ▷ **nervy**

nerviest adj ▷ **nervy**

nervous adj apprehensive or worried > **nervously** adv > **nervousness** n (pl -**es**)

nervously adv ▷ **nervous**

nervousness n ▷ **nervous**

nervousnesses n ▷ **nervous**

nervy adj (-**vier**, -**viest**) excitable or nervous

nest n (pl -**s**) place or structure in which birds or certain animals lay eggs or give birth to young ▶ v (-**s**, -**ing**, -**ed**) make or inhabit a nest

nested v ▷ **nest**

nesting v ▷ **nest**

nests v, n ▷ **nest**

nestle v (-**les**, -**ling**, -**led**) snuggle

nestled v ▷ **nestle**

nestles v ▷ **nestle**

nestling n (pl -**s**) bird too young to leave the nest ▶ v ▷ **nestle**

nestlings n ▷ **nestling**

net[1] n (pl -**s**) fabric of meshes of string, thread, or wire with many openings ▶ v (-**s**, -**tting**, -**tted**) catch (a fish or animal) in a net

net[2], **nett** adj left after all deductions ▶ v (-**s**, -**tting**, -**tted**) yield or earn as a clear profit

netball n (pl -**s**) team game in which a ball has to be thrown through a net hanging from a ring at the top of a pole

netballs n ▷ **netball**

nether adj lower

nets v ▷ **net**[1, 2]

nets n ▷ **net**[1]

nett adj ▷ **net**[2]

netted v ▷ **net**[1, 2]

netting v ▷ **net**[1, 2] ▶ n (pl -**s**) material made of net

nettings n ▷ **netting**

nettle n (pl -**s**) plant with stinging hairs on the leaves

nettled adj irritated or annoyed

nettles n ▷ **nettle**

network n (pl -**s**) system of intersecting lines, roads, etc.

networks n ▷ **network**

neural adj of a nerve or the nervous system

neuralgia n (pl -**s**) severe pain along a nerve

neuralgias n ▷ **neuralgia**

neuritis [nyoor-rite-tiss] n (pl -**tises**) inflammation of a nerve or nerves

neuritises n ▷ **neuritis**

neurologies n ▷ **neurology**

neurologist n ▷ **neurology**

neurologists n ▷ **neurology**

neurology n (pl -**gies**) scientific study of the nervous system > **neurologist** n (pl -**s**)

neuroses n ▷ **neurosis**

neurosis n (pl -**ses**) mental disorder producing hysteria, anxiety, depression, or obsessive behaviour

neurotic adj emotionally unstable ▶ n (pl -**s**) neurotic person

neurotics n ▷ **neurotic**

neuter adj belonging to a particular class of grammatical inflections in some languages ▶ v (-**s, -ing, -ed**) castrate (an animal)

neutered v ▷ **neuter**

neutering v ▷ **neuter**

neuters v ▷ **neuter**

neutral adj taking neither side in a war or dispute ▶ n (pl -**s**) neutral person or nation > **neutrality** n (pl -**ties**)

neutralities n ▷ **neutral**

neutrality n ▷ **neutral**

neutralize v (-**izes, -izing, -ized**) make ineffective or neutral

neutralized v ▷ **neutralize**

neutralizes v ▷ **neutralize**

neutralizing v ▷ **neutralize**

neutrals n ▷ **neutral**

neutrino [new-tree-no] n (pl -**nos**) elementary particle with no mass or electrical charge

neutrinos n ▷ **neutrino**

neutron n (pl -**s**) electrically neutral elementary particle of about the same mass as a proton

neutrons n ▷ **neutron**

never adv at no time

nevertheless adv in spite of that

new adj (-**er, -est**) not existing before (foll. by **to**) ▶ adv recently

newbie (Informal) n (pl -**s**) person new to a job, club, etc

newbies n ▷ **newbie**

newborn adj recently or just born

newcomer n (pl -**s**) recent arrival or participant

newcomers n ▷ **newcomer**

newel n (pl -**s**) post at the top or bottom of a flight of stairs that supports the handrail

newels n ▷ **newel**

newer adj ▷ **new**

newest adj ▷ **new**

newfangled adj objectionably or unnecessarily modern

newlyweds pl n recently married couple

newness n (pl -**es**) novelty

newnesses n ▷ **newness**

news n important or interesting new happenings

newsagent n (pl -**s**) (BRIT) shopkeeper who sells newspapers and magazines

newsagents n ▷ **newsagent**

newscaster n ▷ **newsreader**

newscasters n ▷ **newsreader**

newsflash n (pl -**es**) brief important news item, which interrupts a radio or television programme

newsflashes n ▷ **newsflash**

newsier adj ▷ **newsy**

newsiest adj ▷ **newsy**

newsletter n (pl -**s**) bulletin issued periodically to members of a group

newsletters n ▷ **newsletter**

newspaper n (pl -**s**) weekly or daily publication containing news

newspapers n ▷ **newspaper**

newsprint n (pl -**s**) inexpensive paper used for newspapers

newsprints n ▷ **newsprint**

newsreader, newscaster n (pl -**s**) person who reads the news on the television or radio

newsreaders n ▷ **newsreader**

newsreel n (pl -**s**) short film giving news

newsreels n ▷ **newsreel**

newsroom n (pl -**s**) room where news is received and prepared for publication or broadcasting

newsrooms n ▷ **newsroom**

newsworthy adj sufficiently interesting to be reported as news

newsy adj (-**sier, -siest**) full of news

newt n (pl -**s**) small amphibious creature with a long slender body and tail

newton n (pl -**s**) unit of force

newtons n ▷ **newton**

newts n ▷ **newt**

next adj, adv immediately following

nexus n (pl **nexus**) connection or link

nib n (pl -**s**) writing point of a pen

nibble v (-**les, -ling, -led**) take little bites (of) ▶ n (pl -**les**) little bite

nibbled v ▷ **nibble**

nibbles v, n ▷ **nibble**

nibbling v ▷ **nibble**

nibs n (pl ▷ **nib**

nibses n ▷ **nibs**

nice adj (-**r, -st**) pleasant > **nicely** adv > **niceness** n (pl -**es**)

nicely adv ▷ **nice**

niceness n ▷ **nice**

nicenesses n ▷ **nice**

nicer adj ▷ **nice**

nicest adj ▷ **nice**

niceties n ▷ **nicety**

nicety n (pl **-ties**) subtle point

niche [neesh] n (pl **-s**) hollow area in a wall

  niches n ▷ **niche**

nick v (**-s, -ing, -ed**) make a small cut in ▶ n (pl **-s**) small cut

  nicked v ▷ **nick**

nickel n (pl **-s**) (CHEM) silvery-white metal often used in alloys

nickelodeon n (pl **-s**) (US) early type of jukebox

  nickelodeons n ▷ **nickelodeon**

  nickels n ▷ **nickel**

  nicking v ▷ **nick**

nickname n (pl **-s**) familiar name given to a person or place ▶ v (**-mes, -ming, -med**) call by a nickname

  nicknamed v ▷ **nickname**

  nicknames n, v ▷ **nickname**

  nicknaming v ▷ **nickname**

  nicks v, n ▷ **nick**

nicotine n (pl **-s**) poisonous substance found in tobacco

  nicotines n ▷ **nicotine**

niece n (pl **-s**) daughter of one's sister or brother

  nieces n ▷ **niece**

  niftier adj ▷ **nifty**

  niftiest adj ▷ **nifty**

nifty adj (**-tier, -tiest**) (Informal) neat or smart

  niggard n ▷ **niggardly**

niggardly adj stingy ▷ **niggard** n (pl **-s**) stingy person

  niggards n ▷ **niggardly**

niggle v (**-les, -ling, -led**) worry slightly ▶ n (pl **-s**) small worry or doubt

  niggled v ▷ **niggle**

  niggles v, n ▷ **niggle**

  niggling v ▷ **niggle**

nigh adv, prep (Lit) near

night n (pl **-s**) time of darkness between sunset and sunrise

nightcap n (pl **-s**) drink taken just before bedtime

  nightcaps n ▷ **nightcap**

nightclub n (pl **-s**) establishment for dancing, music, etc., open late at night

  nightclubs n ▷ **nightclub**

nightdress n (pl **-es**) woman's loose dress worn in bed

  nightdresses n ▷ **nightdress**

nightfall n (pl **-s**) approach of darkness

  nightfalls n ▷ **nightfall**

nightie n (pl **-s**) (Informal) nightdress

  nighties n ▷ **nightie**

nightingale n (pl **-s**) small bird with a musical song usu. heard at night

  nightingales n ▷ **nightingale**

nightjar n (pl **-s**) nocturnal bird with a harsh cry

  nightjars n ▷ **nightjar**

nightlife n (pl **-s**) entertainment and social activities available at night in a town or city

  nightlifes n ▷ **nightlife**

nightly adj, adv (happening) each night

nightmare n (pl **-s**) very bad dream

  nightmares n ▷ **nightmare**

  nights n ▷ **night**

nightshade n (pl **-s**) plant with bell-shaped flowers which are often poisonous

  nightshades n ▷ **nightshade**

nightshirt n (pl **-s**) long loose shirt worn in bed

  nightshirts n ▷ **nightshirt**

nihilism [nye-ill-liz-zum] n (pl **-s**) rejection of all established authority and institutions > **nihilist** n (pl **-s**) > **nihilistic** adj

  nihilisms n ▷ **nihilism**

  nihilist n ▷ **nihilism**

  nihilistic adj ▷ **nihilism**

  nihilists n ▷ **nihilism**

nil n (pl **-s**) nothing, zero

  nils n ▷ **nil**

  nimbi n ▷ **nimbus**

nimble adj (**-r, -st**) agile and quick > **nimbly** adv

  nimbler adj ▷ **nimble**

  nimblest adj ▷ **nimble**

  nimbly adv ▷ **nimble**

nimbus n (pl **-bi, -buses**) dark grey rain cloud

  nimbuses n ▷ **nimbus**

nincompoop n (pl **-s**) (Informal) stupid person

  nincompoops n ▷ **nincompoop**

nine adj, n (pl **-s**) one more than eight

ninepins n game of skittles

  nines n ▷ **nine**

nineteen adj, n (pl **-s**) ten and nine > **nineteenth** adj, n (pl **-s**)

  nineteens n ▷ **nineteen**

nineteenth adj, n ▷ **nineteen**

  nineteenths n ▷ **nineteen**

  nineties n ▷ **ninety**

ninetieth adj, n ▷ **ninety**

  ninetieths n ▷ **ninety**

ninety adj, n (pl **-ties**) ten times nine > **ninetieth** adj, n (pl **-s**)

ninth adj, n (pl **-s**) (of) number nine in a series

  ninths n ▷ **ninth**

niobium n (pl **-s**) (CHEM) white superconductive metallic element

  niobiums n ▷ **niobium**

nip¹ v (**-s, -pping, -pped**) (Informal) hurry ▶ n (pl

-s) pinch or light bite

nip² n (pl **nips**) small alcoholic drink
  nipped v ▷ **nip¹**

nipper n (pl -s) (BRIT, AUST & NZ) (Informal) small child
  nippers n ▷ **nipper**
  nippier adj ▷ **nippy**
  nippiest adj ▷ **nippy**
  nipping v ▷ **nip¹**

nipple n (pl -s) projection in the centre of a breast
  nipples n ▷ **nipple**

nippy adj (Informal) (-pier, -piest) frosty or chilly
  nips v ▷ **nip¹** ▷ n ▷ **nip¹,²**

nirvana [near-vah-na] n (pl -s) (BUDDHISM) (HINDUISM) absolute spiritual enlightenment and bliss
  nirvanas n ▷ **nirvana**

nit n (pl -s) egg or larva of a louse (Informal) ▷ **nitwit**

nitrate n (pl -s) compound of nitric acid, used as a fertilizer
  nitrates n ▷ **nitrate**

nitric, nitrous, nitrogenous adj of or containing nitrogen

nitrogen [nite-roj-jen] n (pl -s) (CHEM) colourless odourless gas that forms four fifths of the air
  nitrogenous n ▷ **nitric**
  nitrogens n ▷ **nitrogen**
  nitroglycerin n ▷ **nitroglycerine**

nitroglycerine, nitroglycerin n (pl -s) explosive liquid
  nitroglycerines n ▷ **nitroglycerine**
  nitroglycerins n ▷ **nitroglycerine**
  nitrous adj ▷ **nitric**
  nits n ▷ **nit**

nitwit n (pl -s) (Informal) stupid person
  nitwits n ▷ **nitwit**

> **nix** n (**nixes**). A nix is a water sprite in Germanic mythology. This is a handy little word, combining X with two of the most common tiles in the game. If you have an X on your rack, look out for opportunities on the board to play this as there's most likely an N or I available. Nix scores 10 points.

no interj expresses denial, disagreement, or refusal ▶ adj not any, not a ▶ adv not at all ▶ n (pl **noes, nos**) answer or vote of 'no'

nob n (pl -s) (CHIEFLY BRIT) (Slang) person of wealth or social distinction
  nobs n ▷ **nob**

nobble v (-les, -ling, -led) (BRIT) (Slang) attract the attention of (someone) in order to talk to him or her

nobbled v ▷ **nobble**
  nobbles v ▷ **nobble**
  nobbling v ▷ **nobble**

nobelium n (pl -s) (CHEM) artificially-produced radioactive element
  nobeliums n ▷ **nobelium**
  nobilities n ▷ **nobility**

nobility n (pl -ties) quality of being noble
  > **nobleman, noblewoman** n (pl -men)

noble adj (-r, -st) showing or having high moral qualities ▶ n (pl -s) member of the nobility
  > **nobly** adv

nobleman n ▷ **nobility**
  noblemen n ▷ **nobility**
  nobler adj ▷ **noble**
  nobles n ▷ **noble**
  noblest adj ▷ **noble**
  noblewoman n ▷ **nobility**
  noblewomen n ▷ **nobility**
  nobly adv ▷ **noble**
  nobodies n ▷ **nobody**

nobody pron no person ▶ n (pl -dies) person of no importance

nocturnal adj of the night

nocturne n (pl -s) short dreamy piece of music
  nocturnes n ▷ **nocturne**

nod v (-s, -dding, -dded) lower and raise (one's head) briefly in agreement or greeting ▶ n (pl -s) act of nodding
  nodded v ▷ **nod**
  nodding v ▷ **nod**

noddle n (pl s) (CHIEFLY BRIT) (Informal) the head
  noddles n ▷ **noddle**

node n (pl -s) point on a plant stem from which leaves grow
  nodes n ▷ **node**
  nods v, n ▷ **nod**

nodule n (pl -s) small knot or lump
  nodules n ▷ **nodule**

noel n (pl -s) Christmas carol
  noels n ▷ **noel**
  noes n ▷ **no**

noggin n (pl -s) (Informal) head
  noggins n ▷ **noggin**

noise n (pl -s) sound, usu. a loud or disturbing one > **noiseless** adj
  noiseless adj ▷ **noise**
  noises n ▷ **noise**
  noisier adj ▷ **noisy**
  noisiest adj ▷ **noisy**
  noisily adv ▷ **noisy**

noisy adj (-sier, -siest) making a lot of noise
  > **noisily** adv

noisome adj (of smells) offensive

nomad n (pl -s) member of a tribe with no fixed

dwelling place, wanderer ▷ **nomadic** *adj*
nomadic *adj* ▷ **nomad**
nomads *n* ▷ **nomad**
nomenclature *n* (*pl* **-s**) system of names used in a particular subject
  nomenclatures *n* ▷ **nomenclature**
nominal *adj* in name only ▷ **nominally** *adv*
  nominally *adv* ▷ **nominal**
nominate *v* (**-tes, -ting, -ted**) suggest as a candidate ▷ **nomination** *n* (*pl* **-s**)
  nominated *v* ▷ **nominate**
  nominates *v* ▷ **nominate**
  nominating *v* ▷ **nominate**
  nomination *n* ▷ **nominate**
  nominations *n* ▷ **nominate**
nominative *n* (*pl* **-s**) form of a noun indicating the subject of a verb
  nominatives *n* ▷ **nominative**
nominee *n* (*pl* **-s**) candidate
  nominees *n* ▷ **nominee**
non- *prefix* indicating: negation
nonagenarian *n* (*pl* **-s**) person aged between ninety and ninety-nine
  nonagenarians *n* ▷ **nonagenarian**
nonaggression *n* (*pl* **-s**) policy of not attacking other countries
  nonaggressions *n* ▷ **nonaggression**
nonagon *n* (*pl* **-s**) geometric figure with nine sides
  nonagons *n* ▷ **nonagon**
nonalcoholic *adj* containing no alcohol
nonaligned *adj* (of a country) not part of a major alliance or power bloc
nonce *n* (*pl* **-s**) for the present
  nonces *n* ▷ **nonce**
  nonchalance *n* ▷ **nonchalant**
  nonchalances *n* ▷ **nonchalant**
nonchalant *adj* casually unconcerned or indifferent ▷ **nonchalantly** *adv*
  ▷ **nonchalance** *n* (*pl* **-s**)
  nonchalantly *adv* ▷ **nonchalant**
noncombatant *n* (*pl* **-s**) member of the armed forces whose duties do not include fighting
  noncombatants *n* ▷ **noncombatant**
noncommittal *adj* not committing oneself to any particular opinion
nonconductor *n* (*pl* **-s**) substance that is a poor conductor of heat, electricity, or sound
  nonconductors *n* ▷ **nonconductor**
nonconformist *n* (*pl* **-s**) person who does not conform to generally accepted patterns of behaviour or thought (**N-**) ▶ *adj* (of behaviour or ideas) not conforming to accepted patterns ▷ **nonconformity** *n* (*pl* **-ties**)
  nonconformists *n* ▷ **nonconformist**

nonconformities *n* ▷ **nonconformist**
  nonconformity *n* ▷ **nonconformist**
noncontributory *adj* (BRIT) denoting a pension scheme for employees, the premiums of which are paid entirely by the employer
nondescript *adj* lacking outstanding features
none *pron* not any
  nonentities *n* ▷ **nonentity**
nonentity [non-**enn**-tit-tee] *n* (*pl* **-ties**) insignificant person or thing
nonetheless *adv* despite that, however
nonevent *n* (*pl* **-s**) disappointing or insignificant occurrence
  nonevents *n* ▷ **nonevent**
nonflammable *adj* not easily set on fire
nonintervention *n* (*pl* refusal to intervene in the affairs of others
nonpareil [non-par-**rail**] *n* (*pl* **-s**) person or thing that is unsurpassed
  nonpareils *n* ▷ **nonpareil**
nonpayment *n* (*pl* **-s**) failure to pay money owed
  nonpayments *n* ▷ **nonpayment**
nonplussed *adj* perplexed
nonsense *n* (*pl* **-s**) something that has or makes no sense ▷ **nonsensical** *adj*
  nonsenses *n* ▷ **nonsense**
  nonsensical *adj* ▷ **nonsense**
nonstandard *adj* denoting language that is not regarded as correct by educated native speakers
nonstarter *n* (*pl* **-s**) person or idea that has little chance of success
  nonstarters *n* ▷ **nonstarter**
nonstick *adj* coated with a substance that food will not stick to when cooked
nonstop *adj, adv* without a stop
nontoxic *adj* not poisonous
noodles *pl n* long thin strips of pasta
nook *n* (*pl* **-s**) sheltered place
  nooks *n* ▷ **nook**
noon *n* (*pl* **-s**) twelve o'clock midday
noonday *adj* happening at noon
  noons *n* ▷ **noon**
noose *n* (*pl* **-s**) loop in the end of a rope, tied with a slipknot
  nooses *n* ▷ **noose**
nor *conj* and not
norm *n* (*pl* **-s**) standard that is regarded as normal
normal *adj* usual, regular, or typical
  ▷ **normally** *adv* ▷ **normality** *n* (*pl* **-ties**)
  ▷ **normalize** *v* (**-izes, -izing, -ized**)
  normalities *n* ▷ **normal**

normality *n* ▷ **normal**
normalized *v* ▷ **normal**
normalizes *v* ▷ **normal**
normalizing *v* ▷ **normal**
normally *adv* ▷ **normal**
norms *n* ▷ **norm**
north *n* (*pl* **-s**) direction towards the North Pole, opposite south ▶ *adj* to or in the north ▶ *adv* in, to, or towards the north ▷ **northerly** *adj* ▷ **northern** *adj* ▷ **northward** *adj*, *adv* ▷ **northwards** *adv*
northerly *adj* ▷ **north**
northern *adj* ▷ **north**
northerner *n* (*pl* **-s**) person from the north of a country or area
northerners *n* ▷ **northerner**
norths *n* ▷ **north**
northward *adj*, *adv* ▷ **north**
northwards *adv* ▷ **north**
nos *n* ▷ **no**
nose *n* (*pl* **-s**) organ of smell, used also in breathing ▶ *v* (**-ses, -sing, -sed**) move forward slowly and carefully
nosed *v* ▷ **nose**
nosegay *n* (*pl* **-s**) small bunch of flowers
nosegays *n* ▷ **nosegay**
noses *n*, *v* ▷ **nose**
nosey, nosy *adj* (*Informal*) (**-sier, -siest**) prying or inquisitive ▷ **nosiness** *n* (*pl* **-es**)
nosier *adj* ▷ **nosey**
nosiest *adj* ▷ **nosey**
nosiness *n* ▷ **nosey**
nosinesses *n* ▷ **nosey**
nosing *v* ▷ **nose**
nosh *n* (*pl* **-es**) (BRIT, AUST & NZ) (*Slang*) food ▶ *v* (**-shes, -shing, -shed**) eat
noshed *v* ▷ **nosh**
noshes *n*, *v* ▷ **nosh**
noshing *v* ▷ **nosh**
nostalgia *n* (*pl* **-s**) sentimental longing for the past ▷ **nostalgic** *adj*
nostalgias *n* ▷ **nostalgia**
nostalgic *adj* ▷ **nostalgia**
nostril *n* (*pl* **-s**) one of the two openings at the end of the nose
nostrils *n* ▷ **nostril**
nostrum *n* (*pl* **-s**) quack medicine
nostrums *n* ▷ **nostrum**
nosy *adj* (**-sier, -siest**) ▷ **nosey**
not *adv* expressing negation, refusal, or denial
notable *adj* worthy of being noted, remarkable ▶ *n* (*pl* **-s**) person of distinction ▷ **notably** *adv*
notabilities *n* ▷ **notability**
notability *n* (*pl* **-ties**)

notables *n* ▷ **notable**
notably *adv* ▷ **notable**
notaries *n* ▷ **notary**
notary *n* (*pl* **-ries**) person authorized to witness the signing of legal documents
notation *n* (*pl* **-s**) representation of numbers or quantities in a system by a series of symbols
notations *n* ▷ **notation**
notch *n* (*pl* **-es**) V-shaped cut ▶ *v* (**-ches, -ching, -ched**) make a notch in (*foll.* by **up**)
notched *v* ▷ **notch**
notches *n*, *v* ▷ **notch**
notching *v* ▷ **notch**
note *n* (*pl* **-s**) short letter ▶ *v* (**-tes, -ting, -ted**) notice, pay attention to
notebook *n* (*pl* **-s**) book for writing in
notebooks *n* ▷ **notebook**
noted *v* ▷ **note** ▶ *adj* well-known
notes *n*, *v* ▷ **note**
noteworthy *adj* worth noting, remarkable
nothing *pron* not anything ▶ *adv* not at all
nothingness *n* (*pl* **-es**) nonexistence
nothingnesses *n* ▷ **nothingness**
notice *n* (*pl* **-s**) observation or attention ▶ *v* (**-ces, -cing, -ced**) observe, become aware of
noticeable *adj* easily seen or detected, appreciable
noticed *v* ▷ **notice**
notices *n*, *v* ▷ **notice**
noticing *v* ▷ **notice**
notifiable *adj* having to be reported to the authorities
notification *n* ▷ **notify**
notifications *n* ▷ **notify**
notified *v* ▷ **notify**
notifies *v* ▷ **notify**
notify *v* (**-fies, -fying, -fied**) inform ▷ **notification** *n* (*pl* **-s**)
notifying *v* ▷ **notify**
noting *v* ▷ **note**
notion *n* (*pl* **-s**) idea or opinion
notional *adj* speculative, imaginary, or unreal
notions *n* ▷ **notion**
notorieties *n* ▷ **notorious**
notoriety *n* ▷ **notorious**
notorious *adj* well known for something bad ▷ **notoriously** *adv* ▷ **notoriety** *n* (*pl* **-ties**)
notoriously *adv* ▷ **notorious**
notwithstanding *prep* in spite of
nougat *n* (*pl* **-s**) chewy sweet containing nuts and fruit
nougats *n* ▷ **nougat**
nought *n* (*pl* **-s**) figure o
noughties *pl n* (*Informal*) decade from 2000 to 2009

noughts n ▷ nought

noun n (pl -s) word that refers to a person, place, or thing

nouns n ▷ noun

nourish v (-shes, -shing, -shed) feed
> **nourishment** n (pl -s)

nourished v ▷ nourish

nourishes v ▷ nourish

nourishing adj providing the food necessary for life and growth ▶ v ▷ nourish

nourishment n ▷ nourish

nourishments n ▷ nourish

nova n (pl -vae, -vas) star that suddenly becomes brighter and then gradually decreases to its original brightness

novae n ▷ nova

novas n ▷ nova

novel¹ n (pl -s) long fictitious story in book form

novel² adj fresh, new, or original > **novelist** n (pl -s) writer of novels

novelists n ▷ novelist

novella n (pl -s, -llae) short novel

novellae n ▷ novella

novellas n ▷ novella

novels n ▷ novel¹

novelties n ▷ novelty

novelty n (pl -ties) newness

novena [no-vee-na] n (pl -s) (RC CHURCH) set of prayers or services on nine consecutive days

novenas n ▷ novena

novice n (pl -s) beginner

novices n ▷ novice

now adv at or for the present time ▶ conj seeing that, since

nowadays adv in these times

nowhere adv not anywhere

nox n (noxes). In chemistry, nox is short for nitrogen oxide. This can come in useful in the later stages of the game when there isn't much space left, or when you have an X but can't form a longer word with it. Nox scores 10 points.

noxious adj poisonous or harmful

nozzle n (pl -s) projecting spout through which fluid is discharged

nozzles n ▷ nozzle

nth adv. In mathematics, nth represents an unspecified ordinal number. Nth is a good word to remember for awkward situations on the board, as it's one of very few three-letter words that doesn't contain a vowel. Nth scores 6 points.

nu n nus. Nu is the 13th letter in the Greek alphabet. This word can be really useful when you want to form short words in the process of playing a longer one. Nu scores 2 points.

nuance [new-ahnss] n (pl -s) subtle difference in colour, meaning, or tone

nuances n ▷ nuance

nub n (pl -s) point or gist (of a story etc.)

nubs n ▷ nub

nubile [new-bile] adj (of a young woman) sexually attractive

nuclear adj of nuclear weapons or energy

nuclei n ▷ nucleus

nucleus n (pl -clei) centre, esp. of an atom or cell

nude adj (-r, -st) naked ▶ n (pl -s) naked figure in painting, sculpture, or photography > **nudity** n (pl -ties)

nuder adj ▷ nude

nudes n ▷ nude

nudest adj ▷ nude

nudge v (-dges, -dging, -dged) push gently, esp. with the elbow ▶ n (pl -s) gentle push or touch

nudged v ▷ nudge

nudges v, n ▷ nudge

nudging v ▷ nudge

nudism n (pl -s) practice of not wearing clothes > **nudist** n (pl -s)

nudisms n ▷ nudism

nudist n ▷ nudism

nudists n ▷ nudism

nudities n ▷ nude

nudity n ▷ nude

nugatory [new-gat-tree] adj of little value

nugget n (pl -s) small lump of gold in its natural state ▶ v (-s, -tting, -tted) (NZ & S AFR) polish footwear

nuggeted v ▷ nugget

nuggeting v ▷ nugget

nuggets n, v ▷ nugget

nuggetted v ▷ nugget

nuggetting v ▷ nugget

nuisance n (pl -s) something or someone that causes annoyance or bother

nuisances n ▷ nuisance

nuke (Slang) v (-kes, -king, -ked) attack with nuclear weapons ▶ n (pl -s) nuclear weapon

nuked v ▷ nuke

nukes v, n ▷ nuke

nuking v ▷ nuke

null adj not legally valid > **nullity** n (pl -s)

nullified v ▷ nullify

nullifies v ▷ nullify

nullify *v* (-fies, -fying, -fied) make ineffective
  nullifying *v* ▷ nullify
  nullities *n* ▷ null
  nullity *n* ▷ null
numb *adj* (-er, -est) without feeling, as through cold, shock, or fear ▶ *v* (-s, -ing, -ed) make numb > **numbly** *adv* > **numbness** *n* (*pl* -es)
numbat *n* (*pl* -s) small Australian marsupial with a long snout and tongue
  numbats *n* ▷ numbat
  numbed *v* ▷ numb
  number[1] *adj* ▷ numb
number[2] *n* (*pl* -s) sum or quantity ▶ *v* (-s, -ing, -ed) count
  numbered *v* ▷ number
  numbering *v* ▷ number
numberless *adj* too many to be counted
numberplate *n* (*pl* -s) plate on a car showing the registration number
  numberplates *n* ▷ numberplate
  numbers *n, v* ▷ number
  numbest *adj* ▷ numb
  numbing *v* ▷ numb
  numbly *adv* ▷ numb
  numbness *n* ▷ numb
  numbnesses *n* ▷ numb
  numbs *v* ▷ numb
numbskull *n* (*pl* -s) stupid person
  numbskulls *n* ▷ numbskull
  numeracies *n* ▷ numerate
  numeracy *n* ▷ numerate
numeral *n* (*pl* -s) word or symbol used to express a sum or quantity
  numerals *n* ▷ numeral
numerate *adj* able to do basic arithmetic > **numeracy** *n* (*pl* -cies)
numeration *n* (*pl* -s) act or process of numbering or counting
  numerations *n* ▷ numeration
numerator *n* (*pl* -s) (MATHS) number above the line in a fraction
  numerators *n* ▷ numerator
numerical *adj* measured or expressed in numbers > **numerically** *adv*
  numerically *adv* ▷ numerical
numerous *adj* existing or happening in large numbers
numismatist *n* (*pl* -s) coin collector
  numismatists *n* ▷ numismatist
numskull *n* (*pl* -s) ▷ numbskull
  numskulls *n* ▷ numskull
nun *n* (*pl* -s) female member of a religious order
nuncio *n* (*pl* -s) (RC CHURCH) pope's ambassador
  nuncios *n* ▷ nuncio

  nunneries *n* ▷ nunnery
nunnery *n* (*pl* -ries) convent
  nuns *n* ▷ nun
nuptial *adj* relating to marriage
nuptials *pl n* wedding
nurse *n* (*pl* -s) person employed to look after sick people, usu. in a hospital ▶ *v* (-ses, -sing, -sed) look after (a sick person)
  nursed *v* ▷ nurse
  nurseries *n* ▷ nursery
nursery *n* (*pl* -ries) room where children sleep or play
nurseryman *n* (*pl* -men) person who raises plants for sale
  nurserymen *n* ▷ nurseryman
  nurses *n, v* ▷ nurse
  nursing *v* ▷ nurse
nurture *n* (*pl* -s) act or process of promoting the development of a child or young plant ▶ *v* (-res, -ring, -red) promote or encourage the development of
  nurtured *v* ▷ nurture
  nurtures *n, v* ▷ nurture
  nurturing *v* ▷ nurture
nut *n* (*pl* -s) fruit consisting of a hard shell and a kernel
nutcracker *n* (*pl* -s) device for cracking the shells of nuts
  nutcrackers *n* ▷ nutcracker
nuthatch *n* (*pl* -es) small songbird
  nuthatches *n* ▷ nuthatch
nutmeg *n* (*pl* -s) spice made from the seed of a tropical tree
  nutmegs *n* ▷ nutmeg
nutria *n* (*pl* -s) fur of the coypu
  nutrias *n* ▷ nutria
nutrient *n* (*pl* -s) substance that provides nourishment
  nutrients *n* ▷ nutrient
nutriment *n* (*pl* -s) food or nourishment required by all living things to grow and stay healthy
  nutriments *n* ▷ nutriment
nutrition *n* (*pl* -s) process of taking in and absorbing nutrients > **nutritional** *adj*
  nutritional *adj* ▷ nutrition
  nutritions *n* ▷ nutrition
nutritious, nutritive *adj* nourishing
  nutritive *adj* ▷ nutritious
  nuts *n* ▷ nut
nutter *n* (*pl* -s) (BRIT) (*Slang*) insane person
  nutters *n* ▷ nutter
  nuttier *adj* ▷ nutty
  nuttiest *adj* ▷ nutty
nutty *adj* (-ttier, -ttiest) containing or

resembling nuts

nuzzle v (**-les, -ling, -led**) push or rub gently with the nose or snout
  nuzzled v ▷ **nuzzle**
  nuzzles v ▷ **nuzzle**
  nuzzling v ▷ **nuzzle**

  ny *adj, adv*. Ny is an old spelling of **nigh.** This word can be useful when you're forming one word adjacent to another, and so need to form two-letter words where the two words meet. Ny is also unusual in that it doesn't contain a vowel. Ny scores 5 points.

nylon n (*pl* **-s**) synthetic material used for clothing etc.
  nylons n ▷ **nylon** ▶ *pl* n stockings made of nylon

nymph n (*pl* **-s**) mythical spirit of nature, represented as a beautiful young woman
  nymphs n ▷ **nymph**

nymphet n (*pl* **-s**) sexually precocious young girl
  nymphets n ▷ **nymphet**

Oo

With eight Os in the bag, you're likely to have at least one on your rack during a game. There are plenty of good two-letter words starting with O. It's worth knowing that O will form a two-letter word in front of every other vowel except A, as well as in front of Y. O also combines well with X, with **ox** (9 points) as the obvious starting point, and several words that refer to **oxygen** (17). Don't forget the short everyday words that begin with O. While **on** and **or** (2 each) won't earn you many points, they can be very helpful when you are trying to score in more than one direction at a time. **Of** and **oh** (5 each) can also prove very useful.

oaf n (pl **-s**) stupid or clumsy person ▷ **oafish** adj
  oafish adj ▷ **oaf**
  oafs n ▷ **oaf**
oak n (pl **-s**) deciduous forest tree ▷ **oaken** adj
  oaken adj ▷ **oak**
  oaks n ▷ **oak**
oakum n (pl **-s**) fibre obtained by unravelling old rope
  oakums n ▷ **oakum**
oar n (pl **-s**) pole with a broad blade, used for rowing a boat
  oars n ▷ **oar**
oasis n (pl **-ses**) fertile area in a desert
  oases n ▷ **oasis**
oast n (pl **-s**) (CHIEFLY BRIT) oven for drying hops
  oasts n ▷ **oast**
oat n (pl **-s**) hard cereal grown as food ▶ pl grain of this cereal
oath n (pl **-s**) solemn promise, esp. to be truthful in court
  oaths n ▷ **oath**
oatmeal adj pale brownish-cream
  oats n ▷ **oat**
obbligato [ob-lig-**gah**-toe] n (pl **-os**) (MUSIC) essential part or accompaniment
  obbligatos n ▷ **obbligato**
  obduracies n ▷ **obdurate**
  obduracy n ▷ **obdurate**
obdurate adj hardhearted or stubborn ▷ **obduracy** n (pl **-cies**)
  obedience n ▷ **obedient**
  obediences n ▷ **obedient**
obedient adj obeying or willing to obey ▷ **obedience** n (pl **-s**) ▷ **obediently** adv
  obediently adv ▷ **obedient**
obeisance [oh-**bay**-sanss] n (pl **-s**) attitude of respect
  obeisances n ▷ **obeisance**
obelisk [ob-bill-isk] n (pl **-s**) four-sided stone column tapering to a pyramid at the top
  obelisks n ▷ **obelisk**
obese [oh-**beess**] adj (**-r**, **-st**) very fat ▷ **obesity** n (pl **-ties**)
  obeser adj ▷ **obese**
  obesest adj ▷ **obese**
  obesities n ▷ **obese**
  obesity n ▷ **obese**
obey v (**-s**, **-ing**, **-ed**) carry out instructions or orders
  obeyed v ▷ **obey**
  obeying v ▷ **obey**
  obeys v ▷ **obey**
obfuscate v (**-tes**, **-ting**, **-ted**) make (something) confusing
  obfuscated v ▷ **obfuscate**
  obfuscates v ▷ **obfuscate**
  obfuscating v ▷ **obfuscate**
  obituaries n ▷ **obituary**
  obituarist n ▷ **obituary**
  obituarists n ▷ **obituary**
obituary n (pl **-ies**) announcement of someone's death, esp. in a newspaper ▷ **obituarist** n (pl **-s**)
object[1] n (pl **-s**) physical thing
object[2] v (**-s**, **-ing**, **-ed**) express disapproval ▷ **objection** n (pl **-s**) ▷ **objector** n (pl **-s**)
  objected v ▷ **object**[2]
  objecting v ▷ **object**[2]
  objection n ▷ **object**[2]
objectionable adj unpleasant
  objections n ▷ **object**[2]
objective n (pl **-s**) aim or purpose ▶ adj not

biased > **objectively** adv > **objectivity** n (pl -ties)
objectively adv ▷ objective
objectives n ▷ objective
objectivities n ▷ objective
objectivity n ▷ objective
objector n ▷ object²
objectors n ▷ object²
objects n, v ▷ object¹, ²
oblation n (pl -s) religious offering
oblations n ▷ oblation
obligated adj obliged to do something
obligation n (pl -s) duty
obligations n ▷ obligation
obligatory adj required by a rule or law
oblige v (-ges, -ging, -ged) compel (someone) morally or by law to do something
obliged v ▷ oblige
obliges v ▷ oblige
obliging adj ready to help other people ▶ v ▷ oblige > **obligingly** adv
obligingly adv ▷ oblige
oblique [oh-bleak] adj (-r, -st) slanting ▶ n (pl -s) the symbol (/) > **obliquely** adv
obliquely adv ▷ oblique
obliquer adj ▷ oblique
obliques n ▷ oblique
obliquest adj ▷ oblique
obliterate v (-tes, -ting, -ted) wipe out, destroy > **obliteration** n (pl -s)
obliterated v ▷ obliterate
obliterates v ▷ obliterate
obliterating v ▷ obliterate
obliteration n ▷ obliterate
obliterations n ▷ obliterate
oblivion n (pl -s) state of being forgotten
oblivions n ▷ oblivion
oblivious adj unaware
oblong adj having two long sides, two short sides, and four right angles ▶ n (pl -s) oblong figure
oblongs n ▷ oblong
obloquies n ▷ obloquy
obloquy [ob-lock-wee] n (pl -quies) verbal abuse
obnoxious adj offensive
oboe n (pl -s) double-reeded woodwind instrument > **oboist** n (pl -s)
oboes n ▷ oboe
oboist n ▷ oboe
oboists n ▷ oboe
obscene adj (-r, -st) portraying sex offensively > **obscenity** n (pl -ies)
obscener adj ▷ obscene
obscenest adj ▷ obscene
obscenities n ▷ obscene

obscenity n ▷ obscene
obscure adj (-r, -st) not well known ▶ v (-res, -ring, -red) make (something) obscure > **obscurity** n (pl -ties)
obscured v ▷ obscure
obscurer adj ▷ obscure
obscures v ▷ obscure
obscurest adj ▷ obscure
obscuring v ▷ obscure
obscurities n ▷ obscure
obscurity n ▷ obscure
obsequies [ob-sick-weez] pl n funeral rites
obsequious [ob-seek-wee-uss] adj overattentive in order to gain favour > **obsequiousness** n
obsequiousness n ▷ obsequious
observe v (-ves, -ving, -ved) see or notice > **observable** adj
observable adj ▷ observe
observance n (pl -s) observing of a custom
observances n ▷ observance
observant adj quick to notice things
observation n (pl -s) action or habit of observing
observations n ▷ observation ()
observatories n ▷ observatory
observatory n (pl -ries) building equipped for studying the weather and the stars
observed v ▷ observe
observer n (pl -s) person who observes, esp. one who watches someone or something carefully
observers n ▷ observer
observes v ▷ observe
observing v ▷ observe
obsess v (-es, -ing, -ed) preoccupy (someone) compulsively > **obsessed** adj > **obsessive** adj > **obsession** n (pl -s)
obsessed v, adj ▷ obsess
obsesses v ▷ obsess
obsessing v ▷ obsess
obsession n ▷ obsess
obsessions n ▷ obsess
obsessive adj ▷ obsess
obsidian n (pl -s) dark glassy volcanic rock
obsidians n ▷ obsidian
obsolescence n ▷ obsolescent
obsolescences n ▷ obsolescent
obsolescent adj becoming obsolete > **obsolescence** n (pl -s)
obsolete adj no longer in use
obstacle n (pl -s) something that makes progress difficult
obstacles n ▷ obstacle
obstetric adj ▷ obstetrics

obstetrician n ▷ obstetrics
obstetricians n ▷ obstetrics
obstetrics n branch of medicine concerned with pregnancy and childbirth > **obstetric** adj
> **obstetrician** n (pl -s)
obstinacy n ▷ obstinate
obstinacies n ▷ obstinate
obstinate adj stubborn > **obstinately** adv
> **obstinacy** n (pl -cies)
obstinately adv ▷ obstinate
obstreperous adj unruly, noisy
obstruct v (-s, -ing, -ed) block with an obstacle
> **obstruction** n (pl -s) > **obstructive** adj
obstructed v ▷ obstruct
obstructing v ▷ obstruct
obstruction n ▷ obstruct
obstructions n ▷ obstruct
obstructive adj ▷ obstruct
obstructs v ▷ obstruct
obtain v (-s, -ing, -ed) acquire intentionally
> **obtainable** adj
obtainable adj ▷ obtain
obtained v ▷ obtain
obtaining v ▷ obtain
obtains v ▷ obtain
obtrude v (-des, -ding, -ded) push oneself or one's ideas on others
obtruded v ▷ obtrude
obtrudes v ▷ obtrude
obtruding v ▷ obtrude
obtuse adj (-r, -st) mentally slow > **obtuseness** n (pl -es)
obtuseness n ▷ obtuse
obtusenesses n ▷ obtuse
obtuser adj ▷ obtuse
obtusest adj ▷ obtuse
obtrusive adj unpleasantly noticeable
> **obtrusively** adv
obtrusively adv ▷ obtrusive
obverse n (pl -s) opposite way of looking at an idea
obverses n ▷ obverse
obviate v (-tes, -ting, -ted) make unnecessary
obviated v ▷ obviate
obviates v ▷ obviate
obviating v ▷ obviate
obvious adj easy to see or understand, evident
> **obviously** adv
obviously adv ▷ obvious
ocarina n (pl -s) small oval wind instrument
ocarinas n ▷ ocarina
occasion n (pl -s) time at which a particular thing happens ▶ v (-s, -ing, -ed) cause
occasional adj happening sometimes
> **occasionally** adv

occasionally adv ▷ occasional
occasioned v ▷ occasion
occasioning v ▷ occasion
occasions n, v ▷ occasion
occident n (pl occidents) (Lit) west
> **occidental** adj
occidental adj ▷ occident
occidents n ▷ occident
occiput [ox-sip-put] n (pl -s) back of the head
occiputs n ▷ occiput
occlude v (-des, -ding, -ded) obstruct
> **occlusion** n (pl -s)
occluded v ▷ occlude
occludes v ▷ occlude
occluding v ▷ occlude
occlusion n ▷ occlude
occlusions n ▷ occlude
occult adj relating to the supernatural
occupancies n ▷ occupancy
occupancy n (pl -cies) (length of) a person's stay in a specified place
occupant n (pl -s) person occupying a specified place
occupants n ▷ occupant
occupation n (pl -s) profession > **occupational** adj
occupational adj ▷ occupation
occupations n ▷ occupation
occupied v ▷ occupy
occupier n ▷ occupy
occupiers n ▷ occupy
occupies v ▷ occupy
occupy v (-pies, -pying, -pied) live or work in (a building) > **occupier** n (pl -s)
occur v (-s, -rring, -rred) happen
occurrence n (pl -s) something that occurs
occurrences n ▷ occurrence
occurred v ▷ occur
occurring v ▷ occur
occurs v ▷ occur
ocean n (pl -s) vast area of sea between continents > **oceanic** adj
oceanic adj ▷ ocean
oceanographies n ▷ oceanography
oceanography n (pl -phies) scientific study of the oceans
oceans n ▷ ocean
ocelot [oss-ill-lot] n (pl -s) American wild cat with a spotted coat
ocelots n ▷ ocelot
oche [ok-kee] n (pl -s) (DARTS) mark on the floor behind which a player must stand
oches n ▷ oche
ochre [oak-er] adj, n (pl -s) brownish-yellow (earth)

ochres n ▷ **ochre**
octagon n (pl -s) geometric figure with eight sides > **octagonal** adj
  octagonal adj ▷ **octagon**
  octagons n ▷ **octagon**
  octahedra n ▷ **octahedron**
octahedron [ok-ta-**heed**-ron] n (pl **-drons, -dra**) three-dimensional geometric figure with eight faces
  octahedrons n ▷ **octahedra**
octane n (pl -s) hydrocarbon found in petrol
  octanes n ▷ **octane**
octave n (pl -s) (MUSIC) (interval between the first and) eighth note of a scale
  octaves n ▷ **octave**
octet n (pl -s) group of eight performers
  octets n ▷ **octet**
octogenarian n (pl -s) person aged between eighty and eighty-nine
  octogenarians n ▷ **octogenarian**
octopus n (pl -es) sea creature with a soft body and eight tentacles
  octopuses n ▷ **octopus**
ocular adj relating to the eyes or sight
odd (-er, -est) adj unusual
  odder adj ▷ **odd**
  oddest adj ▷ **odd**
  oddities n ▷ **oddity**
oddity n (pl -ties) odd person or thing
oddments pl n things left over
oddness n (pl -es) quality of being odd
  oddnesses n ▷ **oddness**
odds n (ratio showing) the probability of something happening
ode n (pl -s) lyric poem, usu. addressed to a particular subject
  odes n ▷ **ode**
odious adj offensive
odium [oh-dee-um] n (pl -s) widespread dislike
  odiums n ▷ **odium**
  odorous adj ▷ **odour**
odour n (pl -s) particular smell > **odorous** adj > **odourless** adj
  odourless adj ▷ **odour**
  odours n ▷ **odour**
odyssey [**odd**-iss-ee] n (pl -s) long eventful journey
  odysseys n ▷ **odyssey**

> **oe** n (**oes**). Oe is a Scots word for a grandchild. This is a good word to remember, as it combines two of the most common letters in the game without using any consonants. Oe scores 2 points.

oedema [id-**deem**-a] n (pl -mata) (MED) abnormal swelling
  oedemata n ▷ **oedema**
  oesophagi n ▷ **oesophagus**
oesophagus [ee-**soff**-a-guss] n (pl -gi) passage between the mouth and stomach
oestrogen [ee-stra-jen] n (pl -s) female hormone that controls the reproductive cycle
  oestrogens n ▷ **oestrogen**
of prep belonging to
off prep away from ▶ adv away ▶ adj not operating ▶ n (pl -s) (CRICKET) side of the field to which the batsman's feet point
offal n (pl -s) edible organs of an animal, such as liver or kidneys
  offals n ▷ **offal**
offcut n (pl -s) piece remaining after the required parts have been cut out
  offcuts n ▷ **offcut**
offend v (-s, -ing, -ed) hurt the feelings of, insult
offence n (pl -s) (cause of) hurt feelings or annoyance
  offences n ▷ **offence**
  offended v ▷ **offend**
offender n (pl -s) person who commits a crime
  offenders n ▷ **offender**
  offending v ▷ **offend**
  offends v ▷ **offend**
offensive adj disagreeable ▶ n (pl -s) position or action of attack
  offensives n ▷ **offensive**
offer v (-s, -ing, -ed) present (something) for acceptance or rejection ▶ n (pl -s) instance of offering something
offering n (pl -s) thing offered
  offered v ▷ **offer**
  offering v ▷ **offer**
  offerings n ▷ **offer**
  offers v, n ▷ **offer**
  offertories n ▷ **offertory**
offertory n (-ries) (CHRISTIANITY) offering of the bread and wine for Communion
offhand adj casual, curt ▶ adv without preparation
office n (pl -s) room or building where people work at desks
officer n (pl -s) person in authority in the armed services
  officers n ▷ **officer**
  offices n ▷ **office**
official adj of a position of authority ▶ n (pl -s) person who holds a position of authority > **officially** adv
officialdom n (pl -s) officials collectively
  officialdoms n ▷ **officialdom**

officially adv ▷ official
officials n ▷ official
officiate v (**-tes, -ting, -ted**) act in an official role
  officiated v ▷ officiate
  officiates v ▷ officiate
  officiating v ▷ officiate
officious adj interfering unnecessarily
offing n (pl **-s**) area of the sea visible from the shore
  offings n ▷ offing
  offs n ▷ off
offset v (**-sets, -setting, -set**) cancel out, compensate for
  offsets v ▷ offset
  offsetting v ▷ offset
offshoot n (pl **-s**) something developed from something else
  offshoots n ▷ offshoot
offside adj, adv (SPORT) (positioned) illegally ahead of the ball
offspring n (pl **-s**) child
  offsprings n ▷ offspring
oft adv (Poetic) often
often adv frequently, much of the time
ogle v (**-les, -ling, -led**) stare at (someone) lustfully
  ogled v ▷ ogle
  ogles v ▷ ogle
  ogling v ▷ ogle
ogre n (pl **-s**) giant that eats human flesh
  ogres n ▷ ogre
oh interj exclamation of surprise, pain, etc.
ohm n (pl **-s**) unit of electrical resistance
  ohms n ▷ ohm

> **oi** interj. Oi is something people shout to attract attention. This is a good word to remember, as it combines two of the most common letters in the game without using any consonants. Oi scores 2 points.

oil n (pl **-s**) viscous liquid, insoluble in water and usu. flammable ▷ **petroleum** ► pl oil-based paints used in art ► v (**-s, -ing, -ed**) lubricate (a machine) with oil > **oily** adj (**-lier, -liest**)
  oiled v ▷ oil
oilfield n (**-s**) area containing oil reserves
  oilfields n ▷ oilfield
  oilier adj ▷ oil
  oiliest adj ▷ oil
  oiling v ▷ oil
  oils n, v ▷ oil
oilskin n (pl **-s**) (garment made from) waterproof material

oilskins n ▷ oilskin
oily adj ▷ oil
ointment n (pl **-s**) greasy substance used for healing skin or as a cosmetic
  ointments n ▷ ointment
okapi [ok-kah-pee] n (pl **-s**) African animal related to the giraffe but with a shorter neck
  okapis n ▷ okapi
okra n (pl **-s**) tropical plant with edible green pods
  okras n ▷ okra
okay (Informal) interj expression of approval ► v (**-s, -ing, -ed**) approve (something) ► n (pl **-s**) approval
  okayed v ▷ okay
  okaying v ▷ okay
  okays v, n ▷ okay
old adj (**-er, -est**) having lived or existed for a long time
  olden adj old
  older adj ▷ old
  oldest adj ▷ old
oldie n (pl **-s**) (Informal) old but popular song or film
  oldies n ▷ oldie
oleaginous [ol-lee-aj-in-uss] adj oily, producing oil
oleander [ol-lee-ann-der] n (pl **-s**) Mediterranean flowering evergreen shrub
  oleanders n ▷ oleander
olfactory adj relating to the sense of smell
  oligarchic adj ▷ oligarchy
  oligarchical adj ▷ oligarchy
  oligarchies n ▷ oligarchy
oligarchy [ol-lee-gark-ee] n (pl **-ies**) government by a small group of people > **oligarchic, oligarchical** adj
olive n (pl **-s**) small green or black fruit used as food or pressed for its oil ► adj greyish-green
  olives n ▷ olive
ombudsman n (pl **-men**) official who investigates complaints against government organizations
  ombudsmen n ▷ ombudsman
omelette n (pl **-s**) dish of eggs beaten and fried
  omelettes n ▷ omelette
omen n (pl (pl **-s**) happening or object thought to foretell success or misfortune
  omens n ▷ omen
ominous adj worrying, seeming to foretell misfortune
omit v (**-s, -tting, -tted**) leave out > **omission** n (pl **-s**)
  omission n ▷ omit
  omissions n ▷ omit

omits v ▷ omit
omitted v ▷ omit
omitting v ▷ omit
omnibus n (pl -es) several books or TV or radio programmes made into one
omnibuses n ▷ omnibus
omnipotence n ▷ omnipotent
omnipotences n ▷ omnipotent
omnipotent adj having unlimited power
 > **omnipotence** n (pl -s)
omnipresence n ▷ omnipresent
omnipresences n ▷ omnipresent
omnipresent adj present everywhere
 > **omnipresence** n (pl -s)
omniscience n ▷ omniscient
omnisciences n ▷ omniscient
omniscient [om-niss-ee-ent] adj knowing everything > **omniscience** n (pl -s)
omnivore n (pl -s) omnivorous animal
omnivores n ▷ omnivore
omnivorous [om-niv-vor-uss] adj eating food obtained from both animals and plants
on prep indicating position above, attachment, closeness, etc. ▶ adv in operation ▶ adj operating ▶ n (pl -s) (CRICKET) side of the field on which the batsman stands
once adv on one occasion ▶ conj as soon as
oncogene [on-koh-jean] n (pl -s) gene that can cause cancer when abnormally activated
oncogenes n ▷ oncogene
oncoming adj approaching from the front
one adj single, lone ▶ n (pl -s) number or figure 1 ▶ pron any person
oneness n (pl -es) unity
onenesses n ▷ oneness
onerous [own-er-uss] adj (of a task) difficult to carry out
ones n ▷ one
oneself pron ▷ one
ongoing adj in progress, continuing
onion n (pl -s) strongly flavoured edible bulb
onions n ▷ onion
online adj (of a computer) directly controlled by a central processor
onlooker n (pl -s) person who watches without taking part
onlookers n ▷ onlooker
only adj alone of its kind ▶ adv exclusively ▶ conj but
onomatopoeia [on-a-mat-a-pee-a] n (pl -s) use of a word which imitates the sound it represents, such as hiss > **onomatopoeic** adj
onomatopoeias n ▷ onomatopoeia
onomatopoeic adj ▷ onomatopoeia
onset n (pl -s) beginning

onsets n ▷ onset
onslaught n (pl -s) violent attack
onslaughts n ▷ onslaught
onto prep to a position on
ontological adj ▷ ontology
ontologies n ▷ ontology
ontology n (pl -gies) branch of philosophy concerned with existence > **ontological** adj
onus [own-uss] n (pl -es) responsibility or burden
onuses n ▷ onus
onward adj directed or moving forward ▶ adv (also **onwards**) ahead, forward
onwards see ▷ onward
onyx n (pl -es) type of quartz with coloured layers
onyxes n ▷ onyx

> **oo** n (oos). Oo is a Scots word for **wool**. This is a good word to remember, as it combines two of the most common letters in the game without using any consonants. Oo scores two points.

oodles pl n (Informal) great quantities
ooze[1] v (-zes, -zing, -zed) flow slowly ▶ n (pl -s) sluggish flow > **oozy** adj (-zier, -ziest)
ooze[2] n (-s) soft mud at the bottom of a lake or river
oozed v ▷ ooze
oozes v, n ▷ ooze[1, 2]
oozier adj ▷ oozy[1]
ooziest adj ▷ oozy[1]
oozing v ▷ ooze
oozy adj ▷ ooze[1]
opacities n ▷ opaque
opacity n ▷ opaque
opal n (pl -s) iridescent precious stone
opalescent adj iridescent like an opal
opals n ▷ opal
opaque adj (-r, -st) not able to be seen through, not transparent > **opacity** n (-ties)
opaquer adj ▷ opaque
opaquest adj ▷ opaque
open adj (-er, -est) not closed ▶ v (-s, -ing, -ed) (cause to) become open ▶ n (pl -s) (SPORT) competition which all may enter
opened v ▷ open
opener n instrument for opening containers
openest adj ▷ open
opening n (pl -s) opportunity ▶ adj first ▶ v ▷ open
openings n ▷ opening
openly adv without concealment
opens v, n ▷ open
opera[1] n (pl -s) drama in which the text is sung to an orchestral accompaniment > **operatic**

adj

opera² *n* ▷ **opus**

operas *n* ▷ **opera**

operate *v* (**-tes, -ting, -ted**) (cause to) work
> **operator** *n* (*pl* **-s**)

operated *v* ▷ **operate**

operates *v* ▷ **operate**

operatic *adj* ▷ **opera¹**

operating *v* ▷ **operate**

operation *n* (*pl* **-s**) method or procedure of
working

operational *adj* in working order

operations *n* ▷ **operation**

operative *adj* working ▶ *n* (*pl* **-s**) worker with
a special skill

operatives *n* ▷ **operative**

operator *n* ▷ **operate**

operators *n* ▷ **operate**

operetta *n* (*pl* **-s**) light-hearted comic opera

operettas *n* ▷ **operetta**

ophthalmic *adj* relating to the eye

ophthalmologies *n* ▷ **ophthalmology**

ophthalmologist *n* ▷ **ophthalmology**

ophthalmologists *n* ▷ **ophthalmology**

ophthalmology *n* (*pl* **-gies**) study of the eye
and its diseases > **ophthalmologist** *n* (*pl* **-s**)

opiate *n* (*pl* **-s**) narcotic drug containing
opium

opiates *n* ▷ **opiate**

opine *v* (**-nes, -ning, -ned**) (*Old-fashioned*)
express an opinion

opined *v* ▷ **opine**

opines *v* ▷ **opine**

opining *v* ▷ **opine**

opinion *n* (*pl* **-s**) personal belief or judgment

opinionated *adj* having strong opinions

opinions *n* ▷ **opinion**

opium *n* (*pl* **-s**) addictive narcotic drug made
from poppy seeds

opiums *n* ▷ **opium**

opossum *n* (*pl* **-s**) small marsupial of America
or Australasia

opossums *n* ▷ **opossum**

opponent *n* (*pl* **-s**) person one is working
against in a contest, battle, or argument

opponents *n* ▷ **opponent**

opportune *adj* happening at a suitable time

opportunism *n* ▷ **opportunist**

opportunisms , ▷ **opportunist**

opportunist *n* (*pl* **-s**) ▶ *adj* (person) doing
whatever is advantageous without regard for
principles > **opportunism** *n* (*pl* **-s**)

opportunists *n* ▷ **opportunist**

opportunities *n* ▷ **opportunity**

opportunity *n* (*pl* **-ties**) favourable time or

condition

oppose *v* (**-ses, -sing, -sed**) work against

opposed *v* ▷ **oppose**

opposes *v* ▷ **oppose**

opposing *v* ▷ **oppose**

opposition *n* (*pl* **-s**) obstruction or hostility

oppositions *n* ▷ **opposition**

opposite *adj* situated on the other side ▶ *n*
(*pl* **-s**) person or thing that is opposite ▶ *prep*
facing ▶ *adv* on the other side

opposites *n* ▷ **opposite**

oppress *v* (**-es, -ing, -ed**) control by cruelty or
force > **oppression** *n* (*pl* **-s**) > **oppressor** *n* (*pl* **-s**)

oppressed *v* ▷ **oppress**

oppresses *v* ▷ **oppress**

oppressing *v* ▷ **oppress**

oppression *n* ▷ **oppress**

oppressions *n* ▷ **oppress**

oppressive *adj* tyrannical > **oppressively** *adv*

oppressively *adv* ▷ **oppressive**

oppressor *n* ▷ **oppress**

oppressors *n* ▷ **oppress**

opprobrium [op-**probe**-ree-um] *n* (*pl* **-s**) state
of being criticized severely for wrong one
has done

opprobriums *n* ▷ **opprobrium**

opt *v* (**-s, -ing, -ed**) show a preference, choose

opted *v* ▷ **opt**

opting *v* ▷ **opt**

opts *v* ▷ **opt**

optic *adj* relating to the eyes or sight > **optical**
adj

optical *adj* ▷ **optic**

optics *n* science of sight and light

optician *n* (*pl* **-s**) (*also* **ophthalmic optician**)
person qualified to prescribe glasses (*also*
dispensing optician)

opticians *n* ▷ **optician**

optimism *n* (*pl* **-s**) tendency to take the most
hopeful view > **optimist** *n* (*pl* **-s**) > **optimistic**
adj > **optimistically** *adv*

optimisms *n* ▷ **optimism**

optimist *n* ▷ **optimism**

optimistic *adj* ▷ **optimism**

optimistically *adv* ▷ **optimism**

optimists *n* ▷ **optimism**

optima *n* ▷ **optimum**

optimal *adj* ▷ **optimum**

optimize *v* (**-zes, -zing, -zed**) make the most of

optimized *v* ▷ **optimize**

optimizes *v* ▷ **optimize**

optimizing *v* ▷ **optimize**

optimum *n* (*pl* **-ma, -mums**) best possible
conditions ▶ *adj* most favourable > **optimal**
adj

optimums n ▷ **optimum**

option n (pl -**s**) choice

optional adj possible but not compulsory

options n ▷ **option**

optometries n ▷ **optometry**

optometrist n (pl -**s**) person qualified to prescribe glasses > **optometry** n (-**ries**)

optometrists n ▷ **optometrist**

optometry n ▷ **optometrist**

opulence n ▷ **opulent**

opulences n ▷ **opulent**

opulent [op-pew-lent] adj having or indicating wealth > **opulence** n (-**s**)

opus n (pl **opuses, opera**) artistic creation, esp. a musical work

opuses n ▷ **opus**

or conj used to join alternatives

oracle n (pl -**s**) shrine of an ancient god > **oracular** adj

oracles n ▷ **oracle**

oracular adj ▷ **oracle**

oral adj spoken ▶ n (pl -**s**) spoken examination > **orally** adv

orally adv ▷ **oral**

orals n ▷ **oral**

orange n (pl -**s**) reddish-yellow citrus fruit ▶ adj reddish-yellow

orangeade n (BRIT) orange-flavoured, usu. fizzy drink

orangeades n ▷ **orangeade**

orangeries n ▷ **orangery**

orangery n (pl -**ries**) greenhouse for growing orange trees

oranges n ▷ **orange**

oration n (pl -**s**) formal speech

orations n ▷ **oration**

orator [or-rat-tor] n (pl -**s**) skilful public speaker

oratorical adj ▷ **oratory**

oratories n ▷ **oratory**¹, ²

oratorio [or-rat-**tor**-ee-oh] n (pl -**s**) musical composition for choir and orchestra, usu. with a religious theme

oratorios n ▷ **oratorio**

orators n ▷ **orator**

oratory¹ [or-rat-tree] n (pl -**ries**) art of making speeches > **oratorical** adj

oratory² n (pl -**ries**) small private chapel

orb n (pl -**s**) ceremonial decorated sphere with a cross on top, carried by a monarch

orbs n ▷ **orb**

orbit n (pl -**s**) curved path of a planet, satellite, or spacecraft around another body ▶ v (-**s, -ing, -ed**) move in an orbit around > **orbital** adj

orbital adj ▷ **orbit**

orbited v ▷ **orbit**

orbiting v ▷ **orbit**

orbits n, v ▷ **orbit**

orchard n (pl -**s**) area where fruit trees are grown

orchards n ▷ **orchard**

orchestra n (pl -**s**) large group of musicians, esp. playing a variety of instruments (also **orchestra pit**) > **orchestral** adj

orchestral adj ▷ **orchestra**

orchestras n ▷ **orchestra**

orchestrate v (-**tes, -ting, -ted**) arrange (music) for orchestra > **orchestration** n (pl -**s**)

orchestrated v ▷ **orchestrate**

orchestrates v ▷ **orchestrate**

orchestrating v ▷ **orchestrate**

orchestration n ▷ **orchestrate**

orchestrations n ▷ **orchestrate**

orchid n (pl -**s**) plant with flowers that have unusual lip-shaped petals

orchids n ▷ **orchid**

ordain v (-**s, -ing, -ed**) make (someone) a member of the clergy

ordained v ▷ **ordain**

ordaining v ▷ **ordain**

ordains v ▷ **ordain**

ordeal n (pl -**s**) painful or difficult experience

ordeals n ▷ **ordeal**

order n (pl -**s**) instruction to be carried out ▶ v (-**s, -ing, -ed**) give an instruction to

orderlies n ▷ **orderly**

orderliness n ▷ **orderly**

orderlinesses n ▷ **orderly**

orderly adj well-organized ▶ n (pl -**lies**) male hospital attendant > **orderliness** n (pl -**es**)

ordered v ▷ **order**

ordering v ▷ **order**

orders n, v ▷ **order**

ordinance n (pl -**s**) official rule or order

ordinances n ▷ **ordinance**

ordinarily adv ▷ **ordinary**

ordinary adj usual or normal > **ordinarily** adv

ordination n (pl -**s**) act of making someone a member of the clergy

ordinations n ▷ **ordination**

ordnance n (pl -**s**) weapons and military supplies

ordnances n ▷ **ordnance**

ordure n (pl -**s**) excrement

ordures n ▷ **ordure**

ore n (pl -**s**) (rock containing) a mineral which yields metal

ores n ▷ **ore**

oregano [or-rig-**gah**-no] n (pl -**nos**) sweet-smelling herb used in cooking

oreganos n ▷ **oregano**

organ n (pl -**s**) part of an animal or plant that has a particular function, such as the heart or lungs

organdie n (pl -**s**) fine cotton fabric
  organdies n ▷ **organdie**

organic adj of or produced from animals or plants (CHEM) > **organically** adv
  organically adv ▷ **organic**

organism n (-**s**) any living animal or plant
  organisms n ▷ **organism**

organist n (pl -**s**) organ player
  organists n ▷ **organist**

organization n (pl -**s**) group of people working together > **organizational** adj
  organizational adj ▷ **organization**
  organizations n ▷ **organization**

organize v (-**zes**, -**zing**, -**zed**) make arrangements for > **organizer** n (pl -**s**)
  organized v ▷ **organize**
  organizer n ▷ **organize**
  organizers n ▷ **organize**
  organizes v ▷ **organize**
  organizing v ▷ **organize**
  organs n ▷ **organ**

orgasm n (pl -**s**) most intense point of sexual pleasure > **orgasmic** adj
  orgasmic adj ▷ **orgasm**
  orgasms n ▷ **orgasm**
  orgiastic adj ▷ **orgy**
  orgies n ▷ **orgy**

orgy n (pl -**gies**) party involving promiscuous sexual activity > **orgiastic** adj

orient¹, orientate v (-**s**, -**ing**, -**ed**) position (oneself) according to one's surroundings > **orientation** n (pl -**s**)

orient² n (pl -**s**) (Lit) east > **oriental** adj
  oriental adj ▷ **orient²**
  orientate v ▷ **orient**
  orientated v ▷ **orient**
  orientates v ▷ **orient**
  orientating v ▷ **orient**
  orientation n ▷ **orient**
  orientations n ▷ **orient**
  oriented v ▷ **orient**

orienteering n (pl -**s**) sport in which competitors hike over a course using a compass and map
  orienteerings n ▷ **orienteering**
  orienting v ▷ **orient**
  orients v ▷ **orient**
  Orients n ▷ **Orient**

Orientalist n (pl -**s**) specialist in the languages and history of the Far East
  Orientalists n ▷ **Orientalist**

orifice [or-rif-fiss] n (pl -**s**) opening or hole

orifices n ▷ **orifice**

origami [or-rig-**gah**-mee] n (pl -**mis**) Japanese decorative art of paper folding
  origamis n ▷ **origami**

origin n (pl -**s**) point from which something develops

original adj first or earliest ▶ n (pl -**s**) first version, from which others are copied > **originality** n (pl -**ies**) > **originally** adv
  originalities n ▷ **original**
  originality n ▷ **original**
  originally adv ▷ **original**
  originals n ▷ **original**

originate v (-**tes**, -**ting**, -**ted**) come or bring into existence > **origination** n (pl -**s**) > **originator** n (pl -**s**)
  originated v ▷ **originate**
  originates v ▷ **originate**
  originating v ▷ **originate**
  origination n ▷ **origination**
  originations n ▷ **originate**
  originator n ▷ **originate**
  originator n ▷ **originate**
  origins n ▷ **origin**

oriole n (pl -**s**) tropical or American songbird
  orioles n ▷ **oriole**

ormolu n (pl -**lus**) gold-coloured alloy used for decoration
  ormulus n ▷ **ormulu**

ornament n (pl -**s**) decorative object ▶ v (-**s**, -**ing**, -**ed**) decorate > **ornamental** adj > **ornamentation** n (pl -**s**)
  ornamental adj ▷ **ornament**
  ornamentation n ▷ **ornament**
  ornamentations n ▷ **ornament**
  ornamented v ▷ **ornament**
  ornamenting v ▷ **ornament**
  ornaments n, v ▷ **ornament**

ornate adj highly decorated, elaborate
  ornithological adj ▷ **ornithology**
  ornithologies n ▷ **ornithology**
  ornithologist n ▷ **ornithology**
  ornithologists n ▷ **ornithology**

ornithology n (pl -**gies**) study of birds > **ornithological** adj > **ornithologist** n (pl -**s**)

orphan n (pl -**s**) child whose parents are dead

orphanage n (pl -**s**) children's home for orphans
  orphanages n ▷ **orphanage**

orphaned adj having no living parents
  orphans n ▷ **orphan**
  orreries n ▷ **orrery**

orrery n (pl -**ries**) mechanical model of the solar system

orris n (pl -**es**) kind of iris (also **orris root**)

orrises n ▷ orris
orthodontics n (pl branch of dentistry concerned with correcting irregular teeth
> **orthodontist** n (pl -s)
orthodontist n ▷ orthodontics
orthodontists n ▷ orthodontics
orthodox adj conforming to established views
> **orthodoxy** n (pl -ies)
orthodoxies n ▷ orthodox
orthodoxy n ▷ orthodox
orthography n (pl -phies) correct spelling
orthographies n ▷ orthography
orthopaedic adj ▷ orthopaedics
orthopaedics n (pl branch of medicine concerned with disorders of the bones or joints > **orthopaedic** adj
oryx n (pl -es) large African antelope
oryxes n ▷ oryx

os n (**ossa**). Os is a technical word for **bone.** This word won't score many points on its own, but will allow you to connect a word beginning with O to one ending in S (e.g. most plurals). Os scores 2 points.

oscillate [oss-ill-late] v (-**tes, -ting, -ted**) swing back and forth > **oscillation** n (pl -s)
> **oscillator** n (pl -s)
oscillated v ▷ oscillate
oscillates v ▷ oscillate
oscillating v ▷ oscillate
oscillation n ▷ oscillate
oscillations n ▷ oscillate
oscillator n ▷ oscillate
oscillators n ▷ oscillate
oscilloscope [oss-sill-oh-scope] n (pl -s) instrument that shows the shape of a wave on a cathode-ray tube
oscilloscopes n ▷ oscilloscope
osier [oh-zee-er] n (pl -s) willow tree
osiers n ▷ osier
osmium n (pl -s) (CHEM) heaviest known metallic element
osmiums n ▷ osmium
osmosis n (pl -ses) movement of a liquid through a membrane from a lower to a higher concentration > **osmotic** adj
osmoses n ▷ osmosis
osmotic adj ▷ osmosis
osprey n (pl -s) large fish-eating bird of prey
ospreys n ▷ osprey
ossification n ▷ ossify
ossifications n ▷ ossify
ossified v ▷ ossify
ossifies v ▷ ossify

ossify v (-**fies, -fying, -fied**) (cause to) become bone, harden > **ossification** n (pl -s)
ossifying v ▷ ossify
ostensible adj apparent, seeming > **ostensibly** adv
ostensibly adv ▷ ostensible
ostentation n (pl -s) pretentious display
> **ostentatious** adj > **ostentatiously** adv
ostentations n ▷ ostentation
ostentatious adj ▷ ostentation
ostentatiously adv ▷ ostentation
osteopath n ▷ osteopathy
osteopathies n ▷ osteopathy
osteopaths n ▷ osteopathy
osteopathy n (pl -thies) medical treatment involving manipulation of the joints
> **osteopath** n (pl -s)
osteoporosis n (pl -ses) brittleness of the bones, caused by lack of calcium
osteoporoses n ▷ osteoporosis
ostracism n ▷ ostracize
ostracisms n ▷ ostracize
ostracize v (-**zes, -zing, -zed**) exclude (a person) from a group > **ostracism** n (pl -s)
ostracized v ▷ ostracize
ostracizes v ▷ ostracize
ostracizing v ▷ ostracize
ostrich n (pl -es) large African bird that runs fast but cannot fly
ostriches n ▷ ostrich
other adj remaining in a group of which one or some have been specified ▶ n (pl -s) other person or thing
others n ▷ other
otherwise conj or else, if not ▶ adv differently, in another way
otherworldly adj concerned with spiritual rather than practical matters
otiose [oh-tee-ooze] adj not useful
otter n (pl -s) small brown freshwater mammal that eats fish
otters n ▷ otter
ottoman n (pl -mans) storage chest with a padded lid for use as a seat
ottomans n ▷ ottoman

ou n (**ous**). Ou is a South African slang word for a man. This word doesn't score many points, but is very useful when you are trying to form words in more than one direction. Ou scores 2 points.

oubliette [oo-blee-ett] n (pl -s) dungeon entered only by a trapdoor
oubliettes n ▷ oubliette
ouch interj exclamation of sudden pain

ought *v* used to express: obligation
ounce *n* (*pl* -s) unit of weight equal to one sixteenth of a pound (28.4 grams)
  ounces *n* ▷ **ounce**
our *adj* belonging to us
ours *pron* thing(s) belonging to us
  ourselves *pron* ▷ **we, us**
  ousel *n* (*pl* -s) ▷ **dipper**
  ousels *n* ▷ **ousel**
oust *v* (-s, -ing, -ed) force (someone) out, expel
  ousted *v* ▷ **oust**
  ousting *v* ▷ **oust**
  ousts *v* ▷ **oust**
out *adv, adj* denoting movement or distance away from, a state of being used up or extinguished, public availability, etc. ▶ *v* (-s, -ing, -ed) (*Informal*) name (a public figure) as being homosexual
outback *n* (*pl* -s) remote bush country of Australia
  outbacks *n* ▷ **outback**
outbid *v* (-bids, -bidding, -bid, -bidden) offer a higher price than
  outbid *v* ▷ **outbid**
  outbidden *v* ▷ **outbid**
  outbidding *v* ▷ **outbid**
  outbids *v* ▷ **outbid**
outbreak *n* (*pl* -s) sudden occurrence (of something unpleasant)
  outbreaks *n* ▷ **outbreak**
outburst *n* (*pl* -s) sudden expression of emotion
  outbursts *n* ▷ **outburst**
outcast *n* (*pl* -s) person rejected by a particular group
  outcasts *n* ▷ **outcast**
outclass *v* (-es, -ing, -ed) surpass in quality
  outclassed *v* ▷ **outclass**
  outclasses *v* ▷ **outclass**
  outclassing *v* ▷ **outclass**
outcome *n* (*pl* -s) result
  outcomes *n* ▷ **outcome**
  outcries *n* ▷ **outcry**
outcrop *n* (*pl* -s) part of a rock formation that sticks out of the earth
  outcrops *n* ▷ **outcrop**
outcry *n* (*pl* -ries) vehement or widespread protest
outdo *v* (-does, -doing, -did, -done) surpass in performance
  outdid *v* ▷ **outdo**
  outdoes *v* ▷ **outdo**
  outdoing *v* ▷ **outdo**
  outdone *v* ▷ **outdo**
  outdoor *adj* ▷ **outdoors**

outdoors *adv* in(to) the open air ▶ *n* (*pl* the open air > **outdoor** *adj*
  outed *v* ▷ **out**
outer *adj* on the outside
outermost *adj* furthest out
outface *v* (-ces, -cing, -ced) subdue or disconcert (someone) by staring
  outfaced *v* ▷ **outface**
  outfaces *v* ▷ **outface**
  outfacing *v* ▷ **outface**
outfield *n* (*pl* -s) (CRICKET) area far from the pitch
  outfields *n* ▷ **outfield**
outfit *n* (*pl* -s) matching set of clothes
  outfits *n* ▷ **outfit**
outfitter *n* (*pl* -s) supplier of men's clothes
  outfitters *n* ▷ **outfitter**
outflank *v* (-s, -ing, -ed) get round the side of (an enemy army)
  outflanked *v* ▷ **outflank**
  outflanking *v* ▷ **outflank**
  outflanks *v* ▷ **outflank**
outgoing *adj* leaving
outgoings *pl n* expenses
outgrow *v* (-grows, -growing, -grew, -grown) become too large or too old for
  outgrew *v* ▷ **outgrow**
  outgrowing *v* ▷ **outgrow**
  outgrown *v* ▷ **outgrow**
  outgrows *v* ▷ **outgrow**
outgrowth *n* natural development
  outgrowths *n* ▷ **outgrowth**
outhouse *n* (*pl* -s) building near a main building
  outhouses *n* ▷ **outhouse**
outing *n* (*pl* -s) leisure trip ▶ *v* ▷ **out**
  outings *n* ▷ **outing**

> **outjinx** *v* (outjinxes, outjinxing, outjinxed). Outjinx means to outmanoeuvre. If someone else plays **jinx,** you can outjinx them by adding O, U and T! If you can form the whole word using all of your letters, you'll get a 50-point bonus. Outjinx scores 21 points.

outlandish *adj* extremely unconventional
outlaw *n* (*pl* -s) (HIST) criminal deprived of legal protection, bandit ▶ *v* (-s, -ing, -ed) make illegal (HIST)
  outlawed *v* ▷ **outlaw**
  outlawing *v* ▷ **outlaw**
  outlaws *n, v* ▷ **outlaw**
outlay *n* (*pl* -s) expenditure
  outlays *n* ▷ **outlay**
outlet *n* (*pl* -s) means of expressing emotion
  outlets *n* ▷ **outlet**

outline n (pl -s) short general explanation ▶ v (-nes, -ning, -ned) summarize
outlined v ▷ outline
outlines n, v ▷ outline
outlining v ▷ outline
outlook n (pl -s) attitude
outlooks n ▷ outlook
outlying adj distant from the main area
outmanoeuvre v (-res, -ring, -red) get an advantage over
outmanoeuvred v ▷ outmanoeuvre
outmanoeuvres v ▷ outmanoeuvre
outmanoeuvring v ▷ outmanoeuvre
outmoded adj no longer fashionable or accepted
outnumber v (-s, -ing, -ed) exceed in number
outnumbered v ▷ outnumber
outnumbering v ▷ outnumber
outnumbers n ▷ outnumber
outpatient n (pl -s) patient who does not stay in hospital overnight
outpatients n ▷ outpatient
outpost n (pl -s) outlying settlement
outposts n ▷ outpost
outpouring n (pl -s) passionate outburst
outpourings n ▷ outpouring
output n (pl -s) amount produced ▶ v (-puts, -putting, -putted) (COMPUTERS) produce (data) at the end of a process
outputted v ▷ output
outputting v ▷ output
outputs n, v ▷ output
outrage n (pl -s) great moral indignation ▶ v (-s, -ing, -ed) offend morally
outraged v ▷ outrage
outrageous adj shocking > **outrageously** adv
outrageously adv ▷ outrageous
outrages n, v ▷ outrage
outraging v ▷ outrage
outré [oo-tray] adj shockingly eccentric
outrider n (pl -s) motorcyclist acting as an escort
outriders n ▷ outrider
outrigger n (pl -s) stabilizing frame projecting from a boat
outriggers n ▷ outrigger
outright adj, adv absolute(ly)
outrun v (-runs, -running, -ran, -run) run faster than
outran v ▷ outrun
outrun v ▷ outrun
outrunning v ▷ outrun
outruns v ▷ outrun
outs v ▷ out
outset n (pl -s) beginning

outsets n ▷ outset
outshine v (-shines, -shining, -shone) surpass (someone) in excellence
outshines v ▷ outshine
outshining v ▷ outshine
outshone v ▷ outshine
outside prep, adj adv indicating movement to or position on the exterior ▶ adj unlikely ▶ n (pl -s) external area or surface
outsider n (pl -s) person outside a specific group
outsiders n ▷ outsider
outsides n ▷ outside
outsize, outsized adj larger than normal
outsized adj ▷ outsize
outskirts pl n outer areas, esp. of a town
outsmart v (-s, -ing, -ed) (Informal) outwit
outsmarted v ▷ outsmart
outsmarting v ▷ outsmart
outsmarts v ▷ outsmart
outspan v (-s, -nning, -nned) (S AFR) relax
outspanned v ▷ outspan
outspanning v ▷ outspan
outspans v ▷ outspan
outspoken adj tending to say what one thinks
outstanding adj excellent
outstrip v (-s, -pping, -pped) surpass
outstripped v ▷ outstrip
outstripping v ▷ outstrip
outstrips v ▷ outstrip
outtake n (pl -s) unreleased take from a recording session, film, or TV programme
outtakes n ▷ outtake
outward adj apparent ▶ adv (also **outwards**) away from somewhere > **outwardly** adv
outwardly adv ▷ outward
outweigh v (-s, -ing, -ed) be more important, significant, or influential than
outweighed v ▷ outweigh
outweighing v ▷ outweigh
outweighs v ▷ outweigh
outwit v (-s, -tting, -tted) get the better of (someone) by cunning
outwits v ▷ outwit
outwitted v ▷ outwit
outwitting v ▷ outwit
ouzel [ooze-el] n (pl -s) ▷ dipper
ouzels n ▷ ouzel
ova n ▷ ovum
oval adj egg-shaped ▶ n (pl -s) anything that is oval in shape
ovals n ▷ oval
ovarian adj ▷ ovary
ovaries n ▷ ovary
ovary n (pl -ries) female egg-producing organ

> **ovarian** *adj*

ovation *n* (*pl* -**s**) enthusiastic round of applause

 ovations *n* ▷ **ovation**

oven *n* (*pl* -**s**) heated compartment or container for cooking or for drying or firing ceramics

 ovens *n* ▷ **oven**

over *prep, adv* indicating position on the top of, movement to the other side of, amount greater than, etc. ▶ *adj* finished ▶ *n* (*pl* -**s**) (CRICKET) series of six balls bowled from one end

overall *adj, adv* in total ▶ *n* (*pl* -**s**) coat-shaped protective garment ▶ *pl* protective garment consisting of trousers with a jacket or bib and braces attached

 overalls *n* ▷ **overall**

overarm *adj, adv* (thrown) with the arm above the shoulder

overawe *v* (-**wes**, -**wing**, -**wed**) affect (someone) with an overpowering sense of awe

 overawed *v* ▷ **overawe**
 overawes *v* ▷ **overawe**
 overawing *v* ▷ **overawe**

overbalance *v* (-**ces**, -**cing**, -**ced**) lose balance

 overbalanced *v* ▷ **overbalance**
 overbalances *v* ▷ **overbalance**
 overbalancing *v* ▷ **overbalance**

overbearing *adj* unpleasantly forceful

overblown *adj* excessive

overboard *adv* from a boat into the water

 overcame *v* ▷ **overcome**

overcast *adj* (of the sky) covered by clouds

overcoat *n* (*pl* -**s**) heavy coat

 overcoats *n* ▷ **overcoat**

overcome *v* (-**comes**, -**coming**, -**came**, -**come**) gain control over after an effort

 overcomes *v* ▷ **overcome**
 overcoming *v* ▷ **overcome**

overcrowded *adj* containing more people or things than is desirable

 overdid *v* ▷ **overdo**

overdo *v* (-**does**, -**doing**, -**did**, -**done**) do to excess

 overdoes *v* ▷ **overdo**
 overdoing *v* ▷ **overdo**
 overdone *v* ▷ **overdo**

overdose *n* (*pl* -**s**) excessive dose of a drug ▶ *v* (-**ses**, -**sing**, -**sed**) take an overdose

 overdosed *n* ▷ **overdose**
 overdoses *n, v* ▷ **overdose**
 overdosing *v* ▷ **overdose**

overdraft *n* (*pl* -**s**) overdrawing

 overdrafts *n* ▷ **overdraft**

overdraw *v* (-**draws**, -**drawing**, -**drew**, -**drawn**) withdraw more money than is in (one's bank account)

 overdrawing *v* ▷ **overdraw**
 overdrawn *v* ▷ **overdraw**
 overdraws *v* ▷ **overdraw**
 overdrew *v* ▷ **overdraw**

overdrawn *adj* having overdrawn one's account

overdrive *n* (*pl* -**s**) very high gear in a motor vehicle

 overdrives *n* ▷ **overdrive**

overdue *adj* still due after the time allowed

overgrown *adj* thickly covered with plants and weeds

overhaul *v* (-**s**, -**ing**, -**ed**) examine and repair ▶ *n* (*pl* -**s**) examination and repair

 overhauled *v* ▷ **overhaul**
 overhauling *v* ▷ **overhaul**
 overhauls *v, n* ▷ **overhaul**

overhead *adv, adj* above one's head

overheads *pl n* general cost of maintaining a business

overhear *v* (-**hears**, -**hearing**, -**heard**) hear (a speaker or remark) unintentionally or without the speaker's knowledge

 overheard *v* ▷ **overhear**
 overhearing *v* ▷ **overhear**
 overhears *v* ▷ **overhear**

overjoyed *adj* extremely pleased

overkill *n* (*pl* -**s**) treatment that is greater than required

 overkills *n* ▷ **overkill**

overland *adj, adv* by land

overlap *v* (-**s**, -**pping**, -**pped**) share part of the same space or period of time (as) ▶ *n* (*pl* -**s**) area overlapping

 overlapped *v* ▷ **overlap**
 overlapping *v* ▷ **overlap**
 overlaps *v, n* ▷ **overlap**

overleaf *adv* on the back of the current page

overlook *v* (-**s**, -**ing**, -**ed**) fail to notice

 overlooked *v* ▷ **overlook**
 overlooking *v* ▷ **overlook**
 overlooks *v* ▷ **overlook**

overly *adv* excessively

overnight *adj, adv* (taking place) during one night

overpower *v* (-**s**, -**ing**, -**ed**) subdue or overcome (someone)

 overpowered *v* ▷ **overpower**
 overpowering *v* ▷ **overpower**
 overpowers *v* ▷ **overpower**

overran *v* ▷ **overrun**

overreach v (-es, -ing, -ed) fail by trying to be too clever
　overreached v ▷ overreach
　overreaches v ▷ overreach
　overreaching v ▷ overreach
override v (-rides, -riding, -rode, -ridden) overrule
　overridden v ▷ override
　overrides v ▷ override
　overriding v ▷ override
　overrode v ▷ override
overrule v (-les, -ling, -led) reverse the decision of (a person with less power)
　overruled v ▷ overrule
　overrules v ▷ overrule
　overruling v ▷ overrule
overrun v (-runs, -running, -ran, -run) spread over (a place) rapidly
　overrunning v ▷ overrun
　overruns v ▷ overrun
　overs n ▷ over
　oversaw v ▷ oversee
overseas adv, adj to, of, or from a distant country
oversee v (-sees, -seeing, -saw, -seen) watch over from a position of authority > **overseer** n (-s)
　overseeing v ▷ oversee
　overseen v ▷ oversee
　overseer n ▷ oversee
　overseers n ▷ oversee
　oversees v ▷ oversee
overshadow v (-s, -ing, -ed) reduce the significance of (a person or thing) by comparison
　overshadowed v ▷ overshadow
　overshadowing v ▷ overshadow
　overshadows v ▷ overshadow
oversight n (pl -s) mistake caused by not noticing something
　oversights n ▷ oversight
overspill n (pl -s) (BRIT) rehousing of people from crowded cities in smaller towns
　overspills n ▷ overspill
overstay v (-s, -ing, -ed) stay longer than one's host or hostess would like
　overstayed v ▷ overstay
overstayer n (-s) (NZ) person who remains in New Zealand after their permit has expired
　overstayers n ▷ overstyer
　overstaying v ▷ overstay
　overstays v ▷ overstay
overt adj open, not hidden > **overtly** adv
　overtly adv ▷ overt
overtake v (-takes, -taking, -took, -taken) move past (a vehicle or person) travelling in the same direction
　overtaken v ▷ overtake
　overtakes v ▷ overtake
　overtaking v ▷ overtake
　overtook v ▷ overtake
　overthrew v ▷ overthrow
overthrow v (-throws, -throwing, -threw, -thrown) defeat and replace ▶ n (pl -s) downfall, destruction
　overthrowing v ▷ overthrow
　overthrown v ▷ overthrow
　overthrows v, n ▷ overthrow
overtime n, adv (pl -s) (paid work done) in addition to one's normal working hours
　overtimes n ▷ overtime
overtone n (pl -s) additional meaning
　overtones n ▷ overtone
overture n (pl -s) (MUSIC) orchestral introduction ▶ pl opening moves in a new relationship
　overtures n ▷ overture
overturn v (-s, -ing, -ed) turn upside down
　overturned v ▷ overturn
　overturning v ▷ overturn
　overturns v ▷ overturn
overweight adj weighing more than is healthy
overwhelm v (-s, -ing, -ed) overpower, esp. emotionally > **overwhelming** adj > **overwhelmingly** adv
　overwhelmed v ▷ overwhelm
　overwhelming v, adj ▷ overwhelm
　overwhelmingly adv ▷ overwhelm
　overwhelms v ▷ overwhelm
overwrought adj nervous and agitated
ovoid [oh-void] adj egg-shaped
ovulate [ov-yew-late] v (-tes, -ting, -ted) produce or release an egg cell from an ovary > **ovulation** n (-s)
　ovulated v ▷ ovulate
　ovulates v ▷ ovulate
　ovulating v ▷ ovulate
　ovulation n ▷ ovulate
　ovulations n ▷ ovulate
ovum [oh-vum] n (pl **ova**) unfertilized egg cell
owe v (owes, owing, owed) be obliged to pay (a sum of money) to (a person)
　owed v ▷ owe
　owes v ▷ owe
　owing v ▷ owe
owl n (pl -s) night bird of prey > **owlish** adj
　owlish adj ▷ owl
　owls n ▷ owl
own adj used to emphasize possession

▶ v (-s, -ing, -ed) possess > **owner** n (pl -s)
> **ownership** n (pl -s)

owned v ▷ own

owner n ▷ own

owners n ▷ own

ownership n ▷ own

ownerships n ▷ own

owning v ▷ own

owns v ▷ own

ox n (pl **oxen**) castrated bull

oxen n ▷ ox

oxide n (pl -s) compound of oxygen and one other element

oxides n ▷ oxide

oxidize v (-zes, -zing, -zed) combine chemically with oxygen, as in burning or rusting

oxidized v ▷ oxidize

oxidizes v ▷ oxidize

oxidizing v ▷ oxidize

oxygen n (pl -s) (CHEM) gaseous element essential to life and combustion

oxygenate v (-tes, -ting, -ted) add oxygen to

oxygenated v ▷ oxygenate

oxygenates v ▷ oxygenate

oxygenating v ▷ oxygenate

oxygens n ▷ oxygen

oxymora n ▷ oxymoron

oxymoron [ox-see-**more**-on] n (pl -**mora**, -**morons**) figure of speech that combines two apparently contradictory ideas

oxymorons n ▷ oxymoron

oyez interj (HIST) shouted three times by a public crier, listen

oyster n (pl -s) edible shellfish

oystercatcher n (pl -s) wading bird with black-and-white feathers

oystercatchers n ▷ oystercatcher

oysters n ▷ oyster

ozone n (pl -s) strong-smelling form of oxygen

ozones n ▷ ozone

Pp

P forms a two-letter word in front of every vowel except U, which makes it very useful for joining a new word to one already on the board. It also forms several three-letter words with X: **pax, pix, pox** (12 points each) and **pyx** (15). You should also remember one of the strangest words in Scrabble – **pH** (7), which is valid because it doesn't start with a capital letter. When you have the letter P on your rack, look for an H on the board, as they may allow you to play a word beginning or ending in PH, adding to your options.

pa n (pl **-s**) (NZ) (formerly) a fortified Maori settlement

pace n (pl **-s**) single step in walking ▶ v (**-ces, -cing, -ced**) walk up and down, esp. in anxiety
  paced v ▷ **pace**

pacemaker n (pl **-s**) electronic device surgically implanted in a person with heart disease to regulate the heartbeat
  pacemakers n ▷ **pacemaker**
  paces n, v ▷ **pace**

pachyderm [pak-ee-durm] n (pl **-s**) thick-skinned animal such as an elephant
  pachyderms n ▷ **pachyderm**
  pacification n ▷ **pacify**
  pacifications n ▷ **pacify**
  pacified v ▷ **pacify**
  pacifies v ▷ **pacify**
  pacifism n ▷ **pacifist**
  pacifisms n ▷ **pacifist**

pacifist n (pl **-s**) person who refuses on principle to take part in war > **pacifism** n (pl **-s**)
  pacifists n ▷ **pacifist**

pacify v (**-fies, -fying, -fied**) soothe, calm > **pacification** n (pl **-s**)
  pacifying v ▷ **pacify**
  pacing v ▷ **pace**

pack v (**-s, -ing, -ed**) put (clothes etc.) together in a suitcase or bag ▶ n (pl **-s**) bag carried on a person's or animal's back
  packed v ▷ **pack**
  packing v ▷ **pack**
  packs v, n ▷ **pack**

package n (pl **-s**) small parcel ▶ v (**-ges, -ging, -ged**) put into a package > **packaging** n (pl **-s**)
  packaged v ▷ **package**

packages n, v ▷ **package**
  packaging v, n ▷ **package**
  packagings n ▷ **package**

packet n (pl **-s**) small container (and contents)
  packets n ▷ **packet**

packhorse n (pl **-s**) horse used for carrying goods
  packhorses n ▷ **packhorse**

pact n (pl **-s**) formal agreement
  pacts n ▷ **pact**

pad n (pl **-s**) piece of soft material used for protection, support, absorption of liquid, etc. ▶ v (**padding, padded**) protect or fill with soft material
  padded v ▷ **pad**
  paddies n ▷ **paddy**

padding n (pl **-s**) soft material used to pad something ▶ v ▷ **pad**
  paddings n ▷ **padding**

paddle¹ n (pl **-s**) short oar with a broad blade at one or each end ▶ v (**-les, -ling, -led**) move (a canoe etc.) with a paddle

paddle² v (**-les, -ling, -led**) walk barefoot in shallow water
  paddled v ▷ **paddle¹, ²**
  paddles n, v ▷ **paddle¹, ²**
  paddling v ▷ **paddle¹, ²**

paddock n (pl **-s**) small field or enclosure for horses
  paddocks n ▷ **paddock**

paddy n (pl **-ies**) (BRIT) (Informal) fit of temper
  paddymelons n ▷ **pademelon**

pademelon, paddymelon [pad-ee-mel-an] n (pl **-s**) small Australian wallaby
  pademelons n ▷ **pademelon**

padlock n (pl **-s**) detachable lock with a hinged

hoop fastened over a ring on the object to be secured

padlocks n ▷ **padlock**

padre [**pah**-dray] n (pl **-s**) chaplain to the armed forces

padres n ▷ **padre**

pads v, n ▷ **pad**

paean [**pee**-an] n (pl **-s**) song of triumph or thanksgiving

paeans n ▷ **paean**

paediatrics n branch of medicine concerned with diseases of children ▷ **paediatrician** n

paella [pie-**ell**-a] n (pl **-s**) Spanish dish of rice, chicken, shellfish, and vegetables

paellas n ▷ **paella**

pagan n (pl **-s**) ▶ adj (person) not belonging to one of the world's main religions

pagans n ▷ **pagan**

page¹ n (pl **-s**) (one side of) a sheet of paper forming a book etc.

page² n (also **pageboy**) small boy who attends a bride at her wedding ▶ v (**-ges**, **-ging**, **-ged**) summon (someone) by bleeper or loudspeaker, in order to pass on a message

pageant n (pl **-s**) parade or display of people in costume, usu. illustrating a scene from history ▷ **pageantry** n (pl **-ries**)

pageantries n ▷ **pageant**

pageantry n ▷ **pageant**

pageants n ▷ **pageant**

paged v ▷ **page²**

pages n, v ▷ **page¹, ²**

pagination n (pl **-s**) numbering of the pages of a book etc.

paginations n ▷ **pagination**

paging v ▷ **page²**

pagoda n (pl **-s**) pyramid-shaped Asian temple or tower

pagodas n ▷ **pagoda**

paid v ▷ **pay**

pail n (pl **-s**) (contents of) a bucket

pails n ▷ **pail**

pain n (pl **-s**) physical or mental suffering ▶ pl trouble, effort ▷ **painful** adj ▷ **painfully** adv ▷ **painless** adj ▷ **painlessly** adv

painful adj ▷ **pain**

painfully adv ▷ **pain**

painkiller n (pl **-s**) drug that relieves pain

painkillers n ▷ **painkiller**

painless adj ▷ **pain**

painlessly adv ▷ **pain**

pains n ▷ **pain**

painstaking adj extremely thorough and careful

paint n (pl **-s**) coloured substance, spread on a surface with a brush or roller ▶ v (**-s**, **-ing**, **-ed**) colour or coat with paint ▷ **painter** n (pl **-s**) ▷ **painting** n (pl **-s**)

painted v ▷ **paint**

painter¹ n ▷ **paint**

painter² n (pl **-s**) rope at the front of a boat, for tying it up

painters n ▷ **paint painter²**

painting v, n ▷ **paint**

paintings n ▷ **paint**

paints n, v ▷ **paint**

pair n (pl **-s**) set of two things matched for use together ▶ v (**-s**, **-ing**, **-ed**) group or be grouped in twos

paired v ▷ **pair**

pairing v ▷ **pair**

pairs n, v ▷ **pair**

pakeha [**pah**-kee-ha] n (pl **-s**) (NZ) New Zealander who is not of Maori descent

pakehas n ▷ **pakeha**

pal n (pl **-s**) (Informal) (Old-fashioned in NZ) friend

pals n ▷ **pal**

palace n (pl **-s**) residence of a king, bishop, etc.

palaces n ▷ **palace**

palaeographies n ▷ **palaeography**

palaeography [pal-ee-**og**-ra-fee] n (pl **-ies**) study of ancient manuscripts

palaeolithic [pal-ee-oh-**lith**-ik] adj of the Old Stone Age

palaeontologies n ▷ **palaeontology**

palaeontology [pal-ee-on-**tol**-a-jee] n (pl **-ies**) study of past geological periods and fossils

palagi [pa-**lang**-gee] n (pl **-s**) (NZ) Samoan name for a pakeha

palagis n ▷ **palagi**

palatable adj pleasant to taste

palate n (pl **-s**) roof of the mouth

palates n ▷ **palate**

palatial adj like a palace, magnificent

palaver [pal-**lah**-ver] n (pl **-s**) time-wasting fuss

palavers n ▷ **palaver**

pale¹ adj (**-er**, **-est**) light, whitish ▶ v (**-les**, **-ling**, **-led**) become pale

pale² n (pl **-s**) wooden or metal post used in fences

paled v ▷ **pale**

paler adj ▷ **pale¹**

pales n ▷ **pale¹, ²**

palest adj ▷ **pale¹**

paling v ▷ **pale**

palette n (pl **-s**) artist's flat board for mixing colours on

palettes n ▷ **palette**

palindrome n (pl **-s**) word or phrase that reads the same backwards as forwards

palindromes *n* ▷ palindrome

paling *n* (*pl* -s) wooden or metal post used in fences

palings *n* ▷ paling

palisade *n* (*pl* -s) fence made of wooden posts driven into the ground

palisades *n* ▷ palisade

pall¹ *n* (*pl* -s) cloth spread over a coffin

pall² *v* (-s, -ing, -ed) become boring

pallbearer *n* (*pl* -s) person who helps to carry the coffin at a funeral

pallbearers *n* ▷ pallbearer

palled *v* ▷ pall²

palling *v* ▷ pall²

palls *n* ▷ pall¹ ▶ *v* ▷ pall²

palladium *n* (*pl* -s) (CHEM) silvery-white element of the platinum metal group

palladiums *n* ▷ palladium

pallet¹ *n* (*pl* -s) portable platform for storing and moving goods

pallet² *n* straw-filled mattress or bed

pallets *n* ▷ pallet¹, ²

palliate *v* (-tes, -ting, -ted) lessen the severity of (something) without curing it

palliated *v* ▷ palliate

palliates *v* ▷ palliate

palliating *v* ▷ palliate

palliative *adj* giving temporary or partial relief ▶ *n* (*pl* -s) something, for example a drug, that palliates

palliatives *n* ▷ palliative

pallid *adj* (-er, -est) pale, esp. because ill or weak > **pallor** *n* (*pl* -s)

pallider *adj* ▷ pallid

pallidest *adj* ▷ pallid

pallier *adj* ▷ pally

palliest *adj* ▷ pally

pallor *n* ▷ pallid

pallors *n* ▷ pallid

pally *adj* (-lier, -lliest) (*Informal*) on friendly terms

palm¹ *n* (*pl* -s) inner surface of the hand

palm² *n* (*pl* -s) tropical tree with long pointed leaves growing out of the top of a straight trunk

palmist *n* ▷ palmistry

palmistries *n* ▷ palmistry

palmistry *n* (*pl* -ries) fortune-telling from lines on the palm of the hand > **palmist** *n* (*pl* -s)

palmists *n* ▷ palmistry

palms *n* ▷ palm¹, ²

palmtop *adj* (of a computer) small enough to be held in the hand ▶ *n* (*pl* -s) computer small enough to be held in the hand

palmtops *n* ▷ palmtop

palomino *n* (*pl* -s) gold-coloured horse with a white mane and tail

palominos *n* ▷ palomino

palpable *adj* obvious > **palpably** *adv*

palpably *adv* ▷ palpable

palpate *v* (-tes, -ting, -ted) (MED) examine (an area of the body) by touching

palpated *v* ▷ palpate

palpates *v* ▷ palpate

palpating *v* ▷ palpate

palpitate *v* (-tes, -ting, -ted) (of the heart) beat rapidly > **palpitation** *n* (*pl* -s)

palpitated *v* ▷ palpitate

palpitates *v* ▷ palpitate

palpitating *v* ▷ palpitate

palpitation *n* ▷ palpitate

palpitations *n* ▷ palpitate

palsied *adj* affected with palsy

palsies *n* ▷ palsy

palsy [pawl-zee] *n* (*pl* -sies) paralysis

paltrier *adj* ▷ paltry

paltriest *adj* ▷ paltry

paltry *adj* (-rier, -riest) insignificant

pampas *pl n* vast grassy plains in S America

pamper *v* (-s, -ing, -ed) treat (someone) with great indulgence, spoil

pampered *v* ▷ pamper

pampering *v* ▷ pamper

pampers *v* ▷ pamper

pamphlet *n* (*pl* -s) thin paper-covered booklet

pamphleteer *n* (*pl* -s) writer of pamphlets

pamphleteers *n* ▷ pamphleteer

pamphlets *n* ▷ pamphlet

pan¹ *n* (*pl* -s) wide long-handled metal container used in cooking ▶ *v* (-s, -nning, -nned) sift gravel from (a river) in a pan to search for gold (*Informal*)

pan² *v* (-s, -nning, -nned) (of a film camera) be moved slowly so as to cover a whole scene or follow a moving object

panacea [pan-a-**see**-a] *n* (*pl* -s) remedy for all diseases or problems

panaceas *n* ▷ panacea

panache [pan-**ash**] *n* (*pl* -s) confident elegant style

panaches *n* ▷ panache

panatella *n* (*pl* -s) long slender cigar

panatellas *n* ▷ panatella

pancake *n* (*pl* -s) thin flat circle of fried batter

pancakes *n* ▷ pancake

panchromatic *adj* (PHOTOG) sensitive to light of all colours

pancreas [**pang**-kree-ass] *n* (*pl* -es) large gland behind the stomach that produces insulin and helps digestion > **pancreatic** *adj*

pancreases *n* ▷ pancreas
pancreatic *adj* ▷ pancreas
panda *n* (*pl* -s) large black-and-white bearlike mammal from China
pandas *n* ▷ panda
pandemic *adj* (of a disease) occurring over a wide area
pandemonium *n* (*pl* -s) wild confusion, uproar
pandemoniums *n* ▷ pandemonium
pander¹ *v* (-s, -ing, -ed) (*foll. by* **to**) indulge (a person his or her desires)
pander² *n* (*pl* -s) (*Old-fashioned*) person who procures a sexual partner for someone
pandered *v* ▷ pander
pandering *v* ▷ pander
panders *v, n* ▷ pander¹, ²
pane *n* (*pl* -s) sheet of glass in a window or door
panes *n* ▷ pane
panegyric [pan-ee-**jire**-ik] *n* (*pl* -s) formal speech or piece of writing in praise of someone or something
panegyrics *n* ▷ panegyric
panel *n* (*pl* -s) flat distinct section of a larger surface, for example in a door ▶ *v* (-s, -lling, -lled) cover or decorate with panels
panelled *v* ▷ panel
panelling *n* (*pl* -s) panels collectively, esp. on a wall ▶ *v* ▷ panel
panellings *n* ▷ panelling
panellist *n* (*pl* -s) member of a panel
panellists *n* ▷ panellist
panels *n* ▷ panel
pang *n* (*pl* -s) sudden sharp feeling of pain or sadness
pangs *n* ▷ pang
pangolin *n* (*pl* -s) animal of tropical countries with a scaly body and a long snout for eating ants and termites (*also* **scaly anteater**)
pangolins *n* ▷ pangolin
panic *n* (*pl* -s) sudden overwhelming fear, often affecting a whole group of people ▶ *v* (-s, -cking, -cked) feel or cause to feel panic ▶ **panicky** *adj* (-ier, -iest)
panicked *v* ▷ panic
panickier *adj* ▷ panic
panickiest *adj* ▷ panic
panicking *v* ▷ panic
panicky *adj* ▷ panic
panics *n, v* ▷ panic
panic-stricken *adj* ▷ panic
pannier *n* (*pl* -s) bag fixed on the back of a cycle
panniers *n* ▷ pannier
panoplies *n* ▷ panoply
panoply *n* (*pl* -ies) magnificent array
panorama *n* (*pl* -s) wide unbroken view of a

scene > **panoramic** *adj*
panoramas *n* ▷ panorama
panoramic *adj* ▷ panorama
pansies *n* ▷ pansy
pansy *n* (*pl* -sies) small garden flower with velvety purple, yellow, or white petals
pant *v* (-s, -ing, -ed) breathe quickly and noisily during or after exertion
pantaloons *pl n* baggy trousers gathered at the ankles
pantechnicon *n* (*pl* -s) large van for furniture removals
pantechnicons *n* ▷ pantechnicon
panted *v* ▷ pant
pantheism *n* (*pl* -s) belief that God is present in everything > **pantheist** *n* (*pl* -s) > **pantheistic** *adj*
pantheisms *n* ▷ pantheism
pantheist *n* ▷ pantheism
pantheistic *adj* ▷ pantheism
pantheists *n* ▷ pantheism
pantheon *n* (*pl* -s) (in ancient Greece and Rome) temple built to honour all the gods
pantheons *n* ▷ pantheon
panther *n* (*pl* -s) leopard, esp. a black one
panthers *n* ▷ panther
panties *pl n* women's underpants
pantile *n* (*pl* -s) roofing tile with an S-shaped cross section
pantiles *n* ▷ pantile
panting *v* ▷ pant
pantomime *n* (*pl* -s) play based on a fairy tale, performed at Christmas time
pantomimes *n* ▷ pantomime
pantries *n* ▷ pantry
pantry *n* (*pl* -ries) small room or cupboard for storing food
pants *v* ▷ pant
pants *pl n* undergarment for the lower part of the body
pap *n* (*pl* -s) soft food for babies or invalids
papacies *n* ▷ papacy
paps *n* ▷ pap
papacy [**pay**-pa-see] *n* (*pl* -cies) position or term of office of a pope
papal *adj* of the pope
paparazzi *n* ▷ paparazzo
paparazzo [pap-a-**rat**-so] *n* (*pl* -razzi) photographer specializing in candid photographs of famous people
papaya [pa-**pie**-ya] *n* (*pl* -s) large sweet West Indian fruit
papayas *n* ▷ papaya
paper *n* (*pl* -s) material made in sheets from wood pulp or other fibres ▶ *pl* personal

documents ▶ v (-s, -ing, -ed) cover (walls)
with wallpaper

paperback n (pl -s) book with covers made of
flexible card

paperbacks n ▷ paperback

papering v ▷ paper

papered v ▷ paper

papers n, v ▷ paper

paperweight n (pl -s) heavy decorative object
placed on top of loose papers

paperweights n ▷ paperweight

paperwork n (pl -s) clerical work, such as
writing reports and letters

paperworks n ▷ paperwork

papoose n (pl -s) Native American child

papooses n ▷ papoose

paprika n (pl -s) mild powdered seasoning
made from red peppers

paprikas n ▷ paprika

papyri n ▷ papyrus

papyrus [pap-ire-uss] n (pl -ri, -ruses) tall water
plant

papyruses n ▷ papyrus

par n (pl -s) usual or average condition

parable n (pl -s) story that illustrates a
religious teaching

parables n ▷ parable

parabola [par-ab-bol-a] n (pl -s) regular curve
resembling the course of an object thrown
forward and up > **parabolic** adj

parabolas n ▷ parabola

parabolic adj ▷ parabola

paracetamol n (pl -s) mild pain-relieving drug

paracetamols n ▷ paracetamol

parachute n (pl -s) large fabric canopy that
slows the descent of a person or object from
an aircraft ▶ v (-tes, -ting, -ted) land or drop by
parachute > **parachutist** n (pl -s)

parachuted n, v ▷ parachute

parachutes v ▷ parachute

parachuting v ▷ parachute

parachutist n ▷ parachute

parachutists n ▷ parachute

parade n (pl -s) procession or march ▶ v (-des,
-ding, -ded) display or flaunt

paraded v ▷ parade

parades n, v ▷ parade

parading v ▷ parade

paradigm [par-a-dime] n (pl -s) example or
model

paradigms n ▷ paradigm

paradise n (pl -s) heaven

paradises n ▷ paradise

paradox n (pl -xes) statement that seems self-
contradictory but may be true > **paradoxical**

adj > **paradoxically** adv

paradoxes n ▷ paradox

paradoxical adj ▷ paradox

paradoxically adv ▷ paradox

paraffin n (pl -s) (BRIT & S AFR) liquid mixture
distilled from petroleum and used as a fuel
or solvent

paraffins n ▷ paraffin

paragliding n (pl -s) cross-country gliding
wearing a parachute shaped like wings

paraglidings n ▷ paragliding

paragon n (pl -s) model of perfection

paragons n ▷ paragon

paragraph n (pl -s) section of a piece of writing
starting on a new line

paragraphs n ▷ paragraph

parakeet n (pl -s) small long-tailed parrot

parakeets n ▷ parakeet

parallax n (pl -es) apparent change in an
object's position due to a change in the
observer's position

parallaxes n ▷ parallax

parallel adj separated by an equal distance
at every point ▶ n (pl -s) line separated from
another by an equal distance at every point
▶ v (-s, -ing, -ed) correspond to

paralleled n ▷ parallel

paralleling v ▷ parallel

parallels n, v ▷ parallel

parallelogram n (pl -s) four-sided geometric
figure with opposite sides parallel

parallelograms n ▷ parallelogram

paralyse v (-ses, -sing, -sed) affect with
paralysis

paralysed v ▷ paralyse

paralyses v ▷ paralyse ▶ n ▷ paralysis

paralysing v ▷ paralyse

paralysis n (pl -ses) inability to move or feel,
because of damage to the nervous system

paralytic n (pl -s) ▶ adj (person) affected with
paralysis

paralytics n ▷ paralytic

paramedic n (pl -s) person working in support
of the medical profession > **paramedical** adj

paramedical n ▷ paramedic

paramedics n ▷ paramedic

parameter [par-am-it-er] n (pl -s) limiting
factor, boundary

parameters n ▷ parameter

paramilitary adj organized on military lines

paramount adj of the greatest importance

paramour n (pl -s) (Old-fashioned) lover, esp. of a
person married to someone else

paramours n ▷ paramour

paranoia n (pl -s) mental illness causing

delusions of grandeur or persecution
(*Informal*) > **paranoid, paranoiac** *adj, n (pl -s)*
paranoiac *adj, n ▷* paranoia
paranoiacs *n ▷* paranoia
paranoias *n ▷* paranoia
paranoid *adj, n ▷* paranoia
paranoids *n ▷* paranoia
paranormal *adj* beyond scientific explanation
parapet *n (pl -s)* low wall or railing along the
edge of a balcony or roof
parapets *n ▷* parapet
paraphernalia *n (pl -s)* personal belongings or
bits of equipment
paraphernalias *n ▷* paraphernalia
paraphrase *v (-ses, -sing, -sed)* put (a
statement or text) into other words
paraphrased *v ▷* paraphrase
paraphrases *v ▷* paraphrase
paraphrasing *v ▷* paraphrase
paraplegia [par-a-**pleej**-ya] *n (pl -s)* paralysis
of the lower half of the body > **paraplegic**
adj, n (pl -s)
paraplegias *n ▷* paraplegia
paraplegic *adj, n ▷* paraplegia
paraplegics *n ▷* paraplegia
parapsychologies *n ▷* parapsychology
parapsychology *n (pl -gies)* study of mental
phenomena such as telepathy
parasite *n (pl -s)* animal or plant living in or on
another > **parasitic** *adj*
parasites *n ▷* parasite
parasitic *adj ▷* parasite
parasol *n (pl -s)* umbrella-like sunshade
parasols *n ▷* parasol
paratrooper *n (pl -s)* soldier trained to be
dropped by parachute into a battle area
> **paratroops** *pl n*
paratroopers *n ▷* paratrooper
paratroops *n ▷* paratrooper
parboil *v (-s, -ing, -ed)* boil until partly cooked
parboiled *v ▷* parboil
parboiling *v ▷* parboil
parboils *v ▷* parboil
parcel *n (pl -s)* something wrapped up,
package ▶ *v (-s, -lling, -lled) (often foll. by* **up**)
wrap up
parcelled *v ▷* parcel
parcelling *v ▷* parcel
parcels *n, v ▷* parcel
parch *v (-es, -ing, -ed)* make very hot and dry
parched *v ▷* parch
parches *v ▷* parch
parching *v ▷* parch
parchment *n (pl -s)* thick smooth writing
material made from animal skin

parchments *n ▷* parchment
pardon *v (-s, -ing, -ed)* forgive, excuse ▶ *n (pl -s)*
forgiveness > **pardonable** *adj*
pardonable *adj ▷* pardon
pardoned *v ▷* pardon
pardoning *v ▷* pardon
pardons *v, n ▷* pardon
pare *v (-res, -ring, -red)* cut off the skin or top
layer of *(often foll. by* **down**)
pared *v ▷* pare
pares *v ▷* pare
paring *v ▷* pare ▶ *n (pl -s)* piece pared off
parings *n ▷* pareing
parent *n (pl -s)* father or mother > **parental** *adj*
> **parenthood** *n (pl -s)*
parentage *n (pl -s)* ancestry or family
parentages *n ▷* parentage
parental *adj ▷* parent
parenthood *n ▷* parent
parenthoods *n ▷* parent
parenting *n (pl -s)* activity of bringing up
children
parentings *n ▷* parenting
parents *n ▷* parent
parenthesis [par-en-**thiss**-iss] *n (pl -ses)* word or
sentence inserted into a passage, marked off
by brackets or dashes ▶ *pl* round brackets, ( )
> **parenthetical** *adj*
parentheses *n ▷* parenthesis
parenthetical *adj ▷* parenthesis
pariah [par-**rye**-a] *n (pl -s)* social outcast
pariahs *n ▷* pariah
parietal [par-**rye**-it-al] *adj* of the walls of a body
cavity such as the skull
parish *n (pl -es)* area that has its own church
and a priest or pastor
parishes *n ▷* parish
parishioner *n (pl -s)* inhabitant of a parish
parishioners *n ▷* parishioner
parities *n ▷* parity
parity *n (pl -ties)* equality or equivalence
park *n (pl -s)* area of open land for recreational
use by the public ▶ *v (-s, -ing, -ed)* stop and
leave (a vehicle) temporarily
parked *v ▷* park
parking *v ▷* park
parks *n, v ▷* park
parka *n (pl -s)* large waterproof jacket with
a hood
parkas *n ▷* parka
parkier *adj ▷* parky
parkiest *adj ▷* parky
parky *adj (-kier, -kiest)* (BRIT) (*Informal*) (of the
weather) chilly
parlance *n (pl -s)* particular way of speaking,

idiom

parlances n ▷ parlance

parley n (pl -s) meeting between leaders or representatives of opposing forces to discuss terms ▶ v (-s, -ing, -ed) have a parley

parleyed v ▷ parley

parleying v ▷ parley

parleys n, v ▷ parley

parliament n (pl -s) law-making assembly of a country > **parliamentary** adj

parliamentary adj ▷ parliament

parliaments n ▷ parliament

parlour n (pl -s) (Old-fashioned) living room for receiving visitors

parlours n ▷ parlour

parlous adj (Old-fashioned) dire

parochial adj narrow in outlook > **parochialism** n (pl -s)

parochialism n ▷ parochial

parochialisms n ▷ parochial

parodied v ▷ parody

parodies n, v ▷ parody

parody n (pl -dies) exaggerated and amusing imitation of someone else's style ▶ v (-ies, -ying, -ied) make a parody of

parodying v ▷ parody

parole n (pl -s) early freeing of a prisoner on condition that he or she behaves well ▶ v (-les, -ling, -led) put on parole

paroled v ▷ parole

paroles n, v ▷ parole

paroling v ▷ parole

paroxysm n (pl -s) uncontrollable outburst of rage, delight, etc.

paroxysms n ▷ paroxysm

parquet [par-kay] n (pl -s) floor covering made of wooden blocks arranged in a geometric pattern > **parquetry** n (pl -ies)

parquetries n ▷ parquet

parquetry n ▷ parquet

parquets n ▷ parquet

parricide n (pl -s) crime of killing either of one's parents

parricides n ▷ parricide

parried v ▷ parry

parries v ▷ parry

parrot n (pl -s) tropical bird with a short hooked beak and an ability to imitate human speech ▶ v (-s, -ing, -ed) repeat (someone else's words) without thinking

parroted v ▷ parrot

parroting v ▷ parrot

parrots n, v ▷ parrot

parry v (-rries, -rrying, -rried) ward off (an attack)

parrying v ▷ parry

pars n ▷ par

parse [parz] v (-ses, -sing, -sed) analyse (a sentence) in terms of grammar

parsed v ▷ parse

parses v ▷ parse

parsing v ▷ parse

parsimonies n ▷ parsimony

parsimonious adj ▷ parsimony

parsimony n (pl -nies) extreme caution in spending money > **parsimonious** adj

parsley n (pl -s) herb used for seasoning and decorating food

parsleys n ▷ parsley

parsnip n (pl -s) long tapering cream-coloured root vegetable

parsnips n ▷ parsnip

parson n (pl -s) Anglican parish priest

parsons n ▷ parson

parsonage n (pl -s) parson's house

parsonages n ▷ parsonage

part n (pl -s) one of the pieces that make up a whole ▶ v (-s, -ing, -ed) divide or separate

partake v (-takes, -taking, -took, -taken) (foll. by **of**) take (food or drink)

partaken v ▷ partake

partakes v ▷ partake

partaking v ▷ partake

partial adj not complete > **partiality** n (pl -ties) > **partially** adv

partialities n ▷ partial

partiality n ▷ partial

partially adv ▷ partial

parted v ▷ part

participate v (-tes, -ting, -ted) become actively involved > **participant** n (pl -s) > **participation** n (pl -s)

participant n ▷ participate

participants n ▷ participate

participated v ▷ participate

participates v ▷ participate

participating v ▷ participate

participation n ▷ participation

participations n ▷ participations

participle n (pl -s) form of a verb used in compound tenses or as an adjective

participles n ▷ participle

particle n (pl -s) extremely small piece or amount

particles n ▷ particle

particular adj relating to one person or thing, not general ▶ n (pl -s) item of information, detail > **particularly** adv

particularize v (-zes, -zing, -zed) give details about

particularized v ▷ particularize
particularizes v ▷ particularize
particularizing v ▷ particularize
particularly adv ▷ particular
particulars n ▷ particular
parties n ▷ party
parting n (pl -s) occasion when one person leaves another ▶ v ▷ part
partings n ▷ parting
partisan n (pl -s) strong supporter of a party or group ▶ adj prejudiced or one-sided
partisans n ▷ partisan
partition n (pl -s) screen or thin wall that divides a room ▶ v (-s, -ing, -ed) divide with a partition
partitioned v ▷ partition
partitioning v ▷ partition
partitions n, v ▷ partition
partly adv not completely
partner n (pl -s) either member of a couple in a relationship or activity ▶ v (-s, -ing, -ed) be the partner of
partnered v ▷ partner
partnering v ▷ partner
partners n, v ▷ partner
partnership n (pl -s) joint business venture between two or more people
partnerships n ▷ partnership
partook v ▷ partake
partridge n (pl -s) game bird of the grouse family
partridges n ▷ partridge
parts n, v ▷ part
parturition n (pl -s) act of giving birth
party n (pl -ties) social gathering for pleasure
parvenu [par-ven-new] n (pl -s) person newly risen to a position of power or wealth
parvenus n ▷ parvenu
pas n ▷ pa
pascal n (pl -s) unit of pressure
pascals n ▷ pascal
paspalum [pass-**pale**-um] n (pl -s) (AUST & NZ) type of grass with wide leaves
paspalums n ▷ paspalum
pass v (-es, -ing, -ed) go by, past, or through (SPORT) ▶ n (pl -es) successful result in a test or examination
passable adj (just) acceptable
passage n (pl -s) channel or opening providing a way through
passages n ▷ passage
passageway n (pl -s) passage or corridor
passageways n ▷ passageway
passbook n (pl -s) book issued by a bank or building society for keeping a record of deposits and withdrawals
passbooks n ▷ passbook
passé [pas-say] adj out-of-date
passed v ▷ pass
passenger n (pl -s) person travelling in a vehicle driven by someone else
passengers n ▷ passenger
passes v, n ▷ pass
passim adv (LATIN) everywhere, throughout
passing adj brief or transitory ▶ v ▷ pass
passion n (pl -s) intense sexual love
 >**passionate** adj
passionate adj ▷ passion
passionflower n (pl -s) tropical American plant
passionflowers n ▷ passionflower
passions n ▷ passion
passive adj not playing an active part
 >**passivity** n (pl -ties)
passivities n ▷ passive
passivity n ▷ passive
passport n (pl -s) official document of nationality granting permission to travel abroad
passports n ▷ passport
password n (pl -s) secret word or phrase that ensures admission
passwords n ▷ password
past adj of the time before the present ▶ n (pl -s) period of time before the present ▶ adv by, along ▶ prep beyond
pasta n (pl -s) type of food, such as spaghetti, that is made in different shapes from flour and water
pastas n ▷ pasta
paste n (pl -s) moist soft mixture, such as toothpaste ▶ v (-tes, -ting, -ted) fasten with paste
pasteboard n (pl -s) stiff thick paper
pasteboards n ▷ pasteboard
pasted v ▷ paste
pastel n (pl -s) coloured chalk crayon for drawing ▶ adj pale and delicate in colour
pastels n ▷ pastel
pastes n, v ▷ paste
pasteurize v (-zes, -zing, -zed) sterilize by heating >**pasteurization** n (pl -s)
pasteurization n ▷ pasteurize
pasteurizations n ▷ pasteurize
pasteurized v ▷ pasteurize
pasteurizes v ▷ pasteurize
pasteurizing v ▷ pasteurize
pastiche [pass-**teesh**] n (pl -s) work of art that mixes styles or copies the style of another artist
pastiches n ▷ pastiche

pastier adj ▷ pasty¹
pasties n ▷ pasty²
pastiest adj ▷ pasty¹
pastille n (pl -s) small fruit-flavoured and sometimes medicated sweet
pastilles n ▷ pastille
pastime n (pl -s) activity that makes time pass pleasantly
pastimes n ▷ pastime
pasting n (pl -s) (Informal) heavy defeat ▶ v ▷ paste
pastings n ▷ pasting
pastor n (pl -s) member of the clergy in charge of a congregation
pastoral adj of or depicting country life
pastors n ▷ pastor
pastrami n (pl -s) highly seasoned smoked beef
pastramis n ▷ pastrami
pastries n ▷ pastry
pastry n (pl -ries) baking dough made of flour, fat, and water
pasts n ▷ past
pasture n (pl -s) grassy land for farm animals to graze on
pastures n ▷ pasture
pasty¹ [pay-stee] adj (-tier, -tiest) (of a complexion) pale and unhealthy
pasty² [pass-tee] n (pl -ties) round of pastry folded over a savoury filling
pat¹ v (-s, -tting, -tted) tap lightly ▶ n (pl -s) gentle tap or stroke
pat² adj quick, ready, or glib
patch n (pl -es) piece of material sewn on a garment ▶ v (-es, -ing, -ed) mend with a patch
patched v ▷ patch
patches n, v ▷ patch
patchier adj ▷ patchy
patchiest adj ▷ patchy
patching v ▷ patch
patchwork n (pl -s) needlework made of pieces of different materials sewn together
patchworks n ▷ patchwork
patchy adj (-hier, -hiest) of uneven quality or intensity
pate n (pl -s) (Old-fashioned) head
pates n ▷ pate
pâté [pat-ay] n (pl -s) spread of finely minced liver etc.
pâtés n ▷ pâté
patella n (pl -ae) kneecap
patellae n ▷ patella
patent n (pl -s) document giving the exclusive right to make or sell an invention ▶ adj open to public inspection ▶ v (-s, -ing, -ed) obtain

a patent for
patented v ▷ patent
patenting v ▷ patent
patently adv obviously
patents n, v ▷ patent
paternal adj fatherly
paternities n ▷ paternity
paternity n (pl -ties) fact or state of being a father
paternalism n (pl -s) authority exercised in a way that limits individual responsibility > **paternalistic** adj
paternalisms n ▷ paternalism
paternalistic adj ▷ paternalism
path n (pl -s) surfaced walk or track
pathname n (pl -s) (COMPUTERS) file name listing the sequence of directories leading to a particular file or directory
pathnames n ▷ pathname
paths n ▷ path
pathetic adj causing feelings of pity or sadness > **pathetically** adv
pathetically adv ▷ pathetic
pathogen n (pl -s) thing that causes disease > **pathogenic** adj
pathogenic adj ▷ pathogen
pathogens n ▷ pathogen
pathologies n ▷ pathology
pathology n (pl -gies) scientific study of diseases > **pathologist** n (pl -s)
pathological adj of pathology
pathologist n ▷ pathology
pathologists n ▷ pathology
pathos n (pl -es) power of arousing pity or sadness
pathoses n ▷ pathos
patience n (pl -s) quality of being patient
patiences n ▷ patience
patient adj enduring difficulties or delays calmly ▶ n (pl -s) person receiving medical treatment
patients n ▷ patient
patina n (pl -s) fine layer on a surface
patinas n ▷ patina
patio n (pl -os) paved area adjoining a house
patios n ▷ patio
patois [pat-wah] n (pl patois) [pat-wahz] regional dialect, esp. of French
patriarch n (pl -s) male head of a family or tribe > **patriarchal** adj
patriarchal adj ▷ patriarch
patriarchies n ▷ patriarchy
patriarchs n ▷ patriarch
patriarchy n (pl -hies) society in which men have most of the power

patrician n (pl -s) member of the nobility ▶ adj of noble birth
  patricians n ▷ patrician
patricide n (pl -s) crime of killing one's father
  patricides n ▷ patricide
  patrimonies n ▷ patrimony
patrimony n (pl -nies) property inherited from ancestors
patriot n (pl -s) person who loves his or her country and supports its interests > **patriotic** adj > **patriotism** n (pl -s)
  patriotic adj ▷ patriot
  patriotism n ▷ patriot
  patriotisms n ▷ patriot
  patriots n ▷ patriot
patrol n (pl -s) regular circuit by a guard ▶ v (-s, -lling, -lled) go round on guard, or reconnoitring
  patrolled v ▷ patrol
  patrolling v ▷ patrol
  patrols n, v ▷ patrol
patron n (pl -s) person who gives financial support to charities, artists, etc.
patronage n (pl -s) support given by a patron
  patronages n ▷ patronage
patronize v (-zes, -zing, -zed) treat in a condescending way
  patronized v ▷ patronize
  patronizes v ▷ patronize
  patronizing v ▷ patronize
  patrons n ▷ patron
patronymic n (pl -s) name derived from one's father or a male ancestor
  patronymics n ▷ patronymic
  pats v, n ▷ pat[1]
  patted v ▷ pat[1]
patter[1] v (-s, -ing, -ed) make repeated soft tapping sounds ▶ n (pl -s) quick succession of taps
patter[2] n (pl -s) glib rapid speech
  pattered v ▷ patter[1]
  pattering v ▷ patter[1]
  patters v, n ▷ patter[1, 2]
pattern n (pl -s) arrangement of repeated parts or decorative designs
patterned adj decorated with a pattern
  patterns n ▷ pattern
  patties n ▷ patty
  patting v ▷ pat[1]
patty n (pl -tties) small flattened cake of minced food
  paucities n ▷ paucity
paucity n (pl -ties) scarcity
paunch n (pl -es) protruding belly
  paunches n ▷ paunch

pauper n (pl -s) very poor person
  paupers n ▷ pauper
pause v (-ses, -sing, -sed) stop for a time ▶ n (pl -s) stop or rest in speech or action
  paused v ▷ pause
  pauses v, n ▷ pause
  pausing v ▷ pause
pave v (-ves, -ving, -ved) form (a surface) with stone or brick
  paved v ▷ pave
pavement n (pl -s) paved path for pedestrians
  pavements n ▷ pavement
  paves v ▷ pave
  paving v ▷ pave
pavilion n (pl -s) building on a playing field etc.
  pavilions n ▷ pavilion
paw n (pl -s) animal's foot with claws and pads ▶ v (-s, -ing, -ed) scrape with the paw or hoof
  pawed v ▷ paw
  pawing v ▷ paw
  paws n, v ▷ paw
pawn[1] v (-s, -ing, -ed) deposit (an article) as security for money borrowed
pawn[2] n (pl -s) chessman of the lowest value
pawnbroker n (pl -s) lender of money on goods deposited
  pawnbrokers n ▷ pawnbroker
  pawned v ▷ pawn[1]
  pawning v ▷ pawn[1]
  pawns v, n ▷ pawn[1, 2]
pay v (-s, -ing, paid) give money etc. in return for goods or services ▶ n (pl -s) wages or salary
payable adj due to be paid
payee n (pl -s) person to whom money is paid or due
  payees n ▷ payee
  paying v ▷ pay
payload n (pl -s) passengers or cargo of an aircraft
  payloads n ▷ payload
payment n (pl -s) act of paying
  payments n ▷ payment
payola n (pl -s) (CHIEFLY US) (Informal) bribe to get special treatment, esp. to promote a commercial product
  pays v, n ▷ pay
  payolas n ▷ payola

pax n (paxes). A pax is a period of peace, especially when there is one dominant nation. If you have a P and an X on your rack, there is likely to be an A available on the board. Pax gives a decent score for a three-letter word, so watch out for chances to play it on a bonus square. Pax scores 12 points.

pe *n* (**pes**). Pe is the 17th letter in the Hebrew alphabet. This is a very handy word because it allows you to connect words beginning with P to those ending in E, or vice versa and E is the most common tile in the game. Pe scores 4 points.

pea *n* (*pl* -s) climbing plant with seeds growing in pods

peas *n* ▷ pea

peace *n* (*pl* -s) calm, quietness ▷ **peaceful** *adj* ▷ **peacefully** *adv*

peaceable *adj* inclined towards peace ▷ **peaceably** *adv*

peaceably *adv* ▷ peaceable

peaceful *adj* ▷ peace

peacefully *adv* ▷ peace

peaces *n* ▷ peace

peach *n* (*pl* -es) soft juicy fruit with a stone and a downy skin ▶ *adj* pinkish-orange

peaches *n* ▷ peach

peacock *n* (*pl* -s) large male bird with a brilliantly coloured fanlike tail ▷ **peahen** *n fem* (*pl* -s)

peacocks *n* ▷ peacock

peahen *n* ▷ peacock

peahens *n* ▷ peacock

peak *n* (*pl* -s) pointed top, esp. of a mountain ▶ *v* (-s, -ing, -ed) form or reach a peak ▶ *adj* of or at the point of greatest demand ▷ **peaked** *adj*

peaked *adj*, *v* ▷ peak

peakier *adj* ▷ peaky

peakiest *adj* ▷ peaky

peaking *v* ▷ peak

peaks *n*, *v* ▷ peak

peaky *adj* (-kier, -kiest) pale and sickly

peal *n* (*pl* -s) long loud echoing sound, esp. of bells or thunder ▶ *v* (-s, -ing, -ed) sound with a peal or peals

pealed *v* ▷ peal

pealing *v* ▷ peal

peals *n*, *v* ▷ peal

peanut *n* (*pl* -s) pea-shaped nut that ripens underground ▶ *pl* (*Informal*) trifling amount of money

peanuts *n* ▷ peanut

pear *n* (*pl* -s) sweet juicy fruit with a narrow top and rounded base

pears *n* ▷ pear

pearl *n* (*pl* -s) hard round shiny object found inside some oyster shells and used as a jewel ▷ **pearly** *adj* (-lier, -liest)

pearlier *adj* ▷ pearl

pearliest *adj* ▷ peral

pearls *n* ▷ pearl

pearly *adj* ▷ pearl

peasant *n* (*pl* -s) person working on the land, esp. in poorer countries or in the past

peasantries *n* ▷ peasantry

peasantry *n* (*pl* -ries) peasants collectively

peasants *n* ▷ peasant

peat *n* (*pl* -s) decayed vegetable material found in bogs, used as fertilizer or fuel

peats *n* ▷ peat

pebble *n* (*pl* -s) small roundish stone ▷ **pebbly** *adj* (-lier, -liest)

pebbles *n* ▷ pebble

pebblier *adj* ▷ pebble

pebbliest *adj* ▷ pebble

pebbly *adj* ▷ pebble

pecan [pee-kan] *n* (*pl* -s) edible nut of a N American tree

pecans *n* ▷ pecan

peccadillo *n* (*pl* -lloes, -llos) trivial misdeed

peccadilloes *n* ▷ peccadillo

peccadillos *n* ▷ peccadillo

peck *v* (-s, -ing, -ed) strike or pick up with the beak ▶ *n* (*pl* -s) pecking movement

pecked *v* ▷ peck

pecking *v* ▷ peck

peckish *adj* (*Informal*) slightly hungry

pecks *v*, *n* ▷ peck

pecs *pl n* (*Informal*) pectoral muscles

pectin *n* (*pl* -s) substance in fruit that makes jam set

pectins *n* ▷ pectin

pectoral *adj* of the chest or thorax ▶ *n* (*pl* -s) pectoral muscle or fin

pectorals *n* ▷ pectoral

peculiar *adj* strange

peculiarities *n* ▷ peculiarity

peculiarity *n* (*pl* -ties) oddity, eccentricity

pecuniary *adj* relating to, or consisting of, money

pedagogue *n* (*pl* -s) schoolteacher, esp. a pedantic one

pedagogues *n* ▷ pedagogue

pedal *n* (*pl* -s) foot-operated lever used to control a vehicle or machine, or to modify the tone of a musical instrument ▶ *v* (-s, -lling, -lled) propel (a bicycle) by using its pedals

pedalled *v* ▷ pedal

pedalling *v* ▷ pedal

pedals *n* ▷ pedal

pedant *n* (*pl* -s) person who is excessively concerned with details and rules, esp. in academic work ▷ **pedantic** *adj* ▷ **pedantry** *n* (*pl* -ries)

pedantic *adj* ▷ pedant

pedantries n ▷ pedant
pedantry n ▷ pedant
pedants n ▷ pedant
peddle v (-les, -ling, -led) sell (goods) from door to door
peddled v ▷ peddle
peddles v ▷ peddle
peddling v ▷ peddle
peddler n (pl -s) person who sells illegal drugs
peddlers n ▷ peddler
pedestal n (pl -s) base supporting a column, statue, etc.
pedestals n ▷ pedestal
pedestrian n (pl -s) person who walks ▶ adj dull, uninspiring
pedestrians n ▷ pedestrian
pedicure n (pl -s) medical or cosmetic treatment of the feet
pedicures n ▷ pedicure
pedigree n (pl -s) register of ancestors, esp. of a purebred animal
pedigrees n ▷ pedigree
pediment n (pl -s) triangular part over a door etc.
pediments n ▷ pediment
pedlar n (pl -s) person who sells goods from door to door
pedlars n ▷ pedlar
pee (Informal) v (-s, -ing, peed) urinate ▶ n (-s) act of urinating
peed v ▷ pee
peeing v ▷ pee
pees v, n ▷ pee
peek v, n (pl -s) peep or glance
peeks n ▷ peek
peel v (-s, -ing, -ed) remove the skin or rind of (a vegetable or fruit) ▶ n (pl -s) rind or skin
> **peelings** pl n
peeled v ▷ peel
peeling v ▷ peel
peelings n ▷ peel
peels v, n ▷ peel
peep¹ v (-s, -ing, -ed) look slyly or quickly ▶ n (pl -s) peeping look
peep² v (-s, -ing, -ed) make a small shrill noise ▶ n (-s) small shrill noise
peeped v ▷ peep¹, ²
peeping v ▷ peep¹, ²
peeps v, n ▷ peep¹, ²
peer¹ n (pl -s), fem **peeress** (pl -es) (in Britain) member of the nobility
peer² v (-s, -ing, -ed) look closely and intently
peerage n (BRIT) whole body of peers
peerages n ▷ peerage
peered v ▷ peer²

peeress n ▷ peer
peeresses n ▷ peer
peering v ▷ peer²
peerless adj unequalled, unsurpassed
peers n, v ▷ peer¹, ²
peers v ▷ peer
peering v ▷ peer
peered v ▷ peer
peeved adj (Informal) annoyed
peevish adj fretful or irritable > **peevishly** adv
peevishly adv ▷ peevish
peewee n (pl -s) black-and-white Australian bird
peewees n ▷ peewee
peewit n (pl -s) ▷ lapwing
peewits n ▷ peewit
peg n (pl -s) pin or clip for joining, fastening, marking, etc. ▶ v (-s, -gging, -gged) fasten with pegs
pegged v ▷ peg
pegging v ▷ peg
pegs n, v ▷ peg
peignoir [pay-nwahr] n (pl -s) woman's light dressing gown
peignoirs n ▷ peignoir
pejorative [pij-jor-a-tiv] adj (of words etc.) with an insulting or critical meaning
pelargonium n (pl -s) plant with red, white, purple, or pink flowers
pelargoniums n ▷ pelargonium
pelican n (pl -s) large water bird with a pouch beneath its bill for storing fish
pelicans n ▷ pelican
pellagra n (pl -s) disease caused by lack of vitamin B
pellagras n ▷ pellagra
pellet n (pl -s) small ball of something
pellets n ▷ pellet
pellucid adj very clear
pelmet n (pl -s) ornamental drapery or board, concealing a curtain rail
pelmets n ▷ pelmet
pelt¹ v (-s, -ing, -ed) throw missiles at
pelt² n (pl -s) skin of a fur-bearing animal
pelted v ▷ pelt¹
pelting v ▷ pelt¹
pelts v, n ▷ pelt¹, ²
pelvic adj ▷ pelvis
pelvis n (pl -es) framework of bones at the base of the spine, to which the hips are attached
> **pelvic** adj
pelvises n ▷ pelvis
pen¹ n (pl -s) instrument for writing in ink ▶ v (-s, -nning, -nned) write or compose
pen² n small enclosure for domestic animals

▶ v (-s, -nning, -nned) put or keep in a pen
pen³ n (pl -s) female swan
penal [pee-nal] adj of or used in punishment
penalize (-zes, -zing, -zed) v impose a penalty on
 penalized v ▷ penalize
 penalizes v ▷ penalize
 penalizing v ▷ penalize
 penalties n ▷ penalty
penalty n (pl -ties) punishment for a crime or offence
penance n (pl (pl -s) voluntary self-punishment to make amends for wrongdoing
 penances n ▷ penance
pence n (BRIT) ▷ penny
penchant [pon-shon] n (pl -s) inclination or liking
 penchants n ▷ penchant
pencil n (pl -s) thin cylindrical instrument containing graphite, for writing or drawing
 ▶ v (-s, -lling, -lled) draw, write, or mark with a pencil
 pencilled v ▷ pencil
 pencilling v ▷ pencil
 pencils n, v ▷ pencil
pendant n (pl -s) ornament worn on a chain round the neck
 pendants n ▷ pendant
pendent adj hanging
pending prep while waiting for ▶ adj not yet decided or settled
pendulous adj hanging, swinging
pendulum n (pl -s) suspended weight swinging to and fro, esp. as a regulator for a clock
 pendulums n ▷ pendulum
penetrate v (-tes, -ting, -ted) find or force a way into or through ▷ **penetration** n (pl -s)
penetrable adj capable of being penetrated
 penetrated v ▷ penetrate
 penetrates v ▷ penetrate
penetrating adj (of a sound) loud and unpleasant ▶ v ▷ penetrate
 penetration n ▷ penetrate
 penetrations n ▷ penetrate
penguin n (pl -s) flightless black-and-white sea bird of the southern hemisphere
 penguins n ▷ penguin
penicillin n (pl -s) antibiotic drug effective against a wide range of diseases and infections
 penicillins n ▷ penicillin
peninsula n (pl -s) strip of land nearly surrounded by water ▷ **peninsular** adj
 penisular adj ▷ penisula

 peninsulas n ▷ peninsula
penis n (pl -es) organ of copulation and urination in male mammals
 penises n ▷ penis
 penitence n ▷ penitent
 penitences n ▷ penitent
penitent adj feeling sorry for having done wrong ▶ n (pl -s) someone who is penitent
 ▷ **penitence** n (pl -s)
 penitentiaries n ▷ penitentiary
penitentiary n (pl -ries) (US) prison ▶ adj (also **penitential**) relating to penance
 penitents n ▷ penitent
penknife n (pl -knives) small knife with blade(s) that fold into the handle
 penknives n ▷ penknife
pennant n (pl -s) long narrow flag
 pennants n ▷ pennant
 penned v ▷ pen¹, ²
 pennies n ▷ penny
penniless adj very poor
 penning v ▷ pen¹, ²
penny n (pl pence, pennies) British bronze coin worth one hundredth of a pound
 pens n ▷ pen¹, ², ³
pension¹ n (pl -s) regular payment to people above a certain age, retired employees, widows, etc. ▷ **pensionable** adj
pension² [pon-syon] n (pl -s) boarding house in Europe
 pensionable adj ▷ pension
pensioner n (pl -s) person receiving a pension
 pensioners n ▷ pension
 pensions n ▷ pension¹, ²
pensive adj deeply thoughtful, often with a tinge of sadness
pentagon n (pl -s) geometric figure with five sides ▷ **pentagonal** adj
 pentagonal adj ▷ pentagon
 pentagons n ▷ pentagon
pentameter [pen-tam-it-er] n (pl -s) line of poetry with five metrical feet
 pentameters n ▷ pentameter
penthouse n (pl -s) flat built on the roof or top floor of a building
 penthouses n ▷ penthouse
penultimate adj second last
penumbra n (pl -brae, -bras) (in an eclipse) the partially shadowed region which surrounds the full shadow
 penumbrae n ▷ penumbra
 penumbras n ▷ penumbra
 penuries n ▷ penury
 penurious adj ▷ penury
penury n (pl -ries) extreme poverty

> **penurious** adj
peonies n ▷ peony
peony n (pl -nies) garden plant with showy red, pink, or white flowers
people pl n persons generally ▶ n (pl -s) race or nation ▶ v (-les, -ling, -led) provide with inhabitants
  peopled v ▷ people
  peoples n, v ▷ people
  peopling v ▷ people
pep n (pl -s) (Informal) high spirits, energy, or enthusiasm
pepper n (pl -s) sharp hot condiment made from the fruit of an East Indian climbing plant ▶ v (-s, -ing, -ed) season with pepper
peppercorn n dried berry of the pepper plant
  peppercorns n ▷ peppercorn
  peppered v ▷ pepper
  pepperier adj ▷ peppery
  pepperiest adj ▷ peppery
  peppering v ▷ pepper
peppermint n (pl -s) plant that yields an oil with a strong sharp flavour
  peppermints n ▷ peppermint
  peppers n, v ▷ pepper
peppery adj (-rier, -riest) tasting of pepper
  peps n ▷ pep
peptic adj relating to digestion or the digestive juices
per prep for each
perambulate v (-tes, -ting, -ted) (Old-fashioned) walk through or about (a place)
  > **perambulation** n (pl -s)
  perambulated v ▷ perambulate
  perambulates v ▷ perambulate
  perambulating v ▷ perambulate
  perambulation n ▷ perambulate
  perambulations n ▷ perambulate
perambulator n (pl -s) pram
  perambulators n ▷ perambulator
perceive v (-ves, -ving, -ved) become aware of (something) through the senses
  perceived v ▷ perceive
  perceives v ▷ perceive
  perceiving v ▷ perceive
perceptible adj discernible, recognizable
perception n (pl -s) act of perceiving
  > **perceptive** adj
  perceptions n ▷ perception
  perceptive adj ▷ perception
perch[1] n (pl -es) resting place for a bird ▶ v (-es, -ing, -ed) alight, rest, or place on or as if on a perch
perch[2] n (pl -es) any of various edible fishes
perchance adv (Old-fashioned) perhaps

perches n, v ▷ perch[1, 2]
perching v ▷ perch[1, 2]
perched v ▷ perch[1, 2]
percipient adj quick to notice things, observant
percolate v (-tes, -ting, -ted) pass or filter through small holes > **percolation** n
  percolated v ▷ percolate
  percolates v ▷ percolate
  percolating v ▷ percolate
  percolation n ▷ percolate
  percolations n ▷ percolate
percolator n (pl -s) coffeepot in which boiling water is forced through a tube and filters down through coffee
  percolators n ▷ percolator
percussion n (pl -s) striking of one thing against another
  percussions n ▷ percussion
perdition n (pl -s) (CHRISTIANITY) spiritual ruin
  perditions n ▷ perdition
peregrination n (pl -s) (Obs) travels, roaming
  peregrinations n ▷ peregrination
peremptory adj authoritative, imperious
perennial adj lasting through many years ▶ n (pl -s) plant lasting more than two years
  > **perennially** adv
  perennially adv ▷ perennial
  perennials n ▷ perennial
perfect adj (-er, -est) having all the essential elements ▶ n (pl -s) (GRAMMAR) perfect tense ▶ v (-s, -ing, -ed) improve > **perfectly** adv
  perfected n ▷ perfect
  perfecter adj ▷ perfect
  perfectest adj ▷ perfect
  perfecting v ▷ perfect
perfection n (pl -s) state of being perfect
perfectionist n (pl -s) person who demands the highest standards of excellence
  > **perfectionism** n (pl -s)
  perfectionism n ▷ perfectionist
  perfectionisms n ▷ perfectionist
  perfectionists n ▷ perfectionist
  perfections n ▷ perfection
  perfectly adv ▷ perfect
  perfects n, v ▷ perfect
perfidious adj (Lit) treacherous, disloyal
  > **perfidy** n (pl -ies)
  perfidies n ▷ perfidious
  perfidy n ▷ perfidious
perforate v (-es, -ing, -ed) make holes in
  > **perforation** n (pl -s)
  perforated v ▷ perforate
  perforates v ▷ perforate
  perforating v ▷ perforate

perforation n ▷ perforate
perforations n ▷ perforate
perforce adv of necessity
perform v (-s, -ing, -ed) carry out (an action)
> **performance** n (pl -s) > **performer** n (pl -s)
performance n ▷ perform
performances n ▷ perform
performed v ▷ perform
performer n ▷ perform
performers n ▷ perform
performing v ▷ perform
performs v ▷ perform
perfume n (pl -s) liquid cosmetic worn for
its pleasant smell ▶ v (-es, -ing, -ed) give a
pleasant smell to
perfumed v ▷ perfume
perfumeries n ▷ perfumery
perfumery n (pl -ries) perfumes in general
perfumes n, v ▷ perfume
perfuming v ▷ perfume
perfunctorily adv ▷ perfunctory
perfunctory adj done only as a matter of
routine, superficial > **perfunctorily** adv
pergola n (pl -s) arch or framework of trellis
supporting climbing plants
pergolas n ▷ pergola
perhaps adv possibly, maybe
pericardia n ▷ pericardum
pericardium n (pl -dia) membrane enclosing
the heart
perihelia n ▷ perihelion
perihelion n (pl -lia) point in the orbit of a
planet or comet that is nearest to the sun
peril n (pl -s) great danger > **perilous** adj
> **perilously** adv
perilous adj ▷ peril
perilously adv ▷ peril
perils n ▷ peril
perimeter [per-**rim**-it-er] n (pl -s) (length of) the
outer edge of an area
perimeters n ▷ perimeter
perinatal adj of or in the weeks shortly before
or after birth
period n (pl -s) particular portion of time (us)
▶ adj (of furniture, dress, a play, etc.) dating
from or in the style of an earlier time
periodic adj recurring at intervals
periodical n (pl -s) magazine issued at regular
intervals ▶ adj periodic
periodicals n ▷ periodical
periods n ▷ period
peripatetic [per-rip-a-**tet**-ik] adj travelling
about from place to place
peripheral [per-**if**-er-al] adj unimportant, not
central

peripheries n ▷ periphery
periphery [per-**if**-er-ee] n (pl -ries) boundary
or edge
periscope n (pl -s) instrument used, esp. in
submarines, to give a view of objects on a
different level
periscopes n ▷ periscope
perish v (-es, -ing, -ed) be destroyed or die
perishable adj liable to rot quickly
perished v ▷ perish
perishes v ▷ perish
perishing adj (Informal) very cold ▶ v ▷ perish
peritonea n ▷ peritoneum
peritoneum [per-rit-toe-**nee**-um] n (pl -nea,
-neums) membrane lining the internal
surface of the abdomen
peritoneums n ▷ peritoneum
peritonitis [per-rit-tone-**ite**-iss] n (pl -tises)
inflammation of the peritoneum
peritonitises n ▷ peritonitis
periwinkle[1] n (pl -s) small edible shellfish,
the winkle
periwinkle[2] n (pl -s) plant with trailing stems
and blue flowers
periwinkles n ▷ periwinkle[1, 2]
perjuries n ▷ perjury
perjury n (pl -ies) act or crime of lying while
under oath in a court
perk n (pl -s) (Informal) incidental benefit
gained from a job, such as a company car
perkier adj ▷ perk
perkiest adj ▷ perk
perks n ▷ perk
perky adj (-kier, -kiest) lively or cheerful
perlemoen n (pl -s) (S AFR) edible sea creature
with a shell lined with mother of pearl
perlemoens n ▷ perlemoen
perm n (pl -s) long-lasting curly hairstyle
produced by treating the hair with chemicals
▶ v (-s, -ing, -ed) give (hair) a perm
permafrost n (pl -s) permanently frozen
ground
permafrosts n ▷ permafrost
permanence n ▷ permanent
permanences n ▷ permanent
permanent adj lasting forever > **permanence**
n (pl -s) > **permanently** adv
permanently adv ▷ permanent
permeate v (-tes, -ting, -ted) pervade or pass
through the whole of (something)
permeable adj able to be permeated, esp.
by liquid
permeated v ▷ permeate
permeates v ▷ permeate
permeating v ▷ permeate

permed *v* ▷ perm

perming *v* ▷ perm

permissible *adj* ▷ permit

permission *n* (*pl* -s) authorization to do something

permissions *n* ▷ permission

permissive *adj* (excessively) tolerant, esp. in sexual matters

permit *v* (-s, -tting, -tted) give permission, allow ▶ *n* (*pl* -s) document giving permission to do something > **permissible** *adj*

permits *v*, *n* ▷ permit

permitted *v* ▷ permit

permitting *v* ▷ permit

perms *n*, *v* ▷ perm

permutation *n* (*pl* -s) any of the ways a number of things can be arranged or combined

permutations *n* ▷ permutation

pernicious *adj* wicked

pernickety *adj* (*Informal*) (excessively) fussy about details

peroration *n* (*pl* -s) concluding part of a speech, usu. summing up the main points

perorations *n* ▷ peroration

peroxide *n* (*pl* -s) hydrogen peroxide used as a hair bleach

peroxides *n* ▷ peroxide

perpendicular *adj* at right angles to a line or surface ▶ *n* (*pl* -s) line or plane at right angles to another

perpendiculars *n* ▷ perpendicular

perpetrate *v* (-tes, -ting, -ted) commit or be responsible for (a wrongdoing) > **perpetration** *n* (*pl* -s) > **perpetrator** *n* (*pl* -s)

perpetrated *v* ▷ perpetrate

perpetrates *v* ▷ perpetrate

perpetrating *v* ▷ perpetrate

perpetration *n* ▷ perpetrate

perpetrations *n* ▷ perpetrate

perpetrator *n* ▷ perpetrate

perpetrators *n* ▷ perpetrate

perpetual *adj* lasting forever > **perpetually** *adv*

perpetually *adv* ▷ perpetual

perpetuate *v* (-tes, -ting, -ted) cause to continue or be remembered > **perpetuation** *n* (*pl* -s)

perpetuated *v* ▷ perpetuate

perpetuates *v* ▷ perpetuate

perpetuating *v* ▷ perpetuate

perpetuation *n* ▷

perpetuations *n* ▷

perplex *v* (-es, -ing, -ed) puzzle, bewilder > **perplexity** *n* (*pl* -ties)

perplexed *v* ▷ perplex

perplexes *v* ▷ perplex

perplexing *v* ▷ perplex

perplexities *n* ▷ perplex

perplexity *n* ▷ perplex

perquisite *n* (*pl* -s) (*Formal*) ▷ perk

perquisites *n* ▷ perquisite

perries *n* ▷ perry

perry *n* (*pl* -rries) alcoholic drink made from fermented pears

persecute *v* (-tes, -ting, -ted) treat cruelly because of race, religion, etc. > **persecution** *n* (*pl* -s) > **persecutor** *n* (*pl* -s)

persecuted *v* ▷ persecute

persecutes *v* ▷ persecute

persecuting *v* ▷ persecute

persecution *n* ▷ persecute

persecutions *n* ▷ persecute

persecutor *n* ▷ persecute

persecutors *n* ▷ persecute

persevere *v* (-res, -ring, -red) keep making an effort despite difficulties > **perseverance** *n* (*pl* -s)

perseverance *n* ▷ persevere

perseverances *n* ▷ persevere

persevered *v* ▷ persevere

perseveres *v* ▷ persevere

persevering *v* ▷ persevere

persimmon *n* (*pl* -s) sweet red tropical fruit

persimmons *n* ▷ persimmon

persist *v* (-s, -ing, -ed) continue to be or happen, last > **persistent** *adj* > **persistently** *adv* > **persistence** *n* (*pl* -s)

persisted *v* ▷ persist

persistence *adj* ▷ persist

persistences *adj* ▷ persist

persistent *adj* ▷ persist

persistently *adv* ▷ persist

persisting *v* ▷ persist

persists *v* ▷ persist

person *n* (*pl* -s) human being

persons *n* ▷ person

persona [per-soh-na] *n* (*pl* -nae) [-nee] someone's personality as presented to others

personable *adj* pleasant in appearance and personality

personae *n* ▷ persona

personage *n* (*pl* -s) important person

personages *n* ▷ personage

personal *adj* individual or private

personalities *n* ▷ personality

personality *n* (*pl* -ties) person's distinctive characteristics

personally *adv* directly, not by delegation to others

personification *n* ▷ personify

personifications n ▷ personify
personified v ▷ personify
personifies v ▷ personify
personify v (-fies, -fying, -fied) give human characteristics to > **personification** n (pl -s)
personifying v ▷ personify
personnel n (pl -s) people employed in an organization
personnels n ▷ personnel
perspective n (pl -s) view of the relative importance of situations or facts
perspectives n ▷ perspective
perspicacious adj having quick mental insight > **perspicacity** n (pl -ties)
perspicacities n ▷ perspicacious
perspicacity n ▷ perspicacious
perspiration n ▷ perspire
perspirations n ▷ perspire
perspire v (-res, -ring, -red) sweat > **perspiration** n (pl -s)
perspired v ▷ perspire
perspires v ▷ perspire
perspiring v ▷ perspire
persuade v (-des, -ding, -ded) make (someone) do something by argument, charm, etc. > **persuasive** adj
persuasion n (pl -s) act of persuading
persuasions n ▷ persuasion
persuasive adj ▷ persuade
persuaded v ▷ persuade
persuades v ▷ persuade
persuading v ▷ persuade
pert adj (-er, -est) saucy and cheeky
pertain v (-s, -ing, -ed) belong or be relevant (to)
pertained v ▷ pertain
pertaining v ▷ pertain
pertains v ▷ pertain
perter adj ▷ pert
pertest adj ▷ pert
pertinacious adj (Formal) very persistent and determined > **pertinacity** n (pl -ties)
pertinacities n ▷ pertinacious
pertinacity n ▷ pertinacious
pertinence n ▷ pertinent
pertinences n ▷ pertinent
pertinent adj relevant > **pertinence** n (pl -s)
perturb v (-s, -ing, -ed) disturb greatly > **perturbation** n (pl -s)
perturbation n ▷ perturb
perturbation n ▷ perturb
perturbed v ▷ perturb
perturbing v ▷ perturb
perturbs v ▷ perturb
perusal n ▷ peruse

perusals n ▷ peruse
peruse v (-ses, -sing, -sed) read in a careful or leisurely manner > **perusal** n (pl -s)
perused v ▷ peruse
peruses v ▷ peruse
perusing v ▷ peruse
pervade v (-des, -ding, -ded) spread right through (something) > **pervasive** adj
pervaded v ▷ pervade
pervades v ▷ pervade
pervading v ▷ pervade
pervasive adj ▷ pervade
perverse adj (-r, -st) deliberately doing something different from what is thought normal or proper > **perversely** adv > **perversity** n (pl -ties)
perversely adv ▷ perverse
perverser adj ▷ perverse
perversest adj ▷ perverse
perversion n (pl -s) sexual act or desire considered abnormal
perversions n ▷ perversion
perversities n ▷ perverse
perversity n ▷ perverse
pervert v (-s, -ing, -ed) use or alter for a wrong purpose ▶ n (pl -s) person who practises sexual perversion
perverted v ▷ pervert
perverting v ▷ pervert
perverts v, n ▷ pervert
pervious adj able to be penetrated, permeable
peseta [pa-**say**-ta] n (pl -s) former monetary unit of Spain
pesetas n ▷ peseta
pessaries n ▷ pessary
pessary n (pl -ries) appliance worn in the vagina, either to prevent conception or to support the womb
pessimism n (pl -s) tendency to expect the worst in all things > **pessimist** n (pl -s) > **pessimistic** adj > **pessimistically** adv
pessimisms n ▷ pessimism
pessimist n ▷ pessimism
pessimistic adj ▷ pessimism
pessimistically adv ▷ pessimism
pessimists n ▷ pessimism
pest n (pl -s) annoying person
pesticide n (pl -s) chemical for killing insect pests
pesticides n ▷ pesticide
pester v (-s, -ing, -ed) annoy or nag continually
pestered v ▷ pester
pestering v ▷ pester
pesters v ▷ pester
pestilence n (pl -s) deadly epidemic disease

pestilences n ▷ **pestilence**
pestilent adj annoying, troublesome
  > **pestilential** adj
  pestilential adj ▷ **pestilent**
pestle n (pl **-s**) club-shaped implement for grinding things to powder in a mortar
  pestles n ▷ **pestle**
  pests n ▷ **pest**
pet n (pl **-s**) animal kept for pleasure and companionship ▶ adj particularly cherished
  ▶ v (**-s**, **-tting**, **-tted**) treat as a pet
petal n (pl **-s**) one of the brightly coloured outer parts of a flower > **petalled** adj
  petalled adj ▷ **petal**
  petals n ▷ **petal**
petard n (pl **-s**) being the victim of one's own schemes
  petards n ▷ **petard**
petite adj (of a woman) small and dainty
petition n (pl **-s**) formal request, esp. one signed by many people and presented to parliament ▶ v (**-s**, **-ing**, **-ed**) present a petition to > **petitioner** n (pl **-s**)
  petitioned v ▷ **petition**
  petitioner n ▷ **petition**
  petitioners n ▷ **petition**
  petitioning v ▷ **petition**
  petitions n, v ▷ **petition**
petrel n (pl **-s**) sea bird with a hooked bill and tubular nostrils
  petrels n ▷ **petrel**
  petrification n ▷ **petrify**
  petrifications n ▷ **petrify**
  petrified v ▷ **petrify**
  petrifies v ▷ **petrify**
petrify v (**-fies**, **-fying**, **-fied**) frighten severely
  > **petrification** n (pl **-s**)
petrochemical n (pl **-s**) substance, such as acetone, obtained from petroleum
  petrochemicals n ▷ **petrochemical**
petrol n (pl **-s**) flammable liquid obtained from petroleum, used as fuel in internal-combustion engines
petroleum n (pl **-s**) thick dark oil found underground
  petroleums n ▷ **petroleum**
  petrols n ▷ **petrol**
  pets n, v ▷ **pet**
  petted v ▷ **pet**
petticoat n (pl **-s**) woman's skirt-shaped undergarment
  petticoats n ▷ **petticoat**
  pettier adj ▷ **petty**
  pettiest adj ▷ **petty**
pettifogging adj excessively concerned with

unimportant detail
  pettiness n ▷ **petty**
  pettinesses n ▷ **petty**
  petting v ▷ **pet**
petty adj (**-ttier**, **-ttiest**) unimportant, trivial
  > **pettiness** n (pl **-es**)
  petulance n ▷ **petulant**
  petulances n ▷ **petulant**
petulant adj childishly irritable or peevish
  > **petulance** n (pl **-s**) > **petulantly** adv
  petulantly adv ▷ **petulant**
petunia n (pl **-s**) garden plant with funnel-shaped flowers
  petunias n ▷ **petunia**
pew n (pl **-s**) fixed benchlike seat in a church
  pews n ▷ **pew**
pewter n (pl **-s**) greyish metal made of tin and lead
  pewters n ▷ **pewter**
phalanger n (pl **-s**) long-tailed Australian tree-dwelling marsupial
  phalangers n ▷ **phalanger**
phalanx n (pl **-es**) closely grouped mass of people
  phalanxes n ▷ **phalanx**
  phalli n ▷ **phallus**
  phallic adj ▷ **phallic**
phallus n (pl **-lluses**, **-lli**) penis, esp. as a symbol of reproductive power in primitive rites
  > **phallic** adj
  phalluses n ▷ **phallus**
phantasm n (pl **-s**) unreal vision, illusion
  > **phantasmal** adj
  phantasmal adj ▷ **phantasm**
  phantasms n ▷ **phantasm**
phantasmagoria n (pl **-s**) shifting medley of dreamlike figures
  phantasmagorias n ▷ **phantasmagoria**
phantom n (pl **-s**) ghost
  phantoms n ▷ **phantom**
pharmaceutical adj of pharmacy
  pharmacies n ▷ **pharmacy**
pharmacist n (pl **-s**) person qualified to prepare and sell drugs and medicines
  pharmacists n ▷ **pharmacist**
  pharmacological adj ▷ **pharmacology**
  pharmacologies n ▷ **pharmacology**
  pharmacologist n ▷ **pharmacology**
  pharmacologists n ▷ **pharmacology**
pharmacology n (pl **-gies**) study of drugs
  > **pharmacological** adj > **pharmacologist** n (pl **-s**)
pharmacopoeia [far-ma-koh-**pee**-a] n (pl **-s**) book with a list of and directions for the use of drugs

pharmacopeias *n* ▷ pharmacopoeia
pharmacy *n* (*pl* -cies) preparation and
dispensing of drugs and medicines
pharynges *n* ▷ pharynx
pharyngitis [far-rin-**jite**-iss] *n* (*pl* -tes)
inflammation of the pharynx
pharyngitises *n* ▷ pharynx
pharynx [**far**-rinks] *n* (*pl* -nges, -nxes) cavity
forming the back part of the mouth
pharynxes ▷ pharynx
phase *n* (*pl* -s) any distinct or characteristic
stage in a development or chain of events
▶ *v* (-ses, -sing, -sed) arrange or carry out in
stages or to coincide with something else
phased *v* ▷ phase
phases *n*, *v* ▷ phase
phasing *v* ▷ phase
pheasant *n* (*pl* -s) game bird with bright
plumage
pheasants *n* ▷ pheasant
phenobarbitone *n* (*pl* -s) drug inducing sleep
or relaxation
phenobarbitones *n* ▷ phenobarbitone
phenol *n* (*pl* -s) chemical used in disinfectants
and antiseptics
phenols *n* ▷ phenol
phenomena *n* ▷ phenomenon
phenomenal *adj* extraordinary, outstanding
> **phenomenally** *adv*
phenomenally *adv* ▷ phenomenal
phenomenon *n* (*pl* -mena) anything
appearing or observed
phial *n* (*pl* -s) small bottle for medicine etc.
phials *n* ▷ phial
philadelphus *n* (*pl* -es) shrub with sweet-
scented flowers
philadelphuses *n* ▷ philadelphus
philanderer *n* (*pl* -s) man who flirts or has
many casual love affairs > **philandering** *adj*,
n (*pl* -s)
philanderers *n* ▷ philanderer
philandering *n* ▷ philanderer
philanderings *n* ▷ philanderer
philanthropic *adj* ▷ philanthropy
philanthropies *n* ▷ philanthropy
philanthropist *n* ▷ philanthropy
philanthropists *n* ▷ philanthropy
philanthropy *n* (*pl* -pies) practice of
helping people less well-off than oneself
> **philanthropic** *adj* > **philanthropist** *n* (*pl* -s)
philatelies *n* ▷ philately
philatelist *n* ▷ philately
philatelists *n* ▷ philately
philately [fill-**lat**-a-lee] *n* (*pl* -lies) stamp
collecting > **philatelist** *n* (*pl* -s)

philharmonic *adj* (in names of orchestras etc.)
music-loving
philistine *adj*, *n* (*pl* -s) boorishly uncultured
(person) > **philistinism** *n* (*pl* -s)
philistines *n* ▷ philistine
philistinism *n* ▷ philistine
philistinisms *n* ▷ philistine
philological *adj* ▷ philology
philologies *n* ▷ philology
philologist *n* ▷ philology
philologists *n* ▷ philology
philology *n* (*pl* -gies) science of the structure
and development of languages > **philological**
adj > **philologist** *n* (*pl* -s)
philosopher *n* (*pl* -s) person who studies
philosophy
philosophers *n* ▷ philosopher
philosophize *v* (-zes, -zing, -zed) discuss in a
philosophical manner
philosophized *v* ▷ philosophize
philosophizes *v* ▷ philosophize
philosophizing *v* ▷ philosophize
philosophic *adj* ▷ philosophy
philosophical *adj* ▷ philosophy
philosophically *adv* ▷ philosophy
philosophies *n* ▷ philosophy
philosophy *n* (*pl* -phies) study of the
meaning of life, knowledge, thought,
etc. > **philosophical, philosophic** *adj* of
philosophy > **philosophically** *adv*
philtre *n* (*pl* -s) magic drink supposed to
arouse love in the person who drinks it
philtres *n* ▷ philtre
phlebitis [fleb-**bite**-iss] *n* (*pl* -es) inflammation
of a vein
phlebitises *n* ▷ phlebitis
phlegm [flem] *n* (*pl* -s) thick yellowish
substance formed in the nose and throat
during a cold
phlegmatic [fleg-**mat**-ik] *adj* not easily excited,
unemotional > **phlegmatically** *adv*
phlegmatically *adv* ▷ phlegmatic
phlegms *n* ▷ phlegm
phlox *n* (*pl* phlox, -xes) flowering garden plant
phloxes *n* ▷ phlox
phobia *n* (*pl* -s) intense and unreasoning fear
or dislike
phobias *n* ▷ phobia
phoenix *n* (*pl* -es) legendary bird said to set fire
to itself and rise anew from its ashes
phoenixes *n* ▷ phoenix
phone *n*, *v* (-nes, -ning, -ned) (*Informal*)
telephone
phonecard *n* (*pl* -s) card used to operate
certain public telephones

phonecards *n* ▷ phonecard

phoned *v* ▷ phone

phones *v* ▷ phone

phonetic *adj* of speech sounds > **phonetically** *adv*

phonetically *adv* ▷ phonetic

phonetics *n* science of speech sounds

phoney, phony (*Informal*) *adj* (**-nier, -niest**) not genuine ▶ *n* (*pl* **-neys, -nies**) phoney person or thing

phoneys *n* ▷ phoney

phonier *adj* ▷ phoney

phonies *n* ▷ phoney

phoniest *adj* ▷ phoney

phoning *v* ▷ phone

phonograph *n* (*pl* **-s**) (US) (*old-fashioned*) record player

phonographs *n* ▷ phonograph

phony *adj* ▷ phoney

phosphorescence *n* (*pl* **-s**) faint glow in the dark > **phosphorescent** *adj*

phosphorescences *n* ▷ phosphorescence

phosphorescent *adj* ▷ phosphorescence

phosphate *n* (*pl* **-s**) compound of phosphorus

phosphates *n* ▷ phosphate

phosphorus *n* (*pl* **-es**) (CHEM) toxic flammable nonmetallic element which appears luminous in the dark

phosphoruses *n* ▷ phosphorus

photo *n* (*pl* **-s**) ▷ photograph

photocopied *v* ▷ photocopy

photocopier *n* ▷ photocopy

photocopiers *n* ▷ photocopy

photocopies *n, v* ▷ photocopy

photocopy *n* (*pl* **-pies**) photographic reproduction ▶ *v* (**-pies, -pying, -pied**) make a photocopy of > **photocopier** *n* (*pl* **-s**)

photocopying *v* ▷ photocopy

photoelectric *adj* using or worked by electricity produced by the action of light

photogenic *adj* always looking attractive in photographs

photograph *n* (*pl* **-s**) picture made by the chemical action of light on sensitive film ▶ *v* (**-s, -ing, -ed**) take a photograph of > **photographic** *adj*

photographed *v* ▷ photograph

photographer *n* (*pl* **-s**) person who takes photographs, esp. professionally

photographers *n* ▷ photographer

photographic *adj* ▷ photograph

photographing *v* ▷ photograph

photographs *n, v* ▷ photograph

photographies *n* ▷ photography

photography *n* (*pl* **-s**) art of taking photographs

photos *n* ▷ photo

photostat *n* (*pl* **-s**) copy made by photocopying machine

photostats *n* ▷ photostat

photosyntheses *n* ▷ photosynthesis

photosynthesis *n* (*pl* **-ses**) process by which a green plant uses sunlight to build up carbohydrate reserves

phrase *n* (*pl* **-s**) group of words forming a unit of meaning, esp. within a sentence ▶ *v* (**-ses, -sing, -sed**) express in words

phrased *v* ▷ phrase

phrases *n, v* ▷ phrase

phrasing *v* ▷ phrase

phraseologies *n* ▷ phraseology

phraseology *n* (*pl* **-gies**) way in which words are used

physical *adj* of the body, as contrasted with the mind or spirit > **physically** *adv*

physically *adv* ▷ physical

physician *n* (*pl* **-s**) doctor of medicine

physicians *n* ▷ physician

physics *n* science of the properties of matter and energy

physicist *n* (*pl* **-s**) person skilled in or studying physics

physicists *n* ▷ physicist

physiognomies *n* ▷ physiognomy

physiognomy [fiz-ee-on-om-ee] *n* (*pl* **-mies**) face

physiological *adj* ▷ physiology

physiologies *n* ▷ physiology

physiologist *n* ▷ physiology

physiologists *n* ▷ physiology

physiology *n* (*pl* **-gies**) science of the normal function of living things > **physiological** *adj* > **physiologist** *n* (*pl* **-s**)

physiotherapies *n* ▷ physiotherapy

physiotherapist *n* ▷ physiotherapy

physiotherapists *n* ▷ physiotherapy

physiotherapy *n* (*pl* **-pies**) treatment of disease or injury by physical means such as massage, rather than by drugs > **physiotherapist** *n* (*pl* **-s**)

physique *n* (*pl* **-s**) person's bodily build and muscular development

physiques *n* ▷ physique

pi *n* (*pl* **-s**) (MATHS) ratio of the circumference of a circle to its diameter

pis *n* ▷ pi

pianissimo *adv* (MUSIC) very quietly

piano¹ *n* (*pl* **-os**) musical instrument with strings which are struck by hammers worked by a keyboard (*also* **pianoforte**) (*pl* **-s**) > **pianist**

n (*pl* **-s**)

pianist *n* ▷ **piano¹**

pianists *n* ▷ **piano¹**

piano² *adv* (MUSIC) quietly

pianoforte *n* ▷ **piano¹**

pianofortes *n* ▷ **piano¹**

pianos *n* ▷ **piano¹**

piazza *n* (*pl* **-s**) square or marketplace, esp. in Italy

piazzas *n* ▷ **piazza**

pic *n* (*pl* **-s, pix**) (*Informal*) photograph or illustration

picador *n* (*pl* **-s**) mounted bullfighter with a lance

picadors *n* ▷ **picador**

picaresque *adj* denoting a type of fiction in which the hero, a rogue, has a series of adventures

piccalilli *n* (*pl* **-s**) pickle of vegetables in mustard sauce

piccalillis *n* ▷ **piccalilli**

piccolo *n* (*pl* **-os**) small flute

piccolos *n* ▷ **piccolo**

pick¹ *v* (**-s, -ing, -ed**) choose ▶ *n* (*pl* **-s**) choice

pick² *n* (*pl* **-s**) tool with a curved iron crossbar and wooden shaft, for breaking up hard ground or rocks

pickaxe *n* (*pl* **-s**) large pick

pickaxes *n* ▷ **pickaxe**

picked *v* ▷ **pick¹**

picket *n* (*pl* **-s**) person or group standing outside a workplace to deter would-be workers during a strike ▶ *v* (**-s, -ing, -ed**) form a picket outside (a workplace)

picketed *v* ▷ **picket**

picketing *v* ▷ **picket**

pickets *n, v* ▷ **picket**

picking *v* ▷ **pick¹**

pickings *pl n* money easily acquired

pickle *n* (*pl* **-s**) food preserved in vinegar or salt water ▶ *v* (**-les, -ling, -led**) preserve in vinegar or salt water

pickled *adj* (of food) preserved ▶ *n* ▷ **pickle**

pickles *n, v* ▷ **pickle**

pickling *v* ▷ **pickle**

pickpocket *n* (*pl* **-s**) thief who steals from someone's pocket

pickpockets *n* ▷ **pickpocket**

picks *n, v* ▷ **pick¹, ²**

picnic *n* (*pl* **-s**) (*Informal*) meal out of doors ▶ *v* (**-s, -cking, -cked**) have a picnic

picnicked *v* ▷ **picnic**

picnicking *v* ▷ **picnic**

picnics *n, v* ▷ **picnic**

pics *n* ▷ **pic**

pictorial *adj* of or in painting or pictures

picture *n* (*pl* **-s**) drawing or painting ▶ *pl* cinema ▶ *v* (**-res, -ring, -red**) visualize, imagine

pictured *v* ▷ **picture**

pictures *n, v* ▷ **picture**

picturesque *adj* (of a place or view) pleasant to look at

picturing *v* ▷ **picture**

piddle *v* (**-les, -ling, -led**) (*Informal*) urinate

piddled *v* ▷ **piddle**

piddles *v* ▷ **piddle**

piddling *v* ▷ **piddle**

pidgin *n* (*pl* **-s**) language, not a mother tongue, made up of elements of two or more other languages

pidgins *n* ▷ **pidgin**

pie *n* (*pl* **-s**) dish of meat, fruit, etc. baked in pastry

pies *n* ▷ **pie**

piebald *adj*, *n* (*pl* **-s**) (horse) with irregular black-and-white markings

piebalds *n* ▷ **piebald**

piece *n* (*pl* **-s**) separate bit or part

pieces *n* ▷ **piece**

piecemeal *adv* bit by bit

piecework *n* (*pl* **-s**) work paid for according to the quantity produced

pieceworks *n* ▷ **piecework**

pied *adj* having markings of two or more colours

pier *n* (*pl* **-s**) platform on stilts sticking out into the sea

piers *n* ▷ **pier**

pierce *v* (**-ces, -cing, -ced**) make a hole in or through with a sharp instrument

pierced *v* ▷ **pierce**

pierces *v* ▷ **pierce**

piercing *adj* (of a sound) shrill and high-pitched ▶ *v* ▷ **pierce**

pierrot [pier-roe] *n* (*pl* **-s**) pantomime clown with a whitened face

pierrots *n* ▷ **pierrot**

pieties *n* ▷ **piety**

piety *n* (*pl* **-ties**) deep devotion to God and religion

piffle *n* (*pl* **-s**) (*Informal*) nonsense

piffles *n* ▷ **piffle**

pig *n* (*pl* **-s**) animal kept and killed for pork, ham, and bacon

pigeon¹ *n* (*pl* **-s**) bird with a heavy body and short legs, sometimes trained to carry messages

pigeon² *n* (*Informal*) concern or responsibility

pigeonhole *n* (-s) compartment for papers in a desk etc. ▶ *v* (-les, -ling, -led) classify
pigeonholed *v* ▷ pigeonhole
pigeonholing *v* ▷ pigeonhole
pigeonholes *n, v* ▷ pigeonhole
pigeons *n* ▷ pigeon[1, 2]
piggeries *n* ▷ piggery
piggery *n* (*pl* -ries) place for keeping and breeding pigs
piggier *adj* ▷ piggy
piggiest *adj* ▷ piggy
piggish, piggy (-ggier, -ggiest) *adj* (*Informal*) dirty
piggy *adj* ▷ piggish
piggyback *n* (*pl* -s) ride on someone's shoulders ▶ *adv* carried on someone's shoulders
piggybacks *n* ▷ piggyback
pigment *n* (*pl* -s) colouring matter, paint or dye > **pigmentation** *n* (*pl* -s)
pigmentation *n* ▷ pigment
pigmentations *n* ▷ pigment
pigments *n* ▷ pigment
pigmies *n* ▷ pygmy
pigmy *n* (*pl* -mies) ▷ pygmy
pigs *n* ▷ pig
pigtail *n* (*pl* -s) plait of hair hanging from the back or either side of the head
pigtails *n* ▷ pigtail
pike[1] *n* (*pl* -s) large predatory freshwater fish
pike[2] *n* (*pl* -s) (HIST) long-handled spear
pikes *n* ▷ pike[1, 2]
pikelet *n* (*pl* -s) (AUST & NZ) small thick pancake
pikelets *n* ▷ pikelet
piker *n* (*pl* -s) (AUST & NZ) (*Slang*) shirker
pikers *n* ▷ piker
pilaster *n* (*pl* -s) square column, usu. set in a wall
pilasters *n* ▷ pilaster
pilau, pilaf, pilaff *n* (*pl* -s) Middle Eastern dish of meat, fish, or poultry boiled with rice, spices, etc.
pilaffs *n* ▷ pilaff
pilafs *n* ▷ pilaf
pilchard *n* (*pl* -s) small edible sea fish of the herring family
pilchards *n* ▷ pilchard
pile[1] *n* (*pl* -s) number of things lying on top of each other ▶ *v* (-les, -ling, -led) collect into a pile
pile[2] *n* (*pl* -s) beam driven into the ground, esp. as a foundation for building
pile[3] *n* (*pl* -s) fibres of a carpet or a fabric, esp. velvet, that stand up from the weave
piled *v* ▷ pile[1]

piling *v* ▷ pile[1]
piles *pl n* swollen veins in the rectum, haemorrhoids ▶ *v, n* ▷ pile[1, 2, 3]
pilfer *v* (-s, -ing, -ed) steal in small quantities
pilfered *v* ▷ pilfer
pilfering *v* ▷ pilfer
pilfers *v* ▷ pilfer
pilgrim *n* (*pl* -s) person who journeys to a holy place > **pilgrimage** *n* (*pl* -s)
pilgrimage *n* ▷ pilgrim
pilgrimages *n* ▷ pilgrim
pilgrims *n* ▷ pilgrim
pill *n* (*pl* -s) small ball of medicine swallowed whole
pills *n* ▷ pill
pillage *v* (-s, -ging, -ged) steal property by violence in war ▶ *n* (*pl* -s) violent seizure of goods, esp. in war
pillaged *v* ▷ pillage
pillages *v, n* ▷ pillage
pillaging *v* ▷ pillage
pillar *n* (*pl* -s) upright post, usu. supporting a roof
pillars *n* ▷ pillar
pillion *n* (*pl* -s) seat for a passenger behind the rider of a motorcycle
pillions *n* ▷ pillion
pilloried *v* ▷ pillory
pillories *n, v* ▷ pillory
pillory *n* (*pl* -ries) (HIST) frame with holes for the head and hands in which an offender was locked and exposed to public abuse ▶ *v* (-ies, -ying, -ied) ridicule publicly
pillow *n* (*pl* -s) stuffed cloth bag for supporting the head in bed ▶ *v* (-s, -ing, -ed) rest as if on a pillow
pillowcase, pillowslip *n* (*pl* -s) removable cover for a pillow
pillowcases *n* ▷ pillowcase
pillowed *v* ▷ pillow
pillowing *v* ▷ pillow
pillows *n, v* ▷ pillow
pillowslip *n* ▷ pillowcase
pillowslips *n* ▷ pillowcase
pilot *n* (*pl* -s) person qualified to fly an aircraft or spacecraft ▶ *adj* experimental and preliminary ▶ *v* (-s, -ing, -ed) act as the pilot of
piloted *v* ▷ pilot
piloting *v* ▷ pilot
pilots *n, v* ▷ pilot
pimento *n* (*pl* -tos) mild-tasting red pepper
pimentos *n* ▷ pimento
pimp *n* (*pl* -s) man who gets customers for a prostitute in return for a share of his or her earnings ▶ *v* (-s, -ing, -ed) act as a pimp

pimped v ▷ pimp

pimpernel n (pl -s) wild plant with small star-shaped flowers

pimpernels n ▷ pimpernel

pimping v ▷ pimp

pimple n (pl -s) small pus-filled spot on the skin > **pimply** adj (-lier, -liest)

pimples n ▷ pimple

pimplier v ▷ pimple

pimpliest v ▷ pimple

pimply v ▷ pimple

pimps n, v ▷ pimp

pin n (pl -s) short thin piece of stiff wire with a point and head, for fastening things ▶ v (-s, pinning, pinned) fasten with a pin

pinafore n (pl -s) apron

pinafores n ▷ pinafore

pinball n (pl -s) electrically operated table game in which a small ball is shot through various hazards

pinballs n ▷ pinball

pincers pl n tool consisting of two hinged arms, for gripping

pinch v (-es, -ing, -ed) squeeze between finger and thumb ▶ n (pl -es) act of pinching

pinchbeck n (pl -s) alloy of zinc and copper, used as imitation gold

pinchbecks n ▷ pinchbeck

pinched v ▷ pinch

pinches v, n ▷ pinch

pinching v ▷ pinch

pinned v ▷ pin

pinning v ▷ pin

pins n, v ▷ pin

pine¹ n (pl -s) evergreen coniferous tree

pine² v (-nes, -ning, -ned) (foll. by **for**) feel great longing (for)

pineapple n (pl -s) large tropical fruit with juicy yellow flesh and a hard skin

pineapples n ▷ pineapple

pined v ▷ pine²

pines n, v ▷ pine¹, ²

ping v (-s, -ing, -ed) ▶ n (pl -s) (make) a short high-pitched sound

pinged v ▷ ping

pinging v ▷ ping

pings v, n ▷ ping

pining v ▷ pine²

pinion¹ n (pl -s) bird's wing ▶ v (-s, -ing, -ed) immobilize (someone) by tying or holding his or her arms

pinion² n (pl -s) small cogwheel

pinioned v ▷ pinion

pinioning v ▷ pinion

pinions n, v ▷ pinion¹, ²

pink n (pl -s) pale reddish colour ▶ adj (-er, -est) of the colour pink ▶ v (-s, -ing, -ed) (of an engine) make a metallic noise because not working properly, knock

pinked v ▷ pink

pinker adj ▷ pink

pinkest adj ▷ pink

pinking v ▷ pink

pinks n, v ▷ pink

pinnacle n (pl -s) highest point of fame or success

pinnacles n ▷ pinnacle

pinotage [pin-no-tajj] n (pl -s) blended red wine of S Africa

pinotages n ▷ pinotage

pinpoint v (-s, -ing, -ed) locate or identify exactly

pinpointed v ▷ pinpoint

pinpointing v ▷ pinpoint

pinpoints v ▷ pinpoint

pinstripe n (pl -s) very narrow stripe in fabric

pinstripes n ▷ pinstripe

pint n (pl -s) liquid measure, 1/8 gallon (.568 litre)

pints n ▷ pint

pioneer n (pl -s) explorer or early settler of a new country ▶ v (-s, -ing, -ed) be the pioneer or leader of

pioneered v ▷ pioneer

pioneering v ▷ pioneer

pioneers n, v ▷ pioneer

pious adj deeply religious, devout

pip¹ n (pl -s) small seed in a fruit

pip² n high-pitched sound used as a time signal on radio (Informal)

pips n ▷ pip¹, ²

pipe n (pl -s) tube for conveying liquid or gas ▶ pl bagpipes ▶ v (-pes, -ping, -ped) play on a pipe

piped v ▷ pipe

piper n (pl -s) player on a pipe or bagpipes

pipers n ▷ piper

piping n (pl -s) system of pipes ▶ v ▷ pipe

pipings n ▷ piping

pipeline n (pl -s) long pipe for transporting oil, water, etc.

pipelines n ▷ pipeline

pipes n, v ▷ pipe

pipette n (pl -s) slender glass tube used to transfer or measure fluids

pipettes n ▷ pipette

pipi n (pl -s) (AUST) mollusc often used as bait

pipit n (pl -s) small brownish songbird

pipits n ▷ pipit

pippin n (pl -s) type of eating apple

pippins n ▷ pippin

pips n ▷ pip[1, 2]

piquancies n ▷ piquant

piquancy n ▷ piquant

piquant [pee-kant] adj having a pleasant spicy taste > **piquancy** n (pl -cies)

pique [peek] n (pl -s) feeling of hurt pride, baffled curiosity, or resentment ▶ v (-ques, -quing, -qued) hurt the pride of

piqué [pee-kay] n (pl -s) stiff ribbed cotton fabric

piqued v ▷ pique

piques n, v ▷ pique

piqués n ▷ piqué

piquing v ▷ pique

piquet [pik-ket] n (pl -s) card game for two

piquets n ▷ piquet

piracies n ▷ pirate

piracy n ▷ pirate

piranha n (pl -s) small fierce freshwater fish of tropical America

piranhas n ▷ piranha

pirate n (pl -s) sea robber ▶ v (-tes, -ting, -ted) sell or reproduce (artistic work etc.) illegally > **piracy** n (pl -cies) > **piratical** adj

pirated v ▷ pirate

pirates n, v ▷ pirate

piratical adj ▷ pirate

pirating v ▷ pirate

pirouette v, n (pl -s) (make) a spinning turn balanced on the toes of one foot

pirouettes n ▷ pirouette

pistachio n (pl -s) edible nut of a Mediterranean tree

pistachios n ▷ pistachio

piste [peest] n (pl -s) ski slope

pistes n ▷ piste

pistil n (pl -s) seed-bearing part of a flower

pistils n ▷ pistil

pistol n (pl -s) short-barrelled handgun

pistols n ▷ pistol

piston n (pl -s) cylindrical part in an engine that slides to and fro in a cylinder

pistons n ▷ piston

pit n (pl -s) deep hole in the ground ▷ orchestra pit ▶ v (-s, -tting, -tteds) mark with small dents or scars

pitch[1] v (-es, -ing, -ed) throw, hurl ▶ n (pl -es) area marked out for playing sport

pitch[2] n dark sticky substance obtained from tar

pitched v ▷ pitch[1]

pitches v, n ▷ pitch[1]

pitching v ▷ pitch[1]

pitchblende n (pl -s) mineral composed largely of uranium oxide, yielding radium

pitchblendes n ▷ pitchblende

pitcher n (pl -s) large jug with a narrow neck

pitchers n ▷ pitcher

pitchfork n (pl -s) large long-handled fork for lifting hay ▶ v (-s, -ing, -ed) thrust abruptly or violently

pitchforked v ▷ pitchfork

pitchforking v ▷ pitchfork

pitchforks n, v ▷ pitchfork

piteous, pitiable adj arousing pity

pitfall n (pl -s) hidden difficulty or danger

pitfalls n ▷ pitfall

pith n (pl -s) soft white lining of the rind of oranges etc.

pithier adj ▷ pithy

pithiest adj ▷ pithy

piths n ▷ pith

pithy adj (-thier, -thiest) short and full of meaning

pitiable adj ▷ piteous

pitied v ▷ pity

pities n, v ▷ pity

pitiful adj arousing pity > **pitifully** adv

pitifully adv ▷ pitiful

pitiless adj feeling no pity or mercy > **pitilessly** adv

pitilessly adv ▷ pitiless

piton [peet-on] n (pl -s) metal spike used in climbing to secure a rope

pitons n ▷ piton

pits n, v ▷ pit

pittance n (pl -s) very small amount of money

pittances n ▷ pittance

pitted v ▷ pit

pitting v ▷ pit

pituitaries n ▷ pituitary

pituitary n (pl -ies) gland at the base of the brain, that helps to control growth

pity n (pl -ties) sympathy or sorrow for others' suffering ▶ v (-ies, -ying, -ied) feel pity for

pitying v ▷ pity

pivot n (pl -s) central shaft on which something turns ▶ v (-s, -ing, -ed) provide with or turn on a pivot

pivotal adj of crucial importance

pivoted v ▷ pivot

pivoting v ▷ pivot

pivots n, v ▷ pivot

pix n (Informal) ▷ pic

pixie n (pl -s) (in folklore) fairy

pixies n ▷ pixie

pizza n (pl -s) flat disc of dough covered with a wide variety of savoury toppings and baked

pizzas n ▷ pizza

pizzazz n (pl -es) (Informal) attractive combination of energy and style
pizzazzes n ▷ pizzazz
pizzicato [pit-see-kah-toe] adj (MUSIC) played by plucking the string of a violin etc. with the finger
placard n (pl -s) notice that is carried or displayed in public
placards n ▷ placard
placate v (-tes, -ting, -ted) make (someone) stop feeling angry or upset > **placatory** adj
placated v ▷ placate
placates v ▷ placate
placating v ▷ placate
placatory adj ▷ placate
place n (pl -s) particular part of an area or space ▶ v (-ces, -cing, -ced) put in a particular place
placed v ▷ place
places n, v ▷ place
placebo [plas-see-bo] n (pl -bos, -boes) sugar pill etc. given to an unsuspecting patient instead of an active drug
placeboes n ▷ placebo
placebos n ▷ placebo
placenta [plass-ent-a] n (pl -tas, -tae) organ formed in the womb during pregnancy, providing nutrients for the fetus > **placental** adj
placentae n ▷ placenta
placental adj ▷ placenta
placentas n ▷ placenta
placid adj (-er, -est) not easily excited or upset, calm > **placidity** n (pl -ties)
placider adj ▷ placid
placidest adj ▷ placid
placidities n ▷ placid
placidity n ▷ placid
placing v ▷ place
plagiarize [play-jer-ize] v (-zes, -zing, -zed) steal ideas, passages, etc. from (someone else's work) and present them as one's own > **plagiarism** n (pl -s)
plagiarism n ▷ plagiarize
plagiarisms n ▷ plagiarize
plagiarized v ▷ plagiarize
plagiarizes v ▷ plagiarize
plagiarizing v ▷ plagiarize
plague n (pl -s) fast-spreading fatal disease ▶ v (-gues, -guing, -gued) trouble or annoy continually
plagued v ▷ plague
plagues n, v ▷ plague
plaguing v ▷ plague
plaice n (pl plaice) edible European flatfish

plaid n (pl -s) long piece of tartan cloth worn as part of Highland dress
plaids n ▷ plaid
plain (-er, -est) adj easy to see or understand ▶ n (pl -s) large stretch of level country > **plainly** adv > **plainness** n (pl -es)
plainer adj ▷ plain
plainest adj ▷ plain
plainly adj ▷ plain
plainness n ▷ plain
plainnesses n ▷ plain
plains n ▷ plain
plainsong n (pl -s) unaccompanied singing, esp. in a medieval church
plainsongs n ▷ plainsong
plaintiff n (pl -s) person who sues in a court of law
plaintiffs n ▷ plaintiff
plaintive adj sad, mournful > **plaintively** adv
plaintively adv ▷ plaintive
plait [platt] n (pl -s) intertwined length of hair ▶ v (-s, -ing, -ed) intertwine separate strands in a pattern
plaited v ▷ plait
plaiting v ▷ plait
plaits n, v ▷ plait
plan n (pl -s) way thought out to do or achieve something ▶ v (-s, -nning, -nned) arrange beforehand > **planner** n (pl -s)
plane[1] n (pl -s) aeroplane ▶ adj perfectly flat or level ▶ v (-nes, -ning, -ned) glide or skim
plane[2] n (pl -s) tool for smoothing wood ▶ v (-nes, -ning, -ned) smooth (wood) with a plane
plane[3] n (pl -s) tree with broad leaves
planed v ▷ plane[1, 2]
planes n, v ▷ plane[1, 2, 3]
planet n (pl -s) large body in space that revolves round the sun or another star > **planetary** adj
planetaria n ▷ planetarium
planetarium n (pl -iums, -ia) building where the movements of the stars, planets, etc. are shown by projecting lights on the inside of a dome
planetariums n ▷ planetarium
planetary adj ▷ planet
planets n ▷ planet
plangent adj (of sounds) mournful and resounding
planing v ▷ plane[1, 2]
plank n (pl -s) long flat piece of sawn timber
planks n ▷ plank
plankton n (pl -s) minute animals and plants floating in the surface water of a sea or lake

planktons *n* ▷ plankton
planned *v* ▷ plan
planner *n* ▷ plan
planners *n* ▷ plan
planning *v* ▷ plan
plans *n, v* ▷ plan
plant *n* (*pl* -s) living organism that grows in the ground and has no power to move ▶ *v* (-s, -ing, -ed) put in the ground to grow
plantain¹ *n* (*pl* -s) low-growing wild plant with broad leaves
plantain² *n* (-s) tropical fruit like a green banana
plantains *n* ▷ plantain¹, ²
plantation *n* (*pl* -s) estate for the cultivation of tea, tobacco, etc.
plantations *n* ▷ plantation
planted *v* ▷ plant
planter *n* (*pl* -s) owner of a plantation
planters *n* ▷ planter
planting *v* ▷ plant
plants *n, v* ▷ plant
plaque *n* (*pl* -s) inscribed commemorative stone or metal plate
plaques *n* ▷ plaque
plasma *n* (*pl* -s) clear liquid part of blood
plasmas *n* ▷ plasma
plaster *n* (*pl* -s) mixture of lime, sand, etc. for coating walls ▶ *v* (-s, -ing, -ed) cover with plaster
plastered *adj* (*Slang*) drunk ▶ *v* ▷ plaster
plastering *v* ▷ plaster
plasters *n, v* ▷ plaster
plastic *n* (*pl* -s) synthetic material that can be moulded when soft but sets in a hard long-lasting shape ▶ *adj* made of plastic
plasticities *n* ▷ plasticity
plasticity *n* (*pl* -ties) ability to be moulded
plastics *n* ▷ plastic
plate *n* (*pl* -s) shallow dish for holding food ▶ *v* (-tes, -ting, -ted) cover with a thin coating of gold, silver, or other metal ▷ plateful *n* (*pl* -s)
plateau *n* (*pl* -teaus, -teaux) area of level high land
plateaus *n* ▷ plateau
plateaux *n* ▷ plateau
plated *v* ▷ plate
plateful *n* ▷ plate
platefuls *n* ▷ plate
platen *n* (*pl* -s) roller of a typewriter, against which the paper is held
platens *n* ▷ platen
plates *n, v* ▷ plate
platform *n* (*pl* -s) raised floor
platforms *n* ▷ platform

plating *v* ▷ plate
platinum *n* (*pl* -s) (CHEM) valuable silvery-white metal
platinums *n* ▷ platinum
platitude *n* (*pl* -s) remark that is true but not interesting or original ▷ platitudinous *adj*
platitudes *n* ▷ platitude
platitudinous *adj* ▷ platitude
platonic *adj* (of a relationship) friendly or affectionate but not sexual
platoon *n* (*pl* -s) smaller unit within a company of soldiers
platoons *n* ▷ platoon
platteland *n* (*pl* -s) (S AFR) rural district
plattelands *n* ▷ plattelands
platter *n* (*pl* -s) large dish
platters *n* ▷ platter
platypus *n* (*pl* -es) Australian egg-laying amphibious mammal, with dense fur, webbed feet, and a ducklike bill (also **duck-billed platypus**)
platypuses *n* ▷ platypus
plaudits *pl n* expressions of approval
plausible *adj* apparently true or reasonable ▷ plausibly *adv* ▷ plausibility *n* (*pl* -ties)
plausibilities *n* ▷ plausible
plausibility *n* ▷ plausible
plausibly *adj* ▷ plausible
play *v* (-s, -ing, -ed) occupy oneself in (a game or recreation) ▶ *n* (*pl* -s) story performed on stage or broadcast
playboy *n* (*pl* -s) rich man who lives only for pleasure
playboys *n* ▷ playboy
playcentre *n* (*pl* -s) (NZ & S AFR) centre for preschool children run by parents
playcentres *n* ▷ playcentre
played *v* ▷ play
player *n* (*pl* -s) person who plays a game or sport
players *n* ▷ player
playful *adj* lively
playgroup *n* (*pl* -s) regular meeting of very young children for supervised play
playgroups *n* ▷ playgroup
playhouse *n* theatre
playhouses *n* ▷ playhouse
playing *v* ▷ play
plays *v, n* ▷ play
playschool *n* (*pl* -s) nursery group for young children
playschools *n* ▷ playschool
plaything *n* toy
playthings *n* ▷ plaything
playwright *n* author of plays

playwrights n ▷ playwright

plaza n (pl -s) open space or square

  plazas n ▷ plaza

plea n (pl -s) serious or urgent request, entreaty

  pleas n ▷ plea

plead v (-s, -ing, -ed) ask urgently or with deep feeling (LAW)

  pleaded v ▷ plead

  pleading v ▷ plead

  pleads v ▷ plead

pleasant adj (-er, -est) pleasing, enjoyable > **pleasantly** adv

  pleasanter adj ▷ pleasant

  pleasantest adj ▷ pleasant

  pleasantly adv ▷ pleasant

  pleasantries n ▷ pleasantry

pleasantry n (pl -ries) polite or joking remark

please v (-ses, -sing, -sed) give pleasure or satisfaction to ▶ adv polite word of request > **pleased** adj > **pleasing** adj

  pleased v, adj ▷ please

  pleasing v, adj ▷ please

  pleases v ▷ please

pleasurable adj giving pleasure > **pleasurably** adv

  pleasurably adv ▷ pleasurable

pleasure n (pl -s) feeling of happiness and satisfaction

  pleasures n ▷ pleasure

pleat n (pl -s) fold made by doubling material back on itself ▶ v (-s, -ing, -ed) arrange (material) in pleats

  pleated v ▷ pleat

  pleating v ▷ pleat

  pleats n, v ▷ pleat

plebeian [pleb-ee-an] adj of the lower social classes ▶ n (pl -s) (also **pleb**) member of the lower social classes

  plebeians n ▷ plebeian

plebiscite [pleb-iss-ite] n (pl -s) decision by direct voting of the people of a country

  plebiscites n ▷ plebiscite

  plectra n ▷ plectrum

plectrum n (pl -rums, -ra) small implement for plucking the strings of a guitar etc.

  plectrums n ▷ plectrum

pledge n (pl -s) solemn promise ▶ v (-ges, -ging, -ged) promise solemnly

  pledged v ▷ pledge

  pledges n, v ▷ pledge

  pledging v ▷ pledge

plenary adj (of a meeting) attended by all members

plenipotentiary adj having full powers

▶ n diplomat or representative having full powers

plenitude n (pl -s) completeness, abundance

  plenitudes n ▷ plenitude

plenteous adj plentiful

  plenties n ▷ plenty

plenty n (pl -ties) large amount or number

plentiful adj existing in large amounts or numbers > **plentifully** adv

  plentifully adv ▷ plentiful

pleonasm n (pl -s) use of more words than necessary

  pleonasms n ▷ pleonasm

plethora n (pl -s) excess

  plethoras n ▷ plethora

  pleurisies n ▷ pleurisy

pleurisy n (pl -sies) inflammation of the membrane covering the lungs

  pliabilities n ▷ pliable

  pliability n ▷ pliable

pliable adj easily bent > **pliability** n (pl -ties)

  pliancies n ▷ pliant

  pliancy n ▷ pliant

pliant adj pliable > **pliancy** n (pl -cies)

  plied v ▷ ply

  plies v, n ▷ ply

pliers pl n tool with hinged arms and jaws for gripping

plight[1] n (pl -s) difficult or dangerous situation

plight[2] v (-s, -ing, -ed) pledge

  plighted v ▷ plight[2]

  plighting v ▷ plight[2]

  plights n, v ▷ plight[1], [2]

plimsolls pl n (BRIT) rubber-soled canvas shoes

plinth n (pl -s) slab forming the base of a statue, column, etc.

  plinths n ▷ plinth

plod v (-s, -dding, -dded) walk with slow heavy steps > **plodder** n (pl -s)

  plodded v ▷ plod

  plodder n ▷ plod

  plodders n ▷ plod

  plodding v ▷ plod

  plods v ▷ plod

plonk[1] v (-s, -ing, -ed) put (something) down heavily and carelessly

plonk[2] n (pl -s) (Informal) cheap inferior wine

  plonked v ▷ plonk[1]

  plonking v ▷ plonk[1]

  plonks v, n ▷ plonk[1], [2]

plop n (pl -s) sound of an object falling into water without a splash ▶ v (-s, -pping, -pped) make this sound

  plopped v ▷ plop

  plopping v ▷ plop

plops *n, v* ▷ plop

plot¹ *n (pl -s)* secret plan to do something illegal or wrong ▶ *v (-s, -tting, -tted)* plan secretly, conspire

plot² *n (-s)* small piece of land

plotted *v* ▷ plot¹

plotting *v* ▷ plot¹

plots *n, v* ▷ plot¹, ²

plough *n (pl -s)* agricultural tool for turning over soil ▶ *v (-s, -ing, -ed)* turn over (earth) with a plough > **ploughman** *n (pl -men)*

ploughed *v* ▷ plough

ploughing *v* ▷ plough

ploughman *n* ▷ plough

ploughmen *n* ▷ plough

ploughs *n, v* ▷ plough

ploughshare *n (pl -s)* blade of a plough

ploughshares *n* ▷ ploughshare

plover *n (pl -s)* shore bird with a straight bill and long pointed wings

plovers *n* ▷ plover

ploy *n (pl -s)* manoeuvre designed to gain an advantage

ploys *n* ▷ ploy

pluck *v (-s, -ing, -ed)* pull or pick off ▶ *n (pl -s)* courage

plucked *v* ▷ pluck

pluckier *adj* ▷ plucky

pluckiest *adj* ▷ plucky

pluckily *adj* ▷ plucky

plucking *v* ▷ pluck

plucks *v, n* ▷ pluck

plucky *adj (-kier, -kiest)* brave > **pluckily** *adv*

plug *n (pl -s)* thing fitting into and filling a hole ▶ *v (-s, -gging, -gged)* block or seal (a hole or gap) with a plug

plugged *v* ▷ plug

plugging *v* ▷ plug

plugs *n, v* ▷ plug

plum *n (pl -s)* oval usu. dark red fruit with a stone in the middle ▶ *adj* dark purplish-red

plumage *n (pl -s)* bird's feathers

plumages *n* ▷ plumage

plumb *v (-s, -ing, -ed)* understand (something obscure) ▶ *adv* exactly

plumbed *v* ▷ plumb

plumber *n (pl -s)* person who fits and repairs pipes and fixtures for water and drainage systems

plumbers *n* ▷ plumber

plumbing *n* pipes and fixtures used in water and drainage systems ▶ *v* ▷ plumb

plumbs *v* ▷ plumb

plume *n (pl -s)* feather, esp. one worn as an ornament

plumes *n* ▷ plume

plummet *v (-s, -ing, -ed)* plunge downward

plummeted *v* ▷ plummet

plummeting *v* ▷ plummet

plummets *v* ▷ plummet

plump¹ *adj (-er, -est)* moderately or attractively fat > **plumpness** *n (pl -es)*

plump² *v (-s, -ing, -ed)* sit or fall heavily and suddenly

plumper *adj* ▷ plump¹

plumpest *adj* ▷ plump¹

plumped *v* ▷ plump²

plumping *v* ▷ plump²

plumpness *n* ▷ plump¹

plumpnesses *n* ▷ plump

plumps *v* ▷ plump²

plums *n* ▷ plum

plunder *v (-s, -ing, -ed)* take by force, esp. in time of war ▶ *n (pl -s)* things plundered, spoils

plundered *v* ▷ plunder

plundering *v* ▷ plunder

plunders *v, n* ▷ plunder

plunge *v (-ges, -ging, -ged)* put or throw forcibly or suddenly (into) ▶ *n (pl -s)* plunging, dive

plunged *v* ▷ plunge

plunger *n (pl -s)* rubber suction cup used to clear blocked pipes

plungers *n* ▷ plunger

plunges *v, n* ▷ plunge

plunging *v* ▷ plunge

pluperfect *adj, n (pl -s)* (GRAMMAR) (tense) expressing an action completed before a past time, e.g. *had gone* in *his wife had gone already*

pluperfects *n* ▷ pluperfect

plural *adj* of or consisting of more than one ▶ *n (pl -s)* word indicating more than one

plurals *n* ▷ plural

pluralism *n (pl -s)* existence and toleration of a variety of peoples, opinions, etc. in a society > **pluralist** *n (pl -s)* > **pluralistic** *adj*

pluralisms *n* ▷ pluralism

pluralist *n* ▷ pluralism

pluralists *n* ▷ pluralism

pluralistic *adj* ▷ pluralism

plus *prep, adj* indicating addition ▶ *adj* more than zero ▶ *n (pl -es)* sign (+) denoting addition

pluses *n* ▷ plus

plush *n (pl -es)* fabric with long velvety pile ▶ *adj (-er, -est)* (*also* **plushy**) (-ier, -iest) luxurious

plusher *adj* ▷ plush

plushest *adj* ▷ plush

plushes *n* ▷ plush

plushier adj ▷ plush
plushiest adj ▷ plush
plutocrat n (pl -s) person who is powerful because of being very rich > **plutocratic** adj
plutocratic adj ▷ plutocrat
plutocrats n ▷ plutocrat
plutonium n (pl -s) (CHEM) radioactive metallic element used esp. in nuclear reactors and weapons
plutoniums n ▷ plutonium
ply¹ v (-ies, -ying, -ied) work at (a job or trade)
ply² n (pl -ies) thickness of wool, fabric, etc.
plying v ▷ ply¹
plywood n (pl -s) board made of thin layers of wood glued together
plywoods n ▷ plywood
pneumatic adj worked by or inflated with wind or air
pneumonia n (pl -s) inflammation of the lungs
pneumonias n ▷ pneumonia

> **po** n (pos). A po is an informal word for a chamber pot. This is a good word to have ready in case you see an opportunity to play a good word beginning with P next to a word ending in O, or vice versa. Po scores 4 points.

poach¹ v (-es, -ing, -ed) catch (animals) illegally on someone else's land
poach² v (-es, -ing, -ed) simmer (food) gently in liquid
poached v ▷ poach
poacher n (pl -s) person who catches animals illegally on someone else's land
poachers n ▷ poacher
poaches v ▷ poach
poaching v ▷ poach
pocket n (pl -s) small bag sewn into clothing for carrying things ▶ v (-s, -ing, -ed) put into one's pocket ▶ adj small
pocketed v ▷ pocket
pocketing v ▷ pocket
pockets n, v ▷ pocket
pockmarked adj (of the skin) marked with hollow scars where diseased spots have been
pod n (pl -s) long narrow seed case of peas, beans, etc.
podgier adj ▷ podgy
podgiest adj ▷ podgy
pods n ▷ pod
podgy adj (-gier, -giest) short and fat
podia n ▷ podium
podium n (pl -diums, -dia) small raised platform for a conductor or speaker
podiums n ▷ podium

poem n (pl -s) imaginative piece of writing in rhythmic lines
poems n ▷ poem
poep n (pl -s) (S AFR) (Slang) emission of gas from the anus
poeps n ▷ poep
poesies n ▷ poesy
poesy n (pl -sies) (Obs) poetry
poet n (pl -s) writer of poems
poetic, poetical adj of or like poetry > **poetically** adv
poetical adj ▷ poetic
poetically adv ▷ poetic
poetries n ▷ poetry
poetry n (pl -ries) poems
poets n ▷ poet
pogrom n (pl -s) organized persecution and massacre
pogroms n ▷ pogrom
poignancies n ▷ poignant
poignancy n ▷ poignant
poignant adj sharply painful to the feelings
> **poignancy** n (pl -cies)
poinsettia n (pl -s) Central American shrub widely grown for its clusters of scarlet leaves, which resemble petals
poinsettias n ▷ poinsettia
point n (pl -s) main idea in a discussion, argument, etc. ▶ v (-s, -ing, -ed) show the direction or position of something or draw attention to it by extending a finger or other pointed object towards it
pointed adj having a sharp end ▶ v ▷ point > **pointedly** adv
pointedly adv ▷ pointed
pointer n (pl -s) helpful hint
pointers n ▷ pointer
pointing v ▷ point
pointless adj meaningless, irrelevant
points n, v ▷ point
poise n (pl -s) calm dignified manner
poised adj absolutely ready
poises n ▷ poise
poison n (pl -s) substance that kills or injures when swallowed or absorbed ▶ v (-s, -ing, -ed) give poison to > **poisoner** n (pl -s) > **poisonous** adj
poisoned v ▷ poison
poisoner n ▷ poison
poisoners n ▷ poison
poisoning v ▷ poison
poisonous adj ▷ poison
poisons n, v ▷ poison
poke v (-kes, -king, -ked) jab or prod with one's finger, a stick, etc. ▶ n (pl -s) poking

poked v ▷ poke

poker[1] n (pl -s) metal rod for stirring a fire

poker[2] n (pl -s) card game in which players bet on the hands dealt

pokers n ▷ poker[1, 2]

pokier adj ▷ poky

pokiest adj ▷ poky

poking v ▷ poke

pokes v, n ▷ poke

poky adj (-kier, -kiest) small and cramped

polar adj of or near either of the earth's poles

polarize v (-zes, -zing, -zed) form or cause to form into groups with directly opposite views > **polarization** n (pl -s)

polarization n ▷ polarize

polarizations n ▷ polarize

polarized v ▷ polarize

polarizes v ▷ polarize

polarizing v ▷ polarize

polder n (pl -s) land reclaimed from the sea, esp. in the Netherlands

polders n ▷ polder

pole[1] n (pl -s) long rounded piece of wood etc.

pole[2] n (pl -s) point furthest north or south on the earth's axis of rotation

poleaxe v (-xes, -xing, -xed) hit or stun with a heavy blow

poleaxed v ▷ poleaxe

poleaxes v ▷ poleaxe

poleaxing v ▷ poleaxe

polecat n (pl -s) small animal of the weasel family

polecats n ▷ polecat

polemic [pol-**em**-ik] n (pl -s) fierce attack on or defence of a particular opinion, belief, etc. > **polemical** adj

polemical adj ▷ polemic

polemics n ▷ polemic

poles n ▷ pole[1, 2]

police n organized force in a state which keeps law and order ▶ v (-ces, -cing, -ced) control or watch over with police or a similar body

policed v ▷ police

policeman, policewoman n (pl -men, -women) member of a police force

policemen n ▷ policeman

polices v ▷ police

policewomen n ▷ policeman

policies n ▷ policy[1, 2]

policing v ▷ police

policy[1] n (pl -cies) plan of action adopted by a person, group, or state

policy[2] n (pl -cies) document containing an insurance contract

polio n (pl -s) disease affecting the spinal cord, which often causes paralysis (also **poliomyelitis**)

polios n ▷ polio

polish v (-es, -ing, -ed) make smooth and shiny by rubbing ▶ n (pl -es) substance used for polishing

polished adj accomplished ▶ v ▷ polish

polishing v ▷ polish

polishes v, n ▷ polish

polite adj showing consideration for others in one's manners, speech, etc. > **politely** adv > **politeness** n (pl -es)

politely adv ▷ polite

politeness n ▷ polite

politenesses n ▷ politeness

politic adj wise and likely to prove advantageous

political adj of the state, government, or public administration > **politically** adv

politically adv ▷ political

politician n (pl -s) person actively engaged in politics, esp. a member of parliament

politicians n ▷ politician

politics n winning and using of power to govern society

polka n (pl -s) lively 19th-century dance

polkas n ▷ polka

poll n (pl -s) (also **opinion poll**) questioning of a random sample of people to find out general opinion ▶ v (-s, -ing, -ed) receive (votes)

pollarded adj (of a tree) growing very bushy because its top branches have been cut short

polled v ▷ poll

pollen n (pl -s) fine dust produced by flowers to fertilize other flowers

pollens ▷

pollinate v (-tes, -ting, -ted) fertilize with pollen

pollinated v ▷ pollinate

pollinates v ▷ pollinate

pollinating v ▷ pollinate

polling v ▷ poll

polls n, v ▷ poll

pollster n (pl -s) person who conducts opinion polls

pollsters n ▷ pollster

pollute v (-tes, -ting, -ted) contaminate with something poisonous or harmful > **pollution** n (pl -s)

pollutant n (pl -s) something that pollutes

pollutants n ▷ pollutant

polluted v ▷ pollute

pollutes v ▷ pollute

polluting v ▷ pollute

pollution n ▷ pollute

pollutions n ▷ pollute

polo n (pl -s) game like hockey played by teams of players on horseback

polonaise n (pl -s) old stately dance

polonaises n ▷ polonaise

polonium n (pl -s) (CHEM) radioactive element that occurs in trace amounts in uranium ores

poloniums n ▷ polonium

polos n ▷ polo

poltergeist n (pl -s) spirit believed to move furniture and throw objects around

poltergeists n ▷ poltergeist

poltroon n (pl -s) (Obs) utter coward

poltroons n ▷ poltroon

polyandries n ▷ polyandry

polyandry n (pl -ries) practice of having more than one husband at the same time

polyanthus n (pl -es) garden primrose

polyanthuses n ▷ polyanthus

polychromatic adj many-coloured

polyester n (pl -s) synthetic material used to make plastics and textile fibres

polyesters n ▷ polyester

polygamies n ▷ polygamy

polygamist n ▷ polygamy

polygamists n ▷ polygamy

polygamous adj ▷ polygamy

polygamy [pol-ig-a-mee] n (pl -mies) practice of having more than one husband or wife at the same time > **polygamous** adj > **polygamist** n (pl -s)

polyglot adj, n (pl -s) (person) able to speak or write several languages

polyglots n ▷ polyglot

polygon n (pl -s) geometrical figure with three or more angles and sides > **polygonal** adj

polygonal adj ▷ polygon

polygons n ▷ polygon

polyhedra n ▷ polyhedron

polyhedron n (pl -rons, -ra) solid figure with four or more sides

polyhedrons n ▷ polyhedron

polymer n (pl -s) chemical compound with large molecules made of simple molecules of the same kind

polymerize v (-zes, -zing, -zed) form into polymers > **polymerization** n (pl -s)

polymerization n ▷ polymerize

polymerizations n ▷ polymerize

polymerized v ▷ polymerize

polymerizes v ▷ polymerize

polymerizing v ▷ polymerize

polymers n ▷ polymer

polyp n (pl -s) small simple sea creature with a hollow cylindrical body

polyps n ▷ polyp

polyphonic adj (MUSIC) consisting of several melodies played simultaneously

polystyrene n (pl -s) synthetic material used esp. as white rigid foam for packing and insulation

polystyrenes n ▷ polystyrene

polytechnic n (pl -s) (in New Zealand and formerly in Britain) college offering courses in many subjects at and below degree level

polytechnics n ▷ polytechnic

polytheism n (pl -s) belief in many gods > **polytheistic** adj

polytheisms n ▷ polytheism

polytheistic n ▷ polytheism

polythene n (pl -s) light plastic used for bags etc.

polythenes n ▷ polythene

polyunsaturated adj of a group of fats that do not form cholesterol in the blood

polyurethane n (pl -s) synthetic material used esp. in paints

polyurethanes n ▷ polyurethane

pom n (pl -s) (AUST & NZ) (Slang) person from England (also **pommy**) (pl -mmies)

pomander n (pl -s) (container for) a mixture of sweet-smelling petals, herbs, etc.

pomanders n ▷ pomander

pomegranate n (pl -s) round tropical fruit with a thick rind containing many seeds in a red pulp

pomegranates n ▷ pomegranate

pommel n (pl -s) raised part on the front of a saddle

pommels n ▷ pommel

pommies n ▷ pom

pommy n ▷ pom

poms n ▷ pom

pomp n (pl -s) stately display or ceremony

pomps n ▷ pomp

pompom n (pl -s) decorative ball of tufted wool, silk, etc.

pompoms n ▷ pompom

pomposities n ▷ pompous

pomposity n ▷ pompous

pompous adj foolishly serious and grand, self-important > **pompously** adv > **pomposity** n (pl -ties)

pompously adv ▷ pompous

poncho n (pl -os) loose circular cloak with a hole for the head

ponchos n ▷ poncho

pond n (pl -s) small area of still water

ponds n ▷ pond

ponder v (-s, -ing, -ed) think thoroughly or

deeply (about)

pondered v ▷ ponder

pondering v ▷ ponder

ponderous adj serious and dull > **ponderously** adv

ponderously adv ▷ ponderous

ponders v ▷ ponder

pong v, n (pl -s) (Informal) (give off) a strong unpleasant smell

pongs n ▷ pong

ponies n ▷ pony

pontiff n (pl -s) the Pope

pontiffs n ▷ pontiff

pontificate v (-tes, -ting, -ted) state one's opinions as if they were the only possible correct ones ▶ n (pl -s) period of office of a Pope

pontificated v ▷ pontificate

pontificates v, n ▷ pontificate

pontificating v ▷ pontificate

pontoon[1] n (pl -s) floating platform supporting a temporary bridge

pontoon[2] n (pl -s) gambling card game

pontoons n ▷ pontoon[1, 2]

pony n (pl -nies) small horse

ponytail n (pl -s) long hair tied in one bunch at the back of the head

ponytails n ▷ ponytail

poodle n (pl -s) dog with curly hair often clipped fancifully

poodles n ▷ poodle

pool[1] n (pl -s) small body of still water

pool[2] n (pl -s) shared fund or group of workers or resources ▶ pl (BRIT) ▷ football pools ▶ v (-s, -ing, -ed) put in a common fund

pooled v ▷ pool[2]

pooling v ▷ pool[2]

pools n, v ▷ pool[1, 2]

poop n (pl -s) raised part at the back of a sailing ship

poops n ▷ poop

poor adj having little money and few possessions

poorlier adj ▷ poorly

poorliest adj ▷ poorly

poorly adv in a poor manner ▶ adj (-lier, -liest) not in good health

pop[1] v (-s, -pping, -pped) make or cause to make a small explosive sound (Informal) ▶ n small explosive sound (BRIT)

pop[2] n (pl -s) music of general appeal, esp. to young people

pop[3] n (pl -s) (Informal) father

popcorn n (pl -s) grains of maize heated until they puff up and burst

popcorns n ▷ popcorn

pope n (pl -s) head of the Roman Catholic Church

popes n ▷ pope

poplar n (pl -s) tall slender tree

poplars n ▷ poplar

poplin n (pl -s) ribbed cotton material

poplins n ▷ poplin

poppadom n (pl -s) thin round crisp Indian bread

poppadoms n ▷ poppadom

popped v ▷ pop[1]

poppies n ▷ poppy

popping v ▷ pop[1]

poppy n (pl -ppies) plant with a large red flower

pops n ▷ pop

populace n (pl -s) the ordinary people

populaces n ▷ populace

popular adj widely liked and admired > **popularly** adv > **popularity** n (pl -ties)

popularize v (-zes, -zing, -zed) make popular

popularized v ▷ popularize

popularizes v ▷ popularize

popularizing v ▷ popularize

popularities n ▷ popular

popularity n ▷ popular

popularly adv ▷ popular

populate v (-tes, -ting, -ted) live in, inhabit

populated v ▷ populate

populates v ▷ populate

populating v ▷ populate

population n (pl -s) all the people who live in a particular place

populations n ▷ population

populous adj densely populated

porbeagle n (pl -s) kind of shark

porbeagles n ▷ porbeagle

porcelain n (pl -s) fine china

porcelains n ▷ porcelain

porch n (pl -es) covered approach to the entrance of a building

porches n ▷ porch

porcine adj of or like a pig

porcupine n (pl -s) animal covered with long pointed quills

porcupines n ▷ porcupine

pore n (pl -s) tiny opening in the skin or in the surface of a plant

pores n ▷ pore

pork n (pl -s) pig meat

porker n (pl -s) pig raised for food

porkers n ▷ porker

porks n ▷ pork

porn, porno adj, n (pl -s) (Informal) ▷ pornography, pornographic

pornographies n ▷ pornography
pornography n (pl -**hies**) writing, films, or pictures designed to be sexually exciting > **pornographic** adj
pornographer n (pl -**s**) producer of pornography
pornographers n ▷ pornographer
pornographic n ▷ pornography
pornos n ▷ porn
porns n ▷ porn
porosities n ▷ porous
porosity n ▷ porous
porous adj allowing liquid to pass through gradually > **porosity** n (pl -**ties**)
porphyries n ▷ porphyry
porphyry [por-fir-ee] n (pl -**ries**) reddish rock with large crystals in it
porpoise n (pl -**s**) fishlike sea mammal
porpoises n ▷ porpoise
porridge n (pl -**s**) breakfast food made of oatmeal cooked in water or milk
porridges n ▷ porridge
port[1] n (pl -**s**) (town with) a harbour
port[2] n (pl -**s**) left side of a ship or aircraft when facing the front of it
port[3] n (pl -**s**) sweet wine, usu. red
port[4] n (pl -**s**) opening in the side of a ship
portabilities n ▷ portable
portability n ▷ portable
portable adj easily carried > **portability** n (pl -**ties**)
portal n (pl -**s**) large imposing doorway or gate
portals n ▷ portal
portcullis n (pl -**es**) grating suspended above a castle gateway, that can be lowered to block the entrance
portcullises n ▷ portcullis
portend v (-**s**, -**ing**, -**ed**) be a sign of
portended v ▷ portend
portending v ▷ portend
portends v ▷ portend
portent n (pl -**s**) sign of a future event
portentous adj of great or ominous significance
portents n ▷ portent
porter[1] n (pl -**s**) man who carries luggage
porter[2] n (pl -**s**) doorman or gatekeeper of a building
porters n ▷ porter[1, 2]
portfolio n (pl -**s**) (flat case for carrying) examples of an artist's work
portfolios n ▷ portfolio
porthole n (pl -**s**) small round window in a ship or aircraft
portholes n ▷ porthole

portico n (pl -**coes**, -**cos**) porch or covered walkway with columns supporting the roof
porticoes n ▷ portico
porticos n ▷ portico
portion n (pl -**s**) part or share
portions n ▷ portion
portlier adj ▷ portly
portliest adj ▷ portly
portly adj (-**lier**, -**liest**) rather fat
portmanteau n (pl -**eaus**, -**eaux**) (Old-fashioned) large suitcase that opens into two compartments ▶ adj combining aspects of different things
portmanteaus n ▷ portmanteau
portmanteaux n ▷ portmanteau
portrait n (pl -**s**) picture of a person
portraits n ▷ portrait
portray v (-**s**, -**ing**, -**ed**) describe or represent by artistic means, as in writing or film > **portrayal** n (pl -**s**)
portrayal n ▷ portray
portrayals n ▷ portray
portrayed v ▷ portray
portraying v ▷ portray
portrays v ▷ portray
ports n ▷ port[1, 2, 3, 4]
pose v (-**ses**, -**sing**, -**sed**) place in or take up a particular position to be photographed or drawn ▶ n (pl -**s**) position while posing
posed v ▷ pose
poser n (pl -**s**) puzzling question
posers n ▷ poser
poses v, n ▷ pose
poseur n (pl -**s**) person who behaves in an affected way to impress others
poseurs n ▷ poseur
posies n ▷ posy
posing v ▷ pose
posh adj (Informal) smart, luxurious
posit [pozz-it] v (-**s**, -**ing**, -**ed**) lay down as a basis for argument
posited v ▷ posit
positing v ▷ posit
position n (pl -**s**) place ▶ v (-**s**, -**ing**, -**ed**) place
positioned v ▷ position
positioning v ▷ position
positions n, v ▷ position
posits v ▷ posit
positive adj feeling no doubts, certain (MATHS) > **positively** adv
positively adv ▷ positive
positron n (pl -**s**) (PHYSICS) particle with same mass as electron but positive charge
positrons n ▷ positron
posse [poss-ee] n (pl -**s**) (US) group of men

organized to maintain law and order

posses n ▷ posse

possess v (-es, -ing, -ed) have as one's property ▸ **possessor** n (pl -s)

possessed v ▷ possess

possesses v ▷ possess

possessing v ▷ possess

possession n (pl -s) state of possessing, ownership ▸ pl things a person possesses

possessions n ▷ possession

possessive adj wanting all the attention or love of another person ▸ **possessiveness** n

possessiveness n ▷ possessive

possessor n ▷ possess

possessors n ▷ possess

possibilities n ▷ possibility

possibility n ▷ possible

possible adj able to exist, happen, or be done ▸ n (pl -s) person or thing that might be suitable or chosen ▸ **possibility** n (pl -ties)

possibles n ▷ possible

possibly adv perhaps, not necessarily

possum n (pl -s) ▷ opossum (AUST & NZ) ▷ phalanger

possums n ▷ possum

post[1] n (pl -s) official system of delivering letters and parcels ▸ v (-s, -ing, -ed) send by post ▸ **postal** adj

post[2] n (pl -s) length of wood, concrete, etc. fixed upright to support or mark something ▸ v (-s, -ing, -ed) put up (a notice) in a public place

post[3] n (pl -s) job ▸ v (-s, -ing, -ed) send (a person) to a new place to work

postage n charge for sending a letter or parcel by post

postages n ▷ postage

postal adj ▷ post[1]

postbag n (pl -s) postman's bag

postbags n ▷ postbag

postcard n (pl -s) card for sending a message by post without an envelope

postcards n ▷ postcard

postcode n system of letters and numbers used to aid the sorting of mail

postcodes n ▷ postcode

postdate v (-tes, -ting, -ted) write a date on (a cheque) that is later than the actual date

postdated v ▷ postdate

postdates v ▷ postdate

postdating v ▷ postdate

posted v ▷ post[1, 2, 3]

poster n (pl -s) large picture or notice stuck on a wall

posterior n (pl -s) buttocks ▸ adj behind, at

the back of

posteriors n ▷ posterior

posterities n ▷ posterity

posterity n (pl -ties) future generations, descendants

postern n (pl -s) small back door or gate

posterns n ▷ postern

posters n ▷ poster

postgraduate n (pl -s) person with a degree who is studying for a more advanced qualification

postgraduates n ▷ postgraduate

posthaste adv with great speed

posthumous [poss-tume-uss] adj occurring after one's death ▸ **posthumously** adv

posthumously adv ▷ posthumous

postie n (pl -s) (SCOT, AUST & NZ) (Informal) postman

posties n ▷ postie

postilion, postillion n (pl -s) (HIST) person riding one of a pair of horses drawing a carriage

postilions n ▷ postilion

postillion n ▷ postilion

postillions n ▷ postilion

posting v ▷ post[1, 2, 3]

postman, postwoman n (pl -men, -women) person who collects and delivers post

postmark n (pl -s) official mark stamped on letters showing place and date of posting

postmarks n ▷ postmark

postmen n ▷ postman

postmaster, postmistress n (pl -s, -es) (in some countries) official in charge of a post office

postmasters n ▷ postmaster

postmistress n ▷ postmaster

postmistresses n ▷ postmaster

postmortem ▸ n (pl -s) medical examination of a body to establish the cause of death

postmortems n ▷ postmortem

postnatal adj occurring after childbirth

postpone v (-es, -ning, -ned) put off to a later time ▸ **postponement** n (pl -s)

postponed v ▷ postpone

postponement n ▷ postpone

postponements n ▷ postpone

postpones v ▷ postpone

postponing v ▷ postpone

posts n, v ▷ post[1, 2, 3]

postscript n (pl -s) passage added at the end of a letter

postscripts n ▷ postscript

postulant n (pl -s) candidate for admission to a religious order

postulants n ▷ postulant
postulate v (-tes, -ting, -ted) assume to be true as the basis of an argument or theory
  postulated v ▷ postulate
  postulates v ▷ postulate
  postulating v ▷ postulate
posture n (pl -s) position or way in which someone stands, walks, etc. ▶ v (-res, -ring, -red) behave in an exaggerated way to get attention
  postured v ▷ posture
  postures n, v ▷ posture
  posturing v ▷ posture
  postwomen n ▷ postman
posy n (pl -sies) small bunch of flowers
pot¹ n (pl -s) round deep container ▶ pl (informal) large amount ▶ v (-s, -tting, -tted) plant in a pot
pot² n (Slang) cannabis
potted adj grown in a pot ▶ v ▷ pot¹
  potting v ▷ pot¹
  pots n ▷ pot¹
potable [pote-a-bl] adj drinkable
potash n (pl -es) white powdery substance obtained from ashes and used as fertilizer
  potashes n ▷ potash
potassium n (pl -s) (CHEM) silvery metallic element
  potassiums n ▷ potassium
potato ▶ n (pl -oes) roundish starchy vegetable that grows underground
  potatoes n ▷ potato
poteen n (pl -s) (in Ireland) illegally made alcoholic drink
  poteens n ▷ poteen
  potencies n ▷ potent
  potency n ▷ potent
potent adj having great power or influence
  > **potency** n (pl -cies)
potentate n (pl -s) ruler or monarch
  potentates n ▷ potentate
potential adj possible but not yet actual ▶ n (pl -s) ability or talent not yet fully used
  > **potentially** adv > **potentiality** n (pl -ties)
  potentialities n ▷ potential
  potentiality n ▷ potential
  potentially adv ▷ potential
  potentials n ▷ potential
pothole n (pl -s) hole in the surface of a road
  potholer n ▷ potholing
  potholers n ▷ potholing
  potholes n ▷ pothole
potholing n (pl -s) sport of exploring underground caves > **potholer** n (pl -s)
  potholings n ▷ potholing

potion n (pl -s) dose of medicine or poison
  potions n ▷ potion
potoroo n (pl -s) Australian leaping rodent
  potoroos n ▷ potoroo
potpourri [po-poor-ee] n (pl -s) fragrant mixture of dried flower petals
  potpourris n ▷ potpourri
pottage n (pl -s) (Old-fashioned) thick soup or stew
  pottages n ▷ pottage
potter¹ n (pl -s) person who makes pottery
potter² v (-s, -ing, -ed) be busy in a pleasant but aimless way
  pottered v ▷ potter²
  potteries n ▷ pottery
  pottering v ▷ potter²
  potters n, v ▷ potter¹,²
pottery n (pl -ries) articles made from baked clay
  pottier adj ▷ potty
  potties n ▷ potty²
  pottiest adj ▷ potty
potty¹ adj (-ttier, -ttiest) (Informal) crazy or silly
potty² n (pl -tries) bowl used by a small child as a toilet
pouch n (pl -es) small bag
  pouches n ▷ pouch
pouf, pouffe [poof] n (pl -s) large solid cushion used as a seat
  pouffe n ▷ pouf
  pouffes n ▷ pouf
  poufs n ▷ pouf
poulterer n (pl -s) (BRIT) person who sells poultry
  poulterers n ▷ poulterer
poultice [pole-tiss] n (pl -s) moist dressing, often heated, applied to inflamed skin
  poultices n ▷ poultice
  poultries n ▷ poultry
poultry n (pl -ries) domestic fowls
pounce v (-ces, -cing, -ced) spring upon suddenly to attack or capture ▶ n (pl -s)
  pouncing
  pounced v ▷ pounce
  pouncing v ▷ pounce
  pounces v, n ▷ pounce
pound¹ n (pl -s) monetary unit of Britain and some other countries
pound² v (-s, -ing, -ed) hit heavily and repeatedly
pound³ n (pl -s) enclosure for stray animals or officially removed vehicles
  pounded v ▷ pound²
  pounding v ▷ pound²
  pounds n, v ▷ pound¹,³

pour v (-s, -ing, -ed) flow or cause to flow out in a stream
  poured v ▷ pour
  pouring v ▷ pour
  pours v ▷ pour
pout v (-s, -ing, -ed) thrust out one's lips, look sulky ▶ n (pl -s) pouting look
  pouted v ▷ pout
  pouting v ▷ pout
  pouts v, n ▷ pout
  poverties n ▷ poverty
poverty n (pl -ties) state of being without enough food or money
powder n (pl -s) substance in the form of tiny loose particles ▶ v (-s, -ing, -ed) apply powder to > **powdery** adj (-rier, -riest)
powdered adj, v ▷ powder
  powderier adj ▷ powder
  powderiest adj ▷ powder
  powdering v ▷ powder
  powders n, v ▷ powder
power n (pl -s) ability to do or act > **powerful** adj > **powerless** adj
powered adj having or operated by mechanical or electrical power
  powerful adj ▷ power
  powerless adj ▷ power
  powers n ▷ power
powwow n (pl -s) (Informal) talk or conference
  powwows n ▷ powwow
pox n (pl -es) disease in which skin pustules form
  poxes n ▷ pox

> **poz** adj. Poz is an old-fashioned short form of **positive**. This is a good word for a crowded board towards the end of the game, especially if you can form another word in the process, or form it on a bonus square. Poz scores 24 points.

  practicabilities n ▷ practicable
  practicability n ▷ practicable
practicable adj capable of being done successfully > **practicability** n (pl -ties)
practical adj involving experience or actual use rather than theory ▶ n (pl -s) examination in which something has to be done or made > **practically** adv
  practically adv ▷ practical
  practicals n ▷ practical
practice n (pl -s) something done regularly or habitually
  practices n ▷ practice
practise v (-ses, -sing, -sed) do repeatedly so as to gain skill

  practised v ▷ practise
  practises v ▷ practise
  practising v ▷ practise
practitioner n (pl -s) person who practises a profession
  practitioners n ▷ practitioner
pragmatic adj concerned with practical consequences rather than theory
  > **pragmatism** n (pl -s) > **pragmatist** n (pl -s)
  pragmatism n ▷ pragmatic
  pragmatisms n ▷ pragmatic
  pragmatist n ▷ pragmatic
  pragmatists n ▷ pragmatic
prairie n (pl -s) large treeless area of grassland, esp. in N America and Canada
  prairies n ▷ prairie
praise v (-ses, -sing, -sed) express approval or admiration of (someone or something) ▶ n (pl -s) something said or written to show approval or admiration > **praiseworthy** adj
  praised v ▷ praise
  praises v, n ▷ praise
  praiseworthy adj ▷ praise
  praising v ▷ praise
praline [prah-leen] n (pl -s) sweet made of nuts and caramelized sugar
  pralines n ▷ praline
pram n (pl -s) four-wheeled carriage for a baby, pushed by hand
  prams n ▷ pram
prance v (-ces, -cing, -ced) walk with exaggerated bouncing steps
  pranced v ▷ prance
  prances v ▷ prance
  prancing v ▷ prance
prang v, n (pl -s) (Slang) (have) a crash in a car or aircraft
  prangs n ▷ prang
prank n (pl -s) mischievous trick
  pranks n ▷ prank
prat n (pl -s) (BRIT, AUST & NZ) (Informal) stupid person
  prats n ▷ prat
prattle v (-les, -ling, -led) chatter in a childish or foolish way ▶ n (pl -s) childish or foolish talk
  prattled v ▷ prattle
  prattles v, n ▷ prattle
  prattling v ▷ prattle
prawn n (pl -s) edible shellfish like a large shrimp
  prawns n ▷ prawn
praxis n (pl praxises) practice as opposed to theory
  praxises n ▷ praxis
pray v (-s, -ing, -ed) say prayers

prayed v ▷ pray

prayer n (pl -s) thanks or appeal addressed to one's God

prayers n ▷ prayer

praying v ▷ pray

prays v ▷ pray

preach v (-es, -ing, -ed) give a talk on a religious theme as part of a church service

preached v ▷ preach

preaches v ▷ preach

preaching v ▷ preach

preacher n (pl -s) person who preaches, esp. in church

preachers n ▷ preacher

preamble n (pl -s) introductory part to something said or written

preambles n ▷ preamble

prearranged adj arranged beforehand

prebendaries n ▷ prebendary

prebendary n (pl -ries) clergyman who is a member of the chapter of a cathedral

precarious adj insecure, unsafe, likely to fall or collapse > **precariously** adv

precariously adv ▷ precarious

precaution n (pl -s) action taken in advance to prevent something bad happening > **precautionary** adj

precautionary adj ▷ precaution

precautions n ▷ precaution

precede v (-des, -ding, -ded) go or be before

preceded v ▷ precede

precedence [press-ee-denss] n (pl -s) formal order of rank or position

precedences n ▷ precedence

precedent n (pl -s) previous case or occurrence regarded as an example to be followed

precedents n ▷ precedent

precedes v ▷ precede

preceding v ▷ precede

precentor n (pl -s) person who leads the singing in a church

precentors n ▷ precentor

precept n (pl -s) rule of behaviour > **preceptive** adj

preceptive adj ▷ precept

precepts n ▷ precept

precinct n (pl -s) (BRIT, AUST & S AFR) area in a town closed to traffic ▶ pl surrounding region

precincts n ▷ precinct

precious adj of great value and importance

precipice n (pl -s) very steep face of cliff or rockface

precipices n ▷ precipice

precipitate v (-tes, -ting, -ted) cause to happen suddenly ▶ adj done rashly or hastily

▶ n (pl -s) (CHEM) substance precipitated from a solution > **precipitately** adv > **precipitation** n (pl -s) precipitating

precipitated v, n ▷ precipitate

precipitately adv ▷ precipitate

precipitates v, n ▷ precipitate

precipitating v ▷ precipitate

precipitation n ▷ precipitate

precipitations n ▷ precipitate

precipitous adj sheer

précis [pray-see] n (pl précis) short written summary of a longer piece ▶ v (-ses, -sing, -sed) make a précis of

precise adj (-r, -st) exact, accurate in every detail > **precisely** adv > **precision** n (pl -s)

précised v ▷ précis

précises v ▷ précis

precisely adv ▷ precise

preciser adj ▷ precise

precisest adj ▷ precise

précising v ▷ précis

precision n ▷ precise

precisions n ▷ precise

preclude v (-des, -ding, -ded) make impossible to happen

precluded v ▷ preclude

precludes v ▷ preclude

precluding v ▷ preclude

precocious adj having developed or matured early or too soon > **precocity** n (pl -ties)

precocities n ▷ precocious

precocity n ▷ precocious

precognition n (pl -s) alleged ability to foretell the future

precognitions n ▷ precognition

preconceived adj (of an idea) formed without real experience or reliable information > **preconception** n (pl -s)

preconception n ▷ preconceived

preconceptions n ▷ preconceive

precondition n (pl -s) something that must happen or exist before something else can

preconditions n ▷ precondition

precursor n (pl -s) something that precedes and is a signal of something else, forerunner

precursors n ▷ precursor

predate v (-tes, -ting, -ted) occur at an earlier date than

predated v ▷ predate

predates v ▷ predate

predating v ▷ predate

predator n (pl -s) predatory animal

predators n ▷ predators

predatory [pred-a-tree] adj habitually hunting and killing other animals for food

predecease v (**-ses, -sing, -sed**) die before (someone else)
  predeceased v ▷ predecease
  predeceases v ▷ predecease
  predeceasing v ▷ predecease
predecessor n (pl **-s**) person who precedes another in an office or position
  predecessors n ▷ predecessor
predestination n (pl **-s**) (THEOLOGY) belief that future events have already been decided by God or fate ▷ **predestined** adj
  predestinations n ▷ predestine
  predestined adj ▷ predestination
predetermined adj decided in advance
predicament n (pl **-s**) embarrassing or difficult situation
  predicaments n ▷ predicament
predicate n (pl **-tes**) (GRAMMAR) part of a sentence in which something is said about the subject, e.g. went home in I went home ▶ v (**-tes, -ting, -ted**) declare or assert
  predicated v ▷ predicate
  predicates n, v ▷ predicate
  predicating v ▷ predicate
predict v (**-s, -ing, -ed**) tell about in advance, prophesy > **predictable** adj > **prediction** n (pl **-s**)
  predictable adj ▷ predict
  predicted v ▷ predict
  predicting v ▷ predict
  prediction n ▷ predict
  predictions n ▷ predict
predictive adj relating to or able to make predictions
  predicts v ▷ predict
predilection n (pl **-s**) (Formal) preference or liking
  predilections n ▷ predilection
predispose v (**-ses, -sing, -sed**) influence (someone) in favour of something > **predisposition** n (pl **-s**)
  predisposed v ▷ predispose
  predisposes v ▷ predispose
  predisposing v ▷ predispose
  predisposition n ▷ predispose
  predispositions n ▷ predispose
predominate v (**-tes, -ting, -ted**) be the main or controlling element > **predominance** n (pl **-s**) > **predominant** adj > **predominantly** adv
  predominance n ▷ predominate
  predominances n ▷ predominance
  predominant n ▷ predominate
  predominantly adv ▷ predominate
  predominated v ▷ predominate
  predominates v ▷ predominate

predominating v ▷ predominate
preen v (**-s, -ing, -ed**) (of a bird) clean or trim (feathers) with the beak
  preened v ▷ preen
  preening v ▷ preen
  preens v ▷ preen
prefab n (pl **-s**) prefabricated house
prefabricated adj (of a building) manufactured in shaped sections for rapid assembly on site
  prefabs n ▷ prefab
preface [**pref-iss**] n (pl **-s**) introduction to a book ▶ v (**-ces, -cing, -ced**) serve as an introduction to (a book, speech, etc.) > **prefatory** adj
  prefaced v ▷ preface
  prefaces n, v ▷ preface
  prefacing v ▷ preface
  prefatory adj ▷ preface
prefect n (pl **-s**) senior pupil in a school, with limited power over others
  prefects n ▷ prefect
prefecture n (pl **-s**) office or area of authority of a prefect
  prefectures n ▷ prefecture
prefer v (**-s, -rring, -rred**) like better > **preference** n (pl **-s**)
preferable adj more desirable > **preferably** adv
  preferably adv ▷ preferable
  preference n ▷ prefer
  preferences n ▷ prefer
preferential adj showing preference
preferment n (pl **-s**) promotion or advancement
  preferments n ▷ preferment
  preferred v ▷ prefer
  preferring v ▷ prefer
  prefers v ▷ prefer
prefigure v (**-res, -ring, -red**) represent or suggest in advance
  prefigured v ▷ prefigure
  prefigures v ▷ prefigure
  prefiguring v ▷ prefigure
prefix n (pl **-es**) letter or group of letters put at the beginning of a word to make a new word, such as un- in unhappy ▶ v (**-es, -ing, -ed**) put as an introduction or prefix (to)
  prefixed v ▷ prefix
  prefixes n, v ▷ prefix
  prefixing v ▷ prefix
  pregnacies n ▷ pregnant
  pregnancy n ▷ pregnant
pregnant adj carrying a fetus in the womb > **pregnancy** n (pl **-cies**)
prehensile adj capable of grasping

prehistoric *adj* of the period before written history begins > **prehistory** *n* (*pl* -ries)
  prehistories *n* ▷ prehistory
  prehistory *n* ▷ prehistoric
prejudice *n* (*pl* -s) unreasonable or unfair dislike or preference ▶ *v* (-ces, -cing, -ced) cause (someone) to have a prejudice
  > **prejudicial** *adj* disadvantageous, harmful
  prejudiced *v* ▷ prejudice
  prejudicial *adj* ▷ prejudice
  prejudicing *v* ▷ prejudice
  prejudices *n*, *v* ▷ prejudice
prelate [**prel**-it] *n* (*pl* -s) bishop or other churchman of high rank
  prelates *n* ▷ prelate
  preliminaries *n* ▷ preliminary
preliminary *adj* happening before and in preparation, introductory ▶ *n* (*pl* -ries) preliminary remark, contest, etc.
prelude *n* (*pl* -s) introductory movement in music
  preludes *n* ▷ prelude
premarital *adj* occurring before marriage
premature *adj* happening or done before the normal or expected time > **prematurely** *adv*
  prematurely *adv* ▷ premature
premeditated *adj* planned in advance
  > **premeditation** *n* (*pl* -s)
  premeditation *n* ▷ premeditated
  premeditations *n* ▷ premeditated
premenstrual *adj* occurring or experienced before a menstrual period
premier *n* (*pl* -s) prime minister ▶ *adj* chief, leading > **premiership** *n* (*pl* -s)
première *n* (*pl* -s) first performance of a play, film, etc.
  premières *n* ▷ première
  premiers *n* ▷ premier
  premiership *n* ▷ premier
  premierships *n* ▷ premier
premise, premiss *n* (*pl* -s, -es) statement assumed to be true and used as the basis of reasoning
  premises *n* ▷ premise
premises *pl n* house or other building and its land
  premisses *n* ▷ premise
premium *n* (*pl* -s) additional sum of money, as on a wage or charge
  premiums *n* ▷ premium
premonition *n* (*pl* -s) feeling that something unpleasant is going to happen; foreboding
  > **premonitory** *adj*
  premonitions *n* ▷ premonition
  premonitory *adj* ▷ premonition

prenatal *adj* before birth, during pregnancy
  preoccupied *v* ▷ preoccupy
  preoccupies *v* ▷ preoccupy
preoccupy *v* (-pied, -pying, -pied) fill the thoughts or attention of (someone) to the exclusion of other things > **preoccupation** *n* (*pl* -s)
  preoccupation *n* ▷ preoccupy
  preoccupations *n* ▷ preoccupy
  preoccupying *v* ▷ preoccupy
preordained *adj* decreed or determined in advance
prep. preparatory
prepacked *adj* sold already wrapped
prepaid *adj* paid for in advance
prepare *v* (-res, -ring, -red) make or get ready
preparation *n* (*pl* -s) preparing
  preparations *n* ▷ preparation
preparatory [prip-**par**-a-tree] *adj* preparing for
prepared *adj* willing ▶ *v* ▷ prepare
  prepares *v* ▷ prepare
  preparing *v* ▷ prepare
preponderance *n* (*pl* -s) greater force, amount, or influence > **preponderant** *adj*
  preponderances *adj* ▷ preponderance
  preponderant *adj* ▷ preponderance
preposition *n* (*pl* -s) word used before a noun or pronoun to show its relationship with other words, such as by in go by bus
  > **prepositional** *adj*
  prepositional *n* ▷ preposition
  prepositions *n* ▷ preposition
prepossessing *adj* making a favourable impression, attractive
preposterous *adj* utterly absurd
prepuce [**pree**-pyewss] *n* (*pl* -s) retractable fold of skin covering the tip of the penis, foreskin
  prepuces *n* ▷ prepuce
prerecorded *adj* recorded in advance to be played or broadcast later
prerequisite *adj*, *n* (*pl* -s) (something) required before something else is possible
  prerequisites *n* ▷ prerequisite
prerogative *n* (*pl* -s) special power or privilege
  prerogatives *n* ▷ prerogative
presage [**press**-ij] *v* (-ges, -ging, -ged) be a sign or warning of
  presaged *v* ▷ presage
  presages *v* ▷ presage
  presaging *v* ▷ presage
  presbyteries *n* ▷ presbytery
presbytery *n* (*pl* -ies) (PRESBYTERIAN CHURCH) local church court
prescience [**press**-ee-enss] *n* (*pl* -s) knowledge of events before they happen > **prescient** *adj*

presciences n ▷ prescience
prescient adj ▷ prescience
prescribe v (-bes, -bing, -bed) recommend the use of (a medicine)
prescribed v ▷ prescribe
prescribes v ▷ prescribe
prescribing v ▷ prescribe
prescription n written instructions from a doctor for the making up and use of a medicine
prescriptions n ▷ prescription
prescriptive adj laying down rules
presence n (pl -s) fact of being in a specified place
presences n ▷ presence
present¹ adj being in a specified place ▶ n (pl -s) present time or tense
present² n something given to bring pleasure to another person ▶ v (-s, -ing, -ed) introduce formally or publicly > **presentation** n (pl -s)
presentable adj attractive, neat, fit for people to see
presented n ▷ present²
presenter n (pl -s) person introducing a TV or radio show
presenters n ▷ presenter
presentiment [priz-**zen**-tim-ent] n (pl -s) sense of something unpleasant about to happen
presentiments n ▷ presentiment
presenting v ▷ present²
presently adv soon (US & SCOT)
presents n, v ▷ present¹, ²
preserve v (-ves, -ving, -ved) keep from being damaged, changed, or ended ▶ n (pl -s) area of interest restricted to a particular person or group > **preservation** n (pl -s)
preservation n ▷ preserve
preservations n ▷ preserve
preservative n (pl -s) chemical that prevents decay
preservatives n ▷ preservative
preserved v ▷ preserve
preserves v, n ▷ preserve
preserving v ▷ preserve
preshrunk adj (of fabric or a garment) having been shrunk during manufacture so that further shrinkage will not occur when washed
preside v (-des, -ding, -ded) be in charge, esp. of a meeting
presided v ▷ preside
presidencies n ▷ president
presidency n ▷ president
president n (pl -s) head of state in many countries > **presidential** adj > **presidency** n

(pl -cies)
presidential n ▷ president
presidents n ▷ president
presides v ▷ preside
presiding v ▷ preside
press v (-es, -ing, -ed) apply force or weight to ▶ n (pl -es) printing machine
pressed v ▷ press
presses v, n ▷ press
pressing adj urgent ▶ v ▷ press
presses n ▷ press
pressure n (pl -s) force produced by pressing
pressures n ▷ pressure
prestidigitation n (pl -s) skilful quickness with the hands, conjuring
prestidigitations n ▷ prestidigitation
prestige n (pl -s) high status or respect resulting from success or achievements > **prestigious** adj
prestiges n ▷ prestige
prestigious adj ▷ prestige
presumed v ▷ presume
presto adv (MUSIC) very quickly
prestressed adj (of concrete) containing stretched steel wires to strengthen it
presume v (-mes, -ing, -med) suppose to be the case
presumably adv one supposes (that)
presumed v ▷ presume
presumes v ▷ presume
presuming v ▷ presume
presumption (pl -s) n bold insolent behaviour
presumption n ▷ presumption
presumptive adj assumed to be true or valid until the contrary is proved
presumptuous adj doing things one has no right to do
presuppose v (-ses, -sing, -sed) need as a previous condition in order to be true > **presupposition** n (pl -s)
presupposed v ▷ presuppose
presupposes v ▷ presuppose
presupposing v ▷ presuppose
presupposition v ▷ presuppose
presuppositions v ▷ presuppose
pretence n (pl -s) behaviour intended to deceive, pretending
pretences n ▷ pretence
pretend v (-s, -ing, -ed) claim or give the appearance of (something untrue) to deceive or in play
pretended v ▷ pretend
pretender n (pl -s) person who makes a false or disputed claim to a position of power
pretenders n ▷ pretender

pretending v ▷ pretend
pretends v ▷ pretend
pretension n ▷ pretentious
pretensions n ▷ pretentious
pretentious adj making (unjustified) claims to special merit or importance > **pretension** n (pl -s)
preternatural adj beyond what is natural, supernatural
pretext n (pl -s) false reason given to hide the real one
pretexts n ▷ pretext
prettier adj ▷ pretty
prettiest adj ▷ pretty
prettily adv ▷ pretty
prettiness n ▷ pretty
prettinesses n (pl -es)
pretty adj (-tier, -tiest) pleasing to look at ▶ adv fairly, moderately > **prettily** adv > **prettiness** n (pl -es)
pretzel n (pl -s) brittle salted biscuit
pretzels n ▷ pretzel
prevail v (-s, -ing, -ed) gain mastery
prevailed v ▷ prevail
prevailing adj widespread ▶ v ▷ prevail
prevails v ▷ prevail
prevalence n ▷ prevalent
prevalences n ▷ prevalent
prevalent adj widespread, common > **prevalence** n (pl -s)
prevaricate v (-tes, -ting, -ted) avoid giving a direct or truthful answer > **prevarication** n (pl -s)
prevaricated v ▷ prevaricate
prevaricates v ▷ prevaricate
prevaricating v ▷ prevaricate
prevarication n ▷ prevaricate
prevarications n ▷ prevaricate
prevent v (-s, -ing, -ed) keep from happening or doing > **preventable** adj > **prevention** n (pl -s) > **preventive** adj, n (pl -s)
preventable adj ▷ prevent
prevented v ▷ prevent
preventing v ▷ prevent
prevention n ▷ prevent
preventions n ▷ prevent
preventive adj, n ▷ prevent
preventives n ▷ prevent
prevents v ▷ prevent
preview n (pl -s) advance showing of a film or exhibition before it is shown to the public
previews v ▷ preview
previous adj coming or happening before > **previously** adv
previously adv ▷ previous

prey n (pl -s) animal hunted and killed for food by another animal
preys v ▷ prey
price n (pl -s) amount of money for which a thing is bought or sold ▶ v (-ces, -cing, -ced) fix or ask the price of
priced v ▷ price
priceless adj very valuable
prices n, v ▷ price
pricier adj ▷ pricey
priciest adj ▷ pricey
pricing v ▷ price
pricey adj (-cier, -ciest) (Informal) expensive
prick v (-s, -ing, -ed) pierce lightly with a sharp point ▶ n (pl -s) sudden sharp pain caused by pricking
pricked v ▷ prick
pricking v ▷ prick
prickle n (pl -s) thorn or spike on a plant ▶ v (-les, -ling, -led) have a tingling or pricking sensation > **prickly** adj (-lier, -liest)
prickled v ▷ prickle
prickles n, v ▷ prickle
pricklier adj ▷ prickle
prickliest adj ▷ prickle
prickling v ▷ prickle
prickly adj ▷ prickle
pricks v, n ▷ prick
pride n (pl -s) feeling of pleasure and satisfaction when one has done well
prides n ▷ pride
pried v ▷ pry
pries v ▷ pry
priest n (pl -s) (in the Christian church) a person who can administer the sacraments and preach > **priestess** n fem (pl -es) > **priesthood** n (pl -s) > **priestly** adj (-lier, -liest)
priestess n ▷ priest
priestesses n ▷ priest
priesthood n ▷ priest
priesthoods n ▷ priest
priestlier adj ▷ priest
priestliest adj ▷ priest
priestly adj ▷ priest
priests n ▷ priest
prig n (pl -s) self-righteous person who acts as if superior to others > **priggish** adj > **priggishness** n (pl -s)
priggish adj ▷ prig
priggishness n ▷ prig
priggishnesses n ▷ prig
prigs n ▷ prig
prim adj (-mmer, -mmest) formal, proper, and rather prudish > **primly** adv
primacies n ▷ primacy

primacy *n* (*pl* -**ies**) state of being first in rank, grade, etc.
  primaeval *adj* ▷ primeval
primal *adj* of basic causes or origins
  primarily *adv* ▷ primary
primary *adj* chief, most important > **primarily** *adv*
primate[1] *n* (*pl* -**s**) member of an order of mammals including monkeys and humans
primate[2] *n* (*pl* -**s**) archbishop
  primates *n* ▷ primate[1, 2]
prime *adj* main, most important ▶ *n* (*pl* -**s**) time when someone is at his or her best or most vigorous ▶ *v* (-**mes**, -**ming**, -**med**) give (someone) information in advance to prepare them for something
  primed *v* ▷ prime
primer *n* (*pl* -**s**) special paint applied to bare wood etc. before the main paint
  primers *n* ▷ primer
  primes *n*, *v* ▷ prime
  priming *v* ▷ prime
primeval [prime-**ee**-val] *adj* of the earliest age of the world
primitive *adj* of an early simple stage of development
  primly *adv* ▷ prim
  primmer *adj* ▷ prim
  primmest *adj* ▷ prim
primogeniture *n* (*pl* -**s**) system under which the eldest son inherits all his parents' property
  primogenitures *n* ▷ primogeniture
primordial *adj* existing at or from the beginning
primrose *n* (*pl* -**s**) pale yellow spring flower
  primroses *n* ▷ primrose
primula *n* (*pl* -**s**) type of primrose with brightly coloured flowers
  primulas *n* ▷ primula
prince *n* (*pl* -**s**) male member of a royal family, esp. the son of the king or queen
  princelier *adj* ▷ princely
  princeliest *adj* ▷ princely
  princely *adj* (-**lier**, -**liest**) of or like a prince
princess *n* (*pl* -**es**) female member of a royal family, esp. the daughter of the king or queen
  princes *n* ▷ prince
  princesses *n* ▷ princess
principal *adj* main, most important ▶ *n* (*pl* -**s**) head of a school or college > **principally** *adv*
  principalities *n* ▷ principality
principality *n* (*pl* -**ties**) territory ruled by a prince
  principally *adv* ▷ principal

principals *n* ▷ principal
principle *n* (*pl* -**s**) moral rule guiding behaviour
  principles *n* ▷ principle
print *v* (-**s**, -**ing**, -**ed**) reproduce (a newspaper, book, etc.) in large quantities by mechanical or electronic means ▶ *n* (*pl* -**s**) printed words etc. > **printing** *n* (*pl* -**s**)
  printed *v* ▷ print
printer *n* (*pl* -**s**) person or company engaged in printing
  printers *n* ▷ printer
printing *n*, *v* ▷ print
  printings *n* ▷ print
  prints *v* ▷ print
  printing *v* ▷ print
  printed *v* ▷ print
  prints *n* ▷ print
prior[1] *adj* earlier
prior[2] *n* (*pl* -**s**) head monk in a priory
prioress *n* (*pl* -**es**) deputy head nun in a convent
  prioresses *n* ▷ prioress
  priories *n* ▷ priory
  priors *n* ▷ prior[2]
priory *n* (*pl* -**ries**) place where certain orders of monks or nuns live
  priors *n* ▷ prior
  priorities *n* ▷ priority
priority *n* (*pl* -**ties**) most important thing that must be dealt with first
prise *v* (-**ses**, -**sing**, -**sed**) force open by levering
  prised *v* ▷ prise
  prises *v* ▷ prise
  prising *v* ▷ prise
prism *n* (*pl* -**s**) transparent block usu. with triangular ends and rectangular sides, used to disperse light into a spectrum or refract it in optical instruments
prismatic *adj* of or shaped like a prism
  prisms *n* ▷ prism
prison *n* (*pl* -**s**) building where criminals and accused people are held
  prisons *n* ▷ prison
prisoner *n* (*pl* -**s**) person held captive
  prisoners *n* ▷ prisoner
  prissier *adj* ▷ prissy
  prissiest *adj* ▷ prissy
  prissily *adv* ▷ prissy
prissy *adj* (-**ssier**, -**ssiest**) prim, correct, and easily shocked > **prissily** *adv*
pristine *adj* clean, new, and unused
  privacies *n* ▷ private
  privacy *n* ▷ private
private *adj* for the use of one person or group only ▶ *n* (*pl* -**s**) soldier of the lowest rank

> **privately** *adv* ▷ **privacy** *n* (*pl* **-cies**)
privately *adv* ▷ **private**
privates *n* ▷ **private**
privateer *n* (*pl* **-s**) (HIST) privately owned armed vessel authorized by the government to take part in a war
  privateers *n* ▷ **privateer**
privation *n* (*pl* **-s**) loss or lack of the necessities of life
  privations *n* ▷ **privation**
  privatization *n* ▷ **privatize**
  privatizations *n* ▷ **privatize**
privatize *v* (**-zes**, **-zing**, **-zed**) sell (a publicly owned company) to individuals or a private company > **privatization** *n* (*pl* **-s**)
  privatized *v* ▷ **privatize**
  privatizes *v* ▷ **privatize**
  privatizing *v* ▷ **privatize**
privet *n* (*pl* **-s**) bushy evergreen shrub used for hedges
  privets *n* ▷ **privet**
  privier *adj* ▷ **privy**
  privies *n* ▷ **privy**
  priviest *adj* ▷ **privy**
privilege *n* (*pl* **-s**) advantage or favour that only some people have
privileged *adj* enjoying a special right or immunity
  privileges *n* ▷ **privilege**
privy *adj* (**-vier**, **-viest**) sharing knowledge of something secret ▶ *n* (*pl* **-ies**) (Obs) toilet, esp. an outside one
prize[1] *n* (*pl* **-s**) reward given for success in a competition etc. ▶ *adj* winning or likely to win a prize
prize[2] *v* (**-zes**, **-zing**, **-zed**) value highly
prize[3] *v* ▷ **prise**
  prized *v* ▷ **prize**[2]
prizefighter *n* (*pl* **-s**) boxer who fights for money
  prizefighters *n* ▷ **prizefighter**
  prizes *n*, *v* ▷ **prize**[1, 2]
  prizing *v* ▷ **prize**[2]
pro[1] *adv*, *prep* in favour of
pro[2] *n* (*pl* **-s**) (Informal) professional
  probabilities *n* ▷ **probable**
  probabiility *n* ▷ **probable**
probable *adj* likely to happen or be true > **probability** *n* (*pl* **-ties**)
probably *adv* in all likelihood
probate *n* (*pl* **-s**) process of proving the validity of a will
  probates *n* ▷ **probate**
probation *n* (*pl* **-s**) system of dealing with law-breakers, esp. juvenile ones, by placing them under supervision
probationer *n* (*pl* **-s**) person on probation
  probationers *n* ▷ **probationer**
  probations *n* ▷ **probation**
probe *v* (**-bes**, **-bing**, **-bed**) search into or examine closely ▶ *n* (*pl* **-s**) surgical instrument used to examine a wound, cavity, etc.
  probed *v* ▷ **probe**
  probes *v*, *n* ▷ **probe**
  probing *v* ▷ **probe**
probiotic *adj*, *n* (*pl* **-s**) (of) a bacterium that protects the body from harmful bacteria
  probiotics *n* ▷ **probiotic**
  probities *n* ▷ **probity**
probity *n* (*pl* **-ties**) honesty, integrity
problem *n* (*pl* **-s**) something difficult to deal with or solve > **problematic, problematical** *adj*
  problematic *adj* ▷ **problem**
  problematical *adj* ▷ **problem**
  problems *n* ▷ **problem**
proboscis [pro-**boss**-iss] *n* (*pl* **-scises**) long trunk or snout
  proboscises *n* ▷ **proboscis**
  procedural *adj* ▷ **procedure**
procedure *n* (*pl* **-s**) way of doing something, esp. the correct or usual one > **procedural** *adj*
  procedures *n* ▷ **procedure**
proceed *v* (**-s**, **-ing**, **-ed**) start or continue doing
  proceeded *v* ▷ **proceed**
proceeds *pl n* money obtained from an event or activity ▶ *v* ▷ **proceed**
  proceeding *v* ▷ **proceed**
proceedings *pl n* organized or related series of events
process *n* (*pl* **-es**) series of actions or changes ▶ *v* (**-es**, **-ing**, **-ed**) handle or prepare by a special method of manufacture > **processor** *n* (*pl* **-s**)
processed *adj* (of food) treated to prevent it decaying ▶ *v* ▷ **process**
  processes *n*, *v* ▷ **process**
  processing *v* ▷ **process**
procession *n* (*pl* **-s**) line of people or vehicles moving forward together in order
  processions *n* ▷ **procession**
  processor *n* ▷ **process**
  processors *n* ▷ **process**
proclaim *v* (**-s**, **-ing**, **-ed**) declare publicly > **proclamation** *n* (*pl* **-s**)
  proclaimed *v* ▷ **proclaim**
  proclaiming *v* ▷ **proclaim**
  proclaims *v* ▷ **proclaim**
  proclamation *n* ▷ **proclaim**
  proclamations *n* ▷ **proclaim**

proclivities *n* ▷ proclivity
proclivity *n* (*pl* -ties) inclination, tendency
procrastinate *v* (-tes, -ting, -ted) put off
taking action, delay > **procrastination** *n* (*pl* -s)
procrastinated *v* ▷ procrastinate
procrastinates *v* ▷ procrastinate
procrastinating *v* ▷ procrastinate
procrastination *n* ▷ procrastinate
procrastinations *n* ▷ procrastinate
procreate *v* (-tes, -ting, -ted) (*Formal*) produce
offspring > **procreation** *n* (*pl* -s)
procreated *v* ▷ procreate
procreates *v* ▷ procreate
procreating *v* ▷ procreate
procreation *n* ▷ procreate
procreations *n* ▷ procreate
procure *v* (-res, -ring, -red) get, provide
> **procurement** *n* (*pl* -s)
procured *v* ▷ procure
procurement *n* ▷ procure
procurements *n* ▷ procure
procurer, procuress *n* (*pl* -s, -es) person who
obtains people to act as prostitutes
procurers *n* ▷ procurer
procures *v* ▷ procure
procuress *n* ▷ procurer
procuresses *n* ▷ procurer
procuring *v* ▷ procure
prod *v* (-s, -dding, -dded) poke with something
pointed ▶ *n* (*pl* -s) prodding
prodded *v* ▷ prod
prodding *v* ▷ prod
prodigal *adj* recklessly extravagant, wasteful
> **prodigality** *n* (*pl* -s)
prodigalities *n* ▷ prodigal
prodigality *n* ▷ prodigal
prodigies *n* ▷ prodigy
prodigious *adj* very large, immense
> **prodigiously** *adv*
prodigiously *adv* ▷ prodigious
prodigy *n* (*pl* -gies) person with some
marvellous talent
prods *v*, *n* ▷ prod
produce *v* (-ces, -cing, -ced) bring into
existence ▶ *n* (*pl* -s) food grown for sale
produced *v* ▷ produce
producer *n* (*pl* -s) person with control over the
making of a film, record, etc.
producers *n* ▷ producer
produces *v*, *n* ▷ produce
producing *v* ▷ produce
product *n* (*pl* -s) something produced
production *n* (*pl* -s) producing
productions *n* ▷ production
productive *adj* producing large quantities

> **productivity** *n* (*pl* -ies)
productivities *n* ▷ productive
productivity *n* ▷ productive
products *n* ▷ product
profane *adj* showing disrespect for religion
or holy things ▶ *v* (-nes, -ning, -ned) treat
(something sacred) irreverently, desecrate
profanation *n* (*pl* -s) act of profaning
profanations *n* ▷ profanation
profaned *v* ▷ profane
profanes *v* ▷ profane
profaning *v* ▷ profane
profanities *n* ▷ profanity
profanity *n* (*pl* -ties) profane talk or behaviour,
blasphemy
profess *v* (-es, -ing, -ed) state or claim
(something as true), sometimes falsely
> **professed** *adj* supposed
professed *v*, *adj* ▷ profess
professes *v* ▷ profess
professing *v* ▷ profess
profession *n* (*pl* -s) type of work, such as being
a doctor, that needs special training
professional *adj* working in a profession
▶ *n* person who works in a profession
> **professionally** *adv* > **professionalism** *n*
(*pl* -s)
professionally *adv* ▷ professional
professionalism *n* ▷ professional
professionalisms *n* ▷ professional
professions *n* ▷ profession
professor *n* (*pl* -s) teacher of the highest
rank in a university > **professorial** *adj*
> **professorship** *n* (*pl* -s)
professorial *adj* ▷ professor
professors *n* ▷ professor
professorship *n* ▷ professor
professorships *n* ▷ professor
proffer *v* (-s, -ing, -ed) offer
proffered *v* ▷ proffer
proffering *v* ▷ proffer
proffers *v* ▷ proffer
proficiencies *n* ▷ proficient
proficiency *n* ▷ proficient
proficient *adj* skilled, expert > **proficiency** *n*
(*pl* -cies)
profile *n* (*pl* -s) outline, esp. of the face, as seen
from the side
profiles *n* ▷ profile
profit *n* (*pl* -s) money gained ▶ *v* (-s, -ing, -ed)
gain or benefit
profitable *adj* making profit > **profitably** *adv*
> **profitability** *n* (*pl* -ties)
profitabilities *n* ▷ profitable
profitability *n* ▷ profitable

profitably *adv* ▷ profitable
profited *v* ▷ profit
profiteer *n* (*pl* -**s**) person who makes excessive profits at the expense of the public > **profiteering** *n* (*pl* -**s**)
profiteering *n* ▷ profiteer
profiteerings *n* ▷ profiteer
profiteers *n* ▷ profiteer
profiting *v* ▷ profit
profits *n, v* ▷ profit
profligacies *n* ▷ profligate
profligacy *n* ▷ profligate
profligate *adj* recklessly extravagant ▶ *n* (*pl* -**s**) profligate person > **profligacy** *n* (*pl* -**cies**)
profligates *n* ▷ profligate
profound *adj* (-**er**, -**est**) showing or needing great knowledge > **profundity** *n* (*pl* -**ties**)
profounder *adj* ▷ profound
profoundest *adj* ▷ profound
profundities *n* ▷ profound
profundity *n* ▷ profound
profuse *adj* plentiful > **profusion** *n* (*pl* -**s**)
profusion *n* ▷ profuse
profusions *n* ▷ profuse
progenies *n* ▷ progeny
progeny [proj-in-ee] *n* (*pl* -**nies**) children
progenitor [pro-**jen**-it-er] *n* (*pl* -**s**) ancestor
progenitors *n* ▷ progenitor
progesterone *n* (*pl* -**s**) hormone which prepares the womb for pregnancy and prevents further ovulation
progesterones *n* ▷ progesterone
prognoses *n* ▷ prognosis
prognosis *n* (*pl* -**noses**) doctor's forecast about the progress of an illness
prognostication *n* (*pl* -**s**) forecast or prediction
prognostications *n* ▷ prognostication
program *n* (*pl* -**s**) sequence of coded instructions for a computer ▶ *v* (-**s**, -**mming**, --**mmed**) arrange (data) so that it can be processed by a computer > **programmer** *n* (*pl* -**s**) > **programmable** *adj*
programmable *adj* ▷ program
programmed *v* ▷ program
programmer *n* ▷ program
programmers *n* ▷ program
programming *v* ▷ program
programs *n, v* ▷ program
programme *n* (*pl* -**s**) planned series of events
programmes *n* ▷ programme
progress *n* (*pl* -**es**) improvement, development ▶ *v* (-**es**, -**ing**, -**ed**) become more advanced or skilful > **progression** *n* (*pl* -**s**)
progressed *v* ▷ progress

progresses *v* ▷ progress
progressing *v* ▷ progress
progression *n* ▷ progress
progressions *n* ▷ progress
progressive *adj* favouring political or social reform > **progressively** *adv*
progressively *adv* ▷ progressive
prohibit *v* (-**s**, -**ing**, -**ed**) forbid or prevent from happening
prohibited *v* ▷ prohibit
prohibiting *v* ▷ prohibit
prohibition *n* (*pl* -**s**) act of forbidding
prohibitions *n* ▷ prohibition
prohibitive *adj* (of prices) too high to be affordable > **prohibitively** *adv*
prohibitively *adv* ▷ prohibitive
prohibits *v* ▷ prohibit
project *n* (*pl* **projects**) planned scheme to do or examine something over a period ▶ *v* (-**s**, -**ing**, -**ed**) make a forecast based on known data > **projection** *n* (*pl* -**s**)
projected *v* ▷ project
projectile *n* (*pl* -**s**) object thrown as a weapon or fired from a gun
projectiles *n* ▷ projectile
projecting *v* ▷ project
projection *n* ▷ project
projectionist *n* (*pl* -**s**) person who operates a projector
projectionists *n* ▷ projectionist
projections *n* ▷ project
projector *n* (*pl* -**s**) apparatus for projecting photographic images, films, or slides on a screen
projectors *n* ▷ projector
projects *n, v* ▷ project
prolapse *n* (*pl* -**s**) slipping down of an internal organ of the body from its normal position
prolapses *n* ▷ prolapse
prole *adj, n* (*pl* -**s**) (CHIEFLY BRIT) (Slang) proletarian
proles *n* ▷ prole
proletariat [pro-lit-**air**-ee-at] *n* (*pl* -**s**) working class > **proletarian** *adj, n* (*pl* -**s**)
proletarian *n* ▷ proletariat
proletarians *n* ▷ proletariat
proletariats *n* ▷ proletariat
proliferate *v* (-**tes**, -**ting**, -**ted**) grow or reproduce rapidly > **proliferation** *n* (*pl* -**s**)
proliferated *v* ▷ proliferate
proliferates *v* ▷ proliferate
proliferating *v* ▷ proliferate
proliferation *n* ▷ proliferate
proliferations *n* ▷ proliferate
prolific *adj* very productive > **prolifically** *adv*

prolifically *adv* ▷ prolific

prolix *adj* (of speech or a piece of writing) overlong and boring

prologue *n* (*pl* -s) introduction to a play or book

prologues *n* ▷ prologue

prolong *v* (-s, -ing, -ed) make (something) last longer > **prolongation** *n* (*pl* -s)

prolongation *n* ▷ prolong

prolongations *n* ▷ prolong

prolonged *v* ▷ prolong

prolonging *v* ▷ prolong

prolongs *v* ▷ prolong

prom *n* (*pl* -s) ▷ promenade

promenade *n* (*pl* -s) (CHIEFLY BRIT) paved walkway along the seafront at a holiday resort ▶ *v* (-des, -ding, -ded) ▶ *n* (Old-fashioned) (take) a leisurely walk

promenaded *v* ▷ promenade

promenades *n*, *v* ▷ promenade

promenading *v* ▷ promenade

prominence *n* ▷ prominent

prominences *n* ▷ prominent

prominent *adj* very noticeable > **prominently** *adv* ▷ prominently

prominently *adv* ▷ prominent

promiscuities *n* ▷ promiscuous

promiscuity *n* ▷ promiscuous

promiscuous *adj* having many casual sexual relationships > **promiscuity** *n* (*pl* -ties)

promise *v* (-ses, -sing, -sed) say that one will definitely do or not do something ▶ *n* (*pl* -s) undertaking to do or not to do something

promised *v* ▷ promise

promises *v* ▷ promise

promising *adj* likely to succeed or turn out well ▶ *v* ▷ promise

promo *n* (*pl* -os) (Informal) short film to promote a product

promontories *n* ▷ promontory

promontory *n* (*pl* -ries) point of high land jutting out into the sea

promos *n* ▷ promo

promote *v* (-tes, -ting, -ted) help to make (something) happen or increase > **promotion** *n* (*pl* -s) > **promotional** *adj*

promoted *v* ▷ promote

promoter *n* (*pl* -s) person who organizes or finances an event etc.

promoters *n* ▷ promoter

promotes *v* ▷ promote

promoting *v* ▷ promote

promotion *n* ▷ promote

promotional *adj* ▷ promote

promotions *n* ▷ promote

prompt *v* (-s, -ing, -ed) cause (an action) ▶ *adj* done without delay ▶ *adv* exactly > **promptness** *n* (*pl* -es)

prompted *v* ▷ prompt

prompter, prompt *n* (*pl* -s) person offstage who prompts actors

prompter *n* ▷ prompter

prompting *v* ▷ prompt

promptly *adv* immediately, without delay

promptness *n* ▷ prompt

promptnesses *n* ▷ prompt

prompts *v*, *n* ▷ prompt

proms *n* ▷ prom

promulgate *v* (-tes, -ting, -ted) put (a law etc.) into effect by announcing it officially > **promulgation** *n* (*pl* -s)

promulgated *v* ▷ promulgate

promulgates *v* ▷ promulgate

promulgating *v* ▷ promulgate

promulgation *n* ▷ promulgate

promulgations *n* ▷ promulgate

prone *adj* (-r, -st) (foll. by **to**) likely to do or be affected by (something)

proner *adj* ▷ prone

pronest *adj* ▷ prone

prong *n* (*pl* -s) one spike of a fork or similar instrument > **pronged** *adj*

pronged *adj* ▷ prong

prongs *n* ▷ prong

pronoun *n* (*pl* -s) word, such as *she* or *it*, used to replace a noun

pronouns *n* ▷ pronoun

pronounce *v* (-ces, -cing, -ced) form the sounds of (words or letters), esp. clearly or in a particular way > **pronounceable** *adj*

pronouncable *adj* ▷ pronounce

pronounced *adj* very noticeable ▶ *v* ▷ pronounce

pronounces *v* ▷ pronounce

pronouncement *n* (*pl* -s) formal announcement

pronouncements *n* ▷ pronouncement

pronouncing *v* ▷ pronounce

pronunciation *n* (*pl* -s) way in which a word or language is pronounced

pronunciations *n* ▷ pronunciation

pronto *adv* (Informal) at once

proof *n* (*pl* -s) evidence that shows that something is true or has happened ▶ *adj* able to withstand

proofread *v* (-s, -ing, -read) read and correct (printer's proofs) > **proofreader** *n* (*pl* -s)

proofreader *n* ▷ proofread

proofreaders *n* ▷ proofread

proofreading *v* ▷ proofread

proofreads v ▷ proofread

proofs n ▷ proof

prop¹ v (-s, -pping, -pped) support (something) so that it stays upright or in place ▶ n (pl -s) pole, beam, etc. used as a support

prop² n (pl -s) movable object used on the set of a film or play

prop³ n (pl -s) (*Informal*) propeller

propaganda n (pl -s) (organized promotion of) information to assist or damage the cause of a government or movement ▷ **propagandist** n (pl -s)

propagandas n ▷ propaganda

propagandist n ▷ propaganda

propagandists n ▷ propaganda

propagate v (-tes, -ting, -ted) spread (information and ideas) ▷ **propagation** n (pl -s)

propagated v ▷ propagate

propagates v ▷ propagate

propagating v ▷ propagate

propagation n ▷ propagate

propagations n ▷ propagate

propane n (pl -s) flammable gas found in petroleum and used as a fuel

propanes n ▷ propane

propel v (-s, -lling, -lled) cause to move forward

propellant n (pl -s) something that provides or causes propulsion

propellants n ▷ propellant

propelled v ▷ propel

propeller n (pl -s) revolving shaft with blades for driving a ship or aircraft

propellers n ▷ propeller

propelling v ▷ propel

propels v ▷ propel

propped v ▷ prop¹

propping v ▷ prop¹

props v, n ▷ prop¹, ², ³

propulsion n (pl -s) method by which something is propelled

propulsions n ▷ propulsion

propensities n ▷ propensity

propensity n (pl -ties) natural tendency

proper adj (-er, -est) real or genuine ▷ **properly** adv

properer adj ▷ proper

properest adj ▷ proper

properly adv ▷ proper

properties n ▷ property

property n (pl -ties) something owned

prophecies n ▷ prophecy

prophecy n (pl -cies) prediction

prophesied v ▷ prophesy

prophesies v ▷ prophesy

prophesy v (-sies, -sying, -sied) foretell

prophesying v ▷ prophesy

prophet n (pl -s) person supposedly chosen by God to spread His word ▷ **prophetic** adj ▷ **prophetically** adv

prophetic adj ▷ prophet

prophetically adv ▷ prophet

prophets n ▷ prophet

prophylactic n (pl -s) ▶ adj (drug) used to prevent disease

prophylactics n ▷ prophylactic

propitiate v (-tes, -ting, -ted) appease, win the favour of ▷ **propitiation** n

propitiated v ▷ propitiate

propitiates v ▷ propitiate

propitiating v ▷ propitiate

propitiation n ▷ propitiate

propitiations n ▷ propitiate

propitious adj favourable or auspicious

proponent n (pl -s) person who argues in favour of something

proponents n ▷ proponent

proportion n (pl -s) relative size or extent ▶ pl dimensions or size ▶ v (-s, -ing, -ed) adjust in relative amount or size

proportional, proportionate adj being in proportion ▷ **proportionally, proportionately** adv

proportionally adv ▷ proportional

proportionate adj ▷ proportional

proportionately adv ▷ proportional

proportioned v ▷ proportion

proportioning v ▷ proportion

proportions n, v ▷ proportion

propose v (-ses, -sing, -sed) put forward for consideration ▷ **proposal** n (pl -s)

proposal n ▷ propose

proposals n ▷ propose

proposed v ▷ propose

proposes v ▷ propose

proposing v ▷ propose

proposition n (pl -s) offer ▶ v (-s, -ing, -ed) (*Informal*) ask (someone) to have sexual intercourse

propositioned v ▷ proposition

propositioning v ▷ proposition

propositions n, v ▷ proposition

propound v (-s, -ing, -ed) put forward for consideration

propounded v ▷ propound

propounding v ▷ propound

propounds v ▷ propound

proprietor n (pl -s) owner of a business establishment ▷ **proprietress** n fem (pl -es)

proprietary adj made and distributed under

a trade name

proprieties *n* ▷ propriety

proprietors *n* ▷ proprietor

proprietress *n* ▷ proprietor

proprietresses *n* ▷ proprietor

propriety *n* (*pl* -ties) correct conduct

propulsion *n* ▷ propel

prorogue *v* (-gues, -guing, -gued) suspend (parliament) without dissolving it

> **prorogation** *n* (*pl* -s)

prorogation *n* ▷ prorogue

prorogations *n* ▷ prorogue

prorogued *v* ▷ prorogue

prorogues *v* ▷ prorogue

proroguing *v* ▷ prorogue

pros *n* ▷ pro

prosaic [pro-**zay**-ik] *adj* lacking imagination, dull > **prosaically** *adv*

prosaically *adv* ▷ prosaic

proscenia *n* ▷ proscenium

proscenium *n* (*pl* -nia, -niums) arch in a theatre separating the stage from the auditorium

prosceniums *n* ▷ proscenium

proscribe *v* (-bes, -bing, -bed) prohibit, outlaw

> **proscription** *n* (*pl* -s) > **proscriptive** *adj*

proscribed *v* ▷ proscribe

proscribes *v* ▷ proscribe

proscribing *v* ▷ proscribe

proscription *n* ▷ proscribe

proscriptions *n* ▷ proscribe

proscriptive *adj* ▷ proscribe

prose *n* (*pl* -s) ordinary speech or writing in contrast to poetry

proses *n* ▷ prose

prosecute *v* (-tes, -ting, -ted) bring a criminal charge against > **prosecution** *n* (*pl* -s)

> **prosecutor** *n* (*pl* -s)

prosecuted *v* ▷ prosecute

prosecutes *v* ▷ prosecute

prosecuting *v* ▷ prosecute

prosecution *n* ▷ prosecute

prosecutions *n* ▷ prosecute

prosecutor *n* ▷ prosecute

prosecutors *n* ▷ prosecute

proselyte [**pross**-ill-ite] *n* (*pl* -s) recent convert

proselytes *n* ▷ proselyte

proselytize [**pross**-ill-it-ize] *v* (-zes, -zing, -zed) attempt to convert

proselytized *v* ▷ proselytize

proselytized *v* ▷ proselytize

proselytizing *v* ▷ proselytize

prospect *n* (*pl* -s) something anticipated (*Old-fashioned*) ▶ *pl* probability of future success ▶ *v* (-s, -ing, -ed) explore, esp. for gold

> **prospector** *n* (*pl* -s)

prospected *v* ▷ prospect

prospecting *v* ▷ prospect

prospective *adj* future

prospector *n* ▷ prospect

prospectors *n* ▷ prospect

prospects *n*, *v* ▷ prospect

prospectus *n* (*pl* -es) booklet giving details of a university, company, etc.

prospectuses *n* ▷ prospectus

prosper *v* (-s, -ing, -ed) be successful

> **prosperous** *adj*

prospered *v* ▷ prosper

prospering *v* ▷ prosper

prosperities *n* ▷ prosperity

prosperity *n* success and wealth

prosperous *adj* ▷ prosper

prospers *v* ▷ prosper

prostate *n* (*pl* -s) gland in male mammals that surrounds the neck of the bladder

prostates *n* ▷ prostate

prostheses *n* ▷ prosthesis

prosthesis [pross-**theess**-iss] *n* (*pl* -ses) [-seez] artificial body part, such as a limb or breast

> **prosthetic** *adj*

prosthetic *adj* ▷ prosthesis

prostitute *n* (*pl* -s) person who offers sexual intercourse in return for payment ▶ *v* (-tes, -ting, -ted) make a prostitute of

> **prostitution** *n* (*pl* -s)

prostituted *v* ▷ prostitute

prostitutes *n*, *v* ▷ prostitute

prostituting *v* ▷ prostitute

prostitution *n* ▷ prostitute

prostitutions *n* ▷ prostitute

prostrate *adj* lying face downwards ▶ *v* (-tes, -ting, -ted) lie face downwards > **prostration** *n* (*pl* -s)

prostrated *v* ▷ prostrate

prostrates *v* ▷ prostrate

prostrating *v* ▷ prostrate

prostration *n* ▷ prostrate

prostrations *n* ▷ prostrate

protagonist *n* (*pl* -s) supporter of a cause

protagonists *n* ▷ protagonist

protea [**pro**-tee-a] *n* (*pl* -s) African shrub with showy flowers

protean [pro-**tee**-an] *adj* constantly changing

proteas *n* ▷ protea

protect *v* (-s, -ing, -ed) defend from trouble, harm, or loss > **protection** *n* (*pl* -s)

protected *v* ▷ protect

protecting *v* ▷ protect

protection *n* ▷ protect

protectionism *n* policy of protecting

industries by taxing competing imports
> **protectionist** n (pl -**s**) adj
protectionisms n ▷ protectionism
protectionist n ▷ protectionism
protectionists n ▷ protectionism
protections n ▷ protect
protective adj giving protection
protector n (pl -**s**) person or thing that protects
protectorate n (pl -**s**) territory largely controlled by a stronger state
protectorates n ▷ protectorate
protectors n ▷ protector
protects v ▷ protect
protégé, fem **protégée** [pro-ti-zhay] n (pl -**s**) person who is protected and helped by another
protégés n ▷ protégé
protein n (pl -**s**) any of a group of complex organic compounds that are essential for life
proteins n ▷ protein
protest n (pl -**s**) declaration or demonstration of objection ▶ v (-**s**, -**ing**, -**ed**) object, disagree
protestant n (pl -**s**) one who protests
protestants n ▷ protestant
protestation n (pl -**s**) strong declaration
protestations n ▷ protestation
protested v ▷ protest
protesting v ▷ protest
protests n, v ▷ protest
protocol n (pl -**s**) rules of behaviour for formal occasions
protocols n ▷ protocol
proton n (pl -**s**) positively charged particle in the nucleus of an atom
protons n ▷ proton
protoplasm n (pl -**s**) substance forming the living contents of a cell
protoplasms n ▷ protoplasm
prototype n (pl -**s**) original or model to be copied or developed
prototypes n ▷ prototype
protozoa n ▷ protozoan
protozoan [pro-toe-**zoe**-an] n (pl -**zoa**) microscopic one-celled creature
protracted adj lengthened or extended
protractor n (pl -**s**) instrument for measuring angles
protractors n ▷ protractor
protrude v (-**des**, -**ding**, -**ded**) stick out, project
> **protrusion** n (pl -**s**)
protruded v ▷ protrude
protrudes v ▷ protrude
protruding v ▷ protrude
protrusion n ▷ protrude

protrusions n ▷ protrude
protuberance n ▷ protuberant
protuberances n ▷ protuberant
protuberant adj swelling out, bulging
> **protuberance** n (pl -**s**)
proud adj (-**er**, -**est**) feeling pleasure and satisfaction > **proudly** adv
prouder adj ▷ proud
proudest adj ▷ proud
proudly adv ▷ proud
prove v (-**ves**, -**ving**, -**ved** or -**ven**) establish the validity of
proved v ▷ prove
proven adj known from experience to work
▶ v ▷ prove
provenance [**prov**-in-anss] n (pl -**s**) place of origin
provenances n ▷ provenance
provender n (pl -**s**) (Old-fashioned) fodder
provenders n ▷ provender
proverb n (pl -**s**) short saying that expresses a truth or gives a warning > **proverbial** adj
proverbial adj ▷ proverb
proverbs n ▷ proverb
proves v ▷ prove
provide v (-**des**, -**ding**, -**ded**) make available
> **provider** n (pl -**s**)
provided v ▷ provide
providence n (pl -**s**) God or nature seen as a protective force that arranges people's lives
providences n ▷ providence
provident adj thrifty
providential adj lucky
provider n ▷ provide
providers n ▷ provide
provides v ▷ provide
providing v ▷ provide
province n (pl -**s**) area governed as a unit of a country or empire ▶ pl parts of a country outside the capital
provincial adj of a province or the provinces
▶ n (pl -**s**) unsophisticated person
provincialism n (pl -**s**) narrow-mindedness and lack of sophistication
provincialisms n ▷ provincialism
provincials n ▷ provincial
provinces n ▷ province
proving v ▷ prove
provision n (pl -**s**) act of supplying something
▶ pl food ▶ v (-**s**, -**ing**, -**ed**) supply with food
provisional adj temporary or conditional
> **provisionally** adv
provisionally adv ▷ provisional
provisioned v ▷ provision
provisioning v ▷ provision

provisions *n*, *v* ▷ provision
proviso [pro-**vize**-oh] *n* (*pl* -sos, -soes) condition, stipulation
provisoes *n* ▷ proviso
provisos *n* ▷ proviso
provocation *n* ▷ provoke
provocations *n* ▷ provoke
provocative *adj* ▷ provoke
provoke *v* (-kes, -king, -ked) deliberately anger > **provocation** *n* (*pl* -s) > **provocative** *adj*
provoked *v* ▷ provoke
provokes *v* ▷ provoke
provoking *v* ▷ provoke
provost *n* (*pl* -s) head of certain university colleges in Britain
provosts *n* ▷ provost
prow *n* (*pl* -s) bow of a vessel
prows *n* ▷ prow
prowess *n* (*pl* -es) superior skill or ability
prowesses *n* ▷ prowess
prowl *v* (-s, -ing, -ed) move stealthily around a place as if in search of prey or plunder ▶ *n* (*pl* -s) prowling
prowled *v* ▷ prowl
prowler *n* (*pl* -s) person who moves stealthily around a place as if in search of prey or plunder
prowlers *n* ▷ prowler
prowling *v* ▷ prowl
prowls *v*, *n* ▷ prowl
proxies *n* ▷ proxy
proximate *n* ▷ proximity
proximities *n* ▷ proximity
proximity *n* (*pl* -ties) nearness in space or time > **proximate** *adj*
proxy *n* (*pl* -xies) person authorized to act on behalf of someone else
prude *n* (*pl* -s) person who is excessively modest, prim, or proper > **prudish** *adj* > **prudery** *n* (*pl* -ries)
prudence *n* ▷ prudent
prudences *n* ▷ prudent
prudent *adj* cautious, discreet, and sensible > **prudence** *n* (*pl* -s)
prudential *adj* (Old-fashioned) prudent
prudes *n* ▷ prude
pruderies *n* ▷ prude
prudery *n* ▷ prude
prudish *adj* ▷ prude
prune[1] *n* (*pl* -s) dried plum
prune[2] *v* (-nes, -ning, -ned) cut off dead parts or excessive branches from (a tree or plant)
pruned *v* ▷ prune
prunes *n*, *v* ▷ prune[1, 2]
pruning *v* ▷ prune

prurience *n* ▷ prurient
pruriences *n* ▷ prurient
prurient *adj* excessively interested in sexual matters > **prurience** *n* (*pl* -s)
pry *v* (prys, prying, pried) make an impertinent or uninvited inquiry into a private matter
prying *v* ▷ pry
psalm *n* (*pl* -s) sacred song
psalmist *n* (*pl* -s) writer of psalms
psalmists *n* ▷ psalmist
psalms *n* ▷ psalm
psalter *n* (*pl* -s) book containing (a version of) psalms from the Bible
psalteries *n* ▷ psalter
psaltery *n* (*pl* -ries) ancient instrument played by plucking strings
psalters *n* ▷ psalter
psephologies *n* ▷ psephology
psephology [sef-**fol**-a-jee] *n* (*pl* -gies) statistical study of elections
pseud *n* (*pl* -s) (Informal) pretentious person
pseuds *n* ▷ pseud
pseudonym *n* (*pl* -s) fictitious name adopted esp. by an author > **pseudonymous** *adj*
pseudonymous *adj* ▷ pseudonym
pseudonyms *n* ▷ pseudonym

> **psi** *n* (psis). Psi is the 23rd letter of the Greek alphabet. This word can be useful if you have a difficult rack, especially if you can form another word at the same time. Psi scores 5 points.

psittacosis *n* (*pl* -ses) disease of parrots that can be transmitted to humans
psittacoses *n* ▷ psittacosis

> **pst** *interj*. Pst is a sound people make when they want to draw someone's attention to something without making too much noise. This is a useful word to remember because it doesn't use any vowels, and so can be useful if you have no vowels on your rack. Pst scores 5 points.

psyche [**sye**-kee] *n* (*pl* -s) human mind or soul
psychedelic *adj* denoting a drug that causes hallucinations
psyche *n* ▷ psyche
psychiatric *adj* ▷ psychiatry
psychiatries *n* ▷ psychiatry
psychiatrist *n* ▷ psychiatry
psychiatrists *n* ▷ psychiatry
psychiatry *n* (*pl* -ries) branch of medicine concerned with mental disorders > **psychiatric** *adj* > **psychiatrist** *n*

psychic adj (also **psychical**) having mental powers which cannot be explained by natural laws ▸ n (pl -s) person with psychic powers
psychics n ▷ psychic
psycho n (pl -s) (Informal) psychopath
psychoanalyse v ▷ psychoanalysis
psychoanalysed v ▷ psychoanalysis
psychoanalyses n, v ▷ psychoanalysis
psychoanalysing v ▷ psychoanalysis
psychoanalysis n (pl -ses) method of treating mental and emotional disorders by discussion and analysis of one's thoughts and feelings > **psychoanalyse** v (-ses, -sing, -sed) > **psychoanalyst** n (pl -s)
psychoanalyst n ▷ psychoanalysis
psychoanalysts n ▷ psychoanalysis
psychological adj of or affecting the mind > **psychologically** adv
psychologically adv ▷ psychological
psychologies n ▷ psychology
psychologist n ▷ psychology
psychologists n ▷ psychology
psychology n (pl -gies) study of human and animal behaviour > **psychologist** n (pl -s)
psychopath n (pl -s) person afflicted with a personality disorder causing him or her to commit antisocial or violent acts > **psychopathic** adj
psychopathic adj ▷ psychopath
psychopaths n ▷ psychopath
psychos n ▷ psycho
psychoses n ▷ psychosis
psychosis n (pl -ses) severe mental disorder in which the sufferer's contact with reality becomes distorted > **psychotic** adj
psychosomatic adj (of a physical disorder) thought to have psychological causes
psychotherapeutic adj ▷ psychotherapy
psychotherapies n ▷ psychotherapy
psychotherapist n ▷ psychotherapy
psychotherapists n ▷ psychotherapy
psychotherapy n (pl -pies) treatment of nervous disorders by psychological methods > **psychotherapeutic** adj > **psychotherapist** n
psychotic adj ▷ psychosis
ptarmigan [tar-mig-an] n (pl -s) bird of the grouse family which turns white in winter
ptarmigans n ▷ ptarmigan
pterodactyl [terr-roe-**dak**-til] n (pl -s) extinct flying reptile with batlike wings
pterodactyls n ▷ pterodactyl
ptomaine [toe-main] n (pl -s) any of a group of poisonous alkaloids found in decaying matter
ptomaines n ▷ ptomaine

pub n (pl -s) building with a bar licensed to sell alcoholic drinks
pubertal adj ▷ puberty
puberties n ▷ puberty
puberty n (pl -ties) beginning of sexual maturity > **pubertal** adj
pubic adj of the lower abdomen
public adj of or concerning the people as a whole ▸ n (pl -s) the community, people in general > **publicly** adv
publican n (pl -s) (BRIT, AUST & NZ) person who owns or runs a pub
publicans n ▷ publican
publication n ▷ publish
publications n ▷ publish
publicist n (pl -s) person, esp. a press agent or journalist, who publicizes something
publicists n ▷ publicist
publicities n ▷ publicity
publicity n (pl -ties) process or information used to arouse public attention
publicize v (-zes, -zing, -zed) bring to public attention
publicized v ▷ publicize
publicizes v ▷ publicize
publicizing v ▷ publicize
publicly adv ▷ public
publics n ▷ public
publish v (-es, -ing, -ed) produce and issue (printed matter) for sale > **publication** n (pl -s) > **publisher** n (pl -s)
published v ▷ publish
publisher n ▷ publish
publishers n ▷ publish
publishes v ▷ publish
publishing v ▷ publish
pubs n ▷ pub
puce adj (pucer, pucest) purplish-brown
pucer adj ▷ puce
pucest adj ▷ puce
puck¹ n (pl -s) small rubber disc used in ice hockey
puck² n (pl -s) mischievous or evil spirit > **puckish** adj
pucker v (-s, -ing, -ed) gather into wrinkles ▸ n (pl -s) wrinkle or crease
puckered v ▷ pucker
puckering v ▷ pucker
puckers v, n ▷ pucker
puckish adj ▷ puck²
pucks n ▷ puck¹, ²
pudding n (pl -s) dessert, esp. a cooked one served hot
puddings n ▷ pudding
puddle n (pl -s) small pool of water, esp. of rain

puddles n ▷ puddle
puerile adj silly and childish
puerperal [pew-er-per-al] adj concerning the period following childbirth
puff n (pl -s) (sound of) a short blast of breath, wind, etc. ▶ v (-s, -ing, -ed) blow or breathe in short quick draughts > **puffy** adj (-fier, -ffiest)
puffball n (pl -s) ball-shaped fungus
  puffballs n ▷ puffball
  puffed v ▷ puff
  puffier adj ▷ puff
  puffiest adj ▷ puff
puffin n (pl -s) black-and-white sea bird with a brightly-coloured beak
  puffins n ▷ puffin
  puffing v ▷ puff
  puffs n, v ▷ puff
  puffy adj ▷ puff
pug n (pl -s) small snub-nosed dog
  pugs n ▷ pug
pugilist [pew-jil-ist] n (pl -s) boxer > **pugilism** n (pl -s) > **pugilistic** adj
  pugilism n ▷ pugilist
  pugilisms n ▷ pugilist
  pugilistic adj ▷ pugilist
  pugilists n ▷ pugilist
pugnacious adj ready and eager to fight > **pugnacity** n (pl -ties)
  pugnacities n ▷ pugnacious
  pugnacity n ▷ pugnacious
puissance [pwee-sonce] n (pl -s) showjumping competition that tests a horse's ability to jump large obstacles
  puissances n ▷ puissance
puke (Slang) v (-kes, -king, -ked) vomit ▶ n (pl -s) act of vomiting
  puked v ▷ puke
  pukes v, n ▷ puke
  puking v ▷ puke
pulchritude n (pl -s) (Lit) beauty
  pulchritudes n ▷ pulchritude
pull v (-s, -ing, -ed) exert force on (an object) to move it towards the source of the force ▶ n (pl -s) act of pulling
  pulled v ▷ pull
pullet n (pl -s) young hen
  pullets n ▷ pullet
pulley n (pl -s) wheel with a grooved rim in which a belt, chain, or piece of rope runs in order to lift weights by a downward pull
  pulleys n ▷ pulley
  pulling v ▷ pull
pullover n (pl -s) sweater that is pulled on over the head
  pullovers n ▷ pullover

  pulls v, n ▷ pull
pulmonary adj of the lungs
pulp n (pl -s) soft wet substance made from crushed or beaten matter ▶ v (-s, -ing, -ed) reduce to pulp
  pulped v ▷ pulp
  pulping v ▷ pulp
pulpit n (pl -s) raised platform for a preacher
  pulpits n ▷ pulpit
  pulps n, v ▷ pulp
pulsar n (pl -s) small dense star which emits regular bursts of radio waves
  pulsars n ▷ pulsar
  pulsate v ▷ pulse[1]
  pulsated v ▷ pulse[1]
  pulsates v ▷ pulse[1]
  pulsating v ▷ pulse[1]
  pulsation n ▷ pulse[1]
  pulsations n ▷ pulse[1]
pulse[1] n (pl -s) regular beating of blood through the arteries at each heartbeat > **pulsate** v (-s, -ing, -ed) throb, quiver > **pulsation** n (pl -s)
pulse[2] n (-s) edible seed of a pod-bearing plant such as a bean or pea
  pulses n ▷ pulse[1, 2]
pulverize v (-zes, -zing, -zed) reduce to fine pieces
  pulverized v ▷ pulverize
  pulverizes v ▷ pulverize
  pulverizing v ▷ pulverize
puma n (pl -s) large American wild cat with a greyish-brown coat
  pumas n ▷ puma
pumice [pumm-iss] n (pl -s) light porous stone used for scouring
  pumices n ▷ pumice
pummel v (-s, -lling, -lled) strike repeatedly with or as if with the fists
  pummelled v ▷ pummel
  pummelling v ▷ pummel
  pummels v ▷ pummel
pump[1] n (pl -s) machine used to force a liquid or gas to move in a particular direction ▶ v (-s, -ing, -ed) raise or drive with a pump
pump[2] n (pl -s) light flat-soled shoe
  pumped v ▷ pump
  pumping v ▷ pump
pumpkin n (pl -s) large round fruit with an orange rind, soft flesh, and many seeds
  pumpkins n ▷ pumpkin
  pumps n, v ▷ pump[1, 2]
pun n (pl -s) use of words to exploit double meanings for humorous effect ▶ v (-s, -nning, -nned) make puns

punch¹ v (-es, -ing, -ed) strike at with a clenched fist ▸ n (pl -es) blow with a clenched fist (Informal)

punch² n (pl -es) tool or machine for shaping, piercing, or engraving ▸ v (-es, -ing, -ed) pierce, cut, stamp, shape, or drive with a punch

punch³ n (pl -es) drink made from a mixture of wine, spirits, fruit, sugar, and spices

punched v, n ▷ punch¹, ²

punches v, n ▷ punch

punchier adj ▷ punchy

punchiest adj ▷ punchy

punching v ▷ punch¹, ²

punchy adj (-chier, -chiest) forceful

punctilious adj paying great attention to correctness in etiquette

punctual adj arriving or taking place at the correct time > **punctuality** n (pl -ties) > **punctually** adv

punctualities n ▷ punctual

punctuality n ▷ punctual

punctually adv ▷ punctual

punctuate v (-tes, -ting, -ted) put punctuation marks in

punctuated v ▷ punctuate

punctuates v ▷ punctuate

punctuating v ▷ punctuate

punctuation n (pl -s) (use of) marks such as commas, colons, etc. in writing, to assist in making the sense clear

punctuations n ▷ punctuation

puncture n (pl -s) small hole made by a sharp object, esp. in a tyre ▸ v (-res, -ring, -red) pierce a hole in

punctured v ▷ puncture

punctures n, v ▷ puncture

puncturing v ▷ puncture

pundit n (pl -s) expert who speaks publicly on a subject

pundits n ▷ pundit

pungencies n ▷ pungent

pungency n ▷ pungent

pungent adj having a strong sharp bitter flavour > **pungency** n (pl -cies)

punier adj ▷ puny

puniest adj ▷ puny

punish v (-es, -ing, -ed) cause (someone) to suffer or undergo a penalty for some wrongdoing > **punishment** n (pl -s)

punished v ▷ punish

punishes v ▷ punish

punishing adj harsh or difficult ▸ v ▷ punish

punishment n ▷ punish

punishments n ▷ punish

punitive [pew-nit-tiv] adj relating to punishment

punk n (pl -s) anti-Establishment youth movement and style of rock music of the late 1970s

punks n ▷ punk

punned v ▷ pun

punnet n (pl -s) small basket for fruit

punnets n ▷ punnet

punning v ▷ pun

puns n, v ▷ pun

punt¹ n (pl -s) open flat-bottomed boat propelled by a pole ▸ v (-s, -ing, -ed) travel in a punt

punt² (SPORT) n (pl -s) kick of a ball before it touches the ground when dropped from the hands ▸ v (-s, -ing, -ed) kick (a ball) in this way

punt³ n (pl -s) former monetary unit of the Irish Republic

punted v ▷ punt

punter n (pl -s) person who bets

punters n ▷ punter

punting v ▷ punt

punts n, v ▷ punt¹, ², ³

puny adj (-nier, -niest) small and feeble

pup n (pl -s) young of certain animals, such as dogs and seals

pupa n (pl -pae, -pas) insect at the stage of development between a larva and an adult

pupae n ▷ pupa

pupas n ▷ pupa

pupil¹ n (pl -s) person who is taught by a teacher

pupil² n (pl -s) round dark opening in the centre of the eye

pupils n ▷ pupil¹, ²

puppet n (pl -s) small doll or figure moved by strings or by the operator's hand > **puppeteer** n (pl -s)

puppeteer n ▷ puppet

puppeteers n ▷ puppet

puppets n ▷ puppet

puppies n ▷ puppy

puppy n (pl -ppies) young dog

pups n ▷ pup

purchase v (-ses, -sing, -sed) obtain by payment ▸ n (pl -s) thing that is bought > **purchaser** n (pl -s)

purchased v ▷ purchase

purchaser n ▷ purchase

purchasers n ▷ purchase

purchases v, n ▷ purchase

purchasing v ▷ purchase

purdah n (pl -s) Muslim and Hindu custom of keeping women in seclusion, with clothing

that conceals them completely when they go out
purdahs n ▷ purdah
pure adj (-r, -st) unmixed, untainted > **purely** adv > **purity** n (pl -ies)
purely adv ▷ pure
purée [pure-ray] n (pl -s) pulp of cooked food ▶ v (-s, -réeing, -réed) make into a purée
puréed v ▷ purée
puréeing v ▷ purée
purées n, v ▷ purée
purer adj ▷ pure
purest adj ▷ pure
purgatorial adj ▷ purgatory
purgatories n ▷ purgatory
purgatory n (pl -ries) place or state of temporary suffering > **purgatorial** adj
purge v (-ges, -ging, -ged) rid (a thing or place) of (unwanted things or people) ▶ n (pl -s) purging
purgative n, adj (medicine) designed to cause defecation
purgatives n ▷ purgative
purged v ▷ purge
purges v, n ▷ purge
purging v ▷ purge
purification n ▷ purify
purifications n ▷ purify
purified v ▷ purify
purifies v ▷ purify
purify v (-fies, -fying, -fied) make or become pure > **purification** n (pl -s)
purifying v ▷ purify
purist n (pl -s) person concerned with strict obedience to the traditions of a subject
purists n ▷ purist
puritan n (pl -s) person with strict moral and religious principles > **puritanical** adj > **puritanism** n (pl -s)
puritanical adj ▷ puritan
puritanism n ▷ puritan
puritanisms n ▷ puritan
puritans n ▷ puritan
purities n ▷ pure
purity n ▷ pure
purl n (pl -s) stitch made by knitting a plain stitch backwards ▶ v (-s, -ing, -ed) knit in purl
purled v ▷ purl
purlieus [per-lyooz] pl n (Lit) outskirts
purling v ▷ purl
purloin v (-s, -ing, -ed) steal
purloined v ▷ purloin
purloining v ▷ purloin
purloins v ▷ purloin
purls n, v ▷ purl

purple adj, n (pl -s) (of) a colour between red and blue
purples n ▷ purple
purport v (-s, -ing, -ed) claim (to be or do something) ▶ n (pl -s) apparent meaning, significance
purported v ▷ purport
purporting v ▷ purport
purports v, n ▷ purport
purpose n (pl -s) reason for which something is done or exists
purposely adv intentionally
purposes n ▷ purpose
purr v (-s, -ing, -ed) (of cats) make low vibrant sound, usu. when pleased ▶ n (pl -s) this sound
purred v ▷ purr
purring v ▷ purr
purrs v, n ▷ purr
purse n (pl -s) small bag for money (US & NZ) ▶ v (-ses, -sing, -sed) draw (one's lips) together into a small round shape
pursed v ▷ purse
purser n (pl -s) ship's officer who keeps the accounts
pursers n ▷ purser
purses n, v ▷ purse
pursing v ▷ purse
pursue v (-sues, -suing, -sued) chase > **pursuer** n (pl -s)
pursued v ▷ pursue
pursuer n ▷ pursue
pursuers n ▷ pursue
pursues v ▷ pursue
pursuing v ▷ pursue
pursuit n (pl -s) pursuing
pursuits n ▷ pursuit
purulent [pure-yoo-lent] adj of or containing pus
purvey v (-s, -ing, -ed) supply (provisions) > **purveyor** n (pl -s)
purveyed v ▷ purvey
purveying v ▷ purvey
purveyor n ▷ purvey
purveyors n ▷ purvey
purveys v ▷ purvey
purview n (pl -s) scope or range of activity or outlook
purviews n ▷ purview
pus n (pl -es) yellowish matter produced by infected tissue
puses n ▷ pus
push v (-es, -ing, -ed) move or try to move by steady force (Informal) ▶ n (pl -es) act of pushing

pushed v ▷ push
pusher n (pl -s) person who sells illegal drugs
pushers n ▷ pusher
pushes v, n ▷ push
pushier adj ▷ pushy
pushiest adj ▷ pushy
pushing v ▷ push
pushy adj (-shier, -shiest) too assertive or ambitious
pushchair n (pl -s) (BRIT) folding chair on wheels for a baby
pushchairs n ▷ pushchair
pusillanimous adj timid and cowardly
  > **pusillanimity** n (pl -ies)
pusillanimities n ▷ pusillanimous
pusillanimity n ▷ pusillanimous
puss, pussy n (pl -es, -ies) (Informal) cat
pusses n ▷ puss
pussies n ▷ puss
pussyfoot v (-s, -ing, -ed) (Informal) behave too cautiously
pussyfooted v ▷ pussyfoot
pussyfooting v ▷ pussyfoot
pussyfoots v ▷ pussyfoot
pustule n (pl -s) pimple containing pus
pustules n ▷ pustule
put v (puts, putting, put) cause to be (in a position, state, or place) ▶ n (pl -s) throw in putting the shot
putative adj reputed, supposed
putrefied v ▷ putrify
putrefies v ▷ putrify
putrefy v (-fies, -fying, -fied) rot and produce an offensive smell > **putrefaction** n (pl -s)
putrefaction n ▷ putrefy
putrefactions n ▷ putrefy
putrefying v ▷ putrefy
putrescent adj rotting
putrid adj rotten and foul-smelling
puts v, n ▷ put
putsch n (pl -es) sudden violent attempt to remove a government from power
putsches n ▷ putsch
putt (GOLF) n (pl -s) stroke on the putting green to roll the ball into or near the hole ▶ v (-s, -ing, -ed) strike (the ball) in this way
putted n, v ▷ putt
putter n (pl -s) golf club for putting
putters n ▷ putter

putties n ▷ putty
putting v ▷ put putt
putts v, n ▷ putt
putty n (pl -ies) adhesive used to fix glass into frames and fill cracks in woodwork
puzzle v (-les, -ling, -led) perplex and confuse or be perplexed or confused ▶ n (pl -s) problem that cannot be easily solved > **puzzlement** n (pl -s) > **puzzling** adj
puzzled v ▷ puzzle
puzzlement n ▷ puzzle
puzzlements n ▷ puzzle
puzzles v, n ▷ puzzle
puzzling v, adj ▷ puzzle
pygmies n ▷ pygmy
pygmy n (pl -ies) something that is a very small example of its type ▶ adj (p-) very small
pyjamas pl n loose-fitting trousers and top worn in bed
pylon n (pl -s) steel tower-like structure supporting electrical cables
pylons n ▷ pylon
pyramid n (pl -s) solid figure with a flat base and triangular sides sloping upwards to a point > **pyramidal** adj
pyramidal adj ▷ pyramid
pyramids n ▷ pyramid
pyre n (pl -s) pile of wood for burning a corpse on
pyres n ▷ pyre
pyromania n (pl -s) uncontrollable urge to set things on fire > **pyromaniac** n (pl -s)
pyromanias n ▷ pyromania
pyromaniac n ▷ pyromania
pyromaniacs n ▷ pyromania
pyrotechnics n art of making fireworks
  > **pyrotechnic** adj
pyrotechnic adj ▷ pyrotechnics
python n (pl -s) large nonpoisonous snake that crushes its prey
pythons n ▷ python

> **pyx** n (**pyxes**). A **pyx** is a container used for testing the weight of coins. This word can also be spelt **pix**. It's a great word to know as it earns a good score and doesn't use any vowels very helpful if you have a difficult rack. Pyx scores 15 points.

Qq

With a value of 10 points, Q is one of the best tiles to have on your rack. It can, however, be a difficult letter to use, especially if you don't have a U to play it with. It's therefore a good idea to remember the short words beginning with Q that don't need a U. This is easy, as there's only one two-letter word starting with Q: **qi** (11 points). There are three three-letter words, only one of which needs a U: **qua** (12). The other two are **qat** and **qis** (12 each). If you do have a U, remember **quiz** (22), which is a very useful word. If you have a blank tile for the second Z, you may be able to form its plural or verb inflections: **quizzes** (24), **quizzed** (25) and **quizzing** (26). This is especially worth remembering in case someone else plays quiz. Don't forget **quartz** (24) either.

qat *n* (*qats*). Qat is a shrub that grows in Africa and Arabia. This is a great word as it combines Q with two of the most common letters in the game, and thus is very handy if there isn't a U on your rack or the board. Qat scores 12 points.

qi *n* (*qis*). In Chinese medicine, qi is vital energy believed to circulate in the body. This is an exceptionally useful word, as it's the only two-letter word containing Q, and doesn't contain a U. The plural is one of only three three-letter words that begin with Q. As I is one of the more common tiles on the board, it's highly likely that you will be able to play qi if you have a Q. Qi scores 11 points.

qua *prep.* Qua means in the capacity of. This is the only three-letter word beginning with Q that needs a U, and is useful when you have a U, or there is a U on the board, but don't have any promising tiles to go with it. Qua scores 12 points.

quack[1] *v* (*-s, -ing, -ed*) (of a duck) utter a harsh guttural sound ▶ *n* (*pl -s*) sound made by a duck

quack[2] *n* (*pl -s*) unqualified person who claims medical knowledge
    quacked *v* ▷ quack[1]
    quacking *v* ▷ quack[1]
    quacks *v* ▷ quack[1] ▶ *n* ▷ quack[1, 2]

quad *n* (*pl -s*) ▷ **quadrangle** ▶ *adj*
  ▷ **quadraphonic**

quadrangle *n* (*pl -s*) (*also* **quad**) rectangular courtyard with buildings on all four sides
  > **quadrangular** *adj*
    quadrangles *n* ▷ quadrangle
    quadrangular *adj* ▷ quadrangle

quadrant *n* (*pl -s*) quarter of a circle
    quadrants *n* ▷ quadrant

quadraphonic *adj* (*also* **quad**) using four independent channels to reproduce or record sound

quadratic (MATHS) *n* (*pl -s*) equation in which the variable is raised to the power of two, but nowhere raised to a higher power ▶ *adj* of the second power
    quadratics *n* ▷ quadratic

quadrennial *adj* occurring every four years

quadrilateral *adj* having four sides ▶ *n* (*pl -s*) polygon with four sides
    quadrilaterals *n* ▷ quadrilateral

quadrille *n* (*pl -s*) square dance for four couples
    quadrilles *n* ▷ quadrille

quadriplegia *n* (*pl -s*) paralysis of all four limbs
    quadriplegias *n* ▷ quadriplegia

quadruped [**kwod**-roo-ped] *n* (*pl -s*) any animal with four legs
    quadrupeds *n* ▷ quadruped

quadruple *v* (*-les, -ling, -led*) multiply by four ▶ *adj* four times as much or as many
    quadrupled *v* ▷ quadruple
    quadruples *v* ▷ quadruple

quadruplet *n* (*pl -s*) one of four offspring born

at one birth
quadruplets n ▷ quadruplet
quadrupling v ▷ quadruple
quads n ▷ quad
quaff [kwoff] v (-s, -ing, -ed) drink heartily or in one draught
quaffed v ▷ quaff
quaffing v ▷ quaff
quaffs v ▷ quaff
quagmire [kwog-mire] n (pl -s) soft wet area of land
quagmires n ▷ quagmire
quail[1] n (pl -s) small game bird of the partridge family
quail[2] v (-s, -ing, -ed) shrink back with fear
quailed v ▷ quail
quailing v ▷ quail
quails n ▷ quail[1] ▶ v ▷ quail[2]
quaint adj (-er, -est) attractively unusual, esp. in an old-fashioned style > **quaintly** adv
quainter adj ▷ quaint
quaintest adj ▷ quaint
quaintly adv ▷ quaint
quake v (-kes, -king, -ked) shake or tremble with or as if with fear ▶ n (pl -s) (Informal) earthquake
quaked v, n ▷ quake
quakes v ▷ quake
quaking v ▷ quake
qualification n (pl -s) official record of achievement in a course or examination
qualifications n ▷ qualification
qualified v, adj ▷ qualify
qualifies v ▷ qualify
qualify v (-fies, -fying, -fied) provide or be provided with the abilities necessary for a task, office, or duty > **qualified** adj
qualifying v ▷ qualify
qualitative adj of or relating to quality
qualities n ▷ quality
quality n (pl -ties) degree or standard of excellence ▶ adj excellent or superior
qualm [kwahm] n (pl -s) pang of conscience
qualms n ▷ qualm
quandaries n ▷ quandary
quandary n (pl -ries) difficult situation or dilemma
quandong [kwon-dong] n (pl -s) small Australian tree with edible fruit and nuts used in preserves
quandongs n ▷ quandong
quango n (pl -s) (CHIEFLY BRIT) quasi-autonomous nongovernmental organization: any partly independent official body set up by a government

quangos n ▷ quango
quanta n ▷ quantum
quantifiable adj ▷ quantify
quantification n ▷ quantify
quantifications n ▷ quantify
quantified v ▷ quantify
quantifies v ▷ quantify
quantify v (-fies, -fying, -fied) discover or express the quantity of > **quantifiable** adj
> **quantification** n (pl -s)
quantifying v ▷ quantify
quantitative adj of or relating to quantity
quantities n ▷ quantity
quantity n (pl -ties) specified or definite amount or number
quantum n (pl -ta) desired or required amount, esp. a very small one
quarantine n (pl -s) period of isolation of people or animals to prevent the spread of disease ▶ v (-nes, -ning, -ned) isolate in or as if in quarantine
quarantined v ▷ quarantine
quarantines n, v ▷ quarantine
quarantining v ▷ quarantine
quark n (pl -s) (PHYSICS) subatomic particle thought to be the fundamental unit of matter
quarks n ▷ quark
quarrel n (pl -s) angry disagreement ▶ v (-s, -lling, -lled) have a disagreement or dispute
> **quarrelsome** adj
quarrelled v ▷ quarrel
quarrelling v ▷ quarrel
quarrels n, v ▷ quarrel
quarrelsome adj ▷ quarrel
quarried v ▷ quarry[1]
quarries n ▷ quarry[1, 2] ▶ v ▷ quarry[1]
quarry[1] n (pl -rries) place where stone is dug from the surface of the earth ▶ v (-rries, -rrying, -rried) extract (stone) from a quarry
quarry[2] n (pl -rries) person or animal that is being hunted
quart n (pl -s) unit of liquid measure equal to two pints (1.136 litres)
quarter n (pl -s) one of four equal parts of something ▶ v (-s, -ing, -ed) divide into four equal parts
quarterdeck n (pl -s) (NAUT) rear part of the upper deck of a ship
quarterdecks n ▷ quarterdeck
quartered v ▷ quarter
quarterfinal n (pl -s) round before the semifinal in a competition
quarterfinals n ▷ quarterfinal
quartering v ▷ quarter

quarterlies n ▷ quarterly

quarterly adj occurring, due, or issued at intervals of three months ▶ n (pl -lies) magazine issued every three months ▶ adv once every three months

quartermaster n (pl -s) military officer responsible for accommodation, food, and equipment

quartermasters n ▷ quartermaster

quarters n, v ▷ quarter

quartet n (pl -s) group of four performers

quartets n ▷ quartet

quarto n (pl -s) book size in which the sheets are folded into four leaves

quarto n ▷ quarto

quarts n ▷ quart

quartz n (pl -es) hard glossy mineral

quartzes n ▷ quartz

quasar [kway-zar] n (pl -s) extremely distant starlike object that emits powerful radio waves

quasars n ▷ quasar

quash v (-shes, -shing, -shed) annul or make void

quashed v ▷ quash

quashes v ▷ quash

quashing v ▷ quash

quatrain n (pl -s) stanza or poem of four lines

quatrains n ▷ quatrain

quaver v (-s, -ing, -ed) (of a voice) quiver or tremble ▶ n (pl -s) (MUSIC) note half the length of a crotchet

quavered v ▷ quaver

quavering v ▷ quaver

quavers v, n ▷ quaver

quay [kee] n (pl -s) wharf built parallel to the shore

quays n ▷ quay

queasier adj ▷ queasy

queasiest adj ▷ queasy

queasiness n ▷ queasy

queasinesses n ▷ queasy

queasy adj (-sier, -siest) having the feeling that one is about to vomit > **queasiness** n (pl -es)

queen n (pl -s) female sovereign who is the official ruler or head of state > **queenly** adj

queenly adj ▷ queen

queens n ▷ queen

queer adj (-er, -est) not normal or usual

queerer adj ▷ queer

queerest adj ▷ queer

quell v (-s, -ing, -ed) suppress

quelled v ▷ quell

quelling v ▷ quell

quells v ▷ quell

quench v (-es, -ing, -ed) satisfy (one's thirst)

quenched v ▷ quench

quenches v ▷ quench

quenching v ▷ quench

queried v ▷ query

queries n, v ▷ query

quern n (pl -s) stone hand mill for grinding corn

querns n ▷ quern

querulous [kwer-yoo-luss] adj complaining or whining > **querulously** adv

querulously adv ▷ querulous

query n (pl -ries) question, esp. one raising doubt ▶ v (-ries, -rying, -ried) express uncertainty, doubt, or an objection concerning (something)

querying v ▷ query

quest n (pl -s) long and difficult search ▶ v (-s, -ing, -ed) (foll. by for or after) go in search of

quested v ▷ quest

questing v ▷ quest

question n (pl -s) form of words addressed to a person in order to obtain an answer ▶ v (-s, -ing, -ed) put a question or questions to (a person)

questionable adj of disputable value or authority > **questionably** adv

questionably adv ▷ questionable

questioned v ▷ question

questioning v ▷ question

questionnaire n (pl -s) set of questions on a form, used to collect information from people

questionnaires n ▷ questionnaire

questions n, v ▷ question

quests n, v ▷ quest

> **quetzal** or **quezal** n (**quetzals, quezales, quezals**). The quetzal is a crested bird of Central and South America. This is a great word if you can get the tiles for it, so it's well worth remembering both spellings and the three plural forms. If you can use all your letters to play quetzal or quezals, you'll earn a bonus of 50 points. Quetzal scores 25 points.

queue n (pl -s) line of people or vehicles waiting for something ▶ v (**queues, queuing** or **queueing, queued**) (often foll. by **up**) form or remain in a line while waiting

queued v ▷ queue

queueing v ▷ queue

queues n, v ▷ queue

queuing v ▷ queue

quibble v (-les, -ling, -led) make trivial

objections ▶ *n* (*pl* -s) trivial objection
quibbled *v* ▷ quibble
quibbles *v, n* ▷ quibble
quibbling *v* ▷ quibble
quiche [keesh] *n* (*pl* -s) savoury flan with an egg custard filling to which vegetables etc. are added
quiches *n* ▷ quiche
quick *adj* (-er, -est) speedy, fast ▶ *n* (*pl* -s) area of sensitive flesh under a nail ▶ *adv* (*Informal*) in a rapid manner ▷ **quickly** *adv*
quicken *v* (-s, -ing, -ed) make or become faster
quickened *v* ▷ quicken
quickening *v* ▷ quicken
quickens *v* ▷ quicken
quicker *adj* ▷ quick
quickest *adj* ▷ quick
quicklime *n* (*pl* -s) white solid used in the manufacture of glass and steel
quicklimes *n* ▷ quicklime
quickly *adv* ▷ quick
quicks *n* ▷ quick
quicksand *n* (*pl* -s) deep mass of loose wet sand that sucks anything on top of it into it
quicksands *n* ▷ quicksand
quicksilver *n* (*pl* -s) mercury
quicksilvers *n* ▷ quicksilver
quickstep *n* (*pl* -s) fast modern ballroom dance
quicksteps *n* ▷ quickstep
quid *n* (*pl* quid, -s) (BRIT) (*Slang*) pound (sterling)
quids *n* ▷ quid
quiescence *n* ▷ quiescent
quiescences *n* ▷ quiescent
quiescent [kwee-**ess**-ent] *adj* quiet, inactive, or dormant ▷ **quiescence** *n* (*pl* -s)
quiet *adj* (-er, -est) with little noise ▶ *n* (*pl* -s) quietness ▶ *v* (-s, -ing, -ed) make or become quiet ▷ **quietly** *adv* ▷ **quietness** *n* (*pl* -es)
quieted *v* ▷ quiet
quieten *v* (-s, -ing, -ed) (*often foll. by* **down**) make or become quiet
quieter *adj* ▷ quiet
quietest *adj* ▷ quiet
quieting *v* ▷ quiet
quietism *n* (*pl* -s) passivity and calmness of mind towards external events
quietisms *n* ▷ quietism
quietly *adv* ▷ quiet
quietness *n* ▷ quiet
quietnesses *n* ▷ quiet
quiets *v, n* ▷ quiet
quietude *n* (-s) quietness, peace, or tranquillity
quietudes *n* ▷ quietude
quiff *n* (*pl* -s) tuft of hair brushed up above the forehead

quiffs *n* ▷ quiff
quill *n* (*pl* -s) pen made from the feather of a bird's wing or tail
quills *n* ▷ quill
quilt *n* (*pl* -s) padded covering for a bed
quilted *adj* consisting of two layers of fabric with a layer of soft material between them
quilts *n* ▷ quilt
quince *n* (*pl* -s) acid-tasting pear-shaped fruit
quinces *n* ▷ quince
quinine *n* (*pl* -s) bitter drug used as a tonic and formerly to treat malaria
quinines *n* ▷ quinine
quinquennial *adj* occurring every five years
quins *n* ▷ quin
quinsies *n* ▷ quinsy
quinsy *n* (*pl* -sies) inflammation of the throat or tonsils
quintessence *n* (*pl* -s) most perfect representation of a quality or state ▷ **quintessential** *adj*
quintessences *n* ▷ quintessence
quintessential *adj* ▷ quintessence
quintet *n* (*pl* -s) group of five performers
quintets *n* ▷ quintet
quintuplet *n* (*pl* -s) one of five offspring born at one birth
quintuplets *n* ▷ quintuplet

> **quinze** *n* (**quinzes**). Quinze is a card game. This is a high-scoring word, and if you can use all of your tiles to form the plural, you'll get a 50-points bonus. Quinze scores 24 points.

quip *n* (*pl* -s) witty saying ▶ *v* (-s, -pping, -pped) make a quip
quipped *v* ▷ quip
quipping *v* ▷ quip
quips *n, v* ▷ quip
quire *n* (*pl* -s) set of 24 or 25 sheets of paper
quires *n* ▷ quire
quirk *n* (*pl* -s) peculiarity of character ▷ **quirky** *adj* (-kier, -kiest)
quirks *n* ▷ quirk
quirky *adj* ▷ quirk
quisling *n* (*pl* -s) traitor who aids an occupying enemy force
quislings *n* ▷ quisling
quit *v* (quits, quitting, quit) stop (doing something)
quite *adv* somewhat ▶ *interj* expression of agreement
quits *adj* (*Informal*) on an equal footing ▶ *v* ▷ quit
quitter *n* (*pl* -s) person who lacks perseverance

quitters *n* ▷ quitter

quitting *v* ▷ quit

quiver¹ *v* (**-s, -ing, -ed**) shake with a tremulous movement ▶ *n* (*pl* **-s**) shaking or trembling

quiver² *n* (*pl* **-s**) case for arrows

quivered *v* ▷ quiver¹

quivering *v* ▷ quiver¹

quivers *v* ▷ quiver¹ ▶ *n* ▷ quiver¹, ²

> **quixote** *n* (**quixotes**). A quixote is an impractically idealistic person. This is a high-scoring word; if you have all the letters to play it, and can place them on the board, you'll score a 50-point bonus for using all of your tiles. Quixote scores 23 points.

quixotic [kwik-**sot**-ik] *adj* romantic and unrealistic > **quixotically** *adv*

quixotically *adv* ▷ quixotic

quiz *n* (*pl* **-zzes**) entertainment in which the knowledge of the players is tested by a series of questions ▶ *v* (**-zzes, -zzing, -zzed**) investigate by close questioning

quizzed *v* ▷ quiz

quizzes *n*, *v* ▷ quiz

quizzical *adj* questioning and mocking > **quizzically** *adv*

quizzically *adv* ▷ quizzical

quizzing *v* ▷ quiz

quod *n* (*pl* **-s**) (BRIT) (Slang) jail

quods *n* ▷ quod

quoit *n* (*pl* **-s**) large ring used in the game of

quoits ▶ *pl* game in which quoits are tossed at a stake in the ground in attempts to encircle it

quoits *n* ▷ quoit

quokka *n* (*pl* **-s**) small Australian wallaby

quokkas *n* ▷ quokka

quorum *n* (*pl* **-s**) minimum number of people required to be present at a meeting before any transactions can take place

quorums *n* ▷ quorum

quota *n* (*pl* **-s**) share that is due from, due to, or allocated to a group or person

quotable *adj* ▷ quote

quotas *n* ▷ quota

quotation *n* (*pl* **-s**) written or spoken passage repeated exactly in a later work, speech, or conversation

quotations *n* ▷ quotation

quote *v* (**-tes, -ting, -ted**) repeat (words) exactly from (an earlier work, speech, or conversation) ▶ *n* (*pl* **-s**) (*Informal*) quotation > **quotable** *adj*

quoted *v* ▷ quote

quotes *v*, *n* ▷ quote

quoth *v* (*Obs*) said

quotidian *adj* daily

quotient *n* (*pl* **-s**) result of the division of one number or quantity by another

quotients *n* ▷ quotient

quoting *v* ▷ quote

Rr

R is one of the most common consonants in Scrabble, along with N and T. Despite this, however, there is only one two-letter word beginning with R: **re** (2 points). This is worth remembering, as you won't need to waste time trying to think of others. There are some good three-letter words with R, however, some of which are quite unusual: **raj**, **rax**, **rex** (10 each), **rez** and **riz** (12 each). Also, don't forget common words like **raw**, **ray** and **row** (6 each).

rabbi [rab-bye] *n* (*pl* -s) Jewish spiritual leader
> **rabbinical** *adj*
  rabbinical *adj* ▷ rabbi
  rabbis *n* ▷ rabbi
rabbit *n* (*pl* -s) small burrowing mammal with long ears
  rabbits *n* ▷ rabbit
rabble *n* (*pl* -s) disorderly crowd of noisy people
  rabbles *n* ▷ rabble
rabid *adj* (-er, -est) fanatical > **rabidly** *adv*
  rabider *adj* ▷ rabid
  rabidest *adj* ▷ rabid
  rabidly *adv* ▷ rabid
rabies [ray-beez] *n* usu. fatal viral disease transmitted by dogs and certain other animals
raccoon *n* (*pl* -s) small N American mammal with a long striped tail
  raccoons *n* ▷ raccoon
race¹ *n* (*pl* -s) contest of speed ▶ *pl* meeting for horse racing ▶ *v* (-ces, -cing, -ced) compete with in a race > **racer** *n* (*pl* -s) > **racecourse** *n* (*pl* -s) > **racehorse** *n* (*pl* -s) > **racetrack** *n* (*pl* -s)
race² *n* (*pl* -s) group of people of common ancestry with distinguishing physical features, such as skin colour > **racial** *adj*
raced *n*, *v* ▷ race¹
  racecourse *n* ▷ race¹
  racecourses *n* ▷ race¹
  raced *n*, *v* ▷ race¹
racehorse *n* ▷ race¹
  racehorses *n* ▷ race¹
raceme [rass-eem] *n* (*pl* -s) cluster of flowers along a central stem, as in the foxglove
  racemes *n* ▷ raceme
  racer *n* ▷ race¹
  racers *n* ▷ race¹
  races *n* ▷ race¹, ² *v* ▷ race¹

racetrack *n* ▷ race¹
  racetracks *n* ▷ race¹
racial *adj* ▷ race²
racialism *n* ▷ racism
  racialisms *adj*, *n* ▷ racism
  racialist *n* ▷ racism
  racialists *n* ▷ racism
  racier *adj* ▷ racy
  raciest *adj* ▷ racy
  racing *v* ▷ race
racism, racialism *n* (*pl* -s) hostile attitude or behaviour to members of other races, based on a belief in the innate superiority of one's own race > **racist, racialist** *adj*, *n* (*pl* -s)
  racisms *n* ▷ racism
  racist *n* ▷ racism
  racists *n* ▷ racism
rack *n* (*pl* -s) framework for holding particular articles, such as coats or luggage (HIST) ▶ *v* (-s, -ing, -ed) cause great suffering to
  racked *v* ▷ rack
racket¹ *n* (*pl* -s) noisy disturbance
racket², racquet *n* (-s) bat with strings stretched in an oval frame, used in tennis etc.
racketeer *n* (*pl* -s) person making illegal profits
  racketeers *n* ▷ racketeer
rackets *n* ball game played in a paved walled court ▶ *n* ▷ racket¹, ²
  racking *v* ▷ rack
  racks *n*, *v* ▷ rack
raconteur [rak-on-tur] *n* (*pl* -s) skilled storyteller
  raconteurs *n* ▷ raconteur
  racquet *n* ▷ racket²
  racquets *n* ▷ racket²
racy *adj* (-cier, -ciest) slightly shocking
radar *n* (*pl* -s) device for tracking distant objects by bouncing high-frequency radio

pulses off them

radars n ▷ radar

radial adj spreading out from a common central point

radiance n ▷ radiant

radiances n ▷ radiant

radiant adj looking happy > **radiance** n (-s)

radiate v (-tes, -ting, -ted) spread out from a centre

radiated v ▷ radiate

radiates v ▷ radiate

radiating v ▷ radiate .

radiation n (pl -s) transmission of energy from one body to another

radiations n ▷ radiation

radiator n (-s) (BRIT) arrangement of pipes containing hot water or steam to heat a room

radiators n ▷ radiator

radical adj fundamental ▶ n (pl -s) person advocating fundamental (political) change > **radically** adv > **radicalism** n (-s)

radicalism n ▷ radical

radicalisms n ▷ radical

radically adv ▷ radical

radicals n ▷ radical

radicle n (pl -s) small or developing root

radicles n ▷ radicle

radii n ▷ radius

radio n (pl -s) use of electromagnetic waves for broadcasting, communication, etc. ▶ v (-s, -ing, -ed) transmit (a message) by radio

radioactive adj emitting radiation as a result of nuclear decay > **radioactivity** n (pl -ies)

radioactivities n ▷ radioactive

radioactivity n ▷ radioactive

radioed v ▷ radio

radiographer n ▷ radiography

radiographers n ▷ radiography

radiographies n ▷ radiography

radiography [ray-dee-**og**-ra-fee] n (pl -phies) production of an image on a film or plate by radiation > **radiographer** n (pl -s)

radioing v ▷ radio

radiologies n ▷ radiology

radiologist n ▷ radiology

radiologists n ▷ radiology

radiology [ray-dee-**ol**-a-jee] n (pl -gies) science of using x-rays in medicine > **radiologist** n (pl -s)

radios n, v ▷ radio

radiotherapies n ▷ radiotherapy

radiotherapist n ▷ radiotherapy

radiotherapists n ▷ radiotherapy

radiotherapy n (pl -pies) treatment of disease,

esp. cancer, by radiation > **radiotherapist** n (pl -s)

radish n (pl -es) small hot-flavoured root vegetable eaten raw in salads

radishes n ▷ radish

radium n (-s) (CHEM) radioactive metallic element

radiums n ▷ radiums

radius n (pl radii, radiuses) (length of) a straight line from the centre to the circumference of a circle

radiuses n ▷ radius

radon [**ray**-don] n (pl -s) (CHEM) radioactive gaseous element

radons n ▷ radon

raffia n (pl -s) prepared palm fibre for weaving mats etc.

raffias n ▷ raffia

raffish adj slightly disreputable

raffle n (pl -s) lottery with goods as prizes ▶ v (-les, -ling, -led) offer as a prize in a raffle

raffled v ▷ raffle

raffles n, v ▷ raffle

raffling v ▷ raffle

raft n (pl -s) floating platform of logs, etc.

rafter n (pl -s) one of the main beams of a roof

rafters n ▷ rafter

raftings n ▷ raft

rafts n ▷ raft

rag[1] n (pl -s) fragment of cloth ▶ pl tattered clothing

rag[2] (BRIT) v (-s, -gging, -gged) tease ▶ adj, n (pl -s) (of) events organized by students to raise money for charities

rage n (pl -s) violent anger or passion ▶ v (-ges, -ging, -ged) speak or act with fury

raged v ▷ rage

rages n, v ▷ rage

ragamuffin n (pl -s) ragged dirty child

ragamuffins n ▷ ragamuffin

ragged [**rag**-gid] adj dressed in shabby or torn clothes ▶ v ▷ rag[2]

ragging v ▷ rag[2]

raging v ▷ rage

raglan adj (of a sleeve) joined to a garment by diagonal seams from the neck to the underarm

ragout [rag-**goo**] n (pl -s) richly seasoned stew of meat and vegetables

ragouts n ▷ ragout

rags n, v ▷ rag[1, 2]

ragtime n (pl -s) style of jazz piano music

ragtimes n ▷ ragtime

raid n (pl -s) sudden surprise attack or search ▶ v (-s, -ing, -ed) make a raid on > **raider** n

(pl -s)
raided v ▷ raid
raider n ▷ raid
raiders n ▷ raid
raiding v ▷ raid
raidings n ▷ raid
raids n, v ▷ raid
rail¹ n (pl -s) horizontal bar, esp. as part of a fence or track
rail² v (-s, -ing, -ed) (foll. by at or against) complain bitterly or loudly
rail³ n (pl -s) small marsh bird
railed v ▷ rail²
railing n (pl -s) fence made of rails supported by posts ▶ v ▷ rail²
railings n ▷ railing
railleries n ▷ raillery
raillery n (pl -ies) teasing or joking
rails n ▷ rail¹, ², ³ ▷ v ▷ rail²
railway n (pl -s) track of iron rails on which trains run
railways n ▷ railway
raiment n (pl -s) (Obs) clothing
raiments n ▷ raiment
rain n rain falling in drops from the clouds ▶ v (-s, -ing, -ed) fall or pour down as rain > **rainy** adj (-nier, -niest)
rainbow n (pl -s) arch of colours in the sky
rainbows n ▷ rainbow
raincoat n (pl -s) water-resistant overcoat
raincoats n ▷ raincoat
rained v ▷ rain
rainier adj ▷ rainy
rainiest adj ▷ rainy
rainfall n (pl -s) amount of rain
rainfalls n ▷ rainfall
rainforest n (pl -s) dense forest in tropical and temperate areas
rainforests n ▷ rainforest
raining v ▷ rain
rains n, v ▷ rain
rainy adj ▷ rain
raise v (-ses, -sing, -sed) lift up
raised v ▷ raise
raises n ▷ raise
raisin n (pl -s) dried grape
raising v ▷ raise
raisins n ▷ raisin

> **raj** n (**rajes**). Raj is an Indian word for government. This can be very useful when there isn't much space. If you can't play raj, remember it's just **jar** backwards, and you might be able to fit that in. Raj scores 10 points.

raja, rajah n (pl -s) (HIST) Indian prince or ruler

rajah n ▷ raja
rajahs n ▷ raja
rajas n ▷ raja
rake¹ n (pl -s) tool with a long handle and a crosspiece with teeth, used for smoothing earth or gathering leaves, hay, etc. ▶ v (-kes, -king, -ked) gather or smooth with a rake
rake² n (pl -s) dissolute or immoral man
raked v ▷ rake¹
rakes n, v ▷ rake¹, ² ▶ v ▷ rake¹
raking v ▷ rake¹
rakish adj dashing or jaunty
rallied v ▷ rally
rallies n, v ▷ rally
rally n (pl -ies) large gathering of people for a meeting ▶ v (-ies, -ying, -ied) bring or come together after dispersal or for a common cause
rallying v ▷ rally
ram n (pl -s) male sheep ▶ v (-s, -mming, -mmed) strike against with force
ramble v (-les, -ling, -led) walk without a definite route ▶ n (pl -s) walk, esp. in the country
rambled v ▷ ramble
rambler n (pl -s) person who rambles
ramblers n ▷ rambler
rambles v, n ▷ ramble
rambling v ▷ ramble
ramekin [ram-ik-in] n (pl -s) small ovenproof dish for a single serving of food
ramekins n ▷ ramekin
ramifications pl n consequences resulting from an action
rammed v ▷ ram
ramming v ▷ ram
ramp n (pl -s) slope joining two level surfaces
rampage v (-ges, -ging, -ged) dash about violently
rampaged v ▷ rampage
rampages v ▷ rampage
rampaging v ▷ rampage
rampant adj growing or spreading uncontrollably
rampart n (pl -s) mound or wall for defence
ramparts n ▷ rampart
ramps n ▷ ramp
rams n, v ▷ ram
ramshackle adj tumbledown, rickety, or makeshift
ran v ▷ run
ranch n (pl -es) large cattle farm in the American West > **rancher** n (pl -s)
rancher n ▷ ranch
ranchers n ▷ ranch

ranches *n* ▷ ranch
rancid *adj* (of bacon, etc.) stale and having an offensive smell > **rancidity** *n* (*pl* -ies)
rancidities *n* ▷ rancidity
rancidity *n* ▷ rancid
rancorous *adj* ▷ rancour
rancorousnesses *n* ▷ rancour
rancour *n* (*pl* -s) deep bitter hate > **rancorous** *adj*
rancours *n* ▷ rancour
rand *n* (*pl* -s) monetary unit of S Africa
randier *adj* ▷ randy
randiest *adj* ▷ randy
random *adj* made or done by chance or without plan
rands *n* ▷ rand
randy *adj* (-ier, -iest) (*Informal*) sexually aroused
rang *v* ▷ ring¹
range *n* (*pl* -s) limits of effectiveness or variation ▶ *v* (-ges, -ging, -ged) vary between one point and another
ranged *v* ▷ range
ranger *n* (*pl* -s) official in charge of a nature reserve etc.
rangers *n* ▷ ranger
rangefinder *n* (*pl* -s) instrument for finding how far away an object is
rangefinders *n* ▷ rangefinder
ranges *n, v* ▷ range
rangier *adj* ▷ rangy
rangiest *adj* ▷ rangy
ranging *v* ▷ range
rangy [rain-jee] *adj* (-ier, -iest) having long slender limbs
rank¹ *n* (*pl* -s) relative place or position ▶ *v* (-s, -ing, -ed) have a specific rank or position
rank² *adj* complete or absolute
ranked *v* ▷ rank
ranking *v* ▷ rank
rankle *v* (-les, -ling, -led) continue to cause resentment or bitterness
rankled *v* ▷ rankle
rankles *v* ▷ rankle
rankling *v* ▷ rankle
ranks *n, v* ▷ rank¹
ransack *v* (-s, -ing, -ed) search thoroughly
ransacked *v* ▷ ransack
ransacking *v* ▷ ransack
ransacks *v* ▷ ransack
ransom *n* (*pl* -s) money demanded in return for the release of someone who has been kidnapped
ransoms *n* ▷ ransom
rant *v* (-s, -ing, -ed) talk in a loud and excited way > **ranter** *n* (*pl* -s)

ranted *v* ▷ rant
ranter *n* ▷ rant
ranters *n* ▷ rant
ranting *v* ▷ rant
rants *v* ▷ rant
rap *v* (-s, -pping, -pped) hit with a sharp quick blow ▶ *n* (*pl* -s) quick sharp blow > **rapper** *n* (*pl* -s)
rapacious *adj* greedy or grasping > **rapacity** *n* (*pl* -ies)
rapacities *n* ▷ rapacious
rapacity *n* ▷ rapacious
rape¹ *v* (-pes, -ping, -ped) force to submit to sexual intercourse ▶ *n* (*pl* -s) act of raping > **rapist** *n* (*pl* -s)
rape² *n* (*pl* -s) plant with oil-yielding seeds, also used as fodder
raped *v* ▷ rape¹
rapes *v* ▷ rape¹ ▶ *n* ▷ rape¹,²
rapid *adj* (-er, -est) quick, swift > **rapidly** *adv* > **rapidity** *n* (*pl* -ies)
rapider *adj* ▷ rapid
rapidest *adj* ▷ rapid
rapidities *n* ▷ rapid
rapidity *n* ▷ rapid
rapidly *adv* ▷ rapid
rapids *pl n* part of a river with a fast turbulent current
rapier [ray-pyer] *n* (*pl* -s) fine-bladed sword
rapiers *n* ▷ rapier
raping *v* ▷ rape¹
rapist *n* ▷ rape¹
rapists *n* ▷ rape¹
rapped *v* ▷ rap
rapper *n* ▷ rap
rappers *n* ▷ rap
rapping *v* ▷ rap
rapport [rap-pore] *n* (*pl* -s) harmony or agreement
rapports *n* ▷ rapport
rapprochement [rap-prosh-mong] *n* (*pl* -s) re-establishment of friendly relations, esp. between nations
rapprochements *n* ▷ rapprochement
raps *v, n* ▷ rap
rapt *adj* engrossed or spellbound
rapture *n* (*pl* -s) ecstasy > **rapturous** *adj*
raptures *n* ▷ rapture
rapturous *adj* ▷ rapture
rare¹ *adj* (-r, -st) uncommon > **rarity** *n* (*pl* -ies)
rare² *adj* (-r, -st) (of meat) lightly cooked
rarebit *n* (*pl* -s) dish of melted cheese on toast
rarebits *n* ▷ rarebit
rarefied [rare-if-ide] *adj* highly specialized, exalted

rarely *adv* seldom
  rarer *adj* ▷ rare[1,2]
  rarest *adj* ▷ rare[1,2]
raring *adj* enthusiastic, willing, or ready to
  rarities *n* ▷ rare[1]
  rarity *n* ▷ rare[1]
rascal *n* (*pl* -s) rogue > **rascally** *adj* (-ier, -iest)
  rascalliest *adj* ▷ rascal
  rascally *adj* ▷ rascal
  rascals *n* ▷ rascal
rash[1] *adj* (-er, -est) hasty, reckless, or incautious > **rashly** *adv*
rash[2] *n* (*pl* -es) eruption of spots or patches on the skin
rasher *n* (*pl* -s) thin slice of bacon ▶ *adj* ▷ rash[1]
  rashers *n* ▷ rasher
  rashes *n* ▷ rash[2]
  rashest *adj* ▷ rash[1]
  rashly *adv* ▷ rash[1]
rasp *n* (*pl* -s) harsh grating noise ▶ *v* (-s, -ing, -ed) speak in a grating voice
  raspberries *n* ▷ raspberry
raspberry *n* (*pl* -ies) red juicy edible berry (*Informal*)
  rasped *v* ▷ rasp
  rasping *v* ▷ rasp
  rasps *n*, *v* ▷ rasp
rat *n* (*pl* -s) small rodent (*Informal*) ▶ *v* (-s, -tting, -tted) (*Informal*) inform (on)
ratafia [rat-a-**fee**-a] *n* (*pl* -s) fruit liqueur
  ratafias ▷ ratafia
ratatouille [rat-a-**twee**] *n* (*pl* -s) vegetable casserole of tomatoes, aubergines, etc.
  ratatouilles *n* ▷ ratatouille
ratchet *n* (*pl* -s) set of teeth on a bar or wheel allowing motion in one direction only
  ratchets *n* ▷ ratchet
rate *n* (*pl* -s) degree of speed or progress ▶ *pl* local tax on business ▶ *v* (-tes, -ting, -ted) consider or value > **ratepayer** (*pl* -s)
rateable *adj* able to be rated
  rated *v* ▷ rate
  ratepayer *n* ▷ rate
  ratepayers *n* ▷ rate
  rates *n*, *v* ▷ rate
rather *adv* to some extent
  ratification *n* ▷ ratify
  ratifications *n* ▷ ratify
  ratified *v* ▷ ratify
  ratifies *v* ▷ ratify
ratify *v* (-ies, -ying, -ied) give formal approval to > **ratification** *n* (*pl* -s)
  ratifiying *v* ▷ ratify
rating *n* (*pl* -s) valuation or assessment ▶ *pl* size of the audience for a TV programme ▶ *v*
  ▷ **rate**
  ratings *n* ▷ rating
ratio *n* (*pl* -s) relationship between two numbers or amounts expressed as a proportion
ration *n* (*pl* -s) fixed allowance of food etc. ▶ *v* (-s, -ing, -ed) limit to a certain amount per person
rational *adj* reasonable, sensible > **rationally** *adv* > **rationality** *n* (*pl* -ies)
rationale [rash-a-**nahl**] *n* (*pl* -s) reason for an action or decision
  rationales *n* ▷ rationale
rationalism *n* (*pl* -s) philosophy that regards reason as the only basis for beliefs or actions > **rationalist** *n* (*pl* -s)
  rationalisms *n* ▷ rationalism
  rationalist *n* ▷ rationalism
  rationalists *n* ▷ rationalism
  rationalities *n* ▷ rational
  rationality *n* ▷ rational
rationalize *v* (-zes, -zing, -zed) justify by plausible reasoning > **rationalization** *n* (*pl* -s)
  rationalization *n* ▷ rationalize
  rationalizations *n* ▷ rationalize
  rationalized *v* ▷ rationalize
  rationalizes *v* ▷ rationalize
  rationalizing *v* ▷ rationalize
  rationally *adv* ▷ rational
  rationed *v* ▷ ration
  rationing *v* ▷ ration
  rations *n*, *v* ▷ ration
  ratios *n* ▷ ratio
  rats *n* ▷ rat
rattan *n* (*pl* -s) climbing palm with jointed stems used for canes
  rattans *n* ▷ rattan
  ratted *v* ▷ rat
  rattier *adj* ▷ ratty
  rattiest *adj* ▷ ratty
  rattinesses *n* ▷ ratty
  ratting *v* ▷ rat
rattle *v* (-les, -ling, -led) give out a succession of short sharp sounds ▶ *n* (*pl* -s) short sharp sound
  rattled *v* ▷ rattle
rattlesnake *n* (*pl* -s) poisonous snake with loose horny segments on the tail that make a rattling sound
  rattlesnakes *n* ▷ rattlesnake
  rattles *v*, *n* ▷ rattle
  rattling *v* ▷ rattle
ratty *adj* (-ier, -iest) (BRIT G-NZ) (*Informal*) bad-tempered, irritable
raucous *adj* hoarse or harsh

raunchier *adj* ▷ **raunchy**
raunchiest *adj* ▷ **raunchy**
raunchy *adj* (**-chier, -chiest**) (*Slang*) earthy, sexy
ravage *v* (**-ges, -ging, -ged**) cause extensive damage to
  ravaged *v* ▷ **ravage**
  ravages *pl n* damaging effects ► *v* ▷ **ravage**
  ravaging *v* ▷ **ravage**
rave *v* (**-ves, -ving, -ved**) talk wildly or with enthusiasm ► *n* (*pl* **-s**) (*Slang*) large-scale party with electronic dance music
  raved *v* ▷ **rave**
ravel *v* (**-s, -lling, -lled**) tangle or become entangled
  ravelled *v* ▷ **ravel**
  ravelling *v* ▷ **ravel**
  ravels *v* ▷ **ravel**
raven *n* (*pl* **-s**) black bird like a large crow ► *adj* (of hair) shiny black
  ravens *n* ▷ **raven**
ravenous *adj* very hungry
  raves *v, n* ▷ **rave**
ravine [rav-**veen**] *n* (*pl* **-s**) narrow steep-sided valley worn by a stream
  ravines *n* ▷ **ravine**
raving *adj* delirious ► *v* ▷ **rave**
ravioli *pl n* small squares of pasta with a savoury filling
ravish *v* (**-es, -ing, -ed**) enrapture
  ravished *v* ▷ **ravish**
  ravishes *v* ▷ **ravish**
  ravishing *adj, v* ▷ **ravish**
raw *adj* (**-er, -est**) uncooked
  rawer *adj* ▷ **raw**
  rawest *adj* ▷ **raw**
rawhide *n* (*pl* **-s**) untanned hide
  rawhides *n* ▷ **rawhide**

> **rax** *v* (**raxes, raxing, raxed**). Rax is a Scots word that means to stretch or extend. This is a good word to have ready when you have an X on your rack, as there is probably an A or R on the board already. The verb forms can also help you to get a better score. Rax scores 10 points.

ray[1] *n* (*pl* **-s**) single line or narrow beam of light
ray[2] *n* (*pl* **-s**) large sea fish with a flat body and a whiplike tail
  rays *n* ▷ **ray**[1, 2]
rayon *n* (*pl* **-s**) (fabric made of) a synthetic fibre
  rayons *n* ▷ **rayon**
raze *v* (**-zes, -zing, -zed**) destroy (buildings or a town) completely
  razed *v* ▷ **raze**
  razes *v* ▷ **raze**

razing *v* ▷ **raze**
razor *n* (*pl* **-s**) sharp instrument for shaving
razorbill *n* (*pl* **-s**) sea bird of the North Atlantic with a stout sideways flattened bill
  razorbills *n* ▷ **razorbill**
  razors *n* ▷ **razor**

> **re** *n* (**res**). Re is a musical note. This is the only two-letter word beginning with R, and so is a good one to remember. Re is very useful as it allows you to connect a word beginning with R to one ending in E, or vice versa. Re scores 2 points.

reach *v* (**-es, -ing, -ed**) arrive at ► *n* (*pl* **-es**) distance that one can reach; stretch of a river
> **reachable** *adj*
  reachable *adj* ▷ **reach**
  reached *v* ▷ **reach**
  reaches *v, n* ▷ **reach**
  reaching *v* ▷ **reach**
react *v* (**-s, -ing, -ed**) act in response (to) (*foll. by* **against**)
reactance *n* (*pl* **-s**) (ELECTRICITY) resistance to the flow of an alternating current caused by the inductance or capacitance of the circuit
  reactances *n* ▷ **reactance**
  reacted *v* ▷ **react**
  reacting *v* ▷ **react**
reaction *n* (*pl* **-s**) physical or emotional response to a stimulus
  reactionaries *n* ▷ **reactionary**
reactionary *n, adj* (*pl* **-ies**) (person) opposed to change, esp. in politics
  reactionary *n* ▷ **reaction**
  reactionisms *n* ▷ **reactionary**
  reactions *n* ▷ **reaction**
reactive *adj* chemically active
reactor *n* (*pl* **-s**) apparatus in which a nuclear reaction is maintained and controlled to produce nuclear energy
  reactors *n* ▷ **reactor**
  reacts *v* ▷ **react**
read *v* (**-s, -ing, read**) look at and understand or take in (written or printed matter) ► *n* matter suitable for reading > **reading** *n* (*pl* **-s**)
readable *adj* enjoyable to read
reader *n* (*pl* **-s**) person who reads
  readers *n* ▷ **reader**
readership *n* (*pl* **-s**) readers of a publication collectively
  readerships *n* ▷ **readership**
  readier *adj* ▷ **ready**
  readiest *adj* ▷ **ready**
  readily *adv* ▷ **ready**
  readiness *n* ▷ **ready**

readinesses *n* ▷ ready
reading *n*, *v* ▷ read
readings *n* ▷ read
readjust *v* (-s, -ing, -ed) adapt to a new situation > **readjustment** *n* (*pl* -s)
readjusted *v* ▷ readjust
readjusting *v* ▷ readjust
readjustment *n* ▷ readjust
readjustments *n* ▷ readjust
readjusts *v* ▷ readjust
reads *v* ▷ read
ready *adj* (-dier, -diest) prepared for use or action > **readily** *adv* > **readiness** *n* (*pl* -es)
reagent [ree-age-ent] *n* (*pl* -s) chemical substance that reacts with another, used to detect the presence of the other
reagents *n* ▷ reagent
real *adj* (-er, -est) existing in fact
realism *n* ▷ realistic
realisms *n* ▷ realistic
realist *n* ▷ realistic
realistically *adv* ▷ realistic
realists *n* ▷ realistic
realistic *adj* seeing and accepting things as they really are, practical > **realistically** *adv* > **realism** *n* (*pl* -s) > **realist** *n* (*pl* -s)
realities *n* ▷ reality
reality *n* (*pl* -ies) state of things as they are
realize *v* (-zes, -zing, -zed) become aware or grasp the significance of > **realization** *n* (*pl* -s)
realization *n* ▷ realize
realizations *n* ▷ realize
realized *v* ▷ realize
realizes *v* ▷ realize
realizing *v* ▷ realize
really *adv* very ▶ *interj* exclamation of dismay, doubt, or surprise
realm *n* (*pl* -s) kingdom
realms *n* ▷ realm
ream *n* (*pl* -s) twenty quires of paper, generally 500 sheets ▶ *pl* (*Informal*) large quantity (of written matter)
reams *n* ▷ ream
reap *v* (-s, -ing, -ed) cut and gather (a harvest) > **reaper** *n* (*pl* -s)
reaped *v* ▷ reap
reaper *n* ▷ reap
reapers *n* ▷ reap
reaping *v* ▷ reap
reappear *v* (-s, -ing, -ed) appear again > **reappearance** *n* (*pl* -s)
reappearance *n* ▷ reappear
reappearances *n* ▷ reappear
reappeared *v* ▷ reappear
reappearing *v* ▷ reappear

reappears *v* ▷ reappear
reaps *v* ▷ reap
rear[1] *n* (*pl* -s) back part > **rearmost** *adj*
rear[2] *v* (-s, -ing, -ed) care for and educate (children)
reared *v* ▷ rear
rearguard *n* (*pl* -s) troops protecting the rear of an army
rearguards *n* ▷ rearguard
rearing *v* ▷ rear
rearmost *adj* ▷ rear[1]
rearrange *v* (-ges, -ging, -ged) organize differently, alter > **rearrangement** *n* (*pl* -s)
rearranged *v* ▷ rearrange
rearrangement *n* ▷ rearrange
rearrangements *n* ▷ rearrange
rearranges *v* ▷ rearrange
rearranging *v* ▷ rearrange
rears *n* ▷ rear[1] ▶ *v* ▷ rear[2]
reason *n* (*pl* -s) cause or motive ▶ *v* (-s, -ing, -ed) think logically in forming conclusions
reasonable *adj* sensible > **reasonably** *adv*
reasoned *v* ▷ reason
reasoning *v* ▷ reason
reasons *n*, *v* ▷ reason
reassess *v* (-es, -ing, -ed) reconsider the value or importance of
reassessed *v* ▷ reassess
reassesses *v* ▷ reassess
reassessing *v* ▷ reassess
reassure *v* (-res, -ring, -red) restore confidence to > **reassurance** *n* (*pl* -s)
reassurance *n* ▷ reassure
reassurances *n* ▷ reassure
reassured *v* ▷ reassure
reassures *v* ▷ reassure
reassuring *v* ▷ reassure
rebate *n* (*pl* -s) discount or refund
rebates *n* ▷ rebate
rebel *v* (-s, -lling, -lled) revolt against the ruling power ▶ *n* (*pl* -s) person who rebels > **rebellious** *adj*
rebelled *v* ▷ rebel
rebelling *v* ▷ rebel
rebellion *n* (*pl* -s) organized open resistance to authority
rebellions *n* ▷ rebellion
rebellious *adj* ▷ rebel
rebels *v*, *n* ▷ rebel
rebore, reboring *n* (*pl* -s) boring of a cylinder to restore its true shape
rebores *n* ▷ rebore
reboring *n* ▷ rebore
reborings *n* ▷ rebore
rebound *v* (-s, -ing, -ed) spring back

rebounded v ▷ rebound
rebounding v ▷ rebound
rebounds v ▷ rebound
rebuff v (-s, -ing, -ed) reject or snub ▶ n (pl -s) blunt refusal, snub
rebuffed v ▷ rebuff
rebuffing v ▷ rebuff
rebuffs v, n ▷ rebuff
rebuke v (-kes, -king, -ked) scold sternly ▶ n (pl -s) stern scolding
rebuked v ▷ rebuke
rebukes v, n ▷ rebuke
rebuking v ▷ rebuke
rebus n (pl -es) puzzle consisting of pictures and symbols representing words or syllables
rebuses n ▷ rebus
rebut v (-s, -tting, -tted) prove that (a claim) is untrue ▶ **rebuttal** n (pl -s)
rebuts v ▷ rebut
rebuttal n ▷ rebut
rebuttals n ▷ rebut
rebutted v ▷ rebut
rebutting v ▷ rebut
recalcitrant adj wilfully disobedient > **recalcitrance** n (pl -s)
recalcitrance n ▷ recalcitrant
recalcitrances n ▷ recalcitrant
recall v (-s, -ing, -ed) recollect or remember ▶ n (pl (pl -s) ability to remember
recalled v ▷ recall
recalling v ▷ recall
recalls v, n ▷ recall
recant v (-s, -ing, -ed) withdraw (a statement or belief) publicly > **recantation** n (pl -s)
recantation n ▷ recant
recantations n ▷ recant
recanted v ▷ recant
recanting v ▷ recant
recants v ▷ recant
recap (Informal) v (-s, -pping, -pped) recapitulate ▶ n (pl -s) recapitulation
recapitulate v (-tes, -ting, -ted) state again briefly, repeat > **recapitulation** n (pl -s)
recapitulated v ▷ recapitulate
recapitulates v ▷ recapitulate
recapitulating v ▷ recapitulate
recapitulation n ▷ recapitulate
recapitulations n ▷ recapitulate
recapped v ▷ recap
recapping v ▷ recap
recaps v, n ▷ recap
recapture v (-res, -ring, -red) experience again
recaptured v ▷ recapture
recaptures v ▷ recapture
recapturing v ▷ recapture

recce (CHIEFLY BRIT) (Slang) v (-s, -ceing, -ced or -ceed) reconnoitre ▶ n (pl -s) reconnaissance
recced v ▷ recce
recceed v ▷ recce
recceing v ▷ recce
recces v, n ▷ recce
recede v (-des, -ding, -ded) move to a more distant place
receded v ▷ recede
recedes v ▷ recede
receding v ▷ recede
receipt n (pl -s) written acknowledgment of money or goods received
receipts n ▷ receipt
receive v (-ves, -ving, -ved) take, accept, or get
received adj generally accepted ▶ v ▷ receive
receiver n (pl -s) part of telephone that is held to the ear
receivers n ▷ receiver
receivership n (pl -s) state of being administered by a receiver
receiverships n ▷ receivership
receives v ▷ receive
receiving v ▷ receive
recent adj (-er, -est) having happened lately > **recently** adv
recenter adj ▷ recent
recentest adj ▷ recent
recently adv ▷ recent
receptacle n (pl -s) object used to contain something
receptacles n ▷ receptacle
reception n (pl -s) area for receiving guests, clients, etc.
receptionist n (pl -s) person who receives guests, clients, etc.
receptionists n ▷ receptionist
receptions n ▷ reception
receptive adj willing to accept new ideas, suggestions, etc. > **receptivity** n (pl -ies)
receptivities n ▷ receptive
receptivity n ▷ receptive
recess n (pl -es) niche or alcove
recessed adj hidden or placed in a recess
recesses n ▷ recess
recession n (pl -s) period of economic difficulty when little is being bought or sold
recessions n ▷ recession
recessive adj receding
recherché [rish-air-shay] adj refined or elegant
recidivism n (pl -s) habitual relapse into crime > **recidivist** n (pl -s)
recidivisms n ▷ recidivism
recidivist n ▷ recidivism
recidivists n ▷ recidivism

recipe n (pl **-s**) directions for cooking a dish
  recipes n ▷ **recipe**
recipient n (pl **-s**) person who receives
something
  recipients n ▷ **recipient**
reciprocal [ris-**sip**-pro-kl] adj mutual
  > **reciprocally** adv
  reciprocally adv ▷ **reciprocal**
reciprocate v (**-tes, -ting, -ted**) give or feel in
return > **reciprocation** n (pl **-s**) > **reciprocity**
n (pl **-s**)
  reciprocated v ▷ **reciprocate**
  reciprocates v ▷ **reciprocate**
  reciprocating v ▷ **reciprocate**
  reciprocation n ▷ **reciprocate**
  reciprocations n ▷ **reciprocate**
  reciprocities n ▷ **reciprocate**
  reciprocity n ▷ **reciprocate**
recital n (pl **-s**) musical performance by a
soloist or soloists
  recitals n ▷ **recital**
recitation n (pl **-s**) recital, usu. from memory,
of poetry or prose
  recitations n ▷ **recitation**
recitative [ress-it-a-**teev**] n (pl **-s**) speechlike
style of singing, used esp. for narrative
passages in opera
  recitatives n ▷ **recitative**
recite v (**-tes, -ting, -ted**) repeat (a poem etc.)
aloud to an audience
  recited v ▷ **recite**
  recites v ▷ **recite**
  reciting v ▷ **recite**
reckless adj heedless of danger > **recklessly**
adv > **recklessness** n (pl **-s**)
  recklessly adv ▷ **reckless**
  recklessness n ▷ **reckless**
  recklessnesses n ▷ **reckless**
reckon v (**-s, -ing, -ed**) consider or think
> **reckoning** n (pl **-s**)
  reckoned v ▷ **reckon**
  reckoning v, n ▷ **reckon**
  reckonings n ▷ **reckon**
  reckons v ▷ **reckon**
reclaim v (**-s, -ing, -ed**) regain possession of
> **reclamation** n (pl **-s**)
  reclaimed v ▷ **reclaim**
  reclaiming v ▷ **reclaim**
  reclaims v ▷ **reclaim**
  reclamation n ▷ **reclaim**
  reclamations n ▷ **reclaim**
recline v (**-nes, -ning, -ned**) rest in a leaning
position > **reclining** adj
  reclined v ▷ **recline**
  reclines v ▷ **recline**

reclining v, adj ▷ **recline**
recluse n (pl **-s**) person who avoids other
people > **reclusive** adj
  recluses n ▷ **recluse**
  reclusive adj ▷ **recluse**
recognition n ▷ **recognize**
  recognitions n ▷ **recognize**
  recognizable adj ▷ **recognize**
recognizance [rik-og-**nizz**-anss] n (pl **-s**)
undertaking before a court to observe some
condition
  recognizances n ▷ **recognizance**
recognize v (**-zes, -zing, -zed**) identify
as (a person or thing) already known
> **recognition** n (pl **-s**) > **recognizable** adj
  recognized v ▷ **recognize**
  recognizes v ▷ **recognize**
  recognizing v ▷ **recognize**
recoil v (**-s, -ing, -ed**) jerk or spring back ▶ n (pl
-s) backward jerk
  recoiled v ▷ **recoil**
  recoiling v ▷ **recoil**
  recoils v, n ▷ **recoil**
recollect v (**-s, -ing, -ed**) call back to mind,
remember > **recollection** n (pl **-s**)
  recollected v ▷ **recollect**
  recollecting v ▷ **recollect**
  recollection n ▷ **recollect**
  recollections n ▷ **recollect**
  recollects v ▷ **recollect**
recommend v (**-s, -ing, -ed**) advise or counsel
> **recommendation** n (pl **-s**)
  recommendation n ▷ **recommend**
  recommendations n ▷ **recommend**
  recommended v ▷ **recommend**
  recommending v ▷ **recommend**
  recommends v ▷ **recommend**
recompense v (**-ses, -sing, -sed**) pay or reward
▶ n (pl **-s**) compensation
  recompensed v ▷ **recompense**
  recompenses v, n ▷ **recompense**
  recompensing v ▷ **recompense**
reconcile v (**-les, -ling, -led**) harmonize
(conflicting beliefs etc.) > **reconciliation**
n (pl **-s**)
  reconciled v ▷ **reconcile**
  reconciles v ▷ **reconcile**
  reconciliation n ▷ **reconcile**
  reconciliations n ▷ **reconcile**
  reconciling v ▷ **reconcile**
recondite adj difficult to understand
recondition v (**-s, -ing, -ed**) restore to good
condition or working order
  reconditioned v ▷ **recondition**
  reconditioning v ▷ **recondition**

reconditions v ▷ recondition
reconnaissance [rik-**kon**-iss-anss] n (pl -s)
survey for military or engineering purposes
reconnaissances n ▷ reconnaissance
reconnoitre [rek-a-**noy**-ter] v (**-res, -ring, -red**)
make a reconnaissance of
reconnoitred v ▷ reconnoitre
reconnoitres v ▷ reconnoitre
reconnoitring v ▷ reconnoitre
reconsider v (**-s, -ing, -ed**) think about again,
consider changing
reconsidered v ▷ reconsider
reconsidering v ▷ reconsider
reconsiders v ▷ reconsider
reconstitute v (**-tes, -ting, -ted**) reorganize
> **reconstitution** n (pl -s)
reconstituted v ▷ reconstitute
reconstitutes v ▷ reconstitute
reconstituting v ▷ reconstitute
reconstitution n ▷ reconstitute
reconstitutions n ▷ reconstitute
reconstruct v (**-s, -ing, -ed**) rebuild
> **reconstruction** n (pl -s)
reconstructed v ▷ reconstruct
reconstructing v ▷ reconstruct
reconstruction n ▷ reconstruct
reconstructions n ▷ reconstruct
reconstructs v ▷ reconstruct
record n (pl -s) [**rek**-ord] document or other
thing that preserves information ▶ v (**-s, -ing,
-ed**) [rik-**kord**] put in writing > **recording** n
(pl -s)
recorded v ▷ record
recorder n (pl -s) person or machine that
records, esp. a video, cassette, or tape
recorder
recorders n ▷ recorder
recording v ▷ record
records n, v ▷ record
recount v (**-s, -ing, -ed**) tell in detail
recounted v ▷ recount
recounting v ▷ recount
recounts v ▷ recount
recoup [rik-**koop**] v (**-s, -ing, -ed**) regain or
make good (a loss)
recouped v ▷ recoup
recouping v ▷ recoup
recoups v ▷ recoup
recourse n (pl -s) source of help
recourses n ▷ recourse
recover v (**-s, -ing, -ed**) become healthy again
> **recovery** n (pl -ies) > **recoverable** adj
recoverable adj ▷ recover
recovered v ▷ recover
recoveries n ▷ recover

recovering v ▷ recover
recovers v ▷ recover
recovery v ▷ recover
recreation n (pl -s) agreeable or refreshing
occupation, relaxation, or amusement
> **recreational** adj
recreational adj ▷ recreation
recreations n ▷ recreation
recrimination n (pl -s) mutual blame
> **recriminatory** adj
recriminations n ▷ recrimination
recriminatory adj ▷ recrimination
recruit v (**-s, -ing, -ed**) enlist (new soldiers,
members, etc.) ▶ n (pl -s) newly enlisted
soldier > **recruitment** n (pl -s)
recruited v ▷ recruit
recruiting v ▷ recruit
recruitment n ▷ recruit
recruitments n ▷ recruit
recruits v, n ▷ recruit
recta n ▷ rectum
rectangle n (pl -s) oblong four-sided figure
with four right angles > **rectangular** adj
rectangles n ▷ rectangle
rectangular adj ▷ rectangle
rectification n ▷ rectify
rectifications n ▷ rectify
rectified v ▷ rectify
rectifier n ▷ rectify
rectifiers n ▷ rectify
rectifies v ▷ rectify
rectify v (**-ies, -ying, -ied**) put right, correct
(CHEM) (ELECTRICITY) > **rectification** n (pl -s)
rectifying v ▷ rectify
rectilinear adj in a straight line
rectitude n (pl -s) moral correctness
rectitudes n ▷ rectitude
recto n (pl -os) right-hand page of a book
rector n (pl -s) clergyman in charge of a parish
rectories n ▷ rectory
rectors n ▷ rector
rectory n (pl -s) rector's house
rectos n ▷ recto
rectum n (pl -tums, -ta) final section of the
large intestine
rectums n ▷ rectum
recumbent adj lying down
recuperate v (**-tes, -ting, -ted**) recover from
illness > **recuperation** n (pl -s) > **recuperative**
adj
recuperated v ▷ recuperate
recuperates v ▷ recuperate
recuperating v ▷ recuperate
recuperation n ▷ recuperate
recuperations n ▷ recuperate

recuperative adj ▷ recuperate
recur v (-s, -rring, -rred) happen again
> **recurrence** n (pl -s) repetition > **recurrent**
adj
recurred v ▷ recur
recurrence n ▷ recur
recurrences n ▷ recur
recurrent adj ▷ recur
recurring v ▷ recur
recurs v ▷ recur
recycle v (-les, -ling, -led) reprocess (used
materials) for further use > **recyclable** adj
recyclable adj ▷ recycle
recycled v ▷ recycle
recycles v ▷ recycle
recycling v ▷ recycle
red adj (-dder, -ddest) of a colour varying from
crimson to orange and seen in blood, fire, etc.
▶ n (pl -s) red colour > **reddish** adj > **redness**
n (pl -es)
redbrick adj (of a university in Britain)
founded in the late 19th or early 20th century
redcoat n (pl -s) (HIST) British soldier
redcoats n ▷ redcoat
redcurrant n (pl -s) small round edible red
berry
redcurrants n ▷ redcurrant
redden v (-s, -ing, -ed) make or become red
reddened v ▷ redden
reddening v ▷ redden
reddens v ▷ redden
redder adj ▷ red
reddest adj ▷ red
reddish adj ▷ red
redeem v (-s, -ing, -ed) make up for
> **redeemable** adj > **redemption** n (pl -s)
> **redemptive** adj
redeemable adj ▷ reddem
redeemed v ▷ reddem
redeeming v ▷ reddem
redeems v ▷ reddem
redemption adj ▷ reddem
redemptions adj ▷ reddem
redemptive adj ▷ reddem
redeploy v (-s, -ing, -ed) assign to a new
position or task > **redeployment** n (pl -s)
redeployed v ▷ redeploy
redeploying v ▷ redeploy
redeployment n ▷ redeploy
redeployment n ▷ redeploy
redeploys v ▷ redeploy
redevelop v (-s, -ing, -ed) rebuild or renovate
(an area or building) > **redevelopment** n (pl -s)
redeveloped v ▷ redevelop
redeveloping v ▷ redevelop

redevelopment n ▷ redevelop
redevelopments n ▷ redevelop
redevelops v ▷ redevelop
redness n ▷ red
redolent adj reminiscent (of)
redouble v (-les, -ling, -led) increase, multiply,
or intensify
redoubled v ▷ redouble
redoubles v ▷ redouble
redoubling v ▷ redouble
redoubt n (pl -s) small fort defending a hilltop
or pass
redoubtable adj formidable
redoubts n ▷ redoubt
redound v (-s, -ing, -ed) cause advantage or
disadvantage (to)
redounded v ▷ redound
redounding v ▷ redound
redounds v ▷ redound
redox n (pl -es) chemical reaction in which
one substance is reduced and the other is
oxidized
redoxes n ▷ redox
redress v (-es, -ing, -ed) make amends for ▶ n
(pl -es) compensation or amends
redressed v ▷ redress
redresses v, n ▷ redress
redressing v ▷ redress
reds n ▷ red
reduce v (-ces, -cing, -ced) bring down, lower
> **reducible** adj > **reduction** n (pl -s)
reduced v ▷ reduce
reduces v ▷ reduce
reducible adj ▷ reduce
reducing v ▷ reduce
reduction n ▷ reduce
reductions n ▷ reduce
redundancies n ▷ redundant
redundancy n ▷ redundant
redundant adj (of a worker) no longer needed
> **redundancy** n (pl -s)
reed n (pl -s) tall grass that grows in swamps
and shallow water
reedier adj ▷ reedy
reediest ▷ reedy
reeds n ▷ reed
reedy (-dier, -diest) adj harsh and thin in tone
reef¹ n (pl -s) ridge of rock or coral near the
surface of the sea
reef² n (pl -s) part of a sail which can be rolled
up to reduce its area ▶ v (-s, -ing, -ed) take
in a reef of
reefed v ▷ reef²
reefer n (pl -s) short thick jacket worn esp.
by sailors

reefers *n* ▷ reefer
reefing *v* ▷ reef²
reefs *n* ▷ reef¹, ², ▶ *v* ▷ reef²
reek *v* (-s, -ing, -ed) smell strongly ▶ *n* (*pl* -s) strong unpleasant smell
reeked *v* ▷ reek
reeking *v* ▷ reek
reeks *v*, *n* ▷ reek
reel¹ *n* (*pl* -s) cylindrical object on which film, tape, thread, or wire is wound
reel² *v* (-s, -ing, -ed) stagger, sway, or whirl
reel³ *n* (*pl* -s) lively Scottish dance
reeled *v* ▷ reel²
reeling *v* ▷ reel²
reels *n* ▷ reel¹, ³ ▶ *v* ▷ reel²
ref *n* (*pl* -s) (*Informal*) referee in sport
refectories *n* ▷ refectory
refectory *n* (*pl* -ies) room for meals in a college etc.
refer *v* (-s, -rring, -rred) (*foll. by* **to**) allude (to) > **referral** *n* (*pl* -s)
referee *n* (*pl* -s) umpire in sports, esp. soccer or boxing ▶ *v* (-s, -ing, -eed) act as referee of
refereed *v* ▷ referee
refereeing *v* ▷ referee
referees *n*, *v* ▷ referee
reference *n* (*pl* -s) act of referring
references *n* ▷ reference
referenda *n* ▷ referendum
referendum *n* (*pl* -dums, -da) direct vote of the electorate on an important question
referendums *n* ▷ referendum
referral *n* ▷ refer
referrals *n* ▷ refer
referred *v* ▷ refer
referring *v* ▷ refer
refers *v* ▷ refer
refill *v* (-s, -ing, -ed) fill again ▶ *n* (*pl* -s) second or subsequent filling
refilled *v* ▷ refill
refilling *v* ▷ refill
refills *v*, *n* ▷ refill
refine *v* (-nes, -ning, -ned) purify
refined *adj* cultured or polite ▶ *v* ▷ refine
refinement *n* (*pl* -s) improvement or elaboration
refinements *n* ▷ refinement
refineries *n* ▷ refinery
refinery *n* (*pl* -ies) place where sugar, oil, etc. is refined
refines *v* ▷ refine
refining *v* ▷ refine
reflate *v* ▷ reflation
reflated *v* ▷ reflation
reflates *v* ▷ reflation

reflating *v* ▷ reflation
reflation *n* (*pl* -s) increase in the supply of money and credit designed to encourage economic activity > **reflate** *v* (-tes, -ting, -ted) > **reflationary** *adj*
reflationary *adj* ▷ reflation
reflations *n* ▷ reflation
reflect *v* (-s, -ing, -ed) throw back, esp. rays of light, heat, etc.
reflected *v* ▷ reflect
reflecting *v* ▷ reflect
reflection *n* (*pl* -s) act of reflecting
reflections *n* ▷ reflect
reflective *adj* quiet, contemplative
reflector *n* (*pl* -s) polished surface for reflecting light etc.
reflectors *n* ▷ reflector
reflects *v* ▷ reflect
reflex *n* (*pl* -es) involuntary response to a stimulus or situation ▶ *adj* (of a muscular action) involuntary
reflexes *n* ▷ reflex
reflexive *adj* (GRAMMAR) denoting a verb whose subject is the same as its object
reflexologies *n* ▷ reflexology
reflexology *n* (*pl* -ies) foot massage as a therapy in alternative medicine
reform *n* (*pl* -s) improvement ▶ *v* (-s, -ing, -ed) improve > **reformer** *n* (*pl* -s)
reformation *n* (*pl* -s) act or instance of something being reformed
reformations *n* ▷ reformation
reformatories *n* ▷ reformatory
reformatory *n* (*pl* -ies) (formerly) institution for reforming young offenders
reformed *v* ▷ reform
reformer *n* ▷ reform
reformers *n* ▷ reform
reforming *v* ▷ reform
reforms *n*, *v* ▷ reform
refract *v* (-s, -ing, -ed) change the course of (light etc.) passing from one medium to another > **refraction** *n* (*pl* -s) > **refractive** *adj*
refracted *v* ▷ refract
refracting *v* ▷ refract
refraction *n* ▷ refract
refractions *n* ▷ refract
refractive *adj* ▷ refract
refractor *n* ▷ refract
refractors *n* ▷ refract
refractory *adj* unmanageable or rebellious
refracts *v* ▷ refract
refrain¹ *v* (-s, -ing, -ed) keep oneself from doing
refrain² *n* (*pl* -s) frequently repeated part of

a song
refrained v ▷ refrain¹
refraining v ▷ refrain¹
refrains n ▷ refrain¹, ² ▶ v ▷ refrain²
refresh v (-es, -ing, -ed) revive or reinvigorate, as through food, drink, or rest ▷ **refresher** n (pl -s)
refreshed v ▷ refresh
refresher n ▷ refresh
refreshers n ▷ refresh
refreshes v ▷ refresh
refreshing adj having a reviving effect ▶ v ▷ refresh
refreshment n (pl -s) something that refreshes, esp. food or drink
refreshments n ▷ refreshment
refrigerate v (-tes, -ting, -ted) cool or freeze in order to preserve ▷ **refrigeration** n (pl -s)
refrigerated v ▷ refrigerate
refrigerates v ▷ refrigerate
refrigerating v ▷ refrigerate
refrigeration n ▷ refrigerate
refrigerations n ▷ refrigerate
refrigerator n (pl -s) ▷ fridge
refrigerators n ▷ refrigerator
refs n ▷ ref
refuge n (pl -s) (source of) shelter or protection
refugee n (pl -s) person who seeks refuge, esp. in a foreign country
refugees n ▷ refugee
refuges n ▷ refuge
refulgent adj shining, radiant
refund v (-s, -ing, -ed) pay back ▶ n (pl -s) return of money
refunded v ▷ refund
refunding v ▷ refund
refunds v, n ▷ refund
refurbish v (-es, -ing, -ed) renovate and brighten up
refurbished v ▷ refurbish
refurbishes v ▷ refurbish
refurbishing v ▷ refurbish
refusal n (pl -s) denial of anything demanded or offered
refusals n ▷ refusal
refuse¹ v (-ses, -sing, -sed) decline, deny, or reject
refuse² n (pl -s) rubbish or useless matter
refused v ▷ refuse¹
refuses v ▷ refuse¹ ▶ n ▷ refuse²
refusing v ▷ refuse¹
refute v (-tes, -ting, -ted) disprove ▷ **refutation** n (pl -s)
refutation n ▷ refute
refutations n ▷ refute

refuted v ▷ refute
refutes v ▷ refute
refuting v ▷ refute
regain v (-s, -ing, -ed) get back or recover
regained v ▷ regain
regaining v ▷ regain
regains v ▷ regain
regal adj of or like a king or queen ▷ **regally** adv
regalia pl n ceremonial emblems of royalty or high office
regale v (-les, -ling, -led) entertain (someone) with stories etc.
regaled v ▷ regale
regales v ▷ regale
regaling v ▷ regale
regally adv ▷ regal
regard v (-s, -ing, -ed) consider ▶ n (pl -s) respect or esteem ▶ pl expression of goodwill
regarded v ▷ regard
regarding in respect of, concerning v ▷ regard
regardless adj heedless ▶ adv in spite of everything
regards v, n ▷ regard
regatta n (pl -s) meeting for yacht or boat races
regattas n ▷ regatta
regenerate v (-tes, -ting, -ted) (cause to) undergo spiritual, moral, or physical renewal ▷ **regeneration** n (pl -s) ▷ **regenerative** adj
regenerated v ▷ regenerate
regenerates v ▷ regenerate
regenerating v ▷ regenerate
regeneration n ▷ regenerate
regenerations n ▷ regenerate
regenerative adj ▷ regenerate
regencies n ▷ regency
regency n (pl -ies) status or period of office of a regent
regent n (pl -s) ruler of a kingdom during the absence, childhood, or illness of its monarch ▶ adj ruling as a regent
regents n ▷ regent
reggae n (pl -s) style of Jamaican popular music with a strong beat
reggaes n ▷ reggae
regicide n (pl -s) killing of a king
regicides n ▷ regicide
regime [ray-zheem] n (pl -s) system of government
regimen n (pl -s) prescribed system of diet etc.
regimens n ▷ regimen
regiment n (pl -s) organized body of troops as a unit of the army ▷ **regimental** adj ▷ **regimentation** n (pl -s)
regimental adj ▷ regiment
regimentation n ▷ regiment

regimentations n ▷ regiment
regimented adj very strictly controlled
regiments n ▷ regiment
regimes n ▷ regime
region n (pl -s) administrative division of a country > **regional** adj
regional adj ▷ region
regions n ▷ region
register n (pl -s) (book containing) an official list or record of things ▶ v (-s, -ing, -ed) enter in a register or set down in writing > **registration** n (pl -s)
registered v ▷ register
registering v ▷ register
registers n, v ▷ register
registrar n (pl -s) keeper of official records
registrars n ▷ registrar
registration n ▷ register
registrations n ▷ registers
regress v (-es, -ing, -ed) revert to a former worse condition
regressed v ▷ regress
regresses v ▷ regress
regressing v ▷ regress
regression n (pl -s) act of regressing (PSYCHOL) > **regressive** adj
regressions n ▷ regression
regressive adj ▷ regression
regret v (-s, -tting, -tted) feel sorry about ▶ n (pl -s) feeling of repentance, guilt, or sorrow > **regretful** adj > **regrettable** adj
regretful adj ▷ regret
regrets v ▷ regret
regrettable adj ▷ regret
regretted v ▷ regret
regretting v ▷ regret
regular adj normal, customary, or usual ▶ n (pl -s) regular soldier > **regularity** n (pl -s) > **regularize** v (-zes, -zing, -zed) > **regularly** adv
regularities n ▷ regular
regularity n ▷ regular
regularize v ▷ regular
regularized v ▷ regular
regularizes v ▷ regular
regularizing v ▷ regular
regularly adv ▷ regular
regulars n ▷ regular
regulate v (-tes, -ting, -ted) control, esp. by rules
regulated v ▷ regulate
regulates v ▷ regulate
regulating v ▷ regulate
regulation n (pl -s) rule
regulations n ▷ regulation

regulator n (pl -s) device that automatically controls pressure, temperature, etc.
regulators n ▷ regulator
regurgitate v (-tes, -ting, -ted) vomit > **regurgitation** n (pl -s)
regurgitated v ▷ regurgitate
regurgitates v ▷ regurgitate
regurgitating v ▷ regurgitate
regurgitation n ▷ regurgitate
regurgitations n ▷ regurgitate
rehabilitate v (-tes, -ting, -ted) help (a person) to readjust to society after illness, imprisonment, etc. > **rehabilitation** n (pl -s)
rehabilitated v ▷ rehabilitate
rehabilitates n ▷ rehabilitate
rehabilitating v ▷ rehabilitate
rehabilitation n ▷ rehabilitate
rehabilitations n ▷ rehabilitate
rehash v (-es, -ing, -ed) rework or reuse ▶ n (pl -es) old ideas presented in a new form
rehashed v ▷ rehash
rehashes v, n ▷ rehash
rehashing v ▷ rehash
rehearse v (-ses, -sing, -sed) practise (a play, concert, etc.) > **rehearsal** n (pl -s)
rehearsal n ▷ rehearse
rehearsals n ▷ rehearse
rehearsed v ▷ rehearse
rehearses v ▷ rehearse
rehearsing v ▷ rehearse
rehouse v (-ses, -sing, -sed) provide with a new (and better) home
rehoused v ▷ rehouse
rehouses v ▷ rehouse
rehousing v ▷ rehouse
reign n (pl -s) period of a sovereign's rule ▶ v (-s, -ing, -ed) rule (a country)
reigned v ▷ reign
reigning v ▷ reign
reigns n, v ▷ reign
reimburse v (-ses, -sing, -sed) refund, pay back > **reimbursement** n (pl -s)
reimbursed v ▷ reimburse
reimbursement n ▷ reimburse
reimbursements n ▷ reimburse
reimburses v ▷ reimburse
reimbursing v ▷ reimburse
rein v (-s, -ing, -ed) check or manage with reins
reincarnation n (pl -s) rebirth of a soul in successive bodies > **reincarnate** v (-tes, -ting, -ted)
reincarnate v ▷ reincarnation
reincarnated v ▷ reincarnation
reincarnates v ▷ reincarnation
reincarnating v ▷ reincarnation

reincarnations *n* ▷ reincarnation
reindeer *n* (*pl* -deer, -deers) deer of arctic regions with large branched antlers
  reindeers *n* ▷ reindeer
  reined *v* ▷ rein
  reining *v* ▷ rein
reinforce *v* (-ces, -cing, -ced) strengthen with new support, material, or force
  > **reinforcement** *n* (*pl* -s)
  reinforced *v* ▷ reinforce
  reinforcement *n* ▷ reinforce
  reinforcements *n* ▷ reinforce
  reinforces *v* ▷ reinforce
  reinforcing *v* ▷ reinforce
reins *pl n* narrow straps attached to a bit to guide a horse ▶ *v* ▷ rein
reinstate *v* (-tes, -ting, -ted) restore to a former position > **reinstatement** *n* (*pl* -s)
  reinstated *v* ▷ reinstate
  reinstatement *n* ▷ reinstate
  reinstatements *n* ▷ reinstate
  reinstates *v* ▷ reinstate
  reinstating *v* ▷ reinstate
reiterate *v* (-tes, -ting, -ted) repeat again and again > **reiteration** *n* (*pl* -s)
  reiterated *v* ▷ reiterate
  reiterates *v* ▷ reiterate
  reiterating *v* ▷ reiterate
  reiteration *n* ▷ reiterate
  reiterations *n* ▷ reiterate
reject *v* (-s, -ing, -ed) refuse to accept or believe ▶ *n* (*pl* -s) person or thing rejected as not up to standard > **rejection** *n* (*pl* -s)
  rejected *v* ▷ reject
  rejecting *v* ▷ reject
  rejection *n* ▷ reject
  rejections *n* ▷ reject
  rejects *v, n* ▷ reject
rejig *v* (-s, -gging, -gged) re-equip (a factory or plant)
  rejigged *v* ▷ rejig
  rejigging *v* ▷ rejig
  rejigs *v* ▷ rejig
rejoice *v* (-ces, -cing, -ced) feel or express great happiness
  rejoiced *v* ▷ rejoice
  rejoices *v* ▷ rejoice
  rejoicing *v* ▷ rejoice
rejoin¹ *v* (-s, -ing, -ed) join again
rejoin² *v* (-s, -ing, -ed) reply
rejoinder (*pl* -s) *n* answer, retort
  rejoinders *n* ▷ rejoinder
  rejoined *v* ▷ rejoin¹, ²
  rejoining *v* ▷ rejoin¹, ²
  rejoins *v* ▷ rejoin¹, ²

rejuvenate *v* (-tes, -ting, -ted) restore youth or vitality to > **rejuvenation** *n* (*pl* -s)
  rejuvenated *v* ▷ rejuvenate
  rejuvenates *v* ▷ rejuvenate
  rejuvenating *v* ▷ rejuvenate
  rejuvenation *n* ▷ rejuvenate
  rejuvenations *v* ▷ rejuvenate
relapse *v* (-ses, -sing, -sed) fall back into bad habits, illness, etc. ▶ *n* (*pl* -s) return of bad habits, illness, etc.
  relapsed *v* ▷ relapse
  relapses *v, n* ▷ relapse
  relapsing *v* ▷ relapse
relate *v* (-tes, -ting, -ted) establish a relation between > **related** *adj*
  related *adj, v* ▷ relate
  relates *v* ▷ relate
  relating *v* ▷ relate
relation *n* (*pl* -s) connection between things ▶ *pl* social or political dealings
  relations *n* ▷ relation
relationship *n* (*pl* -s) dealings and feelings between people or countries
  relationships *n* ▷ relationship
relative *adj* dependent on relation to something else, not absolute ▶ *n* (*pl* -s) person connected by blood or marriage > **relatively** *adv*
  relatively *adv* ▷ relative
  relatives *n* ▷ relative
  relativities *n* ▷ relativity
relativity *n* (*pl* -ies) subject of two theories of Albert Einstein, dealing with relationships of space, time, and motion, and acceleration and gravity
relax *v* (-es, -ing, -ed) make or become looser, less tense, or less rigid ▶ **relaxing** *adj*
  > **relaxation** *n* (*pl* -s)
  relaxation *n* ▷ relax
  relaxations *n* ▷ relax
  relaxed *v* ▷ relax
  relaxes *v* ▷ relax
  relaxing *v, adj* ▷ relax
relay *n* (*pl* -s) fresh set of people or animals relieving others ▶ *v* (-s, -ing, -ed) pass on (a message)
  relayed *v* ▷ relay
  relaying *v* ▷ relay
  relays *n, v* ▷ relay
release *v* (-ses, -sing, -sed) set free ▶ *n* (*pl* -s) setting free
  released *v* ▷ release
  releases *v, n* ▷ release
  releasing *v* ▷ release
relegate *v* (-tes, -ting, -ted) put in a less

important position > **relegation** n (pl -s)
relegated v ▷ relegate
relegates v ▷ relegate
relegating v ▷ relegate
relegation n ▷ relegate
relegations n ▷ relegate
relent v (-s, -ing, -ed) give up a harsh intention, become less severe
relented v ▷ relent
relenting v ▷ relent
relentless adj unremitting
relents v ▷ relent
relevance n ▷ relevant
relevances n ▷ relevant
relevant adj to do with the matter in hand
>**relevance** n (pl -s)
reliabilities n ▷ reliable
reliability n ▷ reliable
reliable adj able to be trusted, dependable
>**reliably** adv >**reliability** n (pl -ies)
reliably adv ▷ reliable
reliance n (pl -s) dependence, confidence, or trust >**reliant** adj
reliances n ▷ reliance
reliant adj ▷ reliance
relic n (pl -s) something that has survived from the past ▶ pl remains or traces
relics n ▷ relic
relict n (pl -s) (Obs) widow
relicts n ▷ relict
relied v ▷ rely
relief n (pl -s) gladness at the end or removal of pain, distress, etc.
reliefs n ▷ relief
relies v ▷ rely
relieve v (-ves, -ving, -ved) bring relief to
relieved v ▷ relieve
relieves v ▷ relieve
relieving v ▷ relieve
religion n (pl -s) system of belief in and worship of a supernatural power or god
religious adj of religion >**religiously** adv
religiously adv ▷ religious
religions n ▷ religion
relinquish v (-es, -ing, -ed) give up or abandon
relinquished v ▷ relinquish
relinquishes v ▷ relinquish
relinquishing v ▷ relinquish
reliquaries n ▷ reliquary
reliquary n (pl -ies) case or shrine for holy relics
relish v (-es, -ing, -ed) enjoy, like very much ▶ n (pl -es) liking or enjoyment
relished v ▷ relish
relishes v, n ▷ relish
relishing v ▷ relish

relocate v (-tes, -ting, -ted) move to a new place to live or work >**relocation** n (pl -s)
relocated v ▷ relocate
relocates v ▷ relocate
relocating v ▷ relocate
relocation n ▷ relocate
relocations n ▷ relocate
reluctance n ▷ reluctant
reluctances n ▷ reluctant
reluctant adj unwilling or disinclined
>**reluctantly** adv >**reluctance** n (pl -s)
reluctantly adv ▷ reluctant
rely v (-ies, -ying, -ied) depend (on)
relying v ▷ rely
remain v (-s, -ing, -ed) continue
remainder n (pl -s) part which is left ▶ v (-s, -ing, -ed) offer (copies of a poorly selling book) at reduced prices
remaindered v ▷ remainders
remaindering v ▷ remainders
remainders n, v ▷ remainders
remained v ▷ remain
remaining v ▷ remain
remains pl n relics, esp. of ancient buildings ▶ v ▷ remain
remand v (-s, -ing, -ed) send back into custody or put on bail before trial
remanded v ▷ remand
remanding v ▷ remand
remands v ▷ remand
remark v (-s, -ing, -ed) make a casual comment (on) ▶ n (pl -s) observation or comment
remarkable adj worthy of note or attention
>**remarkably** adv
remarkably adv ▷ remarkable
remarked v ▷ remark
remarking v ▷ remark
remarks v, n ▷ remark
remedial adj intended to correct a specific disability, handicap, etc.
remedied v ▷ remedy
remedies n, v ▷ remedy
remedy n (pl -ies) means of curing pain or disease ▶ v (-ies, -ying, -ied) put right
remedying v ▷ remedy
remember v (-s, -ing, -ed) retain in or recall to one's memory
remembered v ▷ remember
remembering v ▷ remember
remembers v ▷ remember
remembrance n (pl -s) memory
remembrances n ▷ remembrance
remind v (-s, -ing, -ed) cause to remember
reminded v ▷ remind
reminder n (pl -s) something that recalls the

past

reminders n ▷ reminder

reminding v ▷ remind

reminds v ▷ remind

reminisce v (-ces, -cing, -ced) talk or write of past times, experiences, etc.

reminisced v ▷ reminisce

reminiscence n (pl -s) remembering ▶ pl memoirs

reminiscences n ▷ reminiscence

reminiscent adj reminding or suggestive (of)

reminisces v ▷ reminisce

reminiscing v ▷ reminisce

remiss adj negligent or careless

remission n (pl -s) reduction in the length of a prison term

remissions n ▷ remission

remit v (-s, -tting, -tted) send (money) for goods, services, etc., esp. by post ▶ n (pl -s) [**ree**-mitt] area of competence or authority

remits v, n ▷ remit

remittance n (pl -s) money sent as payment

remittances n ▷ remittance

remitted v ▷ remit

remitting v ▷ remit

remnant n (pl -s) small piece, esp. of fabric, left over

remnants n ▷ remnant

remonstrance n ▷ remonstrate

remonstrances n ▷ remonstrate

remonstrate v (-tes, -ting, -ted) argue in protest > **remonstrance** n (pl -s)

remonstrated v ▷ remonstrate

remonstrates v ▷ remonstrate

remonstrating v ▷ remonstrate

remorse n (pl -s) feeling of sorrow and regret for something one did > **remorseful** adj

remorseful adj ▷ remorse

remorseless adj pitiless > **remorselessly** adv

remorselessly adv ▷ remorseless

remorses n ▷ remorse

remote adj (-er, -est) far away, distant > **remotely** adv

remoter adj ▷ remote

remotest adj ▷ remote

remotely adv ▷ remote

remould v (-s, -ing, -ed) (BRIT) renovate (a worn tyre) ▶ n (pl -s) (BRIT) renovated tyre

remoulded v ▷ remould

remoulding v ▷ remould

remoulds v, n ▷ remould

removal n (pl -s) removing, esp. changing

residence

removals n ▷ removal

removed v ▷ remove

removes v, n ▷ remove

removing v ▷ remove

remunerate v (-tes, -ting, -ted) reward or pay > **remunerative** adj

remunerated v ▷ remunerate

remunerates v ▷ remunerate

remunerating v ▷ remunerate

remuneration n (pl -s) reward or payment

remunerations n ▷ remuneration

remunerative adj ▷ remuneration

renaissance n (pl -s) revival or rebirth

renaissances n ▷ renaissance

renal [**ree**-nal] adj of the kidneys

renascent adj becoming active or vigorous again

rend v (-s, -ing, rent) tear or wrench apart

render v (-s, -ing, -ed) cause to become

rendered v ▷ render

rendering v ▷ render

renders v ▷ render

rendezvous [**ron**-day-voo] n (pl -vous) appointment ▶ v (-vous, -vousing, -voused) meet as arranged

rendezvoused v ▷ rendezvous

rendezvousing v ▷ rendezvous

rending v ▷ rend

rendition n (pl -s) performance

renditions n ▷ rendition

rends v ▷ rend

renegade n (pl -s) person who deserts a cause

renegades n ▷ renegade

renege [rin-**nayg**] v (-ges, -ging, -ged) go back (on a promise etc.)

reneged v ▷ renege

reneges v ▷ renege

reneging v ▷ renege

renew v (-s, -ing, -ed) begin again > **renewable** adj > **renewal** n (pl -s)

renewable adj ▷ renew

renewal n ▷ renew

renewals n ▷ renew

renewed v ▷ renew

renewing v ▷ renew

renews v ▷ renew

rennet n (pl -s) substance for curdling milk to make cheese

rennets n ▷ rennet

renounce v (-ces, -cing, -ced) give up (a belief, habit, etc.) voluntarily > **renunciation** n (pl -s)

renounced v ▷ renounce

renounces v ▷ renounce

renouncing v ▷ renounce

renovate v (-tes, -ting, -ted) restore to good condition > **renovation** n (pl -s)
renovated v ▷ renovate
renovates v ▷ renovate
renovating v ▷ renovate
renovation n ▷ renovate
renovations n ▷ renovate
renown n (pl -s) widespread good reputation
renowned adj famous
renowns n ▷ renown
rent¹ v (-s, -ing, -ed) give or have use of in return for regular payments ▶ n (pl -s) regular payment for use of land, a building, etc.
rent² n (pl -s) tear or fissure ▶ v ▷ rend
rental n (pl -s) sum payable as rent
rentals n ▷ rental
rented v ▷ rent¹
renting v ▷ rent¹
rentings n ▷ rent¹
rents v ▷ rent¹ ▶ n ▷ rent²
renunciation n ▷ renounce
renunciations n ▷ renounce
reorganize v (-zes, -zing, -zed) organize in a new and more efficient way > **reorganization** n (pl -s)
reorganization n ▷ reorganize
reorganizations n ▷ reorganize
reorganized v ▷ reorganize
reorganizes v ▷ reorganize
reorganizing v ▷ reorganize
rep¹ n (pl -s) repertory company
rep² n (pl -s) ▷ representative
repair¹ v (-s, -ing, -ed) restore to good condition, mend ▶ n (pl -s) act of repairing
repair² v (-s, -ing, -ed) go (to)
repaired v ▷ repair¹, ²
repairing v ▷ repair¹, ²
repairs v ▷ repair¹, ² ▶ n ▷ repair¹
reparation n (pl -s) something done or given as compensation
reparations n ▷ reparation
repartee n (pl -s) interchange of witty retorts
repartees n ▷ repartee
repast n (pl -s) meal
repasts n ▷ repast
repatriate v (-tes, -ting, -ted) send (someone) back to his or her own country > **repatriation** n (pl -s)
repatriated v ▷ repatriate
repatriates v ▷ repatriate
repatriating v ▷ repatriate
repatriation n ▷ repatriate
repatriations n ▷ repatriate
repay v (-s, -ing, -paid) pay back, refund > **repayable** adj > **repayment** n (pl -s)

repayable adj ▷ repay
repaying v ▷ repay
repayment n ▷ repay
repayments n ▷ repay
repays v ▷ repay
repeal v (-s, -ing, -ed) cancel (a law) officially ▶ n (pl -s) act of repealing
repealed v ▷ repeal
repealing v ▷ repeal
repeals v, n ▷ repeal
repeat v (-s, -ing, -ed) say or do again ▶ n (pl -s) act or instance of repeating > **repeatedly** adv
repeated v ▷ repeat
repeatedly adv ▷ repeat
repeater n (pl -s) firearm that may be discharged many times without reloading
repeaters n ▷ repeater
repeating v ▷ repeat
repeats v, n ▷ repeat
repel v (-s, -lling, -lled) be disgusting to
repelled v ▷ repel
repellent adj distasteful ▶ n (pl -s) something that repels, esp. a chemical to repel insects
repellents n ▷ repellent
repelling v ▷ repel
repels v ▷ repel
repent v (-s, -ing, -ed) feel regret for (a deed or omission) > **repentance** n (pl -s) > **repentant** adj
repentance n ▷ repent
repentances n ▷ repent
repentant adj ▷ repent
repented v ▷ repent
repenting v ▷ repent
repents v ▷ repent
repercussions pl n indirect effects, often unpleasant
repertoire n (pl -s) stock of plays, songs, etc. that a player or company can give
repertoires n ▷ repertoire
repertories n ▷ repertory
repertory n (pl -ies) repertoire
repetition n (pl -s) act of repeating
repetitions n ▷ repetition
repetitious adj ▷ repetitive
repetitive, repetitious adj full of repetition
rephrase v (-ses, -sing, -sed) express in different words
rephrased v ▷ rephrase
rephrases v ▷ rephrase
rephrasing v ▷ rephrase
repine v (-nes, -ning, -ned) fret or complain
repined v ▷ repine
repines v ▷ repine
repining v ▷ repine

replace v (-ces, -cing, -ced) substitute for
> **replacement** n (pl -s)
  replaced v ▷ replace
  replacement n ▷ replace
  replacements n ▷ replace
  replaces v ▷ replace
  replacing v ▷ replace
replay n (pl -s) immediate reshowing on TV
of an incident in sport, esp. in slow motion
▶ v (-s, -ing, -ed) play (a match, recording,
etc.) again
  replayed v ▷ replay
  replaying v ▷ replay
  replays n, v ▷ replay
replenish v (-es, -ing, -ed) fill up again,
resupply > **replenishment** n (pl -s)
  replenished v ▷ replenish
  replenishes v ▷ replenish
  replenishing v ▷ replenish
  replenishment n ▷ replenish
  replenishments n ▷ replenish
replete adj filled or gorged
replica n (pl -s) exact copy
  replicas n ▷ replica
replicate v (-s, -ing, -ed) make or be a copy of
  replicated v ▷ replicate
  replicates v ▷ replicate
  replicating v ▷ replicate
  replied v ▷ reply
  replies v, n ▷ reply
reply v (-ies, -ying, -ied) answer or respond ▶ n
(pl -ies) answer or response
  replying v ▷ reply
report v (-s, -ing, -ed) give an account of ▶ n (pl
-s) account or statement
  reported v ▷ report
reportedly adv according to rumour
reporter n (pl -s) person who gathers news for
a newspaper, TV, etc.
  reporters n ▷ reporter
  reporting v ▷ report
  reports v, n ▷ report
repose n (pl -s) peace ▶ v (-ses, -sing, -sed) lie
or lay at rest
  reposed v ▷ repose
  reposes n, v ▷ repose
  reposing v ▷ repose
  repositories n ▷ repository
repository n (pl -ies) place where valuables are
deposited for safekeeping, store
repossess v (-es, -ing, -ed) (of a lender) take
back property from a customer who is behind
with payments > **repossession** n (pl -s)
  repossessed v ▷ repossess
  repossesses v ▷ repossess

  repossessing v ▷ repossess
  repossession n ▷ repossess
  repossessions n ▷ repossess
reprehensible adj open to criticism,
unworthy
represent v (-s, -ing, -ed) act as a delegate or
substitute for > **representation** n (pl -s)
  representation n ▷ represent
  representations n ▷ represent
representative n (pl -s) person chosen to
stand for a group ▶ adj typical
  representatives n ▷ representative
  represented v ▷ represent
  representing v ▷ represent
  represents v ▷ represent
repress v (-es, -ing, -ed) keep (feelings) in
check > **repression** n (pl -s) > **repressive** adj
  repressed v ▷ repress
  represses v ▷ repress
  repressing v ▷ repress
  repression n ▷ repress
  repressions n ▷ repress
  repressive adj ▷ repress
reprieve v (-ves, -ving, -ved) postpone the
execution of (a condemned person) ▶ n (pl
-s) (document granting) postponement or
cancellation of a punishment
  reprieved v ▷ reprieve
  reprieves v, n ▷ reprieve
  reprieving v ▷ reprieve
reprimand v (-s, -ing, -ed) blame (someone)
officially for a fault ▶ n (pl -s) official blame
  reprimanded v ▷ reprimand
  reprimanding v ▷ reprimand
  reprimands v, n ▷ reprimand
reprint v (-s, -ing, -ed) print further copies of (a
book) ▶ n (pl -s) reprinted copy
  reprinted v ▷ reprint
  reprinting v ▷ reprint
  reprints v, n ▷ reprint
reprisal n (pl -s) retaliation
  reprisals n ▷ reprisal
reproach n, v (-es, -ing, -ed) blame, rebuke
> **reproachful** adj > **reproachfully** adv
  reproached v ▷ reproach
  reproaches v ▷ reproach
  reproachful adj ▷ reproach
  reproachfully adv ▷ reproach
  reproaching v ▷ reproach
reprobate adj, n (pl -s) depraved or
disreputable (person)
  reprobates n ▷ reprobate
reproduce v (-ces, -cing, -ced) produce a copy
of > **reproducible** adj
  reproduced v ▷ reproduce

reproduces v ▷ reproduce
reproducible adj ▷ reproduce
reproducing v ▷ reproduce
reproduction n (pl -s) process of reproducing
> **reproductive** adj
reproductions n ▷ reproduction
reproductive adj ▷ reproduction
reproof n (pl -s) severe blaming of someone
for a fault
reproofs n ▷ reproof
reprove v (-ves, -ving, -ved) speak severely to
(someone) about a fault
reproved v ▷ reprove
reproves v ▷ reprove
reproving v ▷ reprove
reps n ▷ rep[1, 2]
reptile n (pl -s) cold-blooded egg-laying
vertebrate with horny scales or plates, such
as a snake or tortoise > **reptilian** adj
reptiles n ▷ reptile
reptilian adj ▷ reptile
republic n (pl -s) form of government in which
the people or their elected representatives
possess the supreme power
republican n (pl -s) supporter or advocate of a
republic > **republicanism** n (pl -s)
republicans n ▷ republican
republicanism n ▷ republican
republicanisms n ▷ republican
republics n ▷ republic
repudiate [rip-**pew**-dee-ate] v (-tes, -ting,
-ted) reject the authority or validity of
> **repudiation** n (pl -s)
repudiated v ▷ repudiate
repudiates v ▷ repudiate
repudiating v ▷ repudiate
repudiation n ▷ repudiate
repudiations n ▷ repudiate
repugnance n ▷ repugnant
repugnances n ▷ repugnant
repugnant adj offensive or distasteful
> **repugnance** n (pl -s)
repulse v (-ses, -sing, -sed) be disgusting to ▶ n
(pl -s) driving back
repulsed v ▷ repulse
repulsing v ▷ repulse
repulses v, n ▷ repulse
repulsion n (pl -s) distaste or aversion
repulsions n ▷ repulsion
repulsive adj loathsome, disgusting
reputable adj of good reputation, respectable
reputation n (pl -s) estimation in which a
person is held
reputations n ▷ reputation
repute n (pl -s) reputation

reputed adj supposed > **reputedly** adv
reputedly adv ▷ reputed
reputes v ▷ repute
request v (-s, -ing, -ed) ask ▶ n (pl -s) asking
requested v ▷ request
requesting v ▷ request
requests v, n ▷ request
requiem [rek-wee-em] n (pl -s) Mass for the
dead
requiems n ▷ requiem
require v (-res, -ring, -red) want or need
required v ▷ require
requirement n (pl -s) essential condition
requirements n ▷ requirement
requires v ▷ require
requiring v ▷ require
requisite [rek-wizz-it] adj necessary, essential
▶ n (pl -s) essential thing
requisites n ▷ requisite
requisition v (-s, -ing, -ed) demand (supplies)
▶ n (pl -s) formal demand, such as for
materials or supplies
requisitioned v ▷ requisition
requisitioning v ▷ requisition
requisitions v, n ▷ requisition
requite v (-tes, -ting, -ted) return to someone
(the same treatment or feeling as received)
requited v ▷ requite
requites v ▷ requite
requiting v ▷ requite
reredos [rear-doss] n (pl -es) ornamental screen
behind an altar
reredoses n ▷ reredos
resat v ▷ resit
rescind v (-s, -ing, -ed) annul or repeal
rescinded v ▷ rescind
rescinding v ▷ rescind
rescinds v ▷ rescind
rescue v (-cues, -cuing, -cued) deliver from
danger or trouble, save ▶ n (pl -s) rescuing
> **rescuer** n (pl -s)
rescued v ▷ rescue
rescuer n ▷ rescue
rescuers n ▷ rescue
rescues v, n ▷ rescue
rescuing v ▷ rescue
research n (pl -es) systematic investigation
to discover facts or collect information
▶ v (-es, -ing, -ed) carry out investigations
> **researcher** n (pl -s)
researched v ▷ research
researcher n ▷ research
researchers n ▷ research
researches n, v ▷ research
researching v ▷ research

resemblance n ▷ resemble
resemblances n ▷ resemble
resemble v (-les, -ling, -led) be or look like
  > **resemblance** n (pl -s)
resembled v ▷ resemble
resembles v ▷ resemble
resembling v ▷ resemble
resent v (-s, -ing, -ed) feel bitter about
  > **resentful** adj > **resentment** n (pl -s)
resented v ▷ resent
resentful adj ▷ resent
resenting v ▷ resent
resentment n ▷ resent
resentments n ▷ resent
resents v ▷ resent
reservation n (pl -s) doubt
reservations n ▷ reservation
reserve v (-ves, -ving, -ved) set aside, keep for
  future use ▶ n (pl -s) something, esp. money
  or troops, kept for emergencies (SPORT)
reserved adj not showing one's feelings,
  lacking friendliness ▶ v ▷ **reserve**
reserves v, n ▷ reserve
reserving v ▷ reserve
reservist n (pl -s) member of a military reserve
reservists n ▷ reservist
reservoir n (pl -s) natural or artificial lake
  storing water for community supplies
reservoirs n ▷ reservoir
reshuffle n (pl -s) reorganization ▶ v (-s, -ing,
  -ed) reorganize
reshuffled n ▷ reshuffle
reshuffles n, v ▷ reshuffle
reshuffling v ▷ reshuffle
reside v (-des, -ding, -ded) dwell permanently
resided v ▷ reside
residence n (pl -s) home or house
residences n ▷ residence
resident n (pl -s) person who lives in a place
  ▶ adj living in a place
residential adj (of part of a town) consisting
  mainly of houses
residents n ▷ resident
resides v ▷ reside
residing v ▷ reside
residue n (pl -s) what is left, remainder
  > **residual** adj
residual adj ▷ residue
residues n ▷ residue
resign v (-s, -ing, -ed) give up office, a job, etc.
resignation n (pl -s) resigning
resignations n ▷ resignation
resigned adj content to endure ▶ v ▷ **resign**
resigning v ▷ resign
resigns v ▷ resign

resilience n ▷ resilient
resiliences n ▷ resilient
resilient adj (of a person) recovering quickly
  from a shock etc. > **resilience** n (pl -s)
resin [rezz-in] n (pl -s) sticky substance from
  plants, esp. pines > **resinous** adj
resinous adj ▷ resin
resins n ▷ resin
resist v (-s, -ing, -ed) withstand or oppose
  > **resistant** adj > **resistible** adj
resistance n (pl -s) act of resisting
resistances n ▷ resistance
resistant adj ▷ resist
resisted v ▷ resist
resistible adj ▷ resist
resisting v ▷ resist
resistor n (pl -s) component of an electrical
  circuit producing resistance
resistors n ▷ resistor
resists v ▷ resist
resit v (-s, -tting, -sat) take (an exam) again ▶ n
  (pl -s) exam that has to be taken again
resitting v ▷ resit
resits v, n ▷ resit
resolute adj firm in purpose > **resolutely** adv
resolutely adv ▷ resolute
resolution n (pl -s) firmness of conduct or
  character
resolutions n ▷ resolution
resolve v (-ves, -ving, -ved) decide with an
  effort of will
resolved adj determined ▶ v ▷ **resolve**
resolves v ▷ resolve
resolving v ▷ resolve
resonance n (pl -s) echoing, esp. with a deep
  sound > **resonant** adj > **resonate** v (-tes,
  -ting, -ted)
resonances n ▷ resonance
resonant adj ▷ resonance
resonate v ▷ resonance
resonated v ▷ resonance
resonates v ▷ resonance
resonating v ▷ resonance
resort v (-s, -ing, -ed) have recourse (to) for
  help etc. ▶ n (pl -s) place for holidays
resorted v ▷ resort
resorting v ▷ resort
resorts v, n ▷ resort
resound [riz-zownd] v (-s, -ing, -ed) echo or ring
  with sound
resounded v ▷ resound
resounding adj echoing ▶ v ▷ **resound**
resounds v ▷ resound
resource n (pl -s) thing resorted to for
  support ▶ pl sources of economic wealth

> **resourceful** *adj* > **resourcefulness** *n*
resourceful *adj* ▷ **resource**
resourcefulness *n* ▷ **resource**
resources *n* ▷ **resource**
respect *n* (*pl* -s) consideration ▶ *v* (-s, -ing, -ed) treat with esteem > **respecter** *n* (*pl* -s) > **respectful** *adj*
respectable *adj* worthy of respect
> **respectably** *adv* > **respectability** *n* (*pl* -ies)
respectables *n* ▷ **respectable**
respectability *n* ▷ **respectable**
respectably *adv* ▷ **respectable**
respected *v* ▷ **respect**
respecter *n* ▷ **respect**
respecters *n* ▷ **respect**
respectful *adj* ▷ **respect**
respecting *prep* concerning ▶ *v* ▷ **respect**
respective *adj* relating separately to each of those in question > **respectively** *adv*
respectively *adv* ▷ **respective**
respects *n*, *v* ▷ **respect**
respiration [ress-per-ray-shun] *n* (*pl* -s) breathing > **respiratory** *adj*
respirations *n* ▷ **respiration**
respirator *n* apparatus worn over the mouth and breathed through as protection against dust, poison gas, etc., or to provide artificial respiration
respirators *n* ▷ **respirator**
respiratory *adj* ▷ **respiration**
respire *v* (-res, -ring, -red) breathe
respired *v* ▷ **respire**
respires *v* ▷ **respire**
respiring *v* ▷ **respire**
respite *n* (*pl* -s) pause, interval of rest
respites *n* ▷ **respite**
resplendence *n* ▷ **resplendent**
resplendences *n* ▷ **resplendent**
resplendent *adj* brilliant or splendid
> **resplendence** *n* (*pl* -s)
respond *v* (-s, -ing, -ed) answer
responded *v* ▷ **respond**
respondent *n* (*pl* -s) (LAW) defendant
respondents *n* ▷ **respondent**
responding *v* ▷ **respond**
responds *v* ▷ **respond**
response *n* (*pl* -s) answer
responses *n* ▷ **response**
responsibilities *n* ▷ **responsibility**
responsibility *n* (*pl* -ies) state of being responsible
responsible *adj* having control and authority
> **responsibly** *adv*
responsibly *adv* ▷ **responsible**
responsive *adj* readily reacting to some

influence > **responsiveness** *n*
responsiveness *n* ▷ **responsive**
rest[1] *n* (*pl* -s) freedom from exertion etc. ▶ *v* (-s, -ing, -ed) take a rest > **restful** *adj* > **restless** *adj*
rest[2] *n* what is left ▶ *v* (-s, -ing, -ed) remain, continue to be
restaurant *n* (*pl* -s) commercial establishment serving meals
restaurants *n* ▷ **restaurant**
restaurateur [rest-er-a-tur] *n* (*pl* -s) person who owns or runs a restaurant
restaurateurs *n* ▷ **restaurateur**
rested *v* ▷ **rest**[1, 2]
restful (-ler, -lest) *adj* ▷ **rest**[1]
restfuller *adj* ▷ **restful**
restfullest *adj* ▷ **restful**
resting *v* ▷ **rest**[1, 2]
restitution *n* (*pl* -s) giving back
restitutions *n* ▷ **restitution**
restive *adj* restless or impatient
restless *adj* ▷ **rest**[1]
restore *v* (-res, -ring, -red) return (a building, painting, etc.) to its original condition
> **restoration** *n* (*pl* -s) > **restorer** *n* (*pl* -s)
restoration *n* ▷ **restore**
restorations *n* ▷ **restore**
restorative *adj* restoring ▶ *n* (*pl* -s) food or medicine to strengthen etc.
restoratives *n* ▷ **restorative**
restored *v* ▷ **restore**
restorer *n* ▷ **restore**
restorers *n* ▷ **restore**
restores *v* ▷ **restore**
restoring *v* ▷ **restore**
restrain *v* (-s, -ing, -ed) hold (someone) back from action
restrained *adj* not displaying emotion ▶ *v* ▷ **restrain**
restraining *v* ▷ **restrain**
restrains *v* ▷ **restrain**
restraint *n* (*pl* -s) control, esp. self-control
restraints *n* ▷ **restraint**
restrict *v* (-s, -ing, -ed) confine to certain limits > **restriction** *n* (*pl* -s) > **restrictive** *adj*
restricted *v* ▷ **restrict**
restricting *v* ▷ **restrict**
restriction *n* ▷ **restrict**
restrictions *n* ▷ **restrict**
restrictive *adj* ▷ **restrict**
restricts *v* ▷ **restrict**
restructure *v* (-res, -ring, -red) organize in a different way
restructured *v* ▷ **restructure**
restructures *v* ▷ **restructure**
restructuring *v* ▷ **restructure**

rests *n, v* ▷ rest[1, 2]

result *n* (*pl* -s) outcome or consequence ▶ *v* (-s, -ing, -ed) (foll. by **from**) be the outcome or consequence (of) > **resultant** *adj*

resultant *adj* ▷ result

resulted *v* ▷ result

resulting *v* ▷ result

results *n, v* ▷ result

resume *v* (-mes, -ming, -med) begin again > **resumption** *n* (*pl* -s)

résumé [rezz-yew-may] *n* (*pl* -s) summary

resumed *v* ▷ resume

resumes *v* ▷ resume

résumés *n* ▷ résumé

resuming *v* ▷ resume

resumption *n* ▷ resume

resumptions *n* ▷ resume

resurgence *n* (*pl* -s) rising again to vigour > **resurgent** *adj*

resurgences *n* ▷ resurgence

resurgent *adj* ▷ resurgence

resurrect *v* (-s, -ing, -ed) restore to life

resurrected *v* ▷ resurrect

resurrecting *v* ▷ resurrect

resurrection *n* (*pl* -s) rising again (esp. from the dead)

resurrections *n* ▷ resurrection

resurrects *v* ▷ resurrect

resuscitate [ris-suss-it-tate] *v* (-tes, -ting, -ted) restore to consciousness > **resuscitation** *n* (*pl* -s)

resuscitated *v* ▷ resuscitate

resuscitates *v* ▷ resuscitate

resuscitating *v* ▷ resuscitate

resuscitation *n* ▷ resuscitate

resuscitations *n* ▷ resuscitate

retail *n* (*pl* -s) selling of goods individually or in small amounts to the public ▶ *adv* by retail ▶ *v* (-s, -ing, -ed) sell or be sold retail

retailed *v* ▷ retail

retailer *n* (*pl* -s) person or company that sells goods to the public

retailers *n* ▷ retailer

retailing *v* ▷ retail

retails *n, v* ▷ retail

retain *v* (-s, -ing, -ed) keep in one's possession

retained *v* ▷ retain

retainer *n* (*pl* -s) fee to retain someone's services

retainers *n* ▷ retainer

retaining *v* ▷ retain

retains *v* ▷ retain

retaliate *v* (-tes, -ting, -ted) repay an injury or wrong in kind > **retaliation** *n* (*pl* -s) > **retaliatory** *adj*

retaliated *v* ▷ retaliate

retaliates *v* ▷ retaliate

retaliating *v* ▷ retaliate

retaliation *n* ▷ retaliate

retaliations *n* ▷ retaliate

retaliatory *adj* ▷ retaliate

retard *v* (-s, -ing, -ed) delay or slow (progress or development) > **retardation** *n* (*pl* -s)

retardation *n* ▷ retard

retardations *n* ▷ retard

retarded *adj* underdeveloped, esp. mentally ▶ *v* ▷ retard

retarding *v* ▷ retard

retards *v* ▷ retard

retch *v* (-es, -ing, -ed) try to vomit

retched *v* ▷ retch

retches *v* ▷ retch

retching *v* ▷ retch

rethink *v* (-s, -ing, -thought) consider again, esp. with a view to changing one's tactics

rethinks *v* ▷ rethink

rethinking *v* ▷ rethink

rethought *v* ▷ rethink

reticence *n* ▷ reticent

reticences *n* ▷ reticent

reticent *adj* uncommunicative, reserved > **reticence** *n* (*pl* -s)

retina *n* (*pl* -nas, -nae) light-sensitive membrane at the back of the eye

retinae *n* ▷ retina

retinas *n* ▷ retina

retinue *n* (*pl* -s) band of attendants

retinues *n* ▷ retinue

retire *v* (-res, -ring, -red) (cause to) give up office or work, esp. through age > **retirement** *n* (*pl* -s)

retired *adj* having retired from work etc. ▶ *v* ▷ retire

retirement *n* ▷ retire

retirements *n* ▷ retire

retires *v* ▷ retire

retiring *adj* shy ▶ *v* ▷ retire

retort[1] *v* (-s, -ing, -ed) reply quickly, wittily, or angrily ▶ *n* (*pl* -s) quick, witty, or angry reply

retort[2] *n* (*pl* -s) glass container with a bent neck used for distilling

retorted *v* ▷ retort[1]

retorting *v* ▷ retort[1]

retorts *v* ▷ retort[1] ▶ *n* ▷ retort[1, 2]

retouch *v* (-es, -ing, -ed) restore or improve by new touches, esp. of paint

retouched *v* ▷ retouch

retouches *v* ▷ retouch

retouching *v* ▷ retouch

retrace *v* (-ces, -cing, -ced) go back over (a

retraced *v* ▷ retrace
retraces *v* ▷ retrace
retracing *v* ▷ retrace
retract *v* (-s, -ing, -ed) withdraw (a statement etc.) > **retraction** *n* (*pl* -s)
retractable, retractile *adj* able to be retracted
retracted *v* ▷ retract
retractile *adj* ▷ retractable
retracting *v* ▷ retract
retracts *v* ▷ retract
retraction *n* ▷ retract
retractions *n* ▷ retract
retread *v* (-s, -ing, -ed) ▶ *n* (*pl* -s) ▷ remould
retreaded *v* ▷ retread
retreading *v* ▷ retread
retreads *v*, *n* ▷ retread
retreat *v* (-s, -ing, -ed) move back from a position, withdraw ▶ *n* (*pl* -s) act of or military signal for retiring or withdrawal
retreated *v* ▷ retreat
retreating *v* ▷ retreat
retreats *v*, *n* ▷ retreat
retrench *v* (-es, -ing, -ed) reduce expenditure, cut back > **retrenchment** *n* (*pl* -s)
retrenched *v* ▷ retrench
retrenches *v* ▷ retrench
retrenching *v* ▷ retrench
retrenchment *n* ▷ retrench
retrenchments *n* ▷ retrench
retrial *n* (*pl* -s) second trial of a case or defendant in a court of law
retrials *n* ▷ retrial
retribution *n* (*pl* -s) punishment or vengeance for evil deeds > **retributive** *adj*
retributions *n* ▷ retribution
retributive *adj* ▷ retributions
retrieve *v* (-ves, -ving, -ved) fetch back again > **retrievable** *adj* > **retrieval** *n* (*pl* -s)
retrievable *adj* ▷ retrieve
retrieval *n* ▷ retrieve
retrievals *n* ▷ retrieve
retrieved *v* ▷ retrieve
retriever *n* (*pl* -s) dog trained to retrieve shot game
retrievers *n* ▷ retrieve
retrieves *v* ▷ retrieve
retrieving *v* ▷ retrieve
retroactive *adj* effective from a date in the past
retrograde *adj* tending towards an earlier worse condition
retrogressive *adj* going back to an earlier worse condition > **retrogression** *n* (*pl* -s)
retrogression *n* ▷ retrogressive

retrogressions *n* ▷ retrogressive
retrorocket *n* (*pl* -s) small rocket engine used to slow a spacecraft
retrorockets *n* ▷ retrorocket
retrospective *adj* looking back in time ▶ *n* (*pl* -s) exhibition of an artist's life's work
retrospectives *n* ▷ retrospective
retroussé [rit-**troo**-say] *adj* (of a nose) turned upwards
retsina *n* (*pl* -s) Greek wine flavoured with resin
retsinas *n* ▷ retsina
return *v* (-s, -ing, -ed) go or come back ▶ *n* (*pl* -s) returning > **returnable** *adj*
returnable *adj* ▷ return
returned *v* ▷ return
returning *v* ▷ return
returns *v*, *n* ▷ return
reunion *n* (*pl* -s) meeting of people who have been apart
reunions *n* ▷ reunion
reunite *v* (-tes, -ting, -ted) bring or come together again after a separation
reunited *v* ▷ reunite
reunites *v* ▷ reunite
reuniting *v* ▷ reunite
reuse *v* (-ses, -sing, -sed) use again > **reusable** *adj*
reusable *adj* ▷ reuse
reused *v* ▷ reuse
reuses *v* ▷ reuse
reusing *v* ▷ reuse
rev (*Informal*) *n* (*pl* -s) revolution (of an engine) ▶ *v* (-s, -vving, -vved) (*foll. by* up) increase the speed of revolution of (an engine)
revalue *v* (-ues, -uing, -ued) adjust the exchange value of (a currency) upwards > **revaluation** *n* (*pl* -s)
revaluation *n* ▷ revalue
revaluations *n* ▷ revalue
revalued *v* ▷ revalue
revalues *v* ▷ revalue
revaluing *v* ▷ revalue
revamp *v* (-s, -ing, -ed) renovate or restore
revamped *v* ▷ revamp
revamping *v* ▷ revamp
revamps *v* ▷ revamp
reveal *v* (-s, -ing, -ed) make known > **revelation** *n* (*pl* -s)
revealed *v* ▷ reveal
revealing *v* ▷ reveal
reveals *v* ▷ reveal
reveille [riv-**val**-ee] *n* (*pl* -s) morning bugle call to waken soldiers
reveilles *n* ▷ reveille

revel v (**-s, -lling, -lled**) take pleasure (in)
> **reveller** n (pl **-s**)
revelation n ▷ revel
revelations n ▷ revel
revelled v ▷ revel
reveller n ▷ revel
revellers n ▷ revel
revelling v ▷ revel
revelries n ▷ revelry
revelry n (pl **-s**) festivity
revels pl n merrymaking ▶ v ▷ revel
revenge n (pl **-s**) retaliation for wrong done
▶ v (**-ges, -ging, -ged**) make retaliation for
> **revengeful** adj
revenged v ▷ revenge
revengeful adj ▷ revenge
revenges n, v ▷ revenge
revenging v ▷ revenge
revenue n (pl **-s**) income, esp. of a state
revenues n ▷ revenue
reverberate v (**-tes, -ting, -ted**) echo or
resound > **reverberation** n (pl **-s**)
reverberated v ▷ reverberate
reverberates v ▷ reverberate
reverberating v ▷ reverberate
reverberation n ▷ reverberate
reverberations n ▷ reverberate
revere v (**-s, -ing, -ed**) be in awe of and respect
greatly
revered v ▷ revere
reverence n (pl **-s**) awe mingled with respect
and esteem
reverences n ▷ reverence
reverent adj showing reverence > **reverently**
adv
reverential adj marked by reverence
reverently adv ▷ reverent
reveres v ▷ revere
revering v ▷ revere
reverie n (pl **-s**) absent-minded daydream
reveries n ▷ reverie
revers [riv-**veer**] n (pl **-s**) turned back part of a
garment, such as the lapel
reverse v (**-ses, -sing, -sed**) turn upside down
or the other way round ▶ n (pl **-s**) opposite
▶ adj opposite or contrary > **reversal** n (pl **-s**)
> **reversible** adj
reversal n ▷ reverse
reversals n ▷ reverse
reversed v ▷ reverse
reverses v, n ▷ reverse
reversible adj ▷ reverse
reversing v ▷ reverse
reversion n ▷ revert
reversions n ▷ revert

revert v (**-s, -ing, -ed**) return to a former state
> **reversion** n (pl **-s**)
reverted v ▷ revert
reverting v ▷ revert
reverts v ▷ revert
review n (pl **-s**) critical assessment of a book,
concert, etc. ▶ v (**-s, -ing, -ed**) hold or write
a review of
reviewed v ▷ review
reviewer n (pl **-s**) writer of reviews
reviewers n ▷ reviewer
reviewing v ▷ review
reviews n, v ▷ review
revile v (**-les, -ling, -led**) be abusively scornful
of
reviled v ▷ revile
reviles v ▷ revile
reviling v ▷ revile
revise v (**-ses, -sing, -sed**) change or alter
> **revision** n (pl **-s**)
revised v ▷ revise
revises v ▷ revise
revising v ▷ revise
revision n ▷ revive
revisions n ▷ revive
revival n (pl **-s**) reviving or renewal
> **revivalism** n (pl **-s**) > **revivalist** n (pl **-s**)
revivalism n ▷ revival
revivalisms n ▷ revival
revivalists n ▷ revival
revivalist n ▷ revival
revivals n ▷ revival
revive v (**-ves, -ving, -ved**) bring or come back
to life, vigour, use, etc.
revived v ▷ revive
revives v ▷ revive
reviving v ▷ revive
revocation n ▷ revoke
revocations n ▷ revoke
revoke v (**-kes, -king, -ked**) cancel (a will,
agreement, etc.) > **revocation** n (pl **-s**)
revoked v ▷ revoke
revokes v ▷ revoke
revoking v ▷ revoke
revolt n (pl **-s**) uprising against authority ▶ v
(**-s, -ing, -ed**) rise in rebellion
revolted v ▷ revolt
revolting adj disgusting, horrible ▶ v ▷ revolt
revolts n, v ▷ revolt
revolution n (pl **-s**) overthrow of a government
by the governed
revolutionaries n ▷ revolutionary
revolutionary adj advocating or engaged in
revolution ▶ n (pl **-ies**) person advocating or
engaged in revolution

revolutionize v (-zes, -zing, -zed) change considerably
  revolutionized v ▷ revolutionize
  revolutionizes v ▷ revolutionize
  revolutionizing v ▷ revolutionize
  revolutions n ▷ revolution
revolve v (-ves, -ving, -ved) turn round, rotate
  revolved v ▷ revolve
revolver n (pl -s) repeating pistol
  revolvers n ▷ revolver
  revolves v ▷ revolve
  revolving v ▷ revolve
  revs n, v ▷ rev
revue n (pl -s) theatrical entertainment with topical sketches and songs
  revues n ▷ revue
revulsion n (pl -s) strong disgust
  revulsions n ▷ revulsion
  revved v ▷ rev
  revving v ▷ rev
reward n (pl -s) something given in return for a service ▶ v (-s, -ing, -ed) pay or give something to (someone) for a service, information, etc.
  rewarded v ▷ reward
  rewarding v ▷ reward
  rewards n, v ▷ reward
rewind v (-s, -ing, -wound) run (a tape or film) back to an earlier point in order to replay
  rewinding v ▷ rewind
  rewinds v ▷ rewind
rewire v (-res, -ring, -red) provide (a house, engine, etc.) with new wiring
  rewired v ▷ rewire
  rewires v ▷ rewire
  rewiring v ▷ rewire
  rewound v ▷ rewind
rewrite v (-tes, -ting, -wrote, -written) write again in a different way ▶ n (pl -s) something rewritten
  rewrites n, v ▷ rewrite
  rewriting v ▷ rewrite
  rewritten v ▷ rewrite
  rewrote v ▷ rewrite

> **rex** n (**rexes**). Rex is a Latin word for king. This is a very useful word, as it combines X with two of the most common letters on the board, making it one to look for when you get an X. Rex scores 10 points.

> **rez** n (**rezes**). Rez is a short informal word for reservation. Combining Z with two of the most common tiles on the board, this is one of the first words to think about when you draw a Z and

don't have the letters for a longer word. Rez scores 12 points.

rhapsodic adj ▷ rhapsody
rhapsodies n ▷ rhapsody
rhapsodize v (-zes, -zing, -zed) speak or write with extravagant enthusiasm
  rhapsodized v ▷ rhapsodize
  rhapsodizes v ▷ rhapsodize
  rhapsodizing v ▷ rhapsodize
rhapsody n (pl -ies) freely structured emotional piece of music > **rhapsodic** adj
rhea [ree-a] n (pl -s) S American three-toed ostrich
  rheas n ▷ rhea
rhenium n (pl -s) (CHEM) silvery-white metallic element with a high melting point
  rheniums n ▷ rhenium
rheostat n (pl -s) instrument for varying the resistance of an electrical circuit
  rheostats n ▷ rheostat
rhesus [ree-suss] n (pl -es) small long-tailed monkey of S Asia
  rhesuses n ▷ rhesus
rhetoric n (pl -s) art of effective speaking or writing
rhetorical adj (of a question) not requiring an answer > **rhetorically** adv
  rhetorically adv ▷ rhetorical
  rhetorics n ▷ rhetoric
rheumatic n, adj (pl -s) (person) affected by rheumatism
  rheumatics n ▷ rheumatic
rheumatism n (pl -s) painful inflammation of joints or muscles
  rheumatisms n ▷ rheumatism
rheumatoid adj of or like rheumatism
rhinestone n (pl -s) imitation diamond
  rhinestones n ▷ rhinestone
rhino n (pl -s) rhinoceros
rhinoceros n (pl -oses, -os) large thick-skinned animal with one or two horns on its nose
  rhinoceroses n ▷ rhinoceros
  rhinos n ▷ rhino
rhizome n (pl -s) thick underground stem producing new plants
  rhizomes n ▷ rhizome

> **rho** n (**rhos**). Rho is the 17th letter of the Greek alphabet. It's useful to remember words that start with RH, as there are quite a few that can come in useful. If you or someone else plays rho, remember that it could be expanded to **rhodium, rhombus** or **rhomboid.** Rho scores 6 points.

rhodium n (pl -s) (CHEM) hard metallic element

rhodiums n ▷ rhodium
rhododendron n (pl -s) evergreen flowering shrub
  rhododendrons n ▷ rhododendron
  rhombi n ▷ rhombus
rhomboid n (pl -s) parallelogram with adjacent sides of unequal length
  rhomboids n ▷ rhomboid
rhombus n (pl -buses, -bi) parallelogram with sides of equal length but no right angles, diamond-shaped figure
  rhombuses n ▷ rhombus
rhubarb n (pl -s) garden plant of which the fleshy stalks are cooked as fruit
  rhubarbs n ▷ rhubarb

> **rhy** n (rhys). Rhy is an alternative spelling of rye. This is a useful word as it doesn't contain a vowel, and so can be helpful when you have a poor combination of tiles on your rack. Rhy scores 9 points.

rhyme n (pl -s) sameness of the final sounds at the ends of lines of verse, or in words ▶ v (-mes, -ming, -med) make a rhyme
  rhymed v ▷ rhyme
  rhymes n, v ▷ rhyme
  rhyming v ▷ rhyme
rhythm n (pl -s) any regular movement or beat > **rhythmic, rhythmical** adj > **rhythmically** adv
  rhythmic adj ▷ rhythm
  rhythmical adj ▷ rhythm
  rhythmically adv ▷ rhythm
  rhythms n ▷ rhythm
rib¹ n (pl -s) one of the curved bones forming the framework of the upper part of the body ▶ v (-s, -bbing, -bbed) provide or mark with ribs > **ribbed** adj > **ribbing** n (pl -s)
rib² v (-s, -bbing, -bbed) (Informal) tease or ridicule > **ribbing** n (pl -s)
ribald adj humorously or mockingly rude or obscene > **ribaldry** n (pl -s)
  ribaldries n ▷ ribald
  ribaldry n ▷ ribald
  ribbed v, adj ▷ rib¹, ²
  ribbing v, n ▷ rib¹, ²
  ribbings n ▷ rib¹, ²
ribbon n (pl -s) narrow band of fabric used for trimming, tying, etc.
  ribbons n ▷ ribbon
ribcage n (pl -s) bony structure of ribs enclosing the lungs
  ribcages n ▷ ribcage
riboflavin [rye-boe-**flay**-vin] n (pl -s) form of vitamin B

riboflavins n ▷ riboflavin
ribs n, v ▷ rib¹, ²
rice n (pl -s) cereal plant grown on wet ground in warm countries
  rices n ▷ rice
rich adj (-er, -est) owning a lot of money or property, wealthy > **richness** n (pl -es)
  richer adj ▷ rich
  riches pl n wealth
  richest adj ▷ rich
  richly adv elaborately
  richness n ▷ rich
  richnesses n ▷ rich
rick¹ n (pl -s) stack of hay etc.
rick² v, n (-s, -ing, -ed) sprain or wrench
  ricked v ▷ rick²
  ricketier adj ▷ rickety
  ricketiest adj ▷ rickety
rickets n disease of children marked by softening of the bones, bow legs, etc., caused by vitamin D deficiency
rickety adj (-tier, -tiest) shaky or unstable
  ricking v ▷ rick¹
  ricks n ▷ rick¹ ▶ v ▷ rick²
rickshaw n (pl -s) light two-wheeled man-drawn Asian vehicle
  rickshaws n ▷ rickshaw
ricochet [**rik**-osh-ay] v (-s, -ing, -ed) (of a bullet) rebound from a solid surface ▶ n (pl -s) such a rebound
  ricocheted v ▷ ricochet
  ricocheting v ▷ ricochet
  ricochets v, n ▷ ricochet
rid v (-s, -dding, rid) clear or relieve (of)
ridden v ▷ ride ▶ adj afflicted or affected by the thing specified
  ridding v ▷ rid
riddle¹ n (pl -s) question made puzzling to test one's ingenuity
riddle² v (-les, -ling, -led) pierce with many holes ▶ n (pl -s) coarse sieve for gravel etc.
  riddled v ▷ riddle²
  riddles n ▷ riddle¹, ² ▶ v ▷ riddle²
  riddling v ▷ riddle²
ride v (-des, -ding, rode, ridden) sit on and control or propel (a horse, bicycle, etc.) ▶ n (pl -s) journey on a horse etc., or in a vehicle
rider n (pl -s) person who rides
  riders n ▷ rider
  rides v, n ▷ ride
ridge n (pl -s) long narrow hill > **ridged** adj
  ridged adj ▷ ridge
  ridges n ▷ ridge
ridicule n (pl -s) treatment of a person or thing as ridiculous ▶ v (-les, -ling, -led) laugh at,

make fun of
ridiculed *v* ▷ ridicule
ridicules *n*, *v* ▷ ridicule
ridiculing *v* ▷ ridicule
ridiculous *adj* deserving to be laughed at, absurd
riding¹ *v* ▷ ride
riding² *n* (*pl* -s) (in Canada) parliamentary constituency
ridings *n* ▷ riding
rids *v* ▷ rid
riesling *n* (*pl* -s) type of white wine
rieslings *n* ▷ riesling
rife *adj* (-r, -st) widespread or common
rifer *adj* ▷ rife
rifest *adj* ▷ rife
riff *n* (*pl* -s) (JAZZ, ROCK) short repeated melodic figure
riffle *v* (-les, -ling, -led) flick through (pages etc.) quickly
riffled *v* ▷ riffle
riffles *v* ▷ riffle
riffling *v* ▷ riffle
riffraff *n* (*pl* -s) rabble, disreputable people
riffraffs *n* ▷ riffraff
riffs *n* ▷ riff
rifle¹ *n* (*pl* -s) firearm with a long barrel
rifle² *v* (-les, -ling, -led) search and rob
rifled *v* ▷ rifle²
rifles *n* ▷ rifle¹ ▶ *v* ▷ rifle²
rifling *v* ▷ rifle²
rift *n* (*pl* -s) break in friendly relations
rifts *n* ▷ rift
rig *v* (-s, -gging, -gged) arrange in a dishonest way ▶ *n* (*pl* -s) apparatus for drilling for oil and gas
rigged *v* ▷ rig
rigging *n* ship's spars and ropes ▶ *v* ▷ rig
right *adj* (-er, -est) just ▶ *adv* properly ▶ *n* (*pl* -s) claim, title, etc. allowed or due ▶ *v* (-s, -ing, -ed) bring or come back to a normal or correct state > **rightly** *adv* > **rightful** *adj* > **rightfully** *adv*
righted *v* ▷ right
righteous [rye-chuss] *adj* upright, godly, or virtuous > **righteousness** *n* (*pl* -s)
righteousness *n* ▷ righteous
righteousnesses *n* ▷ righteous
righter *adj* ▷ right
rightest *adj* ▷ right
rightful *adj* ▷ right
rightfully *adv* ▷ right
righting *v* ▷ right
rightist *n* (*pl* -s) ▶ *adj* (person) on the political right

rightists *n* ▷ rightist
rightly *adv* ▷ right
rights *n*, *v* ▷ right
rigid *adj* (-er, -est) inflexible or strict > **rigidly** *adv* > **rigidity** *n* (*pl* -s)
rigider *adj* ▷ rigid
rigidest *adj* ▷ rigid
rigidities *n* ▷ rigid
rigidity *n* ▷ rigid
rigidly *n* ▷ rigid
rigmarole *n* (*pl* -s) long complicated procedure
rigmaroles *n* ▷ rigmarole
rigorous *adj* harsh, severe, or stern
rigour *n* (*pl* -s) harshness, severity, or strictness
rigours *n* ▷ rigour
rigs *v*, *n* ▷ rig
rile *v* (-les, -ling, -led) anger or annoy
riled *v* ▷ rile
riles *v* ▷ rile
riling *v* ▷ rile
rill *n* (*pl* -s) small stream
rills *n* ▷ rill
rim *n* (*pl* -s) edge or border > **rimmed** *adj*
rime *n* (*pl* -s) (Lit) hoarfrost
rimes *n* ▷ rime
rimmed *adj* ▷ rim
rims *n* ▷ rim
rimu *n* (*pl* -s) (NZ) New Zealand tree whose wood is used for building and furniture
rimus *n* ▷ rimu
rind *n* (*pl* -s) tough outer coating of fruits, cheese, or bacon
rinds *n* ▷ rind
ring¹ *v* (-s, -ing, rang, rung) give out a clear resonant sound, as a bell ▶ *n* (*pl* -s) ringing
ring² *n* (*pl* -s) circle of gold etc., esp. for a finger ▶ *v* (-s, -ing, -ed) put a ring round
ringed *v* ▷ ring²
ringer *n* (*pl* -s) (BRIT, AUST & NZ) (Slang) person or thing apparently identical to another
ringers *n* ▷ ringer
ringing *v* ▷ ring¹, ²
ringleader *n* (*pl* -s) instigator of a mutiny, riot, etc.
ringleaders *n* ▷ ringleader
ringlet *n* (*pl* -s) curly lock of hair
ringlets *n* ▷ ringlet
rings *n*, *v* ▷ ring¹, ²
ringside *n* (*pl* -s) row of seats nearest a boxing or circus ring
ringsides *n* ▷ ringside
ringtail *n* (*pl* -s) (AUST) possum with a curling tail used to grip branches while climbing
ringtails *n* ▷ ringtail

ringtone *n* (*pl* -s) tune played by a mobile phone when it receives a call
  ringtones *n* ▷ ringtone
ringworm *n* (*pl* -s) fungal skin disease in circular patches
  ringworms *n* ▷ ringworm
rink *n* (*pl* -s) sheet of ice for skating or curling
  rinks *n* ▷ rink
rinse *v* (-ses, -sing, -sed) remove soap from (washed clothes, hair, etc.) by applying clean water ▶ *n* (*pl* -s) rinsing
  rinsed *v* ▷ rinse
  rinses *v, n* ▷ rinse
  rinsing *v* ▷ rinse
riot *v* (-s, -ing, -ed) disorderly unruly disturbance ▶ *v* (-s, -ing, -ed) take part in a riot
  rioted *v* ▷ riot
  rioting *v* ▷ riot
riotous *adj* unrestrained
  riots *n, v* ▷ riot
rip *v* (-s, -pping, -pped) tear violently (*Informal*) ▶ *n* (*pl* -s) split or tear
  riparian [rip-**pair**-ee-an] *adj* of or on the banks of a river
ripcord *n* (*pl* -s) cord pulled to open a parachute
  ripcords *n* ▷ ripcord
ripe *adj* (-er, -est) ready to be reaped, eaten, etc.
ripen *v* (-s, -ing, -ed) grow ripe
  ripened *v* ▷ ripen
  ripening *v* ▷ ripen
  ripens *v* ▷ ripen
  riper *adj* ▷ ripe
  ripest *adj* ▷ ripe
riposte [rip-**posst**] *n* (*pl* -s) verbal retort ▶ *v* (-tes, -ting, -ted) make a riposte
  riposted *v* ▷ riposte
  ripostes *n, v* ▷ riposte
  riposting *v* ▷ riposte
  ripped *v* ▷ rip
  ripping *v* ▷ rip
ripple *n* (*pl* -s) slight wave or ruffling of a surface ▶ *v* (-les, -ling, -led) flow or form into little waves (on)
  rippled *v* ▷ ripple
  ripples *n, v* ▷ ripple
  rippling *v* ▷ ripple
  rips *v, n* ▷ rip
rise *v* (-ses, -sing, rose, risen) get up from a lying, sitting, or kneeling position ▶ *n* (*pl* -s) rising
  risen *v* ▷ rise
riser *n* (*pl* -s) person who rises, esp. from bed
  risers *n* ▷ riser
  rises *v, n* ▷ rise

rising *n* (*pl* -s) revolt ▶ *adj* increasing in rank or maturity ▶ *v* ▷ rise
  risings *n* ▷ rising
risible [riz-**zib**-bl] *adj* causing laughter, ridiculous
risk *n* (*pl* -s) chance of disaster or loss ▶ *v* (-s, -ing, -ed) act in spite of the possibility of (injury or loss)
  risked *v* ▷ risk
  riskier *adj* ▷ risky
  riskiest *adj* ▷ risky
  risking *v* ▷ risk
  risks *n, v* ▷ risk
risky *adj* (-kier, -kiest) full of risk, dangerous
risotto *n* (*pl* -s) dish of rice cooked in stock with vegetables, meat, etc.
  risottos *n* ▷ risotto
risqué [risk-**ay**] *adj* bordering on indecency
rissole *n* (*pl* -s) cake of minced meat, coated with breadcrumbs and fried
  rissoles *n* ▷ rissole
rite *n* (*pl* -s) formal practice or custom, esp. religious
  rites *n* ▷ rite
ritual *n* (*pl* -s) prescribed order of rites ▶ *adj* concerning rites > **ritually** *adv*
ritualistic *adj* like a ritual
  ritually *adv* ▷ ritual
  rituals *n* ▷ ritual
  ritzier *adj* ▷ ritzy
  ritziest *adj* ▷ ritzy
ritzy *adj* (-zier, -ziest) (*Slang*) luxurious or elegant
rival *n* (*pl* -s) person or thing that competes with or equals another for favour, success, etc. ▶ *adj* in the position of a rival ▶ *v* (-s, -lling, -lled) (try to) equal
  rivalled *v* ▷ rival
  rivalling *v* ▷ rival
  rivalries *n* ▷ rivalry
rivalry *n* (*pl* -s) keen competition
  rivals *v, n* ▷ rival
riven *adj* split apart
river *n* (*pl* -s) large natural stream of water
  rivers *n* ▷ river
rivet [**riv**-vit] *n* (*pl* -s) bolt for fastening metal plates, the end being put through holes and then beaten flat ▶ *v* (-s, -ing, -ed) fasten with rivets
  riveted *v* ▷ rivet
riveting *adj* very interesting and exciting ▶ *v* ▷ rivet
  rivets *n, v* ▷ rivet
rivulet *n* (*pl* -s) small stream
  rivulets *n* ▷ rivulet

riz *v.* Riz is the past tense of rise in some US dialects. This unusual word can be very useful if you get a Z in the later stages of the game, as you will probably be able to find either I or R on the board already. Riz scores 12 points.

roach *n* (*pl* -**es**) Eurasian freshwater fish
  roaches *n* ▷ roach

road *n* (*pl* -**s**) way prepared for passengers, vehicles, etc.

roadblock *n* (*pl* -**s**) barricade across a road to stop traffic for inspection etc.
  roadblocks *n* ▷ roadblock

roadhouse *n* (*pl* -**s**) (BRIT, AUST & S AFR) pub or restaurant on a country road
  roadhouses *n* ▷ roadhouse

roadie *n* (*pl* -**s**) (BRIT, AUST & NZ) (*Informal*) person who transports and sets up equipment for a band
  roadies *n* ▷ roadie
  roads *n* ▷ road

roadside *n* (*pl* -**s**) ▶ *adj* by the road
  roadsides *n* ▷ roadside

roadway *n* (*pl* -**s**) the part of a road used by vehicles
  roadways *n* ▷ roadway

roadworks *pl n* repairs to a road, esp. blocking part of the road

roadworthy *adj* (of a vehicle) mechanically sound

roam *v* (-**s**, -**ing**, -**ed**) wander about
  roamed *v* ▷ roam
  roaming *v* ▷ roam
  roams *v* ▷ roam

roan *adj* (of a horse) having a brown or black coat sprinkled with white hairs ▶ *n* (*pl* -**s**) roan horse
  roans *n* ▷ roan

roar *v* (-**s**, -**ing**, -**ed**) make or utter a loud deep hoarse sound like that of a lion ▶ *n* (*pl* -**s**) such a sound
  roared *v* ▷ roar
  roaring *v* ▷ roar
  roars *v*, *n* ▷ roar

roast *v* (-**s**, -**ing**, -**ed**) cook by dry heat, as in an oven ▶ *n* (*pl* -**s**) roasted joint of meat ▶ *adj* roasted
  roasted *v* ▷ roast

roasting (*Informal*) *adj* extremely hot ▶ *n* (*pl* -**s**) severe criticism or scolding ▶ *v* ▷ roast
  roastings *n* ▷ roasting
  roasts *v*, *n* ▷ roast

rob *v* (-**s**, -**bing**, -**bed**) steal from > **robber** *n* (*pl* -**s**) > **robbery** *n* (*pl* -**ies**)
  robbed *v* ▷ rob

robber *n* ▷ rob
  robberies *n* ▷ rob
  robbers *n* ▷ rob
  robbery *n* ▷ rob
  robbing *v* ▷ rob

robe *n* (*pl* -**s**) long loose outer garment ▶ *v* (-**bes**, -**bing**, -**bed**) put a robe on
  robed *v* ▷ robe
  robes *v*, *n* ▷ robe

robin *n* (*pl* -**s**) small brown bird with a red breast
  robing *v* ▷ robe
  robins *n* ▷ robin

robot *n* (*pl* -**s**) automated machine, esp. one performing functions in a human manner > **robotic** *adj*
  robotic *adj* ▷ robot

robotics *n* science of designing and using robots
  robots *n* ▷ robot
  robs *v* ▷ rob

robust *adj* (-**er**, -**est**) very strong and healthy > **robustly** *adv* > **robustness** *n* (*pl* -**s**)
  robuster *adj* ▷ robust
  robustest *adj* ▷ robust
  robustly *adv* ▷ robust
  robustness *n* ▷ robust
  robustnesses *n* ▷ robust

roc *n* (*pl* -**s**) monstrous bird of Arabian mythology

rock¹ *n* (*pl* -**s**) hard mineral substance that makes up part of the earth's crust, stone

rock² *v* (-**s**, -**ing**, -**ed**) (cause to) sway to and fro ▶ *n* style of pop music with a heavy beat
  rocked *v* ▷ rock²

rocker *n* (*pl* -**s**) rocking chair
  rockeries *n* ▷ rockery
  rockers *n* ▷ rocker

rockery *n* (*pl* -**ies**) mound of stones in a garden for rock plants

rocket *n* (*pl* -**s**) self-propelling device powered by the burning of explosive contents (used as a firework, weapon, etc.) ▶ *v* (-**s**, -**ing**, -**ed**) move fast, esp. upwards, like a rocket
  rocketed *v* ▷ rocket
  rocketing *v* ▷ rocket
  rockets *n*, *v* ▷ rocket
  rockier *adj* ▷ rocky¹, rocky²
  rockiest *adj* ▷ rocky¹, rocky²
  rocking *v* ▷ rock²
  rocks *n* ▷ rock¹ ▶ *v* ▷ rock²

rocky¹ *adj* (-**ier**, -**iest**) having many rocks

rocky² *adj* (-**ier**, -**iest**) shaky or unstable

rococo [rok-koe-koe] *adj* (of furniture, architecture, etc.) having much elaborate decoration in an early 18th-century style

rocs n ▷ roc

rod n (pl -s) slender straight bar, stick

rode v ▷ ride

rodent n (pl -s) animal with teeth specialized for gnawing, such as a rat, mouse, or squirrel

rodents n ▷ rodent

rodeo n (pl -s) display of skill by cowboys, such as bareback riding

rodeos n ▷ rodeo

rods n ▷ rod

roe¹ n (pl -s) mass of eggs in a fish, sometimes eaten as food

roe² n (pl -s) small species of deer

roentgen [ront-gan] n (pl -s) unit measuring a radiation dose

roentgens n ▷ roentgen

roes n ▷ roe¹, ²

rogue n (pl -s) dishonest or unprincipled person ▶ adj (of a wild beast) having a savage temper and living apart from the herd

> **roguish** adj

rogues n ▷ rogue

roguish adj ▷ rogee

roister v (-s, -ing, -ed) make merry noisily or boisterously

roistered v ▷ roister

roistering v ▷ roister

roisters v ▷ roister

> **rok** n (roks). Rok is an alternative spelling of **roc**. This uncommon word can be helpful if you have a K without the tiles needed for a longer word. Rok scores 7 points.

role n (pl -s) task or function

roles n ▷ role

roll v (-s, -ing, -ed) move by turning over and over ▶ n (pl -s) act of rolling over or from side to side

rolled v ▷ roll

roller n (pl -s) rotating cylinder used for smoothing or supporting a thing to be moved, spreading paint, etc.

rollers n ▷ roller

rollicking adj boisterously carefree

rolling v ▷ roll

rolls v, n ▷ roll

roman n roman type or print

romance n (pl -s) love affair

romances n ▷ romance

romantic adj of or dealing with love ▶ n (pl -s) romantic person or artist > **romantically** adv

> **romanticism** n (pl -s)

romantically adv ▷ romantic

romanticism n ▷ romantic

romanticisms n ▷ romantic

romanticize v (-zes, -zing, -zed) describe or regard in an idealized and unrealistic way

romanticized v ▷ romanticize

romanticizes v ▷ romanticize

romanticizing v ▷ romanticize

romantics n ▷ romantic

romp v (-s, -ing, -ed) play wildly and joyfully ▶ n (pl -s) boisterous activity

romped v ▷ romp

rompers pl n child's overalls

romping v ▷ romp

romps v, n ▷ romp

rondo n (pl -s) piece of music with a leading theme continually returned to

rondos n ▷ rondo

roo n (pl -s) (AUST) (Informal) kangaroo

rood n (pl -s) (CHRISTIANITY) the Cross

roods n ▷ rood

roof n (pl -s) outside upper covering of a building, car, etc. ▶ v put a roof on

roofs n ▷ roofs

rooibos [roy-boss] n (pl -es) (S AFR) tea prepared from the dried leaves of an African plant

rooiboses n ▷ rooibos

rook¹ n (pl -s) Eurasian bird of the crow family

rook² n (pl -s) chess piece shaped like a castle

rookeries n ▷ rookery

rookery n (pl -ies) colony of rooks, penguins, or seals

rookie n (pl -s) (Informal) new recruit

rookies n ▷ rookie

rooks n ▷ rook

room n (pl -s) enclosed area in a building ▶ pl lodgings

roomier adj ▷ roomy

roomiest adj ▷ roomy

rooms n ▷ room

roomy adj (-ier, -iest) spacious

roos n ▷ roo

roost n (pl -s) perch for fowls ▶ v (-s, -ing, -ed) perch

roosted v ▷ roost

rooster n (pl -s) domestic cock

roosters n ▷ rooster

roosting v ▷ roost

roosts v, n ▷ roost

root¹ n (pl -s) part of a plant that grows down into the earth obtaining nourishment ▶ pl person's sense of belonging ▶ v (-s, -ing, -ed) establish a root and start to grow

root² v (-s, -ing, -ed) dig or burrow

rooted v ▷ root¹, ²

rooting v ▷ root¹, ²

rootless adj having no sense of belonging

roots *n* ▷ root[1] ▶ *v* ▷ root[1, 2]
rope *n* (*pl* -s) thick cord
ropes *n* ▷ rope
ropey, ropy *adj* (-pier, -piest) (BRIT) (*Informal*) inferior or inadequate
ropier *adj* ▷ ropy
ropiest *adj* ▷ ropy
ropy *adj* ▷ ropey
rorqual *n* (*pl* -s) toothless whale with a dorsal fin
rorquals *n* ▷ rorqual
rort (AUST) (*Informal*) *n* (*pl* -s) dishonest scheme ▶ *v* (-s, -ing, -ed) take unfair advantage of something
rorted *v* ▷ rort
rorting *v* ▷ rort
rorts *n*, *v* ▷ rort
rosaries *n* ▷ rosary
rosary *n* (*pl* -ies) series of prayers
rose[1] *n* (*pl* -s) shrub or climbing plant with prickly stems and fragrant flowers ▶ *adj* pink
rose[2] *v* ▷ rise
roseate [roe-zee-ate] *adj* rose-coloured
rosehip *n* (*pl* -s) berry-like fruit of a rose plant
rosehips *n* ▷ rosehip
rosella *n* (*pl* -s) type of Australian parrot
rosellas *n* ▷ rosella
rosemaries *n* ▷ rosemary
rosemary *n* (*pl* -ies) fragrant flowering shrub
roses *n* ▷ rose[1]
rosette *n* (*pl* -s) rose-shaped ornament, esp. a circular bunch of ribbons
rosettes *n* ▷ rosette
rosewood *n* (*pl* -s) fragrant wood used to make furniture
rosewoods *n* ▷ rosewood
rosier *adj* ▷ rosy
rosiest *adj* ▷ rosy
rosin [rozz-in] *n* (*pl* -s) resin used for treating the bows of violins etc.
rosins *n* ▷ rosin
roster *n* (*pl* -s) list of people and their turns of duty
rosters *n* ▷ roster
rostra *n* ▷ rostrum
rostrum *n* (*pl* -trums, -tra) platform or stage
rostrums *n* ▷ rostrum
rosy *adj* (-sier, -siest) pink-coloured
rot *v* (-s, -tting, -ted) decompose or decay ▶ *n* (*pl* -s) decay (*Informal*)
rota *n* (*pl* -s) list of people who take it in turn to do a particular task
rotas *n* ▷ rota
rotary *adj* revolving
rotate *v* (-tes, -ting, -ted) (cause to) move

round a centre or on a pivot > **rotation** *n* (*pl* -s)
rotated *v* ▷ rotate
rotates *v* ▷ rotate
rotating *v* ▷ rotate
rotation *n* ▷ rotate
rotations *n* ▷ rotate
rote *n* (*pl* -s) mechanical repetition
rotes *n* ▷ rote
rotisserie *n* (*pl* -s) rotating spit for cooking meat
rotisseries *n* ▷ rotisserie
rotor *n* (*pl* -s) revolving portion of a dynamo, motor, or turbine
rotors *n* ▷ rotor
rots *v*, *n* ▷ rot
rotted *v* ▷ rot
rotten *adj* (-er, -est) decaying (*Informal*)
rottener *adj* ▷ rotten
rottenest *adj* ▷ rotten
rotter *n* (*pl* -s) (CHIEFLY BRIT) (*Slang*) despicable person
rotters *n* ▷ rotter
rotting *v* ▷ rot
rotund [roe-tund] *adj* round and plump > **rotundity** *n* (*pl* -ies)
rotunda *n* (*pl* -s) circular building or room, esp. with a dome
rotundas *n* ▷ rotunda
rotundities *n* ▷ rotund
rotundity *n* ▷ rotund
rouble [roo-bl] *n* (*pl* -s) monetary unit of Russia, Belarus, and Tajikistan
roubles *n* ▷ rouble
roué [roo-ay] *n* (*pl* -s) man given to immoral living
roués *n* ▷ roué
rouge *n* (*pl* -s) red cosmetic used to colour the cheeks
rouges *n* ▷ rouge
rough *adj* (-er, -est) uneven or irregular ▶ *v* (-s, -ing, -ed) make rough ▶ *n* (*pl* -s) rough state or area > **roughen** *v* (-s, -ing, -ed) > **roughly** *adv* > **roughness** *n* (*pl* -s)
roughage *n* (*pl* -s) indigestible constituents of food which aid digestion
roughages *n* ▷ roughage
roughcast *n* (*pl* -s) mixture of plaster and small stones for outside walls ▶ *v* (-s, -ing, -cast) coat with this
roughcasting *v* ▷ roughcast
roughcasts *n*, *v* ▷ roughcast
roughed *v* ▷ rough
roughen *v* ▷ rough
roughened *v* ▷ rough
roughening *v* ▷ rough

roughens v ▷ rough
rougher adj ▷ rough
roughest adj ▷ rough
roughhouse n (pl -s) (CHIEFLY US) (Slang) fight
roughhouses n ▷ roughhouse
roughing v ▷ rough
roughly adv ▷ rough
roughness n ▷ rough
roughnesses n ▷ rough
roughs v, n ▷ rough
roughshod adv with total disregard
roulette n (pl -s) gambling game played with a revolving wheel and a ball
roulettes n ▷ roulette
round adj (-er, -est) spherical, cylindrical, circular, or curved ▶ adv, prep indicating an encircling movement, presence on all sides, etc. ▶ v (-s, -ing, -ed) move round ▶ n (pl -s) customary course, as of a milkman
roundabout n (pl -s) road junction at which traffic passes round a central island ▶ adj not straightforward
roundabouts n ▷ roundabout
rounded v ▷ round
roundel n (pl -s) small disc
roundelay n (pl -s) simple song with a refrain
roundelays n ▷ roundelay
roundels n ▷ roundel
rounder adj ▷ round
roundest adj ▷ round
rounders n bat-and-ball team game
rounding v ▷ round
roundly adv thoroughly
rounds v, n ▷ round
rouse¹ [rhymes with cows] v (-ses, -sing, -sed) wake up
rouse² [rhymes with mouse] v (-ses, -sing, -sed) (foll. by **on**) (AUST) scold or rebuke
rouseabout n (pl -s) (AUST & NZ) labourer in a shearing shed
rouseabouts n ▷ rouseabout
roused v ▷ rouse¹, ²
rouses v ▷ rouse¹, ²
rousing v ▷ rouse¹, ²
roustabout n (pl -s) labourer on an oil rig
roustabouts n ▷ roustabout
rout n (pl -s) overwhelming defeat ▶ v (-s, -ing, -ed) defeat and put to flight
route n (pl -s) roads taken to reach a destination
routed v ▷ rout
routes n ▷ route
routine n (pl -s) usual or regular method of procedure ▶ adj ordinary or regular
routines n ▷ routine

routing v ▷ rout
routs n, v ▷ rout
roux [roo] n (pl roux) fat and flour cooked together as a basis for sauces
rove v (-ves, -ving, -ved) wander
roved v ▷ rove
rover n (pl -s) wanderer, traveller
rovers n ▷ rover
roves v ▷ rove
roving v ▷ rove
row¹ [rhymes with go] n (pl -s) straight line of people or things
row² [rhymes with go] v (-s, -ing, -ed) propel (a boat) by oars ▶ n (-s) spell of rowing
row³ [rhymes with now] (Informal) n (-s) dispute ▶ v (-s, -ing, -ed) quarrel noisily
rowan n (pl -s) tree producing bright red berries, mountain ash
rowans n ▷ rowan
rowdier adj ▷ rowdy
rowdiest adj ▷ rowdy
rowdies n ▷ rowdy
rowdy adj (-dier, -diest) disorderly, noisy, and rough ▶ n (pl -ies) person like this
rowed v ▷ row², ³
rowel [rhymes with towel] n (pl -s) small spiked wheel on a spur
rowels n ▷ rowel
rowing v ▷ row², ³
rowlock [rol-luk] n (pl -s) device on a boat that holds an oar in place
rowlocks n ▷ rowlock
rows n ▷ row¹, ², ³ ▶ v ▷ row², ³
royal adj (-ler, -lest) of, befitting, or supported by a king or queen ▶ n (pl -s) (Informal) member of a royal family > **royally** adv
royalist n (pl -s) supporter of monarchy
royalists n ▷ royalist
royaller adj ▷ royal
royallest adj ▷ royal
royally adv ▷ royal
royals n ▷ royal
royalties n ▷ royalty
royalty n (pl -ies) royal people
rub v (-s, -bbing, -bbed) apply pressure and friction to (something) with a circular or backwards-and-forwards movement ▶ n (-s) act of rubbing
rubato adv, n (pl -s) (MUSIC) (with) expressive flexibility of tempo
rubatos n ▷ rubato
rubbed v ▷ rub
rubber¹ n (pl -s) strong waterproof elastic material, orig. made from the dried sap of a tropical tree, now usu. synthetic ▶ adj made

of or producing rubber > **rubbery** adj (**-rier,
-riest**)
rubber² n (pl **-s**) match consisting of three
games of bridge, whist, etc.
  rubberier adj ▷ **rubber¹**
  rubberiest adj ▷ **rubber¹**
rubberneck v (**-s, -ing, -ed**) stare with
unthinking curiosity
  rubbernecked v ▷ **rubberneck**
  rubbernecking v ▷ **rubberneck**
  rubbernecks v ▷ **rubberneck**
  rubbers n ▷ **rubber¹, ²**
  rubbery adj ▷ **rubber¹**
  rubbing v ▷ **rub**
rubbish n (pl **-es**) waste matter > **rubbishy** adj
  rubbishes n ▷ **rubbish**
  rubbishy adj ▷ **rubbish**
rubble n (pl **-s**) fragments of broken stone,
brick, etc.
  rubbles n ▷ **rubble**
rubella n (pl **-s**) ▷ **German measles**
  rubellas n ▷ **rubella**
rubicund adj ruddy
rubidium n (pl **-s**) (CHEM) soft highly reactive
radioactive element
  rubidiums n ▷ **rubidium**
  rubies n ▷ **ruby**
rubric n (pl **-s**) heading or explanation inserted
in a text
  rubrics n ▷ **rubric**
  rubs v, n ▷ **rub**
ruby n (pl **-ies**) red precious gemstone ▶ adj
deep red
ruck¹ n (pl **-s**) rough crowd of common people
ruck² n, v (**-s, -ing, -ed**) wrinkle or crease
  rucked v ▷ **ruck²**
  rucking v ▷ **ruck²**
  rucks n ▷ **ruck¹, ²** ▶ v ▷ **ruck²**
rucksack n (pl **-s**) (BRIT, AUST & S AFR) large pack
carried on the back
  rucksacks n ▷ **rucksack**
ructions pl n (Informal) noisy uproar
rudder n (pl **-s**) vertical hinged piece at the
stern of a boat or at the rear of an aircraft,
for steering
  rudders n ▷ **rudder**
  ruddier adj ▷ **ruddy**
  ruddiest adj ▷ **ruddy**
ruddy adj (**-dier, -diest**) of a fresh healthy red
colour
rude adj (**-r, -st**) impolite or insulting > **rudely**
adv > **rudeness** n (pl **-s**)
  rudely adv ▷ **rude**
  rudeness n ▷ **rude**
  rudenesses n ▷ **rude**

  ruder adj ▷ **rude**
  rudest adj ▷ **rude**
rudimentary adj basic, elementary
rudiments pl n simplest and most basic stages
of a subject
rue¹ v (**rues, ruing, rued**) feel regret for
rue² n (pl **-s**) plant with evergreen bitter leaves
rueful adj regretful or sorry > **ruefully** adv
  ruefully adv ▷ **rueful**
  rued v ▷ **rue¹**
  rues v ▷ **rue¹** ▶ n ▷ **rue²**
ruff n (pl **-s**) starched and frilled collar
ruffian n (pl **-s**) violent lawless person
  ruffians n ▷ **ruffian**
ruffle v (**-les, -ling, -led**) disturb the calm of ▶ n
(pl **-s**) frill or pleat
  ruffled v ▷ **ruffle**
  ruffles v, n ▷ **ruffle**
  ruffling v ▷ **ruffle**
  ruffs n ▷ **ruff**
rug n (pl **-s**) small carpet
  rugbies n ▷ **rugby**
rugby n (pl **-ies**) form of football played with an
oval ball which may be handled by the players
rugged [rug-gid] adj rocky or steep
rugger n (pl **-s**) (CHIEFLY BRIT) (Informal) rugby
  ruggers n ▷ **rugger**
  rugs n ▷ **rug**
ruin v (**-s, -ing, -ed**) destroy or spoil completely
▶ n (pl **-s**) destruction or decay
ruination n (pl **-s**) act of ruining
  ruinations n ▷ **ruination**
  ruined v ▷ **ruin**
  ruing v ▷ **rue¹**
  ruining v ▷ **ruin**
ruinous adj causing ruin > **ruinously** adv
  ruinously adv ▷ **ruinous**
  ruins v, n ▷ **ruin**
rule n (pl **-s**) statement of what is allowed,
for example in a game or procedure ▶ v (**-les,
-ling, -led**) govern
  ruled v ▷ **rule**
ruler n (pl **-s**) person who governs
  rulers n ▷ **ruler**
  rules n, v ▷ **rule**
ruling n (pl **-s**) formal decision ▶ v ▷ **rule**
  rulings n ▷ **ruling**
rum n (pl **-s**) alcoholic drink distilled from
sugar cane
rumba n (pl **-s**) lively ballroom dance of Cuban
origin
  rumbas n ▷ **rumba**
rumble v (**-les, -ling, -led**) make a low
continuous noise (BRIT) (Informal) ▶ n (pl **-s**)
deep resonant sound

rumbled v ▷ rumble

rumbles v, n ▷ rumble

rumbling v ▷ rumble

rumbustious adj boisterous or unruly

ruminate v (-tes, -ting, -ted) chew the cud

ruminant adj, n (pl -s) cud-chewing (animal, such as a cow, sheep, or deer)

ruminants n ▷ ruminant

ruminated v ▷ ruminate

ruminates v ▷ ruminate

ruminating v ▷ ruminate

rumination n (pl -s) quiet meditation and reflection > **ruminative** adj

ruminations n ▷ rumination

ruminative adj ▷ rumination

rummage v (-ges, -ging, -ged) search untidily and at length ▶ n (pl -s) untidy search through a collection of things

rummaged v ▷ rummage

rummages v, n ▷ rummage

rummaging v ▷ rummage

rummies n ▷ rummy

rummy n (pl -ies) card game in which players try to collect sets or sequences

rumour n (pl -s) unproved statement

rumoured adj suggested by rumour

rumours n ▷ rumour

rump n (pl -s) buttocks

rumple v (-les, -ling, -led) make untidy, crumpled, or dishevelled

rumpled v ▷ rumple

rumples v ▷ rumple

rumpling v ▷ rumple

rumps n ▷ rump

rumpus n (pl -es) noisy commotion

rumpuses n ▷ rumpus

rums n ▷ rum

run v (runs, running, ran, run) move with a more rapid gait than walking ▶ n (pl -s) act or spell of running

rune n (pl -s) any character of the earliest Germanic alphabet > **runic** adj

runes n ▷ rune

rung¹ n (pl -s) crossbar on a ladder

rung² v ▷ ring¹

rungs n ▷ rung¹

runic adj ▷ rune

runnel n (pl -s) small brook

runnels n ▷ runnel

runner n (pl -s) competitor in a race

runners n ▷ runner

runnier adj ▷ runny

runniest adj ▷ runny

running adj continuous ▶ n (pl -s) act of moving or flowing quickly ▶ v ▷ run

runnings n ▷ running

runny adj (-nier, -niest) tending to flow

runs v, n ▷ run

runt n (pl -s) smallest animal in a litter

runts n ▷ runt

runway n (pl -s) hard level roadway where aircraft take off and land

runways n ▷ runway

rupee n (pl -s) monetary unit of India and Pakistan

rupees n ▷ rupee

rupture n (pl -s) breaking, breach ▶ v (-res, -ring, -red) break, burst, or sever

ruptured v ▷ rupture

ruptures n, v ▷ rupture

rupturing v ▷ rupture

rural adj in or of the countryside

ruse [rooz] n (pl -s) stratagem or trick

ruses n ▷ ruse

rush¹ v (-es, -ing, -ed) move or do very quickly ▶ n (pl -es) sudden quick or violent movement ▶ pl first unedited prints of a scene for a film ▶ adj done with speed, hasty

rush² n (pl -es) marsh plant with a slender pithy stem

rushed v ▷ rush¹

rushes v, n ▷ rush¹, ²

rushier adj ▷ rushy

rushiest adj ▷ rushy

rushing v ▷ rush¹

rushy adj (-shier, -shiest) full of rushes

rusk n (pl -s) hard brown crisp biscuit, used esp. for feeding babies

rusks n ▷ rusk

russet adj reddish-brown ▶ n (pl -s) apple with rough reddish-brown skin

russets n ▷ russet

rust n (pl -s) reddish-brown coating formed on iron etc. that has been exposed to moisture ▶ adj reddish-brown ▶ v (-s, -ing, -ed) become coated with rust

rusted v ▷ rust

rustic adj of or resembling country people ▶ n (pl -s) person from the country

rustics n ▷ rustic

rustier adj ▷ rusty

rustiest adj ▷ rusty

rusting v ▷ rust

rustle¹ v, n (pl -s) (make) a low whispering sound

rustle² v (-les, -ling, -led) (US) steal (cattle)

rustled v ▷ rustle

rustler n (pl -s) (US) cattle thief

rustlers n ▷ rustler

rustles n, v ▷ rustle

rustling *v* ▷ rustle
rusts *n, v* ▷ rust
rusty *adj* (**-tier, -tiest**) coated with rust
rut¹ *n* (*pl* **-s**) furrow made by wheels
rut² *n* recurrent period of sexual excitability in
    male deer ▶ *v* (**-s, -tting, -tted**) be in a period
    of sexual excitability
ruthenium *n* (*pl* **-s**) (CHEM) rare hard brittle
    white element
    rutheniums *n* ▷ ruthenium
ruthless *adj* pitiless, merciless > **ruthlessly** *adv*

> **ruthlessness** *n* (*pl* **-es**)
ruthlessly *adv* ▷ ruthless
ruthlessness *n* ▷ ruthless
ruthlessnesses *n* ▷ ruthless
ruts *n* ▷ rut¹, ² ▶ *v* ▷ rut²
rutted *v* ▷ rut²
rutting *v* ▷ rut²
rye *n* (*pl* **-s**) kind of grain used for fodder and
    bread
    ryes *n* ▷ rye

Ss

S begins only four two-letter words, **sh** (5 points), **si**, **so** and **st** (2 each). These are easy to remember, and it's worth noting that two of them, **sh** and **st**, don't use any vowels. Interestingly, there are quite a few three-letter words beginning with S that don't contain vowels, some of which give good scores. These are **shh** (9), **shy** (9), **sky** (10), **sly** (6), **sny** (6), **spy** (8), **sty** (6), **swy** (9) and **syn** (6). S also forms a number of three-letter words with X. These are easy to remember as they use every vowel except U: **sax, sex, six** and **sox** (10 each). Apart from the two- and three-letter words, don't forget **squeeze** (25), which uses the two highest-scoring tiles in the game.

sabbath n (pl -s) day of worship and rest: Saturday for Jews, Sunday for Christians
   sabbaths n ▷ **sabbath**
sabbatical adj, n (pl -s) (denoting) leave for study
   sabbaticals n ▷ **sabbatical**
sable n (pl -s) dark fur from a small weasel-like Arctic animal ▶ adj black
   sables n ▷ **sable**
sabot [sab-oh] n (pl -s) wooden shoe traditionally worn by peasants in France
sabotage n (pl -s) intentional damage done to machinery, systems, etc. ▶ v (-ges, -ging, -ged) damage intentionally
   sabotaged v ▷ **sabotage**
   sabotages n, v ▷ **sabotage**
   sabotaging v ▷ **sabotage**
saboteur n (pl -s) person who commits sabotage
   saboteurs n ▷ **saboteur**
   sabots n ▷ **sabot**
sabre n (pl -s) curved cavalry sword
   sabres n ▷ **sabre**
sac n (pl -s) pouchlike structure in an animal or plant
saccharin n (pl -s) artificial sweetener
   > **saccharine** adj excessively sweet
   saccharine adj ▷ **saccharin**
   saccharins n ▷ **saccharin**
sacerdotal adj of priests
sachet n (pl -s) small envelope or bag containing a single portion
   sachets n ▷ **sachet**
sack[1] n (pl -s) large bag made of coarse material ▶ v (-s, -ing, -ed) (Informal) dismiss

sack[2] n (pl -s) plundering of a captured town ▶ v (-s, -ing, -ed) plunder (a captured town)
sackcloth n (pl -s) coarse fabric used for sacks, formerly worn as a penance
   sackcloths n ▷ **sackcloth**
   sacked v ▷ **sack**[1, 2]
   sacking v ▷ **sack**[1, 2]
   sacks v, n ▷ **sack**[1, 2]
   sacra n ▷ **sacrum**
sacrament n (pl -s) ceremony of the Christian Church, esp. Communion > **sacramental** adj
   sacramental adj ▷ **sacrament**
   sacraments n ▷ **sacrament**
sacred adj holy
sacrifice n (pl -s) giving something up ▶ v (-es, -ing, -ced) offer as a sacrifice > **sacrificial** adj
   sacrificed v ▷ **sacrifice**
   sacrifices n, v ▷ **sacrifice**
   sacrificial adj ▷ **sacrifice**
   sacrificing v ▷ **sacrifice**
sacrilege n (pl -s) misuse or desecration of something sacred > **sacrilegious** adj
   sacrileges n ▷ **sacrilege**
   sacrilegious adj ▷ **sacrilege**
sacristan n (pl -s) person in charge of the contents of a church
   sacristans n ▷ **sacristan**
   sacristies n ▷ **sacristy**
sacristy n (pl -ties) room in a church where sacred objects are kept
sacrosanct adj regarded as sacred, inviolable
sacrum [say-krum] n (pl -cra) wedge-shaped bone at the base of the spine
   sacs n ▷ **sac**
sad adj (-dder, -ddest) sorrowful, unhappy

> **sadly** adv > **sadness** n (pl **-es**)
sadden v (-s, -ing, -ed) make sad
  saddened v ▷ sadden
  saddening v ▷ sadden
  saddens v ▷ sadden
  sadder adj ▷ sad
  saddest adj ▷ sad
saddle n (pl **-les**) rider's seat on a horse or bicycle ▶ v (**-les, -ling, -led**) put a saddle on (a horse)
  saddled v ▷ saddle
saddler n (pl **-s**) maker or seller of saddles
  saddlers n ▷ saddler
  saddles n, v ▷ saddle
  saddling v ▷ saddle
saddo n (pl **-s, -es**) (BRIT) (Informal) socially inadequate or pathetic person
  saddoes n ▷ saddo
  saddos n ▷ saddo
sadism [say-dizz-um] n (pl **-s**) gaining of (sexual) pleasure from inflicting pain > **sadist** n (pl **-s**) > **sadistic** adj > **sadistically** adv
  sadisms n ▷ sadism
  sadist n ▷ sadism
  sadistic adj ▷ sadism
  sadistically adv ▷ sadism
  sadists n ▷ sadism
  sadly adv ▷ sad
  sadness n ▷ sad
  sadnesses n ▷ sad
sadomasochism n (pl **-s**) combination of sadism and masochism > **sadomasochist** n (pl **-s**)
  sadomasochisms n ▷ sadomasochism
  sadomasochist n ▷ sadomasochism
  sadomasochists n ▷ sadomasochism
safari n (pl **-s**) expedition to hunt or observe wild animals, esp. in Africa
  safaris n ▷ safari
safe adj (-r, -st) secure, protected ▶ n (pl **-s**) strong lockable container > **safely** adv
safeguard v (-s, -ing, -ed) protect ▶ n (pl **-s**) protection
  safeguarded v ▷ safeguard
  safeguarding v ▷ safeguard
  safeguards v, n ▷ safeguard
safekeeping n (pl **-s**) protection
  safekeepings n ▷ safekeeping
  safely adv ▷ safe
  safer adj ▷ safe
  safes n ▷ safe
  safest adj ▷ safe
  safeties n ▷ safety
safety n (pl **-ties**) state of being safe
saffron n (pl **-s**) orange-coloured flavouring obtained from a crocus ▶ adj orange
  saffrons n ▷ saffron
sag v (**sags, sagging, sagged**) sink in the middle ▶ n (pl **-s**) droop
saga [sah-ga] n (pl **-s**) legend of Norse heroes
sagacious adj wise > **sagacity** n (pl **-ties**)
  sagacities n ▷ sagacious
  sagacity n ▷ sagacious
  sagas n ▷ saga
sage¹ n (pl **-s**) very wise man ▶ adj (-r, -st) (Lit) wise > **sagely** adv
sage² n (pl **-s**) aromatic herb with grey-green leaves
  sagely adv ▷ sage¹
  sager adj ▷ sage¹
  sages n ▷ sage¹, ²
  sagest adj ▷ sage¹
  sagged v ▷ sag
  sagging v ▷ sag
sago n (pl **-s**) starchy cereal from the powdered pith of the sago palm tree
  sagos n ▷ sago
  sags v, n ▷ sag
  said v ▷ say
sail n (pl **-s**) sheet of fabric stretched to catch the wind for propelling a sailing boat ▶ v (-s, -ing, -ed) travel by water
sailboard n (pl **-s**) board with a mast and single sail, used for windsurfing
  sailboards n ▷ sailboard
  sailed v ▷ sail
  sailing v ▷ sail
sailor n (pl **-s**) member of a ship's crew
  sailors n ▷ sailor
  sails n, v ▷ sail
saint n (pl **-s**) (CHRISTIANITY) person venerated after death as specially holy > **saintly** adj > **saintliness** n (pl **-es**)
  saintliness n ▷ saint
  saintlinesses n ▷ saint
  saintly adj ▷ saint
  saints n ▷ saint
sake¹ n (pl **-s**) benefit
sake², saki [sah-kee] n (pl **-s**) Japanese alcoholic drink made from fermented rice
  sakes n ▷ sake¹, ²
  saki n ▷ sake²
  sakis n ▷ sake²
salaam [sal-ahm] n (pl **-s**) low bow of greeting among Muslims
  salaams n ▷ salaam
salacious adj excessively concerned with sex
salad n (pl **-s**) dish of raw vegetables, eaten as a meal or part of a meal
  salads n ▷ salad

salamander n (pl -s) amphibian which looks like a lizard
  salamanders n ▷ salamander
salami n (pl -s) highly spiced sausage
  salamis n ▷ salami
salaried adj ▷ salary
salaries n ▷ salary
salary n (pl -ries) fixed regular payment, usu. monthly, to an employee > **salaried** adj
sale n (pl -s) exchange of goods for money > **saleable** adj fit or likely to be sold
  saleable adj ▷ sale
  sales n ▷ sale
salesman, saleswoman (pl -men, -women) > **salesperson** (pl -people) n person who sells goods
salesmanship n (pl -s) skill in selling
  salesmanships n ▷ salesmanship
  salesmen n ▷ salesman
  salespeople n ▷ salesman
  salesperson n ▷ salesman
  saleswoman n ▷ salesman
  saleswomen n ▷ salesman
salient [say-lee-ent] adj prominent, noticeable ▶ n (pl -s) (MIL) projecting part of a front line
  salients n ▷ salient
saline [say-line] adj containing salt > **salinity** n (pl -ties)
  salinities n ▷ saline
  salinity n ▷ saline
saliva n (pl -s) liquid that forms in the mouth, spittle > **salivary** adj
  salivary adj ▷ saliva
  salivas n ▷ saliva
salivate v (-tes, -ting, -ted) produce saliva
  salivated v ▷ salivate
  salivates v ▷ salivate
  salivating v ▷ salivate
sallee n (pl -s) (AUST) SE Australian eucalyptus with a pale grey bark
  sallees n ▷ sallee
  sallied v ▷ sally
  sallies n, v ▷ sally
sallow adj (-er, -est) of an unhealthy pale or yellowish colour
  sallower adj ▷ sallow
  sallowest adj ▷ sallow
sally n (pl -lies) witty remark ▶ v (-lies, -lying, -lied) (foll. by **forth**) rush out
  sallying v ▷ sally
salmon n (pl -s) large fish with orange-pink flesh valued as food ▶ adj orange-pink
salmonella n (pl -lae) bacterium causing food poisoning
  salmonellae n ▷ salmonella

  salmons n ▷ salmon
salon n (pl -s) commercial premises of a hairdresser, beautician, etc.
  salons n ▷ salon
saloon n (pl -s) two-door or four-door car with body closed off from rear luggage area
  saloons n ▷ saloon
salt n (pl -s) white crystalline substance used to season food ▶ v (-s, -ing, -ed) season or preserve with salt > **salty** adj (-tier, -tiest)
saltbush n (pl -es) shrub that grows in alkaline desert regions
  saltbushes n ▷ saltbush
  salted v ▷ salt
  saltier adj ▷ salt
  saltiest adj ▷ salt
  salting v ▷ salt
saltire n (pl -s) (HERALDRY) diagonal cross on a shield
  saltires n ▷ saltire
saltpetre n (pl -s) compound used in gunpowder and as a preservative
  saltpetres n ▷ saltpetre
  salts n, v ▷ salt
  salty adj ▷ salt
salubrious adj favourable to health
saluki n (pl -s) tall hound with a silky coat
  salukis n ▷ saluki
salutary adj producing a beneficial result
salutation n (pl -s) greeting by words or actions
  salutations n ▷ salutation
salute n (pl -s) motion of the arm as a formal military sign of respect ▶ v (-tes, -ting, -ted) greet with a salute
  saluted v ▷ salute
  salutes n, v ▷ salute
  saluting v ▷ salute
salvage n (pl -s) saving of a ship or other property from destruction ▶ v (-ges, -ging, -ged) save from destruction or waste
  salvaged v ▷ salvage
  salvages n, v ▷ salvage
  salvaging v ▷ salvage
salvation n (pl -s) fact or state of being saved from harm or the consequences of sin
  salvations n ▷ salvation
salve n (pl -s) healing or soothing ointment ▶ v (-ves, -ving, -ved) soothe or appease
  salved v ▷ salve
salver n (pl -s) (silver) tray on which something is presented
  salvers n ▷ salver
  salves n, v ▷ salve
salvia n (pl -s) plant with blue or red flowers

salvias *n* ▷ salvia

salving *v* ▷ salve

salvo *n* (*pl* **-s**, **-es**) simultaneous discharge of guns etc.

salvoes *n* ▷ salvo

salvos *n* ▷ salvo

samaritan *n* (*pl* **-s**) person who helps people in distress

samaritans *n* ▷ samaritan

samba *n* (*pl* **-s**) lively Brazilian dance

sambas *n* ▷ samba

same *adj* identical, not different, unchanged > **sameness** *n* (*pl* **-es**)

sameness *n* ▷ same

samenesses *n* ▷ same

samovar *n* (*pl* **-s**) Russian tea urn

samovars *n* ▷ samovar

sampan *n* (*pl* **-s**) small boat with oars used in China

sampans *n* ▷ sampan

samphire *n* (*pl* **-s**) plant found on rocks by the seashore

samphires *n* ▷ samphire

sample *n* (*pl* **-s**) part taken as representative of a whole ▶ *v* (**-les**, **-ling**, **-led**) take and test a sample of > **sampling** *n* (*pl* **-s**)

sampled *v* ▷ sample

sampler *n* (*pl* **-s**) piece of embroidery showing the embroiderer's skill

samplers *n* ▷ sampler

samples *v*, *n* ▷ sample

sampling *v*, *n* ▷ sample

samplings *n* ▷ sample

samurai *n* (*pl* **-rai**) member of an ancient Japanese warrior caste

sanatoria *n* ▷ sanatorium

sanatorium *n* (*pl* **-riums**, **-ria**) institution for invalids or convalescents

sanatoriums *n* ▷ sanatorium

sancta *n* ▷ sanctum

sanctified *v* ▷ sanctify

sanctifies *v* ▷ sanctify

sanctify *v* (**-fies**, **-fying**, **-fied**) make holy

sanctifying *v* ▷ sanctify

sanctimonious *adj* pretending to be religious and virtuous

sanction *n* (*pl* **-s**) permission, authorization ▶ *v* (**-s**, **-ing**, **-ed**) allow, authorize

sanctioned *v* ▷ sanction

sanctioning *v* ▷ sanction

sanctions *n*, *v* ▷ sanction

sanctities *n* ▷ sanctity

sanctity *n* (*pl* **-ties**) sacredness, inviolability

sanctuaries *n* ▷ sanctuary

sanctuary *n* (*pl* **-ries**) holy place

sanctum *n* (*pl* **-tums**, **-ta**) sacred place

sanctums *n* ▷ sanctum

sand *n* (*pl* **-s**) substance consisting of small grains of rock, esp. on a beach or in a desert ▶ *v* (**-s**, **-ing**, **-ed**) smooth with sandpaper

sandal *n* (*pl* **-s**) light shoe consisting of a sole attached by straps

sandals *n* ▷ sandal

sandalwood *n* (*pl* **-s**) sweet-scented wood

sandalwoods *n* ▷ sandalwood

sandbag *n* (*pl* **-s**) bag filled with sand, used as protection against gunfire or flood water

sandbags *n* ▷ sandbag

sandblast *v* (**-s**, **-ing**, **-ed**) ▶ *n* (*pl* **-s**) (clean with) a jet of sand blown from a nozzle under pressure

sandblasted *v* ▷ sandblast

sandblasting *v* ▷ sandblast

sandblasts *v*, *n* ▷ sandblast

sanded *v* ▷ sand

sander *n* (*pl* **-s**) power tool for smoothing surfaces

sanders *n* ▷ sander

sandier *adj* ▷ sandy

sandiest *adj* ▷ sandy

sanding *v* ▷ sand

sandpaper *n* (*pl* **-s**) paper coated with sand for smoothing a surface

sandpapers *n* ▷ sandpaper

sandpiper *n* (*pl* **-s**) shore bird with a long bill and slender legs

sandpipers *n* ▷ sandpiper

sands *n*, *v* ▷ sand ▶ *pl n* stretches of sand forming a beach or desert

sandstone *n* (*pl* **-s**) rock composed of sand

sandstones *n* ▷ sandstone

sandstorm *n* (*pl* **-s**) desert wind that whips up clouds of sand

sandstorms *n* ▷ sandstorm

sandwich *n* (*pl* **-es**) two slices of bread with a layer of food between ▶ *v* (**-es**, **-ing**, **-ed**) insert between two other things

sandwiched *v* ▷ sandwich

sandwiches *n*, *v* ▷ sandwich

sandwiching *v* ▷ sandwich

sandy *adj* (**-dier**, **-diest**) covered with sand

sane *adj* (**-r**, **-st**) of sound mind > **sanity** *n* (*pl* **-ties**)

saner *adj* ▷ sane

sanest *adj* ▷ sane

sang *v* ▷ sing

sangoma *n* (*pl* **-s**) (*s AFR*) witch doctor or herbalist

sangomas *n* ▷ sangoma

sanguinary *adj* accompanied by bloodshed

sanguine adj cheerful, optimistic
sanitary adj promoting health by getting rid of dirt and germs
sanitation n (pl -s) sanitary measures, esp. drainage or sewerage
  sanitations n ▷ sanitation
  sanities n ▷ sane
  sanity n ▷ sane
  sank v ▷ sink
sap¹ n (pl -s) moisture that circulates in plants
sap² v (saps, sapping, sapped) undermine
sapient [say-pee-ent] adj (Lit) wise, shrewd
sapling n (pl -s) young tree
  saplings n ▷ sapling
  sapped v ▷ sap²
sapper n (pl -s) soldier in an engineering unit
  sappers n ▷ sapper
sapphire n (pl -s) blue precious stone ▶ adj deep blue
  sapphires n ▷ sapphire
  sapping v ▷ sap²
  saps n ▷ sap¹ ▶ v ▷ sap²
  saraband n ▷ sarabande
sarabande, saraband n (pl -s) slow stately Spanish dance
  sarabandes n ▷ sarabande
  sarabands n ▷ sarabande
sarcasm n (pl -s) (use of) bitter or wounding ironic language > **sarcastic** adj > **sarcastically** adv
  sarcasms n ▷ sarcasm
  sarcastic adj ▷ sarcasm
  sarcastically adv ▷ sarcasm
  sarcophagi n ▷ sarcophagus
sarcophagus n (pl -gi, -guses) stone coffin
  sarcophaguses n ▷ sarcophagus
sardine n (pl -s) small fish of the herring family, usu. preserved tightly packed in tins
  sardines n ▷ sardine
sardonic adj mocking or scornful > **sardonically** adv
  sardonically adv ▷ sardonic
  saree n ▷ sari
  sarees n ▷ sari
  sargasso n ▷ sargassum
  sargassos n ▷ sargassum
sargassum, sargasso n (pl -s) type of floating seaweed
  sargassums n ▷ sargassum
sari, saree n (pl -s) long piece of cloth draped around the body and over one shoulder, worn by Hindu women
  saris n ▷ sari
sarmie n (pl -s) (S AFR) (Slang) sandwich
  sarmies n ▷ sarmie

sarong n (pl -s) long piece of cloth tucked around the waist or under the armpits, worn esp. in Malaysia
  sarongs n ▷ sarong
sarsaparilla n (pl -s) soft drink, orig. made from the root of a tropical American plant
  sarsaparillas n ▷ sarsaparilla
sartorial adj of men's clothes or tailoring
sash¹ n (pl -es) decorative strip of cloth worn round the waist or over one shoulder
sash² n (pl -es) wooden frame containing the panes of a window
  sashes n ▷ sash¹, ²
sassafras n (pl -rases) American tree with aromatic bark used medicinally
  sassafrases n ▷ sassafras
  sat v ▷ sit
satanic adj of Satan
satanism n (pl -s) worship of Satan
  satanisms n ▷ satanism
satay, saté [sat-ay] n (pl -s) Indonesian and Malaysian dish consisting of pieces of chicken, pork, etc., grilled on skewers and served with peanut sauce
  satays n ▷ satay
satchel n (pl -s) bag, usu. with a shoulder strap, for carrying books
  satchels n ▷ satchel
sate v (-tes, -ting, -ted) satisfy (a desire or appetite) fully
  sated v ▷ sate
satellite n (pl -s) man-made device orbiting in space ▶ adj of or used in the transmission of television signals from a satellite to the home
  satellites n ▷ satellite
  sates v ▷ sate
satiate [say-she-ate] v (-tes, -ting, -ted) provide with more than enough, so as to disgust
  satiated v ▷ satiate
  satiates v ▷ satiate
  satiating v ▷ satiate
  satieties n ▷ satiety
satiety [sat-**tie**-a-tee] n (pl -ties) feeling of having had too much
satin n (pl -s) silky fabric with a glossy surface on one side
  sating v ▷ sate
  satins n ▷ satin
satinwood n (pl -s) tropical tree yielding hard wood
  satinwoods n ▷ satinwood
satiny adj of or like satin
satire n (pl -s) use of ridicule to expose vice or folly > **satirical** adj > **satirist** n (pl -s)

satires n ▷ satire

satirical adj ▷ satire

satirist n ▷ satire

satirists n ▷ satire

satirize v (-zes, -zing, -zed) ridicule by means of satire

satirized v ▷ satirize

satirizes v ▷ satirize

satirizing v ▷ satirize

satisfaction n ▷ satisfy

satisfactions n ▷ satisfy

satisfactory adj ▷ satisfy

satisfied v ▷ satisfy

satisfies v ▷ satisfy

satisfy v (-fies, -fying, -fied) please, content > **satisfaction** n (pl -s) > **satisfactory** adj

satisfying v ▷ satisfy

satnav n (pl -s) (MOTORING) (Informal) satellite navigation

satnavs n ▷ satnav

satsuma n (pl -s) kind of small orange

satsumas n ▷ satsuma

saturate v (-tes, -ting, -ted) soak thoroughly > **saturation** n (pl -s)

saturated v ▷ saturate

saturates v ▷ saturate

saturating v ▷ saturate

saturation n ▷ saturate

saturations n ▷ saturate

saturnalia n (pl -s) wild party or orgy

saturnalias n ▷ saturnalia

saturnine adj gloomy in temperament or appearance

satyr n (pl -s) woodland god, part man, part goat

satyrs n ▷ satyr

sauce n (pl -s) liquid added to food to enhance flavour

saucepan n (pl -s) cooking pot with a long handle

saucepans n ▷ saucepan

saucer n (pl -s) small round dish put under a cup

saucers n ▷ saucer

sauces n ▷ sauce

saucier adj ▷ saucy

sauciest adj ▷ saucy

saucily adv ▷ saucy

saucy adj (-cier, -ciest) impudent > **saucily** adv

sauerkraut n (pl -s) shredded cabbage fermented in brine

sauerkrauts n ▷ sauerkraut

sauna n (pl -s) Finnish-style steam bath

saunas n ▷ sauna

saunter v (-s, -ing, -ed) walk in a leisurely manner, stroll ▶ n (pl -s) leisurely walk

sauntered v ▷ saunter

sauntering v ▷ saunter

saunters v, n ▷ saunter

sausage n (pl -s) minced meat in an edible tube-shaped skin

sausages n ▷ sausage

sauté [so-tay] v (-tés, -téing or -téeing, -téed) fry quickly in a little fat

sautéed v ▷ sauté

sautéeing v ▷ sauté

sautéing v ▷ sauté

sautés v ▷ sauté

savage adj (-r, -st) wild, untamed ▶ n (pl -s) uncivilized person ▶ v (-ges, -ging, -ged) attack ferociously > **savagely** adv > **savagery** n (pl -ries)

savaged v ▷ savage

savagely adv ▷ savage

savager adj ▷ savage

savageries n ▷ savage

savagery n ▷ savage

savages n, v ▷ savage

savagest adj ▷ savage

savaging v ▷ savage

savanna n ▷ savannah

savannah, savanna n (pl -s) extensive open grassy plain in Africa

savannahs n ▷ savannah

savannas n ▷ savanna

savant n (pl -s) learned person

savants n ▷ savant

save v (-ves, -ving, -ved) rescue or preserve from harm, protect ▶ n (pl -s) (SPORT) act of preventing a goal > **saver** n (pl -s)

saved v ▷ save

saveloy n (pl -s) (BRIT, AUST & NZ) spicy smoked sausage

saveloys n ▷ saveloy

saver n ▷ save

savers n ▷ save

saves v, n ▷ save

saving v ▷ save ▶ n (pl -s) economy

savings n pl money put by for future use

saviour n (pl -s) person who rescues another

saviours n ▷ saviour

savories n ▷ savory

savory n (pl -ries) aromatic herb used in cooking

savour v (-s, -ing, -ed) enjoy, relish (foll. by of) ▶ n (pl -s) characteristic taste or odour

savoured v ▷ savour

savourier adj ▷ savoury

savouries n ▷ savoury

savouriest adj ▷ savoury

savouring v ▷ savour

savours v, n ▷ savour

savoury adj (-rier, -riest) salty or spicy ▶ n (pl -ries) savoury dish served before or after a meal

savoy n (pl -s) variety of cabbage

savoys n ▷ savoy

savvied v ▷ savvy

savvies v, n ▷ savvy

savvy (Slang) v (-vies, -vying, -vied) understand ▶ n (pl -vies) understanding, intelligence

savvying v ▷ savvy

saw¹ n (pl -s) cutting tool with a toothed metal blade ▶ v (-s, -ing, -ed, -ed or sawn) cut with a saw

saw² ▷ see¹

saw³ n (pl -s) wise saying, proverb

sawdust n (pl -s) fine wood fragments made in sawing

sawdusts n ▷ sawdust

sawed v ▷ saw¹

sawfish n (pl -es) fish with a long toothed snout

sawfishes n ▷ sawfish

sawing v ▷ saw¹

sawmill n (pl -s) mill where timber is sawn into planks

sawmills n ▷ sawmill

sawn v ▷ saw¹

saws n ▷ saw¹, ³ ▶ v ▷ saw¹

sawyer n (pl -s) person who saws timber for a living

sawyers n ▷ sawyer

sax n (pl -es) (Informal) ▷ saxophone

saxes n ▷ sax

saxifrage n (pl -s) alpine rock plant with small flowers

saxifrages n ▷ saxifrage

saxophone n (pl -s) brass wind instrument with keys and a curved body > **saxophonist** n (pl -s)

saxophones n ▷ saxophone

saxophonist n ▷ saxophone

saxophonists n ▷ saxophone

say v (-s, -ing, said) speak or utter ▶ n (pl -s) right or chance to speak

saying n (pl -s) maxim, proverb ▶ v ▷ say

sayings n ▷ saying

says v, n ▷ say

> **saz** n (**sazes**). A saz is a Turkish musical instrument. This is a very useful word, and one to remember for when you get a Z in the later stages of the game, with little space left on the board. Saz scores 12 points.

scab n (pl -s) crust formed over a wound

scabbard n (pl -s) sheath for a sword or dagger

scabbards n ▷ scabbard

scabbier adj ▷ scabby

scabbiest adj ▷ scabby

scabby adj (-bbier, -bbiest) covered with scabs

scabies [skay-beez] n itchy skin disease

scabrous [skay-bruss] adj rough and scaly

scabs n ▷ scab

scaffold n (pl -s) temporary platform for workmen

scaffolding n (pl -s) (materials for building) scaffolds

scaffoldings n ▷ scaffolding

scaffolds n ▷ scaffold

scalar n (pl -s) ▶ adj (variable quantity) having magnitude but no direction

scalars n ▷ scalar

scald v (-s, -ing, -ed) burn with hot liquid or steam ▶ n (pl -s) injury by scalding

scalded v ▷ scald

scalding v ▷ scald

scalds v, n ▷ scald

scale¹ n (pl -s) one of the thin overlapping plates covering fishes and reptiles ▶ v (-les, -ling, -led) remove scales from > **scaly** adj (-lier, -liest)

scale² n (pl -s) (often pl) weighing instrument

scale³ n (pl -s) graduated table or sequence of marks at regular intervals, used as a reference in making measurements ▶ v (-les, -ling, -led) climb

scaled v ▷ scale¹, ³

scalene adj (of a triangle) with three unequal sides

scales n ▷ scale¹, ², ³ ▶ v ▷ scale¹, ³

scalier adj ▷ scale¹

scaliest adj ▷ scale¹

scaling v ▷ scale¹, ³

scallop n (pl -s) edible shellfish with two fan-shaped shells

scalloped adj decorated with small curves along the edge

scallops n ▷ scallop

scallywag n (pl -s) (Informal) scamp, rascal

scallywags n ▷ scallywag

scalp n (pl -s) skin and hair on top of the head ▶ v (-s, -ing, -ed) cut off the scalp of

scalped v ▷ scalp

scalpel n (pl -s) small surgical knife

scalpels n ▷ scalpel

scalping v ▷ scalp

scalps n, v ▷ scalp

scaly adj ▷ scale¹

scam n (pl -s) (Informal) dishonest scheme

scamp n (pl -s) mischievous child

scamper v (-s, -ing, -ed) run about hurriedly or in play ▶ n (pl -s) scampering

scampered v ▷ scamper

scampering v ▷ scamper

scampers v, n ▷ scamper

scampi pl n large prawns

scamps n ▷ scamp

scams n ▷ scam

scan v (-s, -nning, -nned) scrutinize carefully ▶ n (pl -s) scanning

scandal n (pl -s) disgraceful action or event > **scandalous** adj

scandalize v (-zes, -zing, -zed) shock by scandal

scandalized v ▷ scandalize

scandalizes v ▷ scandalize

scandalizing v ▷ scandalize

scandalous adj ▷ scandal

scandals n ▷ scandal

scandium n (pl -s) (CHEM) rare silvery-white metallic element

scandiums n ▷ scandium

scanned v ▷ scan

scanner n (pl -s) electronic device used for scanning

scanners n ▷ scanner

scanning v ▷ scan

scans v, n ▷ scan

scansion n (pl -s) metrical scanning of verse

scansions n ▷ scansion

scant adj (-er, -est) barely sufficient, meagre

scanter adj ▷ scant

scantest adj ▷ scant

scantier adj ▷ scanty

scantiest adj ▷ scanty

scantily adv ▷ scanty

scanty adj (-tier, -tiest) barely sufficient or not sufficient > **scantily** adv

scapegoat n (pl -s) person made to bear the blame for others

scapegoats n ▷ scapegoat

scapula n (pl -lae, -las) shoulder blade > **scapular** adj

scapulae n ▷ scapula

scapular adj ▷ scapula

scapulas n ▷ scapula

scar n (pl -s) mark left by a healed wound ▶ v (-s, -rring, -rred) mark or become marked with a scar

scarab n (pl -s) sacred beetle of ancient Egypt

scarabs n ▷ scarab

scarce adj (-r, -st) insufficient to meet demand > **scarcity** n (pl -ties)

scarcely adv hardly at all

scarcer adj ▷ scarce

scarcest adj ▷ scarce

scarcities n ▷ scarce

scarcity n ▷ scarce

scare v (-res, -ring, -red) frighten or be frightened ▶ n (pl -s) fright, sudden panic

scarecrow n (pl -s) figure dressed in old clothes, set up to scare birds away from crops

scarecrows n ▷ scarecrow

scared v ▷ scare

scaremonger n (pl -s) person who spreads alarming rumours

scaremongers n ▷ scaremonger

scares v, n ▷ scare

scarf[1] n (pl scarves, -s) piece of material worn round the neck, head, or shoulders

scarf[2] n (pl -s) joint between two pieces of timber made by notching the ends and fastening them together ▶ v (-s, -ing, -ed) join in this way

scarfed v ▷ scarf[2]

scarfing v ▷ scarf[2]

scarfs n ▷ scarf[1, 2] ▶ v ▷ scarf[2]

scarier adj ▷ scary

scariest adj ▷ scary

scarification n ▷ scarify

scarifications n ▷ scarify

scarified v ▷ scarify

scarifies v ▷ scarify

scarify v (-fies, -fying, -fied) scratch or cut slightly all over > **scarification** n (pl -s)

scarifying v ▷ scarify

scaring v ▷ scare

scarlatina n (pl -s) scarlet fever

scarlatinas n ▷ scarlatina

scarlet adj, n (pl -s) brilliant red

scarlets n ▷ scarlet

scarp n (pl s) steep slope

scarper v (-s, -ing, -ed) (BRIT) (Slang) run away

scarpered v ▷ scarper

scarpering v ▷ scarper

scarpers v ▷ scarper

scarps n ▷ scarp

scarred v ▷ scar

scarring v ▷ scar

scars n, v ▷ scar

scarves n ▷ scarf[1]

scary adj (-rier, -riest) (Informal) frightening

scat[1] v (-s, -tting, -tted) (Informal) go away

scat[2] n (pl -s) jazz singing using improvised vocal sounds instead of words

scathing adj harshly critical

scatological adj preoccupied with obscenity, esp. with references to excrement > **scatology** n (pl -gies)

scatologies n ▷ scatology
scatology n ▷ scatological
scats n ▷ scat² ▶ v ▷ scat¹
scatted v ▷ scat¹
scatter v (-s, -ing, -ed) throw about in various directions
scatterbrain n (pl -s) empty-headed person
  scatterbrains n ▷ scatterbrain
  scattered v ▷ scatter
  scattering v ▷ scatter
  scatters v ▷ scatter
  scattier adj ▷ scatty
  scattiest adj ▷ scatty
  scatting v ▷ scat¹
scatty adj (-tier, -tiest) (Informal) empty-headed
scavenge v (-ges, -ging, -ged) search for (anything usable) among discarded material
  scavenged v ▷ scavenge
scavenger n (pl -s) person who scavenges
  scavengers n ▷ scavenger
  scavenges v ▷ scavenge
  scavenging v ▷ scavenge
scenario n (pl -rios) summary of the plot of a play or film
  scenarios n ▷ scenario
scene n (pl -s) place of action of a real or imaginary event
  sceneries n ▷ scenery
scenery n (pl -ries) natural features of a landscape
  scenes n ▷ scene
scenic adj picturesque
scent n (pl -s) pleasant smell ▶ v (-s, -ing, -ed) detect by smell
  scented v ▷ scent
  scenting v ▷ scent
  scents n, v ▷ scent
sceptic [skep-tik] n (pl -s) person who habitually doubts generally accepted beliefs > **sceptical** adj > **sceptically** adv > **scepticism** n (pl -s)
  sceptical adj ▷ sceptic
  sceptically adv ▷ sceptic
  scepticism n ▷ sceptic
  scepticisms n ▷ sceptic
  sceptics n ▷ sceptic
sceptre n (pl -s) ornamental rod symbolizing royal power
  sceptres n ▷ sceptre
schedule n (pl -s) plan of procedure for a project ▶ v (-les, -ling, -led) plan to occur at a certain time
  scheduled v ▷ schedule
  schedules n, v ▷ schedule

  scheduling v ▷ schedule
schema n (pl -mata) overall plan or diagram
schematic adj presented as a plan or diagram
scheme n (pl -s) systematic plan ▶ v (-mes, -ming, -med) plan in an underhand manner > **scheming** adj, n (pl -s)
  schemed v ▷ scheme
  schemes n, v ▷ scheme
  scheming v, adj n ▷ scheme
  schemings n ▷ scheme
  scherzi n ▷ scherzo
scherzo [skairt-so] n (pl -zos, -zi) brisk lively piece of music
  scherzos n ▷ scherzo
schism [skizz-um] n (pl -s) (group resulting from) division in an organization > **schismatic** adj, n (pl -s)
  schismatic adj, n ▷ schism
  schismatics n ▷ schism
  schisms n ▷ schism
schist [shist] n (pl -s) crystalline rock which splits into layers
  schists n ▷ schist
schizoid adj abnormally introverted ▶ n (pl -s) schizoid person
  schizoids n ▷ schizoid
schizophrenia n (pl -s) mental disorder involving deterioration of or confusion about the personality > **schizophrenic** adj, n (pl -s)
  schizophrenias n ▷ schizophrenia
  schizophrenic adj, n ▷ schizophrenia
  schizophrenics n ▷ schizophrenia
schmaltz n (pl -es) excessive sentimentality > **schmaltzy** adj (-zier, -ziest)
  schmaltzes n ▷ schmaltz
  schmaltzier adj ▷ schmaltz
  schmaltziest adj ▷ schmaltz
  schmaltzy adj ▷ schmaltz
schnapps n (pl -es) strong alcoholic spirit
  schnappses n ▷ schnapps
schnitzel n (pl -s) thin slice of meat, esp. veal
  schnitzels n ▷ schnitzel
scholar n (pl -s) learned person
scholarly adj learned
  scholars n ▷ scholar
scholarship n (pl -s) learning
  scholarships n ▷ scholarship
scholastic adj of schools or scholars
school¹ n (pl -s) place where children are taught or instruction is given in a subject ▶ v (-s, -ing, -ed) educate or train
school² n (pl -s) shoal of fish, whales, etc.
  schooled v ▷ school¹
schoolie n (pl -s) (AUST) schoolteacher or high-school student

schoolies n ▷ schoolie
schooling v ▷ school[1]
schools n ▷ school[1, 2] ▶ v ▷ school[1]
schooner n (pl -s) sailing ship rigged fore-and-aft
schooners n ▷ schooner
sciatic adj of the hip
sciatica n (pl -s) severe pain in the large nerve in the back of the leg
sciaticas n ▷ sciatica
science n (pl -s) systematic study and knowledge of natural or physical phenomena
sciences n ▷ science
scientific adj of science > **scientifically** adv
scientifically adv ▷ scientific
scientist n (pl -s) person who studies or practises a science
scientists n ▷ scientist
scimitar n (pl -s) curved oriental sword
scimitars n ▷ scimitar
scintillate v (-tes, -ting, -ted) give off sparks
scintillated v ▷ scintillate
scintillates v ▷ scintillate
scintillating adj very lively and amusing ▶ v ▷ scintillate
scion [sy-on] n (pl -s) descendant or heir
scions n ▷ scion
scissors pl n cutting instrument with two crossed pivoted blades
scleroses n ▷ sclerosis
sclerosis n (pl -ses) abnormal hardening of body tissues
scoff[1] v (-s, -ing, -ed) express derision
scoff[2] v (-s, -ing, -ed) (Informal) eat rapidly
scoffed v ▷ scoff[1, 2]
scoffing v ▷ scoff[1, 2]
scoffs v ▷ scoff[1, 2]
scold v (-s, -ing, -ed) find fault with, reprimand ▶ n (pl -s) person who scolds > **scolding** n (pl -s)
scolded v ▷ scold
scolding v, n ▷ scold
scoldings n ▷ scold
scolds v, n ▷ scold
sconce n (pl -s) bracket on a wall for holding candles or lights
sconces n ▷ sconce
scone n (pl -s) small plain cake baked in an oven or on a griddle
scones n ▷ scone
scoop n (pl -s) shovel-like tool for ladling or hollowing out ▶ v (-s, -ing, -ed) take up or hollow out with or as if with a scoop
scooped v ▷ scoop
scooping v ▷ scoop
scoops n, v ▷ scoop

scoot v (-s, -ing, -ed) (Slang) leave or move quickly
scooted v ▷ scoot
scooter n (pl -s) child's vehicle propelled by pushing on the ground with one foot
scooters n ▷ scooter
scooting v ▷ scoot
scoots v ▷ scoot
scope n (pl -s) opportunity for using abilities
scopes n ▷ scope
scorch v (-es, -ing, -ed) burn on the surface ▶ n (pl -es) slight burn
scorched v ▷ scorch
scorcher n (pl -s) (Informal) very hot day
scorchers n ▷ scorcher
scorches v, n ▷ scorch
scorching v ▷ scorch
score n (pl -s) points gained in a game or competition ▶ v (-res, -ring, -red) gain (points) in a game
scored v ▷ score
scores n, v ▷ score ▶ pl n lots
scoring v ▷ score
scorn n (pl -s) open contempt ▶ v (-s, -ing, -ed) despise > **scornful** adj > **scornfully** adv
scorned v ▷ scorn
scornful adj ▷ scorn
scornfully adv ▷ scorn
scorning v ▷ scorn
scorns n, v ▷ scorn
scorpion n (pl -s) small lobster-shaped animal with a sting at the end of a jointed tail
scorpions n ▷ scorpion
scotch v (-es, -ing, -ed) put an end to
scotched v ▷ scotch
scotches v ▷ scotch
scotching v ▷ scotch
scoundrel n (pl -s) (Old-fashioned) cheat or deceiver
scoundrels n ▷ scoundrel
scour[1] v (-s, -ing, -ed) clean or polish by rubbing with something rough
scour[2] v (-s, -ing, -ed) search thoroughly and energetically
scoured v ▷ scour[1, 2]
scourer n (pl -s) small rough nylon pad used for cleaning pots and pans
scourers n ▷ scourer
scourge n (pl -s) person or thing causing severe suffering ▶ v (-ges, -ging, -ged) cause severe suffering to
scourged v ▷ scourge
scourges n, v ▷ scourge
scourging v ▷ scourge
scouring v ▷ scour[1, 2]

scours v ▷ scour[1, 2]

scout n (pl -s) person sent out to reconnoitre ▶ v (-s, -ing, -ed) act as a scout

scouted v ▷ scout

scouting v ▷ scout

scouts n, v ▷ scout

scowl v (-s, -ing, -ed) ▶ n (pl -s) (have) an angry or sullen expression

scowled v ▷ scowl

scowling v ▷ scowl

scowls v, n ▷ scowl

scrabble v (-les, -ling, -led) scrape at with the hands, feet, or claws

scrabbled v ▷ scrabble

scrabbles v ▷ scrabble

scrabbling v ▷ scrabble

scrag n (pl -s) thin end of a neck of mutton

scraggier adj ▷ scraggy

scraggiest adj ▷ scraggy

scraggy adj (-gier, -giest) thin, bony

scrags n ▷ scrag

scram v (-s, -mming, -mmed) (Informal) go away quickly

scramble v (-les, -ling, -led) climb or crawl hastily or awkwardly ▶ n (pl -les) scrambling

scrambled v ▷ scramble

scrambler n (pl -s) electronic device that makes transmitted speech unintelligible

scramblers n ▷ scrambler

scrambles v, n ▷ scramble

scrambling v ▷ scramble

scrammed v ▷ scram

scramming v ▷ scram

scrams v ▷ scram

scrap[1] n (pl -s) small piece ▶ v (-s, -pping, -pped) discard as useless

scrap[2] n (pl -s) ▶ v (-s, -pping, -pped) (Informal) fight or quarrel

scrapbook n (pl -s) book with blank pages in which newspaper cuttings or pictures are stuck

scrapbooks n ▷ scrapbook

scrape v (-pes, -ping, -ped) rub with something rough or sharp ▶ n (pl -s) act or sound of scraping > **scraper** n (pl -s)

scraped v ▷ scrape

scraper n ▷ scrape

scrapers n ▷ scrape

scrapes v, n ▷ scrape

scraping v ▷ scrape

scrapped v ▷ scrap[1, 2]

scrappier adj ▷ scrappy

scrappiest adj ▷ scrappy

scrapping v ▷ scrap[1, 2]

scrappy adj (-pier, -piest) fragmentary, disjointed

scraps v ▷ scrap[1, 2] ▶ n ▷ scrap[1, 2] ▶ pl n leftover food

scratch v (-es, -ing, -ed) mark or cut with claws, nails, or anything rough or sharp ▶ n (pl -es) wound, mark, or sound made by scratching ▶ adj put together at short notice > **scratchy** adj (-chier, -chiest)

scratchcard n (pl -s) ticket that reveals whether or not the holder has won a prize when the surface is removed by scratching

scratchcards n ▷ scratchcard

scratched v ▷ scratch

scratches v, n ▷ scratch

scratchier adj ▷ scratch

scratchiest adj ▷ scratch

scratching v ▷ scratch

scratchy adj ▷ scratch

scrawl v (-s, -ing, -ed) write carelessly or hastily ▶ n (pl -s) scribbled writing

scrawled v ▷ scrawl

scrawling v ▷ scrawl

scrawls v, n ▷ scrawl

scrawnier adj ▷ scrawny

scrawniest adj ▷ scrawny

scrawny adj (-nier, -niest) thin and bony

scream v (-s, -ing, -ed) utter a piercing cry, esp. of fear or pain ▶ n (pl -s) shrill piercing cry

screamed v ▷ scream

screaming v ▷ scream

screams v, n ▷ scream

scree n (pl -s) slope of loose shifting stones

screech v (-es, -ing, -ed) ▶ n (pl -es) (utter) a shrill cry

screeched v ▷ screech

screeches v, n ▷ screech

screeching v ▷ screech

screed n (pl -s) long tedious piece of writing

screeds n ▷ screed

screen n (pl -s) surface of a television set, VDU, etc., on which an image is formed ▶ v (-s, -ing, -ed) shelter or conceal with or as if with a screen

screened v ▷ screen

screening v ▷ screen

screens n, v ▷ screen

screes n ▷ scree

screw n (pl -s) metal pin with a spiral ridge along its length, twisted into materials to fasten them together ▶ v (-s, -ing, -ed) turn (a screw)

screwdriver n (pl -s) tool for turning screws

screwdrivers n ▷ screwdriver

screwed v ▷ screw

screwier adj ▷ screwy

screwiest *adj* ▷ screwy

screwing *v* ▷ screw

screws *n, v* ▷ screw

screwy *adj* (**-wier, -wiest**) (*Informal*) crazy or eccentric

scribble *v* (**-les, -ling, -led**) write hastily or illegibly ▶ *n* (*pl* **-s**) something scribbled

scribbled *v* ▷ scribble

scribbles *v, n* ▷ scribble

scribbling *v* ▷ scribble

scribe *n* (*pl* **-s**) person who copied manuscripts before the invention of printing

scribes *n* ▷ scribe

scrimmage *n* (*pl* **-s**) rough or disorderly struggle

scrimmages *n* ▷ scrimmage

scrimp *v* (**-s, -ing, -ed**) be very economical

scrimped *v* ▷ scrimp

scrimping *v* ▷ scrimp

scrimps *v* ▷ scrimp

scrip *n* (*pl* **-s**) certificate representing a claim to stocks or shares

scrips *n* ▷ scrip

script *n* (*pl* **-s**) text of a film, play, or TV programme

scripts *n* ▷ script

scriptural *adj* ▷ scripture

scripture *n* (*pl* **-s**) sacred writings of a religion > **scriptural** *adj*

scriptures *n* ▷ scripture

scrofula *n* (*pl* **-s**) tuberculosis of the lymphatic glands > **scrofulous** *adj*

scrofulas *n* ▷ scrofula

scrofulous *adj* ▷ scrofula

scroggin *n* (*pl* **-s**) (NZ) mixture of nuts and dried fruits

scroggins *n* ▷ scroggin

scroll *n* (*pl* **-s**) roll of parchment or paper ▶ *v* (**-s, -ing, -ed**) move (text) up or down on a VDU screen

scrolled *v* ▷ scroll

scrolling *v* ▷ scroll

scrolls *n, v* ▷ scroll

scrota *n* ▷ scrotum

scrotum *n* (*pl* **-ta, -tums**) pouch of skin containing the testicles

scrotums *n* ▷ scrotum

scrounge *v* (**-ges, -ging, -ged**) (*Informal*) get by cadging or begging > **scrounger** *n* (*pl* **-s**)

scrounged *v* ▷ scrounge

scrounger *n* ▷ scrounge

scroungers *n* ▷ scrounge

scrounges *v* ▷ scrounge

scrounging *v* ▷ scrounge

scrub[1] *v* (**-s, -bbing, -bbed**) clean by rubbing, often with a hard brush and water ▶ *n* (*pl* **-s**) scrubbing

scrub[2] *n* (*pl* **-s**) stunted trees

scrubbed *v* ▷ scrub[1]

scrubbier *adj* ▷ scrubby

scrubbiest *adj* ▷ scrubby

scrubbing *v* ▷ scrub[1]

scrubby *adj* (**-bbier, -bbiest**) covered with scrub

scrubs *v* ▷ scrub[1] ▶ *n* ▷ scrub[1, 2]

scruff[1] *n* (*pl* **-s**) nape (of the neck)

scruff[2] *n* (*pl* **-s**) (*Informal*) untidy person

scruffier *adj* ▷ scruffy

scruffiest *adj* ▷ scruffy

scruffs *n* ▷ scruff[1, 2]

scruffy *adj* (**-ffier, -ffiest**) unkempt or shabby

scrum, scrummage *n* (*pl* **-s**) (RUGBY) restarting of play in which opposing packs of forwards push against each other to gain possession of the ball

scrummage *n* ▷ scrum

scrummages *n* ▷ scrum

scrumptious *adj* (*Informal*) delicious

scrums *n* ▷ scrum

scrunch *v* (**-es, -ing, -ed**) crumple or crunch or be crumpled or crunched ▶ *n* (*pl* **-es**) act or sound of scrunching

scrunched *v* ▷ scrunch

scrunches *v, n* ▷ scrunch

scrunching *v* ▷ scrunch

scruple *n* (*pl* **-s**) doubt produced by one's conscience or morals ▶ *v* (**-les, -ling, -led**) have doubts on moral grounds

scrupled *v* ▷ scruple

scruples *n, v* ▷ scruple

scrupling *v* ▷ scruple

scrupulous *adj* very conscientious > **scrupulously** *adv*

scrupulously *adv* ▷ scrupulous

scrutinies *n* ▷ scrutiny

scrutinize *v* (**-zes, -zing, -zed**) examine closely

scrutinized *v* ▷ scrutinize

scrutinizes *v* ▷ scrutinize

scrutinizing *v* ▷ scrutinize

scrutiny *n* (*pl* **-nies**) close examination

scud *v* (**-s, -dding, -dded**) move along swiftly

scudded *v* ▷ scud

scudding *v* ▷ scud

scuds *v* ▷ scud

scuff *v* (**-s, -ing, -ed**) drag (the feet) while walking ▶ *n* (*pl* **-s**) mark caused by scuffing

scuffed *v* ▷ scuff

scuffing *v* ▷ scuff

scuffle *v* (**-les, -ling, -led**) fight in a disorderly manner ▶ *n* (*pl* **-s**) disorderly struggle

scuffled v ▷ scuffle
scuffles v, n ▷ scuffle
scuffling v ▷ scuffle
scuffs v, n ▷ scuff
scull n (pl -s) small oar ▸ v (-s, -ing, -ed) row (a boat) using sculls
sculled v ▷ scull
sculleries n ▷ scullery
scullery n (pl -ries) small room where washing-up and other kitchen work is done
sculling v ▷ scull
sculls n, v ▷ scull
sculptor n ▷ sculpture
sculptors n ▷ sculpture
sculptress n ▷ sculpture
sculptresses n ▷ sculpture
sculptural adj ▷ sculpture
sculpture n (pl -s) art of making figures or designs in wood, stone, etc. ▸ v (-res, -ring, -red) (also **sculpt**) represent in sculpture > **sculptor, sculptress** n (pl -s, -es) > **sculptural** adj
sculptured v ▷ sculpture
sculptures n, v ▷ sculpture
sculpturing v ▷ sculpture
scum n (pl -s) impure or waste matter on the surface of a liquid > **scummy** adj (-mmier, -mmiest)
scummier adj ▷ scum
scummiest adj ▷ scum
scummy adj ▷ scum
scums n ▷ scum
scungier adj ▷ scungy
scungiest adj ▷ scungy
scungy adj (-ier, -iest) (AUST & NZ) (Informal) sordid or dirty
scupper v (-s, -ing, -ed) (Informal) defeat or ruin
scuppered v ▷ scupper
scuppering v ▷ scupper
scuppers v ▷ scupper
scurf n (pl -s) flaky skin on the scalp
scurfs n ▷ scurf
scurried v ▷ scurry
scurries v, n ▷ scurry
scurrilous adj untrue and defamatory
scurry v (-ries, -rying, -ried) move hastily ▸ n (pl -ries) act or sound of scurrying
scurrying v ▷ scurry
scurvies n ▷ scurvy
scurvy n (pl -vies) disease caused by lack of vitamin C
scut n (pl -s) short tail of the hare, rabbit, or deer
scuts n ▷ scut
scuttle¹ n (pl -s) fireside container for coal

scuttle² v (-les, -ling, -led) run with short quick steps ▸ n (pl -s) hurried run
scuttle³ v (-les, -ling, -ed) make a hole in (a ship) to sink it
scuttled v ▷ scuttle²,³
scuttles n ▷ scuttle¹; v ▷ scuttle²,³
scuttling v ▷ scuttle²,³
scythe n (pl -s) long-handled tool with a curved blade for cutting grass ▸ v (-thes, -thing, -thed) cut with a scythe
scythed v ▷ scythe
scythes n, v ▷ scythe
scything v ▷ scythe
sea n (pl -s) mass of salt water covering three quarters of the earth's surface
seaboard n (pl -s) coast
seaboards n ▷ seaboard
seafaring adj working or travelling by sea
seafood n (pl -s) edible saltwater fish or shellfish
seafoods n ▷ seafood
seagull n (pl -s) gull
seagulls n ▷ seagull
seal¹ n (pl -s) piece of wax, lead, etc. with a special design impressed upon it, attached to a letter or document as a mark of authentication ▸ v (-s, -ing, -ed) close with or as if with a seal
seal² n (pl -s) amphibious mammal with flippers as limbs > **sealskin** n (pl -s)
sealant n (pl -s) any substance used for sealing
sealants n ▷ sealant
sealed v ▷ seal¹
sealing v ▷ seal¹
seals n ▷ seal¹,²; v ▷ seal¹
sealskin n ▷ seal²
sealskins n ▷ seal²
seam n (pl -s) line where two edges are joined, as by stitching ▸ v (-s, -ing, -ed) mark with furrows or wrinkles > **seamless** adj
seaman n (pl -men) sailor
seamed v ▷ seam
seamen n ▷ seaman
seamier adj ▷ seamy
seamiest adj ▷ seamy
seaming v ▷ seam
seamless adj ▷ seam
seams n, v ▷ seam
seamstress n (pl -es) woman who sews, esp. professionally
seamstresses n ▷ seamstress
seamy adj (-mier, -miest) sordid
seance [say-anss] n (pl -s) meeting at which spiritualists attempt to communicate with the dead

seances n ▷ seance
seaplane n (pl -s) aircraft designed to take off from and land on water
  seaplanes n ▷ seaplane
sear v (-s, -ing, -ed) scorch, burn the surface of
search v (-es, -ing, -ed) examine closely in order to find something ▶ n (pl -es) searching
  searched v ▷ search
  searches v, n ▷ search
searching adj keen or thorough ▶ v ▷ search
searchlight n (pl -s) powerful light with a beam that can be shone in any direction
  searchlights n ▷ searchlight
  seared v ▷ sear
searing adj (of pain) very sharp ▶ v ▷ sear
  sears v ▷ sear
  seas n ▷ sea
seasick adj suffering from nausea caused by the motion of a ship ▶ **seasickness** n (pl -es)
  seasickness n ▷ seasick
  seasicknesses n ▷ seasick
seaside n (pl -s) area, esp. a holiday resort, on the coast
  seasides n ▷ seaside
season n (pl -s) one of four divisions of the year, each of which has characteristic weather conditions ▶ v (-s, -ing, -ed) flavour with salt, herbs, etc.
seasonable adj appropriate for the season
seasonal adj depending on or varying with the seasons
seasoned adj experienced ▶ v ▷ season
seasoning v ▷ season ▶ n (pl -s) salt, herbs, etc. added to food to enhance flavour
  seasonings n ▷ seasoning
  seasons n, v ▷ season
seat n (pl -s) thing designed or used for sitting on ▶ v (-s, -ing, -ed) cause to sit
  seated v ▷ seat
  seating v ▷ seat
  seats n, v ▷ seat
seaweed n (pl -s) plant growing in the sea
  seaweeds n ▷ seaweed
seaworthy adj (of a ship) in fit condition for a sea voyage
sebaceous adj of, like, or secreting fat or oil
secateurs pl n small pruning shears
secede v (-des, -ding, -ded) withdraw formally from a political alliance or federation
  > **secession** n (pl -s)
  seceded v ▷ secede
  secedes v ▷ secede
  seceding v ▷ secede
  secession n ▷ secede
  secessions n ▷ secede

seclude v (-des, -ding, -ded) keep (a person) from contact with others
secluded adj private, sheltered ▶ v ▷ seclude
  > **seclusion** n (pl -s)
  secludes v ▷ seclude
  secluding v ▷ seclude
  seclusion n ▷ secluded
  seclusions n ▷ secluded
second[1] adj coming directly after the first ▶ n (pl -s) person or thing coming second ▶ v (-s, -ing, -ed) express formal support for (a motion proposed in a meeting) > **secondly** adv
second[2] n (pl -s) sixtieth part of a minute of an angle or time
second[3] [si-kond] v (-s, -ing, -ed) transfer (a person) temporarily to another job
  > **secondment** n (pl -s)
secondary adj of less importance
  seconded v ▷ second[1, 3]
secondhand adj bought after use by another
  seconding v ▷ second[1, 3]
  secondly adv ▷ second[1]
  secondment n ▷ second[3]
  secondments n ▷ second[3]
seconds v ▷ second[1, 3] ▶ n ▷ second[1, 2] ▶ pl n inferior goods
  secrecies n ▷ secret
  secrecy n ▷ secret
secret adj kept from the knowledge of others ▶ n (pl -s) something kept secret > **secretly** adv
  > **secrecy** n (pl -cies)
secretarial adj ▷ secretary
secretariat n (pl -s) administrative office or staff of a legislative body
  secretariats n ▷ secretariat
  secretaries n ▷ secretary
secretary n (pl -ries) person who deals with correspondence and general clerical work
  > **secretarial** adj
secrete[1] v (-tes, -ting, -ted) (of an organ, gland, etc.) produce and release (a substance)
  > **secretion** n (pl -s) > **secretory** [sek-reet-or-ee] adj
secrete[2] v (-tes, -ting, -ted) hide or conceal
  secreted v ▷ secrete[1, 2]
  secretes v ▷ secrete[1, 2]
  secreting v ▷ secrete[1, 2]
  secretion n ▷ secrete[1]
  secretions n ▷ secrete[1]
secretive adj inclined to keep things secret
  > **secretiveness** n (pl -es)
  secretiveness n ▷ secretive
  secretivenesses n ▷ secretive
  secretly adv ▷ secret

secretory adj ▷ secrete¹

secrets n ▷ secret

sect n (pl -s) subdivision of a religious or political group, esp. one with extreme beliefs

sectarian adj of a sect

section n (pl -s) part cut off ▶ v (-s, -ing, -ed) cut or divide into sections > **sectional** adj

sectional adj ▷ section

sectioned v ▷ section

sectioning v ▷ section

sections n, v ▷ section

sector n (pl -s) part or subdivision

sectors n ▷ sector

sects n ▷ sect

secular adj worldly, as opposed to sacred

secure adj (-r, -st) free from danger ▶ v (-res, -ring, -red) obtain > **securely** adv

secured v ▷ secure

securely adv ▷ secure

securer adj ▷ secure

secures v ▷ secure

securest adj ▷ secure

securing v ▷ secure

securities n ▷ security

security n (pl -ties) precautions against theft, espionage, or other danger

sedan n (pl -s) (US, AUST & NZ) two-door or four-door car with the body closed off from the rear luggage area

sedans n ▷ sedan

sedate¹ adj (-r, -st) calm and dignified > **sedately** adv

sedate² v (-tes, -ting, -ted) give a sedative drug to > **sedation** n (pl -s)

sedated v ▷ sedate²

sedately adv ▷ sedate¹

sedater adj ▷ sedate¹

sedates v ▷ sedate²

sedatest adj ▷ sedate¹

sedating v ▷ sedate²

sedation n ▷ sedate²

sedations n ▷ sedate²

sedative adj having a soothing or calming effect ▶ n (pl -s) sedative drug

sedatives n ▷ sedative

sedentary adj done sitting down, involving little exercise

sedge n (pl -s) coarse grasslike plant growing on wet ground

sedges n ▷ sedge

sediment n (pl -s) matter which settles to the bottom of a liquid > **sedimentary** adj

sedimentary adj ▷ sediment

sediments n ▷ sediment

sedition n (pl -s) speech or action encouraging rebellion against the government > **seditious** adj

seditions n ▷ sedition

seditious adj ▷ sedition

seduce v (-ces, -cing, -ced) persuade into sexual intercourse > **seducer, seductress** n (pl -s, -es) > **seduction** n (pl -s) > **seductive** adj

seduced v ▷ seduce

seducer n ▷ seduce

seducers n ▷ seduce

seduces v ▷ seduce

seducing v ▷ seduce

seduction n ▷ seduce

seductions n ▷ seduce

seductive adj ▷ seduce

seductress n ▷ seduce

seductresses n ▷ seduce

sedulous adj diligent or persevering > **sedulously** adv

sedulously adv ▷ sedulous

see¹ v (-s, -ing, saw, seen) perceive with the eyes or mind

see² n (pl -s) diocese of a bishop

seed n (pl -s) mature fertilized grain of a plant ▶ v (-s, -ing, -ed) sow with seed

seeded v ▷ seed

seedier adj ▷ seedy

seediest adj ▷ seedy

seeding v ▷ seed

seedling n (pl -s) young plant raised from a seed

seedlings n ▷ seedling

seeds n, v ▷ seed

seedy adj (-dier, -diest) shabby

seeing conj in view of the fact that ▶ v ▷ see¹

seek v (-s, -ing, sought) try to find or obtain

seeking v ▷ seek

seeks v ▷ seek

seem v (-s, -ing, -ed) appear to be

seemed v ▷ seem

seeming adj apparent but not real > **seemingly** adv, v ▷ seem

seemingly adv ▷ seeming

seemlier adj ▷ seemly

seemliest adj ▷ seemly

seemly adj (-lier, -liest) proper or fitting

seems v ▷ seem

seen v ▷ see¹

seep v (-s, -ing, -ed) trickle through slowly, ooze > **seepage** n (pl -s)

seepage n ▷ seep

seepages n ▷ seep

seeped v ▷ seep

seeping v ▷ seep

seeps v ▷ seep

seer *n* (*pl* -s) prophet
  seers *n* ▷ seer
seersucker *n* (*pl* -s) light cotton fabric with a slightly crinkled surface
  seersuckers *n* ▷ seersucker
  sees *n* ▷ see² ▶ *v* ▷ see¹
seesaw *n* (*pl* -s) plank balanced in the middle so that two people seated on either end ride up and down alternately ▶ *v* (-s, -ing, -ed) move up and down
  seesawed *v* ▷ seesaw
  seesawing *v* ▷ seesaw
  seesaws *n*, *v* ▷ seesaw
seethe *v* (-thes, -thing, -thed) be very agitated
  seethed *v* ▷ seethe
  seethes *v* ▷ seethe
  seething *v* ▷ seethe
segment *n* (*pl* -s) one of several sections into which something may be divided ▶ *v* (-s, -ing, -ed) divide into segments > **segmentation** *n* (*pl* -s)
  segmentation *n* ▷ segment
  segmentations *n* ▷ segment
  segmented *v* ▷ segment
  segmenting *v* ▷ segment
  segments *n*, *v* ▷ segment
segregate *v* (-tes, -ting, -ted) set apart > **segregation** *n* (*pl* -s)
  segregated *v* ▷ segregate
  segregates *v* ▷ segregate
  segregating *v* ▷ segregate
  segregation *n* ▷ segregate
  segregations *n* ▷ segregate
seine [sane] *n* (*pl* -s) large fishing net that hangs vertically from floats
  seines *n* ▷ seine
seismic *adj* relating to earthquakes
seismograph, seismometer *n* (*pl* -s) instrument that records the strength of earthquakes
  seismographs *n* ▷ seismograph
  seismological *adj* ▷ seismology
  seismologies *n* ▷ seismology
  seismologist *n* ▷ seismology
  seismologists *n* ▷ seismology
seismology *n* (*pl* -gies) study of earthquakes > **seismological** *adj* > **seismologist** *n* (*pl* -s)
  seismometer *n* ▷ seismograph
  seismometers *n* ▷ seismograph
seize *v* (-zes, -zing, -zed) take hold of forcibly or quickly (*usu. foll. by* **up**)
  seized *v* ▷ seize
  seizes *v* ▷ seize
  seizing *v* ▷ seize
seizure *n* (*pl* -s) sudden violent attack of an illness
  seizures *n* ▷ seizure
seldom *adv* not often, rarely
select *v* (-s, -ing, -ed) pick out or choose ▶ *adj* chosen in preference to others > **selector** *n* (*pl* -s)
  selected *v* ▷ select
  selecting *v* ▷ select
selection *n* (*pl* -s) selecting
  selections *n* ▷ selection
selective *adj* chosen or choosing carefully > **selectively** *adv* > **selectivity** *n* (*pl* -ties)
  selectively *adv* ▷ selective
  selectivities *n* ▷ selective
  selectivity *n* ▷ selective
  selector *n* ▷ select
  selectors *n* ▷ select
  selects *v* ▷ select
selenium *n* (*pl* -s) (CHEM) nonmetallic element with photoelectric properties
  seleniums *n* ▷ selenium
self *n* (*pl* selves) distinct individuality or identity of a person or thing
selfish *adj* caring too much about oneself and not enough about others > **selfishly** *adv* > **selfishness** *n* (*pl* -es)
  selfishly *adv* ▷ selfish
  selfishness *n* ▷ selfish
  selfishnesses *n* ▷ selfish
selfless *adj* unselfish
selfsame *adj* the very same
sell *v* (-s, -ing, sold) exchange (something) for money (*foll. by* **for**) ▶ *n* (*pl* -s) manner of selling > **seller** *n* (*pl* -s)
  seller *n* ▷ sell
  sellers *n* ▷ sell
  selling *v* ▷ sell
sellotape *n* (*pl* -s)® type of adhesive tape ▶ *v* (-pes, -ping, -ped) stick with sellotape
  sellotaped *v* ▷ sellotape
  sellotapes *n*, *v* ▷ sellotape
  sellotaping *v* ▷ sellotape
sellout *n* (*pl* -s) performance of a show etc. for which all the tickets are sold
  sellouts *n* ▷ sellout
  sells *v*, *n* ▷ sell
selvage, selvedge *n* (*pl* -s) edge of cloth, woven so as to prevent unravelling
  selvages *n* ▷ selvage
  selvedge *n* ▷ selvage
  selvedges *n* ▷ selvage
  selves *n* ▷ self
semantic *adj* relating to the meaning of words
semantics *n* study of linguistic meaning
semaphore *n* (*pl* -s) system of signalling by

holding two flags in different positions to represent letters of the alphabet

semaphores n ▷ semaphore

semblance n (pl -s) outward or superficial appearance

semblances n ▷ semblance

semen n (pl -s) sperm-carrying fluid produced by male animals

semens n ▷ semen

semester n (pl -s) either of two divisions of the academic year

semesters n ▷ semester

semi n (pl -s) (BRIT & S AFR) (Informal) semidetached house

semibreve n (pl -s) musical note four beats long

semibreves n ▷ semibreve

semicolon n (pl -s) the punctuation mark (;)

semicolons n ▷ semicolon

semiconductor n (pl -s) substance with an electrical conductivity that increases with temperature

semiconductors n ▷ semiconductor

semidetached adj (of a house) joined to another on one side

semifinal n (pl -s) match or round before the final ▷ **semifinalist** n (pl -s)

semifinalist n ▷ semifinal

semifinalists n ▷ semifinal

semifinals n ▷ semifinal

seminal adj original and influential

seminar n (pl -s) meeting of a group of students for discussion

seminaries n ▷ seminary

seminars n ▷ seminar

seminary n (pl -ries) college for priests

semiprecious adj (of gemstones) having less value than precious stones

semiquaver n (pl -s) musical note half the length of a quaver

semiquavers n ▷ semiquaver

semis n ▷ semi

semitone n (pl -s) smallest interval between two notes in Western music

semitones n ▷ semitone

semitrailer n (pl -s) (AUST) large truck in two separate sections joined by a pivoted bar

semitrailers n ▷ semitrailer

semolina n (pl -s) hard grains of wheat left after the milling of flour, used to make puddings and pasta

semolinas n ▷ semolina

senate n (pl -s) upper house of some parliaments; governing body of some universities

senates n ▷ senate

senator n (pl -s) member of a senate
> **senatorial** adj

senatorial adj ▷ senator

senators n ▷ senator

send v (-s, -ing, sent) cause (a person or thing) to go to or be taken or transmitted to a place

sending v ▷ send

sendoff n (pl -s) demonstration of good wishes at a person's departure

sendoffs n ▷ sendoff

sends v ▷ send

sendup n (pl -s) (Informal) imitation

sendups n ▷ sendup

senile adj mentally or physically weak because of old age ▷ **senility** n (pl -ties)

senilities n ▷ senile

senility n ▷ senile

senior adj superior in rank or standing ▶ n (pl -s) senior person > **seniority** n (pl -ties)

seniorities n ▷ senior

seniority n ▷ senior

seniors n ▷ senior

senna n (pl -s) tropical plant

sennas n ▷ senna

señor [sen-**nyor**] n (pl -ores) Spanish term of address equivalent to sir or Mr

señora [sen-**nyor**-a] n (pl -s) Spanish term of address equivalent to madam or Mrs

señoras n ▷ señora

señorita [sen-nyor-**ee**-ta] n (pl -s) Spanish term of address equivalent to madam or Miss

señoritas n ▷ señorita

señors n ▷ señor

sensation n (pl -s) ability to feel things physically

sensational adj causing intense shock, anger, or excitement

sensationalism n (pl -s) deliberate use of sensational language or subject matter
> **sensationalist** adj, n (pl -s)

sensationalisms n ▷ sensationalism

sensationalist adj, n ▷ sensationalism

sensationalists n ▷ sensationalism

sensations n ▷ sensation

sense n (pl -s) any of the faculties of perception or feeling (sight, hearing, touch, taste, or smell ▶ v (-ses, -sing, -sed) perceive
> **senseless** adj

sensed v ▷ sense

senseless adj ▷ sense

senses n, v ▷ sense

sensibilities n ▷ sensibility

sensibility n (pl -ties) ability to experience deep feelings

sensible *adj* (**-r, -st**) having or showing good sense > **sensibly** *adv*
  sensibler *adj* ▷ sensible
  sensiblest *adj* ▷ sensible
  sensibly *adv* ▷ sensible
  sensing *v* ▷ sense
sensitive *adj* easily hurt or offended
  > **sensitively** *adv* > **sensitivity** *n* (*pl* -**s**)
  sensitively *adv* ▷ sensitive
  sensitivities *n* ▷ sensitive
  sensitivity *n* ▷ sensitive
sensitize *v* (**-zes, -zing, -zed**) make sensitive
  sensitized *v* ▷ sensitize
  sensitizes *v* ▷ sensitize
  sensitizing *v* ▷ sensitize
sensor *n* (*pl* -**s**) device that detects or measures the presence of something, such as radiation
  sensors *n* ▷ sensor
sensory *adj* of the senses or sensation
sensual *adj* giving pleasure to the body and senses rather than the mind > **sensually** *adv*
  > **sensuality** *n* (*pl* -**ties**) > **sensualist** *n* (*pl* -**s**)
  sensualist *n* ▷ sensual
  sensualists *n* ▷ sensual
  sensualities *n* ▷ sensual
  sensuality *n* ▷ sensual
  sensually *adv* ▷ sensual
sensuous *adj* pleasing to the senses
  > **sensuously** *adv*
  sensuously *adv* ▷ sensuous
  sent *v* ▷ send
sentence *n* (*pl* -**s**) sequence of words capable of standing alone as a statement, question, or command ▶ *v* (**-ces, -cing, -ced**) pass sentence on (a convicted person)
  sentenced *v* ▷ sentence
  sentences *n, v* ▷ sentence
  sentencing *n, v* ▷ sentence
sententious *adj* trying to sound wise
  sentience *n* ▷ sentient
  sentiences *n* ▷ sentient
sentient [**sen**-tee-ent] *adj* capable of feeling
  > **sentience** *n* (*pl* -**s**)
sentiment *n* (*pl* -**s**) thought, opinion, or attitude
sentimental *adj* excessively romantic or nostalgic > **sentimentalism** *n* (*pl* -**s**)
  > **sentimentality** *n* (*pl* -**ties**)
  sentimentalism *n* ▷ sentimental
  sentimentalisms *n* ▷ sentimental
  sentimentalities *n* ▷ sentimentality
  sentimentality *n* ▷ sentimental
sentimentalize *v* (**-zes, -zing, -zed**) make sentimental
  sentimentalized *v* ▷ sentimentalize

  sentimentalizes *v* ▷ sentimentalize
  sentiments *n* ▷ sentiment
sentinel *n* (*pl* -**s**) sentry
  sentinels *n* ▷ sentinel
  sentries *n* ▷ sentry
sentry *n* (*pl* -**tries**) soldier on watch
sepal *n* (*pl* -**s**) leaflike division of the calyx of a flower
  sepals *n* ▷ sepal
  separable *adj* ▷ separate
separate *v* (**-tes, -ting, -ted**) act as a barrier between ▶ *adj* not the same, different
  > **separable** *adj* > **separately** *adv*
  separated *v* ▷ separate
  separately *adv* ▷ separate
  separates *v* ▷ separate
  separating *v* ▷ separate
separation *n* (*pl* -**s**) separating or being separated
  separations *n* ▷ separation
  separatism *n* ▷ separatist
  separatisms *n* ▷ separatist
separatist *n* (*pl* -**s**) person who advocates the separation of a group from an organization or country > **separatism** *n* (*pl* -**s**)
  separatists *n* ▷ separatist
sepia *adj, n* (*pl* -**s**) reddish-brown (pigment)
  sepias *n* ▷ sepia
  sepses *n* ▷ sepsis
sepsis *n* (*pl* -**ses**) poisoning caused by pus-forming bacteria
septet *n* (*pl* -**s**) group of seven performers
  septets *n* ▷ septet
septic *adj* (of a wound) infected
septicaemia [sep-tis-**see**-mee-a] *n* (*pl* -**s**) infection of the blood
  septicaemias *n* ▷ septicaemia
septuagenarian *n* (*pl* -**s**) person aged between seventy and seventy-nine
  septuagenarians *n* ▷ septuagenarian
sepulchral [sip-**pulk**-ral] *adj* gloomy
sepulchre [**sep**-pull-ker] *n* (*pl* -**s**) tomb or burial vault
  sepulchres *n* ▷ sepulchre
sequel *n* (*pl* -**s**) novel, play, or film that continues the story of an earlier one
  sequels *n* ▷ sequel
sequence *n* (*pl* -**s**) arrangement of two or more things in successive order > **sequential** *adj*
  sequences *n* ▷ sequence
  sequential *adj* ▷ sequence
sequester *v* (**-s, -ing, -ed**) seclude
  sequestered *v* ▷ sequester
  sequestering *v* ▷ sequester
  sequesters *v* ▷ sequester

sequestrate v (-tes, -ting, -ted) confiscate (property) until its owner's debts are paid or a court order is complied with > **sequestration** n (pl -s)

sequestrated v ▷ sequestrate

sequestrates v ▷ sequestrate

sequestrating v ▷ sequestrate

sequestration n ▷ sequestrate

sequestrations n ▷ sequestrate

sequin n (pl -s) small ornamental metal disc on a garment > **sequined** adj

sequined adj ▷ sequin

sequins n ▷ sequin

sequoia n (pl -s) giant Californian coniferous tree

sequoias n ▷ sequoia

seraglio [sir-ah-lee-oh] n (pl -s) harem of a Muslim palace

seraglios n ▷ seraglio

seraph n (pl -s, -aphim) member of the highest order of angels > **seraphic** adj

seraphic adj ▷ seraph

seraphim n ▷ seraph

seraphs n ▷ seraph

serenade n (pl -s) music played or sung to a woman by a lover ▶ v (-des, -ding, -ded) sing or play a serenade to (someone)

serenaded v ▷ serenade

serenades n, v ▷ serenade

serenading v ▷ serenade

serendipities n ▷ serendipity

serendipity n (pl -ties) gift of making fortunate discoveries by accident

serene adj (-r, -st) calm, peaceful > **serenely** adv > **serenity** n (pl -ties)

serenely adv ▷ serene

serener adj ▷ serene

serenest adj ▷ serene

serenities n ▷ serene

serenity n ▷ serene

serf n (pl -s) medieval farm labourer who could not leave the land he worked on > **serfdom** n (pl -s)

serfdom n ▷ serf

serfdoms n ▷ serf

serfs n ▷ serf

serge n (pl -s) strong woollen fabric

sergeant n (pl -s) noncommissioned officer in the army

sergeants n ▷ sergeant

serges n ▷ serge

serial n (pl -s) story or play produced in successive instalments ▶ adj of or forming a series

serialize v (-zes, -zing, -zed) publish or present

as a serial

serialized v ▷ serialize

serializes v ▷ serialize

serializing v ▷ serialize

serials n ▷ serial

series n (pl series) group or succession of related things, usu. arranged in order

serious adj giving cause for concern > **seriously** adv > **seriousness** n (pl -es)

seriously adv ▷ serious

seriousness n ▷ serious

seriousnesses n ▷ serious

sermon n (pl -s) speech on a religious or moral subject by a clergyman in a church service

sermonize v (-zes, -zing, -zed) make a long moralizing speech

sermonized v ▷ sermonize

sermonizes v ▷ sermonize

sermonizing v ▷ sermonize

sermons n ▷ sermon

serpent n (pl -s) (Lit) snake

serpentine adj twisting like a snake

serpents n ▷ serpent

serrated adj having a notched or sawlike edge

serried adj in close formation

serum [seer-um] n (pl -s) watery fluid left after blood has clotted

serums n ▷ serum

servant n (pl -s) person employed to do household work for another

servants n ▷ servant

serve v (-s, -ing, -ed) work for (a person, community, or cause) ▶ n (pl -s) (TENNIS ETC.) act of serving the ball

served v ▷ serve

server n (pl -s) player who serves in racket games

servers n ▷ server

serves n, v ▷ serve

service n (pl -s) system that provides something needed by the public ▶ v (-ces, -cing, -ced) overhaul (a machine or vehicle)

serviceable adj useful or helpful

serviced v ▷ service

serviceman, servicewoman n (pl -men, -women) member of the armed forces

servicemen n ▷ serviceman

services n, v ▷ service ▶ pl n armed forces

servicewoman n ▷ serviceman

servicewomen n ▷ serviceman

servicing v ▷ service

serviette n (pl -s) table napkin

serviettes n ▷ serviette

servile adj too eager to obey people, fawning > **servility** n (pl -s)

servilities *n* ▷ servile
servility *n* ▷ servile
serving *v* ▷ serve
servitude *n* (*pl* -s) bondage or slavery
servitudes *n* ▷ servitude
sesame [sess-am-ee] *n* (*pl* -s) plant cultivated for its seeds and oil, which are used in cooking
sesames *n* ▷ sesame
session *n* (*pl* -s) period spent in an activity
sessions *n* ▷ session
set¹ *v* (-s, -tting, set) put in a specified position or state ▶ *n* (*pl* -s) scenery used in a play or film ▶ *adj* fixed or established beforehand
set² *n* (*pl* -s) number of things or people grouped or belonging together
setback *n* (*pl* -s) anything that delays progress
setbacks *n* ▷ setback
sets *v* ▷ set¹ ▶ *n* ▷ set²
sett, set *n* (*p* -s) badger's burrow
settee *n* (*pl* -s) couch
settees *n* ▷ settee
setter *n* (*pl* -s) long-haired gun dog
setters *n* ▷ setter
setting *n* (*pl* -s) background or surroundings ▶ *v* ▷ set
settings *n* ▷ setting
settle¹ *v* (-les, -ling, -led) arrange or put in order
settle² *n* (*pl* -s) long wooden bench with high back and arms
settled *v* ▷ settle¹
settlement *n* (*pl* -s) act of settling
settlements *n* ▷ settlement
settler *n* (*pl* -s) colonist
settlers *n* ▷ settler
settles *v* ▷ settle¹ ▶ *n* ▷ settle²
settling *v* ▷ settle¹
setts *n* ▷ sett
setup *n* (*pl* -s) way in which anything is organized or arranged
setups *n* ▷ setup
seven *adj*, *n* (*pl* -s) one more than six
sevens *n* ▷ seven
seventeen *adj*, *n* (*pl* -s) ten and seven ▷ **seventeenth** *adj*, *n* (*pl* -s)
seventeens *n* ▷ seventeen
seventeenth *n* ▷ seventeen
seventeenths *n* ▷ seventeen
seventh *adj*, *n* (*pl* -s) (of) number seven in a series
sevenths *n* ▷ seventh
seventies *n* ▷ seventy
seventieth *n* ▷ seventy
seventieths *n* ▷ seventy

seventy *adj*, *n* (*pl* -ties) ten times seven ▷ **seventieth** *adj*, *n* (*pl* -s)
sever *v* (-s, -ing, -ed) cut through or off ▷ **severance** *n* (*pl* -s)
several *adj* some, a few
severally *adv* separately
severance *n* ▷ sever
severances *n* ▷ sever
severe *adj* (-r, -st) strict or harsh ▷ **severely** *adv* ▷ **severity** *n* (*pl* -ties)
severed *v* ▷ sever
severely *adv* ▷ severe
severer *adj* ▷ severe
severest *adj* ▷ severe
severing *v* ▷ sever
severities *n* ▷ severe
severity *n* ▷ severe
severs *v* ▷ sever
sew *v* (-s, -ing, -ed, sewn *or* -ed) join with thread repeatedly passed through with a needle
sewage *n* (*pl* -s) waste matter or excrement carried away in sewers
sewages *n* ▷ sewage
sewed *v* ▷ sew
sewer *n* (*pl* -s) drain to remove waste water and sewage ▷ **sewerage** *n* (*pl* -s) system of sewers
sewerage *n* ▷ sewer
sewerages *n* ▷ sewer
sewers *n* ▷ sewer
sewing *v* ▷ sew
sewn *v* ▷ sew
sews *v* ▷ sew
sex *n* (*pl* -es) state of being male or female ▶ *v* (-es, -ing, -ed) find out the sex of ▷ **sexual** *adj* ▷ **sexually** *adv* ▷ **sexuality** *n* (*pl* -ties)
sexagenarian *n* (*pl* -s) person aged between sixty and sixty-nine
sexagenarians *n* ▷ sexagenarian
sexed *v* ▷ sex
sexes *n*, *v* ▷ sex
sexier *adj* ▷ sexy
sexiest *adj* ▷ sexy
sexing *v* ▷ sex
sexism *n* (*pl* -s) discrimination on the basis of a person's sex ▷ **sexist** *adj*, *n* (*pl* -s)
sexisms *n* ▷ sexism
sexist *n* ▷ sexism
sexists *n* ▷ sexism
sextant *n* (*pl* -s) navigator's instrument for measuring angles, as between the sun and horizon, to calculate one's position
sextants *n* ▷ sextant
sextet *n* (*pl* -s) group of six performers

sextets n ▷ sextet
sexton n (pl -s) official in charge of a church and churchyard
sextons n ▷ sexton
sexual adj ▷ sex
sexualities n ▷ sex
sexuality n ▷ sex
sexually adv ▷ sex
sexy adj (-xier, -xiest) sexually exciting or attractive

> **sez** v. Sez is an short informal form of **says**. This word can be very useful when there isn't much space on the board, as it gives a good score. Sez scores 12 points.
>
> **sh** interj. Sh is a sound people make to request silence or quiet. This is one of two two-letter words beginning with S that do not contain a vowel. It's useful when you want to connect a word beginning with H to one ending in S or vice versa. Sh scores 5 points.

shabbier adj ▷ shabby
shabbiest adj ▷ shabby
shabbily adv ▷ shabby
shabbiness n ▷ shabby
shabbinesses n ▷ shabby
shabby adj (-bier, -biest) worn or dilapidated in appearance > **shabbily** adv > **shabbiness** n (pl -es)
shack n (pl -s) rough hut
shackle n (pl -s) one of a pair of metal rings joined by a chain, for securing a person's wrists or ankles ▶ v (-les, -ling, -led) fasten with shackles
shackled v ▷ shackle
shackles n, v ▷ shackle
shackling v ▷ shackle
shacks n ▷ shack
shad n (pl -s) herring-like fish
shade n (pl -s) relative darkness ▶ v (-des, -ding, -ded) screen from light ▷ **shady** adj (-dier, -diest) situated in or giving shade
shaded v ▷ shade
shades n, v ▷ shade ▶ pl n (Slang) sunglasses
shadier adj ▷ shade
shadiest adj ▷ shade
shading v ▷ shade
shadow n (pl -s) dark shape cast on a surface when something stands between a light and the surface ▶ v (-s, -ing, -ed) cast a shadow over > **shadowy** adj (-wier, -wiest)
shadowboxing n (pl -s) boxing against an imaginary opponent for practice
shadowboxings n ▷ shadowboxing

shadowed v ▷ shadow
shadowier adj ▷ shadow
shadowiest adj ▷ shadow
shadowing v ▷ shadow
shadows n, v ▷ shadow
shadowy adj ▷ shadow
shads n ▷ shad
shady adj ▷ shade
shaft n (pl -s) long narrow straight handle of a tool or weapon
shafts n ▷ shaft
shag[1] n (pl -s) coarse shredded tobacco ▶ adj (of a carpet) having a long pile
shag[2] n (pl -s) kind of cormorant
shaggier adj ▷ shaggy
shaggiest adj ▷ shaggy
shaggy adj (-ggier, -ggiest) covered with rough hair or wool
shagreen n (pl -s) sharkskin
shagreens n ▷ shagreen
shags n ▷ shag[1, 2]
shah n (pl -s) formerly, ruler of Iran
shahs n ▷ shah
shake v (-kes, -king, shook, -en) move quickly up and down or back and forth ▶ n (pl -s) shaking (Informal)
shaken v ▷ shake
shakes v, n ▷ shake
shakier adj ▷ shaky
shakiest adj ▷ shaky
shakily adv ▷ shaky
shaking v ▷ shake
shaky adj (-kier, -kiest) unsteady > **shakily** adv
shale n (pl -s) flaky sedimentary rock
shales n ▷ shale
shall v (past tense **should**) used as an auxiliary to make the future tense or to indicate intention, obligation, or inevitability
shallot n (pl -s) kind of small onion
shallots n ▷ shallot
shallow adj (-er, -est) not deep > **shallowness** n (pl -es)
shallower adj ▷ shallow
shallowest adj ▷ shallow
shallowness n ▷ shallow
shallownesses n ▷ shallow
shallows pl n area of shallow water
sham n (pl -s) thing or person that is not genuine ▶ adj not genuine ▶ v (-s, -mming, -mmed) fake, feign
shamble v (-les, -ling, -led) walk in a shuffling awkward way
shambled v ▷ shamble
shambles n (pl disorderly event or place ▶ v ▷ shamble

shambling v ▷ shamble

shame n (pl -s) painful emotion caused by awareness of having done something dishonourable or foolish ▶ v (-mes, -ming, -med) cause to feel shame ▶ interj (S AFR) (Informal) exclamation of sympathy or endearment

shamed v ▷ shame

shamefaced adj looking ashamed

shameful adj causing or deserving shame > **shamefully** adv

shamefully adv ▷ shameful

shameless adj with no sense of shame

shames n, v ▷ shame

shaming v ▷ shame

shammed v ▷ sham

shammies n ▷ shammy

shamming v ▷ sham

shammy n (pl -mies) (Informal) piece of chamois leather

shampoo n (pl -s) liquid soap for washing hair, carpets, or upholstery ▶ v (-s, -ing, -ed) wash with shampoo

shampooed v ▷ shampoo

shampooing v ▷ shampoo

shampoos n, v ▷ shampoo

shamrock n (pl -s) clover leaf, esp. as the Irish emblem

shamrocks n ▷ shamrock

shams n, v ▷ sham

shandies n ▷ shandy

shandy n (pl -dies) drink made from beer and lemonade

shanghai v (-hais, -haiing, -haied) force or trick (someone) into doing something ▶ n (pl -s) (AUST & NZ) catapult

shanghaied v ▷ shanghai

shanghaiing v ▷ shanghai

shanghais v, n ▷ shanghai

shank n (pl -s) lower leg

shanks n ▷ shank

shanties n ▷ shanty[1, 2]

shantung n (pl -s) soft Chinese silk with a knobbly surface

shantungs n ▷ shantung

shanty[1] n (pl -ties) shack or crude dwelling

shanty[2] n (pl -ties) sailor's traditional song

shantytown n (pl -s) slum consisting of shanties

shantytowns n ▷ shantytown

shape n (pl -s) outward form of an object ▶ v (-pes, -ping, -ped) form or mould > **shapeless** adj

shaped v ▷ shape

shapeless adj ▷ shape

shapelier adj ▷ shapely

shapeliest adj ▷ shapely

shapely adj (-lier, -liest) having an attractive shape

shapes n, v ▷ shape

shaping v ▷ shape

shard n (pl -s) broken piece of pottery or glass

shards n ▷ shard

share[1] n (pl -s) part of something that belongs to or is contributed by a person ▶ v (-res, -ring, -red) give or take a share of (something) > **shareholder** n (pl -s)

share[2] n (pl -s) blade of a plough

shared v ▷ share[1]

shareholder n ▷ share[1]

shareholders n ▷ share[1]

sharemilker n (pl -s) (NZ) person who works on a dairy farm belonging to someone else

sharemilkers n ▷ sharemilker

shares v ▷ share[1] ▶ n ▷ share[1, 2]

sharing v ▷ share[1]

shark n (pl -s) large usu. predatory sea fish

sharks n ▷ shark

sharkskin n (pl -s) stiff glossy fabric

sharkskins n ▷ sharkskin

sharp adj having a keen cutting edge or fine point ▶ adv promptly ▶ n (pl -s) (MUSIC) symbol raising a note one semitone above natural pitch > **sharply** adv > **sharpness** n (pl -es)

sharpen v (-s, -ing, -ed) make or become sharp or sharper > **sharpener** n (pl -s)

sharpened v ▷ sharpen

sharpener n ▷ sharpen

sharpeners n ▷ sharpen

sharpening v ▷ sharpen

sharpens v ▷ sharpen

sharply adv ▷ sharp

sharpness n ▷ sharp

sharpnesses n ▷ sharp

sharps n ▷ sharp

sharpshooter n (pl -s) marksman

sharpshooters n ▷ sharpshooter

shatter v (-s, -ing, -ed) break into pieces

shattered adj (Informal) completely exhausted ▶ v ▷ shatter

shattering v ▷ shatter

shatters v ▷ shatter

shave v (-ves, -ving, -ved, -ved or shaven) remove (hair) from (the face, head, or body) with a razor or shaver ▶ n (pl -s) shaving

shaved v ▷ shave

shaven v ▷ shave

shaver n (pl -s) electric razor

shavers n ▷ shaver

shaves v, n ▷ shave

shaving v ▷ shave
shavings pl n parings
shawl n (pl -s) piece of cloth worn over a woman's head or shoulders or wrapped around a baby
shawls n ▷ shawl
she pron refers to: female person or animal previously mentioned
sheaf n (pl sheaves) bundle of papers
shear v (-s, -ing, -ed, -ed or shorn) clip hair or wool from > **shearer** n (pl -s)
sheared v ▷ shear
shearer n ▷ shear
shearers n ▷ shear
shearing v ▷ shear
shears pl n large scissors or a cutting tool shaped like these ▶ v ▷ shear
shearwater n (pl -s) medium-sized sea bird
shearwaters n ▷ shearwater
sheath n (pl -s) close-fitting cover, esp. for a knife or sword
sheathe v (-thes, -thing, -thed) put into a sheath
sheathed v ▷ sheathe
sheathes v ▷ sheathe
sheathing v ▷ sheathe
sheaths n ▷ sheath
sheaves n ▷ sheaf
shebeen n (pl -s) (SCOT, IRISH & S AFR) place where alcohol is sold illegally
shebeens n ▷ shebeen
shed[1] n (pl -s) building used for storage or shelter or as a workshop
shed[2] v (-s, -dding, shed) pour forth (tears)
shedding v ▷ shed[2]
sheds n ▷ shed[1] ▶ v ▷ shed[2]
sheen n (pl -s) glistening brightness on the surface of something
sheens n ▷ sheen
sheep n (pl sheep) ruminant animal bred for wool and meat
sheepdog n (pl -s) dog used for herding sheep
sheepdogs n ▷ sheepdog
sheepish adj embarrassed because of feeling foolish > **sheepishly** adv
sheepishly adv ▷ sheepish
sheepskin n (pl -s) skin of a sheep with the fleece still on, used for clothing or rugs
sheepskins n ▷ sheepskin
sheer[1] adj (-er, -est) absolute, complete
sheer[2] v (-s, -ing, -ed) change course suddenly
sheered v ▷ sheer[2]
sheerer adj ▷ sheer[1]
sheerest adj ▷ sheer[1]
sheering v ▷ sheer[2]

sheers v ▷ sheer[2]
sheet[1] n (pl -s) large piece of cloth used as an inner bed cover
sheet[2] n (pl -s) rope for controlling the position of a sail
sheets n ▷ sheet[1, 2]
sheikdom n ▷ sheikh
sheikdoms n ▷ sheikh
sheikh, sheik [shake] n (pl -s) Arab chief > **sheikhdom, sheikdom** n (pl -s)
sheikhdoms n ▷ sheikh
sheikhs n ▷ sheikh
sheiks n ▷ sheikh
sheila n (pl -s) (AUST & NZ) (Slang) girl or woman
sheilas n ▷ sheila
shekel n (pl -s) monetary unit of Israel
shekels n ▷ shekel ▶ pl n (Informal) money
shelf n (pl -ves) board fixed horizontally for holding things
shell n (pl -s) hard outer covering of an egg, nut, or certain animals ▶ v (-s, -lling, -lled) take the shell from
shellac n (pl -s) resin used in varnishes ▶ v (-cs, -cking, -cked) coat with shellac
shellacked v ▷ shellac
shellacking v ▷ shellac
shellacs n, v ▷ shellac
shelled v ▷ shell
shellfish n (pl -s) sea-living animal, esp. one that can be eaten, with a shell
shellfishes n ▷ shellfish
shelling v ▷ shell
shells n, v ▷ shell
shelter n (pl -s) structure providing protection from danger or the weather ▶ v (-s, -ing, -ed) give shelter to
sheltered v ▷ shelter
sheltering v ▷ shelter
shelters n, v ▷ shelter
shelve[1] v (-ves, -ving, -ved) put aside or postpone
shelve[2] v (-ves, -ving, -ved) slope
shelved v ▷ shelve[1, 2]
shelves v ▷ shelve[1, 2] ▶ n ▷ shelf
shelving n (pl -s) (material for) shelves ▶ v ▷ shelve[1, 2]
shenanigans pl n (Informal) mischief or nonsense
shepherd n (pl -s) person who tends sheep ▶ v (-s, -ing, -ed) guide or watch over (people) > **shepherdess** n fem (pl -s)
shepherded v ▷ shepherd
shepherdess n ▷ shepherd
shepherdesses n ▷ shepherd
shepherding v ▷ shepherd

shepherds *n, v* ▷ shepherd

sherbet *n* (*pl* -s) (BRIT, AUST & NZ) fruit-flavoured fizzy powder

sherbets *n* ▷ sherbet

sheriff *n* (*pl* -s) (in the US) chief law enforcement officer of a county

sheriffs *n* ▷ sheriff

sherries *n* ▷ sherry

sherry *n* (*pl* -ries) pale or dark brown fortified wine

shh *interj.* Shh is a sound people make to request silence or quiet. As it doesn't contain a vowel, shh can help you to clear an unpromising rack. Shh scores 9 points.

shibboleth *n* (*pl* -s) slogan or principle, usu. considered outworn, characteristic of a particular group

shibboleths *n* ▷ shibboleth

shied *v* ▷ shy¹, ²

shield *n* (*pl* -s) piece of armour carried on the arm to protect the body from blows or missiles ▶ *v* (-s, -ing, -ed) protect

shielded *v* ▷ shield

shielding *v* ▷ shield

shields *n, v* ▷ shield

shies *v* ▷ shy¹, ² ▶ *n* ▷ shy²

shift *v* (-s, -ing, -ed) move ▶ *n* (*pl* -s) shifting

shifted *v* ▷ shift

shiftier *adj* ▷ shifty

shiftiest *adj* ▷ shifty

shiftiness *n* ▷ shifty

shiftinesses *n* ▷ shifty

shifting *v* ▷ shift

shiftless *adj* lacking in ambition or initiative

shifts *v, n* ▷ shift

shifty *adj* (-tier, -tiest) evasive or untrustworthy ▶ **shiftiness** *n* (*pl* -es)

shillelagh [shil-**lay**-lee] *n* (*pl* -s) (in Ireland) a cudgel

shillelaghs *n* ▷ shillelagh

shilling *n* (*pl* -s) former British coin, replaced by the 5p piece

shillings *n* ▷ shilling

shillyshallied *v* ▷ shillyshally

shillyshallies *v* ▷ shillyshally

shillyshally *v* (-lies, -lying, -lied) (*Informal*) be indecisive

shillyshallying *v* ▷ shillyshally

shimmer *v* (-s, -ing, -ed) ▶ *n* (*pl* -s) (shine with) a faint unsteady light

shimmered *v* ▷ shimmer

shimmering *v* ▷ shimmer

shimmers *v, n* ▷ shimmer

shin *n* (*pl* -s) front of the lower leg ▶ *v* (-s,

-nning, -nned) climb by using the hands or arms and legs

shinbone *n* (*pl* -s) tibia

shinbones *n* ▷ shinbone

shindig *n* (*pl* -s) (*Informal*) noisy party

shindigs *n* ▷ shindig

shine *v* (-s, -ing, shone) give out or reflect light ▶ *n* (*pl* -s) brightness or lustre > **shiny** *adj* (-nier, -niest)

shiner *n* (*pl* -s) (*Informal*) black eye

shiners *n* ▷ shiner

shines *v, n* ▷ shine

shingle¹ *n* (*pl* -s) wooden roof tile ▶ *v* (-les, -ling, -led) cover (a roof) with shingles

shingle² *n* (*pl* -s) coarse gravel found on beaches

shingled *v* ▷ shingle¹

shingles *n* disease causing a rash of small blisters along a nerve ▷ shingle¹, ² ▶ *v* ▷ shingle¹

shingling *v* ▷ shingle¹

shinier *adj* ▷ shine

shiniest *adj* ▷ shine

shining *v* ▷ shine

shinned *v* ▷ shin

shinning *v* ▷ shin

shins *n, v* ▷ shin

shinties *n* ▷ shinty

shinty *n* (*pl* -ties) game like hockey

shiny *adj* ▷ shine

ship *n* (*pl* -s) large seagoing vessel ▶ *v* (-s, -pping, -pped) send or transport by carrier, esp. a ship

shipment *n* (*pl* -s) act of shipping cargo

shipments *n* ▷ shipment

shipped *v* ▷ ship

shipping *n* (*pl* -s) freight transport business ▶ *v* ▷ ship

shippings *n* ▷ shipping

ships *n, v* ▷ ship

shipshape *adj* orderly or neat

shipwreck *n* (*pl* -s) destruction of a ship through storm or collision ▶ *v* (-s, -ing, -ed) cause to undergo shipwreck

shipwrecked *v* ▷ shipwreck

shipwrecking *v* ▷ shipwreck

shipwrecks *n, v* ▷ shipwreck

shipyard *n* (*pl* -s) place where ships are built

shipyards *n* ▷ shipyard

shire *n* (*pl* -s) (BRIT) county

shires *n* ▷ shire

shirk *v* (-s, -ing, -ed) avoid (duty or work) > **shirker** *n* (*pl* -s)

shirked *v* ▷ shirk

shirker *n* ▷ shirk

shirkers n ▷ shirk

shirking v ▷ shirk

shirks v ▷ shirk

shirt n (pl -s) garment for the upper part of the body

shirtier adj ▷ shirty

shirtiest adj ▷ shirty

shirts n ▷ shirt

shirty adj (-tier, -tiest) (CHIEFLY BRIT) (Slang) bad-tempered or annoyed

shiver¹ v (-s, -ing, -ed) tremble, as from cold or fear ▶ n (pl -s) shivering

shiver² v (-s, -ing, -ed) splinter into pieces

shivered v ▷ shiver¹, ²

shivering v ▷ shiver¹, ²

shivers v ▷ shiver¹, ² ▶ n ▷ shiver¹

shoal¹ n (pl -s) large number of fish swimming together

shoal² n (pl -s) stretch of shallow water

shoals n ▷ shoal¹, ²

shock¹ v (-s, -ing, -ed) horrify, disgust, or astonish ▶ n (pl -s) sudden violent emotional disturbance > **shocker** n (pl -s)

shock² n (pl -s) bushy mass (of hair)

shocked v ▷ shock¹

shocker n ▷ shock¹

shockers n ▷ shock¹

shocking adj causing horror, disgust, or astonishment ▶ v ▷ shock¹

shocks v ▷ shock¹ ▶ n ▷ shock¹, ²

shod v ▷ shoe

shoddier adj ▷ shoddy

shoddiest adj ▷ shoddy

shoddy adj (-dier, -diest) made or done badly

shoe n (pl -s) outer covering for the foot, ending below the ankle ▶ v (**shoes, shoeing, shod**) fit with a shoe or shoes

shoehorn n (pl -s) smooth curved implement inserted at the heel of a shoe to ease the foot into it

shoehorns n ▷ shoehorn

shoeing v ▷ shoe

shoes n, v ▷ shoe

shoestring n (pl -s) (foll. by **on a**) using a very small amount of money

shoestrings n ▷ shoestring

shone v ▷ shine

shonkier adj ▷ shonky

shonkiest adj ▷ shonky

shonky adj (-kier, -kiest) (AUST & NZ) (Informal) unreliable or unsound

shoo interj go away! ▶ v (-s, -ing, -ed) drive away as by saying 'shoo'

shooed v ▷ shoo

shooing v ▷ shoo

shook v ▷ shake

shoos v ▷ shoo

shoot v (-s, -ing, **shot**) hit, wound, or kill with a missile fired from a weapon ▶ n (pl -s) new branch or sprout of a plant

shooting v ▷ shoot

shoots v, n ▷ shoot

shop n (pl -s) place for sale of goods and services ▶ v (-s, -pping, -pped) visit a shop or shops to buy goods

shoplifter n (pl -s) person who steals from a shop

shoplifters n ▷ shoplifter

shopped v ▷ shop

shopping v ▷ shop

shops n, v ▷ shop

shopsoiled adj soiled or faded from being displayed in a shop

shore¹ n (pl -s) edge of a sea or lake

shore² v (-res, -ring, -red) (foll. by **up**) prop or support

shored v ▷ shore²

shores n ▷ shore¹ ▶ v ▷ shore²

shoring v ▷ shore²

shorn v ▷ shear

short adj (-er, -est) not long ▶ adv abruptly ▶ n (pl -s) drink of spirits

shortage n (pl -s) deficiency

shortages n ▷ shortage

shortbread, shortcake n (pl -s) crumbly biscuit made with butter

shortbreads n ▷ shortbread

shortcake n ▷ shortbread

shortcakes n ▷ shortbread

shortchange v (-ges, -ging, -ed) give (someone) less than the correct amount of change

shortchanged v ▷ shortchange

shortchanges v ▷ shortchange

shortchanging v ▷ shortchange

shortcoming n (pl -s) failing or defect

shortcomings n ▷ shortcoming

shorten v (-s, -ing, -ed) make or become shorter

shortened v ▷ shorten

shortening v ▷ shorten

shortens v ▷ shorten

shorter adj ▷ short

shortest adj ▷ short

shortfall n (pl -s) deficit

shortfalls n ▷ shortfall

shorthand n (pl -s) system of rapid writing using symbols to represent words

shorthanded adj not having enough workers

shorthands n ▷ shorthand

shortlist *v* (**-s, -ing, -ed**) put on a short list
  shortlisted *v* ▷ shortlist
  shortlisting *v* ▷ shortlist
  shortlists *v* ▷ shortlist
shortly *adv* soon
shorts *n* ▷ short ▶ *pl n* short trousers
shortsighted *adj* unable to see distant things clearly
shot *n* (*pl* -s) shooting ▶ *v* ▷ shoot
shotgun *n* (*pl* -s) gun for firing a charge of shot at short range
  shotguns *n* ▷ shotgun
  shots *n* ▷ shot
  should *v* ▷ shall
shoulder *n* (*pl* -s) part of the body to which an arm, foreleg, or wing is attached ▶ *v* (**-s, -ing, -ed**) bear (a burden or responsibility)
  shouldered *v* ▷ shoulder
  shouldering *v* ▷ shoulder
  shoulders *n, v* ▷ shoulder
shout *n* (*pl* -s) loud cry (*Informal*) ▶ *v* (**-s, -ing, -ed**) cry out loudly
  shouted *v* ▷ shout
  shouting *v* ▷ shout
  shouts *n, v* ▷ shout
shove *v* (**-ves, -ving, -ved**) push roughly ▶ *n* (*pl* -s) rough push
  shoved *v* ▷ shove
shovel *n* (*pl* -s) tool for lifting or moving loose material ▶ *v* (**-s, -lling, -lled**) lift or move as with a shovel
  shovelled *v* ▷ shovel
  shovelling *v* ▷ shovel
  shovels *n, v* ▷ shovel
  shoves *n* ▷ shove
  shoving *v* ▷ shove
show *v* (**-s, -ing, -ed, shown** *or* **showed**) make, be, or become noticeable or visible ▶ *n* (*pl* -s) public exhibition
showcase *n* (*pl* -s) situation in which something is displayed to best advantage
  showcases *n* ▷ showcase
showdown *n* (*pl* -s) confrontation that settles a dispute
  showdowns *n* ▷ showdown
  showed *v* ▷ show
shower *n* (*pl* -s) kind of bath in which a person stands while being sprayed with water ▶ *v* (**-s, -ing, -ed**) wash in a shower > **showery** *adj* (**-rier, -riest**)
  showered *v* ▷ shower
  showerier *adj* ▷ shower
  showeriest *adj* ▷ shower
  showering *v* ▷ shower
  showers *n, v* ▷ shower

showery *adj* ▷ shower
showier *adj* ▷ showy
showiest *adj* ▷ showy
showily *adv* ▷ showy
showing *v* ▷ show
showjumping *n* (*pl* -s) competitive sport of riding horses to demonstrate skill in jumping
  showjumpings *n* ▷ showjumping
showman *n* (*pl* -men) man skilled at presenting anything spectacularly > **showmanship** *n* (*pl* -s)
  showmanship *n* ▷ showman
  showmanships *n* ▷ showman
  showmen *n* ▷ showman
  shown *v* ▷ show
showoff *n* (*pl* -s) (*Informal*) person who shows off
  showoffs *n* ▷ showoff
showpiece *n* (*pl* -s) excellent specimen shown for display or as an example
  showpieces *n* ▷ showpiece
showroom *n* (*pl* -s) room in which goods for sale are on display
  showrooms *n* ▷ showroom
  shows *v, n* ▷ show
showy *adj* (**-wier, -wiest**) gaudy > **showily** *adv*
  shrank *v* ▷ shrink
shrapnel *n* (*pl* -s) artillery shell filled with pellets which scatter on explosion
  shrapnels *n* ▷ shrapnel
shred *n* (*pl* -s) long narrow strip torn from something ▶ *v* (**-s, -dding, -dded** *or* **shred**) tear to shreds
  shredded *v* ▷ shred
  shredding *v* ▷ shred
  shreds *n, v* ▷ shred
shrew *n* (*pl* -s) small mouselike animal > **shrewish** *adj*
shrewd *adj* (**-er, -est**) clever and perceptive > **shrewdly** *adv* > **shrewdness** *n* (*pl* -es)
  shrewder *adj* ▷ shrewd
  shrewdest *adj* ▷ shrewd
  shrewdly *adv* ▷ shrewd
  shrewdness *n* ▷ shrewd
  shrewdnesses *n* ▷ shrewd
  shrewish *adj* ▷ shrew
  shrews *n* ▷ shrew
shriek *n* (*pl* -s) shrill cry ▶ *v* (**-s, -ing, -ed**) utter (with) a shriek
  shrieked *v* ▷ shriek
  shrieking *v* ▷ shriek
  shrieks *n, v* ▷ shriek
shrike *n* (*pl* -s) songbird with a heavy hooked bill
  shrikes *n* ▷ shrike

shrill adj (-er, -est) (of a sound) sharp and high-pitched > **shrillness** n (pl -es) > **shrilly** adv
  shriller adj ▷ shrill
  shrillest adj ▷ shrill
  shrillness n ▷ shrill
  shrillnesses n ▷ shrill
  shrilly adv ▷ shrill
shrimp n (pl -s) small edible shellfish (Informal)
shrimping n (pl -s) fishing for shrimps
  shrimpings n ▷ shrimping
  shrimps n ▷ shrimp
shrine n (pl -s) place of worship associated with a sacred person or object
  shrines n ▷ shrine
shrink v (-s, -ing, shrank or shrunk, shrunk or shrunken) become or make smaller ▶ n (pl -s) (Slang) psychiatrist
shrinkage n (pl -s) decrease in size, value, or weight
  shrinkages n ▷ shrinkage
  shrinking v ▷ shrink
  shrinks v, n ▷ shrink
shrivel v (-s, -lling, -lled) shrink and wither
  shrivelled v ▷ shrivel
  shrivelling v ▷ shrivel
  shrivels v ▷ shrivel
shroud n (pl -s) piece of cloth used to wrap a dead body ▶ v (-s, -ing, -ed) conceal
  shrouded v ▷ shroud
  shrouding v ▷ shroud
  shrouds n, v ▷ shroud
shrub n (pl -s) woody plant smaller than a tree
  shrubberies n ▷ shrubbery
shrubbery n (pl -ries) area planted with shrubs
  shrubs n ▷ shrub
shrug v (-s, -gging, -gged) raise and then drop (the shoulders) as a sign of indifference, ignorance, or doubt ▶ n (pl -s) shrugging
  shrugged v ▷ shrug
  shrugging v ▷ shrug
  shrugs v, n ▷ shrug
  shrunk v ▷ shrink
  shrunken v ▷ shrink
shudder v (-s, -ing, -ed) shake or tremble violently, esp. with horror ▶ n (pl -s) shaking or trembling
  shuddered v ▷ shudder
  shuddering v ▷ shudder
  shudders v, n ▷ shudder
shuffle v (-les, -lling, -lled) walk without lifting the feet ▶ n (pl -s) shuffling
  shuffled v ▷ shuffle
  shuffles v, n ▷ shuffle
  shuffling v ▷ shuffle
shun v (-s, -nning, -nned) avoid

  shunned v ▷ shun
  shunning v ▷ shun
  shuns v ▷ shun
shunt v (-s, -ing, -ed) move (objects or people) to a different position
  shunted v ▷ shunt
  shunting v ▷ shunt
  shunts v ▷ shunt
shush interj be quiet!
shut v (-s, -tting, shut) bring together or fold, close
shutdown n (pl -s) closing
  shutdowns n ▷ shutdown
  shuts v ▷ shut
shutter n (pl -s) hinged doorlike cover for closing off a window
  shutters n ▷ shutter
  shutting v ▷ shut
shuttle n (pl -s) vehicle going to and fro over a short distance ▶ v (-les, -lling, -led) travel by or as if by shuttle
shuttlecock n (pl -s) small light cone with feathers stuck in one end, struck to and fro in badminton
  shuttlecocks n ▷ shuttlecock
  shuttled v ▷ shuttle
  shuttles n, v ▷ shuttle
  shuttling v ▷ shuttle
shy¹ adj (-er, -est) not at ease in company (foll. by of) ▶ v (shies, shying, shied) start back in fear (foll. by away from) > **shyly** adv > **shyness** n (pl -es)
shy² v (shies, shying, shied) throw ▶ n (pl shies) throw
  shyer adj ▷ shy¹
  shyest adj ▷ shy¹
  shying v ▷ shy¹, ²
  shyly adv ▷ shy¹
  shyness n ▷ shy¹
  shynesses n ▷ shy¹

> **si** n (sis). Si means the same as **te**, a musical note This is an unusual word which can be helpful when you want to form words in more than one direction Si scores 2 points

sibilant adj hissing ▶ n (pl -s) consonant pronounced with a hissing sound
  sibilants n ▷ sibilant
sibling n (pl -s) brother or sister
  siblings n ▷ sibling
sibyl n (pl -s) (in ancient Greece and Rome) prophetess
  sibyls n ▷ sibyl
sic (LATIN) thus: used to indicate that an odd spelling or reading is in fact accurate

sick *adj* (**-er, -est**) vomiting or likely to vomit
> **sickness** *n* (*pl* **-es**)

sicken *v* (**-s, -zing, -ed**) make nauseated or disgusted
  sickened *v* ▷ sicken
  sickening *v* ▷ sicken
  sickens *v* ▷ sicken
  sicker *adj* ▷ sick
  sickest *adj* ▷ sick

sickle *n* (*pl* **-s**) tool with a curved blade for cutting grass or grain
  sickles *n* ▷ sickle
  sicklier *adj* ▷ sickly
  sickliest *adj* ▷ sickly

sickly *adj* (**-lier, -liest**) unhealthy, weak
  sickness *n* ▷ sick
  sicknesses *n* ▷ sick

side *n* (*pl* **-s**) line or surface that borders anything ▶ *adj* at or on the side

sideboard *n* (*pl* **-s**) piece of furniture for holding plates, cutlery, etc. in a dining room
  sideboards *n* ▷ sideboard ▶ *pl n* ▷ sideburns

sideburns, sideboards *pl n* man's side whiskers

sidekick *n* (*pl* **-s**) (*Informal*) close friend or associate
  sidekicks *n* ▷ sidekick

sidelight *n* (*pl* **-s**) either of two small lights on the front of a vehicle
  sidelights *n* ▷ sidelight

sideline *n* (*pl* **-s**) subsidiary interest or source of income
  sidelines *n* ▷ sideline

sidelong *adj* sideways ▶ *adv* obliquely

sidereal [side-**eer**-ee-al] *adj* of or determined with reference to the stars
  sides *n* ▷ side

sidesaddle *n* (*pl* **-s**) saddle designed to allow a woman rider to sit with both legs on the same side of the horse
  sidesaddles *n* ▷ sidesaddle

sidestep *v* (**-s, -pping, -pped**) dodge (an issue)
  sidestepped *v* ▷ sidestep
  sidestepping *v* ▷ sidestep
  sidesteps *v* ▷ sidestep

sidetrack *v* (**-s, -ing, -ed**) divert from the main topic
  sidetracked *v* ▷ sidetrack
  sidetracking *v* ▷ sidetrack
  sidetracks *v* ▷ sidetrack

sidewalk *n* (*pl* **-s**) (US) paved path for pedestrians, at the side of a road
  sidewalks *n* ▷ sidewalk

sideways *adv* to or from the side

siding *n* (*pl* **-s**) short stretch of railway track

on which trains or wagons are shunted from the main line
  sidings *n* ▷ siding

sidle *v* (**-les, -ling, -led**) walk in a furtive manner
  sidled *v* ▷ sidle
  sidles *v* ▷ sidle
  sidling *v* ▷ sidle

siege *n* (*pl* **-s**) surrounding and blockading of a place
  sieges *n* ▷ siege

sienna *n* (*pl* **-s**) reddish- or yellowish-brown pigment made from natural earth
  siennas *n* ▷ sienna

sierra *n* (*pl* **-s**) range of mountains in Spain or America with jagged peaks
  sierras *n* ▷ sierra

siesta *n* (*pl* **-s**) afternoon nap, taken in hot countries
  siestas *n* ▷ siesta

sieve [siv] *n* (*pl* **-s**) utensil with mesh through which a substance is sifted or strained ▶ *v* (**-ves, -ving, -ved**) sift or strain through a sieve
  sieved *v* ▷ sieve
  sieves *n, v* ▷ sieve
  sieving *v* ▷ sieve

sift *v* (**-s, -ing, -ed**) remove the coarser particles from a substance with a sieve
  sifted *v* ▷ sift
  sifting *v* ▷ sift
  sifts *v* ▷ sift

sigh *n* (*pl* **-s**) long audible breath expressing sadness, tiredness, relief, or longing ▶ *v* (**-s, -ing, -ed**) utter a sigh
  sighed *v* ▷ sigh
  sighing *v* ▷ sigh
  sighs *n, v* ▷ sigh

sight *n* (*pl* **-s**) ability to see ▶ *v* (**-s, -ing, -ed**) catch sight of
  sighted *v* ▷ sight
  sighting *v* ▷ sight

sightless *adj* blind
  sights *n, v* ▷ sight

sightseeing *n* (*pl* **-s**) visiting places of interest
> **sightseer** *n* (*pl* **-s**)
  sightseeings *n* ▷ sightseeing
  sightseer *n* ▷ sightseeing
  sightseers *n* ▷ sightseeing

sign *n* (*pl* **-s**) indication of something not immediately or outwardly observable ▶ *v* (**-s, -ing, -ed**) write (one's name) on (a document or letter) to show its authenticity or one's agreement

signal *n* (*pl* **-s**) sign or gesture to convey information ▶ *adj* (*Formal*) very important

▶ v (**-s, -lling, -lled**) convey (information) by signal > **signally** adv

signalled v ▷ signal

signalling v ▷ signal

signally adv ▷ signal

signalman n (pl **-men**) railwayman in charge of signals and points

signalmen n ▷ signalman

signals n, v ▷ signal

signatories n ▷ signatory

signatory n (pl **-ries**) one of the parties who sign a document

signature n (pl **-s**) person's name written by himself or herself in signing something

signatures n ▷ signature

signed v ▷ sign

signet n (pl **-s**) small seal used to authenticate documents

signets n ▷ signet

significance n ▷ significant

significances n ▷ significant

significant adj important > **significantly** adv > **significance** n (pl **-s**)

significantly adv ▷ significant

signification n ▷ signify

significations n ▷ signify

signified v ▷ signify

signifies v ▷ signify

signify v (**-fies, -fying, -fied**) indicate or suggest > **signification** n (pl **-s**)

signifying v ▷ signify

signing n (pl **-s**) system of communication by gestures, as used by deaf people ▶ v ▷ sign

signings n ▷ signing

signor [see-**nyor**] n (pl **-s**) Italian term of address equivalent to *sir* or *Mr*

signora [see-**nyor-a**] n (pl **-s**) Italian term of address equivalent to *madam* or *Mrs*

signoras n ▷ signora

signorina [see-nyor-**ee**-na] n (pl **-s**) Italian term of address equivalent to *madam* or *Miss*

signorinas n ▷ signorina

signors n ▷ signor

signpost n (pl **-s**) post bearing a sign that shows the way

signposts n ▷ signpost

signs n, v ▷ sign

silage [**sile**-ij] n (pl **-s**) fodder crop harvested while green and partially fermented in a silo or plastic bags

silages n ▷ silage

silence n (pl **-s**) absence of noise or speech ▶ v (**-ces, -cing, -ced**) make silent > **silent** adj > **silently** adv

silenced v ▷ silence

silencer n (pl **-s**) device to reduce the noise of an engine exhaust or gun

silencers n ▷ silencer

silences n, v ▷ silence

silencing v ▷ silence

silent adj ▷ silencet

silently adv ▷ silence

silhouette n (pl **-s**) outline of a dark shape seen against a light background ▶ v (**-s, -ing, -ed**) show in silhouette

silhouetted v ▷ silhouette

silhouettes n, v ▷ silhouette

silhouetting v ▷ silhouette

silica n (pl **-s**) hard glossy mineral found as quartz and in sandstone

silicas n ▷ silica

silicon n (pl **-s**) (CHEM) brittle nonmetallic element widely used in chemistry and industry

silicone n (pl **-s**) tough synthetic substance made from silicon and used in lubricants, paints, and resins

silicones n ▷ silicone

silicons n ▷ silicon

silicoses n ▷ silicosis

silicosis n (pl **-ses**) lung disease caused by inhaling silica dust

silk n (pl **-s**) fibre made by the larva of a certain moth

silken adj ▷ silky

silkier adj ▷ silky

silkiest adj ▷ silky

silks n ▷ silk

silky (**-ier, -iest**), **silken** adj of or like silk

sill n (pl **-s**) ledge at the bottom of a window or door

sillier adj ▷ silly

silliest adj ▷ silly

silliness n ▷ silly

sillinesses n ▷ silly

sills n ▷ sill

silly adj (**-lier, -liest**) foolish > **silliness** n (pl **-es**)

silo n (pl **-los**) pit or airtight tower for storing silage or grains

silos n ▷ silo

silt n (pl **-s**) mud deposited by moving water ▶ v (**-s, -ing, -ed**) (foll. by **up**) fill or be choked with silt

silted v ▷ silt

silting v ▷ silt

silts n, v ▷ silt

silvan adj ▷ sylvan

silver n (pl **-s**) white precious metal ▶ adj made of or of the colour of silver

silverbeet n (pl **-s**) (AUST & NZ) leafy green

vegetable with white stalks
silverbeets n ▷ silverbeet
silverfish n (pl **-es**) small wingless silver-coloured insect
silverfishes n ▷ silverfish
silvers n ▷ silver
silverside n (pl **-s**) cut of beef from below the rump and above the leg
silversides n ▷ silverside
sim n (pl **-s**) computer game that simulates an activity such as flying or playing a sport
simian adj, n (pl **-s**) (of or like) a monkey or ape
simians n ▷ simian
similar adj alike but not identical > **similarity** n (pl **-s**) > **similarly** adv
similarities n ▷ similar
similarity n ▷ similar
similarly adv ▷ similar
simile [**sim**-ill-ee] n (pl **-s**) figure of speech comparing one thing to another, using 'as' or 'like'
similes n ▷ simile
similitude n (pl **-s**) similarity, likeness
similitudes n ▷ similitude
simmer v (**-s, -ing, -ed**) cook gently at just below boiling point
simmered v ▷ simmer
simmering v ▷ simmer
simmers v ▷ simmer
simper v (**-s, -ing, -ed**) smile in a silly or affected way ▶ n (pl **-s**) simpering smile
simpered v ▷ simper
simpering v ▷ simper
simpers v, n ▷ simper
simple adj (**-r, -st**) easy to understand or do > **simply** adv > **simplicity** n (pl **-ties**)
simpler adj ▷ simple
simplest adj ▷ simple
simpleton n (pl **-s**) foolish or half-witted person
simpletons n ▷ simpleton
simplicities n ▷ simple
simplicity n ▷ simple
simplification n ▷ simplify
simplifications n ▷ simplify
simplified v ▷ simplify
simplifies v ▷ simplify
simplify v (**-fies, -fying, -fied**) make less complicated > **simplification** n (pl **-s**)
simplifying v ▷ simplify
simplistic adj too simple or naive
simply adv ▷ simpl
sims n ▷ sim
simulate v (**-tes, -ting, -ted**) make a pretence of > **simulation** n (pl **-s**) > **simulator** n (pl **-s**)

simulated v ▷ simulate
simulates v ▷ simulate
simulating v ▷ simulate
simulation n ▷ simulate
simulations n ▷ simulate
simulator n ▷ simulate
simulators n ▷ simulate
simultaneous adj occurring at the same time > **simultaneously** adv
simultaneously adv ▷ simultaneous
sin¹ n (pl **-s**) breaking of a religious or moral law ▶ v (**-s, -nning, -nned**) commit a sin > **sinner** n (pl **-s**)
sin² (MATHS) sine
since prep during the period of time after ▶ conj from the time when ▶ adv from that time
sincere adj (**-r, -st**) without pretence or deceit > **sincerely** adv > **sincerity** n (pl **-ties**)
sincerely adv ▷ sincere
sincerer adj ▷ sincere
sincerest adj ▷ sincere
sincerities n ▷ sincere
sincerity n ▷ sincere
sine n (pl **-s**) (in trigonometry) ratio of the length of the opposite side to that of the hypotenuse in a right-angled triangle
sinecure [**sin**-ee-cure] n (pl **-s**) paid job with minimal duties
sinecures n ▷ sinecure
sines n ▷ sine
sinew n (pl **-s**) tough fibrous tissue joining muscle to bone > **sinewy** adj (**-wier, -wiest**)
sinewier adj ▷ sinew
sinewiest adj ▷ sinew
sinews n ▷ sinew
sinewy adj ▷ sinew
sinful adj guilty of sin > **sinfully** adv
sinfully adv ▷ sinful
sing v (**-s, -ing, sang, sung**) make musical sounds with the voice
singe v (**-ges, -geing, -ged**) burn the surface of ▶ n (pl **-s**) superficial burn
singed v ▷ singe
singeing v ▷ singe
singer n (pl **-s**) person who sings, esp. professionally
singers n ▷ singer
singes v, n ▷ singe
singing v ▷ sing
single adj one only ▶ n (pl **-s**) single thing ▶ v (**-les, -ling, -led**) (foll. by **out**) pick out from others > **singly** adv
singled v ▷ single
singles n, v ▷ single ▶ pl n game between two players

singlet n (pl -s) sleeveless vest
  singlets n ▷ singlet
  singling v ▷ single
  singly adv ▷ single
  sings v ▷ sing
singsong n (pl -s) informal singing session
  ▶ adj (of the voice) repeatedly rising and
  falling in pitch
  singsongs n ▷ singsong
singular adj (of a word or form) denoting one
  person or thing ▶ n (pl -s) singular form of a
  word > **singularity** n (pl -ties) > **singularly** adv
  singularities n ▷ singular
  singularity n ▷ singular
  singularly adv ▷ singular
  singulars n ▷ singular
sinister adj threatening or suggesting evil
  or harm
sink v (-s, -ing, sank, sunk or sunken) submerge
  (in liquid) ▶ n (pl -s) fixed basin with a water
  supply and drainage pipe
sinker n (pl -s) weight for a fishing line
  sinkers n ▷ sinker
  sinking v ▷ sink
  sinks v, n ▷ sink
  sinned v ▷ sin¹
  sinner n ▷ sin¹
  sinners n ▷ sin¹
  sinning v ▷ sin¹
  sins n, v ▷ sin¹
sinuous adj curving > **sinuously** adv
  sinuously adv ▷ sinuous
sinus [sine-uss] n (pl -nuses) hollow space in
  a bone, esp. an air passage opening into
  the nose
  sinuses n ▷ sinus
sip v (-s, -pping, -pped) drink in small
  mouthfuls ▶ n (pl -s) amount sipped
siphon n (pl -s) bent tube which uses air
  pressure to draw liquid from a container ▶ v
  (-s, -ing, -ed) draw off thus
  siphoned v ▷ siphon
  siphoning v ▷ siphon
  siphons n, v ▷ siphon
  sipped v ▷ sip
  sipping v ▷ sip
  sips v, n ▷ sip
sir n (pl -s) polite term of address for a man
sire n (pl -s) male parent of a horse or other
  domestic animal ▶ v (-res, -ring, -red) father
  sired v ▷ sire
siren n (pl -s) device making a loud wailing
  noise as a warning
  sirens n ▷ siren
  sires n, v ▷ sire

  siring v ▷ sire
sirloin n (pl -s) prime cut of loin of beef
  sirloins n ▷ sirloin
sirocco n (pl -s) hot wind blowing from N Africa
  into S Europe
  siroccos n ▷ sirocco
  sirs n ▷ sir
sis interj (S AFR) (Informal) exclamation of disgust
sisal [size-al] n (pl -s) (fibre of) plant used in
  making ropes
  sisals n ▷ sisal
siskin n (pl -s) yellow-and-black finch
  siskins n ▷ siskin
  sissier adj ▷ sissy
  sissies n ▷ sissy
  sissiest adj ▷ sissy
sissy adj (-ssier, -ssiest) ▶ n (pl -ssies) weak or
  cowardly (person)
sister n (pl -s) girl or woman with the same
  parents as another person ▶ adj closely
  related, similar > **sisterly** adj
sisterhood n (pl -s) state of being a sister
  sisterhoods n ▷ sisterhood
  sisterly adj ▷ sister
  sisters n ▷ sister
sit v (-s, -tting, sat) rest one's body upright on
  the buttocks
sitar n (pl -s) Indian stringed musical
  instrument
  sitars n ▷ sitar
sitcom n (pl -s) (Informal) situation comedy
  sitcoms n ▷ sitcom
site n (pl -s) place where something is, was, or
  is intended to be located > **website** ▶ v (-tes,
  -ting, -ted) provide with a site
  sited v ▷ site
  sites n, v ▷ site
  siting v ▷ site
  sits v ▷ sit
  sitting v ▷ sit
situate v (-tes, -ting, -ted) place
  situated v ▷ situate
  situates v ▷ situate
  situating v ▷ situate
situation n (pl -s) state of affairs
  situations n ▷ situation
six adj, n (pl -es) one more than five
  sixes n ▷ six
sixteen adj, n (pl -s) six and ten > **sixteenth**
  adj, n (pl -s)
  sixteens n ▷ sixteen
  sixteenth n ▷ sixteen
  sixteenths n ▷ sixteen
sixth adj, n (pl -s) (of) number six in a series
  sixths n ▷ sixth

sixties n ▷ sixty
sixtieth n ▷ sixty
sixtieths n ▷ sixty
sixty adj, n (pl -ies) six times ten > **sixtieth** adj, n (pl -s)
sizable adj ▷ sizeable
size¹ n (pl -s) dimensions, bigness ▶ v (-zes, -zing, -zed) arrange according to size
size² n (pl -s) gluey substance used as a protective coating
sizeable, sizable adj quite large
sized v ▷ size¹
sizes n ▷ size¹, ² ▶ v ▷ size¹
sizing v ▷ size¹
sizzle v (-les, -ling, -led) make a hissing sound like frying fat
sizzled v ▷ sizzle
sizzles v ▷ sizzle
sizzling v ▷ sizzle
skankier adj ▷ skanky
skankiest adj ▷ skanky
skanky adj (-kier, -kiest) (Slang) dirty or unattractive
skate¹ n (pl -s) boot with a steel blade or sets of wheels attached to the sole for gliding over ice or a hard surface ▶ v (-tes, -ting, -ted) glide on or as if on skates
skate² n (pl -s) large marine flatfish
skateboard n (pl -s) board mounted on small wheels for riding on while standing up
 > **skateboarding** n (pl -s)
skateboarding n ▷ skateboard
skateboardings n ▷ skateboard
skateboards n ▷ skateboard
skated v ▷ skate¹
skates n ▷ skate¹, ² ▶ v ▷ skate¹
skating v ▷ skate¹
skedaddle v (-les, -ling, -led) (Informal) run off
skedaddled v ▷ skedaddle
skedaddles v ▷ skedaddle
skedaddling v ▷ skedaddle
skein n (pl -s) yarn wound in a loose coil
skeins n ▷ skein
skeletal adj ▷ skeleton
skeleton n (pl -s) framework of bones inside a person's or animal's body ▶ adj reduced to a minimum > **skeletal** adj
skeletons n ▷ skeleton
sketch n (pl -es) rough drawing ▶ v (-es, -ing, -ed) make a sketch (of)
sketched v ▷ sketch
sketches n, v ▷ sketch
sketchier adj ▷ sketchy
sketchiest adj ▷ sketchy
sketching v ▷ sketch

sketchy adj (-chier, -chiest) incomplete or inadequate
skew v (-s, -ing, -ed) make slanting or crooked ▶ adj slanting or crooked
skewed v ▷ skew
skewer n (pl -s) pin to hold meat together during cooking ▶ v (-s, -ing, -ed) fasten with a skewer
skewered v ▷ skewer
skewering v ▷ skewer
skewers n, v ▷ skewer
skewing v ▷ skew
skews v ▷ skew
skewwhiff adj (BRIT) (Informal) slanting or crooked
ski n (pl -s) one of a pair of long runners fastened to boots for gliding over snow or water ▶ v (skis, skiing, skied) travel on skis
 > **skier** n (pl -s)
skid v (-s, -dding, -dded) (of a moving vehicle) slide sideways uncontrollably ▶ n (pl -s) skidding
skidded v ▷ skid
skidding v ▷ skid
skids v, n ▷ skid
skied v ▷ ski
skier n ▷ ski
skiers n ▷ ski
skies n ▷ sky
skiff n (pl -s) small boat
skiffs n ▷ skiff
skiing v ▷ ski
skilful adj having or showing skill > **skilfully** adv
skilfully adv ▷ skilful
skill n (pl -s) special ability or expertise
 > **skilled** adj
skilled adj ▷ skill
skillet n (pl -s) small frying pan or shallow cooking pot
skillets n ▷ skillet
skills n ▷ skill
skim v (-s, -mming, -mmed) remove floating matter from the surface of (a liquid)
skimmed v ▷ skim
skimming v ▷ skim
skimp v (-s, -ing, -ed) not invest enough time, money, material, etc.
skimped v ▷ skimp
skimpier adj ▷ skimpy
skimpiest adj ▷ skimpy
skimping v ▷ skimp
skimps v ▷ skimp
skimpy adj (-pier, -piest) scanty or insufficient
skims v ▷ skim

skin n (pl **-s**) outer covering of the body ▶ v (**-s**, **-nning**, **-nned**) remove the skin of ▷ **skinless** adj

skinflint n (pl **-s**) miser
  skinflints n ▷ skinflint
skinhead n (pl **-s**) youth with very short hair
  skinheads n ▷ skinhead
  skinless adj ▷ skin
  skinned v ▷ skin
  skinnier adj ▷ skinny
  skinniest adj ▷ skinny
  skinning v ▷ skin
skinny adj (**-nnier**, **-nniest**) thin
  skins n, v ▷ skin
skint adj (BRIT) (Slang) having no money
skip[1] v (**-s**, **-pping**, **-pped**) leap lightly from one foot to the other ▶ n (pl **-s**) skipping
skip[2] n (pl **-s**) large open container for builders' rubbish
  skipped v ▷ skip[1]
skipper n (pl **-s**) ▶ v (**-s**, **-ing**, **-ed**) captain
  skippered v ▷ skipper
  skippering v ▷ skipper
  skippers n, v ▷ skipper
  skipping v ▷ skip[1]
  skips v ▷ skip[1] ▶ n ▷ skip[1, 2]
skirl n (pl **-s**) sound of bagpipes
  skirls n ▷ skirl
skirmish n (pl **-es**) brief or minor fight or argument ▶ v (**-es**, **-ing**, **-ed**) take part in a skirmish
  skirmished v ▷ skirmish
  skirmishes n, v ▷ skirmish
  skirmishing v ▷ skirmish
skirt n (pl **-s**) woman's garment hanging from the waist ▶ v (**-s**, **-ing**, **-ed**) border
  skirted v ▷ skirt
  skirting v ▷ skirt
  skirts n, v ▷ skirt
  skis n, v ▷ ski
skit n (pl **-s**) brief satirical sketch
skite v (**-tes**, **-ting**, **-ted**) ▶ n (pl **-s**) (AUST & NZ) boast
  skited v ▷ skite
  skites v, n ▷ skite
  skiting v ▷ skite
  skits n ▷ skit
skittish adj playful or lively
skittle n (pl **-s**) bottle-shaped object used as a target in some games
  skittles n ▷ skittle ▶ pl n game in which players try to knock over skittles by rolling a ball at them
skive v (**-ves**, **-ving**, **-ved**) (BRIT) (Informal) evade work or responsibility

  skived v ▷ skive
  skives v ▷ skive
  skiving v ▷ skive
  skivvies n ▷ skivvy
skivvy n (pl **-vies**) (BRIT) female servant who does menial work
skua n (pl **-s**) large predatory gull
  skuas n ▷ skua
  skulduggeries n ▷ skulduggery
skulduggery n (pl **-ries**) (Informal) trickery
skulk v (**-s**, **-ing**, **-ed**) move stealthily
  skulked v ▷ skulk
  skulking v ▷ skulk
  skulks v ▷ skulk
skull n (pl **-s**) bony framework of the head
skullcap n (pl **-s**) close-fitting brimless cap
  skullcaps n ▷ skullcap
  skulls n ▷ skull
skunk n (pl **-s**) small black-and-white N American mammal which emits a foul-smelling fluid when attacked
  skunks n ▷ skunk
sky n (pl **skies**) upper atmosphere as seen from the earth
skydiving n (pl **-s**) sport of jumping from an aircraft and performing manoeuvres before opening one's parachute
  skydivings n ▷ skydiving
skylark n (pl **-s**) lark that sings while soaring at a great height
  skylarks n ▷ skylark
skylight n (pl **-s**) window in a roof or ceiling
  skylights n ▷ skylight
skyscraper n (pl **-s**) very tall building
  skyscrapers n ▷ skyscraper
slab n (pl **-s**) broad flat piece
  slabs n ▷ slab
slack adj (**-er**, **-est**) not tight ▶ n (pl **-s**) slack part ▶ v (**-s**, **-ing**, **-ed**) neglect one's work or duty ▷ **slacker** n (pl **-s**) ▷ **slackness** n (pl **-es**)
  slacked v ▷ slack
slacken v (**-s**, **-ing**, **-ed**) make or become slack
  slackened v ▷ slacken
  slackening v ▷ slacken
  slackens v ▷ slacken
  slacker n, adj ▷ slack
  slackers n ▷ slack
  slackest adj ▷ slack
  slacking v ▷ slack
  slackness n ▷ slack
  slacknesses n ▷ slack
slacks n, v ▷ slack ▶ pl n informal trousers
slag n (pl **-s**) waste left after metal is smelted ▶ v (**-s**, **-gging**, **-gged**) (foll. by **off**) (BRIT, AUST & NZ) (Slang) criticize

slagged v ▷ slag
slagging v ▷ slag
slags n, v ▷ slag
slain v ▷ slay
slake v (-kes, -king, -ked) satisfy (thirst or desire)
slaked v ▷ slake
slakes v ▷ slake
slaking v ▷ slake
slalom n (pl -s) skiing or canoeing race over a winding course
slaloms n ▷ slalom
slam v (-s, -mming, -mmed) shut, put down, or hit violently and noisily ▶ n (pl -s) act or sound of slamming
slammed v ▷ slam
slamming v ▷ slam
slams v, n ▷ slam
slander n (pl -s) false and malicious statement about a person ▶ v (-s, -ing, -ed) utter slander about > **slanderous** adj
slandered v ▷ slander
slandering v ▷ slander
slanderous adj ▷ slander
slanders n, v ▷ slander
slang n (pl -s) very informal language > **slangy** adj (-gier, -giest)
slangier adj ▷ slang
slangiest adj ▷ slang
slangs n ▷ slang
slangy adj ▷ slang
slant v (-s, -ing, -ed) lean at an angle, slope ▶ n (pl -s) slope > **slanting** adj
slanted v ▷ slant
slanting v, adj ▷ slant
slants v, n ▷ slant
slap n (pl -s) blow with the open hand or a flat object ▶ v (-s, -pping, -pped) strike with the open hand or a flat object
slapdash adj careless and hasty
slaphappy adj (Informal) cheerfully careless
slapped v ▷ slap
slapping v ▷ slap
slaps n, v ▷ slap
slapstick n (pl -s) boisterous knockabout comedy
slapsticks n ▷ slapstick
slash v (-es, -ing, -ed) cut with a sweeping stroke ▶ n (pl -es) sweeping stroke
slashed v ▷ slash
slashes v, n ▷ slash
slashing v ▷ slash
slat n (pl -s) narrow strip of wood or metal
slate¹ n (pl -s) rock which splits easily into thin layers

slate² v (-tes, -ting, -ted) (Informal) criticize harshly
slated v ▷ slate²
slates n ▷ slate¹ ▶ v ▷ slate²
slating v ▷ slate²
slats n ▷ slat
slattern n (pl -s) (Old-fashioned) slovenly woman > **slatternly** adj
slatternly adv ▷ slattern
slatterns n ▷ slattern
slaughter v (-s, -ing, -ed) kill (animals) for food ▶ n (pl -s) slaughtering
slaughtered v ▷ slaughter
slaughterhouse n (pl -s) place where animals are killed for food
slaughterhouses n ▷ slaughterhouse
slaughtering v ▷ slaughter
slaughters v, n ▷ slaughter
slave n (pl -s) person owned by another for whom he or she has to work ▶ v (-ves, -ing, -ved) work like a slave
slaved v ▷ slave
slaver n (pl -s) person or ship engaged in the slave trade ▶ v [slav-ver] (-s, -ing, -ed) dribble saliva from the mouth
slavered v ▷ slaver
slaveries n ▷ slaver
slavering v ▷ slaver
slavers n, v ▷ slaver
slavery n (pl -ries) state or condition of being a slave
slaves v, n ▷ slave
slaving v ▷ slave
slavish adj of or like a slave
slay v (-s, -ing, slew, slain) kill
slaying v ▷ slay
slays v ▷ slay
sleazes n ▷ sleaze
sleazier adj ▷ sleazy
sleaziest adj ▷ sleazy
sleazy adj (-zier, -ziest) run-down or sordid > **sleaze** n (pl -s)
sled n (pl -s) ▶ v (-s, -dding, -dded) ▷
sledded v ▷ sled
sledding v ▷ sled
sledge¹ n (pl -s) carriage on runners for sliding on snow ▶ v (-dges, -dging, -dged) travel by sledge
sledge², **sledgehammer** n (pl -s) heavy hammer with a long handle
sledged v ▷ sledge¹
sledgehammer n ▷ sledge
sledgehammers n ▷ sledge
sledges n ▷ sledge¹, ² ▶ v ▷ sledge¹
sledging v ▷ sledge¹

sleds n, v ▷ sled

sleek adj (-er, -est) glossy, smooth, and shiny
sleeker adj ▷ sleek
sleekest adj ▷ sleek

sleep n (pl -s) state of rest characterized by unconsciousness ▶ v (-s, -ing, slept) be in or as if in a state of sleep > **sleepy** adj (-pier, -piest) > **sleepily** adv > **sleepiness** n (pl -es) > **sleepless** adj

sleeper n (pl -s) railway car fitted for sleeping in
sleepers n ▷ sleeper
sleepier adj ▷ sleep
sleepiest adj ▷ sleep
sleepily adv ▷ sleep
sleepiness n ▷ sleep
sleepinesses n ▷ sleep
sleeping v ▷ sleep
sleepless adj ▷ sleep

sleepout n (pl -s) (NZ) small building for sleeping in
sleepouts n ▷ sleepout

sleepover n (pl -s) occasion when a person stays overnight at a friend's house
sleepovers n ▷ sleepover
sleeps n, v ▷ sleep
sleepy adj ▷ sleep

sleet n (pl -s) rain and snow or hail falling together
sleets n ▷ sleet

sleeve n (pl -s) part of a garment which covers the arm > **sleeveless** adj
sleeveless adj ▷ sleeve
sleeves n ▷ sleeve

sleigh n (pl -s) ▶ v (-s, -ing, -ed) sledge
sleighed v ▷ sleigh
sleighing v ▷ sleigh
sleighs n, v ▷ sleigh

slender adj (-er, -est) slim
slenderer adj ▷ slender
slenderest adj ▷ slender
slept v ▷ sleep

sleuth [slooth] n (pl -s) detective
sleuths n ▷ sleuth
slew[1] v ▷ slay

slew[2] v (-s, -ing, -ed) twist or swing round
slewed v ▷ slew[2]
slewing v ▷ slew[2]
slews v ▷ slew[2]

slice n (pl -s) thin flat piece cut from something ▶ v (-ces, -cing, -ced) cut into slices
sliced v ▷ slice
slices n, v ▷ slice
slicing v ▷ slice

slick adj (-er, -est) persuasive and glib ▶ n (pl -s)

patch of oil on water ▶ v (-s, -ing, -ed) make smooth or sleek
slicked v ▷ slick
slicker adj ▷ slick
slickest adj ▷ slick
slicking v ▷ slick
slicks n, v ▷ slick
slid v ▷ slide

slide v (-des, -ding, slid) slip smoothly along (a surface) ▶ n (pl -s) sliding
slides v, n ▷ slide
sliding v ▷ slide
slier adj ▷ sly
sliest adj ▷ sly

slight adj (-er, -est) small in quantity or extent ▶ v (-s, -ing, -ed) ▶ n (pl -s) snub > **slightly** adv
slighted v ▷ slight
slighter adj ▷ slight
slightest adj ▷ slight
slighting v ▷ slight
slightly adv ▷ slight
slights v, n ▷ slight

slim adj (-mmer, -mmest) not heavy or stout, thin ▶ v (-s, -mming, -mmed) make or become slim by diet and exercise > **slimmer** n (pl -s)

slime n (pl -s) unpleasant thick slippery substance
slimes n ▷ slime
slimier adj ▷ slimy
slimiest adj ▷ slimy
slimmed v ▷ slim
slimmer adj, n ▷ slim
slimmers n ▷ slim
slimmest adj ▷ slim
slimming v ▷ slim
slims v ▷ slim

slimy adj (-mier, -miest) of, like, or covered with slime

sling[1] n (pl -s) bandage hung from the neck to support an injured hand or arm ▶ v (-s, -ing, slung) throw

sling[2] n (pl -s) sweetened drink with a spirit base
slinging v ▷ sling[1]
slings n ▷ sling[1, 2] ▶ v ▷ sling[1]

slink v (-s, -ing, slunk) move furtively or guiltily
slinkier adj ▷ slinky
slinkiest adj ▷ slinky
slinking v ▷ slink
slinks v ▷ slink

slinky adj (-kier, -kiest) (of clothes) figure-hugging

slip[1] v (-s, -pping, -pped) lose balance by sliding ▶ n (pl -s) slipping

slip[2] n (pl -s) small piece (of paper)

slip³ *n* (*pl* -s) clay mixed with water used for decorating pottery

slipknot *n* (*pl* -s) knot tied so that it will slip along the rope round which it is made
  slipknots *n* ▷ slipknot
  slipped *v* ▷ slip¹

slipper *n* (*pl* -s) light shoe for indoor wear
  slipperier *adj* ▷ slippery
  slipperiest *adj* ▷ slippery
  slippers *n* ▷ slipper

slippery *adj* (-rier, -riest) so smooth or wet as to cause slipping or be difficult to hold
  slippier *adj* ▷ slippy
  slippiest *adj* ▷ slippy
  slipping *v* ▷ slip¹

slippy *adj* (-pier, -piest) (*Informal*) slippery
  slips *n* ▷ slip¹, ², ³ ▶ *v* ▷ slip¹

slipshod *adj* (of an action) careless

slipstream *n* (*pl* -s) stream of air forced backwards by a fast-moving object
  slipstreams *n* ▷ slipstream

slipway *n* (*pl* -s) launching slope on which ships are built or repaired
  slipways *n* ▷ slipway

slit *n* (*pl* -s) long narrow cut or opening ▶ *v* (-s, -tting, slit) make a long straight cut in

slither *v* (-s, -ing, -ed) slide unsteadily
  slithered *v* ▷ slither
  slithering *v* ▷ slither
  slithers *v* ▷ slither
  slits *n*, *v* ▷ slit
  slitting *v* ▷ slit

sliver [sliv-ver] *n* (*pl* -s) small thin piece
  slivers *n* ▷ sliver

slob *n* (*pl* -s) (*Informal*) lazy and untidy person
  > **slobbish** *adj*

slobber *v* (-s, -ing, -ed) dribble or drool
  > **slobbery** *adj*
  slobbered *v* ▷ slobber
  slobbering *v* ▷ slobber
  slobbers *v* ▷ slobber
  slobbery *adj* ▷ slobber
  slobbish *adj* ▷ slob
  slobs *n* ▷ slob

sloe *n* (*pl* -s) sour blue-black fruit
  sloes *n* ▷ sloe

slog *v* (-s, -gging, -gged) work hard and steadily ▶ *n* (*pl* -s) long and exhausting work or walk

slogan *n* (*pl* -s) catchword or phrase used in politics or advertising
  slogans *n* ▷ slogan
  slogged *v* ▷ slog
  slogging *v* ▷ slog
  slogs *v*, *n* ▷ slog

sloop *n* (*pl* -s) small single-masted ship
  sloops *n* ▷ sloop

slop *v* (-s, -pping, -pped) splash or spill ▶ *n* (*pl* -s) spilt liquid

slope *v* (-pes, -ping, -ped) slant ▶ *n* (*pl* -s) sloping surface
  sloped *v* ▷ slope

slopes *v*, *n* ▷ slope ▶ *pl n* hills
  sloping *v* ▷ slope
  slopped *v* ▷ slop
  sloppier *adj* ▷ sloppy
  sloppiest *adj* ▷ sloppy
  slopping *v* ▷ slop

sloppy *adj* (-ppier, -ppiest) careless or untidy

slops *v*, *n* ▷ slop ▶ *pl n* liquid refuse and waste food used to feed animals

slosh *v* (-s, -ing, -ed) splash carelessly ▶ *n* (*pl* -es) splashing sound

sloshed *adj* (*Slang*) drunk ▶ *v* ▷ slosh
  sloshes *v*, *n* ▷ slosh
  sloshing *v* ▷ slosh

slot *n* (*pl* -s) narrow opening for inserting something ▶ *v* (-s, -tting, -tted) make a slot or slots in

sloth [rhymes with **both**] *n* (*pl* -s) slow-moving animal of tropical America

slothful *adj* lazy or idle
  sloths *n* ▷ sloth
  slots *n*, *v* ▷ slot
  slotted *v* ▷ slot
  slotting *v* ▷ slot

slouch *v* (-es, -ing, -ed) sit, stand, or move with a drooping posture ▶ *n* (*pl* -es) drooping posture
  slouched *v* ▷ slouch
  slouches *v*, *n* ▷ slouch
  slouching *v* ▷ slouch

slough¹ [rhymes with **now**] *n* (*pl* -s) bog

slough² [**sluff**] *v* (-s, -ing, -ed) (of a snake) shed (its skin) or (of a skin) be shed
  sloughed *v* ▷ slough²
  sloughing *v* ▷ slough²
  sloughs *n* ▷ slough¹ ▶ *v* ▷ slough²

sloven *n* (*pl* -s) habitually dirty or untidy person
  slovenlier *adj* ▷ slovenly
  slovenliest *adj* ▷ slovenly

slovenly *adj* (-lier, -liest) dirty or untidy
  slovens *n* ▷ sloven

slow *adj* (-er, -est) taking a longer time than is usual or expected ▶ *v* (-s, -ing, -ed) reduce the speed (of) > **slowly** *adv* > **slowness** *n* (*pl* -es)

slowcoach *n* (*pl* -es) (*Informal*) person who moves or works slowly
  slowcoaches *n* ▷ slowcoach

slowed v ▷ slow
slower adj ▷ slow
slowest adj ▷ slow
slowing v ▷ slow
slowly adv ▷ slow
slowness n ▷ slow
slownesses n ▷ slow
slows v ▷ slow
slowworm n (pl -s) small legless lizard
slowworms n ▷ slowworm
sludge n (pl -s) thick mud
sludges n ▷ sludge
slug[1] n (pl -s) land snail with no shell
slug[2] n (pl -s) bullet (Informal)
slug[3] v (-s, -gging, -gged) hit hard ▶ n (pl -s)
heavy blow
sluggard n (pl -s) lazy person
sluggards n ▷ sluggard
slugged v ▷ slug[3]
slugging v ▷ slug[3]
sluggish adj slow-moving, lacking energy
> **sluggishly** adv > **sluggishness** n (pl -es)
sluggishly adv ▷ sluggish
sluggishness n ▷ sluggish
sluggishnesses n ▷ sluggish
slugs n ▷ slug[1, 2, 3] ▶ v ▷ slug[3]
sluice n (pl -s) channel carrying off water ▶ v
(-ces, -cing, -ced) pour a stream of water over
or through
sluiced v ▷ sluice
sluices n, v ▷ sluice
sluicing v ▷ sluice
slum n (pl -s) squalid overcrowded house or
area ▶ v (-s, -mming, -mmed) temporarily
and deliberately experience poorer places or
conditions than usual
slumber v (-s, -ing, -ed) ▶ n (pl -s) (Lit) sleep
slumbered v ▷ slumber
slumbering v ▷ slumber
slumbers v, n ▷ slumber
slummed v ▷ slum
slumming v ▷ slum
slump v (-s, -ing, -ed) (of prices or demand)
decline suddenly ▶ n (pl -s) sudden decline in
prices or demand
slumped v ▷ slump
slumping v ▷ slump
slumps v, n ▷ slump
slums n, v ▷ slum
slung v ▷ sling[1]
slunk v ▷ slink
slur v (-s, -rring, -rred) pronounce or utter
(words) indistinctly ▶ n (pl -s) slurring of
words
slurp (Informal) v (-s, -ing, -ed) eat or drink

noisily ▶ n (pl -s) slurping sound
slurped v ▷ slurp
slurping v ▷ slurp
slurps v, n ▷ slurp
slurred v ▷ slur
slurries n ▷ slurry
slurring v ▷ slur
slurry n (pl -ries) muddy liquid mixture
slurs v, n ▷ slur
slush n (pl -es) watery muddy substance
> **slushy** adj (-shier, -shiest)
slushes n ▷ slush
slushier adj ▷ slush
slushiest adj ▷ slush
slushy adj ▷ slush
sly adj (slyer, slyest or slier, sliest) crafty > **slyly**
adv > **slyness** n (pl -es)
slyer adj ▷ sly
slyest adj ▷ sly
slyly adv ▷ sly
slyness n ▷ sly
slynesses n ▷ sly
smack[1] v (-s, -ing, -ed) slap sharply ▶ n (pl -s)
sharp slap ▶ adv (Informal) squarely or directly
smack[2] n (pl -s) slight flavour or trace ▶ v (-s,
-ing, -ed) have a slight flavour or trace (of)
smack[3] n (pl -s) small single-masted fishing
boat
smacked v ▷ smack[1, 2]
smacker n (pl -s) (Slang) loud kiss
smackers n ▷ smacker
smacking v ▷ smack[1, 2]
smacks n ▷ smack[1, 2, 3] ▶ v ▷ smack[1, 2]
small adj (-er, -est) not large in size, number,
or amount ▶ n (pl -s) narrow part of the lower
back > **smallness** n (pl -es)
smaller adj ▷ small
smallest adj ▷ small
smallholding n (pl -s) small area of farming
land
smallholdings n ▷ smallholding
smallness n ▷ small
smallnesses n ▷ small
smallpox n (pl -es) contagious disease with
blisters that leave scars
smallpoxes n ▷ smallpox
smalls n ▷ small ▶ pl n (Informal) underwear
smarmier adj ▷ smarmy
smarmiest adj ▷ smarmy
smarmy adj (-mier, -miest) (Informal)
unpleasantly suave or flattering
smart adj (-er, -est) well-kept and neat ▶ v (-s,
-ing, -ed) feel or cause stinging pain ▶ n (pl
-s) stinging pain > **smartly** adv > **smartness**
n (pl -es)

smarted v ▷ smart
smarten v (-s, -ing, -ed) make or become smart
smartened v ▷ smarten
smartening v ▷ smarten
smartens v ▷ smarten
smarter adj ▷ smart
smartest adj ▷ smart
smarting v ▷ smart
smartly adv ▷ smart
smartness n ▷ smart
smartnesses n ▷ smart
smarts v, n ▷ smart
smash v (-es, -ing, -ed) break violently and noisily ▶ n (pl -es) act or sound of smashing
smashed v ▷ smash
smasher n (pl -s) (Informal) attractive person or thing
smashers n ▷ smasher
smashes v, n ▷ smash
smashing adj (Informal) excellent ▶ v ▷ smash
smattering n (pl -s) slight knowledge
smatterings n ▷ smattering
smear v (-s, -ing, -ed) spread with a greasy or sticky substance ▶ n (pl -s) dirty mark or smudge
smeared v ▷ smear
smearing v ▷ smear
smears n, v ▷ smear
smell v (-s, -ing, smelt or -ed) perceive (a scent or odour) by means of the nose ▶ n (pl -s) ability to perceive odours by the nose
smelled v ▷ smell
smellier adj ▷ smelly
smelliest adj ▷ smelly
smelling v ▷ smell
smells v, n ▷ smell
smelly adj (-lier, -liest) having a nasty smell
smelt[1] v (-s, -ing, -ed) extract (a metal) from (an ore) by heating
smelt[2] n (pl smelt) small fish of the salmon family
smelt[3] v ▷ smell
smelted v ▷ smelt[1]
smelter n (pl -s) industrial plant where smelting is carried out
smelters n ▷ smelter
smelting v ▷ smelt[1]
smelts v ▷ smelt[1]
smile n (pl -s) turning up of the corners of the mouth to show pleasure, amusement, or friendliness ▶ v (-les, -ing, -led) give a smile
smiled v ▷ smile
smiles n, v ▷ smile
smiley n (pl -s) symbol depicting a smile or

other facial expression, used in e-mail
smileys n ▷ smiley
smiling v ▷ smile
smirch v (-es, -ing, -ed) ▶ n (pl -es) stain
smirched v ▷ smirch
smirches v, n ▷ smirch
smirching v ▷ smirch
smirk n (pl -s) smug smile ▶ v (-s, -ing, -ed) give a smirk
smirked v ▷ smirk
smirking v ▷ smirk
smirks n, v ▷ smirk
smite v (-tes, -ting, smote, smitten) (Old-fashioned) strike hard
smites v ▷ smite
smith n (pl -s) worker in metal
smithereens pl n shattered fragments
smithies n ▷ smithy
smiths n ▷ smith
smithy n (pl -thies) blacksmith's workshop
smiting v ▷ smite
smitten v ▷ smite
smock n (pl -s) loose overall ▶ v (-s, -ing, -ed) gather (material) by sewing in a honeycomb pattern > **smocking** n (pl -s)
smocked v ▷ smock
smocking v, n ▷ smock
smockings n ▷ smock
smocks n, v ▷ smock
smog n (pl -s) mixture of smoke and fog
smogs n ▷ smog
smoke n (pl -s) cloudy mass that rises from something burning ▶ v (-kes, -king, -ked) give off smoke > **smokeless** adj > **smoker** n (pl -s) > **smoky** adj (-kier, -kiest)
smoked v ▷ smoke
smokeless adj ▷ smoke
smoker n ▷ smok
smokers n ▷ smok
smokes n, v ▷ smoke
smokier adj ▷ smoke
smokiest adj ▷ smoke
smoking v ▷ smoke
smoky adj ▷ smoke
smooch (Informal) v (-es, -ing, -ed) kiss and cuddle ▶ n (pl -es) smooching
smooched v ▷ smooch
smooches v, n ▷ smooch
smooching v ▷ smooch
smooth adj (-er, -est) even in surface, texture, or consistency ▶ v (-s, -ing, -ed) make smooth > **smoothly** adv
smoothed v ▷ smooth
smoother adj ▷ smooth
smoothest adj ▷ smooth

smoothie n (pl -thies) (Informal) charming but possibly insincere man
smoothies n ▷ smoothie
smoothing v ▷ smooth
smoothly adv ▷ smooth
smooths v ▷ smooth
smorgasbord n (pl -s) buffet meal of assorted dishes
smorgasbords n ▷ smorgasbord
smote v ▷ smite
smother v (-s, -ing, -ed) suffocate or stifle
smothered v ▷ smother
smothering v ▷ smother
smothers v ▷ smother
smoulder v (-s, -ing, -ed) burn slowly with smoke but no flame
smouldered v ▷ smoulder
smouldering v ▷ smoulder
smoulders v ▷ smoulder
smudge v (-ges, -ging, -ged) make or become smeared or soiled ▶ n (pl -s) dirty mark
> **smudgy** adj (-gier, -giest)
smudged v ▷ smudge
smudges v, n ▷ smudge
smudgier adj ▷ smudge
smudgiest adj ▷ smudge
smudging v ▷ smudge
smudgy adj ▷ smudge
smug adj (-gger, -ggest) self-satisfied > **smugly** adv > **smugness** n (pl -es)
smugger adj ▷ smug
smuggest adj ▷ smug
smuggle v (-les, -ling, -led) import or export (goods) secretly and illegally > **smuggler** n (pl -s)
smuggled v ▷ smuggle
smuggler n ▷ smuggle
smugglers n ▷ smuggle
smuggles v ▷ smuggle
smuggling v ▷ smuggle
smugly adv ▷ smug
smugness n ▷ smug
smugnesses n ▷ smug
smut n (pl -s) obscene jokes, pictures, etc. > **smutty** adj (-tier, -tiest)
smuts n ▷ smut
smuttier adj ▷ smut
smuttiest adj ▷ smut
smutty adj ▷ smut
snack n (pl -s) light quick meal
snacks n ▷ snack
snaffle n (pl -s) jointed bit for a horse ▶ v (-les, -ling, -led) (BRIT, AUST & NZ) (Slang) steal
snaffled v ▷ snaffle
snaffles n, v ▷ snaffle

snaffling v ▷ snaffle
snag n (pl -s) difficulty or disadvantage ▶ v (-s, -gging, -gged) catch or tear on a point
snagged v ▷ snag
snagging v ▷ snag
snags n, v ▷ snag
snail n (pl -s) slow-moving mollusc with a spiral shell
snails n ▷ snail
snake n (pl -s) long thin scaly limbless reptile ▶ v (-kes, -king, -ked) move in a winding course like a snake
snaked v ▷ snake
snakes n, v ▷ snake
snakier adj ▷ snaky
snakiest adj ▷ snaky
snaking v ▷ snake
snaky adj (-kier, -kiest) twisted or winding
snap v (-s, -pping, -pped) break suddenly ▶ n (pl -s) act or sound of snapping ▶ adj made on the spur of the moment
snapdragon n (pl -s) plant with flowers that can open and shut like a mouth
snapdragons n ▷ snapdragon
snapped v ▷ snap
snapper n (pl -s) food fish of Australia and New Zealand with a pinkish body covered with blue spots
snappers n ▷ snapper
snappier adj ▷ snappy
snappiest adj ▷ snappy
snapping v ▷ snap
snappish adj ▷ snappy
snappy adj (-ppier, -ppiest) (also **snappish**) irritable
snaps v, n ▷ snap
snapshot n (pl -s) informal photograph
snapshots n ▷ snapshot
snare n (pl -s) trap with a noose ▶ v (-res, -ring, -red) catch in or as if in a snare
snared v ▷ snare
snares n, v ▷ snare
snaring v ▷ snare
snarl¹ v (-s, -ing, -ed) (of an animal) growl with bared teeth ▶ n (pl -s) act or sound of snarling
snarl² n (pl -s) tangled mess ▶ v (-s, -ing, -ed) make tangled
snarled v ▷ snarl¹, ²
snarling v ▷ snarl¹, ²
snarls n, v ▷ snarl¹, ²
snatch v (-es, -ing, -ed) seize or try to seize suddenly ▶ n (pl -es) snatching
snatched v ▷ snatch
snatches v, n ▷ snatch
snatching v ▷ snatch

snazzier adj ▷ snazzy
snazziest adj ▷ snazzy
snazzy adj (-zzier, -zziest) (*Informal*) stylish and flashy
sneak v (-s, -ing, -ed) move furtively ▶ n (pl -s) cowardly or underhand person > **sneaky** adj (-kier, -kiest)
sneaked v ▷ sneak
sneakers pl n canvas shoes with rubber soles
sneakier adj ▷ sneak
sneakiest adj ▷ sneak
sneaking adj slight but persistent ▶ v ▷ sneak
sneaks v, n ▷ sneak
sneaky adj ▷ sneak
sneer n (pl -s) contemptuous expression or remark ▶ v (-s, -ing, -ed) show contempt by a sneer
sneered v ▷ sneer
sneering v ▷ sneer
sneers n, v ▷ sneer
sneeze v (-zes, -zing, -zed) expel air from the nose suddenly, involuntarily, and noisily ▶ n (pl -s) act or sound of sneezing
sneezed v ▷ sneeze
sneezes v, n ▷ sneeze
sneezing v ▷ sneeze
snicker n (pl -s) ▶ v (-s, -ing, -ed) ▷ snigger
snickered v ▷ snicker
snickering v ▷ snicker
snickers n, v ▷ snicker
snide adj (-r, -st) critical in an unfair and nasty way
snider adj ▷ snide
snidest adj ▷ snide
sniff v (-s, -ing, -ed) inhale through the nose in short audible breaths ▶ n (pl -s) act or sound of sniffing
sniffed v ▷ sniff
sniffing v ▷ sniff
sniffle v (-les, -ling, -led) sniff repeatedly, as when suffering from a cold ▶ n (pl -s) slight cold
sniffled v ▷ sniffle
sniffles v, n ▷ sniffle
sniffling v ▷ sniffle
sniffs v, n ▷ sniff
snifter n (pl -s) (*Informal*) small quantity of alcoholic drink
snifters n ▷ snifter
snigger n (pl -s) sly disrespectful laugh, esp. one partly stifled ▶ v (-s, -ing, -ed) utter a snigger
sniggered v ▷ snigger
sniggering v ▷ snigger
sniggers n, v ▷ snigger

snip v (-s, -pping, -pped) cut in small quick strokes with scissors or shears ▶ n (pl -s) (*Informal*) bargain
snipe n (pl -s) wading bird with a long straight bill ▶ v (-pes, -ping, -ped) (foll. by **at**) shoot at (a person) from cover
sniped v ▷ snipe
sniper n (pl -s) person who shoots at someone from cover
snipers n ▷ sniper
snipes n, v ▷ snipe
sniping v ▷ snipe
snipped v ▷ snip
snippet n (pl -s) small piece
snippets n ▷ snippet
snipping v ▷ snip
snips v, n ▷ snip
snitch (*Informal*) v (-es, -ing, -ed) act as an informer ▶ n (pl -es) informer
snitched v ▷ snitch
snitches v, n ▷ snitch
snitching v ▷ snitch
snivel v (-s, -ling, -lled) cry in a whining way
snivelled v ▷ snivel
snivelling v ▷ snivel
snivels v ▷ snivel
snob n (pl -s) person who judges others by social rank > **snobbery** n (pl -ries) > **snobbish** adj
snobberies n ▷ snob
snobbery n ▷ snob
snobbish adj ▷ snob
snobs n ▷ snob
snoek n (pl -s) (S AFR) edible marine fish
snoeks n ▷ snoek
snood n (pl -s) pouch, often of net, loosely holding a woman's hair at the back
snoods n ▷ snood
snook n (pl -s) gesture of contempt
snooker n (pl -s) game played on a billiard table ▶ v (-s, -ing, -ed) leave (a snooker opponent) in a position such that another ball blocks the target ball
snookered v ▷ snooker
snookering v ▷ snooker
snookers n, v ▷ snooker
snooks n ▷ snook
snoop (*Informal*) v (-s, -ing, -ed) pry ▶ n (pl -s) snooping > **snooper** n (pl -s)
snooped v ▷ snoop
snooper n ▷ snoop
snoopers n ▷ snoop
snooping v ▷ snoop
snoops v, n ▷ snoop
snootier adj ▷ snooty

snootiest adj ▷ snooty

snooty adj (**-tier, -tiest**) (Informal) haughty

snooze (Informal) v (**-zes, -zing, -zed**) take a brief light sleep ▶ n (pl **-s**) brief light sleep

snoozed v ▷ snooze

snoozes v, n ▷ snooze

snoozing v ▷ snooze

snore v (**-res, -ring, -red**) make snorting sounds while sleeping ▶ n (pl **-s**) sound of snoring

snored v ▷ snore

snores v, n ▷ snore

snoring v ▷ snore

snorkel n (pl **-s**) tube allowing a swimmer to breathe while face down on the surface of the water ▶ v (**-s, -lling, -lled**) swim using a snorkel

snorkelled v ▷ snorkel

snorkelling v ▷ snorkel

snorkels n, v ▷ snorkel

snort v (**-s, -ing, -ed**) exhale noisily through the nostrils ▶ n (pl **-s**) act or sound of snorting

snorted v ▷ snort

snorting v ▷ snort

snorts v, n ▷ snort

snot n (pl **-s**) (Slang) mucus from the nose

snots n ▷ snot

snout n (pl **-s**) animal's projecting nose and jaws

snouts n ▷ snout

snow n (pl **-s**) frozen vapour falling from the sky in flakes ▶ v (**-s, -ing, -ed**) fall as or like snow > **snowy** adj (**-wier, -wiest**)

snowball n (pl **-s**) snow pressed into a ball for throwing ▶ v (**-s, -ing, -ed**) increase rapidly

snowballed v ▷ snowball

snowballing v ▷ snowball

snowballs n, v ▷ snowball

snowboard n (pl **-s**) board on which a person stands to slide across the snow > **snowboarding** n (pl **-s**)

snowboarding n ▷ snowboard

snowboardings n ▷ snowboard

snowboards n ▷ snowboard

snowdrift n (pl **-s**) bank of deep snow

snowdrifts n ▷ snowdrift

snowdrop n (pl **-s**) small white bell-shaped spring flower

snowdrops n ▷ snowdrop

snowed v ▷ snow

snowflake n (pl **-s**) single crystal of snow

snowflakes n ▷ snowflake

snowier adj ▷ snow

snowiest adj ▷ snow

snowing v ▷ snow

snowman n (pl **-men**) figure shaped out of snow

snowmen n ▷ snowman

snowplough n (pl **-s**) vehicle for clearing away snow

snowploughs n ▷ snowplough

snows n, v ▷ snow

snowshoes pl n racket-shaped shoes for travelling on snow

snowy adj ▷ snow

snub v (**-s, -bbing, -bbed**) insult deliberately ▶ n (pl **-s**) deliberate insult ▶ adj (of a nose) short and blunt

snubbed v ▷ snub

snubbing v ▷ snub

snubs v, n ▷ snub

snuff¹ n (pl **-s**) powdered tobacco for sniffing up the nostrils

snuff² v (**-s, -ing, -ed**) extinguish (a candle)

snuffed v ▷ snuff²

snuffing v ▷ snuff²

snuffle v (**-les, -ling, -led**) breathe noisily or with difficulty

snuffled v ▷ snuffle

snuffles v ▷ snuffle

snuffling v ▷ snuffle

snuffs n ▷ snuff¹ n ▷ snuff²

snug adj (**-gger, -ggest**) warm and comfortable ▶ n (pl **-s**) (in Britain and Ireland) small room in a pub > **snugly** adv

snugger adj ▷ snug

snuggest adj ▷ snug

snuggle v (**-les, -ling, -led**) nestle into a person or thing for warmth or from affection

snuggled v ▷ snuggle

snuggles v ▷ snuggle

snuggling v ▷ snuggle

snugly adv ▷ snug

snugs n ▷ snug

> **sny** n (**snys**). Sny is a Canadian word for a side channel of a river. This word doesn't contain a vowel, so it can help you to clear an awkward rack. Sny scores 6 points.

so adv to such an extent ▶ conj in order that ▶ interj exclamation of surprise, triumph, or realization

soak v (**-s, -ing, -ed**) make wet ▶ n (pl **-s**) soaking > **soaking** n (pl **-s**) adj

soaked v ▷ soak

soaking v, n, adj ▷ soak

soakings n ▷ soak

soaks v, n ▷ soak

soap n (pl **-s**) compound of alkali and fat, used with water as a cleaning agent ▶ v (**-s, -ing,**

-ed) apply soap to > **soapy** *adj* (**-pier, -piest**)
soaped *v* ▷ soap
soapier *adj* ▷ soap
soapiest *adj* ▷ soap
soaping *v* ▷ soap
soaps *n, v* ▷ soap
soapy *adj* ▷ soap
soar *v* (**-s, -ing, -ed**) rise or fly upwards
soared *v* ▷ soar
soaring *v* ▷ soar
soars *v* ▷ soar
sob *v* (**-s, -bbing, -bbed**) weep with convulsive gasps ▶ *n* (**pl -s**) act or sound of sobbing
sobbed *v* ▷ sob
sobbing *v* ▷ sob
sober *adj* (**-er, -est**) not drunk ▶ *v* (**-s, -ing, -ed**) make or become sober > **soberly** *adv*
sobered *v* ▷ sober
soberer *adj* ▷ sober
soberest *adj* ▷ sober
sobering *v* ▷ sober
soberly *adv* ▷ sober
sobers *v* ▷ sober
sobrieties *n* ▷ sobriety
sobriety *n* (**pl -ties**) state of being sober
sobriquet [so-brik-ay] *n* (**pl -s**) nickname
sobriquets *n* ▷ sobriquet
sobs *v, n* ▷ sob
soccer *n* (**pl -s**) football played by two teams of eleven kicking a spherical ball
soccers *n* ▷ soccer
sociabilities *n* ▷ sociable
sociability *n* ▷ sociable
sociable *adj* friendly or companionable > **sociability** *n* (**pl -ties**) > **sociably** *adv*
sociably *adv* ▷ sociable
social *adj* living in a community ▶ *n* (**pl -s**) informal gathering > **socially** *adv*
socialism *n* (**pl -s**) political system which advocates public ownership of industries, resources, and transport
socialisms *n* ▷ socialism
socialist *n* (**pl -s**) ▶ *adj*
socialists *n* ▷ socialist
socialite *n* (**pl -s**) member of fashionable society
socialites *n* ▷ socialite
socialize *v* (**-zes, -zing, -zed**) meet others socially
socialized *v* ▷ socialize
socializes *v* ▷ socialize
socializing *v* ▷ socialize
socially *adv* ▷ social
socials *n* ▷ social
societies *n* ▷ society

society *n* (**pl -ties**) human beings considered as a group
sociological *adj* ▷ sociology
sociologies *n* ▷ sociology
sociologist *n* ▷ sociology
sociologists *n* ▷ sociology
sociology *n* (**pl -gies**) study of human societies > **sociological** *adj* > **sociologist** *n* (**pl -s**)
sock[1] *n* (**pl -s**) knitted covering for the foot
sock[2] (*Slang*) *v* (**-s, -ing, -ed**) hit hard ▶ *n* (**pl -s**) hard blow
socked *v* ▷ sock[2]
socket *n* (**pl -s**) hole or recess into which something fits
sockets *n* ▷ socket
socking *v* ▷ sock[2]
socks *v* ▷ sock[2] ▶ *n* ▷ sock[1, 2]
sod *n* (**pl -s**) (piece of) turf
soda *n* (**pl -s**) compound of sodium
sodas *n* ▷ soda
sodden *adj* soaked
sodium *n* (**pl -s**) (CHEM) silvery-white metallic element
sodiums *n* ▷ sodium
sods *n* ▷ sod
sofa *n* (**pl -s**) couch
sofas *n* ▷ sofa
soft *adj* (**-er, -est**) easy to shape or cut > **softly** *adv*
soften *v* (**-s, -ing, -ed**) make or become soft or softer
softened *v* ▷ soften
softening *v* ▷ soften
softens *v* ▷ soften
softer *adj* ▷ soft
softest *adj* ▷ soft
softly *adv* ▷ soft
software *n* (**pl -s**) computer programs
softwares *n* ▷ software
softwood *n* (**pl -s**) wood of a coniferous tree
softwoods *n* ▷ softwood
soggier *adj* ▷ soggy
soggiest *adj* ▷ soggy
sogginess *n* ▷ soggy
sogginesses *n* ▷ soggy
soggy *adj* (**-ggier, -ggiest**) soaked > **sogginess** *n* (**pl -es**)
soigné, *fem* **soignée** [swah-nyay] *adj* well-groomed, elegant
soil[1] *n* (**pl -s**) top layer of earth
soil[2] *v* (**-s, -ing, -ed**) make or become dirty
soiled *v* ▷ soil
soiling *v* ▷ soil
soils *n* ▷ soil[1] ▶ *v* ▷ soil[2]
soiree [swah-ray] *n* (**pl -s**) evening party or gathering

soirees *n* ▷ soiree

sojourn [soj-urn] *n* (*pl* -s) temporary stay ▶ *v* (-s, -ing, -ed) stay temporarily
sojourned *v* ▷ sojourn
sojourning *v* ▷ sojourn
sojourns *n, v* ▷ sojourn

solace [sol-iss] *n, v* (-ces, -cing, -ced) comfort in distress
solaced *v* ▷ solace
solaces *v* ▷ solace
solacing *v* ▷ solace

solar *adj* of the sun
solaria *n* ▷ solarium

solarium *n* (*pl* -riums, -ria) place with beds and ultraviolet lights used for acquiring an artificial suntan
solariums *n* ▷ solarium
sold *v* ▷ sell

solder *n* (*pl* -s) soft alloy used to join two metal surfaces ▶ *v* (-s, -ing, -ed) join with solder
soldered *v* ▷ solder
soldering *v* ▷ solder
solders *n, v* ▷ solder

soldier *n* (*pl* -s) member of an army ▶ *v* (-s, -ing, -ed) serve in an army ▷ soldierly *adj*
soldiered *v* ▷ soldier
soldiering *v* ▷ soldier
soldierly *adj* ▷ soldier
soldiers *n, v* ▷ soldier

sole¹ *adj* one and only

sole² *n* (*pl* -s) underside of the foot ▶ *v* (-les, -ling, -led) provide (a shoe) with a sole

sole³ *n* (*pl* -s) small edible flatfish

solecism [sol-iss-izz-um] *n* (*pl* -s) minor grammatical mistake
solecisms *n* ▷ solecism
soled *v* ▷ sole²

solely *adv* only, completely

solemn *adj* (-er, -est) serious, deeply sincere ▷ solemnly *adv* ▷ solemnity *n* (*pl* -ties)
solemner *adj* ▷ solemn
solemnest *adj* ▷ solemn
solemnities *n* ▷ solemn
solemnity *n* ▷ solemn
solemnly *adv* ▷ solemn

solenoid [sole-in-oid] *n* (*pl* -s) coil of wire magnetized by passing a current through it
solenoids *n* ▷ solenoid
soles *n* ▷ sole², ³ ▶ *v* ▷ sole²

solicit *v* (-s, -ing, -ed) request ▷ solicitation *n* (*pl* -s)
solicitation *n* ▷ solicit
solicitations *n* ▷ solicit
solicited *v* ▷ solicit
soliciting *v* ▷ solicit

solicitor *n* (*pl* -s) (BRIT, AUST & NZ) lawyer who advises clients and prepares documents and cases
solicitors *n* ▷ solicitor

solicitous *adj* anxious about someone's welfare ▷ solicitude *n* (*pl* -s)
solicits *v* ▷ solicit
solicitude *n* ▷ solicitous
solicitudes *n* ▷ solicitous

solid *adj* (-er, -est) (of a substance) keeping its shape ▶ *n* (*pl* -s) three-dimensional shape ▷ solidity *n* (*pl* -ties) ▷ solidly *adv*
solidarities *n* ▷ solidarity

solidarity *n* (*pl* -ties) agreement in aims or interests, total unity
solider *adj* ▷ solid
solidest *adj* ▷ solid
solidified *v* ▷ solidify
solidifies *v* ▷ solidify

solidify *v* (-fies, -fying, -fied) make or become solid or firm
solidifying *v* ▷ solidify
solidities *n* ▷ solid
solidity *n* ▷ solid
solidly *adv* ▷ solid
solids *n* ▷ solid
soliloquies *n* ▷ soliloquy

soliloquy *n* (*pl* -quies) speech made by a person while alone, esp. in a play
soling *v* ▷ sole²

solipsism *n* (*pl* -s) doctrine that the self is the only thing known to exist ▷ solipsist *n* (*pl* -s)
solipsisms *n* ▷ solipsism
solipsist *n* ▷ solipsism
solipsists *n* ▷ solipsism

solitaire *n* (*pl* -s) game for one person played with pegs set in a board
solitaires *n* ▷ solitaire

solitary *adj* alone, single

solitude *n* (*pl* -s) state of being alone
solitudes *n* ▷ solitude

solo *n* (*pl* -s) music for one performer ▶ *adj* done alone ▶ *adv* by oneself, alone ▷ soloist *n* (*pl* -s)
soloist *n* ▷ solo
soloists *n* ▷ solo
solos *n* ▷ solo

solstice *n* (*pl* -s) either the shortest (in winter) or longest (in summer) day of the year
solstices *n* ▷ solstice
solubilities *n* ▷ soluble
solubility *n* ▷ soluble

soluble *adj* able to be dissolved ▷ solubility *n* (*pl* -ties)

solution *n* (*pl* -s) answer to a problem
solutions *n* ▷ solution

solvable adj ▷ solve
solve v (-ves, -ving, -ved) find the answer to (a problem) > **solvable** adj
solved v ▷ solve
solvencies n ▷ solvent
solvency n ▷ solvent
solvent adj having enough money to pay one's debts ▶ n (pl -s) liquid capable of dissolving other substances > **solvency** n (pl -cies)
solvents n ▷ solvent
solves v ▷ solve
solving v ▷ solve
sombre adj (-r, -st) dark, gloomy
sombrer adj ▷ sombre
sombrero n (pl -s) wide-brimmed Mexican hat
sombreros n ▷ sombrero
sombrest adj ▷ sombre
some adj unknown or unspecified (Informal) ▶ pron certain unknown or unspecified people or things
somebodies n ▷ somebody
somebody pron some person ▶ n (pl -dies) important person
somehow adv in some unspecified way
someone pron somebody
somersault n (pl -s) leap or roll in which the trunk and legs are turned over the head ▶ v (-s, -ing, -ed) perform a somersault
somersaulted v ▷ somersault
somersaulting v ▷ somersault
somersaults n, v ▷ somersault
something pron unknown or unspecified thing or amount
sometime adv at some unspecified time ▶ adj former
sometimes adv from time to time, now and then
somewhat adv to some extent, rather
somewhere adv in, to, or at some unspecified or unknown place
somnambulism n ▷ somnambulist
somnambulisms n ▷ somnambulist
somnambulist n (pl -s) person who walks in his or her sleep > **somnambulism** n (pl -s)
somnambulists n ▷ somnambulist
somnolent adj drowsy
son n (pl -s) male offspring
sonar n (pl -s) device for detecting underwater objects by the reflection of sound waves
sonars n ▷ sonar
sonata n (pl -s) piece of music in several movements for one instrument with or without piano
sonatas n ▷ sonata
song n (pl -s) music for the voice

songbird n (pl -s) any bird with a musical call
songbirds n ▷ songbird
songs n ▷ song
songster, songstress n (pl -s, -es) singer
songsters n ▷ songster
songstress n ▷ songster
songstresses n ▷ songster
sonic adj of or producing sound
sonnet n (pl -s) fourteen-line poem with a fixed rhyme scheme
sonnets n ▷ sonnet
sonorities n ▷ sonorous
sonority n ▷ sonorous
sonorous adj (of sound) deep or resonant > **sonorously** adv > **sonority** n (pl -ties)
sonorously adv ▷ sonorous
sons n ▷ son
soon adv in a short time
sooner adv rather
soot n (pl -s) black powder formed by the incomplete burning of an organic substance > **sooty** adj (-tier, -tiest)
soothe v (-thes, -thing, -thed) make calm
soothed v ▷ soothe
soothes v ▷ soothe
soothing v ▷ soothe
soothsayer n (pl -s) seer or prophet
soothsayers n ▷ soothsayer
sootier adj ▷ soot
sootiest adj ▷ soot
soots n ▷ soot
sooty adj ▷ soot
sop n (pl -s) concession to pacify someone ▶ v (-s, -pping, -pped) mop up or absorb (liquid)
sophism n ▷ sophistry
sophisms n ▷ sophistry
sophist n (pl -s) person who uses clever but invalid arguments
sophisticate v (-tes, -ting, -ted) make less natural or innocent ▶ n (pl -s) sophisticated person
sophisticated adj having or appealing to refined or cultured tastes and habits ▶ v ▷ sophisticate > **sophistication** n (pl -s)
sophisticates v, n ▷ sophisticate
sophisticating v ▷ sophisticate
sophistication n ▷ sophisticated
sophistications n ▷ sophisticated
sophistries n ▷ sophistry
sophistry, sophism n (pl -ries, -s) clever but invalid argument
sophists n ▷ sophist
sophomore n (pl -s) (US) student in second year at college
sophomores n ▷ sophomore

soporific *adj* causing sleep ▸ *n* (*pl* **-s**) drug that causes sleep
 soporifics *n* ▷ soporific
sopped *v* ▷ sop
soppier *adj* ▷ soppy
soppiest *adj* ▷ soppy
sopping *adj* completely soaked ▸ *v* ▷ sop
soppy *adj* (**soppier, soppiest**) (*Informal*) oversentimental
soprano *n* (*pl* **-s**) (singer with) the highest female or boy's voice
 sopranos *n* ▷ soprano
 sops *n*, *v* ▷ sop
sorbet *n* (*pl* **-s**) flavoured water ice
 sorbets *n* ▷ sorbet
sorcerer *n* (*pl* **-s**) magician ▸ **sorceress** *n fem* (*pl* **-es**)
 sorcerers *n* ▷ sorcerer
 sorceress *n* ▷ sorcerer
 sorceresses *n* ▷ sorcerer
 sorceries *n* ▷ sorcery
sorcery *n* (*pl* **-ries**) witchcraft or magic
sordid *adj* (**-er, -est**) dirty, squalid ▸ **sordidly** *adv* ▸ **sordidness** *n* (*pl* **-es**)
 sordider *adj* ▷ sordid
 sordidest *adj* ▷ sordid
 sordidly *adv* ▷ sordid
 sordidness *n* ▷ sordid
 sordidnesses *n* ▷ sordid
sore *adj* (**-r, -st**) painful ▸ *n* (*pl* **-s**) painful area on the body ▸ *adv* (*Obs*) greatly ▸ **soreness** *n* (*pl* **-es**)
sorely *adv* greatly
 soreness *n* ▷ sore
 sorenesses *n* ▷ sore
 sorer *adj* ▷ sore
 sores *n* ▷ sore
 sorest *adj* ▷ sore
sorghum *n* (*pl* **-s**) kind of grass cultivated for grain
 sorghums *n* ▷ sorghum
sorrel *n* (*pl* **-s**) bitter-tasting plant
 sorrels *n* ▷ sorrel
 sorrier *adj* ▷ sorry
 sorriest *adj* ▷ sorry
sorrow *n* (*pl* **-s**) grief or sadness ▸ *v* (**-s, -ing, -ed**) grieve ▸ **sorrowful** *adj* ▸ **sorrowfully** *adv*
 sorrowed *v* ▷ sorrow
 sorrowful *adj* ▷ sorrow
 sorrowfully *adv* ▷ sorrow
 sorrowing *v* ▷ sorrow
 sorrows *n*, *v* ▷ sorrow
sorry *adj* (**-rier, -riest**) feeling pity or regret
sort *n* (*pl* **-s**) group all sharing certain qualities or characteristics ▸ *v* (**-s, -ing, -ed**) arrange

according to kind
 sorted *v* ▷ sort
sortie *n* (*pl* **-s**) relatively short return trip
 sorties *n* ▷ sortie
 sorting *v* ▷ sort
 sorts *n*, *v* ▷ sort
sot *n* (*pl* **-s**) habitual drunkard
 sots *n* ▷ sot
soubriquet [so-brik-ay] *n* (*pl* **-s**) ▷ sobriquet
 soubriquets *n* ▷ soubriquet
soufflé [soo-flay] *n* (*pl* **-s**) light fluffy dish made with beaten egg whites and other ingredients
 soufflés *n* ▷ soufflé
sough [rhymes with **now**] *v* (**-s, -ing, -ed**) (of the wind) make a sighing sound
 soughed *v* ▷ sough
 soughing *v* ▷ sough
 soughs *v* ▷ sough
 sought [sawt] *v* ▷ seek
souk [sook] *n* (*pl* **-s**) marketplace in Muslim countries, often open-air
 souks *n* ▷ souk
soul *n* (*pl* **-s**) spiritual and immortal part of a human being
soulful *adj* full of emotion
soulless *adj* lacking human qualities, mechanical
 souls *n* ▷ soul
sound[1] *n* (*pl* **-s**) something heard, noise ▸ *v* (**-s, -ing, -ed**) make or cause to make a sound
sound[2] *adj* (**-er, -est**) in good condition ▸ **soundly** *adv*
sound[3] *v* (**-s, -ing, -ed**) find the depth of (water etc.)
sound[4] *n* (*pl* **-s**) channel or strait
 sounded *v* ▷ sound[1, 3]
 sounder *adj* ▷ sound[2]
 soundest *adj* ▷ sound[2]
 sounding *v* ▷ sound[1, 3]
soundings *pl n* measurements of depth taken by sounding
 soundly *adv* ▷ sound[2]
soundproof *adj* not penetrable by sound ▸ *v* (**-s, -ing, -ed**) make soundproof
 soundproofed *v* ▷ soundproof
 soundproofing *v* ▷ soundproof
 soundproofs *v* ▷ soundproof
 sounds *n* ▷ sound[1, 4] ▸ *v* ▷ sound[1, 3]
soundtrack *n* (*pl* **-s**) recorded sound accompaniment to a film
 soundtracks *n* ▷ soundtrack
soup *n* (*pl* **-s**) liquid food made from meat, vegetables, etc. ▸ **soupy** *adj* (**-pier, -piest**)
soupçon [soop-sonn] *n* (*pl* **-s**) small amount

soupçons n ▷ soupçon

soupier adj ▷ soup

soupiest adj ▷ soup

soups n ▷ soup

soupy adj ▷ soup

sour adj (-er, -est) sharp-tasting ▶ v (-s, -ing, -ed) make or become sour > **sourly** adv > **sourness** n (pl -s)

source n (pl -s) origin or starting point

sources n ▷ source

soured v ▷ sour

sourer adj ▷ sour

sourest adj ▷ sour

souring v ▷ sour

sourly adv ▷ sour

sourness n ▷ sour

sournesses n ▷ sour

sours v ▷ sour

souse v (-ses, -sing, -sed) plunge (something) into liquid

soused v ▷ souse

souses v ▷ souse

sousing v ▷ souse

soutane [soo-tan] n (pl -s) Roman Catholic priest's cassock

soutanes n ▷ soutane

south n (pl -s) direction towards the South Pole, opposite north ▶ adj to or in the south ▶ adv in, to, or towards the south > **southerly** adj > **southern** adj > **southward** adj, adv > **southwards** adv

southerly adj ▷ south

southern adj ▷ south

southerner n (pl -s) person from the south of a country or area

southerners n ▷ southerner

southpaw n (pl -s) (Informal) left-handed person, esp. a boxer

southpaws n ▷ southpaw

souths n ▷ south

southward adj, adv ▷ south

southwards adv ▷ south

souvenir n (pl -s) keepsake, memento

souvenirs n ▷ souvenir

sou'wester n (pl -s) seaman's waterproof hat covering the head and back of the neck

sou'westers n ▷ sou'wester

sovereign n (pl -s) king or queen ▶ adj (of a state) independent > **sovereignty** n (pl -ties)

sovereigns n ▷ sovereign

sovereignties n ▷ sovereign

sovereignty n ▷ sovereign

soviet n (pl -s) formerly, elected council at various levels of government in the USSR ▶ adj

soviets n ▷ soviet

sow[1] [rhymes with **know**] v (-s, -ing, -ed, **sown** or -ed) scatter or plant (seed) in or on (the ground)

sow[2] [rhymes with **cow**] n (pl -s) female adult pig

sowed v ▷ sow[1]

sowing v ▷ sow[1]

sown v ▷ sow[1]

sows n ▷ sow[2] ▶ v ▷ sow[1]

> **sox** pl n. Sox is an informal word for **socks**. This is a good word to remember for when you find an X on your rack without the space or tiles to play a longer word. Sox scores 10 points.

soya n (pl -s) plant whose edible bean is used for food and as a source of oil

soyas n ▷ soya

sozzled adj (BRIT, AUST & NZ) (Slang) drunk

spa n (pl -s) resort with a mineral-water spring

space n (pl -s) unlimited expanse in which all objects exist and move ▶ v (-ces, -cing, -ced) place at intervals

spacecraft, spaceship n (pl -s) vehicle for travel beyond the earth's atmosphere

spacecrafts n ▷ spacecraft

spaced v ▷ space

spaces n, v ▷ space

spaceship n ▷ spacecraft

spaceships n ▷ spacecraft

spacesuit n (pl -s) sealed pressurized suit worn by an astronaut

spacesuits n ▷ spacesuit

spacing v ▷ space

spacious adj having a large capacity or area

spade[1] n (pl -s) tool for digging

spade[2] n (pl -s) playing card of the suit marked with black leaf-shaped symbols

spades n ▷ spade[1, 2]

spadework n (pl -s) hard preparatory work

spadeworks n ▷ spadework

spaghetti n (pl -s) pasta in the form of long strings

spaghettis n ▷ spaghetti

span n (pl -s) space between two points ▶ v (-s, -nning, -nned) stretch or extend across

spangle n (pl -les) small shiny metallic ornament ▶ v (-les, -ling, -led) decorate with spangles

spangled v ▷ spangle

spangles n, v ▷ spangle

spangling v ▷ spangle

spaniel n (pl -s) dog with long ears and silky hair

spaniels n ▷ spaniel

spank v (-s, -ing, -ed) slap with the open hand, on the buttocks or legs ▶ n (pl -s) such a slap
> **spanking** n (pl -s)
spanked v ▷ spank

spanking adj (Informal) outstandingly fine or smart ▶ n (pl -s) ▷ spank ▶ n ▷ spank
spankings n ▷ spank
spanks v, n ▷ spank
spanned v ▷ span

spanner n (pl -s) tool for gripping and turning a nut or bolt
spanners n ▷ spanner
spanning v ▷ span
spans n, v ▷ span

spar[1] n (pl -s) pole used as a ship's mast, boom, or yard

spar[2] v (-s, -rring, -rred) box or fight using light blows for practice

spare adj extra ▶ n (pl -s) duplicate kept in case of damage or loss ▶ v (-res, -ring, -red) refrain from punishing or harming
spared v ▷ spare
spares n, v ▷ spare

sparing adj economical ▶ v ▷ spare

spark n (pl -s) fiery particle thrown out from a fire or caused by friction ▶ v (-s, -ing, -ed) give off sparks
sparked v ▷ spark

sparkie n (pl -s) (NZ) (Informal) electrician
sparkies n ▷ sparkie
sparking v ▷ spark

sparkle v (-les, -ling, -led) glitter with many points of light ▶ n (pl -s) sparkling points of light
sparkled v ▷ sparkle

sparkler n (pl -s) hand-held firework that emits sparks
sparklers n ▷ sparkler
sparkles v, n ▷ sparkle

sparkling adj (of wine or mineral water) slightly fizzy ▶ v ▷ sparkle
sparks v, n ▷ spark
sparred v ▷ spar[2]
sparring v ▷ spar[2]

sparrow n (pl -s) small brownish bird
sparrowhawk n (pl -s) small hawk
sparrowhawks n ▷ sparrowhawk
sparrows n ▷ sparrow
spars n ▷ spar[1] ▶ v ▷ spar[2]

sparse adj (-r, -st) thinly scattered > **sparsely** adv > **sparseness** n (pl -es)
sparsely adv ▷ sparse
sparseness n ▷ sparse
sparsenesses n ▷ sparse
sparser adj ▷ sparse

sparsest adj ▷ sparse

spartan adj strict and austere

spas n ▷ spa

spasm n (pl -s) involuntary muscular contraction

spasmodic adj occurring in spasms
> **spasmodically** adv
spasmodically adv ▷ spasmodic
spasms n ▷ spasm

spastic n (pl -s) person with cerebral palsy ▶ adj suffering from cerebral palsy
spastics n ▷ spastic

spat[1] n (pl -s) slight quarrel
spat[2] v ▷ spit[1]

spate n (pl -s) large number of things happening within a period of time
spates n ▷ spate

spatial adj of or in space

spats pl n coverings formerly worn over the ankle and instep ▶ n ▷ spat[1]

spatter v (-s, -ing, -ed) scatter or be scattered in drops over (something) ▶ n (pl -s) spattering sound
spattered v ▷ spatter
spattering v ▷ spatter
spatters n, v ▷ spatter

spatula n (pl -s) utensil with a broad flat blade for spreading or stirring
spatulas n ▷ spatula

spawn n (pl -s) jelly-like mass of eggs of fish, frogs, or molluscs ▶ v (-s, -ing, -ed) (of fish, frogs, or molluscs) lay eggs
spawned v ▷ spawn
spawning v ▷ spawn
spawns n, v ▷ spawn

spay v (-s, -ing, -ed) remove the ovaries from (a female animal)
spayed v ▷ spay
spaying v ▷ spay
spays v ▷ spay

speak v (-s, -ing, spoke, spoken) say words, talk
speaker n (pl -s) person who speaks, esp. at a formal occasion
speakers n ▷ speaker
speaking v ▷ speak
speaks v ▷ speak

spear[1] n (pl -s) weapon consisting of a long shaft with a sharp point ▶ v (-s, -ing, -ed) pierce with or as if with a spear
spear[2] n (pl -s) slender shoot
speared v ▷ spear[1]

spearhead v (-es, -ing, -ed) lead (an attack or campaign) ▶ n (pl -s) leading force in an attack or campaign
spearheaded v ▷ spearhead

spearheading *v* ▷ spearhead
spearheads *v*, *n* ▷ spearhead
spearing *v* ▷ spear[1]
spearmint *n* (*pl* -s) type of mint
  spearmints *n* ▷ spearmint
spears *n* ▷ spear[1, 2] ▶ *v* ▷ spear[1]
spec *n* (*pl* -s) (*Informal*) speculation
special *adj* distinguished from others of its
  kind > **specially** *adv*
specialist *n* (*pl* -s) expert in a particular
  activity or subject
  specialists *n* ▷ specialist
  specialities *n* ▷ speciality
speciality *n* (*pl* -ties) special interest or skill
  specialization *n* ▷ specialize
  specializations *n* ▷ specialize
specialize *v* (-zes, -zing, -zed) be a specialist
  > **specialization** *n* (*pl* -s)
  specialized *v* ▷ specialize
  specializes *v* ▷ specialize
  specializing *v* ▷ specialize
  specially *adv* ▷ special
specie *n* coins as distinct from paper money
species *n* (*pl* species) group of plants or
  animals that are related closely enough to
  interbreed naturally
specific *adj* particular, definite ▶ *n* (*pl* -s)
  drug used to treat a particular disease
  > **specifically** *adv*
  specifically *adv* ▷ specific
specification *n* (*pl* -s) detailed description of
  something to be made or done
  specifications *n* ▷ specification
specifics *n* ▷ specific ▶ *pl n* particular details
  specified *v* ▷ specify
  specifies *v* ▷ specify
specify *v* (-fies, -fying, -fied) refer to or state
  specifically
  specifying *v* ▷ specify
specimen *n* (*pl* -s) individual or part typifying
  a whole
  specimens *n* ▷ specimen
specious [spee-shuss] *adj* apparently true, but
  actually false
speck *n* (*pl* -s) small spot or particle
speckle *n* (*pl* -s) small spot ▶ *v* (-les, -ling, -led)
  mark with speckles
  speckled *v* ▷ speckle
  speckles *n*, *v* ▷ speckle
  speckling *v* ▷ speckle
  specks *n* ▷ speck
specs *pl n* (*Informal*) ▷ spectacles ▶ *n* ▷ spec
spectacle *n* (*pl* -s) strange, interesting, or
  ridiculous sight
spectacles *n* ▷ spectacle ▶ *pl n* pair of glasses

for correcting faulty vision
  spectacles *n* ▷ spectacle
spectacular *adj* impressive ▶ *n* (*pl* -s)
  spectacular public show > **spectacularly** *adv*
  spectacularly *adv* ▷ spectacular
  spectaculars *n* ▷ spectacular
spectate *v* (-tes, -ting, -ted) watch
  spectated *v* ▷ spectate
  spectates *v* ▷ spectate
  spectating *v* ▷ spectate
spectator *n* (*pl* -s) person viewing anything,
  onlooker
  spectators *n* ▷ spectator
spectra *n* ▷ spectrum
spectral *adj* ▷ spectre
spectre *n* (*pl* -s) ghost > **spectral** *adj*
  spectres *n* ▷ spectre
spectroscope *n* (*pl* -s) instrument for
  producing or examining spectra
  spectroscopes *n* ▷ spectroscope
spectrum *n* (*pl* -tra) range of different
  colours, radio waves, etc. in order of their
  wavelengths
speculate *v* (-tes, -ting, -ted) guess, conjecture
  > **speculation** *n* (*pl* -s) > **speculative** *adj*
  > **speculator** *n* (*pl* -s)
  speculated *v* ▷ speculate
  speculates *v* ▷ speculate
  speculating *v* ▷ speculate
  speculation *n* ▷ speculate
  speculations *n* ▷ speculate
  speculative *adj* ▷ speculate
  speculator *n* ▷ speculate
  speculators *n* ▷ speculate
  sped *v* ▷ speed
speech *n* (*pl* -es) act, power, or manner of
  speaking
  speeches *n* ▷ speech
speechless *adj* unable to speak because of
  great emotion
speed *n* (*pl* -s) swiftness ▶ *v* (-s, -ing, sped or
  -ed) go quickly
speedboat *n* (*pl* -s) light fast motorboat
  speedboats *n* ▷ speedboat
  speeded *v* ▷ speed
  speedier *adj* ▷ speedy
  speediest *adj* ▷ speedy
  speedily *adv* ▷ speedy
  speeding *v* ▷ speed
speedometer *n* (*pl* -s) instrument to show the
  speed of a vehicle
  speedometers *n* ▷ speedometer
  speeds *n*, *v* ▷ speed
speedway *n* (*pl* -s) track for motorcycle racing
  speedways *n* ▷ speedway

speedwell *n* (*pl* -s) plant with small blue flowers
  speedwells *n* ▷ speedwell
speedy *adj* (-dier, -diest) prompt > **speedily** *adv*
  speleologies *n* ▷ speleology
speleology *n* (*pl* -gies) study and exploration of caves
spell[1] *v* (-s, -ing, spelt *or* -ed) give in correct order the letters that form (a word)
spell[2] *n* (*pl* -s) formula of words supposed to have magic power
spell[3] *n* (*pl* -s) period of time of weather or activity
spellbound *adj* entranced
spellchecker *n* (*pl* -s) (COMPUTING) program that highlights wrongly spelled words in a word-processed document
  spellcheckers *n* ▷ spellchecker
  spelled *v* ▷ spell[1]
spelling *n* (*pl* -s) way a word is spelt ▶ *v* ▷ spell[1]
  spellings *n* ▷ spelling
  spells *v* ▷ spell[1] ▶ *n* ▷ spell[2, 3]
  spelt *v* ▷ spell[1]
spend *v* (-s, -ing, spent) pay out (money)
  spending *v* ▷ spend
  spends *v* ▷ spend
spendthrift *n* (*pl* -s) person who spends money wastefully
  spendthrifts *n* ▷ spendthrift
  spent *v* ▷ spend
sperm *n* (*pl* -s *or* sperm) male reproductive cell
spermaceti [sper-ma-**set**-ee] *n* (*pl* -s) waxy solid obtained from the sperm whale
  spermacetis *n* ▷ spermaceti
  spermatozoa *n* ▷ spermatozoon
spermatozoon [sper-ma-toe-**zoe**-on] *n* (*pl* -zoa) sperm
spermicide *n* (*pl* -s) substance that kills sperm
  spermicides *n* ▷ spermicide
  sperms *n* ▷ sperm
spew *v* (-s, -ing, -ed) vomit
  spewed *v* ▷ spew
  spewing *v* ▷ spew
  spews *v* ▷ spew
sphagnum *n* (*pl* -s) moss found in bogs
  sphagnums *n* ▷ sphagnum
sphere *n* (*pl* -s) perfectly round solid object > **spherical** *adj*
  spheres *n* ▷ sphere
  spherical *adj* ▷ sphere
sphincter *n* (*pl* -s) ring of muscle which controls the opening and closing of a hollow organ
  sphincters *n* ▷ sphincter
sphinx *n* (*pl* -es) enigmatic person

  sphinxes *n* ▷ sphinx
spice *n* (*pl* -s) aromatic substance used as flavouring ▶ *v* (-ces, -cing, -ced) flavour with spices
  spiced *v* ▷ spice
  spices *n*, *v* ▷ spice
  spicier *adj* ▷ spicy
  spiciest *adj* ▷ spicy
  spicing *v* ▷ spice
spicy *adj* (-cier, -ciest) flavoured with spices
spider *n* (*pl* -s) small eight-legged creature which spins a web to catch insects for food > **spidery** *adj*
  spiders *n* ▷ spider
  spidery *adj* ▷ spider
  spied *v* ▷ spy
spiel *n* (*pl* -s) speech made to persuade someone to do something
  spiels *n* ▷ spiel
  spies *v*, *n* ▷ spy
spigot *n* (*pl* -s) stopper for, or tap fitted to, a cask
  spigots *n* ▷ spigot
spike *n* (*pl* -s) sharp point ▶ *v* (-kes, -king, -ked) put spikes on > **spiky** *adj* (-kier, -kiest)
  spiked *v* ▷ spike
spikes *n*, *v* ▷ spike ▶ *pl n* sports shoes with spikes for greater grip
  spikier *adj* ▷ spike
  spikiest *adj* ▷ spike
  spiking *v* ▷ spike
  spiky *adj* ▷ spike
spill[1] *v* (-s, -ing, spilt *or* spilled) pour from or as if from a container ▶ *n* (*pl* -s) fall > **spillage** *n* (*pl* -s)
spill[2] *n* (*pl* -s) thin strip of wood or paper for lighting pipes or fires
  spillage *n* ▷ spill[1]
  spillages *n* ▷ spill[1]
  spilled *v* ▷ spill[1]
  spilling *v* ▷ spill[1]
  spills *n* ▷ spill[1, 2] ▶ *v* ▷ spill[1]
  spilt *v* ▷ spill[1]
spin *v* (-s, -nning, spun) revolve or cause to revolve rapidly ▶ *n* (*pl* -s) revolving motion > **spinner** *n* (*pl* -s)
spinach *n* (*pl* -es) dark green leafy vegetable
  spinaches *n* ▷ spinach
spinal *adj* of the spine
spindle *n* (*pl* -s) rotating rod that acts as an axle
  spindles *n* ▷ spindle
  spindlier *adj* ▷ spindly
  spindliest *adj* ▷ spindly
spindly *adj* (-lier, -liest) long, slender, and frail

spine n (pl **-s**) backbone
spineless adj lacking courage
  spines n ▷ spine
spinet n (pl **-s**) small harpsichord
  spinets n ▷ spinet
  spinier adj ▷ spiny
  spiniest adj ▷ spiny
spinifex n (pl **-es**) coarse spiny Australian grass
  spinifexes n ▷ spinifex
spinnaker n (pl **-s**) large sail on a racing yacht
  spinnakers n ▷ spinnaker
  spinner n ▷ spin
  spinners n ▷ spin
spinney n (pl **-s**) (CHIEFLY BRIT) small wood
  spinneys n ▷ spinney
  spinning v ▷ spin
  spins v, n ▷ spin
spinster n (pl **-s**) unmarried woman
  spinsters n ▷ spinster
spiny adj (**-nier**, **-niest**) covered with spines
spiral n (pl **-s**) continuous curve formed by
  a point winding about a central axis at an
  ever-increasing distance from it ▶ v (**-s**, **-lling**,
  -lled) move in a spiral ▶ adj having the form
  of a spiral
  spiralled v ▷ spiral
  spiralling v ▷ spiral
  spirals n, v ▷ spiral
spire n (pl **-s**) pointed part of a steeple
  spires n ▷ spire
spirit[1] n (pl **-s**) nonphysical aspect of a person
  concerned with profound thoughts ▶ v (**-s**,
  -ing, **-ed**) carry away mysteriously
spirit[2] n (pl **-s**) liquid obtained by distillation
spirited adj lively ▶ v ▷ spirit[1]
  spiriting v ▷ spirit[1]
  spirits n ▷ spirit[1, 2] ▶ pl n emotional state ▶ v
  ▷ spirit[1]
spiritual adj relating to the spirit ▶ n (pl **-s**)
  type of religious folk song originating among
  Black slaves in America > **spiritually** adv
  > **spirituality** n (pl **-ties**)
spiritualism n (pl **-s**) belief that the spirits of
  the dead can communicate with the living
  > **spiritualist** n (pl **-s**)
  spiritualisms n ▷ spiritualism
  spiritualist n ▷ spiritualism
  spiritualists n ▷ spiritualism
  spiritualities n ▷ spiritual
  spirituality n ▷ spiritual
  spiritually adv ▷ spiritual
  spirituals n ▷ spiritual
spit[1] v (**-s**, **-tting**, **spat**) eject (saliva or food)
  from the mouth ▶ n (pl **-s**) saliva
spit[2] n (pl **-s**) sharp rod on which meat is
  skewered for roasting
spite n (pl **-s**) deliberate nastiness ▶ v (**-tes**,
  -ting, **-ted**) annoy or hurt from spite > **spiteful**
  adj > **spitefully** adv
  spited v ▷ spite
  spiteful adj ▷ spite
  spitefully adv ▷ spite
  spites n, v ▷ spite
spitfire n (pl **-s**) person with a fiery temper
  spitfires n ▷ spitfire
  spiting v ▷ spite
  spits n ▷ spit[1, 2] ▶ v ▷ spit[1]
  spitting v ▷ spit[1]
spittle n (pl **-s**) fluid produced in the mouth,
  saliva
  spittles n ▷ spittle
spittoon n (pl **-s**) bowl to spit into
  spittoons n ▷ spittoon
spiv n (pl **-s**) (BRIT, AUST & NZ) (Slang) smartly
  dressed man who makes a living by shady
  dealings
  spivs n ▷ spiv
splash v (**-es**, **-ing**, **-ed**) scatter liquid on
  (something) ▶ n (pl **-es**) splashing sound
  splashed v ▷ splash
  splashes v, n ▷ splash
  splashing v, n ▷ splash
splatter v (**-s**, **-ing**, **-ed**) ▶ n (pl **-s**) splash
  splattered v ▷ splatter
  splattering v ▷ splatter
  splatters v, n ▷ splatter
splay v (**-s**, **-ing**, **-ed**) spread out, with ends
  spreading in different directions
  splayed v ▷ splay
  splaying v ▷ splay
  splays v ▷ splay
spleen n (pl **-s**) abdominal organ which filters
  bacteria from the blood
  spleens n ▷ spleen
splendid adj (**-er**, **-est**) excellent > **splendidly**
  adv > **splendour** n (pl **-s**)
  splendider adj ▷ splendid
  splendidest adj ▷ splendid
  splendidly adv ▷ splendid
  splendour n ▷ splendid
  splendours n ▷ splendid
splenetic adj spiteful or irritable
splice v (**-ces**, **-cing**, **-ced**) join by interweaving
  or overlapping ends
  spliced v ▷ splice
  splices v ▷ splice
  splicing v ▷ splice
splint n (pl **-s**) rigid support for a broken bone
splinter n (pl **-s**) thin sharp piece broken off,
  esp. from wood ▶ v (**-s**, **-ing**, **-ed**) break into

fragments
splintered v ▷ splinter
splintering v ▷ splinter
splinters n, v ▷ splinter
splints n ▷ splint
split v (-s, -tting, split) break into separate pieces ▶ n (pl -s) crack or division caused by splitting
splits v ▷ split ▶ n ▷ split ▶ pl n act of sitting with the legs outstretched in opposite directions
splitting v ▷ split
splodge n (pl -s) ▶ v (-ges, -ging, -ged) ▷ splotch
splodged v ▷ splodge
splodges n, v ▷ splodge
splodging v ▷ splodge
splotch n (pl -s) ▶ v (-ches, -ching, -ched) splash, daub
splotched v ▷ splotch
splotches n, v ▷ splotch
splotching v ▷ splotch
splurge v (-ges, -ging, -ged) spend money extravagantly ▶ n (pl -s) bout of extravagance
splurged v ▷ splurge
splurges v, n ▷ splurge
splurging v ▷ splurge
splutter v (-s, -ing, -ed) utter with spitting or choking sounds ▶ n (pl -s) spluttering
spluttered v ▷ splutter
spluttering v ▷ splutter
splutters v, n ▷ splutter
spoil v (-s, -ing, -spoilt or -ed) damage
spoiled v ▷ spoil
spoiling v ▷ spoil
spoils pl n booty ▶ v ▷ spoil
spoilsport n (pl -s) person who spoils the enjoyment of others
spoilsports n ▷ spoilsport
spoilt v ▷ spoil
spoke¹ v ▷ speak
spoke² n (pl -s) bar joining the hub of a wheel to the rim
spoken v ▷ speak
spokes n ▷ spoke²
spokesman, spokeswoman, spokesperson n (pl -men, -women, -persons, -people) person chosen to speak on behalf of a group
spokesmen n ▷ spokesman
spokespeople n ▷ spokesman
spokesperson n ▷ spokesman
spokespersons n ▷ spokesman
spokeswoman n ▷ spokesman
spokeswomen n ▷ spokesman
spoliation n (pl -s) plundering
spoliations n ▷ spoliation

sponge n (pl -s) sea animal with a porous absorbent skeleton ▶ v (-ges, -ging, -ged) wipe with a sponge > **spongy** adj (-gier, -giest)
sponged v ▷ sponge
sponger n (pl -s) (Slang) person who sponges on others
spongers n ▷ sponger
sponges n, v ▷ sponge
spongier adj ▷ sponge
spongiest adj ▷ sponge
sponging v ▷ sponge
spongy adj ▷ sponge
sponsor n (pl -s) person who promotes something ▶ v (-s, -ing, -ed) act as a sponsor for > **sponsorship** n (pl -s)
sponsored v ▷ sponsor
sponsoring v ▷ sponsor
sponsors n, v ▷ sponsor
sponsorship n ▷ sponsor
sponsorships n ▷ sponsor
spontaneities n ▷ spontaneous
spontaneity n ▷ spontaneous
spontaneous adj not planned or arranged > **spontaneously** adv > **spontaneity** n (pl -ties)
spontaneously adv ▷ spontaneous
spoof n (pl -s) mildly satirical parody
spoofs n ▷ spoof
spook n (pl -s) (Informal) ghost > **spooky** adj (-kier, -kiest)
spookier adj ▷ spook
spookiest adj ▷ spook
spooks n ▷ spook
spooky adj ▷ spook
spool n (pl -s) cylinder round which something can be wound
spools n ▷ spool
spoon n (pl -s) shallow bowl attached to a handle for eating, stirring, or serving food ▶ v (-s, -ing, -ed) lift with a spoon > **spoonful** n (pl -s)
spoonbill n (pl -s) wading bird of warm regions with a long flat bill
spoonbills n ▷ spoonbill
spooned v ▷ spoon
spoonerism n (pl -s) accidental changing over of the initial sounds of a pair of words, such as half-warmed fish for half-formed wish
spoonerisms n ▷ spoonerism
spoonful n ▷ spoon
spoonfuls n ▷ spoon
spooning v ▷ spoon
spoons n, v ▷ spoon
spoor n (pl -s) trail of an animal
spoors n ▷ spoor

sporadic *adj* intermittent, scattered
  > **sporadically** *adv*
  sporadically *adv* ▷ sporadic
spore *n* (*pl* -s) minute reproductive body of some plants
  spores *n* ▷ spore
sporran *n* (*pl* -s) pouch worn in front of a kilt
  sporrans *n* ▷ sporran
sport *n* (*pl* -s) activity for pleasure, competition, or exercise *v* (-s, -ing, -ed) wear proudly > **sporty** *adj* (-tier, -tiest)
  sported *v* ▷ sport
  sportier *adj* ▷ sport
  sportiest *adj* ▷ sport
  sporting *adj* of sport *v* ▷ sport
sportive *adj* playful
  sports *n*, *v* ▷ sport
sportsman, sportswoman *n* (*pl* -men, -women) person who plays sports
  > **sportsmanlike** *adj* > **sportsmanship** *n* (*pl* -s)
  sportsmanlike *adj* ▷ sportsman
  sportsmanship *n* ▷ sportsman
  sportsmanships *n* ▷ sportsman
  sportsmen *n* ▷ sportsman
  sportswoman *n* ▷ sportsman
  sportswomen *n* ▷ sportsman
  sporty *adj* ▷ sport
spot *n* (*pl* -s) small mark on a surface (*Informal*) ▶ *v* (-s, -tting, -tted) notice
spotless *adj* absolutely clean > **spotlessly** *adv*
  spotlessly *adv* ▷ spotless
spotlight *n* (*pl* -s) powerful light illuminating a small area
  spotlights *n* ▷ spotlight
  spots *n*, *v* ▷ spot
  spotted *v* ▷ spot
  spottier *adj* ▷ spotty
  spottiest *adj* ▷ spotty
  spotting *v* ▷ spot
spotty *adj* (-ttier, -ttiest) with spots
spouse *n* (*pl* -s) husband or wife
  spouses *n* ▷ spouse
spout *v* (-s, -ing, -ed) pour out in a stream or jet (*Slang*) ▶ *n* (*pl* -s) projecting tube or lip for pouring liquids
  spouted *v* ▷ spout
  spouting *v* ▷ spout
  spouts *v*, *n* ▷ spout
sprain *v* (-s, -ing, -ed) injure (a joint) by a sudden twist ▶ *n* (*pl* -s) such an injury
  sprained *v* ▷ sprain
  spraining *v* ▷ sprain
  sprains *v*, *n* ▷ sprain
  sprang *v* ▷ spring
sprat *n* (*pl* -s) small sea fish

sprats *n* ▷ sprat
sprawl *v* (-s, -ing, -ed) lie or sit with the limbs spread out ▶ *n* (*pl* -s) part of a city that has spread untidily over a large area
  sprawled *v* ▷ sprawl
  sprawling *v* ▷ sprawl
  sprawls *v*, *n* ▷ sprawl
spray¹ *n* (*pl* -s) (device for producing) fine drops of liquid ▶ *v* (-s, -ing, -ed) scatter in fine drops
spray² *n* (*pl* -s) branch with buds, leaves, etc.
  sprayed *v* ▷ spray¹
  spraying *v* ▷ spray¹
  sprayings *n* ▷ spray¹
  sprays *v* ▷ spray¹ ▶ *n* ▷ spray¹,²
spread *v* (-s, -ing, spread) open out or be displayed to the fullest extent ▶ *n* (*pl* -s) spreading (*Informal*)
  spreading *v* ▷ spread
  spreads *v*, *n* ▷ spread
spreadsheet *n* (*pl* -s) computer program for manipulating figures
  spreadsheets *n* ▷ spreadsheet
spree *n* (*pl* -s) session of overindulgence, usu. in drinking or spending money
  sprees *n* ▷ spree
  sprier *adj* ▷ spry
  spriest *adj* ▷ spry
sprig *n* (*pl* -s) twig or shoot
  sprightlier *adj* ▷ sprightly
  sprightliest *adj* ▷ sprightly
  sprightliness *n* ▷ sprightly
  sprightlinesses *n* ▷ sprightly
sprightly *adj* (-lier, -liest) lively and brisk
  > **sprightliness** *n* (*pl* -es)
  sprigs *n* ▷ sprig
spring *v* (-s, -ing, sprang *or* sprung) move suddenly upwards or forwards in a single motion, jump ▶ *n* (*pl* -s) season between winter and summer
springboard *n* (*pl* -s) flexible board used to gain height or momentum in diving or gymnastics
  springboards *n* ▷ springboard
springbok *n* (*pl* -s) S African antelope
  springboks *n* ▷ springbok
springer *n* (*pl* -s) small spaniel
  springers *n* ▷ springer
  springier *adj* ▷ springy
  springiest *adj* ▷ springy
  springing *v* ▷ spring
  springs *v*, *n* ▷ springs
springy *adj* (-gier, -giest) elastic
sprinkle *v* (-les, -ling, -led) scatter (liquid or powder) in tiny drops or particles over (something) > **sprinkler** *n* (*pl* -s)

sprinkled *v* ▷ sprinkle
sprinkler *n* ▷ sprinkle
sprinklers *n* ▷ sprinkle
sprinkles *v* ▷ sprinkle
sprinkling *v* ▷ sprinkle ▶ *n* (*pl* -s) small quantity or number
sprinklings *n* ▷ sprinkling
sprint *n* (*pl* -s) short race run at top speed ▶ *v* (-s, -ing, -ed) run a short distance at top speed
> **sprinter** *n* (*pl* -s)
sprinted *v* ▷ sprint
sprinter *n* ▷ sprint
sprinters *n* ▷ sprint
sprinting *v* ▷ sprint
sprints *v*, *n* ▷ sprint
sprite *n* (*pl* -s) elf
sprites *n* ▷ sprite
sprocket *n* (*pl* -s) wheel with teeth on the rim, that drives or is driven by a chain
sprockets *n* ▷ sprocket
sprout *v* (-s, -ing, -ed) put forth shoots ▶ *n* (*pl* -s) shoot
sprouted *v* ▷ sprout
sprouting *v* ▷ sprout
sprouts *v*, *n* ▷ sprout
spruce¹ *n* (*pl* -s) kind of fir
spruce² *adj* (-r, -st) neat and smart
sprucer *adj* ▷ spruce²
spruces *n* ▷ spruce¹
sprucest *adj* ▷ spruce²
sprung *v* ▷ spring
spry *adj* (-yer, -yest *or* sprier) (spriest) active or nimble
spryer *adj* ▷ spry
spryest *adj* ▷ spry
spud *n* (*pl* -s) (*Informal*) potato
spuds *n* ▷ spud
spume *n* (*pl* -s) ▶ *v* (-mes, -ming, -med) froth
spumed *v* ▷ spume
spumes *v*, *n* ▷ spume
spuming *v* ▷ spume
spun *v* ▷ spin
spunk *n* (*pl* -s) (*Informal*) courage, spirit
> **spunky** *adj* (-kier, -kiest)
spunkier *adj* ▷ spunk
spunkiest *adj* ▷ spunk
spunks *n* ▷ spunk
spunky *adj* ▷ spunk
spur *n* (*pl* -s) stimulus or incentive ▶ *v* (-s, -rring, -rred) urge on, incite (someone)
spurge *n* (*pl* -s) plant with milky sap
spurges *n* ▷ spurge
spurious *adj* not genuine
spurn *v* (-s, -ing, -ed) reject with scorn
spurned *v* ▷ spurn

spurning *v* ▷ spurn
spurns *v* ▷ spurn
spurred *v* ▷ spur
spurring *v* ▷ spur
spurs *n*, *v* ▷ spur
spurt *v* (-s, -ing, -ed) gush or cause to gush out in a jet ▶ *n* (*pl* -s) short sudden burst of activity or speed
spurted *v* ▷ spurt
spurting *v* ▷ spurt
spurts *v*, *n* ▷ spurt
sputa *n* ▷ sputum
sputnik *n* (*pl* -s) early Soviet artificial satellite
sputniks *n* ▷ sputnik
sputter *v* (-es, -ing, -ed) ▶ *n* (*pl* -s) splutter
sputtered *v* ▷ sputter
sputtering *v* ▷ sputter
sputters *v*, *n* ▷ sputter
sputum *n* (*pl* -ta) spittle, usu. mixed with mucus
spy *n* (*pl* spies) person employed to obtain secret information ▶ *v* (spies, spying, spied) act as a spy
spying *v* ▷ spy
squabble *v* (-les, -ling, -led) ▶ *n* (*pl* -s) (engage in) a petty or noisy quarrel
squabbled *v* ▷ squabble
squabbles *v*, *n* ▷ squabble
squabbling *v* ▷ squabble
squad *n* (*pl* -s) small group of people working or training together
squadron *n* (*pl* -s) division of an air force, fleet, or cavalry regiment
squadrons *n* ▷ squadron
squads *n* ▷ squad
squalid *adj* (-er, -est) dirty and unpleasant
squalider *adj* ▷ squalid
squalidest *adj* ▷ squalid
squall¹ *n* (*pl* -s) sudden strong wind
squall² *v* (-s, -ing, -ed) cry noisily, yell ▶ *n* (*pl* -s) harsh cry
squalled *v* ▷ squall²
squalling *v* ▷ squall²
squalls *v* ▷ squall² ▶ *n* ▷ squall¹, ²
squalor *n* (*pl* -s) disgusting dirt and filth
squalors *n* ▷ squalor
squander *v* (-s, -ing, -ed) waste (money or resources)
squandered *v* ▷ squander
squandering *v* ▷ squander
squanders *v* ▷ squander
square *n* (*pl* -s) geometric figure with four equal sides and four right angles ▶ *adj* square in shape ▶ *v* (-res, -ring, -red) multiply (a number) by itself ▶ *adv* squarely, directly

squared v ▷ square
squarely adv in a direct way
squares n, v ▷ square
squaring v ▷ square
squash[1] v (-es, -ing, -ed) crush flat ▶ n (pl -es) sweet fruit drink diluted with water > **squashy** adj (-shier, -shiest)
squash[2] n (pl -es) marrow-like vegetable
squashed v ▷ squash
squashes n ▷ squash[1, 2] v ▷ squash[1]
squashier adj ▷ squash[1]
squashiest adj ▷ squash[1]
squashing v ▷ squash[1]
squashy adj ▷ squash[1]
squat v (-s, -tting, -tted) crouch with the knees bent and the weight on the feet ▶ n (pl -s) place where squatters live ▶ adj (-tter, -ttest) short and broad
squats v, n ▷ squat
squatted v ▷ squat
squatter n (pl -s) illegal occupier of unused premises ▶ adj ▷ squat
squatters n ▷ squatter
squattest n ▷ squat
squatting v ▷ squat
squaw n (pl -s) (Offens) Native American woman
squawk n (pl -s) loud harsh cry ▶ v (-s, -ing, -ed) utter a squawk
squawked v ▷ squawk
squawking v ▷ squawk
squawks v ▷ squawk
squaws n ▷ squaw
squeak n (pl -s) short shrill cry or sound ▶ v (-s, -ing, -ed) make or utter a squeak > **squeaky** adj (-kier, -kiest)
squeaked v ▷ squeak
squeakier adj ▷ squeak
squeakiest adj ▷ squeak
squeaking v ▷ squeak
squeaks n, v ▷ squeak
squeaky adj ▷ squeak
squeal n (pl -s) long shrill cry or sound ▶ v (-s, -ing, -ed) make or utter a squeal (Slang)
squealed v ▷ squeal
squealing v ▷ squeal
squeals n, v ▷ squeal
squeamish adj easily sickened or shocked
squeegee n (pl -s) tool with a rubber blade for clearing water from a surface
squeegees n ▷ squeegee
squeeze v (-zes, -zing, -zed) grip or press firmly ▶ n (pl -s) squeezing
squeezed v ▷ squeeze
squeezes v, n ▷ squeeze

squeezing v ▷ squeeze
squelch v (-es, -ing, -ed) make a wet sucking sound, as by walking through mud ▶ n (pl -es) squelching sound
squelched v ▷ squelch
squelches n ▷ squelch
squelching v ▷ squelch
squib n (pl -s) small firework that hisses before exploding
squibs n ▷ squib
squid n (pl -s) sea creature with a long soft body and ten tentacles
squids n ▷ squid
squiggle n (pl -s) wavy line > **squiggly** adj (-lier, -liest)
squiggles n ▷ squiggle
squigglier adj ▷ squiggle
squiggliest adj ▷ squiggle
squiggly adj ▷ squiggle
squint v (-s, -ing, -ed) have eyes which face in different directions ▶ n (pl -s) squinting condition of the eye ▶ adj crooked (-er, -est)
squinted v ▷ squint
squinter adj ▷ squint
squintest adj ▷ squint
squinting v ▷ squint
squints v, n ▷ squint
squire n (pl -s) country gentleman, usu. the main landowner in a community
squires n ▷ squire
squirm v (-s, -ing, -ed) wriggle, writhe ▶ n (pl -s) wriggling movement
squirmed v ▷ squirm
squirming v ▷ squirm
squirms v, n ▷ squirm
squirrel n (pl -s) small bushy-tailed tree-living animal
squirrels n ▷ squirrel
squirt v (-s, -ing, -ed) force (a liquid) or (of a liquid) be forced out of a narrow opening ▶ n (pl -s) jet of liquid
squirted v ▷ squirt
squirting v ▷ squirt
squirts n, v ▷ squirt
squish v (-es, -ing, -ed) ▶ n (pl -es) (make) a soft squelching sound > **squishy** adj (-shier, -shiest)
squished v ▷ squish
squishes n, v ▷ squish
squishier adj ▷ squish
squishiest adj ▷ squish
squishing v ▷ squish
squishy adj ▷ squish
squiz n (**squizzes**). Squiz is an informal word for a look or glance. This is a

useful word to remember, both for when you have the most of the tiles to form it and when someone else plays **quiz** which you can then add an S to for a good score. Squiz scores 23 points.

st *interj*. St is a sound people make to request silence or quiet. This is one of two two-letter words beginning with S that do not contain a vowel. It's useful when you want to connect a word beginning with H to one ending in T or vice versa. St scores 2 points.

stab v (-s, -bbing, -bbed) pierce with something pointed ▶ n (pl -s) stabbing
  stabbed v ▷ stab
  stabbing v ▷ stab
  stabilities n ▷ stable²
  stability n ▷ stable²
  stabilization n ▷ stabilize
  stabilizations n ▷ stabilize
stabilize v (-zes, -zing, -zed) make or become stable > **stabilization** n (pl -s)
  stabilized v ▷ stabilize
stabilizer n (pl -s) device for stabilizing a child's bicycle, an aircraft, or a ship
  stabilizers n ▷ stabilizer
  stabilizes v ▷ stabilize
  stabilizing v ▷ stabilize
stable¹ n (pl -s) building in which horses are kept ▶ v (-les, -ling, -led) put or keep (a horse) in a stable
stable² adj (-r, -st) firmly fixed or established > **stability** n (pl -ties)
  stabled v ▷ stable¹
  stabler adj ▷ stable²
  stables n, v ▷ stable¹
  stablest adj ▷ stable²
  stabling v ▷ stable¹
  stabs v, n ▷ stab
staccato [stak-ah-toe] adv (MUSIC) with the notes sharply separated ▶ adj consisting of short abrupt sounds
stack n (pl -s) ordered pile ▶ v (-s, -ing, -ed) pile in a stack
  stacked v ▷ stack
  stacking v ▷ stack
  stacks n, v ▷ stack
  stadia n ▷ stadium
stadium n (pl -diums, -dia) sports arena with tiered seats for spectators
  stadiums n ▷ stadium
staff¹ n (pl -s) people employed in an organization ▶ v (-s, -ing, -ed) supply with personnel
staff² n (pl staves) set of five horizontal lines

on which music is written
  staffed v ▷ staff¹
  staffing v ▷ staff¹
  staffs n, v ▷ staff¹
stag n (pl -s) adult male deer
stage n (pl -s) step or period of development ▶ v (-ges, -ging, -ged) put (a play) on stage
stagecoach n (pl -es) large horse-drawn vehicle formerly used to carry passengers and mail
  stagecoaches n ▷ stagecoach
  staged v ▷ stage
  stages n, v ▷ stage
stagey adj (-gier, -giest) overtheatrical
stagger v (-s, -ing, -ed) walk unsteadily ▶ n (pl -s) staggering
  staggered v ▷ stagger
  staggering v ▷ stagger
  staggers v, n ▷ stagger
  stagier adj ▷ stagey
  stagiest adj ▷ stagey
  staging v ▷ stage
stagnant adj (of water or air) stale from not moving
stagnate v (-tes, -ting, -ted) be stagnant > **stagnation** n (pl -s)
  stagnated v ▷ stagnate
  stagnates v ▷ stagnate
  stagnating v ▷ stagnate
  stagnation n ▷ stagnate
  stagnations n ▷ stagnate
  stags n ▷ stag
staid adj (-er, -est) sedate, serious, and rather dull
  staider adj ▷ staid
  staidest adj ▷ staid
stain v (-s, -ing, -ed) discolour, mark ▶ n (pl -s) discoloration or mark > **stainless** adj
  stained v ▷ stain
  staining v ▷ stain
  stainless adj ▷ stain
  stains v, n ▷ stain
staircase, stairway n (pl -s) flight of stairs with a handrail or banisters
  staircases n ▷ staircase
stairs pl n flight of steps between floors, usu. indoors
  stairway n ▷ staircase
  stairways n ▷ staircase
stake¹ n (pl -s) pointed stick or post driven into the ground as a support or marker ▶ v (-kes, -king, -ked) support or mark out with stakes
stake² n (pl -s) money wagered ▶ v (-kes, -king, -ked) wager, risk
  staked v ▷ stake¹, ²

stakeholder *n* (*pl* **-s**) person who has a concern or interest in something, esp. a business
  stakeholders *n* ▷ stakeholder
stakes *v* ▷ stake[1, 2] ▶ *n* ▷ stake[1, 2]
  staking *v* ▷ stake[1, 2]
stalactite *n* (*pl* **-s**) lime deposit hanging from the roof of a cave
  stalactites *n* ▷ stalactite
stalagmite *n* (*pl* **-s**) lime deposit sticking up from the floor of a cave
  stalagmites *n* ▷ stalagmite
stale *adj* (**-r**, **-st**) not fresh ▷ **staleness** *n* (*pl* **-es**)
stalemate *n* (*pl* **-s**) (CHESS) position in which any of a player's moves would put his king in check, resulting in a draw
  stalemates *n* ▷ stalemate
  staleness *n* ▷ stale
  stalenesses *n* ▷ stale
  staler *adj* ▷ stale
  stalest *adj* ▷ stale
stalk[1] *n* (*pl* **-s**) plant's stem
stalk[2] *v* (**-s**, **-ing**, **-ed**) follow or approach stealthily
  stalked *v* ▷ stalk[2]
stalker *n* (*pl* **-s**) person who follows or stealthily approaches a person or an animal
  stalkers *n* ▷ stalker
  stalking *v* ▷ stalk[2]
stalking-horse *n* (*pl* **-s**) pretext
  stalking-horses *n* ▷ stalking-horse
  stalks *n* ▷ stalk[1] ▶ *v* ▷ stalk[2]
stall[1] *n* (*pl* **-s**) small stand for the display and sale of goods ▶ *v* (**-s**, **-ing**, **-ed**) stop (a motor vehicle or engine) or (of a motor vehicle or engine) stop accidentally
stall[2] *v* (**-s**, **-ing**, **-ed**) employ delaying tactics
  stalled *v* ▷ stall[1, 2]
  stalling *v* ▷ stall[1, 2]
stallion *n* (*pl* **-s**) uncastrated male horse
  stallions *n* ▷ stallion
stalls *n* ▷ stall[1] ▶ *v* ▷ stall[1, 2] ▶ *pl n* ground-floor seats in a theatre or cinema
stalwart [stawl-wart] *adj* strong and sturdy ▶ *n* (*pl* **-s**) stalwart person
  stalwarts *n* ▷ stalwart
stamen *n* (*pl* **-s**) pollen-producing part of a flower
  stamens *n* ▷ stamen
stamina *n* (*pl* **-s**) enduring energy and strength
  staminas *n* ▷ stamina
stammer *v* (**-s**, **-ing**, ed) speak or say with involuntary pauses or repetition of syllables ▶ *n* (*pl* **-s**) tendency to stammer
  stammered *v* ▷ stammer
  stammering *v* ▷ stammer

stammers *v*, *n* ▷ stammer
stamp *n* (*pl* **-s**) piece of gummed paper stuck to an envelope or parcel to show that the postage has been paid ▶ *v* (**-s**, **-ing**, **-ed**) bring (one's foot) down forcefully
  stamped *v* ▷ stamp
stampede *n* (*pl* **-s**) sudden rush of frightened animals or of a crowd ▶ *v* (**-des**, **-ding**, **-ded**) (cause to) take part in a stampede
  stampeded *v* ▷ stampede
  stampedes *n*, *v* ▷ stampede
  stampeding *v* ▷ stampede
  stamping *v* ▷ stamp
  stamps *n*, *v* ▷ stamp
stance *n* (*pl* **-s**) attitude
  stances *n* ▷ stance
stanch [stahnch] *v* (**-es**, **-ing**, **-ed**) ▷ staunch[2]
  stanched *v* ▷ stanch
  stanches *v* ▷ stanch
  stanching *v* ▷ stanch
stanchion *n* (*pl* **-s**) upright bar used as a support
  stanchions *n* ▷ stanchion
stand *v* (**-s**, **-ing**, **stood**) be in, rise to, or place in an upright position ▶ *n* (*pl* **-s**) stall for the sale of goods
standard *n* (*pl* **-s**) level of quality ▶ *adj* usual, regular, or average
  standardization *n* ▷ standardize
standardize *v* (**-zes**, **-zing**, **-zed**) cause to conform to a standard ▷ **standardization** *n* (*pl* **-s**)
  standardized *v* ▷ standardize
  standardizes *v* ▷ standardize
  standardizing *v* ▷ standardize
  standards *n* ▷ standard
standing *adj* permanent, lasting ▶ *n* (*pl* **-s**) reputation or status ▶ *v* ▷ stand
  standings *n* ▷ standing
standoffish *adj* reserved or haughty
standpipe *n* (*pl* **-s**) tap attached to a water main to provide a public water supply
  standpipes *n* ▷ standpipe
standpoint *n* (*pl* **-s**) point of view
  standpoints *n* ▷ standpoint
  stands *v*, *n* ▷ stand
standstill *n* (*pl* **-s**) complete halt
  standstills *n* ▷ standstill
  stank *v* ▷ stink
stanza *n* (*pl* **-s**) verse of a poem
  stanzas *n* ▷ stanza
staple[1] *n* (*pl* **-s**) U-shaped piece of metal used to fasten papers or secure things ▶ *v* (**-les**, **-ling**, **-led**) fasten with staples
staple[2] *adj* of prime importance, principal ▶ *n*

(pl -s) main constituent of anything
  stapled v ▷ staple[1]
stapler n (pl -s) small device for fastening
papers together
  staplers n ▷ stapler
  staples n ▷ staple[1, 2] ▶ v ▷ staple[1]
  stapling v ▷ staple[1]
star n (pl -s) hot gaseous mass in space, visible
in the night sky as a point of light ▶ v (-s,
-rring, -rred) feature or be featured in a main
role ▶ adj leading, famous
starboard n (pl -s) right-hand side of a ship,
when facing forward ▶ adj of or on this side
  starboards n ▷ starboard
starch n (pl -es) carbohydrate forming the
main food element in bread, potatoes, etc.,
and used mixed with water for stiffening
fabric ▶ v (-es, -ing, -ed) stiffen (fabric) with
starch
  starched v ▷ starch
  starches n, v ▷ starch
  starchier adj ▷ starchy
  starchiest adj ▷ starchy
  starching v ▷ starch
starchy adj (-chier, -chiest) containing starch
stardom n (pl -s) status of a star in the
entertainment or sports world
  stardoms n ▷ stardom
stare v (-res, -ring, -red) look or gaze fixedly
(at) ▶ n (pl -s) fixed gaze
  stared v ▷ stare
  stares v, n ▷ stare
starfish n (pl -es) star-shaped sea creature
  starfishes n ▷ starfish
  staring v ▷ stare
stark adj (-er, -est) harsh, unpleasant, and
plain ▶ adv completely
  starker adj ▷ stark
  starkest adj ▷ stark
starling n (pl -s) songbird with glossy black
speckled feathers
  starlings n ▷ starling
  starred v ▷ star
  starrier adj ▷ starry
  starriest adj ▷ starry
  starring v ▷ star
starry adj (-rrier, -rriest) full of or like stars
stars n, v ▷ star ▶ pl n astrological forecast,
horoscope
start v (-s, -ing, -ed) take the first step, begin
▶ n (pl -s) first part of something
  started v ▷ start
starter n (pl -s) first course of a meal
  starters n ▷ starter
  starting v ▷ start

startle v (-les, -ling, -led) slightly surprise or
frighten
  startled v ▷ startle
  startles v ▷ startle
  startling v ▷ startle
  starts v, n ▷ start
  starvation n ▷ starve
  starvations n ▷ starve
starve v (-ves, -ving, -ved) die or suffer or cause
to die or suffer from hunger > **starvation**
n (pl -s)
  starved v ▷ starve
  starves v ▷ starve
  starving v ▷ starve
stash (Informal) v (-es, -ing, -ed) store in a secret
place ▶ n (pl -es) secret store
  stashed v ▷ stash
  stashes v, n ▷ stash
  stashing v ▷ stash
state n (pl -s) condition of a person or thing
▶ adj of or concerning the State ▶ v (-tes,
-ting, -ted) express in words
  stated v ▷ state
statehouse n (pl -s) (NZ) publicly-owned house
rented to a low-income tenant
  statehouses n ▷ statehouse
  statelier adj ▷ stately
  stateliest adj ▷ stately
stately adj (-lier, -liest) dignified or grand
statement n (pl -s) something stated
  statements n ▷ statement
stateroom n (pl -s) private cabin on a ship
  staterooms n ▷ stateroom
  states n, v ▷ state
statesman, stateswoman n (pl -men,
-women) experienced and respected political
leader > **statesmanship** n (pl -s)
  statesmanship n ▷ statesman
  statesmanships n ▷ statesman
  statesmen n ▷ statesman
  stateswoman n ▷ statesman
  stateswomen n ▷ statesman
static adj stationary or inactive ▶ n (pl -s)
crackling sound or speckled picture caused
by interference in radio or television
reception
  statics n ▷ static
  stating v ▷ state
station n (pl -s) place where trains stop
for passengers ▶ v (-s, -ing, -ed) assign
(someone) to a particular place
stationary adj not moving
  stationed v ▷ station
stationer n (pl -s) dealer in stationery
  stationeries n ▷ stationery

stationers n ▷ stationer

stationery n (pl **-ries**) writing materials such as paper and pens

stationing v ▷ station

stations n, v ▷ station

statistic n (pl **-s**) numerical fact collected and classified systematically > **statistical** adj > **statistically** adv

statistical adj ▷ statistic

statistically adv ▷ statistic

statistician n (pl **-s**) person who compiles and studies statistics

statisticians n ▷ statistician

statistics n ▷ statistic

statuaries n ▷ statuary

statuary n (pl **-ries**) statues collectively

statue n (pl **-s**) large sculpture of a human or animal figure

statues n ▷ statue

statuesque adj (of a woman) tall and well-proportioned

statuette n (pl **-s**) small statue

statuettes n ▷ statuette

stature n (pl **-s**) person's height

statures n ▷ stature

status n (pl **-ses**) social position

statuses n ▷ status

statute n (pl **-s**) written law > **statutory** adj required or authorized by law

statutes n ▷ statute

statutory adj ▷ statute

staunch[1] adj (**-er, -est**) loyal, firm

staunch[2], **stanch** v (**-ches, -ching, -ched**) stop (a flow of blood)

staunched v ▷ staunch[2]

stauncher adj ▷ staunch[1]

staunches v ▷ staunch[2]

staunchest adj ▷ staunch[1]

staunching v ▷ staunch[2]

stave n (pl **-s**) one of the strips of wood forming a barrel

staves n ▷ staff[2]

stay[1] v (**-s, -ing, -ed**) remain in a place or condition ▶ n (pl **-s**) period of staying in a place

stay[2] n (pl **-s**) prop or buttress

stay[3] n (pl **-s**) rope or wire supporting a ship's mast

stayed v ▷ stay[1]

staying v ▷ stay[1]

stays n ▷ stay[1, 2, 3] ▶ v ▷ stay[1] ▶ pl n corset

stead n (pl **-s**) in someone's place

steadfast adj firm, determined > **steadfastly** adv

steadfastly adv ▷ steadfast

steadied v ▷ steady

steadier adj ▷ steady

steadiest adj ▷ steady

steadily adv ▷ steady

steadiness n ▷ steady

steadinesses n ▷ steady

steads n ▷ stead

steady adj (**-dier, -diest**) not shaky or wavering ▶ v (**-dies, -dying, -died**) make steady ▶ adv in a steady manner > **steadily** adv > **steadiness** n (pl **-es**)

steadying v ▷ steady

steak n (pl **-s**) thick slice of meat, esp. beef

steaks n ▷ steak

steal v (**-s, -ing, stole, stolen**) take unlawfully or without permission

stealing v ▷ steal

steals v ▷ steal

stealth n (pl **-s**) secret or underhand behaviour ▶ adj (of technology) able to render an aircraft almost invisible to radar > **stealthy** adj (**-thier, -thiest**) > **stealthily** adv

stealthier adj ▷ stealth

stealthiest adj ▷ stealth

stealthily adv ▷ stealth

stealths n ▷ stealth

stealthy adj ▷ stealth

steam n (pl **-s**) vapour into which water changes when boiled ▶ v (**-s, -ing, -ed**) give off steam

steamed v ▷ steam

steamer n (pl **-s**) steam-propelled ship

steamers n ▷ steamer

steaming v ▷ steam

steamroller n (pl **-s**) steam-powered vehicle with heavy rollers, used to level road surfaces ▶ v (**-s, -ing, -ed**) use overpowering force to make (someone) do what one wants

steamrollered v ▷ steamroller

steamrollering v ▷ steamroller

steamrollers n, v ▷ steamroller

steams n, v ▷ steam

steed n (pl **-s**) (Lit) horse

steeds n ▷ steed

steel n (pl **-s**) hard malleable alloy of iron and carbon ▶ v (**-s, -ing, -ed**) prepare (oneself) for something unpleasant > **steely** adj (**-lier, -liest**)

steeled v ▷ steel

steelier adj ▷ steel

steeliest adj ▷ steel

steeling v ▷ steel

steels n, v ▷ steel

steely adj ▷ steel

steep[1] adj (**-er, -est**) sloping sharply > **steeply**

adv ▷ **steepness** *n* (*pl* -es)
steep² *v* (-s, -ing, -ed) soak or be soaked in liquid
  steeped *v* ▷ **steep²**
  steeper *adj* ▷ **steep¹**
  steepest *adj* ▷ **steep¹**
  steeping *v* ▷ **steep²**
steeple *n* (*pl* -s) church tower with a spire
steeplechase *n* (*pl* -s) horse race with obstacles to jump
  steeplechases *n* ▷ **steeplechase**
steeplejack *n* (*pl* -s) person who repairs steeples and chimneys
  steeplejacks *n* ▷ **steeplejack**
  steeples *n* ▷ **steeple**
  steeply *n* ▷ **steep¹**
  steepness *n* ▷ **steep¹**
  steepnesses *n* ▷ **steep¹**
  steeps *v* ▷ **steep²**
steer¹ *v* (-s, -ing, -ed) direct the course of (a vehicle and ship)
steer² *n* (*pl* -s) castrated male ox
steerage *n* (*pl* -s) cheapest accommodation on a passenger ship
  steerages *n* ▷ **steerage**
  steered *v* ▷ **steer¹**
  steering *v* ▷ **steer¹**
  steers *v* ▷ **steer¹** ▶ *n* ▷ **steer²**
stein [stine] *n* (*pl* -s) earthenware beer mug
  steins *n* ▷ **stein**
stellar *adj* of stars
stem¹ *n* (*pl* -s) long thin central part of a plant ▶ *v* (-s, -mming, -mmed) originate from
stem² *v* (-s, -mming, -mmed) stop (the flow of something)
  stemmed *v* ▷ **stem¹, ²**
  stemming *v* ▷ **stem¹, ²**
  stems *v* ▷ **stem¹, ²** ▶ *n* ▷ **stem¹**
stench *n* (*pl* -es) foul smell
  stenches *n* ▷ **stench**
stencil *n* (*pl* -s) thin sheet with cut-out pattern through which ink or paint passes to form the pattern on the surface below ▶ *v* (-s, -lling, -lled) make (a pattern) with a stencil
  stencilled *v* ▷ **stencil**
  stencilling *v* ▷ **stencil**
  stencils *n*, *v* ▷ **stencil**
stenographer *n* (*pl* -s) shorthand typist
  stenographers *n* ▷ **stenographer**
stent *n* (*pl* -s) surgical implant used to keep an artery open
stentorian *adj* (of a voice) very loud
  stents *n* ▷ **stent**
step *v* (-s, -pping, -pped) move and set down the foot, as when walking ▶ *n* (*pl* -s) stepping

stepladder *n* (*pl* -s) folding portable ladder with supporting frame
  stepladders *n* ▷ **stepladder**
  stepped *v* ▷ **step**
steppes *pl n* wide grassy treeless plains in Russia and Ukraine
  stepping *v* ▷ **step**
  steps *pl n* stepladder ▶ *n*, *v* ▷ **step**
  stereo *adj* ▷ **stereophonic** ▶ *n* (*pl* -s) stereophonic record player
stereophonic *adj* using two separate loudspeakers to give the effect of naturally distributed sound
  stereos *n* ▷ **stereo**
stereotype *n* (*pl* -s) standardized idea of a type of person or thing ▶ *v* (-pes, -ping, -ped) form a stereotype of
  stereotyped *v* ▷ **stereotype**
  stereotypes *n*, *v* ▷ **stereotype**
  stereotyping *v* ▷ **stereotype**
sterile *adj* free from germs ▷ **sterility** *n* (*pl* -ties)
  sterilities *n* ▷ **sterile**
  sterility *n* ▷ **sterile**
  sterilization *n* ▷ **sterilize**
  sterilizations *n* ▷ **sterilize**
sterilize *v* (-zes, -zing, -zed) make sterile ▷ **sterilization** *n* (*pl* -s)
  sterilized *v* ▷ **sterilize**
  sterilizes *v* ▷ **sterilize**
  sterilizing *v* ▷ **sterilize**
sterling *n* (*pl* -s) British money system ▶ *adj* genuine and reliable
  sterlings *n* ▷ **sterling**
stern¹ *adj* (-er, -est) severe, strict ▷ **sternly** *adv* ▷ **sternness** *n* (*pl* -es)
stern² *n* (*pl* -s) rear part of a ship
  sterna *n* ▷ **sternum**
  sterner *adj* ▷ **stern¹**
  sternest *adj* ▷ **stern¹**
  sternly *adv* ▷ **stern¹**
  sternness *n* ▷ **stern¹**
  sternnesses *n* ▷ **stern¹**
  sterns *n* ▷ **stern²**
sternum *n* (*pl* -na, -nums) ▷ **breastbone**
  sternums *n* ▷ **sternum**
steroid *n* (*pl* -s) organic compound containing a carbon ring system, such as many hormones
  steroids *n* ▷ **steroid**
stethoscope *n* (*pl* -s) medical instrument for listening to sounds made inside the body
  stethoscopes *n* ▷ **stethoscope**
stevedore *n* (*pl* -s) person who loads and unloads ships
  stevedores *n* ▷ **stevedore**

stew n (pl **-s**) food cooked slowly in a closed pot ▶ v (**-s, -ing, -ed**) cook slowly in a closed pot

steward n (pl **-s**) person who looks after passengers on a ship or aircraft > **stewardess** n fem (pl **-es**)

stewardess n ▷ steward

stewardesses n ▷ steward

stewards n ▷ steward

stewed v ▷ stew

stewing v ▷ stew

stews n, v ▷ stew

stick¹ n (pl **-s**) long thin piece of wood

stick² v (**-s, -ing, stuck**) push (a pointed object) into (something)

sticker n (pl **-s**) adhesive label or sign

stickers n ▷ sticker

stickier adj ▷ sticky

stickiest adj ▷ sticky

sticking v ▷ stick²

stickleback n (pl **-s**) small fish with sharp spines on its back

sticklebacks n ▷ stickleback

stickler n (pl **-s**) person who insists on something

sticklers n ▷ stickler

sticks n ▷ stick¹ ▶ v ▷ stick²

stickup n (pl **-s**) (Slang) robbery at gunpoint

stickups n ▷ stickup

sticky adj (**-ckier, -ckiest**) covered with an adhesive substance

sties n ▷ sty

stiff adj (**-er, -est**) not easily bent or moved ▶ n (pl **-s**) (Slang) corpse > **stiffly** adv > **stiffness** n (pl **-es**)

stiffen v (**-s, -ing, -ed**) make or become stiff

stiffened v ▷ stiffen

stiffening v ▷ stiffen

stiffens v ▷ stiffen

stiffer adj ▷ stiff

stiffest adj ▷ stiff

stiffly adv ▷ stiff

stiffness n ▷ stiff

stiffnesses n ▷ stiff

stiffs n ▷ stiff

stifle v (**-les, -ling, -led**) suppress

stifled v ▷ stifle

stifles v ▷ stifle

stifling v ▷ stifle

stigma n (pl **-mas, -mata**) mark of social disgrace

stigmas n ▷ stigma

stigmata pl n marks resembling the wounds of the crucified Christ ▶ n ▷ stigma

stigmatize v (**-zes, -zing, -zed**) mark as being shameful

stigmatized v ▷ stigmatize

stigmatizes v ▷ stigmatize

stigmatizing v ▷ stigmatize

stile n (pl **-s**) set of steps allowing people to climb a fence

stiles n ▷ stile

stiletto n (pl **-s**) high narrow heel on a woman's shoe

stilettos n ▷ stiletto

still¹ adv now or in the future as before ▶ adj (**-er, -est**) motionless ▶ n (pl **-s**) photograph from a film scene ▶ v (**-s, -ing, -ed**) make still > **stillness** n (pl **-es**)

still² n (pl **-s**) apparatus for distilling alcoholic drinks

stillborn adj born dead

stilled v ▷ still¹

stiller adj ▷ still¹

stillest adj ▷ still¹

stilling v ▷ still¹

stillness n ▷ still¹

stillnesses n ▷ still¹

stills n ▷ still¹, ² ▶ v ▷ still¹

stilted adj stiff and formal in manner

stilts pl n pair of poles with footrests for walking raised from the ground

stimulant n (pl **-s**) something, such as a drug, that acts as a stimulus

stimulants n ▷ stimulant

stimulate v (**-tes, -ting, -ted**) act as a stimulus (on) > **stimulation** n (pl **-s**)

stimulated v ▷ stimulate

stimulates v ▷ stimulate

stimulating v ▷ stimulate

stimulation n ▷ stimulate

stimulations n ▷ stimulate

stimuli n ▷ stimulus

stimulus n (pl **-li**) something that rouses a person or thing to activity

sting v (**-s, -ing, stung**) (of certain animals or plants) wound (by injecting with poison) ▶ n (pl **-s**) wound or pain caused by or as if by stinging

stingier adj ▷ stingy

stingiest adj ▷ stingy

stinginess n ▷ stingy

stinginesses n ▷ stingy

stinging v ▷ sting

stings v, n ▷ sting

stingy adj (**-gier, -giest**) mean or miserly > **stinginess** n (pl **-es**)

stink n (pl **-s**) strong unpleasant smell ▶ v (**-s, -ing, stank** or **stunk**) (**stunk**) give off a strong unpleasant smell

stinking v ▷ stink

stinks *n, v* ▷ stink

stint *v* (-s, -ing, -ed) (foll. by **on**) be miserly with (something) ▶ *n* (pl -s) allotted amount of work

stinted *v* ▷ stint

stinting *v* ▷ stint

stints *v, n* ▷ stint

stipend [sty-pend] *n* (pl -s) regular allowance or salary, esp. that paid to a clergyman > **stipendiary** *adj* receiving a stipend

stipendiary *adj* ▷ stipend

stipends *n* ▷ stipend

stipple *v* (-les, -ling, -led) paint, draw, or engrave using dots

stippled *v* ▷ stipple

stipples *v* ▷ stipple

stippling *v* ▷ stipple

stipulate *v* (-tes, -ting, -ted) specify as a condition of an agreement > **stipulation** *n* (pl -s)

stipulated *v* ▷ stipulate

stipulates *v* ▷ stipulate

stipulating *v* ▷ stipulate

stipulation *n* ▷ stipulate

stipulations *n* ▷ stipulate

stir *v* (-s, -rring, -rred) mix up (a liquid) by moving a spoon etc. around in it ▶ *n* (pl -s) a stirring

stirred *v* ▷ stir

stirring *v* ▷ stir

stirrup *n* (pl -s) metal loop attached to a saddle for supporting a rider's foot

stirrups *n* ▷ stirrup

stirs *v, n* ▷ stir

stitch *n* (pl -es) link made by drawing thread through material with a needle ▶ *v* (-es, -ing, -ed) sew

stitched *v* ▷ stitch

stitches *n, v* ▷ stitch

stitching *v* ▷ stitch

stoat *n* (pl -s) small mammal of the weasel family, with brown fur that turns white in winter

stoats *n* ▷ stoat

stock *n* (pl -s) total amount of goods available for sale in a shop ▶ *adj* kept in stock, standard ▶ *v* (-s, -ing, -ed) keep for sale or future use

stockade *n* (pl -s) enclosure or barrier made of stakes

stockades *n* ▷ stockade

stockbroker *n* (pl -s) person who buys and sells stocks and shares for customers

stockbrokers *n* ▷ stockbroker

stocked *v* ▷ stock

stockier *adj* ▷ stocky

stockiest *adj* ▷ stocky

stocking *n* (pl -s) close-fitting covering for the foot and leg ▶ *v* ▷ stock

stockings *n* ▷ stocking

stockist *n* (pl -s) dealer who stocks a particular product

stockists *n* ▷ stockist

stockpile *v* (-les, -ling, -led) store a large quantity of (something) for future use ▶ *n* (pl -s) accumulated store

stockpiled *v* ▷ stockpile

stockpiles *v, n* ▷ stockpile

stockpiling *v* ▷ stockpile

stocks *n pl* (HIST) instrument of punishment consisting of a wooden frame with holes into which the hands and feet of the victim were locked ▶ *n, v* ▷ stock

stocktaking *n* (pl -s) counting and valuing of the goods in a shop

stocktakings *n* ▷ stocktaking

stocky *adj* (-ckier, -ckiest) (of a person) broad and sturdy

stodge *n* (pl -s) (BRIT, AUST & NZ) heavy starchy food

stodges *n* ▷ stodge

stodgier *adj* ▷ stodgy

stodgiest *adj* ▷ stodgy

stodgy *adj* (-gier, -giest) (of food) heavy and starchy

stoep [stoop] *n* (pl -s) (S AFR) verandah

stoeps *n* ▷ stoep

stoic [stow-ik] *n* (pl -s) person who suffers hardship without showing his or her feelings ▶ *adj* (also **stoical**) suffering hardship without showing one's feelings > **stoically** *adv* > **stoicism** [stow-iss-izz-um] *n* (pl -s)

stoical *adj* ▷ stoic

stoically *adv* ▷ stoic

stoicism *n* ▷ stoic

stoicisms *n* ▷ stoic

stoics *n* ▷ stoic

stoke *v* (-kes, -king, -ked) feed and tend (a fire or furnace) > **stoker** *n* (pl -s)

stoked *v* ▷ stoke

stoker *n* ▷ stoke

stokers *n* ▷ stoke

stokes *v* ▷ stoke

stoking *v* ▷ stoke

stole[1] *v* ▷ steal

stole[2] *n* (pl -s) long scarf or shawl

stolen *v* ▷ steal

stoles *n* ▷ stole[2]

stolid *adj* (-er, -est) showing little emotion or interest > **stolidly** *adv*

stolider *adj* ▷ stolid

stolidest *adj* ▷ stolid
stolidly *adv* ▷ stolid
stomach *n* (*pl* -s) organ in the body which digests food ▶ *v* (-s, -ing, -ed) put up with
  stomached *v* ▷ stomach
  stomaching *v* ▷ stomach
  stomachs *n*, *v* ▷ stomach
stomp *v* (-s, -ing, -ed) (*Informal*) tread heavily
  stomped *v* ▷ stomp
  stomping *v* ▷ stomp
  stomps *v* ▷ stomp
stone *n* (*pl* -s) material of which rocks are made ▶ *v* (-nes, -ning, -ned) throw stones at
stoned *adj* (*Slang*) under the influence of alcohol or drugs ▶ *v* ▷ stone
  stones *n*, *v* ▷ stone
stonewall *v* (-s, -ing, -ed) obstruct or hinder discussion
  stonewalled *v* ▷ stonewall
  stonewalling *v* ▷ stonewall
  stonewalls *v* ▷ stonewall
stoneware *n* (*pl* -s) hard kind of pottery fired at a very high temperature
  stonewares *n* ▷ stoneware
  stonier *adj* ▷ stony
  stoniest *adj* ▷ stony
  stonily *adv* ▷ stony
  stoning *v* ▷ stone
stony *adj* (-nier, -niest) of or like stone
  > **stonily** *adv*
  stood *v* ▷ stand
stooge *n* (*pl* -es) actor who feeds lines to a comedian or acts as the butt of his jokes
  stooges *n* ▷ stooge
stool *n* (*pl* -s) chair without arms or back
  stools *n* ▷ stool
stoop *v* (-s, -ing, -ed) bend (the body) forward and downward ▶ *n* (*pl* -s) stooping posture
  stooped *v* ▷ stoop
  stooping *v* ▷ stoop
  stoops *v*, *n* ▷ stoop
stop *v* (-s, -pping, -pped) cease or cause to cease from doing (something) ▶ *n* (*pl* -s) stopping or being stopped > **stoppage** *n* (*pl* -s)
stopcock *n* (*pl* -s) valve to control or stop the flow of fluid in a pipe
  stopcocks *n* ▷ stopcock
stopgap *n* (*pl* -s) temporary substitute
  stopgaps *n* ▷ stopgap
stopover *n* (*pl* -s) short break in a journey
  stopovers *n* ▷ stopover
  stoppage *n* ▷ stop
  stoppages *n* ▷ stop
  stopped *v* ▷ stop
stopper *n* (*pl* -s) plug for closing a bottle etc.

stoppers *n* ▷ stopper
stopping *v* ▷ stop
stops *v*, *n* ▷ stop
stopwatch *n* (*pl* -es) watch which can be stopped instantly for exact timing of a sporting event
  stopwatches *n* ▷ stopwatch
storage *n* (*pl* -s) storing
  storages *n* ▷ storage
store *v* (-res, -ring, -red) collect and keep (things) for future use ▶ *n* (*pl* -s) shop
  stored *v* ▷ store
  stores *v*, *n* ▷ store ▶ *n pl* stock of provisions
storey *n* (*pl* -s) floor or level of a building
  storeys *n* ▷ storey
  stories *n* ▷ story
  storing *v* ▷ store
stork *n* (*pl* -s) large wading bird
  storks *n* ▷ stork
storm *n* (*pl* -s) violent weather with wind, rain, or snow ▶ *v* (-s, -ing, -ed) attack or capture (a place) suddenly
  stormed *v* ▷ storm
  stormier *adj* ▷ stormy
  stormiest *adj* ▷ stormy
  storming *v* ▷ storm
  storms *n*, *v* ▷ storm
stormy *adj* (-mier, -miest) characterized by storms
story *n* (*pl* -ries) description of a series of events told or written for entertainment
stoup [stoop] *n* (*pl* -s) small basin for holy water
  stoups *n* ▷ stoup
stout *adj* (-er, -est) fat ▶ *n* (*pl* -s) strong dark beer > **stoutly** *adv*
  stouter *adj* ▷ stout
  stoutest *adj* ▷ stout
  stoutly *adv* ▷ stout
  stouts *n* ▷ stout
stove *n* (*pl* -s) apparatus for cooking or heating
  stoves *n* ▷ stove
stow *v* (-s, -ing, -ed) pack or store
stowaway *n* (*pl* -s) person who hides on a ship or aircraft in order to travel free
  stowaways *n* ▷ stowaway
  stowed *v* ▷ stow
  stowing *v* ▷ stow
  stows *v* ▷ stow
straddle *v* (-les, -ling, -led) have one leg or part on each side of (something)
  straddled *v* ▷ straddle
  straddles *v* ▷ straddle
  straddling *v* ▷ straddle
strafe *v* (-fes, -fing, -fed) attack (an enemy) with machine guns from the air

strafed v ▷ strafe
strafes v ▷ strafe
strafing v ▷ strafe
straggle v (-les, -ling, -led) go or spread in a rambling or irregular way > **straggler** n (pl -s) > **straggly** adj (-lier, -liest)
straggled v ▷ straggle
straggler n ▷ straggle
stragglers n ▷ straggle
straggles v ▷ straggle
stragglier adj ▷ straggle
straggliest adj ▷ straggle
straggling v ▷ straggle
straggly adj ▷ straggle
straight adj (-er, -est) not curved or crooked ▶ adv in a straight line ▶ n (pl -s) straight part, esp. of a racetrack > **straighten** v (-s, -ing, -ed)
straightaway adv immediately
straighten v ▷ straight
straightened v ▷ straight
straightening v ▷ straight
straightens v ▷ straighn
straighter adj ▷ straight
straightest adj ▷ straight
straightforward adj honest, frank
straightlaced adj ▷ straitlaced
straights n ▷ straight
strain[1] v (-s, -ing, -ed) cause (something) to be used or stretched beyond its limits ▶ n (pl -s) tension or tiredness
strain[2] n (pl -s) breed or race
strained adj not natural, forced ▶ v ▷ strain[1]
strainer n (pl -s) sieve
strainers n ▷ strainer
straining v ▷ strain[1]
strains n ▷ strain[1, 2] ▶ v ▷ strain[1]
strait n (pl -s) position of acute difficulty
straitened adj not having much money
straitjacket n (pl -s) strong jacket with long sleeves used to bind the arms of a violent person
straitjackets n ▷ straitjacket
straitlaced, straightlaced adj prudish or puritanical
straits n ▷ strait ▶ n pl narrow channel connecting two areas of sea
strand[1] v (-s, -ing, -ed) run aground ▶ n (pl -s) (Poetic) shore
strand[2] n (pl -s) single thread of string, wire, etc.
stranded v ▷ strand[1]
stranding v ▷ strand[1]
strands n ▷ strand[1, 2] ▶ v ▷ strand[1]
strange adj (-r, -st) odd or unusual > **strangely** adv > **strangeness** n (pl -es)

strangely adv ▷ strange
strangeness n ▷ strange
strangenesses n ▷ strange
stranger n (pl -s) person who is not known or is new to a place or experience ▶ adj ▷ strange
strangers n ▷ stranger
strangest adj ▷ strange
strangle v (-les, -ling, -led) kill by squeezing the throat > **strangler** n (pl -s)
strangled v ▷ strangle
stranglehold n (pl -s) strangling grip in wrestling
strangleholds n ▷ stranglehold
strangler n ▷ strangle
stranglers n ▷ strangle
strangles v ▷ strangle
strangling v ▷ strangle
strangulation n (pl -s) strangling
strangulations n ▷ strangulation
strap n (pl -s) strip of flexible material for lifting, fastening, or holding in place ▶ v (-s, -pping, -pped) fasten with a strap or straps
strapped n ▷ strap
strapping adj tall and sturdy ▶ v ▷ strap
straps n, v ▷ strap
strata n ▷ stratum
stratagem n (pl -s) clever plan, trick
stratagems n ▷ stratagem
strategic [strat-ee-jik] adj advantageous > **strategically** adv
strategically adv ▷ strategic
strategies n ▷ strategy
strategist n ▷ strategy
strategists n ▷ strategy
strategy n (pl -gies) overall plan > **strategist** n (pl -s)
strathspey n (pl -s) Scottish dance with gliding steps
strathspeys n ▷ strathspey
stratification n ▷ stratified
stratifications n ▷ stratified
stratified adj divided into strata > **stratification** n (pl -s)
stratosphere n (pl -s) atmospheric layer between about 15 and 50 kilometres above the earth
stratospheres n ▷ stratosphere
stratum [strah-tum] n (pl -ta) layer, esp. of rock
straw n (pl -s) dried stalks of grain
strawberries n ▷ strawberry
strawberry n (pl -ries) sweet fleshy red fruit with small seeds on the outside
straws n ▷ straw
stray v (-s, -ing, -ed) wander ▶ adj having strayed ▶ n (pl -s) stray animal

strayed v ▷ stray

straying v ▷ stray

strays v, n ▷ stray

streak n (pl -s) long band of contrasting colour or substance ▶ v (-s, -ing, -ed) mark with streaks > **streaker** n (pl -s) > **streaky** adj (-kier, -kiest)

streaked v ▷ streak

streaker n ▷ streak

streakers n ▷ streak

streakier adj ▷ streak

streakiest adj ▷ streak

streaking v ▷ streak

streaks n, v ▷ streak

streaky adj ▷ streak

stream n (pl -s) small river ▶ v (-s, -ing, -ed) flow steadily

streamed v ▷ stream

streamer n (pl -s) strip of coloured paper that unrolls when tossed

streamers n ▷ streamer

streaming v ▷ stream

streamline v (-nes, -ning, -ned) make more efficient by simplifying

streamlined v ▷ streamline

streamlines v ▷ streamline

streamlining v ▷ streamline

streams n, v ▷ stream

street n (pl -s) public road, usu. lined with buildings

streetcar n (US) tram

streetcars n ▷ streetcar

streets n ▷ street

streetwise adj knowing how to survive in big cities

strength n (pl -s) quality of being strong > **strengthen** v (-s, -ing, -ed)

strengthen v ▷ strength

strengthened v ▷ strength

strengthening v ▷ strength

strengthens v ▷ strength

strengths n ▷ strength

strenuous adj requiring great energy or effort > **strenuously** adv

strenuously adv ▷ strenuous

streptococci n ▷ streptococcus

streptococcus [strep-toe-**kok**-uss] n (pl -cocci) bacterium occurring in chains, many species of which cause disease

stress n (pl -es) tension or strain ▶ v (-es, -ing, -ed) emphasize

stressed v ▷ stress

stresses n, v ▷ stress

stressing v ▷ stress

stretch v (-es, -ing, -ed) extend or be extended

▶ n (pl -es) stretching > **stretchy** adj (-chier, -chiest)

stretched v ▷ stretch

stretcher n (pl -s) frame covered with canvas, on which an injured person is carried

stretchers n ▷ stretcher

stretches v, n ▷ stretch

stretchier adj ▷ stretch

stretchiest adj ▷ stretch

stretching v ▷ stretch

stretchy adj ▷ stretch

strew v (-s, -ing, -ed or strewn) scatter (things) over a surface

strewed v ▷ strew

strewing v ▷ strew

strewn v ▷ strew

strews v ▷ strew

striated adj having a pattern of scratches or grooves

stricken adj seriously affected by disease, grief, pain, etc.

strict adj (-er, -est) stern or severe > **strictly** adv > **strictness** n (pl -es)

stricter adj ▷ strict

strictest adj ▷ strict

strictly adv ▷ strict

strictness n ▷ strict

strictnesses n ▷ strict

stricture n (pl -s) severe criticism

strictures n ▷ stricture

stridden v ▷ stride

stride v (-des, -ding, strode, stridden) walk with long steps ▶ n (pl -s) long step

stridencies n ▷ strident

stridency n ▷ strident

strident adj loud and harsh > **stridently** adv > **stridency** n (pl -cies)

stridently adv ▷ strident

strides v, n ▷ stride ▶ n pl progress

striding v ▷ stride

strife n (pl -s) conflict, quarrelling

strifes n ▷ strife

strike v (-kes, -king, struck) cease work as a protest ▶ n (pl -s) stoppage of work as a protest

striker n (pl -s) striking worker

strikers n ▷ striker

strikes v, n ▷ strike

striking adj impressive ▶ v ▷ strike

string n (pl -s) thin cord used for tying ▶ v (-s, -ing, strung) provide with a string or strings

stringed adj (of a musical instrument) having strings that are plucked or played with a bow

stringencies n ▷ stringent

stringency n ▷ stringent

stringent [strin-jent] *adj* strictly controlled or enforced ▷ **stringently** *adv* ▷ **stringency** *n* (*pl* -**cies**)
  stringently *adv* ▷ stringent
  stringier *adj* ▷ stringy
  stringiest *adj* ▷ stringy
  stringing *v* ▷ string
strings *n*, *v* ▷ string ▶ *n pl* restrictions or conditions
stringy *adj* (-**gier**, -**giest**) like string
stringybark *n* (*pl* -**s**) Australian eucalyptus with a fibrous bark
  stringybarks *n* ▷ stringybark
strip¹ *v* (-**s**, -**pping**, -**pped**) take (the covering or clothes) off
strip² *n* (*pl* -**s**) long narrow piece
stripe *n* (*pl* -**s**) long narrow band of contrasting colour or substance ▷ **striped, stripy, stripey** *adj* (-**pier**, -**piest**)
  striped *adj* ▷ stripe
  stripes *n* ▷ stripe
  stripey *adj* ▷ stripe
  stripier *adj* ▷ stripe
  stripiest *adj* ▷ stripe
stripling *n* (*pl* -**s**) youth
  striplings *n* ▷ stripling
  stripped *v* ▷ strip¹
stripper *n* (*pl* -**s**) person who performs a striptease
  strippers *n* ▷ stripper
  stripping *v* ▷ strip¹
  strips *v* ▷ strip¹ ▶ *n* ▷ strip²
striptease *n* (*pl* -**s**) entertainment in which a performer undresses to music
  stripteases *n* ▷ striptease
stripy *adj* ▷ stripe
strive *v* (-**ves**, -**ving**, **strove**, **striven**) make a great effort
  striven *v* ▷ strive
  strives *v* ▷ strive
  striving *v* ▷ strive
strobe *n* (*pl* -**s**) ▷ stroboscope
  strobes *n* ▷ strobe
stroboscope *n* (*pl* -**s**) instrument producing a very bright flashing light
  stroboscopes *n* ▷ stroboscope
  strode *v* ▷ stride
stroke *v* (-**kes**, -**king**, -**ked**) touch or caress lightly with the hand ▶ *n* (*pl* -**s**) light touch or caress with the hand
  stroked *v* ▷ stroke
  strokes *v*, *n* ▷ stroke
  stroking *v* ▷ stroke
stroll *v* (-**s**, -**ing**, -**ed**) walk in a leisurely manner ▶ *n* (*pl* -**s**) leisurely walk

strolled *v* ▷ stroll
strolling *v* ▷ stroll
strolls *v*, *n* ▷ stroll
strong *adj* (-**er**, -**est**) having physical power ▷ **strongly** *adv*
  stronger *adj* ▷ strong
  strongest *adj* ▷ strong
stronghold *n* (*pl* -**s**) area of predominance of a particular belief
  strongholds *n* ▷ stronghold
  strongly *adv* ▷ strong
  strongnesses *n* ▷ strong
strongroom *n* (*pl* -**s**) room designed for the safekeeping of valuables
  strongrooms *n* ▷ strongroom
strontium *n* (*pl* -**s**) (CHEM) silvery-white metallic element
  strontiums *n* ▷ strontium
strop *n* (*pl* -**s**) leather strap for sharpening razors
  stroppier *adj* ▷ stroppy
  stroppiest *adj* ▷ stroppy
stroppy *adj* (-**pier**, -**piest**) (*Slang*) angry or awkward
  strops *n* ▷ strop
  strove *v* ▷ strive
  struck *v* ▷ strike
structural *adj* ▷ structure
structuralism *n* (*pl* -**s**) approach to literature, etc., which sees changes in the subject as caused and organized by a hidden set of universal rules ▷ **structuralist** *n* (*pl* -**s**) *adj*
  structuralisms *n* ▷ structuralism
  structuralist *n*, *adj* ▷ structuralism
  structuralists *n* ▷ structuralism
structure *n* (*pl* -**s**) complex construction ▶ *v* (-**res**, -**ring**, -**red**) give a structure to ▷ **structural** *adj*
  structured *v* ▷ structure
  structures *n*, *v* ▷ structure
  structuring *v* ▷ structure
strudel *n* (*pl* -**s**) thin sheet of filled dough rolled up and baked, usu. with an apple filling
  strudels *n* ▷ strudel
struggle *v* (-**les**, -**ling**, -**led**) work, strive, or make one's way with difficulty ▶ *n* (*pl* -**s**) striving
  struggled *v* ▷ struggle
  struggles *v*, *n* ▷ struggle
  struggling *v* ▷ struggle
strum *v* (-**s**, -**mming**, -**mmed**) play (a guitar or banjo) by sweeping the thumb or a plectrum across the strings
  strummed *v* ▷ strum
  strumming *v* ▷ strum

strumpet n (pl -s) (Old-fashioned) prostitute
  strumpets n ▷ strumpet
  strums v ▷ strum
  strung v ▷ string
strut v (-s, -tting, -tted) walk pompously, swagger ▶ n (pl -s) bar supporting a structure
  struts v, n ▷ strut
  strutted v ▷ strut
  strutting v ▷ strut
strychnine [strik-neen] n (pl -s) very poisonous drug used in small quantities as a stimulant
  strychnines n ▷ strychnine
stub n (pl -s) short piece left after use ▶ v (-s, -bbing, -bbed) strike (the toe) painfully against an object
  stubbed v ▷ stub
  stubbier adj ▷ stubby
  stubbiest adj ▷ stubby
  stubbing v ▷ stub
stubble n (pl -s) short stalks of grain left in a field after reaping > **stubbly** adj (-lier, -liest)
  stubbles n ▷ stubble
  stubblier adj ▷ stubble
  stubbliest adj ▷ stubble
  stubbly adj ▷ stubble
stubborn adj (-er, -est) refusing to agree or give in > **stubbornly** adv > **stubbornness** n (pl -es)
  stubborner adj ▷ stubborn
  stubbornest adj ▷ stubborn
  stubbornly adv ▷ stubborn
  stubbornness n ▷ stubborn
  stubbornnesses n ▷ stubborn
stubby adj (-bbier, -bbiest) short and broad
  stubs n, v ▷ stub
stucco n (pl -oes) plaster used for coating or decorating walls
  stuccoes n ▷ stucco
  stuck v ▷ stick²
stud¹ n (pl -s) small piece of metal attached to a surface for decoration ▶ v (-s, -dding, -dded) set with studs
stud² n (pl -s) male animal, esp. a stallion, kept for breeding
  studded v ▷ stud¹
  studding v ▷ stud¹
student n (pl -s) person who studies a subject, esp. at university
  students n ▷ student
studied adj carefully practised or planned ▶ v ▷ study
  studies v, n ▷ study
studio n (pl -s) workroom of an artist or photographer
  studios n ▷ studio

studious adj fond of study > **studiously** adv
  studiously adv ▷ studious
  studs n ▷ stud¹, ² v ▷ stud¹
study v (-dies, -dying, -died) be engaged in learning (a subject) ▶ n (pl -dies) act or process of studying
  studying v ▷ study
stuff n (pl -s) substance or material ▶ v (-s, -ing, -ed) pack, cram, or fill completely
  stuffed v ▷ stuff
  stuffier adj ▷ stuffy
  stuffiest adj ▷ stuffy
stuffing n (pl -s) seasoned mixture with which food is stuffed ▶ v ▷ stuff
  stuffings n ▷ stuffing
  stuffs n, v ▷ stuff
stuffy adj (-ffier, -ffiest) lacking fresh air
stultifying adj very boring and repetitive
stumble v (-les, -ling, -led) trip and nearly fall ▶ n (pl -s) stumbling
  stumbled v ▷ stumble
  stumbles n ▷ stumble
  stumbling v ▷ stumble
stump n (pl -s) base of a tree left when the main trunk has been cut away ▶ v (-s, -ing, -ed) baffle
  stumped v ▷ stump
  stumpier adj ▷ stumpy
  stumpiest adj ▷ stumpy
  stumping v ▷ stump
  stumps n, v ▷ stump
stumpy adj (-pier, -piest) short and thick
stun v (-s, -nning, -nned) shock or overwhelm
  stung v ▷ sting
  stunk v ▷ stink
  stunned v ▷ stun
stunning adj very attractive or impressive ▶ v ▷ stun
  stuns v ▷ stun
stunt¹ v (-ts, -ing, -ed) prevent or impede the growth of > **stunted** adj
stunt² n (pl -s) acrobatic or dangerous action
  stunted v, adj ▷ stunt¹
  stunting v ▷ stunt¹
  stunts v ▷ stunt¹, ² n ▷ stunt²
stupefaction n ▷ stupefy
  stupefactions n ▷ stupefy
  stupefied v ▷ stupefy
  stupefies v ▷ stupefy
stupefy v (-fies, -fying, -fied) make insensitive or lethargic > **stupefaction** n (pl -s)
  stupefying v ▷ stupefy
stupendous adj very large or impressive > **stupendously** adv
  stupendously adv ▷ stupendous

stupid adj (**-er, -est**) lacking intelligence
> **stupidity** n (pl **-ties**) > **stupidly** adv
  stupider adj ▷ stupid
  stupidest adj ▷ stupid
  stupidities n ▷ stupid
  stupidity n ▷ stupid
  stupidly adv ▷ stupid
stupor n (pl **-s**) dazed or unconscious state
  stupors n ▷ stupor
  sturdier adj ▷ sturdy
  sturdiest adj ▷ sturdy
  sturdily adv ▷ sturdy
sturdy adj (**-dier, -diest**) healthy and robust
> **sturdily** adv
sturgeon n (pl **-s**) fish from which caviar is
obtained
  sturgeons n ▷ sturgeon
stutter v (**-s, -ing, -ed**) speak with repetition
of initial consonants ▸ n (pl **-s**) tendency to
stutter
  stuttered v ▷ stutter
  stuttering v ▷ stutter
  stutters v, n ▷ stutter
sty n (pl **sties**) pen for pigs
stye n (pl **styes**) inflammation at the base of
an eyelash
  styes n ▷ stye
style n (pl **-s**) shape or design ▸ v (**-les, -ling,
-led**) shape or design
  styled v ▷ style
  styles n, v ▷ style
  styli n ▷ stylus
  styling v ▷ style
stylish adj smart, elegant, and fashionable
> **stylishly** adv
  stylishly adv ▷ stylish
stylist n (pl **-s**) hairdresser
  stylistic adj of literary or artistic style
  stylists n ▷ stylist
stylize v (**-zes, -zing, -zed**) cause to conform to
an established stylistic form
  stylized v ▷ stylize
  stylizes v ▷ stylize
  stylizing v ▷ stylize
stylus n (pl **-li, -luses**) needle-like device on a
record player that rests in the groove of the
record and picks up the sound signals
  styluses n ▷ stylus
stymie v (**-mies, -mieing, -mied**) hinder or
thwart
  stymied v ▷ stymie
  stymieing v ▷ stymie
  stymies v ▷ stymie
styptic n (pl **-s**) ▸ adj (drug) used to stop
bleeding

  styptics n ▷ styptic
suave [swahv] adj smooth and sophisticated in
manner > **suavely** adv
  suavely adv ▷ suave
sub n (pl **-s**) subeditor ▸ v (**-s, -bbing, -bbed**) act
as a substitute
subaltern n (pl **-s**) British army officer below
the rank of captain
  subalterns n ▷ subaltern
subatomic adj of or being one of the particles
which make up an atom
  subbed v ▷ sub
  subbing v ▷ sub
subcommittee n (pl **-s**) small committee
formed from some members of a larger
committee
  subcommittees n ▷ subcommittee
subconscious adj happening or existing
without one's awareness ▸ n (pl **-es**)
(PSYCHOANALYSIS) that part of the mind of which
one is not aware but which can influence
one's behaviour > **subconsciously** adv
  subconsciouses n ▷ subconscious
  subconsciously adv ▷ subconscious
subcontinent n (pl **-s**) large land mass that is a
distinct part of a continent
  subcontinents n ▷ subcontinent
subcontract n (pl **-s**) secondary contract by
which the main contractor for a job puts
work out to others ▸ v (**-s, -ing, -ed**) put out
(work) on a subcontract > **subcontractor**
n (pl **-s**)
  subcontracted v ▷ subcontract
  subcontracting v ▷ subcontract
  subcontractor n ▷ subcontract
  subcontractors n ▷ subcontract
  subcontracts n, v ▷ subcontract
subcutaneous [sub-cute-**ayn**-ee-uss] adj under
the skin
subdivide v (**-des, -ding, -ded**) divide (a part of
something) into smaller parts > **subdivision**
n (pl **-s**)
  subdivided v ▷ subdivide
  subdivides v ▷ subdivide
  subdividing v ▷ subdivide
  subdivision n ▷ subdivide
  subdivisions n ▷ subdivide
subdue v (**-dues, -duing, -dued**) overcome
  subdued v ▷ subdue
  subdues v ▷ subdue
  subduing v ▷ subdue
subeditor n (pl **-s**) person who checks and
edits text for a newspaper or magazine
  subeditors n ▷ subeditor
subject n (pl **-s**) person or thing being dealt

with or studied ▶ *adj* being under the rule of a monarch or government ▶ *v* (**-s, -ing, -ed**) (*foll. by* **to**) cause to undergo > **subjection** *n* (*pl* **-s**)

subjected *v* ▷ subject

subjecting *v* ▷ subject

subjection *n* ▷ subject

subjections *n* ▷ subject

subjective *adj* based on personal feelings or prejudices > **subjectively** *adv*

subjectively *adv* ▷ subjective

subjects *n, v* ▷ subject

subjugate *v* (**-tes, -ting, -ted**) bring (a group of people) under one's control > **subjugation** *n* (*pl* **-s**)

subjugates *v* ▷ subjugate

subjugating *v* ▷ subjugate

subjugation *n* ▷ subjugate

subjugations *n* ▷ subjugate

subjunctive (GRAMMAR) *n* (*pl* **-s**) mood of verbs used when the content of the clause is doubted, supposed, or wished ▶ *adj* in or of that mood

subjunctives *n* ▷ subjunctive

sublet *v* (**-s, -letting, -let**) rent out (property rented from someone else)

sublets *v* ▷ sublet

subletting *v* ▷ sublet

sublimate *v* (**-tes, -ting, -ted**) (PSYCHOL) direct the energy of (a strong desire, esp. a sexual one) into socially acceptable activities > **sublimation** *n* (*pl* **-s**)

sublimated *v* ▷ sublimate

sublimates *v* ▷ sublimate

sublimating *v* ▷ sublimate

sublimation *n* ▷ sublimate

sublimations *n* ▷ sublimate

sublime *adj* (**-r, -st**) of high moral, intellectual, or spiritual value ▶ *v* (**-mes, -ming, -med**) (CHEM) change from a solid to a vapour without first melting > **sublimely** *adv*

sublimed *v* ▷ sublime

sublimely *adv* ▷ sublime

sublimer *adj* ▷ sublime

sublimes *v* ▷ sublime

sublimest *adj* ▷ sublime

subliminal *adj* relating to mental processes of which the individual is not aware

subliming *v* ▷ sublime

submarine *n* (*pl* **-s**) vessel which can operate below the surface of the sea ▶ *adj* below the surface of the sea

submarines *n* ▷ submarine

submerge *v* (**-ges, -ging, -ged**) put or go below the surface of water or other liquid

> **submersion** *n* (*pl* **-s**)

submerged *v* ▷ submerge

submerges *v* ▷ submerge

submerging *v* ▷ submerge

submersion *n* ▷ submerge

submersions *n* ▷ submerge

submission *n* (*pl* **-s**) submitting

submissions *n* ▷ submission

submissive *adj* meek and obedient

submit *v* (**-s, -tting, -tted**) surrender

submits *v* ▷ submit

submitted *v* ▷ submit

submitting *v* ▷ submit

subordinate *adj* of lesser rank or importance ▶ *n* (*pl* **-s**) subordinate person or thing ▶ *v* (**-tes, -ting, -ted**) make or treat as subordinate > **subordination** *n* (*pl* **-s**)

subordinated *v* ▷ subordinate

subordinates *n, v* ▷ subordinate

subordinating *v* ▷ subordinate

subordination *n* ▷ subordinate

subordinations *n* ▷ subordinate

suborn *v* (**-s, -ing, -ed**) (*Formal*) bribe or incite (a person) to commit a wrongful act

suborned *v* ▷ suborn

suborning *v* ▷ suborn

suborns *v* ▷ suborn

subpoena [sub-pee-na] *n* (*pl* **-s**) writ requiring a person to appear before a lawcourt ▶ *v* (**-nas, -naing, -naed**) summon (someone) with a subpoena

subpoenaed *v* ▷ subpoena

subpoenaing *v* ▷ subpoena

subpoenas *n, v* ▷ subpoena

subs *n, v* ▷ sub

subscribe *v* (**-bes, -bing, -bed**) pay (a subscription) > **subscriber** *n* (*pl* **-s**)

subscribed *v* ▷ subscribe

subscriber *n* ▷ subscribe

subscribers *n* ▷ subscribe

subscribes *v* ▷ subscribe

subscribing *v* ▷ subscribe

subscription *n* (*pl* **-s**) payment for issues of a publication over a period

subscriptions *n* ▷ subscription

subsection *n* (*pl* **-s**) division of a section

subsections *n* ▷ subsection

subsequent *adj* occurring after, succeeding > **subsequently** *adv*

subsequently *adv* ▷ subsequent

subservience *n* ▷ subservient

subserviences *n* ▷ subservient

subservient *adj* submissive, servile > **subservience** *n* (*pl* **-s**)

subside *v* (**-des, -ding, -ded**) become less

intense
subsided v ▷ subside
subsidence n (pl -s) act or process of subsiding
subsidences n ▷ subsidence
subsides v ▷ subside
subsidiaries n ▷ subsidiary
subsidiary adj of lesser importance ▶ n (pl -ries) subsidiary person or thing
subsidies n ▷ subsidy
subsiding v ▷ subside
subsidize v (-izes, -izing, -ized) help financially
subsidized v ▷ subsidize
subsidizes v ▷ subsidize
subsidizing v ▷ subsidize
subsidy n (pl -dies) financial aid
subsist v (-s, -ing, -ed) manage to live
> **subsistence** n (pl -s)
subsisted v ▷ subsist
subsistence n ▷ subsist
subsistences n ▷ subsist
subsisting v ▷ subsist
subsists v ▷ subsist
subsonic adj moving at a speed less than that of sound
substance n (pl -s) physical composition of something
substances n ▷ substance
substantial adj of considerable size or value
> **substantially** adv
substantially adv ▷ substantial
substantiate v (-tes, -ting, -ted) support (a story) with evidence > **substantiation** n (pl -s)
substantiated v ▷ substantiate
substantiates v ▷ substantiate
substantiating v ▷ substantiate
substantiation n ▷ substantiate
substantiations n ▷ substantiate
substantive n (pl -s) noun ▶ adj of or being the essential element of a thing
substantives n ▷ substantive
substitute v (-tes, -ting, -ted) take the place of or put in place of another ▶ n (pl -s) person or thing taking the place of (another)
> **substitution** n (pl -s)
substituted v ▷ substitute
substitutes v, n ▷ substitute
substituting v ▷ substitute
substitution n ▷ substitute
substitutions n ▷ substitute
subsume v (-mes, -ming, -med) include (an idea, case, etc.) under a larger classification or group
subsumed v ▷ subsume
subsumes v ▷ subsume
subsuming v ▷ subsume

subterfuge n (pl -s) trick used to achieve an objective
subterfuges n ▷ subterfuge
subterranean adj underground
subtitle n (pl -s) secondary title of a book ▶ v (-les, -ling, -led) provide with a subtitle or subtitles
subtitled v ▷ subtitle
subtitles v, n ▷ subtitle ▶ pl n printed translation at the bottom of the picture in a film with foreign dialogue
subtitling v ▷ subtitle
subtle adj (-r, -st) not immediately obvious
> **subtly** adv > **subtlety** n (pl -ties)
subtler adj ▷ subtle
subtlest adj ▷ subtle
subtleties n ▷ subtle
subtlety n ▷ subtle
subtly adv ▷ subtle
subtract v (-s, -ing, -ed) take (one number or quantity) from another ▶ **subtraction** n (pl -s)
subtracted v ▷ subtract
subtracting v ▷ subtract
subtraction n ▷ subtract
subtractions n ▷ subtract
subtracts v ▷ subtract
subtropical adj of the regions bordering on the tropics
suburb n (pl -s) residential area on the outskirts of a city
suburban adj of or inhabiting a suburb
suburbia n (pl -s) suburbs and their inhabitants
suburbias n ▷ suburbia
suburbs n ▷ suburb
subvention n (pl -s) (Formal) subsidy
subventions n ▷ subvention
subversion n ▷ subvert
subversions n ▷ subvert
subversive adj, n ▷ subvert
subversives n ▷ subvert
subvert v (-s, -ing, -ed) overthrow the authority of > **subversion** n (pl -s)
> **subversive** adj, n (pl -s)
subverted v ▷ subvert
subverting v ▷ subvert
subverts v ▷ subvert
subway n (pl -s) passage under a road or railway
subways n ▷ subway
succeed v (-s, -ing, -ed) accomplish an aim
succeeded v ▷ succeed
succeeding v ▷ succeed
succeeds v ▷ succeed
success n (pl -es) achievement of something

attempted

successes n ▷ success

successful adj having success > **successfully** adv

successfully adv ▷ successful

succession n (pl -s) series of people or things following one another in order

successions n ▷ succession

successive adj consecutive > **successively** adv

successively adv ▷ successive

successor n (pl -s) person who succeeds someone in a position

successors n ▷ successor

succinct adj (-er, -est) brief and clear > **succinctly** adv

succincter adj ▷ succinct

succinctest adj ▷ succinct

succinctly adv ▷ succinct

succour v (-s, -ing, -ed) ▶ n (pl -s) help in distress

succoured v ▷ succour

succouring v ▷ succour

succours v, n ▷ succour

succulence n ▷ succulent

succulences n ▷ succulent

succulent adj juicy and delicious ▶ n (pl -s) succulent plant > **succulence** n (pl -s)

succulent n ▷ succulent

succulents n ▷ succulent

succumb v (-s, -ing, -ed) (foll. by **to**) give way (to something overpowering)

succumbed v ▷ succumb

succumbing v ▷ succumb

succumbs v ▷ succumb

such adj of the kind specified ▶ pron such things

suchlike pron such or similar things

suck v (-s, -ing, -ed) draw (liquid or air) into the mouth ▶ n (pl -s) sucking

sucked v ▷ suck

sucker n (pl -s) (Slang) person who is easily deceived or swindled

suckers n ▷ sucker

sucking v ▷ suck

suckle v (-les, -ling, -led) feed at the breast

suckled v ▷ suckle

suckles v ▷ suckle

suckling n (pl -s) unweaned baby or young animal ▶ v ▷ suckle

sucklings n ▷ suckling

sucks v, n ▷ suck

sucrose [soo-kroze] n (pl -s) chemical name for sugar

sucroses n ▷ sucrose

suction n (pl -s) sucking

suctions n ▷ suction

sudden adj done or occurring quickly and unexpectedly > **suddenly** adv > **suddenness** n (pl -es)

suddenly adv ▷ sudden

suddenness n ▷ suddenness

suddennesses n ▷ suddenness

sudorific [syoo-dor-**if**-ik] n (pl -s) ▶ adj (drug) causing sweating

sudorifics n ▷ sudorific

suds pl n froth of soap and water, lather

sue v (-ues, -uing, -ued) start legal proceedings against

sued v ▷ sue

suede n (pl -s) leather with a velvety finish on one side

suedes n ▷ suede

sues v ▷ sue

suet n (pl -s) hard fat obtained from sheep and cattle, used in cooking

suets n ▷ suet

suffer v (-s, -ing, -ed) undergo or be subjected to > **sufferer** n (pl -s) > **suffering** n (pl -s) > **sufferance** n (pl -s)

sufferance n ▷ suffer

sufferances n ▷ suffer

suffered v ▷ suffer

sufferer n ▷ suffer

sufferers n ▷ suffer

suffering n, v ▷ suffer

sufferings n ▷ suffer

suffers v ▷ suffer

suffice [suf-**fice**] v (-ces, -cing, -ced) be enough for a purpose

sufficed v ▷ suffice

suffices v ▷ suffice

sufficiencies n ▷ sufficiency

sufficiency n (pl -cies) adequate amount

sufficient adj enough, adequate > **sufficiently** adv

sufficiently adv ▷ sufficient

sufficing v ▷ suffice

suffix n (pl -es) letter or letters added to the end of a word to form another word, such as -s and -ness in dogs and softness

suffixes n ▷ suffix

suffocate v (-tes, -ting, -ted) kill or be killed by deprivation of oxygen > **suffocation** n (pl -s)

suffocated v ▷ suffocate

suffocates v ▷ suffocate

suffocating v ▷ suffocate

suffocation n ▷ suffocate

suffocations n ▷ suffocate

suffragan n (pl -s) bishop appointed to assist an archbishop

suffragans n ▷ suffragan
suffrage n (pl -s) right to vote in public
  elections
  suffrages n ▷ suffrage
suffragette n (pl -s) (in Britain in the early
  20th century) a woman who campaigned
  militantly for the right to vote
  suffragettes n ▷ suffragette
suffuse v (-ses, -sing, -sed) spread through or
  over (something) > **suffusion** n (pl -s)
  suffused v ▷ suffuse
  suffuses v ▷ suffuse
  suffusing v ▷ suffuse
  suffusion n ▷ suffuse
  suffusions n ▷ suffuse
sugar n (pl -s) sweet crystalline carbohydrate
  found in many plants and used to sweeten
  food and drinks ▸ v (-s, -ing, -ed) sweeten or
  cover with sugar > **sugary** adj (-rier, -riest)
  sugared v ▷ sugar
  sugarier adj ▷ sugar
  sugariest adj ▷ sugar
  sugaring v ▷ sugar
  sugars n, v ▷ sugar
  sugary adj ▷ sugar
suggest v (-s, -ing, -ed) put forward (an idea)
  for consideration
  suggested v ▷ suggest
suggestible adj easily influenced
  suggesting v ▷ suggest
suggestion n (pl -s) thing suggested
  suggestions n ▷ suggestion
suggestive adj suggesting something
  indecent > **suggestively** adv
  suggestively adv ▷ suggestive
  suggests v ▷ suggest
suicidal adj liable to commit suicide
  > **suicidally** adv
  suicidally adv ▷ suicide
suicide n (pl -s) killing oneself intentionally
  suicides n ▷ suicide
  suing v ▷ sue
suit n (pl -s) set of clothes designed to be worn
  together ▸ v (-s, -ing, -ed) be appropriate for
  suitabilities n ▷ suitable
  suitability n ▷ suitable
suitable adj appropriate or proper > **suitably**
  adv > **suitability** n (pl -ties)
  suitably adv ▷ suitable
suitcase n (pl -s) portable travelling case for
  clothing
  suitcases n ▷ suitcase
suite n (pl -s) set of connected rooms in a hotel
  suited v ▷ suit
  suites n ▷ suite

suiting v ▷ suit
suitor n (pl -s) (Old-fashioned) man who is
  courting a woman
  suitors n ▷ suitor
  suits n, v ▷ suit
sulk v (-s, -ing, -ed) be silent and sullen
  because of resentment or bad temper ▸ n (pl
  -s) resentful or sullen mood > **sulky** adj (-kier,
  -kiest) > **sulkily** adv
  sulked v ▷ sulk
  sulkier adj ▷ sulk
  sulkiest adj ▷ sulk
  sulkily adv ▷ sulk
  sulking v ▷ sulk
  sulks v, n ▷ sulk
  sulky adj ▷ sulk
sullen adj (-er, -est) unwilling to talk or be
  sociable > **sullenly** adv > **sullenness** n (pl -es)
  sullener adj ▷ sullen
  sullenest adj ▷ sullen
  sullenly adv ▷ sullen
  sullenness n ▷ sullen
  sullennesses n ▷ sullen
  sullied v ▷ sully
  sullies v ▷ sully
sully v (-lies, -lying, -lied) ruin (someone's
  reputation)
  sullying v ▷ sully
sulphate n (pl -s) salt or ester of sulphuric acid
  sulphates n ▷ sulphate
sulphide n (pl -s) compound of sulphur with
  another element
  sulphides n ▷ sulphide
sulphite n (pl -s) salt or ester of sulphurous
  acid
  sulphites n ▷ sulphite
sulphonamide [sulf-on-a-mide] n (pl -s) any
  of a class of drugs that prevent the growth
  of bacteria
  sulphonamides n ▷ sulphonamide
sulphur n (pl -s) (CHEM) pale yellow nonmetallic
  element
sulphuric, sulphurous adj of or containing
  sulphur
  sulphurous adj ▷ sulphuric
  sulphurs n ▷ sulphur
sultan n (pl -s) sovereign of a Muslim country
sultana n (pl -s) kind of raisin
  sultanas n ▷ sultana
sultanate n (pl -s) territory of a sultan
  sultanates n ▷ sultanate
  sultans n ▷ sultan
  sultrier n ▷ sultry
  sultriest n ▷ sultry
sultry adj (-trier, -triest) (of weather or

climate) hot and humid

sum *n* (*pl* **-s**) result of addition, total

    summaries *n* ▷ summary

    summarily *adv* ▷ summary

summarize *v* (**-izes, -izing, -ized**) make or be a summary of (something)

    summarized *v* ▷ summarize

    summarizes *v* ▷ summarize

    summarizing *v* ▷ summarize

summary *n* (*pl* **-ries**) brief account giving the main points of something ▶ *adj* done quickly, without formalities > **summarily** *adv*

summation *n* (*pl* **-s**) summary

    summations *n* ▷ summation

summer *n* (*pl* **-s**) warmest season of the year, between spring and autumn > **summery** *adj* (**-rier, -riest**)

summerhouse *n* (*pl* **-s**) small building in a garden

    summerhouses *n* ▷ summerhouse

    summerier *adj* ▷ summer

    summeriest *adj* ▷ summer

    summers *n* ▷ summer

summertime *n* (*pl* **-s**) period or season of summer

    summertimes *n* ▷ summertime

    summery *adj* ▷ summer

summit *n* (*pl* **-s**) top of a mountain or hill

    summits *n* ▷ summit

summon *v* (**-s, -ing, -ed**) order (someone) to come

    summoned *v* ▷ summon

    summoning *v* ▷ summon

summons *n* (*pl* **-es**) command summoning someone ▶ *v* (**-es, -ing, -ed**) order (someone) to appear in court ▶ *v* ▷ summon

    summonsed *n* ▷ summons

    summonses *v, n* ▷ summons

    summonsing *v* ▷ summons

sumo *n* (*pl* **-s**) Japanese style of wrestling

    sumos *n* ▷ sumo

sump *n* (*pl* **-s**) container in an internal-combustion engine into which oil can drain

    sumps *n* ▷ sump

sumptuous *adj* lavish, magnificent

    > **sumptuously** *adv*

    sumptuously *adv* ▷ sumptuous

    sums *n* ▷ sum

sun *n* (*pl* **-s**) star around which the earth and other planets revolve ▶ *v* (**-s, sunning, sunned**) expose (oneself) to the sun's rays > **sunless** *adj*

sunbathe *v* (**-thes, -thing, -thed**) lie in the sunshine in order to get a suntan

    sunbathed *v* ▷ sunbathe

    sunbathes *v* ▷ sunbathe

    sunbathing *v* ▷ sunbathe

sunbeam *n* (*pl* **-s**) ray of sun

    sunbeams *n* ▷ sunbeam

sunburn *n* (*pl* **-s**) painful reddening of the skin caused by overexposure to the sun

    > **sunburnt, sunburned** *adj*

    sunburned *adj* ▷ sunburn

    sunburns *n* ▷ sunburn

    sunburnt *adj* ▷ sunburn

sundae *n* (*pl* **-s**) ice cream topped with fruit etc.

    sundaes *n* ▷ sundae

sundial *n* (*pl* **-s**) device showing the time by means of a pointer that casts a shadow on a marked dial

    sundials *n* ▷ sundial

sundown *n* (*pl* **-s**) sunset

    sundowns *n* ▷ sundown

sundries *pl n* several things of various sorts

sundry *adj* several, various

sunflower *n* (*pl* **-s**) tall plant with large golden flowers

    sunflowers *n* ▷ sunflower

    sung *v* ▷ sing

    sunk *v* ▷ sink

    sunken *v* ▷ sink

    sunless *adj* ▷ sun

    sunned *v* ▷ sun

    sunnier *adj* ▷ sunny

    sunniest *adj* ▷ sunny

    sunning *v* ▷ sun

sunny *adj* (**-nnier, -nniest**) full of or exposed to sunlight

sunrise *n* (*pl* **-s**) daily appearance of the sun above the horizon

    sunrises *n* ▷ sunrise

    suns *n, v* ▷ sun

sunset *n* (*pl* **-s**) daily disappearance of the sun below the horizon

    sunsets *n* ▷ sunset

sunshine *n* (*pl* **-s**) light and warmth from the sun

    sunshines *n* ▷ sunshine

sunspot *n* (*pl* **-s**) dark patch appearing temporarily on the sun's surface

    sunspots *n* ▷ sunspot

sunstroke *n* (*pl* **-s**) illness caused by prolonged exposure to intensely hot sunlight

    sunstrokes *n* ▷ sunstroke

suntan *n* (*pl* **-s**) browning of the skin caused by exposure to the sun

    suntans *n* ▷ suntan

sup *v* (**-s, -pping, -pped**) take (liquid) by sips ▶ *n* (*pl* **-s**) sip

super adj (Informal) excellent

superannuated adj discharged with a pension, owing to old age or illness

superannuation n (pl -s) regular payment by an employee into a pension fund

  superannuations n ▷ superannuation

superb adj excellent, impressive, or splendid > **superbly** adv

  superbly adv ▷ superb

superbug n (pl -s) (Informal) bacterium resistant to antibiotics

  superbugs n ▷ superbug

supercharged adj (of an engine) having a supercharger

supercharger n (pl -s) device that increases the power of an internal-combustion engine by forcing extra air into it

  superchargers n ▷ supercharger

supercilious adj showing arrogant pride or scorn

superconductor n (pl -s) substance which has almost no electrical resistance at very low temperatures

  superconductors n ▷ superconductor

superficial adj not careful or thorough > **superficially** adv > **superficiality** n (pl -ties)

  superficialities n ▷ superficial

  superficiality n ▷ superficial

  superficially adv ▷ superficial

  superfluities n ▷ superfluous

  superfluity n ▷ superfluous

superfluous [soo-per-flew-uss] adj more than is needed > **superfluity** n (pl -ties)

superhuman adj beyond normal human ability or experience

superimpose v (-ses, -sing, -sed) place (something) on or over something else

  superimposed v ▷ superimpose

  superimposes v ▷ superimpose

  superimposing v ▷ superimpose

superintend v (-s, -ing, -ed) supervise (a person or activity)

  superintended v ▷ superintend

superintendent n (pl -s) senior police officer

  superintendents n ▷ superintendent

  superintending v ▷ superintend

  superintends v ▷ superintend

superior adj greater in quality, quantity, or merit ▶ n (pl -s) person of greater rank or status > **superiority** n (pl -ties)

  superiorities n ▷ superior

  superiority n ▷ superior

  superiors n ▷ superior

superlative [soo-per-lat-iv] adj of outstanding quality ▶ n (pl -s) (GRAMMAR) word expressing this

  superlatives n ▷ superlative

superman n (pl -men) man with great physical or mental powers

supermarket n (pl -s) large self-service store selling food and household goods

  supermarkets n ▷ supermarket

  supermen n ▷ superman

supermodel n (pl -s) famous and highly-paid fashion model

  supermodels n ▷ supermodel

supernatural adj of or relating to things beyond the laws of nature

supernova n (pl -vae, -vas) star that explodes and briefly becomes exceptionally bright

  supernovae n ▷ supernova

  supernovas n ▷ supernova

  supernumeraries n ▷ supernumerary

supernumerary adj exceeding the required or regular number ▶ n (pl -ries) supernumerary person or thing

superpower n (pl -s) extremely powerful nation

  superpowers n ▷ superpower

superscript n (pl -s) ▶ adj (character) printed above the line

  superscripts n ▷ superscript

supersede v (-des, -ding, -ded) replace, supplant

  superseded v ▷ supersede

  supersedes v ▷ supersede

  superseding v ▷ supersede

supersonic adj of or travelling at a speed greater than the speed of sound

superstition n (pl -s) belief in omens, ghosts, etc. > **superstitious** adj

  superstitions n ▷ superstition

  superstitious adj ▷ superstition

superstore n (pl -s) large supermarket

  superstores n ▷ superstore

superstructure n (pl -s) structure erected on something else

  superstructures n ▷ superstructure

supervene v (-nes, -ning, -ned) occur as an unexpected development

  supervened v ▷ supervene

  supervenes v ▷ supervene

  supervening v ▷ supervene

supervise v (-ses, -sing, -sed) watch over to direct or check > **supervision** n (pl -s) > **supervisor** n (pl -s) > **supervisory** adj

  supervised v ▷ supervise

  supervises v ▷ supervise

  supervising v ▷ supervise

  supervision n ▷ supervise

supervisions *n* ▷ supervise
supervisor *n* ▷ supervise
supervisors *n* ▷ supervise
supervisory *adj* ▷ supervise
supine *adj* lying flat on one's back
supped *v* ▷ sup
supper *n* (*pl* -s) light evening meal
suppers *n* ▷ supper
supping *v* ▷ sup
supplant *v* (-s, -ing, -ed) take the place of, oust
supplanted *v* ▷ supplant
supplanting *v* ▷ supplant
supplants *v* ▷ supplant
supple *adj* (-r, -st) (of a person) moving and bending easily and gracefully > **suppleness** *n* (*pl* -es)
supplement *n* (*pl* -s) thing added to complete something or make up for a lack ▶ *v* (-s, -ing, -ed) provide or be a supplement to (something) > **supplementary** *adj*
supplementary *adj* ▷ supplement
supplemented *v* ▷ supplement
supplementing *v* ▷ supplement
supplements *n*, *v* ▷ supplement
suppleness *n* ▷ supple
supplenesses *n* ▷ supple
suppler *adj* ▷ supple
supplest *adj* ▷ supple
supplicant *n* (*pl* -s) person who makes a humble request
supplicants *n* ▷ supplicant
supplication *n* (*pl* -s) humble request
supplications *n* ▷ supplication
supplied *v* ▷ supply
supplier *n* ▷ supply
suppliers *n* ▷ supply
supplies *pl n* food or equipment ▶ *v* ▷ supply
supply *v* (-lies, -lying, -lied) provide with something required ▶ *n* (*pl* -lies) supplying > **supplier** *n* (*pl* -s)
supplying *v* ▷ supply
support *v* (-s, -ing, -ed) bear the weight of ▶ *n* (*pl* -s) supporting > **supportive** *adj*
supported *v* ▷ support
supporter *n* (*pl* -s) person who supports a team, principle, etc.
supporters *n* ▷ supporter
supporting *v* ▷ support
supportive *adj* ▷ support
supports *n*, *v* ▷ support
suppose *v* (-ses, -sing, -sed) presume to be true
supposed *adj* presumed to be true without proof, doubtful ▶ *v* ▷ suppose > **supposedly** *adv*
supposedly *adv* ▷ supposed

supposes *v* ▷ suppose
supposing *v* ▷ suppose
supposition *n* (*pl* -s) supposing
suppositions *n* ▷ supposition
suppositories *n* ▷ suppository
suppository *n* (*pl* -ries) solid medication inserted into the rectum or vagina and left to melt
suppress *v* (-es, -ing, -ed) put an end to > **suppression** *n* (*pl* -s)
suppressed *v* ▷ suppress
suppresses *v* ▷ suppress
suppressing *v* ▷ suppress
suppression *n* ▷ suppress
suppressions *n* ▷ suppress
suppurate *v* (-tes, -ting, -ted) (of a wound etc.) produce pus
suppurated *v* ▷ suppurate
suppurates *v* ▷ suppurate
suppurating *v* ▷ suppurate
supremacies *n* ▷ supremacy
supremacy *n* (*pl* -cies) supreme power
supreme *adj* highest in authority, rank, or degree
supremely *adv* extremely
supremo *n* (*pl* -s) (*Informal*) person in overall authority
supremos *n* ▷ supremo
sups *n*, *v* ▷ sup

> **suq** *n* (**suqs**). A suq is an open-air marketplace in Arabic-speaking countries. This unusual word can be very useful. Usually, when you have a Q and a U, you will be looking to play words with QU in them. But look out for opportunities to play suq instead. Suq scores 12 points.

surcharge *n* (*pl* -s) additional charge
surcharges *n* ▷ surcharge
surd *n* (*pl* -s) (MATHS) number that cannot be expressed in whole numbers
surds *n* ▷ surd
sure *adj* (-r, -st) free from uncertainty or doubt ▶ *adv*, *interj* (*Informal*) certainly
surefooted *adj* unlikely to slip or stumble
surely *adv* it must be true that
surer *adj* ▷ sure
surest *adj* ▷ sure
sureties *n* ▷ surety
surety *n* (*pl* -ties) person who takes responsibility, or thing given as a guarantee, for the fulfilment of another's obligation
surf *n* (*pl* -s) foam caused by waves breaking on the shore ▶ *v* (-s, -ing, -ed) take part in surfing > **surfer** *n* (*pl* -s)

surface n (pl -s) outside or top of an object ▶ v (-ces, -cing, -ced) rise to the surface
  surfaced v ▷ surface
  surfaces n, v ▷ surface
  surfacing v ▷ surface
surfboard n (pl -s) long smooth board used in surfing
  surfboards n ▷ surfboard
  surfed v ▷ surf
surfeit n (pl -s) excessive amount
  surfeits n ▷ surfeit
  surfer n ▷ surf
  surfers n ▷ surf
surfing n (pl -s) sport of riding towards the shore on a surfboard on the crest of a wave ▶ v ▷ surf
  surfings n ▷ surfing
  surfs n, v ▷ surf
surge n (pl -s) sudden powerful increase ▶ v (-ges, -ging, -ged) increase suddenly
  surged v ▷ surge
surgeon n (pl -s) doctor who specializes in surgery
  surgeons n ▷ surgeon
  surgeries n ▷ surgery
surgery n (pl -ries) treatment in which the patient's body is cut open in order to treat the affected part > **surgical** adj > **surgically** adv
  surges n, v ▷ surge
  surgical adj ▷ surgery
  surgically adv ▷ surgery
  surging v ▷ surge
  surlier adj ▷ surly
  surliest adj ▷ surly
  surliness n ▷ surly
  surlinesses n ▷ surly
surly adj (-lier, -liest) ill-tempered and rude > **surliness** n (pl -es)
surmise v (-ises, -ising, -ised) ▶ n (pl -s) guess, conjecture
  surmised v ▷ surmise
  surmises n, v ▷ surmise
  surmising v ▷ surmise
surmount v (-s, -ing, -ed) overcome (a problem) > **surmountable** adj
  surmountable adj ▷ surmount
  surmounted v ▷ surmount
  surmounting v ▷ surmount
  surmounts v ▷ surmount
surname n (pl -s) family name
  surnames n ▷ surname
surpass v (-es, -ing, -ed) be greater than or superior to
  surpassed v ▷ surpass
  surpasses v ▷ surpass

  surpassing v ▷ surpass
surplice n (pl -s) loose white robe worn by clergymen and choristers
  surplices n ▷ surplice
surplus n (pl -es) amount left over in excess of what is required
  surpluses n ▷ surplus
surprise n (pl -ses) unexpected event ▶ v (-ses, -sing, -sed) cause to feel amazement or wonder
  surprised v ▷ surprise
  surprises n, v ▷ surprise
  surprising v ▷ surprise
surreal adj bizarre > **surrealist** n (pl -s) adj > **surrealistic** adj
surrealism n (pl -s) movement in art and literature involving the combination of incongruous images, as in a dream
  surrealisms n ▷ surrealism
  surrealist n, adj ▷ surreal
  surrealistic adj ▷ surreal
  surrealists n ▷ surreal
surrender v (-s, -ing, -ed) give oneself up ▶ n (pl -s) surrendering
  surrendered v ▷ surrender
  surrendering v ▷ surrender
  surrenders v, n ▷ surrender
surreptitious adj done secretly or stealthily > **surreptitiously** adv
  surreptitiously adv ▷ surreptitious
surrogate n (pl -s) substitute
  surrogates n ▷ surrogate
surround v (-s, -ing, -ed) be, come, or place all around (a person or thing) ▶ n (pl -s) border or edging
  surrounded v ▷ surround
  surrounding v ▷ surround
surroundings pl n area or environment around a person, place, or thing
  surrounds v, n ▷ surround
surveillance n (pl -s) close observation
  surveillances n ▷ surveillance
survey v (-s, -ing, -ed) view or consider in a general way ▶ n (pl -s) surveying ▶ **surveyor** n (pl -s)
  surveyed v ▷ survey
  surveying v ▷ survey
  surveyor n ▷ survey
  surveyors n ▷ survey
  surveys v, n ▷ survey
survival n (pl -s) condition of having survived
  survivals n ▷ survival
survive v (-ves, -ing, -ved) continue to live or exist after (a difficult experience) > **survivor** n (pl -s)

survived v ▷ survive

survives v ▷ survive

surviving v ▷ survive

survivor n ▷ survive

survivors n ▷ survive

susceptibilities n ▷ susceptible

susceptibility n ▷ susceptible

susceptible adj liable to be influenced or affected by > **susceptibility** n (pl -ties)

sushi [soo-shee] n (pl -s) Japanese dish of small cakes of cold rice with a topping of raw fish

sushis n ▷ sushi

suspect v (-s, -ing, -ed) believe (someone) to be guilty without having any proof ▶ adj not to be trusted ▶ n (pl -s) person who is suspected

suspected v ▷ suspect

suspecting v ▷ suspect

suspects v, n ▷ suspect

suspend v (-s, -ing, -ed) hang from a high place

suspended v ▷ suspend

suspenders pl n straps for holding up stockings

suspending v ▷ suspend

suspends v ▷ suspend

suspense n (pl -s) state of uncertainty while awaiting news, an event, etc.

suspenses n ▷ suspense

suspension n (pl -s) suspending or being suspended

suspensions n ▷ suspension

suspicion n (pl -s) feeling of not trusting a person or thing

suspicions n ▷ suspicion

suspicious adj feeling or causing suspicion > **suspiciously** adv

suspiciously adv ▷ suspicious

sustain v (-s, -ing, -ed) maintain or prolong

sustained v ▷ sustain

sustaining v ▷ sustain

sustains v ▷ sustain

sustenance n (pl -s) food

sustenances n ▷ sustenance

suture [soo-cher] n (pl -s) stitch joining the edges of a wound

sutures n ▷ suture

suzerain n (pl -s) state or sovereign with limited authority over another self-governing state > **suzerainty** n (pl -ties)

suzerains n ▷ suzerain

suzerainties n ▷ suzerain

suzerainty n ▷ suzerain

svelte adj (-r, -st) attractively or gracefully slim

svelter adj ▷ svelte

sveltest adj ▷ svelte

swab n (pl -s) small piece of cotton wool used to apply medication, clean a wound, etc. ▶ v (-s, -bbing, -bbed) clean (a wound) with a swab

swabbed v ▷ swab

swabbing v ▷ swab

swabs n, v ▷ swab

swaddle v (-les, -ling, -led) wrap (a baby) in swaddling clothes

swaddled v ▷ swaddle

swaddles v ▷ swaddle

swaddling v ▷ swaddle

swag n (pl -s) (Slang) stolen property

swagger v (-s, -ing, -ed) walk or behave arrogantly ▶ n (pl -s) arrogant walk or manner

swaggered v ▷ swagger

swaggering v ▷ swagger

swaggers v, n ▷ swagger

swagman n (pl -men) (AUST HIST) tramp who carries his belongings in a bundle on his back

swagmen n ▷ swagman

swags n ▷ swag

swain n (pl -s) (Poetic) suitor

swains n ▷ swain

swallow¹ v (-s, -ing, -ed) cause to pass down one's throat ▶ n (pl -s) swallowing

swallow² n (pl -s) small migratory bird with long pointed wings and a forked tail

swallowed v ▷ swallow¹

swallowing v ▷ swallow¹

swallows v ▷ swallow¹ ▶ n ▷ swallow¹, ²

swam v ▷ swim

swamp n (pl -s) watery area of land, bog ▶ v (-s, -ing, -ed) cause (a boat) to fill with water and sink > **swampy** adj (-pier, -piest)

swamped v ▷ swamp

swampier adj ▷ swamp

swampiest adj ▷ swamp

swamping v ▷ swamp

swamps n, v ▷ swamp

swampy adj ▷ swamp

swan n (pl -s) large usu. white water bird with a long graceful neck ▶ v (-s, -nning, -nned) (informal) wander about idly

swank (Slang) v (-s, -ing, -ed) show off or boast ▶ n (pl -s) showing off or boasting

swanked v ▷ swank

swankier adj ▷ swanky

swankiest adj ▷ swanky

swanking v ▷ swank

swanks v, n ▷ swank

swanky adj (-kier, -kiest) (Slang) expensive and showy, stylish

swanned n ▷ swan

swanning n ▷ swan

swans n, v ▷ swan

swap v (-s, -pping, -pped) exchange (something) for something else ▶ n (pl -s) exchange
   swapped v ▷ swap
   swapping v ▷ swap
   swaps v, n ▷ swap
sward n (pl -s) stretch of short grass
   swards n ▷ sward
swarm[1] n (pl -s) large group of bees or other insects ▶ v (-s, -ing, -ed) move in a swarm
swarm[2] v (-s, -ing, -ed) (foll. by **up**) climb (a ladder or rope) by gripping with the hands and feet
   swarmed v ▷ swarm[1, 2]
   swarming v ▷ swarm[1, 2]
   swarms v ▷ swarm[1, 2] ▶ n ▷ swarm[1]
   swarthier adj ▷ swarthy
   swarthiest adj ▷ swarthy
swarthy adj (-thier, -thiest) dark-complexioned
   swashbuckler n ▷ swashbuckling
   swashbucklers n ▷ swashbuckling
swashbuckling adj having the exciting behaviour of pirates, esp. those depicted in films > **swashbuckler** n (pl -s)
swastika n (pl -s) symbol in the shape of a cross with the arms bent at right angles, used as the emblem of Nazi Germany
   swastikas n ▷ swastika
swat v (-s, -tting, -tted) hit sharply ▶ n (pl -s) sharp blow
swatch n (pl -es) sample of cloth
   swatches n ▷ swatch
swath [swawth] n (pl -s) ▷ swathe
swathe v (-thes, -thing, -thed) wrap in bandages or layers of cloth ▶ n (pl -s) long strip of cloth wrapped around something (also **swath**)
   swathed v ▷ swathe
   swathes v, n ▷ swathe
   swathing v ▷ swathe
   swaths n ▷ swath
   swats v, n ▷ swat
   swatted v ▷ swat
   swatting v ▷ swat
sway v (-s, -ing, -ed) swing to and fro or from side to side ▶ n (pl -s) power or influence
   swayed v ▷ sway
   swaying v ▷ sway
   sways v, n ▷ sway
swear v (-s, -ing, swore, sworn) use obscene or blasphemous language
   swearing v ▷ swear
   swears v ▷ swear
swearword n (pl -s) word considered obscene or blasphemous
   swearwords n ▷ swearword
sweat n (pl -s) salty liquid given off through the pores of the skin ▶ v (-s, -ing, -ed) have sweat coming through the pores > **sweaty** adj (-tier, -tiest)
sweatband n (pl -s) strip of cloth tied around the forehead or wrist to absorb sweat
   sweatbands n ▷ sweatband
   sweated v ▷ sweat
sweater n (pl -s) (woollen) garment for the upper part of the body
   sweaters n ▷ sweater
   sweatier adj ▷ sweat
   sweatiest adj ▷ sweat
   sweating v ▷ sweat
   sweats n, v ▷ sweat
sweatshirt n (pl -s) long-sleeved cotton jersey
   sweatshirts n ▷ sweatshirt
sweatshop n (pl -s) place where employees work long hours in poor conditions for low pay
   sweatshops n ▷ sweatshop
   sweaty adj ▷ sweat
swede n (pl -des) kind of turnip
   swedes n ▷ swede
sweep v (-s, -ing, swept) remove dirt from (a floor) with a broom ▶ n (pl -s) sweeping
sweeping adj wide-ranging ▶ v ▷ sweep
   sweeps v, n ▷ sweep
sweepstake n (pl -s) lottery in which the stakes of the participants make up the prize
   sweepstakes n ▷ sweepstake
sweet adj (-er, -est) tasting of or like sugar ▶ n (pl -s) shaped piece of food consisting mainly of sugar > **sweetly** adv > **sweetness** n (pl -es) > **sweeten** v (-s, -ing, -ed)
sweetbread n (pl -s) animal's pancreas used as food
   sweetbreads n ▷ sweetbread
   sweetened v ▷ sweet
sweetener n (pl -s) sweetening agent that does not contain sugar
   sweeteners n ▷ sweetener
   sweetening v ▷ sweet
   sweetens v ▷ sweet
sweetheart n (pl -s) lover
   sweethearts n ▷ sweetheart
   sweetly adv ▷ sweet
sweetmeat n (pl -s) (Old-fashioned) sweet delicacy such as a small cake
   sweetmeats n ▷ sweetmeat
   sweetness n ▷ sweet
   sweetnesses n ▷ sweet
   sweets n ▷ sweet

swell v (**-lls**, **-lling**, **-lled**, **swollen** or **swelled**) expand or increase ▸ n (pl -s) swelling or being swollen ▸ adj (**-er**, **-est**) (US) (Slang) excellent or fine

swelled v ▷ swell

sweller adj ▷ swell

swellest adj ▷ swell

swelling n (pl -s) enlargement of part of the body, caused by injury or infection ▸ v ▷ swell

swells v, n ▷ swell

swelter v (**-s**, **-ing**, **-ed**) feel uncomfortably hot

sweltered v ▷ swelter

sweltering adj uncomfortably hot ▸ v ▷ swelter

swelters v ▷ swelter

swept v ▷ sweep

swerve v (**-ves**, **-ving**, **-ved**) turn aside from a course sharply or suddenly ▸ n (pl -s) swerving

swerved v ▷ swerve

swerves v, n ▷ swerve

swerving v ▷ swerve

swift adj (**-er**, **-est**) moving or able to move quickly ▸ n (pl -s) fast-flying bird with pointed wings > **swiftly** adv > **swiftness** n (pl -es)

swifter adj ▷ swift

swiftest adj ▷ swift

swiftly adv ▷ swift

swiftness n ▷ swift

swiftnesses n ▷ swift

swifts n ▷ swift

swig n (pl -s) large mouthful of drink ▸ v (**-s**, **-gging**, **-gged**) drink in large mouthfuls

swigged v ▷ swig

swigging v ▷ swig

swigs n, v ▷ swig

swill v (**-s**, **-ing**, **-ed**) drink greedily ▸ n (pl -s) sloppy mixture containing waste food, fed to pigs

swilled v ▷ swill

swilling v ▷ swill

swills v, n ▷ swill

swim v (**-s**, **-mming**, **swam**, **swum**) move along in water by movements of the limbs ▸ n (pl -s) act or period of swimming > **swimmer** n (pl -s)

swimmer n ▷ swim

swimmers n ▷ swim

swimming v ▷ swim

swimmingly adv successfully and effortlessly

swims v, n ▷ swim

swindle v (**-les**, **-ling**, **-led**) cheat (someone) out of money ▸ n (pl -s) instance of swindling > **swindler** n (pl -s)

swindled v ▷ swindle

swindler n ▷ swindle

swindlers n ▷ swindle

swindles v, n ▷ swindle

swindling v ▷ swindle

swine n (pl -s) contemptible person

swines n ▷ swine

swing v (**-s**, **-ing**, **swung**) move to and fro, sway ▸ n (pl -s) swinging

swingeing [swin-jing] adj punishing, severe

swinging v ▷ swing

swings v, n ▷ swing

swipe v (**-ipes**, **-iping**, **-iped**) strike (at) with a sweeping blow ▸ n (pl -s) hard blow

swiped v ▷ swipe

swipes v, n ▷ swipe

swiping v ▷ swipe

swirl v (**-s**, **-ing**, **-ed**) turn with a whirling motion ▸ n (pl -s) whirling motion

swirled v ▷ swirl

swirling v ▷ swirl

swirls v, n ▷ swirl

swish v (**-es**, **-ing**, **-ed**) move with a whistling or hissing sound ▸ n (pl -es) whistling or hissing sound ▸ adj (**-er**, **-est**) (Informal) fashionable, smart

swished v ▷ swish

swisher adj ▷ swish

swishes v, n ▷ swish

swishest adj ▷ swish

swishing v ▷ swish

switch n (pl -es) device for opening and closing an electric circuit ▸ v (**-ches**, **-ching**, **-ched**) change abruptly

switchback n (pl -s) road or railway with many sharp hills or bends

switchbacks n ▷ switchback

switchboard n (pl -s) installation in a telephone exchange or office where telephone calls are connected

switchboards n ▷ switchboard

switched v ▷ switch

switches n, v ▷ switch

switching v ▷ switch

swivel v (**-s**, **-elling**, **-elled**) turn on a central point ▸ n (pl -s) coupling device that allows an attached object to turn freely

swivelled v ▷ swivel

swivelling v ▷ swivel

swivels v, n ▷ swivel

swollen v ▷ swell

swoon v (**-s**, **-ing**, **-ed**) ▸ n (pl -s) faint

swooned v ▷ swoon

swooning v ▷ swoon

swoons v, n ▷ swoon

swoop v (**-s**, **-ing**, **-ed**) sweep down or pounce on suddenly ▸ n (pl -s) swooping

swooped v ▷ swoop

swooping v ▷ swoop

swoops v, n ▷ swoop

swop v (**-s, -pping, -pped**) ▶ n (pl **-s**) ▷ swap

swopped v ▷ swop

swopping v ▷ swop

swops v, n ▷ swop

sword n (pl **-s**) weapon with a long sharp blade

swordfish n (pl **-es**) large fish with a very long upper jaw

swordfishes n ▷ swordfish

swords n ▷ sword

swordsman n (pl **-men**) person skilled in the use of a sword

swordsmen n ▷ swordsman

swore v ▷ swear

sworn v ▷ swear ▶ adj bound by or as if by an oath

swot (Informal) v (**-s, -tting, -tted**) study hard ▶ n (pl **-s**) person who studies hard

swots v, n ▷ swot

swotted v ▷ swot

swotting v ▷ swot

swum v ▷ swim

swung v ▷ swing

swy n (**swys**) Swy is an Australian gambling game. This is a very unusual word which doesn't contain a vowel, so it can be useful in helping you to clear a difficult rack. Swy scores 9 points.

sybarite [sib-bar-ite] n (pl **-s**) lover of luxury > **sybaritic** adj

sybarites n ▷ sybarite

sybaritic adj ▷ sybarite

sycamore n (pl **-s**) tree with five-pointed leaves and two-winged fruits

sycamores n ▷ sycamore

sycophancies n ▷ sycophant

sycophancy n ▷ sycophant

sycophant n (pl **-s**) person who uses flattery to win favour from people with power or influence > **sycophantic** adj > **sycophancy** n (pl **-cies**)

sycophantic adj ▷ sycophant

sycophants n ▷ sycophant

syllabi n ▷ syllabus

syllabic adj ▷ syllable

syllable n (pl **-s**) part of a word pronounced as a unit > **syllabic** adj

syllables n ▷ syllable

syllabub n (pl **-s**) dessert of beaten cream, sugar, and wine

syllabubs n ▷ syllabub

syllabus n (pl **-buses, -bi**) list of subjects for a course of study

syllabuses n ▷ syllabus

syllogism n (pl **-s**) form of logical reasoning consisting of two premises and a conclusion

syllogisms n ▷ syllogism

sylph n (pl **-s**) slender graceful girl or woman > **sylphlike** adj

sylphlike adj ▷ sylph

sylphs n ▷ sylph

sylvan adj (Lit) relating to woods and trees

symbioses n ▷ symbiosis

symbiosis n (pl **-oses**) close association of two species living together to their mutual benefit > **symbiotic** adj

symbiotic adj ▷ symbiosis

symbol n (pl **-s**) sign or thing that stands for something else > **symbolic** adj > **symbolically** adv

symbolic adj ▷ symbol

symbolically adv ▷ symbol

symbolism n (pl **-s**) representation of something by symbols > **symbolist** n (pl **-s**) adj

symbolisms n ▷ symbolism

symbolist n ▷ symbolism

symbolists n ▷ symbolism

symbolize v (**-izes, -izing, -ized**) be a symbol of

symbolized v ▷ symbolize

symbolizes v ▷ symbolize

symbolizing v ▷ symbolize

symbols n ▷ symbol

symmetrical adj ▷ symmetry

symmetrically adv ▷ symmetry

symmetries n ▷ symmetry

symmetry n (pl **-tries**) state of having two halves that are mirror images of each other > **symmetrical** adj > **symmetrically** adv

sympathetic adj feeling or showing sympathy > **sympathetically** adv

sympathetically adv ▷ sympathetic

sympathies n ▷ sympathy

sympathize v (**-zes, -izing, -ized**) feel or express sympathy > **sympathizer** n (pl **-s**)

sympathized v ▷ sympathize

sympathizer n ▷ sympathize

sympathizers n ▷ sympathize

sympathizes v ▷ sympathize

sympathizing v ▷ sympathize

sympathy n (pl **-thies**) compassion for someone's pain or distress

symphonic adj ▷ symphony

symphonies n ▷ symphony

symphony n (pl **-nies**) composition for orchestra, with several movements > **symphonic** adj

symposia n ▷ symposium

symposium n (pl **-iums, -sia**) conference for

discussion of a particular topic
symposiums n ▷ symposium
symptom n (pl -s) sign indicating the presence of an illness > **symptomatic** adj
symptomatic adj ▷ symptom
symptoms n ▷ symptom

syn adv. (Syn) is a Scots word for **since**. This is a good word to remember for when you have a shortage of vowels. Syn scores 6 points.

synagogue n (pl -s) Jewish place of worship and religious instruction
synagogues n ▷ synagogue
sync, synch (Informal) n (pl -s) synchronization ▶ v (-s, -ing, -ed) synchronize
synced v ▷ sync
synched v ▷ sync
synching v ▷ sync
synchromesh adj (of a gearbox) having a device that synchronizes the speeds of gears before they engage
synchronization n ▷ synchronize
synchronizations n ▷ synchronize
synchronize v (-izes, -izing, -ized) (of two or more people) perform (an action) at the same time > **synchronization** n (pl -s)
synchronized v ▷ synchronize
synchronizes v ▷ synchronize
synchronizing v ▷ synchronize
synchronous adj happening or existing at the same time
synchs n, v ▷ sync
syncing v ▷ sync
syncopate v (-tes, -ting, -ted) (MUSIC) stress the weak beats in (a rhythm) instead of the strong ones > **syncopation** n (pl -s)
syncopated v ▷ syncopate
syncopates v ▷ syncopate
syncopating v ▷ syncopate
syncopation n ▷ syncopate
syncopations n ▷ syncopate
syncope [sing-kop-ee] n (pl -s) (MED) a faint
syncopes n ▷ syncope
syncs n, v ▷ sync
syndicate n (pl -s) group of people or firms undertaking a joint business project ▶ v (-tes, -ting, -ted) publish (material) in several newspapers > **syndication** n (pl -s)
syndicated v ▷ syndicate
syndicates n, v ▷ syndicate
syndicating v ▷ syndicate
syndication n ▷ syndicate
syndications n ▷ syndicate
syndrome n (pl -s) combination of symptoms indicating a particular disease

syndromes n ▷ syndrome
synergies n ▷ synergy
synergy n (pl -gies) potential ability for people or groups to be more successful working together than on their own
synod n (pl -s) church council
synods n ▷ synod
synonym n (pl -s) word with the same meaning as another > **synonymous** adj
synonymous adj ▷ synonym
synonyms n ▷ synonym
synopses n ▷ synopsis
synopsis n (pl -ses) summary or outline
syntactic adj ▷ syntax
syntax n (pl -es) (GRAMMAR) way in which words are arranged to form phrases and sentences > **syntactic** adj
syntaxes n ▷ syntax
syntheses n ▷ synthesis
synthesis n (pl -ses) combination of objects or ideas into a whole
synthesize v (-izes, -izing, -ized) produce by synthesis
synthesized v ▷ synthesize
synthesizer n (pl -s) electronic musical instrument producing a range of sounds
synthesizers n ▷ synthesizer
synthesizes v ▷ synthesize
synthesizing v ▷ synthesize
synthetic adj (of a substance) made artificially > **synthetically** adv
synthetically adv ▷ synthetic
syphilis n (pl -es) serious sexually transmitted disease > **syphilitic** adj
syphilises n ▷ syphilis
syphilitic adj ▷ syphilis
syphon n (pl -s) ▶ v (-s, -ing, -ed) ▷ siphon
syphoned v ▷ syphon
syphoning v ▷ syphon
syphons n, v ▷ syphon
syringe n (pl -s) device for withdrawing or injecting fluids, consisting of a hollow cylinder, a piston, and a hollow needle ▶ v (-ges, -ging, -ged) wash out or inject with a syringe
syringed v ▷ syringe
syringes n, v ▷ syringe
syringing v ▷ syringe
syrup n (pl -s) solution of sugar in water > **syrupy** adj (-pier, -piest)
syrupier adj ▷ syrup
syrupiest adj ▷ syrup
syrups n ▷ syrup
syrupy adj ▷ syrup
system n (pl -s) method or set of methods

> **systematic** *adj* > **systematically** *adv*
systematic *adj* ▷ **system**
systematically *adv* ▷ **system**
systematization *n* ▷ **systematize**
systematizations *n* ▷ **systematize**
systematize *v* (**-izes, -izing, -ized**) organize
  using a system
systematization *n* (*pl* **-s**) systemizing
  systematized *v* ▷ **systematize**

systematizes *v* ▷ **systematize**
systematizing *v* ▷ **systematize**
systemic *adj* affecting the entire animal or
  body
  systems *n* ▷ **system**
systole [**siss**-tol-ee] *n* (*pl* **-s**) regular contraction
  of the heart as it pumps blood > **systolic** *adj*
  systoles *n* ▷ **systole**
  systolic *adj* ▷ **systole**

Tt

T is one of the most common consonants in Scrabble. There are only four two-letter words that begin with T, but they are easy to remember as there is one for every vowel except U. Like S, T begins a number of three-letter words that don't use vowels, which are well worth remembering. These are: **thy** (6 points), **try** (6), **tsk** (7), **twp** (8) and **tyg** (7). There are also some useful three-letter words using X: **tax**, **tix** and **tux** (10 each). If you have an X during a game, remember words like **text** (11), **texts** (12), **textile** (14), **textual** (14) and **texture** (14). The last three of these have seven letters, and so will earn you 50-point bonuses if you use all your tiles to form them.

ta *interj* (*Informal*) thank you

tab *n* (*pl* **-s**) small flap or projecting label

tabard *n* (*pl* **-s**) short sleeveless tunic decorated with a coat of arms, worn in medieval times
  tabards *n* ▷ tabard
  tabbies *n* ▷ tabby

tabby *n* (*pl* **-bbies**) ▸ *adj* (cat) with dark stripes on a lighter background

tabernacle *n* (*pl* **-s**) portable shrine of the Israelites
  tabernacles *n* ▷ tabernacle

tabla *n* (*pl* **-bla**, **-blas**) one of a pair of Indian drums played with the hands
  tablas *n* ▷ tabla

table *n* (*pl* **-s**) piece of furniture with a flat top supported by legs ▸ *v* (**-les**, **-ling**, **-led**) submit (a motion) for discussion by a meeting
  tabled *v* ▷ table

tableland *n* (*pl* **-s**) high plateau
  tablelands *n* ▷ tableland

tablespoon *n* (*pl* **-s**) large spoon for serving food
  tablespoons *n* ▷ tablespoon

tableau [tab-loh] *n* (*pl* **-leaux**) silent motionless group arranged to represent some scene
  tableaux *n* ▷ tableau
  tabled *v* ▷ table
  tables *n*, *v* ▷ table

tablet *n* (*pl* **-s**) pill of compressed medicinal substance
  tablets *n* ▷ tablet
  tabling *v* ▷ table

tabloid *n* (*pl* **-s**) small-sized newspaper with many photographs and a concise, usu. sensational style

tabloids *n* ▷ tabloid

taboo *n* (*pl* **-s**) prohibition resulting from religious or social conventions ▸ *adj* forbidden by a taboo
  taboos *n* ▷ taboo
  tabs *n* ▷ tab

tabular *adj* arranged in a table

tabulate *v* (**-tes**, **-ting**, **-ted**) arrange (information) in a table > **tabulation** *n* (*pl* **-s**)
  tabulated *v* ▷ tabulate
  tabulates *v* ▷ tabulate
  tabulating *v* ▷ tabulate
  tabulation *n* ▷ tabulate
  tabulations *n* ▷ tabulate

tachograph *n* (*pl* **-s**) device for recording the speed and distance travelled by a motor vehicle
  tachographs *n* ▷ tachograph

tachometer *n* (*pl* **-s**) device for measuring speed, esp. that of a revolving shaft
  tachometers *n* ▷ tachometer

tacit [tass-it] *adj* implied but not spoken > **tacitly** *adv*
  tacitly *adv* ▷ tacit

taciturn [tass-it-turn] *adj* habitually uncommunicative > **taciturnity** *n* (*pl* **-ties**)
  taciturnities *n* ▷ taciturn
  taciturnity *n* ▷ taciturn

tack¹ *n* (*pl* **-s**) short nail with a large head ▸ *v* (**-s**, **-ing**, **-ed**) fasten with tacks

tack² *n* (*pl* **-s**) course of a ship sailing obliquely into the wind ▸ *v* (**-s**, **-ing**, **-ed**) sail into the wind on a zigzag course

tack³ *n* (*pl* **-s**) riding harness for horses
  tacked *v* ▷ tack¹, ²
  tackier *adj* ▷ tacky¹, ²

tackies, takkies pl n (sing **tacky**) (S AFR)
(Informal) tennis shoes or plimsolls
   tackiest adj ▷ tacky¹, ²
   tacking v ▷ tack¹, ²

tackle v (**-les, -ling, -led**) deal with (a task)
(SPORT) ▶ n (pl **-les**) (SPORT) act of tackling an
opposing player
   tackled v ▷ tackle
   tackles v, n ▷ tackle
   tackling v ▷ tackle
   tacks n ▷ tack¹, ², ³ ▶ v ▷ tack¹, ²

tacky¹ adj (**-kier, -kiest**) slightly sticky

tacky² adj (**-kier, -kiest**) (Informal) vulgar and
tasteless
   tacky³ n ▷ tackies

taco [tah-koh] n (pl **-s**) (MEXICAN COOKERY) tortilla
fried until crisp, served with a filling
   tacos n ▷ taco

tact n (pl **-s**) skill in avoiding giving offence
   > **tactful** adj > **tactfully** adv > **tactless** adj
   > **tactlessly** adv
   tactful adj ▷ tact
   tactfully adv ▷ tact

tactic n (pl **-s**) method or plan to achieve an
end > **tactical** adj > **tactician** n (pl **-s**)
   tactical adj ▷ tactic
   tactician n ▷ tactic
   tacticians n ▷ tactic

tactics pl n art of directing military forces in
battle ▶ n ▷ tactic

tactile adj of or having the sense of touch
   tactless adj ▷ tact
   tactlessly adv ▷ tact
   tacts n ▷ tact

tadpole n (pl **-s**) limbless tailed larva of a frog
or toad
   tadpoles n ▷ tadpole

taffeta n (pl **-s**) shiny silk or rayon fabric
   taffetas n ▷ taffeta

tag¹ n (pl **-s**) label bearing information ▶ v (**-s,
-ging, -gged**) attach a tag to

tag² n (pl **-s**) children's game where the person
being chased becomes the chaser upon being
touched ▶ v (**-s, -gging, -gged**) touch and
catch in this game
   tagged v ▷ tag¹, ²
   tagging v ▷ tag¹, ²

tagliatelle n pasta in long narrow strips
   tags n, v ▷ tag¹, ²

tail n (pl **-s**) rear part of an animal's body, usu.
forming a flexible appendage ▶ adj at the rear
   ▶ v (**-s, -ing, -ed**) (Informal) follow (someone)
secretly > **tailless** adj

tailback n (pl **-s**) (BRIT) queue of traffic
stretching back from an obstruction

tailbacks n ▷ tailback

tailboard n (pl **-s**) removable or hinged rear
board on a truck etc.
   tailboards n ▷ tailboard
   tailed v ▷ tail
   tailing v ▷ tail
   tailless adj ▷ tail

tailor n (pl **-s**) person who makes men's clothes
   ▶ v (**-s, -ing, -ed**) adapt to suit a purpose
   tailored v ▷ tailor
   tailoring v ▷ tailor
   tailors n, v ▷ tailor

tailplane n (pl **-s**) small stabilizing wing at the
rear of an aircraft
   tailplanes n ▷ tailplane

tails adv with the side of a coin uppermost
that does not have a portrait of a head on it
   ▶ pl n (Informal) tail coat ▶ n, v ▷ tail

tailspin n (pl **-s**) uncontrolled spinning dive of
an aircraft
   tailspins n ▷ tailspin

tailwind n (pl **-s**) wind coming from the rear
   tailwinds n ▷ tailwind

taint v (**-s, -ing, -ed**) spoil with a small amount
of decay, contamination, or other bad quality
   ▶ n (pl **-s**) something that taints
   tainted v ▷ taint
   tainting v ▷ taint
   taints v, n ▷ taint

taipan n (pl **-s**) large poisonous Australian
snake
   taipans n ▷ taipan

> **taj** n (**tajes**). A taj is a tall conical
> cap worn by some Muslims. This
> unusual word can be helpful if you
> are struggling to use J because there
> aren't any good opportunities for
> longer words on the board. Taj scores
> 10 points.

take v (**takes, taking, took, taken**) remove
from a place ▶ n (pl **-s**) one of a series of
recordings from which the best will be used

takeaway n (pl **-s**) shop or restaurant selling
meals for eating elsewhere
   takeaways n ▷ takeaway
   taken v ▷ take

takeoff n (pl **-s**) (of an aircraft) act of leaving
the ground
   takeoffs n ▷ takeoff

takeover n (pl **-s**) act of taking control of a
company by buying a large number of its
shares
   takeovers n ▷ takeover
   takes v, n ▷ take

taking adj charming ▶ v ▷ take

takings *pl n* money received by a shop
  takkies *pl n* ▷ **tackies**
talc *n* (*pl* **-s**) talcum powder
  talcs *n* ▷ **talc**
tale *n* (*pl* **-s**) story
talent *n* (*pl* **-s**) natural ability > **talented** *adj*
  talented *adj* ▷ **talent**
  talents *n* ▷ **talent**
  tales *n* ▷ **tale**
talisman *n* (*pl* **-s**) object believed to have
  magic power > **talismanic** *adj*
  talismanic *adj* ▷ **talisman**
  talismans *n* ▷ **talisman**
talk *v* (**-s, -ing, -ed**) express ideas or feelings by
  means of speech ▶ *n* (*pl* **-s**) speech or lecture
  talkative *adj* fond of talking
  talkback *n* (*pl* **-s**) (NZ) broadcast in which
  telephone comments or questions from the
  public are transmitted live
    talkbacks *n* ▷ **talkback**
    talked *v* ▷ **talk**
  talker *n* (*pl* **-s**) person who talks
    talkers *n* ▷ **talker**
    talking *v* ▷ **talk**
    talks *v, n* ▷ **talk**
tall (**-er, -est**) *adj* higher than average
tallboy *n* (*pl* **-s**) high chest of drawers
    tallboys *n* ▷ **tallboy**
    taller *adj* ▷ **tall**
    tallest *adj* ▷ **tall**
    tallied *v* ▷ **tally**
    tallies *v, n* ▷ **tally**
tallow *n* (*pl* **-s**) hard animal fat used to make
  candles
    tallows *n* ▷ **tallow**
tally *v* (**-llies, -llying, -llied**) (of two things)
  correspond ▶ *n* (*pl* **-lies**) record of a debt or
  score
    tallying *v* ▷ **tally**
talon *n* (*pl* **-s**) bird's hooked claw
    talons *n* ▷ **talon**
tamarind *n* (*pl* **-s**) tropical tree
    tamarinds *n* ▷ **tamarind**
tamarisk *n* (*pl* **-s**) evergreen shrub with slender
  branches and feathery flower clusters
    tamarisks *n* ▷ **tamarisk**
tambourine *n* (*pl* **-s**) percussion instrument
  like a small drum with jingling metal discs
  attached
    tambourines *n* ▷ **tambourine**
tame *adj* (**-r, -est**) (of animals) brought under
  human control ▶ *v* (**-mes, -ming, -med**) make
  tame > **tamely** *adv*
    tamed *v* ▷ **tame**
    tamely *adv* ▷ **tame**

tamer *n* (*pl* **-s**) person who tames wild animals
  ▶ *adj* ▷ **tame**
    tamers *n* ▷ **tamer**
    tames *v* ▷ **tame**
    tamest *adj* ▷ **tame**
    taming *v* ▷ **tame**
tamp *v* (**-s, -ing, -ed**) pack down by repeated
  taps
    tamped *v* ▷ **tamp**
tamper *v* (**-s, -ing, -ed**) (*foll. by* **with**) interfere
    tampered *v* ▷ **tamper**
    tampering *v* ▷ **tamper**
    tampers *v* ▷ **tamper**
    tamping *v* ▷ **tamp**
tampon *n* (*pl* **-s**) absorbent plug of cotton
  wool inserted into the vagina during
  menstruation
    tampons *n* ▷ **tampon**
    tamps *v* ▷ **tamp**
tan *n* (*pl* **-s**) brown coloration of the skin from
  exposure to sunlight ▶ *v* (**-s, -nning, -nned**)
  (of skin) go brown from exposure to sunlight
  ▶ *adj* (**-ner, -nest**) yellowish-brown
tandem *n* (*pl* **-s**) bicycle for two riders, one
  behind the other
    tandems *n* ▷ **tandem**
tandoori *adj* (of food) cooked in an Indian
  clay oven
tang *n* (*pl* **-s**) strong taste or smell > **tangy** *adj*
  (**-gier, -giest**)
tangent *n* (*pl* **-s**) line that touches a curve
  without intersecting it
tangential *adj* of superficial relevance only
  > **tangentially** *adv*
    tangentially *adv* ▷ **tangential**
    tangents *n* ▷ **tangent**
tangerine *n* (*pl* **-s**) small orange-like fruit of an
  Asian citrus tree
    tangerines *n* ▷ **tangerine**
tangible *adj* able to be touched > **tangibly** *adv*
    tangibly *adv* ▷ **tangible**
    tangier *adj* ▷ **tang**
    tangiest *adj* ▷ **tang**
tangle *n* (*pl* **-s**) confused mass or situation ▶ *v*
  (**-les, -ling, -led**) twist together in a tangle
    tangled *v* ▷ **tangle**
    tangles *n, v* ▷ **tangle**
    tangling *v* ▷ **tangle**
tango *n* (*pl* **-gos**) S American dance ▶ *v* (**-goes,
  -going, -goed**) dance a tango
    tangoed *v* ▷ **tango**
    tangoes *v* ▷ **tango**
    tangoing *v* ▷ **tango**
    tangos *v* ▷ **tango**
    tangs *n* ▷ **tang**

tangy *adj* ▷ tang

taniwha [tun-ee-fah] *n* (*pl* -s) (NZ) mythical Maori monster that lives in water
　taniwhas *n* ▷ taniwha

tank *n* (*pl* -s) container for liquids or gases

tankard *n* (*pl* -s) large beer-mug, often with a hinged lid
　tankards *n* ▷ tankard

tanker *n* (*pl* -s) ship or truck for carrying liquid in bulk
　tankers *n* ▷ tanker
　tanks *n* ▷ tank
　tanned *v* ▷ tan
　tanner *adj* ▷ tan
　tanneries *n* ▷ tannery

tannery *n* (*pl* -ries) place where hides are tanned
　tannest *adj* ▷ tan

tannin *n* (*pl* -s) vegetable substance used in tanning
　tanning *v* ▷ tan
　tannins *n* ▷ tannin
　tans *n*, *v* ▷ tan
　tansies *n* ▷ tansy

tansy *n* (*pl* -sies) yellow-flowered plant

tantalize *v* (-zes, -zing, -zed) torment by showing but withholding something desired
　▷ **tantalizing** *adj* ▷ **tantalizingly** *adv*
　tantalized *v* ▷ tantalize
　tantalizes *v* ▷ tantalize
　tantalizing *v*, *adj* ▷ tantalize
　tantalizingly *adv* ▷ tantalize

tantalum *n* (*pl* -s) (CHEM) hard greyish-white metallic element
　tantalums *n* ▷ tantalum

tantamount *adj* equivalent in effect to

tantrum *n* (*pl* -s) childish outburst of temper
　tantrums *n* ▷ tantrum

tap[1] *v* (taps, tapping, -pped) knock lightly and usu. repeatedly ▶ *n* (*pl* -s) light knock

tap[2] *n* (*pl* -s) valve to control the flow of liquid from a pipe or cask ▶ *v* (taps, tapping, tapped) listen in on (a telephone call) secretly by making an illegal connection

tape *n* (*pl* -s) narrow long strip of material ▶ *v* (tapes, taping, taped) record on magnetic tape
　taped *v* ▷ tape

taper *v* (-s, -ing, -ed) become narrower towards one end ▶ *n* (*pl* -s) long thin candle
　tapered *v* ▷ taper
　tapering *v* ▷ taper
　tapers *v*, *n* ▷ taper
　tapes *n*, *v* ▷ tape
　tapestries *n* ▷ tapestry

tapestry *n* (*pl* -tries) fabric decorated with coloured woven designs

tapeworm *n* (*pl* -s) long flat parasitic worm living in the intestines of vertebrates
　tapeworms *n* ▷ tapeworm

tapioca *n* (*pl* -s) beadlike starch made from cassava root, used in puddings
　tapiocas *n* ▷ tapioca
　taping *v* ▷ tape

tapir [tape-er] *n* (*pl* -s) piglike mammal of tropical America and SE Asia, with a long snout
　tapirs *n* ▷ tapir
　tapped *v* ▷ tap[1, 2]

tappet *n* (*pl* -s) short steel rod in an engine, transferring motion from one part to another
　tappets *n* ▷ tappet
　tapping *v* ▷ tap[1, 2]

taproot *n* (*pl* -s) main root of a plant, growing straight down
　taproots *n* ▷ taproot
　taps *n*, *v* ▷ tap[1, 2]

tar *n* (*pl* -rs) thick black liquid distilled from coal etc. ▶ *v* (-s, -rring, -rred) coat with tar

taramasalata *n* (*pl* -s) creamy pink pâté made from fish roe
　taramasalatas *n* ▷ taramasalata

tarantella *n* (*pl* -s) lively Italian dance
　tarantellas *n* ▷ tarantella

tarantula *n* (*pl* -s) large hairy spider with a poisonous bite
　tarantulas *n* ▷ tarantula
　tardier *adj* ▷ tardy
　tardiest *adj* ▷ tardy
　tardily *adv* ▷ tardy
　tardiness *n* ▷ tardy
　tardinesses *n* ▷ tardy

tardy *adj* (-dier, -diest) slow or late ▷ **tardily** *adv*
　▷ **tardiness** *n* (*pl* -es)

tare *n* (*pl* -s) type of vetch plant
　tares *n* ▷ tare

target *n* (*pl* -s) object or person a missile is aimed at ▶ *v* (-gets, -geting, -geted) aim or direct
　targeted *v* ▷ target
　targeting *v* ▷ target
　targets *n*, *v* ▷ target

tariff *n* (*pl* -s) tax levied on imports
　tariffs *n* ▷ tariff

tarn *n* (*pl* -s) small mountain lake

tarnish *v* (-shes, -shing, -shed) make or become stained or less bright ▶ *n* (*pl* -es) discoloration or blemish
　tarnished *v* ▷ tarnish
　tarnishes *v*, *n* ▷ tarnish

tarnishing v ▷ tarnish
tarns n ▷ tarn
tarot [**tarr**-oh] n (pl **-s**) special pack of cards used mainly in fortune-telling
tarots n ▷ tarot
tarpaulin n (pl **-s**) (sheet of) heavy waterproof fabric
tarpaulins n ▷ tarpaulin
tarragon n (pl **-s**) aromatic herb
tarragons n ▷ tarragon
tarred v ▷ tar
tarried v ▷ tarry
tarries v ▷ tarry
tarring v ▷ tar
tarry v (**tarries, tarrying, tarried**) (Old-fashioned) linger or delay
tarrying v ▷ tarry
tars n, v ▷ tar
tarsi n ▷ tarsus
tarsus n (pl **-si**) bones of the heel and ankle collectively
tart[1] n (pl **-s**) pie or flan with a sweet filling
tart[2] adj (**-er, -est**) sharp or bitter ▷ **tartly** adv ▷ **tartness** n (pl **-es**)
tart[3] n (pl **-s**) (Informal) sexually provocative or promiscuous woman
tartan n (pl **-s**) design of straight lines crossing at right angles, esp. one associated with a Scottish clan
tartans n ▷ tartan
tartar[1] n (pl **-s**) hard deposit on the teeth
tartar[2] n (pl **-s**) fearsome or formidable person
tartars n ▷ tartar[1,2]
tarter adj ▷ tart[2]
tartest adj ▷ tart[2]
tartly adv ▷ tart[2]
tartness n ▷ tart[2]
tartnesses n ▷ tart[2]
tartrazine [**tar**-traz-zeen] n (pl **-s**) artificial yellow dye used in food etc.
tartrazines n ▷ tartrazine
tarts n ▷ tart[1,3]
task n (pl **-s**) (difficult or unpleasant) piece of work to be done
taskmaster n (pl **-s**) person who enforces hard work
taskmasters n ▷ taskmaster
tasks n ▷ task
tassel n (pl **-s**) decorative fringed knot of threads
tassels n ▷ tassel
taste n (pl **-s**) sense by which the flavour of a substance is distinguished in the mouth ▷ v (**-tes, -ting, -ted**) distinguish the taste of (a substance)

tasted v ▷ taste
tasteful adj having or showing good taste ▷ **tastefully** adv
tastefully adv ▷ tasteful
tasteless adj bland or insipid ▷ **tastelessly** adv
tastelessly adv ▷ tasteless
tastes n, v ▷ taste
tastier adj ▷ tasty
tastiest adj ▷ tasty
tasting v ▷ taste
tasty adj (**-tier, -tiest**) pleasantly flavoured
tat n (pl **-s**) (BRIT) tatty or tasteless article(s)
tats n ▷ tat
tattered adj ragged or torn
tattier n ▷ tatty
tattiest n ▷ tatty
tattle v (**-les, -ling, -led**), n (pl **-les**) (BRIT, AUST & NZ) gossip or chatter
tattled v ▷ tattle
tattles n ▷ tattle
tattling v ▷ tattle
tattoo[1] n (pl **-s**) pattern made on the body by pricking the skin and staining it with indelible inks ▷ v (**-toos, -tooing, -tooed**) make such a pattern on the skin ▷ **tattooist** n (pl **-s**)
tattoo[2] n (pl **-s**) military display or pageant
tattooed n ▷ tattoo[1]
tattooing n ▷ tattoo[1]
tattooist n ▷ tattoo[1]
tattooists n ▷ tattoo[1]
tattoos n ▷ tattoo[1,2] ▷ v ▷ tattoo[1]
tatty adj (**-tier, -tiest**) shabby or worn out
taught v ▷ teach
taunt v (**-s, -ing, -ed**) tease with jeers ▷ n (pl **-s**) jeering remark
taunted v ▷ taunt
taunting v ▷ taunt
taunts v, n ▷ taunt
taupe adj brownish-grey
taut adj (**-er, -est**) drawn tight
tauten v (**-s, -ing, -ed**) make or become taut
tautened v ▷ tauten
tautening v ▷ tauten
tautens v ▷ tauten
tauter adj ▷ taut
tautest adj ▷ taut
tautological adj ▷ tautology
tautologies n ▷ tautology
tautology n (pl **-gies**) use of words which merely repeat something already stated ▷ **tautological** adj
tavern n (pl **-s**) (Old-fashioned) pub
taverns n ▷ tavern
tawdrier adj ▷ tawdry

tawdriest *adj* ▷ tawdry
tawdry *adj* (**-drier, -driest**) cheap, showy, and of poor quality
tawnier *adj* ▷ tawny
tawniest *adj* ▷ tawny
tawny *adj* (**-nier, -niest**) yellowish-brown
tax *n* (*pl* **-es**) compulsory payment levied by a government on income, property, etc. to raise revenue ▶ *v* (**-es, -ing, -ed**) levy a tax on ▷ **taxable** *adj* ▷ **taxpayer** *n* (*pl* **-s**)
taxable *adj* ▷ tax
taxation *n* (*pl* **-s**) levying of taxes
taxations *n* ▷ taxation
taxed *v* ▷ tax
taxes *n, v* ▷ tax
taxi *n* (*pl* **-s**) car with a driver that may be hired to take people to any specified destination ▶ *v* (**taxis, taxiing, taxied**) (of an aircraft) run along the ground before taking off or after landing
taxidermies *n* ▷ taxidermy
taxidermist *n* ▷ taxidermy
taxidermists *n* ▷ taxidermy
taxidermy *n* (*pl* **-mies**) art of stuffing and mounting animal skins to give them a lifelike appearance ▷ **taxidermist** *n* (*pl* **-s**)
taxied *v* ▷ taxi
taxiing *v* ▷ taxi
taxing *v* ▷ tax
taxis *n, v* ▷ taxi
taxonomic *adj* ▷ taxonomy
taxonomies *n* ▷ taxonomy
taxonomist *n* ▷ taxonomy
taxonomists *n* ▷ taxonomy
taxonomy *n* (*pl* **-mies**) classification of plants and animals into groups ▷ **taxonomic** *adj* ▷ **taxonomist** *n* (*pl* **-s**)
taxpayer *n* ▷ tax
taxpayers *n* ▷ tax

te *n* (**tes**). Te is the seventh note of a musical scale. Although it won't earn you many points on its own, te is extremely useful as it allows you to connect a word beginning with T to one ending in E, or vice versa, which is very helpful as T and E are two of the most common tiles in the game. Te scores 2 points.

tea *n* (*pl* **-s**) drink made from infusing the dried leaves of an Asian bush in boiling water
teapot *n* (*pl* **-s**) container with a lid, spout, and handle for making and serving tea
teapots *n* ▷ teapot
teaspoon *n* (*pl* **-s**) small spoon for stirring tea
teaspoons *n* ▷ teaspoon

teach *v* (**-es, -ing, taught**) tell or show (someone) how to do something ▷ **teaching** *n* (*pl* **-s**)
teacher *n* (*pl* **-s**) person who teaches, esp. in a school
teachers *n* ▷ teacher
teaches *v* ▷ teach
teaching *v, n* ▷ teach
teachings *n* ▷ teach
teak *n* (*pl* **-s**) very hard wood of an E Indian tree
teaks *n* ▷ teak
teal *n* (*pl* **-s**) kind of small duck
teals *n* ▷ teal
team *n* (*pl* **-s**) group of people forming one side in a game
teams *n* ▷ team
teamster *n* (*pl* **-s**) (US) commercial vehicle driver
teamsters *n* ▷ teamster
teamwork *n* (*pl* **-s**) cooperative work by a team
teamworks *n* ▷ teamwork
tear[1], **teardrop** *n* (*pl* **-s**) drop of fluid appearing in and falling from the eye
tear[2] *v* (**-s, -ing, tore, torn**) rip a hole in ▶ *n* (*pl* **-s**) hole or split
tearaway *n* (*pl* **-s**) wild or unruly person
tearaways *n* ▷ tearaway
teardrop *n* ▷ tear[1]
teardrops *n* ▷ tear[1]
tearful *adj* weeping or about to weep
tearing *v* ▷ tear[2]
tears *n* ▷ tear[1, 2] ▶ *v* ▷ tear[2]
teas *n* ▷ tea
tease *v* (**-ses, -sing, -sed**) make fun of (someone) in a provoking or playful way ▶ *n* (*pl* **-s**) person who teases ▷ **teasing** *adj, n* (*pl* **-s**)
teased *v* ▷ tease
teasel, teazel, teazle *n* (*pl* **-s**) plant with prickly leaves and flowers
teasels *n* ▷ teasel
teases *v, n* ▷ tease
teasing *v, adj n* ▷ tease
teasings *n* ▷ tease
teat *n* (*pl* **-s**) nipple of a breast or udder
teats *n* ▷ teat
teazel *n* ▷ teasel
teazels *n* ▷ teasel
teazle *n* ▷ teasel
teazles *n* ▷ teasel
tech *n* (*pl* **-s**) (*Informal*) technical college
techie (*Informal*) *n* (*pl* **-s**) person who is skilled in the use of technology ▶ *adj* relating to or skilled in the use of technology
techies *n* ▷ techie
technetium [tek-**neesh**-ee-um] *n* (*pl* **-s**) (CHEM)

artificially produced silvery-grey metallic element

technetiums *n* ▷ technetium

technical *adj* of or specializing in industrial, practical, or mechanical arts and applied sciences > **technically** *adv*

technicalities *n* ▷ technicality

technicality *n* (*pl* -s) petty point based on a strict application of rules

technically *adv* ▷ technical

technician *n* (*pl* -s) person skilled in a particular technical field

technicians *n* ▷ technician

technicolor *adj* garishly coloured

technique *n* (*pl* -s) method or skill used for a particular task

techniques *n* ▷ technique

techno *n* (*pl* -s) type of electronic dance music with a very fast beat

technocracies *n* ▷ technocracy

technocracy *n* (*pl* -cies) government by technical experts > **technocrat** *n* (*pl* -s)

technocrat *n* ▷ technocracy

technocrats *n* ▷ technocracy

technological *adj* ▷ technology

technologies *n* ▷ technology

technologist *n* ▷ technology

technologists *n* ▷ technology

technology *n* (*pl* -gies) application of practical or mechanical sciences to industry or commerce > **technological** *adj* > **technologist** *n* (*pl* -s)

technos *n* ▷ techno

techs *n* ▷ tech

tectonics *n* study of the earth's crust and the forces affecting it

teddies *n* ▷ teddy

teddy *n* (*pl* -dies) teddy bear

tedious *adj* causing fatigue or boredom > **tediously** *adv*

tediously *adv* ▷ tedious

tedium *n* (*pl* -s) monotony

tediums *n* ▷ tedium

tee *n* (*pl* -s) small peg from which a golf ball can be played at the start of each hole

teem[1] *v* (-s, -ing, -ed) be full of

teem[2] *v* (-s, -ing, -ed) rain heavily

teemed *v* ▷ teem[1,2]

teeming *v* ▷ teem[1,2]

teems *v* ▷ teem[1,2]

teenage *adj* ▷ teenager

teenager *n* (*pl* -s) person aged between 13 and 19 > **teenage** *adj*

teenagers *n* ▷ teenager

teens *pl n* period of being a teenager

teepee *n* (*pl* -s) ▷ tepee

teepees *n* ▷ teepee

tees *n* ▷ tee

teeter *v* (-s, -ing, -ed) wobble or move unsteadily

teetered *v* ▷ teeter

teetering *v* ▷ teeter

teeters *v* ▷ teeter

teeth *n* ▷ tooth

teethe *v* (-thes, -thing, -thed) (of a baby) grow his or her first teeth

teethed *v* ▷ teethe

teethes *v* ▷ teethe

teething *v* ▷ teethe

teetotal *adj* drinking no alcohol > **teetotaller** *n* (*pl* -s)

teetotaller *n* ▷ teetotal

teetotallers *n* ▷ teetotal

telecommunications *n* communications using telephone, radio, television, etc.

telegram *n* (*pl* -s) formerly, a message sent by telegraph

telegrams *n* ▷ telegram

telegraph *n* (*pl* -s) formerly, a system for sending messages over a distance along a cable ▶ *v* (-s, -ing, -ed) communicate by telegraph > **telegraphic** *adj* > **telegraphist** *n* (*pl* -s)

telegraphed *v* ▷ telegraph

telegraphic *adj* ▷ telegraph

telegraphies *n* ▷ telegraphy

telegraphing *v* ▷ telegraph

telegraphist *n* ▷ telegraph

telegraphists *n* ▷ telegraph

telegraphs *n*, *v* ▷ telegraph

telegraphy *n* (*pl* -phies) science or use of a telegraph

telekinesis *n* (*pl* -eses) movement of objects by thought or willpower

telekineses *n* ▷ telekinesis

telemetries *n* ▷ telemetry

telemetry *n* (*pl* -tries) use of electronic devices to record or measure a distant event and transmit the data to a receiver

teleological *adj* ▷ teleology

teleologies *n* ▷ teleology

teleology *n* (*pl* -gies) belief that all things have a predetermined purpose > **teleological** *adj*

telepathic *adj* ▷ telepathy

telepathically *adv* ▷ telepathy

telepathies *n* ▷ telepathy

telepathy *n* (*pl* -thies) direct communication between minds > **telepathic** *adj* > **telepathically** *adv*

telephone *n* (*pl* -s) device for transmitting

sound over a distance ▶ v (**-nes, -ning, -ned**) call or talk to (a person) by telephone > **telephony** n (pl **-nies**) > **telephonic** adj

telephoned v ▷ telephone

telephones n, v ▷ telephone

telephonic adj ▷ telephone

telephonies n ▷ telephone

telephoning v ▷ telephone

telephonist n (pl **-s**) person operating a telephone switchboard

telephonists n ▷ telephonist

telephony n ▷ telephone

teleprinter n (pl **-s**) (BRIT) apparatus like a typewriter for sending and receiving typed messages by wire

teleprinters n ▷ teleprinter

telesales n selling of a product or service by telephone

telescope n (pl **-s**) optical instrument for magnifying distant objects ▶ v (**-pes, -ping, -ped**) shorten > **telescopic** adj

telescoped v ▷ telescope

telescopes n, v ▷ telescope

telescopic adj ▷ telescope

telescoping v ▷ telescope

televise v (**-ses, -sing, -sed**) broadcast on television

televised v ▷ televise

televises v ▷ televise

televising v ▷ televise

television n (pl **-s**) system of producing a moving image and accompanying sound on a distant screen > **televisual** adj

televisions n ▷ television

televisual adj ▷ television

telex n (pl **-es**) international communication service using teleprinters ▶ v (**-es, -ing, -ed**) transmit by telex

telexed v ▷ telex

telexes n, v ▷ telex

telexing v ▷ telex

tell v (**-s, -lling, told**) make known in words

teller n (pl **-s**) narrator

tellers n ▷ teller

tellies n ▷ telly

telling adj having a marked effect ▶ v ▷ tell

tells v ▷ tell

telltale n (pl **-s**) person who reveals secrets ▶ adj revealing

telltales n ▷ telltale

tellurium n (pl **-s**) (CHEM) brittle silvery-white nonmetallic element

telluriums n ▷ tellurium

telly n (pl **-lies**) (Informal) television

temerities n ▷ temerity

temerity [tim-**merr**-it-tee] n (pl **-ties**) boldness or audacity

temp (BRIT) (Informal) n (pl **-s**) temporary employee, esp. a secretary ▶ v (**-s, -ing, -ed**) work as a temp

temped v ▷ temp

temper n (pl **-s**) outburst of anger ▶ v (**-s, -ing, -ed**) make less extreme

tempera n (pl **-s**) painting medium for powdered pigments

temperas n ▷ tempera

temperament n (pl **-s**) person's character or disposition

temperamental adj having changeable moods > **temperamentally** adv

temperamentally adv ▷ temperamental

temperaments n ▷ temperament

temperance n (pl **-s**) moderation

temperances n ▷ temperance

temperate adj (of climate) not extreme

temperature n (pl **-s**) degree of heat or cold

temperatures n ▷ temperature

tempered v ▷ temper

tempering v ▷ temper

tempers n, v ▷ temper

tempest n (pl **-s**) violent storm

tempests n ▷ tempest

tempestuous adj violent or stormy

tempi n ▷ tempo

temping v ▷ temp

template n (pl **-s**) pattern used to cut out shapes accurately

templates n ▷ template

temple[1] n (pl **-s**) building for worship

temple[2] n (pl **-s**) region on either side of the forehead

temples n ▷ temple[1, 2]

tempo n (pl **-pi, -pos**) rate or pace

temporal adj of time

temporarily adv ▷ temporary

temporary adj lasting only for a short time > **temporarily** adv

temporize v (**-zes, -zing, -zed**) gain time by negotiation or evasiveness

temporized v ▷ temporize

temporizes v ▷ temporize

temporizing v ▷ temporize

tempos n ▷ tempo

temps n, v ▷ temp

tempt v (**-s, -ing, -ed**) entice (a person) to do something wrong > **tempter, temptress** n (pl **-s, -es**)

temptation n (pl **-s**) tempting

temptations n ▷ temptation

tempted v ▷ tempt

tempter *n* ▷ tempt

tempters *n* ▷ tempt

tempting *adj* attractive or inviting ▶ *v* ▷ tempt

temptress *n* ▷ tempt

temptresses *n* ▷ tempt

tempts *v* ▷ tempt

ten *adj*, *n* (*pl* -s) one more than nine

tenable *adj* able to be upheld or maintained

tenacious *adj* holding fast > **tenaciously** *adv*
 > **tenacity** *n* (*pl* -ties)

tenaciously *adv* ▷ tenacious

tenacities *n* ▷ tenacious

tenacity *n* ▷ tenacious

tenancies *n* ▷ tenant

tenancy *n* ▷ tenant

tenant *n* (*pl* -s) person who rents land or a
 building > **tenancy** *n* (*pl* -cies)

tenants *n* ▷ tenant

tench *n* (*pl* -es) freshwater game fish of the
 carp family

tenches *n* ▷ tench

tend[1] *v* (-s, -ing, -ed) be inclined

tend[2] *v* (-s, -ing, -ed) take care of

tended *v* ▷ tend[1, 2]

tendencies *n* ▷ tendency

tendency *n* (*pl* -cies) inclination to act in a
 certain way > **tendentious** *adj* biased, not
 impartial

tendentious *adj* ▷ tendency

tender[1] *adj* (-er, -est) not tough > **tenderly** *adv*
 > **tenderness** *n* (*pl* -es)

tender[2] *v* (-s, -ing, -ed) offer ▶ *n* (*pl* -s) such
 an offer

tender[3] *n* (*pl* -s) small boat that brings supplies
 to a larger ship in a port

tendered *v* ▷ tender[2]

tenderer *adj* ▷ tender[1]

tenderest *adj* ▷ tender[1]

tendering *v* ▷ tender[2]

tenderize *v* (-zes, -zing, -zed) soften (meat)
 by pounding or treatment with a special
 substance

tenderized *v* ▷ tenderize

tenderizes *v* ▷ tenderize

tenderizing *v* ▷ tenderize

tenderly *adv* ▷ tender[1]

tenderness *n* ▷ tender[1]

tendernesses *n* ▷ tender[1]

tenders *n* ▷ tender[2, 3] ▶ *v* ▷ tender[2]

tending *v* ▷ tend[1, 2]

tendon *n* (*pl* -s) strong tissue attaching a
 muscle to a bone

tendons *n* ▷ tendon

tendril *n* (*pl* -s) slender stem by which a
 climbing plant clings

tendrils *n* ▷ tendril

tends *v* ▷ tend[1, 2]

tenement *n* (*pl* -s) (esp. in Scotland or the US)
 building divided into several flats

tenements *n* ▷ tenement

tenet [ten-nit] *n* (*pl* -s) doctrine or belief

tenets *n* ▷ tenet

tenner *n* (*pl* -s) (BRIT) (*Informal*) ten-pound note

tenners *n* ▷ tenner

tennis *n* (*pl* -es) game in which players use
 rackets to hit a ball back and forth over a net

tennises *n* ▷ tennis

tenon *n* (*pl* -s) projecting end on a piece of
 wood fitting into a slot in another

tenons *n* ▷ tenon

tenor *n* (*pl* -s) (singer with) the second highest
 male voice ▶ *adj* (of a voice or instrument)
 between alto and baritone

tenors *n* ▷ tenor

tens *n* ▷ ten

tense[1] *adj* (-r, -st) emotionally strained ▶ *v*
 (-ses, -sing, -sed) make or become tense

tense[2] *n* (*pl* -s) (GRAMMAR) form of a verb
 showing the time of action

tensed *v* ▷ tense[1]

tenser *adj* ▷ tense[1]

tenses *n* ▷ tense[2] ▶ *v* ▷ tense[1]

tensest *adj* ▷ tense[1]

tensile *adj* of tension

tensing *v* ▷ tense[1]

tension *n* (*pl* -s) hostility or suspense

tensions *n* ▷ tension

tent *n* (*pl* -s) portable canvas shelter

tentacle *n* (*pl* -s) flexible organ of many
 invertebrates, used for grasping, feeding, etc.

tentacles *n* ▷ tentacle

tentative *adj* provisional or experimental
 > **tentatively** *adv*

tentatively *adv* ▷ tentative

tenterhooks *pl n* tension

tenth *adj*, *n* (*pl* -s) (of) number ten in a series

tenths *n* ▷ tenth

tents *n* ▷ tent

tenuous *adj* slight or flimsy > **tenuously** *adv*

tenuously *adv* ▷ tenuous

tenure *n* (*pl* -s) (period of) the holding of an
 office or position

tenures *n* ▷ tenure

tepee, teepee [tee-pee] *n* (*pl* -s) cone-shaped
 tent, formerly used by Native Americans

tepees *n* ▷ tepee

tepid *adj* (-er, -est) slightly warm

tepider *adj* ▷ tepid

tepidest *adj* ▷ tepid

tequila *n* (*pl* -s) Mexican alcoholic drink

tequilas n ▷ tequila
tercentenaries n ▷ tercentenary
tercentenary adj, n (pl -ries) (of) a three hundredth anniversary
term n (pl -s) word or expression ▶ v (-s, -ing, -ed) name or designate
termed v ▷ term
terminal adj (of an illness) ending in death ▶ n (pl -s) place where people or vehicles begin or end a journey > **terminally** adv
terminally adv ▷ terminal
terminals n ▷ terminal
terminate v (-tes, -ting, -ted) bring or come to an end > **termination** n (pl -s)
terminated v ▷ terminate
terminates v ▷ terminate
terminating v ▷ terminate
termination n ▷ terminate
terminations n ▷ terminate
terming v ▷ term
termini n ▷ terminus
terminologies n ▷ terminology
terminology n (pl -gies) technical terms relating to a subject
terminus n (pl -ni, -nuses) railway or bus station at the end of a line
terminuses n ▷ terminus
termite n (pl -s) white antlike insect that destroys timber
termites n ▷ termite
terms n, v ▷ term ▶ pl n conditions
tern n (pl -s) gull-like sea bird with a forked tail and pointed wings
ternary adj consisting of three parts
terns n ▷ tern
terrace n (pl -s) row of houses built as one block ▶ v (-ces, -cing, -ced) form into or provide with a terrace
terraced v ▷ terrace
terraces n, v ▷ terrace ▶ pl n (also **terracing**) tiered area in a stadium where spectators stand
terracing v ▷ terrace
terracotta adj, n (pl -s) (made of) brownish-red unglazed pottery ▶ adj brownish-red
terracottas n ▷ terracotta
terrain n (pl -s) area of ground, esp. with reference to its physical character
terrains n ▷ terrain
terrapin n (pl -s) small turtle-like reptile
terrapins n ▷ terrapin
terraria n ▷ terrarium
terrarium n (pl -raria, -rariums) enclosed container for small plants or animals
terrariums n ▷ terrarium

terrazzo n (pl -s) floor of marble chips set in mortar and polished
terrazzos n ▷ terrazzo
terrestrial adj of the earth
terrible adj very serious > **terribly** adv
terribly adv ▷ terrible
terrier n (pl -s) any of various breeds of small active dog
terriers n ▷ terrier
terries n ▷ terry
terrific adj great or intense
terrified v, adj ▷ terrify
terrifies v ▷ terrify
terrify v (-fies, -fying, -fied) fill with fear > **terrified** adj > **terrifying** adj
terrifying v, adj ▷ terrify
terrine [terr-reen] n (pl -s) earthenware dish with a lid
terrines n ▷ terrine
territorial adj ▷ territory
territories n ▷ territory
territory n (pl -ries) district > **territorial** adj
terror n (pl -s) great fear
terrorism n (pl -s) use of violence and intimidation to achieve political ends > **terrorist** n (pl -s) adj
terrorisms n ▷ terrorism
terrorist n, adj ▷ terrorism
terrorists n ▷ terrorism
terrorize v (-zes, -zing, -zed) force or oppress by fear or violence
terrorized v ▷ terrorize
terrorizes v ▷ terrorize
terrorizing v ▷ terrorize
terrors n ▷ terror
terry n (pl -ries) fabric with small loops covering both sides, used esp. for making towels
terse adj (-r, -st) neat and concise > **tersely** adv
tersely adv ▷ terse
terser adj ▷ terse
tersest adj ▷ terse
tertiary [tur-shar-ee] adj third in degree, order, etc.
tessellated adj paved or inlaid with a mosaic of small tiles
test v (-s, -ing, -ed) try out to ascertain the worth, capability, or endurance of ▶ n (pl -s) critical examination > **testing** adj
testament n (pl -s) proof or tribute
testaments n ▷ testament
testator [test-**tay**-tor], fem **testatrix** [test-**tay**-triks] n (pl -s, -xes) maker of a will
testators n ▷ testator
testatrix n ▷ testator

testatrixes *n* ▷ testator

tested *v* ▷ test

testes *n* ▷ testis

testicle *n* (*pl* -s) either of the two male reproductive glands

testicles *n* ▷ testicle

testier *adj* ▷ testy

testiest *adj* ▷ testy

testified *v* ▷ testify

testifies *v* ▷ testify

testify *v* (-fies, -fying, -fied) give evidence under oath

testifying *v* ▷ testify

testily *adv* ▷ testy

testimonial *n* (*pl* -s) recommendation of the worth of a person or thing

testimonials *n* ▷ testimonial

testimonies *n* ▷ testimony

testimony *n* (*pl* -nies) declaration of truth or fact

testiness *n* ▷ testy

testinesses *n* ▷ testy

testing *v, adj* ▷ test

testis *n* (*pl* -tes) testicle

testosterone *n* (*pl* -s) male sex hormone secreted by the testes

testosterones *n* ▷ testosterone

tests *v, n* ▷ test

testy *adj* (-tier, -tiest) irritable or touchy
> **testily** *adv* ▷ testy (*pl* -es)

tetanus *n* (*pl* -es) acute infectious disease producing muscular spasms and convulsions

tetanuses *n* ▷ tetanus

tether *n* (*pl* -s) rope or chain for tying an animal to a spot ▶ *v* (-s, -ing, -ed) tie up with rope

tethered *v* ▷ tether

tethering *v* ▷ tether

tethers *n, v* ▷ tether

tetrahedra *n* ▷ tetrahedron

tetrahedron [tet-ra-heed-ron] *n* (*pl* -drons, -dra) solid figure with four faces

tetrahedrons *n* ▷ tetrahedron

tetralogies *n* ▷ tetralogy

tetralogy *n* (*pl* -gies) series of four related works

text *n* (*pl* -s) main body of a book as distinct from illustrations etc. ▶ *v* (-s, -ing, -ed) send a text message to (someone) > **textual** *adj*

textbook *n* (*pl* -s) standard book on a particular subject ▶ *adj* perfect

textbooks *n* ▷ textbook

texted *v* ▷ text

textile *n* (*pl* -s) fabric or cloth, esp. woven

textiles *n* ▷ textile

texting *v* ▷ text

texts *n, v* ▷ text

textual *adj* ▷ text

textural *adj* ▷ texture

texture *n* (*pl* -s) structure, feel, or consistency
> **textured** *adj* ▷ textural *adj*

textured *adj* ▷ texture

textures *n* ▷ texture

thalidomide [thal-**lid**-oh-mide] *n* (*pl* -s) drug formerly used as a sedative, but found to cause abnormalities in developing fetuses

thalidomides *n* ▷ thalidomide

thallium *n* (*pl* -s) (CHEM) highly toxic metallic element

thalliums *n* ▷ thallium

than *conj, prep* used to introduce the second element of a comparison

thane *n* (*pl* -s) (HIST) Anglo-Saxon or medieval Scottish nobleman

thanes *n* ▷ thane

thank *v* (-s, -ing, -ed) express gratitude to

thanked *v* ▷ thank

thankful *adj* grateful

thanking *v* ▷ thank

thankless *adj* unrewarding or unappreciated

thanks *pl n* words of gratitude ▶ *interj* polite expression of gratitude ▶ *v* ▷ thank

that *adj, pron* used to refer to something already mentioned or familiar, or further away ▶ *conj* used to introduce a clause ▶ *pron* used to introduce a relative clause

thatch *n* (*pl* -es) roofing material of reeds or straw ▶ *v* (-ches, -ching, -ched) roof (a house) with reeds or straw

thatched *v* ▷ thatch

thatches *n, v* ▷ thatch

thatching *v* ▷ thatch

thaw *v* (-s, -ing, -ed) make or become unfrozen ▶ *n* (*pl* -s) thawing

thawed *v* ▷ thaw

thawing *v* ▷ thaw

thaws *n, v* ▷ thaw

the *adj* the definite article, used before a noun

theatre *n* (*pl* -s) place where plays etc. are performed

theatres *n* ▷ theatre

theatrical *adj* of the theatre > **theatrically** *adv*
> **theatricality** *n* (*pl* -ties)

theatricalities *n* ▷ theatrical

theatricality *n* ▷ theatrical

theatrically *adv* ▷ theatrical

theatricals *pl n* (amateur) dramatic performances

thee *pron* (Obs) you

theft *n* (*pl* -s) act or an instance of stealing

thefts n ▷ theft

their adj of or associated with them

theirs pron (thing or person) belonging to them

theism [thee-iz-zum] n (pl -s) belief in a God or gods > **theist** n (pl -s) adj > **theistic** adj

theisms n ▷ theism

theist n, adj ▷ theism

theistic adj ▷ theism

theists n ▷ theism

them pron refers to people or things other than the speaker or those addressed

thematic adj ▷ theme

theme n (pl -s) main idea or subject being discussed > **thematic** adj

themes n ▷ theme

themselves pron ▷ they, them

then adv at that time

thence adv from that place or time

theocracies n ▷ theocracy

theocracy n (pl -cies) government by a god or priests > **theocratic** adj

theocratic adj ▷ theocracy

theodolite [thee-odd-oh-lite] n (pl -s) surveying instrument for measuring angles

theodolites n ▷ theodolite

theologian n ▷ theology

theologians n ▷ theology

theological adj ▷ theology

theologically adv ▷ theology

theologies n ▷ theology

theology n (pl -gies) study of religions and religious beliefs > **theologian** n (pl -s) > **theological** adj > **theologically** adv

theorem n (pl -s) proposition that can be proved by reasoning

theorems n ▷ theorem

theoretical adj based on theory rather than practice or fact > **theoretically** adv

theoretically adv ▷ theoretical

theories n ▷ theory

theorist n ▷ theory

theorists n ▷ theory

theorize v (-zes, -zing, -zed) form theories, speculate

theorized v ▷ theorize

theorizes v ▷ theorize

theorizing v ▷ theorize

theory n (pl -ries) set of ideas to explain something > **theorist** n (pl -s)

theosophical adj ▷ theosophy

theosophies n ▷ theosophy

theosophy n (pl -phies) religious or philosophical system claiming to be based on intuitive insight into the divine nature

> **theosophical** adj

therapeutic [ther-rap-pew-tik] adj curing

therapeutics n art of curing

therapies n ▷ therapy

therapist n ▷ therapy

therapists n ▷ therapy

therapy n (pl -pies) curing treatment > **therapist** n (pl -s)

there adv in or to that place

thereby adv by that means

therefore adv consequently, that being so

thereupon adv immediately after that

therm n (pl -s) unit of measurement of heat

thermal adj of heat ▸ n (pl -s) rising current of warm air

thermals n ▷ thermal

thermodynamics n scientific study of the relationship between heat and other forms of energy

thermometer n (pl -s) instrument for measuring temperature

thermometers n ▷ thermometer

thermonuclear adj involving nuclear fusion

thermoplastic adj (of a plastic) softening when heated and resetting on cooling

thermosetting adj (of a plastic) remaining hard when heated

thermostat n (pl -s) device for automatically regulating temperature > **thermostatic** adj

thermostatic adj ▷ thermostat

thermostats n ▷ thermostat

therms n ▷ therm

thesaurus [thiss-sore-uss] n (pl -ruses) book containing lists of synonyms and related words

thesauruses n ▷ thesaurus

these adj, pron ▷ this

theses n ▷ thesis

thesis n (pl theses) written work submitted for a degree

thespian n (pl -s) actor or actress ▸ adj of the theatre

thespians n ▷ thespian

they pron refers to: people or things other than the speaker or people addressed

thiamine n (pl -s) vitamin found in the outer coat of rice and other grains

thiamines n ▷ thiamine

thick adj (-er, -est) of great or specified extent from one side to the other > **thickly** adv

thicken v (-s, -ing, -ed) make or become thick or thicker

thickened v ▷ thicken

thickening v ▷ thicken

thickens v ▷ thicken

thicker *adj* ▷ thick
thickest *adj* ▷ thick
thicket *n* (*pl* **-s**) dense growth of small trees
  thickets *n* ▷ thicket
  thickly *adv* ▷ thick
thickness *n* (*pl* **-es**) state of being thick
  thicknesses *n* ▷ thickness
thickset *adj* stocky in build
thief *n* (*pl* **thieves**) person who steals
thieve *v* (**-ves, -ving, -ved**) steal ▷ **thieving** *adj*
  thieved *v* ▷ thieve
  thieves *v* ▷ thieve ▶ *n* ▷ thief
  thieving *v, adj* ▷ thieve
thigh *n* (*pl* **-s**) upper part of the human leg
  thighs *n* ▷ thigh
thimble *n* (*pl* **-s**) cap protecting the end of the
  finger when sewing
  thimbles *n* ▷ thimble
thin *adj* (**-nner, -nnest**) not thick ▶ *v* (**-s, -nning,
  -nned**) make or become thin ▷ **thinly** *adv*
  ▷ **thinness** *n* (*pl* **-es**)
thine *pron, adj* (*Obs*) (something) of or
  associated with you (thou)
thing *n* (*pl* **-s**) material object
things *n* ▷ thing ▶ *pl n* possessions, clothes,
  etc.
think *v* (**-s, -ing, thought**) consider, judge,
  or believe ▷ **thinker** *n* (*pl* **-s**) ▷ **thinking** *adj,*
  n (*pl* **-s**)
  thinker *n* ▷ think
  thinkers *n* ▷ think
  thinking *v, adj, n* ▷ think
  thinkings *n* ▷ think
  thinks *v* ▷ think
  thinly *adv* ▷ thin
  thinned *v* ▷ thin
  thinner *adj* ▷ thin
  thinness *n* ▷ thin
  thinnesses *n* ▷ thin
  thinnest *adj* ▷ thin
  thinning *v* ▷ thin
  thins *v* ▷ thin
third *adj* of number three in a series ▶ *n* (*pl* **-s**)
  one of three equal parts
  thirds *n* ▷ third
thirst *n* (*pl* **-s**) desire to drink ▶ *v* (**-s, -ing, -ed**)
  feel thirst ▷ **thirsty** *adj* (**-tier, -tiest**) ▷ **thirstily**
  adv
  thirsted *v* ▷ thirst
  thirstier *adj* ▷ thirst
  thirstiest *adj* ▷ thirst
  thirstily *adv* ▷ thirst
  thirsting *v* ▷ thirst
  thirsts *n, v* ▷ thirst
  thirsty *adj* (**-tier, -tiest**) ▷ thirst

thirteen *adj, n* (*pl* **-s**) three plus ten
  ▷ **thirteenth** *adj, n* (*pl* **-s**)
  thirteens *n* ▷ thirteen
  thirteenth *n* ▷ thirteen
  thirteenths *n* ▷ thirteen
  thirties *n* ▷ thirty
  thirtieth *n* ▷ thirty
  thirtieths *n* ▷ thirty
thirty *adj, n* (*pl* **-ties**) three times ten
  ▷ **thirtieth** *adj, n* (*pl* **-s**)
this *adj, pron* used to refer to a thing or person
  nearby, just mentioned, or about to be
  mentioned ▶ *adj* used to refer to the present
  time
thistle *n* (*pl* **-s**) prickly plant with dense flower
  heads
  thistles *n* ▷ thistle
thither *adv* (*Obs*) to or towards that place
thong *n* (*pl* **-s**) thin strip of leather etc.
  thongs *n* ▷ thong
  thoraces *n* ▷ thorax
  thoracic *adj* ▷ thorax
thorax *n* (*pl* **-xes, -races**) part of the body
  between the neck and the abdomen
  ▷ **thoracic** *adj*
  thoraxes *n* ▷ thorax
thorn *n* (*pl* **-s**) prickle on a plant ▷ **thorny** *adj*
  (**-ier, -iest**)
  thornier *adj* ▷ thorn
  thorniest *adj* ▷ thorn
  thorns *n* ▷ thorn
  thorny *adj* ▷ thorn
thorough *adj* complete ▷ **thoroughly** *adv*
  ▷ **thoroughness** *n* (*pl* **-es**)
thoroughbred *n* (*pl* **-s**) ▶ *adj* (animal) of pure
  breed
  thoroughbreds *n* ▷ thoroughbred
thoroughfare *n* (*pl* **-s**) way through from one
  place to another
  thoroughfares *n* ▷ thoroughfare
  thoroughly *adv* ▷ thorough
  thoroughness *n* ▷ thorough
  thoroughnesses *n* ▷ thorough
those *adj, pron* ▷ that
thou *pron* (*Obs*) you
though *conj* despite the fact that ▶ *adv*
  nevertheless
thought *v* ▷ think ▶ *n* (*pl* **-s**) thinking
  ▷ **thoughtful** *adj* considerate
  thoughtful *adj* ▷ thought
thoughtless *adj* inconsiderate
  thoughts *n* ▷ thought
thousand *adj, n* (*pl* **-s**) ten hundred
  thousands *n* ▷ thousand
thousandth *adj, n* (*pl* **-s**) (of) number one

thousand in a series

thousandths *n* ▷ **thousandth**

thrall *n* (*pl* -s) state of being in the power of another person

thralls *n* ▷ **thrall**

thrash *v* (-es, -ing, -ed) beat, esp. with a stick or whip

thrashed *v* ▷ **thrash**

thrashes *v* ▷ **thrash**

thrashing *n* (*pl* -s) severe beating ▶ *v* ▷ **thrash**

thread *n* (*pl* -s) fine strand or yarn ▶ *v* (-s, -ing, -ed) pass thread through

threadbare *adj* (of fabric) with the nap worn off

threaded *v* ▷ **thread**

threading *v* ▷ **thread**

threads *n*, *v* ▷ **thread**

threat *n* (*pl* -s) declaration of intent to harm

threaten *v* (-s, -ing, -ed) make or be a threat to

threatened *v* ▷ **threaten**

threatening *v* ▷ **threaten**

threatens *v* ▷ **threaten**

threats *n* ▷ **threat**

three *adj*, *n* (*pl* -s) one more than two

threes *n* ▷ **three**

threesome *n* (*pl* -s) group of three

threesomes *n* ▷ **threesome**

threnodies *n* ▷ **threnody**

threnody *n* (*pl* -dies) lament for the dead

thresh *v* (-es, -ing, -ed) beat (wheat etc.) to separate the grain from the husks and straw

threshed *v* ▷ **thresh**

threshes *v* ▷ **thresh**

threshing *v* ▷ **thresh**

threshold *n* (*pl* -s) bar forming the bottom of a doorway

thresholds *n* ▷ **threshold**

threw *v* ▷ **throw**

thrice *adv* (Lit) three times

thrift *n* (*pl* -s) wisdom and caution with money > **thrifty** *adj*

thrifts *n* ▷ **thrift**

thrifty *adj* ▷ **thrif**

thrill *n* (*pl* -s) sudden feeling of excitement ▶ *v* (-s, -ing, -ed) (cause to) feel a thrill > **thrilling** *adj*

thrilled *v* ▷ **thrill**

thriller *n* (*pl* -s) book, film, etc. with an atmosphere of mystery or suspense

thrillers *n* ▷ **thriller**

thrilling *v*, *adj* ▷ **thrill**

thrills *n*, *v* ▷ **thrill**

thrive *v* (-ves, -ving, -ved *or* **throve**, **thrived** *or* **thriven**) flourish or prosper

thrived *v* ▷ **thrive**

thriven *v* ▷ **thrive**

thrives *v* ▷ **thrive**

thriving *v* ▷ **thrive**

throat *n* (*pl* -s) passage from the mouth and nose to the stomach and lungs

throatier *adj* ▷ **throaty**

throatiest *adj* ▷ **throaty**

throats *n* ▷ **throat**

throaty *adj* (-tier, -tiest) (of the voice) hoarse

throb *v* (-s, -bbing, -bbed) pulsate repeatedly ▶ *n* (*pl* -s) throbbing

throbbed *v* ▷ **throb**

throbbing *v* ▷ **throb**

throbs *v*, *n* ▷ **throb**

throes *pl n* violent pangs or pains

thrombosis *n* (*pl* -oses) forming of a clot in a blood vessel or the heart

thromboses *n* ▷ **thrombosis**

throne *n* (*pl* -s) ceremonial seat of a monarch or bishop

thrones *n* ▷ **throne**

throng *n* (*pl* -s) ▶ *v* (-s, -ing, -ed) crowd

thronged *v* ▷ **throng**

thronging *v* ▷ **throng**

throngs *n*, *v* ▷ **throng**

throstle *n* (*pl* -s) song thrush

throstles *n* ▷ **throstle**

throttle *n* (*pl* -s) device controlling the amount of fuel entering an engine ▶ *v* (-les, -ling, -led) strangle

throttled *v* ▷ **throttle**

throttles *n*, *v* ▷ **throttle**

throttling *v* ▷ **throttle**

through *prep* from end to end or side to side of ▶ *adj* finished

throughout *prep*, *adv* in every part (of)

throughput *n* (*pl* -s) amount of material processed

throughputs *n* ▷ **throughput**

throve *v* ▷ **thrive**

throw *v* (-s, -ing, **threw**, **thrown**) hurl through the air ▶ *n* (*pl* -s) throwing

throwaway *adj* done or said casually

throwback *n* (*pl* -s) person or thing that reverts to an earlier type

throwbacks *n* ▷ **throwback**

throwing *v* ▷ **throw**

thrown *v* ▷ **throw**

throws *v*, *n* ▷ **throw**

thrush[1] *n* (*pl* -es) brown songbird

thrush[2] *n* (*pl* -es) fungal disease of the mouth or vagina

thrushes *n* ▷ **thrush**[1, 2]

thrust *v* (-s, -ing, **thrust**) push forcefully ▶ *n* (*pl* -s) forceful stab

thrusting v ▷ thrust
thrusts v, n ▷ thrust
thud n (pl -s) dull heavy sound ▶ v (-s, -dding, -dded) make such a sound
thudded v ▷ thud
thudding v ▷ thud
thuds n, v ▷ thud
thug n (pl -s) violent man, esp. a criminal > **thuggery** n (pl -ries) > **thuggish** adj
thuggeries n ▷ thug
thuggery n ▷ thug
thuggish adj ▷ thug
thugs n ▷ thug
thumb n (pl -s) short thick finger set apart from the others ▶ v (-s, -ing, -ed) touch or handle with the thumb
thumbed v ▷ thumb
thumbing v ▷ thumb
thumbs n, v ▷ thumb
thump n (pl -s) (sound of) a dull heavy blow ▶ v (-s, -ing, -ed) strike heavily
thumped v ▷ thump
thumping v ▷ thump
thumps n, v ▷ thump
thunder n (pl -s) loud noise accompanying lightning ▶ v (-s, -ing, -ed) rumble with thunder > **thunderous** adj > **thundery** (-rier, -riest) adj
thunderbolt n (pl -s) lightning flash
thunderbolts n ▷ thunderbolt
thunderclap n (pl -s) peal of thunder
thunderclaps n ▷ thunderclap
thundered v ▷ thunder
thunderier adj ▷ thunder
thunderiest adj ▷ thunder
thundering v ▷ thunder
thunderous adj ▷ thunder
thunders v, n ▷ thunder
thunderstruck adj amazed
thundery adj ▷ thunder
thus adv therefore
thwack v (-s, -ing, -ed) ▶ n (pl -s) whack
thwacked v ▷ thwack
thwacking v ▷ thwack
thwacks v, n ▷ thwack
thwart v (-s, -ing, -ed) foil or frustrate ▶ n (pl -s) seat across a boat
thwarted v ▷ thwart
thwarting v ▷ thwart
thwarts v, n ▷ thwart
thy adj (Obs) of or associated with you (thou)
thylacine n (pl -s) extinct doglike Tasmanian marsupial
thylacines n ▷ thylacine
thyme [time] n (pl -s) aromatic herb

thymes n ▷ thyme
thymi n ▷ thymus
thymus n (pl -muses, -mi) small gland at the base of the neck
thymuses n ▷ thymus
thyroid adj, n (pl -s) (of) a gland in the neck controlling body growth
thyroids n ▷ thyroid
thyself pron (Obs) ▷ thou

> **ti** n (tis). Ti means the same as **te**. This is a useful word when you want to form words in more than one direction. Ti scores 2 points.

tiara n (pl -s) semicircular jewelled headdress
tiaras n ▷ tiara
tibia n (pl -biae, -bias) inner bone of the lower leg > **tibial** adj
tibiae n ▷ tibia
tibial adj ▷ tibia
tibias n ▷ tibia
tic n (pl -s) spasmodic muscular twitch
tick[1] n (pl -s) mark (✓) used to check off or indicate the correctness of something ▶ v (-s, -ing, -ed) mark with a tick
tick[2] n (pl -s) tiny bloodsucking parasitic animal
tick[3] n (pl -s) (Informal) credit or account
ticked v ▷ tick[1]
ticket n (pl -s) card or paper entitling the holder to admission, travel, etc. (CHIEFLY US & NZ) ▶ v (-s, -ing, -ed) attach or issue a ticket to
ticketed v ▷ ticket
ticketing v ▷ ticket
tickets n, v ▷ ticket
ticking n (pl -s) strong material for mattress covers ▶ v ▷ tick[1]
tickings n ▷ ticking
tickle v (-les, -ling, -led) touch or stroke (a person) to produce laughter ▶ n (pl -s) tickling
tickled v ▷ tickle
tickles v, n ▷ tickle
tickling v ▷ tickle
ticklish adj sensitive to tickling
ticks v ▷ tick[1] ▶ n ▷ tick[1, 2, 3]
ticktack n (pl -s) (BRIT) bookmakers' sign language
ticktacks n ▷ ticktack
tics n ▷ tic
tidal adj ▷ tide
tiddler n (pl -s) (Informal) very small fish
tiddlers n ▷ tiddler
tiddlier adj ▷ tiddly[1, 2]
tiddliest adj ▷ tiddly[1, 2]
tiddly[1] adj (-dlier, -dliest) tiny
tiddly[2] adj (-dlier, -dliest) (Informal) slightly

drunk

tiddlywink n small plastic disc

tiddlywinks n game in which players try to flip small plastic discs into a cup

tide n (pl -s) rise and fall of the sea caused by the gravitational pull of the sun and moon > **tidal** adj

tides n ▷ tide

tidied v ▷ tidy

tidier adj ▷ tidy

tidies v ▷ tidy

tidiest adj ▷ tidy

tidily adv ▷ tidy

tidiness n ▷ tidy

tidinesses n ▷ tidy

tidings pl n news

tidy adj (-dier, -diest) neat and orderly ▶ v (-dies, -dying, -died) put in order > **tidily** adv > **tidiness** n (pl -es)

tidying v ▷ tidy

tie v (ties, tying, tied) fasten or be fastened with string, rope, etc. ▶ n (pl -s) long narrow piece of material worn knotted round the neck

tied v ▷ tie ▶ adj (BRIT) (of a cottage etc.) rented to the tenant only as long as he or she is employed by the owner

tier n (pl -s) one of a set of rows placed one above and behind the other

tiers n ▷ tier

ties v, n ▷ tie

tiff n (pl -s) petty quarrel

tiffs n ▷ tiff

tiger n (pl -s) large yellow-and-black striped Asian cat

tigers n ▷ tiger

tight adj (-er, -est) stretched or drawn taut > **tightly** adv

tighten v (-s, -ing, -ed) make or become tight or tighter

tightened v ▷ tighten

tightening v ▷ tighten

tightens v ▷ tighten

tighter adj ▷ tight

tightest adj ▷ tight

tightly adv ▷ tight

tightrope n (pl -s) rope stretched taut on which acrobats perform

tightropes n ▷ tightrope

tights pl n one-piece clinging garment covering the body from the waist to the feet

tigress n (pl -s) female tiger

tigresses n ▷ tigress

tiki n (pl -s) (NZ) small carving of a grotesque person worn as a pendant

tikis n ▷ tiki

tikka adj (INDIAN COOKERY) marinated in spices and dry-roasted

tilde n (pl -s) mark (~) used in Spanish to indicate that the letter 'n' is to be pronounced in a particular way

tildes n ▷ tilde

tile n (pl -s) flat piece of ceramic, plastic, etc. used to cover a roof, floor, or wall ▶ v (-les, -ling, -led) cover with tiles > **tiled** adj

tiled v, adj ▷ tile

tiles n, v ▷ tile

tiling n (pl -s) tiles collectively ▶ v ▷ tile

tilings n ▷ tiling

till[1] conj, prep until

till[2] v (-s, -ing, -ed) cultivate (land) > **tillage** n (pl -s)

till[3] n (pl -s) drawer for money, usu. in a cash register

tillage n ▷ till[2]

tillages n ▷ till[2]

tilled v ▷ till[2]

tiller n (pl -s) lever to move a rudder of a boat

tillers n ▷ tiller

tilling v ▷ till[2]

tills v ▷ till[2] ▶ n ▷ till[3]

tilt v (-s, -ing, -ed) slant at an angle ▶ n (pl -s) slope

tilted v ▷ tilt

tilting v ▷ tilt

tilts v, n ▷ tilt

timber n (pl -s) wood as a building material > **timbered** adj

timbered adj ▷ timber

timbers n ▷ timber

timbre [tam-bra] n (pl -s) distinctive quality of sound of a voice or instrument

timbres n ▷ timbre

time n (pl -s) past, present, and future as a continuous whole ▶ v (-mes, -ming, -med) note the time taken by

timed v ▷ time

timeless adj unaffected by time

timelier adj ▷ timely

timeliest adj ▷ timely

timely adj (-lier, -liest) at the appropriate time

timepiece n (pl -s) watch or clock

timepieces n ▷ timepiece

times n, v ▷ time

timeserver n (pl -s) person who changes his or her views to gain support or favour

timeservers n ▷ timeserver

timetable n (pl -s) plan showing the times when something takes place, the departure and arrival times of trains or buses, etc.

timetables *n* ▷ timetable

timid *adj* (**-er, -est**) easily frightened ▷ **timidly**
adv ▷ **timidity** *n* (*pl* **-dies**)
  timider *adj* ▷ timid
  timidest *adj* ▷ timid
  timidities *n* ▷ timid
  timidity *n* ▷ timid
  timidly *adv* ▷ timid

timing *v* ▷ time

timorous *adj* timid

timpani [tim-pan-ee] *pl n* set of kettledrums
  ▷ **timpanist** *n* (*pl* **-s**)
  timpanist *n* ▷ timpani
  timpanists *n* ▷ timpani

tin *n* (*pl* **-s**) soft metallic element

tincture *n* (*pl* **-s**) medicinal extract in a
solution of alcohol
  tinctures *n* ▷ tincture

tinder *n* (*pl* **-s**) dry easily-burning material
used to start a fire ▷ **tinderbox** *n* (*pl* **-es**)
  tinderbox *n* ▷ tinder
  tinderboxes *n* ▷ tinder
  tinders *n* ▷ tinder

tine *n* (*pl* **-s**) prong of a fork or antler
  tines *n* ▷ tine

ting *n* (*pl* **-s**) high metallic sound, as of a small
bell

tinge *n* (*pl* **-s**) slight tint ▶ *v* (**-ges, -geing, -ged**)
give a slight tint or trace to
  tinged *v* ▷ tinge
  tinges *n*, *v* ▷ tinge
  tinging *v* ▷ tinge

tingle *v* (**-les, -ling, -led**) ▶ *n* (*pl* **-s**) (feel) a
prickling or stinging sensation
  tingled *v* ▷ tingle
  tingles *v*, *n* ▷ tingle
  tingling *v* ▷ tingle
  tings *n* ▷ ting
  tinier *adj* ▷ tiny
  tiniest *adj* ▷ tiny

tinker *n* (*pl* **-s**) travelling mender of pots and
pans ▶ *v* (**-s, -ing, -ed**) fiddle with (an engine
etc.) in an attempt to repair it
  tinkered *v* ▷ tinker
  tinkering *v* ▷ tinker
  tinkers *n*, *v* ▷ tinker

tinkle *v* (**-les, -ling, -led**) ring with a high tinny
sound like a small bell ▶ *n* (*pl* **-s**) this sound
or action
  tinkled *v* ▷ tinkle
  tinkles *v*, *n* ▷ tinkle
  tinkling *v* ▷ tinkle

tinned *adj* (of food) preserved by being sealed
in a tin
  tinnier *adj* ▷ tinny

  tinniest *adj* ▷ tinny

tinny *adj* (**-nnier, -nniest**) (of sound) thin and
metallic

tinpot *adj* (*Informal*) worthless or unimportant
  tins *n* ▷ tin

tinsel *n* (*pl* **-s**) decorative metallic strips or
threads
  tinsels *n* ▷ tinsel

tint *n* (*pl* **-s**) (pale) shade of a colour ▶ *v* (**-s, -ing,
-ed**) give a tint to
  tinted *v* ▷ tint
  tinting *v* ▷ tint
  tints *n*, *v* ▷ tint

tiny *adj* (**-ier, -iest**) very small

tip^1 *n* (*pl* **-s**) narrow or pointed end of anything
▶ *v* (**-s, -pping, -pped**) put a tip on

tip^2 *n* (*pl* **-s**) money given in return for service
▶ *v* (**-s, -pping, -pped**) give a tip to

tip^3 *v* (**-s, -pping, -pped**) tilt or overturn ▶ *n* (*pl*
-s) rubbish dump
  tipped *v* ▷ tip$^{1, 2, 3}$
  tipping *v* ▷ tip$^{1, 2, 3}$

tipple *v* (**-les, -ling, -led**) drink alcohol
habitually, esp. in small quantities ▶ *n* (*pl* **-s**)
alcoholic drink ▷ **tippler** *n* (*pl* **-s**)
  tippled *v* ▷ tipple
  tippler *n* ▷ tipple
  tipplers *n* ▷ tipple
  tipples *v*, *n* ▷ tipple
  tippling *v* ▷ tipple

tips *n*, *v* ▷ tip$^{1, 2, 3}$
  tipsier *adj* ▷ tipsy
  tipsiest *adj* ▷ tipsy

tipster *n* (*pl* **-s**) person who sells tips about
races
  tipsters *n* ▷ tipster

tipsy *adj* (**-sier, -siest**) slightly drunk

tiptoe *v* (**-toes, -toeing, -toed**) walk quietly
with the heels off the ground
  tiptoed *v* ▷ tiptoe
  tiptoeing *v* ▷ tiptoe
  tiptoes *v* ▷ tiptoe

tiptop *adj* of the highest quality or condition

tirade *n* (*pl* **-s**) long angry speech
  tirades *n* ▷ tirade

tire *v* (**-res, -ring, -red**) reduce the energy of, as
by exertion ▷ **tiring** *adj*

tired *adj* (**-er, -est**) exhausted ▶ *v* ▷ **tire**
  tireder *adj* ▷ tired
  tiredest *adj* ▷ tired

tireless *adj* energetic and determined
  tires *v* ▷ tire

tiresome *adj* boring and irritating
  tiring *v*, *adj* ▷ tire

tissue *n* (*pl* **-s**) substance of an animal body

or plant
tissues n ▷ tissue

tit[1] n (pl -s) any of various small songbirds

tit[2] n (pl -s) (SLANG) female breast

titanic adj huge or very important

titanium n (pl -s) (CHEM) strong light metallic element used to make alloys
  titaniums n ▷ titanium

titbit n (pl -s) tasty piece of food
  titbits n ▷ titbit

tithe n (pl -s) esp. formerly, one tenth of one's income or produce paid to the church as a tax
  tithes n ▷ tithe

titian [tish-an] adj (of hair) reddish-gold

titillate v (-tes, -ting, -ted) excite or stimulate pleasurably ▸ **titillating** adj > **titillation** n (pl -s)
  titillated v ▷ titillate
  titillates v ▷ titillate
  titillating v, adj ▷ titillate
  titillation n ▷ titillate
  titillations n ▷ titillate

titivate v (-tes, -ting, -ted) smarten up
  titivated v ▷ titivate
  titivates v ▷ titivate
  titivating v ▷ titivate

title n (pl -s) name of a book, film, etc.

titled adj aristocratic
  titles n ▷ title
  tits n ▷ tit[1, 2]

titter v (-s, -ing, -ed) laugh in a suppressed way ▸ n (pl -s) suppressed laugh
  tittered v ▷ titter
  tittering v ▷ titter
  titters v, n ▷ titter

titular adj in name only
  tizzies n ▷ tizzy

tizzy n (pl -zies) (Informal) confused or agitated state

> **tix** pl n. Tix is an informal word for **tickets**. This is a good word if you are struggling to use an X towards the end of a game.

to prep indicating movement towards, equality or comparison, etc. ▸ adv to a closed position

toad n (pl -s) animal like a large frog
  toadied v ▷ toady
  toadies n, v ▷ toady
  toads n ▷ toad

toadstool n (pl -s) poisonous fungus like a mushroom
  toadstools n ▷ toadstool

toady n (pl -dies) ingratiating person ▸ v (-dies, -dying, -died) be ingratiating

toadying v ▷ toady

toast[1] n (pl -s) sliced bread browned by heat ▸ v (-s, -ing, -ed) brown (bread) by heat

toast[2] n (pl -s) tribute or proposal of health or success marked by people raising glasses and drinking together ▸ v (-s, -ing, -ed) drink a toast to

toasted v, n ▷ toast[1, 2]

toaster n (pl -s) electrical device for toasting bread
  toasters n ▷ toaster
  toasting n, v ▷ toast[1, 2]
  toasts n, v ▷ toast[1, 2]

tobacco n (pl -os, -oes) plant with large leaves dried for smoking
  tobaccoes n ▷ tobacco

tobacconist n (pl -s) person or shop selling tobacco, cigarettes, etc.
  tobacconists n ▷ tobacconist
  tobaccos n ▷ tobacco

toboggan n (pl -s) narrow sledge for sliding over snow ▸ v (-s, -ing, -ed) ride a toboggan
  tobogganed v ▷ toboggan
  tobogganing v ▷ toboggan
  toboggans n, v ▷ toboggan

toccata [tok-kah-ta] n (pl -s) rapid piece of music for a keyboard instrument
  toccatas n ▷ toccata

today n (pl -s) this day ▸ adv on this day
  todays n ▷ today
  toddies n ▷ toddy

toddle v (-les, -ling, -led) walk with short unsteady steps
  toddled v ▷ toddle

toddler n (pl -s) child beginning to walk
  toddlers n ▷ toddler
  toddles v ▷ toddle
  toddling v ▷ toddle

toddy n (pl -dies) sweetened drink of spirits and hot water

toe n (pl -s) digit of the foot ▸ v (toes, toeing, toed) touch or kick with the toe
  toed v ▷ toe
  toeing v ▷ toe
  toes n, v ▷ toe

toff n (pl -s) (BRIT) (Slang) well-dressed or upper-class person

toffee n (pl -s) chewy sweet made of boiled sugar
  toffees n ▷ toffee
  toffs n ▷ toff

tofu n (pl -s) soft food made from soya-bean curd
  tofus n ▷ tofu

tog n (pl -s) unit for measuring the insulating

power of duvets

toga [**toe**-ga] *n* (*pl* -s) garment worn by citizens of ancient Rome

togas *n* ▷ toga

together *adv* in company ▶ *adj* (*Informal*) organized

toggle *n* (*pl* -s) small bar-shaped button inserted through a loop for fastening

toggles *n* ▷ toggle

togs *n* ▷ tog

toil *n* (*pl* -s) hard work ▶ *v* (-s, -ing, -ed) work hard

toiled *v* ▷ toil

toilet *n* (*pl* -s) (room with) a bowl connected to a drain for receiving and disposing of urine and faeces

toiletries *n* ▷ toiletry

toiletry *n* (*pl* -ries) object or cosmetic used to clean or groom oneself

toilets *n* ▷ toilet

toiling *v* ▷ toil

toils *n*, *v* ▷ toil

token *n* (*pl* -s) sign or symbol ▶ *adj* nominal or slight

tokenism *n* (*pl* -s) policy of making only a token effort, esp. to comply with a law

tokenisms *n* ▷ tokenism

tokens *n* ▷ token

told *v* ▷ tell

tolerable *adj* bearable > **tolerably** *adv*

tolerably *adv* ▷ tolerable

tolerance *n* (*pl* -s) acceptance of other people's rights to their own opinions or actions > **tolerant** *adj* > **tolerantly** *adv* > **toleration** *n* (*pl* -s)

tolerances *n* ▷ tolerance

tolerant *adj* ▷ tolerance

tolerantly *adv* ▷ tolerance

tolerate *v* (-tes, -ting, -ted) allow to exist or happen

tolerated *v* ▷ tolerate

tolerates *v* ▷ tolerate

tolerating *v* ▷ tolerate

toleration *n* ▷ tolerance

tolerations *n* ▷ tolerance

toll[1] *v* (-s, -ing, -ed) ring (a bell) slowly and regularly, esp. to announce a death ▶ *n* (*pl* -s) tolling

toll[2] *n* (*pl* -s) charge for the use of a bridge or road

tolled *v* ▷ toll[1]

tolling *v* ▷ toll[1]

tolls *n* ▷ toll[1, 2] ▶ *v* ▷ toll[1]

tom *n* (*pl* -s) male cat

tomahawk *n* (*pl* -s) fighting axe of the Native Americans

tomahawks *n* ▷ tomahawk

tomato *n* (*pl* -es) red fruit used in salads and as a vegetable

tomatoes *n* ▷ tomato

tomb *n* (*pl* -s) grave

tombola *n* (*pl* -s) lottery with tickets drawn from a revolving drum

tombolas *n* ▷ tombola

tomboy *n* (*pl* -s) girl who acts or dresses like a boy

tomboys *n* ▷ tomboy

tombs *n* ▷ tomb

tombstone *n* (*pl* -s) gravestone

tombstones *n* ▷ tombstone

tome *n* (*pl* -s) large heavy book

tomes *n* ▷ tome

tomfooleries *n* ▷ tomfoolery

tomfoolery *n* (*pl* -ries) foolish behaviour

tomorrow *adv*, *n* (*pl* -s) (on) the day after today

tomorrows *n* ▷ tomorrow

toms *n* ▷ tom

ton *n* (*pl* -s) unit of weight equal to 2240 pounds or 1016 kilograms or, in the US, 2000 pounds or 907 kilograms

tonal *adj* (MUSIC) written in a key > **tonality** *n* (*pl* -ties)

tonalities *n* ▷ tonal

tonality *n* ▷ tonal

tone *n* (*pl* -s) sound with reference to its pitch, volume, etc. ▶ *v* (-nes, -ning, -ned) harmonize (with) > **toneless** *adj*

toned *v* ▷ tone

toneless *adj* ▷ tone

tones *n*, *v* ▷ tone

tongs *pl n* large pincers for grasping and lifting

tongue *n* (*pl* -s) muscular organ in the mouth, used in speaking and tasting

tongues *n* ▷ tongue

tonic *n* (*pl* -s) medicine to improve body tone ▶ *adj* invigorating

tonics *n* ▷ tonic

tonight *adv*, *n* (*pl* -s) (in or during) the night or evening of this day

tonights *n* ▷ tonight

toning *v* ▷ tone

tonnage *n* (*pl* -s) weight capacity of a ship

tonnages *n* ▷ tonnage

tonne [tunn] *n* (*pl* -s) unit of weight equal to 1000 kilograms

tonnes *n* ▷ tonne

tons *n* ▷ ton

tonsil *n* (*pl* -s) small gland in the throat

tonsillectomies *n* ▷ tonsillectomy

tonsillectomy *n* (*pl* -mies) surgical removal

of the tonsils

tonsillitis n (pl -tises) inflammation of the tonsils

tonsillitises n ▷ tonsillitis

tonsils n ▷ tonsil

tonsure n (pl -s) shaving of all or the top of the head as a religious or monastic practice > tonsured adj

tonsured adj ▷ tonsure

tonsures n ▷ tonsure

too adv also, as well

took v ▷ take

tool n (pl -s) implement used by hand

tools n ▷ tool

toot n (pl -s) short hooting sound ▶ v (-s, -ing, -ed) (cause to) make such a sound

tooted v ▷ toot

tooth n (pl teeth) bonelike projection in the jaws of most vertebrates for biting and chewing > toothless adj

toothless adj ▷ tooth

toothpaste n (pl -s) paste used to clean the teeth

toothpastes n ▷ toothpaste

toothpick n (pl -s) small stick for removing scraps of food from between the teeth

toothpicks n ▷ toothpick

tooting v ▷ toot

toots n, v ▷ toot

top¹ n (pl -s) highest point or part ▶ adj at or of the top ▶ v (-s, -pping, -pped) form a top on

top² n (pl -s) toy which spins on a pointed base

topaz [toe-pazz] n (pl -es) semiprecious stone in various colours

topazes n ▷ topaz

topee, topi [toe-pee] n (pl -s) lightweight hat worn in tropical countries

topees n ▷ topee

topi n ▷ topee

topiaries n ▷ topiary

topiary [tope-yar-ee] n (pl -ries) art of trimming trees and bushes into decorative shapes

topic n (pl -s) subject of a conversation, book, etc.

topical adj relating to current events > topicality n (pl -ties)

topicalities n ▷ topical

topicality n ▷ topical

topics n ▷ topic

topis n ▷ topee

topless adj (of a costume or woman) with no covering for the breasts

topmost adj highest or best

topographer n ▷ topography

topographers n ▷ topography

topographical adj ▷ topography

topographies n ▷ topography

topography n (pl -phies) (science of describing) the surface features of a place > topographer n (pl -s) > topographical adj

topological adj ▷ topology

topologies n ▷ topology

topology n (pl -gies) geometry of the properties of a shape which are unaffected by continuous distortion > topological adj

topped n ▷ top¹

topping n (pl -s) sauce or garnish for food ▶ v ▷ top¹

toppings n ▷ topping

topple v (-les, -ling, -led) (cause to) fall over

toppled v ▷ topple

topples v ▷ topple

toppling v ▷ topple

top-notch adj excellent, first-class

tops n ▷ top¹, ² ▶ v ▷ top¹

topsoil n (pl -s) surface layer of soil

topsoils n ▷ topsoil

toque [toke] n (pl -s) small round hat

toques n ▷ toque

tor n (pl -s) high rocky hill

torch n (pl -es) small portable battery-powered lamp ▶ v (-es, -ing, -ed) (Informal) deliberately set (a building) on fire

torched v ▷ torch

torches n, v ▷ torch

torching v ▷ torch

tore v ▷ tear²

toreador [torr-ee-a-dor] n (pl -s) bullfighter

toreadors n ▷ toreador

torment v (-s, -ing, -ed) cause (someone) great suffering ▶ n (pl -s) great suffering > tormentor n (pl -s)

tormented v ▷ torment

tormenting v ▷ torment

tormentor n ▷ torment

tormentors n ▷ torment

torments v, n ▷ torment

torn v ▷ tear²

tornado n (pl -s, -es) violent whirlwind

tornadoes n ▷ tornado

tornados n ▷ tornado

torpedo n (pl -es) self-propelled underwater missile ▶ v (-es, -ing, -ed) attack or destroy with or as if with torpedoes

torpedoed v ▷ torpedo

torpedoes n, v ▷ torpedo

torpedoing v ▷ torpedo

torpid adj sluggish and inactive

torpor n (pl -s) torpid state

torpors n ▷ torpor

torque [tork] *n* (*pl* -s) force causing rotation
  torques *n* ▷ torque
torrent *n* (*pl* -s) rushing stream
torrential *adj* (of rain) very heavy
  torrents *n* ▷ torrent
torrid *adj* (-er, -est) very hot and dry
  torrider *adj* ▷ torrid
  torridest *adj* ▷ torrid
  tors *n* ▷ tor
torsion *n* (*pl* -s) twisting of a part by equal
  forces being applied at both ends but in
  opposite directions
  torsions *n* ▷ torsion
torso *n* (*pl* -s) trunk of the human body
  torsos *n* ▷ torso
tort *n* (*pl* -s) (LAW) civil wrong or injury for
  which damages may be claimed
tortilla *n* (*pl* -s) thin Mexican pancake
  tortillas *n* ▷ tortilla
tortoise *n* (*pl* -s) slow-moving land reptile with
  a dome-shaped shell
  tortoises *n* ▷ tortoise
tortoiseshell *n* (*pl* -s) mottled brown shell of
  a turtle, used for making ornaments ▶ *adj*
  having brown, orange, and black markings
  tortoiseshells *n* ▷ tortoiseshell
  torts *n* ▷ tort
tortuous *adj* winding or twisting
torture *v* (-res, -ring, -red) cause (someone)
  severe pain or mental anguish ▶ *n* (*pl* -s)
  severe physical or mental pain > **torturer**
  n (*pl* -s)
  tortured *v* ▷ torture
  torturer *n* ▷ torture
  torturers *n* ▷ torture
  tortures *v, n* ▷ torture
  torturing *v* ▷ torture
toss *v* (-es, -ing, -ed) throw lightly ▶ *n* (*pl* -es)
  tossing
  tossed *v* ▷ toss
  tosses *v, n* ▷ toss
  tossing *v* ▷ toss
tot[1] *n* (*pl* -s) small child
tot[2] *v* (-s, -tting, -tted) add (numbers) together
total *n* (*pl* -s) whole, esp. a sum of parts ▶ *adj*
  complete ▶ *v* (-s, -lling, -lled) amount to
  > **totally** *adv* > **totality** *n* (*pl* -ties)
totalitarian *adj* of a dictatorial one-party
  government > **totalitarianism** *n* (*pl* -s)
  totalitarianism *n* ▷ totalitarian
  totalitarianisms *n* ▷ totalitarian
  totalities *n* ▷ total
  totality *n* ▷ total
  totalled *v* ▷ total
  totalling *v* ▷ total

  totally *adv* ▷ total
  totals *n, v* ▷ total
tote[1] *v* (-tes, -ting, -ted) carry (a gun etc.)
tote[2] *n* (*pl* -s) ▷ totalizator
  toted *v* ▷ tote[1]
totem *n* (*pl* -s) tribal badge or emblem
  totems *n* ▷ totem
  totes *v* ▷ tote[1] ▶ *n* ▷ tote[2]
  toting *v* ▷ tote[1]
  tots *n* ▷ tot[1] ▶ *v* ▷ tot[2]
  totted *v* ▷ tot[2]
totter *v* (-s, -ing, -ed) move unsteadily
  tottered *v* ▷ totter
  tottering *v* ▷ totter
  totters *v* ▷ totter
  totting *v* ▷ tot[2]
toucan *n* (*pl* -s) tropical American bird with
  a large bill
  toucans *n* ▷ toucan
touch *v* (-es, -ing, -ed) come into contact
  with ▶ *n* (*pl* -es) sense by which an object's
  qualities are perceived when they come into
  contact with part of the body ▶ *adj* of a non-
  contact version of particular sport
touché [too-shay] *interj* acknowledgment of
  the striking home of a remark or witty reply
touched *adj* emotionally moved ▶ *v* ▷ touch
  touches *v, n* ▷ touch
  touchier *adj* ▷ touchy
  touchiest *adj* ▷ touchy
touching *adj* emotionally moving ▶ *v* ▷ touch
touchline *n* (*pl* -s) side line of the pitch in some
  games
  touchlines *n* ▷ touchline
touchstone *n* (*pl* -s) standard by which a
  judgment is made
  touchstones *n* ▷ touchstone
touchy *adj* (-chier, -chiest) easily offended
tough *adj* (-er, -est) strong or resilient ▶ *n* (*pl* -s)
  (*Informal*) rough violent person > **toughness**
  n (*pl* -es)
toughen *v* (-s, -ing, -ed) make or become
  tough or tougher
  toughened *v* ▷ toughen
  toughening *v* ▷ toughen
  toughens *v* ▷ toughen
  tougher *adj* ▷ tough
  toughest *adj* ▷ tough
  toughness *n* ▷ tough
  toughnesses *n* ▷ tough
  toughs *n* ▷ tough
toupee [too-pay] *n* (*pl* -s) small wig
  toupees *n* ▷ toupee
tour *n* (*pl* -s) journey visiting places of interest
  along the way ▶ *v* (-s, -ing, -ed) make a tour

(of)

toured v ▷ tour

touring v ▷ tour

tourism n (pl -s) tourist travel as an industry

tourisms n ▷ tourism

tourist n (pl -s) person travelling for pleasure

tourists n ▷ tourist

touristy adj (Informal) (often derogatory) full of tourists or tourist attractions

tournament n (pl -s) sporting competition with several stages to decide the overall winner

tournaments n ▷ tournament

tourniquet [tour-nick-kay] n (pl -s) something twisted round a limb to stop bleeding

tourniquets n ▷ tourniquet

tours n, v ▷ tour

tousled adj ruffled and untidy

tout [rhymes with **shout**] v (-s, -ing, -ed) seek business in a persistent manner ▶ n (pl -s) person who sells tickets for a popular event at inflated prices

touted v ▷ tout

touting v ▷ tout

touts v, n ▷ tout

tow[1] v (-s, -ing, -ed) drag, esp. by means of a rope ▶ n (pl -s) towing

tow[2] n (pl -s) fibre of hemp or flax

toward n ▷ towards

towards, toward prep in the direction of

towbar n (pl -s) metal bar on a car for towing vehicles

towbars n ▷ towbar

towed v ▷ tow[1]

towel n (pl -s) cloth for drying things

towelling n (pl -s) material used for making towels

towellings n ▷ towelling

towels n ▷ towel

tower n (pl -s) tall structure, often forming part of a larger building

towers n ▷ tower

towing v ▷ tow[1]

town n (pl -s) group of buildings larger than a village

towns n ▷ town

township n (pl -s) small town

townships n ▷ township

towpath n (pl -s) path beside a canal or river, originally for horses towing boats

towpaths n ▷ towpath

tows n ▷ tow[1, 2] ▷ v ▷ tow[1]

toxaemia [tox-seem-ya] n (pl -s) blood poisoning

toxaemias n ▷ toxaemia

toxic adj poisonous > **toxicity** n (pl -ties)

toxicities n ▷ toxic

toxicity n ▷ toxic

toxicologies n ▷ toxicology

toxicology n (pl -gies) study of poisons

toxin n (pl -s) poison of bacterial origin

toxins n ▷ toxin

toy n (pl -s) something designed to be played with ▶ adj (of a dog) of a variety much smaller than is normal for that breed ▶ v (-s, -ing, -ed) play

toyed v ▷ toy

toying v ▷ toy

toys n, v ▷ toy

trace v (-ces, -cing, -ced) track down and find ▶ n (pl -s) track left by something > **traceable** adj

traceable adj ▷ trace

traced v ▷ trace

tracer n (pl -s) projectile which leaves a visible trail

traceries n ▷ tracery

tracers n ▷ tracer

tracery n (pl -ries) pattern of interlacing lines

traces v, n ▷ trace ▶ pl n strap by which a horse pulls a vehicle

trachea [track-kee-a] n (pl -cheae) windpipe

tracheae n ▷ trachea

tracheotomies n ▷ tracheotomy

tracheotomy [track-ee-ot-a-mee] n (pl -mies) surgical incision into the trachea

tracing n (pl -s) traced copy ▶ v ▷ trace

track n (pl -s) rough road or path ▶ v (-s, -ing, -ed) follow the trail or path of

tracked v ▷ track

tracking v ▷ track

tracks n, v ▷ track

tracksuit n (pl -s) warm loose-fitting suit worn by athletes etc., esp. during training

tracksuits n ▷ tracksuit

tract[1] n (pl -s) wide area

tract[2] n (pl -s) pamphlet, esp. a religious one

tractable adj easy to manage or control

traction n (pl -s) pulling, esp. by engine power

tractions n ▷ traction

tractor n (pl -s) motor vehicle with large rear wheels for pulling farm machinery

tractors n ▷ tractor

tracts n ▷ tract[1, 2]

trade n (pl -s) buying, selling, or exchange of goods ▶ v (-des, -ding, -ded) buy and sell > **trader** n (pl -s) > **trading** n (pl -s)

traded v ▷ trade

trademark n (pl -s) (legally registered) name or symbol used by a firm to distinguish its goods

trademarks n ▷ trademark

trader n ▷ trade

traders n ▷ trade

trades n, v ▷ trade

tradesman n (pl -men) skilled worker

tradesmen n ▷ tradesman

trading v, n ▷ trade

tradings n ▷ trad

tradition n (pl -s) body of beliefs, customs, etc. handed down from generation to generation > **traditional** adj > **traditionally** adv

traditional adj ▷ tradition

traditionally adv ▷ tradition

traditions n ▷ tradition

traduce v (-ces, -cing, -ced) slander

traduced v ▷ traduce

traduces v ▷ traduce

traducing v ▷ traduce

traffic n (pl -s) vehicles coming and going on a road ▶ v (-s, -cking, -cked) trade, usu. illicitly > **trafficker** n (pl -s)

trafficked v ▷ traffic

trafficker n ▷ traffic

traffickers n ▷ traffic

trafficking v ▷ traffic

traffics n, v ▷ traffic

tragedian [traj-**jee**-dee-an], **tragedienne** [traj-jee-dee-**enn**] n (pl -s) person who acts in or writes tragedies

tragedians n ▷ tragedian

tragedies n ▷ tragedy

tragedy n (pl -dies) shocking or sad event

tragic adj of or like a tragedy > **tragically** adv

tragically adv ▷ tragic

tragicomedies n ▷ tragicomedy

tragicomedy n (pl -s) play with both tragic and comic elements

trail n (pl -s) path, track, or road ▶ v (-s, -ing, -ed) drag along the ground

trailed v ▷ trail

trailer n (pl -s) vehicle designed to be towed by another vehicle

trailers n ▷ trailer

trailing v ▷ trail

trails n, v ▷ trail

train v (-s, -ing, -ed) instruct in a skill ▶ n (pl -s) line of railway coaches or wagons drawn by an engine

trained v ▷ train

trainee n (pl -s) person being trained

trainees n ▷ trainee

trainer n (pl -s) person who trains an athlete or sportsman

trainers n ▷ trainer

training v ▷ train

trains v, n ▷ train

traipse v (-pses, -psing, -psed) (Informal) walk wearily

traipsed v ▷ traipse

traipses v ▷ traipse

traipsing v ▷ traipse

trait n (pl -s) characteristic feature

traitor n (pl -s) person guilty of treason or treachery > **traitorous** adj

traitorous adj ▷ traitor

traitors n ▷ traitor

traits n ▷ trait

trajectories n ▷ trajectory

trajectory n (pl -ries) line of flight, esp. of a projectile

tram n (pl -s) public transport vehicle powered by an overhead wire and running on rails laid in the road

tramlines pl n track for trams

tramp v (-s, -ing, -ed) travel on foot, hike ▶ n (pl -s) homeless person who travels on foot

tramped v ▷ tramp

tramping v ▷ tramp

trample v (-les, -ling, -led) tread on and crush

trampled v ▷ trample

tramples v ▷ trample

trampling v ▷ trample

trampoline n (pl -s) tough canvas sheet attached to a frame by springs, used by acrobats etc. ▶ v (-nes, -ning, -ned) bounce on a trampoline

trampolined v ▷ trampoline

trampolines n, v ▷ trampoline

trampolining v ▷ trampoline

tramps n ▷ tramp

trams n ▷ tram

trance n (pl -s) unconscious or dazed state

trances n ▷ trance

tranche n (pl -s) portion of something large, esp. a sum of money

tranches n ▷ tranche

tranquil adj (-ler, -lest) calm and quiet > **tranquilly** adv > **tranquillity** n (pl -ties)

tranquiller adj ▷ tough

tranquillest adj ▷ tough

tranquillities n ▷ tranquil

tranquillity n ▷ tranquil

tranquillize v (-zes, -zing, -zed) make calm

tranquillized v ▷ tranquillize

tranquillizer n (pl -s) drug which reduces anxiety or tension

tranquillizers n ▷ tranquillizer

tranquillizes v ▷ tranquillize

tranquillizing v ▷ tranquillize

tranquilly adv ▷ tranquil

transact v (-s, -ing, -ed) conduct or negotiate (a business deal)

  transacted v ▷ transact

  transacting v ▷ transact

transaction n (pl -s) business deal transacted

  transactions n ▷ transaction

  transacts v ▷ transact

transatlantic adj on, from, or to the other side of the Atlantic

transceiver n (pl -s) transmitter and receiver of radio or electronic signals

  transceivers n ▷ transceiver

transcend v (-s, -ing, -ed) rise above
  > **transcendence** n (pl -s) > **transcendent** adj

  transcended v ▷ transcend

  transcendence n ▷ transcend

  transcendences n ▷ transcend

  transcendent adj ▷ transcend

transcendental adj based on intuition rather than experience

  transcending v ▷ transcend

  transcends v ▷ transcend

transcribe v (-bes, -bing, -bed) write down (something said)

  transcribed v ▷ transcribe

  transcribes v ▷ transcribe

  transcribing v ▷ transcribe

transcript n (pl -s) copy

  transcripts n ▷ transcript

transducer n (pl -s) device that converts one form of energy to another

  transducers n ▷ transducer

transept n (pl -s) either of the two shorter wings of a cross-shaped church

  transepts n ▷ transept

transexual n ▷ transsexual

  transexuals n ▷ transsexual

transfer v (-fers, -ferring, -ferred) move or send from one person or place to another ▶ n (pl -s) transferring > **transferable** adj

  transferable adj ▷ transfer

transference n (pl -s) transferring

  transferences n ▷ transference

  transferred v ▷ transfer

  transferring v ▷ transfer

  transfers v, n ▷ transfer

  transfiguration n ▷ transfigure

  transfigurations n ▷ transfigure

transfigure v (-res, -ring, -red) change in appearance > **transfiguration** n (pl -s)

  transfigured v ▷ transfigure

  transfigures v ▷ transfigure

  transfiguring v ▷ transfigure

transfix v (-es, -ing, -ed) astound or stun

  transfixed v ▷ transfix

  transfixes v ▷ transfix

  transfixing v ▷ transfix

transform v (-s, -ing, -ed) change the shape or character of > **transformation** n (pl -s)

  transformation n ▷ transform

  transformations n ▷ transform

  transformed v ▷ transform

transformer n (pl -s) device for changing the voltage of an alternating current

  transformers n ▷ transformer

  transforming v ▷ transform

  transforms v ▷ transform

transfuse v (-ses, -sing, -sed) give a transfusion to

  transfused v ▷ transfuse

  transfuses v ▷ transfuse

  transfusing v ▷ transfuse

transfusion n (pl -s) injection of blood into the blood vessels of a patient

  transfusions n ▷ transfusion

transgress v (-es, -ing, -ed) break (a moral law) > **transgression** n (pl -s) > **transgressor** n (pl -s)

  transgressed v ▷ transgress

  transgresses v ▷ transgress

  transgressing v ▷ transgress

  transgression n ▷ transgress

  transgressions n ▷ transgress

  transgressor n ▷ transgress

  transgressors n ▷ transgress

  transience n ▷ transient

  transiences n ▷ transient

transient adj lasting only for a short time
  > **transience** n (pl -s)

transistor n (pl -s) semiconducting device used to amplify electric currents

  transistors n ▷ transistor

transit n (pl -s) movement from one place to another

transition n (pl -s) change from one state to another > **transitional** adj

  transitional adj ▷ transition

  transitions n ▷ transition

transitive adj (GRAMMAR) (of a verb) requiring a direct object

transitory adj not lasting long

  transits n ▷ transit

translate v (-tes, -ting, -ted) turn from one language into another > **translation** n (pl -s)
  > **translator** n (pl -s)

  translated v ▷ translate

  translates v ▷ translate

  translating v ▷ translate

  translation n ▷ translat

translations n ▷ translat
translator n ▷ translate
translators n ▷ translate
transliterate v (-tes, -ting, -ted) convert to the letters of a different alphabet
> **transliteration** n (pl -s)
transliterated v ▷ transliterate
transliterates v ▷ transliterate
transliterating v ▷ transliterate
transliteration n ▷ transliterate
translucence n ▷ translucence
translucences n ▷ translucent
translucencies n ▷ translucent
translucency n ▷ translucent
translucent adj letting light pass through, but not transparent > **translucency,**
translucence n (pl -cies, -ces)
transmigrate v (-tes, -ting, -ted) (of a soul) pass into another body > **transmigration** n (pl -s)
transmigrated v ▷ transmigrate
transmigrates v ▷ transmigrate
transmigrating v ▷ transmigrate
transmigration n ▷ transmigrate
transmigrations n ▷ transmigrate
transmission n (pl -s) transmitting
transmissions n ▷ transmission
transmit v (-mits, -mitting, -mitted) pass (something) from one person or place to another > **transmittable** adj > **transmitter** n (pl -s)
transmits v ▷ transmit
transmittable adj ▷ transmit
transmitted v ▷ transmit
transmitter n ▷ transmit
transmitters n ▷ transmit
transmitting v ▷ transmit
transmogrified v ▷ transmogrify
transmogrifies v ▷ transmogrify
transmogrify v (-fies, -fying, -fied) (Informal) change completely
transmogrifying v ▷ transmogrify
transmutation n ▷ transmute
transmutations n ▷ transmute
transmute v (-tes, -ting, -ted) change the form or nature of > **transmutation** n (pl -s)
transmuted v ▷ transmute
transmutes v ▷ transmute
transmuting v ▷ transmute
transom n (pl -s) horizontal bar across a window
transoms n ▷ transom
transparencies n ▷ transparency
transparency n (pl -cies) transparent quality
transparent adj able to be seen through, clear

> **transparently** adv
transparently adv ▷ transparent
transpiration n ▷ transpire
transpirations n ▷ transpire
transpire v (-res, -ring, -red) become known
> **transpiration** n (pl -s)
transpired v ▷ transpire
transpires v ▷ transpire
transpiring v ▷ transpire
transplant v (-s, -ing, -ed) transfer (an organ or tissue) surgically from one part or body to another ▶ n (pl -s) surgical transplanting
> **transplantation** n (pl -s)
transplantation n ▷ transplant
transplantations n ▷ transplant
transplanted v ▷ transplant
transplanting v ▷ transplant
transplants v, n ▷ transplant
transport v (-s, -ing, -ed) convey from one place to another ▶ n (pl -s) business or system of transporting > **transportation** n (pl -s)
transportation n ▷ transport
transportations n ▷ transport
transported v ▷ transport
transporter n (pl -s) large goods vehicle
transporters n ▷ transporter
transporting v ▷ transport
transports v, n ▷ transport
transpose v (-ses, -sing, -sed) interchange two things > **transposition** n (pl -s)
transposed v ▷ transpose
transposes v ▷ transpose
transposing v ▷ transpose
transposition n ▷ transpose
transpositions n ▷ transpose
transsexual, transexual n (pl -s) person of one sex who believes his or her true identity is of the opposite sex
transsexuals n ▷ transsexual
transuranic [tranz-yoor-ran-ik] adj (of an element) having an atomic number greater than that of uranium
transverse adj crossing from side to side
transvestite n (pl -s) person who seeks sexual pleasure by wearing the clothes of the opposite sex > **transvestism** n (pl -s)
transvestism n ▷ transvestite
transvestisms n ▷ transvestite
transvestites n ▷ transvestite
trap n (pl -s) device for catching animals ▶ v (-s, -pping, -pped) catch
trapdoor n (pl -s) door in floor or roof
trapdoors n ▷ trapdoor
trapeze n (pl -s) horizontal bar suspended from two ropes, used by circus acrobats

trapezes n ▷ trapeze

trapezia n ▷ trapezium

trapezium n (pl -ziums, -zia) quadrilateral with two parallel sides of unequal length

trapeziums n ▷ trapezium

trapezoid [trap-piz-zoid] n (pl -s) quadrilateral with no sides parallel

trapezoids n ▷ trapezoid

trapped n ▷ trap

trapper n (pl -s) person who traps animals for their fur

trappers n ▷ trapper

trapping n ▷ trap

trappings pl n accessories that symbolize an office or position

traps n, v ▷ trap

trash n (pl -es) anything worthless > **trashy** adj (-shier, -shiest)

trashes n ▷ trash

trashier adj ▷ trash

trashiest adj ▷ trash

trashy adj ▷ trash

trauma [traw-ma] n (pl -mata, -s) emotional shock > **traumatic** adj > **traumatize** v (-zes, -zing, -zed)

traumas n ▷ trauma

traumata n ▷ trauma

traumatic adj ▷ trauma

traumatized v ▷ trauma

traumatizes v ▷ trauma

traumatizing v ▷ trauma

travail n (pl -s) (Lit) labour or toil

travails n ▷ travail

travel v (-s, -lling, -lled) go from one place to another, through an area, or for a specified distance ▶ n (pl -s) travelling, esp. as a tourist > **traveller** n (pl -s)

travelled v ▷ travel

traveller n ▷ travel

travellers n ▷ travel

travelling v ▷ travel

travelogue n (pl -s) film or talk about someone's travels

travelogues n ▷ travelogue

travels v, n ▷ travel ▶ pl n (account of) travelling

traverse v (-ses, -sing, -sed) move over or back and forth over

traversed v ▷ traverse

traverses v ▷ traverse

traversing v ▷ traverse

travesties n ▷ travesty

travesty n (pl -ties) grotesque imitation or mockery

trawl n (pl -s) net dragged at deep levels behind a fishing boat ▶ v (-s, -ing, -ed) fish with such a net

trawled v ▷ trawl

trawler n (pl -s) trawling boat

trawlers n ▷ trawler

trawling v ▷ trawl

trawls n, v ▷ trawl

tray n (pl -s) flat board, usu. with a rim, for carrying things

trays n ▷ tray

treacheries n ▷ treachery

treacherous adj disloyal > **treacherously** adv

treacherously adv ▷ treacherous

treachery n (pl -ries) wilful betrayal

treacle n (pl -s) thick dark syrup produced when sugar is refined > **treacly** adj (-lier, -liest)

treacles n ▷ treacle

treaclier adj ▷ treacle

treacliest adj ▷ treacle

treacly adj ▷ treacle

tread v (-s, -ing, trod, trodden or trod) set one's foot on ▶ n (pl -s) way of walking or dancing

treading v ▷ tread

treadle [tred-dl] n (pl -s) lever worked by the foot to turn a wheel

treadles n ▷ treadle

treadmill n (pl -s) (HIST) cylinder turned by treading on steps projecting from it

treadmills n ▷ treadmill

treads v, n ▷ tread

treason n (pl -s) betrayal of one's sovereign or country > **treasonable** adj

treasonable adj ▷ treason

treasons n ▷ treason

treasure n (pl -s) collection of wealth, esp. gold or jewels ▶ v (-res, -ring, -red) prize or cherish

treasured v ▷ treasure

treasurer n (pl -s) official in charge of funds

treasurers n ▷ treasurer

treasures n, v ▷ treasure

treasuries n ▷ treasury

treasuring v ▷ treasure

treasury n (pl -ries) storage place for treasure

treat v (-s, -ing, -ed) deal with or regard in a certain manner ▶ n (pl -s) pleasure, entertainment, etc. given or paid for by someone else

treated v ▷ treat

treaties n ▷ treaty

treating v ▷ treat

treatise [treat-izz] n (pl -s) formal piece of writing on a particular subject

treatises n ▷ treatise

treatment n (pl -s) medical care

treatments *n* ▷ treatment

treats *v*, *n* ▷ treat

treaty *n* (*pl* -ties) signed contract between states

treble *adj* triple (MUSIC) ▶ *n* (*pl* -s) (singer with or part for) a soprano voice ▶ *v* (-les, -ling, -led) increase three times > **trebly** *adv*

trebled *v* ▷ treble

trebles *n*, *v* ▷ treble

trebling *v* ▷ treble

trebly *adv* ▷ treble

tree *n* (*pl* -s) large perennial plant with a woody trunk > **treeless** *adj*

treeless *adj* ▷ tree

trees *n* ▷ tree

trefoil [tref-foil] *n* (*pl* -s) plant, such as clover, with a three-lobed leaf

trefoils *n* ▷ trefoil

trek *n* (*pl* -s) long difficult journey, esp. on foot ▶ *v* (-s, -kking, -kked) make such a journey

trekked *v* ▷ trek

trekking *v* ▷ trek

treks *n*, *v* ▷ trek

trellis *n* (*pl* -ises) framework of horizontal and vertical strips of wood

trellises *n* ▷ trellis

tremble *v* (-les, -ling, -led) shake or quiver ▶ *n* (*pl* -les) trembling > **trembling** *adj*

trembled *v* ▷ tremble

trembles *v*, *n* ▷ tremble

trembling *v*, *adj* ▷ tremble

tremendous *adj* huge > **tremendously** *adv*

tremendously *adv* ▷ tremendous

tremolo *n* (*pl* -s) (MUSIC) quivering effect in singing or playing

tremolos *n* ▷ tremolo

tremor *n* (*pl* -s) involuntary shaking

tremors *n* ▷ tremor

tremulous *adj* trembling, as from fear or excitement

trench *n* (*pl* -es) long narrow ditch, esp. one used as a shelter in war

trenchant *adj* incisive

trencher *n* (*pl* -s) (HIST) wooden plate for serving food

trencherman *n* (*pl* -men) hearty eater

trenchermen *n* ▷ trencherman

trenchers *n* ▷ trencher

trenches *n* ▷ trench

trend *n* (*pl* -s) general tendency or direction

trendier *adj* ▷ trendy

trendies *n* ▷ trendy

trendiest *adj* ▷ trendy

trendiness *n* ▷ trendy

trendinesses *n* ▷ trendy

trends *n* ▷ trend

trendy *adj* (-dier, -diest) ▶ *n* (*pl* -dies) (*Informal*) consciously fashionable (person) > **trendiness** *n* (*pl* -es)

trepidation *n* (*pl* -s) fear or anxiety

trepidations *n* ▷ trepidation

trespass *v* (-es, -ing, -ed) go onto another's property without permission ▶ *n* (*pl* -es) trespassing > **trespasser** *n* (*pl* -s)

trespassed *v* ▷ trespass

trespasser *n* ▷ trespass

trespassers *n* ▷ trespass

trespasses *v*, *n* ▷ trespass

trespassing *v* ▷ trespass

tresses *pl n* long flowing hair

trestle *n* (*pl* -s) board fixed on pairs of spreading legs, used as a support

trestles *n* ▷ trestle

trevallies *n* ▷ trevally

trevally *n* (*pl* -lies) (AUST & NZ) any of various food and game fishes

trews *pl n* close-fitting tartan trousers

triad *n* (*pl* -s) group of three

triads *n* ▷ triad

trial *n* (*pl* -s) investigation of a case before a judge

trials *n* ▷ trial ▶ *pl n* sporting competition for individuals

triangle *n* (*pl* -s) geometric figure with three sides > **triangular** *adj*

triangles *n* ▷ triangle

triangular *adj* ▷ triangle

tribal *adj* ▷ tribe

tribalism *n* (*pl* -s) loyalty to a tribe

tribalisms *n* ▷ tribalism

tribe *n* (*pl* -s) group of clans or families believed to have a common ancestor > **tribal** *adj*

tribes *n* ▷ tribe

tribulation *n* (*pl* -s) great distress

tribulations *n* ▷ tribulation

tribunal *n* (*pl* -s) board appointed to inquire into a specific matter

tribunals *n* ▷ tribunal

tribune *n* (*pl* -s) people's representative, esp. in ancient Rome

tribunes *n* ▷ tribune

tributaries *n* ▷ tributary

tributary *n* (*pl* -ries) stream or river flowing into a larger one ▶ *adj* (of a stream or river) flowing into a larger one

tribute *n* (*pl* -s) sign of respect or admiration

tributes *n* ▷ tribute

trice *n* (*pl* -s) moment

triceps *n* (*pl* -pses) muscle at the back of the upper arm

tricepses n ▷triceps
trices n ▷trice
trichologies n ▷trichology
trichologist n ▷trichology
trichologists n ▷trichology
trichology [trick-ol-a-jee] n (pl -gies) study and treatment of hair and its diseases > **trichologist** n (pl -s)
trick n (pl -s) deceitful or cunning action or plan ▶ v (-s, -ing, -ed) cheat or deceive > **trickery** n (pl -ries) > **trickster** n (pl -s)
tricked v ▷trick
trickeries n ▷trick
trickery n ▷trick
trickier adj ▷tricky
trickiest adj ▷tricky
tricking v ▷trick
trickle v (-les, -ling, -led) (cause to) flow in a thin stream or drops ▶ n (pl -s) gradual flow
trickled v ▷trickle
trickles v, n ▷trickle
trickling v ▷trickle
tricks n, v ▷trick
trickster n ▷trick
tricksters n ▷trick
tricky adj (-kier, -kiest) difficult, needing careful handling
tricolour [trick-kol-lor] n (pl -s) three-coloured striped flag
tricolours n ▷tricolour
tricycle n (pl -s) three-wheeled cycle
tricycles n ▷tricycle
trident n (pl -s) three-pronged spear
tridents n ▷trident
tried v ▷try
triennial adj happening every three years
tries v, n ▷try
trifle n (pl -s) insignificant thing or amount
trifles n ▷trifle
trifling adj insignificant
trigger n (pl -s) small lever releasing a catch on a gun or machine ▶ v (-s, -ing, -ed) (usu. foll. by **off**) set (an action or process) in motion
triggered v ▷trigger
triggering v ▷trigger
triggers n, v ▷trigger
trigonometries n ▷trigonometry
trigonometry n (pl -ries) branch of mathematics dealing with relations of the sides and angles of triangles
trike n (pl -s) (Informal) tricycle
trikes n ▷trike
trilateral adj having three sides
trilbies n ▷trilby
trilby n (pl -bies) man's soft felt hat

trill n (pl -s) (MUSIC) rapid alternation between two notes ▶ v (-s, -ing, -ed) play or sing a trill
trilled v ▷trill
trilling v ▷trill
trillion n (pl -s) one million million, 10^{12}
trillions n ▷trillion
trills n, v ▷trill
trilobite [trile-oh-bite] n (pl -s) small prehistoric sea animal
trilobites n ▷trilobite
trilogies n ▷trilogy
trilogy n (pl -gies) series of three related books, plays, etc.
trim adj (-mmer, -mmest) neat and smart ▶ v (-s, -mming, -mmed) cut or prune into good shape ▶ n (pl -s) decoration
trimaran [trime-a-ran] n (pl -s) three-hulled boat
trimarans n ▷trimaran
trimmed v ▷trim
trimmer adj ▷trim
trimmest adj ▷trim
trimming n (pl -s) decoration ▶ v ▷trim
trimmings n ▷trimming ▶ pl n usual accompaniments
trims v, n ▷trim
trinities n ▷trinity
trinitrotoluene n (pl -s) TNT
trinitrotoluenes n ▷trinitrotoluene
trinity n (pl -ties) group of three
trinket n (pl -s) small or worthless ornament or piece of jewellery
trinkets n ▷trinket
trio n (pl -s) group of three
trios n ▷trio
trip n (pl -s) journey to a place and back, esp. for pleasure ▶ v (-s, -pping, -pped) (cause to) stumble
tripe n (pl -s) stomach of a cow used as food
tripes n ▷tripe
triple adj having three parts ▶ v (-les, -ling, -led) increase three times
tripled v ▷triple
triples v ▷triple
triplet n (pl -s) one of three babies born at one birth
triplets n ▷triplet
triplicate adj triple
tripling v ▷triple
tripod [tripe-pod] n (pl -s) three-legged stand, stool, etc.
tripods n ▷tripod
tripos [tripe-poss] n (pl -poses) final examinations for an honours degree at Cambridge University
triposes n ▷tripos

tripped v ▷ trip
tripper n (pl **-s**) tourist
  trippers n ▷ tripper
  tripping v ▷ trip
  trips n, v ▷ trip
triptych [trip-tick] n (pl **-s**) painting or carving on three hinged panels, often forming an altarpiece
  triptychs n ▷ triptych
trite adj (of a remark or idea) commonplace and unoriginal
tritium n (pl **-s**) radioactive isotope of hydrogen
  tritiums n ▷ tritium
triumph n (pl **-s**) (happiness caused by) victory or success ▶ v (**-s, -ing, -ed**) be victorious or successful
triumphal adj celebrating a triumph
triumphant adj feeling or showing triumph
  triumphed v ▷ triumph
  triumphing v ▷ triumph
  triumphs n, v ▷ triumph
triumvirate [try-**umm**-vir-rit] n (pl **-s**) group of three people in joint control
  triumvirates n ▷ triumvirate
trivet [triv-vit] n (pl **-s**) metal stand for a pot or kettle
  trivets n ▷ trivet
trivia pl n trivial things or details
trivial adj of little importance > **trivially** adv > **triviality** n (pl **-ties**)
  trivialities n ▷ trivial
  triviality n ▷ trivial
trivialize v (**-zes, -zing, -zed**) make (something) seem less important or complex than it is
  trivialized v ▷ trivialize
  trivializes v ▷ trivialize
  trivializing v ▷ trivialize
  trivially adv ▷ trivial
  trod v ▷ tread
  trodden v ▷ tread
troglodyte n (pl **-s**) cave dweller
  troglodytes n ▷ troglodyte
troika n (pl **-s**) Russian vehicle drawn by three horses abreast
  troikas n ▷ troika
troll n (pl **-s**) giant or dwarf in Scandinavian folklore
trolley n (pl **-s**) small wheeled table for food and drink
  trolleys n ▷ trolley
trollop n (pl **-s**) (Old-fashioned) promiscuous or slovenly woman
  trollops n ▷ trollop

  trolls n ▷ troll
trombone n (pl **-s**) brass musical instrument with a sliding tube > **trombonist** n (pl **-s**)
  trombones n ▷ trombone
  trombonist n ▷ trombone
  trombonists n ▷ trombone
troop n (pl **-s**) large group ▶ v (**-s, -ing, -ed**) move in a crowd
  trooped v ▷ troop
trooper n (pl **-s**) cavalry soldier
  troopers n ▷ trooper
  trooping v ▷ troop
troops n, v ▷ troop▶ pl n soldiers
trope n (pl **-s**) figure of speech
  tropes n ▷ trope
  trophies n ▷ trophy
trophy n (pl **-phies**) cup, shield, etc. given as a prize
tropic n (pl **-s**) either of two lines of latitude at $23\frac{1}{2}°$N (**tropic of Cancer**) or $23\frac{1}{2}°$S (**tropic of Capricorn**) ▶ pl n part of the earth's surface between these lines
tropical adj of or in the tropics
  tropics n ▷ tropic
trot v (**-s, -tting, -tted**) (of a horse) move at a medium pace, lifting the feet in diagonal pairs ▶ n (pl **-s**) trotting
troth [rhymes with **growth**] n (pl **-s**) (Obs) pledge of devotion, esp. a betrothal
  troths n ▷ troth
  trots v, n ▷ trot
  trotted v ▷ trot
trotter n (pl **-s**) pig's foot
  trotters n ▷ trotter
  trotting v ▷ trot
troubadour [troo-bad-oor] n (pl **-s**) medieval travelling poet and singer
  troubadours n ▷ troubadour
trouble n (pl **-s**) (cause of) distress or anxiety ▶ v (**-les, -ling, -led**) (cause to) worry > **troubled** adj > **troublesome** adj
  troubled v, adj ▷ trouble
  troubles n, v ▷ trouble
troubleshooter n (pl **-s**) person employed to locate and deal with faults or problems
  troubleshooters n ▷ troubleshooter
  troublesome adj ▷ trouble
  troubling v ▷ trouble
trough [troff] n (pl **-s**) long open container, esp. for animals' food or water
  troughs n ▷ trough
trounce v (**-ces, -cing, -ced**) defeat utterly
  trounced v ▷ trounce
  trounces v ▷ trounce
  trouncing v ▷ trounce

troupe [troop] n (pl -s) company of performers
> **trouper** n (pl -s)
  trouper n ▷ troupe
  troupers n ▷ troupe
  troupes n ▷ troupe
trouser adj of trousers
trousers pl n two-legged outer garment with legs reaching usu. to the ankles
trousseau [troo-so] n (pl -seaux, -seaus) bride's collection of clothing etc. for her marriage
  trousseaus n ▷ trousseau
  trousseaux n ▷ trousseau
trout n (pl trout, trouts) game fish related to the salmon
  trouts n ▷ trout
trowel n (pl -s) hand tool with a wide blade for spreading mortar, lifting plants, etc.
  trowels n ▷ trowel
  truancies n ▷ truant
  truancy n ▷ truant
truant n (pl -s) pupil who stays away from school without permission > **truancy** n (pl -cies)
  truants n ▷ truant
truce n (pl -s) temporary agreement to stop fighting
  truces n ▷ truce
truck[1] n (pl -s) railway goods wagon
truck[2] n (pl -s) commercial goods
trucker n (pl -s) truck driver
  truckers n ▷ trucker
  trucks n ▷ truck[1, 2]
  truculence n ▷ truculent
  truculences n ▷ truculent
truculent [truck-yew-lent] adj aggressively defiant > **truculence** n (pl -s)
trudge v (-dges, -dging, -dged) walk heavily or wearily ▶ n (pl -s) long tiring walk
  trudged v ▷ trudge
  trudges v, n ▷ trudge
  trudging v ▷ trudge
true adj (truer, truest) in accordance with facts > **truly** adv
  truer adj ▷ true
  truest adj ▷ true
truffle n (pl -s) edible underground fungus
  truffles n ▷ truffle
trug n (pl -s) (BRIT) long shallow basket used by gardeners
  trugs n ▷ trug
truism n (pl -s) self-evident truth
  truisms n ▷ truism
  truly adv ▷ true
trump[1] n (pl -s) ▶ adj (card) of the suit outranking the others ▶ v (-s, -ing, -ed) play a trump card on (another card)

trump[2] n (pl -s) (Lit) (sound of) a trumpet
  trumped v ▷ trump[1]
trumpet n (pl -s) valved brass instrument with a flared tube ▶ v (-s, -ing, -ed) proclaim loudly > **trumpeter** n (pl -s)
  trumpeted v ▷ trumpet
  trumpeter n ▷ trumpet
  trumpeters n ▷ trumpet
  trumpeting v ▷ trumpet
  trumpets n, v ▷ trumpet
  trumping v ▷ trump[1]
  trumps n ▷ trump[1, 2] ▶ pl n suit outranking the others ▶ v ▷ trump[1]
truncate v (-tes, -ting, -ted) cut short
  truncated v ▷ truncate
  truncates v ▷ truncate
  truncating v ▷ truncate
truncheon n (pl -s) club carried by a policeman
  truncheons n ▷ truncheon
trundle v (-les, -ling, -led) move heavily on wheels
  trundled v ▷ trundle
  trundles v ▷ trundle
  trundling v ▷ trundle
trunk n (pl -s) main stem of a tree
  trunks n ▷ trunk ▶ pl n man's swimming shorts
truss v (-es, -ing, -ed) tie or bind up ▶ n (pl -es) device for holding a hernia in place
  trussed v ▷ truss
  trusses v, n ▷ truss
  trussing v ▷ truss
trust v (-s, -ing, -ed) believe in and rely on ▶ n (pl -s) confidence in the truth, reliability, etc. of a person or thing
  trusted v ▷ trust
trustee n (pl -s) person holding property on another's behalf
  trustees n ▷ trustee
trustful, trusting adj inclined to trust others
  trustier adj ▷ trusty
  trustiest adj ▷ trusty
  trusting v ▷ trust ▶ adj ▷ trustful
  trusts n, v ▷ trust
trustworthy adj reliable or honest
trusty adj (-tier, -tiest) faithful or reliable
truth n (pl -s) state of being true
truthful adj honest > **truthfully** adv
  truthfully adv ▷ truthful
  truths n ▷ truth
try v (tries, trying, tried) make an effort or attempt ▶ n (pl tries) attempt or effort
trying adj (Informal) difficult or annoying ▶ v ▷ try
tryst n (pl -s) arrangement to meet
  trysts n ▷ tryst

tsar, czar [zahr] n (pl -s) (HIST) Russian emperor

tsars n ▷ tsar

tsk interj. Tsk is a sound people make to show disapproval. This is a useful word because it enables you to play K without using vowels, which is handy if your rack is low on vowel tiles. Tsk scores 7 points.

tsunami n (pl -mis, -mi) tidal wave, usu. caused by an earthquake under the sea

tsunamis n ▷ tsunami

tuatara n (pl -s) large lizard-like New Zealand reptile

tuataras n ▷ tuatara

tub n (pl -s) open, usu. round container

tuba [tube-a] n (pl -s) valved low-pitched brass instrument

tubas n ▷ tuba

tubbier adj ▷ tubby

tubbiest adj ▷ tubby

tubby adj (tubbier, tubbiest) (of a person) short and fat

tube n (pl -s) hollow cylinder

tuber [tube-er] n (pl -s) fleshy underground root of a plant such as a potato > **tuberous** adj

tubercle [tube-er-kl] n (pl -s) small rounded swelling

tubercles n ▷ tubercle

tubercular adj ▷ tuberculosis

tuberculin n (pl -s) extract from a bacillus used to test for tuberculosis

tuberculins n ▷ tuberculin

tuberculosis [tube-berk-yew-lohss-iss] n (pl -ses) infectious disease causing tubercles, esp. in the lungs > **tubercular** adj

tuberculoses n ▷ tuberculosis

tuberous adj ▷ tuber

tubers n ▷ tuber

tubes n ▷ tube

tubing n (pl -s) length of tube

tubings n ▷ tubing

tubs n ▷ tub

tubular [tube-yew-lar] adj of or shaped like a tube

tuck v (-s, -ing, -ed) push or fold into a small space ▶ n (pl -s) stitched fold

tucked v ▷ tuck

tucker n (pl -s) (AUST & NZ) (Informal) food

tuckers n ▷ tucker

tucking v ▷ tuck

tucks v, n ▷ tuck

tufa [tew-fa] n (pl -s) porous rock formed as a deposit from springs

tufas n ▷ tufa

tuffet n (pl -s) small mound or seat

tuffets n ▷ tuffet

tuft n (pl -s) bunch of feathers, grass, hair, etc. held or growing together at the base

tufts n ▷ tuft

tug v (-s, -gging, -gged) pull hard ▶ n (pl -s) hard pull

tugged v ▷ tug

tugging v ▷ tug

tugs v, n ▷ tug

tuition n (pl -s) instruction, esp. received individually or in a small group

tuitions n ▷ tuition

tulip n (pl -s) plant with bright cup-shaped flowers

tulips n ▷ tulip

tulle [tewl] n (pl -s) fine net fabric of silk etc.

tulles n ▷ tulle

tumble v (-les, -ling, -led) (cause to) fall, esp. awkwardly or violently ▶ n (pl -s) fall

tumbled v ▷ tumble

tumbledown adj dilapidated

tumbler n (pl -s) stemless drinking glass

tumblers n ▷ tumbler

tumbles v, n ▷ tumble

tumbling v ▷ tumble

tumbrel n ▷ tumbril

tumbrels n ▷ tumbril

tumbril, tumbrel n (pl -s) farm cart used during the French Revolution to take prisoners to the guillotine

tumbrils n ▷ tumbril

tumescent [tew-mess-ent] adj swollen or becoming swollen

tummies n ▷ tummy

tummy n (pl -mies) (Informal) stomach

tumour [tew-mer] n (pl -s) abnormal growth in or on the body

tumours n ▷ tumour

tumuli n ▷ tumulus

tumult n (pl -s) uproar or commotion > **tumultuous** [tew-mull-tew-uss] ▶ adj

tumults n ▷ tumult

tumultuous adj ▷ tumult

tumulus n (pl -li) burial mound

tun n (pl -s) large beer cask

tuna n (pl -s) large marine food fish

tunas n ▷ tuna

tundra n (pl -s) vast treeless Arctic region with permanently frozen subsoil

tundras n ▷ tundra

tune n (pl -s) (pleasing) sequence of musical notes ▶ v (-nes, -ning, -ned) adjust (a musical instrument) so that it is in tune > **tuneful** adj > **tunefully** adv > **tuneless** adj > **tuner** n (pl -s)

tuned v ▷ tune

tuneful adj ▷ tune
tunefully adv ▷ tune
tuneless adj ▷ tune
tuner n ▷ tune
tuners n ▷ tune
tunes n, v ▷ tune
tungsten n (pl -s) (CHEM) greyish-white metal
tungstens n ▷ tungsten
tunic n (pl -s) close-fitting jacket forming part of some uniforms
tunics n ▷ tunic
tuning v ▷ tune
tunnel n (pl -s) underground passage ▶ v (-s, -lling, -lled) make a tunnel (through)
tunnelled v ▷ tunnel
tunnelling v ▷ tunnel
tunnels n, v ▷ tunnel
tunnies n ▷ tunny
tunny n (pl -nies, -ny) tuna
tuns n ▷ tun
tup n (pl -s) male sheep
tups n ▷ tup
turban n (pl -s) Muslim, Hindu, or Sikh man's head covering, made by winding cloth round the head
turbans n ▷ turban
turbid adj muddy, not clear
turbine n (pl -s) machine or generator driven by gas, water, etc. turning blades
turbines n ▷ turbine
turbot n (pl -s) large European edible flatfish
turbots n ▷ turbot
turbulence n (pl -s) confusion, movement, or agitation > **turbulent** adj
turbulences n ▷ turbulence
turbulent adj ▷ turbulence
tureen n (pl -s) serving dish for soup
tureens n ▷ tureen
turf n (pl -s, turves) short thick even grass ▶ v (-s, -ing, -ed) cover with turf
turfed v ▷ turf
turfing v ▷ turf
turfs n, v ▷ turf
turgid [tur-jid] adj (-er, -est) (of language) pompous
turgider adj ▷ turgid
turgidest adj ▷ turgid
turkey n (pl -s) large bird bred for food
turkeys n ▷ turkey
turmeric n (pl -s) yellow spice obtained from the root of an Asian plant
turmerics n ▷ turmeric
turmoil n (pl -s) agitation or confusion
turmoils n ▷ turmoil
turn v (-s, -ing, -ed) change the position or

direction (of) ▶ n (pl -s) turning > **turner** n (pl -s)
turncoat n (pl -s) person who deserts one party or cause to join another
turncoats n ▷ turncoat
turned v ▷ turn
turner n ▷ turn
turners n ▷ turn
turning n (pl -s) road or path leading off a main route ▶ v ▷ turn
turnings n ▷ turning
turnip n (pl -s) root vegetable with orange or white flesh
turnips n ▷ turnip
turnout n (pl -s) number of people appearing at a gathering
turnouts n ▷ turnout
turnover n (pl -s) total sales made by a business over a certain period
turnovers n ▷ turnover
turnpike n (pl -s) (BRIT) road where a toll is collected at barriers
turnpikes n ▷ turnpike
turns v, n ▷ turn
turnstile n (pl -s) revolving gate for admitting one person at a time
turnstiles n ▷ turnstile
turntable n (pl -s) revolving platform
turntables n ▷ turntable
turnup n (pl -s) turned-up fold at the bottom of a trouser leg
turnups n ▷ turnup
turpentine n (pl -s) (oil made from) the resin of certain trees
turpentines n ▷ turpentine
turpitude n (pl -s) wickedness
turpitudes n ▷ turpitude
turps n turpentine oil
turquoise adj blue-green ▶ n (pl -s) blue-green precious stone
turquoises n ▷ turquoise
turret n (pl -s) small tower
turrets n ▷ turret
turtle n (pl -s) sea tortoise
turtledove n (pl -s) small wild dove
turtledoves n ▷ turtledove
turtleneck n (pl -s) (sweater with) a round high close-fitting neck
turtlenecks n ▷ turtleneck
turtles n ▷ turtle
turves n ▷ turf
tusk n (pl -s) long pointed tooth of an elephant, walrus, etc.
tusks n ▷ tusk
tussle n (pl -s) ▶ v (-les, -ling, -led) fight or

scuffle
tussled v ▷ tussle
tussles n, v ▷ tussle
tussling v ▷ tussle
tussock n (pl **-s**) tuft of grass
tussocks n ▷ tussock
tutelage [tew-till-lij] n (pl **-s**) instruction or guidance, esp. by a tutor > **tutelary** [tew-till-lar-ee] ▶ adj
tutelages n ▷ tutelage
tutelary adj ▷ tutelage
tutor n (pl **-s**) person teaching individuals or small groups ▶ v (**-s, -ing, -ed**) act as a tutor to
tutored v ▷ tutor
tutorial n (pl **-s**) period of instruction with a tutor
tutorials n ▷ tutorial
tutoring v ▷ tutor
tutors n, v ▷ tutor
tutu n (pl **-s**) short stiff skirt worn by ballerinas
tutus n ▷ tutu

> **tux** n (**tuxes**). Tux is a short form of **tuxedo**. This is a very useful word, as U and T are common tiles, so look for opportunities to play it when you get an X. Tux scores 10 points.

tuxedo n (pl **-s**) (US & AUST) dinner jacket
tuxedos n ▷ tuxedo
twaddle n (pl **-s**) silly or pretentious talk or writing
twaddles n ▷ twaddle
twain n (pl **-s**) (Obs) two
twains n ▷ twain
twang n (pl **-s**) sharp ringing sound ▶ v (**-s, -ing, -ed**) (cause to) make a twang
twanged v ▷ twang
twanging v ▷ twang
twangs n, v ▷ twang
tweak v (**-s, -ing, -ed**) pinch or twist sharply ▶ n (pl **-s**) tweaking
tweaked v ▷ tweak
tweaking v ▷ tweak
tweaks v, n ▷ tweak
twee adj (Informal) (**-r, -st**) too sentimental, sweet, or pretty
tweed n (pl **-s**) thick woollen cloth > **tweedy** adj (**-dier, -diest**)
tweedier adj ▷ tweed
tweediest adj ▷ tweed
tweeds n ▷ tweed ▶ pl n suit of tweed
tweedy adj ▷ tweed
tweer adj ▷ twee
tweest adj ▷ twee
tweet n (pl **-s**) ▶ v (**-s, -ing, -ed**) chirp
tweeted v ▷ tweet

tweeter n (pl **-s**) loudspeaker reproducing high-frequency sounds
tweeters n ▷ tweeter
tweeting v ▷ tweet
tweets n, v ▷ tweet
tweezers pl n small pincer-like tool
twelfth adj, n (pl **-s**) (of) number twelve in a series
twelfths n ▷ twelfth
twelve adj, n (pl **-s**) two more than ten
twelves n ▷ twelve
twenties n ▷ twenty
twentieth adj, n ▷ twenty
twentieths n ▷ twenty
twenty adj, n (pl **-ties**) two times ten > **twentieth** adj, n (pl **-s**)
twerp n (pl **-s**) (Informal) silly person
twerps n ▷ twerp
twice adv two times
twiddle v (**-les, -ling, -led**) fiddle or twirl in an idle way
twiddled v ▷ twiddle
twiddles v ▷ twiddle
twiddling v ▷ twiddle
twig¹ n (pl **-s**) small branch or shoot
twig² v (**-s, -gging, -gged**) (Informal) realize or understand
twigged v ▷ twig¹
twigging v ▷ twig¹
twigs n ▷ twig¹ ▶ v ▷ twig²
twilight n (pl **-s**) soft dim light just after sunset
twilights n ▷ twilight
twill n (pl **-s**) fabric woven to produce parallel ridges
twills n ▷ twill
twin n (pl **-s**) one of a pair, esp. of two children born at one birth ▶ v (**-s, -nning, -nned**) pair or be paired
twine n (pl **-es**) string or cord ▶ v (**-nes, -ning, -ned**) twist or coil round
twined v ▷ twine
twines n, v ▷ twine
twining v ▷ twine
twinge n (pl **-s**) sudden sharp pain or emotional pang
twinges n ▷ twinge
twinkle v (**-les, -ling, -led**) shine brightly but intermittently ▶ n (pl **-les**) flickering brightness
twinkled v ▷ twinkle
twinkles v, n ▷ twinkle
twinkling v ▷ twinkle
twinned v ▷ twin
twinning v ▷ twin
twins n, v ▷ twin

twirl v (**-s, -ing, -ed**) turn or spin around quickly
  twirled v ▷ twirl
  twirling v ▷ twirl
  twirls v ▷ twirl
twist v (**-s, -ing, -ed**) turn out of the natural
  position ▸ n (pl **-s**) twisting
twisted adj (of a person) cruel or perverted
  ▸ v ▷ twist
twister n (pl **-s**) (BRIT) (Informal) swindler
  twisters n ▷ twister
  twisting v ▷ twist
  twists v, n ▷ twist
twit¹ v (**-s, -tting, -tted**) poke fun at (someone)
twit² n (pl **-s**) (Informal) foolish person
twitch v (**-es, -ing, -ed**) move spasmodically ▸ n
  (pl **-es**) nervous muscular spasm
  twitched v ▷ twitch
  twitches v, n ▷ twitch
  twitching v ▷ twitch
  twits n ▷ twit² ▸ v ▷ twit¹
  twitted v ▷ twit¹
twitter v (**-s, -ing, -ed**) (of birds) utter chirping
  sounds ▸ n (pl **-s**) act or sound of twittering
  twittered v ▷ twitter
  twittering v ▷ twitter
  twitters v, n ▷ twitter
  twitting v ▷ twit¹
two adj, n (pl **-s**) one more than one
  twos n ▷ two

  twp adj. This is a Welsh word that
  means stupid or daft. This is a useful
  word because it contains no vowels,
  and can thus help when you have an
  awkward rack. Twp scores 8 points.

tycoon n (pl **-s**) powerful wealthy businessman
  tycoons n ▷ tycoon

  tyg n (**tygs**). A tyg is a cup with more
  than one handle. This word is useful
  because it uses no vowels, and can
  thus help when you are short of them.
  Tyg scores 7 points.

  tying v ▷ tie
tyke n (pl **-s**) (BRIT, AUST & NZ) (Informal) small
  cheeky child
  tykes n ▷ tyke
type n (pl **-s**) class or category ▸ v (**-pes, -ping,
  -ped**) print with a typewriter or word processor
typecast v (**-s, -ing, -ed**) continually cast (an
  actor or actress) in similar roles
  typecasted v ▷ typecast
  typecasting v ▷ typecast
  typecasts v ▷ typecast
  typed v ▷ type

types n, v ▷ type
typewriter n (pl **-s**) machine which prints a
  character when the appropriate key is pressed
  typewriters n ▷ typewriter
  typing v ▷ type
typist n (pl **-s**) person who types with a
  typewriter or word processor
  typists n ▷ typist
typhoon n (pl **-s**) violent tropical storm
  typhoons n ▷ typhoon
typhus n (pl **-uses**) infectious feverish disease
  typhuses n ▷ typhus
typical adj true to type, characteristic
  > **typically** adv
  typically adv ▷ typical
  typified v ▷ typify
  typifies v ▷ typify
typify v (**-fies, -fying, -fied**) be typical of
  typifying v ▷ typify
  typographer n ▷ typography
  typographers n ▷ typography
  typographical adj ▷ typography
  typographies n ▷ typography
typography n (pl **-phies**) art or style of printing
  > **typographical** adj > **typographer** n (pl **-s**)
tyrannical adj like a tyrant, oppressive
  tyrannies n ▷ tyranny
tyrannize v (**-zes, -zing, -zed**) exert power
  (over) oppressively or cruelly > **tyrannous** adj
  tyrannized v ▷ tyrannize
  tyrannizes v ▷ tyrannize
  tyrannizing v ▷ tyrannize
tyrannosaurus [tirr-ran-oh-**sore**-uss] n (pl **-es**)
  large two-footed flesh-eating dinosaur
  tyrannosauruses n ▷ tyrannosaurus
  tyrannous n ▷ tyrannosaurus
tyranny n (pl **-nies**) tyrannical rule
tyrant n (pl **-s**) oppressive or cruel ruler
  tyrants n ▷ tyrant
tyre n (pl **-s**) rubber ring, usu. inflated, over the
  rim of a vehicle's wheel to grip the road
  tyres n ▷ tyre
tyro n (pl **-ros**) novice or beginner
  tyros n ▷ tyro

  tzaddiq n (**tzaddiqim, tzaddiqs**). A
  tzaddiq is a Hasidic Jewish leader.
  This is a fantastic word if you can get
  the necessary tiles. If someone has
  played add, you might be able to form
  it around that; if you can form the
  whole word using all your tiles you'll
  earn a 50-point bonus. Tzaddiq scores
  27 points.

U u

U can be a difficult tile to use effectively. Although there are quite a few two-letter words beginning with U, most of them are quite unusual, and so difficult to remember. Only **up** (4 points) and **us** (2) are immediately obvious, so it's well worth learning words like **ug** (3), **uh** (5), **um** (4), and **un**, **ur** and **ut** (2 each). Three-letter words beginning with U can also be difficult to remember. If you are trying to use a Q, X or Z, bear in mind that there aren't any valid three-letter words with these letters that start with U. Knowing this can save you valuable time. It's also helpful to remember that there aren't any particularly high-scoring two- or three-letter words starting with U.

ubiquities n ▷ ubiquitous

ubiquitous [yew-**bik**-wit-uss] adj being or seeming to be everywhere at once > **ubiquity** n (pl -**ties**)

  ubiquity n ▷ ubiquitous

udder n (pl -**s**) large baglike milk-producing gland of cows, sheep, or goats

  udders n ▷ udder

> **ug** v (**ugs, ugging, ugged**). Ug is an old word meaning to loathe. The different verb forms of this word can be useful, and remember that if someone plays ug or its inflections, you can put B, L, M or T in front of it to form another valid word. Ug scores 3 points.
>
> **ugh** interj. Ugh is a sound that people make when they dislike something or are disgusted by it. Together with uke, this is the highest-scoring three-letter word starting with U. Ugh scores 7 points.

uglier adj ▷ ugly

ugliest adj ▷ ugly

ugliness n ▷ ugly

  uglinesses n ▷ ugly

ugly adj (-**lier, -liest**) of unpleasant appearance > **ugliness** n (pl -**es**)

> **uh** interj. Uh is a sound that people make when they are unsure about something. This useful little word can help when you are trying to form words in more than one direction. Uh scores 5 points.
>
> **uke** n (**ukes**). Uke is a short form of ukulele. Together with ugh, this is the highest-scoring three-letter word

starting with U. Uke scores 7 points.

ukelele n ▷ ukulele

  ukeleles n ▷ ukulele

ukulele, ukelele [yew-kal-**lay**-lee] n (pl -**s**) small guitar with four strings

  ukuleles n ▷ ukulele

ulcer n (pl -**s**) open sore on the surface of the skin or mucous membrane. > **ulceration** n (pl -**s**)

ulcerated adj made or becoming ulcerous

  ulceration n ▷ ulcer

  ulcerations n ▷ ulcer

ulcerous adj of, like, or characterized by ulcers

  ulcers n ▷ ulcer

ulna n (pl -**nae, -nas**) inner and longer of the two bones of the human forearm

  ulnae n ▷ ulna

  ulnas n ▷ ulna

ulterior adj (of an aim, reason, etc.) concealed or hidden

ultimate adj final in a series or process > **ultimately** adv

  ultimately adv ▷ ultimate

ultimatum [ult-im-**may**-tum] n (pl -**s**) final warning stating that action will be taken unless certain conditions are met

  ultimatums n ▷ ultimatum

ultramarine adj vivid blue

ultrasonic adj of or producing sound waves with a higher frequency than the human ear can hear

ultraviolet adj, n (pl -**s**) (of) light beyond the limit of visibility at the violet end of the spectrum

  ultraviolets n ▷ ultraviolet

ululate [**yewl**-yew-late] v (-**tes, -ting, -ted**) howl

or wail ▷ **ululation** n (pl -s)
ululated v ▷ ululate
ululates v ▷ ululate
ululating v ▷ ululate
ululation n ▷ ululate
ululations n ▷ ululate

um interj. Um is a sound people make when hesitating in speech. If someone plays this word, remember that lots of words end in UM (dictum, podium and rostrum, for example) and look out for chances to play them. Um scores 4 points.

umber adj dark brown to reddish-brown
umbilical adj of the navel
umbrella n (pl -s) portable device used for protection against rain, consisting of a folding frame covered in material attached to a central rod
umbrellas n ▷ umbrella
umpire n (pl -s) official who rules on the playing of a game ▸ v (-res, -ring, -red) act as umpire in (a game)
umpired v ▷ umpire
umpires n, v ▷ umpire
umpiring v ▷ umpire
umpteen adj (Informal) very many
> **umpteenth** n (pl -s) adj
umpteenth n, adj ▷ umpteen
umpteenths n ▷ umpteen

un pron. Un is a dialect word for one. If someone plays this, remember that you can form lots of words by placing letters after UN. Un scores 2 points.

unable adj lacking the necessary power, ability, or authority to (do something)
unaccountable adj unable to be explained
> **unaccountably** adv
unaccountably adv ▷ unaccountable
unadulterated adj with nothing added, pure
unanimities n ▷ unanimous
unanimity n ▷ unanimous
unanimous [yew-nan-im-uss] adj in complete agreement > **unanimity** n (pl -ties)
unarmed adj without weapons
unassuming adj modest or unpretentious
unaware adj not aware or conscious
unawares adv by surprise
unbalanced adj biased or one-sided
unbearable adj not able to be endured
> **unbearably** adv
unbearably adv ▷ unbearable
unbeknown adv without the knowledge of (a person)
unbend v (-s, -ing, unbent) (Informal) become

less strict or more informal in one's attitudes or behaviour > **unbending** adj
unbending v, adj ▷ unbend
unbends v ▷ unbend
unbent v ▷ unbend
unbidden adj not ordered or asked
unborn adj not yet born
unbosom v (-s, -ing, -ed) relieve (oneself) of (secrets or feelings) by telling someone
unbosomed v ▷ unbosom
unbosoming v ▷ unbosom
unbosoms v ▷ unbosom
unbridled adj (of feelings or behaviour) not controlled in any way
unburden v (-s, -ing, -ed) relieve (one's mind or oneself) of a worry by confiding in someone
unburdened v ▷ unburden
unburdening v ▷ unburden
unburdens v ▷ unburden
uncannier adj ▷ uncanny
uncanniest adj ▷ uncanny
uncannily adv ▷ uncanny
uncanny adj (-nnier, -nniest) weird or mysterious > **uncannily** adv
unceremonious adj relaxed and informal
> **unceremoniously** adv
unceremoniously adv ▷ unceremonious
uncertain adj not able to be accurately known or predicted > **uncertainty** n (pl -ties)
uncertainties n ▷ uncertain
uncertainty n ▷ uncertain
uncle n (pl -s) brother of one's father or mother
unclean adj lacking moral, spiritual, or physical cleanliness
uncles n ▷ uncle
uncomfortable adj not physically relaxed
uncommon adj (-er, -est) not happening or encountered often > **uncommonly** adv
uncommoner adj ▷ uncommon
uncommonest adj ▷ uncommon
uncommonly adv ▷ uncommon
uncompromising adj not prepared to compromise
unconcerned adj lacking in concern or involvement > **unconcernedly** adv
unconcernedly adv ▷ unconcerned
unconditional adj without conditions or limitations
unconscionable adj having no principles, unscrupulous
unconscious adj lacking normal awareness through the senses ▸ n (pl -es) part of the mind containing instincts and ideas that exist without one's awareness
> **unconsciously** adv > **unconsciousness** n

(pl -es)
unconsciouses n ▷ unconscious
unconsciously adv ▷ unconscious
unconsciousness n ▷ unconscious
unconsciousnesses n ▷ unconscious
uncooperative adj not willing to help other
people with what they are doing
uncouth adj (-er, -est) lacking in good
manners, refinement, or grace
uncouther adj ▷ uncouth
uncouthest adj ▷ uncouth
uncover v (-s, -ing, -ed) reveal or disclose
uncovered v ▷ uncover
uncovering v ▷ uncover
uncovers v ▷ uncover
unction n (pl -s) act of anointing with oil in
sacramental ceremonies
unctions n ▷ unction
unctuous adj pretending to be kind and
concerned
undecided adj not having made up one's mind
undeniable adj unquestionably true
> **undeniably** adv
undeniably adv ▷ undeniable
under prep, adv indicating movement to or
position beneath the underside or base ▶ prep
less than
underage adj below the required or standard
age
underarm adj (SPORT) denoting a style of
throwing, bowling, or serving in which the
hand is swung below shoulder level ▶ adv
(SPORT) in an underarm style
undercarriage n (pl -s) landing gear of an
aircraft
undercarriages n ▷ undercarriage
underclass n (pl -es) class consisting of the
most disadvantaged people, such as the
long-term unemployed
underclasses n ▷ underclass
undercoat n (pl -s) coat of paint applied before
the final coat
undercoats n ▷ undercoat
undercover adj done or acting in secret
undercurrent n (pl -s) current that is not
apparent at the surface
undercurrents n ▷ undercurrent
undercut v (-cuts, -cutting, -cut) charge less
than (a competitor) to obtain trade
undercuts v ▷ undercut
undercutting v ▷ undercut
underdog n (pl -s) person or team in a weak or
underprivileged position
underdogs n ▷ underdog
underdone adj not cooked enough

underestimate v (-tes, -ting, -ted) make too
low an estimate of
underestimated v ▷ underestimate
underestimates v ▷ underestimate
underestimating v ▷ underestimate
underfoot adv under the feet
undergarment n (pl -s) any piece of
underwear
undergarments n ▷ undergarment
undergo v (-goes, -going, -went, -gone)
experience, endure, or sustain
undergoes v ▷ undergo
undergoing v ▷ undergo
undergone v ▷ undergo
undergraduate n (pl -s) person studying in a
university for a first degree
undergraduates n ▷ undergraduate
underground adj occurring, situated, used,
or going below ground level ▶ n (pl -s) electric
passenger railway operated in underground
tunnels
undergrounds n ▷ underground
undergrowth n (pl -s) small trees and bushes
growing beneath taller trees in a wood or
forest
undergrowths n ▷ undergrowth
underhand adj sly, deceitful, and secretive
underlain v ▷ underlie
underlay v ▷ underlie
underlie v (-lies, -lying, -lay, underlain)
lie or be placed under > **underlying** adj
fundamental or basic
underlies v ▷ underlie
underline v (-s, -ning, -d) draw a line under
underlined v ▷ underline
underlines v ▷ underline
underling n (pl -s) subordinate
underlings n ▷ underling
underlining v ▷ underline
underlying v, adj ▷ underlie
undermine v (-nes, -ning, -ned) weaken
gradually
undermined v ▷ undermine
undermines v ▷ undermine
undermining v ▷ undermine
underneath prep, adv under or beneath ▶ adj, n
(pl -s) lower (part or surface)
underneaths n ▷ underneath
underpants pl n man's undergarment for the
lower part of the body
underpass n (pl -es) section of a road that
passes under another road or a railway line
underpasses n ▷ underpass
underpin v (-pins, -pinning, -pinned) give
strength or support to

underpinned v ▷ underpin

underpinning v ▷ underpin

underpins v ▷ underpin

underprivileged adj lacking the rights and advantages of other members of society

underrate v (-tes, -ting, -ted) not realize the full potential of > **underrated** adj

underrated v, adj ▷ underrate

underrates v ▷ underrate

underrating v ▷ underrate

underseal n (pl -s) (CHIEFLY BRIT) coating of tar etc. applied to the underside of a motor vehicle to prevent corrosion

underseals n ▷ underseal

underside n (pl -s) bottom or lower surface

undersides n ▷ underside

understand v (-s, -ing, -stood) know and comprehend the nature or meaning of > **understandable** adj > **understandably** adv

understandable adj ▷ understand

understandably adj ▷ understand

understanding n (pl -s) ability to learn, judge, or make decisions ▶ adj kind and sympathetic ▶ v ▷ understand

understandings n ▷ understanding

understands v ▷ understand

understate v (-tes, -ting, -ted) describe or represent (something) in restrained terms > **understatement** n (pl -s)

understated v ▷ understate

understatement n ▷ understate

understatements n ▷ understate

understates v ▷ understate

understating v ▷ understate

understood v ▷ understand

understudied v ▷ understudy

understudies n, v ▷ understudy

understudy n (pl -dies) actor who studies a part in order to be able to replace the usual actor if necessary ▶ v (-dies, -dying, -died) act as an understudy for

understudying v ▷ understudy

undertake v (-takes, -taking, -took, -taken) agree or commit oneself to (something) or to do (something)

undertaken v ▷ undertake

undertaker n (pl -s) person whose job is to prepare corpses for burial or cremation and organize funerals

undertakers n ▷ undertaker

undertakes v ▷ undertake

undertaking n (pl -s) task or enterprise ▶ v ▷ undertake

undertakings n ▷ undertaking

undertone n (pl -s) quiet tone of voice

undertones n ▷ undertone

undertook v ▷ undertake

undertow n (pl -s) strong undercurrent flowing in a different direction from the surface current

undertows n ▷ undertow

underwear n (pl -s) clothing worn under the outer garments and next to the skin

underwears n ▷ underwear

underwent v ▷ undergo

underworld n (pl -s) criminals and their associates

underworlds n ▷ underworld

underwrite v (-writes, -writing, -wrote, -written) accept financial responsibility for (a commercial project)

underwriter n (pl -s) person who underwrites (esp. an insurance policy)

underwriters n ▷ underwriter

underwrites v ▷ underwrite

underwriting v ▷ underwrite

underwritten v ▷ underwrite

underwrote v ▷ underwrite

undesirable adj not desirable or pleasant, objectionable ▶ n (pl -s) objectionable person

undesirables n ▷ undesirable

undid v ▷ undo

undo v (-does, -doing, -did, -done) open, unwrap > **undone** adj

undoes v ▷ undo

undoing n (pl -s) cause of someone's downfall ▶ v ▷ undo

undoings n ▷ undoing

undone v, adj ▷ undo

undoubted adj certain or indisputable > **undoubtedly** adv

undoubtedly adv ▷ undoubted

undue adj greater than is reasonable, excessive > **unduly** adv

undulate v (-tes, -ting, -ted) move in waves > **undulation** n (pl -s)

undulated v ▷ undulate

undulates v ▷ undulate

undulating v ▷ undulate

undulation n ▷ undulate

undulations n ▷ undulate

unduly adv ▷ undue

undying adj never ending, eternal

unearth v (-s, -ing, -ed) reveal or discover by searching

unearthed v ▷ unearth

unearthing v ▷ unearth

unearthly adj ghostly or eerie

unearths v ▷ unearth

unease n (pl -s) feeling of anxiety

uneases n ▷ unease
uneasier adj ▷ uneasy
uneasiest adj ▷ uneasy
uneasily adv ▷ uneasy
uneasiness n ▷ uneasy
uneasinesses n ▷ uneasy
uneasy adj (-sier, -siest) (of a person) anxious or apprehensive > **uneasily** adv > **uneasiness** n (pl -es)
unemployed adj out of work
   > **unemployment** n (pl -s)
unemployment n ▷ unemployed
unemployments n ▷ unemployed
unequivocal adj completely clear in meaning
   > **unequivocally** adv
unequivocally adv ▷ unequivocal
unerring adj never mistaken, consistently accurate
unexceptionable adj beyond criticism or objection
unfailing adj continuous or reliable
   > **unfailingly** adv
unfailingly adv ▷ unfailing
unfair adj (-er, -est) not right, fair, or just
   > **unfairly** adv > **unfairness** n (pl -es)
unfairer adj ▷ unfair
unfairest adj ▷ unfair
unfairly adv ▷ unfair
unfairness n ▷ unfair
unfairnesses n ▷ unfair
unfaithful adj having sex with someone other than one's regular partner > **unfaithfulness** n (pl -es)
unfaithfulness n ▷ unfaithful
unfaithfulnesses n ▷ unfaithful
unfeeling adj without sympathy
unfit adj unqualified or unsuitable
unflappabilities n ▷ unflappable
unflappability n ▷ unflappable
unflappable adj (Informal) not easily upset
   > **unflappability** n (pl -ties)
unfold v (-s, -ing, -ed) open or spread out from a folded state
unfolded v ▷ unfold
unfolding v ▷ unfold
unfolds v ▷ unfold
unforgettable adj impossible to forget, memorable
unfortunate adj unlucky, unsuccessful, or unhappy > **unfortunately** adv
unfortunately adv ▷ unfortunate
unfrock v (-s, -ing, -ed) deprive (a priest in holy orders) of his or her priesthood
unfrocked v ▷ unfrock
unfrocking v ▷ unfrock

unfrocks v ▷ unfrock
ungainlier adj ▷ ungainly
ungainliest adj ▷ ungainly
ungainly adj (-lier, -liest) lacking grace when moving
ungodlier adj ▷ ungodly
ungodliest adj ▷ ungodly
ungodly adj (-lier, -liest) (Informal) unreasonable or outrageous
ungrateful adj not grateful or thankful
unguarded adj not protected
unguent [ung-gwent] n (pl -s) (Lit) ointment
unguents n ▷ unguent
unhand v (-s, -ing, -ed) (Old-fashioned or lit) release from one's grasp
unhanded v ▷ unhand
unhanding v ▷ unhand
unhands v ▷ unhand
unhappier adj ▷ unhappy
unhappiest adj ▷ unhappy
unhappily adv ▷ unhappy
unhappiness n ▷ unhappy
unhappinesses n ▷ unhappy
unhappy adj (-ppier, -ppiest) sad or depressed
   > **unhappily** adv > **unhappiness** n (pl -es)
unhealthier adj ▷ unhealthy
unhealthiest adj ▷ unhealthy
unhealthy adj (-thier, -thiest) likely to cause poor health
unhinge v (-ges, -ging, -ged) derange or unbalance (a person or his or her mind)
unhinged v ▷ unhinge
unhinges v ▷ unhinge
unhinging v ▷ unhinge
unicorn n (pl -s) imaginary horselike creature with one horn growing from its forehead
unicorns n ▷ unicorn
unification n ▷ unify
unifications n ▷ unify
unified v ▷ unify
unifies v ▷ unify
uniform n (pl -s) special identifying set of clothes for the members of an organization, such as soldiers ▶ adj regular and even throughout, unvarying > **uniformly** adv
   > **uniformity** n (pl -ties)
uniformities n ▷ uniform
uniformity n ▷ uniform
uniformly adv ▷ uniform
uniforms n ▷ uniform
unify v (-fies, -fying, -fied) make or become one > **unification** n (pl -s)
unifying v ▷ unify
unilateral adj made or done by only one person or group > **unilaterally** adv

unilaterally adv ▷ unilateral

unimpeachable adj completely honest and reliable

uninterested adj having or showing no interest in someone or something

union n (pl -s) uniting or being united

unionist n (pl -s) member or supporter of a trade union

unionists n ▷ unionist

unionization n ▷ unionize

unionizations n ▷ unionize

unionize v (-zes, -zing, -zed) organize (workers) into a trade union ▷ **unionization** n (pl -s)

unionized v ▷ unionize

unionizes v ▷ unionize

unionizing v ▷ unionize

unions n ▷ union

unique [yoo-neek] adj being the only one of a particular type ▷ **uniquely** adv

uniquely adv ▷ unique

unisex adj designed for use by both sexes

unison n (pl -s) complete agreement

unisons n ▷ unison

unit n (pl -s) single undivided entity or whole

unitary adj consisting of a single undivided whole

unite v (-tes, -ting, -ted) make or become an integrated whole

united v ▷ unite

unites v ▷ unite

unities n ▷ unity

uniting v ▷ unite

units n ▷ unit

unity n (pl -ties) state of being one

universal adj or of typical of the whole of mankind or of nature ▷ **universally** adv ▷ **universality** n (pl -ties)

universalities n ▷ universal

universality n ▷ universal

universally adv ▷ universal

universe n (pl -s) whole of all existing matter, energy, and space

universes n ▷ universe

universities n ▷ university

university n (pl -ties) institution of higher education with the authority to award degrees

unkempt adj (of the hair) not combed

unknown adj not known ▶ n (pl -s) unknown person, quantity, or thing

unknowns n ▷ unknown

unleaded adj (of petrol) containing less tetraethyl lead, in order to reduce environmental pollution

unless conj except under the circumstances that

unlike adj dissimilar or different ▶ prep not like or typical of

unlikely adj improbable

unload v (-s, -ing, -ed) remove (cargo) from (a ship, truck, or plane)

unloaded v ▷ unload

unloading v ▷ unload

unloads v ▷ unload

unmask v (-s, -ing, -ed) remove the mask or disguise from

unmasked v ▷ unmask

unmasking v ▷ unmask

unmasks v ▷ unmask

unmentionable adj unsuitable as a topic of conversation

unmistakable, unmistakeable adj not ambiguous, clear ▷ **unmistakably, unmistakeably** adv

unmistakably adv ▷ unmistakable

unmistakeable adj ▷ unmistakable

unmistakeably adv ▷ unmistakable

unmitigated adj not reduced or lessened in severity etc.

unmoved adj not affected by emotion, indifferent

unnatural adj strange and frightening because not usual

unnerve v (-ves, -ving, -ved) cause to lose courage, confidence, or self-control

unnerved v ▷ unnerve

unnerves v ▷ unnerve

unnerving v ▷ unnerve

unnumbered adj countless

unorthodox adj (of ideas, methods, etc.) unconventional and not generally accepted

unpack v (-s, -ing, -ed) remove the contents of (a suitcase, trunk, etc.)

unpacked v ▷ unpack

unpacking v ▷ unpack

unpacks v ▷ unpack

unparalleled adj not equalled, supreme

unpick v (-s, -ing, -ed) undo (the stitches) of (a piece of sewing)

unpicked v ▷ unpick

unpicking v ▷ unpick

unpicks v ▷ unpick

unpleasant adj not pleasant or agreeable ▷ **unpleasantly** adv ▷ **unpleasantness** n (pl -s)

unpleasantly adv ▷ unpleasant

unpleasantness n ▷ unpleasant

unpleasantnesses n ▷ unpleasant

unprintable adj unsuitable for printing for reasons of obscenity or libel

unprofessional *adj* contrary to the accepted code of a profession ⊳ **unprofessionally** *adv*
  unprofessionally *adv* ⊳ unprofessional
unqualified *adj* lacking the necessary qualifications
unravel *v* (**-vels, -velling, -velled**) reduce (something knitted or woven) to separate strands
  unravelled *v* ⊳ unravel
  unravelling *v* ⊳ unravel
  unravels *v* ⊳ unravel
unremitting *adj* never slackening or stopping
unrequited *adj* not returned
unrest *n* (*pl* **-s**) rebellious state of discontent
  unrests *n* ⊳ unrest
unrivalled *adj* having no equal
unroll *v* (**-s, -ing, -ed**) open out or unwind (something rolled or coiled) or (of something rolled or coiled) become opened out or unwound
  unrolled *v* ⊳ unroll
  unrolling *v* ⊳ unroll
  unrolls *v* ⊳ unroll
  unrulier *adj* ⊳ unruly
  unruliest *adj* ⊳ unruly
unruly *adj* (**-lier, -liest**) difficult to control or organize
unsavoury *adj* distasteful or objectionable
unscathed *adj* not harmed or injured
unscrupulous *adj* prepared to act dishonestly, unprincipled
unseat *v* (**-s, -ing, -ed**) throw or displace from a seat or saddle
  unseated *v* ⊳ unseat
  unseating *v* ⊳ unseat
  unseats *v* ⊳ unseat
unsettled *adj* lacking order or stability
  unsightlier *adj* ⊳ unsightly
  unsightliest *adj* ⊳ unsightly
unsightly *adj* (**-lier, -liest**) unpleasant to look at
  unsociable *adj* ⊳ unsocial
unsocial *adj* (*also* **unsociable**) avoiding the company of other people
unsound *adj* unhealthy or unstable
unstable *adj* (**-r, -st**) lacking stability or firmness
  unstabler *adj* ⊳ unstable
  unstablest *adj* ⊳ unstable
unsuitable *adj* not right or appropriate for a particular purpose ⊳ **unsuitably** *adv*
  unsuitably *adv* ⊳ unsuitable
unsuited *adj* not appropriate for a particular task or situation
unswerving *adj* firm, constant, not changing

unthinkable *adj* out of the question, inconceivable
  untidier *adj* ⊳ untidy
  untidiest *adj* ⊳ untidy
  untidily *adv* ⊳ untidy
  untidiness *n* ⊳ untidy
  untidinesses *n* ⊳ untidy
untidy *adj* (**-dier, -diest**) messy and disordered ⊳ **untidily** *adv* ⊳ **untidiness** *n* (*pl* **-es**)
untie *v* (**-ties, -tying, -tied**) open or free (something that is tied)
  untied *v* ⊳ untie
  unties *v* ⊳ untie
until *conj* up to the time that ▶ *prep* in or throughout the period before
  untimelier *adj* ⊳ untimely
  untimeliest *adj* ⊳ untimely
untimely *adj* (**-lier, -liest**) occurring before the expected or normal time
unto *prep* (*Old-fashioned*) to
untold *adj* incapable of description
untouchable *adj* above reproach or suspicion ▶ *n* (*pl* **-s**) member of the lowest Hindu caste in India
  untouchables *n* ⊳ untouchable
untoward *adj* causing misfortune or annoyance
untrue *adj* (**-r, -st**) incorrect or false
  untruer *adj* ⊳ untrue
  untruest *adj* ⊳ untrue
untruth *n* (*pl* **-s**) statement that is not true, lie
  untruths *n* ⊳ untruth
  untying *v* ⊳ untie
unusual *adj* uncommon or extraordinary ⊳ **unusually** *adv*
  unusually *adv* ⊳ unusual
unutterable *adj* incapable of being expressed in words ⊳ **unutterably** *adv*
  unutterably *adv* ⊳ unutterable
unvarnished *adj* not elaborated upon
  unwieldier *adj* ⊳ unwieldy
  unwieldiest *adj* ⊳ unwieldy
unwieldy *adj* (**-dier, -diest**) too heavy, large, or awkward to be easily handled
unwind *v* (**-s, -ing, unwound**) relax after a busy or tense time
  unwinding *v* ⊳ unwind
  unwinds *v* ⊳ unwind
unwitting *adj* not intentional ⊳ **unwittingly** *adv*
  unwittingly *adv* ⊳ unwitting
unwonted *adj* out of the ordinary
  unworthier *adj* ⊳ unworthy
  unworthiest *adj* ⊳ unworthy
unworthy *adj* (**-thier, -thiest**) not deserving

or worthy

unwound v ▷ unwind

unwrap v (-s, -pping, -pped) remove the wrapping from (something)
unwrapped v ▷ unwrap
unwrapping v ▷ unwrap
unwraps v ▷ unwrap

unwritten adj not printed or in writing

up prep, adv indicating movement to or position at a higher place ▶ adv indicating readiness, intensity or completeness, etc. ▶ adj of a high or higher position ▶ v (-s, -pping, -pped) increase or raise ▶ adv (also **upwards**) from a lower to a higher place, level, or condition

upbeat adj (Informal) cheerful and optimistic ▶ n (pl -s) (MUSIC) unaccented beat
upbeats n ▷ upbeat

upbraid v (-s, -ing, -ded) scold or reproach
upbraided v ▷ upbraid
upbraiding v ▷ upbraid
upbraids v ▷ upbraid

upbringing n (pl -s) education of a person during the formative years
upbringings n ▷ upbringing

update v (-tes, -ting, -ted) bring up to date
updated v ▷ update
updates v ▷ update
updating v ▷ update

upend v (-s, -ing, -ed) turn or set (something) on its end
upended v ▷ upend
upending v ▷ upend
upends v ▷ upend

upfront adj open and frank ▶ adv, adj (of money) paid out at the beginning of a business arrangement

upgrade v (-des, -ding, -ded) promote (a person or job) to a higher rank
upgraded v ▷ upgrade
upgrades v ▷ upgrade
upgrading v ▷ upgrade

upheaval n (pl -s) strong, sudden, or violent disturbance
upheavals n ▷ upheaval
upheld v ▷ uphold

uphill adj sloping or leading upwards ▶ adv up a slope ▶ n (pl -s) (S AFR) difficulty
uphills n ▷ uphill

uphold v (-s, -ing, upheld) maintain or defend against opposition > **upholder** n (pl -s)
upholder n ▷ uphold
upholders n ▷ uphold
upholding v ▷ uphold
upholds v ▷ uphold

upholster v (-s, -ing, -ed) fit (a chair or sofa) with padding, springs, and covering > **upholsterer** n (pl -s)
upholstered v ▷ upholster
upholsterer n ▷ upholster
upholsterers n ▷ upholster
upholsteries n ▷ upholstery
upholstering v ▷ upholster
upholsters v ▷ upholster

upholstery n (pl -ries) soft covering on a chair or sofa

upkeep n (pl -s) act, process, or cost of keeping something in good repair
upkeeps n ▷ upkeep

upland adj of or in an area of high or relatively high ground > **uplands** pl n area of high or relatively high ground
uplands pl n ▷ upland

uplift v (-s, -ing, -ed) raise or lift up ▶ n (pl -s) act or process of improving moral, social, or cultural conditions > **uplifting** adj
uplifted v ▷ uplift
uplifting v, adj ▷ uplift
uplifts v, n ▷ uplift

upload v (-s, -ing, -ed) transfer (data or a program) from one's own computer into the memory of another computer
uploaded v ▷ upload
uploading v ▷ upload
uploads v ▷ upload

upon prep on
upped v ▷ up

upper adj higher or highest in physical position, wealth, rank, or status ▶ n (pl -s) part of a shoe above the sole

uppermost adj highest in position, power, or importance ▶ adv in or into the highest place or position
uppers n ▷ upper
upping v ▷ up

uppish, uppity adj (BRIT) (Informal) snobbish, arrogant, or presumptuous
uppity adj ▷ uppish

upright adj vertical or erect ▶ adv vertically or in an erect position ▶ n (pl -s) vertical support, such as a post > **uprightness** n (pl -s)
uprightness n ▷ upright
uprightnesses n ▷ upright
uprights n ▷ upright

uprising n (pl -s) rebellion or revolt
uprisings n ▷ uprising

uproar n (pl -s) disturbance characterized by loud noise and confusion

uproarious adj very funny > **uproariously** adv
uproariously adv ▷ uproarious

uproars n ▷ uproar
uproot v (-s, -ing, -ed) pull up by or as if by the roots
uprooted v ▷ uproot
uprooting v ▷ uproot
uproots v ▷ uproot
ups v ▷ up
upset adj emotionally or physically disturbed or distressed ▶ v (-s, -tting, upset) tip over ▶ n (pl -s) unexpected defeat or reversal > **upsetting** adj
upsets v, n ▷ upset
upsetting v, adj ▷ upset
upshot n (pl -s) final result or conclusion
upshots n ▷ upshot
upstage adj at the back half of the stage ▶ v (-ges, -ging, -ged) (Informal) draw attention to oneself from (someone else)
upstaged v ▷ upstage
upstages v ▷ upstage
upstaging v ▷ upstage
upstairs adv to or on an upper floor of a building ▶ n upper floor
upstanding adj of good character
upstart n (pl -s) person who has risen suddenly to a position of power and behaves arrogantly
upstarts n ▷ upstart
upstream adv, adj in or towards the higher part of a stream
upsurge n (pl -s) rapid rise or swell
upsurges n ▷ upsurge
uptake n (pl -s) (Informal) quick or slow to understand or learn
uptakes n ▷ uptake
uptight adj (Informal) nervously tense, irritable, or angry
upturn n (pl -s) upward trend or improvement > **upturned** adj facing upwards
upturned adj ▷ upturn
upturns n ▷ upturn
upward adj directed or moving towards a higher place or level
upwards adv ▷ up

> **ur** interj. Ur is a sound people make when hesitating in speech. If someone plays this, you may be able to use it to form words that begin with UR. Ur is also handy for connecting words beginning with U to those ending in R. Ur scores 2 points.

uranium n (pl -s) (CHEM) radioactive silvery-white metallic element, used chiefly as a source of nuclear energy
uraniums n ▷ uranium

urban adj of or living in a city or town
urbane adj (-r, -st) characterized by courtesy, elegance, and sophistication > **urbanity** n (pl -ties)
urbaner adj ▷ urbane
urbanest adj ▷ urbane
urbanities n ▷ urbane
urbanity n ▷ urbane
urbanization n ▷ urbanize
urbanizations n ▷ urbanize
urbanize v (-zes, -zing, -zed) make (a rural area) more industrialized and urban > **urbanization** n (pl -s)
urbanized v ▷ urbanize
urbanizes v ▷ urbanize
urbanizing v ▷ urbanize
urchin n (pl -s) mischievous child
urchins n ▷ urchin
urethra [yew-reeth-ra] n (pl -rae) canal that carries urine from the bladder out of the body
urethrae n ▷ urethra
urge n (pl -s) strong impulse, inner drive, or yearning ▶ v (-urges, -urging, -urged) plead with or press (a person to do something)
urged v ▷ urge
urgencies n ▷ urgent
urgency n ▷ urgent
urgent adj requiring speedy action or attention > **urgency** n (pl -cies) > **urgently** adv
urgently adv ▷ urgent
urges n, v ▷ urge
urging v ▷ urge
urinal n (pl -s) sanitary fitting used by men for urination
urinals n ▷ urine
urinary adj ▷ urine
urinate v (-tes, -ting, -ted) discharge urine > **urination** n (pl -s)
urinated v ▷ urinate
urinates v ▷ urinate
urinating v ▷ urinate
urination n ▷ urinate
urinations n ▷ urinate
urine n (pl -s) pale yellow fluid excreted by the kidneys to the bladder and passed as waste from the body > **urinary** adj
urines n ▷ urine
urn n (pl -s) vase used as a container for the ashes of the dead
urns n ▷ urn
ursine adj of or like a bear
us pron ▷ we
usable adj able to be used
usage n (pl -s) regular or constant use
usages n ▷ usage

use v (-ses, -sing, -sed) put into service or action ▶ n (pl -s) using or being used > **user** n (pl -s) > **useful** adj > **usefully** adv > **usefulness** n (pl -es) > **useless** adj > **uselessly** adv > **uselessness** n (pl -es)

used adj second-hand ▶ v ▷ use

useful adj ▷ use

usefully adv ▷ use

usefulness n ▷ use

usefulnesses n ▷ use

useless adj ▷ use

uselessly adv ▷ use

uselessness n ▷ use

uselessnesses n ▷ use

user n ▷ use

username n (pl -s) (COMPUTERS) name entered into a computer for identification purposes

usernames n ▷ username

users n ▷ use

uses v, n ▷ use

usher n (pl -s) official who shows people to their seats, as in a church ▶ v (-s, -ing, -ed) conduct or escort

ushered v ▷ usher

usherette n (pl -s) female assistant in a cinema who shows people to their seats

usherettes n ▷ usherette

ushering v ▷ usher

ushers n, v ▷ usher

using v ▷ use

usual adj of the most normal, frequent, or regular type

usually adv most often, in most cases

usurer n ▷ usury

usurers n ▷ usury

usuries n ▷ usury

usurp [yewz-zurp] v (-s, -ing, -ed) seize (a position or power) without authority > **usurpation** n (pl -s) > **usurper** n (pl -s)

usurpation n ▷ usurp

usurpations n ▷ usurp

usurped v ▷ usurp

usurper n ▷ usurp

usurpers n ▷ usurp

usurping v ▷ usurp

usurps v ▷ usurp

usury n (pl -ries) practice of lending money at an extremely high rate of interest > **usurer** [yewz-yoor-er] ▶ n (pl -s)

> **ut** n (uts). Ut is a musical note. This unusual word is useful for connecting words beginning with U to those ending with T. Ut scores 2 points.

ute [yoot] n (pl -s) (AUST & NZ) (Informal) utility truck

utensil n (pl -s) tool or container for practical use

utensils n ▷ utensil

uteri n ▷ uterus

uterine adj ▷ uterus

uterus [yew-ter-russ] n (pl uteri) womb > **uterine** adj

utes n ▷ ute

utilitarian adj useful rather than beautiful

utilitarianism n (pl -s) (ETHICS) doctrine that the right action is the one that brings about the greatest good for the greatest number of people

utilitarianisms n ▷ utilitarianism

utilities n ▷ utility

utility n (pl -ties) usefulness ▶ adj designed for use rather than beauty

utilization n ▷ utilize

utilizations n ▷ utilize

utilize v (-zes, -zing, -zed) make practical use of > **utilization** n (pl -s)

utilized v ▷ utilize

utilizes v ▷ utilize

utilizing v ▷ utilize

utmost, uttermost adj, n (pl -s) (of) the greatest possible degree or amount

utmosts n ▷ utmost

utopia [yew-tope-ee-a] n (pl -s) any real or imaginary society, place, or state considered to be perfect or ideal > **utopian** adj

utopian adj ▷ utopia

utopias n ▷ utopia

utter[1] v (-s, -ing, -ed) express (something) in sounds or words

utter[2] adj total or absolute > **utterly** adv

utterance n (pl -s) something uttered

utterances n ▷ utterance

uttered v ▷ utter[1]

uttering v ▷ utter[1]

utterly adv ▷ utter[2]

uttermost adj, n (pl -s) ▷ utmost

uttermosts n ▷ uttermost

utters v ▷ utter[1]

uvula [yew-view-la] n (pl -s) small fleshy part of the soft palate that hangs in the back of the throat > **uvular** adj

uvular adj ▷ uvula

uvulas n ▷ uvula

uxorious [ux-or-ee-uss] adj excessively fond of or dependent on one's wife

Vv

If you have a V on your rack, the first thing to remember is that there are no valid two-letter words beginning with V. In fact, there are no two-letter words that end in V either, so you can't form any two-letter words using V. Remembering this will stop you wasting time trying to think of some. While V is useless for two-letter words, it does start some good three-letter words. **Vex** and **vox** (13 points each) are the best of these, while **vaw, vow** and **vly** (9 each) are also useful.

vac n (**vacs**). Vac is a short form of vacuum cleaner. This word can prove useful when you have a V but not much space to play it in. Remember that if you have the letters for vac, you might be able to form **cave** using an E that is already on the board. Vac scores 8 points.

vacancies n ▷ vacancy
vacancy n (pl -**cies**) unfilled job
vacant adj (of a toilet, room, etc.) unoccupied > **vacantly** adv
vacantly adv ▷ vacant
vacate v (-**tes**, -**ting**, -**ted**) cause (something) to be empty by leaving
vacated v ▷ vacate
vacates v ▷ vacate
vacating v ▷ vacate
vacation n time when universities and law courts are closed
vacations n ▷ vacation
vaccinate v (-**tes**, -**ting**, -**ted**) inject with a vaccine > **vaccination** n (pl -**s**)
vaccinated v ▷ vaccinate
vaccinates v ▷ vaccinate
vaccinating v ▷ vaccinate
vaccination n ▷ vaccinate
vaccinations n ▷ vaccinate
vaccine n (pl -**s**) substance designed to cause a mild form of a disease to make a person immune to the disease itself
vaccines n ▷ vaccine
vacillate [vass-ill-late] v (-**tes**, -**ting**, -**ted**) keep changing one's mind or opinions > **vacillation** n (pl -**s**)
vacillated v ▷ vacillate
vacillates v ▷ vacillate
vacillating v ▷ vacillate

vacillation n ▷ vacillate
vacillations n ▷ vacillate
vacua n ▷ vacuum
vacuous adj not expressing intelligent thought > **vacuity** n (pl -**ties**)
vacuum n (pl -**cuums**, -**cua**) empty space from which all or most air or gas has been removed ▶ v (-**s**, -**ing**, -**ed**) clean with a vacuum cleaner
vacuumed v ▷ vacuum
vacuuming v ▷ vacuum
vacuums n ▷ vacuum
vagabond n (pl -**s**) person with no fixed home, esp. a beggar
vagabonds n ▷ vagabond
vagaries n ▷ vagary
vagary [vaig-a-ree] n (pl -**ries**) unpredictable change
vagina [vaj-jine-a] n (pl -**s**) (in female mammals) passage from the womb to the external genitals > **vaginal** adj
vaginal adj ▷ vagina
vaginas n ▷ vagina
vagrancies n ▷ vagrancy
vagrancy n ▷ vagrant
vagrant [vaig-rant] n (pl -**s**) person with no settled home ▶ adj wandering > **vagrancy** n (pl -**cies**)
vagrants n ▷ vagrant
vague adj (-**guer**, -**guest**) not clearly explained > **vaguely** adv
vaguely adv ▷ vague
vaguer adj ▷ vague
vaguest adj ▷ vague
vain adj (-**er**, -**est**) excessively proud, esp. of one's appearance
vainer adj ▷ vain
vainest adj ▷ vain
vainglorious adj (Lit) boastful

valance [**val**-lenss] *n* (*pl* **-s**) piece of drapery round the edge of a bed
  valances *n* ▷ valance
vale *n* (*pl* **-s**) (*Lit*) valley
valediction *n* (*pl* **-s**) farewell speech
  valedictions *n* ▷ valediction
valedictory [val-lid-**dik**-tree] *adj* (of a speech, performance, etc.) intended as a farewell
valence [**vale**-ence] *n* (*pl* **-s**) molecular bonding between atoms
  valences *n* ▷ valence
  valencies *n* ▷ valency
valency *n* (*pl* **-cies**) power of an atom to make molecular bonds
valentine *n* (*pl* **-s**) (person to whom one sends) a romantic card on Saint Valentine's Day, 14th February
  valentines *n* ▷ valentine
valerian *n* (*pl* **-s**) herb used as a sedative
  valerians *n* ▷ valerian
  vales *n* ▷ vale
valet *n* (*pl* **-s**) man's personal male servant
  valets *n* ▷ valet
valetudinarian [val-lit-yew-din-**air**-ee-an] *n* (*pl* **-s**) person with a long-term illness
  valetudinarians *n* ▷ valetudinarian
valiant *adj* brave or courageous
valid *adj* (**-er, -est**) soundly reasoned > **validity** *n* (*pl* **-ies**)
validate *v* (**-tes, -ting, -ted**) make valid > **validation** *n* (*pl* **-s**)
  validated *v* ▷ validate
  validates *v* ▷ validate
  validating *v* ▷ validate
  validation *n* ▷ validate
  validations *n* ▷ validate
  valider *adj* ▷ valid
  validest *adj* ▷ valid
  validities *n* ▷ valid
  validity *n* ▷ valid
valise [val-**leez**] *n* (*pl* **-s**) (*Old-fashioned*) small suitcase
  valises *n* ▷ valise
valley *n* (*pl* **-s**) low area between hills, often with a river running through it
  valleys *n* ▷ valley
valour *n* (*pl* **-s**) (*Lit*) bravery
  valours *n* ▷ valour
valuable *adj* having great worth
  valuables *pl n* valuable personal property
valuation *n* (*pl* **-s**) assessment of worth
  valuations *n* ▷ valuation
value *n* (*pl* **-s**) importance, usefulness ▶ *pl* moral principles ▶ *v* (**-ues, -uing, -ued**) assess the worth or desirability of > **valueless** *adj*

  > **valuer** *n* (*pl* **-s**)
  valued *v* ▷ value
  valueless *adj* ▷ value
  valuer *n* ▷ value
  valuers *n* ▷ value
  values *n, v* ▷ value
  valuing *v* ▷ value
valve *n* (*pl* **-s**) device to control the movement of fluid through a pipe > **valvular** *adj*
  valves *n* ▷ valve
  valvular *adj* ▷ valve
vamp[1] *n* (*pl* **-s**) (*Informal*) sexually attractive woman who seduces men
vamp[2] *v* (**-s, -ing, -ed**) make (a story, piece of music, etc.) seem new by inventing additional parts
  vamped *v* ▷ vamp[2]
  vamping *v* ▷ vamp[2]
vampire *n* (*pl* **-s**) (in folklore) corpse that rises at night to drink the blood of the living
  vampires *n* ▷ vampire
  vamps *n, v* ▷ vamp[1, 2]
van[1] *n* (*pl* **-s**) motor vehicle for transporting goods
van[2] *n* (*pl* **-s**) ▷ vanguard
vanadium *n* (*pl* **-s**) (CHEM) metallic element, used in steel
  vanadiums *n* ▷ vanadium
vandal *n* (*pl* **-s**) person who deliberately damages property > **vandalism** *n* (*pl* **-s**) > **vandalize** *v* (**-zes, -zing, -zed**)
  vandalism *n* ▷ vandal
  vandalisms *n* ▷ vandal
  vandalize *n* ▷ vandal
  vandalized *v* ▷ vandal
  vandalizes *v* ▷ vandal
  vandalizing *v* ▷ vandal
  vandals *n* ▷ vandal
vane *n* (*pl* **-s**) flat blade on a rotary device such as a weathercock or propeller
  vanes *n* ▷ vane
vanguard *n* (*pl* **-s**) unit of soldiers leading an army
  vanguards *n* ▷ vanguard
vanilla *n* (*pl* **-s**) seed pod of a tropical climbing orchid, used for flavouring
  vanillas *n* ▷ vanilla
vanish *v* (**-es, -ing, -ed**) disappear suddenly or mysteriously
  vanished *v* ▷ vanish
  vanishes *v* ▷ vanish
  vanishing *v* ▷ vanish
  vanities *n* ▷ vanity
vanity *n* (*pl* **-ies**) (display of) excessive pride
vanquish *v* (**-es, -ing, -ed**) (*Lit*) defeat

(someone) utterly

vanquished v ▷ vanquish

vanquishes v ▷ vanquish

vanquishing v ▷ vanquish

vans n ▷ van[1, 2]

vantage n (pl -s) position that gives one an overall view

vantages n ▷ vantage

vapid adj (-er, -est) lacking character, dull

vapider adj ▷ vapid

vapidest adj ▷ vapid

vaporize v ▷ vapour

vaporized v ▷ vapour

vaporizer n ▷ vapour

vaporizers n ▷ vapour

vaporizes v ▷ vapour

vaporizing v ▷ vapour

vaporous adj ▷ vapour

vapour n (pl -s) moisture suspended in air as steam or mist > **vaporize** v (-zes, -zing, -zed) > **vaporizer** n (pl -s) > **vaporous** adj

vapours n ▷ vapour

variabilities n ▷ variable

variability n ▷ variable

variable adj not always the same, changeable ▶ n (pl -s) (MATHS) expression with a range of values > **variability** n (pl -ties)

variables n ▷ variable

variant adj differing from a standard or type ▶ n (pl -s) something that differs from a standard or type

variants n ▷ variant

variation n (pl -s) something presented in a slightly different form

variations n ▷ variation

varied v, adj ▷ vary

variegated adj having patches or streaks of different colours > **variegation** n (pl -s)

variegation n ▷ variegate

variegations n ▷ variegate

varies v ▷ vary

varieties n ▷ variety

variety n (pl -ies) state of being diverse or various

various adj of several kinds > **variously** adv

variously adv ▷ various

varnish n (pl -es) solution of oil and resin, put on a surface to make it hard and glossy ▶ v (-es, -ing, -ed) apply varnish to

varnished v ▷ varnish

varnishes n, v ▷ varnish

varnishing v ▷ varnish

vary v (-ries, -rying, -ried) change > **varied** adj

varying v ▷ vary

vascular adj (BIOL) relating to vessels

vase n (pl -s) ornamental jar, esp. for flowers

vasectomies n ▷ vasectomy

vasectomy n (pl -mies) surgical removal of part of the vas deferens, as a contraceptive method

vases n ▷ vase

vassal n (pl -s) (HIST) man given land by a lord in return for military service > **vassalage** n (pl -s)

vassalage n ▷ vassal

vassalages n ▷ vassal

vassals n ▷ vassal

vast adj (-er, -est) extremely large > **vastly** adv > **vastness** n (pl -es)

vaster adj ▷ vast

vastest adj ▷ vast

vastly adv ▷ vast

vastness n ▷ vast

vastnesses n ▷ vast

vat n (pl -s) large container for liquids

vats n ▷ vat

vaudeville n (pl -s) variety entertainment of songs and comic turns

vaudevilles n ▷ vaudeville

vault[1] n (pl -s) secure room for storing valuables

vault[2] v (-s, -ing, -ed) jump over (something) by resting one's hand(s) on it. ▶ n such a jump

vaulted adj having an arched roof ▶ v ▷ vault[2]

vaulting v ▷ vault[1, 2]

vaults n, v ▷ vault[1, 2]

vaunt v (-s, -ing, -ed) describe or display (success or possessions) boastfully > **vaunted** adj

vaunted adj, v ▷ vaunt

vaunting v ▷ vaunt

vaunts v ▷ vaunt

> **vaw** n (**vaws**). Vaw is a letter of the Hebrew alphabet. This is a very unusual word that can be useful when you are short of options. If you have the tiles for vaw, look out for opportunities to play **wave** or **wavy** using an E or Y that is already on the board. Vaw scores 9 points.

veal n (pl -s) calf meat

veals n ▷ veal

vector n (pl -s) (MATHS) quantity that has size and direction, such as force

vectors n ▷ vector

veer v (-s, -ing, -ed) change direction suddenly

veered v ▷ veer

veering v ▷ veer

veers v ▷ veer

> **veg** n (**veges**). Veg is a short form of **vegetable**. If someone plays this, look

out for opportunities to form **vegan** or **vegetate** from it. Veg scores 7 points.

vegan [vee-gan] n (pl -s) person who eats no meat, fish, eggs, or dairy products ▶ adj suitable for a vegan > **veganism** n (pl -s)
  veganism n ▷ vegan
  veganisms n ▷ vegan
  vegans n ▷ vegan

vegetable n (pl -s) edible plant ▶ adj of or like plants or vegetables
  vegetables n ▷ vegetable

vegetarian n (pl -s) person who eats no meat or fish ▶ adj suitable for a vegetarian > **vegetarianism** n (pl -s)
  vegetarianism n ▷ vegetarian
  vegetarianisms n ▷ vegetarian
  vegetarians n ▷ vegetarian

vegetate v (-tes, -ting, -ted) live a dull boring life with no mental stimulation
  vegetated v ▷ vegetate
  vegetates v ▷ vegetate
  vegetating v ▷ vegetate

vegetation n (pl -s) plant life of a given place
  vegetations n ▷ vegetation
  vehemence n ▷ vehement
  vehemences n ▷ vehement

vehement adj expressing strong feelings > **vehemence** n (pl -s) > **vehemently** adv
  vehemently adv ▷ vehement

vehicle n (pl -s) machine, esp. with an engine and wheels, for carrying people or objects > **vehicular** adj
  vehicles n ▷ vehicle
  vehicular adj ▷ vehicle

veil n (pl -s) piece of thin cloth covering the head or face ▶ v (-s, -ing, -ed) cover with or as if with a veil
  veiled adj disguised ▶ v ▷ veil
  veiling v ▷ veil
  veils n, v ▷ veil

vein n (pl -s) tube that takes blood to the heart > **veined** adj
  veined adj ▷ vein
  veins n ▷ vein

veld, veldt n (pl -s) high grassland in southern Africa
  velds n ▷ veld

veldskoen, velskoen n (pl -s) (S AFR) leather ankle boot
  veldskoens n ▷ veldskoen
  veldts n ▷ veld

vellum n (pl -s) fine calfskin parchment
  vellums n ▷ vellum
  velocities n ▷ velocity

velocity n (pl -ties) speed of movement in a given direction

velour, velours [vel-loor] n (pl -s) fabric similar to velvet
  velours n ▷ velour
  velskoen n ▷ veldskoen
  velskoens n ▷ veldskoen

velvet n (pl -s) fabric with a thick soft pile

velveteen n (pl -s) cotton velvet
  velveteens n ▷ velveteen
  velvetier adj ▷ velvety
  velvetiest adj ▷ velvety
  velvets n ▷ velvet

velvety adj (-tier, -tiest) soft and smooth

venal adj easily bribed

vend v (-s, -ing, -ed) sell > **vendor** n (pl -s)
  vended v ▷ vend

vendetta n (pl -s) prolonged quarrel between families, esp. one involving revenge killings
  vendettas n ▷ vendetta
  vending v ▷ vend
  vendor n ▷ vend
  vendors n ▷ vend
  vends v ▷ vend

veneer n (pl -s) thin layer of wood etc. covering a cheaper material
  veneers n ▷ veneer

venerable adj worthy of deep respect

venerate v (-tes, -ting, -ted) hold (a person) in deep respect > **veneration** n (pl -s)
  venerated v ▷ venerate
  venerates v ▷ venerate
  venerating v ▷ venerate
  veneration n ▷ venerate
  venerations n ▷ venerate

vengeance n (pl -s) revenge
  vengeances n ▷ vengeance

vengeful adj wanting revenge

venial [veen-ee-al] adj (of a sin or fault) easily forgiven

venison n (pl -s) deer meat
  venisons n ▷ venison

venom n (pl -s) malice or spite > **venomous** adj
  venomous adj ▷ venom
  venoms n ▷ venom

venous adj (ANAT) of veins

vent[1] n (pl -s) outlet releasing fumes or fluid ▶ v (-s, -ing, -ed) express (an emotion) freely

vent[2] n (pl -s) vertical slit in a jacket
  vented v ▷ vent[1]

ventilate v (-tes, -ting, -ted) let fresh air into > **ventilation** n (pl -s) > **ventilator** n (pl -s)
  ventilated v ▷ ventilate
  ventilates v ▷ ventilate
  ventilating v ▷ ventilate
  ventilation n ▷ ventilate

ventilations *n* ▷ ventilate
ventilator *n* ▷ ventilate
ventilators *n* ▷ ventilate
venting *v* ▷ vent[1]
ventral *adj* relating to the front of the body
ventricle *n* (*pl* -s) (ANAT) one of the four cavities of the heart or brain
ventricles *n* ▷ ventricle
ventriloquism *n* ▷ ventriloquist
ventriloquisms *n* ▷ ventriloquist
ventriloquist *n* (*pl* -s) entertainer who can speak without moving his or her lips, so that a voice seems to come from elsewhere
> **ventriloquism** *n* (*pl* -s)
ventriloquists *n* ▷ ventriloquist
vents *n*, *v* ▷ vent[1, 2]
venture *n* (*pl* -s) risky undertaking, esp. in business ▶ *v* (-res, -ring, -red) do something risky
ventured *v* ▷ venture
ventures *n*, *v* ▷ venture
venturesome *adj* daring
venturing *v* ▷ venture
venue *n* (*pl* -s) place where an organized gathering is held
venues *n* ▷ venue
veracious *adj* ▷ veracity
veracities *n* ▷ veracity
veracity *n* (*pl* -ties) habitual truthfulness
> **veracious** *adj*
veranda *n* ▷ verandah
verandah, veranda *n* (*pl* -s) open porch attached to a house
verandahs *n* ▷ verandah
verandas *n* ▷ verandah
verb *n* (*pl* -s) word that expresses the idea of action, happening, or being
verbal *adj* spoken > **verbally** *adv*
verbalize *v* (-s, -ing, -ed) express (something) in words
verbalized *v* ▷ verbalize
verbalizes *n* ▷ verbalize
verbalizing *v* ▷ verbalize
verbally *adv* ▷ verbal
verbatim [verb-**bait**-im] *adv*, *adj* word for word
verbena *n* (*pl* -s) plant with sweet-smelling flowers
verbenas *n* ▷ verbena
verbiage *n* (*pl* -s) excessive use of words
verbiages *n* ▷ verbiage
verbose [verb-**bohss**] *adj* (-r, -st) speaking at tedious length > **verbosity** *n* (*pl* -ties)
verboser *adj* ▷ verbose
verbosest *adj* ▷ verbose
verbosities *n* ▷ verbose

verbosity *n* ▷ verbose
verbs *n* ▷ verb
verdant *adj* (Lit) covered in green vegetation
verdict *n* (*pl* -s) decision of a jury
verdicts *n* ▷ verdict
verdigris [**ver**-dig-riss] *n* (*pl* -es) green film on copper, brass, or bronze
verdigrises *n* ▷ verdigris
verdure *n* (*pl* -s) (Lit) flourishing green vegetation
verdures *n* ▷ verdure
verge *n* (*pl* -s) grass border along a road
verger *n* (*pl* -s) (C OF E) church caretaker
vergers *n* ▷ verger
verges *n* ▷ verge
verifiable *adj* ▷ verify
verification *n* ▷ verify
verifications *n* ▷ verify
verified *v* ▷ verify
verifies *v* ▷ verify
verify *v* (-fies, -fying, -fied) check the truth or accuracy of > **verifiable** *adj* > **verification** *n* (*pl* -s)
verifying *v* ▷ verify
verily *adv* (Obs) in truth
verisimilitude *n* (*pl* -s) appearance of being real or true
verisimilitudes *n* ▷ verisimilitude
veritable *adj* rightly called, without exaggeration > **veritably** *adv*
veritably *adv* ▷ veritable
verities *n* ▷ verity
verity *n* (*pl* -ies) true statement or principle
vermicelli [ver-me-**chell**-ee] *n* (*pl* -s) fine strands of pasta
vermicellis *n* ▷ vermicelli
vermiform *adj* shaped like a worm
vermilion *adj* orange-red
vermin *pl n* (*pl* -s) animals, esp. insects and rodents, that spread disease or cause damage > **verminous** *adj*
verminous *adj* ▷ vermin
vermins *n* ▷ vermin
vermouth [**ver**-muth] *n* (*pl* -s) wine flavoured with herbs
vermouths *n* ▷ vermouth
vernacular [ver-**nak**-yew-lar] *n* (*pl* -s) most widely spoken language of a particular people or place
vernaculars *n* ▷ vernacular
vernal *adj* occurring in spring
vernier [**ver**-nee-er] *n* (*pl* -s) movable scale on a graduated measuring instrument for taking readings in fractions
verniers *n* ▷ vernier

veronica n (pl -s) plant with small blue, pink, or white flowers
 veronicas n ▷ veronica

verruca [ver-roo-ka] n (pl -s) wart, usu. on the foot
 verrucas n ▷ verruca

versatile adj having many skills or uses
 > **versatility** n (pl -ties)
 versatilities n ▷ versatile
 versatility n ▷ versatile

verse n (pl -s) group of lines forming part of a song or poem
 verses n ▷ verse

versification n (pl -s) writing in verse
 versifications n ▷ versification

version n (pl -s) form of something, such as a piece of writing, with some differences from other forms
 versions n ▷ version

verso n (pl -s) left-hand page of a book
 versos n ▷ verso

versus prep in opposition to or in contrast with

vertebra n (pl -rae) one of the bones that form the spine > **vertebral** adj
 vertebrae n ▷ vertabra
 vertebral adj ▷ vertebra

vertebrate n, adj (pl -s) (animal) having a spine
 vertebrates n ▷ vertebrate

vertex n (pl -texes, -tices) (MATHS) point on a geometric figure where the sides form an angle
 vertexes n ▷ vertex

vertical adj straight up and down ▶ n (pl -s) vertical direction
 verticals n ▷ vertical
 vertices n ▷ vertex
 vertiginous adj ▷ vertigo

vertigo n (pl -s) dizziness, usu. when looking down from a high place > **vertiginous** adj
 vertigoes n ▷ vertigo

vervain n (pl -s) plant with spikes of blue, purple, or white flowers
 vervains n ▷ vervain

verve n (pl -s) enthusiasm or liveliness
 verves n ▷ verve

very adv more than usually, extremely ▶ adj absolute, exact

vesicle n (pl -s) (BIOL) sac or small cavity, esp. one containing fluid
 vesicles n ▷ vesicle

vespers pl n (RC CHURCH) (service of) evening prayer

vessel n (pl -s) ship
 vessels n ▷ vessel

vest n (pl -s) undergarment worn on the top half of the body ▶ v (-s, -ing, -ed) (foll. by in or with) give (authority) to (someone)
 vested v ▷ vest

vestibule n (pl -s) small entrance hall
 vestibules n ▷ vestibule

vestige [vest-ij] n (pl -s) small amount or trace
 > **vestigial** adj
 vestiges n ▷ vestige
 vestigial adj ▷ vestige
 vesting v ▷ vest

vestments pl n priest's robes
 vestries n ▷ vestry

vestry n (pl -ies) room in a church used as an office by the priest or minister
 vests n, v ▷ vest

vet[1] n (pl -s) ▷ **veterinary surgeon** ▶ v (-s, -tting, -tted) check the suitability of

vet[2] n (pl -s) (US, AUST & NZ) military veteran

vetch n (pl -es) climbing plant with a beanlike fruit used as fodder
 vetches n ▷ vetch

veteran n (pl -s) person with long experience in a particular activity, esp. military service ▶ adj long-serving
 veterans n ▷ veteran

veterinary adj concerning animal health

veto n (pl -es) official power to cancel a proposal ▶ v (-es, -ing, -ed) enforce a veto against
 vetoed v ▷ veto
 vetoes n, v ▷ veto
 vetoing v ▷ veto
 vets n, v ▷ vet[1, 2]
 vetted v ▷ vet[1]
 vetting v ▷ vet[1]

vex v (-es, -ing, -ed) frustrate, annoy

vexation n (pl -s) something annoying
 > **vexatious** adj
 vexations n ▷ vexation
 vexatious adj ▷ vexation
 vexed v ▷ vex
 vexes v ▷ vex
 vexing v ▷ vex

via prep by way of
 viabilities n ▷ viable
 viability n ▷ viable

viable adj able to be put into practice
 > **viability** n (pl -ties)

viaduct n (pl -s) bridge over a valley
 viaducts n ▷ viaduct

vial n (pl -s) ▷ phial
 vials n ▷ vial

viands pl n (Obs) food

vibes pl n (Informal) emotional reactions

between people

vibrant [**vibe**-rant] *adj* vigorous in appearance, energetic

vibraphone *n* (*pl* -**s**) musical instrument with metal bars that resonate electronically when hit

 vibraphones *n* ▷ vibraphone

vibrate *v* (-**tes**, -**ting**, -**ted**) move back and forth rapidly > vibration *n* (*pl* -**s**)

 vibrated *v* ▷ vibrate
 vibrates *v* ▷ vibrate
 vibrating *v* ▷ vibrate
 vibration *n* ▷ vibrate
 vibrations *n* ▷ vibrate

vibrato *n* (*pl* -**s**) (MUSIC) rapid fluctuation in the pitch of a note

vibrator *n* (*pl* -**s**) device that produces vibratory motion, used for massage or as a sex aid > vibratory *adj*

 vibrators *n* ▷ vibrate
 vibratos *n* ▷ vibrato

vicar *n* (*pl* -**s**) (C of E) member of the clergy in charge of a parish

vicarage *n* (*pl* -**s**) vicar's house

 vicarages *n* ▷ vicarage

vicarious [vick-**air**-ee-uss] *adj* felt indirectly by imagining what another person experiences > vicariously *adv*

 vicariously *adv* ▷ vicarious
 vicars *n* ▷ vicar

vice[1] *n* (*pl* -**s**) immoral or evil habit or action

vice[2] *n* (*pl* -**s**) tool with a pair of jaws for holding an object while working on it

vice[3] *adj* serving in place of

viceregal *adj* ▷ viceroy

viceroy *n* (*pl* -**s**) governor of a colony who represents the monarch > viceregal *adj*

 viceroys *n* ▷ viceroy
 vices *n* ▷ vice[1, 2]
 vicinities *n* ▷ vicinity

vicinity [viss-**in**-it-ee] *n* (*pl* -**ties**) surrounding area

vicious *adj* cruel and violent > viciously *adv*

 viciously *adv* ▷ vicious

vicissitudes [viss-**iss**-it-yewds] *pl n* changes in fortune

victim *n* (*pl* -**s**) person or thing harmed or killed

 victimization *n* ▷ victimize
 victimizations *n* ▷ victimize

victimize *v* (-**zes**, -**zing**, -**zed**) punish unfairly > victimization *n* (*pl* -**s**)

 victimized *v* ▷ victimize
 victimizes *v* ▷ victimize
 victimizing *v* ▷ victimize
 victims *n* ▷ victim

victor *n* (*pl* -**s**) person who has defeated an opponent, esp. in war or in sport

 victories *n* ▷ victory
 victorious *adj* ▷ victory
 victors *n* ▷ victor

victory *n* (*pl* -**ries**) winning of a battle or contest > victorious *adj*

victuals [**vit**-tals] *pl n* (Old-fashioned) food and drink

vicuña [vik-**koo**-nya] *n* (*pl* -**s**) S American animal like the llama

 vicuñas *n* ▷ vicuña

video *n* (*pl* -**s**) ▷ video cassette (recorder) ▶ *v* (-**s**, -**ing**, -**ed**) record (a TV programme or event) on video ▶ *adj* relating to or used in producing television images

 videoed *v* ▷ video
 videoing *v* ▷ video
 videos *n*, *v* ▷ video

videotext *n* (*pl* -**s**) means of representing on a TV screen information that is held in a computer

 videotexts *n* ▷ videotext

vie *v* (**vies**, **vying**, **vied**) compete (with someone)

 vied *v* ▷ vie
 vies *v* ▷ vie

view *n* (*pl* -**s**) opinion or belief ▶ *v* (-**s**, -**ing**, -**ed**) think of (something) in a particular way

viewdata *n* (*pl* -**as**)® videotext service linking users to a computer by telephone

 viewdatas *n* ▷ viewdata
 viewed *v* ▷ view

viewer *n* person who watches television

 viewers *n* ▷ viewer

viewfinder *n* (*pl* -**s**) window on a camera showing what will appear in a photograph

 viewfinders *n* ▷ viewfinder
 viewing *v* ▷ view
 views *n*, *v* ▷ view

vigil [**vij**-ill] *n* (*pl* -**s**) night-time period of staying awake to look after a sick person, pray, etc.

 vigilance *n* ▷ vigilant
 vigilances *n* ▷ vigilant

vigilant *adj* watchful in case of danger > vigilance *n* (*pl* -**s**)

vigilante [vij-ill-**ant**-ee] *n* (*pl* -**s**) person, esp. as one of a group, who takes it upon himself or herself to enforce the law

 vigilantes *n* ▷ vigilante
 vigils *n* ▷ vigil

vignette [vin-**yet**] *n* (*pl* -**s**) concise description of the typical features of something

 vignettes *n* ▷ vignette

vigorous *adj* ▷ vigour

vigorously *adv* ▷ vigour

vigour *n* (*pl* -s) physical or mental energy
> **vigorous** *adj* > **vigorously** *adv*

vigours *n* ▷ vigour

viking *n* (*pl* -s) (HIST) seafaring raider and settler from Scandinavia

vikings *n* ▷ viking

vile (-r, -st) *adj* very wicked > **vilely** *adv*
> **vileness** *n* (*pl* -s)

vilely *adv* ▷ vile

vileness *n* ▷ vile

vilenesses *n* ▷ vile

viler *adj* ▷ vile

vilest *adj* ▷ vile

vilification *n* ▷ vilify

vilifications *n* ▷ vilify

vilified *v* ▷ vilify

vilifies *v* ▷ vilify

vilify *v* (-fies, -fying, -fied) attack the character of > **vilification** *n* (*pl* -s)

vilifying *v* ▷ vilify

villa *n* (*pl* -s) large house with gardens

village *n* (*pl* -s) small group of houses in a country area > **villager** *n* (*pl* -s)

villager *n* ▷ village

villagers *n* ▷ village

villages *n* ▷ village

villain *n* (*pl* -s) wicked person > **villainous** *adj*
> **villainy** *n* (*pl* -nies)

villianies *n* ▷ villian

villainous *adj* ▷ villain

villains *n* ▷ villain

villas *n* ▷ villa

villein [vill-an] *n* (*pl* -s) (HIST) peasant bound in service to his lord

villeins *n* ▷ villein

villiany *n* ▷ villian

> **vim** *n* (**vims**). Vim means vigour or energy. This word can be helpful when you're stuck with unpromising letters, and gives a reasonable score for a three-letter word. Vim scores 8 points.

vinaigrette *n* (*pl* -s) salad dressing of oil and vinegar

vinaigrettes *n* ▷ vinaigrette

vindicate *v* (-tes, -ting, -ted) clear (someone) of guilt > **vindication** *n* (*pl* -s)

vindicated *v* ▷ vindicate

vindicates *v* ▷ vindicate

vindicating *v* ▷ vindicate

vindication *n* ▷ vindicate

vindications *n* ▷ vindicate

vindictive *adj* maliciously seeking revenge
> **vindictiveness** *n* (*pl* -es) > **vindictively** *adv*

vindictively *adv* ▷ vindictive

vindictiveness *n* ▷ vindictive

vindictivenesses *n* ▷ vindictive

vine *n* (*pl* -s) climbing plant, esp. one producing grapes

vinegar *n* (*pl* -s) acid liquid made from wine, beer, or cider > **vinegary** *adj*

vinegars *n* ▷ vinegar

vinegary *adj* ▷ vinegar

vines *n* ▷ vine

vineyard [vinn-yard] *n* (*pl* -s) plantation of grape vines, esp. for making wine

vineyards *n* ▷ vineyard

vino [vee-noh] *n* (*pl* -s) (*Informal*) wine

vinos *n* ▷ vino

vintage *n* (*pl* -s) wine from a particular harvest of grapes ▸ *adj* best and most typical

vintages *n* ▷ vintage

vintner *n* (*pl* -s) dealer in wine

vintners *n* ▷ vintner

vinyl [vine-ill] *n* (*pl* -s) type of plastic, used in mock leather and records

vinyls *n* ▷ vinyl

viol [vie-oll] *n* (*pl* -s) early stringed instrument preceding the violin

viola¹ [vee-oh-la] *n* (*pl* -s) stringed instrument lower in pitch than a violin

viola² [vie-ol-la] *n* (*pl* -s) variety of pansy

violas *n* ▷ viola¹, ²

violate *v* (-tes, -ting, -ted) break (a law or agreement) > **violation** *n* > **violator** *n*

violated *v* ▷ violate

violates *v* ▷ violate

violating *v* ▷ violate

violation *n* ▷ violate

violations *n* ▷ violate

violator *n* ▷ violate

violators *n* ▷ violate

violence *n* (*pl* -s) use of physical force, usu. intended to cause injury or destruction
> **violent** *adj* > **violently** *adv*

violences *n* ▷ violence

violent *adj* ▷ violence

violently *adv* ▷ violent

violet *n* (*pl* -s) plant with bluish-purple flowers ▸ *adj* bluish-purple

violets *n* ▷ violet

violin *n* (*pl* -s) small four-stringed musical instrument played with a bow. > **violinist** *n* (*pl* -s)

violinist *n* ▷ violin

violinists *n* ▷ violin

violins *n* ▷ violin

viols *n* ▷ viol

viper *n* (*pl* -s) poisonous snake

vipers n ▷ viper
virago [vir-**rah**-go] n (pl **-goes, -gos**) aggressive woman
  viragoes n ▷ virago
  viragos n ▷ virago
viral adj of or caused by a virus
virgin n (pl **-s**) person, esp. a woman, who has not had sexual intercourse ▶ adj not having had sexual intercourse > **virginity** n (pl **-ties**)
virginal adj like a virgin ▶ n early keyboard instrument like a small harpsichord
  virginities n ▷ virgin
  virginity n ▷ virgin
  virgins n ▷ virgin
virile adj having the traditional male characteristics of physical strength and a high sex drive > **virility** n (pl **-ties**)
  virilities n ▷ virile
  virility n ▷ virile
  virologies n ▷ virology
  virologies n ▷ virology
virology n (pl **-gies**) study of viruses
virtual adj having the effect but not the form of > **virtually** adv practically, almost
  virtually adv ▷ virtual
virtue n (pl **-s**) moral goodness
  virtues n ▷ virtue
  virtuosi n ▷ virtuoso
  virtuosities n ▷ virtuoso
  virtuosity n ▷ virtuoso
virtuoso n (pl **-sos, -si**) person with impressive esp. musical skill > **virtuosity** n (pl **-ies**)
  virtuosos n ▷ virtuoso
virtuous adj morally good > **virtuously** adv
  virtuously adv ▷ virtuous
virulent [vir-yew-lent] adj very infectious
virus n (pl **-es**) microorganism that causes disease in humans, animals, and plants
  viruses n ▷ virus
visa n (pl **-s**) permission to enter a country, granted by its government and shown by a stamp on one's passport
visage [viz-zij] n (pl **-s**) (Lit) face
  visages n ▷ visage
  visas n ▷ visa
viscera [viss-er-a] pl n large abdominal organs
visceral [viss-er-al] adj instinctive
viscid [viss-id] adj sticky
viscose n (pl **-s**) synthetic fabric made from cellulose
  viscoses n ▷ viscose
  viscosities n ▷ viscous
  viscosity n ▷ viscous
viscount [vie-count] n (pl **-s**) British nobleman ranking between an earl and a baron

viscountess [vie-count-iss] n (pl **-es**) woman holding the rank of viscount in her own right
  viscountesses n ▷ viscountess
  viscounts n ▷ viscount
viscous adj thick and sticky > **viscosity** n (pl **-ties**)
  visibilities n ▷ visibility
visibility n (pl **-ties**) range or clarity of vision
visible adj able to be seen > **visibly** adv
  visibly adv ▷ visible
vision n (pl **-s**) ability to see
  visionaries n ▷ visionary
visionary adj showing foresight ▶ n (pl **-ries**) visionary person
  visions n ▷ vision
visit v (**-s, -ing, -ed**) go or come to see ▶ n instance of visiting > **visitor** n (pl **-s**)
visitation n (pl **-s**) formal visit or inspection
  visitations n ▷ visitation
  visited v ▷ visit
  visiting v ▷ visit
  visitor n ▷ visit
  visitors n ▷ visit
  visits v ▷ visit
visor [vize-or] n (pl **-s**) transparent part of a helmet that pulls down over the face
  visors n ▷ visor
vista n (pl **-s**) (beautiful) extensive view
  vistas n ▷ vista
visual adj done by or used in seeing
  visualization n ▷ visualize
  visualizations n ▷ visualize
visualize v (**-zes, -zing, -zed**) form a mental image of > **visualization** n (pl **-s**)
  visualized v ▷ visualize
  visualizes v ▷ visualize
  visualizing v ▷ visualize
vital adj essential or highly important > **vitally** adv
  vitalities n ▷ vitality
vitality n (pl **-ties**) physical or mental energy
  vitally adv ▷ vital
vitals pl n bodily organs necessary to maintain life
vitamin n (pl **-s**) one of a group of substances that are essential in the diet for specific body processes
  vitamins n ▷ vitamin
vitiate [vish-ee-ate] v (**-tes, -ting, -ted**) spoil the effectiveness of
  vitiated v ▷ vitiate
  vitiates v ▷ vitiate
  vitiating v ▷ vitiate
viticulture n (pl **-s**) cultivation of grapevines
  viticultures n ▷ viticulture

vitreous *adj* like or made from glass
vitriol *n (pl -s)* language expressing bitterness and hatred > **vitriolic** *adj*
  vitriolic *adj* ▷ vitriol
  vitriols *n* ▷ vitriol
  vituperation *n* ▷ vituperative
  vituperations *n* ▷ vituperative
vituperative [vite-tyew-pra-tiv] *adj* bitterly abusive > **vituperation** *n (pl -s)*
viva¹ *interj* long live (a person or thing)
viva² *n (pl -s)* (BRIT) examination in the form of an interview
vivace [viv-vah-chee] *adv* (MUSIC) in a lively manner
vivacious *adj* full of energy and enthusiasm > **vivacity** *n (pl -ties)*
  vivacities *n* ▷ vivacious
  vivacity *n* ▷ vivacious
  vivas *n* ▷ viva²
vivid *adj (-er, -est)* very bright > **vividly** *adv* > **vividness** *n (pl -es)*
  vivider *adj* ▷ vivd
  vividest *adj* ▷ vivd
  vividly *adv* ▷ vivd
  vividness *n* ▷ vivid
  vividnesses *n* ▷ vivid
vivisection *n (pl -s)* performing surgical experiments on living animals > **vivisectionist** *n (pl -s)*
  vivisectionist *n* ▷ vivisection
  vivisectionists *n* ▷ vivisection
  vivisections *n* ▷ vivisection
vixen *n (pl -s)* female fox
  vixens *n* ▷ vixen
vizier [viz-zeer] *n (pl -s)* high official in certain Muslim countries
  viziers *n* ▷ vizier
vizor *n (pl -s)* ▷ visor
  vizors *n* ▷ vizor

> **vly** *n (vlys)*. Vly is a South African word meaning an area of low marshy ground. This is a good word to remember because it doesn't contain any vowels, making it useful when you are short of vowel tiles. Vly scores 9 points.

  vocabularies *n* ▷ vocabulary
vocabulary *n (pl -ries)* all the words that a person knows
vocal *adj* relating to the voice
vocalist *n (pl -s)* singer
  vocalists *n* ▷ vocalist
  vocalization *n* ▷ vocalize
  vocalizations *n* ▷ vocalize
vocalize *v (-zes, -zing, -zed)* express with or use the voice > **vocalization** *n (pl -s)*
  vocalizes *v* ▷ vocalize
  vocalizes *v* ▷ vocalize
  vocalizing *v* ▷ vocalize
  vocally *adv* ▷ vocal
vocals *pl n* singing part of a piece of pop music > **vocally** *adv*
vocation *n (pl -s)* profession or trade
vocational *adj* directed towards a particular profession or trade
  vocations *n* ▷ vocation
vociferous *adj* shouting, noisy
vodka *n (pl -s)* (Russian) spirit distilled from potatoes or grain
  vodkas *n* ▷ vodka
vogue *n (pl -s)* popular style
  vogues *n* ▷ vogue
voice *n (pl -s)* (quality of) sound made when speaking or singing ▶ *v (-ces, -cing, -ced)* express verbally > **voiceless** *adj*
  voiced *v* ▷ voice
  voiceless *adj* ▷ voice
  voices *n, v* ▷ voice
  voicing *v* ▷ voice
void *adj* not legally binding ▶ *n (pl -s)* empty space ▶ *v (-s, -ing, -ed)* make invalid
  voided *v* ▷ void
  voiding *v* ▷ void
  voids *n, v* ▷ void
voile [voyl] *n (pl -s)* light semitransparent fabric
  voiles *n* ▷ voile
volatile *adj* liable to sudden change, esp. in behaviour > **volatility** *n (pl -ties)*
  volatilities *n* ▷ volatile
  volatility *n* ▷ volatile
  volcanic *adj* ▷ volcano
volcano *n (pl -noes, -nos)* mountain with a vent through which lava is ejected > **volcanic** *adj*
  volcanoes *n* ▷ volcano
  volcanos *n* ▷ volcano
vole *n (pl -s)* small rodent
  voles *n* ▷ vole
volition *n (pl -s)* ability to decide things for oneself
  volitions *n* ▷ volition
volley *n (pl -s)* simultaneous discharge of ammunition ▶ *v (-s, -ing, -ed)* discharge (ammunition) in a volley
volleyball *n (pl -s)* team game where a ball is hit with the hands over a high net
  volleyballs *n* ▷ volleyball
  volleyed *v* ▷ volley
  volleying *v* ▷ volley

volleys n, v ▷ volley
volt n (pl -s) unit of electric potential
voltage n (pl -s) electric potential difference expressed in volts
voltages n ▷ voltage
voltmeter n instrument for measuring voltage
voltmeters n ▷ voltmeter
volts n ▷ volt
volubilities n ▷ voluble
volubility n ▷ voluble
voluble adj talking easily and at length > **volubility** n (pl -ties) > **volubly** adv
volubly adv ▷ voluble
volume n (pl -s) size of the space occupied by something
volumes n ▷ volume
volumetric adj relating to measurement by volume
voluminous adj (of clothes) large and roomy
voluntaries n ▷ voluntary
voluntarily adv ▷ voluntary
voluntary adj done by choice ▶ n (pl -ries) organ solo in a church service > **voluntarily** adv
volunteer n (pl -s) person who offers voluntarily to do something ▶ v (-s, -ing, -ed) offer one's services
volunteered v ▷ volunteer
volunteering v ▷ volunteer
volunteers n, v ▷ volunteer
voluptuaries n ▷ voluptuary
voluptuary n (pl -ries) person devoted to sensual pleasures
voluptuous adj (of a woman) sexually alluring through fullness of figure
volute n (pl -s) spiral or twisting turn, form, or object
volutes n ▷ volute
vomit v (-s, -ing, -ed) eject (the contents of the stomach) through the mouth ▶ n (pl -s) matter vomited
vomited v ▷ vomit
vomiting v ▷ vomit
vomits v, n ▷ vomit
voodoo n (pl -s) religion involving ancestor worship and witchcraft, practised by Black people in the West Indies, esp. in Haiti.
voodoos n ▷ voodoo
voracious adj craving great quantities of food > **voraciously** adv > **voracity** n (pl -ties)
voraciously adv ▷ voracious
voracities n ▷ voracious
voracity n ▷ voracious
vortex n (pl -texes, -tices) whirlpool

vortexes n ▷ vortex
vortices n ▷ vortex
vote n (pl -s) choice made by a participant in a shared decision, esp. in electing a candidate ▶ v (-tes, -ting, -ted) make a choice by a vote > **voter** n (pl -s)
voted v ▷ vote
voter n ▷ vote
voters n ▷ vote
votes n, v ▷ vote
voting v ▷ vote
votive adj done or given to fulfil a vow
vouch v (-es, -ing, -ed) give one's personal assurance about
vouched v ▷ vouch
voucher n (pl -s) ticket used instead of money to buy specified goods
vouchers n ▷ voucher
vouches v ▷ vouch
vouching v ▷ vouch
vouchsafe v (-fes, -fing, -fed) (Old-fashioned) give, entrust
vouchsafed v ▷ vouchsafe
vouchsafes v ▷ vouchsafe
vouchsafing v ▷ vouchsafe
vow n (pl -s) solemn and binding promise ▶ pl formal promises made when marrying or entering a religious order ▶ v (-s, -ing, -ed) promise solemnly
vowed v ▷ vow
vowel n (pl -s) speech sound made without obstructing the flow of breath
vowels n ▷ vowel
vowing v ▷ vow
vows n, v ▷ vow

> **vox** n (**voces**) Vox means a voice or sound. Along with **vex**, this is the highest-scoring three-letter word beginning with V. Vox scores 13 points.

voyage n (pl -s) long journey by sea or in space ▶ v (-ges, -ging, -ged) make a voyage > **voyager** n (pl -s)
voyaged v ▷ voyage
voyager n ▷ voyage
voyagers n ▷ voyager
voyages n, v ▷ voyage
voyaging v ▷ voyage
voyeur n (pl -s) person who obtains pleasure from watching people undressing or having sex > **voyeurism** n (pl -s)
voyeurism n ▷ voyeur
voyeurisms n ▷ voyeur
voyeurs n ▷ voyeur

> **vug** n (**vugs**). A vug is a small cavity in a rock. This is a very unusual word

that can be useful when you have an
uninspiring combination of letters.
Vug scores 7 points.

vulcanize v (**-zes, -zing, -zed**) strengthen
(rubber) by treating it with sulphur
  vulcanized v ▷ vulcanize
  vulcanizes v ▷ vulcanize
  vulcanizing v ▷ vulcanize
vulgar adj (**-er, -est**) showing lack of good
taste, decency, or refinement > **vulgarly** adv
> **vulgarity** n (pl **-ies**)
  vulgarer adj ▷ vulgar
  vulgarest adj ▷ vulgar
vulgarian n (pl **-s**) vulgar (rich) person
  vulgarians n ▷ vulgarian

  vulgarities n ▷ vulgar
  vulgarities n ▷ vulgar
  vulgarly adv ▷ vulgar
  vulnerabilities n ▷ vulnerable
  vulnerability n ▷ vulnerable
vulnerable adj liable to be physically or
emotionally hurt > **vulnerability** n (pl **-s**)
vulpine adj of or like a fox
vulture n (pl **-s**) large bird that feeds on the
flesh of dead animals
  vultures n ▷ vulture
vulva n (pl **-vae**) woman's external genitals
  vulvae n ▷ vulva
  vying v ▷ vie.

Ww

W is a useful tile to have on your rack as it earns 4 points on its own and produces a number of high-scoring short words. There are, however, only two two-letter words begin with W: **we** and **wo** (5 points each). If you know this, though, you won't waste time looking for others. There are lots of everyday three-letter words that earn good scores: **wax** (13) with its two old-fashioned variants **wex** and **wox** (also 13 each) and **way, who, why, wow** and **wry** (9 each). Don't forget **wok** (10) either, which can be as useful on the Scrabble board as in the kitchen!

wackier *adj* ▷ wacky
wackiest *adj* ▷ wacky
wackiness *n* ▷ wacky
wackinesses *n* ▷ wacky
wacky *adj* (**-ckier, -ckiest**) (*Informal*) eccentric or funny > **wackiness** *n* (*pl* **-es**)
wad *n* (*pl* **-s**) small mass of soft material
waddies *n* ▷ waddy
wadding *n* (*pl* **-s**) soft material used for padding or stuffing
waddings *n* ▷ wadding
waddle *v* (**-les, -ling, -led**) walk with short swaying steps ▸ *n* (*pl* **-s**) swaying walk
waddled *v, n* ▷ waddle
waddles *v* ▷ waddle
waddling *v* ▷ waddle
waddy *n* (*pl* **-ies**) heavy wooden club used by Australian Aborigines
wade *v* (**-des, -ding, -ded**) walk with difficulty through water or mud
waded *v* ▷ wade
wader *n* (*pl* **-s**) long-legged water bird ▸ *pl* angler's long waterproof boots
waders *n* ▷ wader
wades *v* ▷ wade
wadi [wod-dee] *n* (*pl* **-s**) (in N Africa and Arabia) river which is dry except in the wet season
wading *v* ▷ wade
wadis *n* ▷ wadi
wads *n* ▷ wad
wafer *n* (*pl* **-s**) thin crisp biscuit
wafers *n* ▷ wafer
waffle[1] (*Informal*) *v* (**-les, -ling, -led**) speak or write in a vague wordy way ▸ *n* (*pl* **-s**) vague wordy talk or writing
waffle[2] *n* (*pl* **-s**) square crisp pancake with a gridlike pattern

waffled *v* ▷ waffle[1]
waffles *v, n* ▷ waffle[1, 2]
waffling *v* ▷ waffle[1]
waft *v* (**-s, -ing, -ed**) drift or carry gently through the air ▸ *n* (*pl* **-s**) something wafted
wafted *v* ▷ waft
wafting *v* ▷ waft
wafts *v, n* ▷ waft
wag *v* (**-s, -gging, -gged**) move rapidly from side to side ▸ *n* (*pl* **-s**) wagging movement
wage *n* (*pl* **-s**) (*often pl* payment for work done, esp. when paid weekly ▸ *v* (**-ges, -ging, -ged**) engage in (an activity)
waged *v* ▷ wage
wager *n, v* (**-s, -ing, -ed**) bet on the outcome of something
wagered *v* ▷ wager
wagering *v* ▷ wager
wagers *n, v* ▷ wager
wages *n, v* ▷ wage
wagged *v* ▷ wag
wagging *v* ▷ wag
waggle *v* (**-les, -ling, -led**) move with a rapid shaking or wobbling motion
waggled *v* ▷ waggle
waggles *v* ▷ waggle
waggling *v* ▷ waggle
waggon *n* ▷ wagon
waggons *n* ▷ wagon
waging *v* ▷ wage
wagon, waggon *n* (*pl* **-s**) four-wheeled vehicle for heavy loads
wagons *n* ▷ wagon
wags *v* ▷ wag
wagtail *n* (*pl* **-s**) small long-tailed bird
wagtail *n* ▷ wagtails
wahoo *n* (*pl* **-s**) food and game fish of tropical

seas
wahoos *n* ▷ wahoo
waif *n* (*pl* -s) young person who is, or seems, homeless or neglected
waifs *n* ▷ waif
wail *v* (-s, -ing, -ed) cry out in pain or misery ▶ *n* (*pl* -s) mournful cry
wailed *v* ▷ wail
wailing *v* ▷ wail
wails *v, n* ▷ wail
wain *n* (*pl* -s) (*Poetic*) farm wagon
wains *n* ▷ wain
wainscot, wainscoting *n* (*pl* -s) wooden lining of the lower part of the walls of a room
wainscoting *n* ▷ wainscot
wainscotings *n* ▷ wainscot
wainscots *n* ▷ wainscot
waist *n* (*pl* -s) part of the body between the ribs and hips
waistband *n* (*pl* -s) band of material sewn on to the waist of a garment to strengthen it
waistbands *n* ▷ waistband
waistcoat *n* (*pl* -s) sleeveless garment which buttons up the front, usu. worn over a shirt and under a jacket
waistcoats *n* ▷ waistcoat
waistline *n* (*pl* -s) (size of) the waist of a person or garment
waistlines *n* ▷ waistline
waists *n* ▷ waist
wait *v* (-s, -ing, -ed) remain inactive in expectation (of something) ▶ *n* (*pl* -s) act or period of waiting
waited *v* ▷ wait
waiter *n* (*pl* -s) man who serves in a restaurant etc. > **waitress** *n fem* (*pl* -es)
waiters *n* ▷ waiter
waiting *v* ▷ wait
waitress *n* ▷ waiter
waitresses *n* ▷ waiter
waits *v, n* ▷ wait
waive *v* (-ves, -ving, -ved) refrain from enforcing (a law, right, etc.)
waived *v* ▷ waive
waiver *n* (*pl* -s) act or instance of voluntarily giving up a claim, right, etc.
waivers *n* ▷ waiver
waives *v* ▷ waive
waiving *v* ▷ waive
waka *n* (*pl* -s) (NZ) Maori canoe
wakas *n* ▷ waka
wake[1] *v* (-kes, -king, woke, woken) rouse from sleep or inactivity ▶ *n* (*pl* -s) vigil beside a corpse the night before the funeral > **wakeful** *adj*

wake[2] *n* (*pl* -s) track left by a moving ship
wakeful *adj* ▷ wake[1]
waken *v* (-s, -ing, -ed) wake
wakened *v* ▷ waken
wakening *v* ▷ waken
wakens *v* ▷ waken
wakes *n* ▷ wake[1, 2]
waking *v* ▷ wake[1]
walk *v* (-s, -ing, -ed) move on foot with at least one foot always on the ground ▶ *n* (*pl* -s) act or instance of walking > **walker** *n* (*pl* -s)
walkabout *n* (*pl* -s) informal walk among the public by royalty etc.
walkabouts *n* ▷ walkabout
walked *v* ▷ walk
walker *n* ▷ walk
walkers *n* ▷ walk
walking *v* ▷ walk
walkout *n* (*pl* -s) strike
walkouts *n* ▷ walkout
walkover *n* (*pl* -s) easy victory
walkovers *n* ▷ walkover
walks *v, n* ▷ walk
wall *n* (*pl* -s) structure of brick, stone, etc. used to enclose, divide, or support ▶ *v* (-s, -ing, -ed) enclose or seal with a wall or walls
wallabies *n* ▷ wallaby
wallaby *n* (*pl* -bies) marsupial like a small kangaroo
wallaroo *n* (*pl* -s) large stocky Australian kangaroo of rocky regions
wallaroos *n* ▷ wallaroo
walled *v* ▷ wall
wallet *n* (*pl* -s) small folding case for paper money, documents, etc.
wallets *n* ▷ wallet
walleye *n* (*pl* -s) fish with large staring eyes (*also* **dory**)
walleyes *n* ▷ walleye
wallflower *n* (*pl* -s) fragrant garden plant
wallflowers *n* ▷ wallflower
wallies *n* ▷ wally
walling *v* ▷ wall
wallop (*Informal*) *v* (-s, -ing, -ed) hit hard ▶ *n* (*pl* -s) hard blow
walloped *v* ▷ wallop
walloping (*Informal*) *n* thrashing ▶ *adj* large or great ▶ *v* ▷ wallop
wallops *v, n* ▷ wallop
wallow *v* (-s, -ing, -ed) revel in an emotion ▶ *n* (*pl* -s) act or instance of wallowing
wallowed *v* ▷ wallow
wallowing *v* ▷ wallow
wallows *v, n* ▷ wallow
wallpaper *n* (*pl* -s) decorative paper to cover

interior walls

wallpapers n ▷ wallpaper

walls n, v ▷ wall

wally n (pl -ies) (BRIT) (Slang) stupid person

walnut n (pl -s) edible nut with a wrinkled shell

walnuts n ▷ walnut

walrus n (pl -ruses, -rus) large sea mammal with long tusks

walruses n ▷ walrus

waltz n (pl -es) ballroom dance ▶ v (-zes, -zing, -zed) dance a waltz

waltzed v ▷ waltz

waltzes n, v ▷ waltz

waltzing v ▷ waltz

wampum [wom-pum] n (pl -s) shells woven together, formerly used by Native Americans for money and ornament

wampums n ▷ wampum

wan [rhymes with swan] adj (-nner, -nnest) pale and sickly looking

wand n (pl -s) thin rod, esp. one used in performing magic tricks

wander v (-s, -ing, -ed) move about without a definite destination or aim ▶ n (pl -s) act or instance of wandering > **wanderer** n (pl -s)

wandered v ▷ wander

wanderer n ▷ wander

wanderers n ▷ wander

wandering v ▷ wander

wanderlust n (pl -s) great desire to travel

wanderlusts n ▷ wanderlust

wanders v, n ▷ wander

wands n ▷ wand

wane v (-nes, -ning, -ned) decrease gradually in size or strength

waned v ▷ wane

wanes v ▷ wane

wangle v (-les, -ling, -led) (Informal) get by devious methods

wangled v ▷ wangle

wangles v ▷ wangle

wangling v ▷ wangle

waning v ▷ wane

wanner adj ▷ wan

wannest adj ▷ wan

want v (-s, -ing, -ed) need or long for ▶ n (pl -s) act or instance of wanting

wanted adj sought by the police ▶ v ▷ want

wanting adj lacking ▶ v ▷ want

wanton adj (-er, -est) without motive, provocation, or justification

wantoner adj ▷ wanton

wantonest adj ▷ wanton

wants v, n ▷ want

war n (pl -s) fighting between nations ▶ adj

of, like, or caused by war ▶ v (-s, -rring, -rred) conduct a war > **warring** adj

waratah n (pl -s) Australian shrub with crimson flowers

waratahs n ▷ waratah

warble v (-les, -ling, -led) sing in a trilling voice

warbled v ▷ warble

warbler n (pl -s) any of various small songbirds

warblers n ▷ warbler

warbles v ▷ warble

warbling v ▷ warble

ward n (pl -s) room in a hospital for patients needing a similar kind of care

warden n (pl -s) person in charge of a building and its occupants

wardens n ▷ warden

warder n (pl -s) prison officer > **wardress** n fem (pl -es)

warders n ▷ warder

wardress n ▷ warder

wardresses n ▷ warder

wardrobe n (pl -s) cupboard for hanging clothes in

wardrobes n ▷ wardrobe

wardroom n (pl -s) officers' quarters on a warship

wardrooms n ▷ wardroom

wards n ▷ ward

ware n (pl -s) articles of a specified type or material ▶ pl goods for sale

warehouse n (pl -s) building for storing goods prior to sale or distribution

warehouses n ▷ warehouse

wares n ▷ ware

warfare n (pl -s) fighting or hostilities

warfares n ▷ warfare

warhead n (pl -s) explosive front part of a missile

warheads n ▷ warhead

warier adj ▷ wary

wariest n ▷ wary

warily adv ▷ wary

wariness n ▷ wary

warinesses n ▷ wary

warlike adj of or relating to war

warlock n (pl -s) man who practises black magic

warlocks n ▷ warlock

warm adj (-er, -est) moderately hot ▶ v (-s, -ing, -ed) make or become warm > **warmly** adv

warmed v ▷ warm

warmer adj ▷ warm

warmest adj ▷ warm

warming v ▷ warm

warmly adv ▷ warm

warmonger n (pl -s) person who encourages war
warmongers n ▷ warmonger
warms v ▷ warm
warmth n (pl -s) mild heat
warmths n ▷ warmth
warn v (-s, -ing, -ed) make aware of possible danger or harm
warned v ▷ warn
warning n (pl -s) something that warns ▶ v ▷ warn
warnings n ▷ warning
warns v ▷ warn
warp v (-s, -ing, -ed) twist out of shape ▶ n (pl -s) state of being warped
warped v ▷ warp
warping v ▷ warp
warps v, n ▷ warp
warrant n (pl -s) (document giving) official authorization ▶ v (-s, -ing, -ed) make necessary
warranted v ▷ warrant
warranties n ▷ warranty
warranting v ▷ warrant
warrants n, v ▷ warrant
warranty n (pl -ties) (document giving) a guarantee
warred v ▷ war
warren n (pl -s) series of burrows in which rabbits live
warrens n ▷ warren
warrigal (AUST) n (pl -s) dingo ▶ adj wild
warrigals n ▷ warrigal
warring v ▷ war
warrior n (pl -s) person who fights in a war
warriors n ▷ warrior
wars n, v ▷ war
warship n (pl -s) ship designed and equipped for naval combat
warships n ▷ warship
wart n (pl -s) small hard growth on the skin
warts n ▷ wart
wary [ware-ree] adj (-rier, -riest) watchful or cautious > **warily** adv > **wariness** n (pl -es)
was v ▷ be
wash v (-es, -ing, -ed) clean (oneself, clothes, etc.) with water and usu. soap (Informal) ▶ n (pl -es) act or process of washing > **washable** adj
washable adj ▷ wash
washed v ▷ wash
washer n (pl -s) ring put under a nut or bolt or in a tap as a seal
washers n ▷ washer
washes v, n ▷ wash
washing n (pl -s) clothes to be washed ▶ v ▷ wash

washings n ▷ washing
washout n (pl -s) (Informal) complete failure
washouts n ▷ washout
wasp n (pl -s) stinging insect with a slender black-and-yellow striped body
waspish adj bad-tempered
wasps n ▷ wasp
wastage n (pl -s) loss by wear or waste
wastages n ▷ wastage
waste v (-tes, -ting, -ted) use pointlessly or thoughtlessly ▶ n (pl -s) act of wasting or state of being wasted ▶ pl desert ▶ adj rejected as worthless or surplus to requirements
wasted v ▷ waste
wasteful adj extravagant > **wastefully** adv
wastefully adv ▷ waste
waster, wastrel n (pl -s) layabout
wasters n ▷ waster
wastes v, n ▷ waste
wasting v ▷ waste
wastrel n ▷ waster
wastrels n ▷ waster
watch v (-es, -ing, -ed) look at closely ▶ n (pl -es) portable timepiece for the wrist or pocket > **watchable** adj > **watcher** n (pl -s)
watchable adj ▷ watch
watchdog n (pl -s) dog kept to guard property
watchdogs n ▷ watchdog
watched v ▷ watch
watcher n ▷ watch
watchers n ▷ watch
watches v, n ▷ watch
watchful adj vigilant or alert > **watchfully** adv
watchfully adv ▷ watchful
watching v ▷ watch
watchman n (pl -men) man employed to guard a building or property
watchmen n ▷ watchman
watchword n (pl -s) word or phrase that sums up the attitude of a particular group
watchwords n ▷ watchword
water n (pl -s) clear colourless tasteless liquid that falls as rain and forms rivers etc. ▶ v (-s, -ing, -ed) put water on or into ▶ **watery** adj (-rier, -riest)
watercolour n (pl -s) paint thinned with water
watercolours n ▷ watercolour
watercourse n (pl -s) bed of a stream or river
watercourses n ▷ watercourse
watercress n (pl -es) edible plant growing in clear ponds and streams
watercresses n ▷ watercress
watered v ▷ water
waterfall n (pl -s) place where the waters of a

river drop vertically
  waterfalls *n* ▷ waterfall
waterfront *n* (*pl* -s) part of a town alongside a body of water
  waterfronts *n* ▷ waterfront
  waterier *adj* ▷ watery
  wateriest *adj* ▷ watery
  watering *v* ▷ water
watermark *n* (*pl* -s) faint translucent design in a sheet of paper
  watermarks *n* ▷ watermark
watermelon *n* (*pl* -s) melon with green skin and red flesh
  watermelons *n* ▷ watermelon
waterproof *adj* not letting water through ▶ *n* (*pl* -s) waterproof garment ▶ *v* (-s, -ing, -ed) make waterproof
  waterproofed *v* ▷ waterproof
  waterproofing *v* ▷ waterproof
  waterproofs *n*, *v* ▷ waterproof
  waters *n*, *v* ▷ water
watershed *n* (*pl* -s) important period or factor serving as a dividing line
  watersheds *n* ▷ watershed
watersider *n* (*pl* -s) (NZ) person employed to load and unload ships
  watersiders *n* ▷ watersider
waterskiing *n* (*pl* -s) sport of riding over water on skis towed by a speedboat
  waterskiings *n* ▷ waterskiing
watertight *adj* not letting water through
  watery *adj* ▷ water
watt [wott] *n* (*pl* -s) unit of power
wattage *n* (*pl* -s) electrical power expressed in watts
  wattages *n* ▷ wattage
wattle [wott-tl] *n* (*pl* -s) branches woven over sticks to make a fence making fences
  wattles *n* ▷ wattle
  watts *n* ▷ watt
wave *v* (-ves, -ving, -ved) move the hand to and fro as a greeting or signal ▶ *n* (*pl* -s) moving ridge on water > **wavy** *adj* (-vier, -viest)
  waved *v* ▷ wave
wavelength *n* (*pl* -s) distance between the same points of two successive waves
  wavelengths *n* ▷ wavelength
waver *v* (-s, -ing, -ed) hesitate or be irresolute > **waverer** *n* (*pl* -s)
  wavered *v* ▷ waver
  waverer *n* ▷ waver
  waverers *n* ▷ waver
  wavering *v* ▷ waver
  wavers *v* ▷ waver
  waves *v*, *n* ▷ wave

  wavier *adj* ▷ wave
  waviest *adj* ▷ wave
  waving *v* ▷ wave
  wavy *adj* ▷ wave
wax¹ *n* (*pl* -es) solid shiny fatty or oily substance used for sealing, making candles, etc. ▶ *v* (-es, -ing, -ed) coat or polish with wax > **waxy** *adj* (-xier, -xiest)
wax² *v* (-es, -ing, -ed) increase in size or strength
  waxed *v* ▷ wax¹, ²
waxen *adj* made of or like wax
  waxes *n*, *v* ▷ wax¹, ²
  waxier *adj* ▷ wax
  waxiest *adj* ▷ wax
  waxing *v* ▷ wax¹, ²
waxwork *n* (*pl* -s) lifelike wax model of a (famous) person ▶ *pl* place exhibiting these
  waxworks *n* ▷ waxwork
  waxy *adj* ▷ wax¹
way *n* (*pl* -s) manner or method
wayfarer *n* (Lit) traveller
  wayfarers *n* ▷ wayfarer
  waylaid *v* ▷ waylay
waylay *v* (-lays, -laying, -laid) lie in wait for and accost or attack
  waylaying *v* ▷ waylay
  waylays *v* ▷ waylay
  ways *n* ▷ way
wayside *adj*, *n* (*pl* -s) (situated by) the side of a road
  waysides *n* ▷ wayside
wayward *adj* erratic, selfish, or stubborn > **waywardness** *n* (*pl* -es)
  waywardness *n* ▷ wayward
  waywardnesses *n* ▷ wayward
we *pron* (used as the subject of a verb) the speaker or writer and one or more others
weak *adj* (-er, -est) lacking strength
weaken *v* (-s, -ing, -ed) make or become weak
  weakened *v* ▷ weaken
  weakening *v* ▷ weaken
  weakens *v* ▷ weaken
  weaker *adj* ▷ weak
  weakest *adj* ▷ weak
weakling *n* feeble person or animal
  weaklings *n* ▷ weakling
weakly *adv* feebly
weakness *n* (-es) being weak
  weaknesses *n* ▷ weakness
weal *n* (*pl* -s) raised mark left on the skin by a blow
  weals *n* ▷ weal
wealth *n* (*pl* -s) state of being rich > **wealthy** *adj* (-thier, -thiest)

wealthier adj ▷ wealth
wealthiest adj ▷ wealth
wealthy adj ▷ wealth
wean v (-s, -ing, -ed) accustom (a baby or young mammal) to food other than mother's milk
weaned v ▷ wean
weaning v ▷ wean
weans v ▷ wean
weapon n (pl -s) object used in fighting
weaponries n ▷ weapon
weaponry n (pl -ries) weapons collectively
weapons n ▷ weapon
wear v (-s, -ing, wore, worn) have on the body as clothing or ornament ▶ n (pl -s) clothes suitable for a particular time or purpose
> **wearer** n (pl -s)
wearer n ▷ wear
wearers n ▷ wear
wearied v ▷ weary
wearier adj ▷ weary
wearies v ▷ weary
weariest adj ▷ weary
wearily adv ▷ weary
weariness n ▷ weary
wearinesses n ▷ weary
wearing v ▷ wear
wearisome adj tedious
wears n, v ▷ wear
weary adj (-rier, -riest) tired or exhausted ▶ v (-ries, -rying, -ried) make or become weary
> **wearily** adv > **weariness** n (pl -es)
wearying v ▷ weary
weasel n (pl -s) small carnivorous mammal with a long body and short legs
weasels n ▷ weasel
weather n (pl -s) day-to-day atmospheric conditions of a place ▶ v (-s, -ing, -ed) (cause to) be affected by the weather
weathercock, weathervane n device that revolves to show the direction of the wind
weathercocks n ▷ weathercock
weathered v ▷ weather
weathering v ▷ weather
weathers v, n ▷ weather
weathervanes n ▷ weathervane
weave v (-s, -ving, wove or weaved, woven or weaved) make (fabric) by interlacing (yarn) on a loom ▶ weaver n (pl -s)
weaved v ▷ weave
weaver n ▷ weave
weavers n ▷ weave
weaves v ▷ weave
web n (pl -s) net spun by a spider > **webbed** adj
webbed adj ▷ web

webbing n (pl -s) strong fabric woven in strips
webbings n ▷ web
webcam n (pl -s) camera that transmits images over the Internet
webcams n ▷ webcam
webcast n (pl -s) broadcast of an event over the Internet
webcasts n ▷ webcast
weblog n (pl -s) person's online journal (also blog)
weblogs n ▷ weblog
webs n ▷ web
website n (pl -s) group of connected pages on the World Wide Web
websites n ▷ website
wed v (-s, -dding, -dded or wed) marry
wedded v ▷ wed
wedding n (pl -s) act or ceremony of marriage ▶ v ▷ wed
weddings n ▷ wedding
wedge n (pl wedges) piece of material thick at one end and thin at the other ▶ v (-ges, -ging, -ged) fasten or split with a wedge
wedged v ▷ wedge
wedges n, v ▷ wedge
wedging v ▷ wedge
wedlock n (pl -s) marriage
wedlocks n ▷ wedlock
wee adj (-r, -st) (BRIT, AUST & NZ) (Informal) small or short
weed n (pl -s) plant growing where undesired (Informal) ▶ v (-s, -ing, -ed) clear of weeds
weeded v ▷ weed
weedier adj ▷ weedy
weediest adj ▷ weddy
weeding v ▷ weed
weeds n, v ▷ weed ▶ pl n (Obs) widow's mourning clothes
weedy adj (-dier, -diest) (Informal) (of a person) thin and weak
week n (pl -s) period of seven days, esp. one beginning on a Sunday
weekday n (pl -s) any day of the week except Saturday or Sunday
weekdays n ▷ weekday
weekend n (pl -s) Saturday and Sunday
weekends n ▷ weekend
weeklies n ▷ weekly
weekly adj, adv happening, done, etc. once a week ▶ n (pl -lies) newspaper or magazine published once a week
weeks n ▷ week
weep v (-s, -ing, wept) shed tears
weepier adj ▷ weepy
weepiest adj ▷ weepy

weeping v ▷ **weep**

weeps v ▷ **weep**

weepy adj (**-pier, -piest**) liable to cry

weer adj ▷ **wee**

weest adj ▷ **wee**

weevil n (pl **-s**) small beetle which eats grain etc.

weevils n ▷ **weevil**

weft n (pl **-s**) cross threads in weaving

wefts n ▷ **weft**

weigh v (**-s, -ing, -ed**) have a specified weight

weighbridge n (pl **-s**) machine for weighing vehicles by means of a metal plate set into the road

weighbridges n ▷ **weighbridge**

weighed v ▷ **weigh**

weighing v ▷ **weigh**

weighs v ▷ **weigh**

weight n (pl **-s**) heaviness of an object ▶ v (**-s, -ing, -ed**) add weight to ▷ **weightless** adj ▷ **weightlessness** n

weighted v ▷ **weight**

weightier adj ▷ **weighty**

weightiest adj ▷ **weighty**

weightily adv ▷ **weighty**

weighting v ▷ **weight** ▶ n (pl **-s**) (BRIT) extra allowance paid in special circumstances

weightings n ▷ **weighting**

weightless adj ▷ **weight**

weightlessness n ▷ **weight**

weights n, v ▷ **weight**

weighty adj (**-tier, -tiest**) important or serious ▷ **weightily** adv

weir n (pl **-s**) river dam

weird (**-er, -est**) adj strange or bizarre

weirder adj ▷ **weird**

weirdest adj ▷ **weird**

weirdo n (pl **-s**) (Informal) peculiar person

weirdos n ▷ **weirdo**

weirs n ▷ **weir**

welch v (**-es, -ing, -ed**) ▷ **welsh**

welched v ▷ **welch**

welches v ▷ **welch**

welching v ▷ **welch**

welcome v (**-mes, -ming, -med**) greet with pleasure ▶ n (pl **-s**) kindly greeting ▶ adj received gladly

welcomed v ▷ **welcome**

welcomes v, n ▷ **welcome**

welcoming v ▷ **welcome**

weld v (**-s, -ing, -ed**) join (pieces of metal or plastic) by softening with heat ▶ n (pl **-s**) welded joint ▷ **welder** n (pl **-s**)

welded v ▷ **weld**

welder n ▷ **weld**

welders n ▷ **weld**

welding v ▷ **weld**

welds v, n ▷ **weld**

welfare n (pl **-s**) wellbeing

welfares n ▷ **welfare**

well[1] adv (**better, best**) satisfactorily ▶ adj in good health ▶ interj exclamation of surprise, interrogation, etc.

well[2] n (pl **-s**) hole sunk into the earth to reach water, oil, or gas ▶ v (**-s, -ing, -ed**) flow upwards or outwards

wellbeing n (pl **-s**) state of being well, happy, or prosperous

wellbeings n ▷ **wellbeing**

welled v ▷ **well**[2]

wellies pl n (BRIT & AUST) (Informal) wellingtons

welling v ▷ **well**[2]

wellingtons pl n (BRIT & AUST) high waterproof rubber boots

wells n, v ▷ **well**[2]

welsh v (**-es, -ing, -ed**) fail to pay a debt or fulfil an obligation

welshed v ▷ **welsh**

welshes v ▷ **welsh**

welshing v ▷ **welsh**

welt n (pl **-s**) raised mark on the skin produced by a blow

welter n (pl **-s**) jumbled mass

welters n ▷ **welter**

welterweight n (pl **-s**) boxer weighing up to 147lb (professional) or 67kg (amateur)

welterweights n ▷ **welterweight**

welts n ▷ **welt**

wen n (pl **-s**) cyst on the scalp

wench n (pl **-es**) (facetious) young woman

wenches n ▷ **wench**

wend v (**-s, -ing, -ed**) go or travel

wended v ▷ **wend**

wending v ▷ **wend**

wends v ▷ **wend**

wens n ▷ **wen**

went v ▷ **go**

wept v ▷ **weep**

were v form of the past tense of **be** used after we, you, they, or a plural noun ▷ **be**

werewolf n (pl **-wolves**) (in folklore) person who can turn into a wolf

werewolves n ▷ **werewolf**

west n (pl **-s**) (direction towards) the part of the horizon where the sun sets ▶ adj to or in the west ▶ adv in, to, or towards the west ▷ **westerly** adj ▷ **westward** adj, adv ▷ **westwards** adv

westerly adj ▷ **west**

western adj of or in the west ▶ n (pl **-s**) film or

story about cowboys in the western US

westernize v (-zes, -zing, -zed) adapt to the customs and culture of the West

westernizes v ▷ westernize

westernizes v ▷ westernize

westernizing v ▷ westernize

westerns n ▷ western

wests n ▷ west

westward adj ▷ west

westwards adv ▷ west

wet adj (-tter, -ttest) covered or soaked with water or another liquid (BRIT) (Informal) ▶ n moisture or rain (BRIT) (Informal) ▶ v (-s, -tting, **wet** or **wetted**) make wet

wetland n (pl -s) area of marshy land

wetlands n ▷ wetland

wetted v ▷ wet

wetter adj ▷ wet

wettest adj ▷ wet

wetting v ▷ wet

> **wex** n (**wexes**). Wex is an old word for **wax**. This gives a very good score for a three-letter word, and is a good one to look for when you have an X. Wex scores 13 points.

whack v (-s, -ing, -ed) strike with a resounding blow ▶ n (pl -s) such a blow

whacked adj exhausted ▶ v ▷ whack

whacking adj (Informal) huge ▶ v ▷ whack

whacks v, n ▷ whack

whale n (pl -s) large fish-shaped sea mammal

whaler n ship or person involved in whaling

whalers n ▷ whaler

whales n ▷ whale

whaling n (pl -s) hunting of whales for food and oil

whalings n ▷ whaling

wharf n (pl **wharves**, **wharfs**) platform at a harbour for loading and unloading ships

wharfie n (pl -s) (AUST) person employed to load and unload ships

wharfies n ▷ wharfie

wharfs n ▷ wharf

wharves n ▷ wharf

what pron which thing ▶ interj exclamation of anger, surprise, etc. ▶ adv in which way, how much

whatnot n (pl -s) (Informal) similar unspecified things

whatnots n ▷ whatnot

whatsoever adj at all

wheat n (pl -s) grain used in making flour, bread, and pasta > **wheaten** adj

wheatear n (pl -s) small songbird

wheatears n ▷ wheatear

wheaten adj ▷ wheat

wheats n ▷ wheat

wheedle v (-les, -ling, -led) coax or cajole

wheedled v ▷ wheedle

wheedles v ▷ wheedle

wheedling v ▷ wheedle

wheel n (pl -s) disc that revolves on an axle ▶ v (-s, -ing, -ed) push or pull (something with wheels)

wheelbarrow n (pl -s) shallow box for carrying loads, with a wheel at the front and two handles

wheelbarrows n ▷ wheelbarrow

wheelbase n (pl -s) distance between a vehicle's front and back axles

wheelbases n ▷ wheelbase

wheelchair n (pl -s) chair mounted on wheels for use by people who cannot walk

wheelchairs n ▷ wheelchair

wheeled v ▷ wheel

wheeling v ▷ wheel

wheels n, v ▷ wheel

wheeze v (-zes, -zing, -zed) breathe with a hoarse whistling noise ▶ n (pl -s) wheezing sound (Informal) > **wheezy** adj (-zier, -ziest)

wheezed v ▷ wheeze

wheezes v, n ▷ wheeze

wheezier adj ▷ wheeze

wheeziest adj ▷ wheeze

wheezing v ▷ wheeze

wheezy adj ▷ wheeze

whelk n (pl -s) edible snail-like shellfish

whelks n ▷ whelk

whelp n (pl -s) pup or cub ▶ v (-s, -ing, -ed) (of an animal) give birth

whelped v ▷ whelp

whelping v ▷ whelp

whelps n, v ▷ whelp

when adv at what time? ▶ conj at the time that ▶ pron at which time

whence adv, conj (Obs) from what place or source

whenever adv, conj at whatever time

where adv in, at, or to what place? ▶ pron in, at, or to which place ▶ conj in the place at which

whereabouts n present position ▶ adv at what place

whereas conj but on the other hand

whereby pron by which

wherefore (Obs) adv why ▶ conj consequently

whereupon conj at which point

wherever conj, adv at whatever place

wherewithal n (pl -s) necessary funds, resources, etc.

wherewithals n ▷ wherewithals

whet v (-s, -tting, -tted) sharpen (a tool)

whether conj used to introduce an indirect question or a clause expressing doubt or choice

whets v ▷ whet

whetstone n (pl -s) stone for sharpening tools

whetstones n ▷ whetstone

whetted v ▷ whet

whetting v ▷ whet

whey [way] n (pl -s) watery liquid that separates from the curd when milk is clotted

wheys n ▷ whey

which adj, pron used to request or refer to a choice from different possibilities ▶ pron used to refer to a thing already mentioned

whichever adj, pron any out of several

whiff n (pl -s) puff of air or odour

whiffs n ▷ whiff

whig n (pl -s) member of a British political party of the 18th–19th centuries that sought limited reform

whigs n ▷ whig

while conj at the same time that ▶ n (pl -s) period of time

whiles n ▷ while

whilst conj while

whim n (pl -s) sudden fancy

whimper v (-s, -ing, -ed) cry in a soft whining way ▶ n (pl -s) soft plaintive whine

whimpered v ▷ whimper

whimpering v ▷ whimper

whimpers v, n ▷ whimper

whims n ▷ whim

whimsical adj unusual, playful, and fanciful

whimsies n ▷ whimsy

whimsy n (pl -ies) capricious idea

whin n (pl -s) (BRIT) gorse

whine n (pl -s) high-pitched plaintive cry ▶ v (-nes, -ning, -ned) make such a sound > whining n, adj (pl -s)

whined v ▷ whine

whines n, v ▷ whine

whinge (BRIT, AUST & NZ) (Informal) v (-ges, -geing, -ged) complain ▶ n (pl -s) complaint

whinged v ▷ whinge

whingeing v ▷ whinge

whinges v, n ▷ whinge

whining v, n adj ▷ whine

whinings n ▷ whine

whinnied v ▷ whinny

whinnies v, n ▷ whinny

whinny v (-nnies, -nnying, -nnied) neigh softly ▶ n (pl -nnies) soft neigh

whinnying v ▷ whinny

whins n ▷ whin

whip n (pl -s) cord attached to a handle, used for beating animals or people ▶ v (-s, -pping, -pped) strike with a whip, strap, or cane

whipped v ▷ whip

whippet n (pl -s) racing dog like a small greyhound

whippets n ▷ whippet

whipping v ▷ whip

whips v, n ▷ whip

whir v ▷ whirr

whirl v (-s, -ing, -ed) spin or revolve ▶ n (pl -s) whirling movement

whirled v ▷ whirl

whirling v ▷ whirl

whirlpool n (pl -s) strong circular current of water

whirlpools n ▷ whirlpool

whirls v, n ▷ whirl

whirlwind n (pl -s) column of air whirling violently upwards in a spiral ▶ adj much quicker than normal

whirlwinds n ▷ whirlwind

whirr, whir n (pl -s) prolonged soft buzz ▶ v (-s, -rring, -rred) (cause to) make a whirr

whirred v ▷ whirr

whirring v ▷ whirr

whirrs n, v ▷ whirr

whirs n ▷ whirr

whisk v (-s, -ing, -ed) move or remove quickly ▶ n (pl -s) egg-beating utensil

whisked v ▷ whisk

whisker n (pl -s) any of the long stiff hairs on the face of a cat or other mammal ▶ pl hair growing on a man's face

whiskers n ▷ whisker

whiskey n (pl -s) Irish or American whisky

whiskeys n ▷ whiskey

whiskies n ▷ whisky

whisking v, v ▷ whisk

whisks n ▷ whisk

whisky n (pl -ies) spirit distilled from fermented cereals

whisper v (-s, -ing, -ed) speak softly, without vibration of the vocal cords ▶ n (pl -s) soft voice (Informal)

whispered v ▷ whisper

whispering v ▷ whisper

whispers v, n ▷ whisper

whist n (pl -s) card game in which one pair of players tries to win more tricks than another pair

whistle v (-les, -ling, -led) produce a shrill sound, esp. by forcing the breath through pursed lips ▶ n (pl -s) whistling sound > whistling n, adj (pl -s)

whistled v ▷ whistle
whistles v, n ▷ whistle
whistling v, n ▷ whistle
whistlings n ▷ whistle
whists n ▷ whist
whit n (pl -s) not the slightest amount
white adj (-r, -st) of the colour of snow ▶ n (pl -s) colour of snow > **whiteness** n (pl -es) > **whitish** adj
whitebait n (pl -s) small edible fish
whitebaits n ▷ whitebait
whiten v (-s, -ing, -ed) make or become white or whiter
whitened v ▷ whiten
whiteness n ▷ white
whitenesses n ▷ white
whitening v ▷ whiten
whitens v ▷ whiten
whiter adj ▷ white
whites n ▷ white
whitest adj ▷ white
whitewash n (pl -es) substance for whitening walls ▶ v (-es, -ing, -ed) cover with whitewash
whitewashed v ▷ whitewash
whitewashes n, v ▷ whitewash
whitewashing v ▷ whitewash
whither adv (Obs) to what place
whiting n (pl -s) edible sea fish
whitings n ▷ whiting
whitish adj ▷ white
whittle v (-les, -ling, -led) cut or carve (wood) with a knife
whittled v ▷ whittle
whittles v ▷ whittle
whittling v ▷ whittle
whiz v ▷ whizz
whizz, whiz v (-es, -ing, -ed) make a loud buzzing sound (Informal) ▶ n (pl -es) loud buzzing sound (Informal)
whizzed v ▷ whizz
whizzes v, n ▷ whizz
whizzing v ▷ whizz
who pron which person
whodunnit, whodunit [hoo-**dun**-nit] n (pl -s) (Informal) detective story, play, or film
whodunnits n ▷ whodunnit
whoever pron any person who
whole adj containing all the elements or parts ▶ n (pl -s) complete thing or system > **wholly** adv
wholefood n (pl -s) food that has been processed as little as possible
wholefoods n ▷ wholefood
wholehearted adj sincere or enthusiastic
wholemeal adj (of flour) made from the whole

wheat grain
wholes n ▷ whole
wholesale adj, adv dealing by selling goods in large quantities to retailers > **wholesaler** n (pl -s)
wholesaler n ▷ wholesale
wholesalers n ▷ wholesale
wholesome adj physically or morally beneficial
wholly adv ▷ whole
whom pron ▷ who
whoop v, n (pl -s) shout or cry to express excitement
whoopee interj (Informal) cry of joy
whoops n ▷ whoop
whopper n (pl -s) (Informal) anything unusually large > **whopping** adj
whoppers n ▷ whopper
whopping adj ▷ whopper
whore [hore] n (pl -s) prostitute
whores n ▷ whore
whorl n (pl -s) ring of leaves or petals
whorls n ▷ whorl
whose pron of whom or of which
why adv for what reason ▶ pron because of which
wick n (pl -s) cord through a lamp or candle which carries fuel to the flame
wicked (-er, -est) adj morally bad > **wickedly** adv > **wickedness** n (pl -s)
wickedly adv ▷ wicked
wickedness n ▷ wicked
wickednesses n ▷ wicked
wicker adj made of woven cane > **wickerwork** n (pl -s)
wickerwork n ▷ wicker
wickerworks n ▷ wicker
wicket n (pl -s) set of three cricket stumps and two bails
wickets n ▷ wicket
wicks n ▷ wick
wide adj (-r, -st) large from side to side ▶ adv to the full extent > **widely** adv
widely adv ▷ wide
widen v (-s, -ing, -ed) make or become wider
widened v ▷ widen
widening v ▷ widen
widens v ▷ widen
wider adj ▷ wide
widespread adj affecting a wide area or a large number of people
widest adj ▷ wide
widgeon n (pl -s) ▷ wigeon
widgeons n ▷ widgeon
widow n (pl -s) woman whose husband is dead

and who has not remarried > **widowed** *adj*
> **widowhood** *n* (*pl* -s)
  widowed *adj* ▷ **widow**
widower *n* (*pl* -s) man whose wife is dead and
who has not remarried
  widowers *n* ▷ **widower**
  widowhood *n* ▷ **widow**
  widowhoods *n* ▷ **widow**
  widows *n*, *v* ▷ **widow**
width *n* (*pl* -s) distance from side to side
  widths *n* ▷ **width**
wield *v* (-s, -ing, -ed) hold and use (a weapon)
  wielded *v* ▷ **wield**
  wielding *v* ▷ **wield**
  wields *v* ▷ **wield**
wife *n* (*pl* **wives**) woman to whom a man is
married
wig *n* (*pl* -s) artificial head of hair
wigeon *n* (*pl* -s) duck found in marshland
  wigeons *n* ▷ **wigeon**
wiggle *v* (-les, -ling, -led) move jerkily from
side to side ▶ *n* (*pl* -les) wiggling movement
  wiggled *v* ▷ **wiggle**
  wiggles *v*, *n* ▷ **wiggle**
  wiggling *v* ▷ **wiggle**
  wigs *n* ▷ **wig**
wigwam *n* (*pl* -s) Native American's tent
  wigwams *n* ▷ **wigwam**
wild *adj* (-er, -est) (of animals) not tamed or
domesticated > **wildly** *adv* > **wildness** *n* (*pl*
-es)
wildcat *n* (*pl* -s) European wild animal like a
large domestic cat
  wildcats *n* ▷ **wildcat**
wildebeest *n* (*pl* -s) gnu
  wildebeests *n* ▷ **wildebeest**
  wilder *adj* ▷ **wild**
wilderness *n* (*pl* -es) uninhabited uncultivated
region
  wildernesses *n* ▷ **wilderness**
  wildest *adj* ▷ **wild**
wildlife *n* (*pl* -s) wild animals and plants
collectively
  wildlifes *n* ▷ **wildlife**
  wildly *adv* ▷ **wild**
  wildness *n* ▷ **wild**
  wildnesses *n* ▷ **wild**
wilds *pl n* desolate or uninhabited place
wiles *pl n* tricks or ploys
wilful *adj* headstrong or obstinate > **wilfully**
adv
  wilfully *adv* ▷ **wilful**
  wilier *adj* ▷ **wily**
  wiliest *adj* ▷ **wily**
will¹ *v* (*past* **would**) used as an auxiliary to form

the future tense or to indicate intention,
ability, or expectation
will² *n* (*pl* -s) strong determination ▶ *v* (-s,
-ing, -ed) use one's will in an attempt to do
(something)
  willed *v* ▷ **will²**
willing *adj* ready or inclined (to do something)
▶ *v* ▷ **will²** > **willingly** *adv* > **willingness** *n*
(*pl* -es)
  willingly *adv* ▷ **willing**
  willingness *n* ▷ **willing**
  willingnesses *n* ▷ **willing**
willow *n* (*pl* -s) tree with thin flexible branches
  willowier *adj* ▷ **willowy**
  willowiest *adj* ▷ **willowy**
  willows *n* ▷ **willow**
willowy *adj* (-wier, -wiest) slender and graceful
willpower *n* (*pl* -s) ability to control oneself
and one's actions
  willpowers *n* ▷ **willpower**
  wills *n*, *v* ▷ **will²**
wilt *v* (-s, -ing, -ed) (cause to) become limp or
lose strength
  wilted *v* ▷ **wilt**
  wilting *v* ▷ **wilt**
  wilts *v* ▷ **wilt**
wily *adj* (-lier, -liest) crafty or sly
wimp *n* (*pl* -s) (*Informal*) feeble ineffectual
person
wimple *n* (*pl* -s) garment framing the face,
worn by medieval women and now by nuns
  wimples *n* ▷ **wimple**
  wimps *n* ▷ **wimp**
win *v* (-s, -nning, **won**) come first in (a
competition, fight, etc.) ▶ *n* (*pl* -s) victory, esp.
in a game > **winner** *n* (*pl* -s)
wince *v* (-ces, -cing, -ced) draw back, as if in
pain ▶ *n* (*pl* -s) wincing
  winced *v* ▷ **wince**
  winces *v*, *n* ▷ **wince**
winch *n* (*pl* -es) machine for lifting or hauling
using a cable or chain wound round a drum
▶ *v* (-es, -ing, -ed) lift or haul using a winch
  winched *v* ▷ **winch**
  winches *n*, *v* ▷ **winch**
  winching *v* ▷ **winch**
  wincing *v* ▷ **wince**
wind¹ *n* (*pl* -s) current of air ▶ *v* (-s, -ing, -ed)
render short of breath > **windy** *adj* (-dier,
-diest)
wind² *v* (-s, -ing, **wound**) coil or wrap around
  winded *v* ▷ **wind¹**
windfall *n* (*pl* -s) unexpected good luck
  windfalls *n* ▷ **windfall**
  windier *adj* ▷ **wind¹**

windiest adj ▷ wind¹
winding v ▷ wind¹, ²
windlass n (pl -es) winch worked by a crank
windlasses n ▷ windlass
windmill n (pl -s) machine for grinding or pumping driven by sails turned by the wind
windmills n ▷ windmill
window n (pl -s) opening in a wall to let in light or air
windows n ▷ window
windpipe n (pl -s) tube linking the throat and the lungs
windpipes n ▷ windpipe
winds n, v ▷ wind¹, ²
windscreen n (pl -s) front window of a motor vehicle
windscreens n ▷ windscreen
windsock n (pl -s) cloth cone on a mast at an airfield to indicate wind direction
windsocks n ▷ windsock
windsurfing n (pl -s) sport of riding on water using a surfboard propelled and steered by a sail
windsurfings n ▷ windsurfing
windward adj, n (pl -s) (of or in) the direction from which the wind is blowing
windwards n ▷ windward
windy adj ▷ wind¹
wine n (pl -s) alcoholic drink made from fermented grapes
wines n ▷ wine
wing n (pl -s) one of the limbs or organs of a bird, insect, or bat that are used for flying ▶ pl sides of a stage ▶ v (-s, -ing, -ed) fly > **winged** adj
winged v, adj ▷ wing
winger n (pl -s) (SPORT) player positioned on the side of the pitch
wingers n ▷ winger
winging v ▷ wing
wings n, v ▷ wing
wink v (-s, -ing, -ed) close and open (an eye) quickly as a signal ▶ n (pl -s) winking
winked v ▷ wink
winking v ▷ wink
winkle n (pl -s) shellfish with a spiral shell
winkles n ▷ winkle
winks v, n ▷ wink
winner n ▷ win
winners n ▷ win
winning adj gaining victory ▶ v ▷ win
winnings pl n sum won, esp. in gambling
winnow v (-s, -ing, -ed) (pl -s) separate (chaff) from (grain)
winnowed v ▷ winnow

winnowing v ▷ winnow
winnows v, n ▷ winnow
winsome adj (-r, -st) charming or winning
winsomer adj ▷ winsome
winsomest adj ▷ winsome
winter n (pl -s) coldest season ▶ v (-s, -ing, -ed) spend the winter
wintered v ▷ winter
wintering v ▷ winter
winters n, v ▷ winter
wintrier adj ▷ wintry
wintriest adj ▷ wintry
wintry adj (-rier, -riest) of or like winter
wipe v (-pes, -ping, -ped) clean or dry by rubbing ▶ n (pl -s) wiping
wiped v ▷ wipe
wipes v, n ▷ wipe
wiping v ▷ wipe
wire n (pl -s) thin flexible strand of metal (Obs) ▶ v (-res, -ring, -red) equip with wires
wired v ▷ wire
wirehaired adj (of a dog) having a stiff wiry coat
wireless n (pl -es) (Old-fashioned) ▷ radio ▶ adj (of a computer network) connected by radio rather than by cables or fibre optics
wirelesses n ▷ wireless
wires n, v ▷ wire
wirier adj ▷ wiry
wiriest adj ▷ wiry
wiring n (pl -s) system of wires ▶ v ▷ wire
wirings n ▷ wiring
wiry adj (-rier, -riest) lean and tough
wisdom n (pl -s) good sense and judgment
wisdoms n ▷ wisdom
wise¹ adj (-r, -st) having wisdom > **wisely** adv
wise² n (pl -s) (Obs) manner
wiseacre n (pl -s) person who wishes to seem wise
wiseacres n ▷ wiseacres
wisecrack (Informal) n (pl -s) clever, sometimes unkind, remark ▶ v (-s, -ing, -ed) make a wisecrack
wisecracked v ▷ wisecrack
wisecracking v ▷ wisecrack
wisecracks n, v ▷ wisecrack
wisely adv ▷ wise¹
wiser adj ▷ wise¹
wises n ▷ wise²
wisest adj ▷ wise¹
wish v (-es, -ing, -ed) want or desire ▶ n (pl -es) expression of a desire
wishbone n (pl -s) V-shaped bone above the breastbone of a fowl
wishbones n ▷ wishbone

wished v ▷ wish

wishes v, n ▷ wish

wishful adj too optimistic

wishing v ▷ wish

wisp n (pl -s) light delicate streak > **wispy** adj (-pier, -piest)

wispier adj ▷ wisp

wispiest adj ▷ wisp

wisps n ▷ wisp

wispy adj ▷ wisp

wisteria n (pl -s) climbing shrub with blue or purple flowers

wisterias n ▷ wisteria

wistful adj sadly longing > **wistfully** adv

wistfully adv ▷ wistful

wit n (pl -s) ability to use words or ideas in a clever and amusing way

witch n (pl -es) person, usu. female, who practises (black) magic

witchcraft n (pl -s) use of magic

witchcrafts n ▷ witchcraft

witches n ▷ witch

with prep indicating presence alongside, possession, means of performance, characteristic manner, etc.

withdraw v (-drawing, -drew, -drawn) take or move out or away > **withdrawal** n (pl -s)

withdrawal n ▷ withdraw

withdrawals n ▷ withdraw

withdrawn adj unsociable ▶ v ▷ withdraw

withdraws v ▷ withdraw

withdrew v ▷ withdraw

wither v (-s, -ing, -ed) wilt or dry up

withered v ▷ wither

withering adj (of a look or remark) scornful ▶ v ▷ wither

withers v ▷ wither ▶ pl n ridge between a horse's shoulder blades

withheld v ▷ withhold

withhold v (-s, -ing, -held) refrain from giving

withholding v ▷ withhold

withholds v ▷ withhold

within prep, adv in or inside

without prep not accompanied by, using, or having

withstand v (-s, -ing, -stood) oppose or resist successfully

withstanding v ▷ withstand

withstands v ▷ wwithstand

withstood v ▷ wwithstand

witless adj foolish

witness n (pl -es) person who has seen something happen ▶ v (-es, -ing, -ed) see at first hand

witnessed v ▷ witness

witnesses n, v ▷ witness

witnessing v ▷ witness

wits n ▷ wit

witter v (-s, -ing, -ed) (CHIEFLY BRIT) chatter pointlessly or at unnecessary length

wittered v ▷ witter

wittering v ▷ witter

witters v ▷ witter

witticism n (pl -s) witty remark

witticisms n ▷ witticism

wittier adj ▷ witty

wittiest adj ▷ witty

wittily adv ▷ witty

wittingly adv intentionally

witty adj (-ttier, -ttiest) clever and amusing > **wittily** adv

wives n ▷ wife

wiz n (**wizzes**). Wiz is a short form of **wizard**. This is the highest-scoring three-letter word beginning with W, and can be especially useful when there isn't much room to manoeuvre. Wiz scores 15 points.

wizard n (pl -s) magician > **wizardry** n (pl -ies)

wizardries n ▷ wizard

wizardry n ▷ wizard

wizards n ▷ wizard

wizened [wiz-zend] adj shrivelled or wrinkled

wo n (**wos**). Wo is an old-fashioned spelling of **woe**. This unusual word is handy for joining words ending in W to those beginning in O. Wo scores 5 points.

woad n (pl -s) blue dye obtained from a plant, used by the ancient Britons as a body dye

woads n ▷ woad

wobbegong n (pl -s) Australian shark with brown-and-white skin

wobbegongs n ▷ wobbegong

wobble v (-les, -ling, -led) move unsteadily ▶ n (pl -s) wobbling movement or sound > **wobbly** adj (-lier, -liest)

wobbled v ▷ wobble

wobbles v, n ▷ wobble

wobblier adj ▷ wobble

wobbliest adj ▷ wobble

wobbling v ▷ wobble

wobbly adj ▷ wobble

wodge n (pl -s) (Informal) thick lump or chunk

wodges n ▷ wodge

woe n (pl -s) grief

woebegone adj looking miserable

woeful adj extremely sad > **woefully** adv

woefully adv ▷ woeful

woes n ▷ woe

wok n (pl -s) bowl-shaped Chinese cooking pan, used for stir-frying
woke v ▷ wake¹
woken v ▷ wake¹
woks n ▷ wok
wold n (pl -s) high open country
wolds n ▷ wold
wolf n (pl wolves) wild predatory canine mammal ▶ v eat ravenously
wolverine n (pl -s) carnivorous mammal of Arctic regions
wolverines n ▷ wolverine
wolves n ▷ wolf
woman n (pl women) adult human female > **womanhood** n (pl -s)
womanhood n ▷ woman
womanhoods n ▷ woman
womanish adj effeminate
womanizer n ▷ womanizing
womanizers n ▷ womanizing
womanizing n (pl -s) practice of indulging in casual affairs with women > **womanizer** n (pl -s)
womanizings n ▷ womanizing
womanly adj having qualities traditionally associated with a woman
womb n (pl -s) hollow organ in female mammals where babies are conceived and develop
wombat n (pl -s) small heavily-built burrowing Australian marsupial
wombats n ▷ wombat
wombs n ▷ womb
women n ▷ woman
won v ▷ win
wonder v (-s, -ing, -ed) be curious about ▶ n (pl -s) wonderful thing ▶ adj spectacularly successful > **wonderment** n (pl -s)
wondered v ▷ wonder
wonderful adj very fine > **wonderfully** adv
wonderfully adv ▷ wonderful
wondering v ▷ wonder
wonderment n ▷ wonder
wonderments n ▷ wonder
wonders v, n ▷ wonder
wondrous adj (Old-fashioned) wonderful
wonkier adj ▷ wonky
wonkiest adj ▷ wonky
wonky adj (-kier, -kiest) (BRIT, AUST & NZ) (Informal) shaky or unsteady
wont [rhymes with **don't**] adj accustomed ▶ n (pl -s) custom
wonts n ▷ wont
woo v (-s, -ing, -ed) try to persuade (Old-fashioned)

wood n (pl -s) substance trees are made of, used in carpentry and as fuel > **woody** adj (-dier, -diest)
woodbine n (pl -s) honeysuckle
woodbines n ▷ woodbine
woodcock n (pl -s) game bird
woodcocks n ▷ woodcock
woodcut n (pl -s) (print made from) an engraved block of wood
woodcuts n ▷ woodcut
wooded adj covered with trees
wooden adj made of wood
woodier adj ▷ wood
woodiest adj ▷ wood
woodland n (pl -s) forest
woodlands n ▷ woodland
woodlice n ▷ woodlouse
woodlouse n (pl -lice) small insect-like creature with many legs
woodpecker n (pl -s) bird which searches tree trunks for insects
woodpeckers n ▷ woodpecker
woods n ▷ wood
woodwind adj, n (pl -s) (of) a type of wind instrument made of wood
woodwinds n ▷ woodwind
woodworm n insect larva that bores into wood
woodworms n ▷ woodworm
woody adj ▷ wood
wooed v ▷ woo
woof¹ n (pl -s) cross threads in weaving
woof² n (pl -s) barking noise made by a dog
woofer n (pl -s) loudspeaker reproducing low-frequency sounds
woofers n ▷ woofer
woofs n ▷ woof¹, ²
wooing v ▷ woo
wool n (pl -s) soft hair of sheep, goats, etc. > **woollen** adj
woollen adj ▷ wool
woollier adj ▷ woolly
woolliest adj ▷ woolly
woolly adj (-llier, -lliest) of or like wool ▶ n knitted woollen garment
wools n ▷ wool
woomera n (pl -s) notched stick used by Australian Aborigines to aid the propulsion of a spear
woomeras n ▷ woomera
woos v ▷ woo
woozier adj ▷ woozy
wooziest adj ▷ woozy
woozy adj (-zier, -ziest) (Informal) weak, dizzy, and confused

rd n (pl -s) smallest single meaningful unit of speech or writing ▶ v (-s, -ing, -ed) express in words

worded v ▷ word
wordier adj ▷ wordy
wordiest adj ▷ wordy
wording n (pl -s) choice and arrangement of words ▶ v ▷ word
wordings n ▷ wording
words n, v ▷ word
wordy adj (-dier, -diest) using too many words
wore v ▷ wear
work n (pl -s) physical or mental effort directed to making or doing something ▶ pl factory (Informal) ▶ adj of or for work ▶ v (-s, -ing, -ed) (cause to) do work > **workable** adj > **worker** n (pl -s)
workable adj ▷ work
workaholic n (pl -s) person obsessed with work
workaholics n ▷ workaholic
worked v ▷ work
worker n ▷ work
workers n ▷ work
workhorse n (pl -s) person or thing that does a lot of dull or routine work
workhorses n ▷ workhorse
workhouse n (pl -s) (in England, formerly) institution where the poor were given food and lodgings in return for work
workhouses n ▷ workhouse
working v ▷ work
workman n (pl -men) manual worker
workmanship n (pl -s) skill with which an object is made
workmanships n ▷ workmanship
workmen n ▷ workman
works n, v ▷ work
workshop n (pl -s) room or building for a manufacturing process
workshops n ▷ w
worktop n (pl -s) surface in a kitchen, used for food preparation
worktops n ▷ worktop
world n (pl -s) the planet earth ▶ adj of the whole world
worldlier adj ▷ worldly
worldliest adj ▷ worldly
worldly adj (-ier, -iest) not spiritual
worlds n ▷ world
worm n (pl -s) small limbless invertebrate animal ▶ pl illness caused by parasitic worms in the intestines ▶ v (-s, -ing, -ed) rid of worms > **wormy** adj (-mier, -miest)
wormed v ▷ worm

wormier adj ▷ worm
wormiest adj ▷ worm
worming v ▷ worm
worms n, v ▷ worm
wormwood n (pl -s) bitter plant
wormwoods n ▷ wormwood
wormy adj ▷ worm
worn v ▷ wear
worried v, adj ▷ worry
worries v, n ▷ worry
worry v (-ies, -ying, -ied) (cause to) be anxious or uneasy ▶ n (pl -ies) (cause of) anxiety or concern > **worried** adj > **worrying** adj, n
worrying v, adj ▷ worry
worse adj, adv ▷ bad, badly
worsen v (-s, -ing, -ed) make or grow worse
worsened v ▷ worsen
worsening v ▷ worsen
worsens v ▷ worsen
worship v (-s, -pping, -pped) show religious devotion to ▶ n (pl -s) act or instance of worshipping > **worshipper** n (pl -s)
worshipful adj worshipping
worshipped v ▷ worship
worshipper n ▷ worship
worshippers n ▷ worship
worshipping v ▷ worship
worships v, n ▷ worship
worst adj, adv ▷ bad, badly ▶ n worst thing
worsted [wooss-tid] n (pl -s) type of woollen yarn or fabric
worsteds n ▷ worsted
worth prep having a value of ▶ n (pl -s) value or price > **worthless** adj
worthier adj ▷ worthy
worthiest adj ▷ worthy
worthily adv ▷ worthy
worthiness n ▷ worthy
worthinesses n ▷ worthy
worthless adj ▷ worth
worths n ▷ worth
worthwhile adj worth the time or effort involved
worthy adj (-thier, -thiest) deserving admiration or respect ▶ n (Informal) notable person > **worthily** adv > **worthiness** n (pl -e
would v ▷ will¹
wound¹ n (pl -s) injury caused by violence ▶ (-s, -ing, -ed) inflict a wound on
wound² v ▷ wind²
wounded v ▷ wound¹
wounding v ▷ wound¹
wounds n, v ▷ wound¹
wove v ▷ weave
woven v ▷ weave

wow *interj* exclamation of astonishment ▶ *n* (*pl -s*) (*Informal*) astonishing person or thing
wows *n* ▷ wow
wowser *n* (*pl -s*) (AUST & NZ) (*Slang*) puritanical person
wowsers *n* ▷ wowser

wox *n* (**woxes**). Wox is an old past tense of the verb **wax**. This gives a very good score for a three-letter word, and is a good one to look for when you have an X. Wox scores 13 points.

wrack *n* (*pl -s*) seaweed
wracks *n* ▷ wrack
wraith *n* (*pl -s*) ghost
wraiths *n* ▷ wraith
wrangle *v* (**-les, -ling, -led**) argue noisily ▶ *n* (*pl -s*) noisy argument
wrangled *v* ▷ wrangle
wrangles *v*, *n* ▷ wrangle
wrangling *v* ▷ wrangle
wrap *v* (**-s, -pping, -pped**) fold (something) round (a person or thing) so as to cover ▶ *n* (*pl -s*) garment wrapped round the shoulders
wrapped *v* ▷ wrap
wrapper *n* (*pl -s*) cover for a product
wrappers *n* ▷ wrapper
wrapping *n* (*pl -s*) material used to wrap ▶ *v* ▷ wrap
wrappings *n* ▷ wrapping
wraps *v*, *n* ▷ wrap
wrasse *n* (*pl -s*) colourful sea fish
wrasses *n* ▷ wrasse
wrath [roth] *n* (*pl -s*) intense anger > **wrathful** *adj*
wrathful *adj* ▷ wrath
wraths *n* ▷ wrath
wreak *v* (**-s, -ing, -ed**) cause (chaos)
wreaked *v* ▷ wreak
wreaking *v* ▷ wreak
wreaks *v* ▷ wreak
wreath *n* (*pl -s*) twisted ring or band of flowers or leaves used as a memorial or tribute
wreathed *adj* surrounded or encircled
wreaths *n* ▷ wreath
wreck *v* (**-s, -ing, -ed**) destroy ▶ *n* (*pl -s*) remains of something that has been destroyed or badly damaged, esp. a ship > **wrecker** *n* (*pl -s*)
wreckage *n* (*pl -s*) wrecked remains
wreckages *n* ▷ wreckage
wrecked *v* ▷ wreck
wrecker *n* ▷ wreck
wreckers *n* ▷ wreck
wrecking *v* ▷ wreck
wrecks *v*, *n* ▷ wreck
wren *n* (*pl -s*) small brown songbird

wrench *v* (**-es, -ing, -ed**) t˙ ▶ *n* (*pl -es*) violent twist o.
wrenched *v* ▷ wrench
wrenches *v*, *n* ▷ wrench
wrenching *v* ▷ wrench
wrens *n* ▷ wren
wrest *v* (**-s, -ing, -ed**) twist violently
wrested *v* ▷ wrest
wresting *v* ▷ wrest
wrestle *v* (**-les, -ling, -led**) fight, esp. as a sport, by grappling with and trying to throw down an opponent > **wrestler** *n* (*pl -s*) > **wrestling** *n* (*pl -s*)
wrestled *v* ▷ wrestle
wrestler *n* ▷ wrestle
wrestlers *n* ▷ wrestle
wrestles *v* ▷ wrestle
wrestling *v*, *n* ▷ wrestle
wrestlings *n* ▷ wrestle
wrests *v* ▷ wrest
wretch *n* (*pl -es*) despicable person
wretched [retch-id] *adj* (**-er, -est**) miserable or unhappy > **wretchedly** *adv* > **wretchedness** *n* (*pl -es*)
wretcheder *adj* ▷ wretched
wretchedest *adj* ▷ wretched
wretchedly *adv* ▷ wretched
wretchedness *n* ▷ wretched
wretchednesses *n* ▷ wretched
wretches *n* ▷ wretch
wrier *adj* ▷ wry
wriest *adj* ▷ wry
wriggle *v* (**-les, -ling, -led**) move with a twisting action ▶ *n* (*pl -s*) wriggling movement
wriggled *v* ▷ wriggle
wriggles *v*, *n* ▷ wriggle
wriggling *v* ▷ wriggle
wright *n* (*pl -s*) maker
wrights *n* ▷ wright
wring *v* (**-s, -ing, wrung**) twist, esp. to squeeze liquid out of
wringing *v* ▷ wring
wrings *v* ▷ wring
wrinkle *n* (*pl -s*) slight crease, esp. one in the skin due to age ▶ *v* (**-les, -ling, -led**) make or become slightly creased > **wrinkly** *adj* (**-lier, -liest**)
wrinkled *v* ▷ wrinkle
wrinkles *n*, *v* ▷ wrinkle
wrinklier *adj* ▷ wrinkle
wrinkliest *adj* ▷ wrinkle
wrinkling *v* ▷ wrinkle
wrinkly *adj* ▷ wrinkle
wrist *n* (*pl -s*) joint between the hand and

the arm

wrists *n* ▷ **wrist**

wristwatch *n* (*pl* **-es**) watch worn on the wrist

wristwatches *n* ▷ **wristwatch**

writ *n* (*pl* **-s**) written legal command

write *v* (**-tes, -ting, wrote, written**) mark paper etc. with symbols or words > **writing** *n* (*pl* **-s**)

writer *n* (*pl* **-s**) author

writers *n* ▷ **writer**

writhe *v* (**-thes, -thing, -thed**) twist or squirm in or as if in pain

writhed *v* ▷ **writhe**

writhes *v* ▷ **writhe**

writhing *v* ▷ **writhe**

writing *v, n* ▷ **write**

writings *n* ▷ **write**

writs *n* ▷ **writ**

written *v* ▷ **write**

wrong *adj* incorrect or mistaken ▶ *adv* in a wrong manner ▶ *n* (*pl* **-s**) something immoral or unjust ▶ *v* (**-s, -ing, -ed**) treat unjustly > **wrongly** *adv* > **wrongful** *adj* > **wrongfully** *adv*

wrongdoer *n* ▷ **wrongdoing**

wrongdoers *n* ▷ **wrongdoing**

wrongdoing *n* (*pl* **-s**) immoral or illegal behaviour > **wrongdoer** *n* (*pl* **-s**)

wrongdoings *n* ▷ **wrongdoing**

wronged *v* ▷ **wrong**

wrongful *adj* ▷ **wrong**

wrongfully *adv* ▷ **wrong**

wronging *v* ▷ **wrong**

wrongly *adv* ▷ **wrong**

wrongs *n, v* ▷ **wrong**

wrought [rawt] *v* (Lit) ▷ **work** ▶ *adj* (of metals) shaped by hammering or beating

wrung *v* ▷ **wring**

wry *adj* (**wrier, wriest** or **wryer**) (**wryest**) drily humorous > **wryly** *adv*

wryer *adj* ▷ **wry**

wryest *adj* ▷ **wry**

wryly *adv* ▷ **wry**

wye *n* (**wyes**). Wye is the letter Y. If you have W and Y on your rack, look for an E on the board that will allow you to play this especially if you can land on a bonus square as a result. Wye scores 9 points.

Xx

Worth 8 points on its own, X is one of the best tiles in the game. It doesn't, however, start many two- and three-letter words. There are only two valid two-letter words, **xi** and **xu** (9 points each), beginning with X, and only one three-letter word, **xis**. Therefore, if you have an X on your rack and need to play short words, you're probably better off thinking of words that end in X or have X in them rather than those that start with X.

xebec *n* (**xebecs**). A xebec is an Algerian ship. This is a good high-scoring word. If you have an X, you'll probably only need one E as well as B and C to play it, as there is likely to be an available E on the board already. Xebec scores 16 points.

xenon *n* (*pl* **-s**) (CHEM) colourless odourless gas found in very small quantities in the air
xenons *n* ▷ xenon

xenophobia [zen-oh-**fobe**-ee-a] *n* (*pl* **-s**) fear or hatred of people from other countries
xenophobias *n* ▷ xenophobia

xi *n* (**xis**). Xi is the 14th letter of the Greek alphabet. The plural of this word is the only three-letter word that starts with X. Xi scores 9 points.

xoanon *n* (**xoanons**) A xoanon is a primitive carving of a god. If you have all the tiles for the plural, and are able to place them all on the board, you'll earn a 50-point bonus. Xoanon scores 13 points.

xu *n* (**xu**). The xu is a unit of currency in Vietnam. The plural form of this word is the same as its singular, so be sure to challenge anyone who adds an S to it! Xu scores 9 points.

xylem [**zy**-lem] *n* (*pl* **-s**) plant tissue that conducts water and minerals from the roots to all other parts
xylems *n* ▷ xylem

xylophone [**zile**-oh-fone] *n* (*pl* **-s**) musical instrument made of a row of wooden bars played with hammers
xylophones *n* ▷ xylophone

Yy

Y is a useful tile to have on your rack. It's worth 4 points on its own, and so often gives you good scores. There are only four two-letter words beginning with Y, but these are easy to remember as there's one for every vowel except I: **ya**, **ye**, **yo** and **yu** (5 points each). There are quite a few useful three-letter words: **yew** (9) and **yob** (8) and remember that yob was originally **boy** backwards: if you can't fit in yob, you may be able to use boy instead. And while his half-brother the **zo** (or **dzo** or **dso** or **zho**) gets all the attention, don't forget that the **yak** (10) earns quite a decent score!

ya *interj* (S AFR) yes
  yabbies *n* ▷ yabby
yabby *n* (*pl* -bbies) (AUST) small freshwater crayfish
yacht [yott] *n* (*pl* -s) large boat with sails or an engine, used for racing or pleasure cruising > **yachting** *n* (*pl* -s) > **yachtsman** *n* (*pl* -men) > **yachtswoman** *n* (*pl* -women)
  yachting *n* ▷ yacht
  yachtings *n* ▷ yacht
  yachts *n* ▷ yacht
  yachtsman *n* ▷ yacht
  yachtsmen *n* ▷ yacht
  yachtswoman *n* ▷ yacht
  yachtswomen *n* ▷ yacht
yak¹ *n* (*pl* -s) Tibetan ox with long shaggy hair
yak² *v* (yaks, yakking, yakked) (*Slang*) talk continuously about unimportant matters
yakka *n* (*pl* -s) (AUST & NZ) (*Informal*) work
  yakkas *n* ▷ yakka
  yakked *v* ▷ yak²
  yakking *v* ▷ yak²
  yaks *n* ▷ yak¹ ▶ *v* ▷ yak²
yam *n* (*pl* -s) tropical root vegetable
  yams *n* ▷ yam
yank *v* (-s, -ing, -ed) pull or jerk suddenly ▶ *n* (*pl* -s) sudden pull or jerk
  yanked *v* ▷ yank
  yanking *v* ▷ yank
  yanks *v*, *n* ▷ yank
yap *v* (-s, -pping, -pped) bark with a high-pitched sound (*Informal*) ▶ *n* (*pl* -s) high-pitched bark
  yapped *v* ▷ yap
  yapping *v* ▷ yap

  yaps *v* ▷ yap
yard¹ *n* (*pl* -s) unit of length equal to 36 inches or about 91.4 centimetres > **yardstick** *n* (*pl* -s) standard against which to judge other people or things
yard² *n* (*pl* -s) enclosed area, usu. next to a building and often used for a particular purpose
  yards *n* ▷ yard¹, ²
  yardstick *n* ▷ yard¹
  yardsticks *n* ▷ yard¹
yarmulke [yar-mull-ka] *n* (*pl* -s) skullcap worn by Jewish men
  yarmulkes *n* ▷ yarmulke
yarn *n* (*pl* -s) thread used for knitting or making cloth
  yarns *n* ▷ yarn
yashmak *n* (*pl* -s) veil worn by a Muslim woman to cover her face in public
  yashmaks *n* ▷ yashmak
yaw *v* (-s, -ing, -ed) (of an aircraft or ship) turn to one side or from side to side while moving
  yawed *v* ▷ yaw
  yawing *v* ▷ yaw
yawl *n* (*pl* -s) two-masted sailing boat
  yawls *n* ▷ yawl
yawn *v* (-s, -ing, -ed) open the mouth wide and take in air deeply, often when sleepy or bored ▶ *n* (*pl* -s) act of yawning > **yawning** *adj*
  yawned *v* ▷ yawn
  yawning ▷ yawn
  yawns *v*, *n* ▷ yawn
  yaws *v* ▷ yaw
ye [yee] *pron* (Obs) you
year *n* (*pl* -s) time taken for the earth to make

one revolution around the sun, about 365 days

yearling n (pl -s) animal between one and two years old
  yearlings n ▷ yearling
yearly adj, adv (happening) every year or once a year
yearn v (-s, -ing, -ed) want (something) very much > **yearning** n (pl -s) adj
  yearned v ▷ yearn
  yearning v, n ▷ yearn
  yearnings n ▷ yearn
  yearns v ▷ yearn
  years n ▷ year
yeast n (pl -s) fungus used to make bread rise and to ferment alcoholic drinks > **yeasty** adj
  yeasts n ▷ yeast
yebo interj (S AFR) (Informal) yes
yell v (-s, -ing, -ed) shout or scream in a loud or piercing way ▶ n (pl -s) loud cry of pain, anger, or fear
  yelled v ▷ yell
  yelling v ▷ yell
yellow n (pl -s) the colour of gold, a lemon, etc. ▶ adj (-er, -est) of this colour ▷ v (-s, -ing, -ed) make or become yellow
  yellowed v ▷ yellow
  yellower adj ▷ yellow
  yellowest adj ▷ yellow
yellowhammer n (pl -s) European songbird with a yellow head and body
  yellowhammers n ▷ yellowhammer
  yellowing v ▷ yellow
  yellows n, v ▷ yellow
  yells v, n ▷ yell
yelp v (-s, -ing, -ed) ▶ n (pl -s) (give) a short sudden cry
  yelped v ▷ yelp
  yelping v ▷ yelp
  yelps v, n ▷ yelp
yen¹ n (pl yen) monetary unit of Japan
yen² n (pl yen) (Informal) longing or desire
yeoman [yo-man] n (pl -men) (HIST) farmer owning and farming his own land
  yeomen n ▷ yeoman
yes interj expresses consent, agreement, or approval
yesterday adv, n (pl -s) (on) the day before today
  yesterdays n ▷ yesterday
yet conj nevertheless, still ▶ adv up until then or now
yeti n (pl yetis) large apelike creature said to live in the Himalayas
  yetis n ▷ yeti

yew n (pl -s) evergreen tree with needle-like leaves and red berries
  yews n ▷ yew

> **yex** v (**yexes, yexing, yexed**). Yex is a Scots word that means to hiccup or cough. This word gives you a good score, and the verb forms offer the chance to expand it if someone else plays it, or if you get the chance later on. Yex scores 13 points.

yield v (-s, -ing, -ed) produce or bear ▶ n (pl -s)
  yielded v ▷ yield
yielding adj submissive ▶ v ▷ yield
  yields v, n ▷ yield

> **yo** interj. Yo is an informal greeting. This is useful for connecting words ending in Y with ones beginning in O. Yo scores 5 points.

yob n (pl -s) (Slang) bad-mannered aggressive youth
yobbo n (pl -bboes or -bbos) yob
  yobboes n ▷ yobbo
  yobbos n ▷ yobbo
  yobs n ▷ yob
yodel v (-s, -lling, -lled) sing with abrupt changes between a normal and a falsetto voice
  yodelled v ▷ yodel
  yodelling v ▷ yodel
  yodels v ▷ yodel
yoga n (pl -s) Hindu method of exercise and discipline aiming at spiritual, mental, and physical wellbeing
  yogas n ▷ yoga
  yoghurt n ▷ yogurt
  yoghurts n ▷ yogurt
yogi n (pl -s) person who practises yoga
  yogis n ▷ yogi
yogurt, yoghurt n (pl -s) slightly sour custard-like food made from milk that has had bacteria added to it, often sweetened and flavoured with fruit
  yogurts n ▷ yogurt

> **yok** n (**yoks**). A yok is a noisy laugh. This unusual word is useful if there isn't much space on the board, as there's likely to be an O available to form it around. Yok scores 10 points.

yoke n (pl -s) wooden bar put across the necks of two animals to hold them together (Lit) ▶ v (-kes, -king, -ked) put a yoke on
  yoked v ▷ yoke
yokel n (pl yokels) (Offens) person who lives in the country and is usu. simple and old-fashioned